DEAR ADAM,

FUN, FACTS, AND FIGURES FOR OUR FAVORITE NEPHEW!

BEST WISHES FOR A FABULOUS YEAR IN SEVENTH GRADE!

LOVE,

Aunt Joan

Uncle Fred

THE MACMILLAN
VISUAL DESK REFERENCE

THE MACMILLAN VISUAL DESK REFERENCE

The Diagram Group

Macmillan Publishing Company
New York

Maxwell Macmillan Canada
Toronto

Maxwell Macmillan International
New York Oxford Singapore Sydney

Project Director
Jane Robertson

Editors
Louise Bostock
Helen Varley

Copy Editors
Margaret Doyle
John Hampson
Moira Johnson
Patricia Johnson
Theodore Rowland-Entwistle
Shunil Roy-Chaudhuri
Richard Shaw

Art Director
Darren Bennett

Designers
Brian Hewson
Richard Hummerstone
Edward Kinsey
Philip Patenall
Tim Scrivens

Design Staff and Artists
Bournetype Typesetting
Chapman Bounford Associates
James Dallas
Andrew Huxstep
Elly King
Susan Kinsey
Pavel Kostal
Kyri Kyriacou
Lee Lawrence
Ali Marshall
Jane Parker
Johnny Pau
Mike Ricketts
Nick Rowland

Indexers
David Harding
Susan Thompson

Contributors
Arthur Butterfield
Mike Darton
David Lambert
Howard Loxton
Edward Miller
Edwin Moore
Anne Morley-Priestman
Dr Richard Walker

Researchers
Cailey Barker
Ben Barkow

Macmillan Publishing Company
866 Third Avenue
New York, NY 10022

Maxwell Macmillan Canada, Inc
1200 Eglinton Avenue East
Suite 200
Don Mills, Ontario M3C 3N1

Macmillan Publishing Company is part of the Maxwell Communication Group of Companies

Library of Congress Cataloging–in–Publication Data

The Macmillan Visual Desk Reference / Diagram Group.
p. cm.
ISBN 0-02-531310-X
1. Encyclopedias and dictionaries.
I. Diagram Group.
AE6. M273 19938 91-38184
031--dc20 CIP

A Diagram Book first created by Diagram Visual Information Limited of 195 Kentish Town Road, London NW5 8SY, England

Macmillan books are available at special discounts for bulk purchases for sales promotions, premiums, fund-raising, or educational use. For details contact
Special Sales Director
Macmillan Publishing Company
866 Third Avenue
New York, NY 10022

10 9 8 7 6 5 4 3 2 1

Printed in the United States of America

Introduction

Each new generation requires a new way of carrying out old activities. The traditional alphabetical one-volume encyclopedia is no longer relevant to readers' needs. Alphabetically structured reference volumes isolate each item of information from related items so that, for example, the entry on the planet Jupiter is far away from the entry on Uranus; agoraphobia (fear of open or public spaces) is far from xenophobia (fear of foreigners or strangers); Braque (the French artist) from Velázquez (the Spanish artist); and DNA (the main constituent of chromosomes) from genetics (the study of heredity).

The Macmillan Visual Desk Reference is organized into eight thematic chapters. Within each chapter, common subjects are grouped under section headings; and within each section, the topics are arranged in panels of information designed to provide quick access to essential information on each subject.

Each subject includes a glossary of key words, definitions of important concepts, and brief biographies of famous people.

To make every subject easier to understand, all sections have explanatory diagrams. Key events in world history, concepts in philosophy and religion, principles of physics and astronomy, are presented in pictures and words. Wherever possible, information is conveyed through diagrams, illustrations, charts, and other graphics. This is intended to make the information in *The Macmillan Visual Desk Reference* clear, quick to find, simple to understand, and memorable.

The book begins with a contents listing of how the topics are grouped, followed by a topic finder in alphabetical order to enable the reader to find where in the book the topic occurs, then a word finder locating the individual entries. Finally, to provide speedy access to names, there is a people finder of the 2,000 biographies in the book.

QUICK ACCESS

How to use the book

The Macmillan Visual Desk Reference uses an innovative method of accessing information.

The book begins with a contents listing panel (a panel is an item of information between rules) showing how over 1,000 panels are grouped.

Then there is a topic finder. This is an alphabetical listing of all the topics, which are identified by a heavy black band across the page.

The word finder which follows enables you to locate the major entry on whatever subject interests you, and the next section is a people finder, listing over 2,000 biographical entries.

How the Numbering System Works

The first digit of the number represents the chapter (there are eight chapters); for example,

1 The Physical World

The second digit represents a subject within the chapter; for example,

1**1** ASTRONOMY

The third digit represents the group of topics within a subject. These are marked by strong black bands; for example,

11**2 STARS**

The fourth digit is the entry number directing you to a specific piece of information; for example,

112**6 Identifying constellations**

An Example of the Numbering System

112**6**

1	=	Chapter 1: **The Physical World**
1**1**	=	1**1** ASTRONOMY
11**2**	=	11**2 STARS**
112**6**	=	112**6 Identifying constellations**

CONTENTS

TOPIC FINDER

WORLD FINDER

PEOPLE FINDER

1 THE PHYSICAL WORLD

2 SCIENCE AND TECHNOLOGY

3 COMMUNICATIONS

4 HISTORY

CONTENTS

6 RELIGION AND PHILOSOPHY

CONTENTS

7 BODY AND HEALTH

8 SPORTS

TOPIC FINDER

A

C

TOPIC FINDER

WORD FINDER

D

E

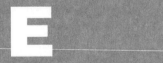

F

G

H

I

L

N

O

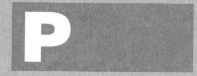

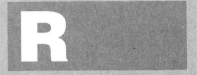

S

U

V

X

Y

Z

PEOPLE FINDER

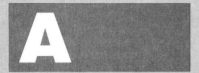

C

D

H

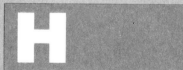

N

T

U

W

111 THE UNIVERSE

Age and size

1111 Astronomers estimate that the universe is 13 billion to 20 billion years old. No one knows how large the universe is or how large it will become – it is still expanding as the galaxies and clusters of galaxies move further away from each other.

The scale of the universe
The cubes in these diagrams give some idea of the enormous scale of the universe. Each cube has sides 100 times as long as the sides of the cube before it. The length of the cube sides is given in light years (ly); see box below for explanations of this and other astronomical abbreviations.

1 Cube side 950 au (0.015 ly) Contains the whole solar system.
2 Cube side 1.5 ly Contains the solar system surrounded by the Oort cloud of comets. This cloud is believed to be the original source of many of the comets that pass through the solar system. It surrounds the Sun at an average distance of 40,000 au ($^2/_3$ ly).
3 Cube side 150 ly Contains the solar system and the nearer stars.
4 Cube side 15,000 ly Contains the nearer spiral arms of our galaxy.
5 Cube side 1.5 million ly Contains the whole of our galaxy, the large and small Magellanic Clouds and other nearby galaxies in the local group.
6 Cube side 150 million ly Contains the whole of the local group and the Pisces, Cancer, and Virgo clusters of galaxies.
7 Cube side 15 billion ly Contains all the known clusters and superclusters of galaxies and all other known objects in space, and represents the limits of our current knowledge of the size of the universe.

1
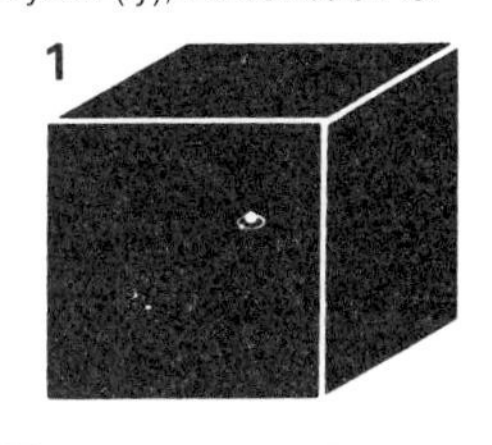
2
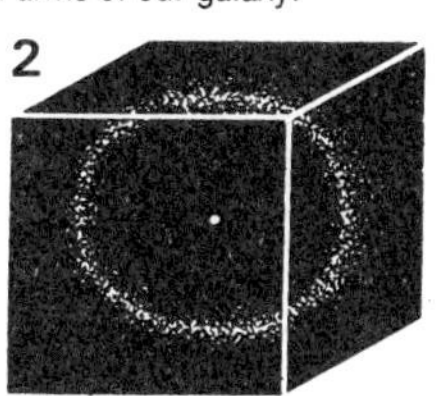
3
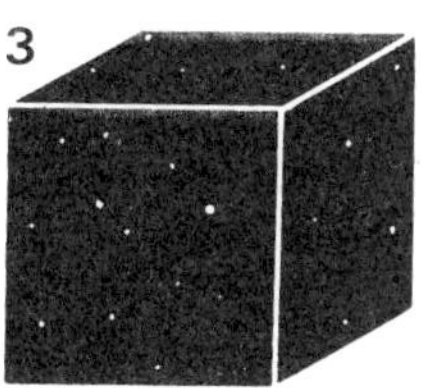
4
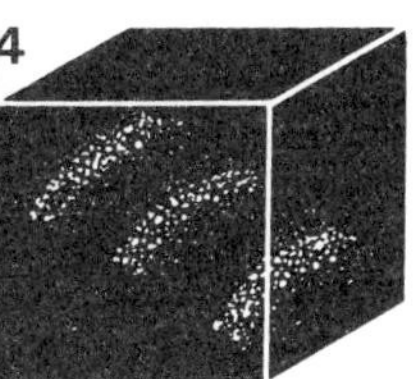
5
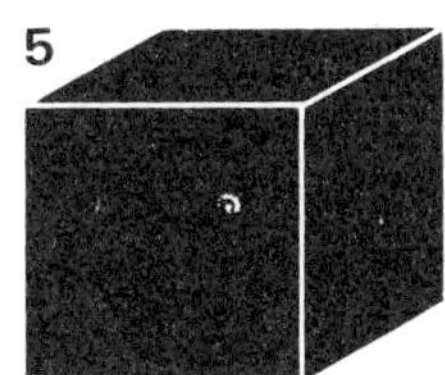
6
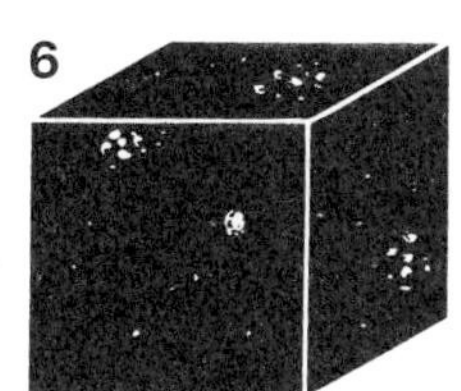
7
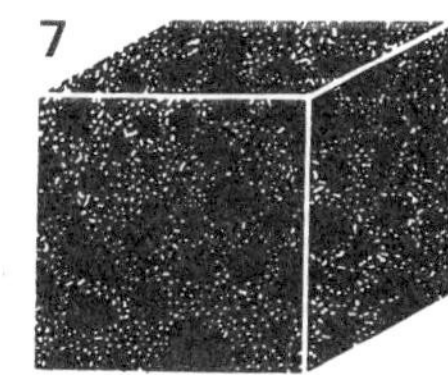

Units of space measurement

1112 **Astronomical unit (au)**
Mean Sun to Earth distance = 92,955,807 mi (149,597,870 km). Agreed internationally in 1964 but value has altered.

Galactic coordinates
Relative location of our galaxy's components in latitude and longitude (degrees and min) measured in relation to the celestial equator which is itself a projection of the Earth's equator.

Light year (ly)
Distance traveled by light in a year = 5.878 trillion mi (9.4605 trillion km) or 63,290 au. Defined in 1888.

Parsec (pc)
The distance at which 1 au would measure 1 sec of arc = 19.16 trillion mi (30.857 trillion km) or 206,265 au or 3.26 ly (**1**).

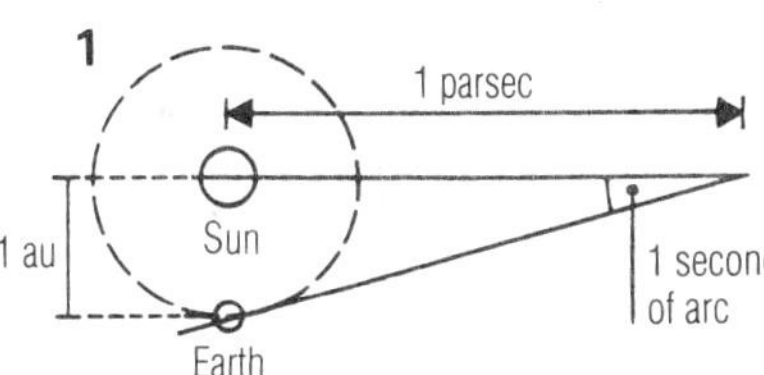

Galaxies

1113

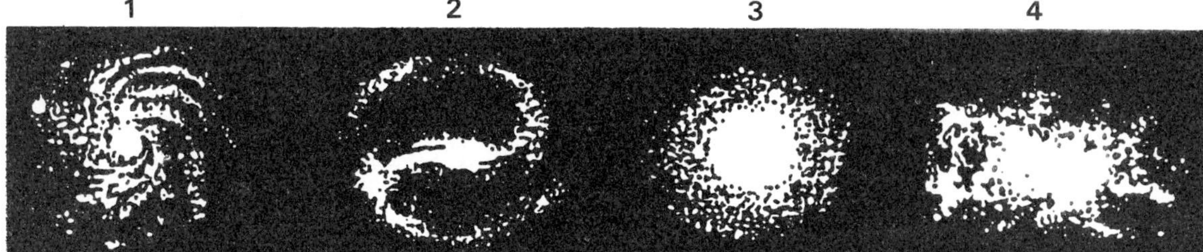

Galaxies are collections of stars and planets and clouds of gas or dust that form "islands" in the emptiness of space. A recent theory claims much of this is occupied by invisible dark matter. Most galaxies are found in groups; very few are found on their own.

Galactic shapes
Galaxies are classified by their shape. The four main classes are:

1 Spiral These galaxies resemble pinwheels, with spiral arms trailing out from a bright center. Our galaxy is a spiral galaxy at the center of which is a cluster of stars called the Milky Way.
2 Barred spiral Here, the spiral arms trail from the ends of a central bar.
About 30% of galaxies are spirals or barred spirals.
3 Elliptical These galaxies do not have spiral arms. About 60% of galaxies are elliptical, varying in shape from almost spherical (like a soccer ball) to very flattened (like a football).
4 Irregular About 10% of galaxies are irregular with no definite shape.

112 STARS

Life cycle

1121

1
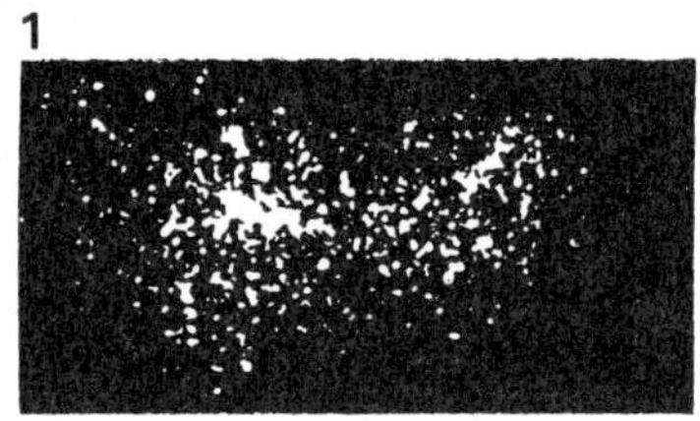

2
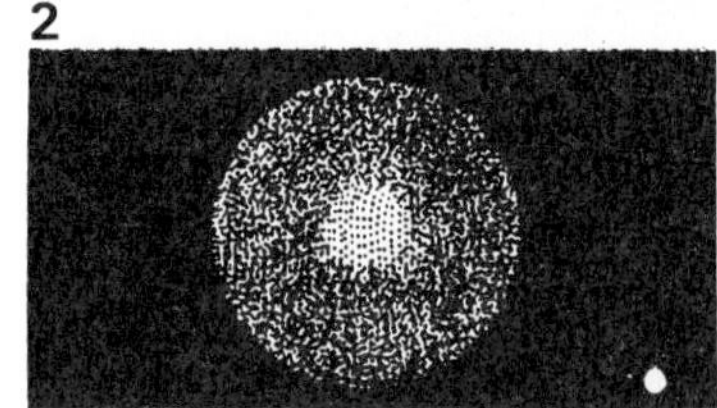

3
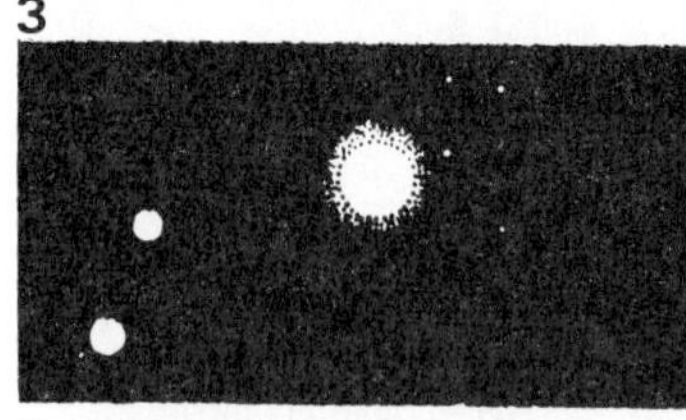

4
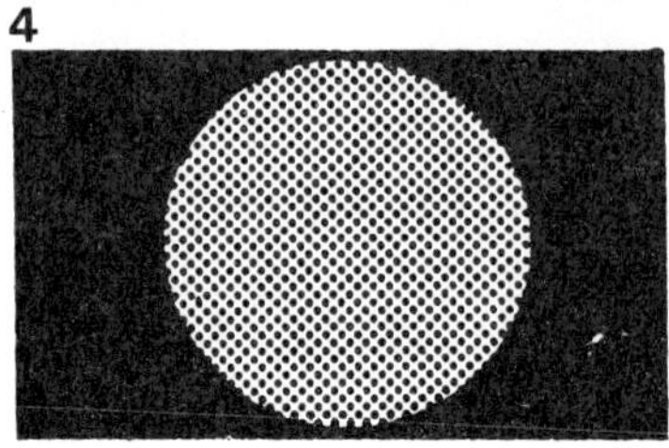

5
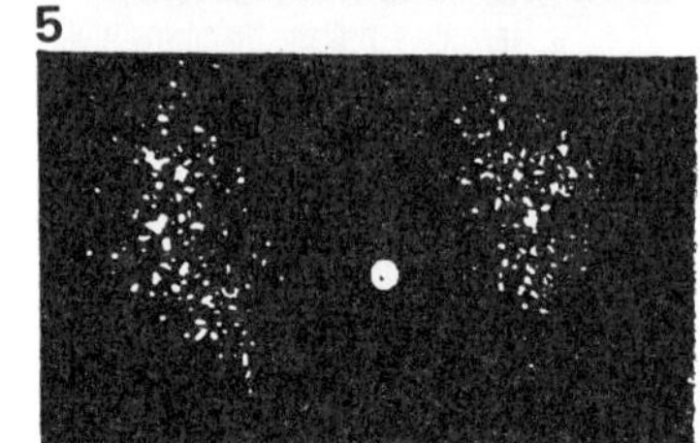

The following describe the life cycle of a star with a mass similar to that of the Sun.
1 All stars form in nebulae (clouds of gas and dust). Denser, smaller clouds called globules gradually form within a nebula. (A globule the size of the solar system will form a star the size of the Sun.)
2 The globule becomes smaller and hotter, begins to shine faintly, and forms a large, red "protostar" (star ancestor). "Protoplanets" may form around the protostar.
3 The protostar contracts further, gets hotter, and becomes an ordinary star (one producing energy by converting hydrogen to helium). The star and any planets remain stable for a few billion years. (This is the current state of the Sun.)
4 Eventually the star's core gets hotter while its outer layers expand and become cooler and redder. The star becomes a red giant, destroying any planets close to it. (The Sun is expected to become a red giant, 100 times its present size, in about 5 billion years. It will engulf Mercury, Venus, and possibly the Earth.)
5 When the red giant reaches its maximum size it becomes unstable and pulsates (swells and shrinks). The outer layers break away to form a ring nebula. The core shrinks to form a white dwarf star.

Color and size

1122 Stars are often referred to in terms of their color (red, orange, yellow, blue, white), comparative size (dwarf, giant, supergiant), and brightness. Blue and white stars are hotter than the yellow Sun; orange and red stars are cooler. Compared here are six types of star.
1 Sirius B A white dwarf: diameter 100 times smaller than the Sun's.
2 Barnard's Star A red dwarf: diameter 10 times smaller than the Sun's.
3 Sun A yellow dwarf.
4 Capella A yellow giant: diameter 16 times larger and brightness 150 times greater than the Sun's.
5 Rigel A blue-white giant: diameter 80 times larger and brightness 60,000 times greater than the Sun's.
6 Betelgeuse A red supergiant: diameter 300–400 times larger and brightness 15,000 times greater than the Sun's.

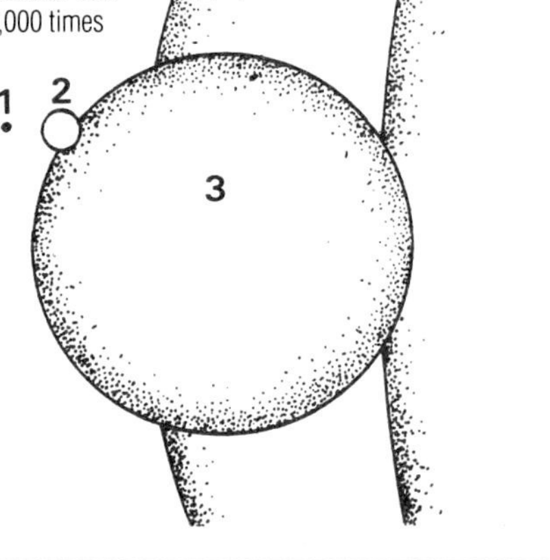

Celestial poles

1123

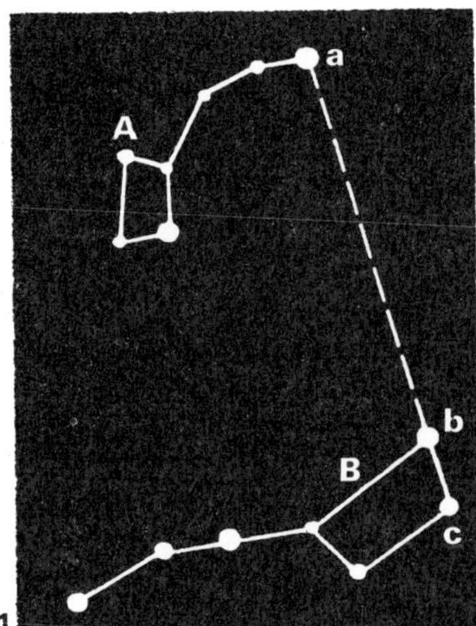

The North and South Celestial Poles are the equivalents in the sky of the North and South Poles on Earth. Earth's axis joins the North and South Poles: extended northward it points to the North Celestial Pole, and extended southward it points to the South Celestial Pole.
1 North Celestial Pole The North Celestial Pole is roughly marked by the star Polaris (**a**) in the constellation Ursa Minor (the Little Dipper) (**A**). Polaris is only three-quarters of one degree away from the true pole. To find Polaris, find Ursa Major (the Big Dipper) (**B**) and extend the imaginary line joining the two stars known as the Pointers (**b** and **c**).
2 South Celestial Pole There is no star marking the South Celestial Pole; the nearest star visible to the naked eye is Sigma Octantis (**d**). To find the South Celestial Pole, find the constellation of the Southern Cross (**C**) and extend the imaginary line joining the two stars that form its longer arm (**e** and **f**).

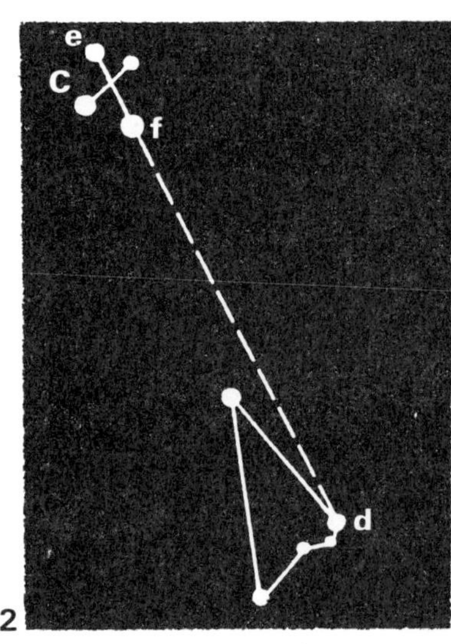

Sky maps

1124

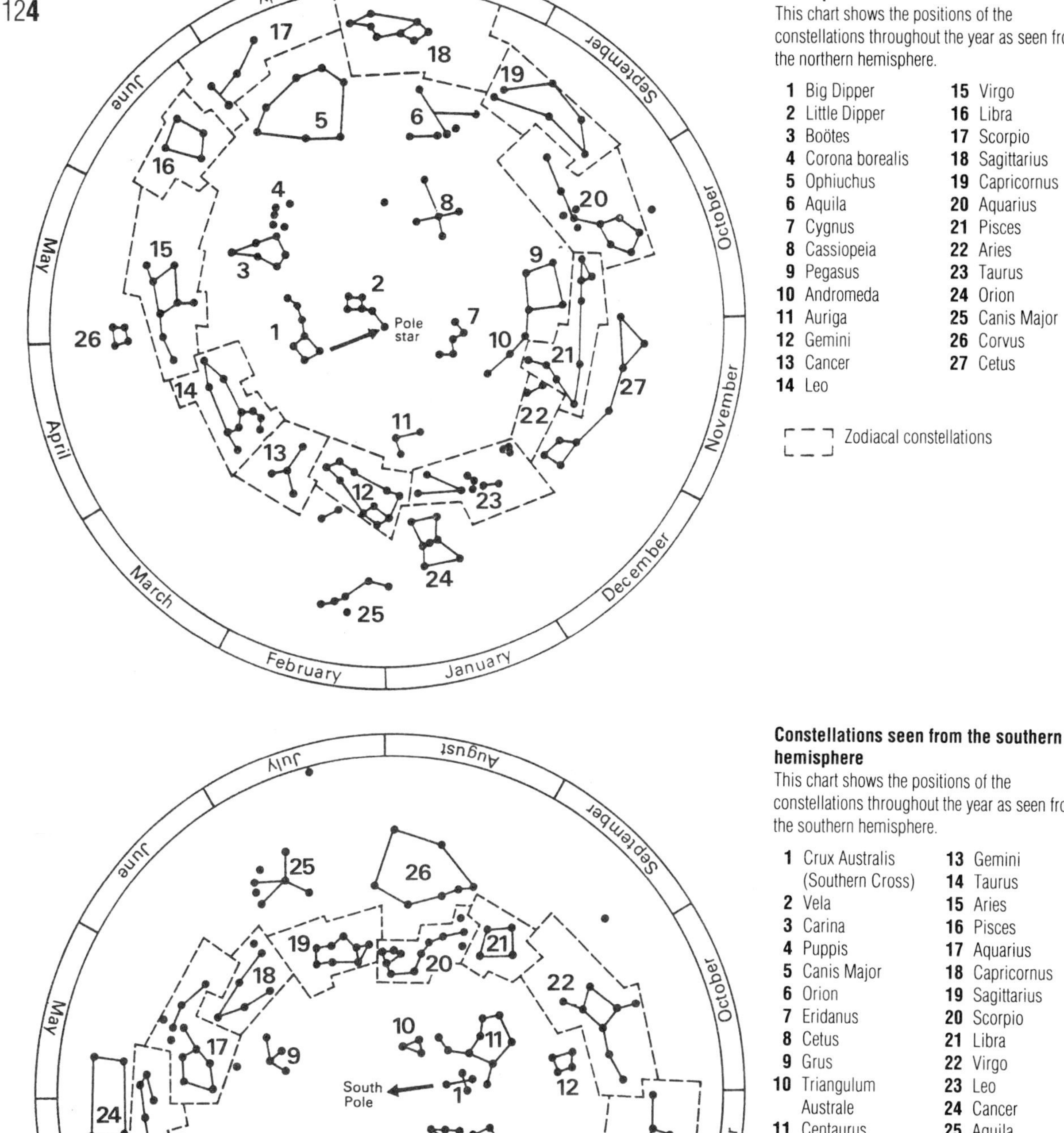

Constellations seen from the northern hemisphere
This chart shows the positions of the constellations throughout the year as seen from the northern hemisphere.

- **1** Big Dipper
- **2** Little Dipper
- **3** Boötes
- **4** Corona borealis
- **5** Ophiuchus
- **6** Aquila
- **7** Cygnus
- **8** Cassiopeia
- **9** Pegasus
- **10** Andromeda
- **11** Auriga
- **12** Gemini
- **13** Cancer
- **14** Leo
- **15** Virgo
- **16** Libra
- **17** Scorpio
- **18** Sagittarius
- **19** Capricornus
- **20** Aquarius
- **21** Pisces
- **22** Aries
- **23** Taurus
- **24** Orion
- **25** Canis Major
- **26** Corvus
- **27** Cetus

Zodiacal constellations (dashed outline)

Constellations seen from the southern hemisphere
This chart shows the positions of the constellations throughout the year as seen from the southern hemisphere.

- **1** Crux Australis (Southern Cross)
- **2** Vela
- **3** Carina
- **4** Puppis
- **5** Canis Major
- **6** Orion
- **7** Eridanus
- **8** Cetus
- **9** Grus
- **10** Triangulum Australe
- **11** Centaurus
- **12** Corvus
- **13** Gemini
- **14** Taurus
- **15** Aries
- **16** Pisces
- **17** Aquarius
- **18** Capricornus
- **19** Sagittarius
- **20** Scorpio
- **21** Libra
- **22** Virgo
- **23** Leo
- **24** Cancer
- **25** Aquila
- **26** Ophiuchus

Zodiacal constellations (dashed outline)

Constellations

1125 Stars have been divided into the artificial groups called constellations for over 2,000 years. Listed here are the Latin names and English equivalents of 88 constellations recognized by astronomers.

N = Northern
E = Ecliptic or zodiacal
S = Southern

Andromeda, Andromeda (N)
Antlia, the air pump (S)
Apus, the bird of paradise (S)
Aquarius, the water-bearer (E)
Aquila, the eagle (N)
Ara, the altar (S)
Aries, the ram (E)
Auriga, the charioteer (N)
Boötes, the herdsman (N)
Caelum, the chisel (S)
Camelopardus, the giraffe (N)
Cancer, the crab (E)
Canes Venatici, the hunting dogs (N)
Canis Major, the great dog (S)
Canis Minor, the little dog (S)
Capricornus, the goat (E)
Carina, the keel (S)
Cassiopeia, lady in the chair (N)
Centaurus, the centaur (S)
Cepheus, the king (N)
Cetus, the sea monster, the whale (S)
Chamaeleon, the chameleon (S)
Circinus, the compasses (S)
Columba, the dove (S)
Coma Berenices, Berenice's hair (N)
Corona Australis, the southern crown (S)
Corona Borealis, the northern crown (N)
Corvus, the crow (S)
Crater, the cup (S)
Crux Australis, the southern cross (S)
Cygnus, the swan (N)
Delphinus, the dolphin (N)
Dorado, the swordfish (S)
Draco, the dragon (N)
Equuleus, the foal (N)
Eridanus, the river Eridanus or the river Po (S)
Fornax, the furnace (S)
Gemini, the twins (E)
Grus, the crane (S)
Hercules, Hercules (N)
Horologium, the clock (S)
Hydra, the water snake (S)
Hydrus, the sea serpent (S)
Indus, the Indian (S)
Lacerta, the lizard (N)
Leo, the lion (E)
Leo Minor, the little lion (N)
Lepus, the hare (S)
Libra, the scales, the balance (E)
Lupus, the wolf (S)
Lynx, the lynx (N)
Lyra, the lyre (N)
Mensa, the table (S)
Microscorpium, the microscope (S)
Monoceros, the unicorn (S)
Musca Australis, the southern fly (S)
Norma, the ruler (S)
Octans, the octant (S)
Ophiuchus, the serpent-bearer (N)
Orion, Orion the hunter (S)
Pavo, the peacock (S)
Pegasus, the winged horse (N)
Perseus, Perseus (N)
Phoenix, the phoenix (S)
Pictor, the painter's easel (S)
Pisces, the fishes (E)
Piscis Austrinus, the southern fish (S)
Puppis, the ship's stern (S)
Pyxis, the mariner's compass (S)
Reticulum, the net (S)
Sagitta, the arrow (N)
Sagittarius, the archer (E)
Scorpio, the scorpion (E)
Sculptor, the sculptor (S)
Scutum, the shield (N)
Serpens, the serpent (N)
Sextans, the sextant (S)
Taurus, the bull (E)
Telescopium, the telescope (S)
Triangulum, the triangle (N)
Triangulum Australe, the southern triangle (S)
Tucana, the toucan (S)
Ursa Major, the great bear, the Big Dipper (N)
Ursa Minor, the little bear, the Little Dipper (N)
Vela, the sails (S)
Virgo, the virgin (E)
Volans, the flying fish (S)
Vulpecula, the fox (N)

Identifying constellations

1126 **How to use the sky maps**
To use the maps on the previous page, turn the page around until the current month is at the bottom. Choose a clear night to look for the stars. Below are some examples.

1 From the northern hemisphere
a The position of the Big Dipper in April
b The position of the Big Dipper in October

a

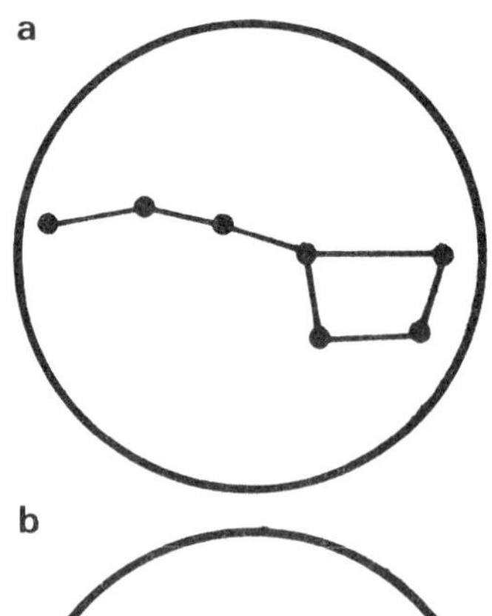

b

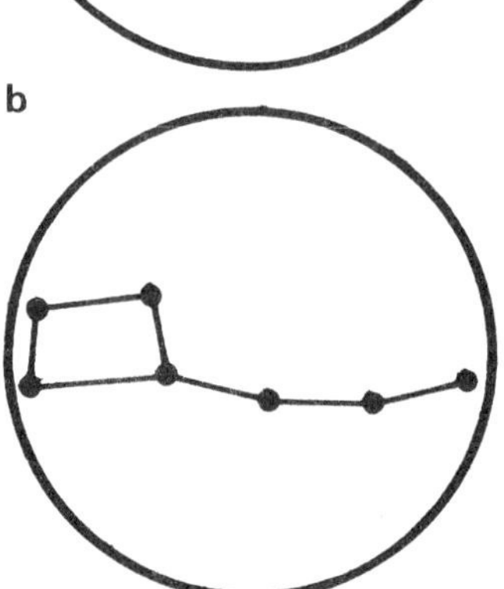

2 From the southern hemisphere
a The position of the Southern Cross in April
b The position of the Southern Cross in January

a

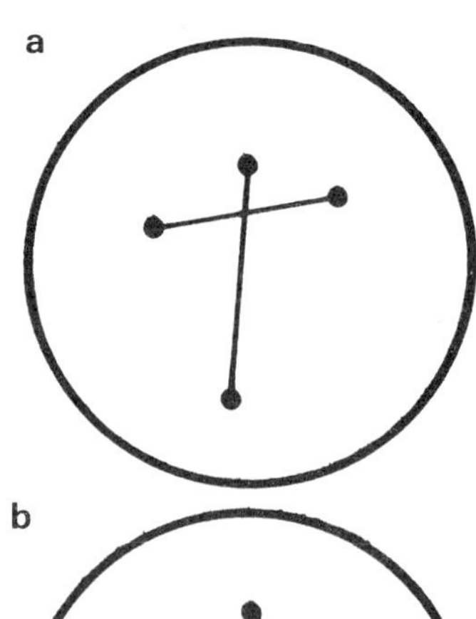

b

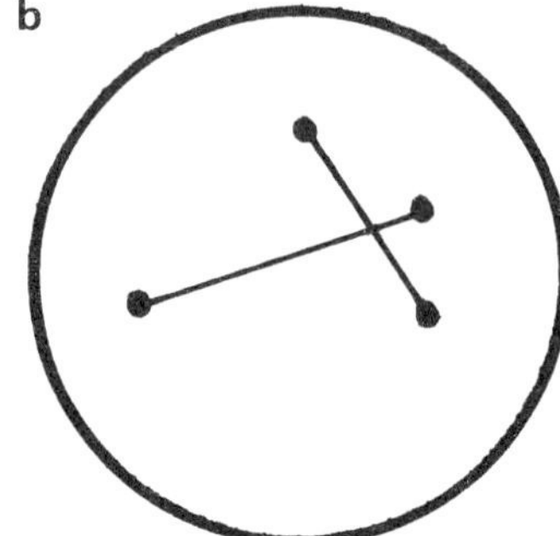

113 SUN, EARTH, MOON

Age

1131 Astronomers believe the Earth and its moon (referred to as the Moon) were formed separately but at the same time and close to each other in space. Tests on Moon rocks brought back to Earth show that the Earth and the Moon are about the same age – 4.6 billion years old. The Sun is thought to be about 5 billion years old.

Rotations

1132 Here is shown the relationship between the Earth, the Sun, and the Moon. Arrows indicate the direction of rotation.
1 The Earth The Earth's mean distance from the Sun is 93 million mi (150 million km) (**a**). The Earth orbits the Sun in 365.25 days. Meanwhile, the Earth rotates every 23 hr 56 min.
2 The Moon It takes 27.3 days for the Moon to complete one orbit of the Earth. Because it takes exactly the same time for the Moon to turn once on its own axis, the same side of the Moon always faces the Earth. The far side of the Moon can be seen only from space.
3 The Sun The Sun, like the Earth, rotates on its axis. Because the Sun is made of gas it can rotate at different speeds at different latitudes: it rotates more slowly at its poles than at its equator. Rotation periods are approximately 34–7 days at its poles and 24–6 days at its equator.

a

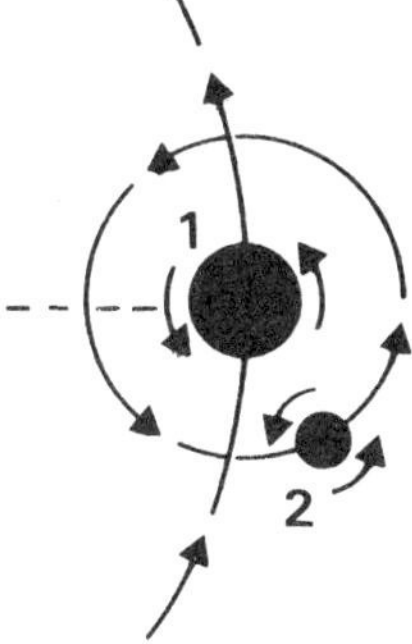

Tides

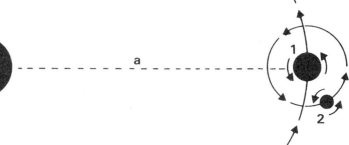

1133 The pull of the Moon's gravity is the main cause of the tides in the Earth's seas and oceans, although the Sun also has an influence. The highest ("spring") tides occur when the Moon and Sun pull along the same line (**1** and **2**); the lowest ("neap") tides occur when they pull at right angles (**3** and **4**).

1

3
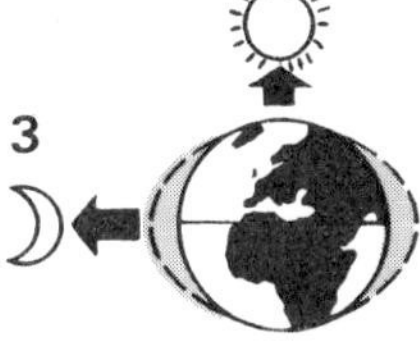

2

4
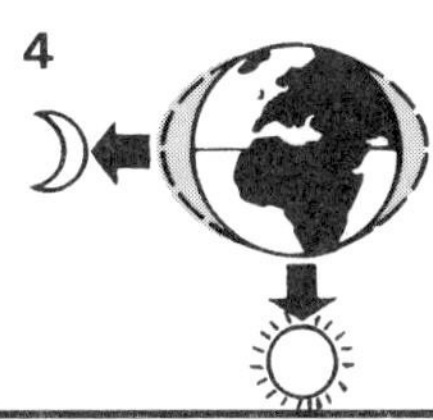

Phases of the Moon

1134

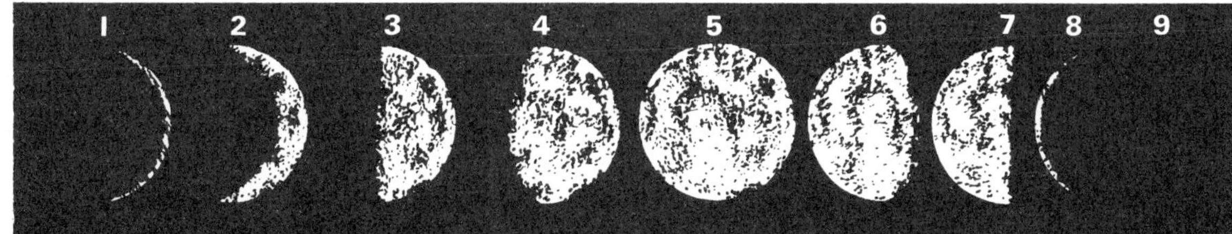

The Moon produces no light of its own: it shines because it reflects sunlight. The amount of the lit half that can be seen from the Earth changes from day to day. These regular changes are known as phases of the Moon. Here we show how the Moon appears from the Earth at different stages during the month. The interval between one new Moon and the next is 29 days, 12 hr, 44 min, 3 sec.

Names of the phases
A waxing Moon is one that becomes increasingly visible; a waning Moon becomes less visible; a gibbous ("humped") Moon is between the half and full phases.
1 New Moon
2 Waxing crescent Moon
3 Half Moon, first quarter
4 Waxing gibbous Moon
5 Full Moon
6 Waning gibbous Moon
7 Half Moon, last quarter
8 Waning crescent Moon
9 New Moon

Eclipses

1135 **1 Eclipse of the Moon** This occurs when the Earth (**a**) is in a direct line between the Sun (**b**) and Moon (**c**). The Moon is then in the Earth's shadow and cannot receive any direct sunlight. It becomes dim and appears coppery-red in color. There are never more than three eclipses of the Moon in a year.

2 Eclipse of the Sun From the Earth, the Sun and Moon appear to be about the same size: the Sun is about 400 times as big as the Moon but is also 400 times farther away from the Earth. When the Moon (**c**) is in a direct line between the Sun (**b**) and the Earth (**a**), the Moon's disk-shaped outline appears to cover the Sun's bright surface, or photosphere. The part of the Earth directly in the Moon's shadow (**d**) sees a total eclipse of the Sun; areas around it (**e**) see a partial eclipse.

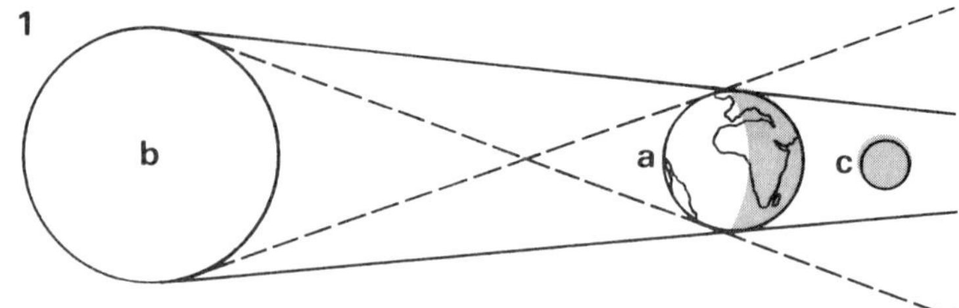

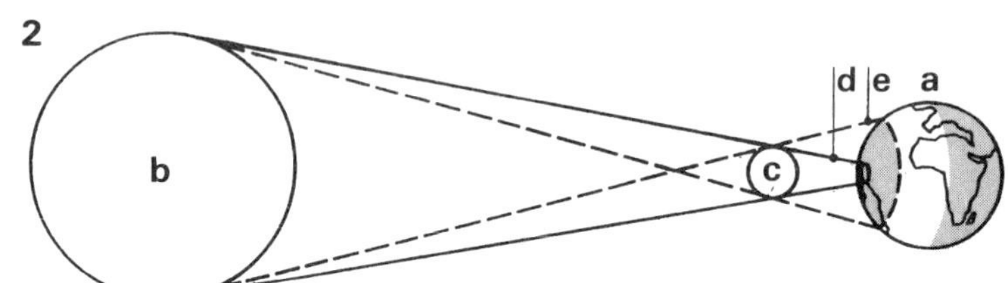

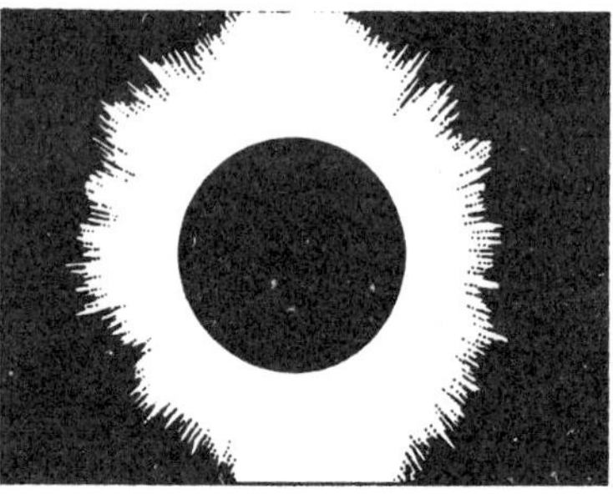

Total This can last from a split second up to a maximum of 7 min 31 sec. The area over which it is seen may have a maximum width of 169 mi (272 km), but is usually much less. The corona – the circle of light that appears as a halo around the Moon's disk during this type of eclipse – is visible to the naked eye.

Partial In this type of eclipse, the Moon's disk obscures only part of the photosphere.

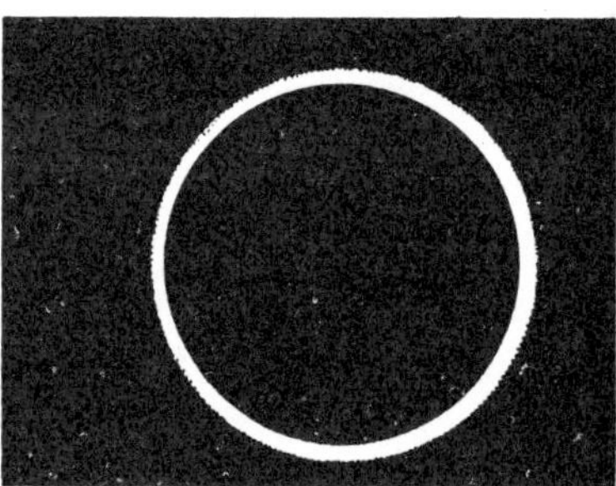

Annular This type of eclipse, named from the Latin word *annulus*, meaning ring, occurs if the Moon is at its farthest point from the Earth and the Earth is at its nearest point to the Sun. The Moon's disk then appears slightly smaller than the photosphere.

114 THE PLANETS

Sizes

1141 The illustrations below indicate the comparative sizes of the nine planets in our solar system. The diameter of each planet, at its equator, is given here.

A Mercury 3,031 mi (4,878 km)
B Venus 7,521 mi (12,104 km)
C Earth 7,926 mi (12,756 km)
D Mars 4,222 mi (6,795 km)
E Jupiter 88,732 mi (142,800 km)
F Saturn 74,565 mi (120,000 km)
G Uranus 31,566 mi (50,800 km)
H Neptune 30,137 mi (48,500 km)
I Pluto 3,725 mi (5,995 Km)

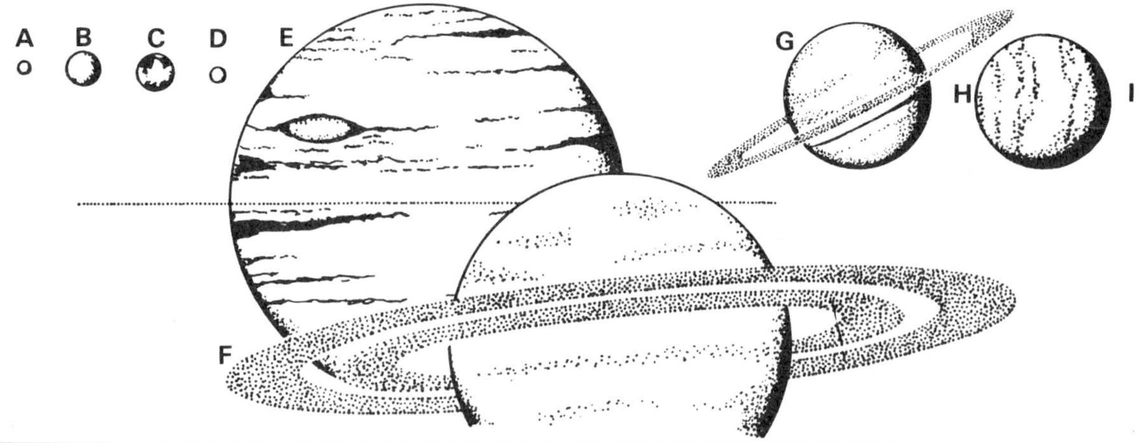

Paths of the planets

1142 Shown here are the paths taken by the nine planets.

1 Planets closest to the Sun
A Mercury
B Venus
C Earth
D Mars
2 Planets farthest from the Sun
E Jupiter
F Saturn
G Uranus
H Neptune
I Pluto

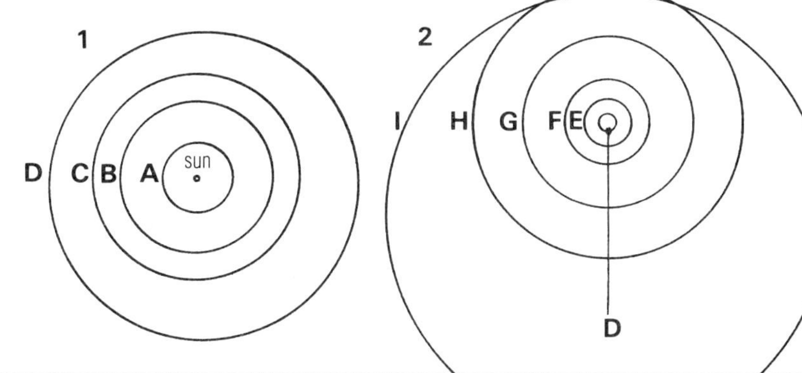

Planetary rings

1143 Planetary rings, made up of millions of particles, are known to orbit the planets Jupiter, Saturn, Uranus, and Neptune. They are rarely more than a few hundred yards in thickness but may be many thousands of yards wide. Saturn (**a**) is thought to have more than 1,000 separate rings (**b**).

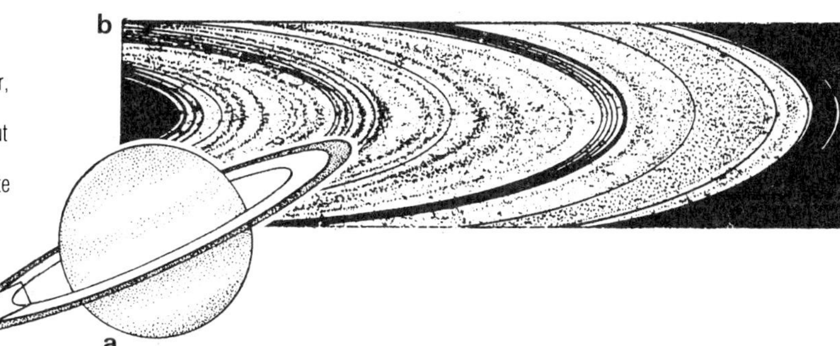

Planetary satellites

1144

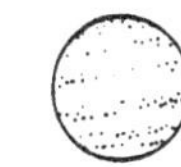

Earth
- Moon

Mars
- Phobos
- Deimos

Jupiter
- Metis
- Adrastea
- Amalthea
- Thebe
- Io
- Europa
- Ganymede
- Callisto
- Leda
- Himalia
- Lysithea
- Elara
- Ananke
- Carme
- Pasiphae
- Sinope

Saturn
- 1980 S.28
- 1980 S.27
- 1980 S.26
- Epimetheus
- Janus
- Mimas
- Mimas co-orbital
- Enceladus
- Tethys
- Calypso
- Telesto
- Dione
- 1980 S.6
- Dione co-orbital
- Rhea
- Titan
- Hyperion
- Iapetus
- Phoebe

Uranus
- Miranda
- Ariel
- Umbriel
- Titania
- Oberon

Neptune
- Triton
- Nereid
- ○ unconfirmed but suspected satellite

Pluto
- Charon

A satellite is a companion body that orbits a planet. Earth's satellite is the Moon. Listed here, – in order of their distance from the planet, closest first – are the known satellites orbiting each planet. Venus and Mercury do not have satellites.

Extraterrestrials

1145 Some scientists calculate that our civilization stands alone in the universe. Others contend that there could be many thousands of worlds inhabited by intelligent beings. Even so, all would be too distant to reach by astronaut-controlled space exploration. Longwave radio signals, though, might reveal them. Reasoning that water (formed from hydrogen and oxygen) is essential to life everywhere, some scientists think that intelligent beings would broadcast in the narrow band of "water-hole" frequencies: the band between those at which oxygen and hydrogen naturally radiate radio energy. Water-hole radio searches have already begun, so far without success. Hundreds of years' probing millions of stars might be needed before we make contact, if indeed there is any intelligence there.

Another approach would be to use radio telescopes to pick up the din of radio noise broadcast by a planet's radio, television, and radar transmitters. (Such signals already make our own world a more powerful radio transmitter than the Sun.)

Schemes such as Project Cyclops would call for a massive array of radio telescopes that are able to eavesdrop on radio noise from planets 1,000 light years from ours. But the huge cost makes such grandiose schemes unlikely to happen.

Comparisons

1146

	Mercury	Venus	Earth	Mars	Jupiter	Saturn
Average distance from Sun	0.39au	0.72au	1.00au	1.52au	5.20au	9.54au
Distance at perihelion	0.31au	0.72au	0.98au	1.38au	4.95au	9.01au
Distance at aphelion	0.47au	0.73au	1.02au	1.67au	5.46au	10.07au
Closest distance to Earth	0.54au	0.27au		0.38au	3.95au	8.00au
Average orbital speed	29.76 mi/sec (47.9 km/sec)	21.75 mi/sec (35.0 km/sec)	18.52 mi/sec (29.8 km/sec)	14.98 mi/sec (24.1 km/sec)	8.14 mi/sec (13.1 km/sec)	5.98 mi/sec (9.6 km/sec)
Rotation period	58 days 15 hr	243 days	23 hr 56 min	24 hr 37 min	9 hr 50 min	10 hr 14 min
Sidereal period	88 days	224.7 days	365.3 days	687 days	11.86 years	29.46 years
Diameter at equator	3,031 mi (4,878 km)	7,521 mi (12,104 km)	7,926 mi (12,756 km)	4,222 mi (6,795 km)	88,732 mi (142,800 km)	74,565 mi (120,000 km)
Mass (Earth's mass = 1)	0.06	0.82	1	0.11	317.9	95.1
Surface temperature	662°F,day-338°F,night (350° C,day-170° C,night)	896° F (480° C)	71.6° F (22° C)	-9.4° F (-23° C)	-238° F (-150° C)	-292° F (-180° C)
Surface gravity (Earth's gravity = 1)	0.38	0.88	1	0.38	2.64	1.15
Density (density of water = 1)	5.5	5.25	5.52	3.94	1.33	0.71
Number of satellites known	0	0	1	2	16	19
Number of rings known	0	0	0	0	1	1,000-
Main gases in atmosphere	No atmosphere	Carbon dioxide	Nitrogen oxide	Carbon dioxide	Hydrogen helium	Hydrogen helium

115 SPACE EXPLORATION 1957–90

US

1958 National Aeronautics and Space Adminstration (NASA) founded. First US satellite, Explorer 1 (**a**), finds Van Allen radiation belts.
1960 First weather satellite: Tiros (**b**).
1961 First US-crewed spaceflight (Alan Shepard).
1962 John Glenn is first American to orbit the Earth. First TV-relay satellite: Telstar (**c**).
1963 Quasars first identified from Mt Palomar Observatory, California.
1965 Gemini (**d**) missions practice two-person flight, space walks, and docking (–1966).
1966 Surveyor 1 (uncrewed) lands on Moon.
1967 First astronauts die (in ground fire). Apollo program delayed 18 months.
1968 Apollo 8 (**e**) makes first crewed orbit of Moon.
1969 First humans walk on the Moon: Neil Armstrong and Buzz Aldrin from Apollo 11 (July 21). Five more Apollo Moon landings (–1972).
1973 First US space station: Skylab (4 missions).
1975 First international space docking: Apollo 18 and Soyuz 19.
1976 First Mars surface landing, by uncrewed Viking 1.
1979 First spacecraft to visit Saturn: Pioneer 11.
1981 First space shuttle flight (**f**).
1983 First US woman in space: Sally Ride aboard shuttle Columbia. First probe to leave solar system: Pioneer 10 (launched 1972).
1986 24th space shuttle flight: Challenger explodes (Jan 28), killing crew of seven. Voyager 2 (launched 1977) reaches Uranus, finds ten more moons.
1988 Discovery resumes space shuttle flights.

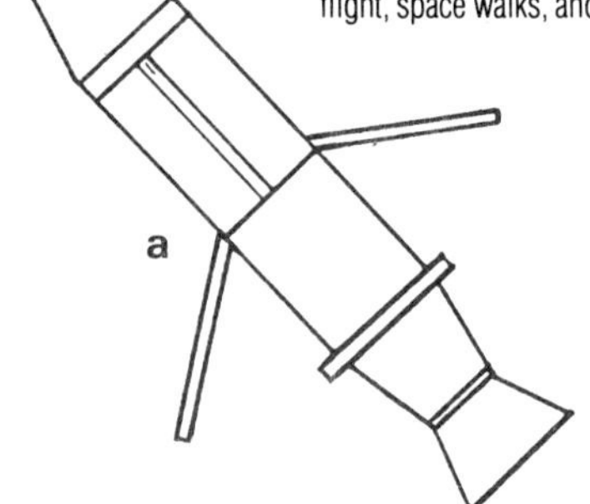

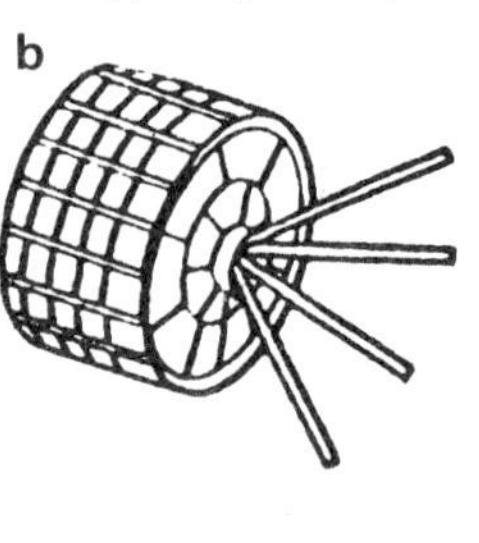

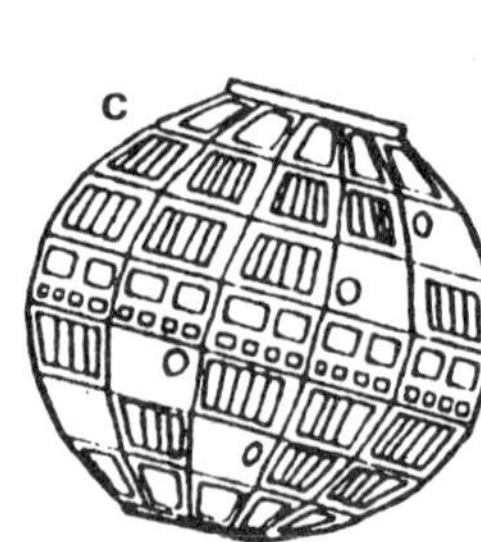

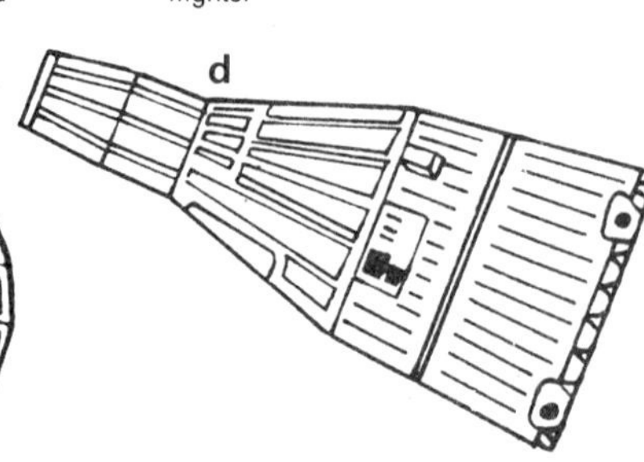

continued

Uranus	Neptune	Pluto	Sun	Moon	
19.18au	30.06au	39.36au		1.00au	**Average distance from Sun**
18.28au	29.80au	29.58au			**Distance at perihelion**
20.09au	30.32au	49.14au			**Distance at aphelion**
17.28au	28.80au	28.72au	0.98au	0.0024au	**Closest distance to Earth**
4.23 mi/sec (6.8 km/sec)	3.36 mi/sec (5.4 km/sec)	2.92 mi/sec (4.7 km/sec)		0.621 mi/sec (1 km/sec)	**Average orbital speed**
16 hr 10 min	18 hr 26 min	6 days 9 hr	1 month	27 days 7 hr 43 min	**Rotation period**
84.01 years	164.8 years	247.7 years			**Sidereal period**
31,566 mi (50,800 Km)	30,137 mi (48,500 Km)	3,725 mi (5,995 Km)	863,746 mi (1.39 million km)	2,160 mi (3,476 km)	**Diameter at equator**
14.6	17.2	0.002–0.003	333,000	0.012	**Mass (Earth's mass = 1)**
-346° F (-210° C)	-364° F (-220° C)	-382° F (-230° C)	9,932° F (5,500° C)	260–536° F (127–280° C)	**Surface temperature**
1.17	1.2	not known		0.165	**Surface gravity (Earth's gravity = 1)**
1.2	1.67	not known	0.1–100	3.34	**Density (density of water = 1)**
5	3	1	9 planets	0	**Number of satellites known**
9	0	0	0	0	**Number of rings known**
Hydrogen helium, methane	Hydrogen helium, methane	Methane	Hydrogen helium		**Main gases in atmosphere**

1989 Galileo probe taken up by shuttle Atlantis for Jupiter 1995 mission.
1990 Hubble Space Telescope launched by Discovery has many flaws.

USSR
1957 First satellite, Sputnik 1, launched (Oct 4) to start the space age (**g**).
1959 Rocket Luna 2 hits the Moon.
1961 First crewed space flight by Yuri Gagarin in Vostok 1: single orbit (**h**).
1962 First dual mission: Vostok 3 and 4.
1963 First woman in space: Valentina Tereshkova in Vostok 6.
1965 First space walk: Alexei Leonov from Voskhod 6.
1966 Venera 3 (uncrewed) hits Venus.
1969 First space walk transfer between Soyuz 5 and 4.
1970 First space station launched: Salyut 1; but three cosmonauts die on return flight.
1975 First double docking. First photos from Venus's surface by Venera 9.
1987 First permanently crewed space station, Mir, sets 326-day crew duration record.

OTHERS
1961 Parkes radio telescope completed west of Sydney, Australia.
1965 First French satellite: A-1 Astérix.
1970 First Chinese and Japanese satellites: China 1 and Osumi.
1975 European Space Agency (ESA) founded.
1979 Ariane satellite launcher first used.
1980 First satellite launched by India.
1985 First Arab in space: Saudi prince aboard US shuttle Discovery.

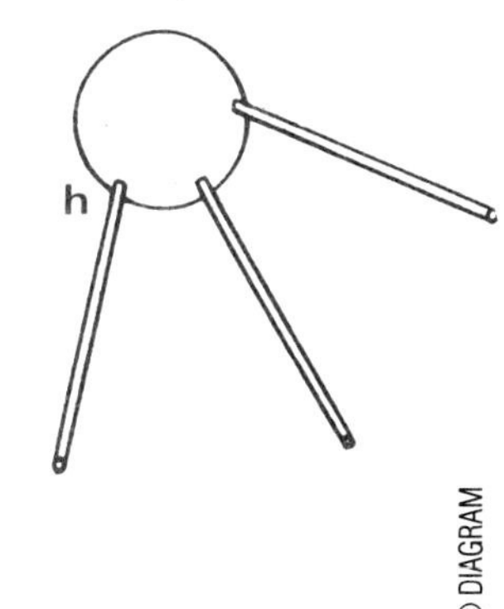

116 ASTRONOMY GLOSSARY

aberration Apparent changes in the position of a celestial body, brought about by the movement of the earth in relation to it.
absolute magnitude A star's size when seen from 10 pc.
albedo The proportion of incoming light reflected – e.g. the Moon reflects 7% of sunlight received.
aphelion The point in a planet's orbit farthest from the Sun.
asteroids Lumps of metal or rock in many sizes concentrated in parts of the solar system.
aurora Northern and southern "polar lights" sometimes seen in Earth's upper atmosphere and created by solar particles striking atoms.
big bang theory The explosive birth of the universe reputedly 13–20 billion years ago. According to the theory, formulated in 1927, the universe is still expanding. It is now obsolete to some extent. Compare with "steady state theory."
black hole Object with large mass but small size, from which no light can escape. Formed in the first moments in the life of the universe.
comet A dust, gas, and ice body that orbits the Sun and develops a long, bright tail on nearing the Sun.
constellation An apparent grouping of prominent stars.
corona The Sun's gaseous outer layer that emits solar wind and is visible as a halo during a total solar eclipse.
cosmology The study of the universe.
critical density The amount of matter and energy in the universe which if exceeded will delay and even reverse the universe's expansion.
curved space The concept that light takes a curved path through space near massive objects
declination A star's angular distance in degrees N or S of the celestial equator. Equivalent to the Earth's latitude.
ecliptic The Sun's apparent path across the sky.
elongation angle As seen from the Earth, the angle between the Sun and a planet or the latter and a satellite.
equinox "Equal night," the two points at which the ecliptic intersects the celestial equator to produce the seasonal spring (vernal) equinox and autumnal (fall) equinox.
Fraunhofer lines Dark lines seen on the Sun and other stars, named after their 1814 Bavarian discoverer.
gravitational collapse Action of a star when its hydrogen and other energy supplies are unable to maintain gravitation. The collapse's result can be a black hole, white dwarf, neutron star, or supernova.
Halley's comet A comet that orbits the Sun about every 76 years (first recorded 240 BC, last seen 1986, next due 2061).
HR (Hertzsprung–Russell) diagram A graph (devised 1911–13) plotting stars' colors against their brightness in descending order, with the Sun midway in the sequence.
Hubble's Constant/Law, Hubble flow In 1924, Edwin P. Hubble discovered that the farther away a galaxy is, the faster its apparent speed. The speed-to-distance ratio is the constant, now measured at 30–60 mi/sec (50–100 km/sec) per million pc.
International Astronomical Union (IAU) A world body founded in 1919.
Kepler's laws Three laws (1609–19) formulated by German astronomer Johann Kepler. (1) The planetary orbits are elliptical. (2) A planet's velocity is greater the nearer it is to the Sun. (3) The square of a planet's orbital period is proportional to the cube of its distance from the Sun.
local group of galaxies Cluster of more than 24 galaxies, including our Milky Way. Andromeda is the largest galaxy.
luminosity A star's essential brightness.
Magellanic Clouds Two Milky Way satellite galaxies visible to the human eye in the southern hemisphere and found by Europeans during the first circumnavigation of the world (1519–22).
magnetosphere The region near the planet possessing a magnetic field, which determines the motion of the charged particles in this region. Earth, Saturn, Jupiter, Uranus, and Mercury are the solar system planets known to have magnetospheres.
magnitude A star's brightness measured as either absolute magnitude or apparent magnitude. The latter states brightness in the sky on a scale from -26.8 (the Sun, brightest) to +25 (the faintest).
meteor Tiny cometary fragments observable as "shooting stars" when burning up in the Earth's atmosphere. About 100 million meteors a day enter the Earth's atmosphere.
meteorite A rock or metal lump that has fallen to Earth; thought to be asteroid debris.
Milky Way Spiral galaxy home of our solar system. Its 150 billion stars extend for 500,000 light years and have existed for about 12 billion years.
nebula A dust and gas cloud formed in space: a source of stars.
neutron star The smallest but densest kind of star, apparently resulting from a supernova explosion that compressed the star's particles into subatomic neutrons. A neutron star 15 mi (25 km) across can equal the Sun's mass.
nova A star that briefly grows intensely bright.
orbit Curving path of one space object around another.
perihelion A planet's closest orbital position to the Sun.
perturbation One space body's gravitational effect on another's orbit.
pulsar Rapidly rotating neutron star that gives off regular bursts of radio waves.
quasars Short for "quasi-stellar radio source," very remote but extremely bright objects, thought to be at the hearts of galaxies existing on the fringes of the universe. The first of more than 600 was discovered in 1963.
radar astronomy Use of radar to track solar system objects. Beyond Saturn, the signal is too weak.
radio astronomy Collection and analysis of radio waves from space, a technique that began in 1937.
red giant A star 10–100 times the Sun's size.
red shift The faster an object moves away from Earth the redder its light spectrum becomes.
reflector Telescope with a concave mirror to focus light back to an eyepiece. Isaac Newton built the first one in about 1668.
refractor Telescope with a lens that refracts light onto a particular point that is magnified for the eye.
right ascension (ra) A space object's angular distance to the east of the vernal equinox.
sidereal period The time taken for a planet to orbit the Sun once.
sidereal time Time measured by Earth's rotation against the stars.
star An object maintained by its own gravity and shining due to the radiant energy produced by the nuclear fusion at its core.
steady state theory The universe has always existed and been expanding. This theory, formulated in 1954, has been largely rejected in favour of the big bang theory.
stellar aberration A star's apparent elliptical course around its true position as Earth orbits the Sun.
supernova An exploding star that leaves a neutron star remnant.
white dwarf (star) Roughly Earth-sized and compacted remnant of a star that has collapsed but is not yet a neutron star.
zodiac A zone divided into 12 constellations along the ecliptic.

117 ASTRONOMERS

Adams, John Couch 1819–92, English professor of astronomy at Cambridge University from 1858, director of Cambridge Observatory from 1861. In 1845, almost simultaneously with Leverrier, mathematically deduced existence and location of planet Neptune.

Baade, (Wilhelm Heinrich) Walter 1893–1960, German-born American astronomer whose work, involving new ways of identifying and classifying stars, led him to increase and improve Hubble's values for size and age of universe. Also worked on supernovae and on radiostars.

Bessel, Friedrich Wilhelm 1784–1846, German astronomer and mathematician who cataloged stars, predicted planets beyond Uranus as well as existence of dark stars, and systematized the mathematical functions (bearing his name) involved in Kepler's problem of heliocentricity.

Bode, Johann Elert 1747–1826, German. Became director of Berlin Observatory. In 1772, publicized Bode's Law, attempting to describe mathematical relationship between the planets and Sun. Law, however, does not hold for most distant planet, Pluto, and has no theoretical significance.

Bradley, James 1693–1762, English. In 1729, published discovery of aberration of light, first observational proof of Copernican hypothesis. In 1748, discovered that inclination of Earth's axis to ecliptic is not constant. Succeeded Halley as Regius professor of astronomy at Greenwich.

Brahe, Tycho or Tyge 1546–1601, Danish. In 1563, discovered serious errors in existing astronomical tables and, in 1572, observed new star in Cassiopeia, nova now known as Tycho's star. From 1576, developed accurate catalog of positions of 777 stars.

Cassini, Giovanni Domenico (Jean Dominique) 1625–1712, Italian-born French. Became professor of astronomy at Bologna in 1560 and first director of observatory at Paris in 1669. Greatly extended knowledge of Sun's parallax, periods of Jupiter, Mars, and Venus, zodiacal light, etc.

Copernicus, Nicolas 1473–1543, Polish founder of modern astronomy. In 1500, in Rome, lectured on astronomy and is said to have observed an eclipse of the moon. His *De Revolutionibus*, proving the Sun to be the center of the universe, was completed in 1530 and published just before his death.

Flamsteed, John 1646–1719, English clergyman who was appointed first astronomer-royal of England in 1675. The following year, he began observations that initiated modern practical astronomy and formed the first trustworthy catalog of fixed stars.

Fraunhofer, Joseph von 1787–1826, German physicist. Founded an optical institute in Munich in1807, and improved prisms and telescopes, enabling him to discover the dark lines in the Sun's spectrum, called Fraunhofers lines. Became a professor and academician in 1823 in Munich.

Galilei, Galileo 1564–1642, Italian astronomer, mathematician, and natural philosopher whose series of astronomical investigations convinced him of correctness of Copernican heliocentric theory and of illumination of Moon by reflection. Perfected refracting telescope.

Galle, Johann Gottfried 1812–1910, German director of Breslau Observatory from 1851 to 1857. In September 1846, at Berlin Observatory discovered planet Neptune, whose existence had already been postulated in calculations made by Leverrier.

Halley, Edmund 1656–1742, English astronomer and mathematician famous for work in cometary astronomy. Correctly predicted return (in 1758, 1835, and 1910) of comet, now named after him. First to make complete observation of transit of Mercury.

Herschel, Caroline 1750–1848, German astronomer. Discovered eight comets and several nebulae and clusters of stars. Published a star catalog in 1798.

Herschel, John Frederick William 1792–1871, English. Continued and expanded researches of father, William Herschel, discovering 525 nebulae and clusters. Pioneered celestial photography and carried out research on photo-active chemicals and wave theory of light.

Herschel, (Frederick) William 1738–1822, German-born British astronomer who greatly added to knowledge of solar system, Milky Way, and nebulae. In 1781, using his own reflecting telescope, discovered planet Uranus. Also made a famous catalog of double stars.

Hertzsprung, Ejnar 1873-1967, Danish. All later work on evolution of stars began with his work on relationships between color and brightness of stars. Also greatly developed Leavitt's method for finding stellar distances, using it to find distances outside our own galaxy.

Hevelius, Johannes 1611–87, German astronomer who cataloged 1,500 stars, discovered four comets, and was one of the first to observe transit of Mercury. Made map of Moon and gave names to many lunar features in his 1647 *Selenographia*.

Hipparchus *fl* 146–127 BC, Greek astronomer and inventor of trigonometry. Discovered precession of equinoxes and eccentricity of the Sun's path, determined length of solar year, estimated distances of Sun and Moon from Earth, and drew catalog of 1,080 stars.

Hubble, Edwin Powell 1889–1953, American. Identified some nebulae as independent galaxies. In 1929, discovered "red shift" and announced Hubble's Constant for expansion of universe, showing that the more distant the galaxy the greater the speed with which it is receding.

Huggins, William 1824–1910, English astronomer who began study of physical constitution of stars, planets, comets, and nebulae. Ascertained that luminous properties of Sun and Moon and certain comets are not the same, and determined amount of heat reaching Earth from some fixed stars.

Kepler, Johann 1571–1630, German astronomer who also made discoveries in optics, general physics, and geometry. Proved that the planets do not orbit in circles but in ellipses. His First and Second Laws are starting point of Newton's discoveries and of modern astronomy.

Kuiper, Gerard Peter 1905–73, Dutch-born American astronomer, involved with early American spaceflights, who discovered two new satellites: Miranda, fifth satellite of Uranus, and Nereid, second satellite of Neptune (1948–49).

Leavitt, Henrietta Swan 1868–1921, American astronomer who showed that apparent magnitude of brightness of Cepheid variable stars decreases linearly with logarithm of period of light variation. Work laid basis for method of measuring distance of stars.

Leverrier, Urbain Jean Joseph 1811–77, French. From disturbances in motions of planets, inferred existence of undiscovered planet and calculated point in heavens where, a few days later, Neptune was discovered by Galle (1846).

Lockyer, Joseph Norman 1836–1920, English astronomer who wrote much on solar chemistry and physics, on meteorite hypothesis, and on orientation of stone circles. Detected and named helium in Sun's chromosphere in 1868.

Lovell, (Alfred Charles) Bernard b. 1913, English radio astronomer who, in late 1940s and early 1950s, made observations on sporadic meteors using radar and succeeded in determining meteor trail heights and velocities.

Lowell, Percival 1855–1916, American astronomer best known for his observations of Mars which were intended to prove existence of artificial Martian canals, and for his prediction of existence of planet Pluto, discovered by Tombaugh in 1930.

Messier, Charles 1730–1817, French. Mapped faint unmoving objects in sky which he could discard in comet-searching, thus producing first nebula catalog in 1784. Prefix "M" still applied to these objects, which are either nebulae or star clusters.

Ptolemy, or Claudius Ptolemaeus c. 90–168, Egyptian astronomer and geographer who influenced scientists into the seventeenth century. Ptolemaic system attempts to reduce to scientific form the common notions of movement of heavenly bodies.

Russell, Henry Norris 1877–1957, American. Became professor of astronomy at Princeton University in 1911. Suggested a now superseded theory of stellar evolution in which stars begin as dim dull objects, shrink and heat up, and then cool again to become red stars once more.

Sagan, Carl Edward b.1934, American astronomer who, through books and television program, has done much to popularize this aspect of science. Has done work on physics and chemistry of planetary atmospheres and surfaces, and on origin of life on Earth.

Schiaparelli, Giovanni Virginio 1835–1910, Italian. Head of Brera Observatory in Milan. Studied meteors and double stars and discovered "canals" of Mars (1877) and asteroid Hesperia (1861).

Tombaugh, Clyde William b.1906, American astronomer. Professor at California University, where he discovered Pluto (1930) and galactic star clusters.

121 EARTH'S ORIGIN

Evolution of the Earth

1211

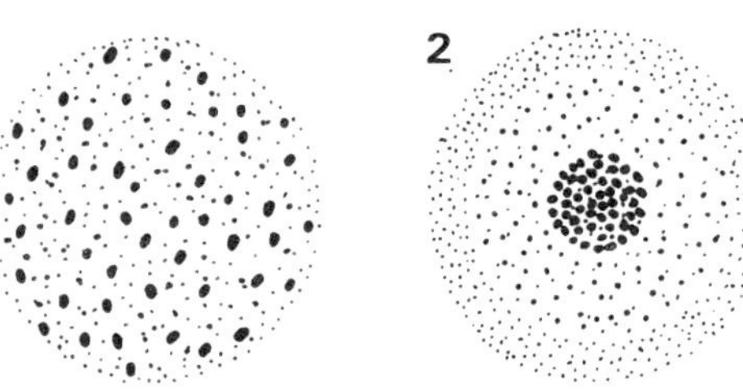

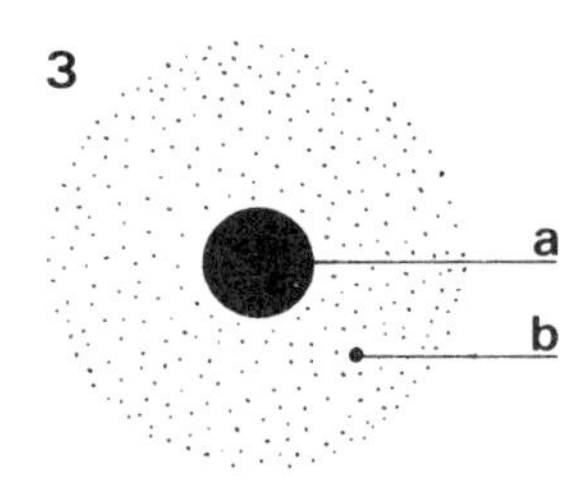

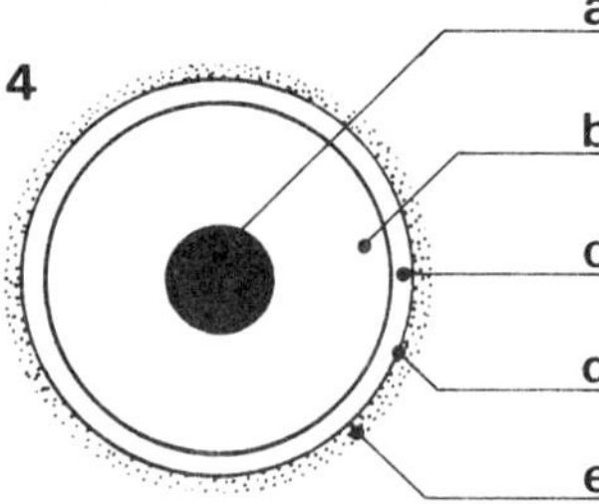

The Earth may have formed in the following four stages:
1 Cloud of particles of various chemical compounds.
2 Densest particles sink inward.
3 Continued sorting of particles leads to primeval planet Earth:
a Dense core of iron and nickel
b Less dense matter similar to that of the meteorites known as carbonaceous chondrites
4 Formation of the Earth's major layers:
a Dense core
b Less dense mantle (melted chondrite)
c Crust
d Ocean
e Primeval atmosphere

Evolving continents

1212

1 200 million years ago, the supercontinent Pangaea ("All Earth") was breaking up and its components had just begun to drift apart.
2 140 million years ago, break-up had produced a northern landmass, Laurasia, and a southern landmass, Gondwanaland, separated by a narrow ocean called the Tethys Sea. Each landmass was breaking up to form the continents we know today.
3 65 million years ago, the widening Atlantic Ocean had separated the Americas from Africa, and continents were gaining their present shapes and positions. India had broken free from Africa but not yet docked with Asia.
4 This shows the current shapes and positions of the seven continents: North and South America, Europe, Asia (Eurasia), Africa, Australia, and Antarctica. The Atlantic Ocean is still widening.

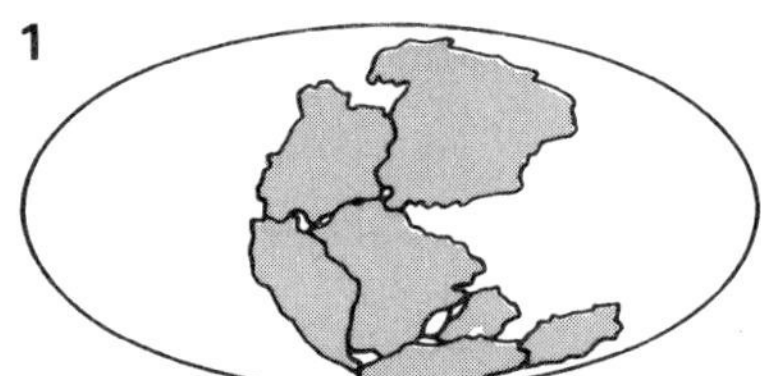

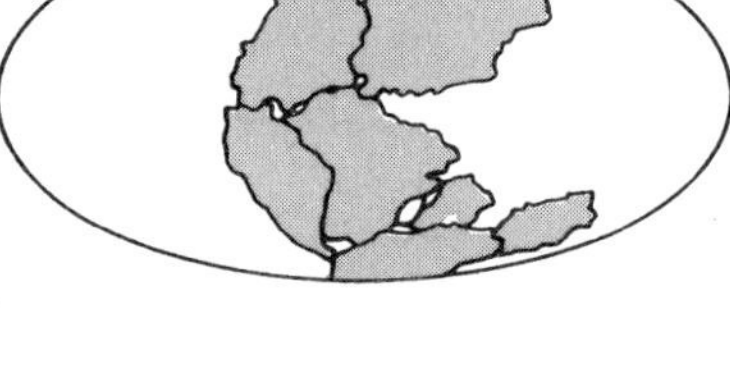

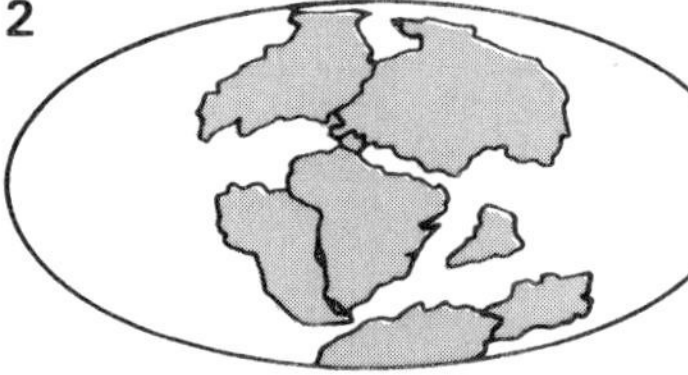

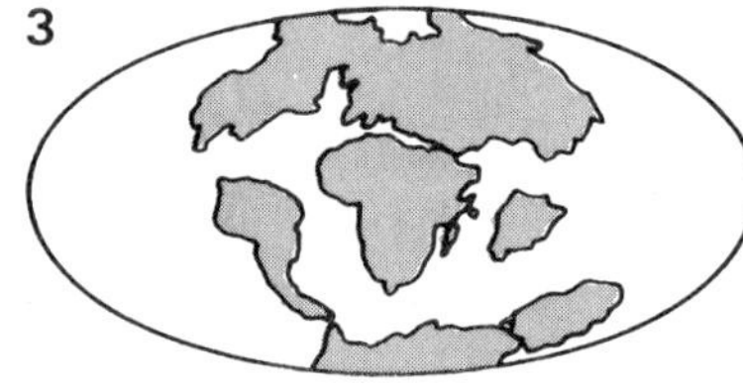

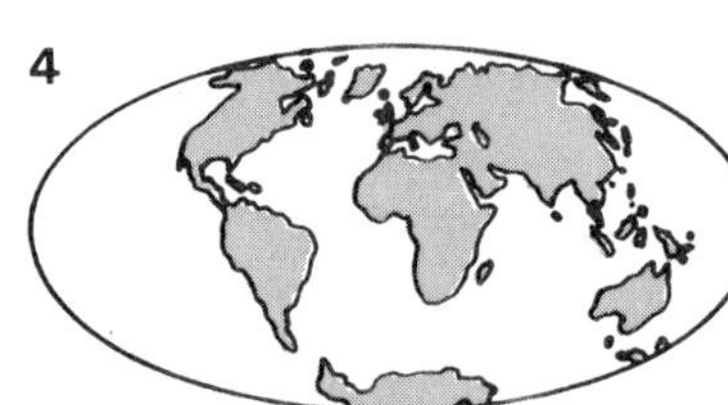

122 EARTH'S COMPOSITION

Layers

1221

The Earth comprises three major layers:
1 Crust: a thin skin of hard rock 6 – 40 mi (10 – 64 km) thick. Continental crust is less dense but thicker than oceanic crust.
2 Mantle: dense, semi-molten rock 1,800 mi (2,900 km) thick. Parts flow sluggishly as convection currents rise through the mantle.
3 Core: the densest, hottest layer, 4,340 mi (6,985 km) in diameter, made mainly of iron and nickel. The outer core is molten; the inner core is solid.

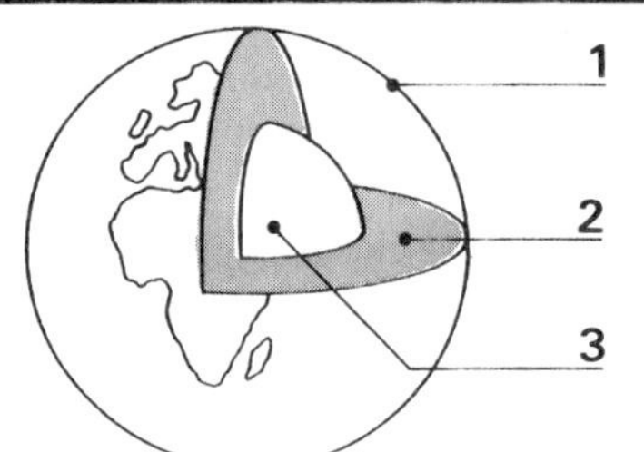

Elements in the crust

1222

The relative abundance of different elements making up the Earth's crust is shown. Of the Earth's 92 naturally occuring elements, eight account for 98% of the weight of the Earth's crust. These combine to become the "rock forming" minerals.

1 Oxygen 46.6%
2 Silicon 27.72%
3 Aluminum 8.13%
4 Iron 5.0%
5 Calcium 3.63%
6 Sodium 2.83%
7 Potassium 2.59%
8 Magnesium 2.09%
9 Other elements 1.41%

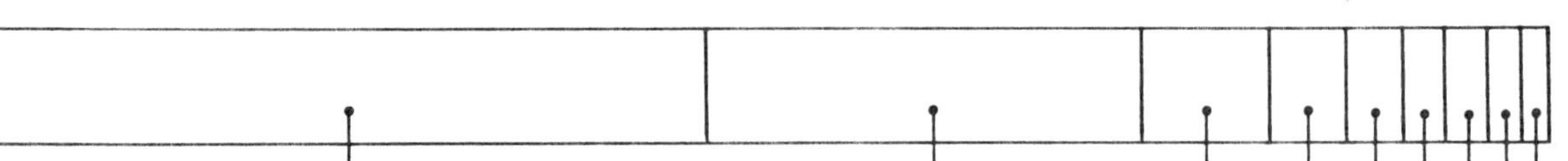

Crystal systems

1223

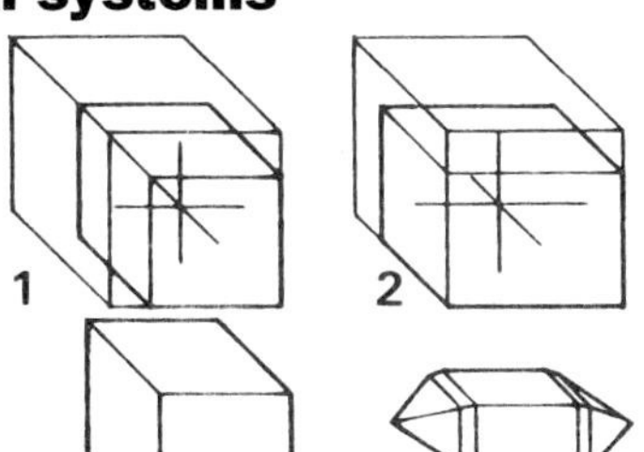
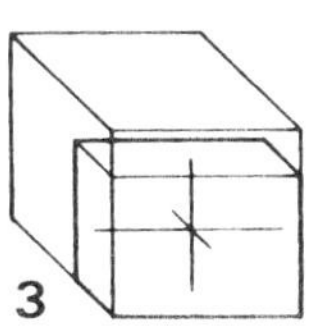
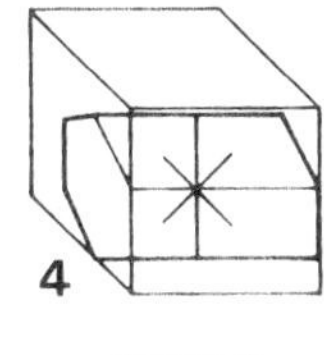
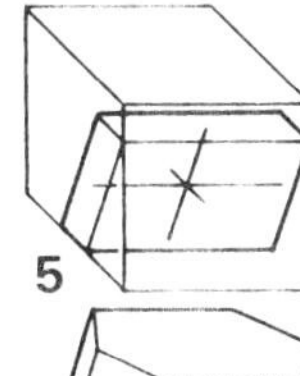
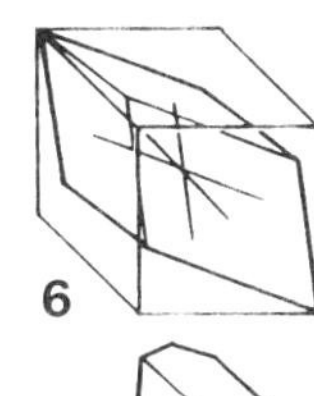
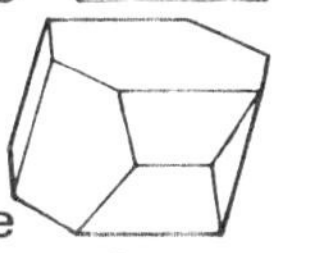

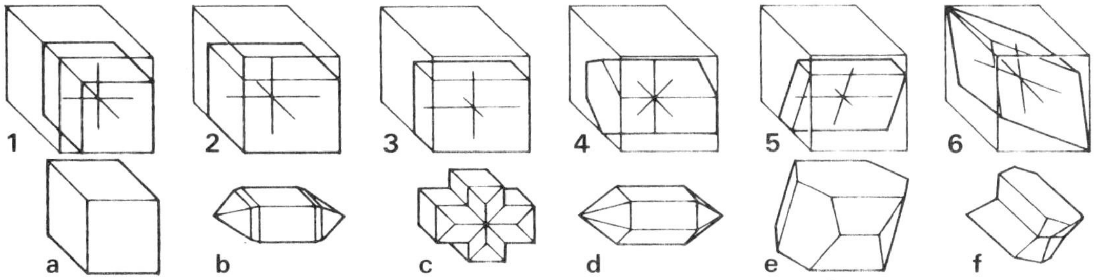

Elements can occur as minerals–within the crust there are approximately 2,000 kinds, but the bulk of it is made up of rock forming minerals (e.g. silicates, carbonates, oxides sulfates, chlorides,and phosphates).
Most rock forming minerals crystallize from fluids. This happens when molten rock cools or when water containing dissolved substances evaporates and leaves those substances behind.

The resulting minerals can be grouped in six systems, each with different axes of symmetry. Crystals in each system have distinctive shapes. Shown here are the six different systems and an example of each.

1 Cubic
a Halite
2 Tetragonal
b Zircon
3 Orthorhombic
c Staurolite
4 Hexagonal
d Quartz
5 Monoclinic
e Orthoclase
6 Triclinic
f Albite

Major rock types

1224 Magnified sections through the three main rock types reveal differences in their crystal textures.

1 Igneous (formed from molten magma): clearly defined crystals.
2 Sedimentary (formed from sediments): worn, weathered, and eroded grains (typical examples, not all rocks display these textures).
3 Metamorphic (recrystallized by heat or pressure): stress-aligned crystals.

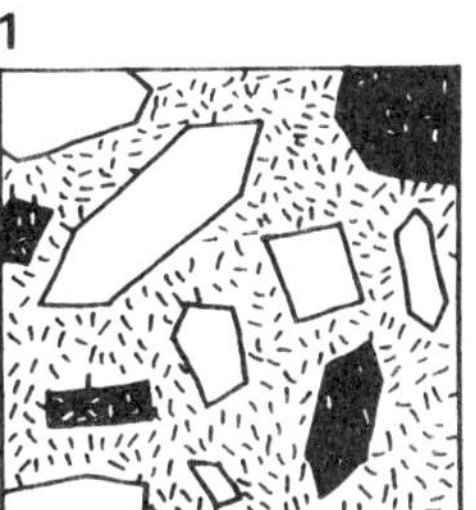
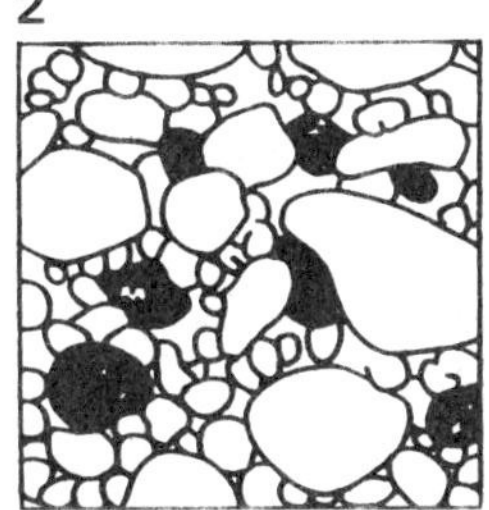
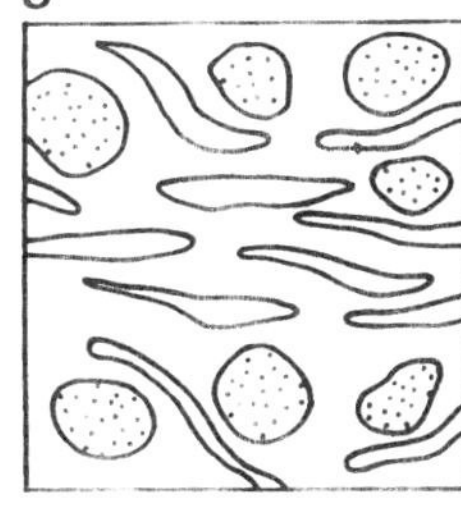

The rock cycle

1225 Natural processes produce, break down, and recycle crustal rocks.

1 Magma: molten rock formed deep down.
2 Igneous rock formed from magma that has cooled below or on the surface.
3 Sedimentary rock formed from sediments: the weathered, eroded, and sometimes biologically reconstituted (e.g. limestone) remains of igneous or metamorphic rock.
4 Metamorphic rock: igneous or sedimentary rock reformed under intense heat or pressure.

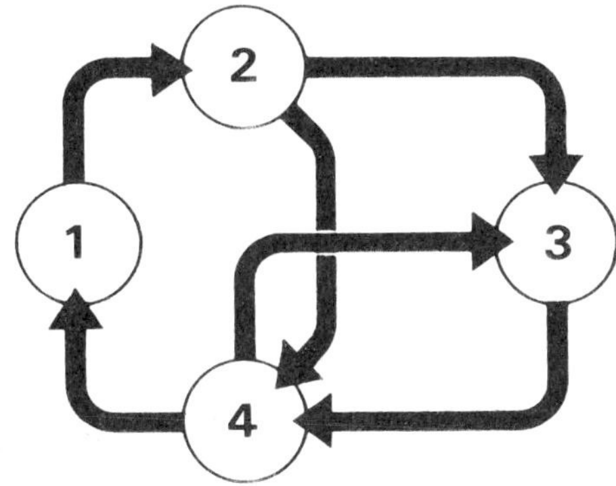

Identifying minerals

1226 Hardness is one of the characteristics used to identify minerals. On the Mohs' scale each numbered mineral scratches, and is therefore harder than, all those with a lower number. The scale is not regular. The field scale of hardness is less precise than the Mohs' scale but it offers collectors in the field a rough guide to the hardness of different minerals. By using everyday materials to scratch minerals they encounter in the field, collectors can estimate the hardness of the minerals and so possibly identify them. More sophisticated mineral identification tests involve spectral analysis and X rays.

a Hard file: Mohs 8–9
b Penknife: Mohs 7
c Window glass: Mohs 6
d Teeth, copper coin: Mohs 5
e Fingernail: Mohs 2–3

Mohs' scale

10	9	8	7	6	5	4	3	2	1
Diamond	Corundum	Topaz	Quartz	Orthoclase	Apatite	Fluorite	Calcite	Gypsum	Talc

Field scale of hardness

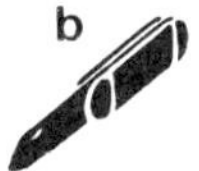

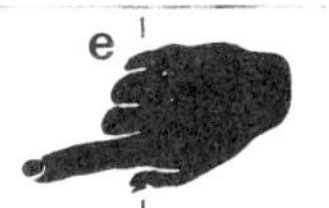

123 **Earth's Crust**
1231 Faults
1232 Folds
1233 Lithospheric plates
1234 Volcanoes
1235 Earthquakes
124 **Geochronology**
1241 Geochronological time scale
1242 Time periods (continued over)

123 EARTH'S CRUST

Faults

1231

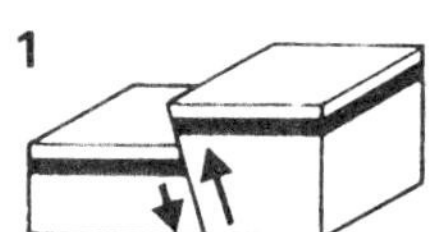

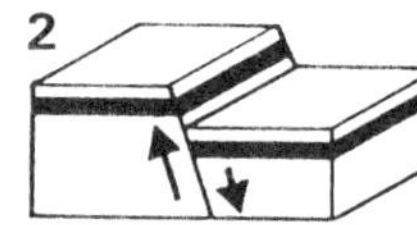

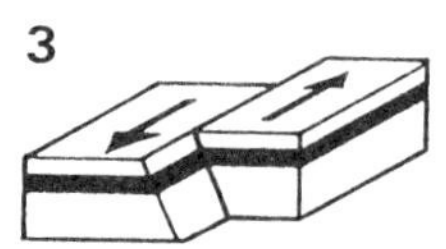

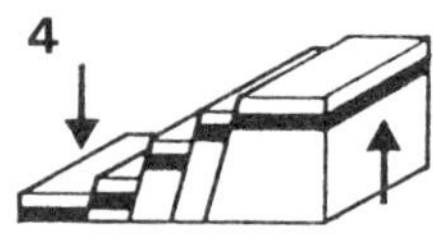

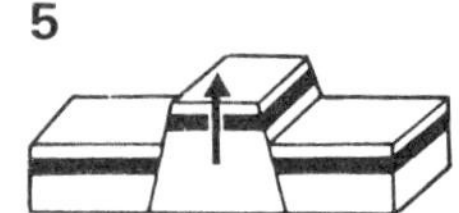

Faults are breaks in the Earth's crust caused by two parts of the crust shifting against one another, as where moving lithospheric plates abut.

1 Reverse fault (compressional)
2 Normal fault (stretching)
3 Tear fault (horizontal shearing)
4 Graben (a sunken valley)
5 Horst (a raised mountain block)

Folds

1232

Folds in the Earth's crust occur where rocks bend under pressure rather than breaking.

The four main types of fold

1 Anticline
2 Syncline
3 Overfold
4 Nappe

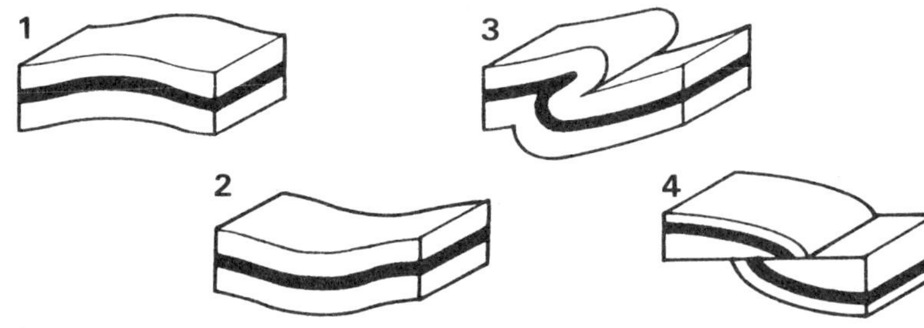

Lithospheric plates

1233

The Earth's crust comprises several different sections, called lithospheric plates. These plates are still shifting.

1 African plate
2 Antarctic plate
3 Eurasian plate
4 Indo-Australian plate
5 Nazca plate
6 North American plate
7 Pacific plate
8 South American plate

Kinds of plate boundary

Collision zone
Direction of plate movement

Subduction zone
Spreading ridge

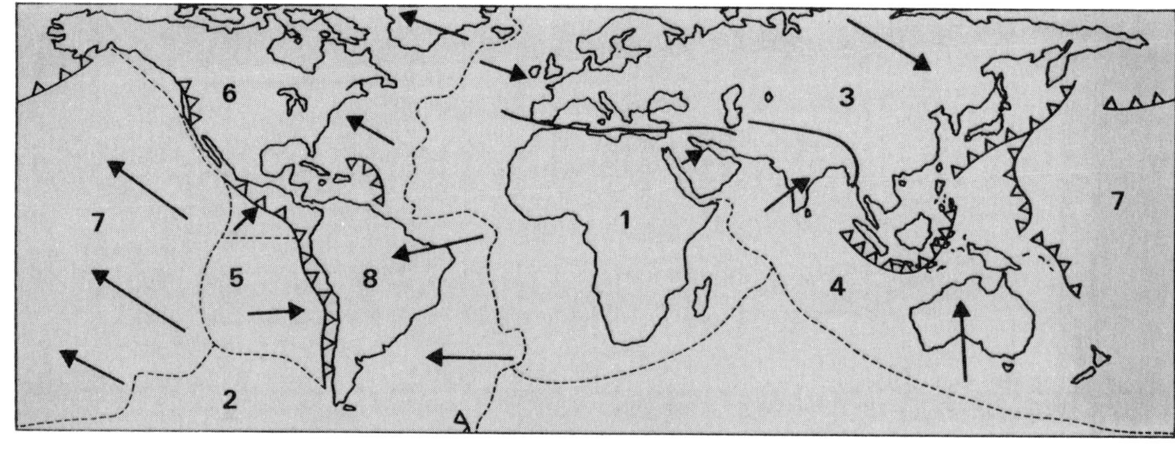

Volcanoes

1234

Volcanoes are holes or cracks in the Earth's crust that release molten lava, ash, or other products from magma chambers underground. Runny volcanic outpourings build thick basalt beds; viscous (sticky) lavas form steep-sided volcanoes. Ash builds cone-shaped peaks. Most volcanoes erupt where one lithospheric plate is forced beneath another, or where two plates diverge. There are between 500 and 800 active volcanoes. In any year, only 30 may erupt on land.

Dormant and extinct volcanoes

Inactive volcanoes are either dormant ("sleeping") or extinct. A dormant volcano is capable of erupting; an extinct volcano is not.

Volcano types

1 Ash and cinder cone
2 Lava cone
3 Lava cone
4 Composite cone

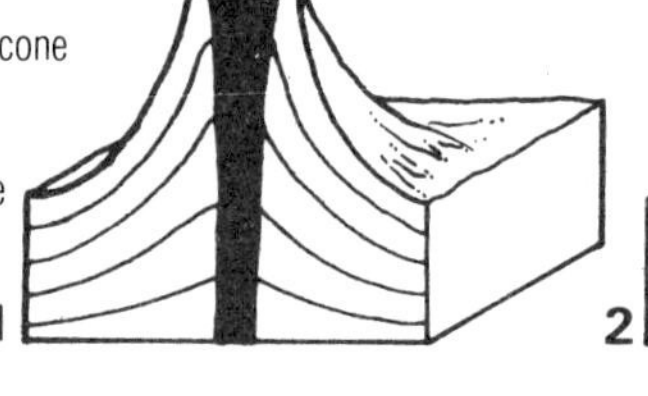

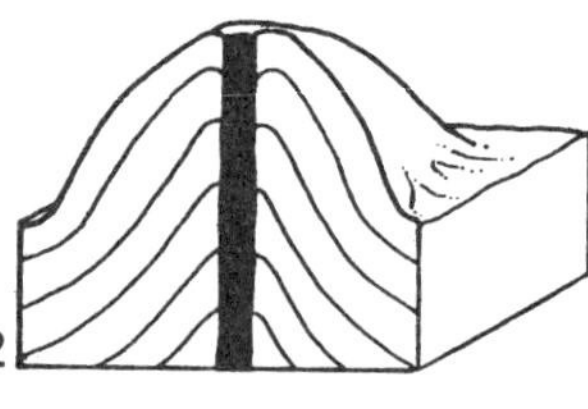

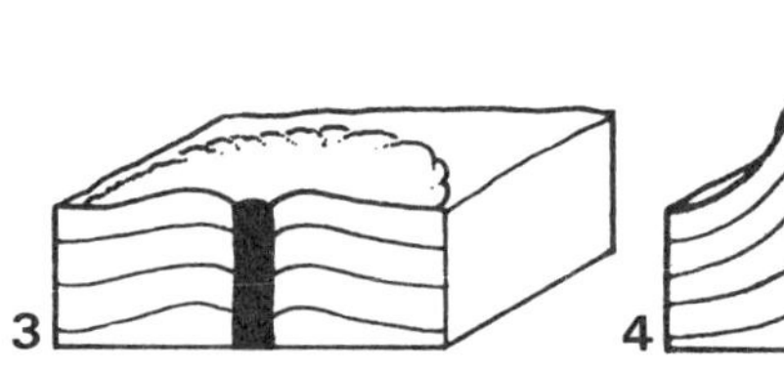

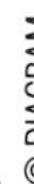

Earthquakes

1235 Earthquakes are sudden shakings of the ground where stressed rocks break along a fault line then snap back, but in a fresh position. Most major earthquakes happen where lithospheric plates collide or one plate overrides another. Earthquakes occur too at spreading ridges where rising molten rock plugs the gap between diverging plates.

Measuring earthquakes
The Richter scale records an earthquake's magnitude–i.e. the energy produced. The scale numbers run logarithmically: each represents 10 times the magnitude of the number below it. The greatest recorded number is 8.6.
The Mercalli scale measures the felt intensity of earthquakes at particular locations on the Earth's surface. Roman numeral I represents the weakest intensity, XII the strongest.

Mercalli and Richter scales

Mercalli number	Intensity	Effects	Richter number
I	Instrumental	Detected by seismographs and some animals.	< 3.5
II	Feeble	Noticed by a few sensitive people at rest.	3.5
III	Slight	Similar to vibrations from a passing truck.	4.2
IV	Moderate	Felt generally indoors; parked cars rock.	4.5
V	Rather strong	Felt generally; most sleepers wake.	4.8
VI	Strong	Trees shake; chairs fall over; some damage.	5.4
VII	Very strong	General alarm; walls crack; plaster falls.	6.1
VIII	Destructive	Chimneys, columns, monuments, weak walls fall.	6.5
IX	Ruinous	Some houses collapse as ground cracks.	6.9
X	Disastrous	Many buildings destroyed; railway lines bend.	7.3
XI	Very disastrous	Few buildings survive; bad landslides and floods.	8.1
XII	Catastrophic	Total destruction; ground forms waves.	> 8.1

124 GEOCHRONOLOGY

Geochronological time scale

1241

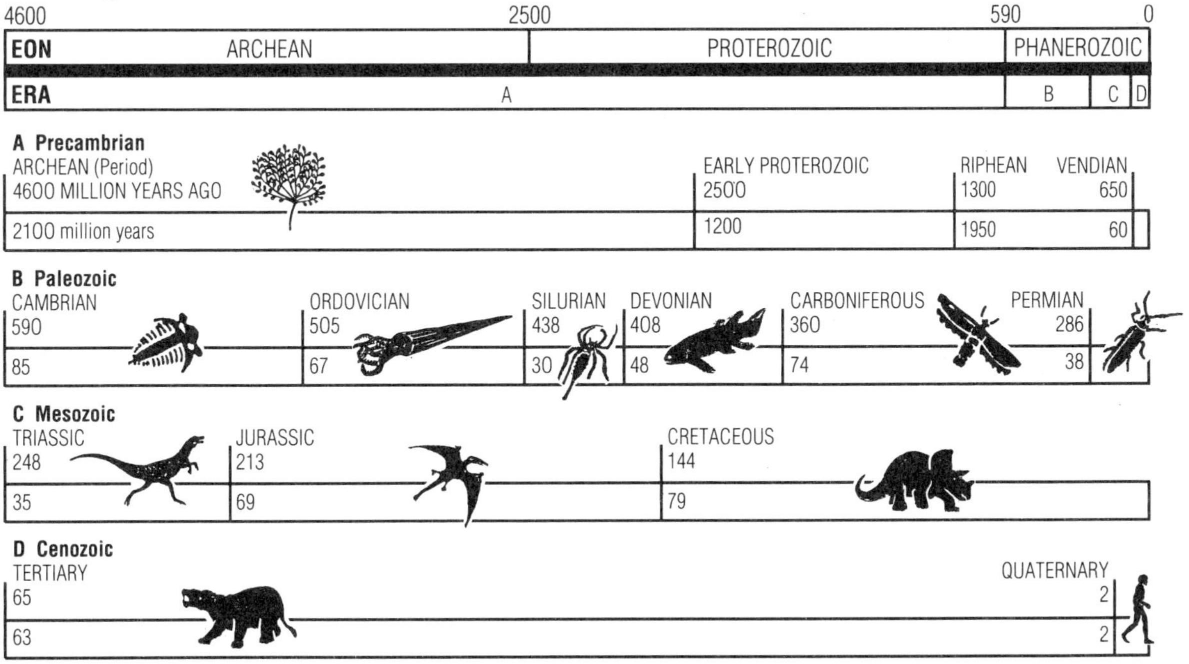

	4600	2500	590	0
EON	ARCHEAN	PROTEROZOIC	PHANEROZOIC	
ERA	A		B	C D

A Precambrian

ARCHEAN (Period)	EARLY PROTEROZOIC	RIPHEAN	VENDIAN
4600 MILLION YEARS AGO	2500	1300	650
2100 million years	1200	1950	60

B Paleozoic

CAMBRIAN	ORDOVICIAN	SILURIAN	DEVONIAN	CARBONIFEROUS	PERMIAN
590	505	438	408	360	286
85	67	30	48	74	38

C Mesozoic

TRIASSIC	JURASSIC	CRETACEOUS
248	213	144
35	69	79

D Cenozoic

TERTIARY	QUATERNARY
65	2
63	2

Time periods

1242 **PRECAMBRIAN EONS (4600–591)**

Archean
During this earliest and longest unit of geological time, the first small continents coalesced, volcanoes erupted on the early active surface, and the first bacteria appeared.

Proterozoic
As the Earth's crust cooled, larger continents took shape, mountains rose, and their eroded sediments accumulated below the sea. Complex living cells gave rise to early plants and animals.

PALEOZOIC PERIODS (590–249)

Cambrian
Most continents, including a southern supercontinent, lay near the equator. Shallow seas teemed with early complex life forms, such as brachiopods, gastropods, graptolites, and trilobites.

Ordovician
A shrinking pre-Atlantic ocean brought proto-North America, Greenland, and Europe close together. Ice covered some southern lands. Coral, dolomite, and limestone covered the shallow sea floor.

Silurian
Colliding northern proto-continents thrust up a mountain range from Scandinavia, through Scotland, to the Appalachians. Eroded debris formed thick sediments below the sea.

continued

Time periods continued

1242

Devonian
Sandstone formed from the eroding arid Old Red Continent (eastern North America and Greenland fused with western Europe). Fish abounded and the world's first forests were formed.

Carboniferous
Limestone formed below a shallow North American sea, followed by warm, swampy coal forests (a source of coal beds), inhabited by early amphibians and reptiles.

Permian
All the continents lay jammed together as Pangaea. In arid inland areas, salt lakes produced evaporites and desert sandstones were formed. The drying up of shallow seas contributed to mass extinctions.

MESOZOIC PERIODS (248–66)

Triassic
Pangaea showed early signs of breaking up. Lands were mild or warm and largely dry. The dinosaurs, pterosaurs, and crocodilians all evolved from other reptiles in the group known as "archosaurs" ("ruling reptiles").

Jurassic
The Atlantic was opening up. The Tethys Sea divided northern and southern supercontinents, Laurasia and Gondwanaland, which were already splitting up into the continents we know today.

Cretaceous
Thick chalk deposits formed below shallow seas, covering parts of North America and Europe. Continental drift was under way and climates cooled. Dinosaurs and pterosaurs died out.

CENOZOIC PERIODS (65–2)

Tertiary
India docked with Asia, and colliding lithospheric plates thrust up the Rockies, Alps, and Himalayas. Birds and mammals evolved and multiplied, to occupy the gaps left by the vanished dinosaurs and pterosaurs. Flowering plants now dominated other kinds.

Quaternary
As temperatures dropped, ice sheets covered Antarctica and large parts of the northern hemisphere, and the ocean level fell. In warm phases, ice retreated and the ocean level rose. The present warm interval began about 10,000 years ago.

Relative dating

1243

Sedimentary rocks hold fossil remains of organisms that evolved and became extinct in the last 600 million years or so. Different kinds of organism lived in different periods. Some left fossils in rocks that were laid down when they existed. Some distinctive fossils overlapped in time. Comparing overlaps in different rock layers helps paleontologists to work out the relative ages of the rocks. Times of peak abundance for eight groups of marine fossil invertebrates during three eras (**A** to **C**) are shown:

A Paleozoic
B Mesozoic
C Cenozoic
1 Trilobites
2 Graptolites
3 Corals
4 Ostracods
5 Ammonoids
6 Belemnites
7 Foraminiferans
8 Gastropods

Peak abundance of fossils

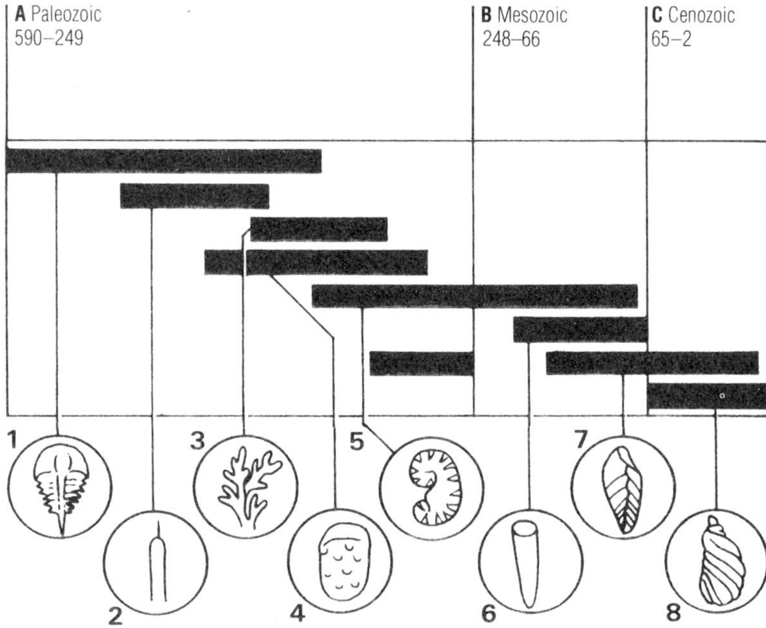

Radiometric dating

1244

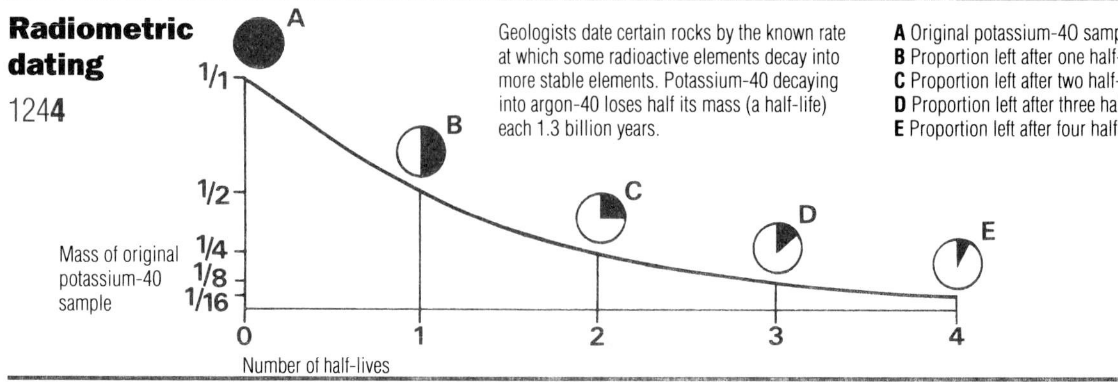

Geologists date certain rocks by the known rate at which some radioactive elements decay into more stable elements. Potassium-40 decaying into argon-40 loses half its mass (a half-life) each 1.3 billion years.

A Original potassium-40 sample.
B Proportion left after one half-life.
C Proportion left after two half-lives.
D Proportion left after three half-lives.
E Proportion left after four half-lives.

Superposition

1245 Relative dating is based on the law of superposition: in an undisturbed sequence of rock strata, the lowest are the oldest and the highest are the youngest. In this cross-section, stratum 1 was formed before 2, 2 before 3, and so on. Between strata 1 and 2, an unconformity is apparent (i.e. the older rock's surface was partly eroded before the second layer was formed).

1 Metamorphic rock
2 Conglomerate
3 Sandstone
4 Limestone
5 Alluvium

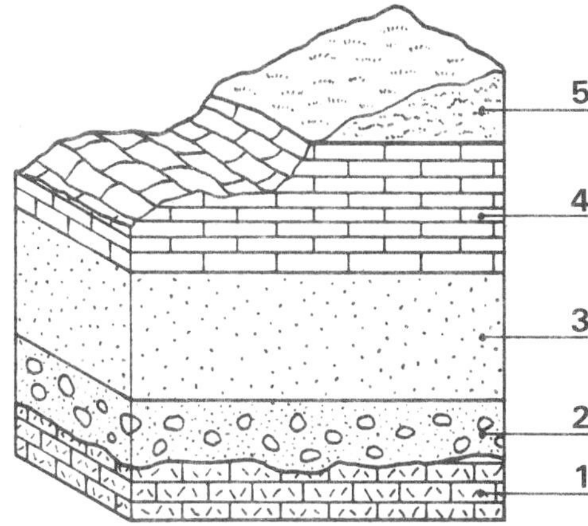

Sea-floor spreading

1246 The sea floor is relatively young geographically due to being constantly made and destroyed by a process called "sea-floor spreading". This is where oceanic crustal plates move away from a central mid-oceanic ridge, causing new crust to form by basalt intruding into fissures as the plates move apart.
As the upwelling basalt forms a new sea floor it takes on the polarity of the magnetic field at that time. As the sea floor spreads it records geomagnetic reversals occurring every few hundred thousand years. The study of this "Paleomagnetism" helped scientists to determine this theory and the date of the sea floor.

1 Astheno-sphere (partly melted mantle)
2 Peridotite upper mantle
3 Gabbroic lower ocean crust
4 Basalt and doerite
5 Normally magnetized basalt, newly formed at spreading ridge
6 Reversely magnetized basalt (older than **5**)
7 Normally magnetized basalt (older than **6**)

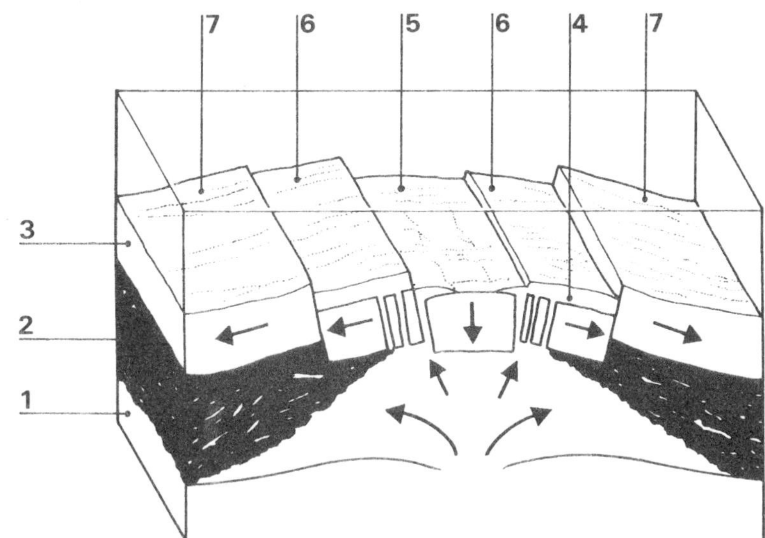

125 GEOLOGICAL MAP SYMBOLS

1 Horizontal strata
2 Inclined strata with a 30-degree dip
3 Anticline
4 Syncline
5 Minor fold, with a 30-degree plunge
6 Base of a lava flow (dots above base)
7 Fault with downthrow
8 Mineral vein (copper)

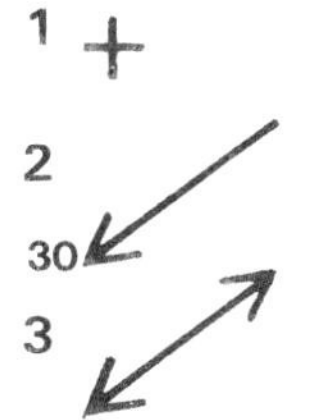

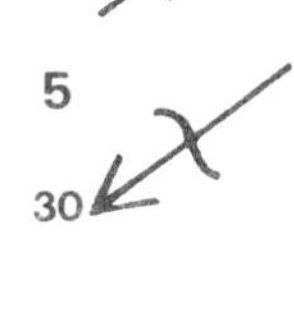

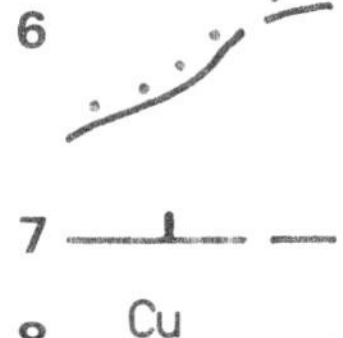

7

8 Cu

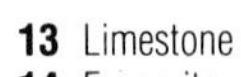

Types of rock (not all symbols are standardized)

9 Igneous rock
10 Sand/sandstone
11 Extrusive igneous rock
12 Clay/shale
13 Limestone
14 Evaporite

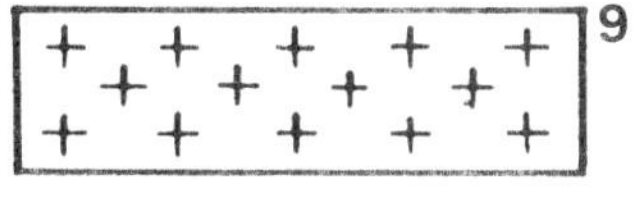
9

11

13

10

12

14

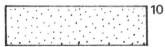

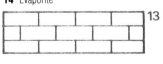

126 GEOLOGY GLOSSARY

age A subdivision of geological time.
amphibole Any group of rock-forming ferromagnesian silicates.
andesites A dark, fine-grained rock, taking its name from the Andes Mountains.
anticline An upfold in the rocks.
Archean eon The first eon in Earth's history (4.6–2.5 billion years ago).
arenit A sandstone with sedimentary particles of between 0.06 mm and 2 mm across.
asthenosphere A dense, plastic layer of mantle below the lithosphere.
basalt A fine-grained extrusive rock. Oceanic crust is largely basalt.
batholith An immense, dome-shaped, deep-seated mass of intrusive igneous rock.
bauxite The main ore from which aluminum is extracted.
bed A sedimentary layer more than 1/2 in (1 cm) thick.
bedding plane/surface The surface between two beds of sedimentary rock.
bedrock The mass of solid rock that lies beneath the regolith.
boss A small mass of intrusive igneous rock with a circular surface.
breccia A sedimentary rock made of sharp-edged fragments naturally cemented together.
Cambrian period The first part of the Paleozoic era: 590 to 505 million years ago.
carbonates Plentiful minerals that contain metal combined with oxygen and carbon. They include calcite, aragonite, and dolomite.
Carboniferous period The penultimate period of the Paleozoic era: 360 to 249 million years ago.
Cenozoic era The geological era after the Mesozoic era. It is sometimes known as the age of mammals and began 65 million years ago.
chalk A white, soft form of limestone.
chert A sedimentary rock formed of tiny quartz crystals.
clasts Rock fragments, such as those that form mud, sand, and gravel.
clay Sheetlike silicates held together by water. Clays tend to be plastic when wet and hard or powdery when dry.
climatology The study of climate.
coal A rock that is mostly carbon and readily burns. It consists of layered plant remains compacted by pressure over millions of years.
conglomerate A sedimentary rock formed of pebbles and larger rounded stones, cemented together by sandy material.
continental drift The theory that continents have drifted around the face of the Earth.
core The dense, intensely hot ball of rock below the Earth's mantle. The outer core, 1,400 mi (2,240 km) thick, is probably molten iron and nickel with some silicon. The inner core, 1,540 mi (2,440 km) across, may be iron and nickel at 3,700 °C. Extreme pressure prevents it from becoming liquid.
craton An ancient part of a continent that has remained undeformed by mountain-building activity.
Cretaceous period The third and last period of the Mesozoic era: 144 to 65 million years ago.
crust The hard outer skin of rock forming the ocean floor and the continents. Continental crust averages 20 mi (33 km) thick. Oceanic crust is less than 6.2 mi (10 km) thick.
crystal A mineral that has solidified with geometrically arranged atoms and external symmetry.
Devonian period The fourth period of the Paleozoic era: 408 to 360 million years ago.
diagenesis The process by which sediment is converted to rock.
dike A vertical sheet of igneous rock intruded across older rocks.
diorite A coarse-textured igneous rock, mainly comprising feldspar and pyroxene.
dolomite A mineral or sedimentary rock made of calcium magnesium carbonate.
earthquake A sudden shaking of the ground when stressed rocks move along a fault. Volcanic eruptions trigger some earthquakes.
Eocene epoch The second part of the Tertiary period: 55 to 38 million years ago.
epoch A time unit within a geological period.
era A time unit within an eon. An era contains at least two periods.
erathem The rocks formed during a geological era.
evaporite Rock formed of crystals precipitated by the evaporation of salt-saturated water.
evolution The process of change by which organisms give rise to new species.
facies Features of a rock representing a local environment.
fault A fracture zone where one rock mass has moved against another.
feldspar Any of a group of minerals comprising aluminum silicates and a metal (calcium, potassium, or sodium).
flint Dark, smooth, shiny chert.
fold A bend in rock layers, formed when pressure has made them plastic.
foliated Formed of leaves of platy minerals aligned during metamorphism.
foredeep A long basin filling with sediment eroded from an active mountain system nearby.
fossil The remains or trace of an organism preserved in sedimentary rocks.
gabbro A dense, dark, coarse-grained, intrusive igneous rock largely consisting of feldspar (plagioclase) and pyroxene.
gangue Valueless minerals in ore.
gemstone A mineral valued for its beauty, durability, scarcity, and suitability for cutting into a gem.
geochemistry The study of substances in the Earth and their chemical changes.
geochronology Earth's history.
geode A hollow nodule of rock lined inside with crystals.
geology The study of the Earth, especially its rocks and minerals and their development.
geophysics The study of the structure and development of the Earth.
gneiss A coarse-grained metamorphic rock with minerals in wavy layers.
granite An intrusive igneous rock rich in quartz and feldspar, often with mica or hornblende.
gypsum A mineral or rock made of calcium sulfate and water.
halite Rock salt: sodium chloride.
hematite Iron oxide.
Holocene epoch The second (present) part of the Quaternary period: 10,000 to the present.
hornblende A variety of amphibole.
hornfels A granular, fine-grained metamorphic rock.
ice age A time when ice sheets covered much of the Earth. The present Ice Age is only one of several ice ages.
igneous rock A rock formed when molten rock cools and hardens. Extrusive, or volcanic, igneous rock cools on the surface as lava. Intrusive igneous rock cools underground.
isostasy The state of balance of the Earth's crust as it floats on the denser mantle. Mountains are balanced by deep roots of crustal rock.
joint A crack in rock, formed along a line of weakness.
Jurassic period The second (middle) period of the Mesozoic era: 213 to 144 million years ago.
laccolith A lens-shaped mass of intrusive igneous rock that pushes overlying rocks into a dome.
lava Molten rock when it appears at the Earth's surface.
limestone Sedimentary rock made mainly of calcium carbonate.
limnology The study of bodies of water that are inland, such as lakes.
lithification A process that changes sediments into solid rocks, i.e. compaction and the precipitation of a mineral cement.
lithosphere The Earth's crust coupled to the rigid upper mantle.
lopolith A saucer-shaped intrusion (some are huge) between rock strata.
magma Molten rock formed below the Earth's surface.
mantle The dense, hot rock layer, 1,800 mi (2,900 km) thick, below the crust. Parts are semi-molten and flow.
marble A metamorphic rock formed from recrystallized limestone or dolomite.
Mesozoic era The geological era between the Paleozoic and Cenozoic eras: 248 to 65 million years ago. It is sometimes called the "Age of Dinosaurs."
metamorphic rock Sedimentary or igneous rock altered by great heat or pressure, e.g. limestone changed to marble.
meteorology The study of weather and atmosphere.
mica A rock-forming silicate.
mineral A natural inorganic substance with distinct chemical composition and internal structure.
mineralogy The study of minerals.
Miocene epoch The fourth part of the Tertiary period.
Mississippian period In North America, the first part of what is generally called the Carboniferous period: 360 to 321 million years ago.
nappe A recumbent (flopped over) fold that has sheared through, with its upper limb forced far forward.
Neogene period The second part of a revised two-part division of the Cenozoic era. It runs from the Miocene epoch to the Holocene: 24.6

continued

Geology glossary continued

million to 2 million years ago.

obsidian A glassy volcanic rock.

oceanography The study of oceans and their life.

Oligocene epoch The third part of the Tertiary period: 38 to 24.6 million years ago.

olivine A dark green silicate.

oolite Sand consisting of rounded grains of carbonate known as ooids.

Ordovician period The second period in the Paleozoic era: 505 to 438 million years ago.

ore A metal-rich mineral deposit.

orogeny A phase of mountain building.

Paleocene epoch The first part of the Tertiary period: 65 to 55 million years ago

paleoecology The study of the relationship between prehistoric plants, animals, and their surroundings.

Paleogene period The first part of a revised two-part division of the Cenozoic era: 65 to 24 million years ago.

paleogeography The study of the Earth's past geography.

paleomagnetism The magnetic alignment of particles in rock that occurred when the rock formed. It reflects the Earth's magnetic field at the time.

paleontology The study of fossilized prehistoric plants and animals.

Paleozoic era The first part of the Phanerozoic eon, 509 to 248 million years ago.

pangaea The prehistoric supercontinent that formed late in the Paleozoic era and broke up in the Cenozoic era.

Pennsylvanian period In North America, the second part of what is generally called the Carboniferous period: 320 to 286 million years ago.

peridotite A coarse-grained igneous rock, mainly of olivine and pyroxene.

period A geological time unit within an era.

Permian period The last period of the Paleozoic era: 286 to 248 million years ago.

petroleum Mineral oil: hydrocarbons formed in the Earth's crust.

petrology The study of rocks.

Phanerozoic eon The "age of visible life" – the fossil-rich past 590 million years of Earth's history.

plate tectonics The study of how lithospheric plates move around.

plate, lithospheric An independently moving slab of lithosphere.

Pleistocene epoch The first (ice age) part of the Quaternary period: 2 to 0.1 million years ago.

Pliocene epoch The last part of the Tertiary period: 5 to 2 million years ago.

Precambrian All Earth's history predating the Cambrian period.

Proterozoic eon The second eon in Earth's history: 2.5 billion to 590 million years ago.

pyroxene Any of a group of rock-forming silicate minerals.

quartz A hard silicate mineral.

quartzite Sandstone that has been changed to solid quartz rock.

Quaternary period The second (present) period of the Cenozoic era: 2 million to the present.

radiocarbon dating Radiometric dating based on the decay of the isotope carbon 14. It is used to date organic materials less than 70,000 years old.

radiometric dating Dating rocks by the known rate of decay of radioactive elements that they contain.

regolith Soil and broken rock covering the bedrock.

rock Any solid mass that is composed of minerals, forming a part of the Earth's crust.

rock units Rocks grouped by their characteristics, not by time. The units include (from major to minor) groups, formations, and members.

sandstone A sedimentary rock formed of naturally cemented sand grains.

schist A metamorphic rock rich in flattened, aligned minerals. It comes from slate and basalt.

sedimentary rock Rock formed from accumulated sediments. Examples are clay, sandstone, and limestone.

seismology The study of Earth tremors.

series The rocks formed during a geological epoch.

shale A layered sedimentary rock formed chiefly from clay.

silicates The most plentiful group of rock-forming minerals, usually consisting of silicon and oxygen combined with a metal. They include feldspar, mica, and quartz.

sill A horizontal sheet of igneous rock intruded between sedimentary rock layers.

Silurian period The third period of the Paleozoic era: 438 to 408 million years ago.

slate A fine-grained metamorphic rock formed from shale. It splits along lines of weakness produced by deformational pressure.

soil Broken rock fragments, often mixed with decayed organic matter.

spreading ridge A submarine mountain chain built by magma that rises to plug a widening gap between two diverging lithospheric plates.

stage The rocks formed during a geological age.

stock Like a batholith but smaller.

stratigraphy The study of stratified (layered) rocks.

stratum A single sedimentary layer.

subduction The sinking of one lithospheric plate's leading edge below another lithospheric plate. This occurs below deep ocean trenches.

superposition The principle that, in undisturbed layered rocks, the higher a stratum, the younger it is.

syncline A downfold in the rocks, creating a trough.

system The rocks formed during a geological period.

tectonics The geological study of large structures such as mountains.

tektites Small, black, glassy pieces of sedimentary rock, melted by the impact of an ancient meteorite.

Tertiary period The first period of the Cenozoic era, comprising the epochs from the Paleocene to the Pliocene: 65 to 2 million years ago.

tillite Rock formed from till – sediment dumped by a glacier.

travertine Calcium carbonate deposited by water, as in stalactites.

Triassic period The first period of the Mesozoic era: 248 to 213 million years ago.

unconformity A level where sedimentary rocks cover an older rock surface partly removed by erosion. The level marks a time gap.

uniformitarianism The principle that present geological processes are the key to past events in Earth's history.

varves Paired (fine and coarse) layers annually deposited in a glacial lake.

vein A crack in rock containing a mineral deposit.

volcano A hole or fissure in the ground from which lava and other volcanic products emerge.

131 EARTH

Angle of inclination

1311 The angle of inclination refers to the Earth's tilt. There is a 23.5° angle (**a**) between the plane of the Equator and the plane of the Earth's orbit around the Sun, and 66.5°(**b**) between the plane of the orbit and the polar axis.

A-B polar diameter
C-D equatorial diameter
E equatorial circumference

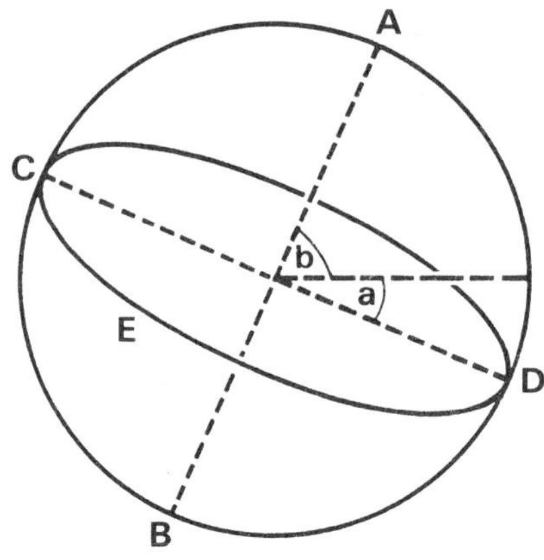

Latitude and longitude

1312

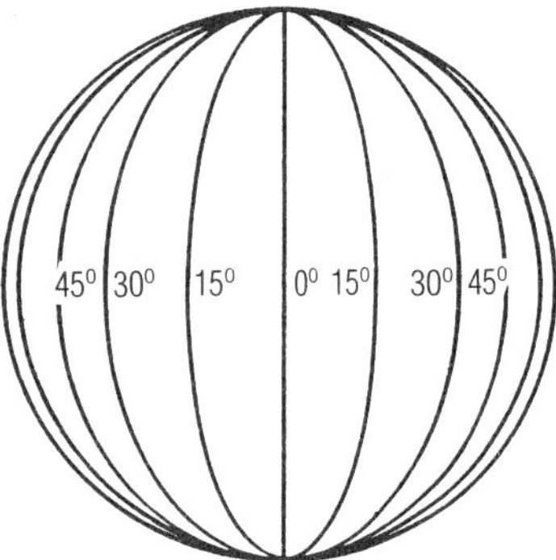

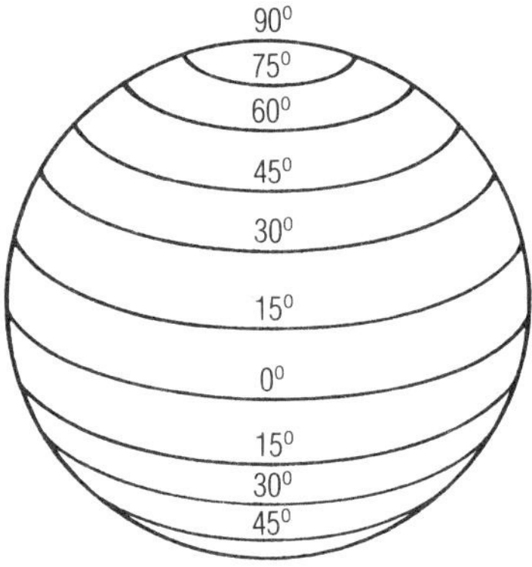

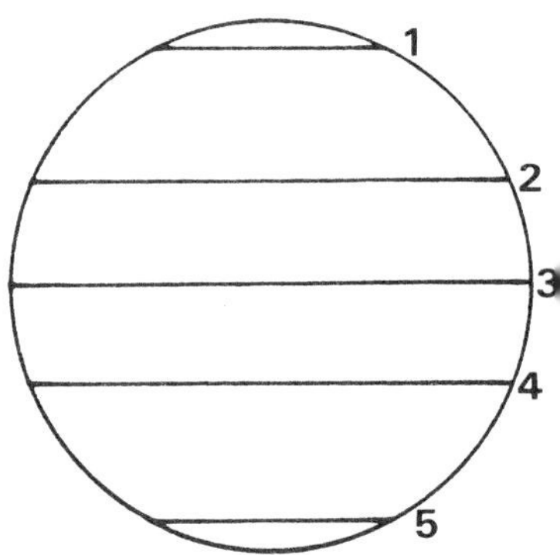

Longitude
On a map or globe, longitude is position east or west of an imaginary north-south line between the North and South Poles. This so-called Prime Meridian passes through Greenwich in England. Precise longitude measurements are given in degrees, minutes, and seconds, e.g. 3°08'24" W (west). (The distance between two degrees of latitude or longitude is 60 minutes, and the distance between two minutes of latitude or longitude is 60 seconds.) The diagram above labels the Prime Meridian (0°) and meridians at 15° intervals east and west of it.

Latitude
On a map or globe, latitude is position north or south of the equator. This is an imaginary east-west line around the world halfway between the poles. Precise latitude measurements are given in degrees, minutes, and seconds – e.g. 52°51'02" N (north). The diagram above labels the equator (0°) and parallels at 15° intervals north and south. The North Pole is 90° N and the South Pole is 90° S.

Key latitudes
Numbers indicate important lines of latitude. Between the tropics the Sun shines down vertically at least once a year. North of the Arctic Circle and south of the Antarctic Circle the Sun does not rise at least once a year.
1 Arctic Circle: 66°30' N
2 Tropic of Cancer: 23°27' N
3 Equator: 0°
4 Tropic of Capricorn: 23°27' S
5 Antarctic Circle: 66°30' S

Locating a point on the globe

1313 **Pinpointing Washington DC**
To find the latitude of a place, measure the number of degrees north or south of the Equator (**A**). Washington DC's approximate latitude (**1**) is 39° N. A more precise measurement would be 38°55' N, or 38 degrees, 55 minutes. To find the longitude of a place, measure the number of degrees west or east of the Prime Meridian (**B**). Washington DC's approximate longitude (**2**) is 77° W. A more precise measurement would be 77°0 or 77 degrees, 0 minutes.

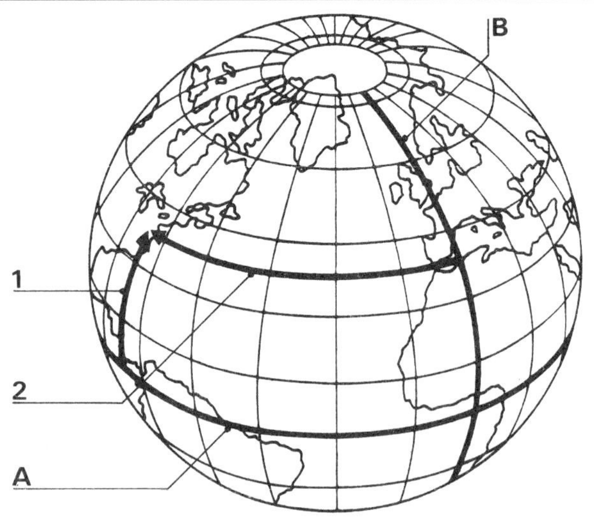

Surface temperatures

1314 Surface temperatures vary largely with the angle at which the Sun's rays strike different parts of the Earth's curved surface. Rays reaching polar regions (**a**, **c**) are more spread out than those reaching near the Equator (**b**). Thus an area near the Equator receives more concentrated solar heat than an area of the same size near the North or South Pole.

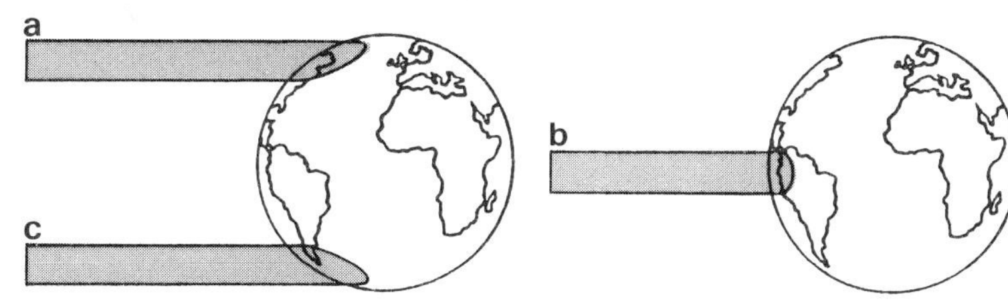

Surface features

1315 **Land**
Land covers about 30% of the Earth's surface. During ice ages, sea level falls and more land is exposed. When ice sheets melt, sea levels rise and shallow seas invade low-lying plains.

Land 30%

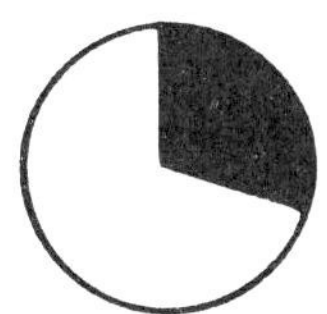

Continents
Relative surface areas of all land:
a Asia: 29.4%
b Africa: 20.2%
c North America: 16.3%
d South America: 11.9%
e Antarctica: 9.0%
f Europe: 7.1%
g Oceania: 6.1%

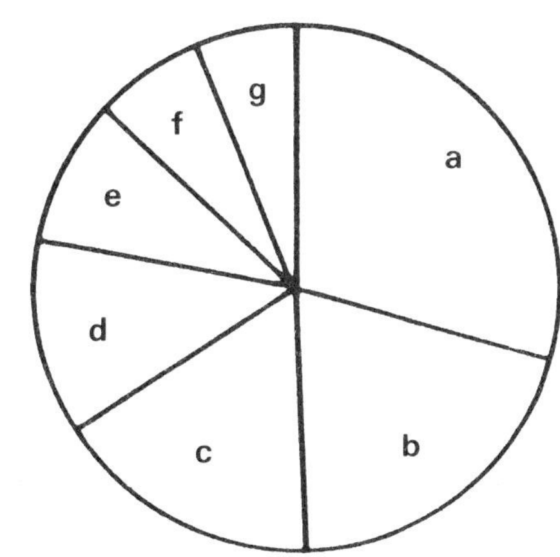

Water
Water covers about 70% of the Earth's surface, distributed in several forms:
Oceans and seas: 97.2%
Ice and snow: 2.15%
Ground water and soil water: 0.625%
Lakes and rivers: 0.017%
Air: 0.001%

Water 70%

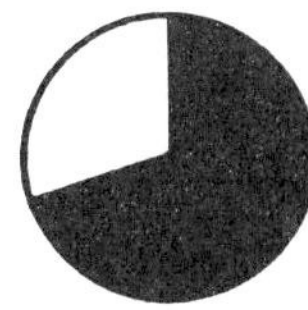

Oceans
Relative surface areas of all oceans:
a Pacific Ocean: 49.7%
b Atlantic Ocean: 24.6%
c Indian Ocean: 22.1%
d Arctic Ocean: 3.6%

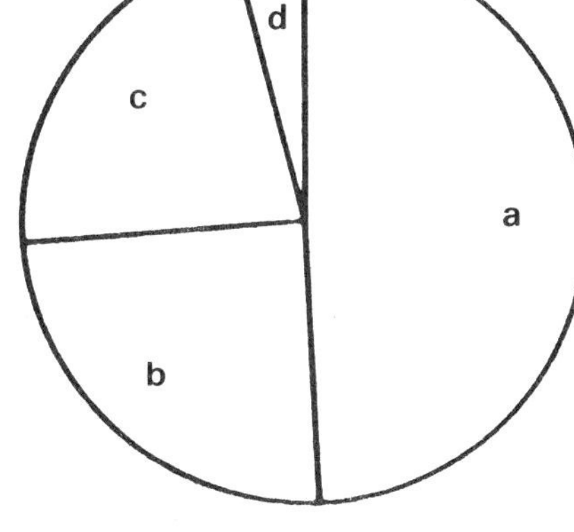

Air
Relative depths of layers of the atmosphere are shown. Life and weather are concentrated in the troposphere, the densest layer nearest to the Earth's surface, about 11 mi (17 km) high.

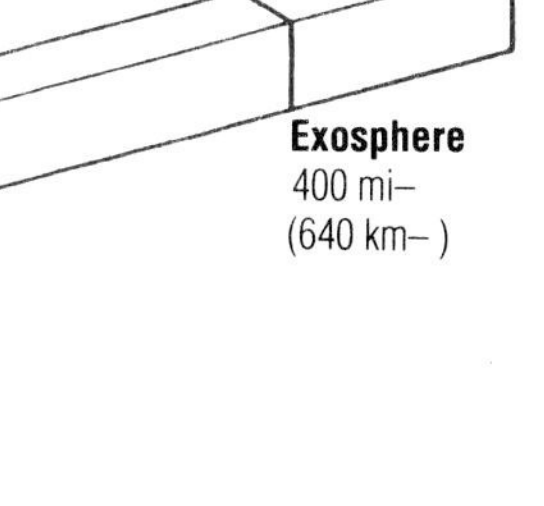

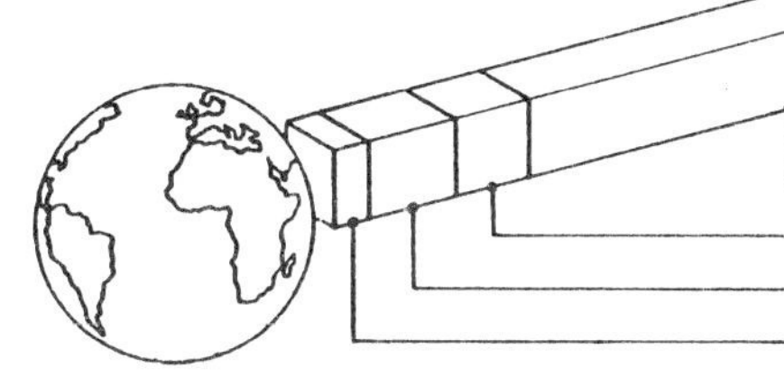

The seasons

1316 The year is divided into four seasons, each determined by the Earth's position relative to the sun. Summer and winter begin at the summer and winter solstices, spring and autumn at the spring and autumn equinoxes. At the summer solstice, the days are longest and the nights shortest, at winter solstice this is reversed. At the equinoxes, the days and nights are equally long. Each season is associated with different weather conditions but varies according to where you are in the world. This figure shows the attitude (position) of the Earth to the Sun at different times of the year. For example, when it is summer in the northern hemisphere – with the north-south axis of the Earth leaning toward the Sun – it is winter in the southern hemisphere.

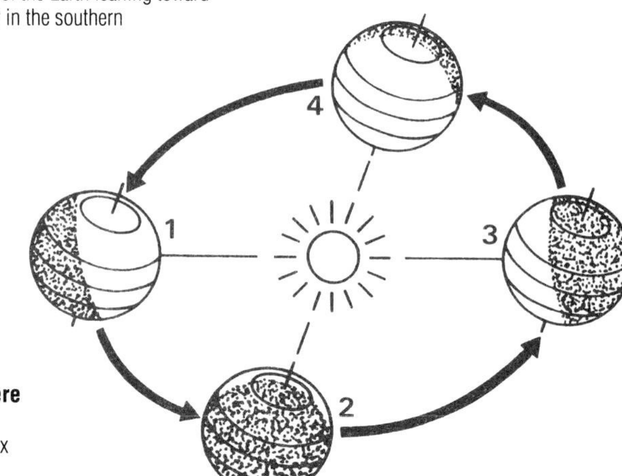

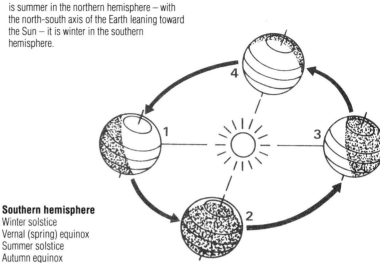

Date	**Northern hemisphere**	**Southern hemisphere**
1 June 21	Summer solstice	Winter solstice
2 September 23	Autumn equinox	Vernal (spring) equinox
3 December 21	Winter solstice	Summer solstice
4 March 21	Vernal (spring) equinox	Autumn equinox

132 EARTH'S LANDFORMS

Largest seas

1321 The relative areas of the Earth's ten largest seas are shown here as circles above a location map. Below, actual areas of the seas are rounded off in millions of sq mi (sq km).

1 Coral Sea 1.85 (4.79)
2 Arabian Sea 1.49 (3.86)
3 South China Sea 1.42 (3.69)
4 Mediterranean Sea 0.97 (2.52)
5 Bering Sea 0.89 (2.30)
6 Bay of Bengal 0.84 (2.17)
7 Sea of Okhotsk 0.61 (1.59)
8 Gulf of Mexico 0.60 (1.54)
9 Gulf of Guinea 0.59 (1.53)
10 Barents Sea 0.54 (1.41)

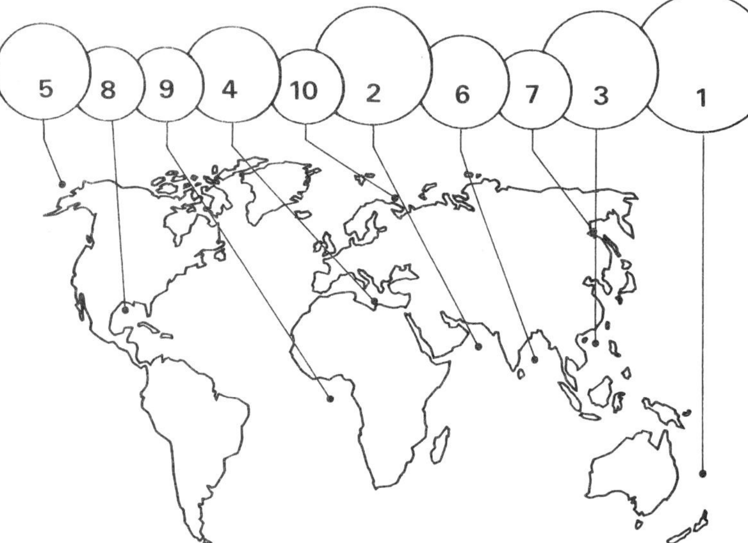

Largest islands

1322 The areas of the Earth's ten largest islands are listed below, rounded off in thousands of sq mi (sq km). This list excludes the giant island-continent Australia.

1 Greenland 840 (2,176)
2 New Guinea 317 (821)
3 Borneo 287 (743)
4 Madagascar 227 (588)
5 Baffin Island (Canada) 184 (476)
6 Sumatra (Indonesia) 183 (474)
7 Honshu (Japan) 89 (230)
8 Great Britain 88 (229)
9 Victoria Island (Canada) 82 (213)
10 Ellesmere Island (Canada) 82 (213)

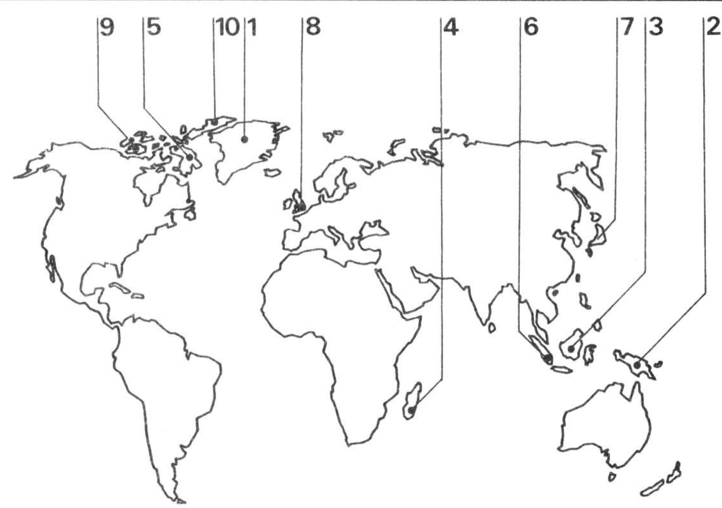

The continents

1323 The areas of the world's seven continents are listed below, rounded off in millions of sq mi (sq km).

1 Asia 17.1 (44.2)
2 Africa 11.7 (30.2)
3 North America 9.4 (24.4)
4 South America 6.9 (17.8)
5 Antarctica 5.1 (13.2)
6 Europe 3.8 (9.9)
7 Oceania 3.3 (8.5)

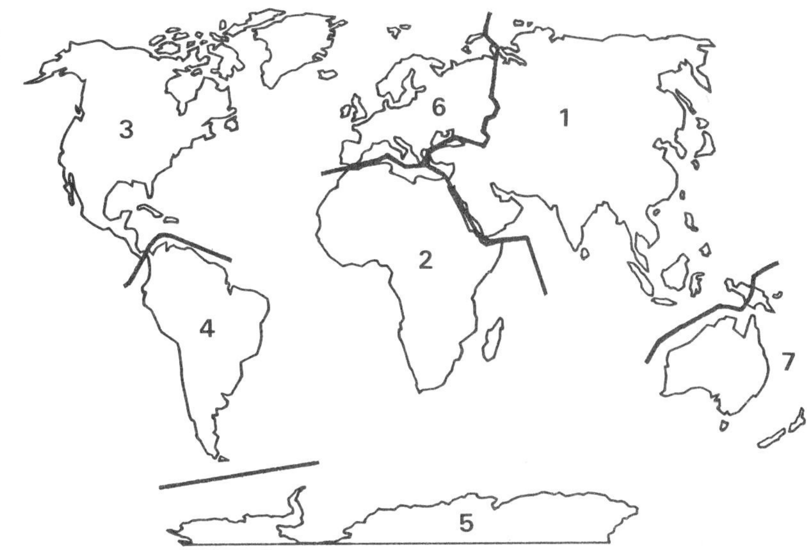

Relative surface areas (%)

1 Asia 29.4%
2 Africa 20.2%
3 North America 16.3%
4 South America 11.9%
5 Antarctica 9.0%
6 Europe 7.1%
7 Oceania 6.1%

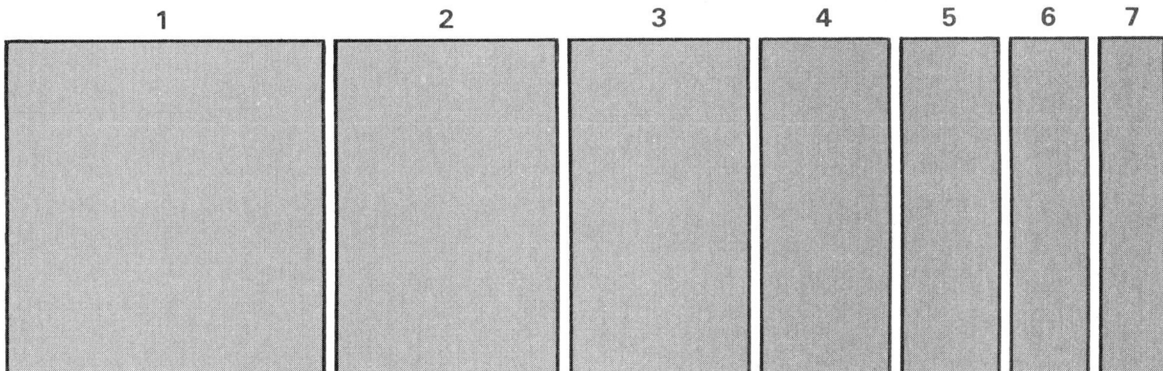

Largest freshwater lakes

1324 The relative areas of freshwater lakes are shown here as circles on a location map. The areas are listed below, rounded off in thousands of sq mi (sq km).

1 Superior 31.8 (82.4)
2 Victoria 26.8 (69.5)
3 Huron 23.0 (59.6)
4 Michigan 22.4 (58.0)
5 Great Bear 12.3 (31.8)
6 Baykal 12.2 (31.5)
7 Great Slave 11.0 (28.4)
8 Tanganyika 11.0 (28.4)
9 Malawi 10.9 (28.2)
10 Erie 9.9 (25.7)

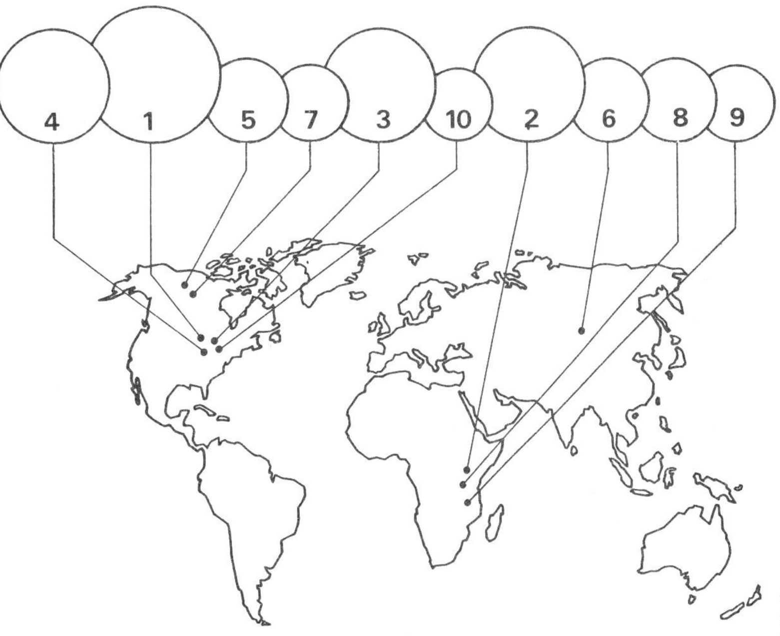

World distribution of deserts

1325 The list gives the major deserts with their areas rounded off in thousands of sq mi (sq km). (These sizes are all approximate).

1 Sahara Desert 3,242 (8,397)
2 Great Australian Desert 598 (1,549)
3 Arabian Desert 502 (1,300)
4 Gobi Desert 401 (1,039)
5 Patagonian Desert 260 (673)
6 Kalahari Desert 201 (521)
7 Turkestan Desert 139 (360)
8 Takla Makan Desert 124 (321)
9 Namib Desert 120 (311)
10 Sonoran Desert 120 (311)
11 Thar Desert 100 (259)
12 Somali Desert 100 (259)
13 Atacama Desert 31 (80)

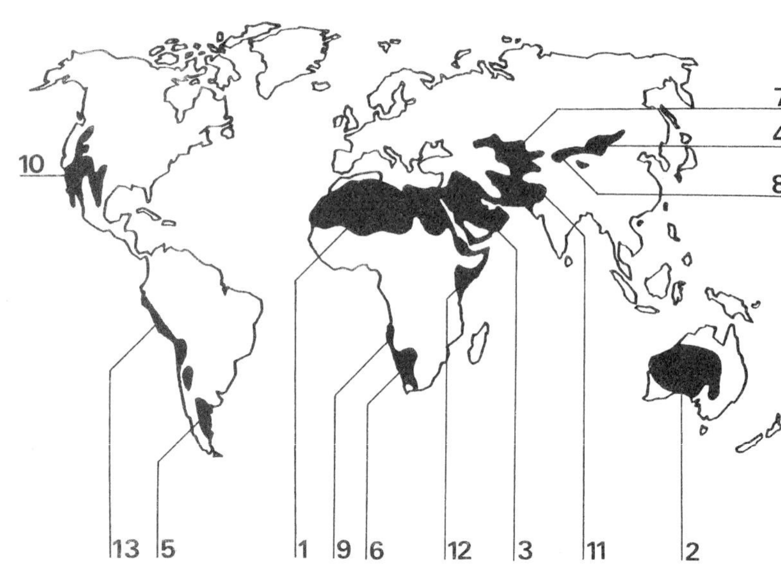

Mountains and volcanoes

1326

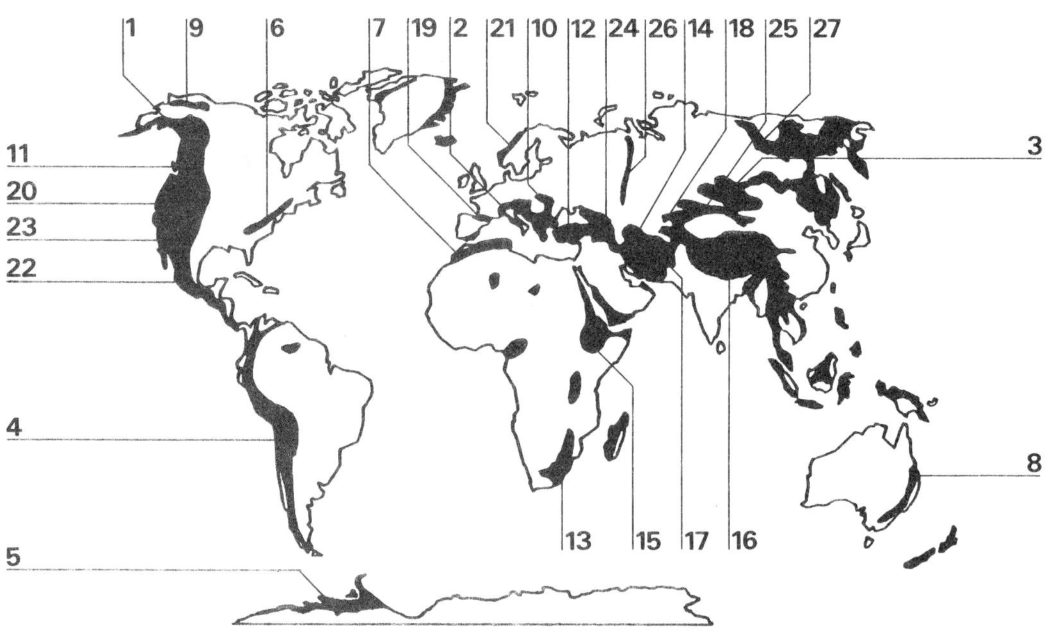

Selected mountain groups

The list gives the major mountain ranges of the world (shown above) and the highest peak in each of the ranges, with its height shown in thousands of ft (m).

1 Alaska Range: Mt McKinley 20.3 (6.2)
2 Alps: Mont Blanc 15.8 (4.8)
3 Altai Range: Gora Belucha 14.8 (4.5)
4 Andes: Aconcagua 22.8 (6.9)
5 Antarctic Peninsula: Vinson Massif 16.9 (5.1)
6 Appalachian Mountains: Mt Mitchell 6.6 (2.0)
7 Atlas Mountains: Jbel Toubkal 13.5 (4.2)
8 Australian Alps: Mt Kosciusko 7.3 (2.2)
9 Brooks Range: Mt Isto 8.9 (2.8)
10 Carpathian Mountains: Moldoveanul 8.2 (2.5)
11 Cascade Range: Mt Rainier 14.2 (4.4)
12 Caucasus Mountains: Mt Elbrus 18.5 (5.6)
13 Drakensberg Mountains: Thabana Ntlenyana 11.4 (3.5)
14 Elburz Mountains: Mt Demavend 18.4 (5.6)
15 Ethiopian Highlands: Ras Dachan 15.2 (4.6)
16 Himalaya: Mt Everest 29 (8.8)
17 Hindu Kush: Tirich Mir 25.2 (7.7)
18 Pamirs: Pik Kommunizma 24.6 (7.5)
19 Pyrenees: Pic d'Aneto 11.2 (3.4)
20 Rocky Mountains: Mt Elbert 14.4 (4.4)
21 Scandinavian Mountains: Glittertind 7.9 (2.4)
22 Sierra Madre: Citlaltépetl 18.7 (5.7)
23 Sierra Nevada: Mt Whitney 14.5 (4.4)
24 Taurus Mountains: Aladag 12.2 (3.7)
25 Tien Shan: Pik Pohedy 24.4(7.4)
26 Ural Mountains: Mt Narodnaya 6.2 (1.9)
27 Verkhoyansk Range: Gora Pobeda 10.3 (3.1)

Highest mountains

The world's ten highest mountains are listed below, rounded off in thousands of ft (m). All are in the Himalayas.

A Everest 29 (8.8)
B K2 (Godwin Austen) 28.2 (8.6)
C Kanchenjunga 28.2 (8.6)
D Lhotse 27.9 (8.5)
E Yalung Kang 27.9 (8.5)
F Makalu 27.8 (8.5)
G Dhaulagiri 26.8 (8.2)
H Manaslu 26.7 (8.1)
I Cho Oyo 26.7 (8.1)
J Nanga Parbat 26.7 (8.1)

continued

Mountains and volcanoes continued

1326 **Highest mountain in each continent**
The relative height of the highest mountain in each continent is shown here. Note the discontinuity between 5,000 and 15,000 ft (2,000- and 4,000 m) in the chart. The actual height of each is listed below, rounded off in thousands of ft (m).

1 Asia: Everest 29 (8.8)
2 South America: Aconagua 22.8 (6.9)
3 North America: McKinley 20.3 (6.2)
4 Africa: Kilimanjaro 19.3 (5.9)
5 Europe: Elbrus 18.5 (5.6)
6 Antarctica: Vinson Massif 16.9 (5.1)
7 Australia: Kosciusko 7.3 (2.2)

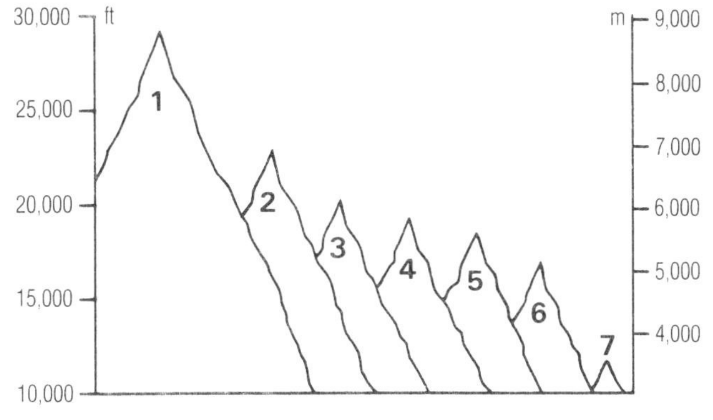

Highest volcanoes
The relative heights of the world's nine highest volcanoes are shown here. Below are listed the actual heights, rounded off in thousands of ft (m).

1 Aconcagua 22.8 (7.0)
2 Llullaillaco 22.1 (6.7)
3 Chimborazo 20.6 (6.3)
4 McKinley 20.3 (6.2)
5 Cotopaxi 19.3 (5.9)
6 Kilimanjaro 19.3 (5.9)
7 Antisana 18.7 (5.7)
8 Citlaltépetl 18.7 (5.7)
9 Elbrus 18.5 (5.6)

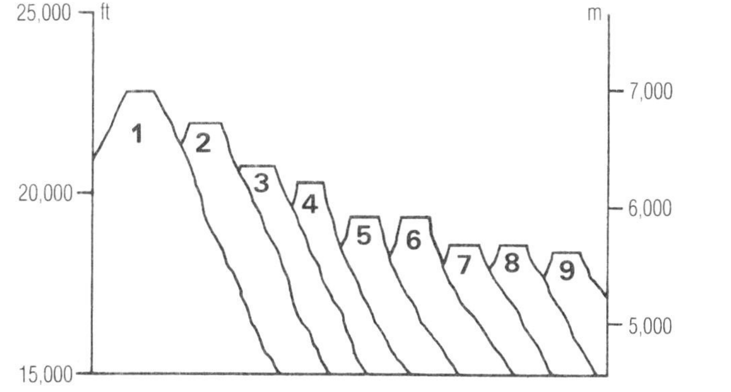

Rivers

1327 **Longest rivers in the world**
The world's longest rivers are compared here. Their actual lenghts are listed below, rounded off in thousands of mi (km).

1 Nile 4.1 (6.6)
2 Amazon 4 (6.4)
3 Mississippi 3.9 (6.2)
4 Ob-Irtysh 3.5 (5.6)
5 Yangtze 3.4 (5.5)
6 Huang He 2.9 (4.7)
7 Congo 2.9 (4.7)
8 Amur 2.8 (4.5)
9 Lena 2.6 (4.3)
10 Mackenzie 2.6 (4.2)

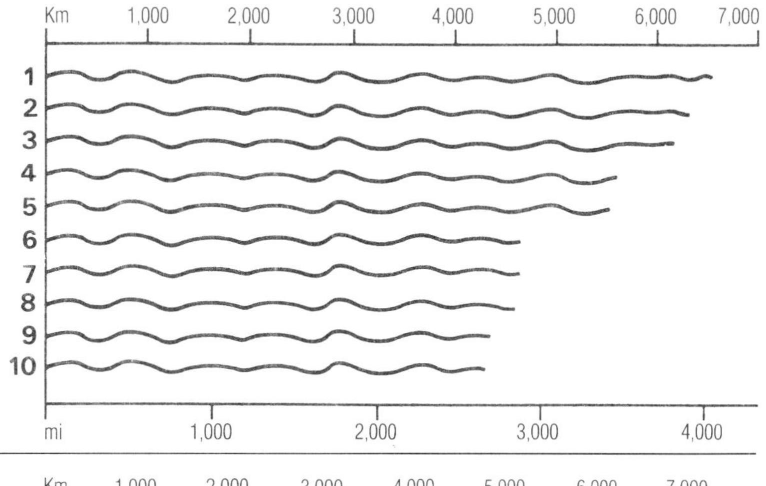

Longest river in each continent
The relative length of the longest river in each continent is shown here. The actual lengths are listed below, rounded off in thousands of mi (km).

1 Africa: Nile 4.1 (6.6)
2 South America: Amazon 4 (6.4)
3 North America: Mississippi 3.9 (6.2)
4 Asia: Ob-Irtysh 3.5 (5.6)
5 Europe: Volga 2.3 (3.7)
6 Australasia: Murray 2 (3.2)

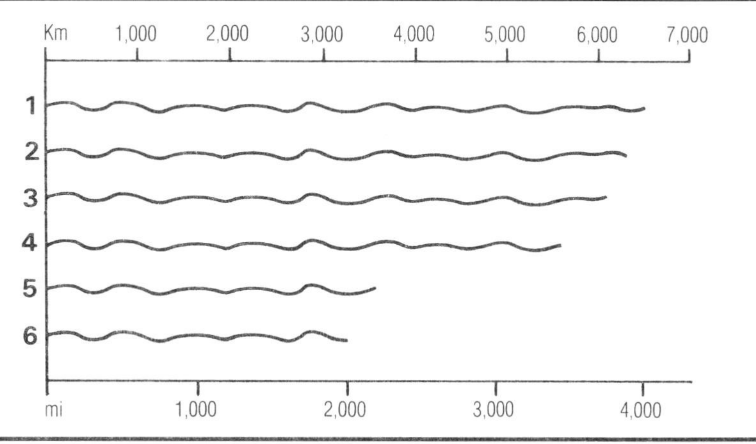

Largest waterfalls

1328 This list gives the largest waterfalls in the world, with their actual height in ft (m).

1 Angel Falls, Venezuela 3,212 ft (979 m)
2 Tugela, S Africa 3,110 ft (948 m)
3 Utigård, Norway 2,625 ft (800 m)
4 Mongefossen, Norway 2,540 ft (774 m)
5 Yosemite, US 2,425 ft (739 m)
6 Østre Mardøla Foss, Norway 2,154 ft (657 m)
7 Tyssestrenggane, Norway 2,120 ft (646 m)
8 Kukenaom, Venezuela 2,000 ft (610 m)
9 Sutherland, N Zealand 1,904 ft (580 m)
10 Kjellfossen, Norway 1,841 ft (561 m)

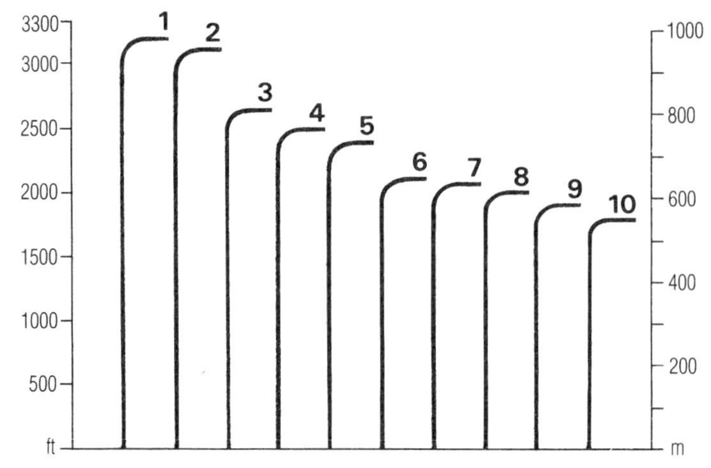

Deepest caves

1329 **1** Pierre St-Martin, France/Spain 4,370 ft (1,332 m)
2 Jean Bernard, France 4,258 ft (1,298 m)
3 Cellagua, Spain 3,182 ft (970 m)
4 Corchia, Italy 3,118 ft (950 m)
5 Kievskaya, Russia 3,114 ft (950 m)
6 Kacherlschact, Austria 2,992 ft (913 m)
7 San Augustin, Mexico 2,819 ft (859 m)
8 Holloch, Switzerland 2,713 ft (827 m)
9 Snieznej, Poland 2,569 ft (783 m)
10 Ghar Parau, Iran 2,464 ft (751 m)

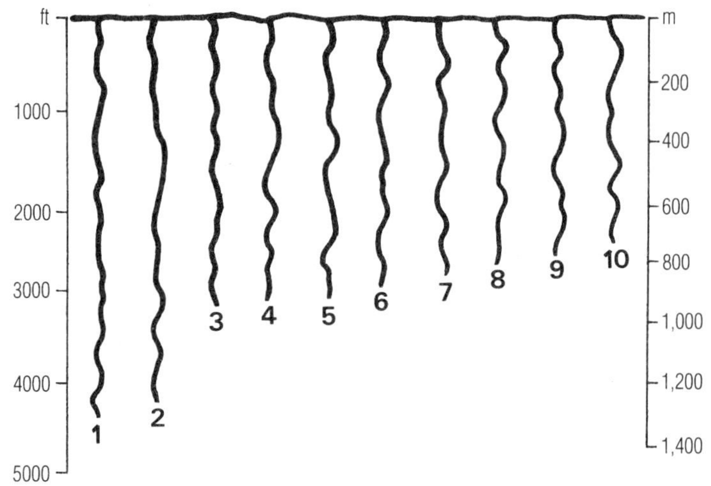

133 CLIMATE AND TEMPERATURE

Factors affecting temperature

1331 These can include altitude, latitude, length of day, aspect, cloud cover, winds, nearness to sea, ocean currents, and the amount of dust or pollutants in the atmosphere.

Polar, temperate, tropical
Lines on the map show the world divided on the basis of temperature into three types of climatic zone: polar (**1**), temperate (**2**), and tropical (**3**). The letters that appear on the map point to six locations with climatic features typical of different parts of the world.

Continental and maritime
These climatic subdivisions depend on distance from the sea. Maritime climates, by an ocean, have less difference between winter and summer temperatures than do continental climates, inland. For the six locations shown on the map the graphs opposite give average daily maximum temperatures for each month (top) and average monthly rainfall (bottom).

Climatic zones
1 Polar
2 Temperate
3 Tropical

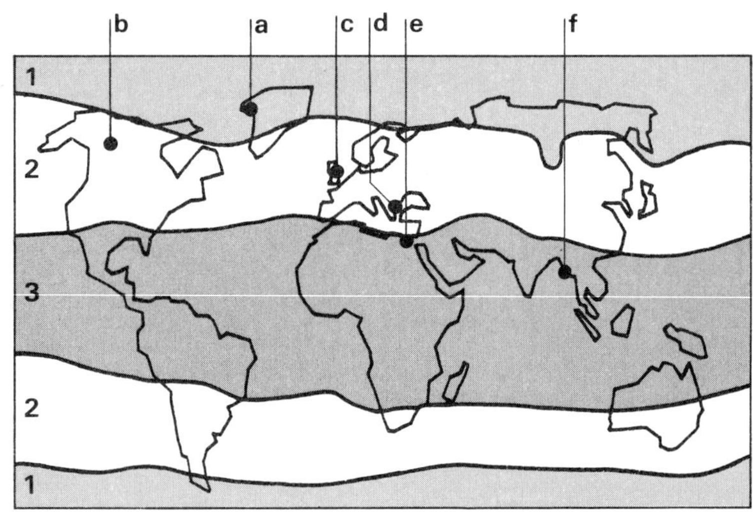

Locations typical of climatic zones
a Polar: Thule, Greenland
b Cold temperate continental: Peace River, Canada
c Cool temperate maritime: London, England
d Warm temperate: Athens, Greece
e Tropical desert: Cairo, Egypt
f Tropical monsoon: Rangoon, Myanmar

Climate graphs

1332

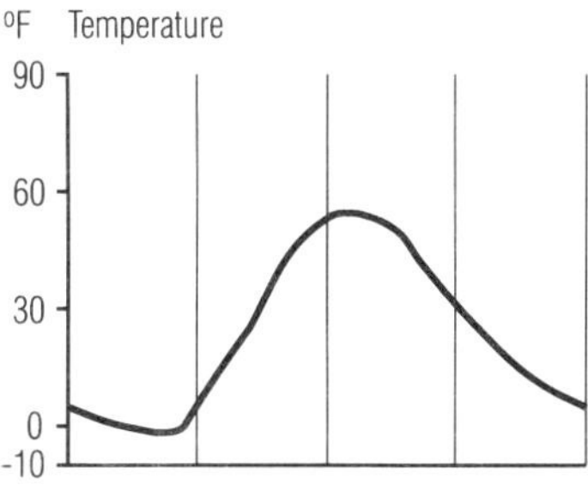

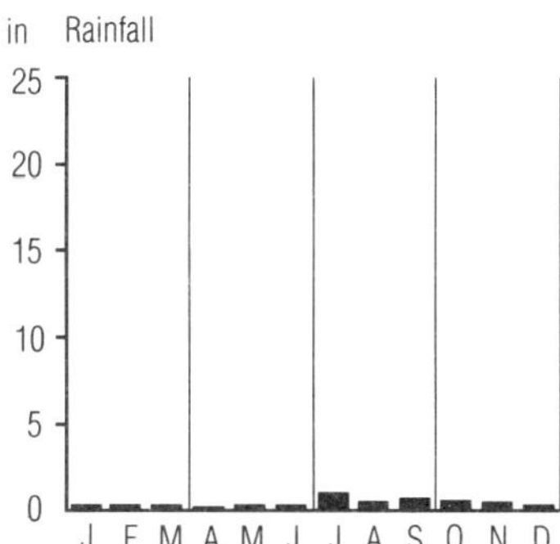

a Polar: Thule, Greenland
A polar climate has cool or cold summers and very cold winters. Precipitation (rain or snow, depending on the time of year) varies considerably from place to place, but is typically low.

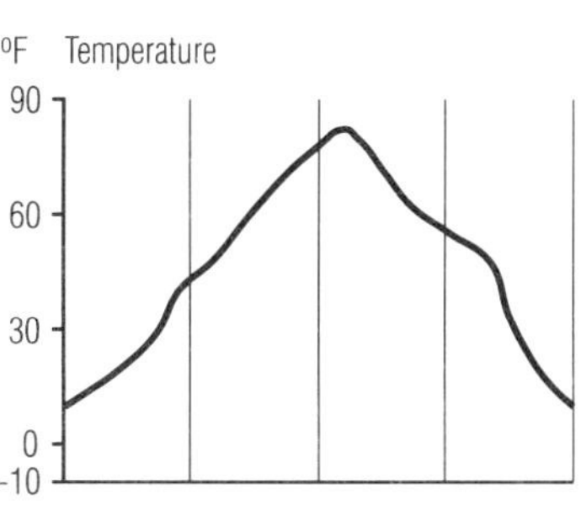

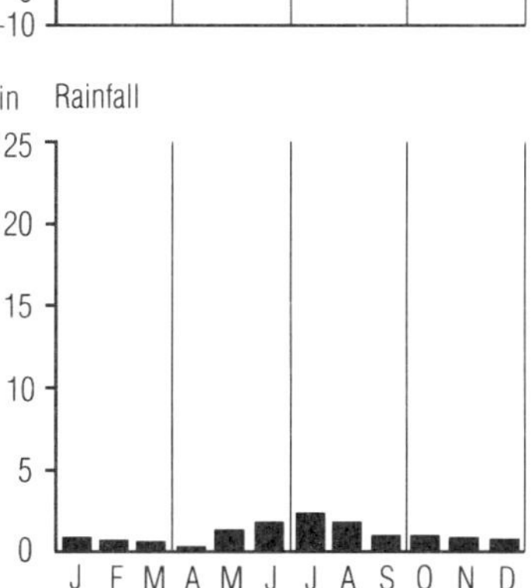

b Cold temperate continental: Peace River, Canada
Averaged over the year, this is less cold than a polar climate. Winters are very cold but summers are warm or hot. Precipitation occurs all year, but is highest in summer when thunderstorms commonly occur.

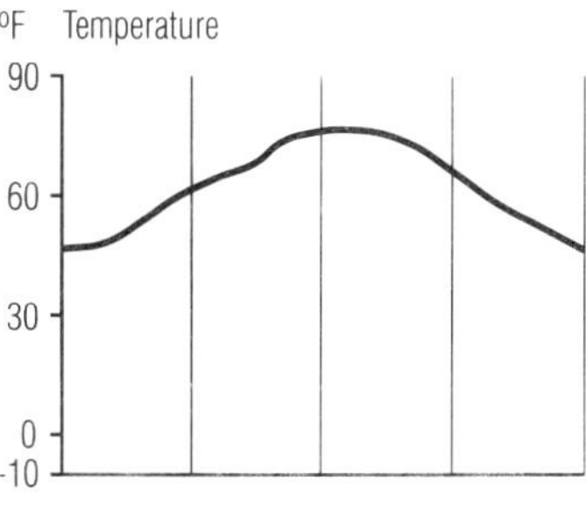

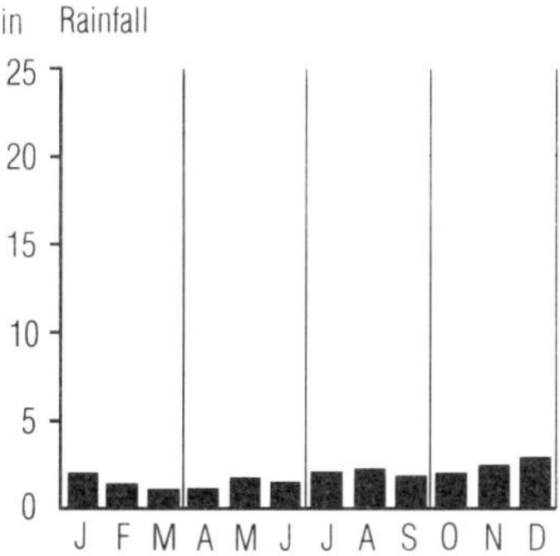

c Cool temperate maritime: London, England
This type of climate is neither very cold nor very hot. Winters are usually fairly mild and summers generally warm rather than hot. Precipitation (usually rain) is fairly evenly spread throughout the year.

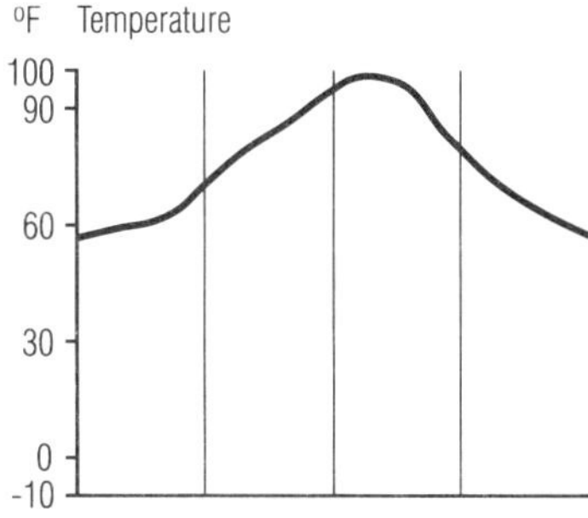

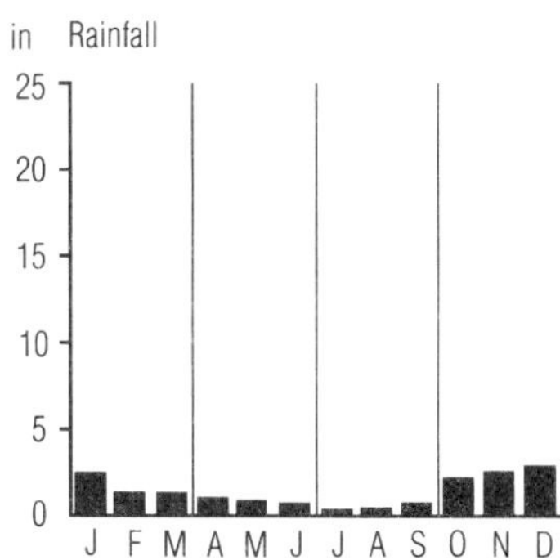

d Warm temperate: Athens, Greece
Warm temperate climate is often called Mediterranean but occurs elsewhere, as in southern California. Its typical features are mild winters and hot, dry summers.

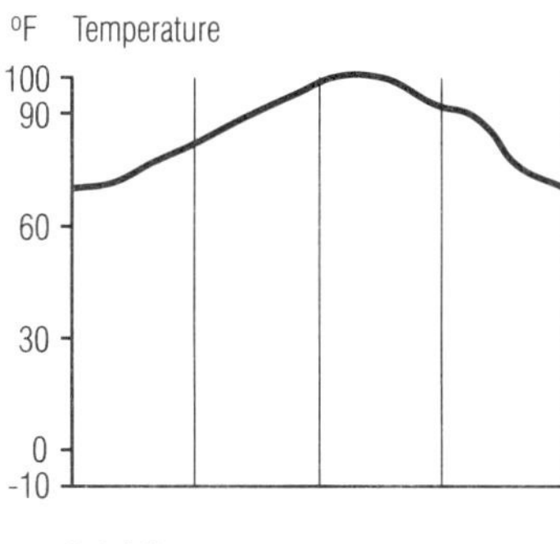

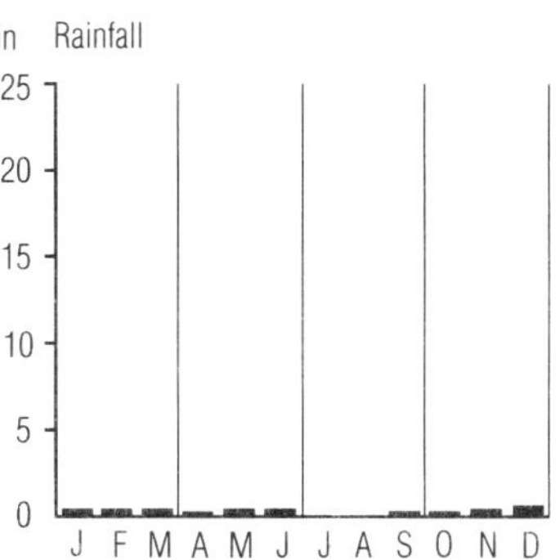

e Tropical desert: Cairo, Egypt
Tropical climates are hotter than temperate ones. Seasonal variations in temperature increase with distance from the equator. In hot deserts there can be a great variation in temperature between day and night.

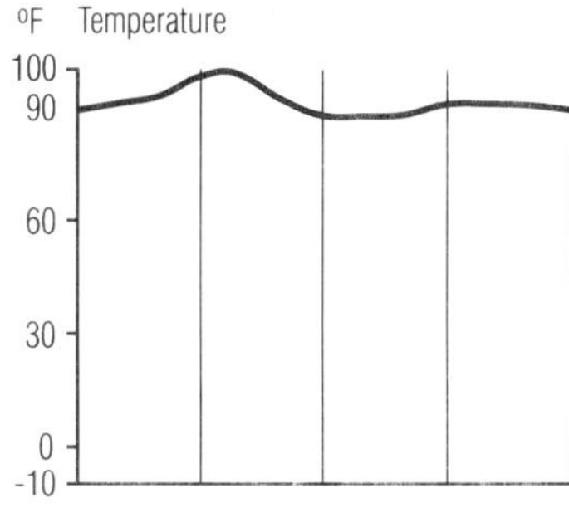

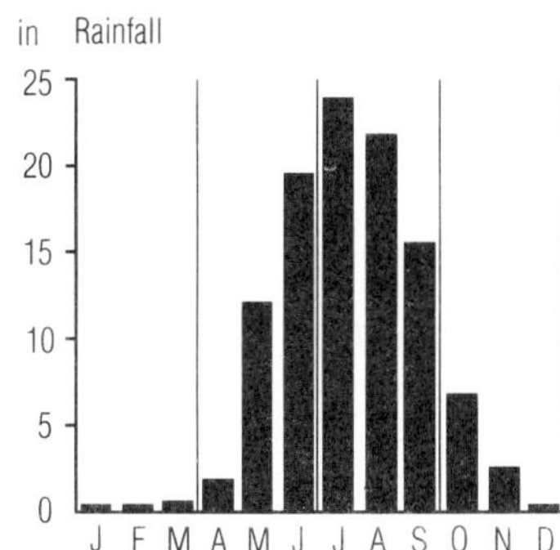

f Tropical monsoon: Rangoon, Myanmar
Near the equator, temperatures are hot all the year. Monsoon climates take their name from monsoon winds blowing onshore or offshore according to season. They bring wet summers and dry winters to parts of southeast Asia.

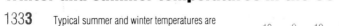

Winter and summer temperatures in the US

1333 Typical summer and winter temperatures are shown here for 23 US cities.

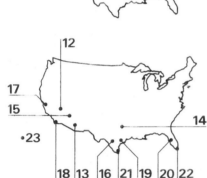

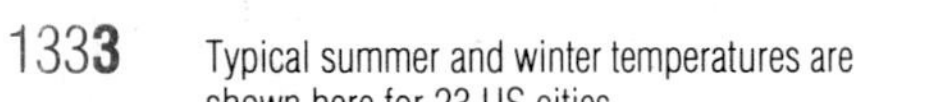

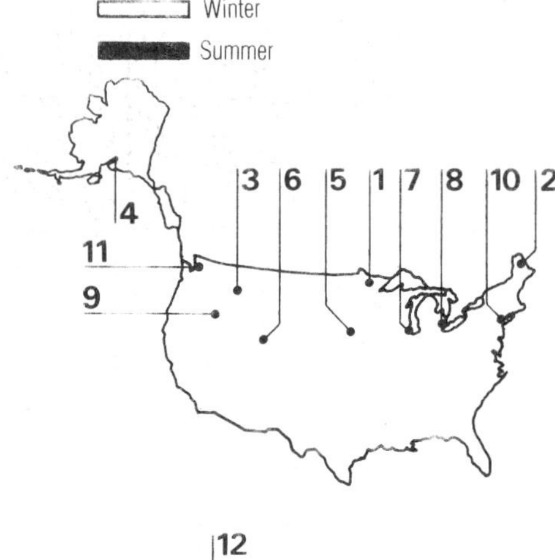

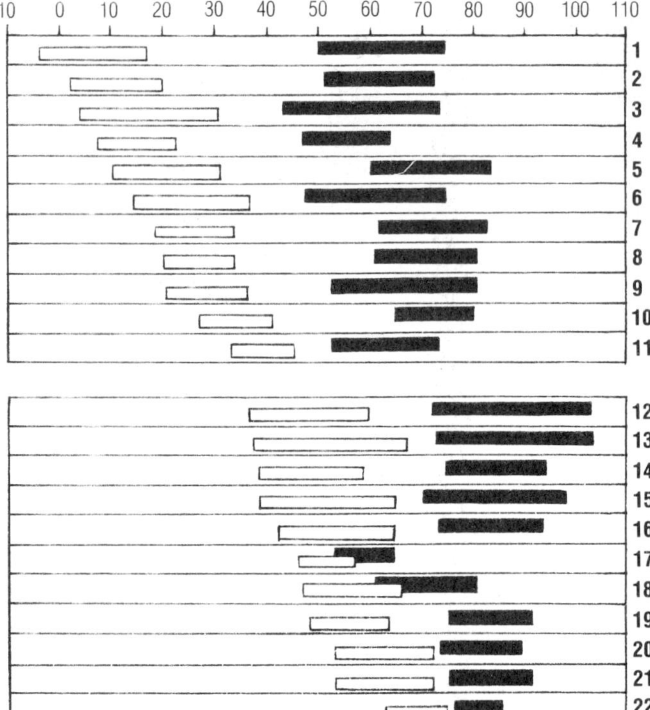

1 International Falls, Minnesota
2 Caribou, Maine
3 Butte, Montana
4 Anchorage, Alaska
5 Omaha, Nebraska
6 Cheyenne, Wyoming
7 Chicago, Illinois
8 Detroit, Michigan
9 Boise, Idaho
10 New York, New York
11 Seattle, Washington
12 Las Vegas, Nevada
13 Phoenix, Arizona
14 Dallas, Texas
15 Tucson, Arizona
16 San Antonio, Texas
17 San Francisco, California
18 Los Angeles, California
19 Houston, Texas
20 Tampa, Florida
21 Brownsville, Texas
22 Miami, Florida
23 Honolulu, Hawaii

Seasonal temperatures

1334 On eight world maps (below and opposite), isotherms (lines joining places with the same temperatures) are used to show the main global temperature zones for the months of January and July.

Jan 80° F+

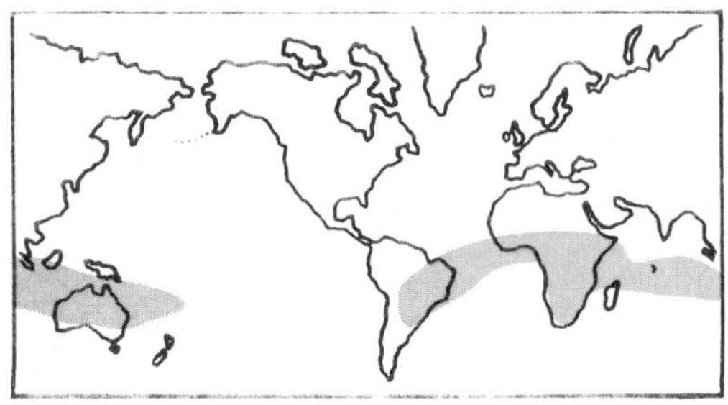

July 80° F+

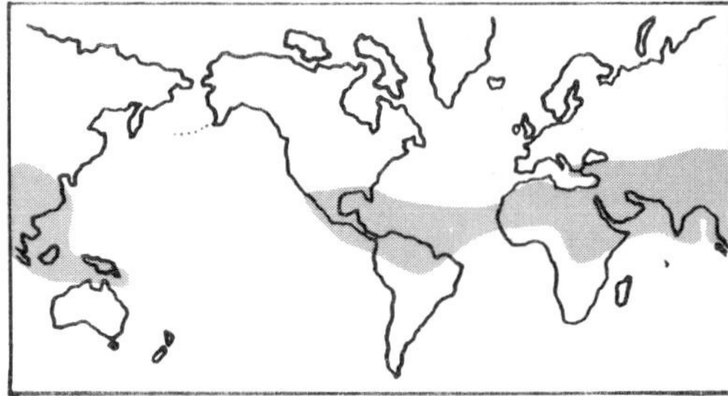

continued

Seasonal temperatures continued

1334 Jan 80° F–50° F

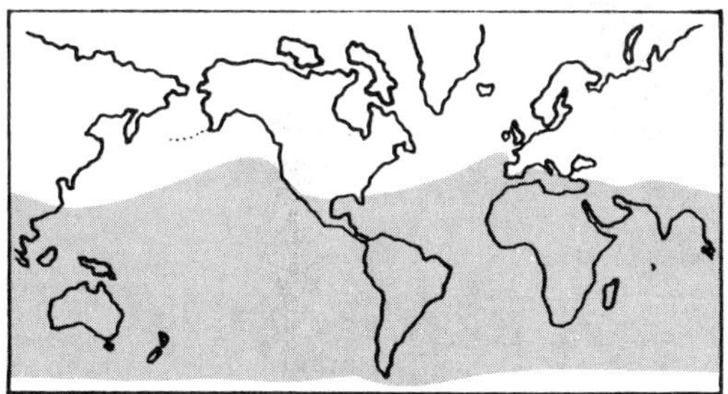

July 80° F–50° F

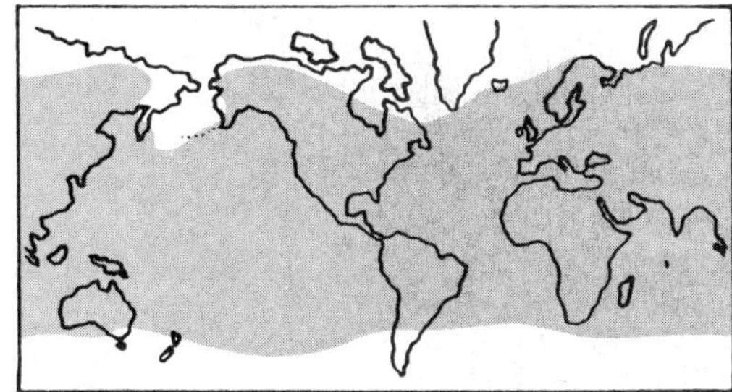

Jan 50° F 0° F

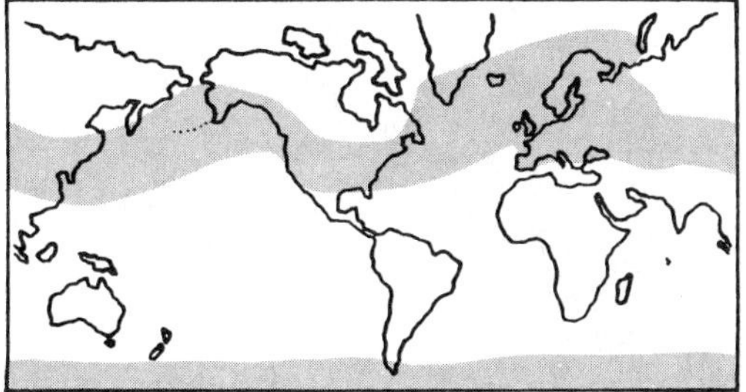

July 50° F– 0° F

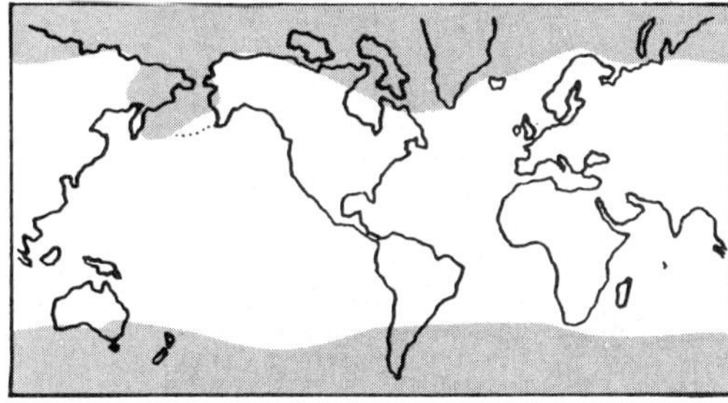

Jan 0° F–below

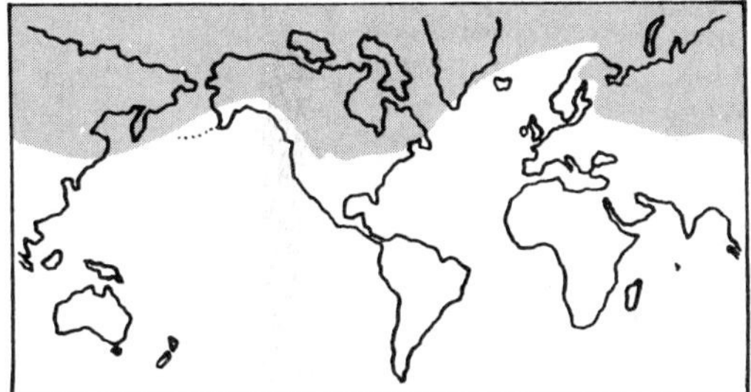

July 20° F–below

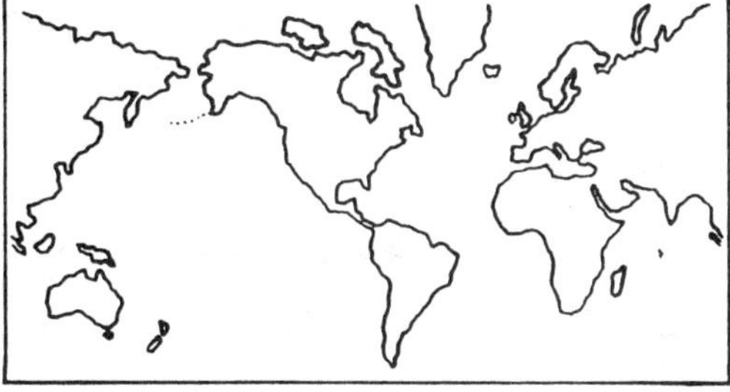

134 WIND AND WEATHER

Wind systems

1341 The Sun's heat and the Earth's spin produce the large-scale atmospheric circulation that we call the world's prevailing winds.

1 Hot air rises from the doldrums near the Equator and thins out. It spreads north and south, cools down, and sinks in the horse latitudes, becoming dense. It then flows back toward the Equator.

2 Prevailing surface winds (**a**–**d**) reflect the atmospheric flow in **1** that produces the surface pressure belts (**e**–**g**). Dense air from the polar highs and the high-pressure horse latitudes flows toward the temperate low-pressure belts and the low-pressure doldrums.

Surface winds
a Polar easterly winds
b Midlatitude westerly winds
c Northeast trade winds
d Southeast trade winds

Surface pressure belts
e Polar high pressure
f Temperate low pressure
g Horse latitudes
h Doldrums

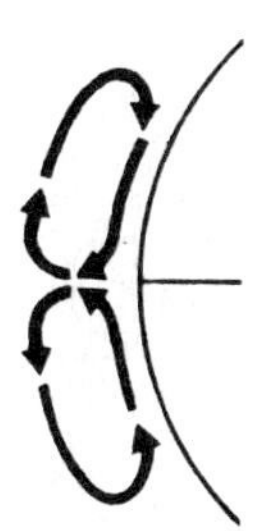

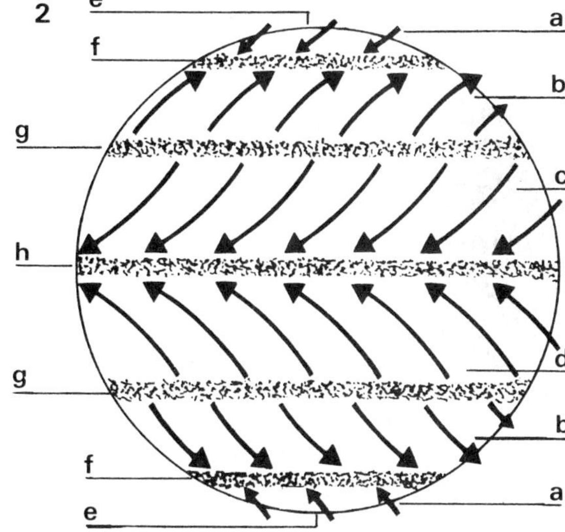

The Beaufort scale

1342 This is an internationally recognized scale for describing wind speeds that are 33 ft (10 m) above ground level. The table gives standard descriptions and wind speeds corresponding to each number in the Beaufort scale. It originated in 1805 when a British admiral, Sir Francis Beaufort, devised a scale of numbers to describe the effects of winds of different speeds on sailing ships.

Number	Description	Speed (mi/hr)	(km/hr)	Characteristics
0	Calm	Below 1	(Below 2)	Smoke goes straight up
1	Light air	1–3	(2–5)	Smoke blown by wind
2	Light breeze	4–7	(6–11)	Wind felt on face
3	Gentle breeze	8–12	(12–19)	Extends a light flag
4	Moderate breeze	13–18	(20–29)	Raises dust and loose paper
5	Fresh breeze	19–24	(30–38)	Small trees begin to sway
6	Strong breeze	25–31	(39–50)	Umbrellas become hard to use
7	Moderate gale	32–38	(51–61)	Difficult to walk into
8	Fresh gale	39–46	(62–74)	Twigs broken off trees
9	Strong gale	47–54	(75–86)	Roof damage
10	Whole gale	55–63	(87–102)	Trees uprooted
11	Storm	64–73	(103–117)	Widespread damage
12–17	Hurricane	74 and up	(118 and up)	Violent destruction

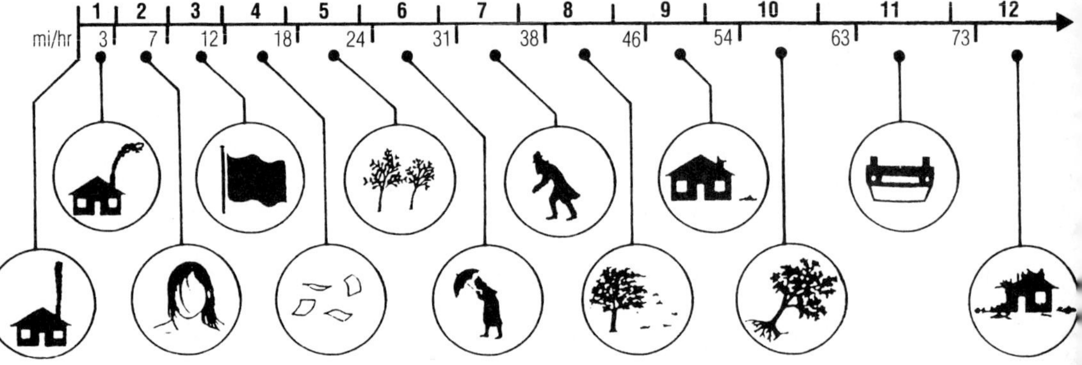

Wind patterns

1343 The maps show wind patterns for January and July and illustrate some interesting features of global wind movement. Winds blowing over North America and Asia are out-blowing during the winter when pressure is high but, are in-blowing during the summer when pressure is low.

Monsoon winds
The word *monsoon* is derived from the Arabic word *mausin* and means *season*. It is always used when describing winds whose direction is reversed completely from one season to the next; these most often develop over Asia.

● high pressure
○ low pressure

January wind pattern

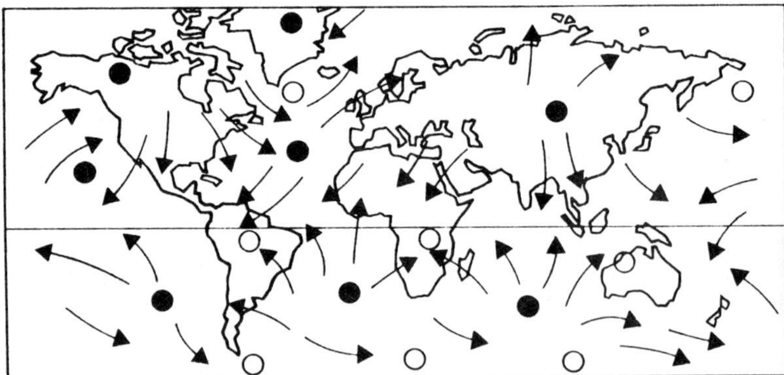

July wind pattern

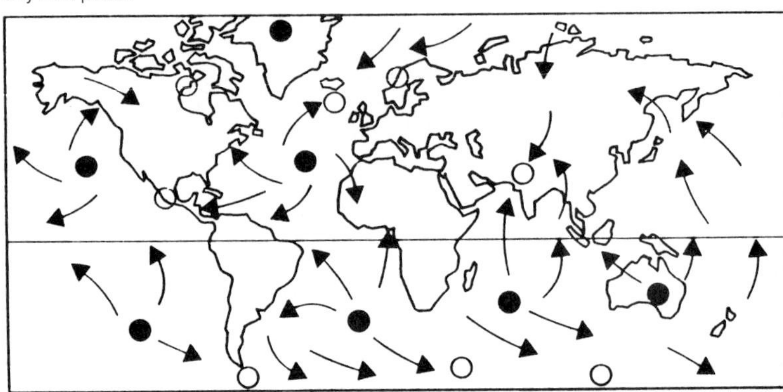

Chief types of cloud

1344 Clouds form when water vapor condenses into water droplets and/or cools to form snowflakes and ice crystals high above the ground.

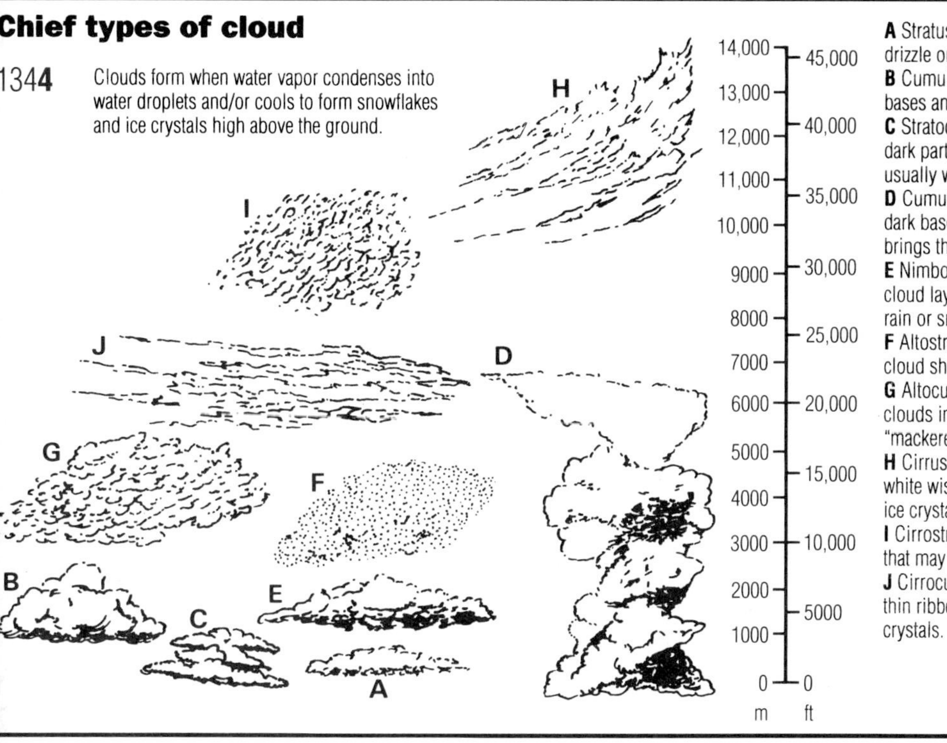

A Stratus: a low gray layer of cloud shedding drizzle or snow grains.
B Cumulus: low detached clouds with dark level bases and white fluffy tops; may bring showers.
C Stratocumulus: low whitish or gray cloud with dark parts, in a wavelike layer or patches; usually without rain.
D Cumulonimbus: towering clouds with a dark base and spreading, anvil-shaped top; brings thunderstorms.
E Nimbostratus: a middle-altitude, dark, dense cloud layer, often ragged beneath; comes with rain or snow.
F Altostratus: middle-altitude, grayish or bluish cloud sheets, thin in parts and rainbearing.
G Altocumulus: middle-altitude white or gray clouds in rolls or rounded masses, fine "mackerel sky" clouds.
H Cirrus: high-altitude thin white or mostly white wispy clouds with a silky sheen; made of ice crystals.
I Cirrostratus: a high, whitish, transparent layer that may cover the entire sky.
J Cirrocumulus: high, white patches of cloud in thin ribbed sheets or layers made up of ice crystals.

Weather fronts

1345 Lows (depressions) bring wind and rain to the temperate midlatitudes. Lows are whirling "pinwheels" of air hundreds of miles across. They form where cold polar air clashes with warm, moist, subtropical air along a boundary called the polar front. Lows bring warm fronts and cold fronts.

1 At a warm front, warm, moist air rides up over cold air, producing sheetlike stratus cloud shedding steady drizzle or snow.

2 At a cold front following a warm front, cold air undercuts the warm air from behind. This may produce dark nimbostratus clouds shedding heavy showers of rain or snow.

a Warm air
b Cold air
c Heavy showers
d Prolonged drizzle

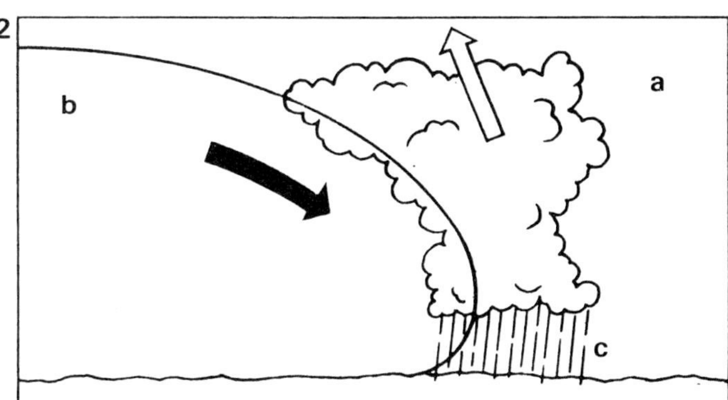

1346 Weather map symbols
135 **Maps**
1351 Topographic map symbols
1352 Map projections
1353 Relief maps

Weather map symbols

1346 **cloud types**

Thick altostratus
Thin altostratus
Scattered cirrus
Dense cirrus patches
Partial cirrus cover
Complete cirrus cover
Bands of thin altostratus
Patches of thin altostratus
Cumulus
Stratocumulus
Bad weather/ fractocumulus
Fair weather stratus

Cloud cover

Clear sky
1/10 or less
2/10 to 3/10
4/10
1/2
6/10
7/10
Mainly overcast
Completely overcast

Wind direction and speed

Calm
1–2 knots
3–7 knots
8–12 knots
13–17 knots
18–22 knots
23–27 knots
28–47 knots
48–52 knots

Precipitation

Mist
Rain
Hail
Fog
Drizzle
Showers
Thunderstorms
Sandstorm
Snow

Fronts and pressure systems

Cold front
Warm front
Occluded front
Stationary front
(H)/(L) High/low pressure center
—29·88— Isobar

135 MAPS

Topographic map symbols

1351

Primary highway (r)
Secondary highway (r)
Light-duty road
Unimproved track
Single-track railroad
Multiple-track railroad
Buildings
Landmark; windmill
Quarry; prospect
X8463 Spot elevation
Index contour
Supplementary contour
Intermediate contour
Embankment
Cutting
National boundary
State boundary
Country parish boundary
Perennial stream (b)
Intermittent stream (b)
Water well; spring (b)
Small rapids (b)
Big rapids (b)
Big falls (b)
Small falls (b)
Intermittent lake (b)
Glacier (w)
Dry lake bed (r-in-b)
Marsh or swamp (b on-w)
Wooded marsh (g)
Woods (g)
Vineyard (g)
Controlled flooding
Submerged marsh (b)
Mangrove swamp (g)
Orchard (g-on-w)
Scrub (g-on-w)
Urban area (p)

Color key
red (r)
green (g)
blue (b)
pink (p)
blue-on-white (b-on-w)
red-in-blue (r-in-b)
green-on-white (g-on-w)

Map projections

1352 These are standard devices for showing the Earth's global surface on a flat sheet of paper. Each projection distorts the Earth in some way.

Azimuthal (zenithal) projection
This projects the Earth as if a flat sheet is touching the globe at the map center. It shows the shortest straight-line distances.

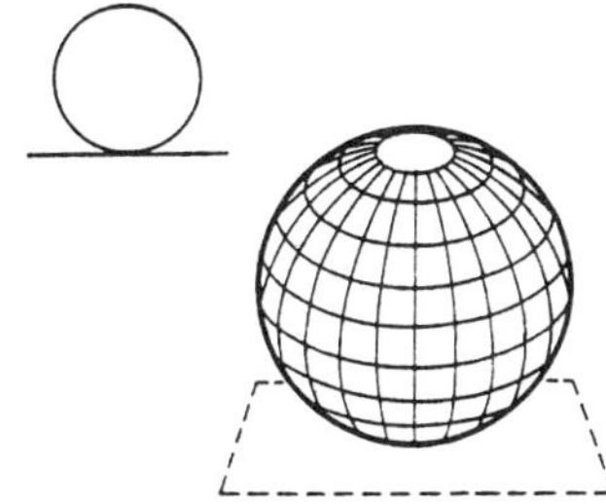

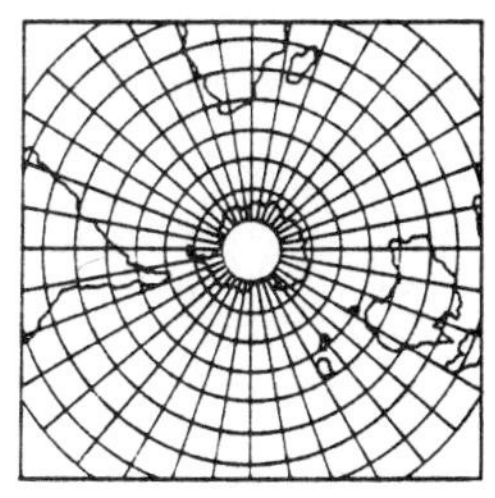

Cylindrical projection
This is made as if wrapping a sheet of paper around a globe's equator to produce a cylinder or tube. On such projections lines of longitude meet lines of latitude at right angles and so do not meet at the poles. The view stretches polar areas but can show a true compass course.

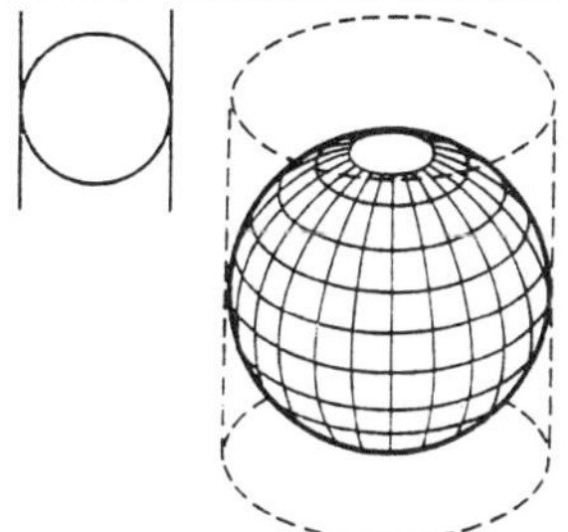

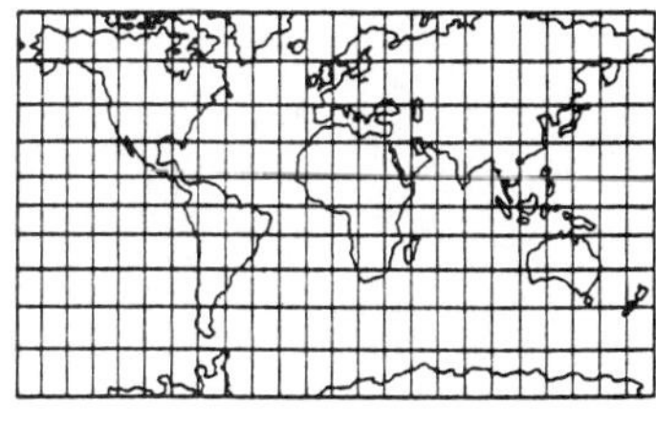

Conic projection
This is made as if a cone of paper is wrapped around a globe so as to touch it along one line of latitude. A conic projection shows lines of latitude as curved and lines of longitude as meeting at a pole. Conic projections show areas, directions, and distances fairly accurately.

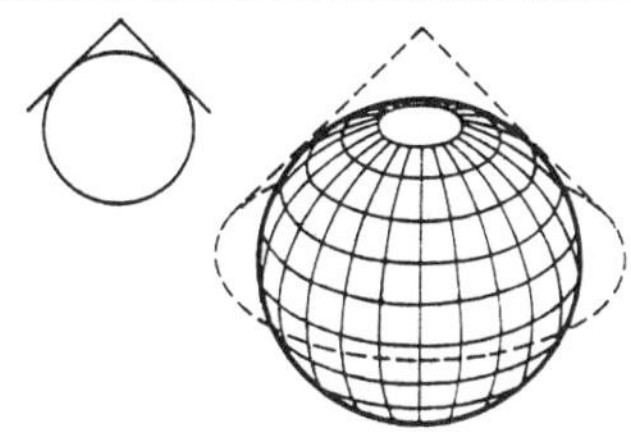

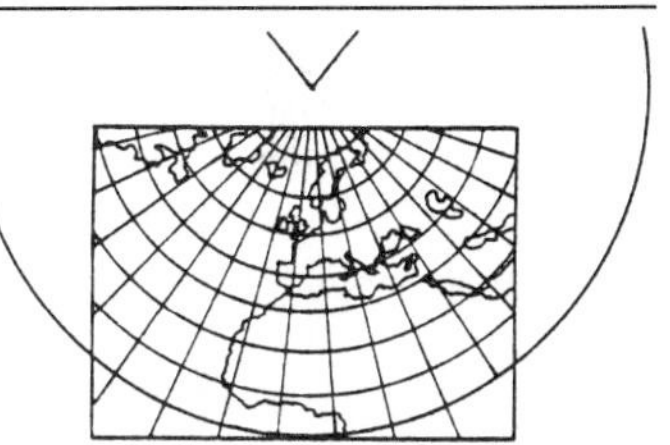

Mathematical projection
Mathematical projections are devised for special purposes. This homolosine equal-area projection is useful for showing the global distributions of different phenomena. Achieving accurate representation of area in this type of projection may involve interruption, as shown here.

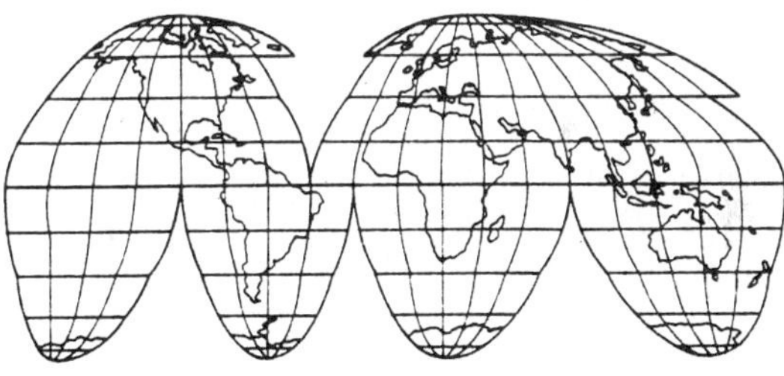

Relief maps

1353 Diagrams show three ways of depicting differences in level (relief) in maps.
1 Contours
a Hills and valleys, shown as if their contour lines could be seen. (A contour line joins places that are the same height above sea level.)
b Contour map with contours at vertical intervals of perhaps 50 ft (15 m).
2 Layered tones or colors show areas that lie between different contour levels.
3 Hachures show slopes as short lines of shading. The thicker the lines and the closer together they are, the steeper the slope they represent.

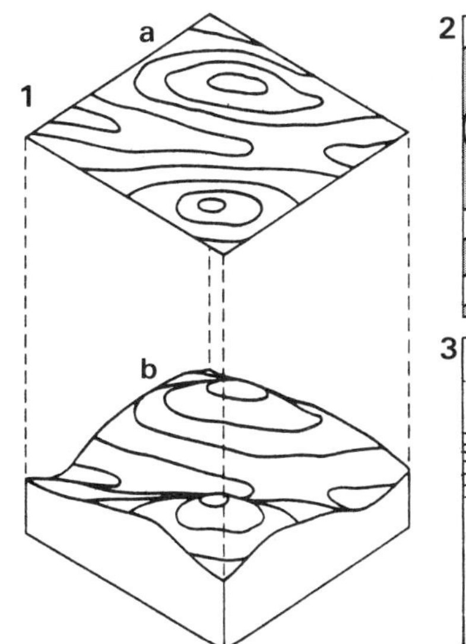

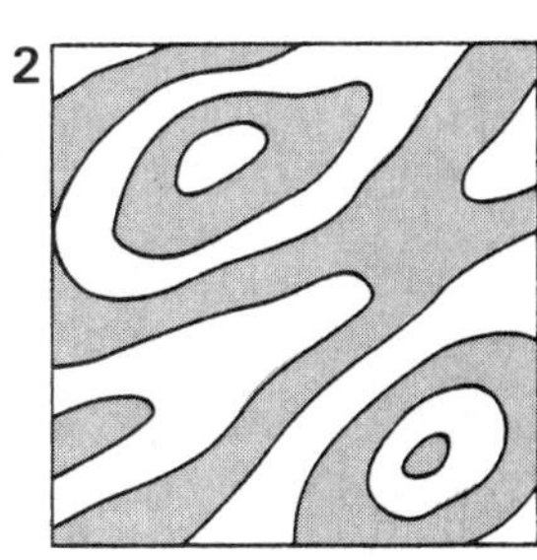

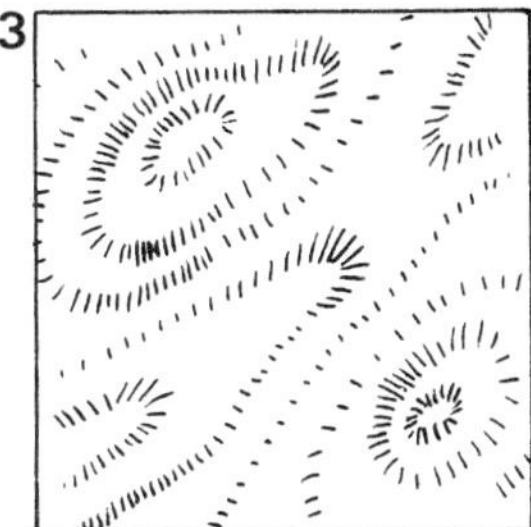

136 GEOGRAPHY GLOSSARY

abyssal plain A level tract of the deep ocean floor.
air mass A fairly uniform mass of air covering a large area and containing air of, for example, polar or tropical origin.
Antarctic Circle A line of latitude approximately 66.5° south of the equator; the southern hemisphere's equivalent of the Arctic Circle.
anticyclone A region of high atmospheric pressure, usually bringing quiet, settled weather.
aquifer A water-bearing, permeable, and porous rock mass or layer.
Arctic Circle A line of latitude, approximately 66° north of the equator, north of which the Sun does not rise at least one day in winter or set at least one day in summer; the northern hemisphere's equivalent of the Antarctic Circle.
atmosphere The envelope of gases that surrounds the Earth.
atoll A ring-shaped coral reef enclosing a lagoon.
aurora An electrical discharge producing curtains of light seen at high latitudes in the night sky.
autumn One of the seasons of temperate climatic zones.
avalanche A great mass of snow that suddenly slides down a slope.
badlands Arid, barren hilly land, deeply eroded by gullies.
bar A sandy or shingly ridge lying across a river mouth or a bay.
barrier island A long, low, narrow, sandy island separated from the mainland by a lagoon.
bay A wide inlet in a sea or lake, but smaller than a gulf.
beach The sloping strip of land between high and low water marks.
butte A flat-topped, steep-sided mountain or hill smaller than a mesa.
cape A pointed mass of land jutting into the sea.
cave A hole in the Earth's crust, produced by water or lava.
cirque A mountain hollow eroded by snow and ice. It may contain snow or a lake.
cliff A steep, erosion-resistant rock face, as in gorges and on some coasts.
climate The average weather of a region or place as measured for all seasons over a number of years.
cloud A mass of water droplets or ice crystals in air, formed by water vapor condensing, usually high above ground.
col A natural pass in a mountain range.
continent One of the world's great unbroken land masses.
continental shelf A shallow sea bed; the submerged edge of a continent.
Coriolis force The tendency of the Earth's rotation to turn winds and currents to the right in the northern hemisphere and to the left in the southern hemishpere.
creep The gradual downslope movement of soil or rock fragments, due to gravity.
cuesta A ridge with a steep slope on one side, and a gentle dip slope on the other.
cyclone A region of low atmospheric pressure, usually bringing windy, rainy, unsettled weather. Temperate regions receive wave cyclones, also called depressions. Violent tropical cyclones include hurricanes and typhoons.
delta Flat, alluvial land at a river mouth where it splits into many streams called distributaries.
denudation The wearing away of the land surface by the sum of such processes as weathering and erosion.
doldrums The low-pressure equatorial belt of calm air and light winds.
drought Prolonged dry weather.
drumlin A half-egg shaped hill of glacial deposits, formed under moving glacial ice.
dune A sand ridge or mound formed where wind heaps up the sand in a desert or on a low sandy coast.
equator An imaginary line around the Earth midway between the poles.
equatorial zone The belt between latitudes 10°N and S of the equator.
erosion The removal of loose mineral particles by wind, water, and moving ice.
estuary A broad, low, river mouth, usually where the coast has sunk or the sea level has risen.
fjord A long, narrow, steep-sided sea inlet invading a glaciated valley.
fog A cloud on the ground or on water.
front The boundary between masses of cold and warm air.
frost Frozen particles of moisture on the ground.
gale A very high wind of force 8 or above on the Beaufort scale.
geyser A periodic fountain forced up by the pressure of steam produced by hot rocks heating underground water.
glaciation (1) The effects on land of ice sheets or glaciers that erode rocks and deposit the rock debris. **(2)** A time when ice sheets develop and spread.
glacier A mass of ice that creeps down a valley, scouring its floor and sides.
gorge A deep, narrow, steep-sided valley, formed where a river erodes the floor far faster than the sides.
ground water Subsurface water filling pores in rock. It flows under gravity.
gulf A very big and deep coastal inlet, larger than a bay.
gully A narrow channel worn in a hillside by running water. Gullies abound in land prone to soil erosion.
guyot A flat-topped submarine mountain formed by a subsiding volcanic island.
hail Pelletlike precipitation made of concentric layers of ice formed as water droplets froze in cumulonimbus clouds. Hail falls during thunderstorms.
hogback A long, narrow ridge that is steep on both sides.
horn A steep-sided, pyramidal mountain peak formed by the backward erosion of the headwalls of several cirques.
horse latitudes Subtropical belts of atmospheric high pressure; calm regions in both hemispheres between the westerlies and the trade winds.

Hemisphere
The Earth can be divided into several hemispheres, or "half spheres." The equator is used to divide the Earth into the northern and southern hemispheres. Although there is no established boundary for the eastern and western hemispheres, it is usually drawn at 20° W and 160° E lines of longitude.

eastern and western hemispheres

eastern hemisphere

western hemisphere

northern and southern hemispheres

northern hemisphere

southern hemisphere

continued

Geography glossary continued

horst A high block of land between parallel faults, caused by the block having risen or the land on either side having sunk.
humidity The (variable) amount of water vapor in the atmosphere.
hurricane The name for a tropical cyclone in the Caribbean Sea and western North Atlantic Ocean.
iceberg A floating mass of ice that has broken off the end of a glacier and fallen into the sea.
ice sheet An immense mass of ice covering a large land area.
international Date Line The line of longitude (with local deviations) 180° E or W, where the date changes by a day. East of the line it is one day earlier than west of the line.
island A piece of land completely surrounded by a river, lake, sea, or ocean.
isobar On a map, a line that passes through places that have the same atmospheric pressure at the same time.
isotherm On a map, a line that passes through places that have the same air temperature at the same time.
isthmus A narrow neck of land joining two larger areas of land.
jet stream A high-altitude, high-speed wind in the upper-air westerlies.
karst Limestone landscape with a largely bare, rocky surface and rivers that flow through underground caves.
lagoon A shallow area of water partly or wholly cut off from the sea by a strip or strips of land.
lake A large sheet of water surrounded by land or, more rarely, ice.
landform A distinctive natural configuration of the land surface.
landslide The sudden slide down a slope or cliff of a mass of rocks or soil.
latitude Location north or south of the equator.
leaching The process by which rainwater washes soluble salts out of the upper soil into a lower soil layer.
lightning A discharge of static electricity during a thunderstorm.
longitude Location east or west of the Prime Meridian.
magnetic poles Points on the Earth's surface sought by a magnetic compass needle. Their positions vary.
map projection A device for showing the Earth's curved surface on a flat sheet.
massif A mountain mass of ancient rocks partly dissected into separate peaks.
meander A curve in a river that swings in wide loops from side to side.
meridian A line of longitude passing between the poles at right angles to the equator.
mesa A relatively small plateau capped by resistant horizontal rocks.
meteorology The study of the atmosphere and its behavior.
midoceanic ridge A submarine mountain chain formed of upwelling molten rock.
mirage An optical illusion caused by the bending of light passing between air layers of differing density.
mist Water droplets in air that reduce visibility, but by less than fog.
monsoon A wind that blows inland in summer and offshore in winter. The summer monsoon brings rain to much of south and southeast Asia.
moraine Rock debris moved or dumped by a melting glacier or ice sheet.
mountain A mass of land higher than a hill and standing significantly above its surroundings. A mountain summit is small compared to its base.
ocean The great sheet of salt water surrounding the Earth's landmasses; also its subdivision into the Pacific, Atlantic, Indian, and Arctic oceans.
ocean current A horizontal flow of water through the ocean. Warm and cold surface currents redistribute the Sun's heat more evenly around the Earth
oceanic trench A deep, narrow trough in an ocean floor.
oceanography The study of oceans, including seawater, the ocean floor, and marine plants and animals.
peneplain A nearly flat land surface almost worn down to sea level.
peninsula A tract of land that is almost surrounded by water.
permafrost Permanently frozen ground found in polar and subpolar zones.
pingo A hillock produced in polar regions by an underground ice "blister" pushing up the surface above.
plain A large tract of almost level land.
plateau A large area of high land with a fairly flat top and steep sides.
polar zones Regions 75–90° N and S of the equator.
poles The ends of the Earth's axis, forming its northernmost and southernmost points: the North Pole and South Pole. Their locations do not correspond exactly with the North and South magnetic poles produced by the Earth's magnetic properties.
precipitation Water deposited from the atmosphere in the forms of rain, hail, sleet, snow, dew, and frost.
prime meridian An imaginary north-south line of longitude that passes through Greenwich, England, and is used as the basis for longitudinal measurements on the globe.
rain Falling water drops formed from droplets coalescing in clouds.
rapids A steep section of river where water flows faster than elsewhere.
ravine A long, narrow, steep-sided depression in the Earth's surface, between a gully and valley in size.
reef A ridge of rocks or coral always or often submerged in the sea.
relief Differences in height for any area of the Earth's surface.
ria A drowned river valley, forming a long, narrow, funnel-shaped inlet at right angles to the sea.
rift valley A long narrow trough where land has sunk between two in-facing parallel faults; also called a graben.
sea A subdivision of an ocean, or a large landlocked expanse of salt water.
seasons Climatically different times of year determined by changes in the angle at which the Sun's rays reach the Earth. Temperate northern regions have four seasons: spring, summer, autumn, and winter, coinciding respectively with autumn, winter, spring, and summer in the temperate southern hemisphere. Some tropical regions have only two seasons: wet and dry.
sleet Precipitation in the form of frozen raindrops or partly melted and then refrozen snow.
snow Precipitation in the form of feathery ice crystals that often stick together as snowflakes.
spit A low strip of sand or shingle, one end joined to land, the other poking into the sea or across a bay.
spring Ground water escaping at the surface, as where a water-saturated rock layer outcrops on a hillside, above a layer of impermeable rock.
stalactite A "stone icicle" formed from dissolved calcium carbonate deposited as dripping water evaporates.
stalagmite A calcium carbonate column formed on a cave floor in the same way as a stalactite.
strait A narrow strip of sea linking two large areas of sea.
stratosphere The layer of atmosphere immediately above the troposphere.
subtropical zones Latitudes between the tropics and temperate zones. They lie about 25–35° N and 25–35° S.
swell A long, symmetrical undulation of the sea surface.
talus Loose rock fragments fallen from a cliff; also called scree.
temperate zones Latitudes broadly between subtropical and polar zones.
thunder The bang produced as the heat from a flash of lightning makes air expand suddenly.
thunderstorm A storm where strong upcurrents of air build a cumulonimbus cloud producing heavy showers (often with hail), lightning, and thunder.
tides The regular rise and fall of sea level mainly due to the Moon's gravitational pull on the Earth.
tornado A fierce whirlwind only a few hundred yards across.
trade winds Constant winds blowing from the subtropics toward the equator.
tropical zones Latitudes lying roughly 10–25° N and 10–25° S.
troposphere The lowest level of the atmosphere, up to 9 mi (14 km) deep.
tsunami A high-speed wave set off by an earthquake, landslide, or volcanic eruption and towering on reaching some coasts; also called seismic sea wave.
valley A long depression worn in the land by a river or ice, or sunk between faults
wadi A normally dry desert watercourse.
water cycle The circulation of water from sea to air and back again. This involves evaporation, condensation, and precipitation, and may include surface runoff, rivers, and glaciers.
waterfall A stream falling over a cliff-like step in the bedrock.
watershed Land drained by a river and its tributaries.
water table The upper surface of rock saturated by ground water. Wet and dry weather make the table rise and fall.
wave A disturbance moving through the surface of land or water.
weather The condition of the atmosphere at a

continued

Geography glossary continued

136 particular time and place.
weathering The decay and break up of rocks on the Earth's surface by natural chemical and mechanical processes.
westerlies The prevailing winds of midlatitudes.
wind An air current parallel to the Earth's surface. North winds blow from the north, for example.

137 GEOLOGY/GEOGRAPHY BIOGRAPHIES

Agassiz, Jean Louis Rodolphe 1807–73, Swiss-born American naturalist and glaciologist. After studying glacial phenomena of Alps, showed that glaciers are not static but move, thus indicating existence of ice age.
Agricola, Georgius Latin name of Georg Bauer, 1494–1555, German. Germany's first systematic mineralogist, as well as metallurgist, who studied ores, recognizing mineral veins as deposits left by rising solutions. *De Re Metallica* published in 1555.
Airy, Sir George Biddell 1801–92, English astronomer and geophysicist who, in 1850s, laid a basis for theory of isostasy-state of balance in the Earth's crust where continents of light material float on a denser substance into which deep continental "roots" project like underwater mass of floating icebergs.
Alberti, Friedrich August von 1795–1878, German geologist who named *Triassic System* in 1824, from a tripartite division of rocks.
Arduino, Giovanni 1714–95, Italian. Founder of Italian geology who coined name *Tertiary*, later given to a rock system and geological period.
Barrell, Joseph 1869–1919, American geologist who declared that much sedimentary rock did not form under oceans. Coined terms *lithosphere* and *asthenosphere* and was first geologist fully to realize potential of radioactive dating.
Beaufort, Sir Francis 1774–1857, English naval officer and hydrographer. From 1829 to 1855, served as hydrographer to navy, devising Beaufort scale of wind force and a tabulated system of weather registration.
Bertrand, Marcel-Alexandre 1847–1907, French geologist who showed that formation of such mountain ranges as Alps involved massive folding of Earth's crust.
Bjerknes, Jacob Aall Bonnevie1897–1975, Norwegian-born American meteorologist, son of Norwegian physicist Vilhelm Bjerknes. With father, formulated theory of cyclones on which modern weather forecasting is based.
Brongniart, Alexandre 1770–1847, French naturalist and geologist who, in 1829, introduced term *Jurassic* for limestones and clays of Cotswolds in England.
Dana, James Dwight 1813–95, American mineralogist and geologist who classified minerals, coined term *geosyncline*, studied coral-rock formation, and theorized about evolution of Earth's crust.
Davis, William Morris 1850–1934, American. A founder of geomorphology (scientific landform studies) who introduced term *peneplain* to describe rolling lowland and was first to formulate doctrine of "cycle of erosion."
Dutton, Clarence Edward 1841–1912, American geologist, seismologist, and vulcanologist who advanced and named theory of isostasy.
Gilbert, Grove Karl 1843–1918, American. A founder of landform studies (geomorphology) who formulated many of the laws of geological processes. Report on Henry mountains became foundation of many modern theories of denudation and river development.
Guettard, Jean Etienne 1715–86, French geologist and mineralogist who studied "weathering" and prepared arguably first geological map of France.
Holmes, Arthur 1890–1965, English geologist and geophysicist who put dates to geological time scale as early as 1913. Determined ages of rocks by measuring their radioactive constituents, and was early scientific supporter of Wegener's continental drift theory.
Hutton, James 1726–97, Scottish geologist who pioneered uniformitarianism, belief that forces still at work had caused geological change over vast span of time, and who contributed to understanding of how igneous rocks are formed. His work formed the basis of modern geology.
Lyell, Sir Charles 1797–1875, Scottish geologist whose *Principles of Geology* (1830-33) had powerful influence on modern scientific thought. It denied necessity of stupendous upheavals, arguing that the greatest geological changes might have been produced by forces still at work.
Mercator, Gerardus Latin name of Gerhard Kremer, 1512-94, Flemish geographer and map-maker. In 1569, introduced map projection that bears his name and has been used ever since. In 1585, published book of maps of Europe, completed by son in 1595, which was first to use the word *atlas*.
Mohorovičić, Andrija 1857–1936, Yugoslavian geophysicist whose earthquake studies led to discovery of Mohorovičić discontinuity, the boundary between crust and mantle.
Mohs, Friedrich 1773–1839, German. mineralogist who wrote *The Natural History System of Mineralogy* (1821), and *Treatise on Mineralogy* (3 vols,1825). The Mohs' scale of hardness he introduced is still in use.
Omalius d'Halloy, Jean-Baptiste-Julien 1783–1875, Belgian geologist who produced systematic subdivisions of geological formations and gave cretaceous rocks their name.
Oppel, Albert 1831–65, German geologist and paleontologist who subdivided stages into zones.
d'Orbigny, Alcide Dessalines 1802–57, French. Founder of micropaleontology who divided geological formations into stages.
Penck, Albrecht 1858–1945, German geographer and geologist. Examined sequence of past ice ages, providing basis for later work on European Pleistocene. Identified six topographic forms and reputedly introduced term *geomorphology*. Classic work *Morphology of the Earth's Surface* produced 1894.
Richter, Charles Francis 1900–85, American seismologist. With Beno Gutenberg, devised absolute scale of earthquake strength-based on logarithm of maximum amplitude of earthquake waves observed on seismograph,adjusted for distance from epicentre of earthquake–which bears his name.
Schlotheim, Ernst von 1764–1832, German paleontologist and pioneer in using fossils to find relative ages of rock layers.
Smith, William 1769–1839, English civil engineer, known as founder of English geology, who used fossils to identify sedimentary rock layers and produced monumental *Geological Map of England* (1815), as well as 21 geologically colored maps of English counties (1819-24).
Stensen, Niels also known as Nicolaus Steno, 1638–86, Danish physician, naturalist, and theologian who did fundamental work in anatomy, geology, crystallography, paleontology, and mineralogy. First to point out true origin of fossil animals (1669), explain structure of Earth's crust, and distinguish between stratified and volcanic rocks.
Suess, Eduard 1831–1914, Austrian geologist, founder of "new geology." His theory that there had once been a great supercontinent made up of the present southern continents led to modern theories of continental drift.
Wegener, Alfred Lothar 1880–1930, German meteorologist and geophysicist who proposed theory of continental drift called the Wegener hypothesis, as outlined in *Origins of Continents and Oceans* (1915). By 1960s, plate tectonics had been established as one of the major tenets of modern geophysics.
Werner, Abraham Gottlob, 1750–1817, German geologist, one of the first to frame classification of rocks. Popularized Neptunism, mistaken theory claiming that almost all rocks had been precipitated from water of early universal ocean.

141 LIFE FORMS

Seven characteristics of life

1411 Most living things display the following seven characteristics:
1 Movement. Even some plants bend toward light.
2 Response to stimuli
3 Reproduction
4 Nutrition
5 Growth
6 Respiration
7 Excretion. Life processes involve metabolism: the biochemical building up and breaking down of organic compounds.

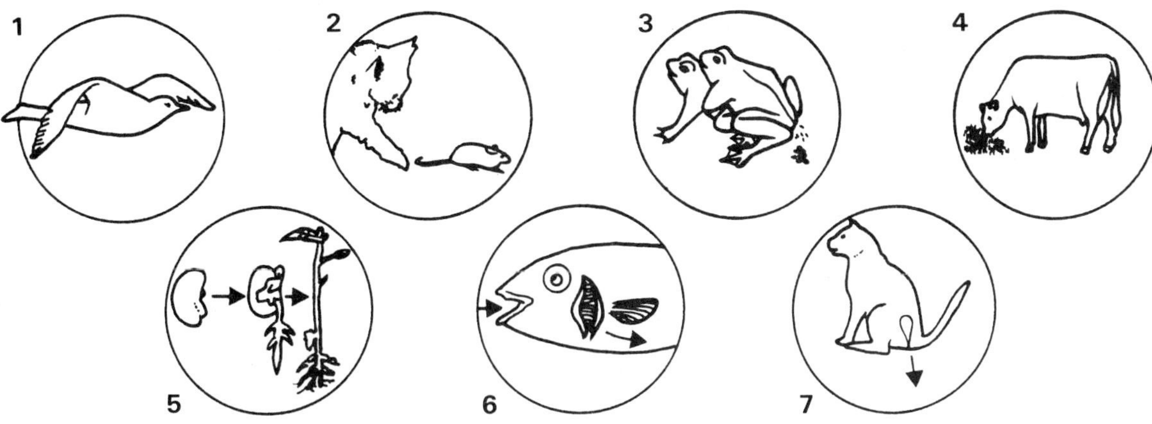

How living things are organized

1412 **1** Organism, made of systems
2 System, made of organs
Some living things lack organs. Some are single cells
3 Organ, made of tissues
4 Tissue, made of cells
5 Cell, made of protoplasm

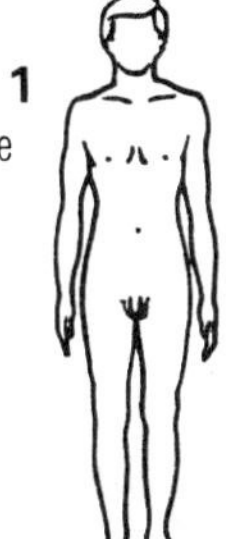

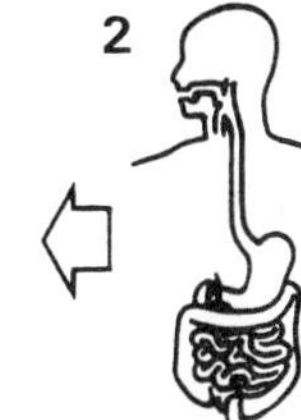

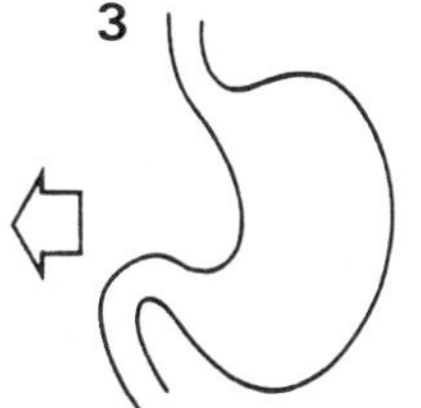

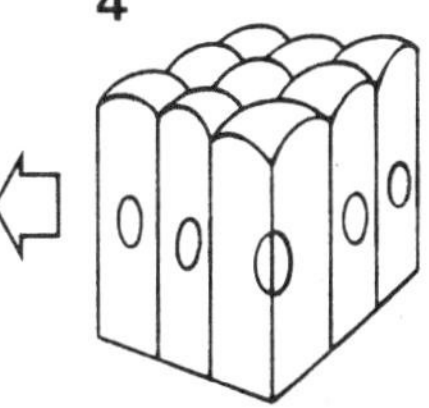

142 CELLS

Types

1421 The diagrams here show the main features of an animal cell (**1**) and a plant cell (**2**).
a Cytoplasm: a transparent, jelly-like substance.
b Cell membrane: a "skin" around the cytoplasm.
c Nucleus, denser than the cytoplasm and acting as the cell's control center.
Plant cells have three additional structures:
d Cell wall surrounding the cell and made of a nonliving substance called cellulose.
e Plastids: units involved in the making and storing of food.
f Vacuoles: cavities filled with the fluid called sap. Many plant cells contain a single large vacuole.

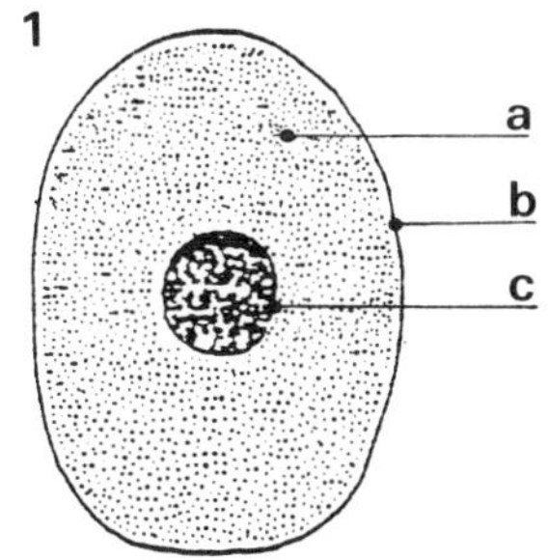

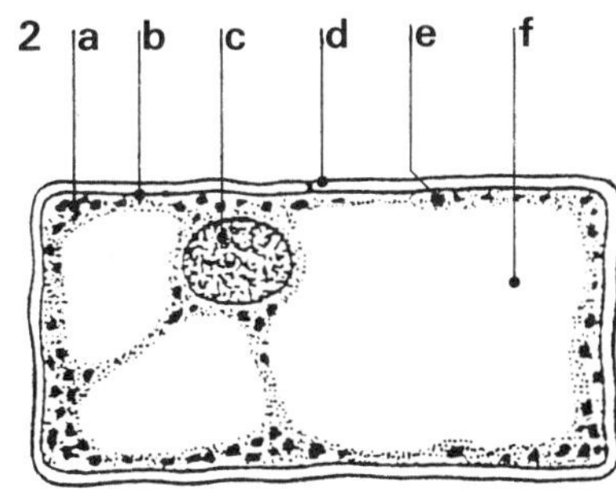

Cell nucleus

1422

1 Cell nucleus, containing chromosomes.

2 Chromosome, consisting largely of protein and DNA (deoxyribonucleic acid). Chromosomes occur in pairs.

3 A DNA helix, one of many in a chromosome. Sections of DNA comprise genes: hereditary factors determining how an organism develops.

Cell variety

1423

Cells have different shapes and perform different tasks. The following are examples of types of cell:
1 Food-conducting plant cells joined by perforated walls.
2 Ciliated cell: a cell with whiplike "hairs" called cilia. Cilia transport fluid called mucus through animals' respiratory tracts and help one-celled organisms called ciliates to move and gather food.
3 Sperm cell: a male sex cell, which lashes its tail to swim toward a female sex cell.
4 Sting cell from a jellyfish, shown with the sting thread extended.
5 Neuron, or nerve cell. Its endings connect with other neurons to carry messages that travel through the nervous system.
6 Red blood cell, or erythrocyte: a cell that transports oxygen and carbon dioxide through the body.
7 White blood cell, or leukocyte: a cell that engulfs bacteria and other harmful agents.
8 Platelets: small disklike cells that assist in the blood-clotting process.

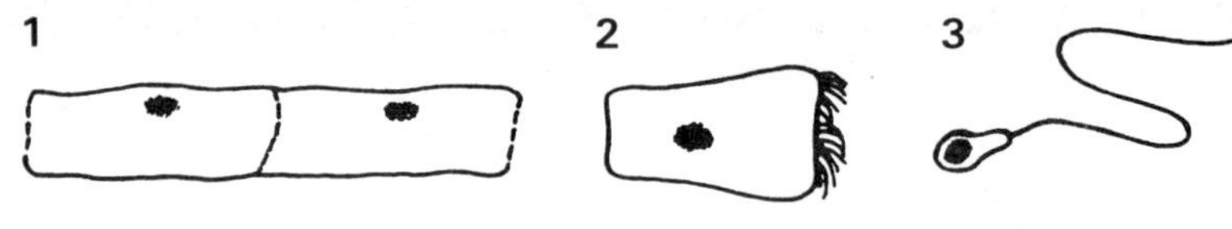

How cells divide

1424

There are five steps in mitosis, the process by which one cell becomes two cells.
1 A single cell before mitosis has begun.
a Cell nucleus
b Nuclear membrane
c Chromosomes
d Centrioles
2 Chromosomes double, forming pairs.
3 Nuclear membrane fades and centrioles diverge, producing fibers.
4 Paired chromosomes line up in the cell's center and are then pulled apart by the fibers.
5 A new cell wall divides the cell into two cells, each with its own nucleus.

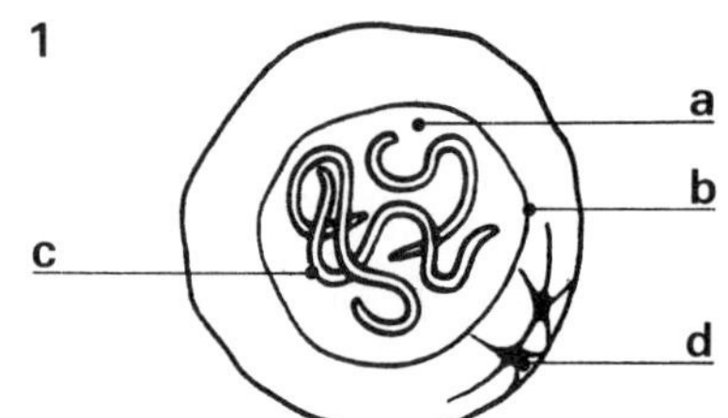

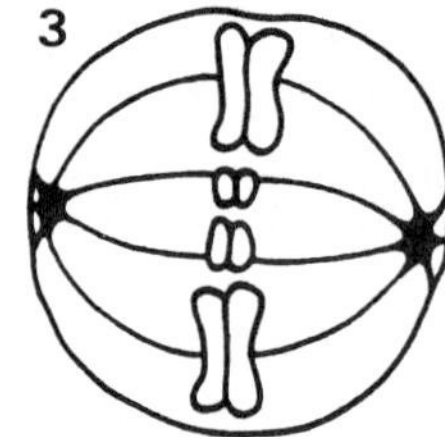

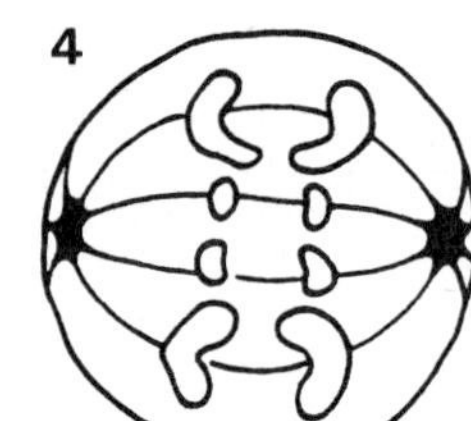

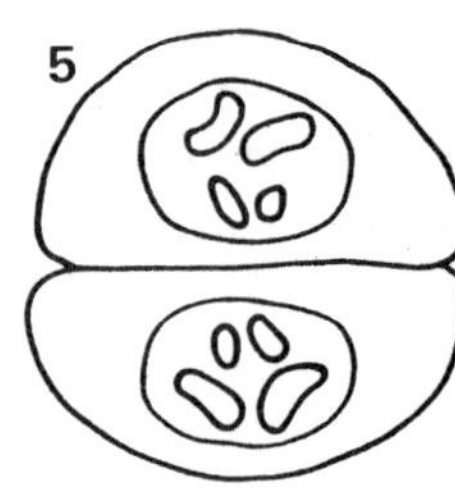

How DNA is copied

1425

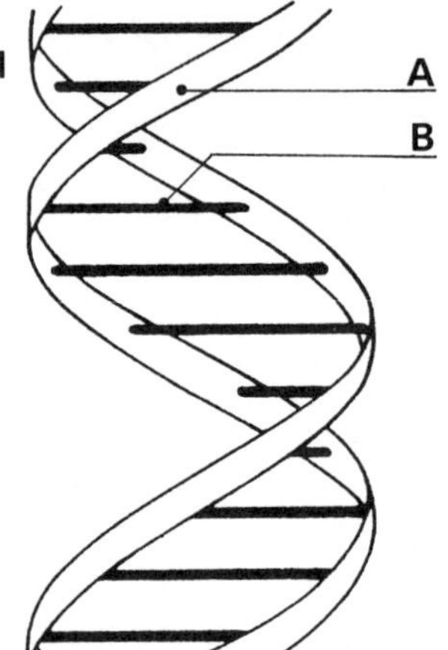

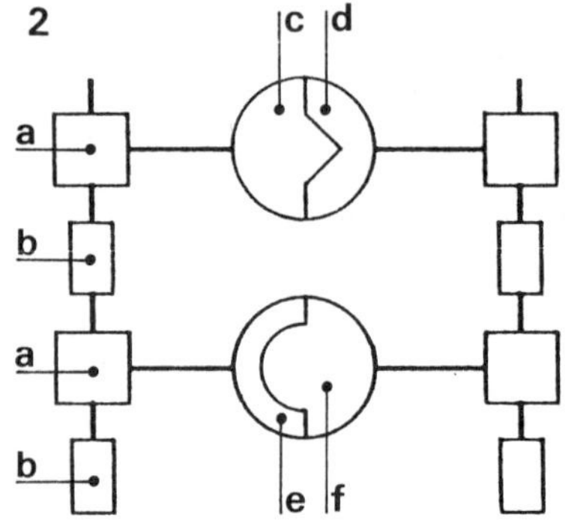

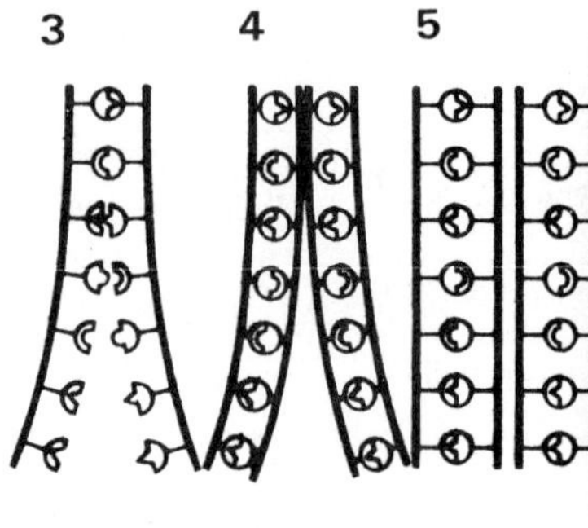

1 A DNA helix resembles a spiral ladder with sides (**A**) and rungs (**B**).
2 Sides comprise sugars (**a**) and acids (**b**). Rungs comprise nitrogen bases (**c**, **d**, **e**, **f**). Sugars, acids, and bases recur in special patterned combinations.
3 When a chromosome begins to duplicate, the DNA ladder "unzips."
4 Each side and its half rungs gain a matching side and half rungs from sugars, acids, and bases available in the cell's nucleus.
5 One ladder thus becomes two ladders.

143 REPRODUCTION

Types of reproduction

1431 There are two types of reproduction:
1 Asexual: reproduction without male and female sex cells, as when a new hydra forms from a bud growing on its parent.
2 Sexual: a female sex cell is fertilized by a male sex cell to produce a fertile seed or egg. This then develops into a young plant or animal that has inherited characteristics from both its parents.

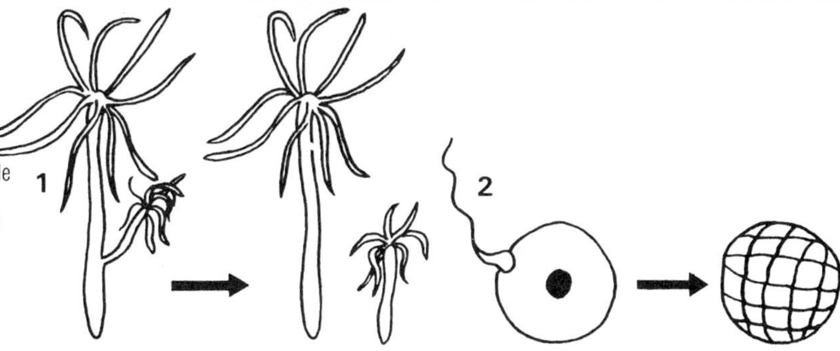

Sex cells and sex

1432 Animal sex cells are produced by meiosis: two separate divisions producing cells with half the chromosomes of other body cells. When a female egg is fertilized by a (male) sperm cell, the egg then has a full complement of chromosomes, each parent having contributed half of every pair of chromosomes. An offspring's sex depends upon the sex chromosome contributed by its father.

1 Sex chromosomes (X or Y) in sperm
2 Sex chromosomes (X) in egg cell
3 Female offspring (XX)
4 Male offspring (XY)

Key
M Male
F Female

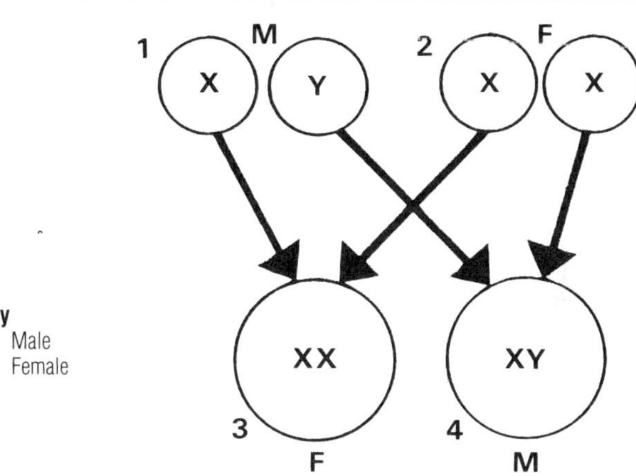

Inherited traits

1433 Plants and animals inherit color, body form, and other traits from parents. Traits depend on genes. Genes, like chromosomes, occur in pairs, one inherited from each parent. In certain gene pairs a dominant gene overpowers a recessive gene. For instance, the brown-eye gene (**B**) is dominant; the blue-eye gene (**b**) is recessive.
1 Inheriting two brown-eye genes produces a brown-eyed child.
2 Inheriting two blue-eye genes produces a blue-eyed child.
3 Inheriting one brown-eye gene and one blue-eye gene produces a brown-eyed child, with a recessive blue-eye gene.

Key Brown eyes (BB) Blue eyes (bb)

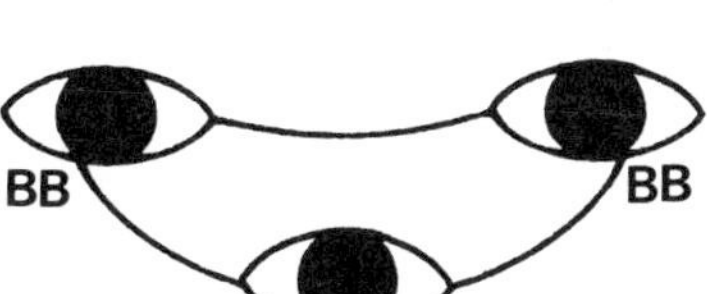

1

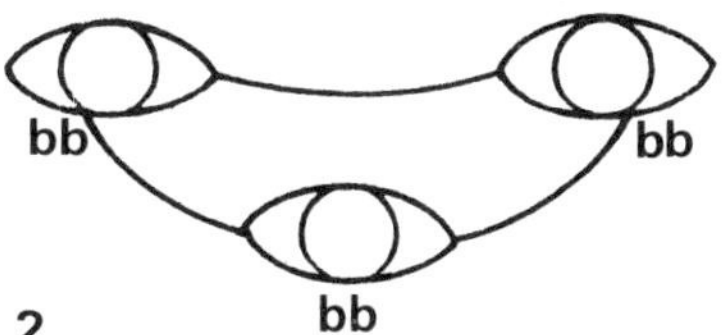

2

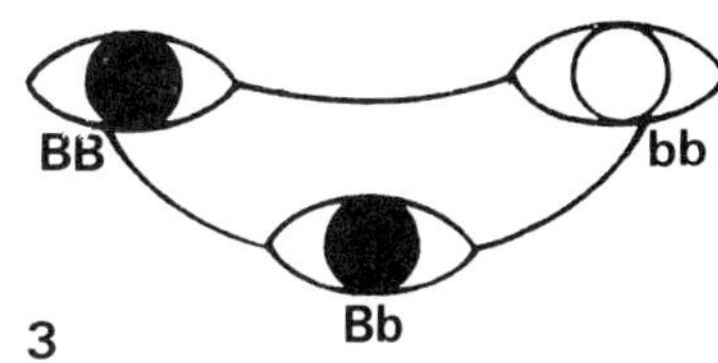

3

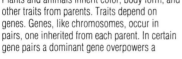

Prolific breeders

1434 **1** Tenrec (mammal): 32 babies
2 Ostrich (bird): 15 eggs
3 Green turtle (reptile): 184 eggs
4 Giant toad (amphibian): 35,000 eggs
5 Sunfish (fish): 300 million eggs
6 Sea hare (mollusk): 478 million eggs
7 Orchid (plant): 4.5 million seeds per capsule
8 Bracket fungus (fungus): 5.5 billion spores

1 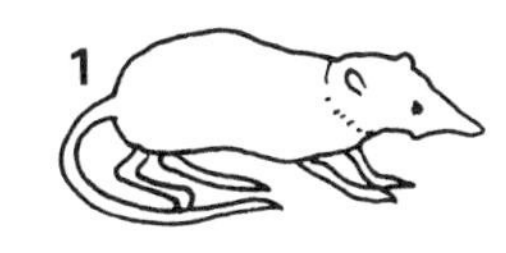
2 
3 
4 
5 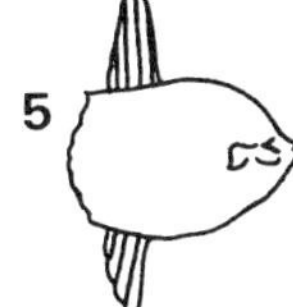
6 
7 
8 

Gestation/incubation (days)

143**5**

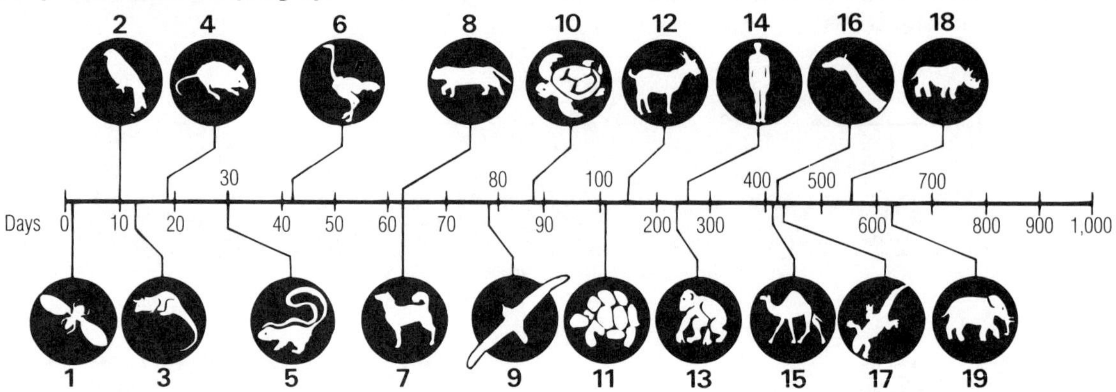

The chart above shows gestation/incubation periods in days

1 Fruit fly: 0.5
2 Some finches: 10
3 Common opossum: 13
4 Mouse: 19
5 Skunk: 30
6 Ostrich: 42
7 Dog: 63
8 Cat: 63
9 Royal albatross: 79
10 Box turtle: 87
11 Tortoise: 105
12 Goat: 151
13 Chimpanzee: 237
14 Human: 265
15 Camel: 406
16 Giraffe: 410
17 Tuatara: 425
18 Rhinoceros: 560
19 Indian elephant: 624

Animal life cycles

143**6**

Butterfly's life cycle

1 Fertilized adult female butterfly
2 Eggs laid by female
3 Caterpillar hatched from egg
4 Full-sized caterpillar
5 Pupa undergoing metamorphosis
6 Adult butterfly emerging from pupa

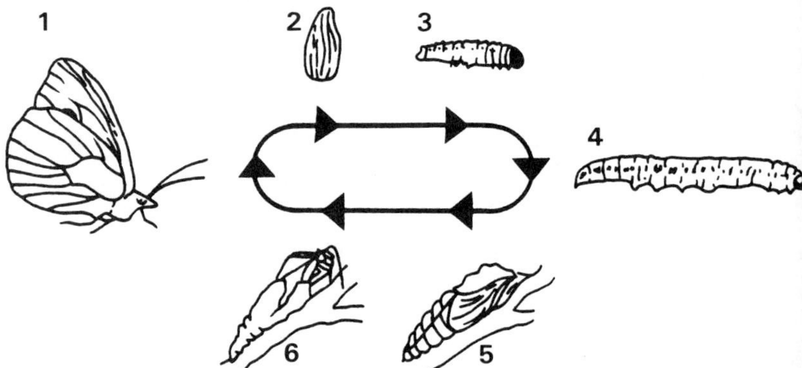

Frog's life cycle

1 Female spawning in water
2 Eggs developing in water
3 Newly hatched tadpole
4 Three-week old tadpole
5 One-month old tadpole
6 Two-month old tadpole
7 Three-month old tadpole
8 Tadpole metamorphosed into frog

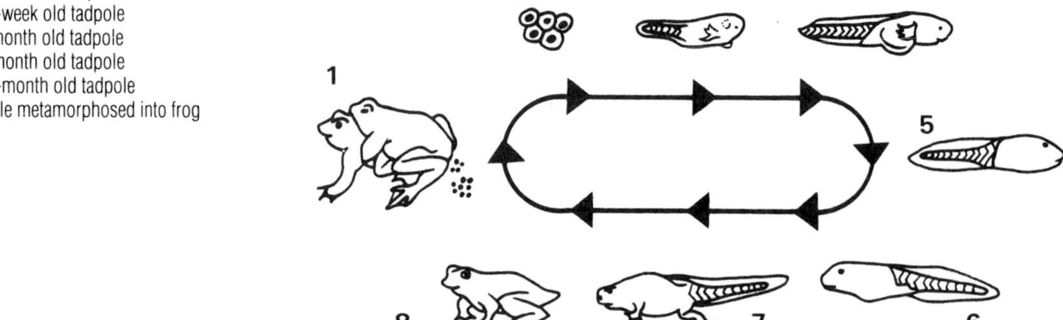

151 PLANT CLASSIFICATION

Traditional groupings

1511

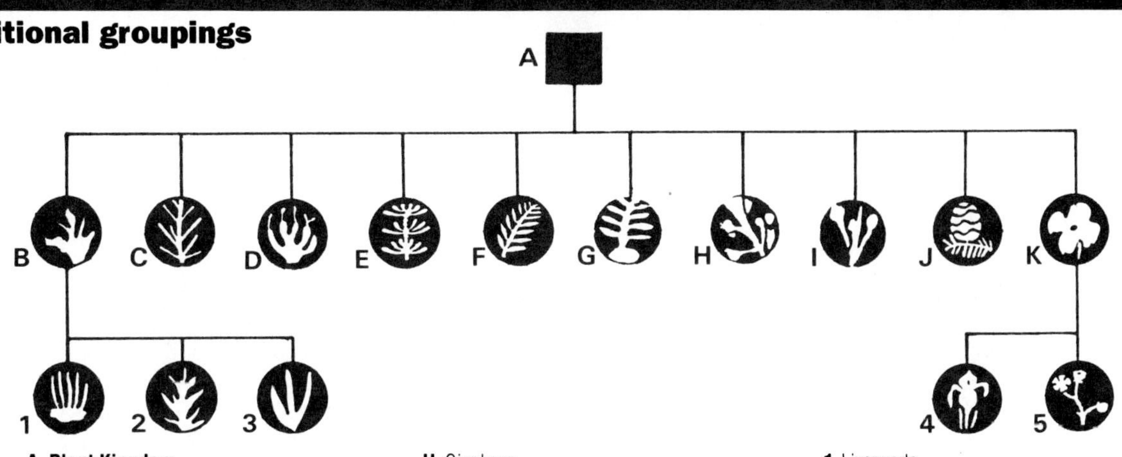

A Plant Kingdom
B Bryophytes
C Psilophyta
D Clubmosses
E Horsetails
F Ferns
G Cycads
H Gingkoes
I Ephedra
J Conifers
K Angiosperms (flowering plants)

1 Liverworts
2 Mosses
3 Hornworts
4 Dicots
5 Monocots

Classifying plants

1512

This diagram shows how botanists split plants into major categories according to their structures.

The monera kingdom (**1**) consists of algae and one-celled organisms. These plants are without phloem or xylem – which provide a network for carrying food and water in other plants. The plant kingdom (**2**) comprises plants with phloem and xylem. They are called the tracheophytes. Tracheophytes are divided into two groups: non-flowering plants that do not form seeds (**3**) like clubmosses, ferns, and horsetails, and seedbearing plants (**4**). This group is further divided. Gymnosperms (**5**) like conifers and cycads have seeds and cones, while angiosperms (**6**) comprise trees and flowering plants bearing seeds protected in an ovary.

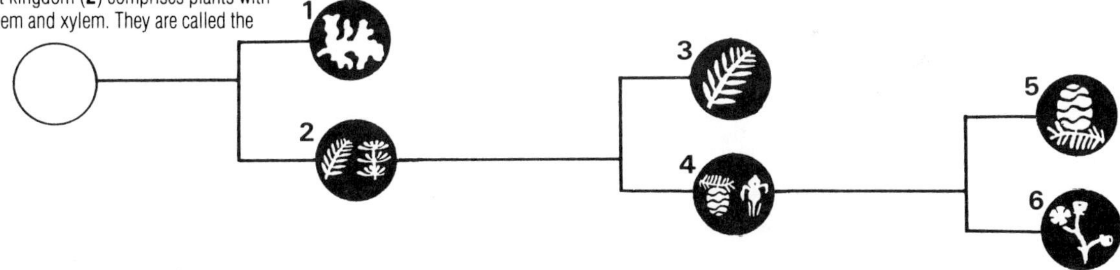

Numbers of species

1513

Circle sizes show comparative numbers of species. Known true plants total about 300,000 species. This diagram includes 12 groups of organisms traditionally placed in the plant kingdom although groups 1, 2, 3, and 4 are now placed in other kingdoms. Group 3 consists of interlinked members of groups 2 and 4.

1 Bacteria
2 Algae
3 Lichens
4 Fungi
5 Liverworts
6 Mosses
7 Clubmosses
8 Horsetails
9 Ferns
10 Gymnosperms
11 Monocots
12 Dicots

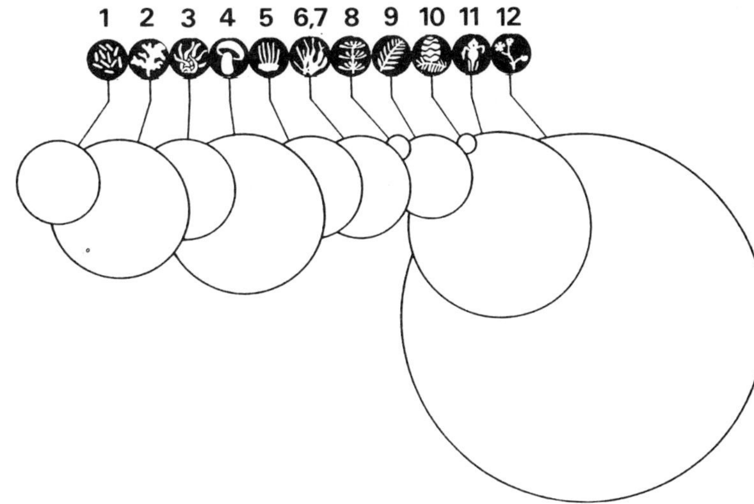

1514 Classifying a plant
1515 Fossil plants
1516 Twelve plant and plantlike groups

Classifying a plant

1514 Plants are classified in successively larger, less closely related groups. The smallest unit shown here is a species. Members of one species normally cannot interbreed with those of another, but many garden plants are hybrids of varieties of one species.

Read upward, this diagram shows that the tea rose (*Rosa odorata*) is one of many species in the genus *Rosa*, one of many genera in the family *Rosaceae*. That family is one of a number in the order *Rosales*, one of many orders in the class *Dicotyledonae* (dicots). Dicots form one of two classes in the subdivision *Angiospermae* (angiosperms or flowering plants). Angiosperms are one of two subdivisions in the division *Spermatophyta*. Spermatophytes (seed plants) are one of 10 divisions in the Plantae (plant kingdom).

1 Kingdom *Plantae*
2 Division: *Spermatophyta*
3 Subdivision: *Angiospermae*
4 Class: *Dicotyledonae*
5 Order: *Rosales*
6 Family: *Rosaceae*
7 Genus: *Rosa*
8 Species: *Rosa odorata*

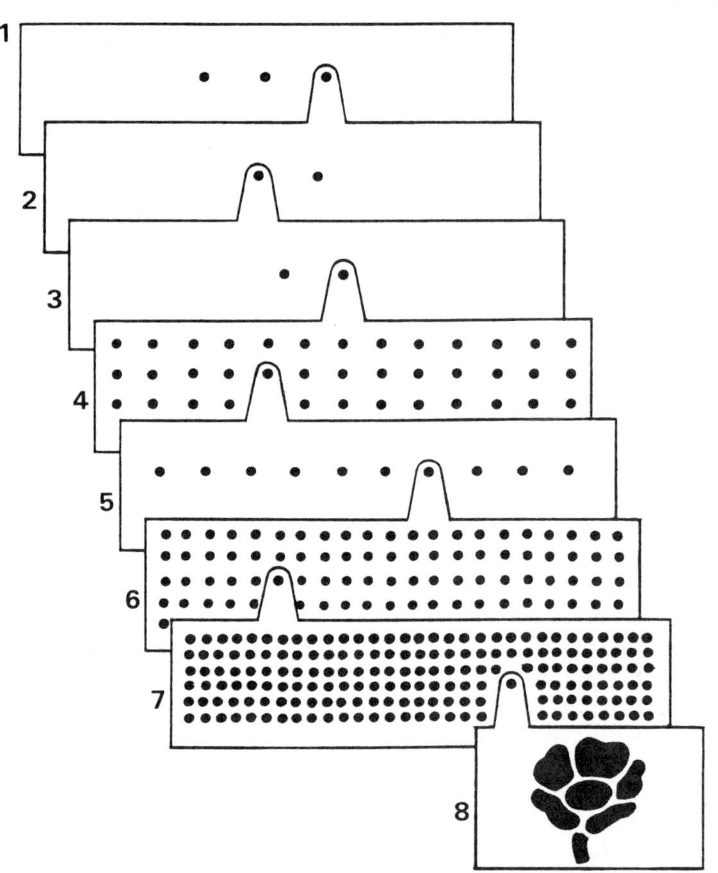

Fossil plants

1515 This family tree shows when eight major groups of plants arose.

A Precambrian
B Paleozoic
C Mesozoic
D Cenozoic

1 Algae
2 Liverworts and mosses
3 Psilophytes (primitive land plants)
4 Clubmosses
5 Horsetails
6 Ferns
7 Gymnosperms
8 Angiosperms

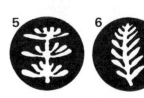

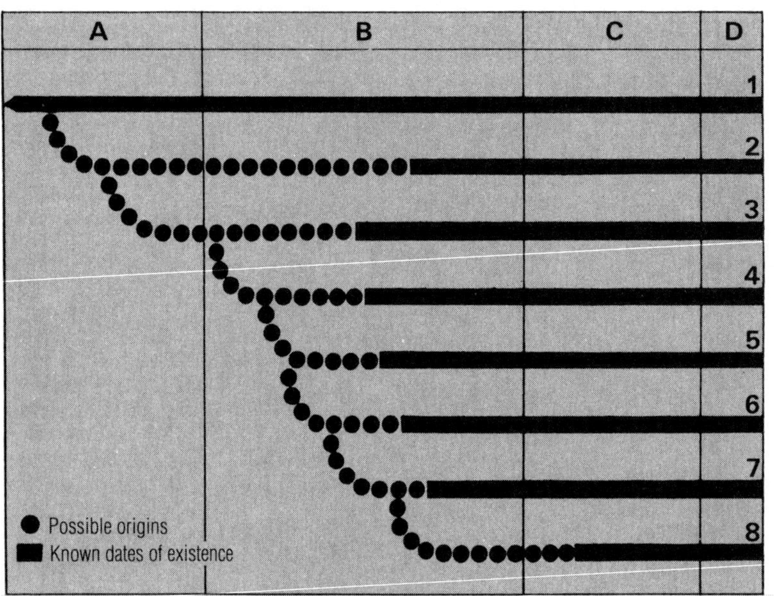

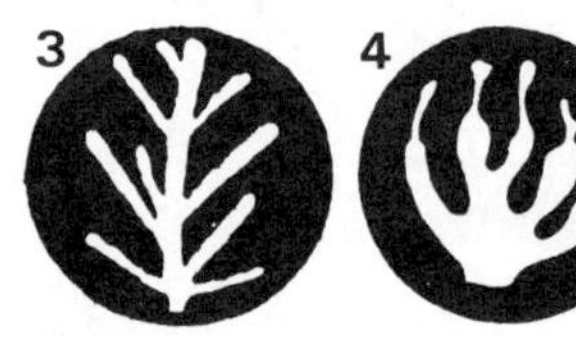

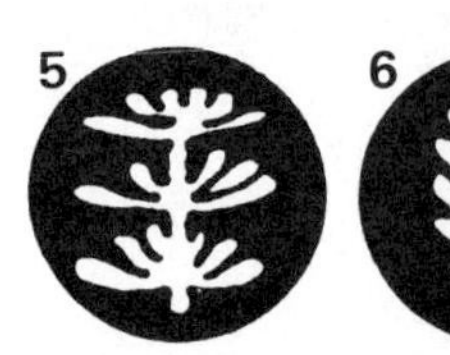

Twelve plant and plantlike groups

1516 **1 Bacteria**

Bacteria are microorganisms without a cell nucleus. Once grouped with plants, bacteria are now placed in a separate kingdom, *Monera*. Many bacteria are one-celled spheres, rods, or spirals, but cyanobacteria (once known as blue-green algae) can occur as filaments. Bacteria occur in water, soil, and air. Some grow only where there is oxygen, others only where there is none. Soil bacteria decompose plant and animal remains, releasing nutrients absorbed by plants. Parasitic bacteria cause diseases such as anthrax, plague, syphilis, and tuberculosis. Like plants, cyanobacteria use the energy in sunlight to manufacture food from carbon dioxide and water.

2 Algae

Algae are plantlike organisms that form part of the kingdom *Protista*. They range from tiny one-celled organisms to seaweeds 200 ft (61 m) long. Most kinds of algae live in water. There are ten major groups:
Bacillariophyta diatoms
Chlorophyta green algae
Chrysophyta golden algae
Cryptophyta cryptomonadi
Dinoflagellata dinoflagellates
Euglenophyta mobile algae
Gamophyta conjugating green algae
Phaeophyta brown algae
Rhodophyta red algae
Xanthophyta yellow-green algae

3 Lichens

A lichen is an alga or cyanophyte living closely connected with a fungus. (Lichens are usually classified with fungi.) In this partnership the alga or bacterium makes food and the fungus collects the moisture that both partners need. Most lichens form small, low, slow-growing patches in soil or on bare rock and bark. They thrive in even the harshest climates.
Crustose lichens form flat crusts.
Foliose lichens appear leafy.
Fruticose lichens resemble tiny shrubs.

4 Clubmosses and quillworts

Clubmosses and quillworts are spore-bearing vascular plants that form the division *Lycopodophyta*. Prehistoric clubmosses included the tall trees *Lepidodendron* and *Sigillaria*, but living forms are small, lowgrowing, and mosslike. Some creep; others stand erect. Stems bear many narrow leaves with unbranched midveins. The lycopsids include three living families.
Isoetaceae Quillworts. Mainly aquatic, with tufted, somewhat grasslike leaves.
Lycopodiaceae Clubmosses, also called "ground pines."
Selaginellaceae Little clubmosses, also called spike mosses. Mainly tropical, with long branching stems that produce four ranks of leaves.

5 Horsetails

Horsetails are sporebearing, herbaceous vascular plants that form the division *Sphenophyta*. Also called scouring rushes, these rushlike plants produce whorls of narrow, sheathlike leaves from nodes along green, grooved, upright stems. Some are evergreen; others annually sprout from rhizomes (underground stems). Horsetails grow in moist, rich soils worldwide, except in Antarctica and Australia. Living forms largely reach about 3 ft (1 m) high, though one flimsy species soars 32 ft (10 m), and sturdy prehistoric forms resembled trees. Extinct and living horsetails form three orders:
Equisetales living horsetails
Hyeniales extinct
Sphenophyllales extinct

6 Ferns

These leafy, sporebearing, vascular plants are related to the horsetails and clubmosses and form the division *Filicinophyta*. Some ferns have simple, rounded leaves, but many produce large lacy leaves called fronds. The leaves unfurl as they grow from a stem that may be upright, creeping, or underground. The leaves' undersides bear spores in (often clustered) structures called sporangia. Most ferns are perennial. They range from tiny filmy plants mere millimeters high to palmlike tree ferns 65 ft (20 m) high. Ferns mainly grow in damp, shady places in warm, humid climates.
A classification gives three living orders:
Marattiales giant ferns
Ophioglossales adder's tongue ferns and their allies
Filicales "true" ferns

7 Fungi

Fungi are plantlike organisms that form their own kingdom: *Fungi*. Unlike most true plants, fungi lack roots, stems, leaves, and the green pigment chlorophyll required for making food; they get this ready-made from dead or living organic substances. Yeasts are fungi with a single cell, but most fungi form a mycelium of tangled, threadlike hyphae that grow in soil or other substances and produce a mushroom or other fruiting body shedding spores. Various fungi recycle plant nutrients, live in useful partnership with plant roots, or cause diseases in plants and animals. There are four main groups.
Ascomycota yeasts, truffles.
Basidiomycota smuts, rusts, mushrooms, puffballs.
Deuteromycota *Pecicillium* mold
Zygomycota black bread mold

continued

Twelve plant and plantlike groups continued

1516

8 Liverworts

These small, nonvascular, spore-producing plants form the class *Hepaticae* in the plant division *Bryophyta*. Liverworts live in moist, shady places and undergo a two-stage, sexual and nonsexual, form of reproduction known as alternation of generations. There are two main groups of liverworts:

Thalloid liverworts have a flattened, leaflike body often shaped like a human liver. Tiny rootlike rhizoids anchor the thallus to moist rocks or trees and suck up minerals dissolved in water.

Foliose liverworts, or leafy liverworts, have two or three rows of leaves on a low, creeping stem.

9 Mosses

These small, nonvascular, spore-producing plants form the class *Musci* in the plant division *Bryophyta*. They produce rootlike rhizoids, stems, and a spiral pattern of little leaves. Mosses form low mats and cushions. Most kinds grow in damp, shady places, but some live on walls. Like liverworts, mosses undergo a two-stage reproduction known as alternation of generations. Mosses contain three orders:

Andreaeales Granite mosses, which often grow on rock. Their species belong to one genus: *Andreaea*.

Bryales True mosses. This group contains most kinds of mosses.

Sphagnales Bog or peat mosses, which grow in bogs. All species belong to one genus: *Sphagnum*.

10 Gymnosperms

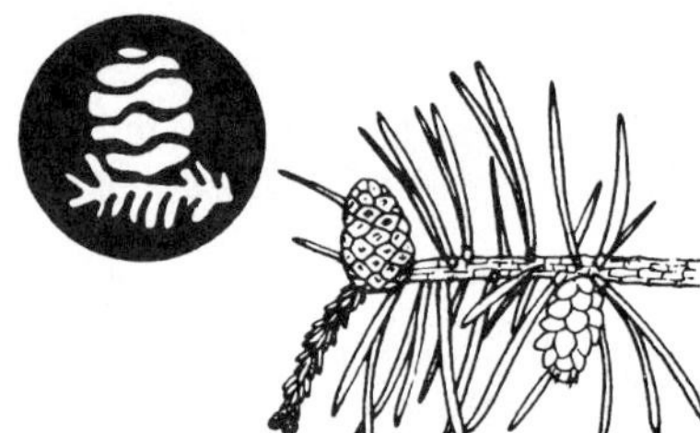

Gymnosperms are plants that are grouped together because they produce "naked" seeds that are unprotected by an outer convering. This grouping is fairly artificial and includes four separate plant divisions:

Coniferophyta The conifers such as fir, larch, pine, and yew. Many have evergreen, needle-shaped leaves.

Cycadophyta Cycads with fern-shaped leaves.

Ginkgophyta Deciduous trees with fan-shaped leaves. One living species.

Gnetophyta Small trees and shrubby plants.

11 Monocots

The *Monocotyledonae* is the smaller of two classes that make up the flowering plants or angiosperms. Seedlings have a single cotyledon (seed leaf). The original root withers, leaving a system of fibrous roots. Leaves have parallel veins, and flowers have parts arranged in threes or multiples of three. The stem's transportation system comprises scattered bundles of tubes. Scientists usually divide the monocots into four subclasses:

Alismidae Mainly aquatic plants including flowering rush, frog's-bit, and the pondweed Potamogeton.

Arecidae Arums, cattails, duckweed, palms and screw pines.

Commelinidae Pineapples, rushes, sedges and grasses (including cereals).

Liliidae Agaves Bananas, irises, lilies, and orchids.

12 Dicot

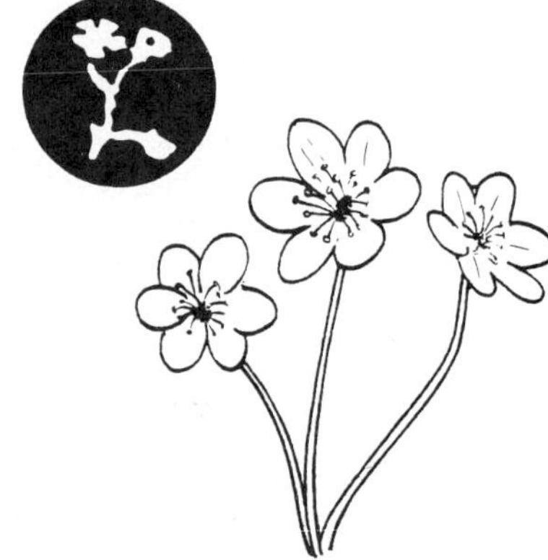

The *Dicotyledonae* is the larger of two classes that make up the flowering plants or angiosperms. Seedlings have two cotyledons (seed leaves). The original root forms a taproot. Leaves have a network of veins, and flowers have parts in fours or fives or their multiples. The stem's transportation system has tubes arranged in a ring. Scientists usually list seven subclasses:

Asteridae Gentians, honeysuckles, lobelias, mints, daisies, etc.

Caryophillidae Amaranths, buckwheats, cacti, leadworts, pinks, etc.

Dilleniidae Begonias, ebonies, mallows, mustards, peonies, teas, violets, etc.

Hamamelididae Beeches, casuarinas, elms, nettles, hemps, planes, etc.

Magnoliidae Laurels, magnolias, peppers, water lilies, rafflesias, etc.

Ranunculidae Buttercups, lotuses, pitcher-plants, poppies, etc.

Rosidae Geraniums, grapes, hollies, maples, mistletoes, olives, peas, roses, saxifrages, sundews, etc.

152 PLANT STRUCTURE AND FUNCTION

A flowering plant

1521 **Each part of a flowering plant performs a different function.**
1 Roots: Anchor the plant in soil and take in water and minerals needed for the plant's life and growth.
2 Root hairs: Absorb water and minerals from soil.
3 Stem: Supports leaves and flowers, holding them up in the air and light; also transports water and minerals from roots to leaves, and food from leaves to the rest of the plant.
4 Leaves: Use light energy to make food from water and gases by photosynthesis.
5 Flowers. Contain the plant's reproductive organs.

A Flow of water and minerals.
B Evaporation of water from leaf (transpiration).

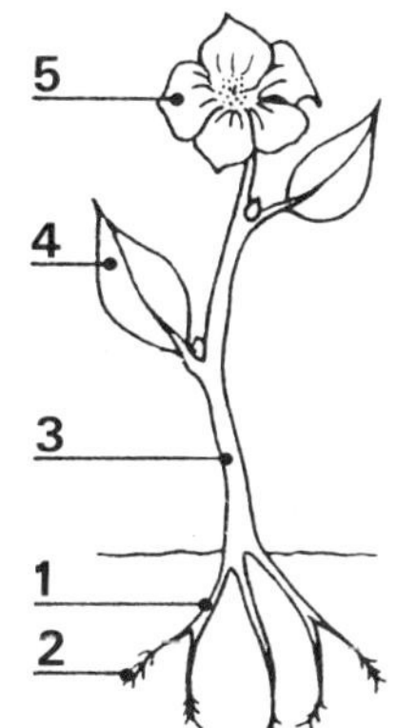

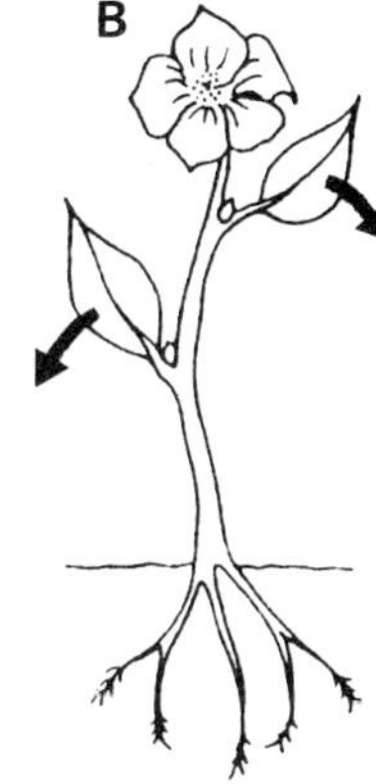

Parts of a leaf

1522 **Dicot leaf**
1 Petiole (leaf stalk)
2 Midrib
3 Leaf blade
4 Vein
5 Margin

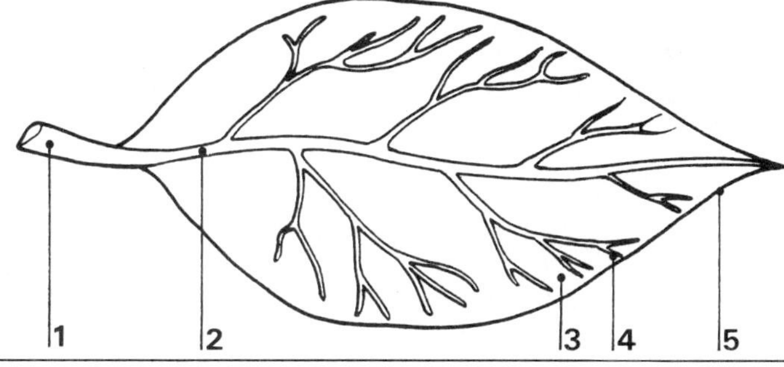

Vein formations
1 Midrib
2 Dichotomous
3 Parallel
4 Pinnate
5 Palmate

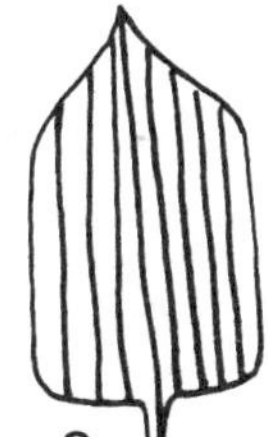

Leaf margins
1 Dentate
2 Serrate (toothed)
3 Doubly serrated
4 Entire
5 Crenate (scalloped)
6 Undulate (sinuate)
7 Pinnately lobed
8 Palmately lobed
9 Ciliate

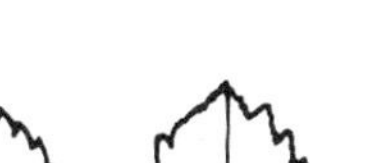
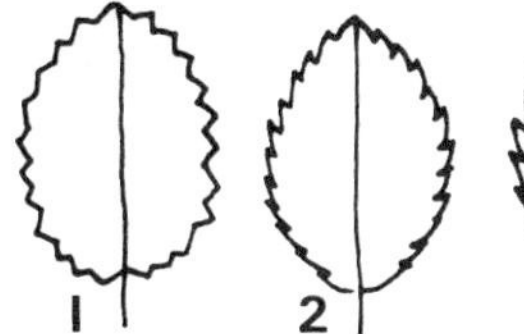
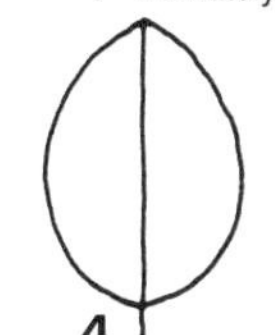

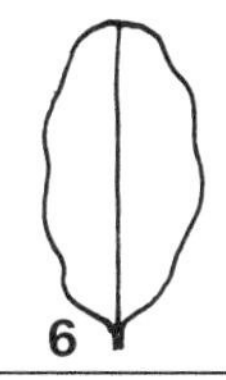
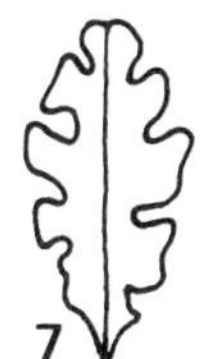

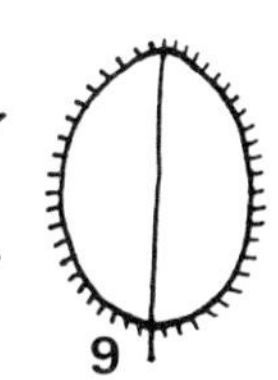

Leaf tips
1 Obcardate
2 Emarginate
3 Truncate
4 Obtuse
5 Acute
6 Mucronate
7 Acuminate
8 Cuspidate
9 Caudate
10 Aristate

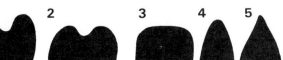

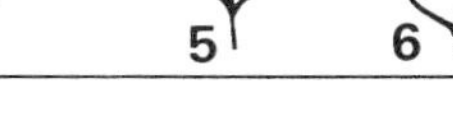
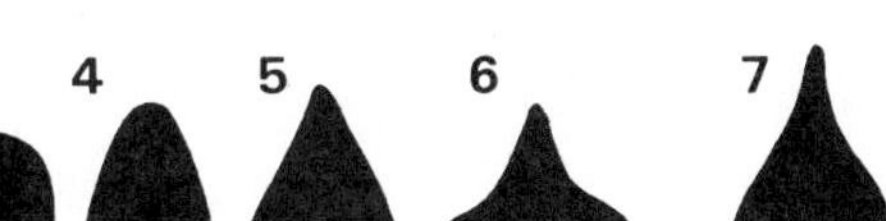

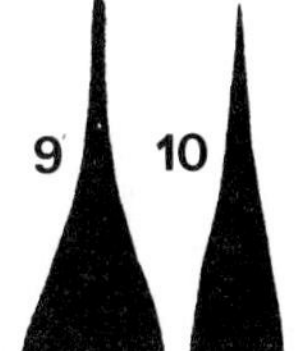

continued

Parts of a leaf continued

1522 **Leaf bases**

1 Rounded
2 Oblique
3 Acute
4 Attenuate
5 Hastate
6 Sagittate
7 Cordate
8 Reniform
9 Auriculate

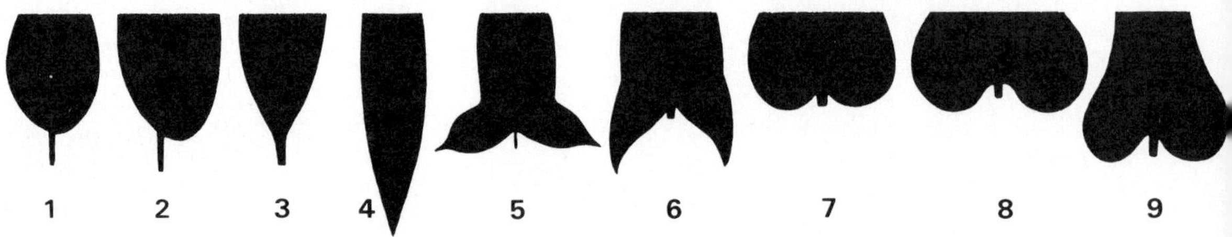

Leaf shapes

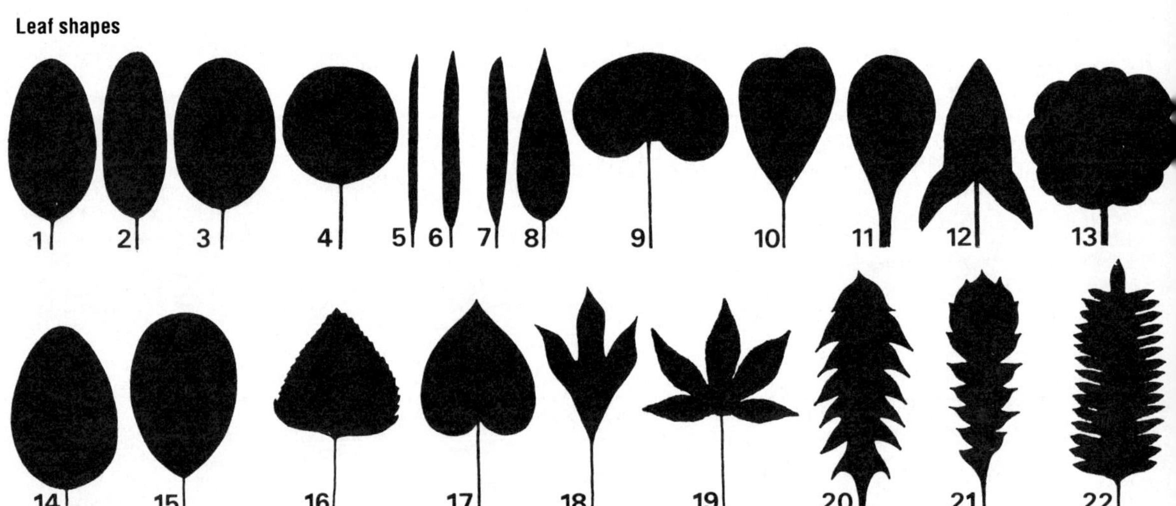

1 Elliptical
2 Oblong
3 Oval
4 Orbiculate
5 Acerose
6 Awl-shaped
7 Linear
8 Lanceolate
9 Reniform
10 Cuneate
11 Sagittate
12 Spatulate
13 Peltate
14 Ovate
15 Obovate
16 Deltoid
17 Cordate
18 Pedate
19 Palmate
20 Runcinate
21 Lyrate
22 Pectinate

Compound leaves

1 Even pinnate
2 Odd pinnate
3 Bipinnate
4 Tripinnate
5 Digitate
6 Palmate
7 Pedate
8 Ternate
9 Biternate

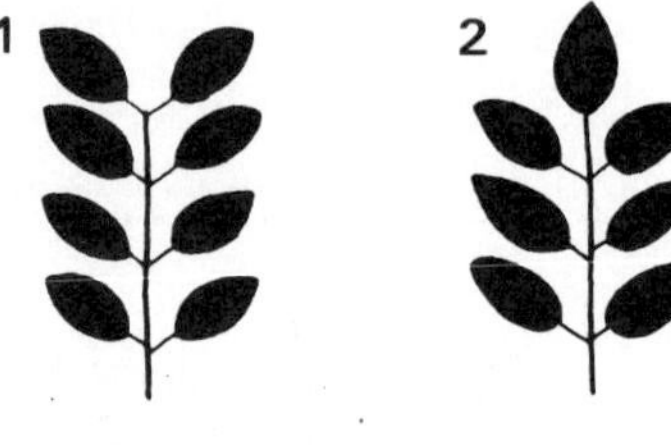

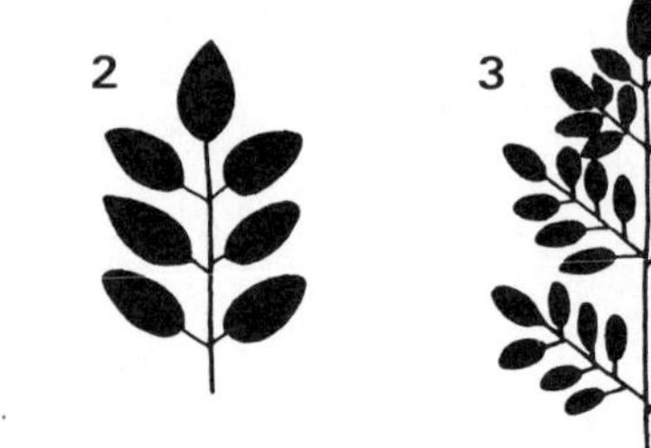

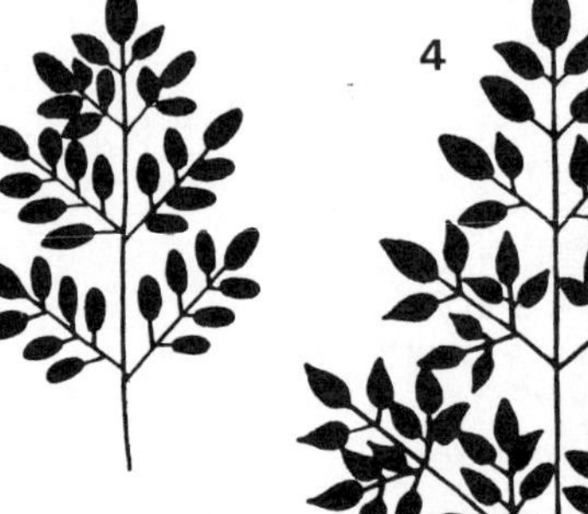

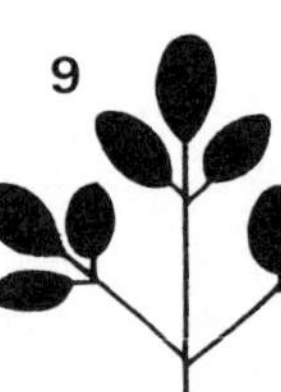

Inside a leaf

1523 **Part of a leaf shown in magnified cross section.**
1 Epidermis
2 Leaf cell
3 Chloroplast: A cell body with chlorophyll, a green pigment that helps plants use light energy to manufacture food from carbon dioxide and water, producing oxygen as waste.
4 Stoma: A hole or pore. Stomata let water vapor and waste oxygen out of the leaf and let in carbon dioxide and oxygen for respiration.
5 Vein transporting water and minerals in and food out.

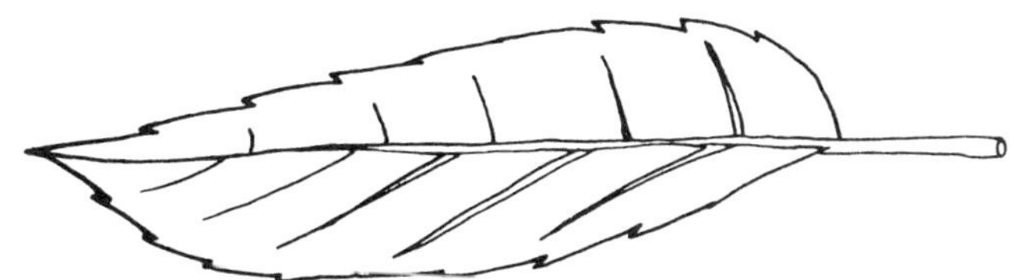

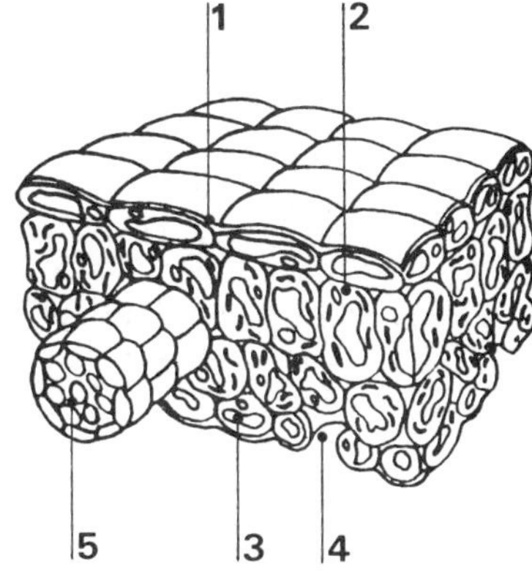

A woody stem

1524 **Part of a woody stem shown in magnified cross section.**
1 Xylem: Tubelike woody cells that provide support, and carry water to leaves.
2 Cambium: A thin layer producing phloem and xylem cells.
3 Phloem: Tubelike cells transporting food down from leaves to roots.
4 Cortex: Cells storing food.
5 Cork: A dead outer layer protecting against pests and water loss.

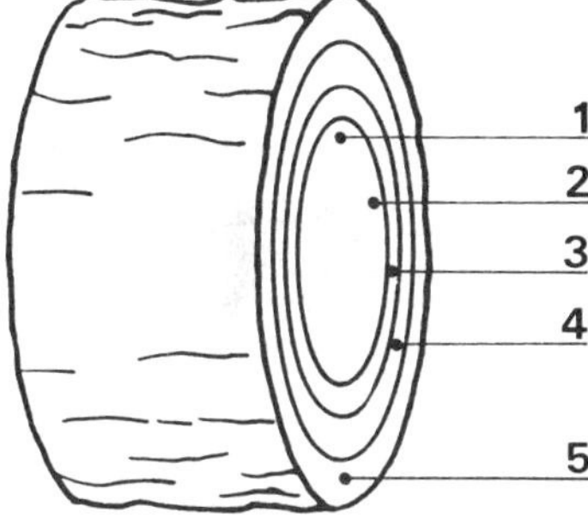

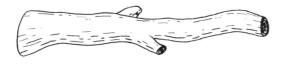

Roots

1525 **Part of a plant root shown in magnified cross section.**
1 Soil particles
2 Root hair
3 Epidermis
4 Parenchyma (cortex)
5 Xylem
6 Water and minerals

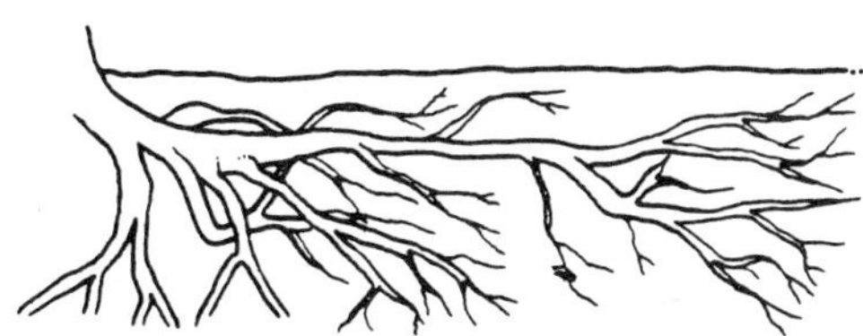

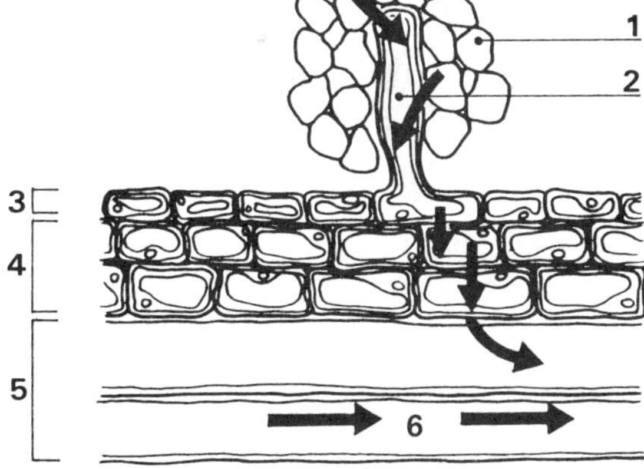

Asexual and sexual reproduction

1526 **Asexual reproduction**
As well as producing seeds, many flowering plants reproduce themselves by runners or rhizomes.
1 Runners are long, low stems that throw off new roots and shoots. Example: strawberries.
2 Rhizomes are underground stems that give off new shoots. Examples: irises and a number of grasses.

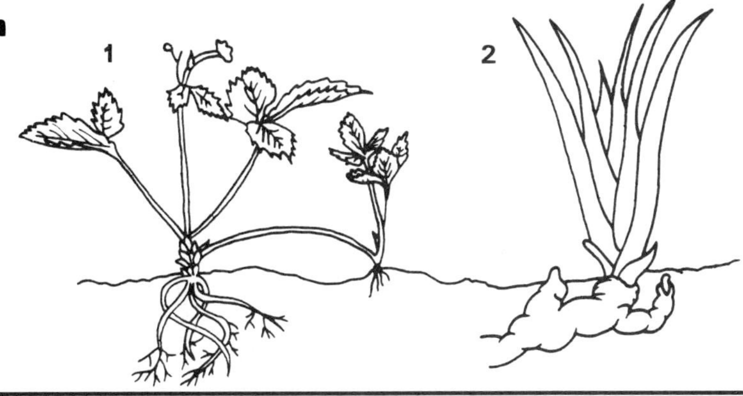

continued

Asexual and sexual reproduction continued

152**6** **Sexual reproduction**
A flower's reproductive organs.
1 Stamen (male)
a Anther producing pollen grains containing sperm (male sex cells).
2 Pistil (female)
b Ovary containing ovules (egg cells).
c Style
d Stigma
Wind-blown or insect-borne pollen lands on a stigma. A pollen grain grows down inside the style to the ovary. Sperm fertilize the ovules. Fertilized ovules become seeds.

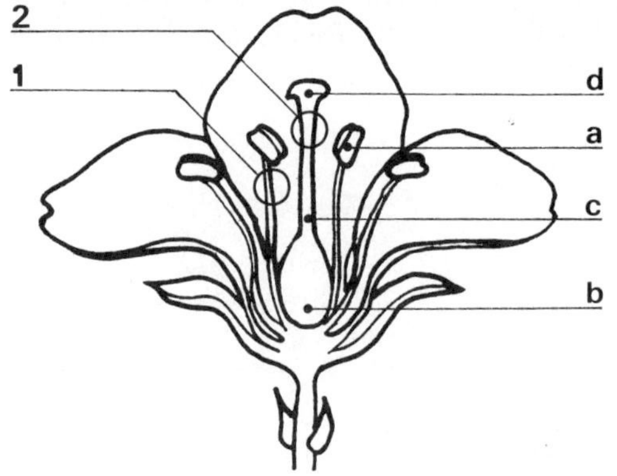

Seed dispersal

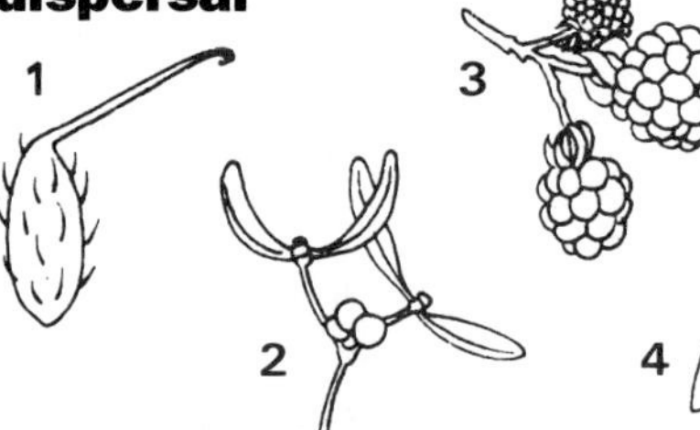

Dispersing seeds helps plants to spread and avoid overcrowding. Various seeds have different dispersal mechanisms. Some examples are shown.
1 Wood avens: fur-borne
2 Mistletoe berry: bird-borne
3 Blackberry: bird and mammal-borne
4 Sycamore "wing": wind-borne
5 Dandelion "parachute": wind-borne
6 *Clematis* "feather": wind-borne
7 Water lily: floating
8 Poppy: wind-shaken
9 Cranesbill: exploding

Growth

152**8** **Ideal conditions for growth**
The diagram shows the composition of a soil providing good plant growth.
1 Minerals: 45%
2 Water: 25%
3 Air: 25%
4 Organic material: 5%

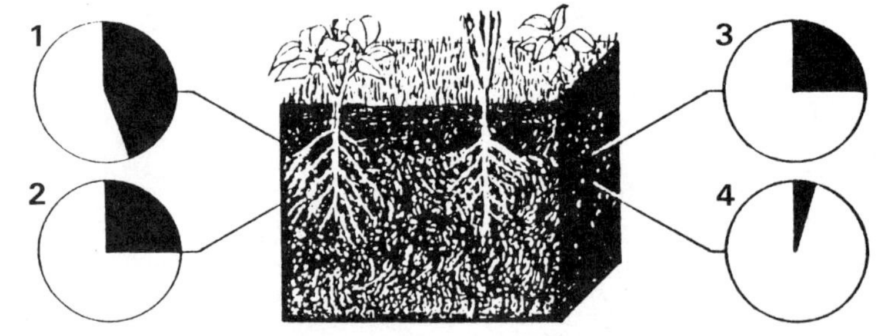

Development

152**9** **Stages in bean seed germination.**
1 The seed coat splits open and the young root starts to grow
2 Root hairs appear
3 The seed splits open completely; lateral roots grow
4 The young shoot grows out of the soil
5 The first leaves appear

Parts of a growing bean seed
a Testa (seed coat)
b Radicle (root of embryo)
c Hypocotyl (seedling stem)
d Root hairs
e Cotyledons (seed leaves)
f Lateral root
g Plumule (embryonic terminal bud)
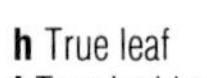
h True leaf
i Terminal bud

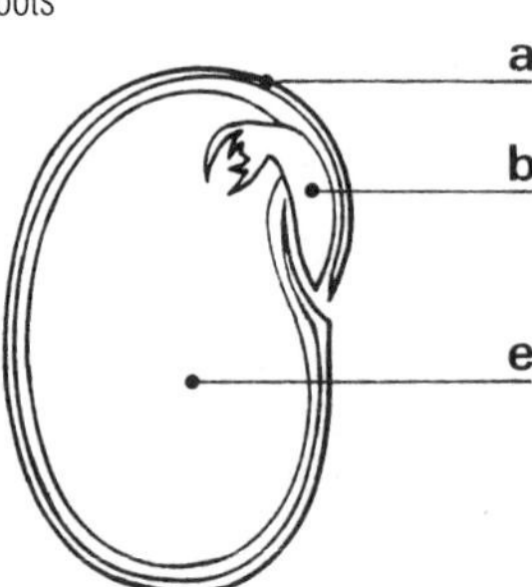

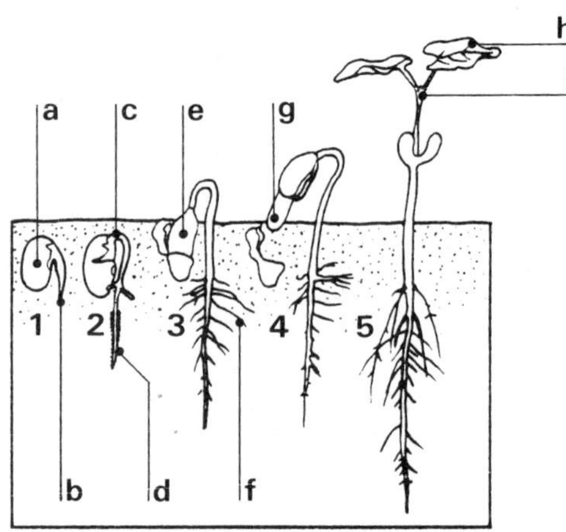

153 TYPES OF VEGETABLE

Brassicas—the cabbage family

1531

1 White/red cabbage
2 Savoy cabbage
3 Chinese cabbage
4 Brussels sprouts
5 Sprouting broccoli
6 Calabrese/Italian broccoli
7 Cauliflower
8 Kale

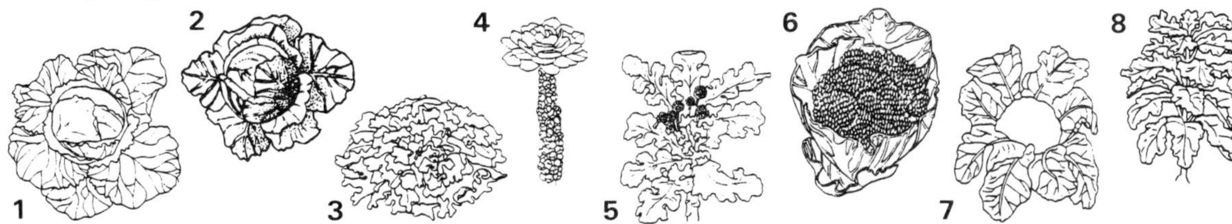

Leaf vegetables

1532

1 Cabbage lettuce
2 Romaine lettuce
3 Swiss chard
4 Spinach
5 Spinach beet
6 Celtuce
7 Corn salad
8 Sorrel
9 Good King Henry
10 Endive
11 Mustard
12 Cress

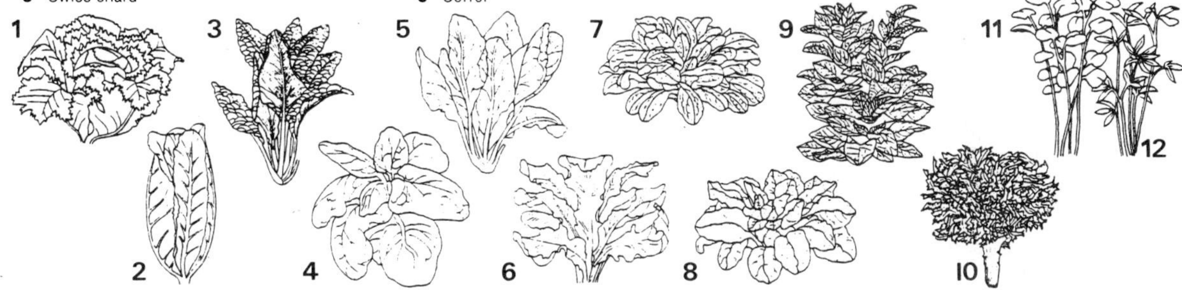

Root and tuber vegetables

1533

1 Carrot
2 Beetroot
3 Parsnip
4 Turnip
5 Swede
6 Radish
7 Potato
8 Sweet potato
9 Celeriac
10 Kohlrabi
11 Jerusalem artichoke
12 Salsify
13 Black salsify
14 Horseradish
15 Chinese artichokes
16 Scorzonera
17 Hamburg parsley
18 Skirret
19 Chervil
20 Rampion
21 Scolymus

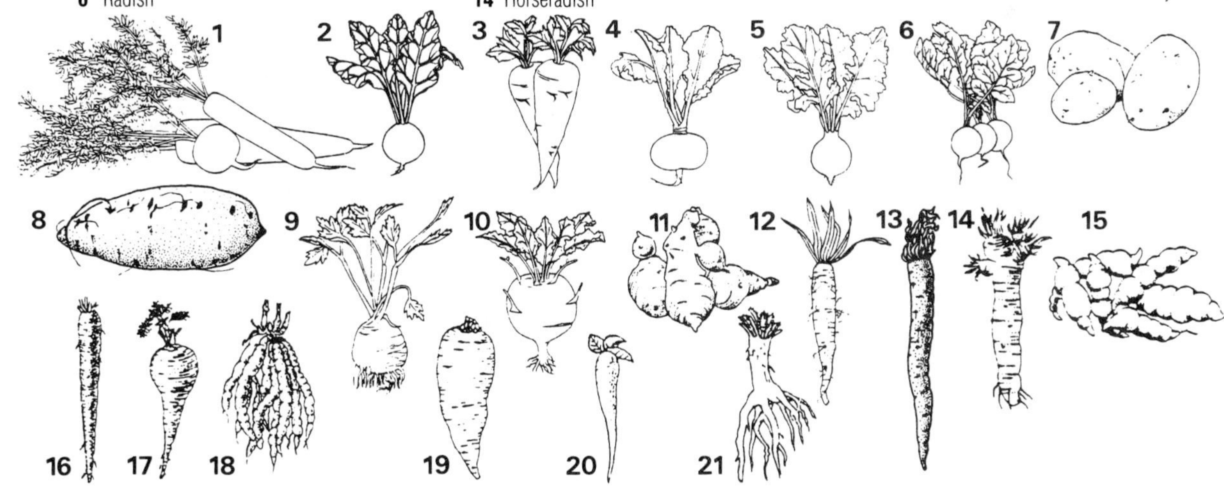

Seed vegetables

1534

1 French beans
2 Broad beans
3 Runner beans
4 Asparagus pea
5 Snow pea
6 Petit pois
7 Sweetcorn

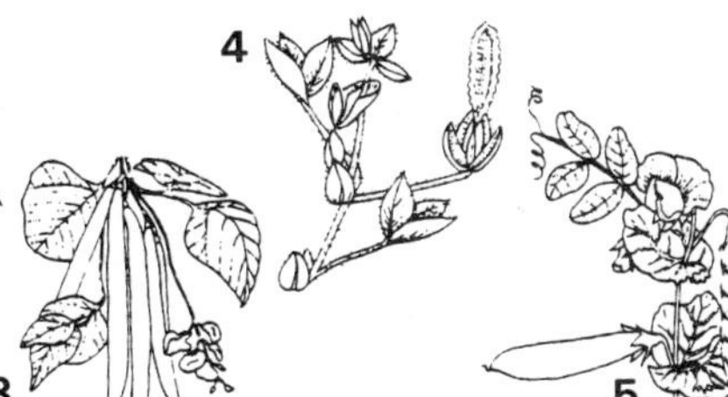

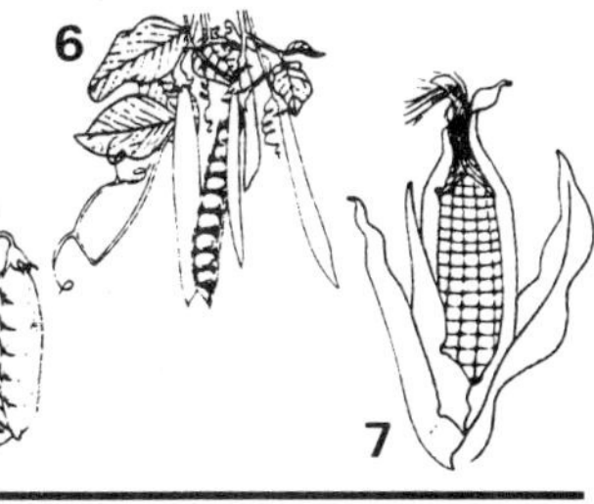

Bulb and stalk vegetables

153**5**

1 Leek
2 Onion
3 Shallot
4 Garlic
5 Celery
6 Rhubarb
7 Sea kale
8 Asparagus
9 Chicory
10 Globe artichoke
11 Cardoon
12 Finocchio
13 Scallion

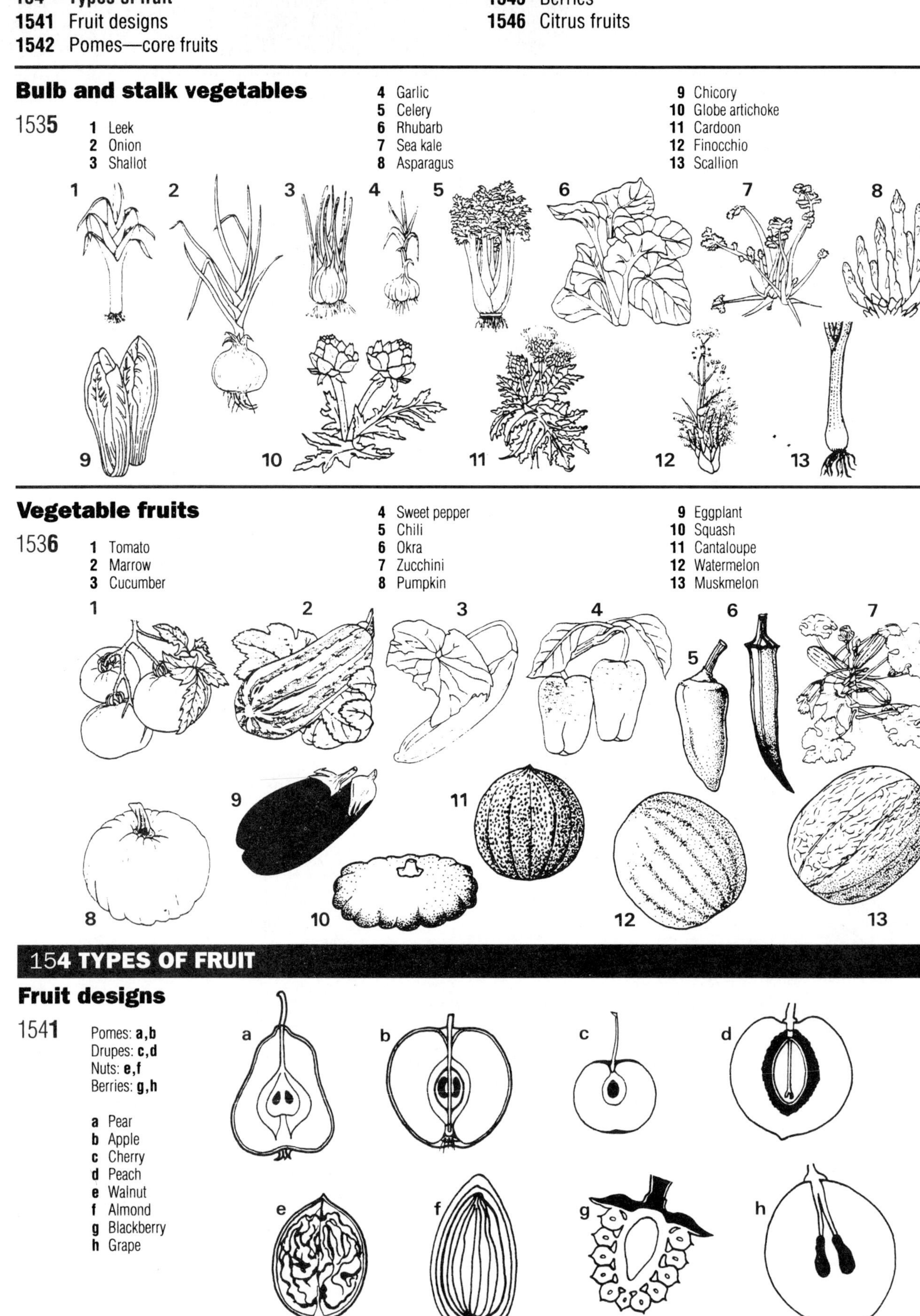

Vegetable fruits

153**6**

1 Tomato
2 Marrow
3 Cucumber
4 Sweet pepper
5 Chili
6 Okra
7 Zucchini
8 Pumpkin
9 Eggplant
10 Squash
11 Cantaloupe
12 Watermelon
13 Muskmelon

15**4** TYPES OF FRUIT

Fruit designs

154**1**

Pomes: **a,b**
Drupes: **c,d**
Nuts: **e,f**
Berries: **g,h**

a Pear
b Apple
c Cherry
d Peach
e Walnut
f Almond
g Blackberry
h Grape

Pomes—core fruits

1542

1 Apple
2 Pear
3 Japanese plum
4 Quince

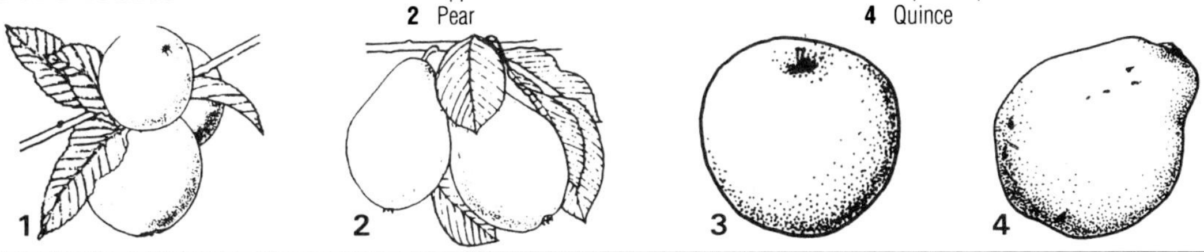

Drupes—stone fruits

1543

1 Cherry
2 Peach
3 Nectarine
4 Apricot
5 Plum
6 Olive
7 Mango
8 Date

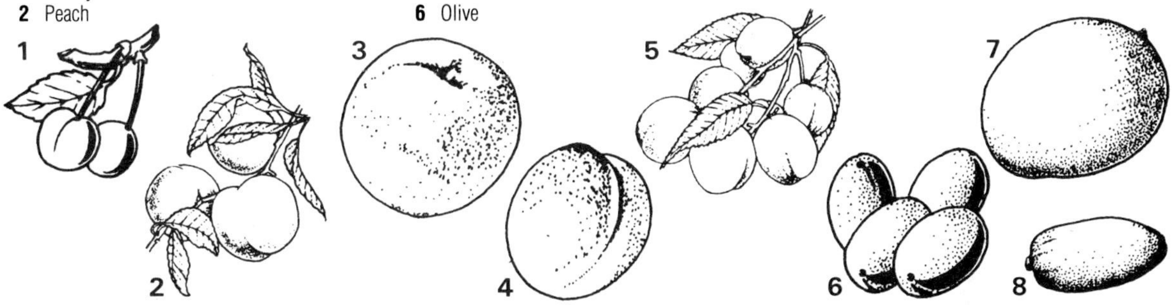

Nuts—dry stone fruits

1544

1 Almond
2 Walnut
3 Hazelnut/cobnut
4 Coconut
5 Chestnut
6 Cashewnut
7 Pine kernel
8 Pistachio
9 Peanut
10 Brazil
11 Pecan

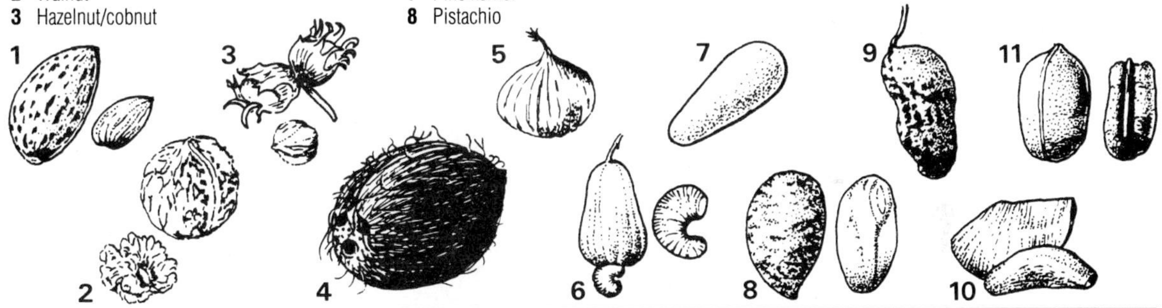

Berries

1545

1 Grape
2 Blueberry
3 Gooseberry
4 Huckleberry
5 Cranberry
6 Blackcurrant
7 Currant
8 Raspberry
9 Strawberry
10 Blackberry
11 Loganberry

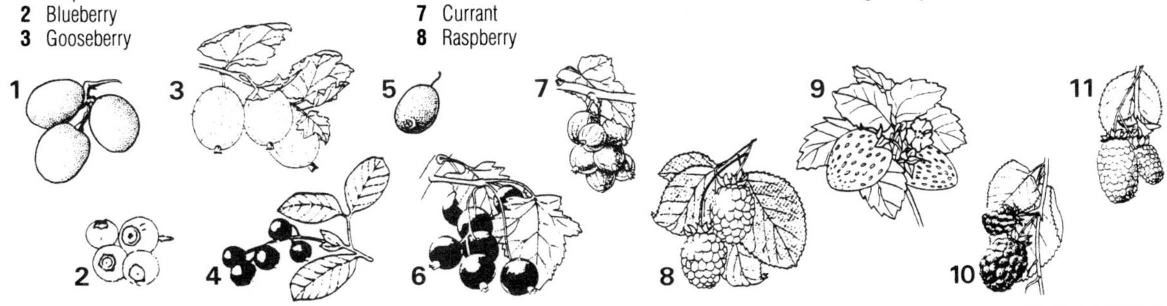

Citrus fruits

1546

1 Grapefruit
2 Orange
3 Lemon
4 Mandarin
5 Kumquat

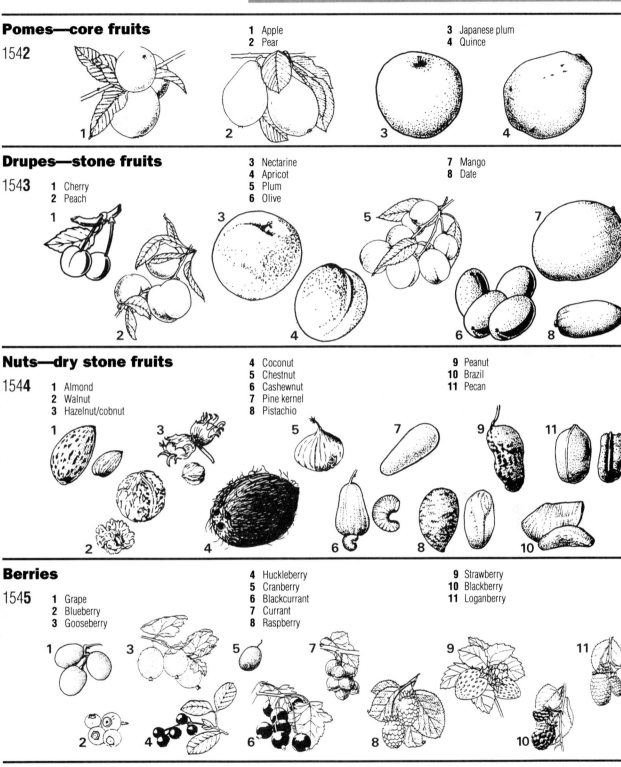

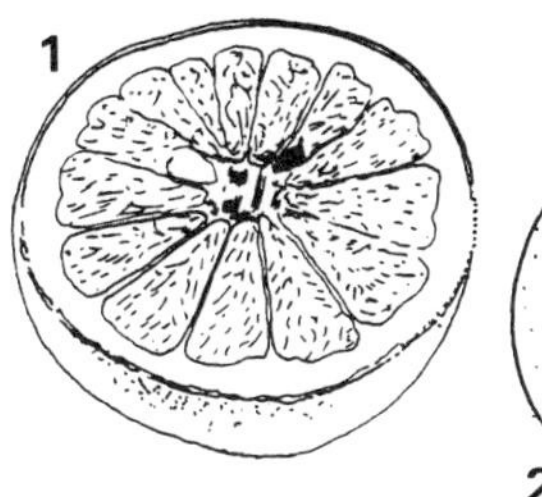
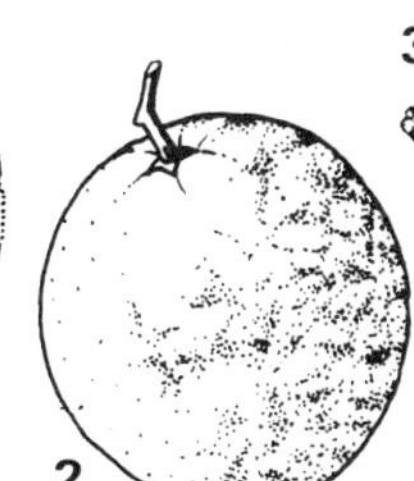
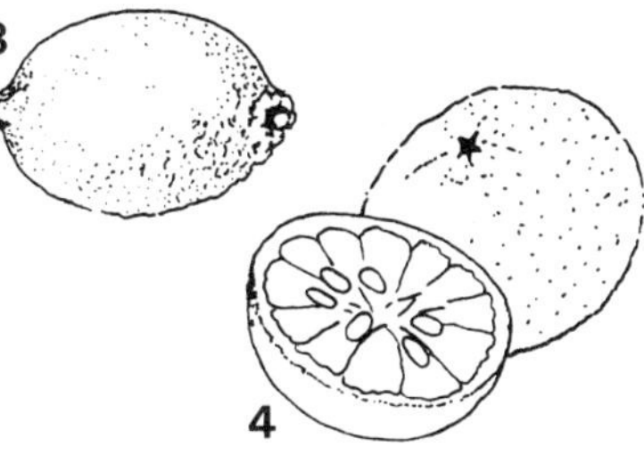
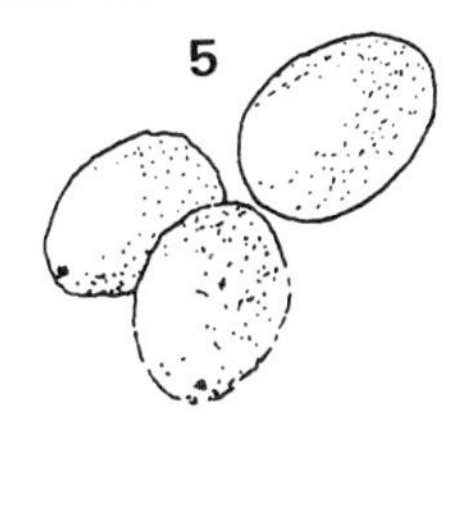

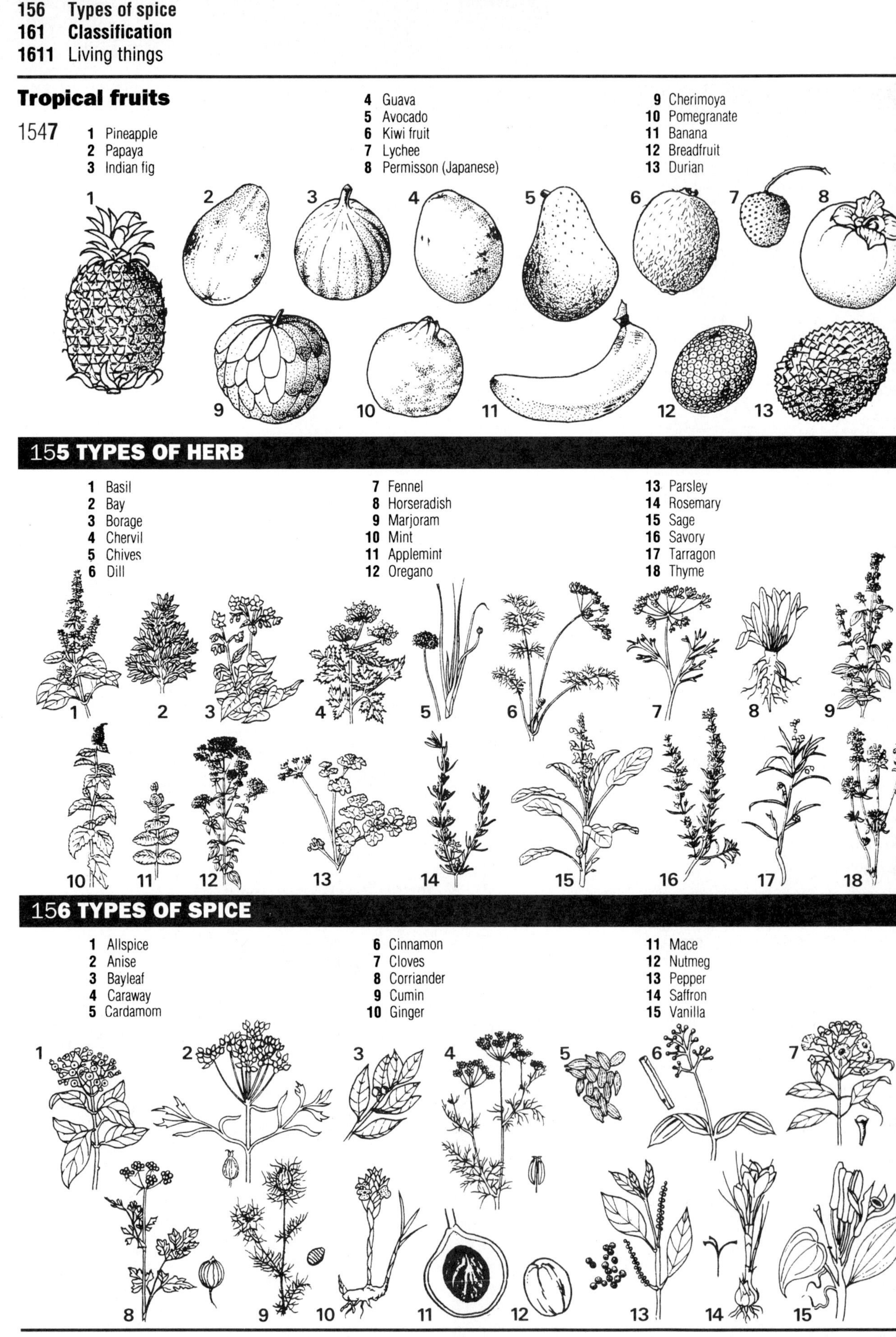

Tropical fruits

1547

1 Pineapple
2 Papaya
3 Indian fig
4 Guava
5 Avocado
6 Kiwi fruit
7 Lychee
8 Permisson (Japanese)
9 Cherimoya
10 Pomegranate
11 Banana
12 Breadfruit
13 Durian

155 TYPES OF HERB

1 Basil
2 Bay
3 Borage
4 Chervil
5 Chives
6 Dill
7 Fennel
8 Horseradish
9 Marjoram
10 Mint
11 Applemint
12 Oregano
13 Parsley
14 Rosemary
15 Sage
16 Savory
17 Tarragon
18 Thyme

156 TYPES OF SPICE

1 Allspice
2 Anise
3 Bayleaf
4 Caraway
5 Cardamom
6 Cinnamon
7 Cloves
8 Corriander
9 Cumin
10 Ginger
11 Mace
12 Nutmeg
13 Pepper
14 Saffron
15 Vanilla

161 CLASSIFICATION

Living things

1611 The animal kingdom is one of the five that include all living things.
1 Monera Bacteria, blue-green algae, and viruses which have procaryotic cells (cells without a nucleus).
2 Protista One-celled eucaryotic organisms (those with a nucleus).
3 Fungi Plant like eucaryotes that absorb ready made food.
4 Plantae (plants) Eucaryotes with a cellulose cell walls, which make food from carbon dioxide and water.
5 Animalia (animals) Many-celled eucaryotes that feed on other organisms. Most can move.

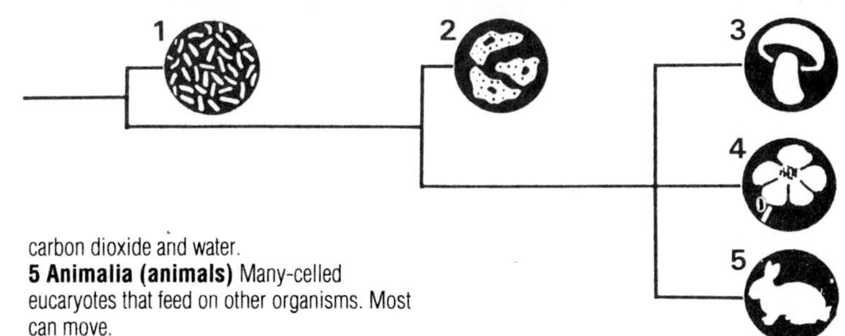

Animal species

1612 The circles of different sizes indicate relative numbers of species of the nine major groups of animals called Phyla and those "animal" protists, the protozoans. Circle 8 would be far larger still if all the world's insects and other arthropods had been included.
1 Protozoa (amoebas, etc).
2 Porifera (sponges).
3 Coelenterata (jellyfish, etc).
4 Platyhelminthes (flatworms).
5 Nematoda (nematode worms).
6 Annelida (segmented worms).
7 Mollusca (mollusks, e.g. snails).
8 Arthropoda (crustaceans, myriapods, insects, spiders, etc).
9 Echinodermata (starfish, etc).
10 Chordata (animals with a notochord or internal skeletal rod, notably vertebrates or backboned animals).

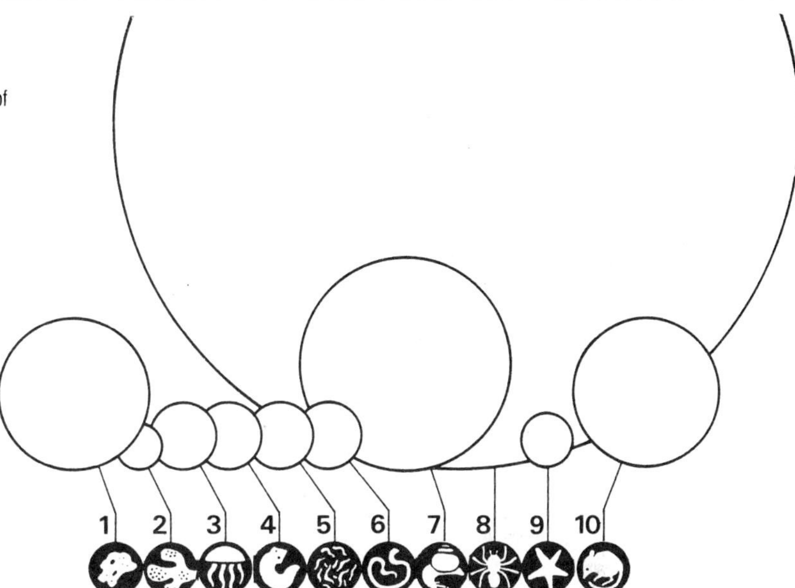

The animal kingdom

1613

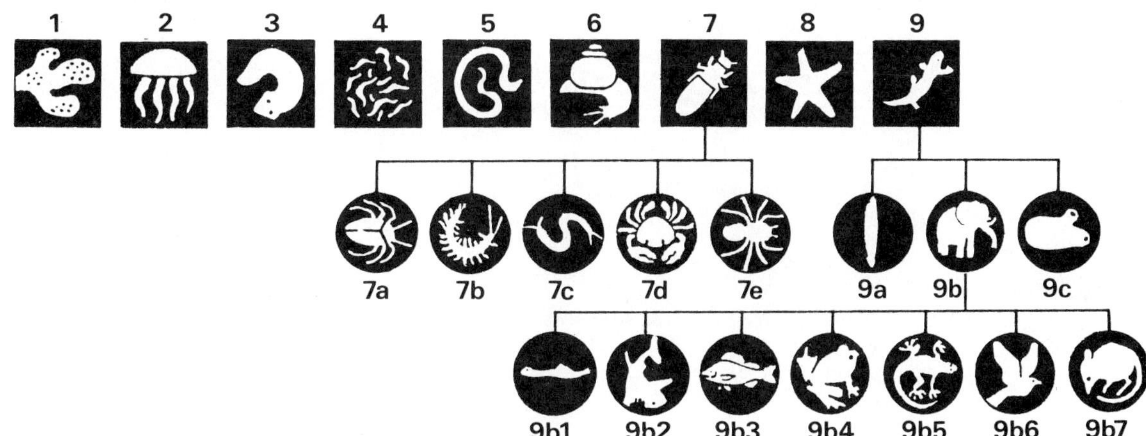

1 Porifera (sponges)
2 Coelenterata (jellyfish, etc.)
3 Platyhelminthes (flatworms)
4 Nematodas (nematode worms)
5 Annelida (segmented worms)
6 Mollusca (mollusks)
7 Arthropoda (arthropods)
7a Insecta (insects)
7b Chilopoda (centipedes)
7c Diplopoda (millipedes)
7d Crustacea (crustaceans)
7e Arachnida (spiders)
8 Echinodermata (starfish, etc.)
9 Chordata (chordates)
9a Cephaldochordata (amphioxus)
9b Vertebrata (vertebrates)
9c Urochordata (sea squirts)
9b1 Cyclostomata (jawless fish)
9b2 Chondrichthyes (cartilaginous fish)
9b3 Osteichthyes (bony fish)
9b4 Amphibia (amphibians)
9b5 Reptilia (reptiles)
9b6 Aves (birds)
9b7 Mammalia (mammals)

Numbers of known species

1614 One estimate of the numbers of all known species gives these totals. Far more species of animals - as much as other forms of life- remain to be identified.
1 Animals: more than 1.2 million
2 Plants: about 300,000
3 Others: more than 100,000

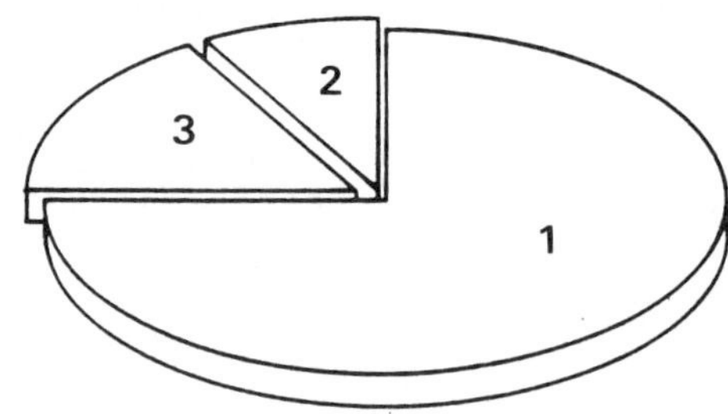

Classifying an animal

1615 Living things are classified in successively larger groups, with successively less close anatomical relationships. The smallest unit usually used is the species. Members of one species normally do not interbreed with members of any other species.
This diagram shows (reading upward) that the lion (*Panthera leo*) is one of several species in the genus *Panthera*. In turn, this genus is one of four genera in the family Felidae. That family is one of seven families in the order Carnivora. This order is one of 17 orders in the class Mammalia. The class Mammalia is one of seven in the subphylum Vertebrata. Vertebrates belong to the phylum Chordata, one of nine phyla making up the animal kingdom.

THE ANIMAL KINGDOM (Example)
1 Kingdom: Animalia
2 Phylum: Chordata
3 Subphylum: Vertebrata
4 Class: Mammalia
5 Order: Carnivora
6 Family: Felidae
7 Genus: *Panthera*
8 Species: *Panthera leo* (lion)

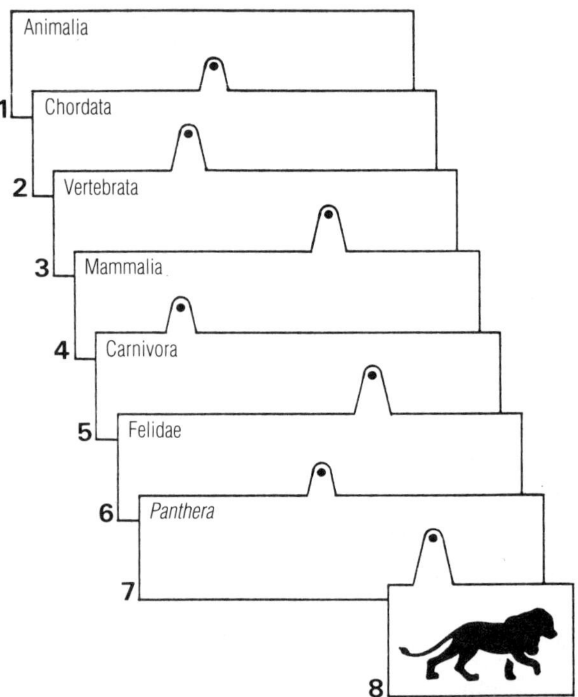

162 INVERTEBRATES AND VERTEBRATES

Invertebrates

1621

About invertebrates
Invertebrates are animals without vertebrae,the interlocking bones or bits of cartilage that form a spine or backbone. Listed below are the animallike protozoans, true invertebrates, and chordates (Chordata). (Only two classes of Chordata are inveretbrates; the remainder are vertebrates).
Protozoa Tiny, mobile, one-celled protists (e.g. amoebas), not now grouped with the true animals.
Mesozoa Tiny, parasitic animals.
Porifera Plantlike aquatic animals without tissues or organs–e.g. sponges.
Coelenterata Jellylike aquatic animals with a central body cavity, tentacles around the mouth, and stinging cells–e.g. jellyfish, sea anemones.
Ctenophora The marine comb jellies.
Platyhelminthes Flatworms, with a head and mouth, which is the body's only opening–e.g. planarians, tapeworms.
Nemertina Ribbon worms.
Aschelminthes Small, wormlike animals, arguably including the *Nematoda*.
Nematoda Roundworms, pointed at both ends–e.g. eelworms, hookworms.
Acanthocephala Thorny-headed worms.
Entoprocta Similar to Bryozoa.
Bryozoa Tiny, tube-dwelling, plantlike aquatic animals that live in colonies.
Phoronida Marine wormlike animals.
Brachiopoda Lamp-shells: marine bivalve animals with whiplike food-gathering appendages called brachia.
Mollusca Animals with a shell and muscular foot or parts derived from them–e.g. clams,

Classes of mollusks

Gastropoda (univalves)

Pelecypoda (bivalves)

Cepalopoda (octopuses and squids)

Scaphoda (tooth shells)

Amphineura (chitons)

Monoplacophora

continued

Invertebrates continued

1621

Sipunculoidea Marine worms with a two-part body. The anus is near the front.
Echiuroidea Marine, sac-shaped, wormlike animals–e.g. spoon-worms.
Annelida Segmented worms seemingly made of cylindrical rings–e.g. earthworms, leeches, lugworms.
Arthropoda Animals with jointed limbs and an outer skeleton–e.g. crabs, millipedes, flies, spiders.
Chaetognatha Arrow worms.
Pogonophora Beard worms.
Echinodermata Aquatic animals with a five-rayed body and chalky plates below the skin–e.g. sea urchins, starfish.
Chordata Animals that at some stage in their lives having a notochord (a flexible internal rod stiffening the body). Only the protochordates or lower chordates are invertebrates. Protochordates include the cephalochordates (lancelets), tunicates (sea squirts), and hemichordates (acorn worms).

Vertebrates

1622

About vertebrates
Vertebrates are chordates (Chordata) with an internal bony or gristly skeleton. Most have a backbone of interlocking vertebrae. Below are described the seven classes of vertebrates: jawless fishes, cartilaginous fishes, bony fishes (all three often collectively called *Pisces*: fishes), amphibians, reptiles, birds, and mammals.

Fishes: jawless

The Cyclostomata; the only living examples of the Agnatha, or jawless fishes, are the most primitive vertebrates. Instead of vertebrae they have a gristly notochord, and they lack paired fins, hinged jaws, or a second nostril. Jawless fishes include lampreys and hagfishes: long, thin, eellike fishes with suckerlike mouths and rasping teeth.

Fishes: cartilaginous

The Chondrichthyes or cartilaginous fishes include the sharks and sharklike fishes. Their skeletons are made of tough, gristly cartilage instead of bone, and their scales are like tiny sharp teeth. There are paired fins but no gill covers and there is no swim bladder to control the depth at which they swim.

Fishes: bony

The Osteichthyes or bony fishes have a bony skeleton, scales, or bony plates covering the slimy skin, gill covers, and a swim bladder. One primitive group contains the paddle-fish and sturgeon. Another holds the coelacanth and lungfish. Barracuda, salmon, tuna, and most other bony fishes belong to a third group, the ray-finned fishes.

Reptiles

The class Reptilia consists of dry-skinned, scaly, and cold-blooded vertebrates that mostly breed on land.

Turtles and tortoises
The Chelonia (turtles and tortoises) are four-legged toothless reptiles with a protective shell. Tortoises live on land; turtles in fresh or salt water. Most tortoises eat plants but some are carnivorous. The largest chelonian is the (marine) leatherback turtle which grows up to 8 ft 4 in (2.5 m) long.

Tuatara
The lizardlike Tuatara has a beaked upper jaw and a scaly crest down its back. It is the sole survivor of the reptile order Sphenodontida and lives only on small, chilly islands off New Zealand. Males grow up to 2 ft (60 cm) long; females are shorter.

Lizards and snakes
Lizards and snakes form the reptile order Squamata. Most lizards have four legs. All snakes are limbless and can "unhinge" their jaws to swallow large prey. The largest lizard is the Komodo monitor, which can be up to 10 ft 2 in (3.10 m) long. The largest snake is the reticulated python, which can be up to 32 ft 9 in (10 m) long.

Crocodiles and Alligators
The Crocodilia (crocodiles and alligators) have long, flattened tails, bulky bodies, four short limbs, and long-jawed heads armed with sharp teeth. The estuarine crocodile is the largest living crocodilian reptile of any kind. Some individuals exceed 23 ft (7 m) long.

continued

Vertebrates continued

1622 Amphibians

The Amphibia are mainly scaleless, cold-blooded vertebrates. Most develop from larvae hatched from eggs laid in water.

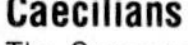

Caecilians
The Gymnophiona form an order of limbless, wormlike amphibians also called caecilians. There are rings around their bodies, and some of them have scales. About 150 species of caecilians burrow in forest floors and river beds of tropical countries around the world. The largest species grow up to 5 ft (1.5 m) long.

Tailed amphibians
The Caudata or tailed amphibians have a long body, long tail, and four legs. They include the salamanders and newts. Most tailed amphibians start as swimming larvae, with feathery gills, but they lose their gills and leave the water as they grow. The axolotl and olm keep their gills and never leave water. The giant salamander, up to 5 ft 11 in (1.8 m) long, is the largest amphibian.

Frogs and toads
Frogs and toads form the Anura or tailless amphibians. These have long hind limbs for leaping or hopping. The majority are also strong swimmers. Most frogs and toads start as swimming, limbless tadpoles with feathery gills, but develop limbs and lose their gills as they grow. The largest anuran is the goliath frog, up to 14 in (35.6 cm) long and weighing up to 7 lb 4 oz (3.3 kg).

Birds

The class Aves contains warm-blooded, feathered, egg-laying vertebrates with arms that have evolved as wings. Most can fly. The largest is the ostrich; the smallest is the bee hummingbird. Scientists group birds into the following orders:

Struthioniformes Ostriches
Rheiformes Rheas
Casuariiformes Emus and cassowaries
Apterygiformes Kiwis
Tinamiformes Tinamous
Gaviiformes Divers
Podicipediformes Grebes
Sphenisciformes Penguins
Procellariiformes Albatrosses, fulmars, petrels, and shearwaters
Pelecaniformes Cormorants, gannets, frigate birds, pelicans, tropic birds
Ciconiiformes Bitterns, herons, ibises, spoonbills, and storks
Phoenicopteriformes Flamingos
Anseriformes Ducks, geese, swans, and screamers
Falconiformes Eagles, falcons, hawks, ospreys, secretary birds, and vultures
Galliformes Curassow fowl, grouse, hoatzin, peafowl, pheasants, turkeys, and quail
Gruiformes Bustards, coots, cranes, and rails
Charadriiformes Gulls and wading birds
Columbiformes Doves, pigeons, and sand grouse
Psittaciformes Cockatoos, lories, macaws, parakeets, and parrots
Cuculiformes Cuckoos and touracos
Strigiformes Owls
Caprimulgiformes Frogmouths, goatsuckers, and oilbirds
Apodiformes Hummingbirds and swifts
Coliiformes Colies
Trogoniformes Trogons
Coraciiformes Bee eaters, hoopoes, hornbills, kingfishers, motmots, rollers, and todies
Piciformes Jacamars, toucans, and woodpeckers
Passeriformes Perching birds, including birds of paradise, broadbills, buntings, crows, dippers, finches, larks, lyre birds, martins, nuthatches, pipits, shrikes, starlings, swallows, thrushes, titmice, warblers, and wrens

Mammals

The class Mammalia consists of warm-blooded, hairy vertebrates whose mothers suckle their young.

Monotremes
The Monotremata are primitive, egg-laying mammals with a toothless beak.They are Australia's aquatic duck-billed platypus and the echidnas of Australia and New Guinea.

Pouched mammals
The Marsupiala or pouched mammals give birth to tiny young that develop in a pouch in the mother's belly. They include Australia's bandicoots, kangaroos, koalas, and wombats, and the American opossums. The largest marsupial is the red kangaroo.

Placental mammals
The Eutheria or placental mammals give birth to babies that develop in the mother's body, nourished by a special organ, the placenta. The largest mammal is the blue whale; it can exceed 108 ft (33 m) in length. Scientists group placentals into these orders:
Insectivora Insectivores
Tupaioidea Tree shrews
Dermoptera Colugos
Chiroptera Bats
Primates Lemurs, monkeys, apes, humans
Edentata Anteaters, sloths
Pholidota Pangolins
Lagomorpha Hares, rabbits, and pikas
Rodentia Nutrias, mice, squirrels
Cetacea Whales
Carnivora Bears, cats, dogs, et.
Pinnipedia Seals, sea lions, walruses
Tubulidentata Aardvarks
Proboscidea Elephants
Hyracoidea Hyraxes
Sirenia Sea cows
Perissodactyla Horses, rhinos
Artiodactyla Antelopes, camels, cattle, deer, giraffes, goats, pigs, sheep

163 BODY SYSTEMS

The bodies of animals are organized into systems that perform certain functions. The support system provides a framework; the respiratory system takes in oxygen; the digestive system digests and absorbs food; the muscular system moves the skeleton; the circulatory system transports materials; and the nervous and regulatory systems, including the brain, coordinate and control all body activities.

Support

1631

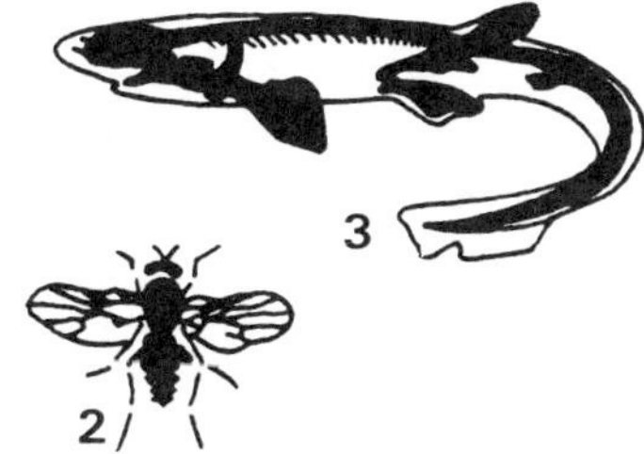

The soft tissues of many animals are supported and protected by a hard, strong (internal) endoskeleton or (external) exoskeleton. Examples:

1 Starfish (echinoderm): calcareous endoskeleton.
2 Fly (arthropod): horny chitin exoskeleton.
3 Shark (fish): cartilaginous endoskeleton.
4 Perch (fish): bony endoskeleton.
5 Cow (mammal): bony endoskeleton.

Respiration

1632 Four animals with different respiratory surfaces are shown. These surfaces admit oxygen for "burning" food to fuel life processes, and they release carbon dioxide, a waste gas of combustion.

1 Hydra (coelenterate): entire body surface.
2 Grasshopper (arthropod): tracheal (tube) system.
3 Carp (fish): gills.
4 Human (mammal): lungs.

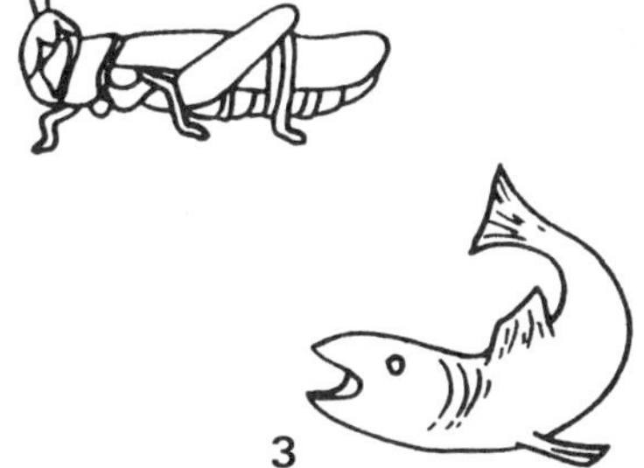

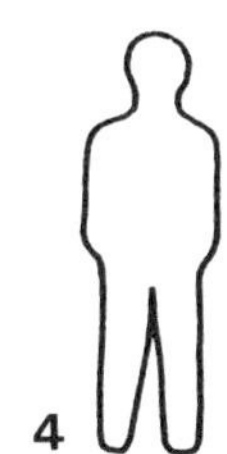

Digestion

1633

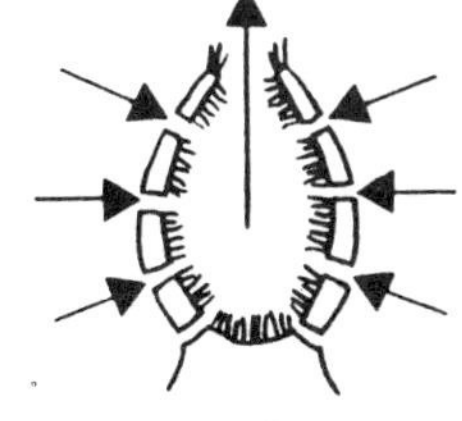

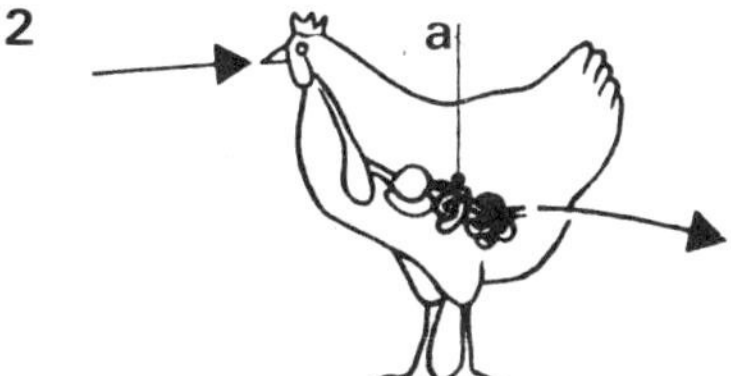

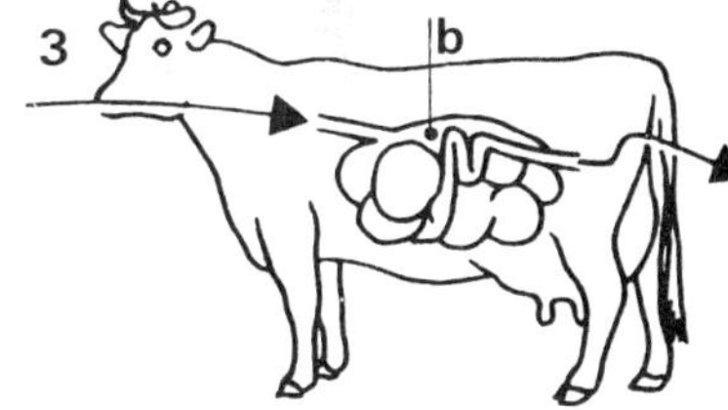

The illustrations compare three animal digestive systems. All systems absorb and break down nutrients and eject indigestible items.

1 Sponge: digestive cavity with many inlets and one outlet.
2 Chicken (bird): digestive tract with an inlet, an outlet, and a gizzard (**a**).
3 Cow (mammal): digestive tract with complex stomach for digesting grass (**b**).

Muscles

1634 The movement of body parts is due to the contraction and expansion of muscles, which consist of elastic tissue. Two examples are shown.

1 Earthworm (annelid): muscular rings around the body contract and then relax to thrust the worm along.
2 Human (mammal): paired muscles contract in turn to move limbs.

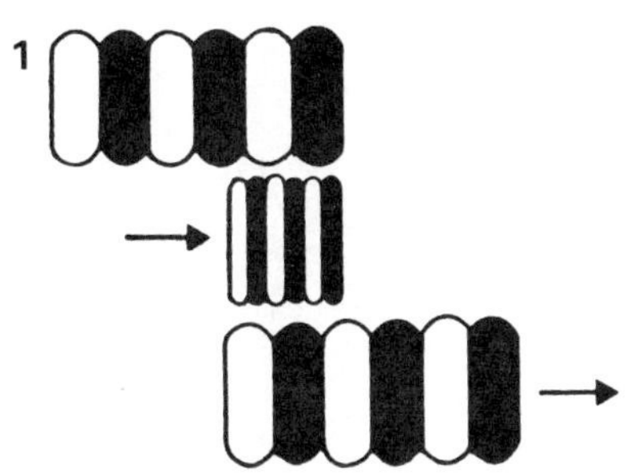

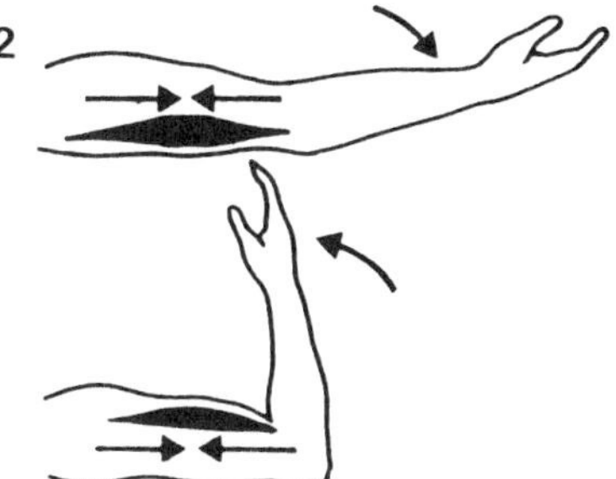

Circulation

1635 The diagrams compare blood circulation in two vertebrates. In each, a heart (**a**) pumps used blood from the body (**b**) to the gills or lungs (**c**) and fresh blood from gills or lungs to the body.
1 Fish, with two-chambered heart.
2 Mammal, with four-chambered heart, separating fresh and stale blood.

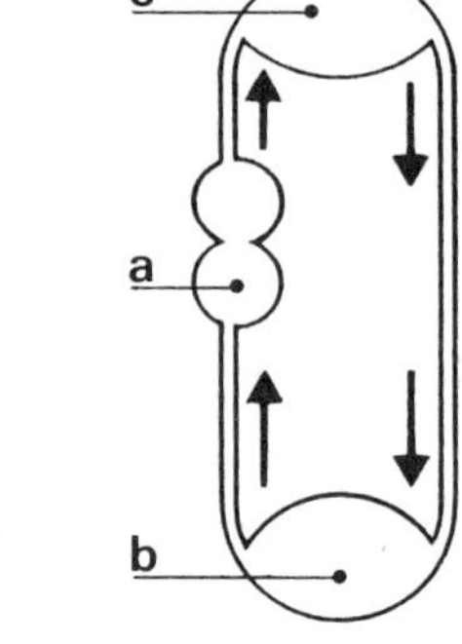

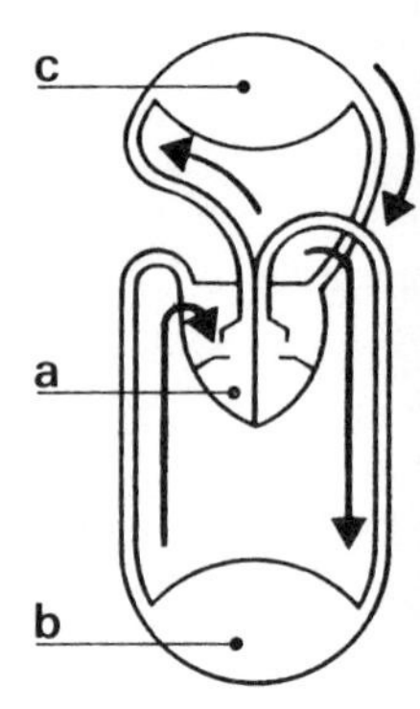

Excretion

1636 Vertebrates have kidneys that filter blood and excrete urine waste. The diagrams compare excretion systems in two types of vertebrate.
1 Lower vertebrate's excretion system (e.g. fish or reptile) .
2 Mammal's excretion system.
a Kidneys: filter out impurities.
b Cloaca: takes urine and solid waste.
c Bladder: takes urine only.

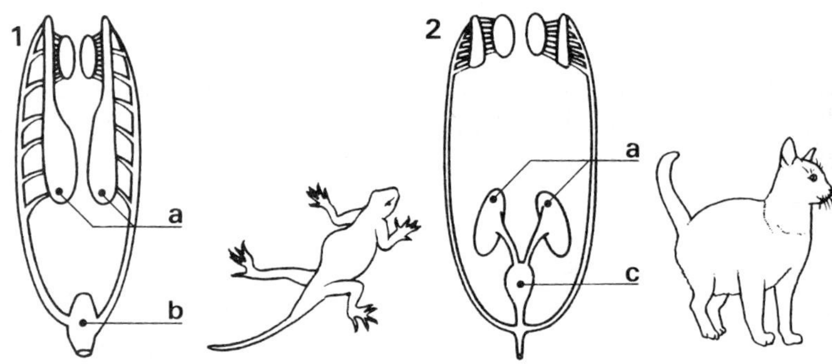

Nervous system

1637 Nerves provide the body with a system for communication and control. Nervous systems range from a loose network to a complex structure with a spinal cord and coordinating center: the brain.
1 Hydra (coelenterate): nerve net.
2 Flatworm (platyhelminth): two nerve cords and a primitive brain.
3 Salamander (amphibian): a brain, a spinal cord relaying signals between the brain and muscles, and nerve endings sensing touch, taste, scent, light, sound, and balance.

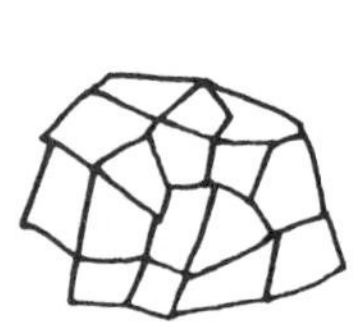

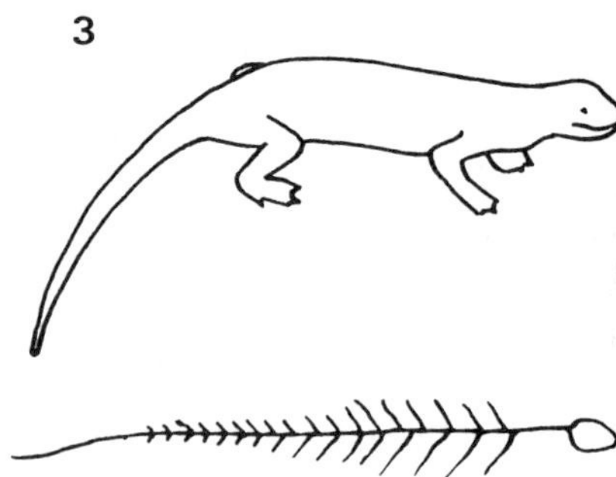

Regulation

1638 Animals regulate their body systems with the help of endocrine glands, which secrete hormones that travel in the blood. In birds and mammals, a thyroid gland regulates body temperature, as shown. Skin receptors (**1**) detect heat and cold, stimulating the brain's hypothalamus (**2**) to make the pituitary gland (**3**) release thyroid-stimulating hormone. This, in turn, makes the thyroid (**4**) secrete hormones that cause tissues (**5**) to adjust their heat output. Feedback (**6**) maintains balance.

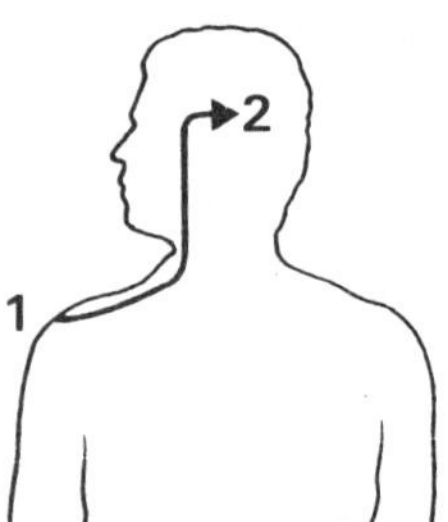

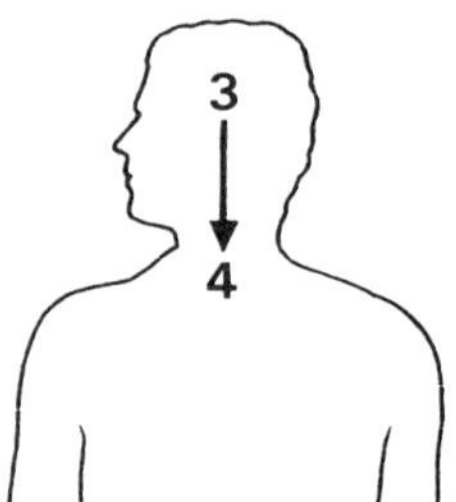

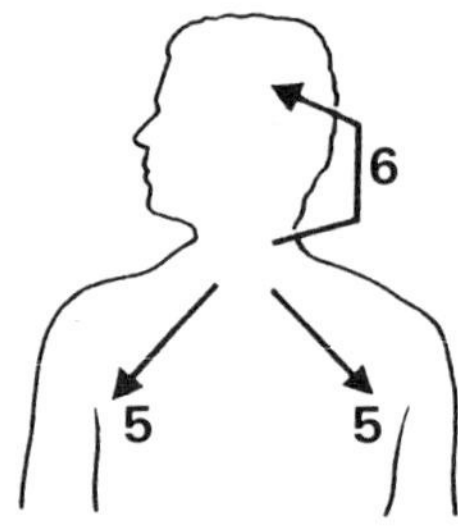

The brain

1639 Development in size and special parts reflects different animals' abilities.
1 Fish's brain
2 Reptile's brain
3 Bird's brain
4 Mammal's (horse's) brain
a Olfactory bulb (smell center)
b Cerebrum (coordinating center; sight of visual center in mammals)
c Optic lobe (visual center)
d Cerebellum (muscular coordination)

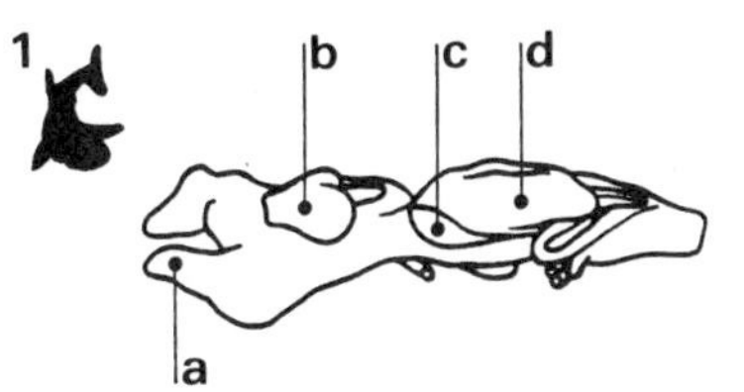

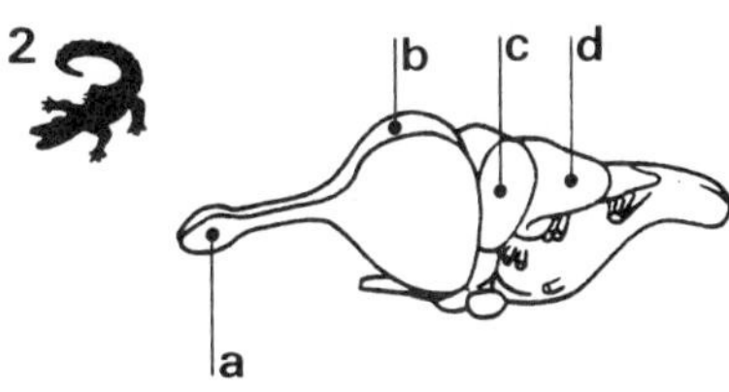

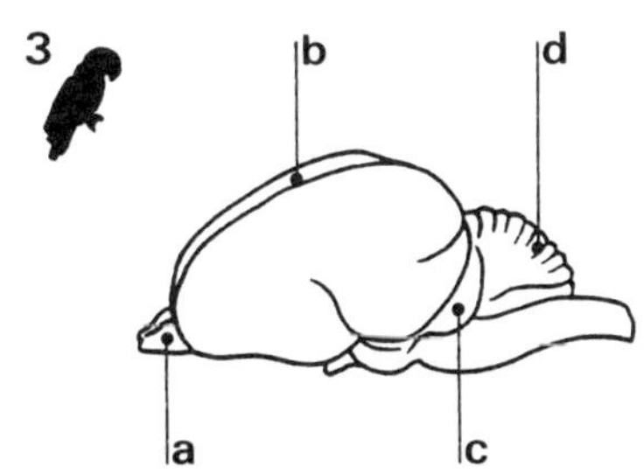

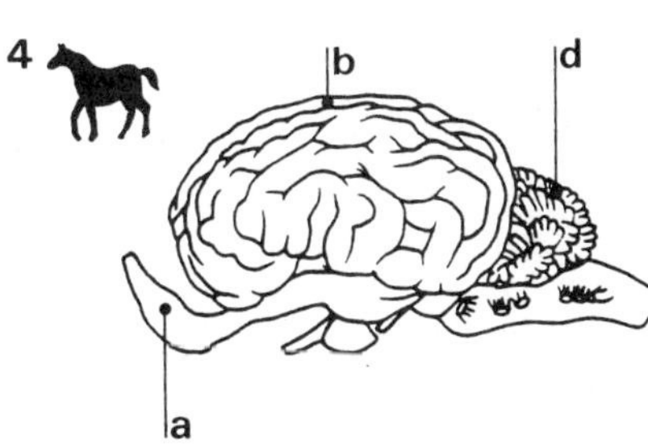

164 SENSES

Internal senses

1641 Internal senses inform animals about their own bodies. Specialized receptor cells inform them of balance, fatigue, hunger, pain, and muscle tension. For example, proprioceptors inform a vertebrate's central nervous system of muscle tension.

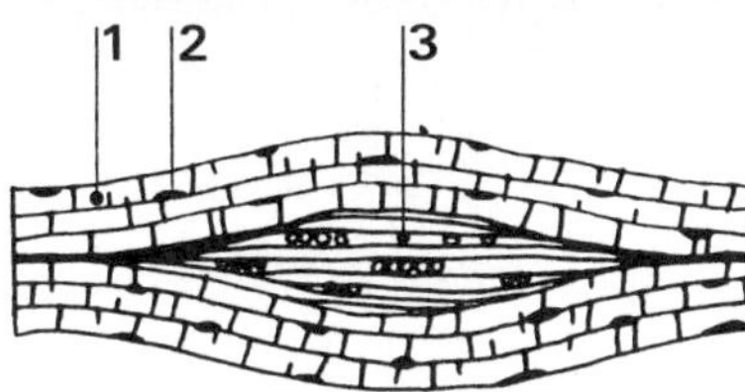

1 Muscle fibers
2 Proprioceptors
3 Nerves from proprioceptors to the central nervous system.

Taste and smell

1642 External senses (taste, smell, hearing, sight, etc.) help animals detect food, danger, and a mate. Two animals with keen smell or taste receptors are shown here.
1 A male moth's antennae (**a**) can detect a sex-attractant chemical released by a female moth over 1 mi (1.6 km) away.

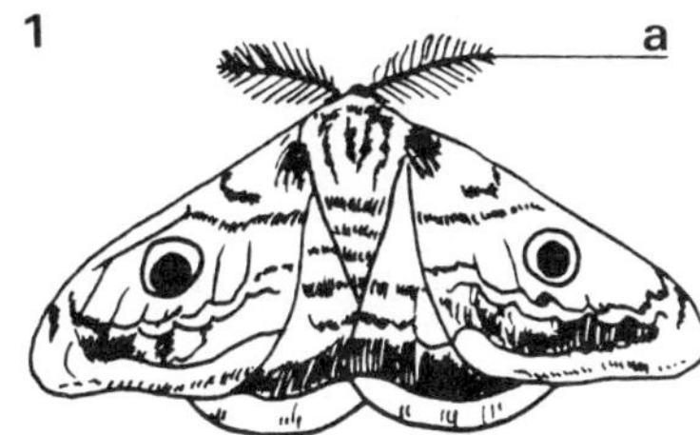

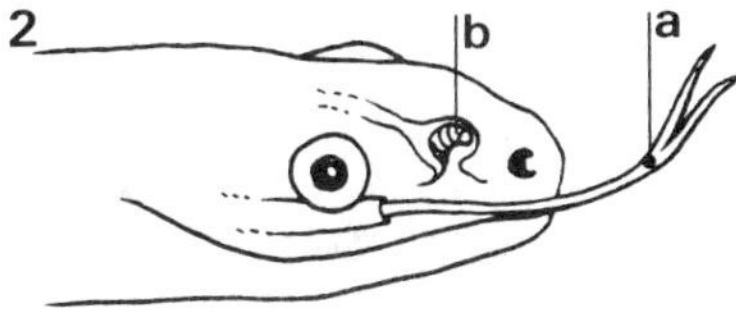

2 A snake "tastes" air with its forked tongue (**a**), taking scent particles to Jacobson's organ (**b**) two sensitive holes in the roof of its mouth.

Touch

1643 Touch organs in the skin and mucous membranes help many creatures sense pressure acting on the body. Touch organs are often linked to sensitive hairs. In a fish, such hairs sprout from canals that run along its sides and head. These "lateral-line" organs inform the fish of nearby still or moving objects.
1 Fish: showing its lateral-line system (**a**) of sensitive hairs.

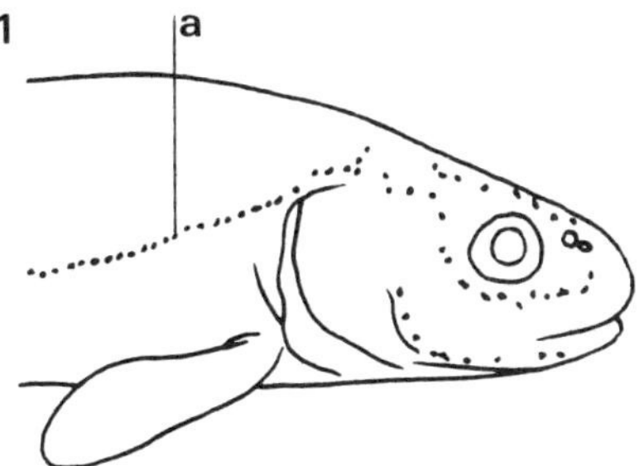

Electroreceptors

1644 Modified lateral-line organs help certain fish to sense an electric field produced by special muscle fibers. Receptor cells note field distortions caused by nearby objects, aiding navigation in dark or muddy water. Four fish with this extra sense are shown.

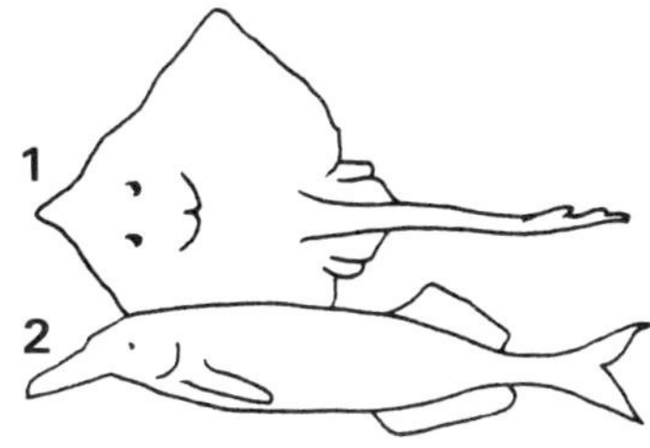

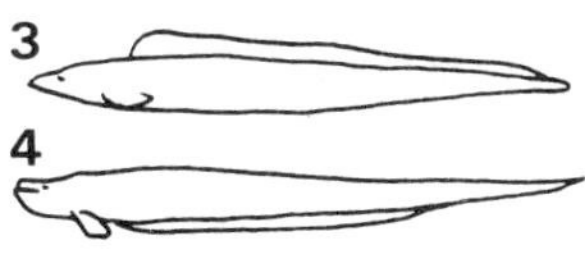

1 *Raja*: a skate
2 *Gnathonemus*
3 *Gymnarchus*
4 *Gymnotus*

Hearing

1645 Creatures are able to hear when receptors respond to membranes vibrated by sound waves moving through air or water. Animals with different kinds of hearing mechanisms (**a**) are shown here.
1 Catfish: a fish with an inner ear on each side of its head.
2 Cricket: an insect with "ears" on its front legs.
3 Frog: an amphibian with large eardrums behind the eyes.
4 Long-eared bat: a mammal with big outer ears to channel sounds.

Sounds heard
The range of pitch in hertz (Hz) that eight animals can hear is compared.
1 Human 20–20,000 Hz (20 = low)
2 Dog 15–50,000 Hz
3 Frog 50–10,000 Hz
4 Cat 60–65,000 Hz
5 Grasshopper 100–15,000 Hz
6 Dolphin 150–150,000 Hz
7 Robin (European) 250–21,000 Hz
8 Bat 1000–120,000 Hz

Sounds made
The range of pitch in hertz (Hz) that eight animals can make is compared
1 Human 80–1100 Hz
2 Dog 452–1080 Hz
3 Frog 50–8000 Hz
4 Cat 760–1520 Hz
5 Grasshopper 7000–100,000 Hz
6 Dolphin 7000–120,000 Hz
7 Robin (European) 2000–13,000 Hz
8 Bat 10,000–120,000 Hz

Sight

1646 **Eye types**
Different types of eye provide varying amounts of information. Three animals with different eye types and visual ability are compared.
1 *Euglena*: a tiny water organism. Its eye spot (**a**) tells light from dark.
2 Honeybee: an insect with three simple eyes (**a**), enabling it to differentiate between light and dark, and two compound eyes (**b**) with many lenses forming many images.
3 Tarsier: a primate with two eyes producing one sharp image.

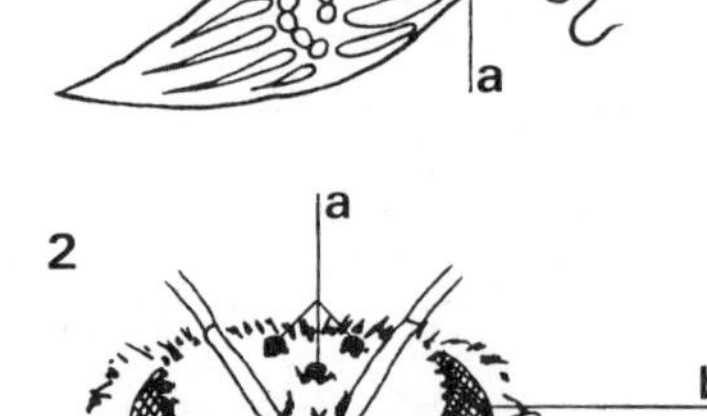

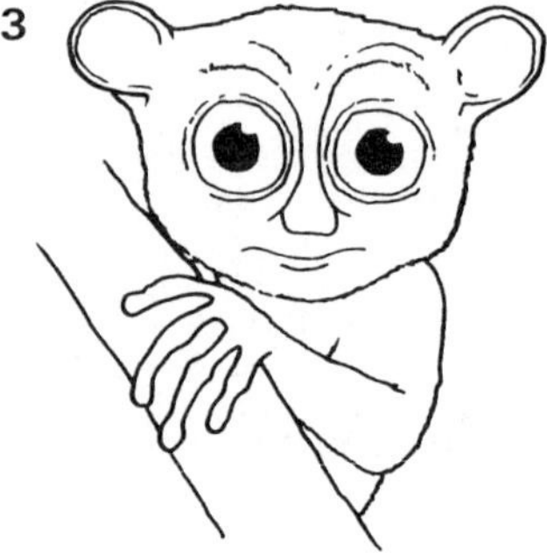

continued

Sight continued

646 **Fields of vision**

Animals with forward-facing eyes can see less far back than ones with eyes at the sides of their heads. The area that an animal sees is called its field of vision. Three fields of vision are compared here.

1 Human's field of vision.
2 Bird's field of vision.
3 Rabbit's field of vision.

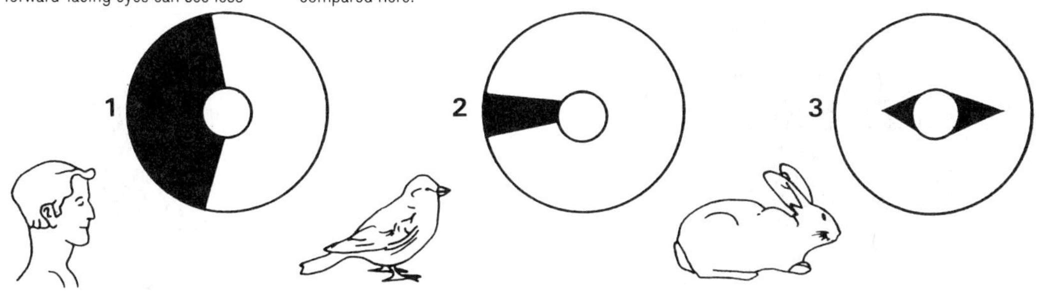

Temperature

647 **Body temperatures**

This diagram shows some of the highest and lowest normal or ideal body temperatures found in each group of backboned mammals. In general, birds have the highest body temperatures, followed by mammals. Few mammals have temperatures below 95°F. Listed here are a selection of animal temperatures, set against that of a human (98.6°F).

1	Western pewee	(bird)	112.6° F	37.0° C
2	Goat	(mammal)	103.8° F	44.8° C
3	Spiny lizard	(reptile)	98.4° F	39.9° C
4	Arctic gull	(bird)	93.2° F	34.0° C
5	Archer fish	(fish)	82.4° F	82.4° C
6	Rain frog	(amphibian)	79.7° F	26.5° C
7	Spiny anteater	(mammal)	73.9° F	23.3° C
8	Ascaphus frog	(amphibian)	51.1° F	10.6° C
9	Tuatara	(reptile)	50.0° F	10.0° C
10	Icefish	(fish)	31.2° F	–0.4° C

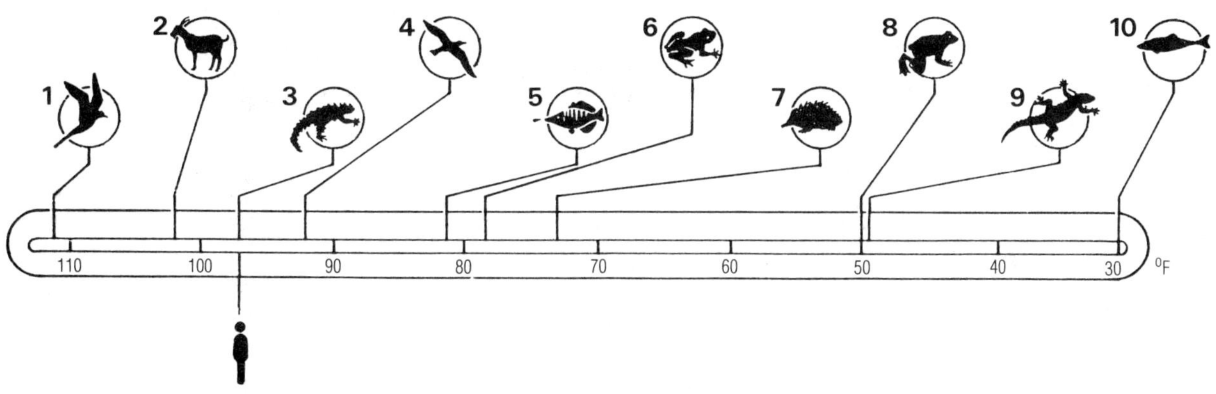

Temperature ranges

Some animals can survive much greater variations in body temperature than others. Bars on the top of this diagram show variations in body temperature that can be survived by four cold-blooded animals.

1 Crocodile 73.4°F to 84.2°F (23–29° C)
2 Garter snake 39.6°F to 102°F (4.2–38.8° C)
3 Ascaphus frog 39.9°F to 60.3°F (4.4–15.7° C)
4 Catfish 42.8°F to 93.2°F (6–34° C)

Hibernating

Bars on the bottom of this diagram show the lowering of body temperature in four mammals that hibernate in cold weather. Letting body temperature fall saves energy and so prevents starvation when plant foods are scarce in winter.

5 Marmot 107°F to 50°F (41.6–10° C)
6 Common hamster 110°F to 43°F (43.3–6.1°C)
7 Opossum 95°F to 50.5°F (35–10.3° C)
8 Dormouse 98.6°F to 35.6°F (37–2° C)

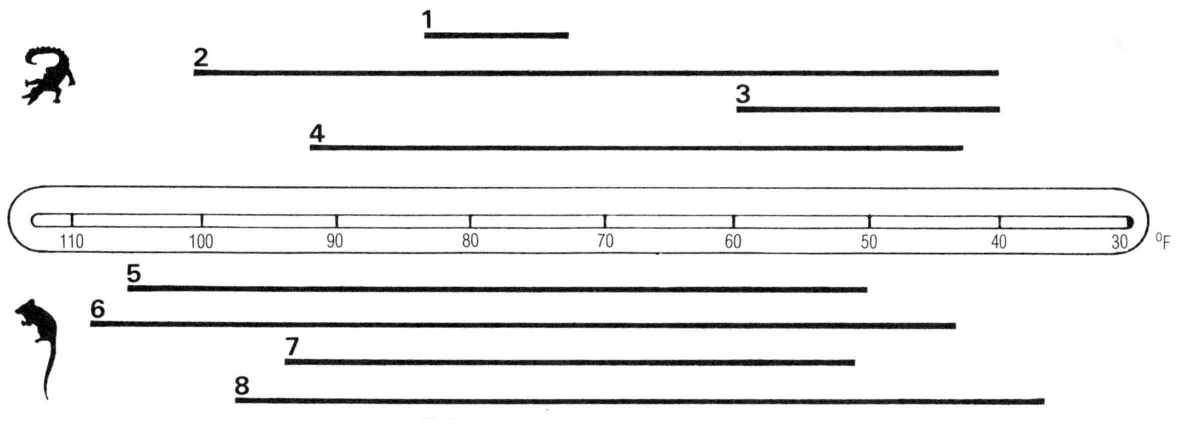

165 PETS

Dogs

1651 Selective breeding from wild wolf or wolflike ancestors produced today's many breeds of dog. Kennel clubs group breeds by the purposes they originally served. The eight groups named here also take account of differences in anatomy. Most measurements give shoulder height.

Greyhounds (1–8)
Lean, long-legged, keen-eyed breeds evolved for hunting and racing.
Borzoi/Russian wolfhound (1) 29 in (74 cm). Coat: long and silky. Various colors.
Greyhound (2) 28–30 in (71–76 cm). Tall, lean, and deep-chested. Coat: short and smooth. Various colors.
Afghan (3) 27–29 in (69–74 cm). Coat: long and thick. Color: often fawn, silver, gray, or tan. A strong, elegant breed.
Italian greyhound (4) 10 in (25 cm). A tiny high-stepping dog. Coat: short and thin. Color: black, blue, fawn, or white.
Whippet (5) 18 in (45 cm). A racing breed. Coat: short and fine. Any color.
Saluki (6) 23–28 in (58–71 cm). Elegant. Coat: smooth and silky. Various colors.
Irish wolfhound (7) 31 in (79 cm) or more. The tallest dog. Coat: rough. Color: gray, brindle, black, fawn, white, or red.
Scottish deerhound (8) 30 in (76 cm) or more. Coat: thick and rough. Color: brindle, blue-gray, reddish, or wheaten.

Mastiffs (9–15)
Heavily built, large-headed guard and rescue dogs, originally bred for use in war.
St. Bernard (9) 25 1/2–29 in (64–74 cm). A big, heavy dog. Coat: rough or smooth. Variety of colors with white patches.
Bulldog (10) 15 in (38 cm). Broad, low and strong with a "squashed" face. Coat: smooth and short. Any colors but black and yellow.
French bulldog (11) 12 in (30 cm). Bat ears. Coat: short. Color: brindle, fawn, or pied.
Boxer (12) 21–24 in (53–61 cm). Powerful. Ears cropped. Coat: short and smooth. Color: fawn, or brindle.
Newfoundland (13) 28 in (71 cm). A fine water dog. Coat: flat and of medium length. Color: usually black.
Bull mastiff (14) 30 in (76 cm). Coat: short and thick. Color: brindle or fawn, with a dark face.
Mastiff (15) 30 in (76 cm). Heavy and strong but gentle. Coat: short. Color: fawn.

Spitz (16–22)
Bred for hauling, herding, and hunting. Most breeds have a rough, thick coat and a curly tail.
Husky (16) 23–28 in (58–71 cm). Coat: dense undercoat below long outer coat. Any color.
Chow chow (17) 18 in (46 cm). Coat: thick with ruff. Any color. Tongue and gums blue-black.
Schipperke (18) 13 in (33 cm). Coat: smooth but rough. Color: usually black. Lively.
Elkhound (19) 20 1/2 in (52 cm). Hunting breed. Coat: long on neck. Color: gray
Pomeranian (20) 7 in (18 cm). A lapdog. Coat: projects from neck and shoulders. Various colors.
Welsh corgi (Pembroke) (21) 10–12 in (25–30 cm). Dense coat. Various colors, some with white. Short tail.
Samoyed (22) 22 in (56 cm). Outer coat long, with ruff. Color: cream or white.

Sheepdogs (23–29)
Physically varied dogs with sheepherding ability.
Old English sheepdog (23) 22in (56 cm). Coat: shaggy, obscuring eyes. Color: blue or gray with white.
Rough collie (24) 20–24 in (51–61 cm). Long, narrow head. Long tail. Dense coat. Several colors.
Shetland sheepdog (25) 14 in (36 cm). Like a rough collie but smaller.
German shepherd dog/Alsatian (26) 24–26 in (61–66 cm). Wolflike. Color variable.
Border collie (27) 18 in (46 cm). Long weatherproof coat, often black and white. Lively. A superb working dog.
Bearded collie (28) 18–24 in (46–61 cm). Somewhat like an Old English sheepdog.
Pyrenean mountain dog (29) 27–32 in (69–81 cm). Big and dignified. Color: mainly white.

Spaniels (30-44)
A large, varied group including toy breeds. Mos

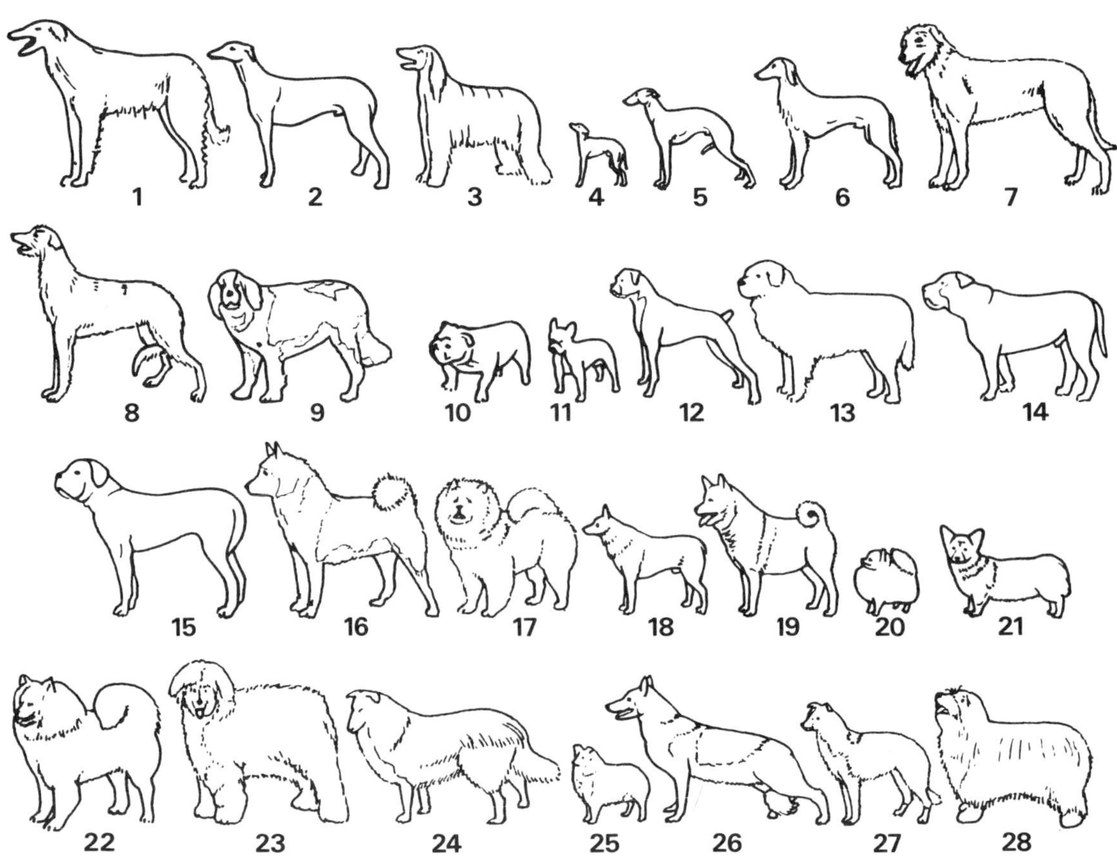

continue

Dogs continued

spaniels were once bred to hunt or retrieve.
Cocker spaniel (30) 16 in (41 cm). Floppy ears. Silky coat in various colors.
American cocker spaniel (31) 15 in (38 cm). Coat: more profuse than the cocker's. Color: black, black and tan, roan, tricolor.
English springer spaniel (32) 20 in (51 cm). Coat: silky. Various colors. Active dog.
Cavalier King Charles spaniel (33) 14 in (36 cm). Distinctive head. Coat: silky. Color: black and tan or tricolor.
King Charles spaniel (34) 11–12 in (28–30 cm). An active toy spaniel. Coat: silky. Color: black and tan, tricolor.
Pekingese (35) 6–9 in (15–23 cm). Toy breed with short head and plumed tail. Coat: long and silky. Any color.
Maltese (36) 10 in (25 cm). Coat: silky and long – almost reaches the ground. Color: white.
Labrador (37) 22 in (56 cm). Good guide dog. Color: usuallly black or yellow.
Golden retriever (38) 23 in (58 cm). Strong and trustworthy. Color: gold or cream.
Pointer (39) 24 in (62 cm). Coat: short and smooth. Color: white with markings. "Points" with its nose and tail at shot game.
Irish setter (40) 23–26 in (58–66 cm). Elegant. Coat: flat and silky. Color: chestnut.
English setter (41) $25^1/2$–27 in (58–66 cm). Coat: silky. Color: white with markings.
Chihuahua (42) 5 in (13 cm). World's tiniest dog. Coat: smooth- or long-haired.
Pug (43) 10–11 in (25–28 cm). Muzzle short and blunt. Coat: short. Color: fawn or black.
Miniature poodle (44) 11–15 in (28–38 cm). One of several breeds. Coat: profuse (clipped). All one color; any color.

Terriers (45–54)
Mainly wirily built, inquisitive dogs originally trained to chase after foxes or badgers.
Wirehaired fox terrier (45) $15^1/2$ in (39 cm). Coat: dense and wiry. Color: white with black and tan. Also a smooth-haired variety.
Airedale (46) 23–24 in (58–61 cm). Coat: wiry. Color: black and tan.
Schnauzer (standard) (47) 18–19 in (46–48 cm). Coat: wiry. Color: white or black.
Doberman pinscher (48) 26 in (66 cm). Alert and muscular. Coat: short. Color: black, blue, or brown with rusty markings.
Boston terrier (49) 16 in (41 cm). Short-headed and compact. Coat: short and smooth. Color: brindle with white.
Bull terrier (50) 16 in (41 cm). Strong and muscular, with powerful jaws. Coat: short. Color: usually white or brindle.
Cairn terrier (51) 10 in (25 cm). Small but game. Coat: rough. Color: gray or sandy.
Skye terrier (52) 10 in (25 cm). Coat: long and silky, reaches the ground. Color: black, cream, fawn, or gray.
Scottish terrier (53) 10–11 in (25–28) cm). Sturdy with short legs and long head. Coat: wiry. Color: black, brindle or wheaten.
Yorkshire terrier (54) 7–8 in (18–20 cm). A toy breed. Coat: long and silky. Color: dark gray and tan.

Hounds (55–62)
Medium to large short-haired hunting dogs with a keen sense of smell; largely kept in packs.
Welsh corgi (Cardigan) (55) 12 in (30 cm). Tail long. Coat: dense. Various colors.
Beagle (56) 13–15 in (33–38 cm). Short-legged. Coat: short and smooth. Various colors.
Smooth-haired dachshund (57) 5–9 in (13–23 cm). Low-bodied. Color: black and tan. Also long- and wire-haired varieties.
English foxhound (58) 23 in (58 cm). Coat: short smooth. Color black, tan, and white.
Dalmation (59) 19–23 in (48–59 cm). Color: short white with black or liver spots.
Basset hound (60) 13–15 in (33-38 cm). Long ears, short legs, loose skin on head. Color often black, white, or tan.
Bloodhound (61) 23–27 cm (71–86 cm). Loose forehead skin. Color: black and tan, red and tan, or red.
Great Dane (62) 28–34 in (71–86 cm). Very large, with short coat. Color: black, blue, brindle, fawn, or "harlequin."

Mixed breeds
Crossbreeds have purebred parents of different breeds. Mongrels have crossbred parents.

Cats

1652

The domestication of cats dates back several thousand years in China and Egypt. Domestic cats include fewer breeds, differing less in shape and size, than dogs. The two main groups are longhairs, with strong body, short legs, broad round head and small ears, and shorthairs. Shorthairs can be subdivided into British/American, with broad heads and strong bodies, and foreign. Most foreign shorthairs are slim with a wedge-shaped head, big ears and long legs.
Persian (1) Medium to large. Broad head, short neck and flowing coat. There are at least 30 color varieties (breeds) recognized.
Ragdoll Large. Heavy and limp when carried. Coat long and silky. Various patterns and colors.
Balinese Medium size. A lithe, dainty, long-haired Siamese. Color: seal, chocolate, blue, and lilac.
Birman (2) Large. It has a strong head, low stocky body, and silky hair. Variuos colors with white feet.
Norwegian Forest Large. Long body, legs, and tail. Can be any color.
Maine coon (3) Large. Rugged with a shaggy coat. Any color or pattern.
Angora (Turkish Angora) Medium size. with a flowing coat. Color: white and auburn.
Turkish (Turkish Van) (4) Medium size. Coat: flowing. Color: white and auburn.
Cymric (longhaired Manx) A tailless, short-backed cat. Medium size. Most colors.
Somali Medium size. A lithe, long-haired Abyssinian. Color: red or ruddy.
British shorthair (5) Medium to large. Sturdy but short-legged. Coat: short and thick. Varieties include black, blue, tabby, white, and tortoiseshell.
American shorthair (6) Medium to large. Strong and lean. Various colors.
Exotic shorthair Medium to large. A "Persian" with a plush, short coat. Various colors.
Scottish Fold (7) Medium size. Forward-folded ears. Various colors.
Manx (8) A short-backed, tailless cat with a glossy coat. Medium size. Various colors.
Japanese bobtail (Mi-Ke) Medium size and slim with a bobbed tail and "oriental" eyes. Shorthaired. Various colors.
Siamese (9) Medium size. Shorthaired. Long, slim and lithe, with narrow head and almond eyes (blue). Color: mainly white with brown, slate-blue, or lilac/gray points (face, ears, legs, and tail).
Snowshoe Medium to large. A Siamese/American shorthair hybrid with a rounder head than a Siamese. Color: fawn or white with brown or gray-blue points; white feet.
Havana brown Medium size. Of Siamese/shorthair ancestry. Color: uniform mahogany.
Oriental shorthair Medium size. Slimly built like a Siamese, but with a shorthaired's pattern and color varieties.
Egyptian Mau (10) Medium size. The only naturally spotted oriental cat, from Egypt. Color: silver, honey, charcoal gray, or fawn.
Burmese (11) Medium size. A lithe, oriental-type cat. Shorthaired. Color: brown, blue, or red.
Tonkinese Medium size. A Burmese/Siamese hybrid. Various colors.
Bombay Medium size. A muscular, Burmese/shorthair hybrid. Color: black with coppery or golden eyes.
Russian Blue (Maltese) (12) Medium to large. An oriental-type cat with a dense, silky, short coat. Color: bluish with green eyes.
Korat (13) Medium size. A muscular oriental cat. Coat short and glossy. Color: silver-blue with green eyes.
Abyssinian (14) Medium size with a triangular face. Color: reddish or blue-gray.
Singapura Small. Large eyes and ears. Hairs have dark tips. Color: fawn or ivory.
Rex (15) Medium size. Slim with large ears and a curly coat. Various colors.
American wirehair Medium to large. Coat springily wiry. Various colors.
Sphynx (Canadian hairless) (16) Medium size. Fine-boned and mostly hairless. Various colors.

Cage birds

653

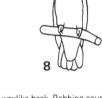

Most cage birds come from the tropics or subtropics. Those shown represent songbirds (1–4), the seed-eating hardbills (5–6), fruit- and/or insect-eating softbills (7–8), and the parrot family (8–10). Measurements are of lengths.
Canary (1) 5–8 in (13–20 cm). Yellow, orange, or greenish. A superb songbird with a number of varieties.
Java sparrow (2) 5½ in (13.5 cm). Gray with black markings and white cheeks. Large, pink, waxlike beak. Bobbing courtship dance.
Hill mynah (3) 13 in (33 cm). Black with yellow wattles. A superb mimic.
Pekin robin (4) 6 in (15 cm). Olive-green and yellow. Has musical song.
Budgerigar (5) 7 in (17.5 cm). A small parakeet. Various colors. Can be taught to speak.
Peach-faced lovebird (6) 6 in (15 cm). Largest of the lovebirds. Green, yellow, blue with pink head. Very tame.
Cockatiel (7) 13 in (33 cm). Gray and white. Orange cheeks. Yellow crest.
Lesser sulfur-crested cockatoo (8) 14 in (36 cm). White. Yellow crest and cheeks. Has a loud shriek.
African gray parrot (9) 14 in (36 cm). Silvery gray with red tail. The best speaking bird.
Blue and yellow macaw (10) 37 in (95 cm). Large. Blue with yellow breast.

Fish

654

Fish kept as pets are divided into three main categories: coldwater, freshwater tropical, and marine tropical; examples of each are shown.
Goldfish (1) Up to 1 ft (30.5 cm). Gold with color varieties. Also fancy forms with unusual shaped head, body, scales, or fins. Coldwater.
Koi carp (2) 1 ft (30.5 cm) or more. White, orange, black. Coldwater.
Swordtail (3) 5 in (13 cm). Males have swordlike tail. Green, red, albino. Freshwater tropical.
Clown triggerfish (4) 20 in (50 cm). Brown or blue and white. Marine tropical.

Small mammals

655

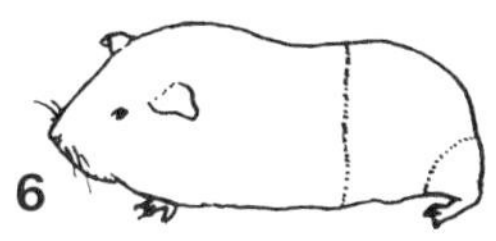

Small mammals most often kept as pets include rabbits (**1**) and five kinds of rodent (**2–6**).
Dutch rabbit (1) 4–5 lb (1.8–2.3 kg). White and colored. One of many breeds.
Domestic mouse (2) 8 in (20 cm) Various colors (up to 40 varieties).
Domestic rat (3) 16 in (41 cm). Various color varieties.
Mongolian gerbil (4) 8 in (20 cm). Gray-brown. Long hind limbs.
Golden hamster (5) 4½ in (11 cm). Stout body. Stumpy tail. Various colors.
Guinea pig/cavy (6) 11 in (28 cm). Stocky body. Short legs. Petal-shaped ears. Lacks visible tail. Color and fancy-coat varieties.

Horses

1656

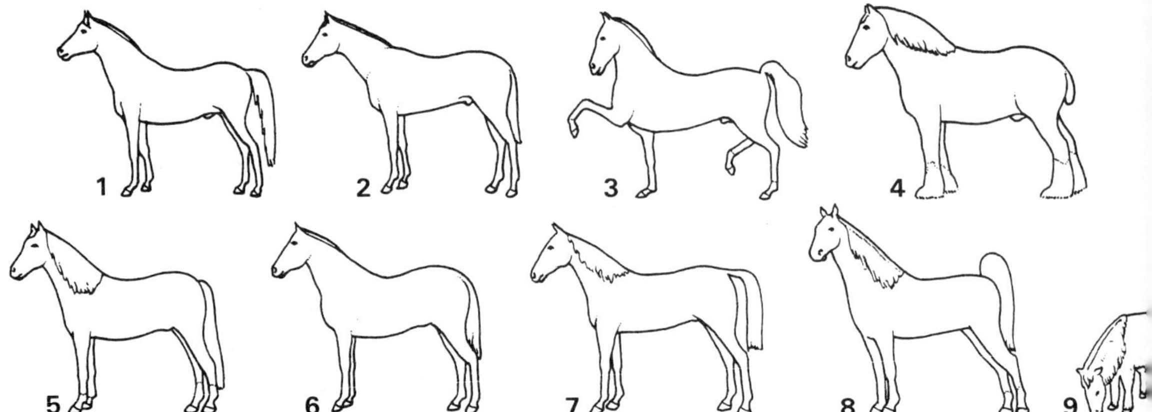

Here, nine modern breeds are shown that differ in height and weight or the tasks that they best perform. Heights are given in hands (hh), measured to the withers (the ridge between the shoulder bones); one hand is 4 in (10 cm). Ponies are horses not exceeding 14.2 hands.
Arab (1) 14.2–15 hh. Small head, arched neck, deep chest, strong legs. Arab blood influences many other breeds.
Thoroughbred (2) 14.2–17 hh. Refined appearance, with sloping shoulders and long lean legs. Champion of the racetrack.
Hackney (3) 14.3–15.3 hh. A harness horse with compact body and strong shoulders.
Shire (4) 16.2–17.3 hh. The largest British draft horse, combining size, weight, strength, and stamina.
Morgan (5) 14–15 hh. Compact, muscular, and elegant. A general-purpose breed.
American quarter horse (6) Approximately 15 hh. Broad chest and strong hindquarters. A fast starter and good sprinter.
Standardbred (7) Approximately 15.2 hh. A more robust version of the thoroughbred. Developed for harness racing.
American saddle horse (8) 15–16 hh. Light and elegant, with head and tail held high. Several show gaits.
Shetland (9) Average 10 hh. A very small pony, with profuse mane and tail.

166 EVOLUTION

Events in evolution

1661 **Key events in evolution**
Key events in the history of evolution appear (**1**) as if on a 12-hour clock.
First appearances
The first animals and plants to evolve are also shown (**2**).

Key events	on the clock	in years
A Earth formed	12 hr ago	4.6 billion years ago
B First life	9 hr 8 min ago	3.5 billion years ago
C First plant	2 hr 36 min ago	By 1.0 billion years ago
D First animal	2 hr 36 min ago	By 1.0 billion years ago
E Many fossils formed	1 hr 32 min ago	590 million years ago

First appearances	time ago	million years ago
a Crustacean	1 hr 42 min	650
b Fish	1 hr 20 min	510
c Land plant	1 hr 6 min	420
d Insect	1 hr 0 min	380
e Seed plant	57 min	360
f Amphibian	57 min	360
g Reptile	53 min	340
h Mammal	33 min	213
i Bird	24 min	150
j Flowering plant	22 min	140
k Human (genus *Homo*)	18.6 sec	2

Mass extinctions

1662 The diagram traces the rise and fall of species among 12 groups of backboned animals: birds, mammals, and ten groups of reptiles including dinosaurs. Experts disagree about why whole groups died out more or less together at the ends of some geological periods.

A Paleozoic era
B Mesozoic era
C Cenozoic era

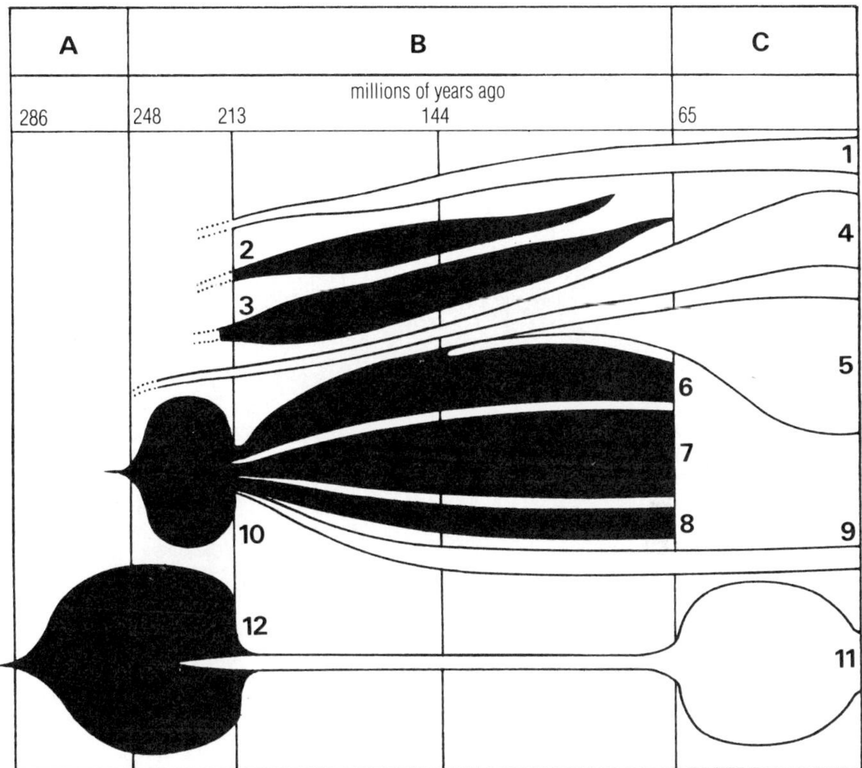

1 Turtles
2 Ichthyosaurs
3 Plesiosaurs
4 Lizards and snakes
5 Birds
6 Sauropod dinosaurs
7 Ornithischian dinosaurs
8 Pterosaurs
9 Crocodilians
10 Thecodonts
11 Mammals
12 Mammal-like reptiles

Species now extinct

Evolving vertebrates

1663 The diagram traces the rise of eight major groups of backboned animals.
A Paleozoic era
B Mesozoic era
C Cenozoic era

1 Jawless vertebrates
2 Placoderms
3 Cartilaginous fishes
4 Bony fishes
5 Amphibians
6 Reptiles
7 Birds
8 Mammals

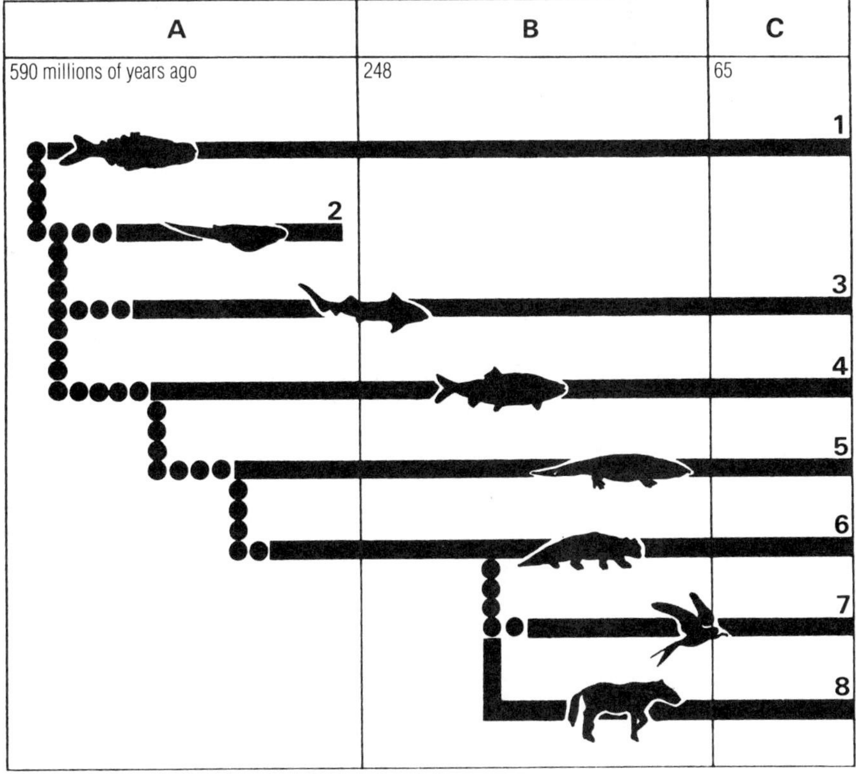

Dinosaurs classified

1664 Traditionally dinosaurs form two orders: Saurischia ("lizard-hipped") and Ornithischia ("bird hipped"). Many experts believe both orders evolved from much earlier dinosaurs, herrerasaurs. Over time ornithiscians outnumbered saurischians and, eventually new species, genera, and families evolved in both groups. These new dinosaurs were better adapted for survival: they were more suited to getting food and escaping enemies.

Ornithischian dinosaurs are identified by a backward-pointing pubis in their pelvis. They were plant eaters with leaf-shaped tooth crownse. Some had no front teeth, but powerful cheek teeth. All had powerful tendons stiffening the spine.

Saurischian dinosaurs included two-legged, flesh-eating theropods; four-legged, plant-eating sauropodomorphs; and segnosaurs. All are identified by a forward-pointing pubis in the hip bone.

1 Saurischia
2 Herrerasauria
3 Ornithischia

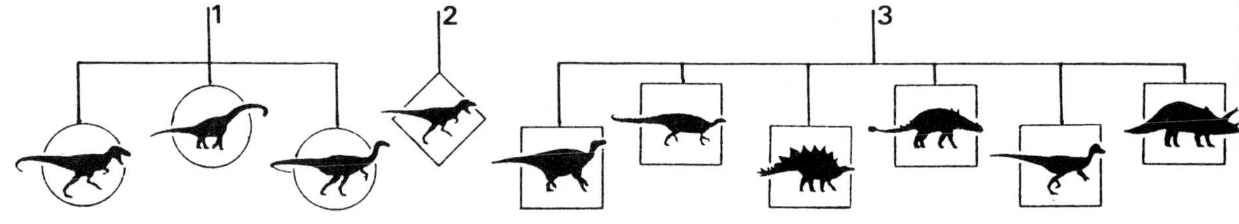

SAURISCHIA

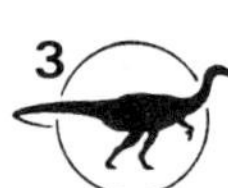

1 Theropods ("beast feet") Bipedal predatory dinosaurs with birdlike bodies and a long bony tail core. Most had sharp teeth (though some had a horny beak instead of teeth). All had scales (except *archaeopteryx,* which had feathers) and arms with clawed fingers. Some were chicken-sized and chased small game, others were larger and weighed the same as an elephant.
2 Sauropodomorphs ("lizard feet"). These animals were characterized by having small heads, long necks, and heavy, bulky bodies. They had long tails and thick, pillarlike limbs. Their teeth were used to crop leaves, which may have been ground up by gizzard stones, then broken down chemically by bacteria in the gut. Like today's gerenuk antelopes and giraffes, sauropodomorphs may have reared on hind legs to browse on tall trees.
3 Segnosaurs ("slow lizards") Dinosaurs with a theropod-type upper hip girdle and ornithiscian-like cheeks, a beak, and a backward-pointing pubic bone.

HERRERASAURIA

Herrerasaurs were early dinosaurs identified by two spinal bones above the hips. They included two families: staurikosauridae and herrerasauridae. They were small to medium in size, predatory, and are thought to have given rise to all other dinosaurs.

ORNITHISCHIA

4 Ornithopods ("bird-feet"). Bipedal and bipedal/quadrupedal bird-hipped, plant-eating diosaurs.
5 Scelidosaurs ("limb lizards"). Dinosaurs with bony studs running down the back. Flourished in Jurassic times.
6 Stegosaurs ("roof lizards"). Four-legged plant eaters with long hind limbs, a short, low head, and a bulky body and low tail.
7 Ankylosaurs ("fused lizards"). Four-legged armoured dinosaurs with plates and studs, and spikes on their back and flanks.
8 Pachycephalosaurs ("thick-headed lizards"). Bipedal and bipedal/quadrpedal dinosaurs that were plant eaters with rigid, thick-rooved skulls, long legs, and short arms. Many also had canine-type front teeth.
9 Ceratops ("horned faces"). Bipedal and four-legged dinosaurs with a triangular shaped skull and bony neck frill. Many had rhinoceros-type heads with bony face horns.

continued

Dinosaurs classified continued

1664 **Dinosaur classification table**

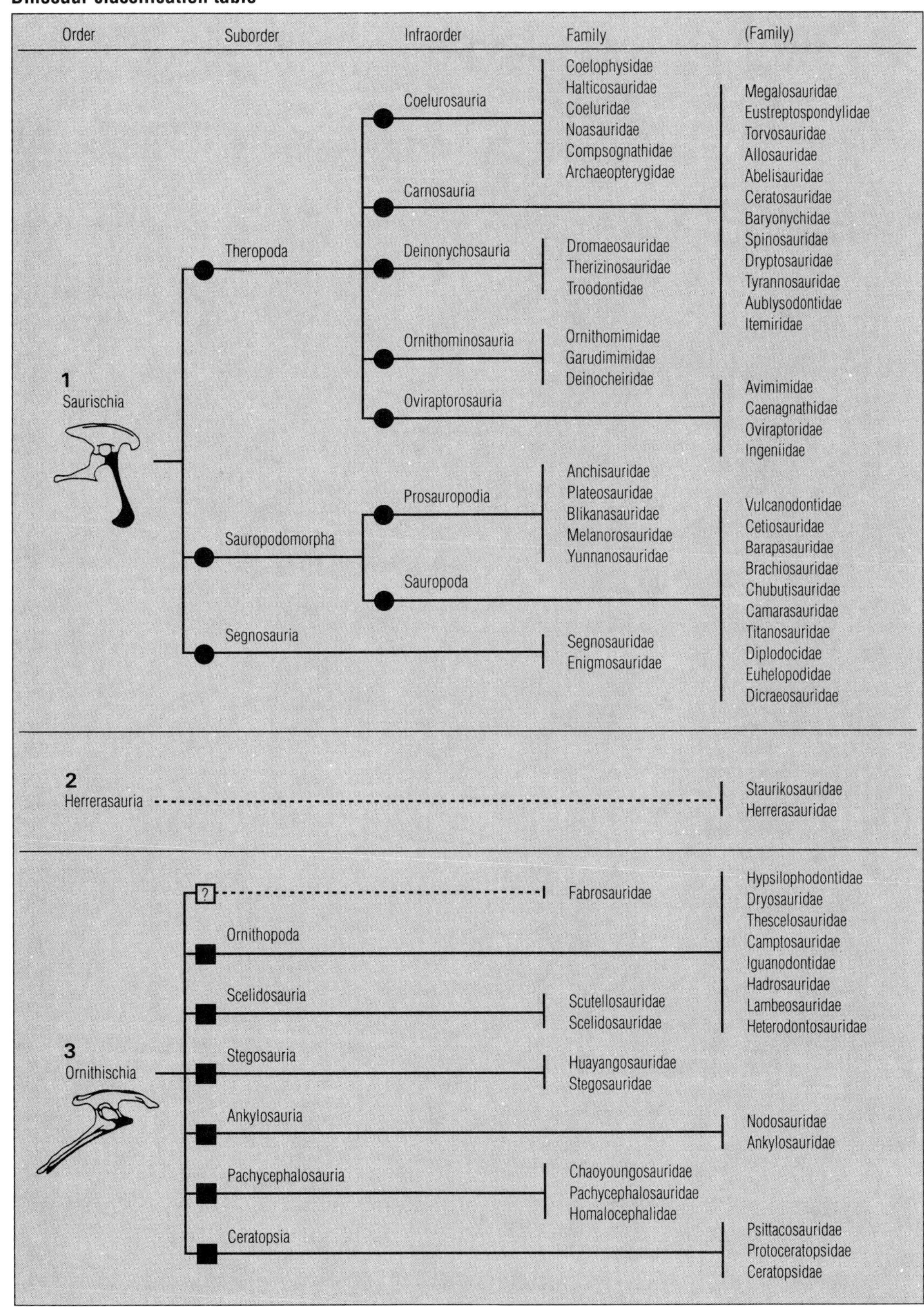
Order
Suborder
Infraorder
Family
(Family)
Coelurosauria
Coelophysidae
Halticosauridae
Coeluridae
Noasauridae
Compsognathidae
Archaeopterygidae
Megalosauridae
Eustreptospondylidae
Torvosauridae
Allosauridae
Abelisauridae
Ceratosauridae
Baryonychidae
Spinosauridae
Dryptosauridae
Tyrannosauridae
Aublysodontidae
Itemiridae
Carnosauria
Theropoda
Deinonychosauria
Dromaeosauridae
Therizinosauridae
Troodontidae
Ornithominosauria
Ornithomimidae
Garudimimidae
Deinocheiridae
1
Saurischia
Oviraptorosauria
Avimimidae
Caenagnathidae
Oviraptoridae
Ingeniidae
Prosauropodia
Anchisauridae
Plateosauridae
Blikanasauridae
Melanorosauridae
Yunnanosauridae
Sauropodomorpha
Sauropoda
Vulcanodontidae
Cetiosauridae
Barapasauridae
Brachiosauridae
Chubutisauridae
Camarasauridae
Titanosauridae
Diplodocidae
Euhelopodidae
Dicraeosauridae
Segnosauria
Segnosauridae
Enigmosauridae
2
Herrerasauria
Staurikosauridae
Herrerasauridae
?
Fabrosauridae
Ornithopoda
Hypsilophodontidae
Dryosauridae
Thescelosauridae
Camptosauridae
Iguanodontidae
Hadrosauridae
Lambeosauridae
Heterodontosauridae
Scelidosauria
Scutellosauridae
Scelidosauridae
3
Ornithischia
Stegosauria
Huayangosauridae
Stegosauridae
Ankylosauria
Nodosauridae
Ankylosauridae
Pachycephalosauria
Chaoyoungosauridae
Pachycephalosauridae
Homalocephalidae
Ceratopsia
Psittacosauridae
Protoceratopsidae
Ceratopsidae

167 ECOLOGY AND THE LIMITS OF TIME

Food paths

1671

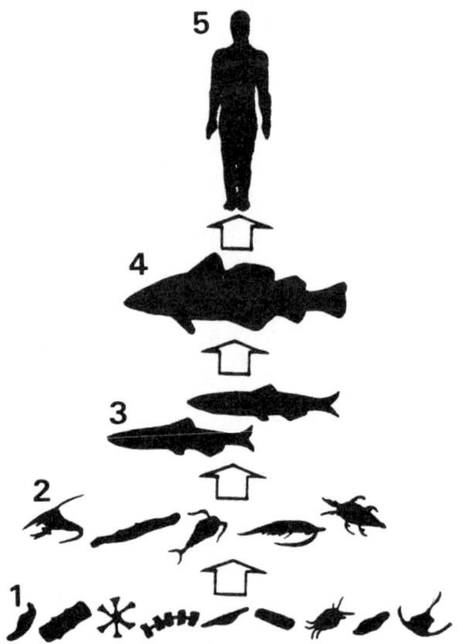

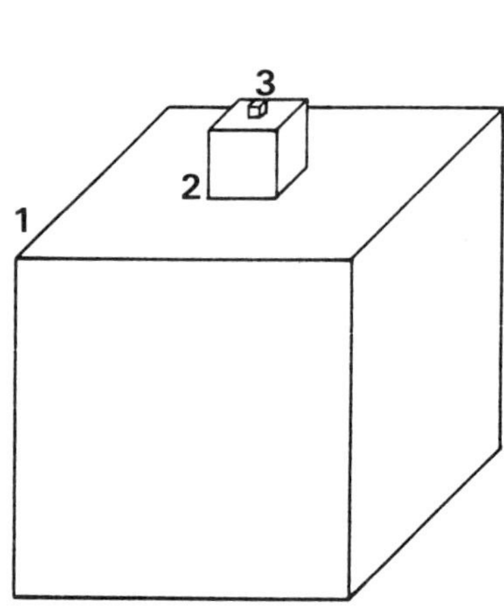

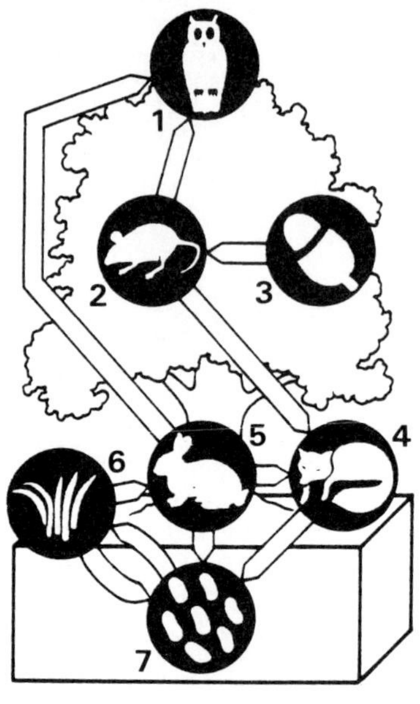

Food chain
A food chain consists of consumers and consumed. Food chains are an important aspect of ecology, the study of plant and animal relationships. In this food chain, arrows show the flow of food energy along a food chain consisting mainly of marine plants and animals.
1 Algae (food producers).
2 Animal plankton (primary consumers).
3 Herring (secondary consumers).
4 Cod (tertiary consumers).
5 Humans (quaternary consumers).

Food pyramid
A food pyramid consists of a broad base of food-producing plants supporting successively higher stages of consumers. Each stage provides food for a smaller weight of animals that form the stage above. The pyramid's apex consists of the top predator. The example given is of a food pyramid in 1 sq mi of East African grassland. (This does not take into account small mammals.)
1 3 million lb of plants.
2 25,000 lb of large mammalian consumers (e.g. wildebeests, antelope).
3 85 lb of secondary mammalian consumers (e.g. lions, hyena, wild dogs).

Food web
A food web consists of interlinking food chains in a natural habitat, as in a lake, marsh, or, here, a wood. Arrows show the flow of food energy.
1 Owl
2 Mouse
3 Acorns
4 Fox
5 Rabbit
6 Grass
7 Bacteria: decomposing dead organic matter which is then reused by plants.

Terrestrial biomes

1672 Biomes are major regional communities of plants and animals. (A community is an interacting group of living things that share the same environment.) The diagrams show the world distribution of six biomes.

1 Tropical forest
2 Desert
3 Grassland
4 Deciduous forest
5 Coniferous forest
6 Mountain and tundra

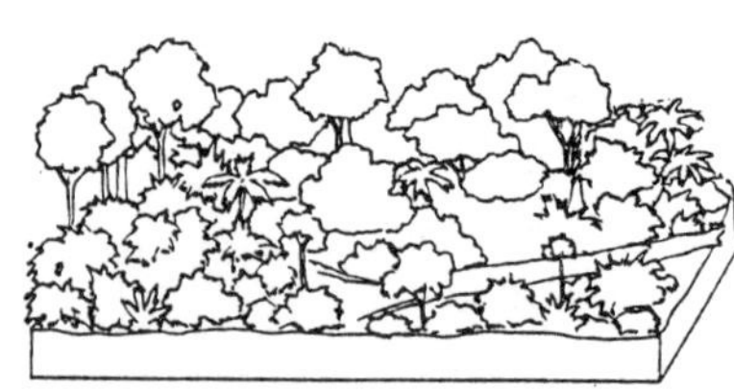

continued

Terrestrial biomes continued

1672

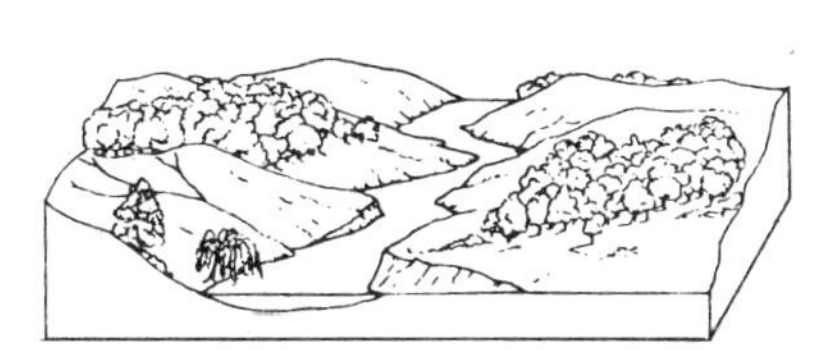

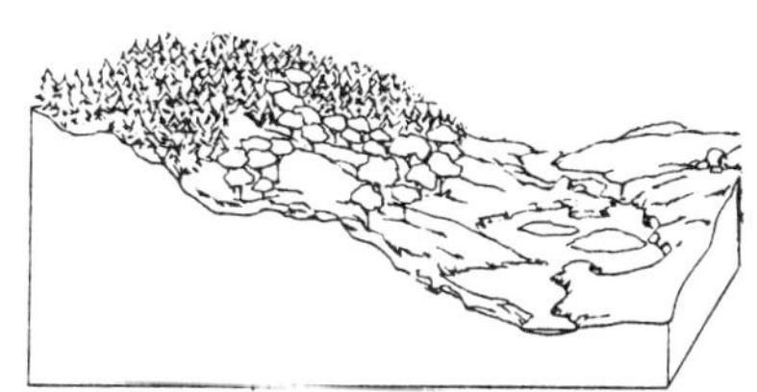

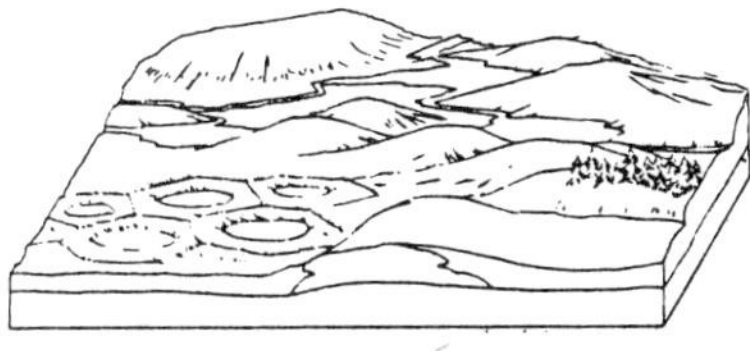

Zoogeographical regions

1673

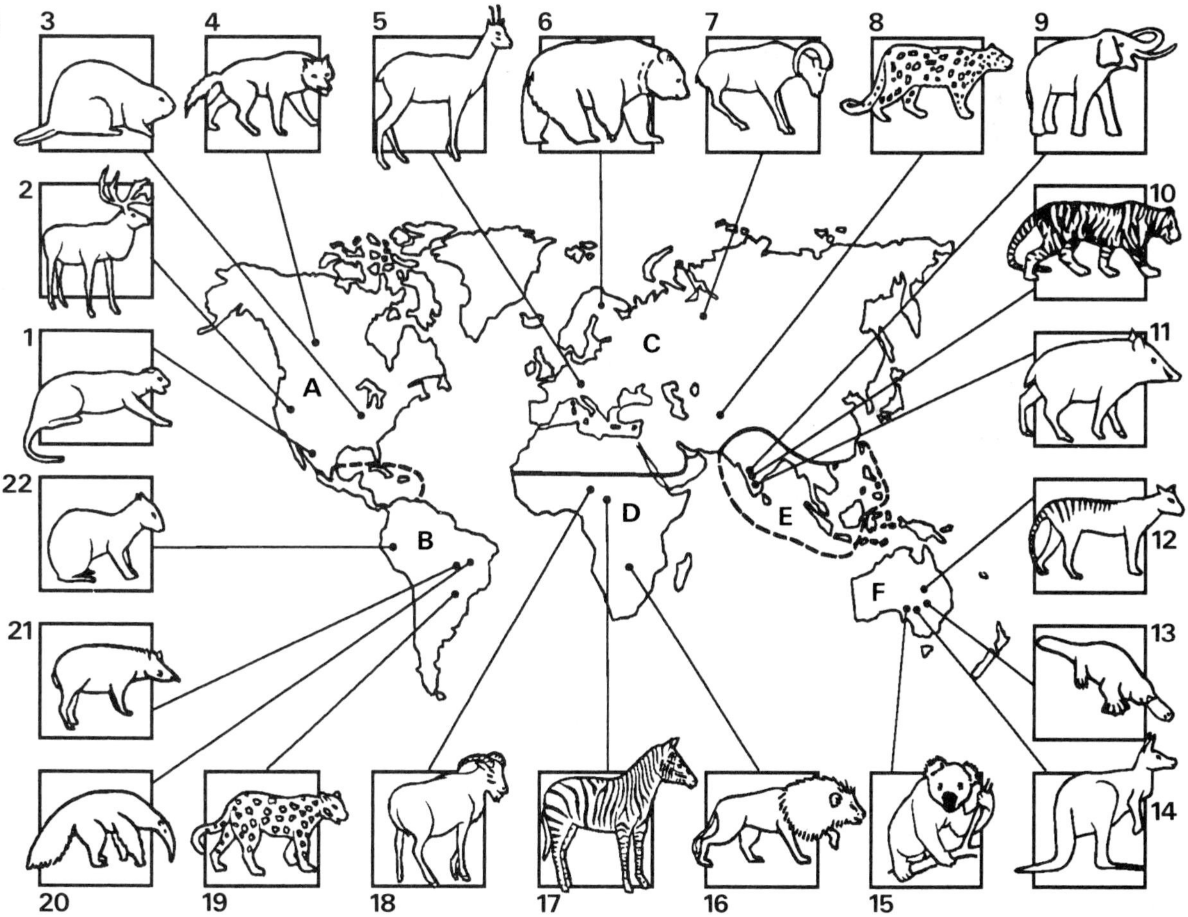

Zoogeography is the branch of biogeography that investigates why animals live in different regions. Zoogeographers divide the Earth into the following regions:

A Nearctic (arctic and temperate parts of North America and Greenland)

B Neotropical (South America, the West Indies, Central America, and tropical Mexico)

C Palearctic (Europe, parts of N. Africa, most of Asia)

D Ethiopian (Afro-tropical; Madagascar, most of Africa)

E Oriental (S.E. Asia south of the Himalayas, the Philippines, Java, Borneo and associated islands)

F Australasian (Australia, New Zealand, New Guinea)

Characteristic animals

1 Cougar
2 Caribou
3 Beaver
4 Wolf
5 Chamois
6 Brown bear
7 Argali
8 Snow leopard
9 Elephant
10 Tiger
11 Indian boar
12 Tasmanian wolf
13 Platypus
14 Kangaroo
15 Koala
16 Lion
17 Zebra
18 Aoudad
19 Jaguar
20 Anteater
21 Tapir
22 Agouti

Typical life spans

1674

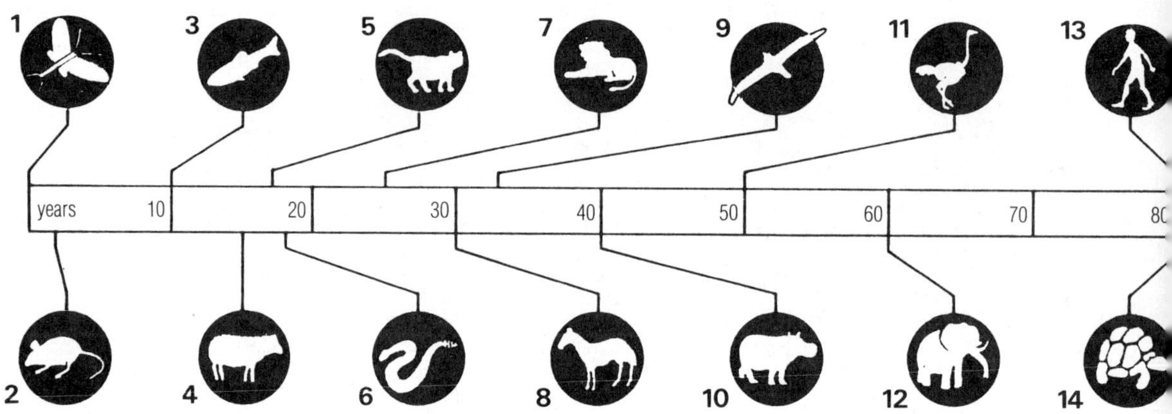

This diagram shows the life spans of 14 kinds of animal. Humans and tortoises may be the only well-known animals whose life spans often exceed 60 years. (Some bacteria and plants far outlive all animals. There are 11,000-year-old bacteria, and the oldest known plant is a bristlecone pine which is 4,600 years old.)

1 Mayfly (adult stage): 1 day
2 Mouse: 2–3 years
3 Trout: 5–10 years
4 Sheep: 10–15 years
5 Cat: 13–17 years
6 Rattlesnake: 18 years
7 Lion: 25 years
8 Horse: 30 years
9 Albatross: 33 years
10 Hippopotamus: 40 years
11 Ostrich: 50 years
12 African elephant: 60 years
13 Human: 70–80 years (oldest 120 years)
14 Tortoise: 80+ years (oldest 152+ years)

Altitude

1675 **Highest**

Shown in feet and meters are the highest altitudes at which the following living things have been observed: 0 is sea level. The bird was flying. The others were on mountainsides.

1 Bird: Ruppell's vulture 37,220 ft (11,280 m).
2 Amphibian: toad 26,240 ft (8,000 m).
3 Arthropod: spider 22,000 ft (6,700 m).
4 Flowering plant: 20,130 ft (6,400 m).
5 Mammal: yak 20,000 ft (6,100 m).
6 Reptile: lizard 18,100 ft (5,500 m).

Lowest

These are the lowest levels at which the following living things have been observed:0 is sea level.

7 Reptile: marine iguana -33 ft (-10 m) (sea turtles may dive deeper).
8 Bird: emperor penguin -872 ft (-265 m) (Sea ducks also dive deep down).
9 Plantlike organism: blue-green algae -1,300 ft (-400 m).
10 Mammal: sperm whale -7,400 ft (-2,250 m).
11 Arthropod: shrimp -35,800 ft (-10,900 m).
12 Fish: flatfish -35,800 ft (-10,900 m).

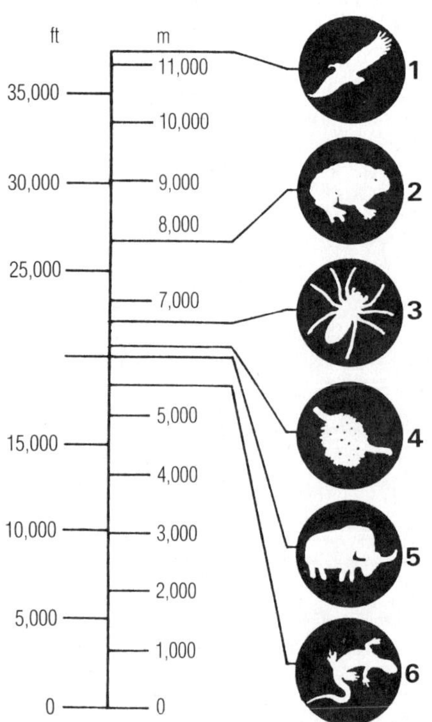

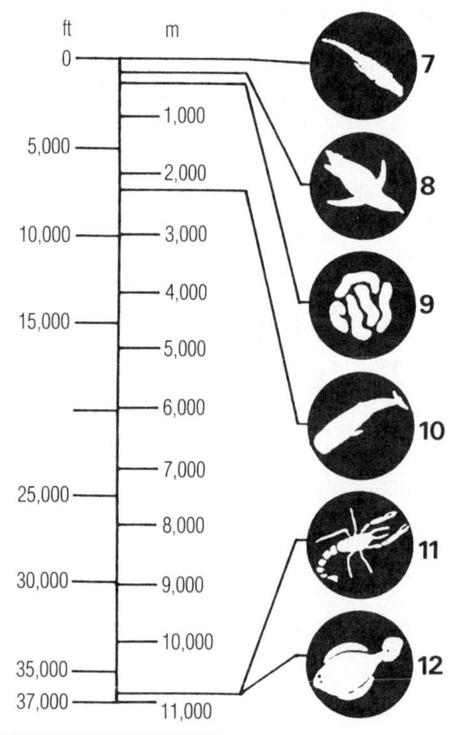

168 NATURE GLOSSARY

See also Glossary for BOTANY and BIOLOGY

absorption Uptake of substances, such as digested food and oxygen, into cells.
active transport Energy-requiring process which carries substances across cell membrane against a concentration gradient.
adaptation Inherited feature that increases organism's chances of survival.
adenosine triphosphate (ATP) Substance supplying immediate energy needs of cell.
aerobic respiration Respiration using oxygen.
algae Group of plantlike organisms, mainly microscopic but also including seaweeds.
alleles Two or more genes which control the same characteristic.
alternation of generations Life cycle (e.g. mosses, ferns) in which a haploid generation alternates with a diploid generation.
amino acids Molecular building blocks of proteins.
anaerobic respiration Respiration without oxygen.
anatomy Study of the structure of organisms.
angiosperms Flowering plants.
annual Plant with one-year life cycle.
anther Pollen-producing part of flower, found at tip of stamen.
antibody Protein released by blood cells to destroy invading foreign organisms or substances.
antigen Molecule recognized as foreign by body's immune system; causes release of antibodies.
artery Blood vessel that carries blood away from heart.
arthropods Largest animal phylum. Have exoskeletons and jointed limbs. Includes insects and crustaceans.
asexual reproduction Reproduction requiring one parent. Offspring are identical to parent.
autotroph Organism (e.g. plant) that can make its own food from simple inorganic molecules.
bacterium (pl. bacteria) Very small, single-celled, prokaryotic organism.
biennial Plant with two-year life cycle.
biochemistry Study of the chemistry of life processes.
biology Study of living things.
botany Study of plants.
bryophytes Group of plants that includes mosses and liverworts.
capillaries Microscopic blood vessels that link arteries to veins.
carbohydrates Compounds composed of carbon, hydrogen, and oxygen; some are energy-rich (e.g. glucose, starch); others are structural (e.g. cellulose).
carnivore Meat-eating organism.
carpel Female sex organ of flowering plants. Consists of stigma, style, and ovary.
cell Basic unit of all living things.
cell membrane Outer boundary of a cell.
cell wall Nonliving covering around cells of plants and some bacteria.
cellulose Carbohydrate of which plant cell walls are made.
central nervous system Brain and spinal cord of vertebrates.
centriole One of two organelles near nucleus involved in cell division.
chlorophyll Green pigment that "traps" sunlight for photosynthesis. Found in plants and some protists.
chloroplast Structure inside a cell that contains chlorophyll.
chromosome Coiled thread of DNA found in nucleus of cell.
cilium (pl. cilia) Microscopic, hairlike projection from some cells.
circadian rhythm Regular recurrence of life activities in 24-hour cycles.
class Group of organisms; subdivision of phylum, e.g. mammals.
conifers Cone-bearing trees and shrubs.
connective tissue Tissue that connects parts of the body, e.g. adipose tissue.
continuous variations Variations within a species that do not fall into distinct categories, e.g. height in humans.
convergent evolution Evolution of similar features in unrelated organisms as adaptations to similar lifestyles, e.g. wings in birds and bats.
cotyledon Seed leaf that provides food for embryo plant.
cuticle Waterproof, waxy outer covering found, for example, on leaves and insects.
cytology Study of cells.
cytoplasm Region of cell between nucleus and membrane. Contains the organelles.
deciduous tree Tree that loses leaves yearly in the autumn.
deoxyribonucleic acid (DNA) Molecule found in cell nucleus that carries genetic information.
dicotyledon Flowering plant with two cotyledons in seed.
digestion Breakdown of large food molecules to smaller ones prior to absorption.
diploid Having two sets of chromosomes in the nucleus.
discontinuous variations Variations within a species that fall into distinct categories, e.g. eye colors.
divergent evolution Evolution of dissimilar features in closely related organisms as adaptations to dissimilar lifestyles, e.g. insect mouth parts.
dominant In genetics, used to describe a trait or gene that suppresses expression of its paired trait or gene.
ecdysis Molting of the exoskeleton of arthropods.
ecology Study of the relationships between living things and their enviroment.
egestion Removal of indigestible food from body.
embryo Plant or animal at early stage of development.
embryology Study of development of embryos.
endocrine gland Ductless gland that secretes hormones.
endoplasmic reticulum System of internal membranes in cell.
endoskeleton Internal skeleton, usually made of bone and cartilage.
entomology Study of insects.
enzyme Biological catalyst.
epidermis Protective outer layer of plants and animals.
epiphyte Plants that grow on other plants without being parasites.
epithelium Type of animal tissue that covers inner and outer surfaces.
ethology Study of animal behavior.
eukaryote Organism whose cells have a nucleus and membrane-bound organelles.
evolution Change in characteristics of population of organisms over time.
excretion Removal of the waste products of cell metabolism.
exoskeleton Hard outer covering of some animals, e.g. insects, crustaceans.
fats Energy-rich compounds; made from one glycerol and three fatty acid molecules.
fauna All animals occupying a major geographical region.
fermentation Breakdown of carbohydrates by anaerobic respiration.
fertilization Union of male and female gametes to form a zygote.
flagellum Whiplike organelle of locomotion in sperm cells and some unicellular organisms.
flora All plants occupying a major geographical region.
flower Specialized reproductive shoot of flowering plants.
fruit Ripened ovary of flowering plant; contains seeds.
fungus (pl. fungi) Member of kingdom Fungi; group of nonmotile saprophytes and parasites.
gamete Sex cell, e.g. sperm, ovum.
gene Piece of DNA molecule that determines a hereditary characteristic.
genetics Study of heredity.
genotype Genetic makeup of an organism.
genus Group of closely related species.
germination Start of development of plant from seed or spore.
gestation period Time between fertilization and birth.
gland Organ that secretes one or more substances along ducts (exocrine) or into bloodstream (endocrine).
haploid Having one set of chromosomes in the nucleus.
hemoglobin Oxygen-carrying pigment found in red blood cells of vertebrate animals.
herbaceous Plant with little or no wood.
herbivore Plant-eating animal.
hermaphrodite Animal producing male and female gametes.
heterotroph Organism that obtains food by feeding on other organisms, e.g. animals, fungi.
heterozygous Possessing two different alleles of a particular gene.
hibernation Dormant state, with reduced metabolic rate, adopted by certain mammals and reptiles to survive winter.
histology Study of tissues.
homeostasis Maintenance of stable internal environment inside organism.
homozygous Possessing identical alleles of a particular gene.
hormone Chemical messenger that is produced in one part of organism and acts in another part.

continued

Nature glossary continued

168

hybrid Offspring of two parents differing in one or more inherited characteristics.
immunity Resistance to disease.
immunology Study of immune systems.
incubation Keeping eggs or embryos warm (e.g. by sitting on them) in preparation for hatching.
inflorescence Flowering shoot.
instinct Inherited behavior, not dependent on experience.
invertebrate Animal without a backbone, e.g. earthworm, locust.
kingdom In biological taxonomy, the highest level in the hierarchy, e.g. plants, animals.
life cycle Sequence of events between start of one generation and start of next.
meiosis Type of cell division that halves number of chromosomes in cell, e.g. production of sex cells.
meristem Plant tissue consisting of rapidly dividing cells.
metabolism All chemical reactions taking place inside organism.
metamorphosis Change in form of certain organisms between juvenile and adult stages, e.g. tadpole and frog.
micro-organism Very small organism, e.g. protist, bacterium.
mimicry Adoption by one species of structure or behavior of another to gain protection.
mitochondrion (pl. mitochondria) Rod-shaped organelle inside cell; site of energy release.
mitosis Type of cell division. Produces two cells identical to parent cell.
monocotyledon Flowering plant with one cotyledon in seed, e.g. grasses.
multicellular Organism composed of many cells.
mutation Inheritable change in a gene's DNA.
mycelium Mass of "threads" (hyphae) that form a fungus.
natural selection Process that favors survival and reproduction of organisms best adapted to their environment.
nitrogen fixation Conversion of nitrogen gas to nitrates by some bacteria.
nucleus Cell organelle that contains the chromosomes; directs cell activities.
omnivore Animal that eats both plants and animals.
organ Structure composed of several tissues that performs specific function, e.g. stomach, leaf.
organelle Specialized structure inside cell, e.g. chloroplast.
organism Individual living thing.
osmosis Movement of water through a selectively permeable membrane, e.g. cell membrane.
ovule Structure inside plant ovary containing female gamete; develops into seed after fertilization.
ovum (pl. ova) Female gamete or egg.
parasite Organism living on or in, and feeding on, another organism.
parthenogenesis Production of young from unfertilized eggs.
pathogen Disease-causing organism.
perennial Plant that lives for several years, e.g. oak.
peristalsis Rhythmic contractions in walls of tubular organs that push contents onward e.g. food in intestine.
phagocytosis Process of cell actively engulfing other cells or food particles.
phenotype Physical appearance of organism; result of interaction between genotype and environment.
phloem Transport tissue in plants; carries food.
photoperiodism Response of plants to changes in day length, e.g. flowering.
photosynthesis Food production by plants and algae using sunlight, carbon dioxide, and water.
phylum Major group of organisms, subdivision of kingdom, e.g. mollusks.
physiology Study of how organisms work.
plankton Microscopic aquatic organisms that float near surface of water.
plasmolysis Shrinkage of plant cell caused by water loss.
pollen Spores produced by plants; contain male gametes.
pollination In flowering plants, transfer of pollen from anther to stigma.
prokaryote Organisms whose cells have no nucleus or membrane-bound organelle, e.g. bacteria.
proteins Molecules made up of long chains of amino acids; important as enzymes and in cell structure.
protist Group of plantlike and animal-like organisms, most unicellular, belonging to kingdom Protista.
pupa A stage in metamorphosis following the larval stage.
recessive In genetics, used to describe a trait or gene that is expressed only when its paired trait or gene is identical.
reflex action Simple behavior in which stimulus evokes response without involving brain, e.g. knee jerk.
respiration Chemical reactions inside cell that break down food molecules to release energy.
ribonucleic acid (RNA) Molecule that transfers information essential for protein synthesis from DNA.
ribosomes Small particles inside cells. Site of protein synthesis.
saprophyte Organism that feeds on dead organic material, e.g. mushroom.
secretion Production and release of useful substance.
seed Embryonic plant and its food supply.
selectively permeable membrane Membrane that allows passage of some molecules but not others through it.
sexual reproduction Reproduction involving fusion of two gametes.
spawn To lay many small eggs, as do fish, for example.
species Group of similar organisms that can interbreed and produce fertile offspring.
spermatozoon (pl. spermatozoa) Male gamete of animals.
stamen Male reproductive organ of flower.
stigma Pollen-receptive tip of female reproductive organ of flower.
stimulus Any change that evokes a response from an organism.
sugar Soluble, sweet-tasting carbohydrates, e.g. sucrose, glucose.
symbiosis Living together of two organisms from different species for mutual benefit.
system Group of organs that function together to perform specific functions, e.g. digestive system.
taxis Response of protist or lower animal to directional stimulus.
taxonomy Classification of organisms.
thallus Type of plant that is not separated into stem, leaves, and roots.
tissue Group of similar cells that performs a particular function, e.g. muscle.
transpiration Evaporation of water from leaves.
tropism Directional growth movement of plant in response to stimulus.
unicellular Organism consisting of one cell.
vacuole Saclike, fluid-filled cell organelle used for storage.
vein Blood vessel that carries blood toward heart.
vertebrate Animal with a backbone, e.g. fish, reptile, mammal.
vestigial organ Organ retained during evolution but no longer useful, e.g. human appendix.
virus Almost lifelike, extremely small particle made of protein and nucleic acid; needs to parasitize a living cell to reproduce.
vitamins Group of substances essential in small amounts in diet.
viviparous Giving birth to live young.
warning coloration Bright pattern of markings indicating animal is unpleasant to eat.
xylem Transport tissue in plants; carries water and mineral salts from roots to rest of plant.
yolk Part of animal egg cell that serves as food source for embryo.
zoology Study of animals.
zygote Fertilized egg cell produced during sexual reproduction.

169 BIOGRAPHIES

Anaximander c. 611–546 BC, Greek philosopher credited with many imaginative scientific speculations, for example that living creatures first emerged from slime and that humans must have developed from some other species that more quickly matured into self-sufficiency.

Baer, Karl Ernst von 1792–1876, German naturalist who discovered mammalian egg (ovum) in ovary and notochord (embryo backbone), and who formulated "biogenetic law" that in embryonic development general characters appear before special ones.

Baltimore, David b. 1938, American biochemist who shared 1975 Nobel Prize for medicine with Temin and Dulbecco by discovering an enzyme that carries out a basic molecular process in a cell.

Brown, Robert 1773–1858, Scottish botanist renowned for investigation into impregnation of plants. He was first to note that, in general, living cells contain a nucleus, and to name it. In 1827, first observed "Brownian movement" of fine particles in liquid.

Burbank, Luther 1849–1926, American horticulturist. Pioneer in improving food plants through grafting, hybridization, etc. Developed Burbank potato and new varieties of plums and berries. Also developed new flowers, including Burbank rose and Shasta daisy.

Burnet, Sir Macfarlane 1899–1985, Australian virologist who worked on immunological tolerance to antigen with Peter Brian Medawar.

Candolle, Augustin Pyrame de 1778–1841, Swiss botanist. First to use word 'taxonomy' for his classification of plants by their morphology, rather than physiology, as set out in his *Elementary Theory of Botany* (1813). His new edition of *Flore Française* appeared in 1805.

Crick, Francis Harry Compton b.1916, English molecular biologist. With Watson, in 1953, built molecular model of complex genetic material deoxyribonucleic acid (DNA). Later work on nucleic acids led to far-reaching disoveries concerning genetic code.

Cuvier, Georges (Léopold Chrétien Frédéric Dagobert) 1769–1832, French anatomist, known as founder of comparative anatomy and paleontology. Originated natural system of animal classification. Studies of animal and fish fossils linked paleontology to comparative anatomy.

Darwin, Charles Robert 1809–82, English naturalist. Originator, with Wallace, of theory of evolution by natural selection. His works on geological and zoological discoveries of his famous voyage on *HMS Beagle* put him in front rank of scientists. *The Origin of Species* published November 1859.

Delbruck, Max 1906–81, German-born American biophysicist. At California Institute of Technology, did much to create bacterial and bacteriophage genetics, and, in 1946, showed that viruses can recombine genetic material.

De Vries, Hugo (Marie) 1848–1935, Dutch botanist and geneticist. From 1890, devoted himself to study of heredity and variation in plants, significantly developing Mendelian genetics and evolutionary theory. *Die Mutationstheorie* (*The Mutation Theory*) was published 1901–03.

Dobzhansky, Theodosius 1900–75, Russian-born American geneticist who showed that genetic variability in population is large, including many potentially lethal genes which nevertheless confer versatility when population exposed to environmental change. Work gave experimental evidence linking Darwinian theory with Mendel's laws of heredity.

Dubois, Marie Eugène François Thomas 1858–1940, Dutch paleontologist. In 1890s, in Java, found humanoid remains, named as *Pithecanthropus erectus* (Java Man), which he claimed to be missing link between apes and humans, a view eventually accepted in 1920s.

Dulbecco, Renato b.1914, Italian-born American molecular biologist who showed how certain viruses can transform some cells into a cancerous state and who gave a valuable, simple model system.

Dutrochet, René Joachim Henri 1776–1847, French physiologist. First to study and to name osmosis. Stated, in 1824, that "all tissues, all animal organs are actually only a cellular tissue variously modified."

Elton, Charles Sutherland 1900–91, English ecologist. Author of classic books on animal ecology. Work on animal communities led to recognition of ability of many animals to counter environmental disadvantages by change of habitats, and to use of concepts of "food chain" and "niche".

Enders, John Franklin 1897–1985, American bacteriologist. Researched antibodies for mumps virus. With Robbins and Weller, achieved cultivation of polio viruses in human cells, thus greatly advancing virology, and in 1962 developed effective vaccine against measles.

Fleming, Alexander 1881–1955, Scottish bacteriologist and discoverer, in 1928, of the antibiotic penicillin. Also, pioneered use of Salvarsan against syphilis, discovered anti-septic powers of lysozyme (present in tears and mucus), and was first to use antityphoid vaccines on humans.

Flemming, Walther 1843–1915, German biologist who, in 1882, gave first modern account of cytology, including process of cell division, which he named mitosis. Also did important work on splitting of chromosomes and on microscopic technique.

Frisch, Karl von 1886–1982, Austrian ethologist and zoologist. Key figure in developing ethology using field observation of animals combined with ingenious experiments. Showed that forager honey bees communicate information (on location of food sources) in part by use of coded dances.

Galvani, Luigi 1737–98, Italian physiologist who investigated role of electrical impulses in animal tissue. In famous experiment connected leg muscle of frog to corresponding nerve, and observed twitching that took place (hence "to galvanize"). Gave name to galvanometer.

Goebel, Karl von 1855–1932, German botanist. Distinguished plant morphologist who wrote *Organographie der Pflanzen* (1898-1901), and founded botanical institute and gardens in Munich.

Goldschmidt, Richard Benedikt 1878–1958, German biologist. Conducted experiments on X-chromosomes and theorized that it is not qualities of individual genes but serial pattern of chromosomes and chemical configuration of chromosome molecules that are decisive hereditary factors.

Goode, George Brown 1851–92, American ichthyologist. US fish commissioner 1887-88, and author of *American Fishes* (1888) and *Oceanic Ichthyology* (1895).

Gray, Asa 1810–88, American botanist. From 1838 to 1842, published *Flora of North America*. Also produced *Genera Florae Americae Boreali-Orientalis Illustrata* (1845–50), *A Free Examination of Darwin's Treatise* (1861), and *Manual of the Botany of the Northern United States* (1848, known as *Gray's Manual*).

Haeckel, Ernst Heinrich Philipp August 1834–1919, German naturalist, and one of first to sketch genealogical tree of animals, explaining that life history of individual is recapitulation of its historic evolution.

Hales, Stephen 1677–1761, English botanist and chemist, founder of plant physiology whose *Vegetable Staticks* (1727) was foundation of vegetable physiology. Also invented machines for ventilating, distilling sea water, preserving meat, etc.

Harrison, Ross Granville 1870–1959, American biologist who introduced hanging-drop culture method (1907) for study of living tissues.

Hershey, Alfred Day b.1908, American biologist who became expert on bacteriophage ("phage") and in early 1950s, with Chase, proved that DNA of this organism is its genetic information-carrying component. Later, with others, they showed that DNA of other organisms fulfils same key genetic role.

Hooker, Sir Joseph Dalton 1817–1911, English botanist and traveller who went on several expeditions that resulted in works on flora of New Zealand, Antarctica, and India, as well as *Himalayan Journals* and monumental *Genera Plantarum*.

Huxley, Thomas Henry 1825–95, English biologist. During *HMS Rattlesnake* expedition to south seas (1846–50), collected and studied specimens of marine animals, particularly plankton. Foremost scientific supporter of Darwin's theory of evolution by natural selection.

Jacob, François b.1920, French biologist. With Monod, demonstrated that function of some genes is to regulate action of others; also with Monod, proposed existence of messenger RNA, which regulates building of enzymes, 1961. Joint Nobel Prize winners in 1965.

Kettlewell, Henry Bernard David 1907–79, English geneticist and entomologist. Demonstrated survival value of dark coloration found on peppered moths in industrial regions and original light coloration in rural areas, thus showing effectiveness of natural selection as evolutionary process.

continued

Biographies continued

169 **Lamarck, Jean (Baptiste Pierre Antoine de Monet) Chevalier de** 1744–1829, French naturalist who made basic distinction between vertebrates and invertebrates. In famous *Philosophie Zoologique* (1809), postulated that acquired characters can be inherited by later generations.

Linnaeus, Carolus (Carl von Linné), 1707–78, Swedish naturalist and physician. Introduced binomial nomenclature of generic and specific names for animals and plants, which permitted hierarchical organization later known as systematics.

Luria, Salvador Edward 1912–91, Italian-born American biologist. Worked with Delbruck and Hershey on role of DNA in viruses infecting bacteria, making basic discoveries in mutation of bacteria and viruses in 1940s.

Malpighi, Marcello 1628–94, Italian anatomist. Discovered capillaries, thus filling in gap between venous and arterial systems. Discovered that blood flows over lungs. First to observe many physiological elements of plant and insect life.

Marsh, Othniel Charles 1831–99, American paleontologist who discovered (mainly in Rocky Mountains) over a thousand species of extinct American vertebrates.

Mayr, Ernst Walter b.1904, German-born American zoologist. Early work was on ornithology of Pacific, but in later career was best known for neo-Darwinian views on evolution, as developed in *Animal Species and Evolution* (1963) and *Evolution and the Diversity of Life* (1976).

Medawar, Sir Peter Brian 1915–87, British. One of world's leading immunologists, who pioneered experiments in prevention of rejection in transplant operations. In 1960, shared Nobel Prize with Burnet for researches on immunological tolerance in relation to skin and organ grafting.

Mendel, Gregor Johann 1822–84, Austrian biologist and botanist whose principle of factorial inheritance and quantitative investigation of single characters have become basis of modern genetics. Experiments in hybridity in plants led to Law of Segregation and Law of Independent Assortment.

Monod, Jacques Lucien 1910–76, French biochemist who worked with François Jacob on messenger RNA. In *Chance and Necessity* (1970) proposed that humans are the product of chance in the universe.

Morgan, Thomas Hunt 1866–1945, American geneticist and biologist. Carried out experiments with *Drosophila* fruit fly, from which he established a chromosome theory of heredity involving genes for specific tasks aligned on chromosomes. This major breakthrough in genetics earned him the 1933 Nobel Prize.

Newton, Alfred 1829–1907, English zoologist. In 1866, appointed first professor of zoology and comparative anatomy at Cambridge University, and wrote valuable works on ornithology, notably *A Dictionary of Birds* (1893-96).

Owen, Sir Richard 1804–92, English zoologist. pre-Darwinian, who maintained hostile attitude to detailed evolutionist theories. Essay on parthenogenesis was pioneer work.

Pasteur, Louis 1822–95, French chemist. Founder of modern bacteriology. Proposed "germ" theory of disease in late 1860s, perhaps greatest single advance in history of medicine. Also discovered "pasteurization": gentle heating to kill harmful bacteria in wine and milk.

Pavlov, Ivan Petrovich 1849–1936, Russian physiologist. Worked on physiology of circulation and digestion, but is most famous for study of "conditioned" or "acquired" reflexes, each associated with some part of brain cortex. Saw brain's functions as mere coupling of neurones to produce reflexes.

Ray, John 1627–1705, English naturalist who originated basic principles of plant classification into cryptogram, monocotyledons, and diocotyledons. Major work was *Historia Generalis Plantarum* (1686–1704), but also wrote on birds, fishes, and insects.

Redi, Francesco 1626–97, Italian physician and poet who wrote book on animal parasites and proved that maggots cannot form on meat which has been covered.

Robbins, Frederick Chapman b. 1916, American virologist who worked with Enders and Weller to develop methods of growing disease viruses.

Schleiden, Matthias Jakob 1804–81, German botanist who did much to establish cell theory. Showed that cells are the units of structure in plants and animals, and that organisms are aggregates of cells arranged according to definite laws.

Schwann, Theodor 1810–82, German physiologist who discovered enzyme pepsin, investigated muscle contraction, demonstrated role of micro-organisms in putrefaction, and extended cell theory (previously applied to plants) to animal tissues.

Spallanzani, Lazaro 1729–99, Italian biologist and naturalist. From 1767–78, did basic experiments to disprove ideas of spontaneous generation of life. Also, demonstrated true nature of digestion and functions of spermatozoa and ova and, in 1785, was first successfully to try artificial insemination.

Spemann, Hans, 1869–1941, German zoologist who worked on embryonic development, discovering "organizer function" of certain tissues.

Temin, Howard Martin b.1934, American virologist. For his work on way viruses can make normal cells malignant, shared Nobel Prize for physiology or medicine with Dulbecco and Baltimore.

Tswett (or Tsvett), Mikhail Semenovich, 1872–1919, Russian botanist who in 1906 devised percolation method of separating plant pigments, thus making first chromatographic analysis.

Wallace, Alfred Russel 1823–1913, Welsh naturalist whose memoir, sent to Darwin in 1858 from the Moluccas, formed important part of Linnaean Society meeting which first promulgated theory of evolution by means of natural selection, in hastening publication of Darwin's *The Origin of Species*, a work extended by Wallace's *Contributions to the Theory of Natural Selection* (1870).

Watson, James Dewey b.1928, American biologist who, in 1951, joined Cavendish Laboratory in Cambridge, where he worked with Crick on structure of DNA; with Wilkins, was awarded 1962 Nobel Prize for physiology or medicine. *The Double Helix* was written 1968.

Wilkins, Maurice Hugh Frederick b. 1916, New Zealand-born British biophysicist. With Crick and Watson determined molecular structure of DNA.

171 AIR

Air pollutants

1711

Main air pollutants
The main air pollutants are carbon dioxide (CO_2), chlorofluorocarbons (CFCs), methane (CH_4), nitrogen oxides (NOx), and sulfur dioxide (SO_2).

Sources of pollution
1 Power stations (CO_2, NOx and SO_2)
2 Factories (CO_2, NOx and SO_2)
3 Forest fires (CO_2, CH_4 and NOx)
4 Automobiles (CO_2 and NOx)
5 Aircraft (CO_2 and NOx)
6 Ships (CO_2 and NOx)
7 Domestic burning (CO_2, CH_4, NOx, SO_2)
8 Air conditioning systems (CFCs)
9 Farm fertilizers (NOx)
10 Refrigerators (CFCs)
11 Some aerosols (CFCs)
12 Foam blowing (CFCs)
13 Rice paddies (CH_4)
14 Garbage dumps (CH_4)

Acid rain

1712 **What is acid rain?**
1 Factories and power stations emit sulfur dioxide and nitrogen oxides.
2 These gases combine with water in the droplets to form clouds.
3 Winds blow acidic clouds far from their source of pollution.
4 Acid rain acidifies the soil and kills trees.
5 Acidified runoff flows into lakes and kills fish.
6 Acidified groundwater seeps into lakes and kills fish.

Contributions to acid rain pollution
A Nitrogen oxides %
B Sulphur dioxides %

	A	B
1 Power stations	36	77
2 Industry	9	12
3 Homes	3	5
4 Commerce	4	3
5 Refineries	2	2
6 Road traffic	42	1
7 Rail traffic	2	
8 Others	2	

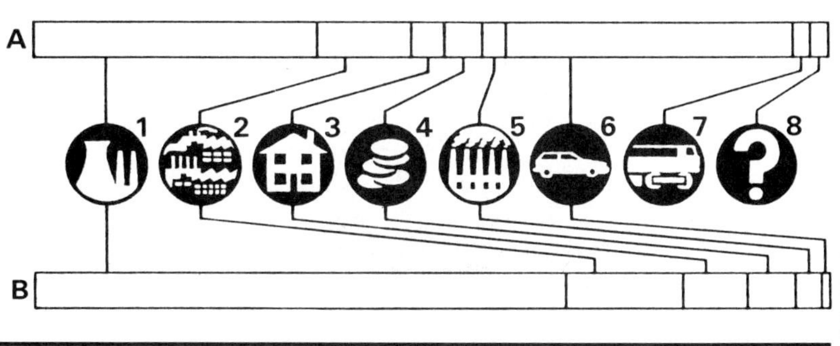

The greenhouse effect

1713**3**

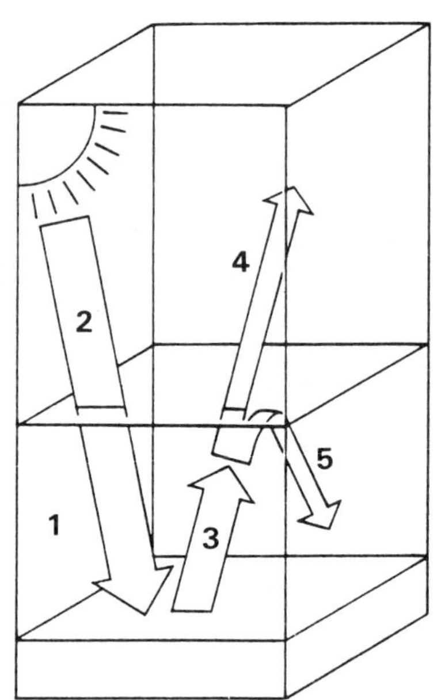

What is the greenhouse effect (left) ?
Largely man-made "greenhouse" gases (carbon dioxide, chlorofluorocarbons, methane) accumulate in air, warming the atmosphere as the diagram shows.
1 Atmosphere
2 Incoming solar radiation
3 Outgoing radiation, reflected by the Earth's surface
4 Heat escaping into space
5 Heat reradiated by gases that, like a greenhouse roof, trap outgoing solar radiation.

Likely future scenario (right)
Three maps show possible rises in temperature in different parts of the world by the mid 21st century, unless nations sharply curb greenhouse gas emissions. Rise of:
A 14.4–18° F (8 –10° C)
B 7.2–14.4° F (4–8° C)
C Less than 3.6–7.2° F (2–4° C)

A

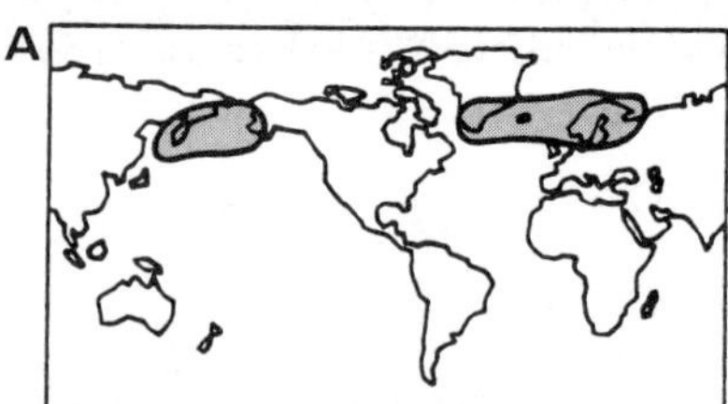

B

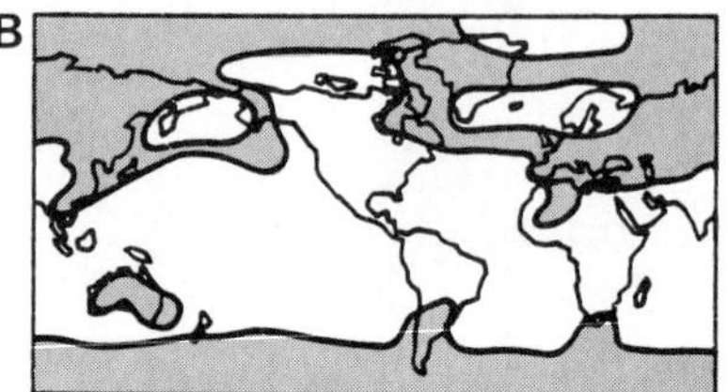

C

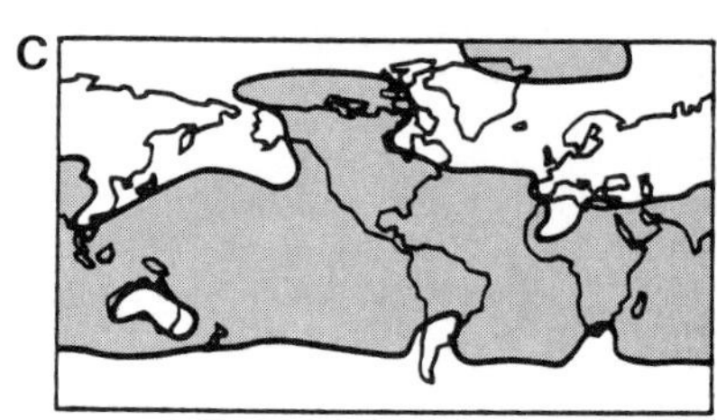

The ozone layer

1714**4**

1 Locating the ozone layer (below)
Stratospheric ozone (a form of oxygen) protects against skin cancers and cataracts by filtering out the Sun's harmful ultraviolet radiation.

	height: mi	km
a Troposphere	0–10	0–16
b Stratosphere	10–30	16–48
c Mesosphere	30–50	48–80
d Ozone layer	9.3–12.4	15–20

2 Antarctica's ozone hole (below)
Four views of Antarctica show growth in the size of the ozone hole appearing over that continent every spring. The hole is due to chlorofluorocarbons "gobbling up" stratospheric ozone. This discovery has led to international action to phase out the use of chlorofluorocarbons.

1

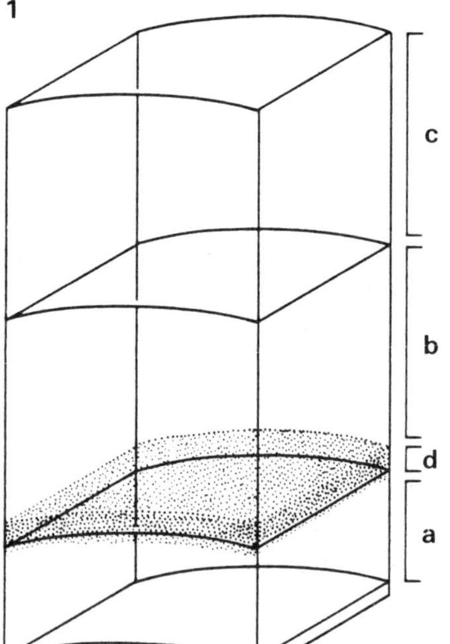

2

1982

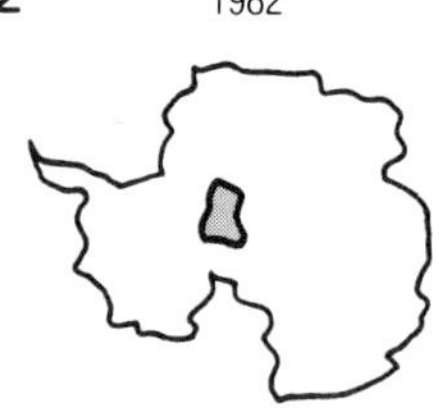

1985

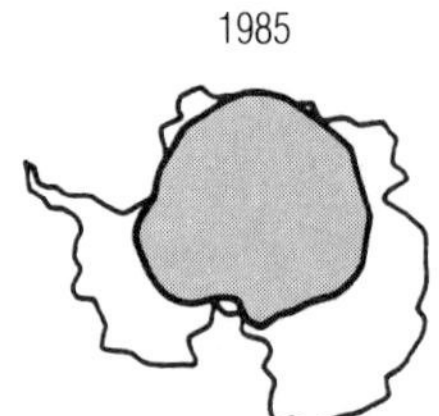

1987

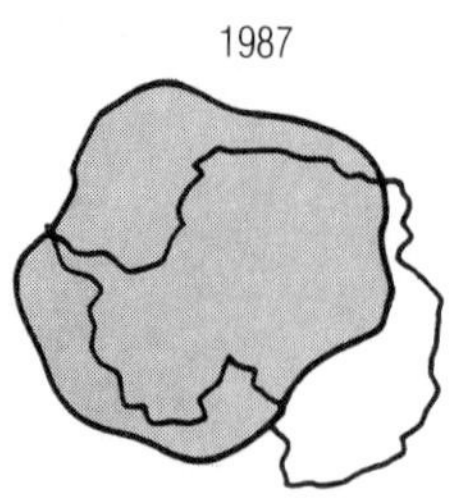

1989

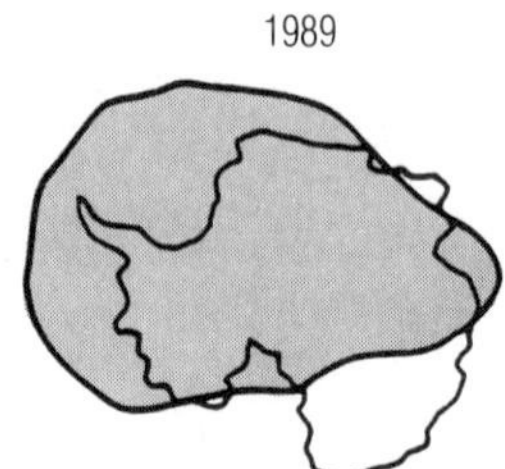

172 WATER

Water usage

1721

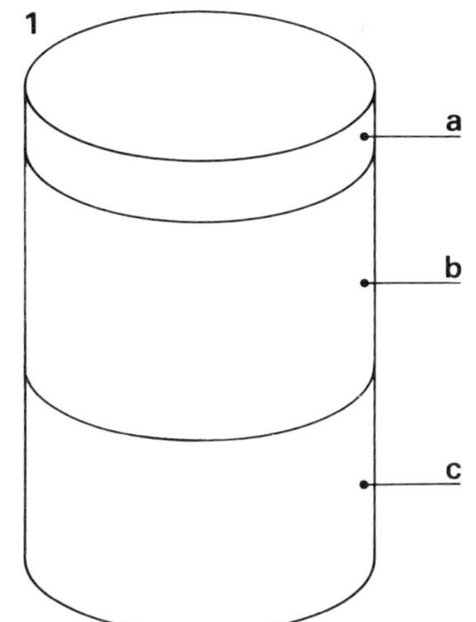

1 Total US usage
Figures show percentages of total US water usage accounted for by the nation's three categories of water consumer.
a Public 12%
b Industry 47%
c Agriculture 41%

2 Domestic usage
Figures show percentages of total US domestic water usage accounted for by six activities.
a Washing and showering 27%
b Toilet flushing 24%
c Running washing machine 17%
d Running dish washer 14%
e Cooking and drinking 10%
f Gardening, washing car, etc 8%

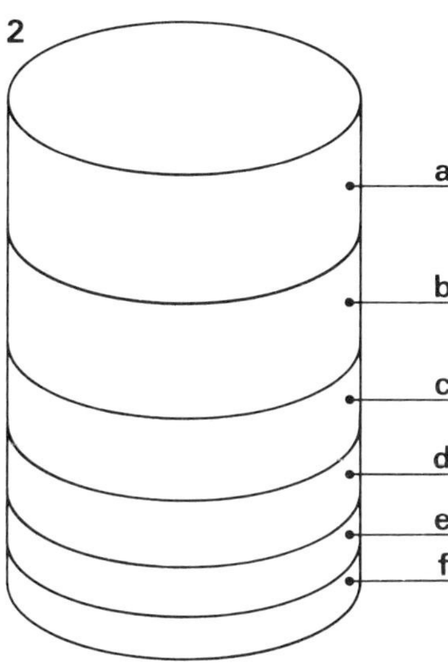

Contaminated seas and oceans

1722

Affected areas
1 Southeast Pacific Ocean
2 North American areas
3 Caribbean Sea
4 Southwest Atlantic Ocean
5 West African areas
6 North Sea
7 Baltic Sea
8 Mediterranean Sea
9 Southern African areas
10 Persian Gulf
11 Indian Ocean
12 Southeast Asian areas
13 Japanese areas
14 Australian areas
15 New Zealand areas

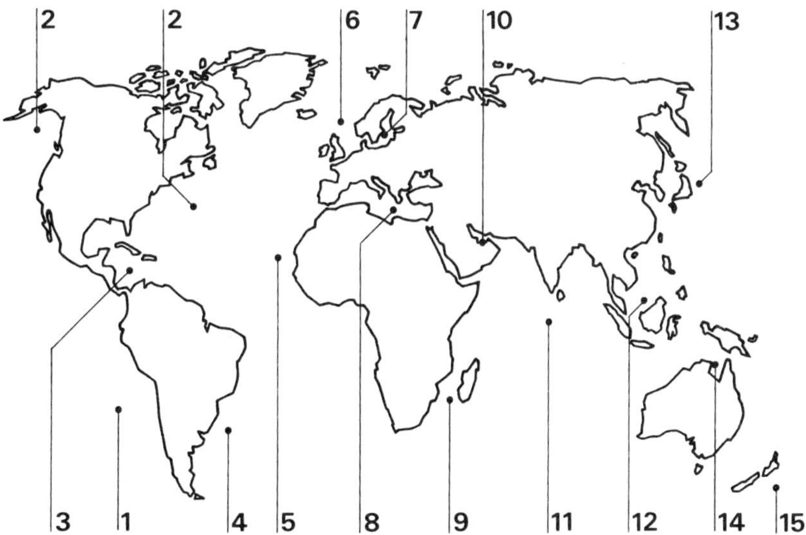

Because of their size and depth, the world's oceans have long been regarded as having an infinite capacity to absorb dumped waste. The assumption has always been that any pollutants are diluted sufficiently so as to pose no threat to human health or the environment. This is now proving to be false. Oceans are affected by pollution from rivers, outfalls, shipping, dumping, and from the air. Most affected are semi-enclosed seas like the Mediterranean and the Baltic. In all areas, however, the effects of pollution are spreading from coastal waters to open ocean.

1	2	3	4	5	6	7	8	9	10	11	12	13	14	15	**Sources of pollution**
●	●	●	●	●	●	●	●	●	●	●	●	●	●	●	Sewage
	●				●			●				●			Sewage and dredge dumping
	●	●	●		●	●	●		●	●		●	●		Thermal effluent
	●	●	●	●		●	●			●	●	●		●	Pesticide and fertilizer runoff
		●		●				●		●	●				Silting from building and agriculture
●	●				●		●				●		●		Mining
		●							●	●					Sea salt extraction
	●				●		●								Radioative waste
●	●	●	●	●	●		●	●	●	●	●	●		●	Metal industries
●	●	●			●	●	●	●	●	●	●	●	●		Chemical industries
●	●			●		●					●	●	●	●	Paper and pulp production
	●	●		●	●		●		●	●	●	●			Petrochemical industry
	●	●		●	●				●		●				Oil extraction
	●	●	●	●	●	●	●	●	●	●	●	●	●		Oil transportation
●	●	●	●	●	●	●	●	●		●	●	●	●	●	Food processing

Polluted rivers

1723**3**

North American polluted rivers

All 23 rivers numbered on this map exceed GEMS (Global Environmental Monitoring System) values for one or more pollutants. Ten rivers (numbered 6-13, 17 and 20) pour water into the Gulf of Mexico. Five rivers (1–5) flow into the Pacific Ocean. Five (18–19 and 21–23) flow into the Atlantic Ocean. Three (14–16) flow into Hudson Bay.

1 Skeena
2 Fraser
3 Columbia
4 Sacramento
5 San Joaquin
6 Rio Grande
7 Brazos
8 Red
9 Arkansas
10 Platte
11 James
12 Missouri
13 Mississippi
14 Nelson
15 Severn
16 Moose
17 Alabama
18 Savannah
19 Roanoke
20 Ohio
21 Delaware
22 Hudson
23 St John

Sources of pollution
1 Agriculture 64%
2 Resource extraction 9%
3 Forestry 6%
4 Urban runoff 5%
5 Hydro-modification 4%
6 Construction 2%
7 Disposal of land 1%
8 Other sources 9%

%

Types of US river pollution
1 Sediment 47%
2 Nutrients from fertilizer and sewage 13%
3 Pathogenic bacteria and viruses 9%
4 Acidity 6%
5 Toxic chemicals 6%
6 Pesticides 3%
7 High salinity 2%
8 Change in environment 9%
9 High biological oxygen demand 4%

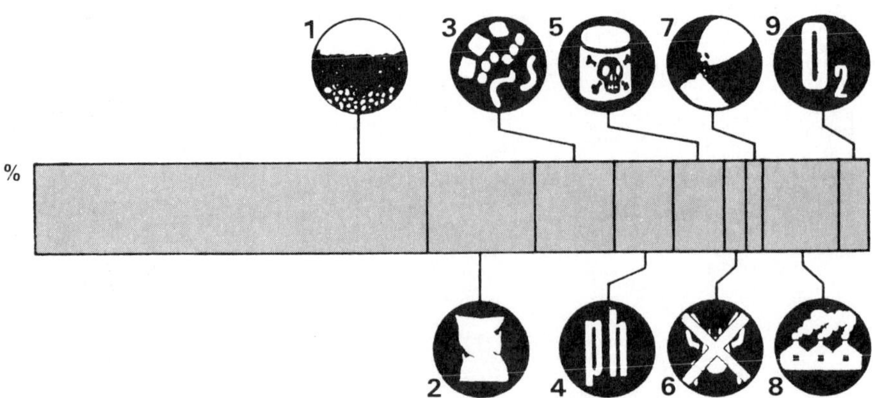

173 LAND

Deforestation

1731 Once-vast tropical rainforests are fast vanishing as people clear the land for logging, farming and ranching. Map (**A**) shows tropical forest area destroyed since 1940. Map (**B**) shows extent of tropical forests 1990. Numbered pie charts show likely percentage forest losses in 16 countries between 1990 and the year 2000.

1	Ivory Coast	100%
2	Nigeria	100%
3	Costa Rica	80%
4	Thailand	60%
5	Ecuador	50%
6	Honduras	50%
7	Nicaragua	50%
8	Brazil	33%
9	Colombia	33%
10	Guatemala	33%
11	Mexico	33%
12	Ghana	26%
13	Malaysia	24%
14	Madagascar	23%
15	Philippines	20%
16	Indonesia	10%

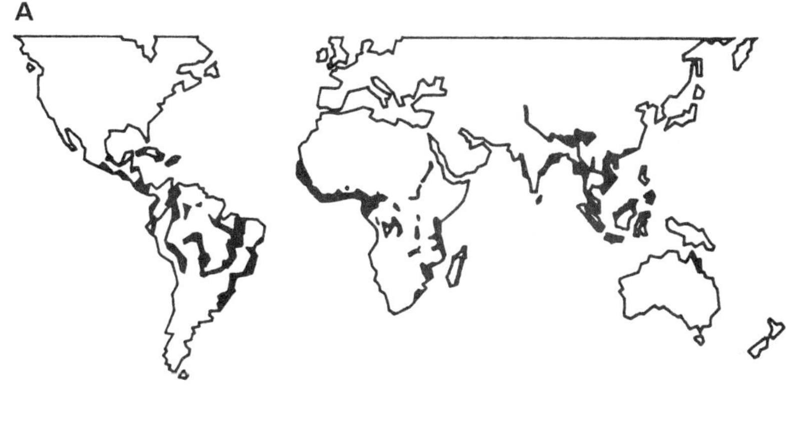

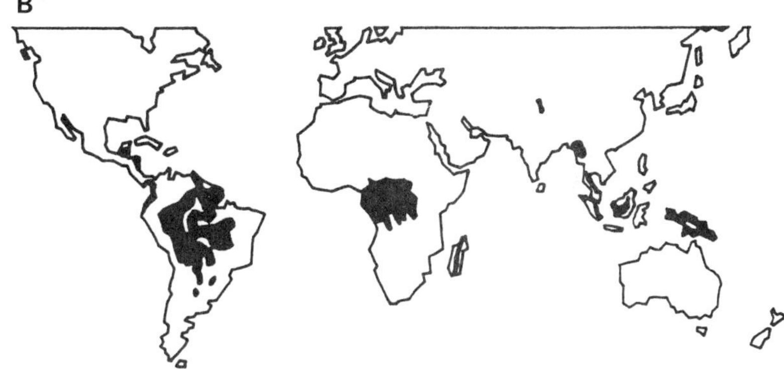

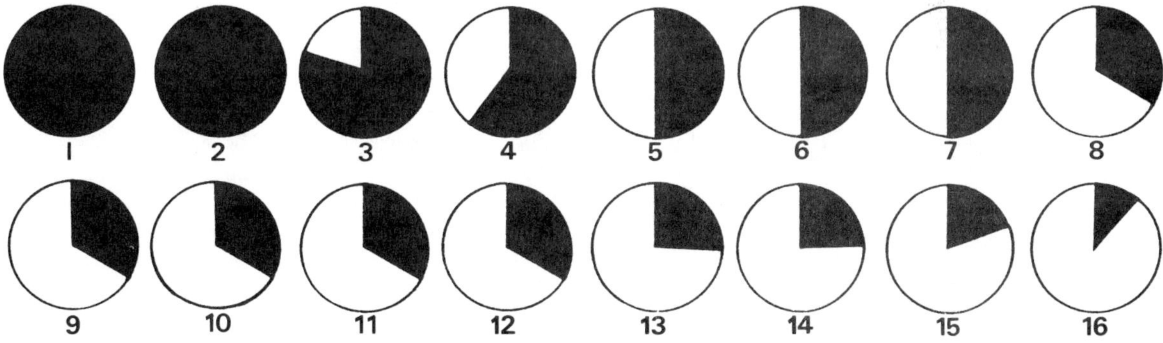

Desertification

1732 Soil misuse threatens to turn huge tracts of mainly semiarid land into deserts. The map shows threatened regions. Most lie in or near tropical or subtropical parts of the world. Deforestation, overcropping and overgrazing expose vulnerable soils to air and rain. Then wind or water erosion strips away the topsoil. Once-productive farmlands and rangelands lose fertility and vegetation and desert takes their place.

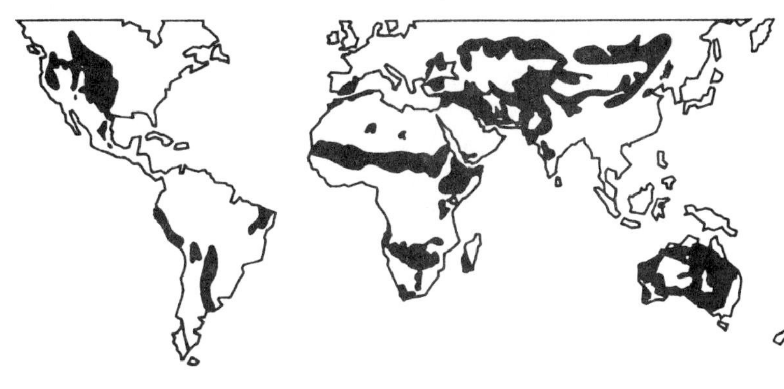

Landfill

1733

Dumping urban wastes consumes vast areas of land with landfill that expands with cities and their mounting waste disposal needs. Comparing eight countries' annual household waste production (in metric, and long, tons) gives an idea of the problem's scale.

1 United States	200,000,000
2 Japan	40,225,000
3 Germany (West)	20,780,000
4 United Kingdom	15,816,000
5 France	15,500,000
6 Italy	14,041,000
7 Canada	12,600,000
8 Australia	10,000,000

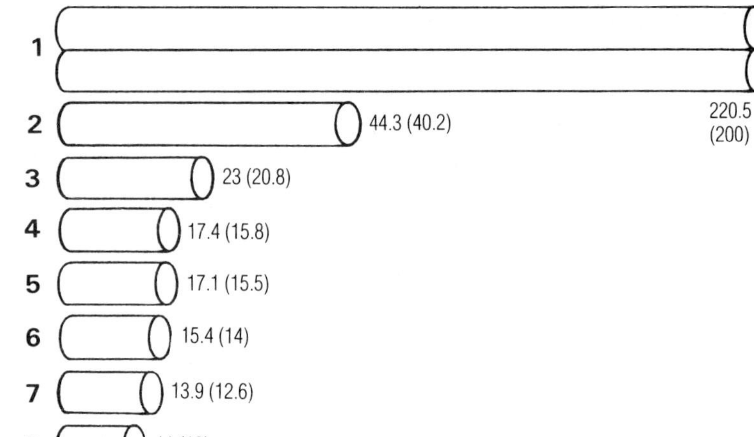

Land at risk to the sea

1734

● affected areas

A predicted global rise in temperatures would melt ice sheets, raising ocean levels and drowning low-lying lands. The world map (**A**) pinpoints vulnerable deltas, marshes and lagoons on continents and major islands. Atolls and low coastal plains worldwide would also be at risk.

The worst scenario (B)
Figures show the highest estimates for worldwide sea-level rise between now and the year 2100. Most of this rise would come from melting of the Antarctic ice sheet. Few experts think the rise will be this great. Even most pessimists think Antarctic melting would raise sea level by no more than 31 in (80 cm).

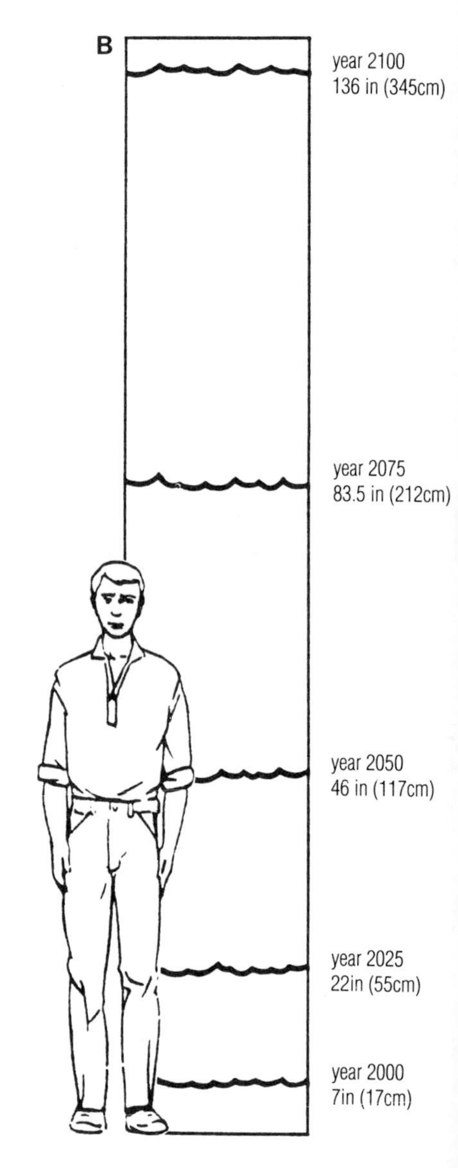

174 ALTERNATIVE ENERGY SOURCES

The need for alternative energy

1741 Most energy consumed in the industrial world comes from burning fossil fuels: coal, oil, and natural gas. As fossil fuel supplies run down, scientists explore alternatives to these and nuclear energy with its risk of major accidents. Renewable sources of energy include sunshine, wind, waves, tides, rivers, and biomass (burnable organic waste and crops). Also, hot rocks yield geothermal energy.

Fuel depletion
1 Oil
2 All fossil fuel

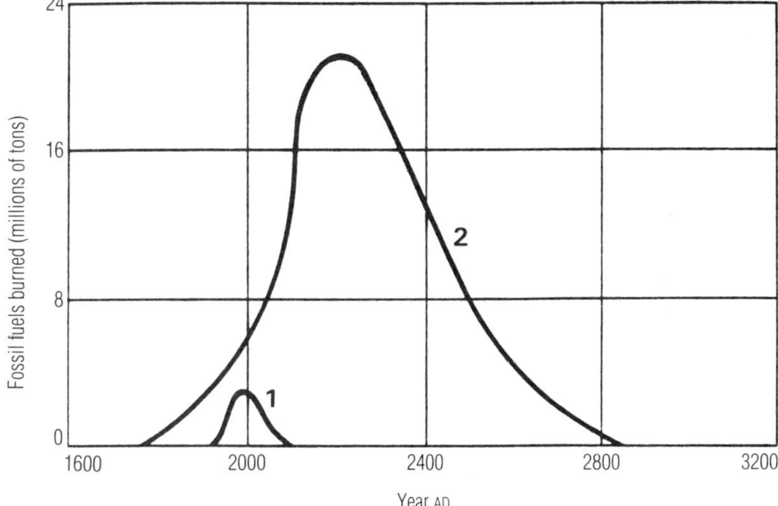

Energy from the Sun

1742 Solar power is the Sun's energy exploited by solar panels, collectors or cells to heat water or air or to generate electricity.

1 Heating domestic water
a Solar collector panels
b Circulating water
c Storage tank
d Pump

2 Domestic space heating
e Transparent glass
f Brick or stone floor
g Radiant and conducted heat
h Convected heat

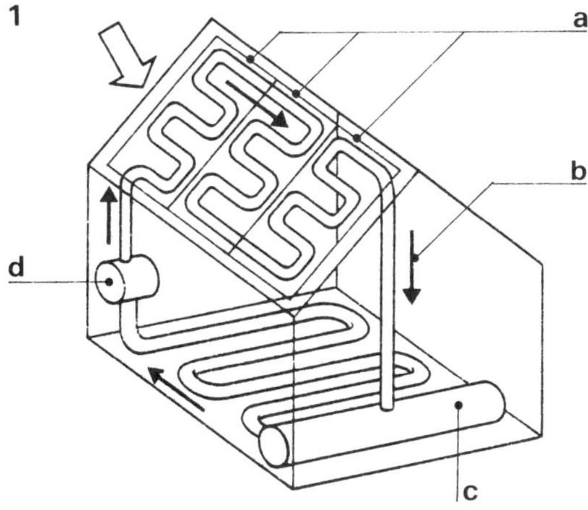

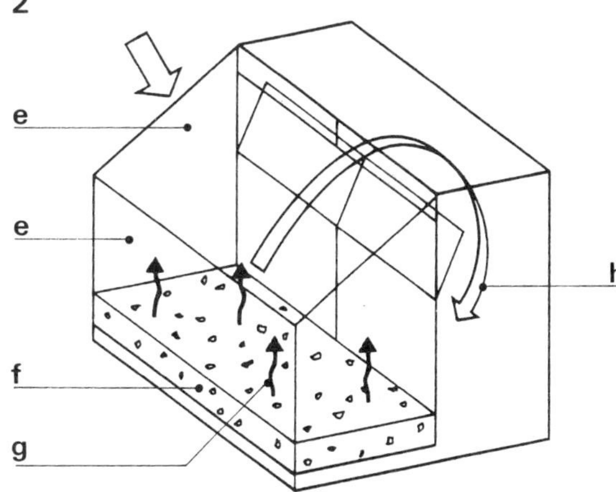

Energy from the wind

1743 Windpower derives from energy in wind exploited by aerogenerators to generate electricity.

Aerogenerators convert the wind's mechanical energy into electricity. Some giant devices generate more than 7,000 kilowatts. Here we show two designs for large aerogenerators.

1 Mod 5B with a horizontal-axis rotor
2 EOLE with a vertical-axis rotor
a Rotor
b Guy cables

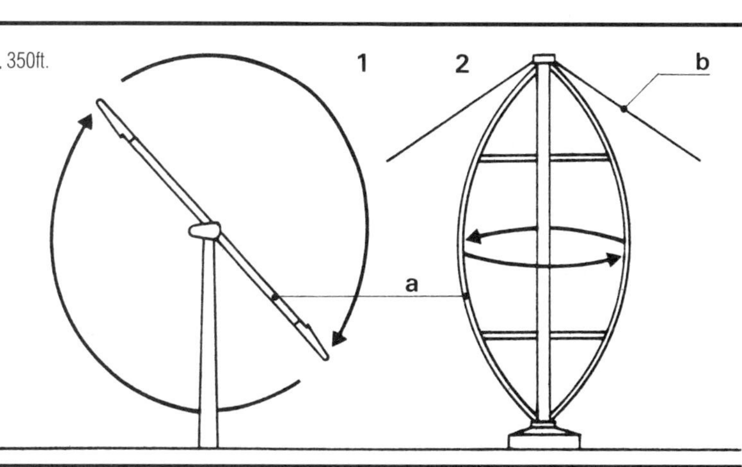

Energy from water

1744

Hydroelectric power stations exploit the flow of rivers. There are now also tidal barrages using the daily tidal flow of water in and out of a river.
1 Flow at low tide
2 Flow at high tide

a River
b Barrage
c Tunnel
d Turbine

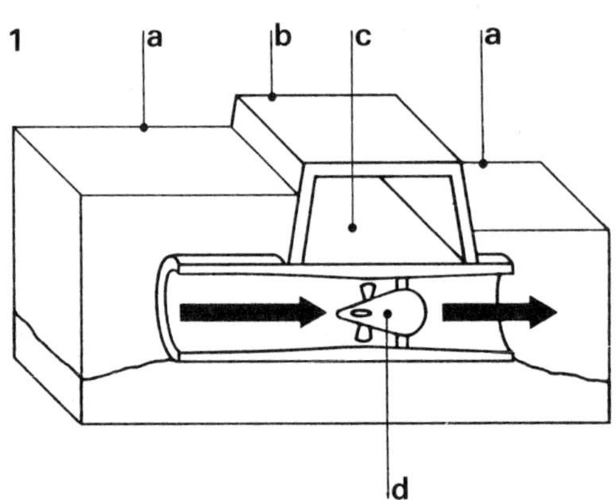

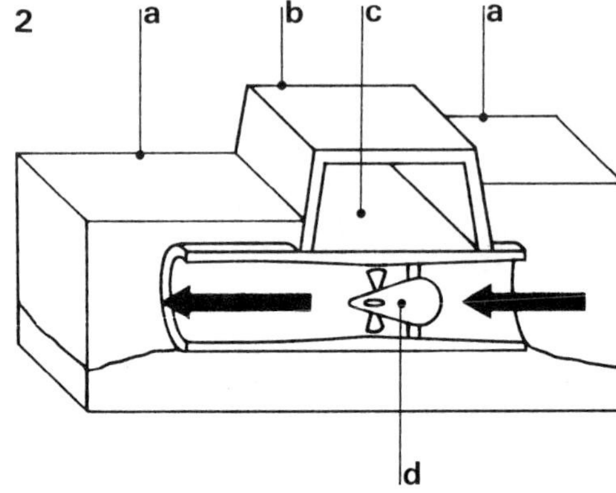

Energy from the Earth

1745

We show two methods of tapping heat trapped in the Earth's crust.

1 Hot-water deposits
a Magma (molten rock)
b Hot solid rock
c Heated water in porous rock
d Impermeable rock
e Pumped up water

2 Hot-rocks technique
a Cold water
b Excavated cavity
c Hot rocks
d High-pressure steam

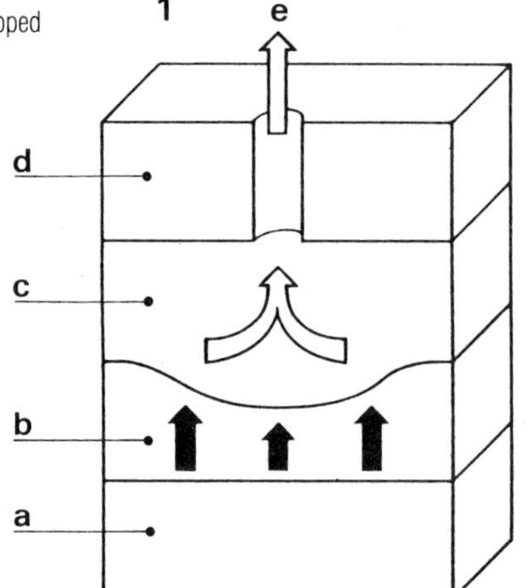

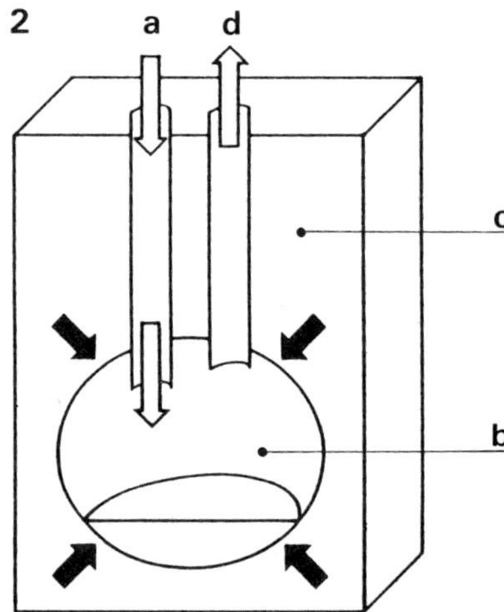

Energy from decomposing organisms

1746

Biogas is gas fuel from living matter, such as ethanol from sugarcane or methane from decaying organic substances. Decomposing organic farm or city waste releases methane gas that can be collected and burned as a fuel.

We show a methane digester converting animal or human waste into fuel to power farm machinery or heat a home.
1 Inlet from pigsty or latrine
2 Solid waste
3 Liquid waste
4 Gas
5 Gas tube

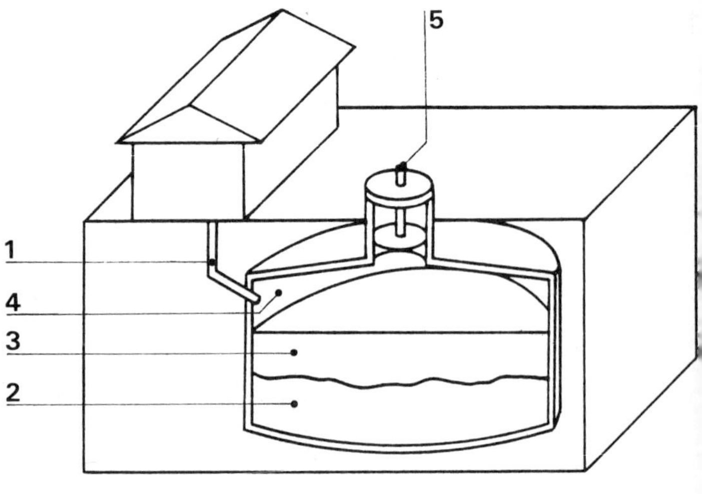

175 ENDANGERED WILDLIFE

Vanished species

1751 Between 1600 and 1990, 310 of 1,400,000 listed animal species became extinct. We show an example from each group.

1 Robert's stonefly, one of 96 extinct invertebrates
2 Pahranagat spinedace, one of 24 extinct fish
3 Réunion skink, one of 20 extinct reptiles and amphibians
4 Dodo, one of 116 extinct birds
5 Quagga, one of 54 extinct mammals

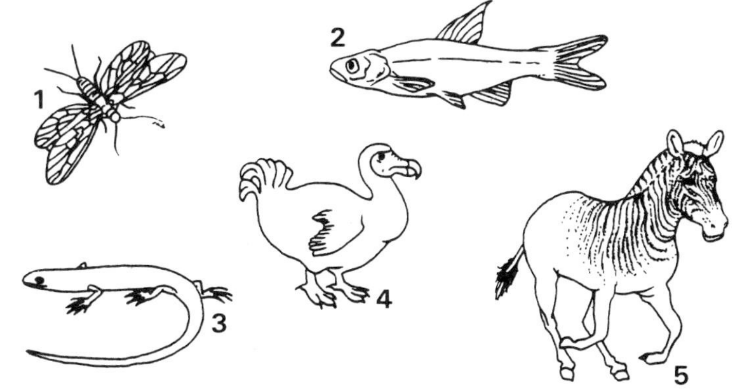

Species at risk

1752 In a century when humans have made great strides in science and technology, we still have no idea how many species of living organisms—animals, plants, fungi, bacteria, and protists—share the Earth with us. About 1.5 million species are listed and cataloged; estimates of the world total number of species as yet unnamed and undiscovered range from 4 million to 100 million. Unfortunately, many of the species will remain unknown because they will become extinct before they can be discovered.

Most people are aware of only large animals becoming extinct—the dodo, for example—and the current threats to large animals such as the blue whale and black rhino. However, there are many smaller plants and animals that face extinction daily through the mass destruction of their habitats: a prime example of this is the destruction of the tropical forests, ecosystems with the richest biological diversity on Earth.

Many of the species at risk could prove to be valuable sources of new medicines, foods or stores of genes to be used in breeding new crops.

The diagram below shows the huge and rapidly increasing numbers of species and subspecies of plants and animals that were at risk of vanishing for good in 1990.

1 Plants 38,000
2 Invertebrates 2,250
3 Birds 1,047
4 Fishes 762
5 Mammals 698
6 Reptiles 191
7 Amphibians 63

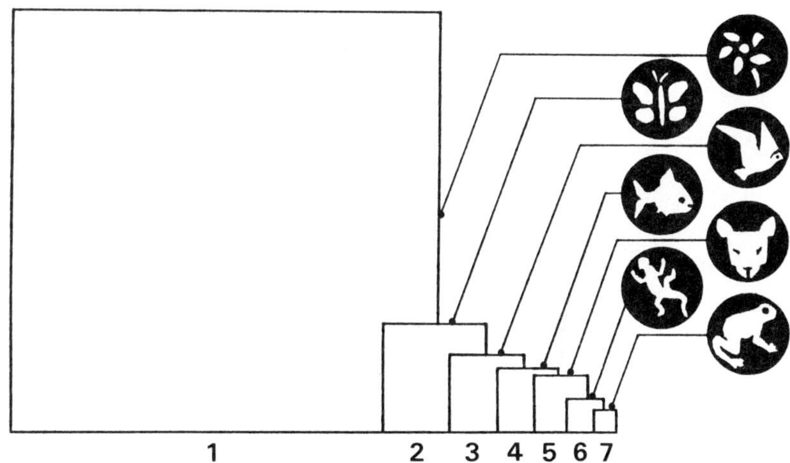

Lost habitat

1753 Habitat destruction is the chief reason why species are becoming extinct. We show percentages of wildlife habitat lost by 1990 for six countries with great biological diversity.

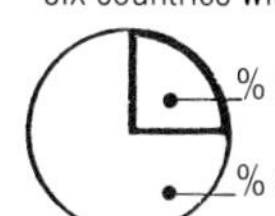

1 Ivory Coast
2 Ethiopia
3 Madagascar
4 Burma
5 Vietnam
6 Philippines

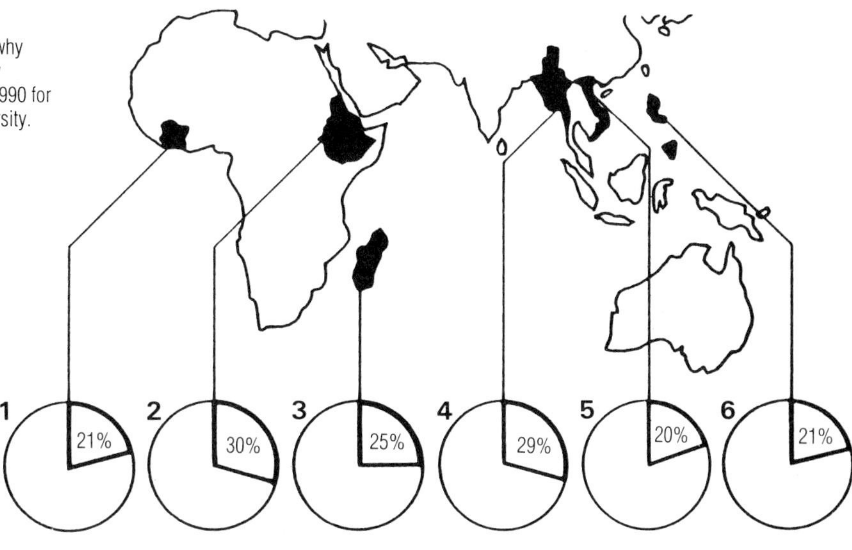

Threats to wildlife

175**4** Six human activities threaten to make many plants and animals extinct.
1 Destroying wildlife habitats
2 Hunting scarce species
3 Overfishing
4 Pollution from factories and farms
5 Trade in endangered species
6 Introducing alien predators

Protected areas

175**5** Wildlife reserves and other legally protected lands, many patrolled by wardens, help prevent numbers of wild plants and animals becoming extinct. Here, squares show relative sizes of protected areas in 1988. The figures below show areas in millions of hectares (1ha = 2.47 ac).
1 North and Central America 172.6
2 South America 66.3
3 Europe 27.2
4 Africa 95.5
5 Asia 60.5
6 Russia 20.2
7 Oceania 38.9

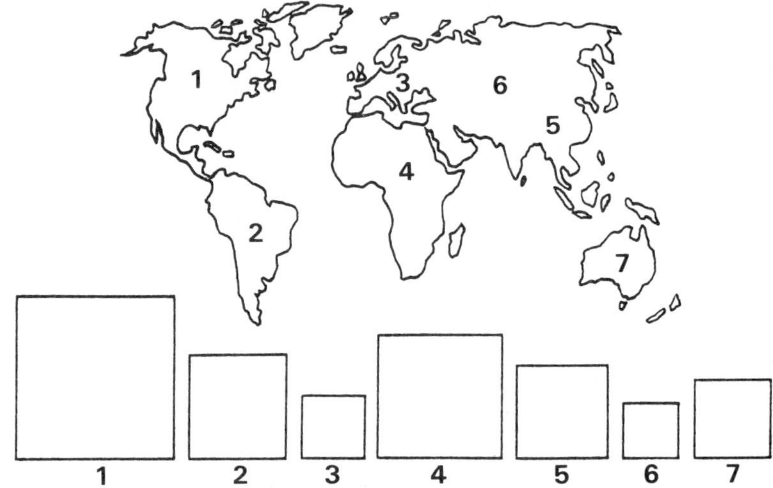

Conservation

175**6** National and international laws and organizations help to save wildlife by setting and monitoring hunting quotas, controlling trade in wildlife, captive-breeding, protecting species-rich habitats, and campaigning against wildlife exploitation. We show logos of some leading conservation bodies.

176 ENVIRONMENTAL ISSUES GLOSSARY

acceptable daily intake (ADI) Human's safe daily intake of any chemical, in milligrams per kilogram of body weight.
acid rain Rain acidified by sulfuric, nitric, and other acids that form when water and sunlight react with sulfur dioxide, nitrogen oxides and other pollutants released by burning fossil fuels. Acid rain can poison lakes, kill forests, and corrode buildings.
additive A chemical added to a food undergoing an industrial process.
agrochemicals The chemical fertilizers and pesticides underpinning modern agriculture.
AIDS Acquired immune deficiency syndrome. A usually fatal disease contracted from body fluids of people with the HIV virus.
air pollution Contamination of the air, especially by smoke or gases from vehicles, factories, and power stations. It can cause disease, kill plants and damage structures.
algal bloom Explosive growth of algae in water overenriched by nutrients from sewage, artificial fertilizers, etc. Effects can include the mass death of fish.
alternative technology Method of using resources more efficiently and with less damage to the environment than orthodox technology.
Antarctic Treaty An international agreement (1959) to ensure the peaceful use of Antarctica and ban waste dumping and nuclear testing.
artificial fertilizer Mineral fertilizer usually containing nitrogen, phosphorus and potassium compounds. Overuse can harm soil structure and pollute water supplies.
bioconcentration The concentration of pollutants, especially pesticides, in the living tissue of organisms at the top end of a food chain.
biodegradable Capable of being broken down

continued

Environmental issues glossary continued

by such living agents as bacteria. Some plastics are biodegradable.
biodiversity Variety of life forms.
biogas Gas fuel from living matter, such as ethanol from sugarcane or methane from decaying organic substances.
biological control Controlling pests by biological not chemical means, as by introducing predators or, as with flies, sterilizing males.
biomass The chemical energy in growing plants, hence biomass fuels (firewood, dried dung, and biogas).
biosphere Earth's living things and their environment.
biosphere reserve A two- (or more) zone conservation area with limited human activity (research, tourism, etc).
calories (kilocalories) Units for measuring the energy content of foods.
cancer Uncontrolled multiplication of cells, a major cause of death in the developed world.
captive breeding Breeding rare animals in zoos or parks, especially to save those threatened by extinction in the wild.
carbon dioxide A gas in air. In the carbon cycle plants make food with carbon dioxide; and breathing, burning, and decay return it to air. See also greenhouse gases.
carcinogen Any cancer-causing agent.
carrying capacity The population of living things that an ecosystem can support without impairing its stability.
catalytic converter A device removing certain pollutants from exhaust gases of vehicles running on unleaded gasoline.
CFCs See chlorofluorocarbons.
Chernobyl Site of the worst nuclear reactor accident, in 1986 in the Ukrainian USSR.
chlorinated hydrocarbons Highly toxic pesticides including Aldrin, DDT and dieldrin, now largely banned in the West.
chlorofluorocarbons (CFCs) Compounds of chlorine and fluorine once much used as aerosol propellants and refrigerants and in foam packaging; now known to deplete the ozone layer and act as greenhouse gases.
conservation Protecting the environment.
contamination Spoiling by contact.
croplands Arable farmlands.
DDT Dichloro-diphenol-trichloroethane. A pesticide with dangerous bioconcentration effects. Banned in much of the West but still used in developing countries.
debt-for-nature swap Cancellation of developing nations' debts in return for environmental conservation commitments.
desertification Fertile land becoming unproductive desert, often due to overcropping and overgrazing.
dioxin Any of dozens of highly toxic contaminants of products including or involving chlorinated phenols.
ecosystem A community of living things and their environment (pond, tree, forest, etc).
endangered species Species of plants and animals in danger of extinction.
eutrophication Over-enrichment of water by nutrients (e.g. chemical fertilizer, sewage), causing plant overgrowth and decay, water deoxygenation and death of its organisms.
food chain A series of different life forms linked by what they eat and what eats them.
food web A mesh of interlinked food chains.
Gaia hypothesis A theory that the biosphere acts as a self-sustaining, self-regulating organism. British scientist James Lovelock named it after a Greek Earth goddess.
genetic diversity The diversity of living species, also of genetic variations within one species. It helps life forms to persist in face of epidemic diseases or harsh climatic change.
geothermal energy Useful heat obtained by pumping water past hot underground rocks.
GNP Gross national product: a measure of national wealth including overseas income.
greenhouse effect Alleged human-made atmospheric warming by accumulating gases trapping solar heat below them rather like a greenhouse roof. See greenhouse gases.
greenhouse gases Carbon dioxide, methane, chlorofluorocarbons, nitrous oxide and low-level ozone. See greenhouse effect.
green movement A popular movement urging production and use of environmentally harmless consumer goods. Green politicians would curb economic and population growth and protect the natural environment.
green revolution A program launched in the 1960s to boost world food supplies with new, high-yielding hybrid cereals.
habitat The type of place where an animal or plant normally lives.
hazardous waste Toxic industrial and other wastes, posing major disposal problems.
heart disease A major cause of death in the developed world, much of it blamed on smoking, overeating, saturated fats and lack of exercise.
heavy metals Elements including cadmium, lead and mercury, all poisonous. Careless dumping can create local health hazards.
herbicides Weed-killing chemicals such as paraquat, a highly toxic contact poison.
HIV Human immunodeficiency virus: a virus causing the disease AIDS.
irradiated food Food preserved by exposure to ionizing radiation. Critics say partly-rotted food would still hold toxins.
landfill Disposal of hazardous or other waste by tipping it in a hole in the ground. Consequences can be an explosive methane build-up and contaminated water supplies.
lean-burn engine An automobile engine that curbs nitrogen oxide exhaust emissions.
London Dumping Convention Agreement (1975) controlling the dumping of waste from ships and aircraft. (Also called the Convention on the Prevention of Marine Pollution by Dumping of Waste and Other Matter.)
low-impact technology Technology with minimal effect on the environment.
migration corridor A protected strip of natural habitat through which wild animals are able to migrate.
monoculture Extensive cultivation of one crop. It maximizes use of farm machinery but increases risks of crop disease, pest infestation and impaired soil structure.
mutagens Chemicals causing mutations, i.e. genetic changes (often harmful) in a living organism's offspring.
national park An area that is preserved chiefly for its outstanding natural beauty or scientific importance.
nature reserve An area set aside chiefly to protect its wild plants and animals.
nitrate A nitrogen compound essential for plant growth, but liable to contaminate water supplies where nitrate fertilizer is washed into rivers or seeps underground.
nitrogen cycle The natural circulation of nitrogen (including nitrogen compounds) from air to consuming organisms (plants, animals and bacteria) and back to air.
noise pollution Persistent loud noise (as from traffic, machinery, audio equipment) causing discomfort and even deafness.
nuclear accident An accident involving a nuclear power plant, perhaps with an escape of harmful radioactivity.
nuclear waste Radioactive waste produced by the nuclear industry. Safe long-term disposal of this waste presents major problems.
nuclear winter The prolonged period of cold, dark weather likely on a global scale if a large-scale nuclear war produced immense dust clouds shutting out the Sun.
organic farming Farming without artificial fertilizers or pesticides. Organic farming involves manuring with plant or animal wastes and the biological control of pests and weeds. See biological control.
organophosphates Organophosphorus compounds, used as pesticides, which act as nerve poisons and can severely affect wildlife.
overfishing Harvesting fish stocks faster than breeding can make good the deficit.
overgrazing Letting livestock graze land so heavily that soil loses fertility, grass grows sparsely and soil erosion may occur.
ozone layer A belt of ozone gas in the upper atmosphere. This ozone filters out incoming ultraviolet radiation liable to damage the chemicals all living things are made of. Holes appearing in the ozone layer above polar regions have been blamed on chlorofluorocarbons (CFCs).
PCBs Polychlorinated biphenyls. Compounds once much used in electrical products, but highly toxic and now difficult to dispose of because extremely stable.
pesticides Chemicals that kill plant, animal and other pests, and may also pollute food and water supplies. Well-known toxic pesticides include Aldrin, Chlordane and DDT. See chlorinated hydrocarbons and organophosphates.
plutonium Element produced in large quantities by nuclear reactors; also used in nuclear weapons.
pollution Introducing harmful substances or other agents into the environment.
population explosion The explosive worldwide growth of human population since the industrial revolution.
population pyramid A diagram showing successive age groups as a pyramid of horizontal bars. Each bar's length shows the relative size of one age group.

continued

Environmental issues glossary continued

176

radioactivity The emission of rays and subatomic particles from the nuclei of certain elements decaying into others, notably uranium and its decay products, down to but excluding lead. Radioactivity from nuclear bombs and installations and even certain rocks can injure living tissues.
Ramsar Convention An international agreement (1971) to protect wetlands. (Also known as the Convention on Wetlands of International Importance especially as Waterfowl Habitat.)
recycling Conserving by reusing (directly or after reprocessing) such used materials as aluminum, glass and paper.
renewable resources Crops, fish, timber, solar, and wind energy and other resources that can be used without exhausting them.
reprocessing Of nuclear fuel, extracting plutonium (for military use) and unused uranium from the nuclear fuel of a reactor.
salinization Making soil too salty for growing land plants. Salinization is a problem in some irrigated soils of hot dry climates. Evaporation concentrates sucked-up salts in the soil's upper levels.
scrubber Equipment curbing air pollution by removing toxic gases from chimneys; used in power stations burning fossil fuels.
smog Air pollution caused by combined smoke and fog or (photochemical smog) by sunlight acting on vehicles' exhaust gases.
solar power The Sun's energy exploited by solar panels, collectors or cells to heat water or air or to generate electricity.
sustainable development Economic progress without damage to ecosystems.
Tropical Forest Action Plan A scheme to conserve tropical forests, devised in 1987 by UN agencies, the World Bank and the World Resources Institute. Critics claim it favors industrial forestry.
unleaded gasoline Lead-free gasoline, promoted to reduce a damaging accumulation of lead in the environment.
uranium Highly radioactive element used in thermal nuclear reactors.
urbanization Growth of towns and cities: a global trend. Huge unsanitary slums are a feature of fast-growing cities in the developing world.
waldsterben (forest death) Damage to trees caused by air pollution and secondary infection.
waste disposal Removing and destroying or storing damaged, used or other unwanted domestic, agricultural or industrial products and substances. Disposal includes burning, burial at landfill sites or at sea, and recycling.
water pollution Contamination of rivers, lakes and seas by fertilizers, pesticides, sewage, and oil or toxic waste from ships and factories.
wave power The energy in sea waves exploited to generate electricity.
wetlands Bogs, marshes, swamps, flood plains, and estuaries. Many have high and varied populations of plants and animals.
wind power The energy in wind exploited by aerogenerators to generate electricity.
World Conservation Strategy A strategy launched (1980) by the IUCN and WWF to help nations protect ecosystems.
World Heritage sites Designated natural and cultural sites internationally recognized as of outstanding importance.

177 ABBREVIATIONS

CITES Convention on International Trade in Endangered Species of Wild Flora and Fauna. An international agreement banning trade in species at risk of extinction, and limiting trade in those endangered by uncontrolled trade.
EC European Community. A group of West European nations working toward economic and political integration.
EPA US Environmental Protection Agency. A US government agency protecting the environment against pollution.
FAO Food and Agriculture Organization. A United Nations agency improving food production, distribution and use worldwide.
GEMS Global Environment Monitoring System. Part of the United Nations Environment Program (UNEP).
ITTO International Tropical Timber Organization, which manages the International Tropical Timber Agreement (ITTA), ratified in 1985 to minimize forest devastation through sustainable management.
IUCN The World Conservation Union. An international body that publishes updated lists of endangered species.
IWC International Whaling Commission. An international body regulating whaling but without power to enforce restrictions.
NGO Non-governmental organization.
TFAP Tropical Forest Action Plan, launched in 1987 to conserve tropical forests.
TRAFFIC Trade Records Analysis of Fauna and Flora in Commerce, a worldwide network which monitors wildlife trade and assists in implementing CITES.
UN The United Nations organization.
UNDP United Nations Development Program. This selects and funds (via UN agencies) technical aid and relief projects.
UNEP United Nations Environment Program. A global program to preserve natural resources and to combat pollution.
UNESCO United Nations Educational Scientific and Cultural Organization. Agency promoting worldwide understanding and cooperation.
UNFPA United Nations Population Fund.
UNICEF United Nations Children's Fund. A UN body promoting child health, nutrition and education in more than 100 nations.
WCMC World Conservation Monitoring Center.
WHO World Health Organization. A UN agency promoting health, mainly through vaccination and improved sanitation and water supplies.
WWF World Wide Fund for Nature. An international group for conserving endangered wildlife and wild places and encouraging sustainable use of natural resources.

211 ENERGY

A man climbing a flight of stairs, a car moving along a road, and a crane lifting a load are all examples of actions that involve energy, work, and power. Each of these terms has a particular scientific meaning. Work is done whenever a force causes movement, i.e. work involves moving something (it could be an object as tiny as an atom or as large as an elephant) from one place to another. Energy is the capacity for doing work. Power is the rate of doing work.

Types of energy

2111 This table lists the six types of energy (**1–6**) and examples of each (**a–o**). The diagram illustrates the relationships between these forms of energy.

Type of energy	Example
1 Mechanical energy: kinetic or potential energy	**a** Dynamo **b** Turbine
2 Electrical energy: the energy produced by electrons moving from atom to atom	**c** Motor **d** Electric heater **e** Light bulb
3 Nuclear energy: the energy stored in the nucleus of an atom	**f** Power station **g** Bomb
4 Heat energy: the energy produced by the random movement of a substance's atoms The faster they move the hotter they become.	**h** Hot air balloon **i** Anything red or white hot
5 Radiant energy: consists of rays, waves or particles, especially forms of electromagnetic radiation such as infra-red radiation, light, ultraviolet radiation, X-rays, gamma rays, and cosmic rays	**j** Solar heating panels **k** Solar cells **l** Photosynthesis
6 Chemical energy: the energy stored in an atom or molecule and released by a chemical reaction	**m** Batteries **n** Gas or oil furnace

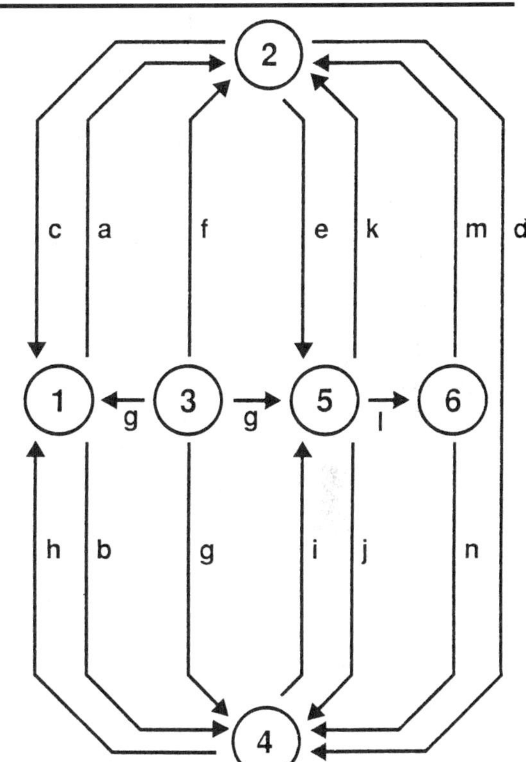

Einstein and energy

2112 In 1905, the German scientist Albert Einstein suggested that matter was a form of energy. This theory was summed up in his famous equation **$E=mc^2$**. **E** represents the amount of energy produced, **m** the mass (i.e. the amount of matter,) and **c** the speed of light in a vacuum – 186,282 mi/sec (2.997925×10^8 m/sec) – which is a constant. The equation is known as the mass–energy equivalence. Einstein's theory was proved by the development of nuclear energy. Nuclear power stations and bombs convert the matter in an atom directly into energy, as do the Sun and other stars. Scientists have also been able to make small amounts of matter from pure energy under specialized laboratory conditions.

Mass into energy
Even in the most efficient nuclear power station, only a tiny amount of the mass of the fuel is converted into energy. The rest remains as matter. Einstein's equation makes it possible to calculate the huge amounts of energy that would be released if the whole of an available mass could be converted into pure energy.

Heat energy

2113 Heating increases the speed at which molecules travel. The more heat energy a substance is given, the faster the molecules travel and the more the molecules bump into one another. Because of this increased movement, heated atoms and molecules (**2**) move around more freely than unheated ones (**1**). Thus a heated substance may change shape. Heating makes various substances expand. On average, gases expand about 100 times more than liquids, and liquids about 10 times more than solids.

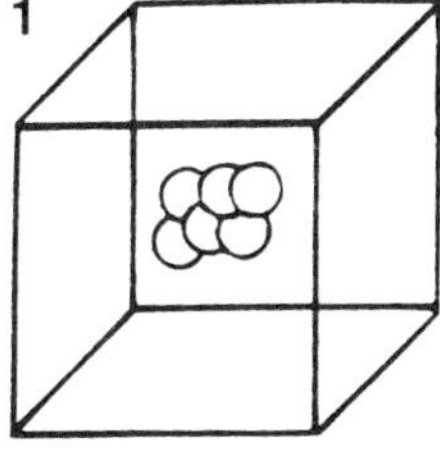

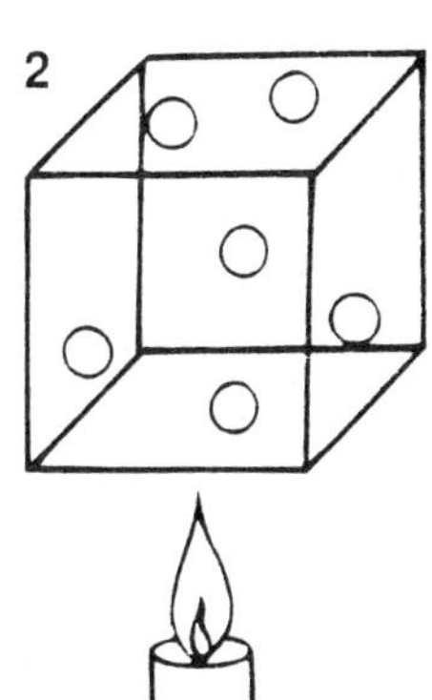

continued

Heat energy continued

2113 **Types of heat transfer**
Heat can be transferred from a hotter to a cooler body in three ways.

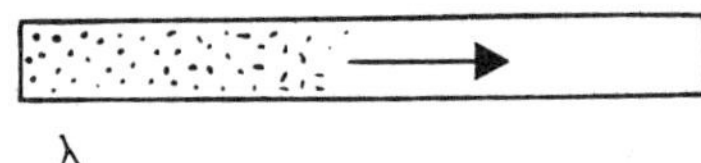

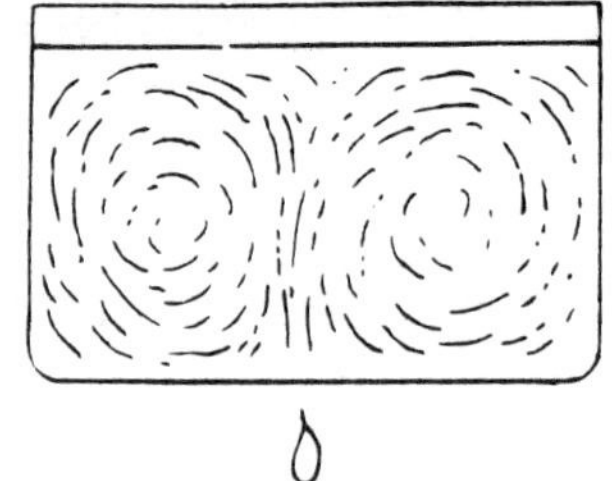

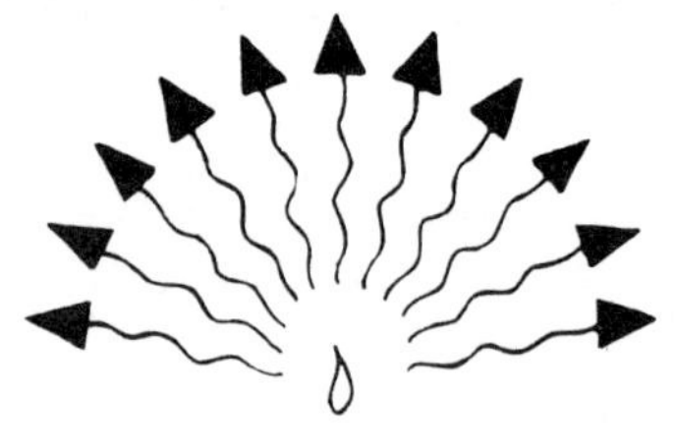

Conduction
Heat is transferred by conduction when it is passed on from molecule to molecule through a substance. The heated molecules transmit their increased vibration to neighboring molecules, so making them hotter. Some substances conduct heat much better than others depending on how well they transmit vibration to their neighbors.

Convection
This form of heat transfer takes place in fluids (liquids and gases) due to the movement of fluid. Heated liquid or gas expands, grows lighter, and rises, while cooler liquid or gas sinks and flows in to take its place. This circulation of a heated fluid creates a convection current.

Radiation
Heat energy can behave like light and other forms of radiant energy, i.e. it can be transferred by radiation. Heat can be radiated even through a vacuum (i.e. where no matter is present). Conduction and convection both only take place when matter is present.

Kinetic and potential energy

2114

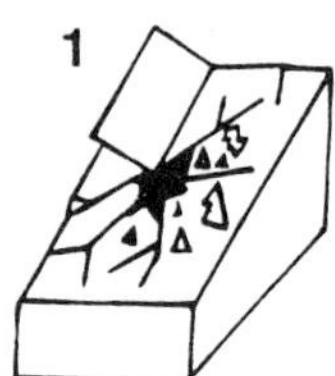

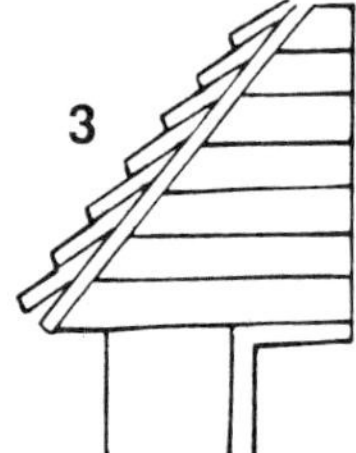

In scientific terms, a slate falling off a roof and breaking a pane of glass is doing work (**1**). The slate therefore has energy. When the slate is actually falling (**2**) it is said to have kinetic energy, from the Greek word *kinesis*, meaning movement. All moving objects have kinetic energy. The slate also has energy before it falls off the roof (**3**), because it has the potential to move, i.e. it has potential energy. The term potential energy describes the energy a stationary object has which can be turned into kinetic energy. The slate has potential energy because of its position above the ground: the force of gravity may act on it to make it move. Potential energy is converted into kinetic energy when an object moves.

Examples of potential and kinetic energy

Potential energy

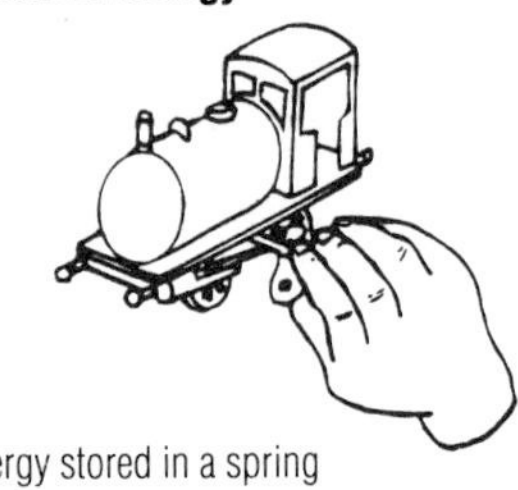
energy stored in a spring

energy stored in a stretched bow

on top of a hill

Kinetic energy

a moving clockwork train

arrow in flight

downhill skier

212 FORCES

A force can change an object's shape, size, speed or direction. The international unit of force is the newton (N): the amount of force needed to give a mass of one kilogram an acceleration of one meter per second per second (1 m/sec^2), i.e. each second the mass travels 1 m/sec faster than the second before. The known forces are:

- Gravity
- Electromagnetism
- The strong and weak nuclear forces in atoms

Gravity

2121 This is the natural force pulling one object toward another. Its strength depends on the mass of the objects involved. Because the Earth is so massive, objects on it are pulled toward it more than they are toward each other. Earth's gravity (surface intensity of gravitation) exerts a pull of 9.8 N on a mass of 1 kg, at the surface.

For example, this apple is pulled toward the center of the Earth. The Earth's mass is greater than the apple's mass, so its pull of gravity is stronger. Earth's mass is 6 million billion billion kilograms.

The mass of an apple is 0.1 kg. The pull of gravity gives it its weight. Weight is measured in newtons:
Gravity = 10 meters per second^2 (m/s^2).
The weight of the apple = mass x gravity.
The weight of this apple is 1 newton.

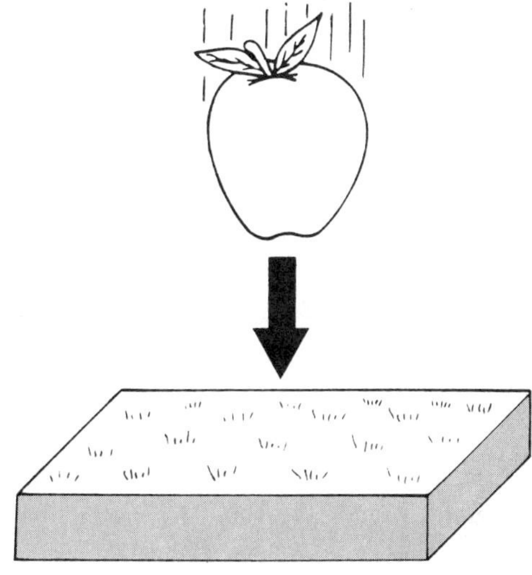

Pressure

2122 A force acting over a small area exerts greater pressure than the same force acting over a large area. Pressure is defined as force per unit area, and it is calculated by dividing the force by the area over which it is acting. Because the Earth's atmosphere has weight (1 m^3 of air weighs about 12 N) it exerts pressure. Atmospheric pressure can be measured with a barometer.

In diagram (**1**) 1lb exerts $^1/_{100}$ lb. In diagram (**2**), the weight is distributed over one square only and therefore exerts the full 1lb of pressure on this square.

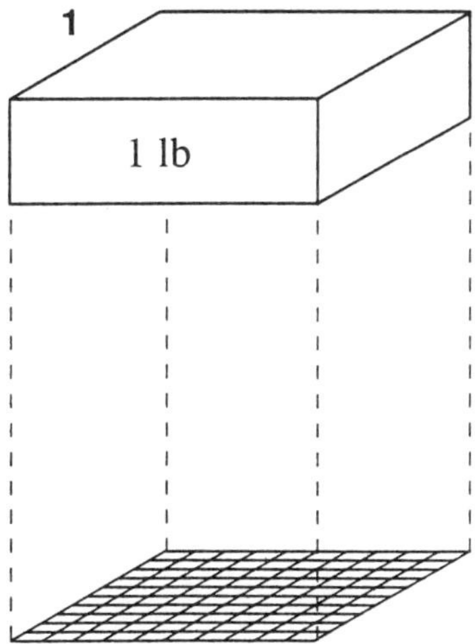

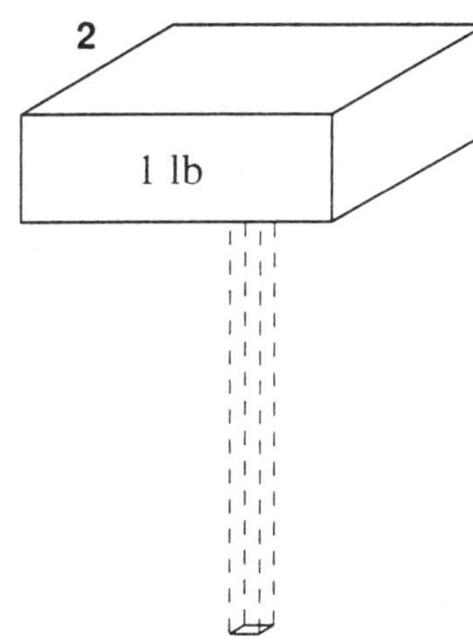

Pushing can change the speed and/or the direction of an object.

Compressing an object to change its shape and size is a form of pushing.

Pulling can change the speed and/or direction of an object.

Stretching an object to change its shape and/or size is a form of pulling.

Bending may be a form of either pulling or pushing.

Twisting is pushing or pulling in a spiral.

Newton

2123 The international unit of force is called the newton (N), named for the great 17th-century English scientist Isaac Newton. Among Newton's many discoveries were the laws governing the universal force of gravity. The idea that led to these laws came to him when he was drinking tea in a garden and noticed an apple fall from a tree. Coincidentally, an apple weighs about 1 N.

Newton's laws of motion

2124 **First law (inertia)**
A body maintains its state of rest or motion in a straight line unless acted on by an external force.
Second law
A body's acceleration depends on its mass and the size of the force that acts on it.
Third law
For every action (**1**) there is an equal and opposite reaction (**2**).

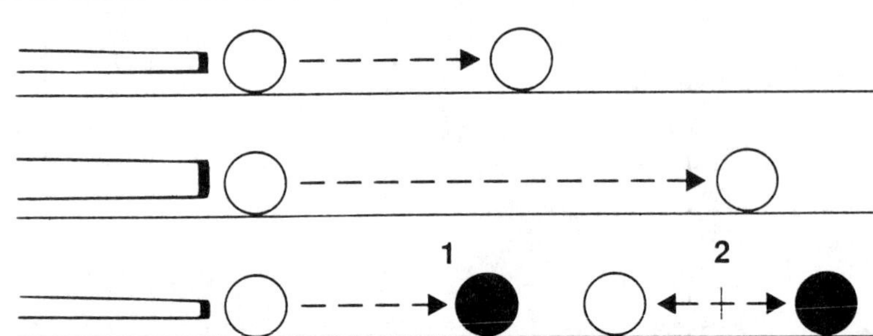

213 MACHINES

Machines are devices that perform work. A machine produces force and controls its direction and motion. Machines cannot create energy, they depend on the input of energy. The ratio of energy output to input determines a machine's efficiency. This is never more than 100% because energy is lost through friction. Some engines convert other forms of energy into mechanical energy. Machines transmitting only mechanical energy produce a mechanical advantage: the ratio of load raised to force applied by the machine. There are six main types of machine. Stone Age peoples unknowingly used three types of these machines. Spear throwers were levers increasing a hunter's throwing range. Sharp pointed sticks and stones served as wedges that pierced skin and dug deep into flesh to kill prey. Hill slopes were the inclined planes that allowed people to raise heavy logs, rocks, and carcasses.

Levers

2131 A lever involves a fulcrum (**1**) supporting a load (**2**) moved by an effort (**3**). Their relative positions create three types of lever. The nearer the fulcrum is to the load, the less the effort required and the greater the machine's mechanical advantage.

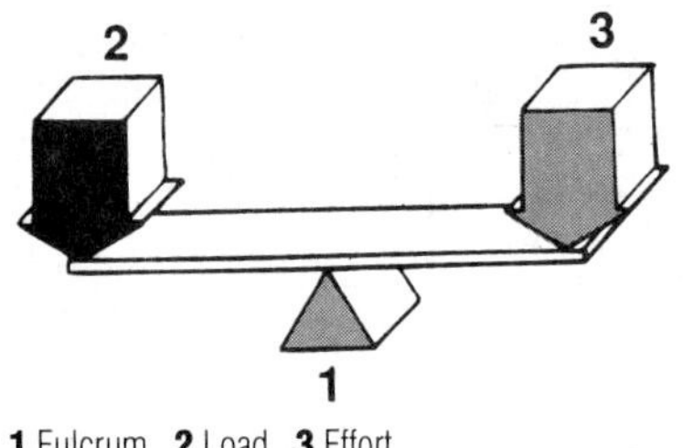

1 Fulcrum **2** Load **3** Effort

seesaw

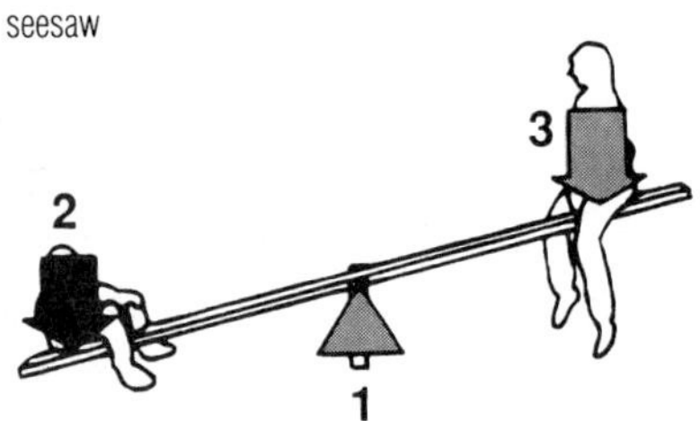

scissors

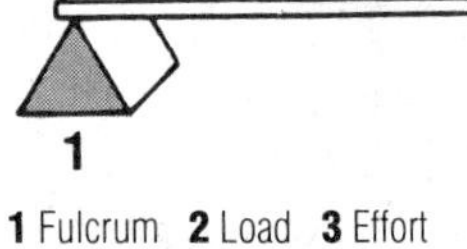

1 Fulcrum **2** Load **3** Effort

wheelbarrow

knife

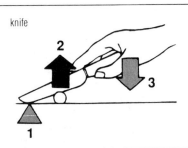

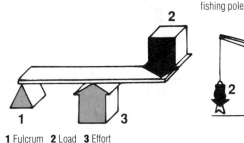

1 Fulcrum **2** Load **3** Effort

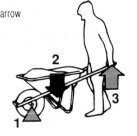

fishing pole

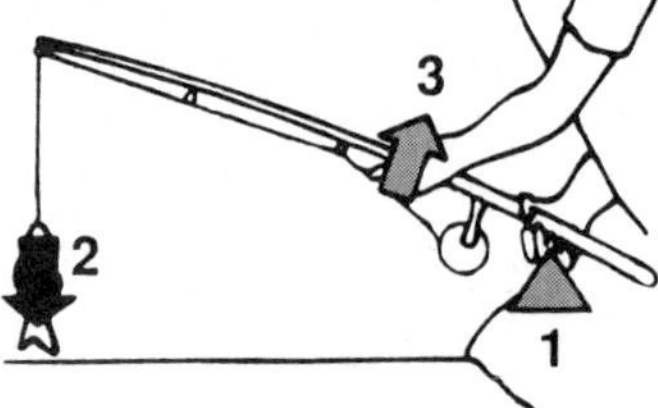

raising your arm to drink

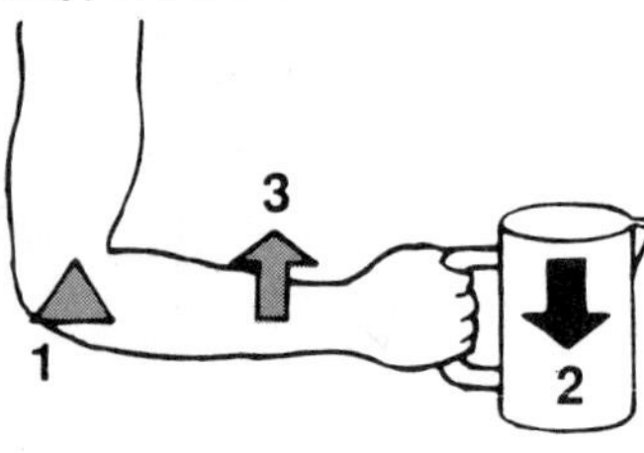

Wheel and axle

2132 A wheel and axle is a form of lever. A lever transmits a force from one place to another. The wheel and axle produces a greater force at one end than at the other. It can move a load further than a lever and can help to move heavy loads overland. There is less friction when rolling than when sliding, so there is less effort required.

1 Wheel
2 Axle

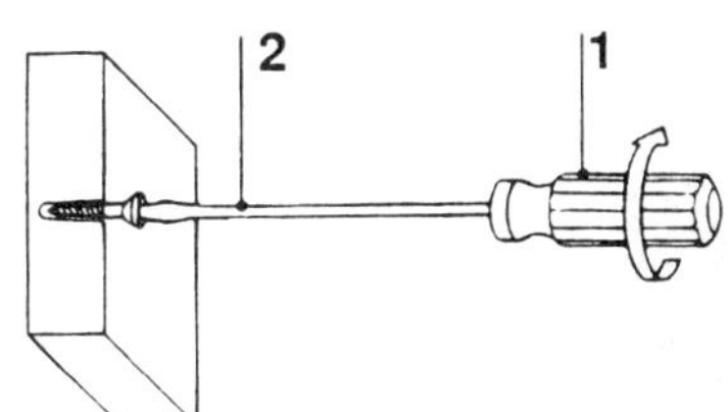

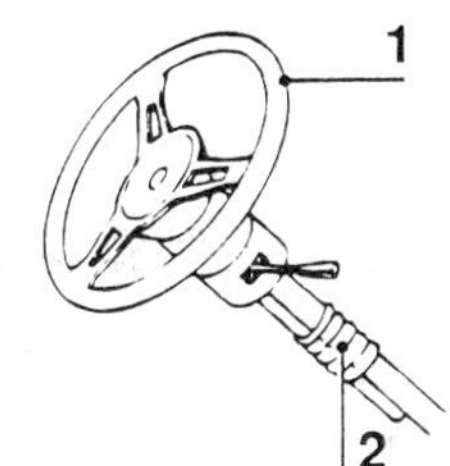

Pulley

2133 A pulley is a wheel and axle that helps to change the direction of force. A rope passes over a groove in the wheel rim. Pulling one end of the rope raises a load attached to the other end.
1 A single pulley (fulcrum) (**a**) changes the direction of force or effort (**b**) needed for raising a load (**c**), but produces a mechanical advantage that is no greater than 1.

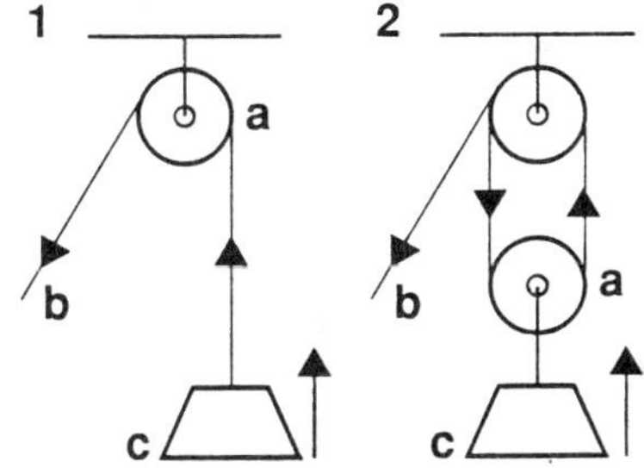

2 A block and tackle has two pulleys, one attached to a fixed support, the other (fulcrum) (**a**) free to move with the load (**c**). This pulley system changes the direction of force and reduces the effort (**b**) required.

Wedge

2134 A wedge is a simple machine made of two inclined planes. The smaller the angle formed by the wedge, the less the force needed for moving the load (i.e. for the wood to be split).

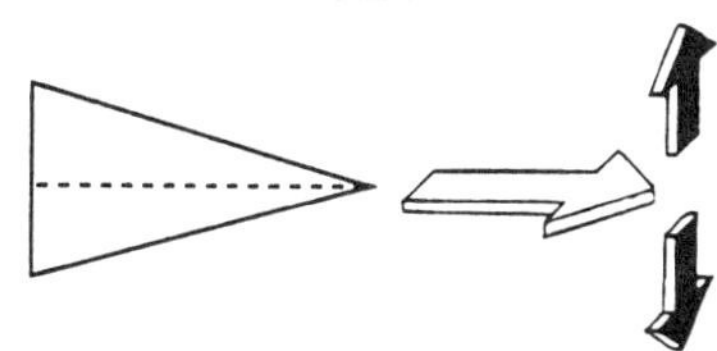

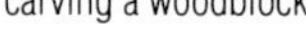
carving a woodblock

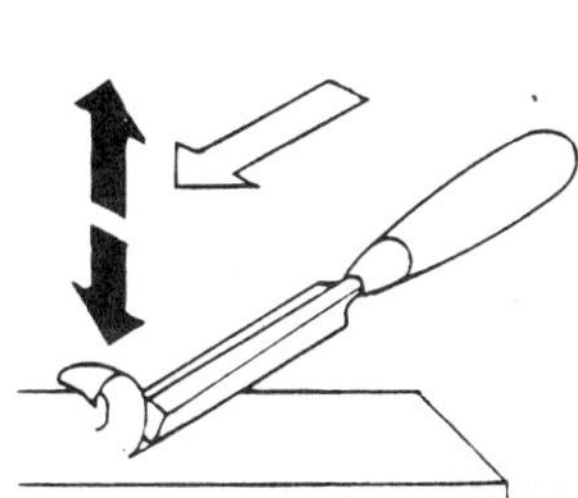

chopping wood

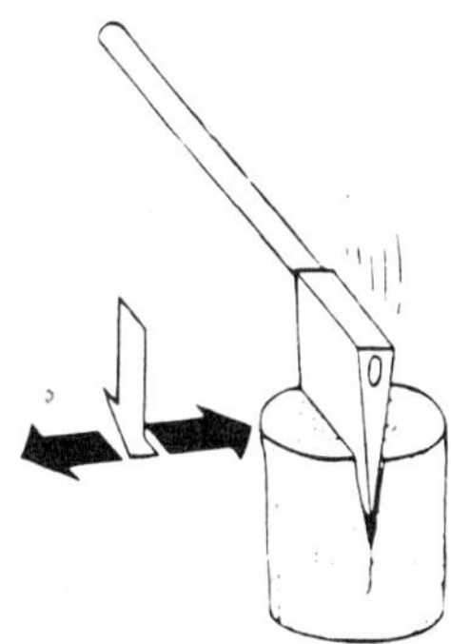

Screw

2135 A screw is simply an inclined plane that spirals around a shaft (**1**). The ratio of the screw's circumference to the distance advanced by the screw in one turn gives this machine's mechanical advantage. An archimedean screw (a screw in a cylinder, **2**) lifts river water to irrigate fields. The ancient Greek mathematician Archimedes was its reputed inventor although it may already have been known in ancient Egypt

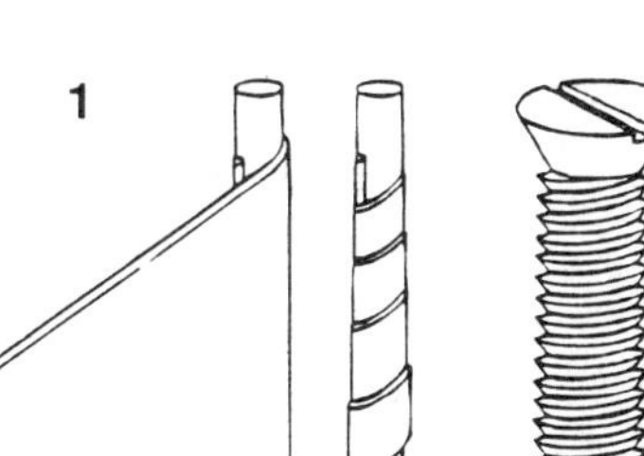

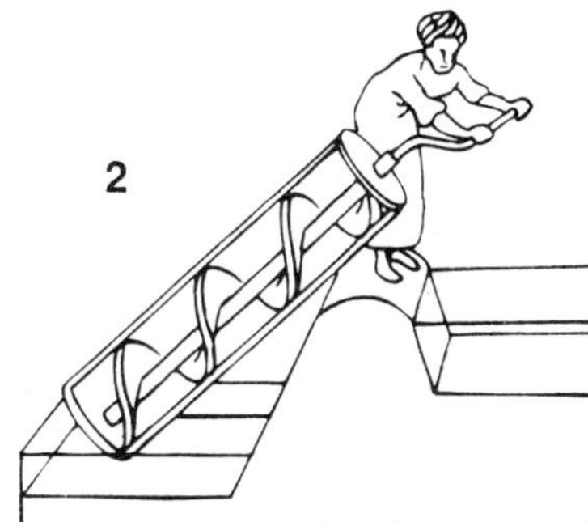

Inclined plane

2136

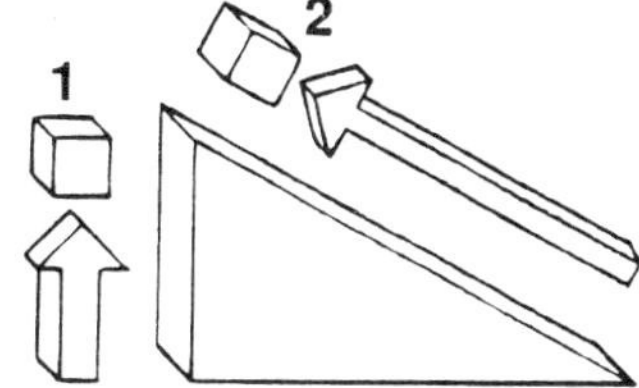

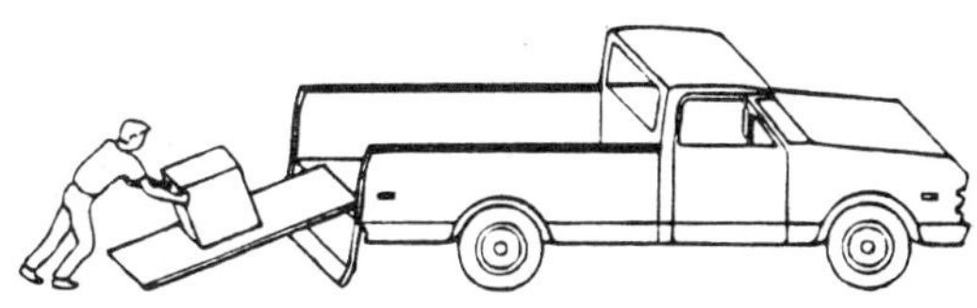

Much more effort is needed to move an object up a vertical face (**1**) than up an inclined plane (**2**). With an inclined plane, the mechanical advantage depends upon the length of the slope divided by the vertical height raised.

214 LIGHT

The light that we see is produced by electromagnetic radiation or electromagnetic waves with a particular range of frequencies and wavelengths. We perceive different wavelengths as different colors, ranging from violet (3.9 x 10^{-7} m) to red (7.8 x 10^{-7} m).

"Ordinary" or white light is a combination of the different wavelengths that produce red, orange, yellow, green, blue, indigo and violet: the seven colors of the rainbow forming what is known as the visible spectrum. Objects such as the Sun and stars or electric light bulbs give off their own light, but objects such as the Moon, rocks and plants only reflect light. Most of the objects around us do not produce light but are seen because they reflect light.

How light travels

2141 A simple test proves that light travels in straight lines. The test involves a light bulb (**1**), and three vertically mounted cards (**2, 3, 4**) each with a pinhole at the same level. The light can be seen through the holes only when all three are in a straight line.

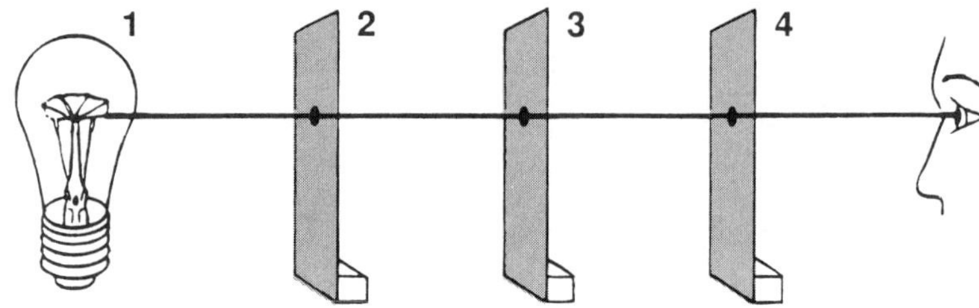

Visible spectrum

2142 A glass prism (**1**) splits a beam of white light into the seven colors of the visible spectrum. A second prism (**2**) will recombine the colors to give white light again.
a White light
b Red end of spectrum
c Violet end of spectrum
A mass of raindrops in air acts as a giant prism, splitting sunlight into the colors of the rainbow.

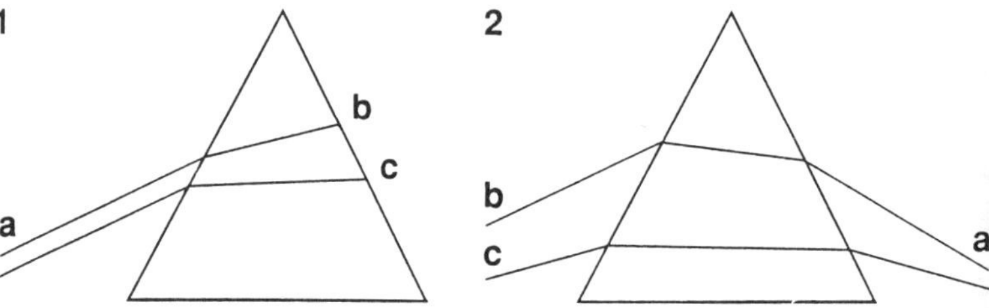

Colored substances
When white light falls on colored substances, most of these substances absorb some wavelengths in the spectrum and reflect others. The wavelengths a substance reflects account for its color.
1 A white substance reflects all the colors of the spectrum
2 A black substance absorbs all the colors of the spectrum
3 A red substance appears red because it reflects the spectrum's red wavelengths but absorbs others

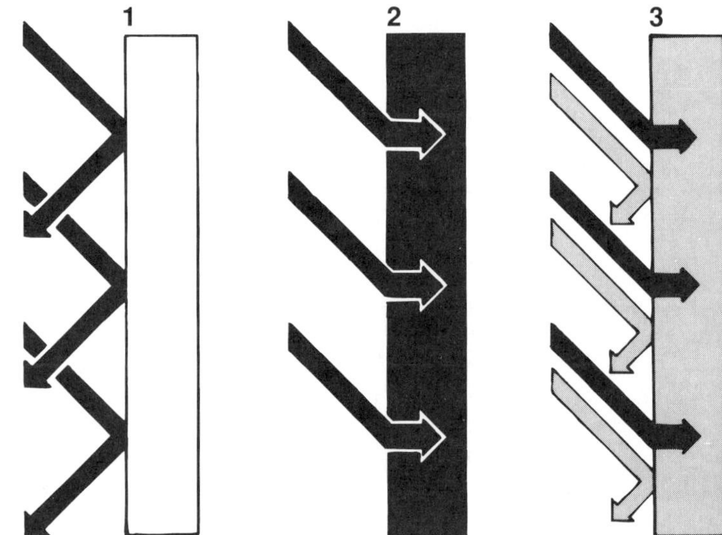

Light intensity

2143 Light intensity varies inversely with the square of the distance between source and lit surface. The amount of light falling onto a square (**1**) from a light source, is spread over four such squares (**2**) that are twice as far from the light or, onto nine squares (**3**), at three times the distance.

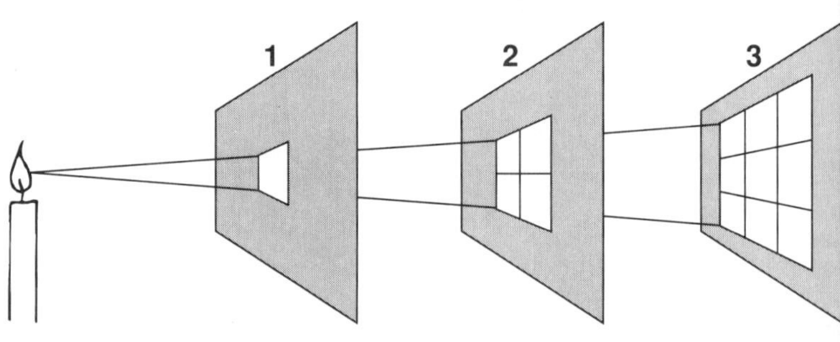

Mirrors

2144

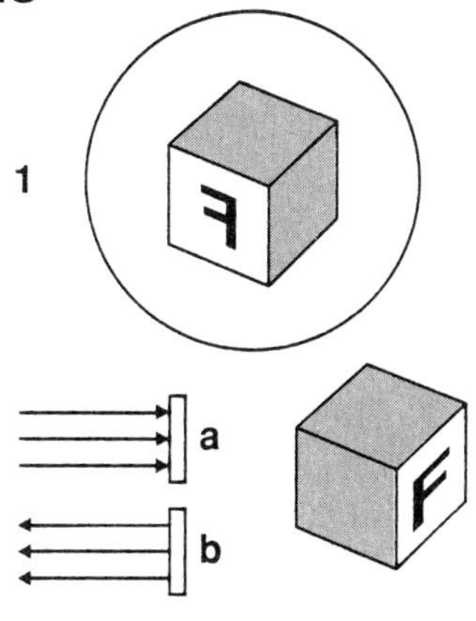

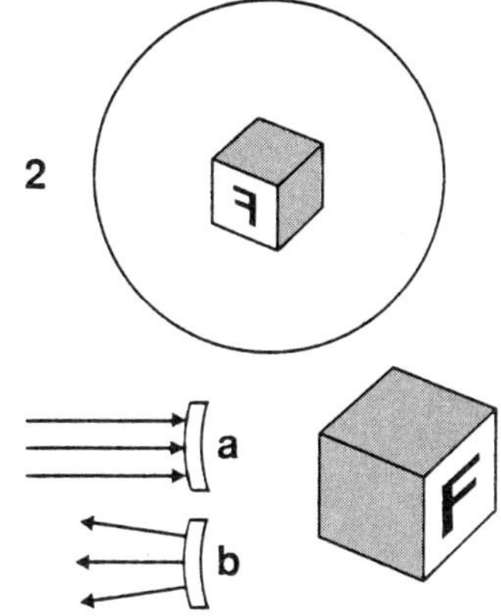

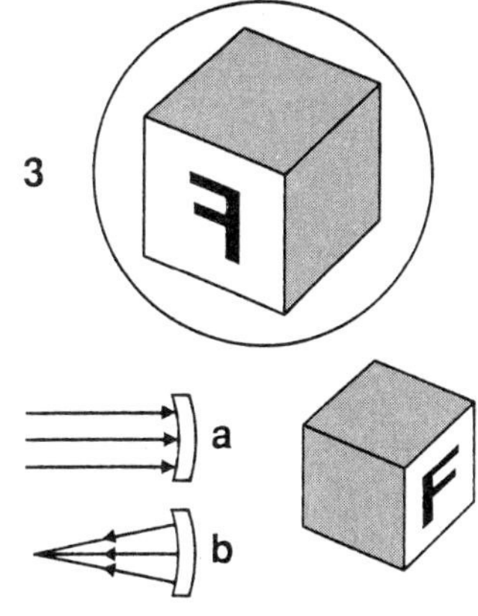

Mirrors and other shiny surfaces change the direction in which rays of light (**a**) travel by reflecting light (**b**).

1 Flat mirror
A flat mirror produces an image that appears as far behind the mirror as the original object is in front. The image is upright and the same size as the object but reversed, i.e. the left of the object becomes the right of the image and vice versa.

2 Convex mirror
A convex mirror gives a larger field of view than the same size flat mirror. For this reason, convex mirrors are often used as rear-view mirrors in cars. The image seen in a convex mirror is upright, reversed, and smaller than the original object.

3 Concave mirror
A concave mirror produces an image that is larger than the object it is reflecting and gives a smaller field of vision.

Lenses

2145 Lenses and other transparent substances change the direction of light by bending (refracting).

Types
1 Double convex: used in magnifying glasses
2 Plano-convex: used in some slide projectors
3 Concavo-convex: used to combat farsightedness
4 Double concave: used to produce reduced images
5 Plano-concave: used with other lenses in cameras
6 Convexo-concave: used to combat nearsightedness

1 2 3 4 5 6

Concave lens
A concave lens is thinner at the center than at the edges. It bends parallel light rays outward as they pass through the lens. A concave lens produces a reduced image that is the right way up and appears on the same side as the original object (**1**). This is a virtual (not real) image and it cannot be focused onto a screen.

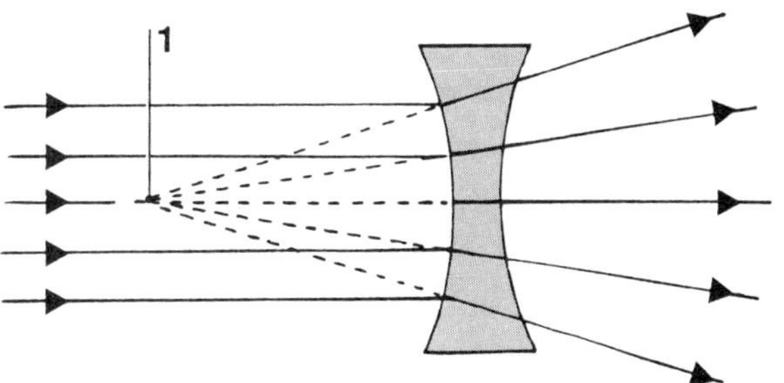

Convex lens
A convex lens is thicker at the center than at the edges. It bends light rays inward to meet at a focal point (**1**) behind the lens, producing a real image. The distance from the center of the lens (**2**) to the focal point is the focal length. An object that is less than one focal length from the lens becomes an enlarged image, the correct way up on the same side of the lens. If the object is moved further away a reduced inverted image is seen on the opposite side of the lens.

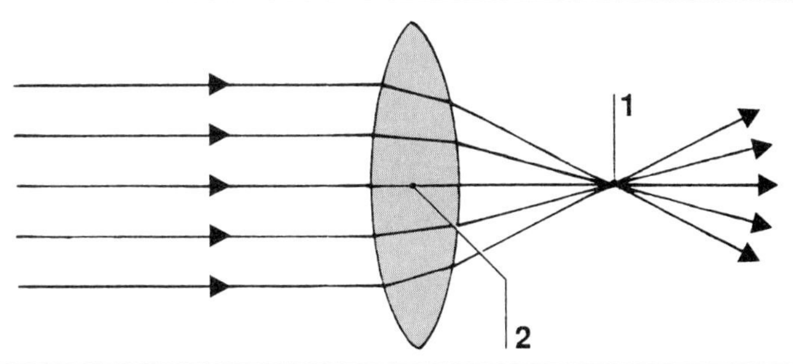

215 SOUND

Properties of sound

2151

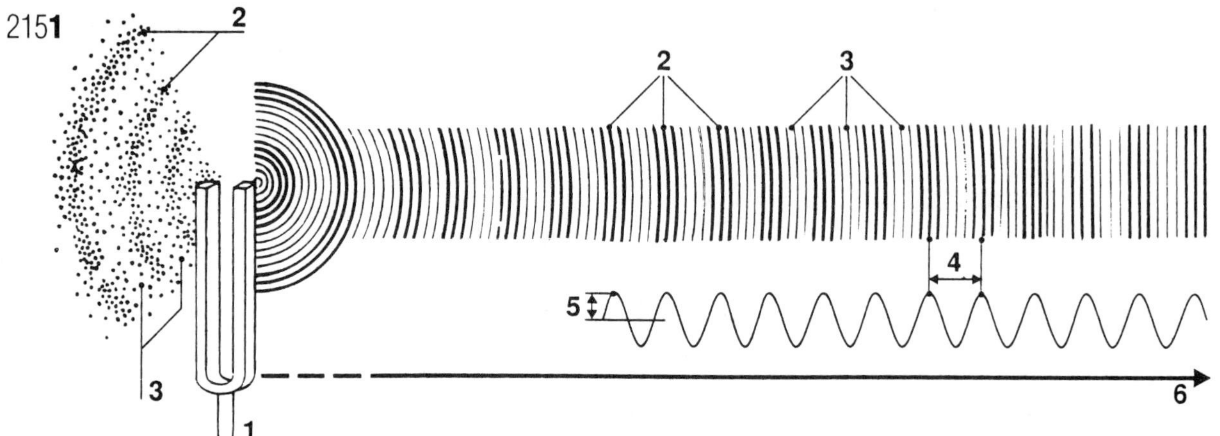

Sound is produced when an object such as a metal bar vibrates back and forth. The bar's vibrations send pressure waves through air. Ears detect waves of certain frequencies as sound.

Sound waves are regions of condensation (contraction) and rarefaction (expansion) which alternate through a medium surrounding a vibrating object, i.e. one that is producing the sound.

1 Tuning fork vibrating in air
2 Condensation: air molecules are compressed as fork vibrates outward
3 Rarefaction: air molecules spread out into the space left as the tuning fork vibrates inward
4 Wavelength
5 Amplitude
6 Frequency: number of waves passing a given point in one second

Pitch and quality

2152

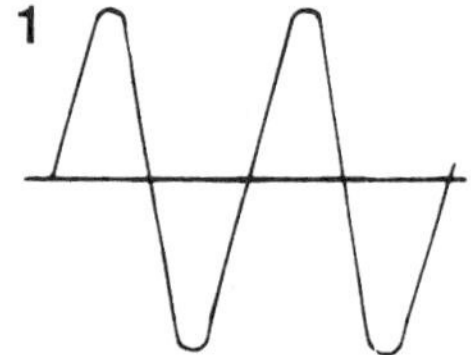

2 3 4

A sound's pitch (highness or lowness) and quality depend upon the nature of its sound waves.

1 Long-interval (low-frequency) waves giving low-pitched sound
2 Short-interval (high-frequency) waves giving high-pitched sound
3 Regular waves giving musical sound
4 Irregular waves giving noise

How sound travels

2153 Sound travels faster through some mediums than others. The chart compares the ability of some mediums to transmit sound.

1 Iron
2 Wood
3 Brick
4 Water
5 Air

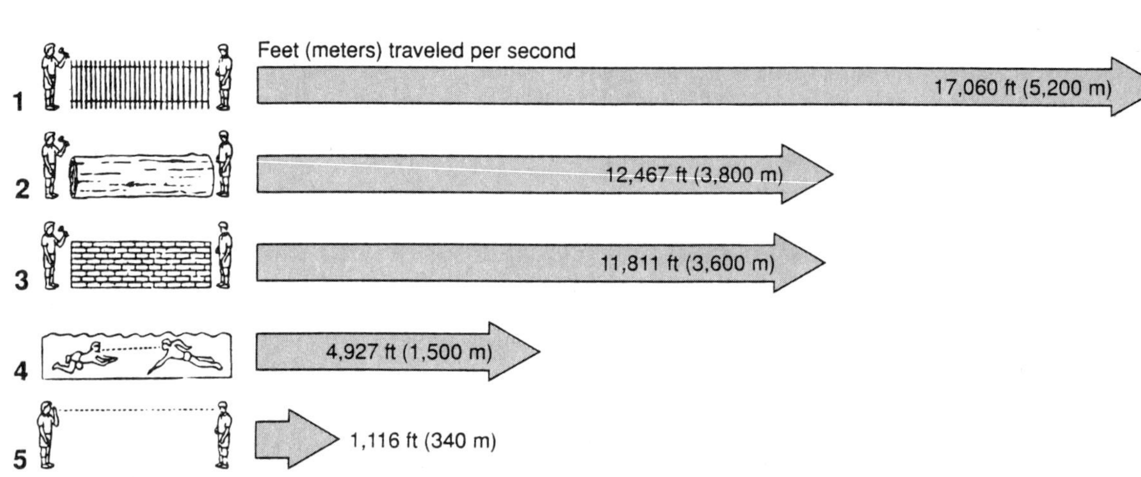

Intensity and loudness

2154

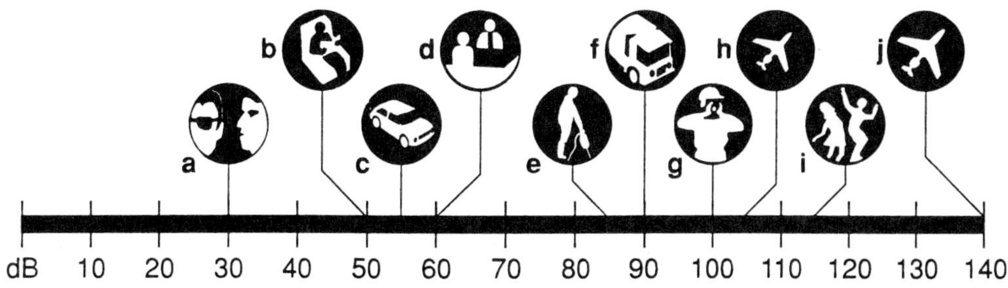

Sound intensity, measured in decibels (dB), increases with the energy of sound-producing vibrations as these, in turn, increase sound waves' amplitude. Loudness is perceived intensity: mid-frequency sounds seem louder to us than high or low sounds of the same intensity.

The chart and scale illustrate common noises and their decibel ratings at certain distances. Noises rated at 120–130 dB cause pain; at above 140 dB they can harm ears permanently.

Noise	Distance ft	Distance m	dB	Noise	Distance ft	Distance m	dB
a Whisper	15	5	30	**f** Heavy traffic	50	15	90
b In an urban home	—	—	50	**g** Loud shout	50	15	100
c Light traffic	50	15	55	**h** Jet taking off	2000	600	105
d Conversation	1	3	60	**i** Full volume disco	—	—	117
e Pneumatic drill	50	15	85	**j** Airplane taking off	200	60	140

216 ELECTRICITY AND MAGNETISM

What is electricity?

2161

Electricity has to do with the way atoms behave. All atoms are made up of subatomic particles: electrons (**1**), protons (**2**), and neutrons (**3**).

1 Electrons are negatively charged (-)
2 Protons are positively charged (+)
3 Neutrons are neutral – they have no charge

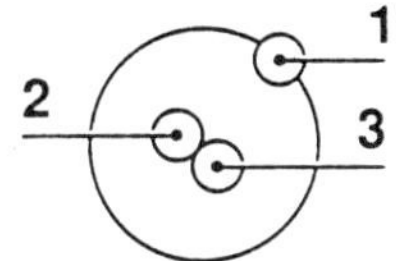
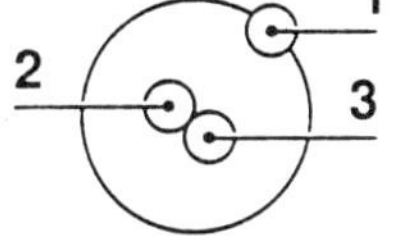

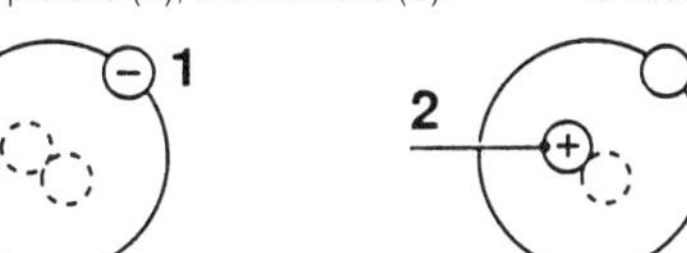

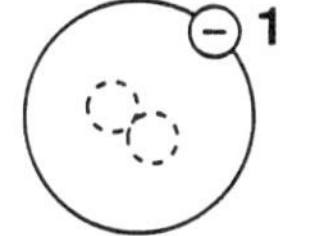

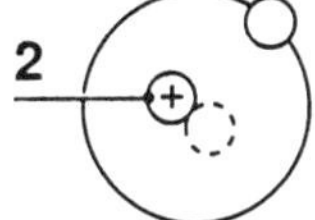

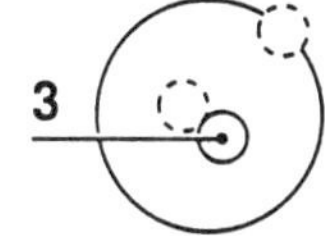

Properties of subatomic particles
The subatomic particles: electrons, protons, and neutrons, react toward each other in a particular way.

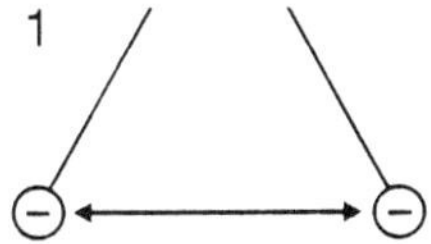

1 Negatively charged particles repel each other

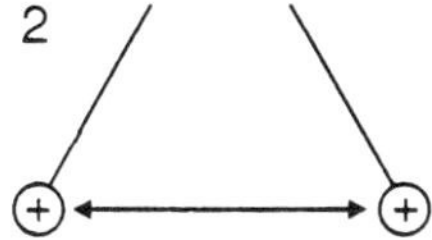

2 Positively charged particles repel each other

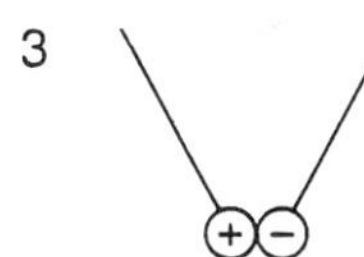

3 Opposite charges will attract each other

Electricity is energy released when negatively charged electrons (**1**) move from atom to atom.

Ions (electrically charged atoms)

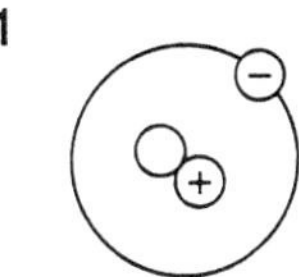

1 In electrically neutral atoms, the numbers of electrons and protons are equal.

2 Removing an electron (**a**) from an electrically neutral atom produces a positively charged ion.

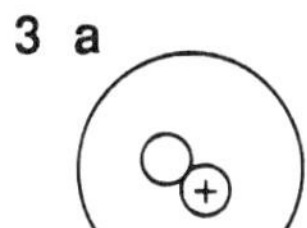

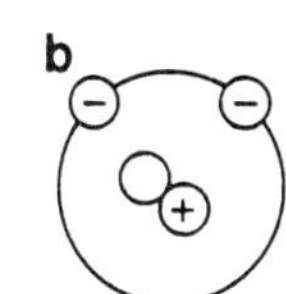

3 In an ion there is a different number of protons than electrons. If there are more protons, it is a positive (or positively-charged) ion (**a**), if there are more electrons it is a negative (or negatively-charged) ion (**b**).

Electric current

2162 An electric current is a continuous flow of electrons through a conductor, such as a copper wire.
1 Static electricity
2 Direct current (DC). Electrons move between atoms in one direction only from the negative to positive terminal within the electric circuit. The electric current produced by a battery is an example of a direct current.
3 Alternating current (AC). Here electrons move between atoms, first one way, then another, and continue to do so very quickly, generating energy as they move.

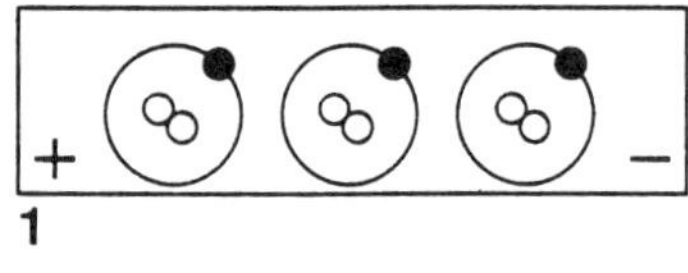

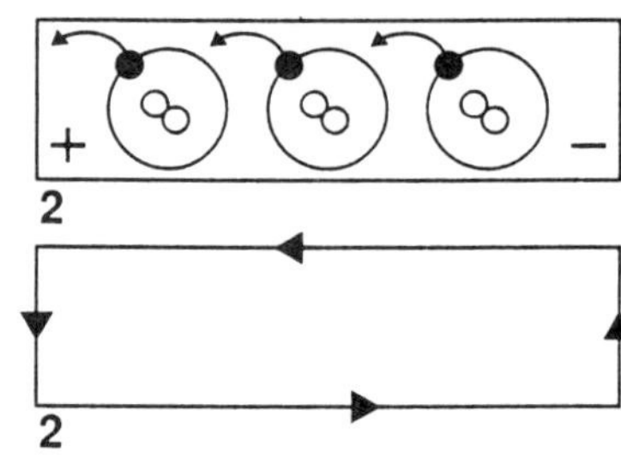

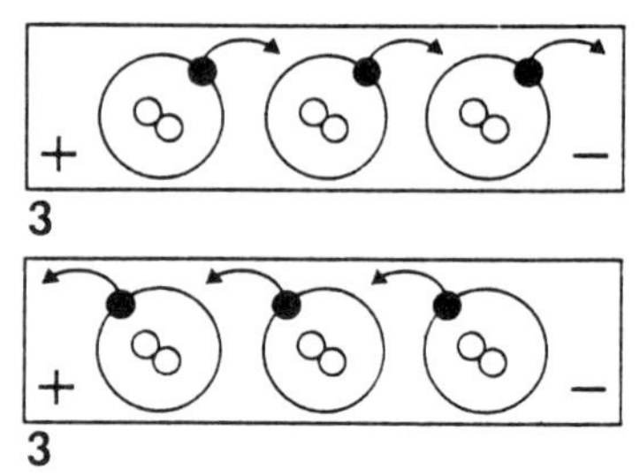

Magnetism

2163 Magnetism is an invisible force that attracts some materials to each other. Most permanent magnets are "ferromagnetic" metals. The tiny molecules within ferromagnetic material each act like miniature magnets and are called dipoles.
1 In an unmagnetized bar they form closed chains – their north and south poles, (the opposite poles) attract and there are no free poles.
2 When the bar is magnetized, the closed chains of dipoles are broken and aligned. This produces free poles at each end of the bar.

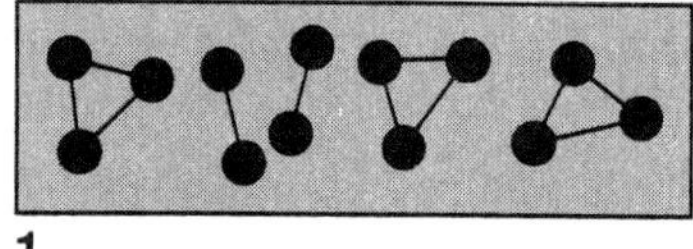

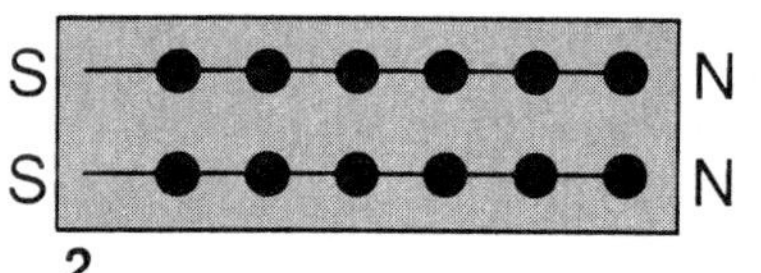

Magnetic objects

2164 **1** Natural magnets include substances such as lodestone
2 Man-made magnets are metal bars

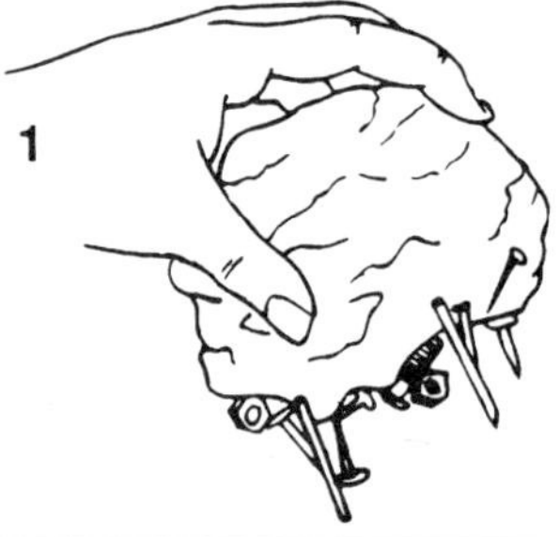

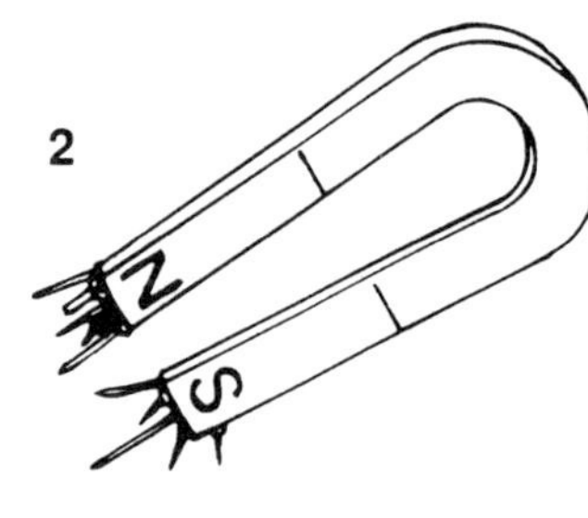

Induced magnets

2165

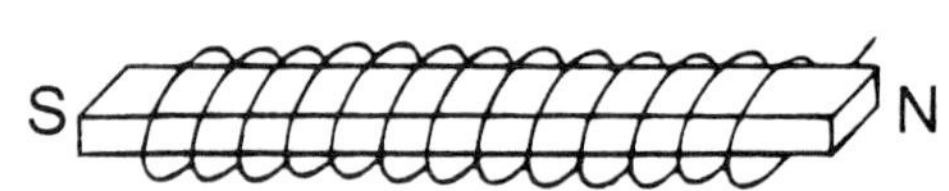

1 When an electric current is passed along a wire, a magnetic field (**a**) is created around it.
2 When this wire is then wrapped around a piece of metal, it causes the metal to become magnetized by lining up its dipoles in such a way as to leave north and south poles free. These are called electromagnets. Scrap metal merchants often use large electromagnets to pick up used vehicles – the magnet loses its power when the electric current is switched off, and the vehicle can be dropped where it is needed.

Magnetic fields

2166 A magnet is surrounded by an invisible magnetic field, strongest at its north and south poles.
1 The unlike poles of two magnets attract one another
2 Like poles repel one another

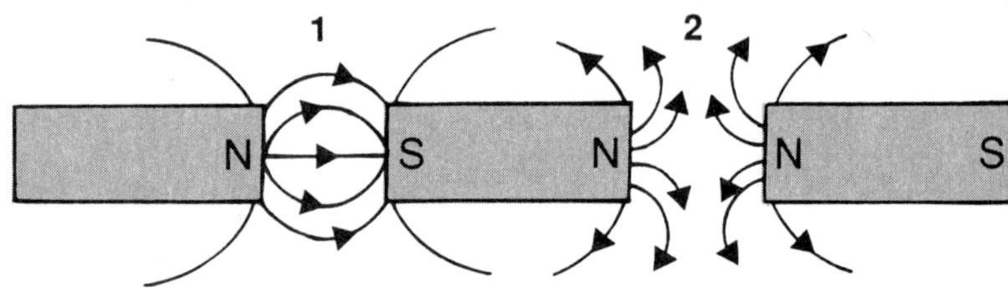

Electromagnetism

2167 Light, radio waves, X-rays, and other forms of radiant energy are transmitted through space as waves of energy called electromagnetic waves. Electromagnetic waves have alternating crests (**1**) and troughs (**2**), like the waves formed when a stone is dropped into a pool of still water. The distance between the crests of the waves is called the wavelength and it is measured in meters. The number of waves per second is called the frequency and is measured in hertz (Hz). All electromagnetic waves travel at the speed of light, which is the frequency of an electromagnetic wave multiplied by its wavelength. Light moves through a vacuum at 186,282 mi (299,792 km) per second.

Types of waves

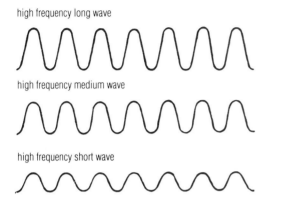

high frequency long wave

high frequency medium wave

high frequency short wave

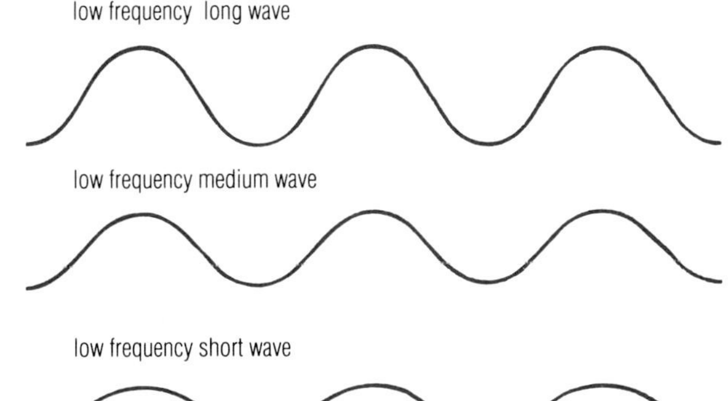

Electromagnetic spectrum

2168

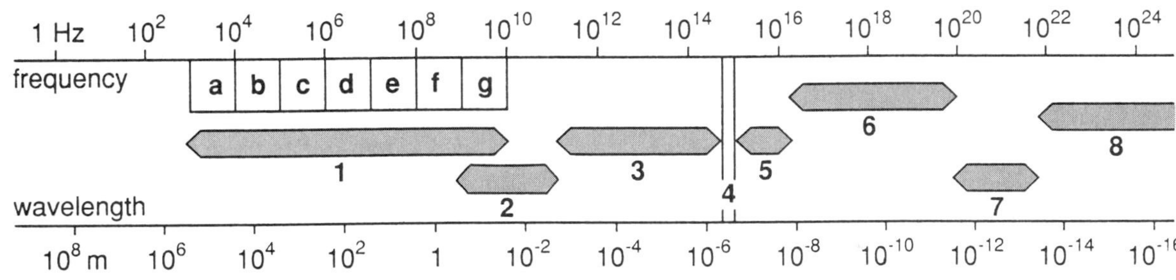

The diagram shows the various forms of radiant energy arranged, in order of their frequency and wavelength, to produce an electromagnetic spectrum. The upper scale gives the frequency in hertz; the lower scale gives the wavelength in meters.

1 Radio waves: used for transmitting radio and television

2 Radar and microwaves: radar devices detect unseen objects at a distance by bouncing radar waves off them. Microwave ovens are used to cook food very quickly

3 Infrared waves: waves of radiant heat emitted by all hot objects

4 Visible light: the part of the electromagnetic spectrum that our eyes can detect

5 Ultraviolet light: invisible radiation that produces vitamin D in the body and causes skin to tan. In large amounts, ultraviolet radiation can harm body cells

6 X-rays: radiation used to photograph the bones in the body and to detect defects in metal structures. Overexposure to X-rays causes harm to the cells of the body

7 Gamma rays: rays emitted during the decay of some radioisotopes

8 Cosmic rays: rays caused by nuclear explosions and nuclear reactions in space. Most cosmic rays reaching the Earth are absorbed by its atmosphere

Radio waves

These comprise the section (**a–g**) of the electromagnetic spectrum shown and described. By international agreement, each radio waveband has specific uses. Each band is named: examples are given of how it might be used

a VLF (very low frequency): special time signals for scientists

b LF (low frequency or "longwave"): ships' radio signals; AM radio

c MF (medium frequency or "medium wave"): police transmissions; AM radio

d HF (high frequency or "shortwave"): amateur "ham" radio

e VHF (very high frequency): FM radio; black and white television

f UHF (ultrahigh frequency): color television

g SHF (superhigh frequency): space and satellite communications

217 MEASUREMENTS IN PHYSICS

Volume

2171 This is the amount of space occupied by an object. The volume of a solid can be found by placing it in a measuring cylinder filled up with water to see by how much the water level rises or is displaced (**1**). The volume of a hollow object can be found by measuring the amount of water needed to fill it.

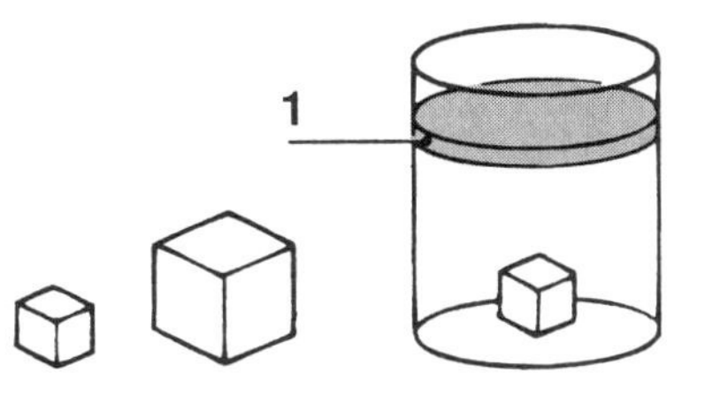

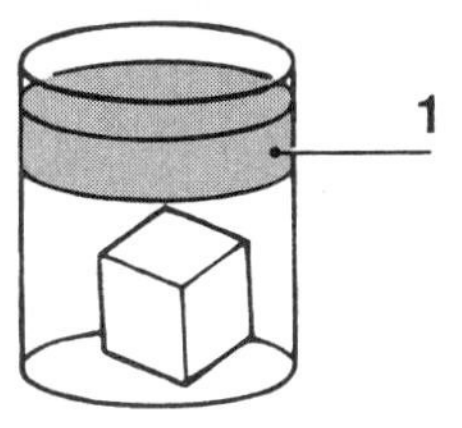

2172 Weight
2173 Mass
2174 Density
218 **Physics glossary**

Weight

2172 On Earth, weight is the force with which gravity pulls an object toward the Earth's center. Gravitational force decreases with distance from the Earth's center, so the further away an object moves from the Earth's center, the lighter the object becomes. Weight can be measured with a spring balance (**1**).

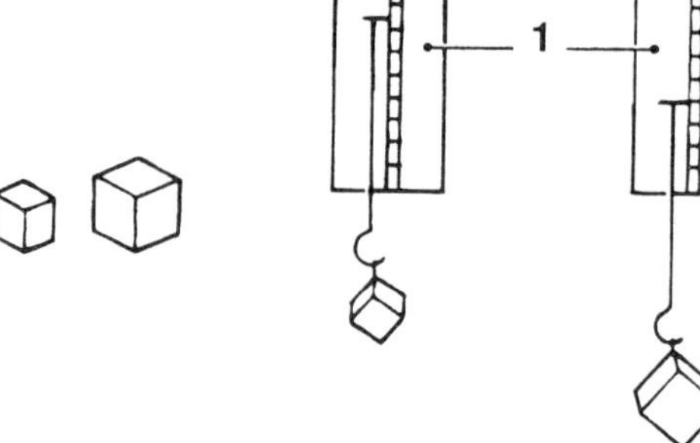

Mass

2173 This is the amount of matter an object contains. The greater its mass, the greater the force needed to alter its speed. Mass is not the same as weight. An astronaut is weightless in space, yet his mass is the same as it was on Earth. An object's mass can be measured by using a beam balance (**1**) to compare it with objects whose mass is known.

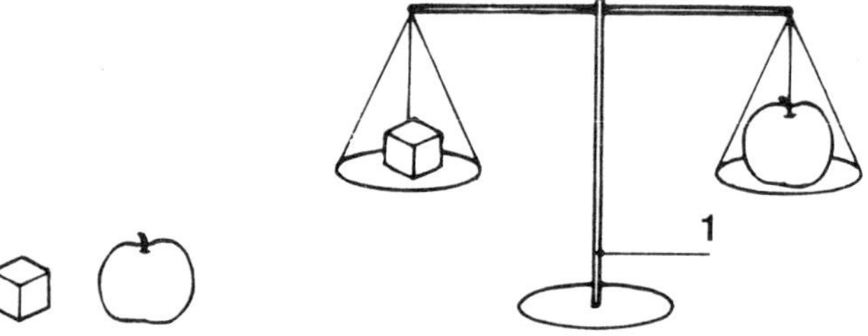

Density

2174 If an object with a small volume has the same mass and contained the same amount of material as an object with a larger volume, the smaller object is said to have the greater density. The definition of density is "mass per unit volume." Density is calculated by dividing an object's mass by its volume.

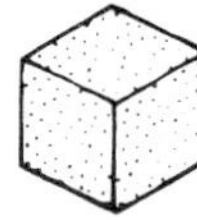

218 PHYSICS GLOSSARY

acceleration Rate of change in velocity, measured in feet (meters) per second per second (ft(m)/sec²).
acoustics The study of sound waves.
adhesion A force of attraction between molecules.
aerodynamics The study of the flow of gases, especially air.
alpha particle A helium nucleus, with a positive electric charge.
alternating current A rapidly reversing electric current.
ampere/amp The unit of electric current in the international system.
amplifier An electronic device that increases the strength of a signal.
amplitude A wave's greatest displacement from equilibrium.
anode A positive electrode.
Archimedes' principle A body submersed in a liquid loses weight equal to that of the volume of liquid that it displaces.
atom The smallest part of an element capable of taking part in a chemical change.
atomic number The number of protons in the nucleus of an atom.
atomic weight *see* relative atomic mass.
barometer An instrument for measuring atmospheric pressure.
beta particle An electron emitted by an isotope undergoing radioactive decay.
boiling point The temperature at which a liquid's vapor pressure equals external pressure.
Boyle's law At a constant temperature the volume of a given mass of gas is inversely proportional to its pressure.
buoyancy The upthrust (upward force) on a body placed in a fluid.
Calorie/calorie A calorie is the amount of heat needed to raise the temperature of a gram of water by 1° C. A Calorie (kilocalorie) is 1,000 calories.
capacitance A system's electrical capacity for storing an electric charge.
capillarity The rise or fall of a liquid in a narrow tube, caused by the relative attraction of its molecules for each other and the tube wall.
cathode A negative electrode.
cathode-ray tube A vacuum tube and cathode forming the picture tube in television receivers.
Celsius The centigrade temperature scale in which water freezes at 0° C and boils at 100° C.
centripetal force A force that acts radially inward on an object moving in a circular path.
concave Curving inward.
condensation The change from vapor into liquid.
conduction 1 Heat transfer from molecule to molecule. **2** Electron flow from atom to atom through a conductor.
conductor 1 An object conducting heat. **2** A substance conducting an electric current.
conservation of mass and energy The principle that, in any system, the sum of mass plus energy is constant.
conservation of momentum The principle that, in any system, linear or angular momentum is constant unless an external force acts on the system.
convection Heat transfer by means of currents circulating through fluids.
convex Curving outward.
coulomb The unit of electric charge, defined as the quantity of electricity conveyed by one ampere in one second.
curie A unit measuring the activity of a radioactive substance.
current The flow of electricity through a conductor.
decay The breakdown of a radioactive substance, producing daughter (decay) products.
decibel A logarithmic unit of sound intensity.
density Mass per unit volume.
diffraction After passing an obstacle or through a narrow slit, waves (e.g. of light) interfere with each other and may bend or spread, giving rise to this effect.
diffusion The mixing of substances due to the motion of their particles.
diode An electronic device with two electrodes; often used as a rectifier.
direct current An electric current that always flows in the same direction.
döppler effect Apparent change in the frequency of light waves or sound waves due to the relative motion of the observer and the source of the waves.
efficiency The ratio of a machine's energy output to energy input.
Einstein's law The law of the equivalence of mass and energy, expressed as $E = mc^2$ or

continued

Physics glossary continued

energy equals mass times the velocity of light squared.
elasticity The ability of a substance that has been deformed to regain its original size and shape when the stress is removed.
electricity Phenomena related to static electric charges and electric currents.
electrode A terminal that conducts electricity toward or away from a conductor in a circuit.
electrolyte A dissolved substance conducting, and decomposed by, an electric current.
electromagnet A temporary magnet produced when electric current flows through wire that has been coiled around soft iron.
electromagnetic radiation Waves of energy associated with electric and magnetic fields.
electromagnetism The study of electric and magnetic fields and their interaction.
electron A subatomic particle carrying a negative charge.
electronics The use and study of electricity in semiconductors.
energy The capacity for doing work.
engine A device converting one form of energy into another, especially mechanical energy.
evaporation Conversion of a liquid to a vapor, below its boiling point.
Fahrenheit scale The temperature scale which measures the melting point of ice at 32° and the boiling point of water at 212°.
fallout Radioactive matter which has fallen to Earth after a nuclear explosion.
farad A unit of capacitance. A conductor has a capacitance of one farad if a charge of one coulomb changes its potential by one volt.
ferromagnetism The magnetic property of cobalt, iron, nickel, and some alloys.
fiber optics The use and study of light transmission through fine, flexible glass, and plastic tubes.
fission The splitting of an atom's nucleus to release subatomic particles and energy.
fluid A (gas or liquid) substance which takes the shape of its container.
flux A flow of particles, fluid, or an electric or magnetic field.
force Something applied which alters a body's state of rest or motion.
freezing Change of state from liquid to solid.
frequency Number of cycles or waves per second.
fundamental particle Theoretically indivisible subatomic particles grouped as matter particles (electrons, muons, taus, neutrinos, and quarks) and force particles (W and Z bosons, gluons, gravitons, and photons).
fusion 1 Melting. **2** A nuclear reaction forming a heavier nucleus from light atomic nuclei and in the process releasing nuclear energy.
g Acceleration in free fall due to gravity: on Earth about 32 feet per second per second (9.81 m/sec^2.
gamma rays Penetrating extreme shortwave radiation emitted in decay of some radioactive substances.
geiger counter A device for measuring radioactivity.
gravitation The mutual attraction between bodies, due to their masses.
gravity Intensity of gravitation measured at the surface of a star, planet or other heavenly body.
half-life The time in which half the atoms in a radioactive isotope decay.
heat A form of energy passed between bodies of differing temperature.
hertz A unit of frequency with a value of one cycle per second.
hydrodynamics The study of moving liquids and fluids.
hydrostatics The study of forces in stationary liquids and fluids.
induction (electromagnetic) Inducing a voltage in an electrical conductor by changing the magnetic field around it.
inertia A body's tendency to maintain a state of rest or of uniform motion.
infrared radiation Invisible heat radiation from hot bodies.
integrated circuit A tiny electrical circuit, comprising a semiconductor chip with many electronic components.
interference The effects of imposing one set of waves on another.
ion An electrically charged atom or group of atoms.
isotope Atoms of an element with an identical number of protons but differing numbers of neutrons.
joule A unit of work or energy transfer. One joule is equal to work done by a force of one newton moved about one yd (1 m) in the direction of the force.
kelvin scale An absolute temperature scale in which 0 K (zero kelvin) equals -459.67° F (-273.15° C), absolute zero, and 273.15 K corresponds to 32° F (0° C).
kinetic energy The energy possessed by moving bodies.
latent heat Heat released or absorbed when a substance changes state without a change in temperature.
lens A device causing light rays or subatomic particles to converge or diverge as they pass through it.
lever A rigid bar turned about a fixed point (fulcrum) to support or move a load; a simple form of machine.
light Electromagnetic radiation with wavelengths visible to the eye.
lux A unit of illumination equal to a luminous flux of one lumen spread over 1 sq m.
machine A device performing work, especially where a smaller force or effort moves a greater load.
mach number A unit of velocity. Mach 1 is the speed of sound; Mach 5 is described as hypersonic.
magnet A substance able to attract iron and which produces a magnetic field.
magnetic field An area of magnetic influence.
magnetism Forces of attraction and repulsion associated with magnets.
mass The amount of matter in a body.
mass–energy equation *see* Einstein's law.
mass number The number of nucleons (protons and neutrons) in the nucleus of an atom.
mechanical advantage The ratio of load to effort produced by a machine.
mechanics The study of how objects move under the influence of forces.
microwaves Electromagnetic radiation between radio and infrared wavelengths.
moment The turning effect produced by a force around a point.
momentum Mass multiplied by velocity.
motor A machine that converts electrical energy into mechanical energy.
neutron A subatomic particle with roughly the mass of a proton and no electric charge.
newton The unit of force giving a mass of about 2.2 lb (1 kg) an acceleration of about 1 yd (1 m) per second per second.
nuclear energy Energy released by the conversion of matter to energy during a chain reaction caused by nuclear fission or fusion in a bomb or reactor.
nucleus An atom's positively charged core of one or more protons and (except in hydrogen) one or more neutrons.
ohm The unit of electrical resistance. *See also* Resistance.
optics The study of light and its uses.
oscillation A repetitive vibration with a regular frequency.
Pascal The unit of pressure produced when one newton acts on about 1 sq m.
Pascal's principle This states that pressure applied to any part of an enclosed fluid acts without loss on all other parts.
pendulum A suspended weight swinging regularly under gravity's influence.
permeability The ability of a substance to let another substance pass through it.
photon A unit or quantum of electromagnetic radiation.
physics The study of matter and energy.
pitch Sound frequency.
Planck's law Electromagnetic radiation consists of units (quanta or photons).
plasma A gas with roughly equal numbers of negative and positive ions.
pneumatics The study of the mechanical properties of gases.
polarization In transverse waves, vibrations confined to one plane.
poles Two points of a magnet where magnetism seems concentrated.
potential difference The energy difference that tends to make an electric charge or current move. It is measured in volts.
power The rate of energy transfer.
pressure Force per unit area.
prism A transparent, solid object, with at least two plane faces, that bends a light beam and splits it into its component colors.
proton A positively charged subatomic particle.
quantum mechanics A system of mechanics that supplanted Newtonian mechanics in the study of subatomic particles.
quantum theory The theory that electromagnetic radiation consists of units called quanta or photons.
rad A unit of radiation absorbed from a radioactive source.
radar A system using reflected radio waves to locate aircraft, etc.
radiation Electromagnetic and radioactive energy emitted as rays, waves, or particles.
radioactivity The emission of subatomic particles and rays due to the disintegration of the atomic nuclei of certain isotopes of some elements.
radioisotope An isotope that is radioactive.

continued

Physics glossary continued

218 **rectifier** An electrical device that converts alternating current into direct current.
refraction The bending of a sound wave or ray of light as it passes from one medium to another.
relative atomic mass (atomic weight) The mass (quantity of matter) of atoms.
relativity, theory of Einstein's two-part theory involving the idea of a four-dimensional space–time continuum.
resistance The ratio between the potential difference across a conductor and the current carried; measured in ohms.
semiconductor A substance with properties between those of an electrical insulator and a conductor at room temperature, but with conductivity modified by temperature and impurities; crucial in modern electronic devices.
SI units International system of units (*Système International d'Unités*) based on the kilogram, meter, and second.
solenoid A wire coil partly surrounding an iron core. When current flows through the wire it produces an electromagnetic effect.
sound The phenomenon produced by certain pressure waves reaching the ear.
spectrum A band of electromagnetic radiation with components separated into their relative wavelengths.
strain Deformation due to stress.
superconductivity The increase in electrical conductivity and decrease in resistance, in certain substances, at very low temperatures.
surface tension The cohesion of a liquid's surface caused by the inward attraction of its molecules.
temperature Degree of "hotness" measured in Celsius, Fahrenheit, etc.
thermodynamics The study of heat and heat-related energy.
transducer A device that converts one kind of wave signal into another.
transformer A device transferring an alternating current from one circuit to another.
transistor A semiconductor device used, as a rectifier, amplifier or switch.
ultrasonics The study of frequencies higher than those we can hear.
ultraviolet radiation Electromagnetic radiation that has a wavelength between visible light and X-rays.
unified field theory A theory still being sought after that will relate electromagnetic, gravitational, and nuclear fields.
vacuum A space without matter.
vapor A gas that becomes a liquid under increased pressure.
vector A quantity that is direction as well as magnitude.
velocity Rate of motion in a particular direction.
viscosity In fluids, the resistance to flow.
volt The unit of potential difference.
watt The unit of power: one watt equals one joule per second.
wave A disturbance or pulse moving through space or a medium.
wavelength The crest-to-crest (or some comparable) distance between two waves.
weight The pull of gravity on an object. Weight is measured in newtons.
work Force multiplied by distance; work is measured in joules.
X-rays Electromagnetic radiation with a wavelength between those of ultraviolet light and gamma rays.

219 PHYSICISTS

Ampère, André Marie 1775–1836, French physicist and mathematician (**1**). Gave name to basic unit of electric current (ampere, amp). Laid foundations of science of electrodynamics through theoretical and experimental work after discovery in 1820 of magnetic effects of electric currents.

1

Becquerel, Antoine Henri 1852–1908, French physicist. Discovered "Becquerel rays," emitted from uranium salts in pitchblende, which led to isolation of radium and beginnings of modern nuclear physics. Shared 1903 Nobel prize for discovery of "radioactivity."
Bohr, Niels Henrik David 1885–1962, Danish physicist. Worked with Thomson at Cambridge and Rutherford at Manchester. Greatly extended theory of atomic structure when he explained spectrum of hydrogen by means of atomic model and quantum theory.
Boyle, Robert 1627–91, Irish physicist and chemist. (**2**) Co-founder of Royal Society. His 1661 *Sceptical Chymist* defines the chemical element as the practical limit of chemical analysis, and his celebrated Boyle's Law (1662) states that the pressure and volume of a gas are inversely proportional.
Broglie, Louis-Victor, 7th Duc de 1892–1987, French physicist. Younger brother of the physicist Maurice Broglie (6th Duc). Did research on quantum theory, and in 1929 won Nobel prize for pioneering work on undulatory theory of matter.
Curie, Marie (née Sklodowska) 1867–1934, Polish-born French physicist. Wife of Pierre Curie, with whom she worked on magnetism and radioactivity (she invented the term in 1898). Isolated polonium and (in 1910) pure radium.
Dirac, Paul Adrien Maurice 1902–84, English mathematical physicist. Worked on quantum mechanics, and gave complete mathematical formulation of Einstein's relativity theory in *The Principles of Quantum Mechanics* (1930).
Einstein, Albert 1879–1955, German-Swiss-American mathematical physicist. Ranks with such figures as Galileo and Newton as one of the great conceptual revisors of humanity's understanding of the universe.World-famous for his Special (1906) and General (1916) Theories of Relativity, and for his formulation of the mass-energy equation.

2

Fahrenheit, Gabriel Daniel 1686–1736, German physicist. Invented alcohol (1709) and mercury thermometers, as well as the temperature scale named after him. Was first to show that boiling point of liquids varies at different atmospheric pressures.
Faraday, Michael 1791–1867, English chemist and physicist. Creator of classical field theory and one of greatest experimental physicists. Discovered electromagnetic induction (1831), laws of electrolysis (1833), and rotation of polarized light by magnetism (1845).
Foucault, Jean Bernard Léon 1819–68, French physicist. Determined velocity of light by revolving mirror method and proved that light travels more slowly in water than in air (1850). In 1851, using freely suspended pendulum, proved that earth rotates.
Galilei, Galileo, known as Galileo 1564–1642, Italian astronomer, mathematician, and natural philosopher (**3**). Proposed and proved theorem that all falling bodies, great or small, descend with equal velocity. Convinced, after astronomical research, of truth of Copernican heliocentric theory.

3

continued

Physicists continued

219

Hertz, Heinrich Rudolf 1857–94, German physicist. Studied under Kirchhoff and von Helmholtz. In 1887, verified Clerk Maxwell's predictions by his fundamental discovery of electromagnetic waves, which, excepting wavelength, behave like light waves.
Hooke, Robert 1635–1703, English physicist, chemist, and architect. One of the most brilliant scientists of his age. Formulated Hooke's Law of extension and compression of elastic bodies, as well as effectively inventing the microscope and building the first Gregorian telescope.
Huygens, Christiaan 1629–93, Dutch physicist. In optics, first propounded undulatory theory of light, and discovered polarization. The "Principle of Huygens" is part of wave theory. Also discovered laws of collision of elastic bodies at same time as Wallis and Wren.
Joule, James Prescott 1818–89, English physicist who laid foundations for theory of conservation of energy. Famous for experiments in heat, which he showed to be a form of energy. The joule, a unit of work or energy, is named after him. With Kelvin, he devised an absolute scale of temperature.
Kelvin, William Thomson, 1st Baron of Largs 1824–1907, Irish-born Scottish physicist and mathematician. Proposed absolute, or Kelvin, temperature scale (1848) and, at same time as Clausius, established second law of thermodynamics. Also invented tide predictor and harmonic analyzer.
Mach, Ernst 1838–1916, Austrian physicist and philosopher whose writings greatly influenced Einstein. Contributed to science of projectiles, and gave name to ratio of speed of flow of gas to speed of sound (Mach number) and to angle of shock wave to direction of motion (Mach angle).
Maxwell, James Clerk 1831–79, Scottish physicist. One of the greatest ever theoretical physicists, whose work on the theory of electromagnetic radiation is considered to have paved the way for Einstein and Planck. Provided the mathematical treatment of Faraday's theory of electrical and magnetic forces.
Michelson, Albert Abraham 1852–1931, German-born American physicist, and first American scientist to win Nobel prize. Chiefly remembered for Michelson-Morley experiment to determine ether drift.
Newton, Sir Isaac 1642–1727, English scientist and mathematician (**4**). By 1684, he had demonstrated the whole of his famous gravitation theory, supposedly inspired by the fall of an apple in his garden in 1665/6. Independently of Leibniz, he discovered differential calculus. He also discovered that white light is composed of many colors.

4

Pauli, Wolfgang 1900–58, Austrian-born American theoretical physicist. In 1924, formulated "exclusion principle" that no two electrons can be in the same energy state simultaneously, and in 1957 carried out experiments confirming nonparity theory of Yang and Lee in nuclear interaction.
Planck, Max Ernst 1858–1947, German theoretical physicist. Work on laws of thermodynamics and black body radiation led him to formulation of quantum theory (1900), postulating energy changes occurring in violently abrupt instalments or quanta.
Rutherford, Ernest Rutherford, 1st Baron of Nelson, 1871–1937, New Zealand-born British pioneer of subatomic physics. Work led to revolutionary concept of atom as miniature universe, with nucleus surrounded by planetary electrons. Predicted existence of neutron.
Schrödinger, Erwin 1887–1961, Austrian physicist. Originated study of wave mechanics as part of quantum theory with his celebrated wave equation, and also made contribution to field theory.
Thomson, Sir Joseph John 1856–1940, English pioneer of nuclear physics, who discovered the electron. Demonstrated that 'corpuscles' (electrons) comprising cathode rays were nearly 2,000 times smaller in mass than lightest-known particle, hydrogen ion.
Torricelli, Evangelista 1608–47, Italian physicist and mathematician (**5**). First to discover fundamental principles of hydromechanics and (1644) to describe barometer or "torricellian tube." Greatly improved telescopes and microscopes, as well as making several mathematical discoveries.
Volta, Alessandro Giuseppe Anastasia, Count 1745–1827, Italian physicist (**6**). Inventor of electric battery, whose name is given to the unit of electrical potential difference, the volt. Developed theory of current electricity and made studies of heat and gases.
Waals, Johannes Diderik van der 1837–1923, Dutch physicist. Famous for discovery (1873) of van der Waal's equation, defining physical state of gas or liquid, and as investigator of weak attractive forces (van der Waal's forces) between molecules.
Wilson, Charles Thomson Rees 1869–1959, Scottish pioneer of atomic and nuclear physics, and researcher of atmospheric electricity. Devised cloud-chamber method of marking track of alpha-particles and electrons, thus allowing movement and interaction of atoms to be followed and photographed.

5

6

2**2**

Chemistry is the scientific study of the composition of matter and changes in its composition, called chemical changes. Matter makes up everything in the universe. Particles of matter can be packed close together, as in a solid, or spread far apart, as in a gas. Here we describe what matter is made of and what forms it most often takes. There are several branches of chemistry.

Major branches of chemistry
- Organic chemistry deals with carbon and its compounds
- Inorganic chemistry deals with non-carbon compounds
- Analytical chemistry determines what substances are made of
- Biochemistry involves the chemical processes of living things
- Physical chemistry uses mathematics to study chemical processes and energy

22**1** ATOMIC STRUCTURE

Atoms

221**1** An atom is the smallest unit of matter. It is the tiniest part of an element containing that element's properties and able to take part in chemical change. Atoms vary in weight more than size. All are so small that many billions form the smallest object anyone can see through an optical microscope. Elements are made up of atoms. Each element is made of one kind of atom.

Atomic structure

221**2** Atoms are made of small units called subatomic particles. Scientists have discovered more than 200 subatomic particles, some of which appear for only a tiny fraction of a second, others of which are stable and do not break down easily. Here we look at three of these stable particles – the proton, the neutron and the electron – which are important in determining the properties of elements.

Proton
This is part of the nucleus (central core) of an atom. The number of protons in an atom (known as the atomic number) determines the identity of an element. If an atom gains or loses a proton it becomes part of a different element. A proton has a mass of 1.6726×10^{-27} kg and a positive electrical charge of one unit.

1 Proton
2 Neutron
3 Electron

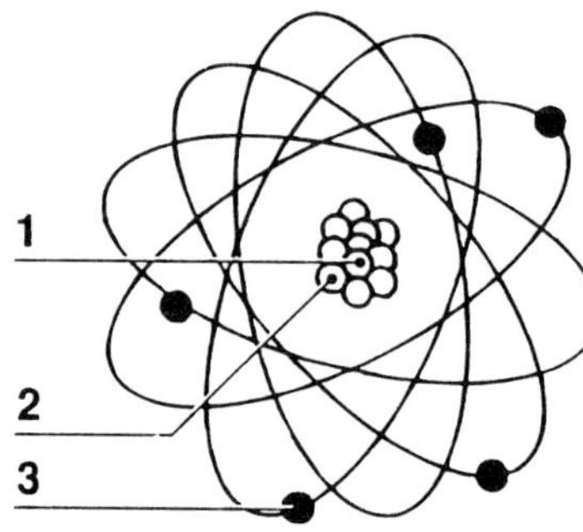

Neutron
This is also part of the atomic nucleus. The number of neutrons in an atom can vary without the element changing its identity. Forms of an element with different numbers of neutrons in the nucleus are called isotopes of the element. A neutron has a mass of 1.6749×10^{-27} kg. It does not carry an electrical charge, so is electrically neutral.

Electron
Electrons move around the nucleus of an atom at high speed, rather like planets orbiting the Sun. The arrangement of electrons in an atom determines an element's chemical behavior. An electron has a mass of 9.1096×10^{-31} kg and a negative electrical charge of one unit. Atoms have the same number of electrons as protons and so are electrically neutral.

Molecules

221**3** Two or more atoms joined together form a molecule. The atoms may be from the same element or from different elements. Molecules containing atoms of two or more elements are the units that make up compounds. If a molecule is broken down, it splits into smaller molecules or a combination of smaller molecules and atoms.

Molecules come in a huge range in sizes. For example:
1 Oxygen molecule: 2 atoms
2 Water molecule: 3 atoms
3 Rubber molecule: 13,000–65,000 atoms

Chemical formulas

221**4** A chemical formula is a kind of shorthand used by scientists to name different molecules. Listed are the formulas for some common molecules.

	Which atoms join?	Formula	Name
	2 oxygen atoms	O_2	oxygen

continued

Chemical formulas continued

2214**4**

Which atoms join?	Formula	Name
2 hydrogen atoms + 1 oxygen atom	H_2O	water
1 carbon atom + 2 oxygen atoms	CO_2	carbon dioxide
1 carbon atom + 4 hydrogen atoms	CH_4	methane
3 oxygen atoms	O_3	ozone
6 carbon atoms + 12 hydrogen atoms + 6 oxygen atoms	$C_6H_{12}O_6$	glucose
9 carbon atoms + 8 hydrogen atoms + 4 oxygen atoms	$C_9H_8O_4$	aspirin

Electrical bonds

2215**5**

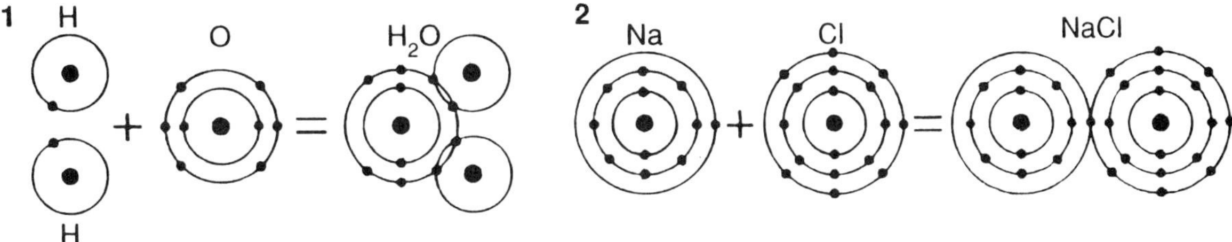

Atoms are linked to each other to make compounds by the sharing or transfer of electrons on the atom's outer shell. Stable compounds are combinations that give a total of eight electrons on the outer shell. Shown here are examples of two main bonding processes.

1 Covalent bonding Two hydrogen (H) atoms each share one positive electron with two negatively charged electrons on an oxygen (O) atom to produce a molecule of water (H_2O).

2 Electrovalent (ionic) bonding An electropositive sodium atom (Na) lends an electron to an electronegative chlorine (Cl) atom to produce a molecule of salt (NaCl).

Acids and alkalis

2216 These substances gain or lose protons. **Acids** give up protons to other substances, turn blue litmus red, and neutralize alkalis. **Alkalis** are bases that are soluble in water. Alkalis turn red litmus paper blue and tend to neutralize acids. Bases accept protons from other substances and react with acids to form salts and water. Salts are compounds that are formed when metals replace all or part of the hydrogen in an acid.

222 MATTER

States of matter

2221 **Element**
This is a single substance that cannot be broken down chemically into simpler substances. Gold, oxygen, and zinc are examples of elements. There are about 90 naturally occurring elements and about 20 more have been produced artificially in nuclear reactors or other machines, but not all of those are officially recognized.

Compound
This is made of two or more elements chemically joined to form a completely new substance. The new substance has different properties (characteristics and behavior) from the elements that went to produce it. For example, water, which is a liquid, is a compound of hydrogen and oxygen, which are gases. In any one compound the same elements always occur in the same proportions by weight.

Mixture
This is made of two or more elements that have not been chemically joined. This means that each substance keeps its own characteristics, and the substances can be separated without involving a chemical change. In a mixture, different ingredients can occur in any proportion.

Examples of mixtures

Type	Substances	States	Result
Solution This is a mixture of two or more substances that cannot be separated by filtering or other mechanical methods. Solutions can be liquid, solid or gaseous. The most common are liquid solutions, where a liquid, solid or gas dissolves in a liquid. The dissolved substance, the solute, spreads evenly through the solvent, the substance or substances in which it dissolves. For example, sugar, solute, dissolves in coffee, solvent.	Nitrogen + Oxygen	gas + gas	= Air
	Salt + Water	solid + liquid	= Brine
	Gasoline + Oil	liquid + liquid	= 2-stroke fuel
Suspension This is a mixture where one substance spreads evenly through another without dissolving. Suspensions include solids in liquids or gases, gases in liquids, and liquids in gases or liquids. Suspensions containing very small particles are colloids. Dust in air is a colloidal suspension. In a colloidal suspension, the suspended particles can be seen in a light beam, but in a solution, the solute cannot be seen in this way.	Air + Water	gas + liquid	= Cloud
	Carbon + Air	solid + gas	= Smoke
Emulsion A liquid evenly spread or dispersed through another liquid is called an emulsion. Emulsions include cosmetic lotions, lubricants, and paints. Droplets of the dispersed liquid remain suspended in the other liquid. In time, however, both liquids separate. This process can be delayed by adding emulsifying agents to an emulsion.	Oil + Vinegar	liquid + liquid	= Salad dressing
	Butterfat + Water	liquid + liquid	= Milk
	Water + Colored resins	liquid + solid	= Paint

Solids, liquids and gases

2222 A substance keeps its identity even when heating changes its state from a solid to a liquid or from a liquid to a gas. The solid, liquid and gas all contain the same molecules, but heat affects how much these move about. The hotter they become the more freely they can move. Molecules in a solid cannot freely move about. But they are never completely still and always vibrating. In a liquid the molecules can move, but only to a limited extent. In a gas they can move around completely freely.

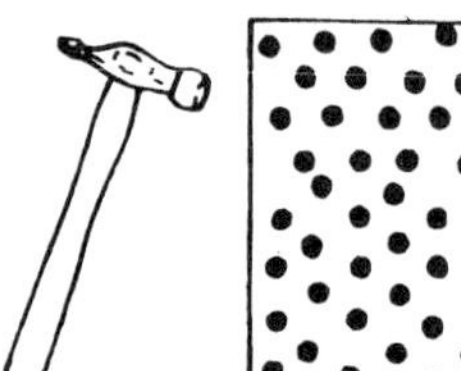

Solid
A solid takes up a definite amount of space. It will not alter its shape unless forced to do so.

Liquid
A liquid usually also takes up a definite amount of space but can alter its shape easily. It will take the shape of any container into which it is poured.

Gas
A gas has no definite size or shape. Because the molecules in a gas can move freely they will spread out to fill the whole of any container, however large. If a gas is not confined in a container it will simply continue to expand.

continued

Solids, liquids and gases continued

2222 A solid that is made hot enough will melt and become a liquid, and a liquid that is made hot enough will vaporize and become a gas. Similarly, a gas that is cooled sufficiently will condense and become a liquid, and a liquid that is cooled sufficiently freezes to become a solid. Below we list temperatures at which these changes take place for various substances.

	Freezing/ melting	boiling point
1 Hydrogen	-489° F (-259° C)	487° F (253° C)
2 Oxygen	-426° F (-219° C)	361° F (183°C)
3 Mercury	-102° F (-39° C)	678° F (359° C)
4 Water	32° F (0° C)	212° F (100° C)
5 Silver	1764° F (962° C)	4010° F (2210° C)
6 Gold	1947° F (1064° C)	5252° F (2900° C)
7 Uranium	267° F (132° C)	6904° F (3818° C)
8 Iron	2797° F (1536° C)	5432° F (3000° C)
9 Carbon	6422° F (3550° C)	8717° F (4825° C)

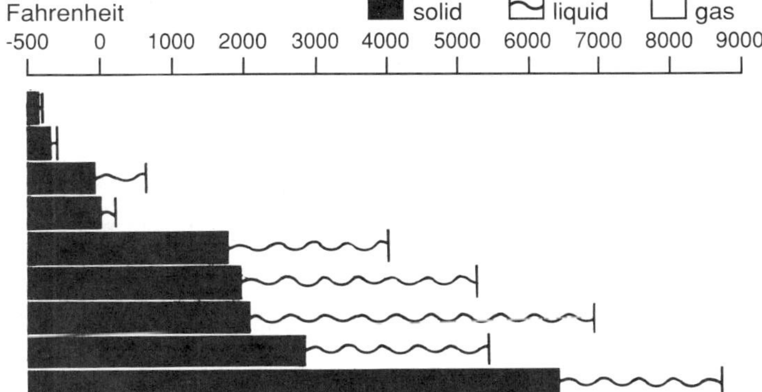

Properties of matter

2223 **Absorption** The ability of a substance to permeate into another, or to be dissolved by another substance (**1**).
Adsorption Sticking of one substance to another's surface (**2**).
Adhesion The sticking together of different substances due to attraction between dissimilar molecules (**3**).
Brownian movement Haphazard motion of tiny particles in a suspension as they are bombarded by molecules agitated by heat energy.
Cohesion Sticking together due to attraction between similar molecules (**4**).
Capillarity Rise or fall of a liquid's surface in contact with a solid, depending on the relative attraction of the liquid's molecules for one another and for the solid: an effect of surface tension.
Condensation Change of a vapor to a liquid. (Also a type of chemical reaction.)
Crystallization A growing process in nonliving substances. It happens as atoms collect on a speck of matter forming a lattice structure of unit cells (**5**).
Diffusion The process by which random collisions spread atoms or particles evenly (**6**).
Evaporation The escape of molecules from a liquid's or solid's surface below its boiling point, producing a vapor.
Osmosis Diffusion of molecules through a semipermeable membrane, equalizing the concentration of a solute on one side and a solvent on the other side.
Surface tension The force that keeps drops of liquid such as water together. The liquid's molecules are pulled toward each other making its surface behave like an elastic skin.

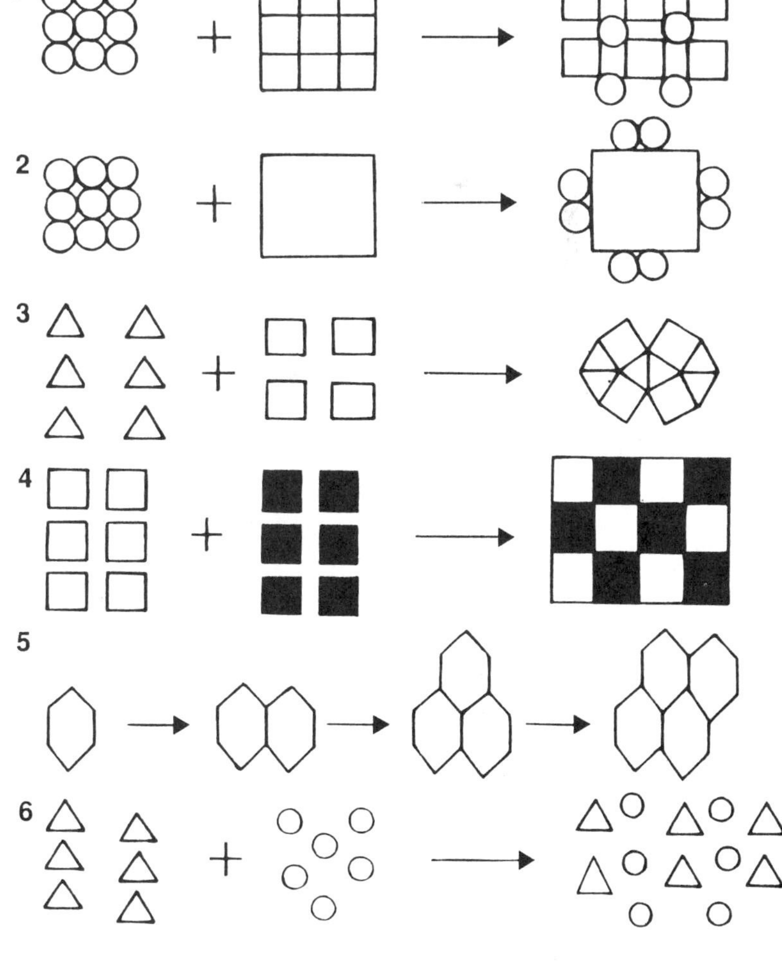

Chemical change

2224

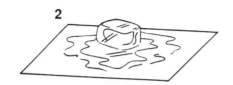

1

2

3

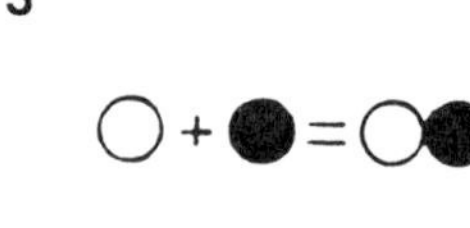

Matter can undergo three kinds of change:
1 Movement

2 Change of form (as from a solid to a liquid)

3 Change of substance. Change of substance is chemical change involving a chemical reaction between two or more substances.

Chemical reactions

2225 In a chemical reaction, the molecules of a substance gain or lose atoms or atoms become rearranged.
There are four main kinds of chemical reaction.
1 Combination Two or more substances combine, forming a compound
2 Decomposition A chemical compound breaks up into simpler substances
3 Replacement (substitution) A compound loses one or more elements but gains other elements instead
4 Double decomposition (double replacement) Two compounds decompose, exchanging atoms to form two new compounds

1

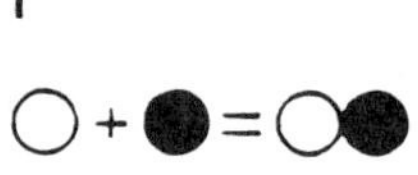

2

3

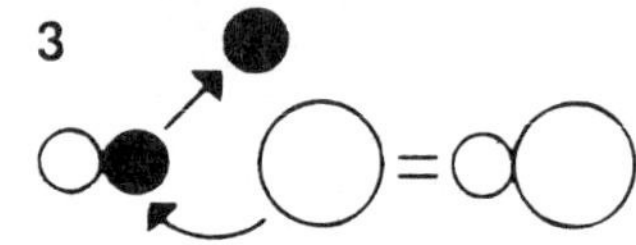

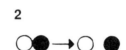

4

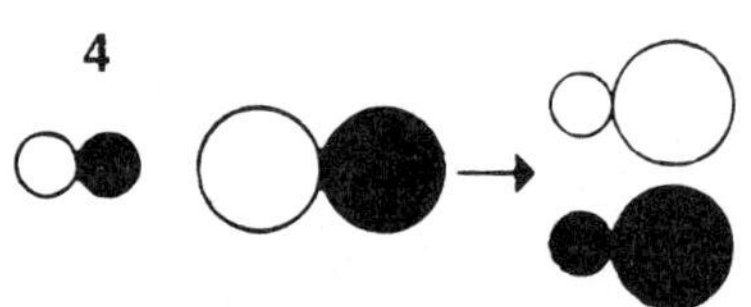

223 THE PERIODIC TABLE

The periodic table is a means of classifying and comparing chemical elements. Substances as different as hydrogen, calcium and gold are all elements; each has distinctive properties and cannot be split chemically into a simpler form.

The table groups elements into seven rows or periods. Elements in the vertical columns, or groups, have similar properties. For example, the first element in any period (called an alkali metal) is reactive; while the last element (a noble, or inert, gas) is almost totally nonreactive. The elements are listed in the table in order of their atomic numbers, from 1 to 104 (appearing in the upper left-hand corner of each box). The atomic number represents the number of protons the element has in its nucleus.

The two bottom rows are the lanthanides (57–71) and the actinides (89–103). These are separate. They have such similar properties that they fit into the space of only two elements in the main table.

1 Atomic number
2 Element symbol

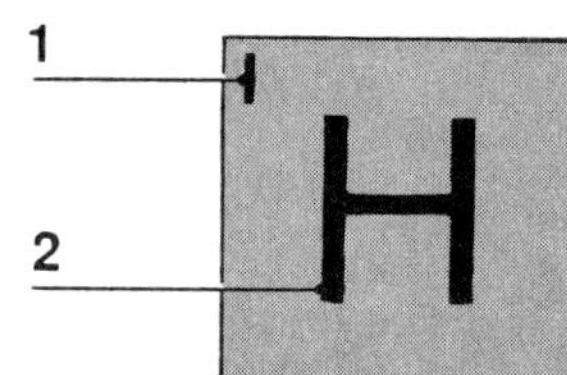

Periods

2231 **1** Each period reads from left to right in a progression from metals to nonmetals and inert (or noble) gases.
2 The seven periods rank elements in order of atomic number (the number of protons (**a**)) in an atom's nucleus (**b**).

Period 1 This consists of the two simplest atoms, hydrogen and helium.
Period 2 Contains eight elements: the silvery metals lithium and beryllium, the black substance boron, carbon (with some properties shared by metals and nonmetals), the colorless gases nitrogen and oxygen, the pale yellow gas fluorine, and the colorless inert (chemically nonreactive) gas neon.
Period 3 Also has eight elements: the silvery metals sodium, magnesium and aluminum; dark, nonmetallic silicon; the nonmetallic solid phosphorus; the yellow nonmetallic solid sulfur; yellow-green chlorine gas; and the colorless inert gas argon.
Period 4 Contains metallic potassium, calcium, gallium and germanium, a group of so-called transition elements (all metals), followed by nonmetallic arsenic, selenium and bromine; and the inert gas krypton.
Period 5 After metallic rubidium and strontium come ten transition elements, three more metallic elements (indium, tin, antimony), the two nonmetals tellurium and iodine, and the inert gas xenon.
Period 6 Its 32 elements make this the largest period of all. Besides the metals cesium, barium, thallium, lead, bismuth and polonium, it holds 10 transition elements with rare earth elements called lanthanides, the nonmetal astatine, and an inert gas, radon.
Period 7 This period seems incomplete. Known elements comprise the metals francium and radium, rare earths called actinides and transition elements.

1

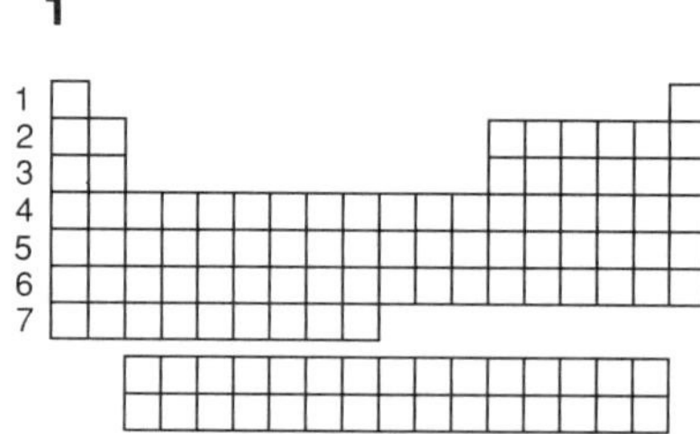

2

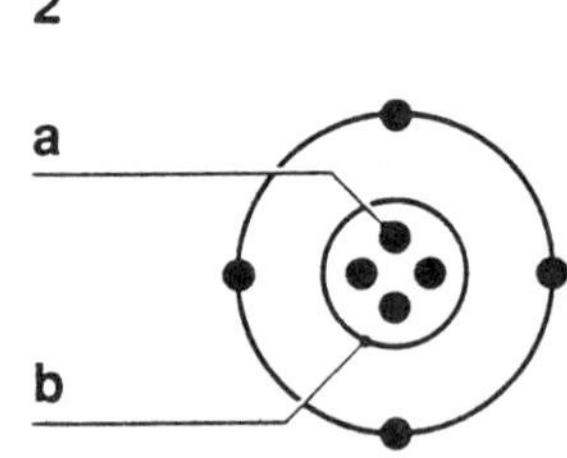

Table of elements

2232

Periods	Group 1	Group 2	Transition Elements										Group 3	Group 4	Group 5	Group 6	Group 7	Group 8
1	1 H																	2 He
2	3 Li	4 Be											5 B	6 C	7 N	8 O	9 F	10 Ne
3	11 Na	12 Mg											13 Al	14 Si	15 P	16 S	17 Cl	18 Ar
4	19 K	20 Ca	21 Sc	22 Ti	23 V	24 Cr	25 Mn	26 Fe	27 Co	28 Ni	29 Cu	30 Zn	31 Ga	32 Ge	33 As	34 Se	35 Br	36 Kr
5	37 Rb	38 Sr	39 Y	40 Zr	41 Nb	42 Mo	43 Tc	44 Ru	45 Rh	46 Pd	47 Ag	48 Cd	49 In	50 Sn	51 Sb	52 Te	53 I	54 Xe
6	55 Cs	56 Ba	57-71 -	72 Hf	73 Ta	74 W	75 Re	76 Os	77 Ir	78 Pt	79 Au	80 Hg	81 Tl	82 Pb	83 Bi	84 Po	85 At	86 Rn
7	87 Fr	88 Ra	89-103 -	104 Unq	105 Unp	106 Unh	107 Uns	108 Uno	109 Une									

Elements 57–51 (Lanthanide series)	57 La	58 Ce	59 Pr	60 Nd	61 Pm	62 Sm	63 Eu	64 Gd	65 Tb	66 Dy	67 Ho	68 Er	69 Tm	70 Yb	71 Lu
Elements 89–103 (Actinide series)	89 Ac	90 Th	91 Pa	92 U	93 Np	94 Pu	95 Am	96 Cm	97 Bk	98 Cf	99 Es	100 Fm	101 Md	102 No	103 Lr

Groups

2233

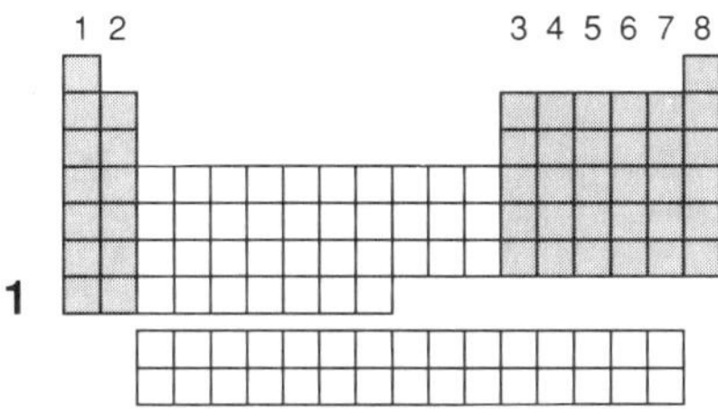

2
a
b

a group 4 element

1 The eight groups read downward.
2 These rank elements according to the number of electrons (**a**) in an atom's outer shell (**b**): Group 1, one electron; Group 2, two electrons and so on through Group 8. Elements with the same number of outer shell electrons broadly share similar properties, for instance the way they form compounds. (Note: hydrogen fits no group, and helium, although placed in Group 8, has only two electrons.)

Group 1 Alkali metals, also called the sodium family, with 1 electron in each atom's outer shell. These are similar, very active metals. The most complex is franconium.
Group 2 Alkaline earth metals, also called the calcium family, with two electrons in each atom's outer shell. The group's' most chemically active element is radium.
Group 3 Nonmetallic through metallic elements, with progressively more complex atoms. All have three electrons in each atom's outer shell, and stable inner shells.
Group 4 Nonmetallic through metallic elements, also with progressively more complex atoms. All have 4 electrons in each atom's outer shell, and stable inner shells.
Group 5 The nitrogen family, ranging from nonmetallic nitrogen and phosphorus via arsenic and antimony with some nonmetallic and metallic properties, to metallic bismuth. All have five electrons in each atom's outer shell, and stable inner shells.
Group 6 The oxygen family, ranging from nonmetallic oxygen through increasingly more complex atoms to metallic polonium. All have six electrons in each atom's outer shell, and stable inner shells.
Group 7 The halogen family of active nonmetals. Chemically the group's most active member is fluorine, but all have seven electrons in each atom's outer shell and stable inner shells.
Group 8 The inert (or noble) gases. None chemically combines with any element. All except helium (with two) have eight electrons in each atom's outer shell. No atom can hold more.

Transition elements

2234 Each of these metallic elements differs from its nearest neighbors in a numbered period only in the number of electrons (**1**) in its next-to-outer electron shell (**2**).

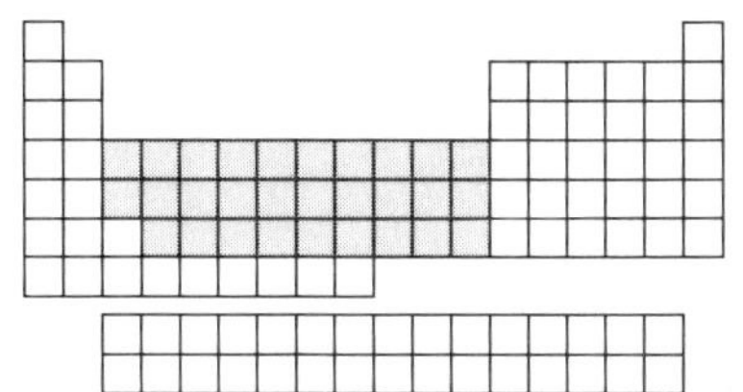

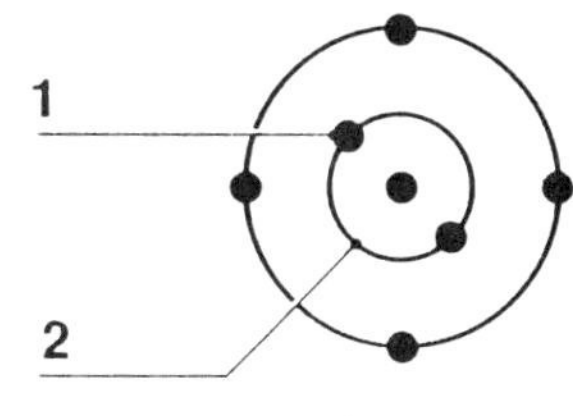

Lanthanide and actinide series

2235 **1 Lanthanide series (57-71)**
These so-called rare earths are rare metallic elements with properties like those of aluminum.

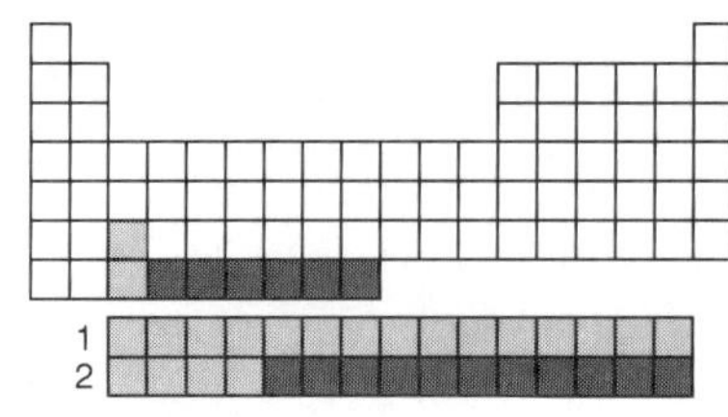

2 Actinide series (89-109)
These elements are chemically similar to lanthanides. All their isotopes are radioactive and most are artificially made. Actinides heavier than uranium are known as the additional transuranium elements, (93-109). Elements 104-109 have not yet been officially recognized.

Elements

2236 On the following pages, the elements are listed in three separate ways: **1** by atomic number; **2** by element name; and **3** by letter symbol. Each listing includes the atomic number, element name, symbol, and atomic weight (or relative atomic mass) of each element.

* Indicates atomic weight of the isotope with the longest known half-life.

1 By atomic number

Atomic No.	Name	Symbol	Atomic weight
1	Hydrogen	H	1.0079
2	Helium	He	4.0026
3	Lithium	Li	6.941
4	Beryllium	Be	9.0128
5	Boron	B	10.81
6	Carbon	C	12.011
7	Nitrogen	N	14.0067
8	Oxygen	O	15.9994
9	Fluorine	F	18.9984
10	Neon	Ne	20.179
11	Sodium	Na	22.98977
12	Magnesium	Mg	24.305
13	Aluminum	Al	26.98154
14	Silicon	Si	28.0855
15	Phosphorus	P	30.9736
16	Sulfur	S	32.064
17	Chlorine	Cl	35.453
18	Argon	Ar	39.948
19	Potassium	K	39.0983
20	Calcium	Ca	40.08
21	Scandium	Sc	44.9559
22	Titanium	Ti	47.88
23	Vanadium	V	50.9415
24	Chromium	Cr	51.996
25	Manganese	Mn	54.938
26	Iron	Fe	55.847
27	Cobalt	Co	58.9332
28	Nickel	Ni	58.69
29	Copper	Cu	63.546
30	Zinc	Zn	65.381
31	Gallium	Ga	69.72
32	Germanium	Ge	72.59
33	Arsenic	As	74.9216
34	Selenium	Se	78.96
35	Bromine	Br	79.904
36	Krypton	Kr	83.8
37	Rubidium	Rb	85.4678
38	Strontium	Sr	87.62
39	Yttrium	Y	88.9059
40	Zirconium	Zr	91.224
41	Niobium	Nb	92.9064
42	Molybdenum	Mo	95.94
43	Technetium	Tc	96.9064*
44	Ruthenium	Ru	101.07
45	Rhodium	Rh	102.9055
46	Palladium	Pd	106.42
47	Silver	Ag	107.868
48	Cadmium	Cd	112.41
49	Indium	In	114.82
50	Tin	Sn	118.69
51	Antimony	Sb	121.75
52	Tellurium	Te	127.6
53	Iodine	I	126.9045
54	Xenon	Xe	131.29
55	Cesium	Cs	132.9054
56	Barium	Ba	137.33
57	Lanthanum	La	138.9055
58	Cerium	Ce	140.12
59	Praseodymium	Pr	140.9077
60	Neodymium	Nd	144.24
61	Promethium	Pm	144.9128*
62	Samarium	Sm	150.36
63	Europium	Eu	151.96
64	Gadolinium	Gd	157.25
65	Terbium	Tb	158.9254
66	Dysprosium	Dy	162.5
67	Holmium	Ho	164.9304
68	Erbium	Er	167.26
69	Thulium	Tm	168.9342
70	Ytterbium	Yb	173.04
71	Lutetium	Lu	174.967
72	Hafnium	Hf	178.49
73	Tantalum	Ta	180.9479
74	Tungsten	W	183.85
75	Rhenium	Re	186.207
76	Osmium	Os	190.2
77	Iridium	Ir	192.22
78	Platinum	Pt	195.08
79	Gold	Au	196.9665
80	Mercury	Hg	200.59
81	Thallium	Tl	204.383
82	Lead	Pb	207.19
83	Bismuth	Bi	208.9804
84	Polonium	Po	208.9824*
85	Astatine	At	209.987*
86	Radon	Rn	222.0176*
87	Francium	Fr	223.0197*
88	Radium	Ra	226.0254*
89	Actinium	Ac	227.0278*
90	Thorium	Th	232.0381
91	Protoactinium	Pa	231.0359
92	Uranium	U	238.029*
93	Neptunium	Np	237.0482*
94	Plutonium	Pu	244.0642*
95	Americium	Am	243.0614*
96	Curium	Cm	247.0703*
97	Berkelium	Bk	247.0703*
98	Californium	Cf	251.0796*
99	Einsteinium	Es	254.088*
100	Fermium	Fm	257.0951*
101	Mendelevium	Md	258.099*
102	Nobelium	No	259.101*
103	Lawrencium	Lr	260.105*
104	Unnilquadium	Unq	261.109*
105	Unnilpentium	Unp	262.114
106	Unnilhexium	Unh	263.12*
107	Unnilseptium	Uns	262.0*
108	Unniloctium	Uno	no data
109	Unnilennium	Une	266

2 By element name

Name	Atomic No.	Symbol	Atomic weight
Actinium	89	Ac	227.0278*
Aluminum	13	Al	26.98154
Americium	95	Am	243.0614*
Antimony	51	Sb	121.75
Argon	18	Ar	39.948
Arsenic	33	As	74.9216
Astatine	85	At	209.987*
Barium	56	Ba	137.33
Berkelium	97	Bk	247.0703*
Beryllium	4	Be	9.0128
Bismuth	83	Bi	208.9804
Boron	5	B	10.81
Bromine	35	Br	79.904
Cadmium	48	Cd	112.41
Calcium	20	Ca	40.08
Californium	98	Cf	251.0796*
Carbon	6	C	12.011
Cerium	58	Ce	140.12
Cesium	55	Cs	132.9054
Chlorine	17	Cl	35.453
Chromium	24	Cr	51.996
Cobalt	27	Co	58.9332
Copper	29	Cu	63.546
Curium	96	Cm	247.703*
Dysprosium	66	Dy	162.5
Einsteinium	99	Es	254.088*
Erbium	68	Er	167.26
Europium	63	Eu	151.96
Fermium	100	Fm	257.0951*
Fluorine	9	F	18.9984
Francium	87	Fr	223.0197*
Gallium	31	Ga	69.72
Gadolinium	64	Gd	157.25

continued

Elements continued

2236

Name	No.	Symbol	Weight
Germanium	32	Ge	72.59
Gold	79	Au	196.9665
Hafnium	72	Hf	78.49
Helium	2	He	4.0026
Holmium	67	Ho	64.9304
Hydrogen	1	H	1.0079
Iodine	53	I	26.9045
Indium	49	In	14.82
Iridium	77	Ir	92.22
Iron	26	Fe	55.847
Krypton	36	Kr	83.8
Lanthanum	57	La	38.9055
Lawrencium	103	Lr	260.105*
Lead	82	Pb	207.19
Lithium	3	Li	6.941
Lutetium	71	Lu	74.967
Magnesium	12	Mg	24.305
Manganese	25	Mn	54.938
Mendelevium	101	Md	258.099*
Mercury	80	Hg	200.59
Molybdenum	42	Mo	95.94
Neodymium	60	Nd	144.24
Neon	10	Ne	20.179
Neptunium	93	Np	237.0482*
Nickel	28	Ni	58.69
Niobium	41	Nb	92.9064
Nitrogen	7	N	14.0067
Nobelium	102	No	259.101*
Oxygen	8	O	15.9994
Osmium	76	Os	190.2
Palladium	46	Pd	106.4
Phosphorus	15	P	30.97376
Platinum	78	Pt	195.08
Plutonium	94	Pu	244.0642*
Polonium	84	Po	208.9824*
Potassium	19	K	39.0983
Praseodymium	59	Pr	140.9077
Promethium	61	Pm	144.9128*
Protoactinium	91	Pa	231.0359
Radium	88	Ra	226.0254*
Radon	86	Rn	222.0176*
Rhenium	75	Re	186.207
Rhodium	45	Rh	102.9055
Rubidium	37	Rb	85.4678
Ruthenium	44	Ru	101.07
Samarium	62	Sm	150.36
Scandium	21	Sc	44.9559
Selenium	34	Se	78.96
Sodium	11	Na	22.98976
Silicon	14	Si	28.0855
Silver	47	Ag	107.868
Strontium	38	Sr	87.62
Sulfur	16	S	32.064
Tantalum	73	Ta	180.9479
Technetium	43	Tc	96.9064*
Tellurium	52	Te	127.6
Terbium	65	Tb	158.9254
Thallium	81	Tl	204.383
Thorium	90	Th	232.0381
Thulium	69	Tm	168.9342
Tin	50	Sn	118.69
Titanium	22	Ti	47.88
Tungsten	74	W	183.85
Unnilhexium	106	Unh	263.12
Unnilennium	109	Une	266.*
Unniloctium	108	Uno	no data
Unnilquadium	104	Unq	261.109*
Unnilseptium	107	Uns	262.*
Unnilpentium	105	Unp	262.114*
Uranium	92	U	238.029*
Vanadium	23	V	50.9415
Xenon	54	Xe	131.3
Ytterbium	70	Yb	173.04
Yttrium	39	Y	88.9059
Zinc	30	Zn	65.381
Zirconium	40	Zr	91.224

3 By letter symbol

Symbol	Atomic No.	Name	Atomic weight
Ac	89	Actinium	227.0278*
Ag	47	Silver	107.868
Al	13	Aluminium	26.98154
Am	95	Americium	243.0614*
Ar	18	Argon	39.948
As	33	Arsenic	74.9216
At	85	Astatine	209.987*
Au	79	Gold	196.9665
B	5	Boron	10.81
Ba	56	Barium	137.33
Be	4	Beryllium	9.0128
Bk	97	Berkelium	247.0703*
Bi	83	Bismuth	208.9804
Br	35	Bromine	79.904
C	6	Carbon	12.011
Ca	20	Calcium	40.08
Cd	48	Cadmium	112.41
Ce	58	Cerium	140.12
Cf	98	Californium	251.0796*
Cl	17	Chlorine	35.453
Cm	96	Curium	247.0703*
Co	27	Cobalt	58.9332
Cr	24	Chromium	51.996
Cs	55	Cesium	132.9054
Cu	29	Copper	63.546
Dy	66	Dysprosium	162.5
Er	68	Erbium	167.26
Es	99	Einsteinium	254.088*
Eu	63	Europium	151.96
F	9	Fluorine	18.9984
Fe	26	Iron	55.847
Fm	100	Fermium	257.0951*
Fr	87	Francium	223.0197*
Ga	31	Gallium	69.72
Gd	64	Gadolinium	157.25
Ge	32	Germanium	72.59
H	1	Hydrogen	1.0079
He	2	Helium	4.0026
Hf	72	Hafnium	178.49
Hg	80	Mercury	200.59
Ho	67	Holmium	164.9304
I	53	Iodine	126.9045
In	49	Indium	114.82
Ir	77	Iridium	192.22
K	19	Potassium	39.0983
Kr	36	Krypton	83.8
La	57	Lanthanum	138.9055
Li	3	Lithium	6.941
Lr	103	Lawrencium	260.105*
Lu	71	Lutetium	174.967
Md	101	Mendelevium	258.099*
Mg	12	Magnesium	24.305
Mn	25	Manganese	54.938
Mo	42	Molybdenum	95.94
N	7	Nitrogen	14.0067
Na	11	Sodium	22.98977
Nb	41	Niobium	92.9064
Nd	60	Neodymium	144.24
Ne	10	Neon	20.179
Ni	28	Nickel	58.69
No	102	Nobelium	259.101*
Np	93	Neptunium	237.0482*
O	8	Oxygen	15.9994
Os	76	Osmium	190.2
P	15	Phosphorus	30.97376
Pa	91	Protoactinium	231.0359
Pb	82	Lead	207.19
Pd	46	Palladium	106.42
Pm	61	Promethium	144.9128*
Po	84	Polonium	208.9824*
Pr	59	Praseodymium	140.9077
Pt	78	Platinum	195.08
Pu	94	Plutonium	244.0642*
Ra	88	Radium	226.0254*
Rb	37	Rubidium	85.4678
Re	75	Rhenium	186.207
Rh	45	Rhodium	102.9055
Rn	86	Radon	222.0176*
Ru	44	Ruthenium	101.07
S	16	Sulfur	32.064
Sb	51	Antimony	121.75
Sc	21	Scandium	44.9559
Se	34	Selenium	78.96
Si	14	Silicon	28.0855
Sm	62	Samarium	150.36
Sn	50	Tin	118.69
Sr	38	Strontium	87.62
Ta	73	Tantalum	180.9479
Tb	65	Terbium	158.9254
Tc	43	Technetium	96.9064*
Te	52	Tellurium	127.6
Th	90	Thorium	232.0381
Ti	22	Titanium	47.88
Tl	81	Thallium	204.383
Tm	69	Thulium	168.9342
U	92	Uranium	238.029*
Une	109	Unnilennium	266
Unh	106	Unnilhexium	263.120
Uno	108	Unniloctium	no data
Unp	105	Unnilpentium	262.114
Unq	104	Unnilquadium	261.109*
Uns	107	Unnilseptium	262
V	23	Vanadium	50.9415
W	74	Tungsten	183.85
Xe	54	Xenon	131.29
Y	39	Yttrium	88.9059
Yb	70	Ytterbium	173.04
Zn	30	Zinc	65.381
Zr	40	Zirconium	91.224

224 KEY CHEMICALS

Metals

2241 All but 25 of the known elements are metals. Metals are elements whose atoms can lose one or more electrons to form electrically positive ions. Most metals are good conductors of heat and electricity. They are malleable (can be beaten or rolled into a new shape) and ductile (can be pulled out into long wires). All metals are shiny, crystalline solids, except mercury which is a liquid.

Activity series

Some metals form positive ions more easily than others, and so are more chemically active. Sixteen common metals are listed in the order of their activity. Lithium is the most active of all the metals, and gold is the least active.

Most active

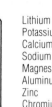

Lithium
Potassium
Calcium
Sodium
Magnesium
Aluminum
Zinc
Chromium
Iron
Nickel
Tin
Lead
Copper
Silver
Platinum
Gold

Least active

Native metals

Only four of the least active metals – copper, silver, platinum and gold – commonly occur in the Earth's crust as native metals (i.e. as free elements). All the others are found in compounds called ores which must be chemically treated to obtain the pure element.

Metalloids

These elements are "half way" between metals and nonmetals. Depending on the way they are treated, they can act as insulators like nonmetals or conduct electricity like metals. This makes several metalloids extremely important as semiconductors in computers and other electronic devices. The eight metalloid elements are boron, silicon, germanium, arsenic, antimony, tellurium, polonium and astatine.

Alloys

An alloy is a mixture of two or more metals. Here we list some everyday alloys, the metals from which they are made, and examples of their use.

Alloy	Metals	Examples of use
Bronze	Copper, tin	"Copper" coins
Brass	Copper, zinc	Doorhandles, buttons
Cupronickel	Copper, nickel	"Silver" coins
Pewter	Tin, lead	Tankards
Stainless steel	Iron, chromium, nickel	Cutlery, pots, etc.
Sterling silver	Silver, copper	Jewelry
9, 18, and 22 carat gold	Gold, silver, copper	Jewelry
Dental amalgam	Silver, tin, copper, zinc, mercury	Filling cavities in teeth
Solder	Lead, tin	Joining metals

Carbon

2242

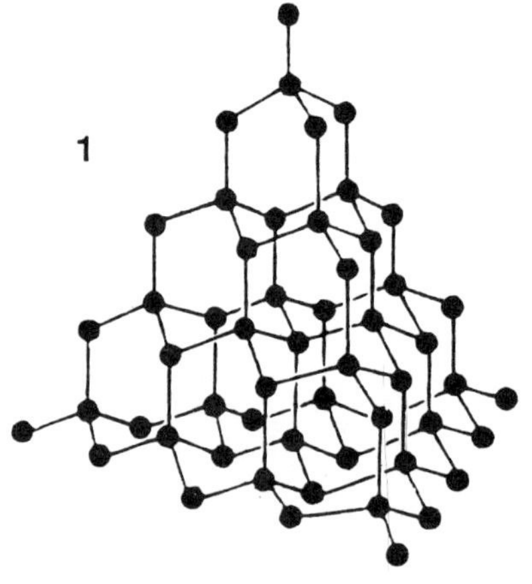

Atomic structure

This nonmetallic element forms only 0.2% of the Earth's crust, yet its importance is immense. Carbon is a major ingredient in living things and combines to form more compounds than all other elements put together. Some forms of carbon are amorphous (their atoms lack a regular, crystalline pattern) but diamond and graphite, the main natural forms of carbon, are both crystalline.

1 Diamond Each atom is surrounded by four others, producing the strong crystal structure shown. This makes diamond the hardest substance known.

2 Graphite Each atom is surrounded by three others, producing flat layers that can slide over each other. This makes graphite soft and "greasy."

Properties

Although diamond and graphite are both made up only of carbon atoms, their very different structures give them very different properties.

Diamond	Graphite
Hard	Soft
Transparent	Greyish-black
Does not conduct electricity	Conducts electricity
Cuts other substances	Easily cut or broken
Abrasive	Good lubricant

Radioactive elements

2243 These are elements in which atoms tend to break up into simpler atoms, at the same time radiating energy. This process is known as radioactive decay. Some naturally occurring elements (those with atomic numbers 84-92) are naturally radioactive, i.e. their nuclei break down of their own accord. Other elements can be made radioactive under special conditions, e.g. by bombarding them with a stream of neutrons in a nuclear reactor. Man-made elements produced in nuclear reactors are also radioactive.

Types of radiation
The three types of radiation given out by radioactive elements are called after letters in the Greek alphabet: α (alpha), ß (beta) and γ (gamma). The type of radiation emitted depends on the radioactive isotope (usually abbreviated to radioisotope): the type of atom giving off the radiation. A chemical element's nucleus (**1**) contains a certain number of protons (**2**) and neutrons (**3**). If the element has five or more forms and has a different number of neutrons in its nucleus, they are isotopes. A radioisotope's nucleus is unstable and it becomes stable by giving off heat and radiation often as alpha or beta particles.

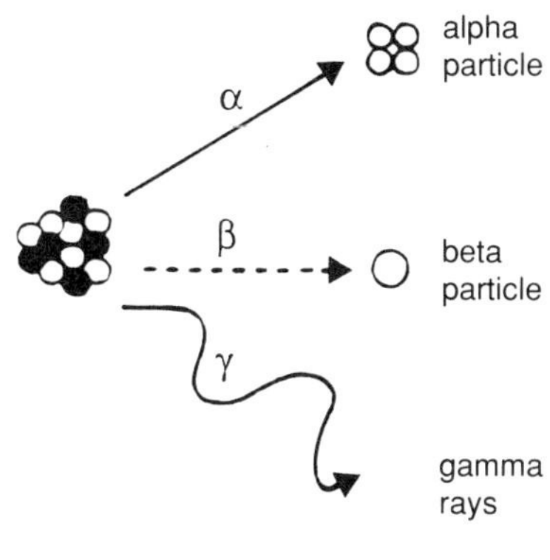

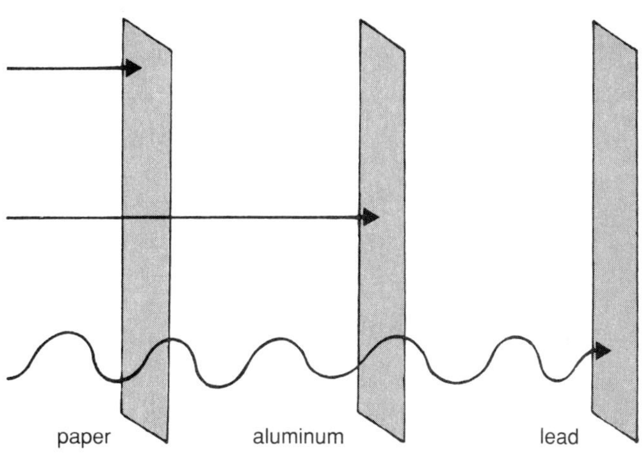

α Alpha radiation
This is the emission of alpha particles, which are the same as helium atoms that have lost their electrons. An alpha particle thus consists of two protons and two neutrons. The speed of a particle is about 5-7 % of the speed of light. Alpha particles can travel through air for no more than 4 in (10 cm) and can barely pass through one sheet of paper (**a**).

ß Beta radiation
This is the emission of negative (-) beta particles, which are the same as electrons. Their speed varies: some almost reach the speed of light. These particles can travel through air about 6 ft (1.8 m). Beta radiation is about 100 times more penetrating than alpha radiation: it can pass through paper (**a**) but not through a sheet of aluminum (**b**).

γ Gamma radiation
Gamma radiation is similar to an X-ray. Gamma rays move at the speed of light and can travel long distances through air. Gamma radiation is about 1,000 times more penetrating than alpha radiation: it can pass through paper (**a**) and aluminum (**b**) and is only stopped by a thick sheet of lead (**c**).

Polymers

2244 Polymers are large molecules consisting of hundreds of identical units comprising small molecules joined together to form long chains. (The word polymer comes from two Greek words: *poly* meaning many and *meros* meaning parts or units.) Some polymers occur naturally, but many others are man-made: many plastics and artificial fibers are man-made polymers. Depending on how they are made, polymers can be soft or hard, stretchy or rigid, easily melted or heat resistant, pressed out into flat sheets, spun into thread, or made into foam. The starting materials for making polymers come from petroleum or coal. The process of making a polymer from monomers (one or more kinds of smaller molecule) is called polymerization.

Natural polymers
Naturally occurring organic and inorganic polymers include cellulose, diamond, feldspar, nucleic acids, proteins, quartz, rubber, starch, and wool.

Man-made polymers

Polymer	Examples of use
Polyethylene	Bottles, shopping bags, containers, electrical insulation
Polypropylene	Carpets, blankets, crates, containers
Polystyrene	Pens, toys, insulating tiles
Polyvinyl chloride (PVC)	Roofs, pipes, toys, luggage, upholstery
Polymethyl methacrylate (Plexiglass)	Aircraft windows, vehicle lights, baths
Polyurethane	Furniture, foam upholstery
Polyvinyl acetate	Emulsion paint
Polytetrafluoroethylene (PTFE, Teflon)	Nonstick pans
Polyformaldehyde	Safety steering columns
Polyamide	Nylon fabrics
Polyethylene terephthalate	Shrink wrapping
Polycarbonate	Safety helmets, computer parts
Polyether urethane	Car seats and armrests
Polychloroprene (neoprene)	Adhesives, shoes, packaging, wet suits
Epoxide resin	Adhesives

225 BIOCHEMICAL CYCLES

Biochemical changes recycle some key elements required by living things. Diagrams show the oxygen, carbon, nitrogen, phosphorus, sulfur cycles, and the Krebs cycle.

Oxygen cycle

2251 Oxygen plays a vital part in the respiration of animals and plants.
1 Oxygen in air
2 Oxygen breathed in by animals
3 Carbon dioxide (a carbon-oxygen compound) breathed out by living things as waste
4 Carbon dioxide absorbed by plants which combine it with water to make carbohydrate foods
5 Surplus oxygen released into the air by plants as waste

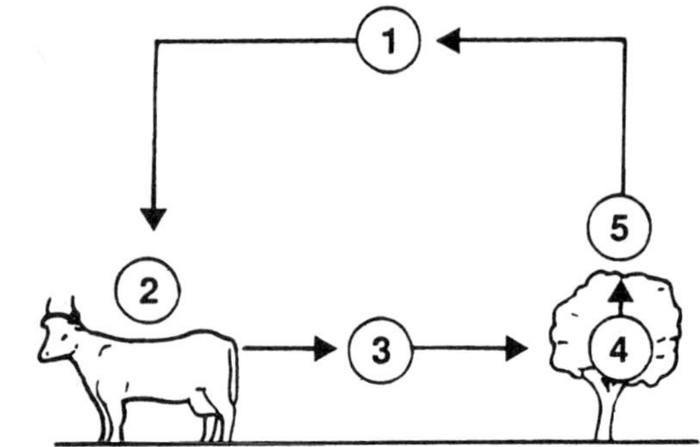

Carbon cycle

2252 Carbon is a valuable source in plant material. Oxidizing carbon compounds provide energy for animals and plants.
1 Carbon dioxide (a carbon-oxygen compound) in air
2 Carbon dioxide absorbed by plants for making food
3 Plants eaten by animals
4 Carbon dioxide waste breathed out by animals and plants
5 Dead organisms broken down by bacteria
6 These give off carbon dioxide waste
7 Remains of long-dead plants and microscopic organisms forming hydrocarbon (hydrogen and carbon) fossil fuels: coal, oil, and gas
8 Volcanoes releasing carbon dioxide into air

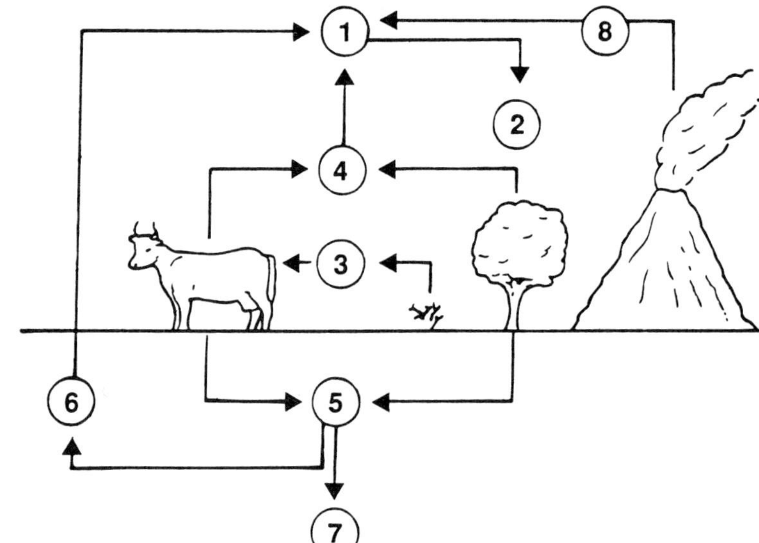

Nitrogen cycle

2253 As an ingredient in proteins and nucleic acids, nitrogen is vital to all living things.
1 Nitrogen in air
2 Atmospheric nitrogen trapped by some plants' roots
3 Nitrogen used by plants for making proteins
4 Plant proteins eaten by animals
5 Proteins in dead organisms and body wastes converted to ammonia by bacteria and fungi
6 Ammonia converted to nitrate by other bacteria
7 Nitrate taken up by plants

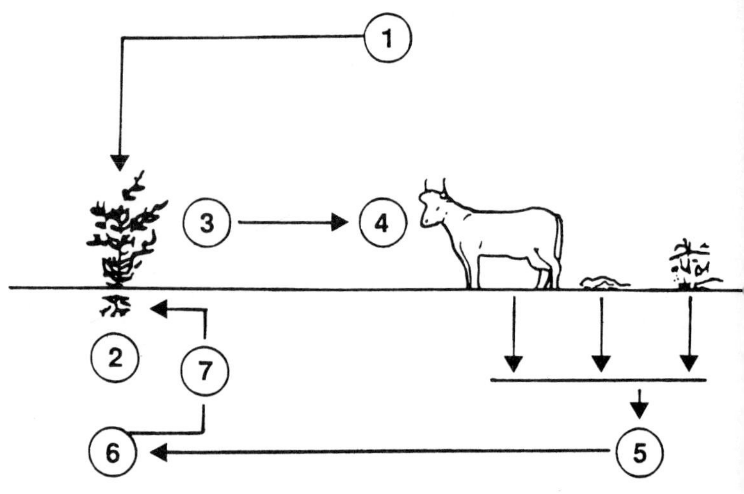

Sulfur cycle

2254 Sulfur is in two of the 20 amino acids which are used by the body to make proteins.
1 Sulfates (sulfur-oxygen compounds) absorbed by plant roots
2 The oxygen in the sulfate is replaced by hydrogen in a plant process that produces certain amino acids
3 Plants eaten by animals
4 Sulfur-containing amino acids of dead plants and animals broken down to hydrogen sulfide (which gives off a rotten egg odor) by decomposer microorganisms
5 Sulfur extracted from sulfides by bacteria
6 Other bacteria combines sulfur with oxygen producing sulfates

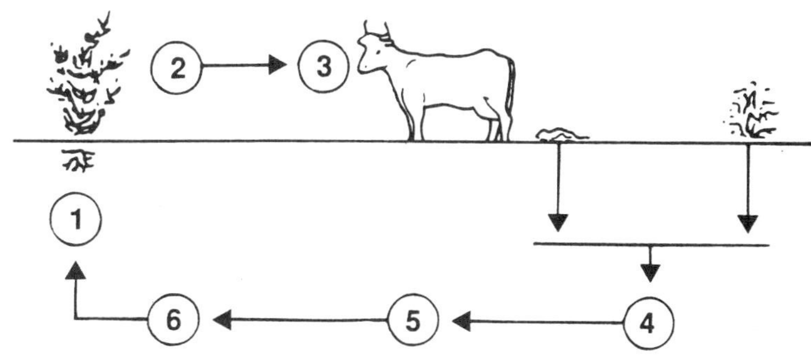

hosphorus cycle

2255 Phosphorus is a vital ingredient of proteins, nucleic acids, and some other compounds found in living things.
1 Phosphates (compounds of phosphorus, hydrogen and oxygen) absorbed by plant roots
2 Phosphates used by plants in making organic phosphorus compounds
3 Plants eaten by animals
4 Compounds in dead plants and animals broken down to phosphates by microorganisms

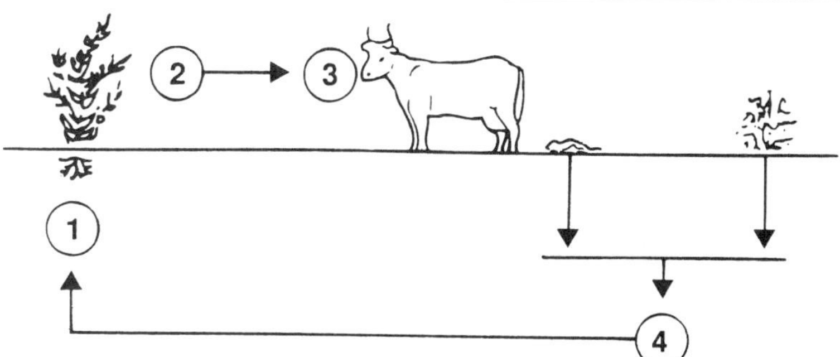

rebs cycle

2256 The Krebs or citric acid cycle is the last part of a process by which living things produce energy from foods. Different enzymes (proteins which promote but are not used up in chemical changes) create successive compounds, so transforming acetic acid to carbon dioxide and water and releasing energy.
1 Acetic acid combines with...
2 Oxaloacetic acid to form...
3 Citric acid. Later changes produce...
4 Aconitic acid
5 Isocitric acid
6 Ketoglutaric acid
7 Succinic acid, carbon dioxide and energy-rich ATP (adenosine triphosphate)
8 Fumaric acid
9 Malic acid
2 Oxaloacetic acid

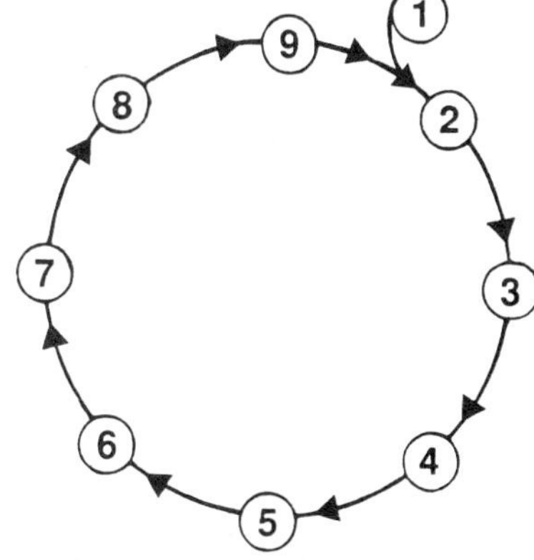

226 CHEMISTRY GLOSSARY

acid Substance that produces hydrogen ions when dissolved in water; the hydrogen may be replaced by metals or bases.
activation energy Energy that must be supplied to reactants before a reaction can take place.
alchemy The forerunner of modern chemistry, alchemy mixed magic and mysticism with a genuine curiosity in the nature and properties of materials.
alcohol Organic compound with one or more hydroxyl (-OH) groups.
aldehyde Organic compound, such as formaldehyde, that contains the CHO group.
aliphatic compound Organic molecule consisting of straight or branched carbon chains.
alkali Solution of a base (usually the oxide of a metal) in water; contains hydroxide ions and reacts with an acid to produce salt and water.
alkali metals Highly reactive elements of group 1 of the periodic table, e.g. sodium, potassium.
alkane Hydrocarbon with general formula C_nH_{2n+2} e.g. ethane.
alkene Hydrocarbon with general formula C_nH_{2n} e.g. ethene.
alkyne Hydrocarbon with general formula C_nH_{2n-2} e.g. ethyne.
allotropes Different physical forms of the same element.
alloy Mixture of two or more metals, e.g. brass (copper and zinc).
alpha radiation Emission of alpha particles (two protons and two neutrons) from the nucleus of a radioactive atom.
amalgam Alloy of mercury with other metals.
amine Organic compounds containing the $-NH_2$ group.
amorphous Describes substance lacking crystalline structure.
amphoteric Describes substance with both alkaline and acidic properties.
analytical chemistry Branch of chemistry concerned with the composition of substances.
anion Negative ion, attracted to anode in electrolysis.
anode Positive electrode, attracted to the anion in electrolysis.
aromatic compound A carbon ring compound having the formula: $C_{4n+2}H_{4n+2}$.
assay Quantitative chemical test to determine composition of a substance.
atom Smallest unit of an element that has properties of that element and can take part in a chemical reaction.
atomic mass Mass of one atom of a particular

continued

Chemistry glossary continued

226

element measured in atomic mass units.
atomic number This is equal to the number of protons in the nucleus of the atom of a particular element.
atomic structure Structure of an atom in terms of the number and arrangement of its constituent protons, neutrons, and electrons.
atomic theory Theory that all matter is made up of atoms.
Avogadro constant Number of atoms or molecules in one mole of a substance (6.02×10^{23}).
base Substance that reacts with an acid to produce a salt; most are oxides of metals.
base metal Metals (e.g. copper) that lose luster on exposure to air.
beta radiation Emission of beta particles (electrons) from the nucleus of a radioactive atom.
bond Force holding together two atoms, ions or molecules, or mixture of these. Bonds are formed or broken during chemical reactions.
bond energy Energy required or released when covalent bond is formed, or energy required to break covalent bond.
catalyst Substance that speeds up a chemical reaction, but which itself is not changed.
chemical change Change through which new substances are produced.
chemical equation Method of representing the changes that take place during a chemical reaction by the use of symbols, e.g. $2H_2 + O_2 \longrightarrow 2H_2O$.
chemistry Study of composition of substances, and the changes in composition that they undergo in certain conditions.

chromatography Technique used for separating mixed soluble substances. A solution of mixed substances poured through an absorbent material creates different bands of substances which are absorbed at different rates. The solvent is collected in a beaker.

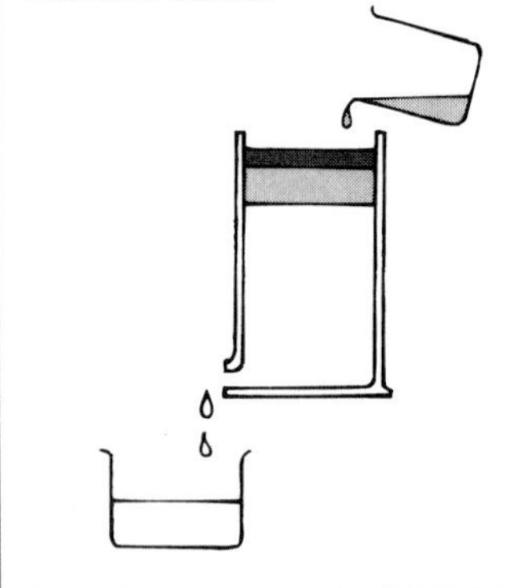

colloid Substances, usually dispersed in liquid form, so that the molecules are not separated, as in a solution, but are grouped together and visible under the microscope, e.g. milk.
combination Joining of two or more substances by chemical bonds to form a compound.
combustion Chemical reaction in which heat is produced.
compound Substance made of two or more elements joined together. It can be decomposed by chemical action into simpler substances.
condensation The change of a vapor to a liquid, or a type of reaction where two organic molecules combine with the elimination of water.
condenser Device for condensing vapor into liquid.
corrosion The eating away of a substance by moisture and/or chemicals.
covalency Measure of ability of atom to form covalent bonds.
covalent bond Bond formed between atoms by sharing electrons.

crystal Solid substance with atoms arranged in a regular polyhedral pattern. Here we show three types of regular shape: (**1**) cubic crystal, (**2**) body-centred crystal, and (**3**) face-centred crystal.

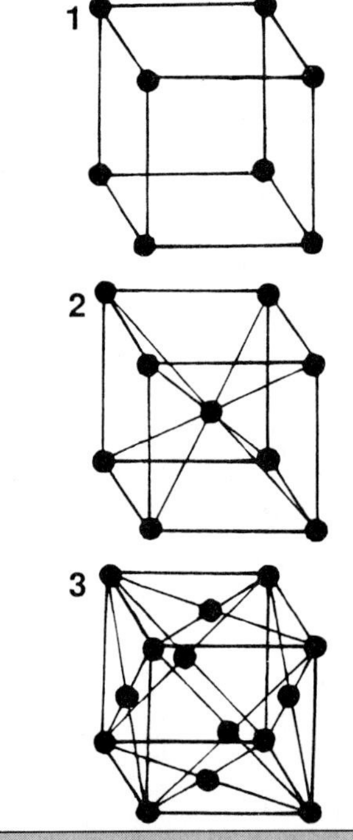

crystallization Formation of crystals in solution of crystalline substance.
decomposition Breaking down of a compound into simpler substances.
decrepitation Crackling sounds produced when crystals explode on heating.
dehydration Process of removing water from a substance.
deliquescent Describes substances which absorb sufficient water from the air to make a solution, e.g. sodium hydroxide.
diffusion Spreading out of liquid or gas caused by random movement of its molecules.
dissociation Reversible separation of compound into simpler components, e.g. sodium chloride into sodium ions and chloride ions.
dissolve To mix gas or solid with a solvent to produce a solution.
distil Process of changing liquid to vapor by heating, then condensing vapor back to liquid.
distillation The act of boiling a liquid while condensing and recovering the resulting vapor. Distillation is used to purify or separate liquids.

effervescent Describes substance which when placed in a liquid causes vigorous release of small gas bubbles, e.g. sodium hydrogen carbonate in water.

electrolysis Chemical decomposition caused by passage of electricity through an electrolyte solution, e.g. electricity through water creates gas bubbles of hydrogen at the negative cathode and oxygen at the positive cathode.

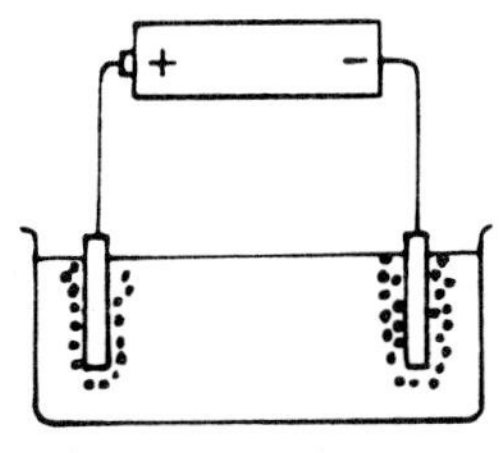

electrolyte Substance which, dissolved in water, will conduct electricity.
electron Subatomic particle with a negative charge.
electrovalency Measure of ability of atom to form ionic bonds.
electrovalent bond *see* ionic bond
element Substance which cannot be broken down into simpler substances by chemical means.
empirical formula Formula showing simplest ratio of elements in a compound, e.g. ethanoic acid: CH_2O.
emulsion Colloidal dispersion of one liquid in another, e.g. milk, paint.
endothermic reaction Reaction where heat energy is taken in.
equation *See* chemical equation
evaporate To heat liquid below boiling point so that vapor is given off.
evaporation Process of turning liquid into vapor below the boiling point of the liquid.
exothermic reaction Reaction where heat energy is released.
explosion Very rapid reaction which releases much energy, and large volumes of gases, heat and light.
filter To separate insoluble substance from a liquid by pouring mixture through filter paper.
filtrate Liquid that passes through a filter leaving insoluble substance behind.
flammable Describes substance which easily

continued

Chemistry glossary continued

226

bursts into flame.

flash point Minimum temperature at which vapor of volatile liquid ignites in the presence of a flame.

formula Means of showing number of atoms of elements in molecules using symbols, e.g. $CaCO_3$ for calcium carbonate.

fuel Substance burned to release heat energy to be used as power, e.g. coal, gas.

gamma radiation Emission of short wavelength, highly penetrative gamma rays from radioactive elements.

gas State of matter, with no definite volume, whose molecules move freely to fill any available space.

halogen Group of nonmetals including fluorine and chlorine.

hydrocarbon Organic compound containing carbon and hydrogen.

hydrolysis Reaction in which water decomposes a substance.

hygroscopic Describes substances which tend to absorb water from the air, e.g. sodium chloride.

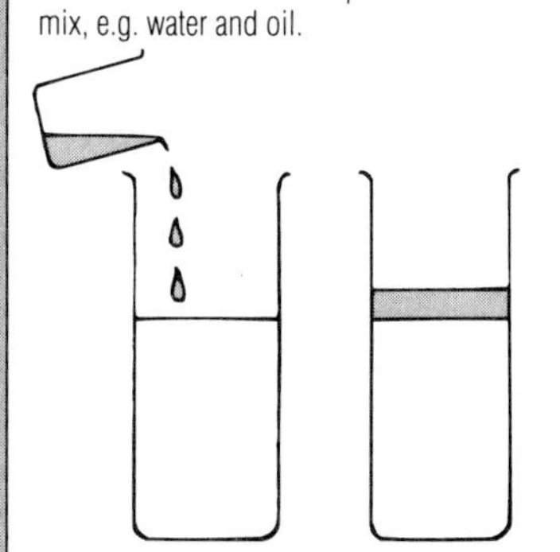

immiscible Describes liquids that do not mix, e.g. water and oil.

inert gas Gas which does not take part in chemical reactions, e.g. helium, argon.

inorganic chemistry Branch of chemistry concerned with substances of mineral origin.

insoluble Describes substance that cannot be dissolved in a particular liquid.

ion Atom or molecule carrying an electric charge. Formed by atom losing (produces positive ion) or gaining (produces negative ion) one or more electrons.

ionic bond Chemical bond formed between ions, e.g. between sodium ion and chloride ion.

ionization Process of ion formation.

isomers Compounds with same empirical formulas but with different molecular structures.

isotopes Atoms of the same element with different atomic masses, e.g. carbon-12 and carbon-13.

liquid State of matter with definite volume, but which takes the shape of its container.

metal An element which forms positive ions during chemical reactions, is a conductor of electricity, and is lustrous, ductile, and malleable.

miscible *see box right*

mixture Two or more substances, put together but not chemically joined, and which can be separated without chemical action.

molarity Number of moles of a solute in one liter of solution.

mole Standard for measuring quantity of a substance. Equals the amount of a substance that contains the same number of atoms or molecules as 12 grams of carbon-12.

molecule Two or more atoms joined by covalent bonds.

monomer Compound consisting of single molecules which may join with other compounds to form polymers.

neutralization Reaction between an acid and an alkaline, or base, to form a salt and water.

neutron Subatomic particle with same mass as proton but no electric charge.

noble metals Metals that resist corrosion by water and acid, e.g. gold, silver, platinum.

organic chemistry Branch of chemistry concerned with carbon and its compounds.

organic compounds Compounds of carbon.

oxidation Removal of electrons from an atom; originally defined as the addition of oxygen to an element or compound. Oxidation is the reverse of reduction.

oxidizing agent Substance which oxidizes other elements or compounds.

periodic table Arrangement of elements, in periods and groups in order of increasing atomic number.

ph Measure of how acid or alkaline a solution is on a scale of 1 (very acid) through 7 (neutral) to 14 (very alkaline).

physical chemistry Branch of chemistry which uses physics to study the physical changes occurring during chemical reactions.

plastic Substance produced synthetically by polymerization of organic compounds.

polymer Compound formed by the joining of many monomers, with high relative molecular mass; produced by polymerization.

polymerization Process in which many molecules combine to form larger molecules.

precipitate Solid substance which separates from a solution during a chemical reaction.

product New substance produced as the result of a chemical reaction.

proton Subatomic particle with positive charge.

radioactive element Element whose nuclei emit subatomic particles (radiation) and which, as a consequence, break up into simpler elements or more stable isotopes of the same element.

reactant Substance that partakes in chemical reaction.

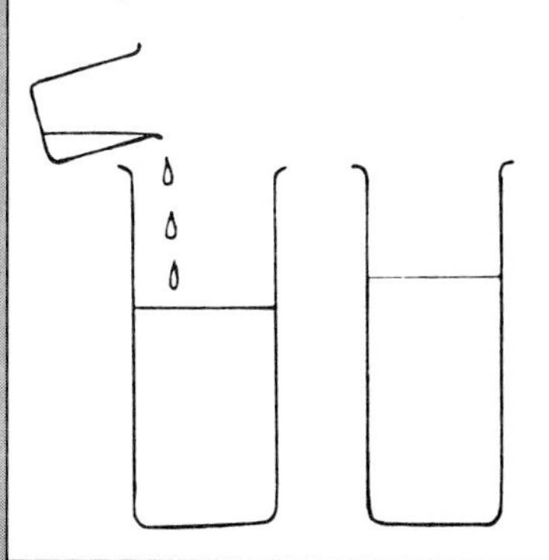

miscible Describes liquids that readily mix, e.g. water and ethanol.

reaction Process whereby substances (reactants) are chemically changed to form new substances (products).

redox reaction Mutual oxidation and reduction, so that when substance X oxidizes substance Y, substance Y reduces substance X.

reducing agent Substance that reduces other compounds by being itself oxidized.

reduction Addition of electrons to an atom; originally defined as reactions involving the removal of oxygen from a compound. Reduction is the reverse of oxidation.

relative atomic mass Measurement of mass of one atom of an element; equals ratio of mass of one atom of a particular element to one atomic mass unit.

relative molecular mass Measurement of the average mass per molecule of a substance. Calculated by adding together the relative atomic masses of its constituent atoms.

salt A compound formed as the result of a reaction in which a metal replaces the hydrogen of an acid, e.g. calcium chloride.

saturated solution Solution in which no further solute can be dissolved.

solid State of matter with a definite volume and definite shape.

soluble Describes property of a substance that can be dissolved in a particular liquid.

solute Substance that dissolves in a particular liquid.

solution Result of dissolving a solute in a solvent; the two cannot be separated by filtration or other mechanical methods.

solvent Liquid in which a particular solute can dissolve.

subatomic particle Small particles that make up atoms.

sublimation Direct change of state from a solid to a vapor by heating.

substance Element or compound with recognizable properties that do not vary, e.g. sugar, tin.

suspension A mixture of small insoluble particles in a liquid which can be removed by filtration, e.g. clay particles in water.

thermochemistry Study of changes in heat energy during a chemical reaction.

thermolabile Describes substances that decompose when heated.

thermostable Describes substances that are stable when heated.

valence electron Electron in outer shell of atom that takes part in bond formation.

valency Measure of ability of an atom to form bonds with other atoms.

van der Waals' bond A type of weak bond that holds molecules together.

227 CHEMISTS

Arrhenius, Svante (August) 1859–1927, Swedish chemist and physicist (**1**), best known for work on dissociation theory of electrolytes, and on reaction rates, who was first to recognize "greenhouse effect" on climate. Nobel prize for chemistry in 1903.

Avogadro, Amedeo 1776–1856, Italian scientist. Professor of physics at Turin (1834-59), who in 1811 formulated the hypothesis known as Avogadro's law: equal volumes of gases contain equal numbers of molecules, when at the same temperature and pressure.
Becher, Johann Joachim 1635–82, German chemist who studied minerals. His *Physica Subterranea* (1669) was the first attempt to bring physics and chemistry into close relation.
Berzelius, Jöns Jakob 1779–1848, Swedish chemist who determined an accurate table of atomic weights. He introduced modern chemical symbols, and worked on electro-chemical theory. He also discovered the elements selenium, thorium, and cerium, and was the first to isolate others.
Bessemer, Sir Henry 1813–98, English chemist, inventor, and engineer. In 1855, in response to the need for guns for the Crimean War, he patented the process by which molten pig-iron can be turned directly into steel by blowing air through it in a Bessemer converter.
Black, Joseph 1728–99, Scottish chemist. Between 1756 and 1761, he evolved the theory of "latent heat" on which his scientific fame chiefly rests. Also showed that the causticity of lime and alkalis is due to the absence of "fixed air" (carbon dioxide) that is present in limestone and carbonates of alkalis.
Bunsen, Robert Wilhelm 1811–99, German chemist and physicist. Shared with Kirchhoff the discovery, in 1859, of spectrum analysis, which led to the discovery of cesium, rubidium and other new elements. Inventions include Bunsen burner and galvanic battery.
Carothers, Wallace Hume 1896–1937, American industrial chemist, working for Du Pont Company at Wilmington, USA, who invented nylon after producing first successful synthetic rubber, neoprene.
Cavendish, Henry 1731–1810, English chemist and natural philosopher. In 1760, he discovered the extreme levity of inflammable air, and later, at the same time as Watt, ascertained that water is the result of the union of two gases. The 'Cavendish Experiment' estimates the density of Earth.
Dalton, John 1766–1844, English chemist, whose atomic theory elevated chemistry to a science. His physical research was chiefly on gases; the law of partial pressures is also known as Dalton's law. In 1794, he first described color blindness ("Daltonism").
Daniell, John Frederic 1790–1845, English chemist. Invented a hygrometer (1820), a pyrometer (1830) and Daniell electric cell (1836). His *Introduction to Chemical Philosophy* was published in 1839.
Davy, Sir Humphry 1778–1829, English chemist and science propagandist. Through his experiments, he discovered the new metals potassium, sodium, barium, strontium, calcium and magnesium. In 1815, invented safe lamp for use in gassy coalmines.
Dewar, Sir James 1842–1923, Scottish chemist and physicist who invented Dewar (or thermos) flask – insulated, double-walled flask with inner space made into a vacuum and silvered to reduce heat loss, by convection and radiation, to minimum. With Abel, he invented cordite.
Frankland, Sir Edward 1825–99, English organic chemist. Became professor at the Royal Institution, London, in 1863. Propounded theory of valency (1852-60) and with Lockyer discovered helium in Sun's atmosphere in 1868. Expert on sanitation.
Graham, Thomas 1805–69, Scottish chemist and physicist. One of the founders of physical chemistry, whose researches on molecular diffusion of gases led him to formulate law "that the diffusion rate of gases is inversely as the square root of their density."
Haber, Fritz 1868–1934, German chemist. With brother-in-law Carl Bosch, invented process for synthesis of ammonia from hydrogen and atmospheric nitrogen in the air, thus overcoming shortage of natural nitrate deposits accessible to German explosives industry in World War I.
Hall, Charles Martin 1863–1914, American chemist. In 1886, discovered, independently of Héroult, first economic method of obtaining aluminum from bauxite (electrolytically). Helped to found Aluminum Company of America (vice-president from 1890).
Hinshelwood, Sir Cyril Norman 1897–1967, English chemist. Simultaneously with Semenov, investigated chemical reaction kinetics in inter-war years, for which they shared Nobel prize in 1956. Linguist, classical scholar. President of Royal Society and Classical Association.
Hofmann, August Wilhelm von 1818–92, German chemist. Obtained aniline from coal products, discovered many other organic compounds, including formaldehyde (1867). Devoted much labor to theory of chemical types.
Kekulé, von Stradonitz, Friedrich August 1829–96, German chemist who made a major contribution to organic chemistry by developing structural theories, including the cyclic structure of benzene.
Lavoisier, Antoine Laurent 1743–94, French chemist. Known as founder of modern chemistry. Discovered and named oxygen, and proved its importance in respiration, combustion and as a compound with metals. His *Traité Elémentaire de Chimie* was published in 1789.
Liebig, Justus, Freiherr von 1803–73, German. One of the most illustrious chemists of his age, equally great in method and in practical applications. Made his name in organic and animal chemistry, and in the study of alcohols. Founder of agricultural chemistry, and discoverer of chloroform.
Mendeleyev, Dmitri Ivanovich 1834–1907, Russian chemist. Formulated periodic law by which he predicted existence of several elements that were subsequently discovered. Element No. 101 is named mendelevium after him.
Pauling, Linus Carl b.1901, American chemist. Awarded Nobel prize in 1954 for work on chemical bonding and on molecular structure. Work also covers inorganic complexes, protein structure, antibodies, and the molecular basis of some genetic diseases.
Perkin, Sir William Henry 1838–1907, English chemist who worked as assistant to August Hofmann and, in 1856, discovered mauve, which led to the foundation of the aniline dye industry.
Priestley, Joseph 1733–1804, English chemist and Presbyterian minister (**2**). Pioneer of chemistry of gases, and one of the discoverers of oxygen.

Ramsay, Sir William 1852–1916, Scottish chemist. In conjunction with Lord Rayleigh, he discovered argon in 1894, and later produced helium, neon, krypton, and xenon. Writings include *The Gases of the Atmosphere* and *Elements and Electrons*.
Scheele, Carl Wilhelm 1742–86, Swedish chemist who discovered several acids, and who first described the pigment called Scheele's green (arsenite of copper) and scheelite (tungsten). In 1777, he showed, independently of Priestley, that atmosphere consists of one gas supporting, and one preventing, combustion.
Swan, Sir Joseph Wilson 1828–1914, English chemist and physicist. Patented the carbon process for photographic printing in 1864, and invented the dry-plate technique (1871) and bromide paper (1879). In 1860, he invented the electric lamp 20 years before Edison. First to produce practicable artificial silk.
Wöhler, Friedrich 1800–82, German chemist whose synthesis of urea from ammonium cyanate in 1828 revolutionized organic chemistry. Also isolated aluminum (1827) and beryllium (1828) and discovered calcium carbide, from which he obtained acetylene.

231 ENGINES

Steam engines

2311 Engines are devices that convert one form of energy into another. By burning coal to boil water, a steam engine turns the chemical energy in coal into heat energy which creates pressure to move the parts of a piston up and down. By using rods or crankshafts (jointed rods) a circular motion can be achieved and this is used to drive the wheels of trains or steam driven engines. By connecting two rods to the same revolving axle, a system of valves can control the supply and extraction of compressed steam.

Double-acting steam engine
1 Compressed steam (**a**) enters the steam chest (**b**).
2 An open valve (**c**) allows steam (**a**) to enter the upper piston cylinder (**d**) and this forces down the piston (**e**). At the same time, steam in the lower cylinder is extracted through an open valve (**f**) to the exhaust (**g**).
3 As the axle (**h**) revolves, the piston (**e**) is forced back up.
4 As the piston (**e**) rises, the lower valve (**f**) opens to allow fresh steam to enter the lower valve chamber, and steam from the upper chamber to empty into the exhaust (**g**).

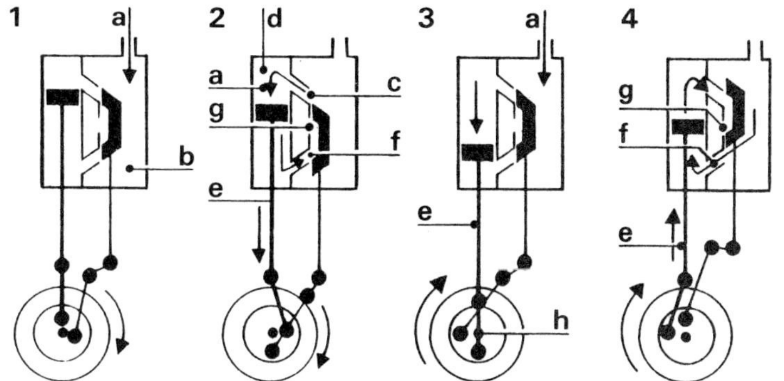

Triple-expansion steam engine
In triple-expansion steam engines the steam (**1**) goes through high (**2**), medium (**3**), and low (**4**) pressure cylinders making the pistons (**5**) rise and fall to turn the axle (**6**).

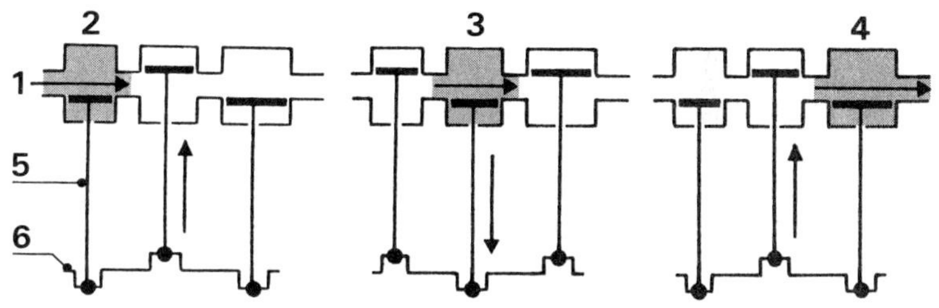

Gasoline engines

2312 **Types of gasoline engine**
There are two types of gasoline engine: a gasoline engine (**1**) and a diesel engine (**2**). In a gasoline engine, a mixture of gasoline and air is drawn into a cylinder (**a**), compressed and heated (**b**), then ignited by a spark (**c**). In a diesel engine, the air is drawn into the cylinder first (**a**) and is compressed to a much greater degree than in the gasoline engine (**b**). Because of this, the air in the diesel engine heats up and when a small amount of diesel fuel is injected, it ignites spontaneously (**c**).

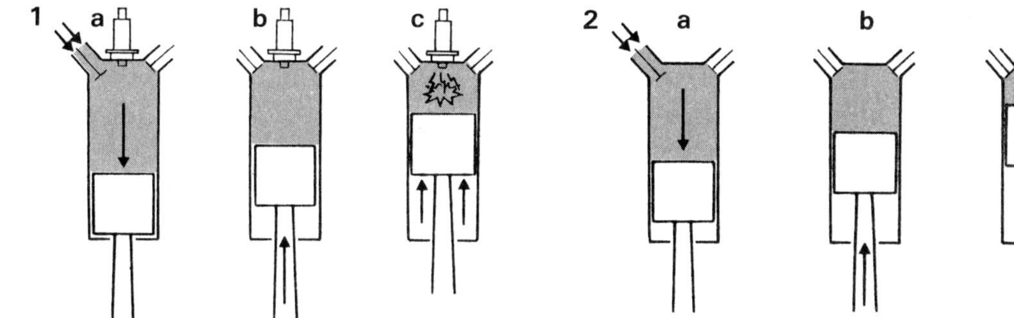

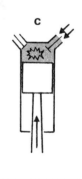

Four stroke engines
These are internal combustion engines, burning a gasoline vapor and air mixture inside a cylinder to move a piston. A four-stroke engine has four piston strokes per cycle.
1 Intake (induction): the piston (**a**) moves down, drawing in the fuel-air mixture (**b**).
2 Compression: the piston rises, compressing the fuel-air mixture.
3 Power: a spark plug (**c**) (in a diesel engine, heat from compressed air,) ignites the fuel, and burning gases force down the piston.
4 Exhaust: as the piston rises, burned gas escapes through an exhaust valve (**d**).

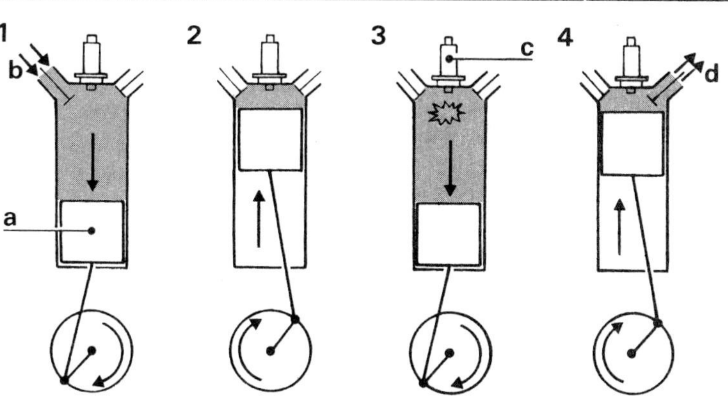

continued

Gasoline engines continued

2312 **Two stroke engines**
These are less efficient than four-stroke engines but they are cheaper and lighter. They deliver a power stroke (shown here as 1–3) for every turn of the crankshaft. A four-stroke engine only does so for every other turn.
1 Power stroke begins: spark plug (**a**) ignites compressed fuel-air mixture (**b**).
2 Piston (**c**) is forced down and burned gases escape through exhaust port (**d**).
3 Descending piston admits fuel-air mixture through inlet port (**e**).
4 Second stroke: piston rises, closing both ports (**d**, **e**) and compressing the fuel-air mixture (**b**).

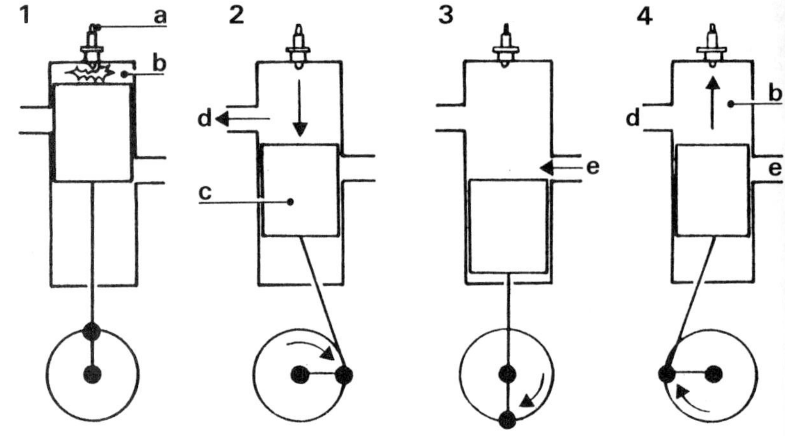

Wankel rotary engine
Invented by Felix Wankel of Germany, this internal combustion engine has a rotor revolving in a chamber instead of a piston moving back and forth in a cylinder. It works smoothly, as shown.
1 Intake (induction): inlet (**a**) admits a fuel-air mixture to the chamber (**b**).
2 Compression: the revolving rotor (**c**) compresses the fuel-air mixture.
3 Combustion: a spark plug (**d**) ignites the compressed fuel-air mixture.
4 Power and exhaust: the burning gases expand, keeping the rotor (**c**) turning. Then the burned gases escape from the exhaust port (**e**).

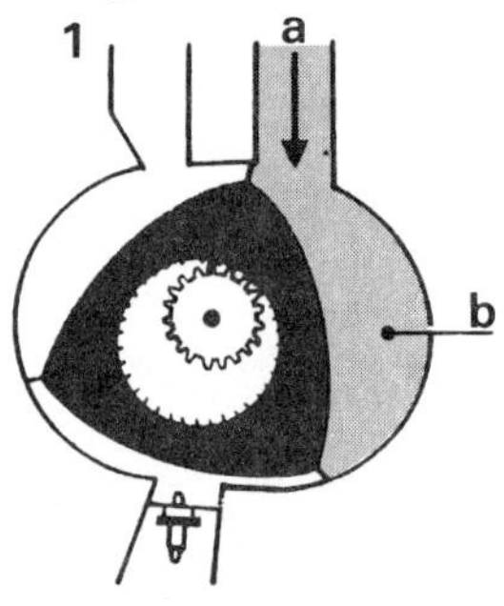

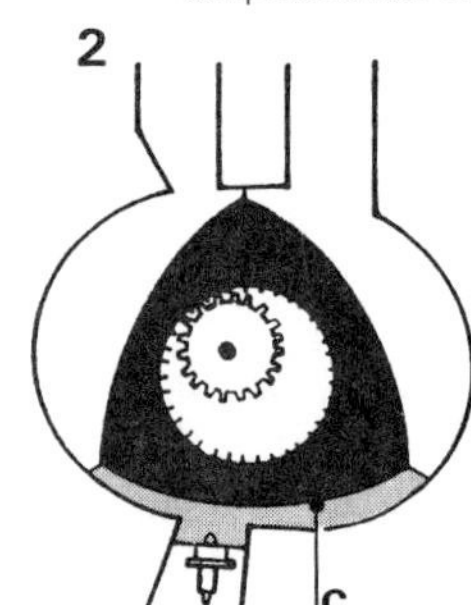

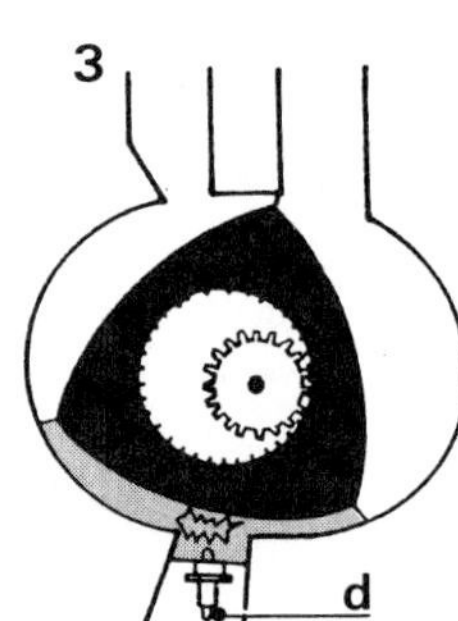

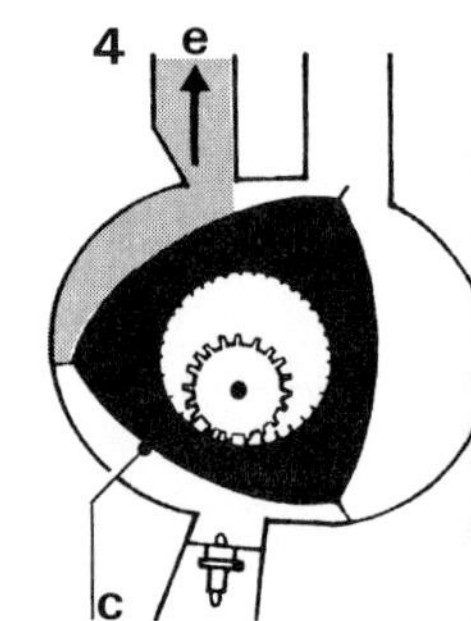

Rocket and jet engines

2313 Jet and rocket engines depend on the law that every action produces an equal and opposite reaction. Hot gases spurting from the back of a jet engine or rocket engine produce the reactive thrust that drives a jet aircraft or a rocket forward. Jet engines obtain oxygen for combustion from the air around them, but rockets carry their own oxygen supply. This is why rockets, but not jets, can travel outside the Earth's atmosphere.
Applications: business aircraft and commuter airliners.

Rocket engines

2314 **Rocket engines**
There are two types of rocket engine: those which burn solid fuel and those which burn liquid fuel.
1 Solid fuel rockets Solid fuel rockets burn fuel in a combustion chamber (**a**) that has an open end (**b**). As the fuel burns it produces gas which forces its way out of the open end of the rocket as it expands, propelling the rocket forward.
2 Liquid-fuel rockets Rockets which burn liquid fuel must also carry oxygen. Liquid hydrogen (**a**) is often used as the fuel, and is fed into a combustion chamber (**b**) where it is mixed with liquid oxygen (**c**). The mixture is then ignited and the gas produced thrusts the rocket along.

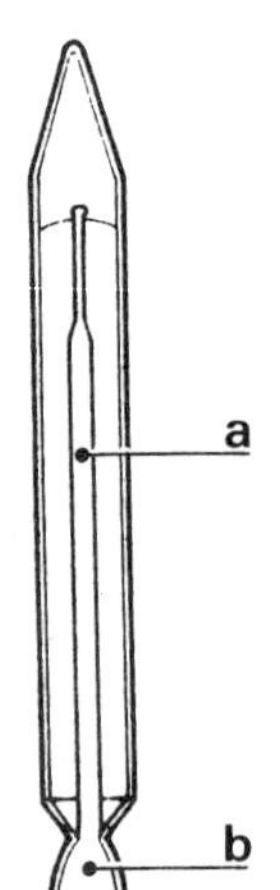

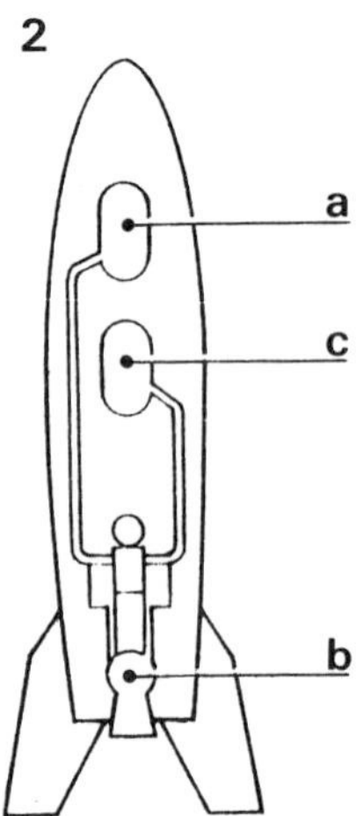

Jet engines

2315 **Jet engines**
Four diagrams show four types of aircraft engine using jet propulsion.

Key
a Air
b Fuel
c Combustion chamber
d Exhaust gases
e Compressor
f Turbine

Ramjet
1 Speed rams air (**a**) under pressure into a tube.

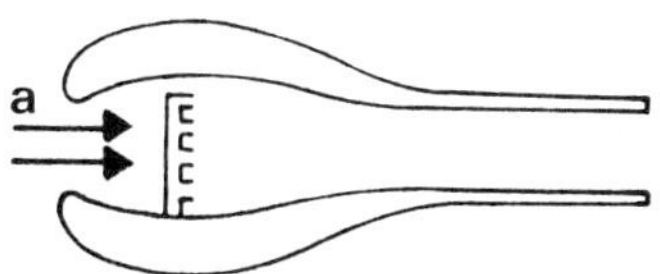

2 Injected fuel (**b**) burns in the tube's combustion chamber (**c**).

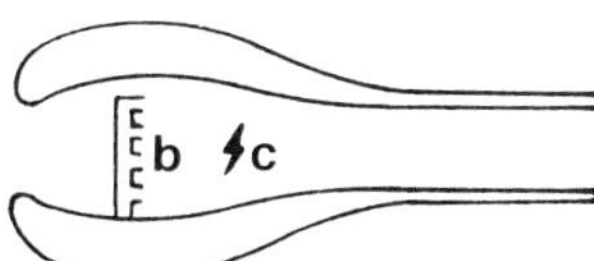

3 Burning gases expand and rush from the back of the tube, forcing it forward (**d**).

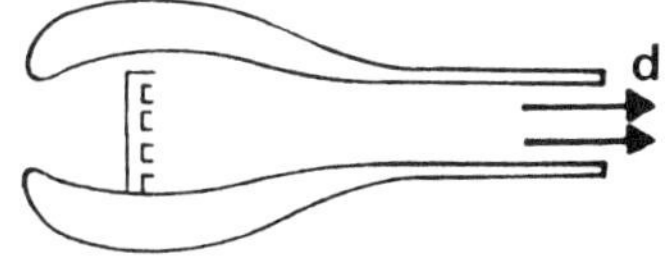

Pulse-jet
1 Air (**a**) rushes into a tube as valves (**g**) within it open.

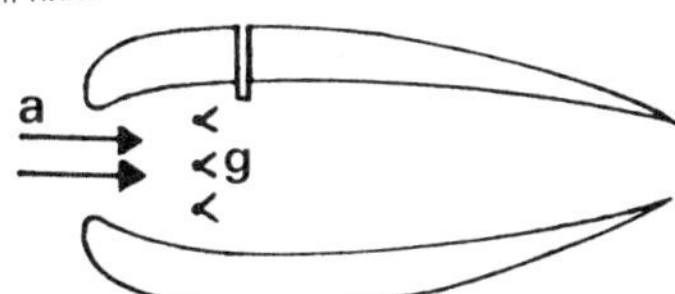

2 Fuel is injected (**b**) and burns in the oxygen contained in the air (**a**).

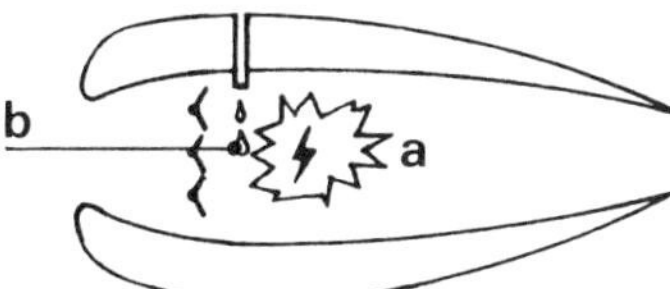

3 The burning mixture rams the valves (**g**) shut and thrusts the tube forward.

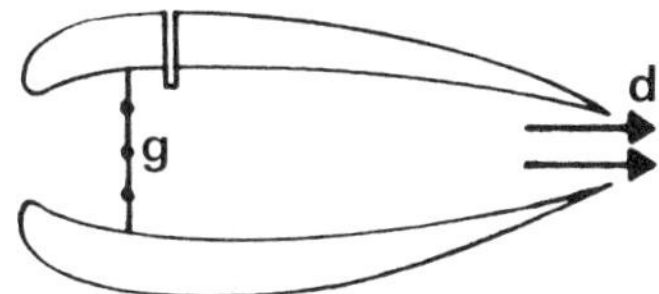

Turbojet
1 Air (**a**) compressed by a compressor (**e**) mixes with fuel (**b**).

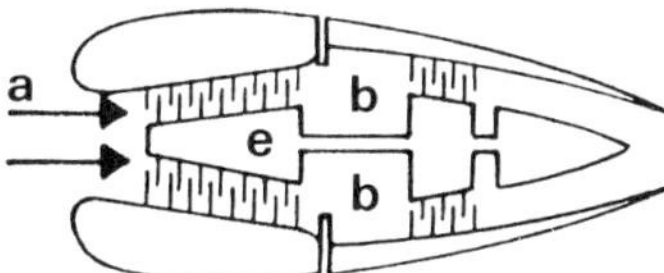

2 Hot gases from the burning fuel produce exhaust gases that spin the blades of a turbine (**f**), which works the compressor.

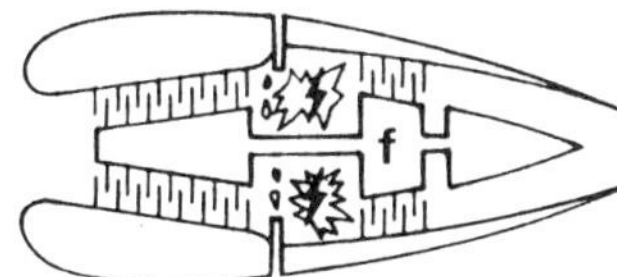

3 Exhaust gases escape thrusting the airplane forward (**d**).

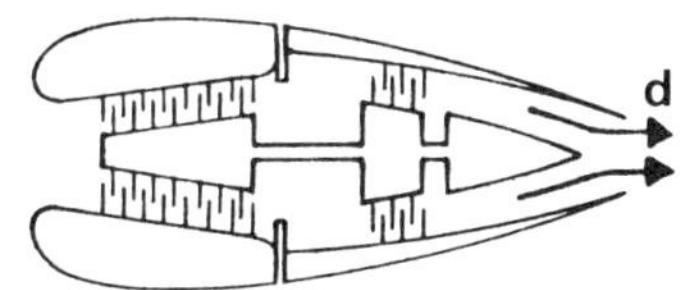

Turboprop

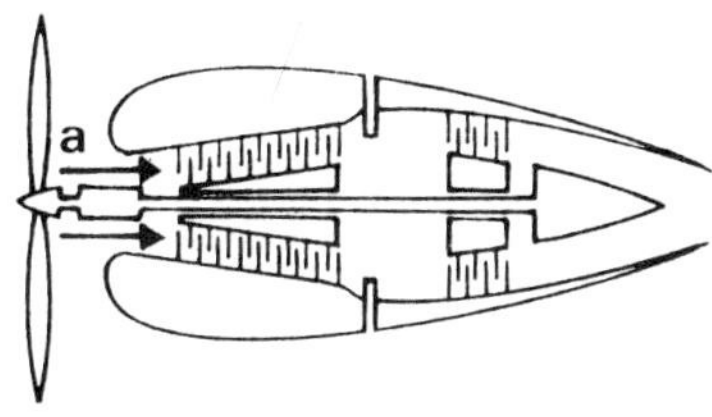

This works in a similar way to the turbojet but most of the exhaust thrust (**d**) is used to spin a

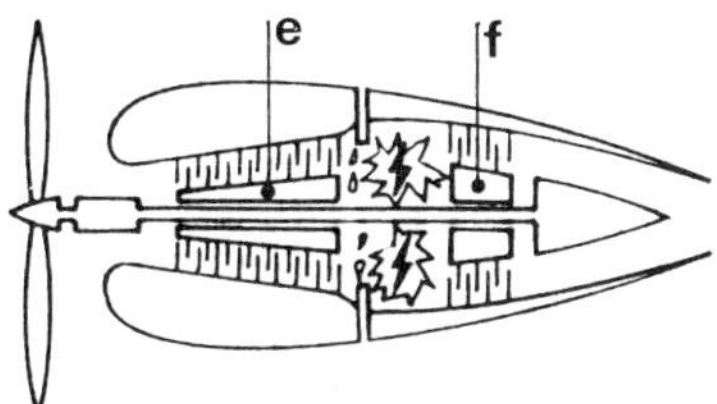

turbine (**f**) which itself spins the compressor(**e**) and a propeller (**h**).

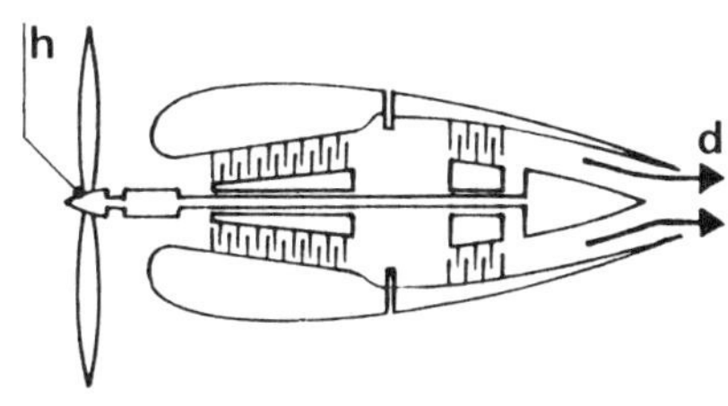

232 FLOATING AND FLYING

Boats

2321 **Why boats float**
In these diagrams arrow sizes indicate relative forces of upthrust (**a**) and displaced water (**b**).
1 A raft floats because water displaced (**b**) by the raft produces an upthrust (buoyancy) (**a**) that is at least equal to the raft's weight.
2 A raft sinks when its weight exceeds upthrust (**a**).
3 A boat floats because the upthrust (**a**) of water is greater than the boat's weight. This boat rides high because bulk for bulk it is much less dense than water.

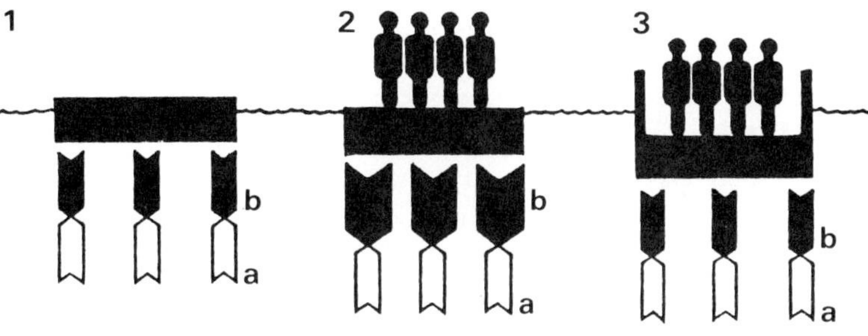

Submarines

232**2** A submarine sinks or rises in water by filling and emptying tanks to alter its density and therefore its buoyancy.
1 Floating on the surface The diving tanks (**a**) are almost empty of water.
2–3 Diving The submarine fills its diving tanks (**a**) with water (**b**).
4–5 Rising Air is pumped into the tanks (**a**) to drive out the water (**b**).

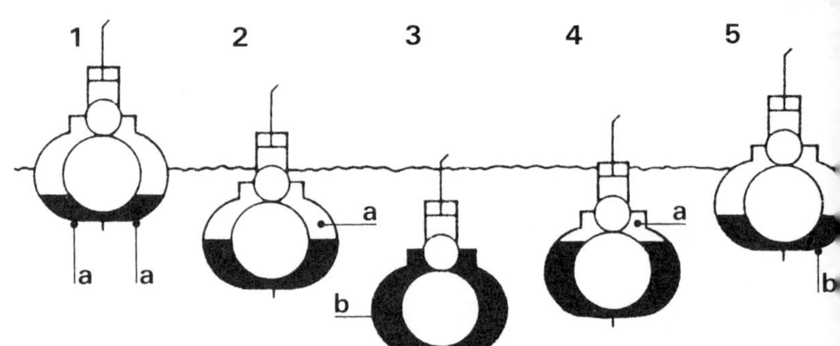

Sailing boats

232**3**

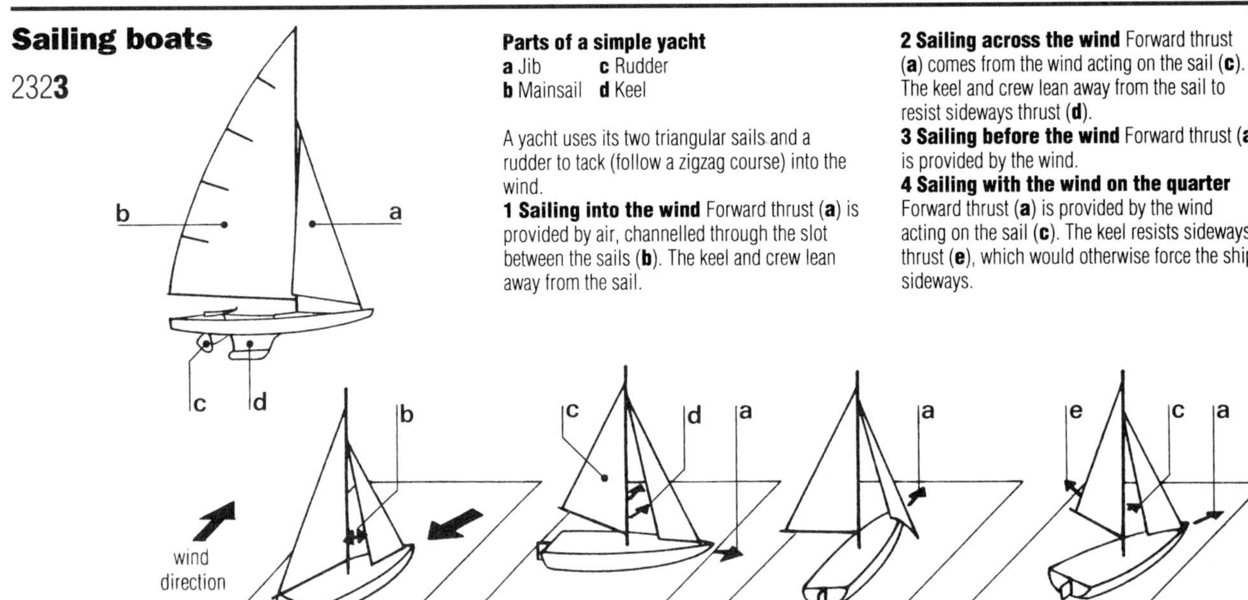

Parts of a simple yacht
a Jib **c** Rudder
b Mainsail **d** Keel

A yacht uses its two triangular sails and a rudder to tack (follow a zigzag course) into the wind.
1 Sailing into the wind Forward thrust (**a**) is provided by air, channelled through the slot between the sails (**b**). The keel and crew lean away from the sail.
2 Sailing across the wind Forward thrust (**a**) comes from the wind acting on the sail (**c**). The keel and crew lean away from the sail to resist sideways thrust (**d**).
3 Sailing before the wind Forward thrust (**a**) is provided by the wind.
4 Sailing with the wind on the quarter Forward thrust (**a**) is provided by the wind acting on the sail (**c**). The keel resists sideways thrust (**e**), which would otherwise force the ship sideways.

Hot-air balloons

232**4** A hot-air balloon rises in air for the same reason that a boat floats on water.
1 Ascent A burner (**a**) heats the air (**b**) which expands in the canopy. Some air escapes (**e**) and the balloon becomes less dense than the air around it, so upthrust (**c**) exceeds weight (**d**).
2 Descent Cooling contracts air in the canopy. Air flows in (**b**). The balloon grows denser and weight (**d**) exceeds upthrust (**c**).

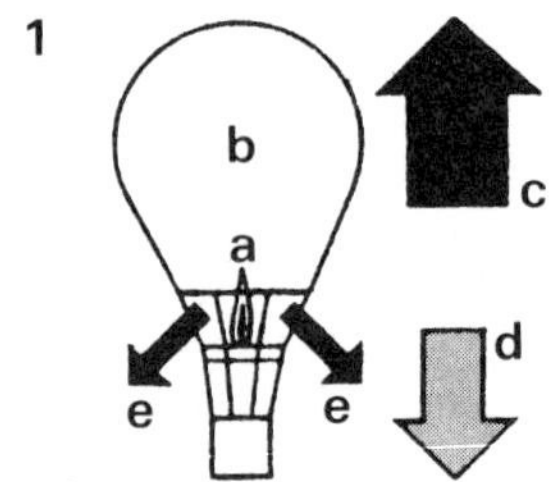

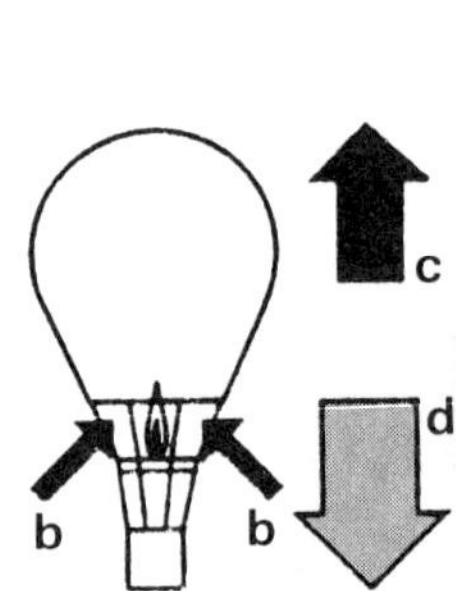

Airships

232**5** Modern airships are filled with a light, nonflammable gas called helium (**1**). Two air-filled compartments (ballonets) (**2**) control the ship's weight. Engines (**3**) at the rear of the ship can be swiveled to assist with maneuverability, as can the rudder (**4**). Passengers travel in a car (**5**).

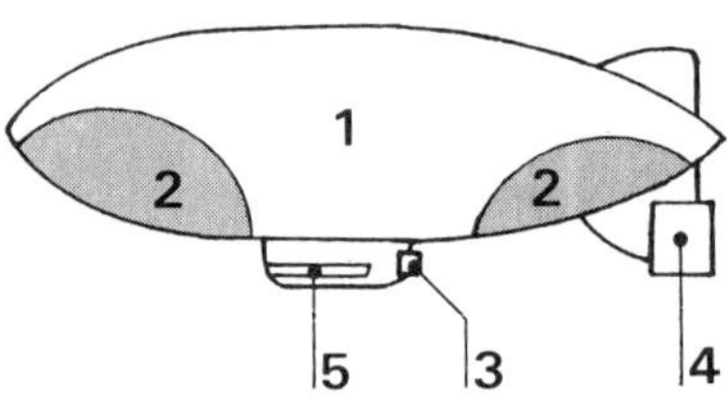

To ascend air is released from the ballonets.
To descend air is pumped into the ballonets.

Parachutes

2326 **1** Because of its domed shape, a parachute canopy has a larger surface area than the area of air through which it is falling. The parachute therefore has a large surface resistance which slows its descent through the air. Drag (**a**) helps to combat the weight (**b**) of the falling parachutist.

2 Stages of a parachute descent:
a Free fall
b Canopy opens
c Canopy retards descent
d Deceleration

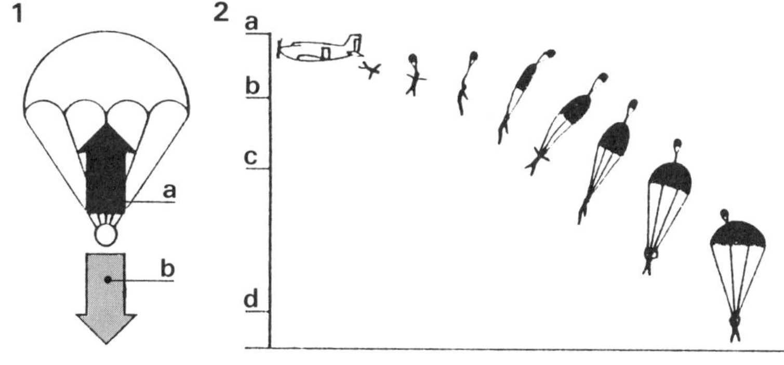

Kites, gliders, and boomerangs

2327

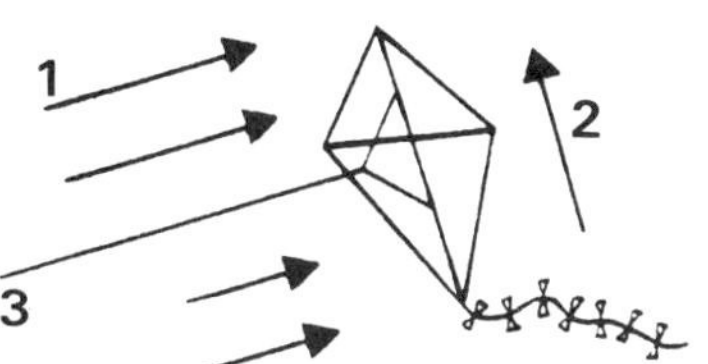

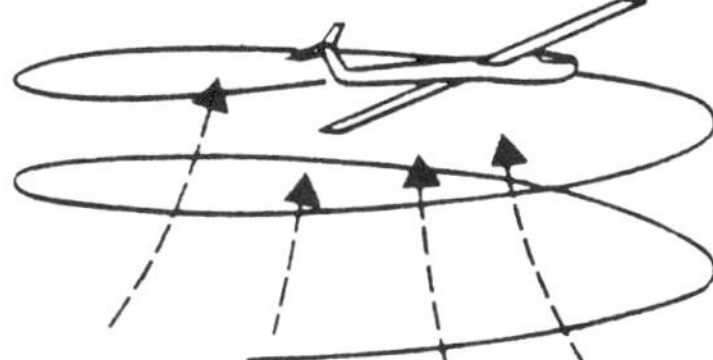

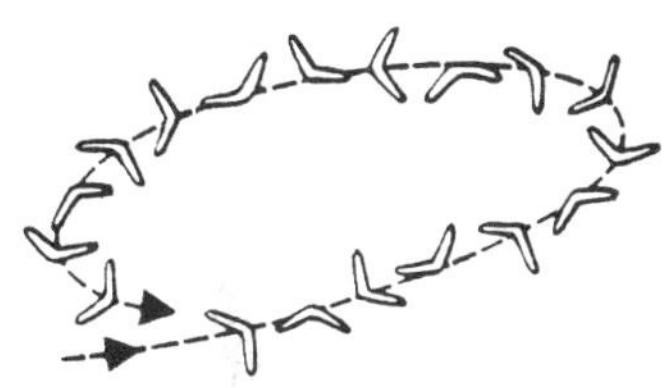

Kites
Kites need a wind to make them fly.
A kite stays airborne if the wind (**1**) produces a reaction force (**2**) as great as the pull of the kite string (**3**).

Gliders
A glider soars upward on rising air if the air rises faster than the glider's rate of descent. Air rises up hills, over warm land and near thunderstorms.

Boomerangs
A boomerang acts similarly to two aircraft wings joined together, flat below and curved above. As a thrown boomerang spins, forces make it curve through the air to return.

Airplanes

2328 **How an airplane flies**
1 Forces of thrust (**a**) from the engines and lift (**b**) from wings and tailplane balance the forces of weight (**c**) and air resistance or drag (**d**).
2 In cross section an aircraft wing is called an aerofoil (**a**), curved so the airflow (**b**) is faster over than under the wing and air above thins out more than air below. This pressure difference forces the wing upward, giving lift (**c**).

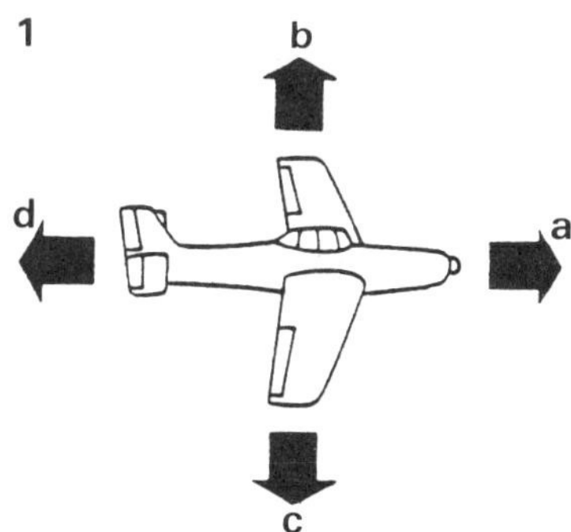

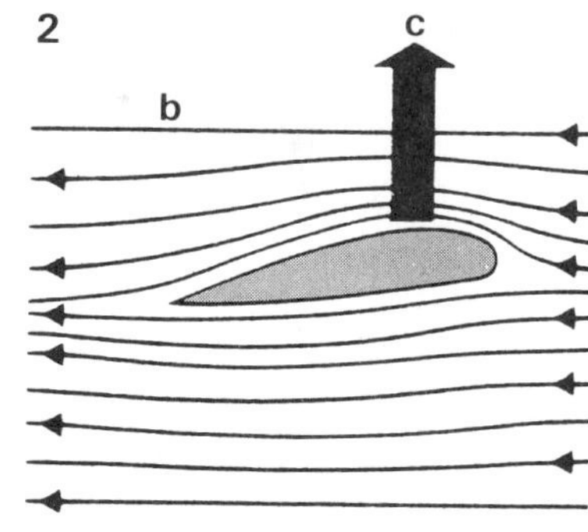

Maneuvering a plane
Pilots maneuver by raising and lowering wing and tail flaps (ailerons and elevators) and turning the rudder.

1 Turning left Left aileron up, right aileron down, rudder turned left.
2 Turning right Left aileron down, right aileron up, rudder turned right.

3 Diving Elevators down.
4 Climbing Elevators up.

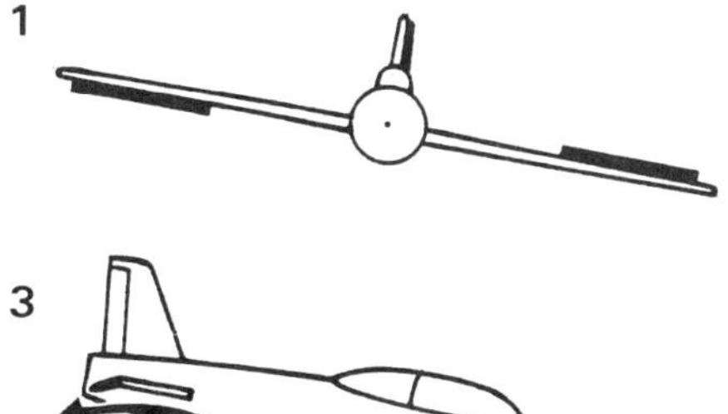

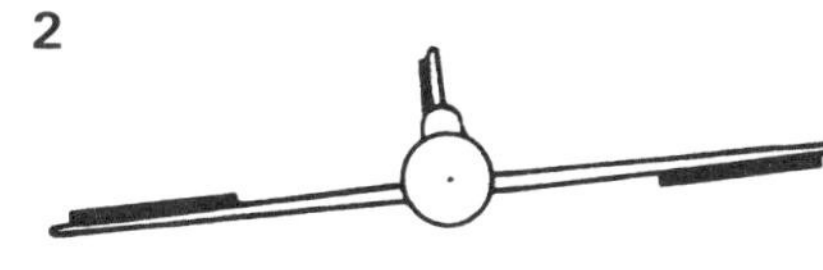

Helicopters

2329 Revolving rotor blades act like a plane's wings to produce lift. A helicopter pilot maneuvers by changing the blades' angle (pitch).
1 Hovering. Lift (**a**) must balance weight (**b**). The blades (shown in cross section) are angled slightly upward.
2 Rising vertically. Lift (**a**) must exceed weight (**b**). The blades' pitch is increased.

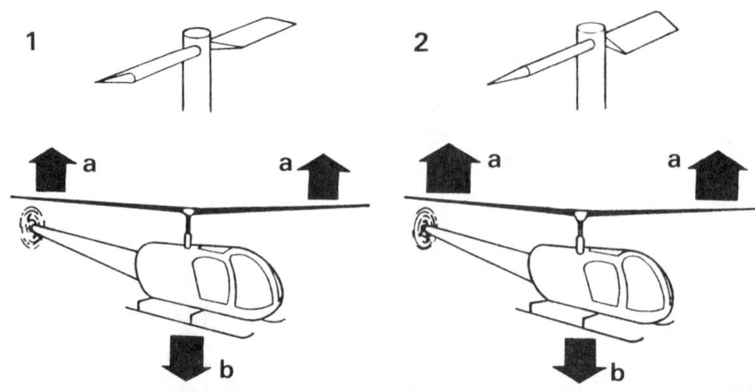

233 ELECTRICAL AND MAGNETIC DEVICES

Making and storing electricity

2331 **Cells and batteries**
A car's wet battery and a flashlight's dry battery convert stored chemical energy into electric current.

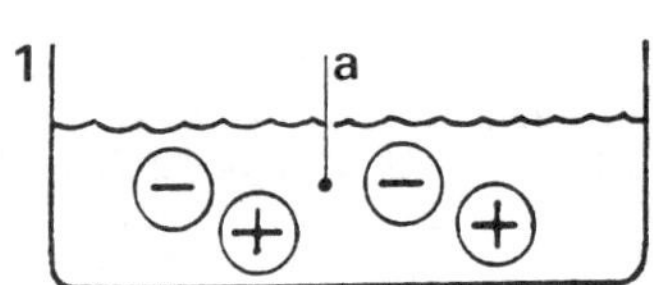

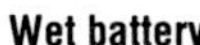

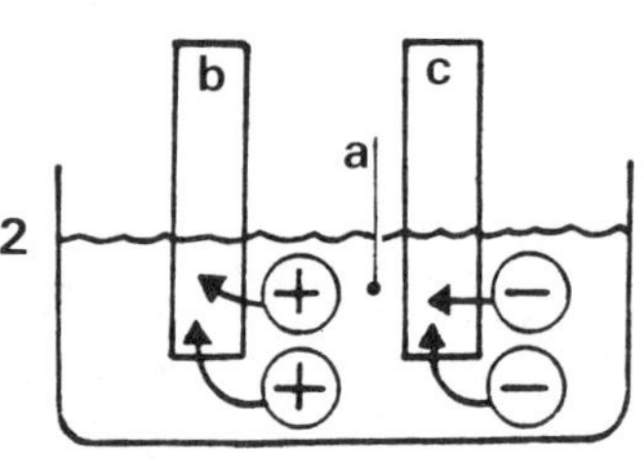

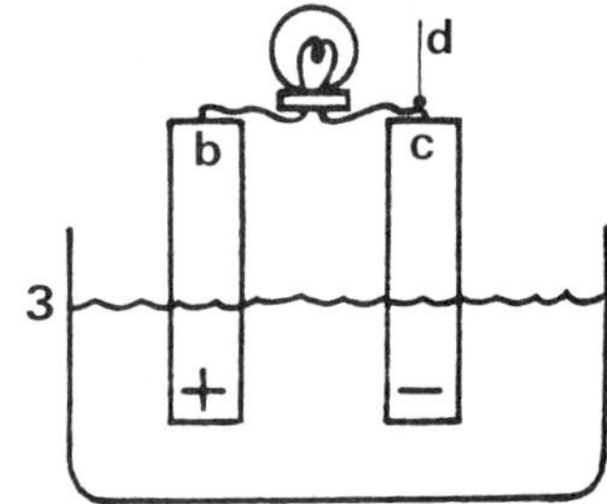

Wet battery
1 A cell from a wet battery has a liquid electrolyte (**a**) with positively and negatively charged particles.

2 A chemical reaction attracts the positive and negative particles to two electrodes (**b**, **c**): rods of different substances placed in the electrolyte (**a**).

3 Electric current then flows through a wire (**d**) between the electrodes (**b**, **c**).

Dry battery
A dry battery works in a similar way to a wet battery, the difference being that instead of having a fluid electrolyte solution, they have a paste electrolyte (**a**). The paste electrolyte is made up of a chemical that reacts to a central rod with the result that some atoms are attracted to one end of the rod, creating positive (**b**) and negative (**c**) anodes at each end of the battery. When both electrodes are connected to make a circuit, a chemical reaction occurs in the electrolyte. Electrons travel from the negative electrode through the connection to the positive electrode, creating a flow of electrons and so current.

Parts of a dry battery
1 Paste electrolyte
2 Positive anode
3 Negative anode
4 Carbon rod
5 Insulating seal
6 Insulating casing

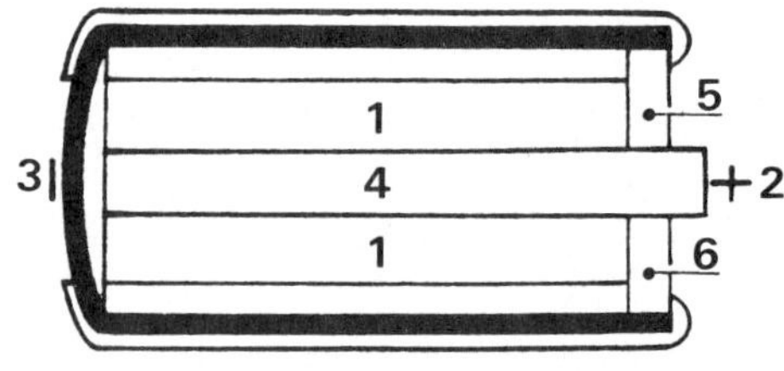

Transformers
Transformers adjust the voltage that alternating current (AC) power lines carry from generators to users.
An iron core (**a**) provides a link between two coils: an input coil, or primary coil (**b**) and an output coil, or secondary coil (**c**). Current in the primary coil (**b**) creates a magnetic field around the iron core (**a**), inducing a current in the secondary coil (**c**).
1 If the secondary coil (**c**) has fewer turns than the primary coil (**b**), voltage (**d**) is reduced.
2 If the secondary coil (**c**) has more turns in it than the primary coil (**b**), voltage (**d**) is increased.

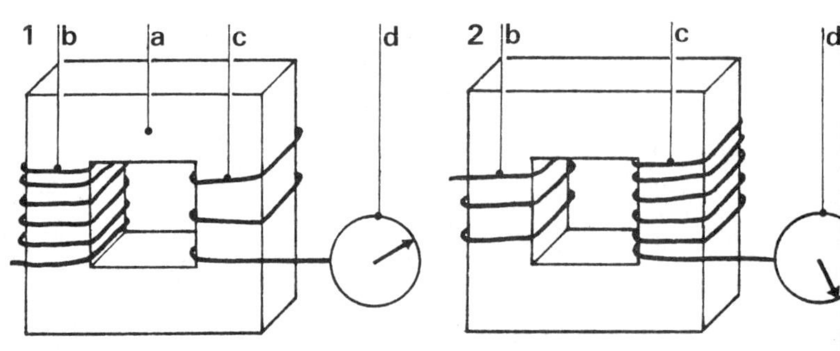

continue

Making and storing electricity continued

2331 **Fuses**

Electric fuses act as circuit breakers, breaking the flow of electricity when the current gets too strong. Their thin wire (**a**) melts when the current increases, breaking the circuit and preventing an excessively high current from setting fire to an appliance as it heats up the wire through which it flows.

There are two types of domestic fuse:
1 Cartridge fuse
2 Plug fuse

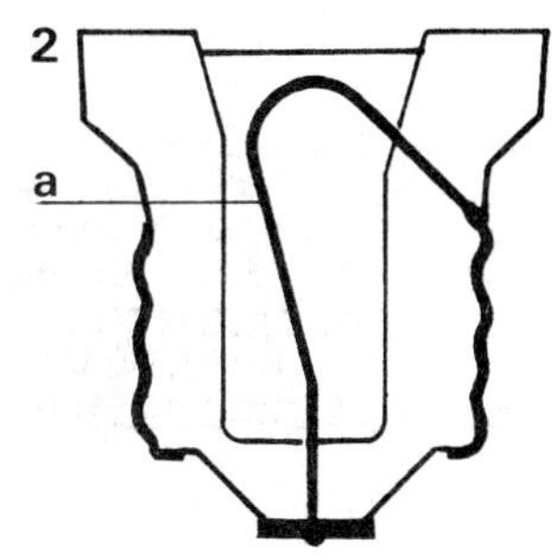

Thermostat

Thermostats regulate temperature. They work on the principal that when an object heats up it expands, and when it cools it contracts.

A simple bimetal thermostat

A bimetallic strip is made of two metals which expand and contract different amounts at different temperatures. One metal expands more than the other and this causes the strip to bend. This reaction can be used to operate a heater switch.

1 Heater on. As the strip cools, it bends back and makes contact with the heater switch. The current can once again flow and the heater is turned on.

2 Heater off. The strip has bent in the heat and opened the contact with the heater and its electricity supply so the current stops flowing and the heater turns off.

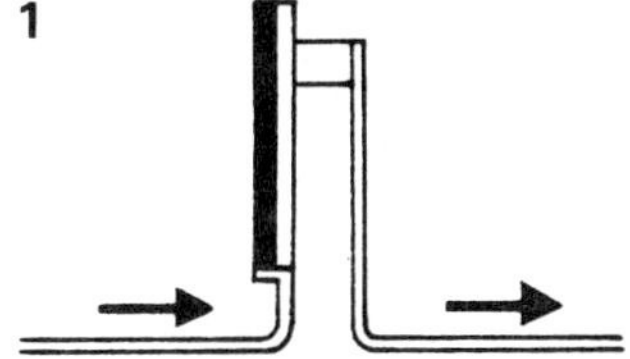

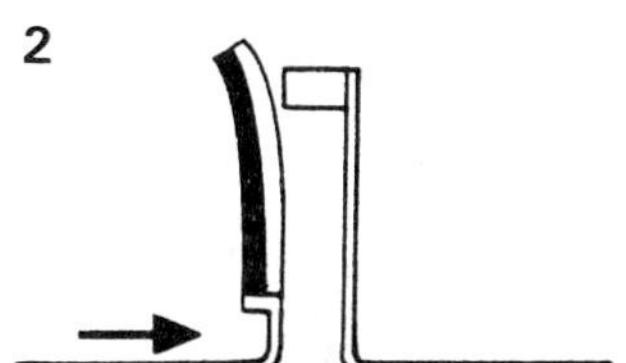

Electric generators (dynamos)

Generators convert mechanical energy into electrical energy through the use of magnets. A spinning wire coil is introduced between the north and south poles of a magnet and electrons within the wire are affected so that they flow along the wire first one way, then another, thus creating an electric current that is alternating in nature.

1 When the wire (**a**) does not interrupt the magnetic field (**c**) between the magnets (**b**) no current flows.

2 When the wire (**a**) interrupts the magnetic field (**c**), electrons (**d**) in the wire are affected and they flow along the wire, creating electricity which has to be channelled off.

3 The wire (**a**) does not interrupt the magnetic field (**c**) as it completes its 180° turn, so electricity does not flow.

4 As the wire (**a**) turns another 90°, it again interrupts the magnetic field and its electrons (**d**) are again affected. They again begin to flow along the wire, creating an electric current, but this time the other way. For each revolution of the coil the current produced by a generator changes direction twice. Generators do not produce electricity from nothing. They are often driven by an outside source of energy such as a steam turbine.

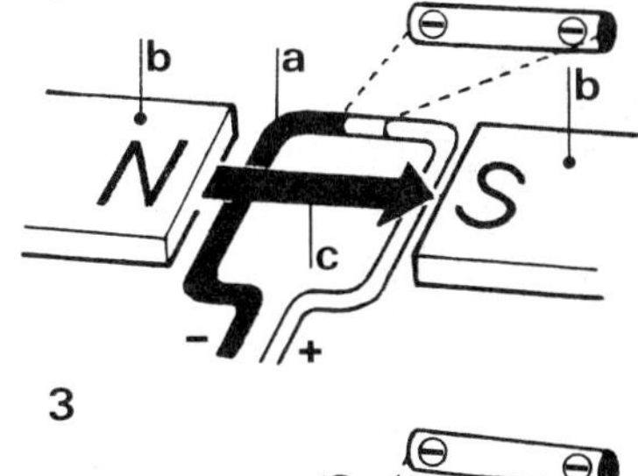

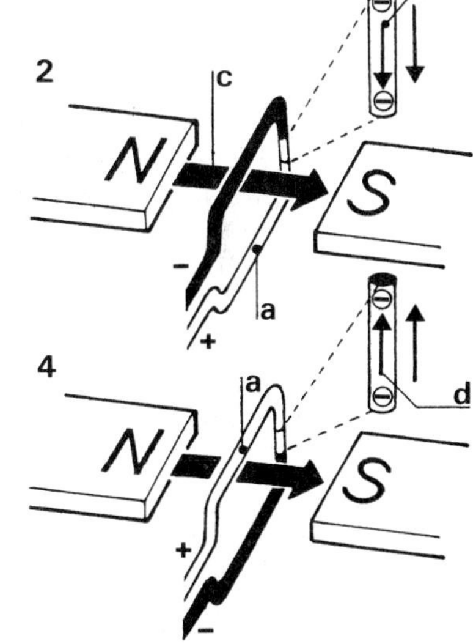

Electric motors

An electric motor is the reverse of a generator: it converts electric energy into mechanical energy by exploiting the force that a magnetic field exerts on a current. Instead of feeding electricity away from a wire loop (as with a generator) electricity is passed to the loop. When the loop is introduced between the magnetic heads, it starts to spin. This spinning movement can then be enhanced and used to power a variety of devices.

In the example, electric current passes through a wire loop (**1**) between the north (**2**) and south (**3**) poles of two magnets. The magnetic force makes the loop spin.

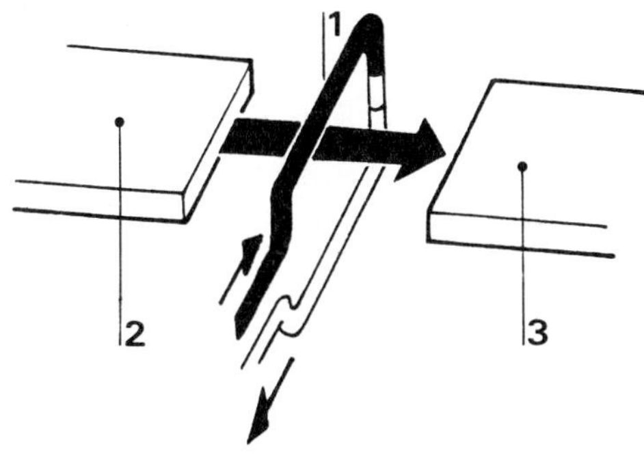

Domestic electrical appliances

2332 Lightning rods

Lightning rods protect buildings from lightning damage by powerful natural discharges of static electricity.

1 In storms, strokes of lightning may hit buildings if a cloud-base gains a negative (-) electric charge and the ground and buildings gain a positive (+) charge. The attraction of opposite charges produces a lightning stroke between the cloud-base and the house.

2 The negative charge in the cloud takes the shortest path to a positive charge. Since a lightning rod produces a positive charge and it is a good conductor of electricity, the lightning will be diverted harmlessly through it to earth.

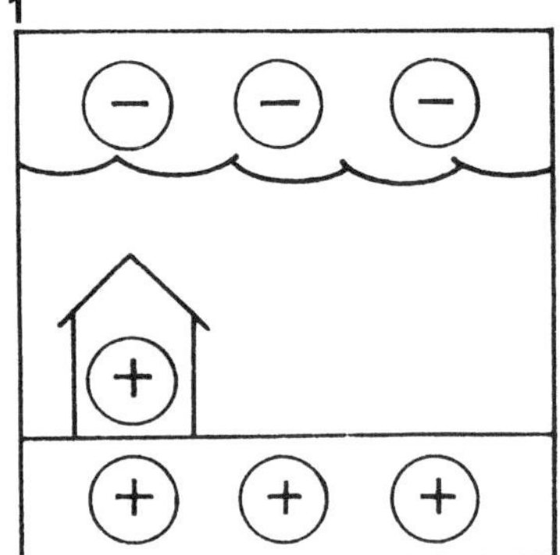

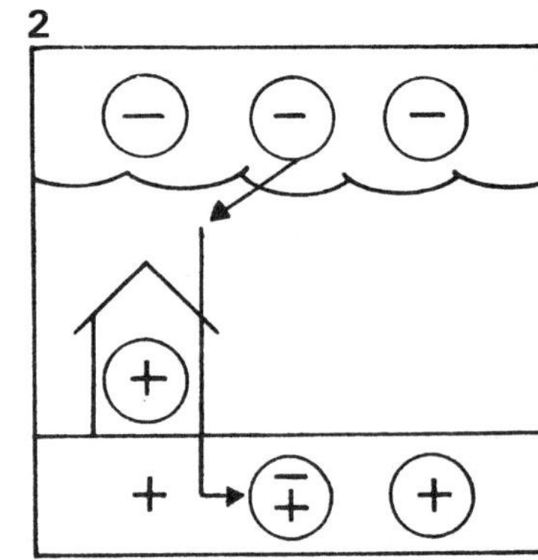

Electric bells

Electric bells employ an electromagnet.

1 Battery
2 Push button
3 Electromagnet
4 Steel plate
5 Contacts
6 Hammer
7 Gong

When you push the button it completes an electric circuit and electricity flows through the coil and contacts. The electromagnet becomes magnetized and attracts the steel plate. Movement of the steel plate and hammer breaks the contacts apart: the electric circuit is broken and the gong is sounded. The electromagnet is demagnetized and the hammer springs back toward the contacts. The process begins again.

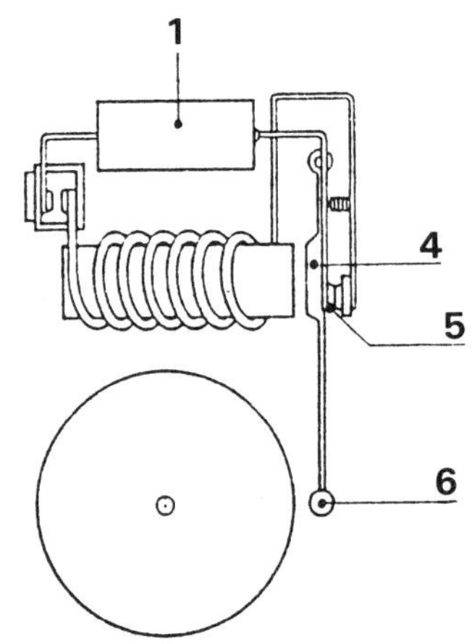

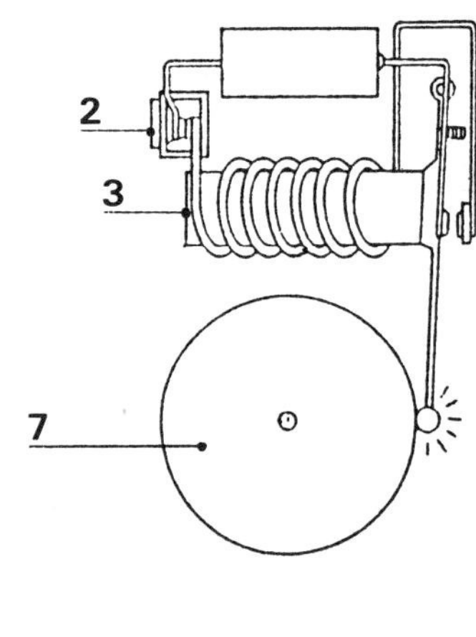

Electric lamps: incandescent

These contain a coiled wire filament, which is part of an electric circuit. The thinner the wire and the greater the number of coils, the more it resists an electric current, so the hotter it gets and the brighter its glow.

Parts of a lamp
1 Fitting
2 Glass bulb
3 Argon gas
4 Glass support
5 Wires
6 Coiled wire filament

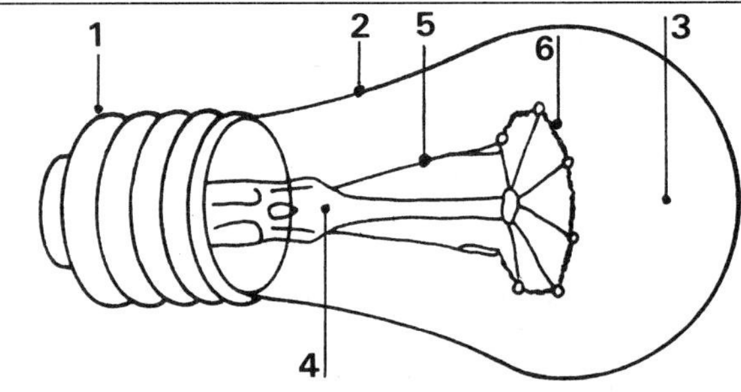

Electric lamps: fluorescent

Fluorescent lamps give the same amount of light, but less heat than incandescent electric lamps, for less cost and they last longer.

1 A fluorescent lamp has a glass tube (**a**) lined with phosphor (**b**) and filled with argon gas and mercury vapor. An electrode at each end (**c**) emits electrons (**d**) into the mercury vapor.

2 When the electrons (**d**) strike the mercury vapor atoms (**e**), the atoms emit rays of ultraviolet light. These rays strike the phospor lining (**b**) and create white light.

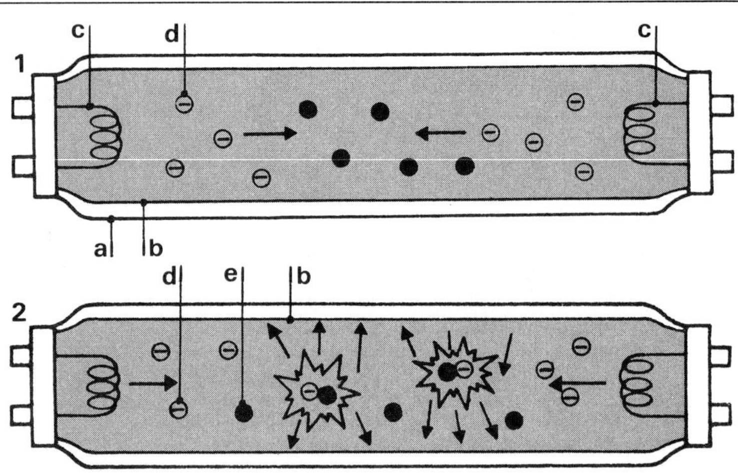

continued

Domestic electrical appliances continued

2332 **Electric kettles and irons**
Electric irons and kettles work in the same way. They both contain coiled wires (**1**) that heat up when an electric current is applied to them. The wire in the base of an iron heats the conductive metal plate, whereas the wire inside a kettle heats water. Both devices are likely to contain a thermostat to prevent the wire from becoming too hot and burning out or causing a fire.

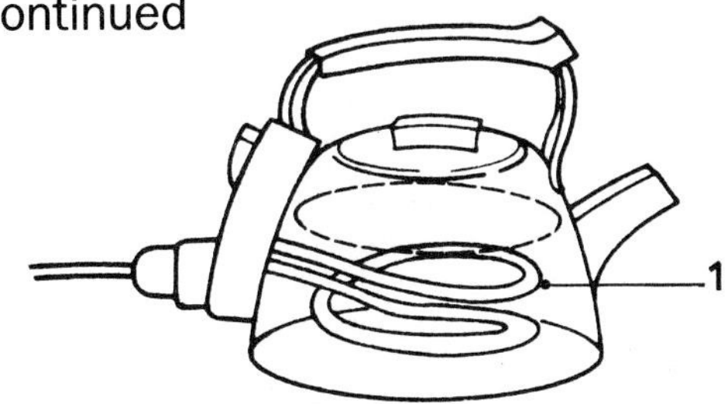

Refrigerators
Refrigerators use a liquid called freon to cool them. **1** Air circulates by convection: cold air sinks, takes heat from food, and slightly warmer air then rises before being cooled again at the top of the refrigerator.

2 This works as freon gas in the pipes (**a**) evaporates in the evaporator (**b**) absorbing heat from the freezer and lowering the temperature at the top of the refrigerator.
The gas flows to an electrically driven compressor (**c**) which compresses the gas and turns it back to a liquid. As this happens heat is released into the room outside the refrigerator and the cycle starts again.

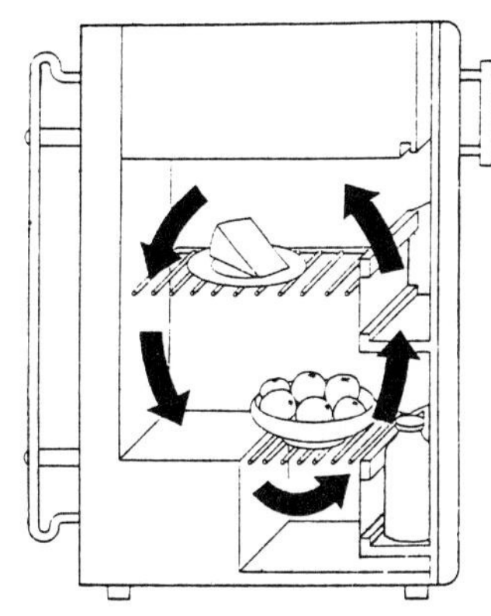

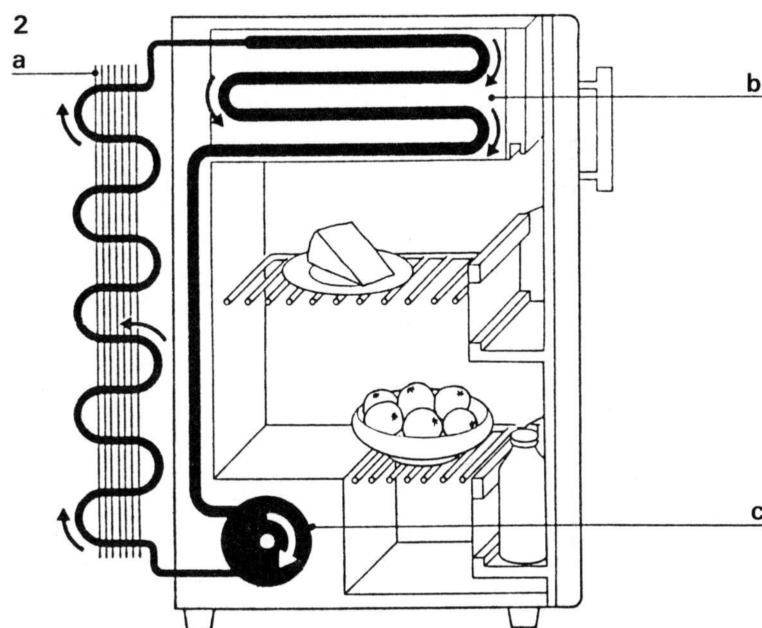

Microwave oven
1 A microwave oven produces a special type of wave that can penetrate food. A device called a magnetron inside the microwave oven produces a beam of microwaves and these are scattered in all directions (and onto the food that is being cooked) by a fan.

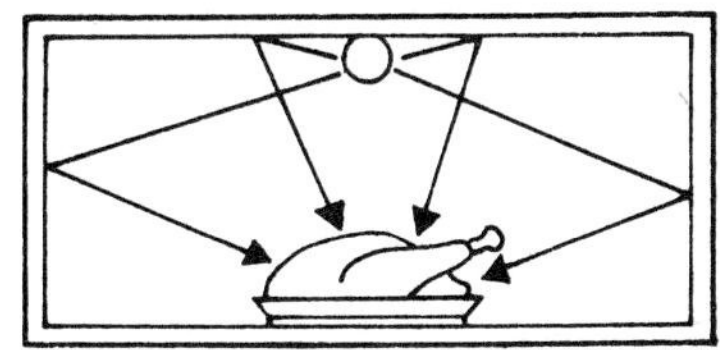

2 Microwaves (**a**) hit water molecules in food (**b**).
3 This causes the water molecules (**b**) to rotate as they reverse their alignment within the food.
4 It is the constant rotating movement of the microscopic molecules in the food that produces the heat, cooking the food (**c**).

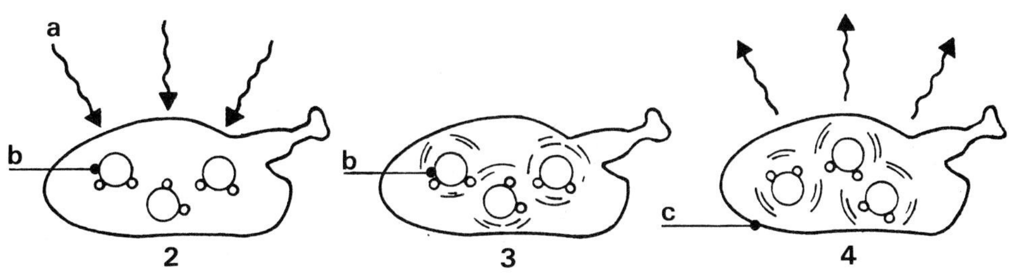

continued

Domestic electrical appliances continued

2332 **Sewing machine**
A sewing machine is powered by an electric motor.
1 The needle (**a**) takes the upper thread (**b**) through the fabric (**c**).
2 The hook (**d**) of the shuttle (**e**) picks up the loop of the upper thread (**b**) as the needle reaches the lowest point.
3 The needle rises and the shuttle (**e**) takes up the loop making it bigger as it rotates.
4 As the loop of the upper thread (**b**) goes around the bobbin (**f**) it goes round the lower thread (**g**) creating a stitch.
5 A take up lever pulls the loop of the upper thread tight.
6 The fabric is moved along by a device called the feed dog and the sequence begins again.

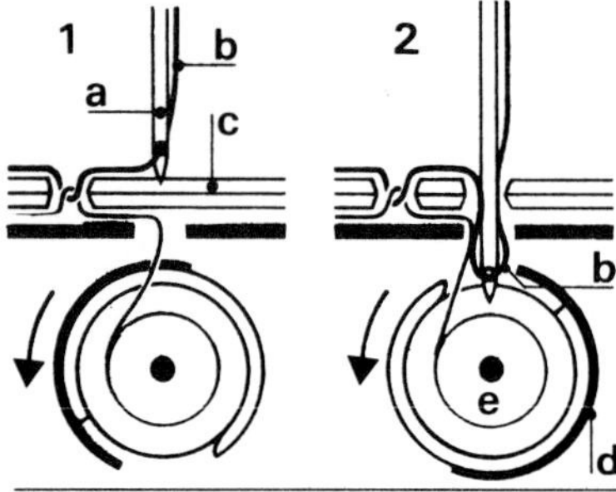

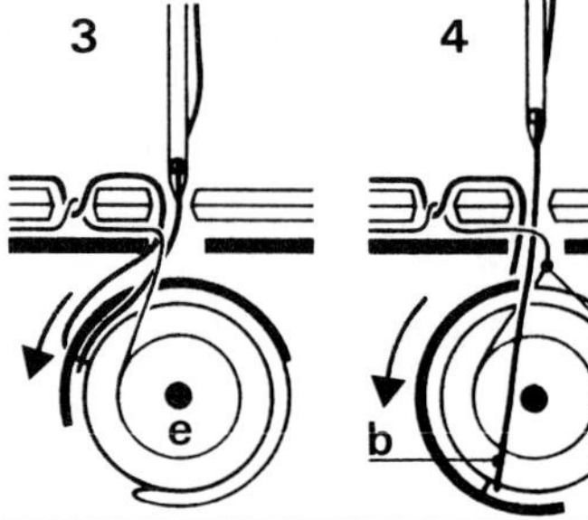

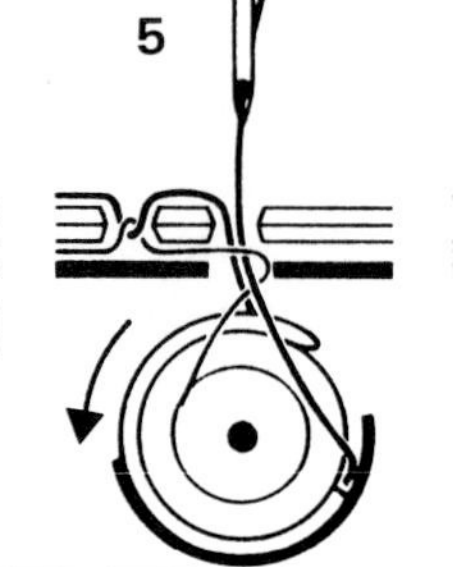

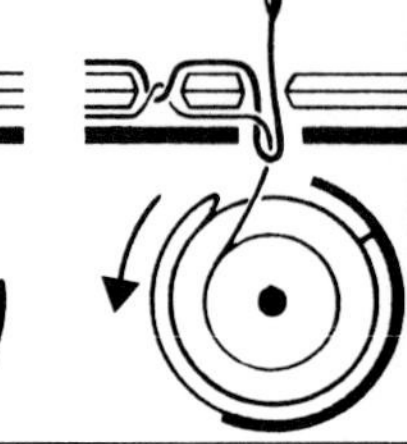

Electrostatic air cleaners
Air cleaners are ionizers: they give airborne dust or smoke particles (**1**) a positive charge (**2**).
A negatively charged collector (**3**) traps the particles, cleaning the air.

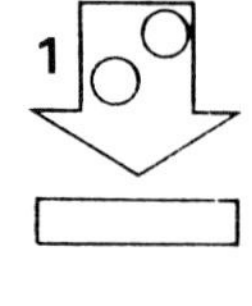

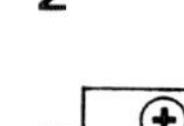

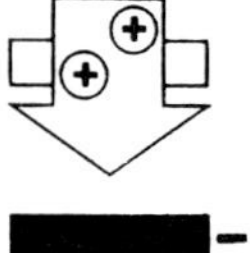
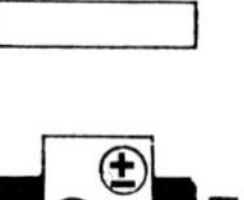

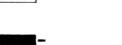

Commercial electrical appliances

2333 **Photocopier**

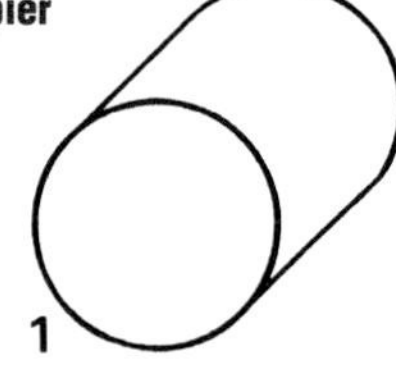

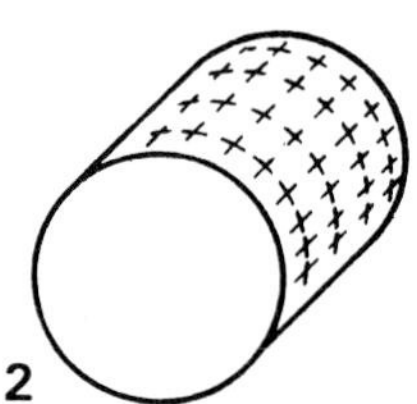

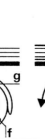

1 A metal plate is wrapped around a cylinder. It conducts electricity only when exposed to light.
2 The plate is given an electric charge.
3 The image to be copied is focused on the plate.
4 Where light falls, the electric charge is conducted away.

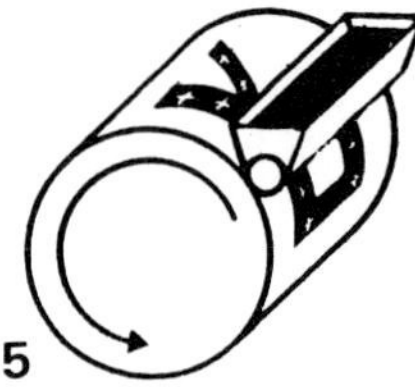

5 Toning powder is dusted over the plate and adheres to the charged image area only.
6 Specially coated paper is pressed against the plate.
7 The powder image adheres to the paper and is fixed using heat.

Maglev trains
Electromagnetism operates these wheelless trains. Magnetic fields move them along and also keep them levitated (raised) above a rail, so eliminating wheel-rail friction.
Electromagnets below the train pull it up toward a "suspension" rail.
Maglev trains use linear motors for propulsion. There are propulsion magnets under the train (**a**). The rail (**b**) has electromagnetic coils. Computers sense where the train is and send electric current to the coils in the rail under the train. As the electromagnetic force travels along the rail it pulls the train along with it.
A second set of electromagnets (**c**) under the train, which are aided by computer sensors, keep it constantly aligned with the rail.

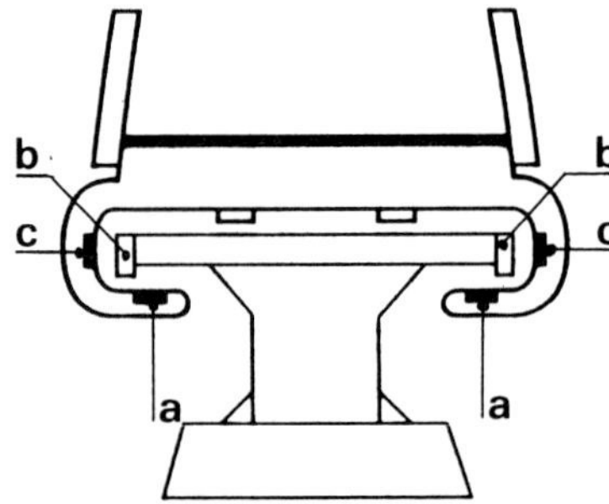

234 PUMPS AND PRESSES

Piston and valved pumps

2341 **Piston pumps**

Pumps use pressure to move fluids. In bicycle pumps or water pistols, a piston moving back and forth in a cylinder sucks a fluid or air in at one end of the pump and forces it out at the other, as shown.

1 The piston (**a**) moves down, forcing air (**b**) from the pump, through the outlet (**c**).

2 As the piston moves back, the outlet valve (**d**) shuts but an inlet valve (**e**) opens, letting water or air (**f**) rush in to fill the low-pressure space that has been emptied of air.

3 The inlet valve (**e**) shuts as the piston moves down, forcing water or air through the outlet valve (**d**).

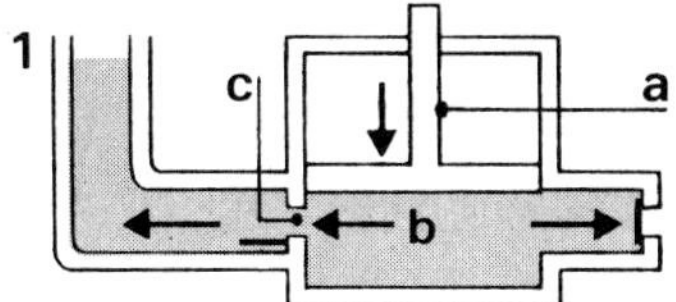

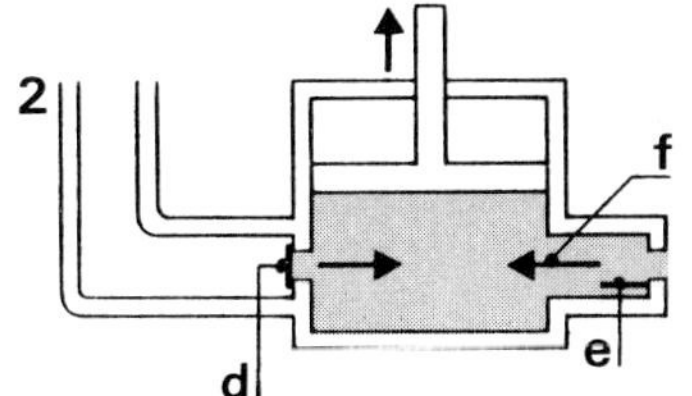

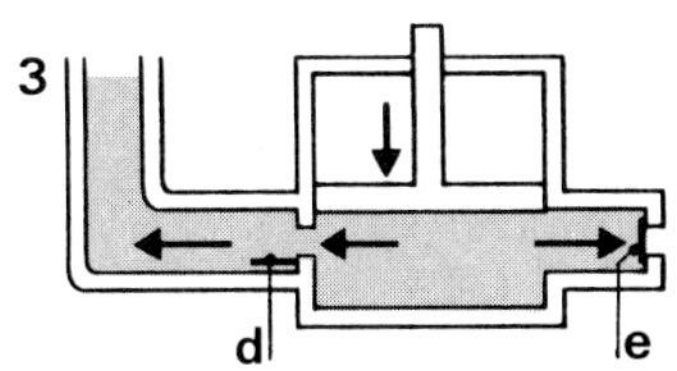

Lifting pumps

Atmospheric pressure helps a piston pump to pump low-level water up through a cylinder, as shown.

1 Raising the pump handle lowers the piston (**a**) and opens its inlet valve (**b**), so that the piston descends into water.

2 Lowering the pump handle raises the piston and closes its valve, so water is lifted up and out of the pump. This leaves a vacuum below the piston, forcing water, under atmospheric pressure (**c**), to open an inlet valve (**d**) and rise to fill the gap.

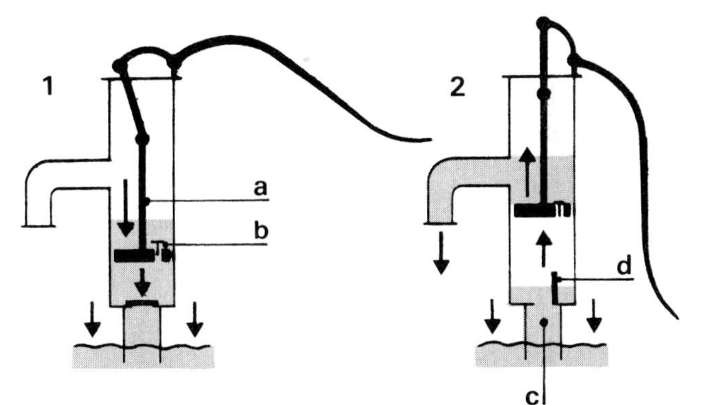

Diaphragm pumps

A car's fuel pump reduces the risk of fuel leaks by using a flexible diaphragm instead of a piston. This pump forces some of the fuel stored in the tank into the engine.

1 A rod (**a**) raised by a spring, lifts the diaphragm (**b**). Its pressure forces fuel (**c**), through an outlet valve (**d**), from the pump to the engine.

2 Operated by a lever, the rod (**a**) lowers the diaphragm, and the outlet valve (**d**) shuts. As fuel pressure falls, fuel from the tank flows into the pump through an inlet valve (**e**).

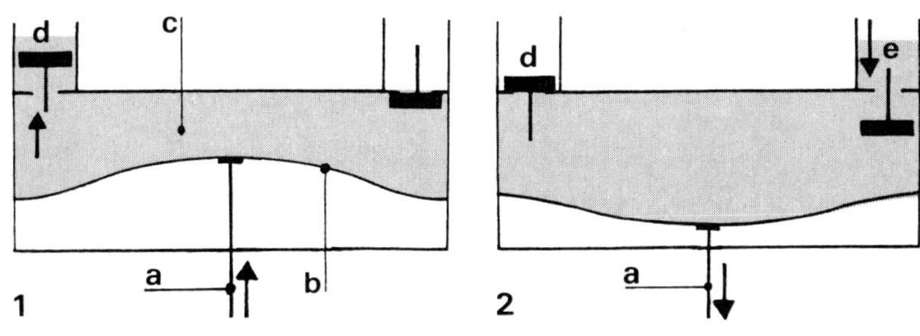

Hydraulic ram

A hydraulic ram uses the kinetic energy of falling water to lift water higher than the level from which it originally fell.

Water from a reservoir (**1**) flows down a pipe (**2**) and along another section of pipe (**3**). This shuts a valve (**4**) causing a build up of pressure. Water is forced up a vertical pipe (**5**) squeezing the air in the air tank (**6**) creating an increase in pressure.

As this pressure increases, the water in the vertical pipe reaches a certain level and closes another valve (**7**). The air pressure forces the water down a discharge pipe (**8**) into a storage tank (**9**).

As pressure decreases, the valves reopen and the process begins again.

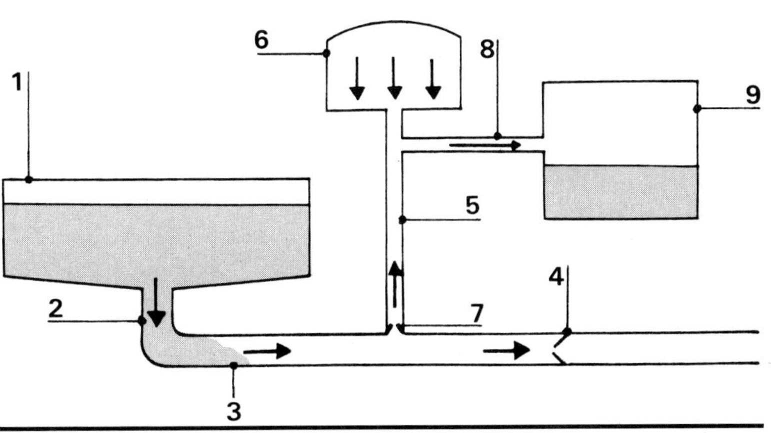

continued

2341 Piston and valved pumps continued
2342 Rotary pumps
2343 Air devices
2344 Liquid devices

Piston and valved pumps continued

2341

Hydraulic presses
Hydraulic presses are machines that magnify the effects of a force acting on a confined liquid. The diagram shows what happens when water pressure is increased and force is transmitted between pistons in connected cylinders of different sizes.
1 A mass of 10 lb placed on a piston within a fluid-filled tube measuring 1 sq in exerts 10 lb per sq in.
2 The same weight applied to the same tube but this time connected to a larger cylinder (of 50 sq in) the pressure of 10 lb acts on 50 sq in to produce a force of 500 lb. In other words, a force of 10 lb has been used to lift a force of 500 lb.

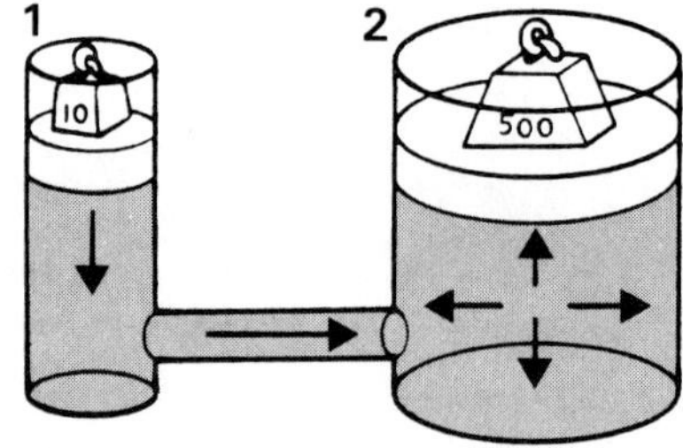

Shock absorbers
Hydraulic systems operate a car's brakes and shock absorbers. Brakes work using the hydraulic press principle. Depressing a brake pedal operates a piston that forces brake fluid through pipes; the brake fluid acts equally upon the brake shoes of all four wheels.
Shock absorbers (**1**) are parts of an automobile's suspension system between the body and the wheels. Each shock absorber includes a piston. As the piston moves, in response to suspension spring movements, oil is forced through a narrow hole, which slows down the action of the piston. In turn, the unwanted vertical movements of the springs (**2**), on bumpy roads, are reduced.

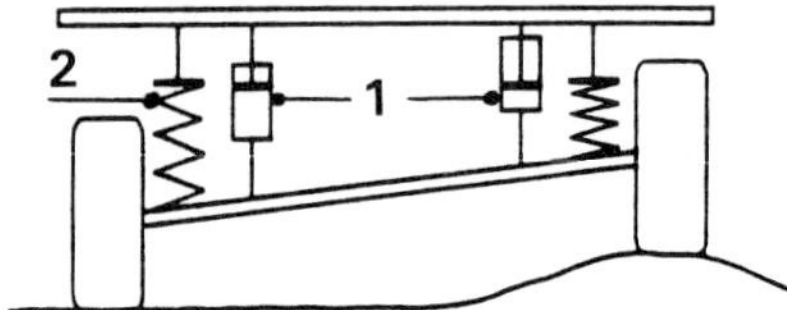

Rotary pumps

2342

Vane pumps
The rotor (**b**) rotates slightly off center and the sliding vanes (**c**) are thrown outward to touch the outer edges of the chamber, creating compartments of differing sizes in which the fuel is transported from **1** through **5**.
At **1** the fuel enters the chamber through an inlet (**a**) and is compressed at **2**, **3**, **4**, and forced out of the chamber at **5** under high pressure through an outlet (**d**). This creates a partial vacuum in compartment **6** before the sequence begins again, drawing in fuel at **1**.
Centrifugal pumps
These are found in chemical factories and car cooling systems. In a centrifugal pump, a fan-like impeller (**1**) revolves in a chamber. The impeller blades suck fluid through an inlet (**2**) into the chamber center. They then fling the fluid outward at high speed, increasing its pressure until it escapes through an outlet (**3**).

Peristaltic pumps
These are used in heart-lung machines where blood might clog up most other pumps. Revolving rollers (**1**) keep pushing blood through a flexible tube (**2**). A peristaltic pump can thus keep blood circulating through a patient's body, while surgeons operate to repair the patient's own pump: the heart.

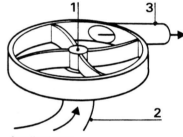

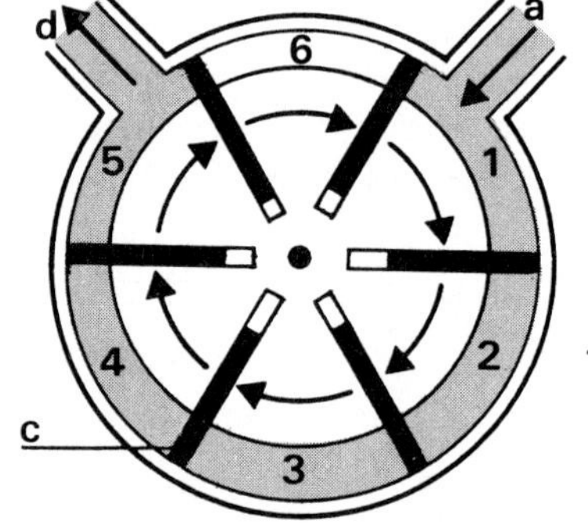

Vane pump

1
3
2

Centrifugal pump

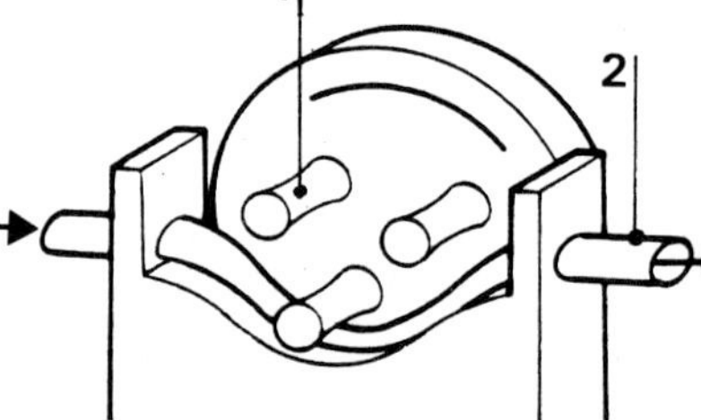

Peristaltic pump

Air devices

2343

Vacuum cleaners
These use atmospheric pressure to remove dirt. In the example shown, the suction fan (**1**) sucks air from the canister (**2**), creating a partial vacuum inside. Air from outside rushes up the hose (**3**) and into the bag in the canister (**4**), carrying dirt picked up by the nozzle (**5**).

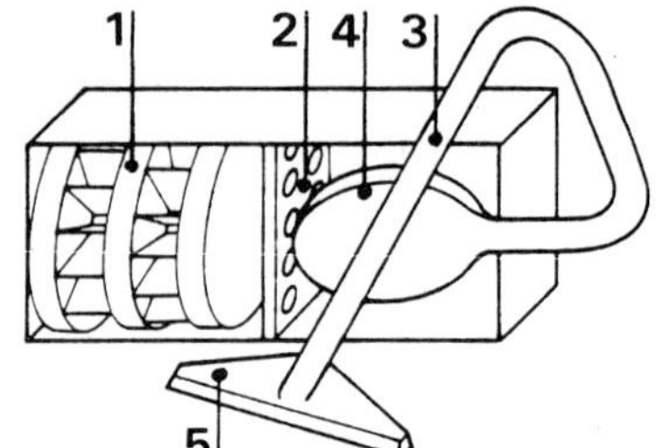

Hovercraft
When under considerable pressure, air can support a weight. Doubling air pressure on area acted upon doubles the weight supported. ACVs (hovercraft) rest on a cushion of compressed air. The air's upward pressure buoys them up so that they float just above land or water; they have to overcome only air resistance as their propellers thrust them along. The cross-section shows an ACV's major features. A fan (**1**) sucks in air (**2**) from above and forces it under the vehicle (**3**), creating a high pressure air cushion trapped close to the surface by a flexible rubberized skirt (**4**).

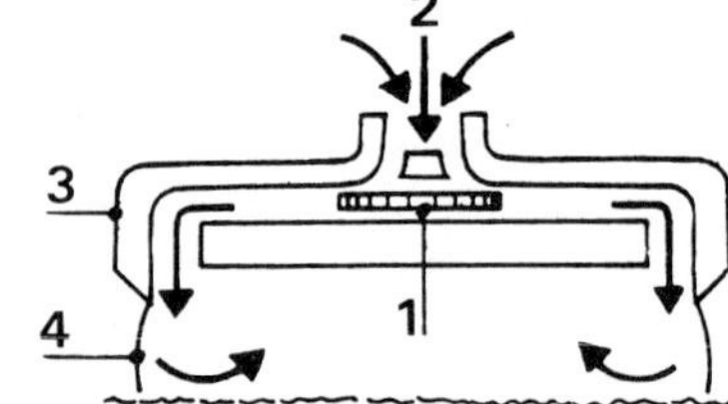

continued

Air devices continued

2343 **Pneumatic machines**

1 The trigger (**a**) is depressed and air enters through the intake tube (**b**) at high pressure. It is guided into the cylinder (**c**) by a rocker valve (**d**), forcing the piston (**e**) down onto the anvil and hammer tool (**f**).
2 When the piston (**e**) passes the exhaust hole (**g**), air escapes lowering the pressure inside the cylinder (**c**).
3 Incoming high-pressure air rocks the valve (**d**) opening the other air passage (**h**). The pressurized air then forces the piston (**e**) up until it again passes the exhaust hole (**g**).
4 The air then escapes through the exhaust hole (**g**), lowering the pressure within the cylinder (**c**) once more and continuing the cycle.

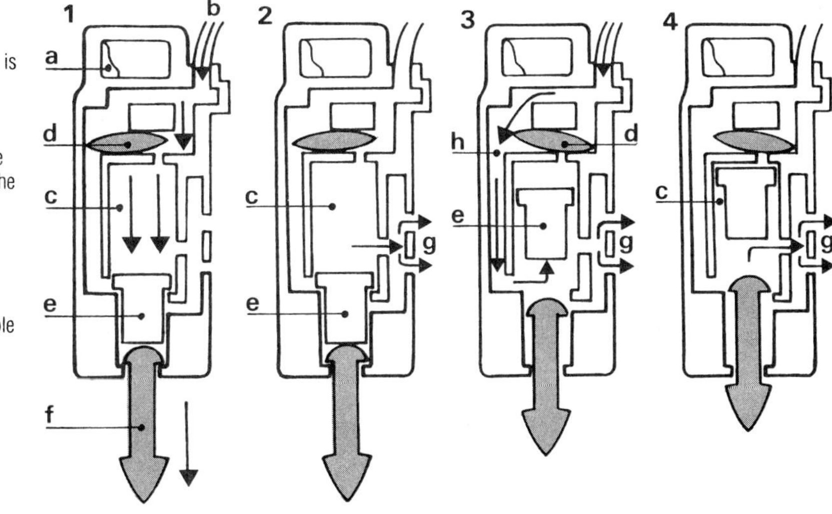

Liquid devices

2344 **Barometers**

These instruments measure atmospheric pressure. In a mercury barometer, atmospheric pressure (**1**), acting on the exposed mercury surface (**2**) balances the weight of a column of mercury (**3**) in a sealed tube (**4**) callibrated in inches or millimeters, at the top of which is a vacuum (**5**).
A rise in atmospheric pressure pushes down on the mercury causing it to rise in the tube. A drop in atmospheric pressure pushes down less on the mercury, providing a smaller counterforce and allowing the mercury to fall in the tube.

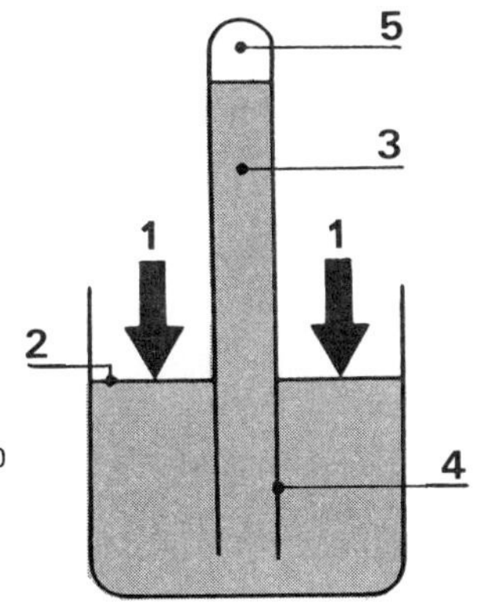

Thermometers

Thermometers measure temperature. They are filled with mercury or alcohol which expands and contracts according to the temperature.
1 When the temperature increases, liquid in the bulb of the thermometer (**a**) expands and is forced up the thin glass tube in which it is cased, thus giving a higher temperature reading.
2 When the temperature drops, the liquid contracts and falls within the glass tube, giving a lower temperature reading.

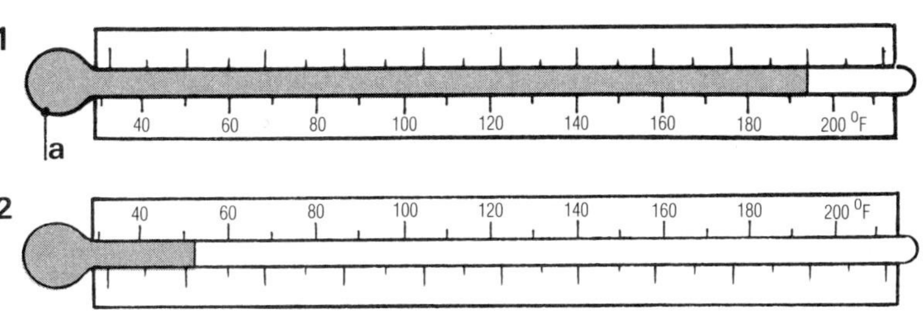

Manometers

These measure differences in fluid pressure. A manometer comprises a liquid reservoir and a tube leading from it, from which pressure can be read.
1 When the pressure in the reservoir (**a**) is low, liquid in the outflow tube (**b**) is also low.
2 But, if pressure within the reservoir increases, it forces fluid higher up into the outflow tube, giving a higher pressure reading.

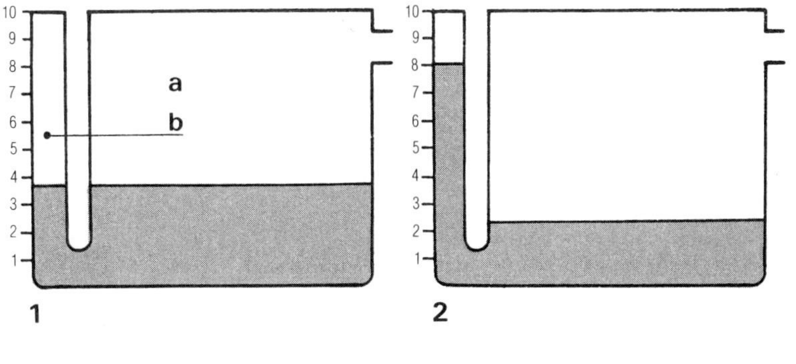

235 DEVICES USING LIGHT

Optical fibers

235**1** These narrow transparent glass or plastic fibers transmit light to show internal parts of the body or to relay long-range telecommunications signals.
1 Much enlarged end of a bundle of individual optic fibers (**a**). Each fiber conveys part of an image.
2 Longitudinal section of a fiber, with a light signal (**b**) moving through the glass core (**c**) as it is bounced back and forth by the core's cladding (**d**).

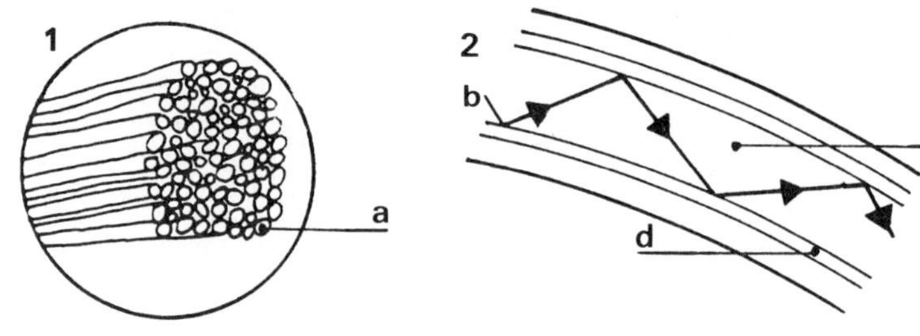

Periscopes

235**2** Periscopes enable the user to see round corners. Simple periscopes consist of two mirrors, positioned in such a way as to let the user see what would otherwise be hidden. Light rays (**1**) are reflected from mirror (**2**) onto mirror (**3**) and it is the image on mirror (**3**) that is viewed.

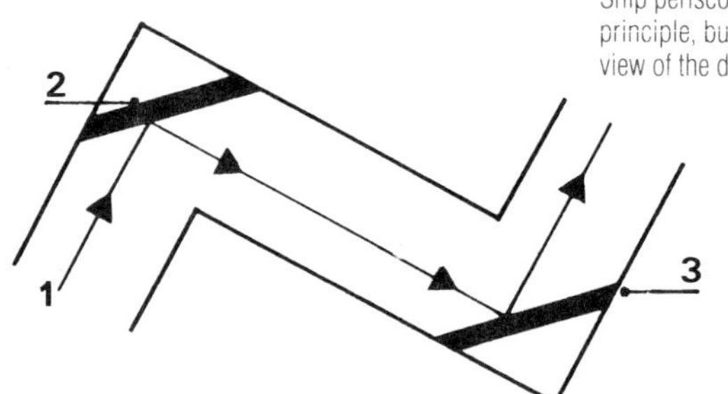

Ship periscopes work on exactly the same principle, but also employ lenses to enlarge the view of the distant objects that they are seeing.

Optical telescopes

235**3** These tubes use lenses or a combination of both lenses and mirrors to magnify distant objects.
1 Refracting telescope: the objective lens (**a**) bends incoming light rays (**b**), producing an image viewed through the eyepiece lens (**c**).
2 Reflecting telescope: the objective mirror (**a**) reflects light rays onto a flat mirror (**b**) that, in turn, reflects light into the eyepiece lens (**c**) at the side of the microscope.

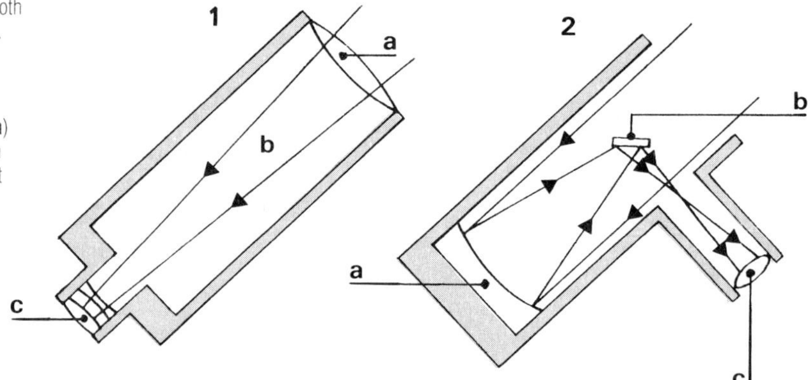

Binoculars

235**4** These give each eye a separate enlarged view of the same distant object to form one three-dimensional image.
Light (**1**) passes through objective lenses (**2**), forming a reversed, inverted image. A prism (**3**) turns this the right way around. A second prism (**4**) turns it the right way up before it passes through the eyepiece lenses (**5**) to the eye.

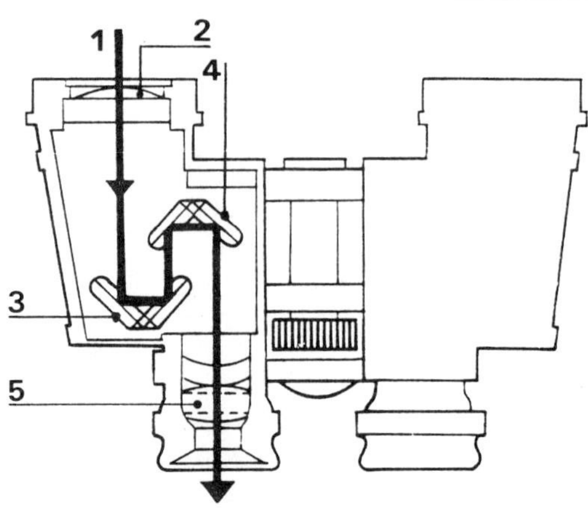

Microscopes

2355 Microscopes magnify minute objects.

Optical microscope
The mirror illuminates the object on the slide then objective lenses produce a magnified image of the object. This is further magnified by the ocular (eyepiece) lenses. Microscopes also employ a light to aid illumination and a variety of control buttons that allow the lenses to be moved nearer and farther from the object, bringing it into focus.

Electron microscopes
These magnify objects as small as atoms and work in the same way as optical microscopes but also employ an electron beam to focus on an object and help to magnify it with a series of lenses.

1 An expanded view of how an image is formed

a Eye
b Eyepiece
c Objective lens
d Specimen
e Condenser lens
f Lamp

2 A standard school microscope

a Eyepiece
b Body tube
c High power objective lens
d Low power objective lens
e Stage
f Condenser
g Mirror
h Base
i Coarse screw adjustment
j Fine screw adjustment
k Arm

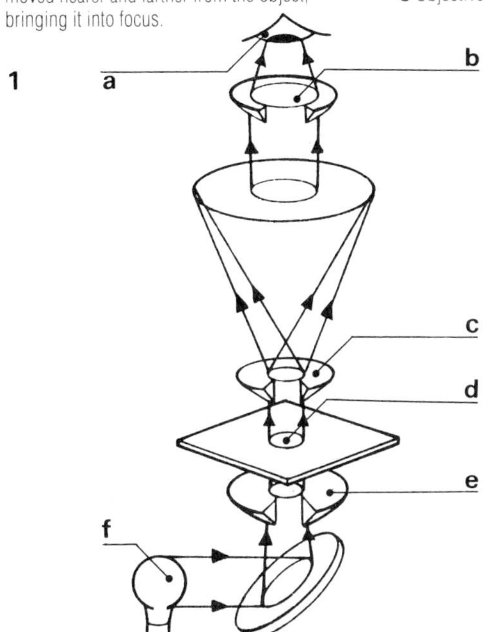

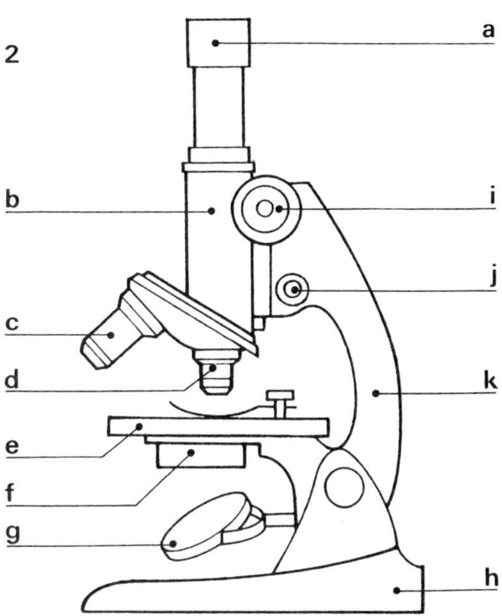

Light polarizers

2356 Ordinary – unpolarized – light consists of vibrations in all directions (**1**) at right angles (transverse) to the direction of travel. A polaroid filter (**2**) works by resolving light into vibrations in a single plane (**3**). A second polaroid filter (**4**) with its polarizing plane at right angles to the first, will block all remaining light.
Much reflected light in our surroundings is partially polarized. Polarizing sunglasses reduce glare by eliminating the light polarized by reflection from horizontal surfaces.

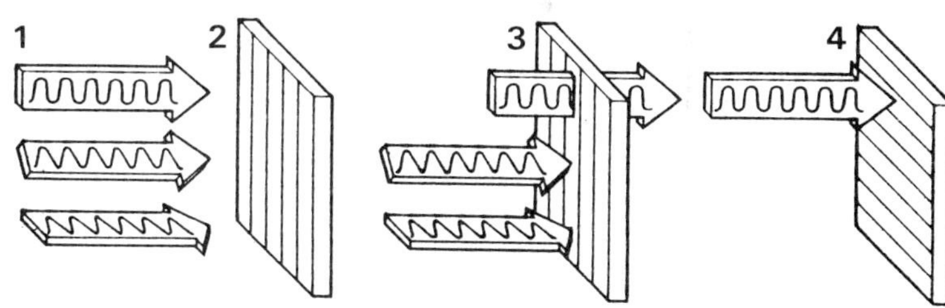

Holography

2357 Holography manipulates light waves to produce a 3-D image of an object.
1 Recording a hologram In reflection holography, light from a laser beam (**a**) is bounced off a mirror (**b**) to form a reference beam (**c**), and is also reflected off (**d**) an object (**e**). The reference and reflected beam interact to form an interference pattern on the photographic plate (**f**). The recorded pattern can be used to re-create a 3-D image of the original object.
2 Reconstructing the image A laser light (**a**) is shone through the transparent hologram (**b**) formed from the photographic plate. A virtual 3-D image (**c**) is seen by the observer (**d**). A real 2-D image is also produced (**e**).

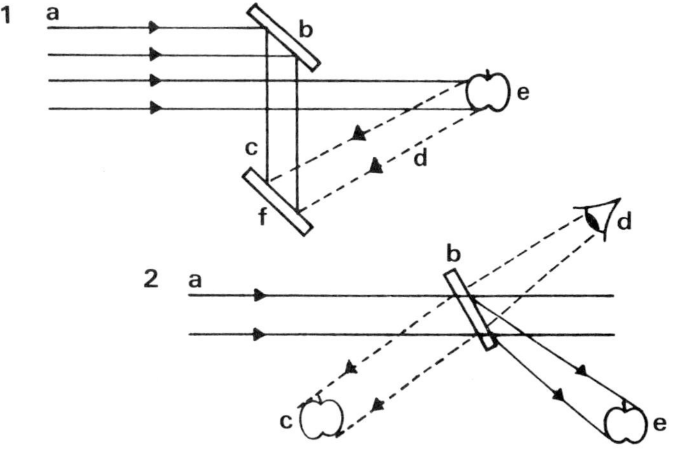

Liquid crystal displays

235**8** Liquid crystals are organic crystals containing rodlike molecules. The crystals change shape when a weak current is applied.
In alphanumeric displays, found in LCD watches and calculators, the crystals (**a**) lie between transparent electrodes (**b**) and sheets of glass (**c**). The glass sheets have polarization planes at right angles to one another.
1 In their normal state, the crystals are slightly twisted, and turn the light (**d**) so that it passes through both sets of glass and reflects off the mirror (**e**). The LCD screen remains clear (**f**).
2 When a current is applied, the crystals align (**g**) and the light is selectively blocked by the second polarizing sheet (**h**). Groups of crystals darken to form digits (**i**) on the LCD screen.

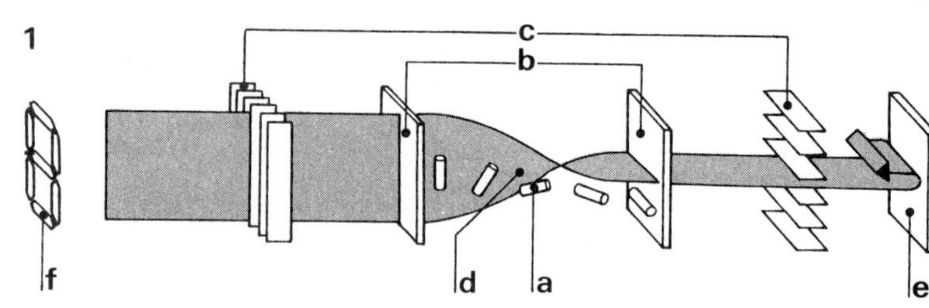

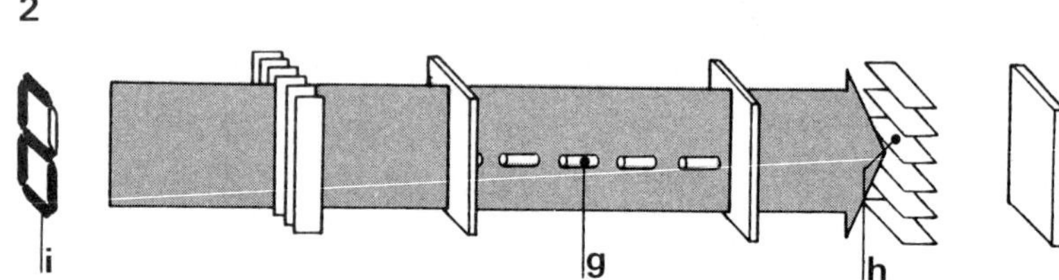

Lasers

235**9** A laser (**L**ight **A**mplification by **S**timulated **E**mission of **R**adiation) produces an intense parallel beam of light of specific wavelength. Laser light is coherent (the light waves are in phase, with the peaks and troughs coinciding). The light-releasing substance can be a solid, liquid or gas. In a gas laser, a high-voltage power source (**a**) excites gas atoms to a high energy state. A gas atom (**b**) spontaneously emits light (**c**) which starts a chain reaction, exciting other atoms (**d**) to emit light of the same wavelength and in phase (**e**). A mirror (**f**; and semi-silvered mirror (**g**) reflect the light back and forth, amplifying it, and the laser beam (**h**) exits through the semi-silvered mirror.

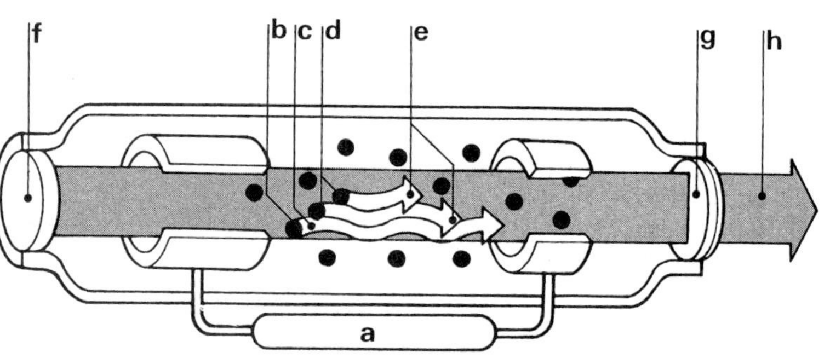

23**6** COMMUNICATIVE DEVICES

Sonar

236**1** Sonar systems use ultrasound (inaudible, high-frequency sound) to detect hidden objects.
A shipborne transducer emits sound pulses (**1**), detects and times echoes (**2**) from the sea floor, then converts these into electric signals to produce a screen image showing water depth.
Similarly, an ultrasound probe produces pulses whose echoes reveal an unborn baby.

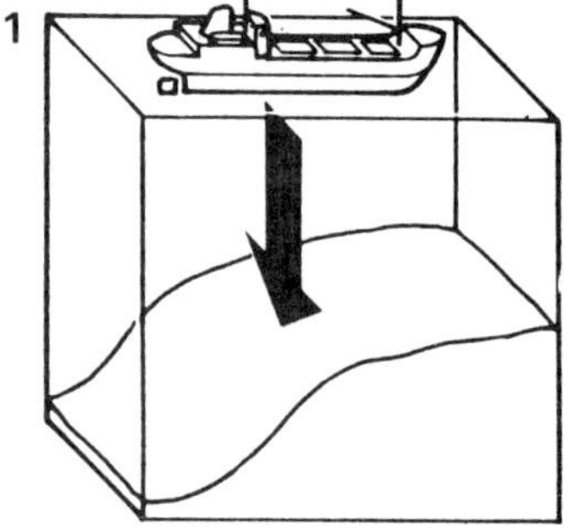

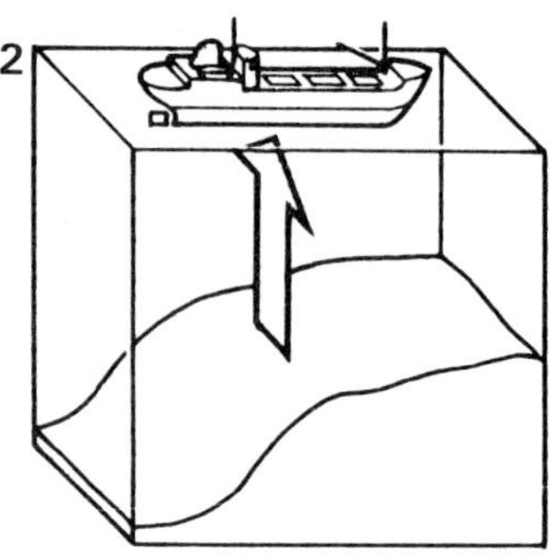

Radar

236**2** Radar systems use reflected radio waves to locate distant objects or objects obscured by fog, rain, or snow. Radar aids weather prediction and navigation. In the diagram, an aircraft's radar antenna (**1**) picks up a strong reflected beam (**2**) from a tall building, a weak reflection (**3**) from bare ground, and none from water (**4**). A receiver converts these reflections into screen images.

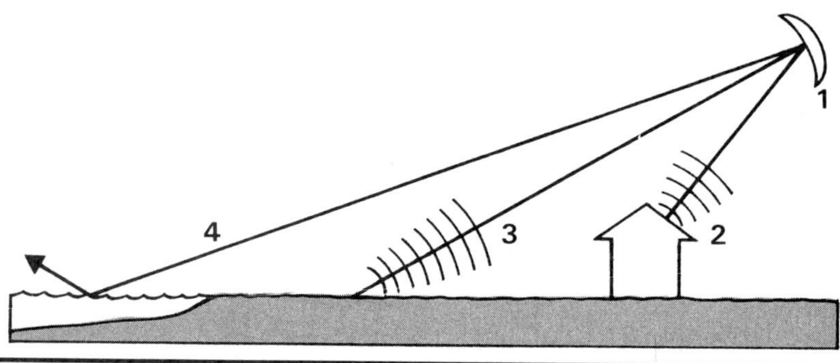

Radio

2363 At a radio transmitter (**1**), a microphone (**a**) converts sounds into electrical signals and a modulator (**b**) imposes these on a carrier wave, which is produced by a radio frequency oscillator (**c**) and beamed out by a transmitting antenna (**d**).
At a receiver (**2**), an antenna (**e**), tuned circuit (**f**), demodulator (**g**), amplifier (**h**), and loudspeaker (**i**) reconvert the radio waves to sounds.

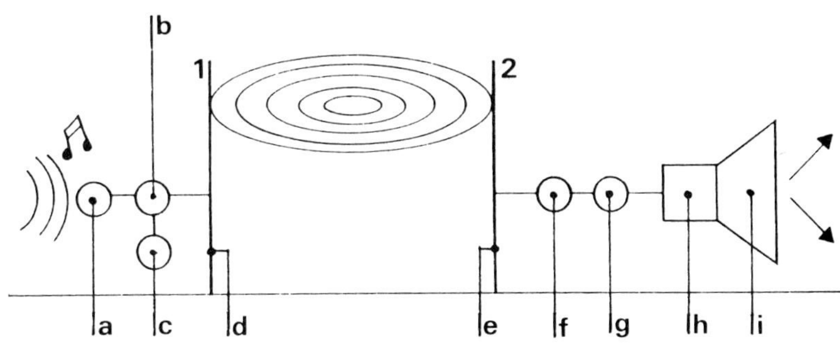

Telephone

2364 A simple electric circuit powered by a battery (**1**) shows how a telephone works. A speaker's voice produces sound waves that vibrate a diaphragm (**2**). The vibrations cause variations in an electric current sent out from the transmitter (**3**), through wires (**4**) to a receiver (**5**), where the varying current creates a varying magnetic field that vibrates another diaphragm (**6**), producing audible sound waves.

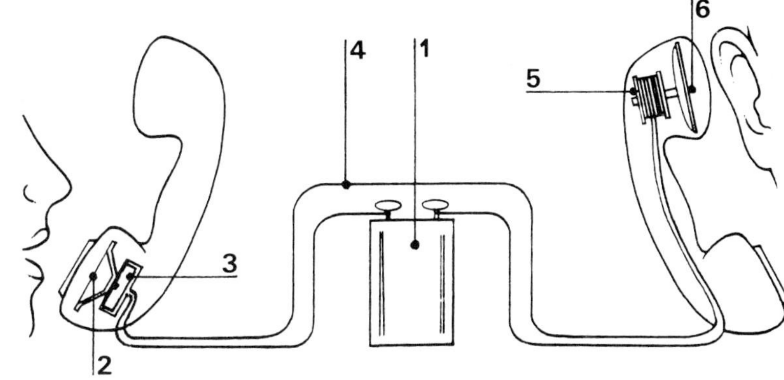

Phonograph (record player)

2365 This reproduces sounds stored on disks (**1**). The record player replays these sounds using the vibration of a stylus (**2**) in the groove (**3**) of a record. As the stylus moves along the groove (**3**), it is vibrated by the sides of the groove (**4**) which provide separate stereo channels. The vibrations travel to a magnet (**5**) which produces electrical signals in fixed coils (**6**) in the stylus. The separate stereo signals are sent to an amplifier (**7**) and speakers (**8**).

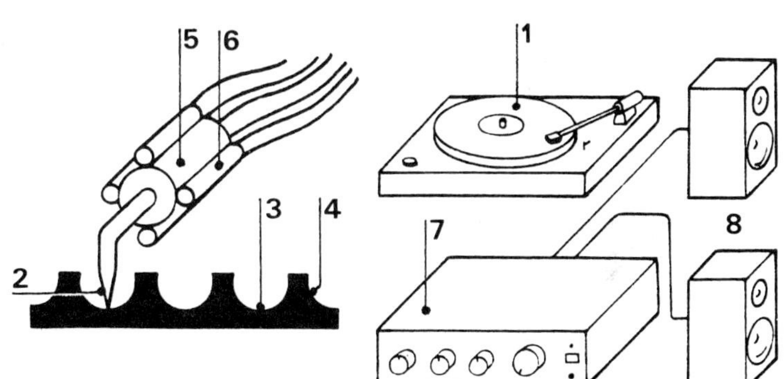

Tape recorder

2366

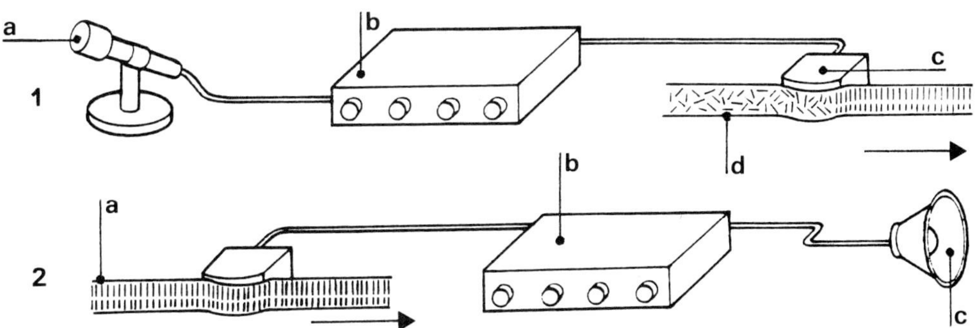

1 A tape recorder records sound when a microphone (**a**) converts the sound to an electric current flowing via an amplifier (**b**) to a recording head (**c**). This produces a varying magnetic field that aligns particles in a magnetic tape (**d**).
2 A tape recorder reproduces sound as the tape (**a**) affects the current flowing via an amplifier (**b**) to a loudspeaker (**c**). This converts current to sound.

Television

2367 Television cameras turn light into electronic video signals that are broadcast by a transmitter and received by the antenna (**1**) of a television receiver. Its tuner (**2**) selects a station. A decoder (**3**) converts video signals into primary color signals. In the picture tube (**4**), three electron guns (**5**), one for each color, rapidly scan the screen (**6**), causing colored dots in the screen to glow forming the picture we see.

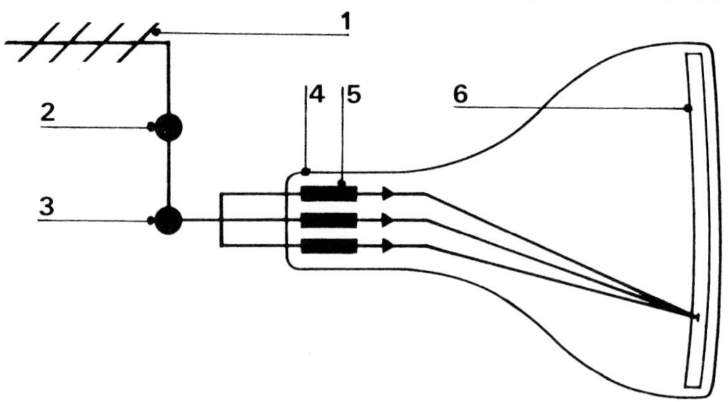

Video recorder

2368 This records pictures and sounds on magnetic videotape with a video, audio, and control track. The video recorder works on the same principle as the tape recorder, but because picture and sound information are recorded together, bigger tapes and faster tape speeds are required. During recording, picture and sound are picked up from the television antenna signal (**1**). The picture is recorded onto tape by a record/playback head (**2**) and the sound by another head (**3**). Picture signals are recorded as a series of sloping tracks (**4**) and the sound signals are recorded along one edge (**5**). During playback, magnetic patterns in the tape affect the current which is converted into video and audio signals.

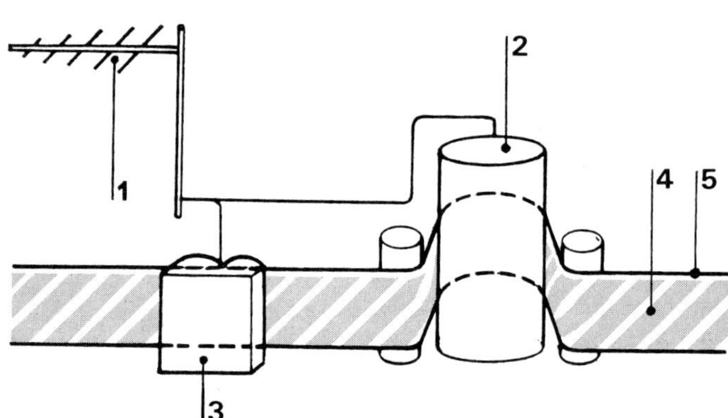

Compact disc

2369 Compact disks are metal disks coated in plastic, on which information is stored in digital form. The tracks which are embossed or melted in the disk can then be read by a laser beam.

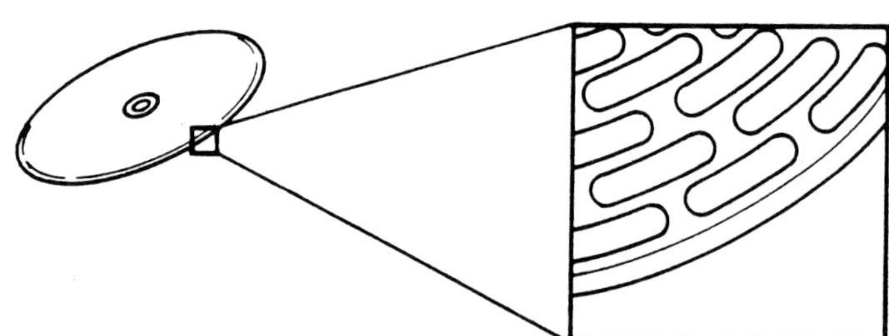

237 FILM AND PHOTOGRAPHY

Cameras

2371 **Simple cameras**
A camera is a lightproof box containing a convex lens and some light-sensitive film (**g**). When exposed to light, the image focused through the lens forms a negative image on the film, from which photographs can be printed. There are three ways of adjusting a camera in order to take a picture.

1 Focusing The lens (**a**) is normally fixed and all distant objects appear reasonably focused. In more advanced cameras the lens can be moved away from the film (for viewing near objects) or closer to the film (for viewing far objects) by adjusting a focus ring (**b**) on the camera.

2 Aperture A hole, or aperture in the diaphragm (**c**) determines the brightness of the light passing through the lens. It is usually marked by *f*-numbers, the larger the *f*-number, the smaller the aperture. A diaphragm adjustment ring (**d**) controls the size of the aperture.

3 Shutter speed The shutter (**e**) opens in order to expose the film to the light which has entered the camera. For many cameras the exposure time can be varied by a dial (**f**) and is expressed in fractions of a second. For example, 1/1000, 1/80. Short exposures are required for fast-moving objects. Aperture setting and shutter speed are balanced to obtain the best image.

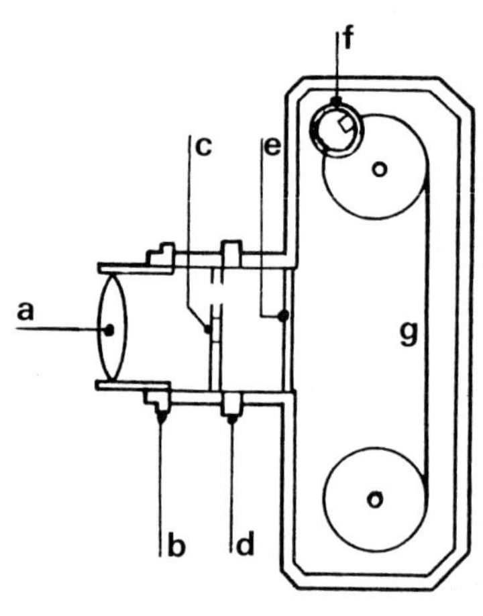

continued

Cameras continued

2371 **Single-lens reflex camera**
This photographs exactly what is seen by using the same lenses for viewing and photographing. Several lens elements (**1**) combine to focus light that comes from the object (**2**). The focused light passes through the hole in the diaphragm (**3**) to a hinged mirror (**4**). This reflects the light onto a focusing screen (**5**), where an image is formed. A pentaprism (**6**) refracts the light from this image to the viewfinder eyepiece (**7**). Pressing a button raises the mirror (**8**), briefly opening the shutter (**9**), letting light from the object fall onto the film (**10**). The longer the shutter is open, the greater the amount of light that falls onto the film.

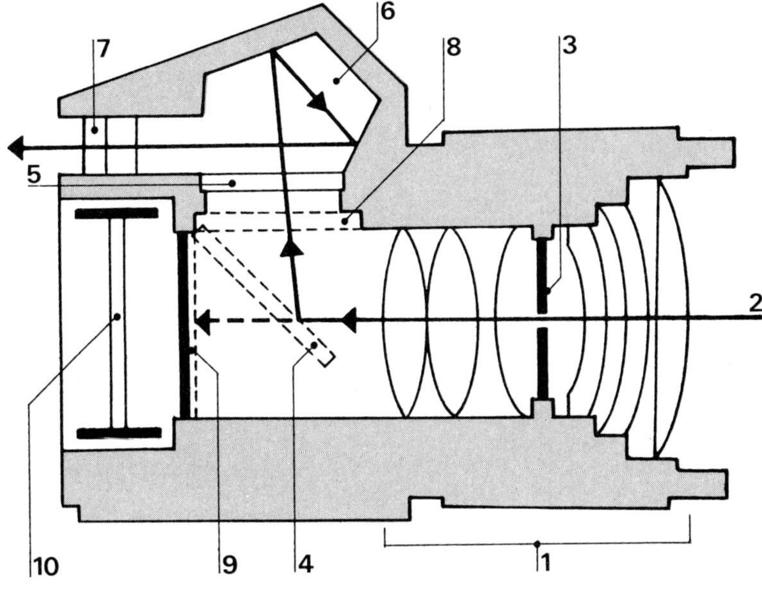

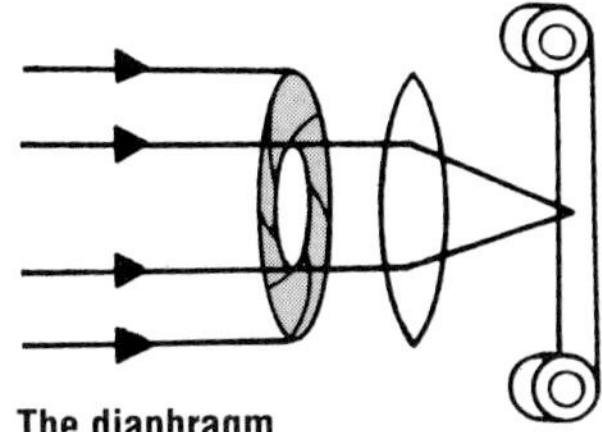

The diaphragm
This set of hinged blades moves to open or close a hole in its center to regulate the lens aperture, and so the amount of light let into the camera.

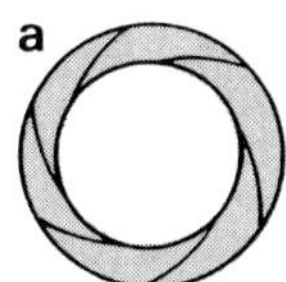

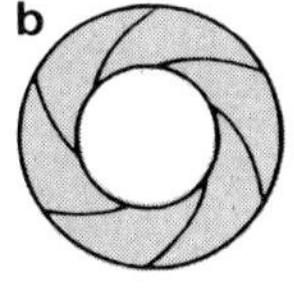

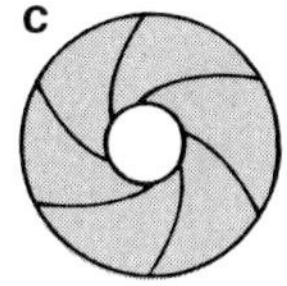

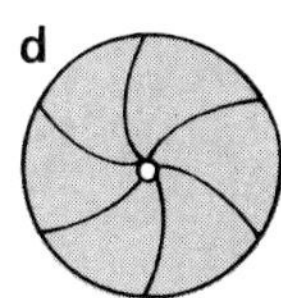

a Large aperture for blurred background and in dim light.
b, **c** Intermediate apertures.
d Small aperture for clear background and in bright light.

A flash
A flash enables you to take pictures when there is poor light. They can only operate within a limited range 4 to 18 ft (1.2 to 5.5 m).

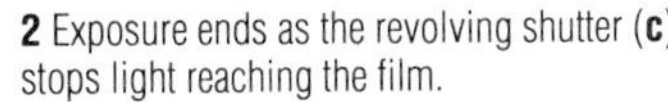

Motion picture (cine) camera
This takes many pictures, in rapid succession, on a strip of film being unwound from a spool.
1 Light from the filmed object produces an image on the piece of film (**a**) exposed at the film gate (**b**).
2 Exposure ends as the revolving shutter (**c**) stops light reaching the film.
3 The feeding claw (**d**) advances the film to bring unexposed film to the film gate. The shutter will move out of the way, allowing a second exposure, and so on.

Thanks to an optical effect called persistence of vision, the film strip seems to show continuous action when played back and projected onto a screen.

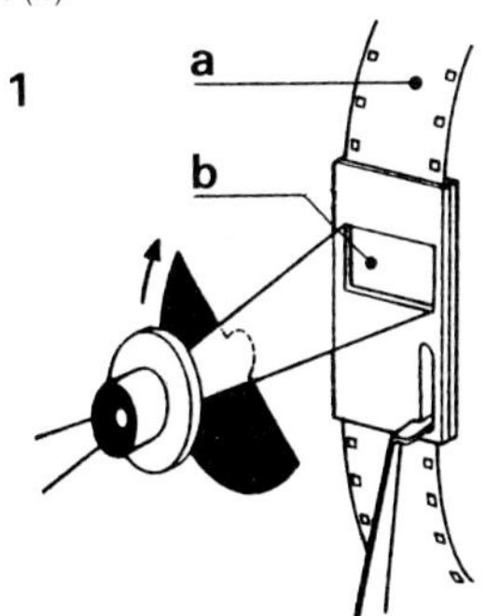

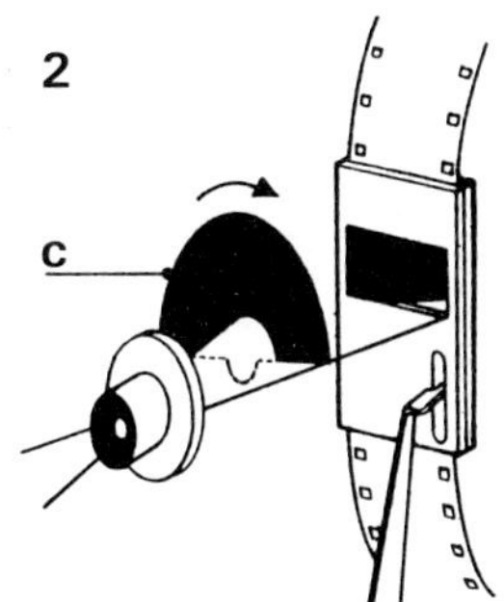

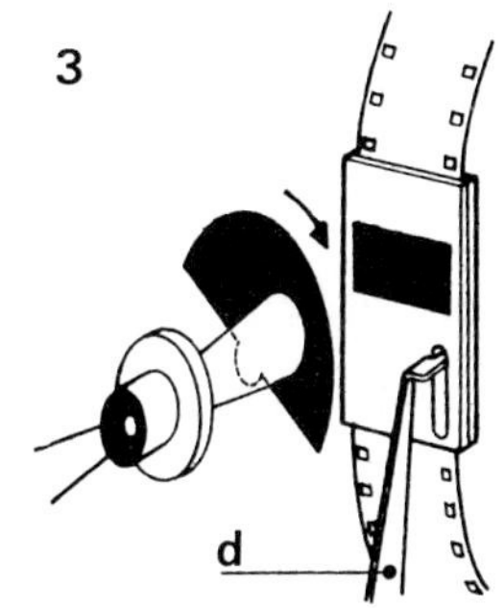

Film

2372 **Composition**
Photographic film (**1**) has one or more layers of light-sensitive emulsion, that can be chemically altered by exposure to light. Shown enlarged, this black-and-white film has a flexible cellulose triacetate base (**2**), an emulsion of silver salts (**3**) and an antihalo layer (**4**) that prevents reflections. Color film has different emulsions sensitive to blue, green, and red light.

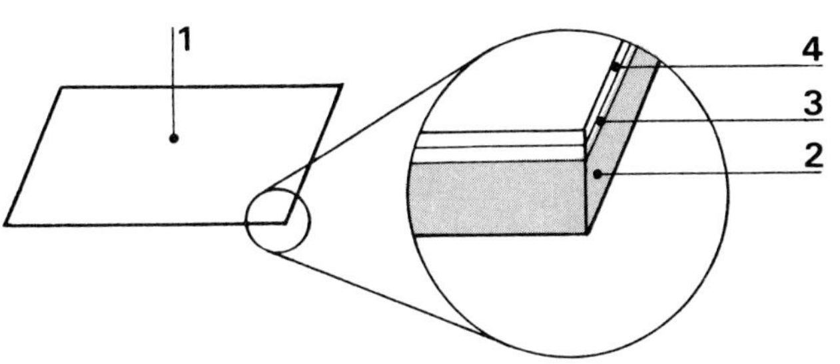

continued

Film continued

2372

Developing film
Before a negative can be produced, film must go through several processes.
1 It is submersed in a developing bath.
2 Washing: this reduces exposed silver salts to black metallic silver and halts the developing process.
3 Fixing: this dissolves the unexposed silver salts.
4 Washing again.
5 Finally the negative is dried.

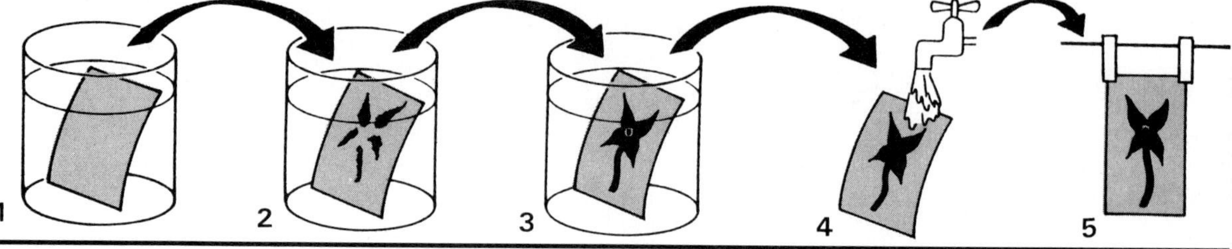

Photographs

2373

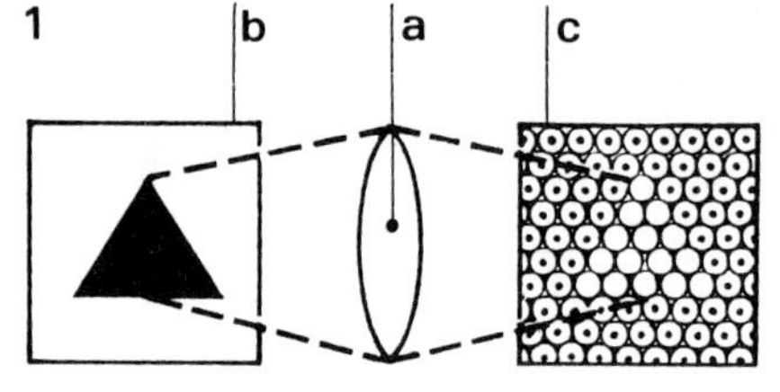

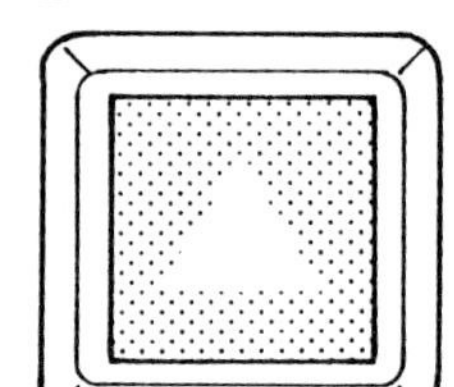

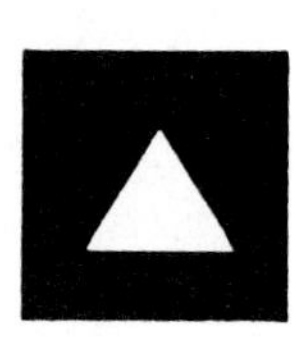

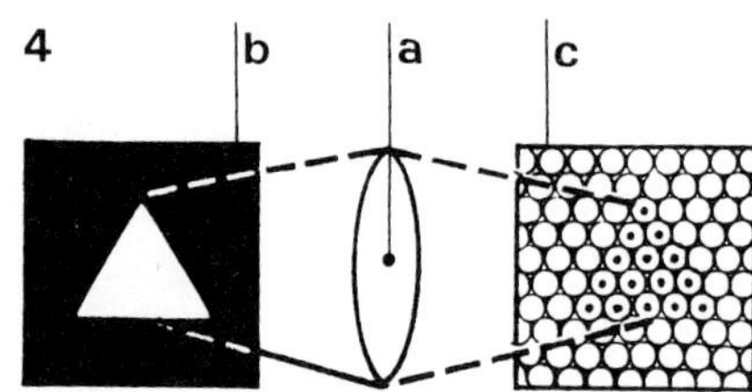

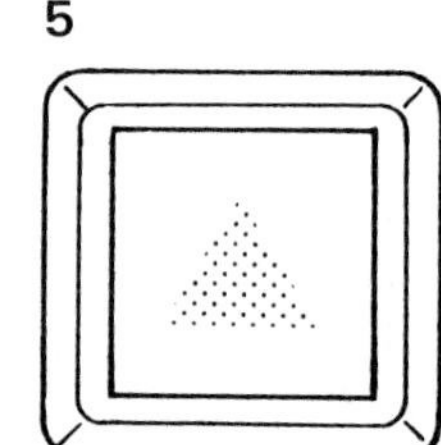

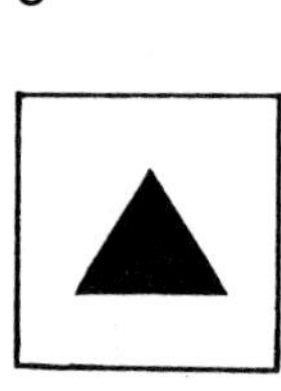

Producing a negative
The production of a negative, from which a positive print is made, is shown here.
1 A lens (**a**) focuses light from bright parts of an image (**b**) onto a black-and-white film's light-sensitive crystals (**c**). They begin to break down.
2 Developer converts exposed crystals to silver. Fixer dissolves those that were unexposed.
3 The negative shows brightly lit film as black silver and dimly lit film as a clearer area.

Producing a print
4 An enlarger's lens (**a**) helps to produce an image of the negative (**b**) on light-sensitive printing paper (**c**).
5 The paper is developed and fixed.
6 The positive print reverses the negative's light and dark areas.

Instant photographs
The Polaroid process produces color photographs in moments from special film, shown enlarged in section.
1 Light (**a**) passes through a clear plastic surface (**b**), acid layer (**c**), timing layer (**d**) and image layer (**e**) to nine chemical layers (**f**), including developer alternating with layers sensitive to red, green, or blue light, all above a black base (**g**).
2 Leaving the camera, the exposed film (**a**) passes through rollers (**b**) that squeeze reagent (**c**), from the film's edge, between its image and chemical layers. The reagent shuts out light long enough to activate developers. These dissolve the dyes which then mix to form a color image (**d**) in the image layer.

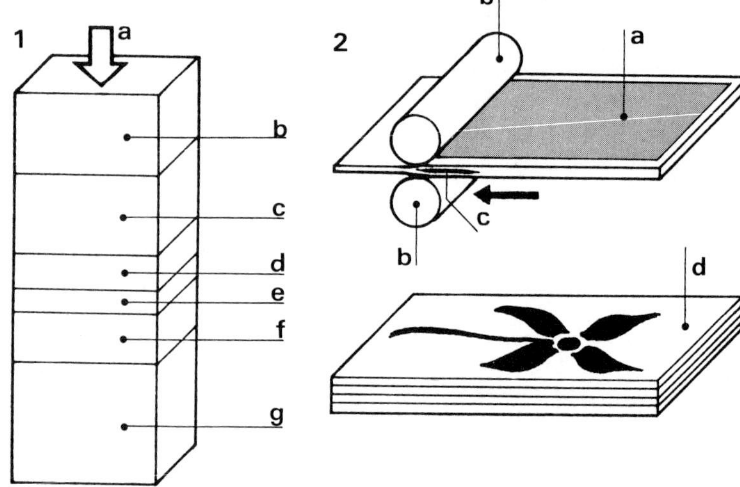

238 INVENTIONS

adding machine Invented in 1623 by Wilhelm Schickard (Ger) and later commercialized by William Burroughs (US) in St Louis, Missouri, in 1885.
adhesive tape Transparent adhesive tape developed from opaque masking tape by Richard Drew (US) in 1930.
air flight In 1709 Father Bartolomeu de Gusmá demonstrates toy hot-air balloon in Portugal. In 1783, Jacques and Joseph Montgolfier (Fr) invent first full-size balloon. In Paris, François Pilâtre de Rozier and Marquis d'Arlandes (Fr) achieve first tethered (Oct 15) then manned free (Nov 21) flight. 1785, Jean-Pierre F. Blanchard (Fr) designs first parachute. 1852, Henri Giffard (Fr) creates non-rigid airship; flown near Paris on Sep 24 using steam-powered propeller. 1853, first glider, by Sir George Cayley (GB), in action near Brompton Hall, Yorkshire. 1903, Orville and Wilbur Wright (US) invent first airplane. Dec 17, first sustained, controlled flight at Kitty Hawk, North Carolina. 1924, Etienne Oehmichen (Fr) invents helicopter. Apr 14, first FAI world record set. 1936, contra-rotating rotors of helicopter developed by Heinriche Focke. 1937, jet engine devised by Sir Frank Whittle (GB). Apr 12, test-bed run at Rugby. 1939, first serviceable helicopter built by Igor Sikorsky (US). Aug 27, first flight of jet engine, made by Heinkel (Ger).
artillery Invented 1326, earliest picture of gun (of kind) shows it being used at siege of Metz in 1324.
ball-point markers Invented by John J. Loud (US) in 1888. Lazlo and Georg Biro (Hungary) develop first cheap and practical writing pens in 1938.
barometer Devised by Evangelista Torricelli (It) in 1643 and first mentioned in letter of June 11.
battery (electric) Invented by Alessandro Volta in 1800 and shown to Napoleon in 1801.
bicycle Invented 1839-40 by Kirkpatrick Macmillan (Scot), using pedal-driven cranks. Mar 1861, Ernest Michaux (Fr) achieves first direct drive.
bifocal lens Invented in 1780 by Benjamin Franklin (US) after experiments dating from 1760.
bronze (copper with tin) First produced c. 3700 BC at Maidum, pre-dynastic Egypt. Copper-smelting practiced earlier.
calculating machine Developed by Wilhelm Schickard in 1623. *See* adding machine.
canal lock First pound lock developed in 983 by Chiao Wei-Yo on West River section of Grand Canal of China near Huai-yin.
car In 1769, Nicolas Cugnot (Fr) devises three-wheeled military steam tractor. Richard Trevithick's eight-seater in Cambourne, Cornwall, tested Dec 22, 1801, was the earliest steam engine for passengers. 1826, Samuel Brown's gas-powered carriage, Blackheath, London, boasted the first internal combustion engine. 1876, first carburettor, by Gottlieb Daimler (Ger). 1885, first petrol engine by Karl Benz (Ger). Nov/Dec, first successful run by Mannheim.
celluloid Developed by John Wesley Hyatt and Isaiah Smith Hyatt in 1869.
cinema Pioneers were Etienne Jules Marey (Fr) and Thomas A. Edison (US).1885, first moving outlines on film by Louis le Prince at Institute for Deaf, Washington Hts, New York City, US. 1888, motion-picture camera invented by William Friese-Greene. 1895, first cinema by Auguste Lumière and Louis Lumière (Fr) shown to public Dec 28 at Blvd des Capucines. Sep 17, 1922, *Der Brandstifter* shown at Alhambra, Berlin by Josef Engl, Josef Mussolle and Hans Vogt (Ger) is first "talking film." In same year, three-dimensional movies developed by Perfect Pictures, US. Mar 13, 1923, demonstration at New York by Dr Lee de Forest of musical sound on film.
clock In AD 725, earliest mechanical model, by I-Hsing and Liang-Tsan (China). Pendulum discovered and demonstrated by Galileo. 1656, Christiaan Huygens (Neth) develops first clock using pendulum.
compact disc First laser beam-read disc developed in 1978 by Philips (Neth) and Sony (Japan). First marketed Oct 1982.
dynamo First Paris demonstration by Hypolite Pixii (Fr) in Paris, Sep 3, 1832. Rotative model demonstrated by Joseph Saxton in June 1833 at Cambridge, England.
electric blanket 1883, first shown at Austria Exhibition, Vienna, in 1883.
electric lamp Carbon filaments first developed by Sir Joseph Swan in 1860. First lamp demonstrated Dec 20, 1879, at Menlo Park, New Jersey, USA, by Thomas A. Edison (US).
electric motor First direct-current model exhibited in Vienna in 1873 by Zénobe Gramme (Belg). In 1888, first alternating-current model by Nikola Tesla (US).
electromagnet Developed in 1824 by William Sturgeon (GB) and improved by Joseph Henry (US).
electronic computer In 1938, John Vincent Atanasoff and Clifford E. Berry (US) build 300-valve ABC machine at Ames, Iowa. 1948, Sir Frederick Williams and Prof T. Kilburn (GB) develop alterable stored program at Manchester University. Point-contact transistor invented by John Bardeen, Dr W. Shockley, and Walter Brattain (US).
elevator Developed in 1852 by Elisha G. Otis (US).
escalator First developed by Jesse W. Reno (US) in 1894.
false limbs Developed in 1540 by Ambrose Paré (Fr).
fire extinguisher Invented by Dr Godfrey (GB) in 1762.
flush toilet Invented 1589 by Sir John Harington.
fountain pen Developed in 1884 by Lewis E. Waterman (US).
galvanometer First measurement of flow of electricity with a free-moving needle demonstrated in 1834 by André Marie Ampère.
gas lighting Invented by William Murdoch (GB) in 1792 and installed in private house in Cornwall. Introduced to factory in Birmingham 1798, and to London streets in 1807.
glass Glassware at Eshanna, Mesopotamia c. 2600 BC. Glass blowing at Sidon, Syria c. 50 BC. First example of stained glass, at St Paul's, Jarrow, Durham dates from before 850. Earliest complete window c. 1080 at Augsburg, Germany.
gramophone Hand-cranked cylinder developed in 1879 at Menlo Park, NJ, by Thomas A. Edison (US).
gyro-compass Jean Foucault (Fr) devises gyroscope in 1852. First gyro-compass invented by Elmer A. Sperry (US) in 1911, tested Aug 28 on USS *Delaware.*
hovercraft Invented 1955 by Sir Christopher Cockerell (GB). May 30, 1959, first "flight" at Cowes, England: Saunders Roe SRN-1.
laser Invented by Dr Charles H. Townes (US) in 1960 and demonstrated by Theodore Maiman (US) at Hughes Research, Malibu, California, in July.
locomotive (railed) Invented 1804 by Richard Trevithick (GB) and run at Penydarren, Wales on Feb 21 for 9 mi (14.4 km).
loom, power Developed in 1785 by Edmund Cartwright (GB).
loudspeaker Horace Short (GB) granted patent in 1900 for compressed air Auxetophone; first used on top of Eiffel Tower in that summer. 1916, June 30, Bell Telephone introduce open-air electric public address system on Staten Island, NY, USA.
machine gun James Puckle (GB) granted patent May 15, 1718. Richard Gatling model dates from 1861.
maps Sumerian clay tablets depicting the River Euphrates date from c. 2250 BC. Earliest measurements attempted by Eratosthenes c. 220 BC. 1477, Bologna, Italy, earliest printed map.
match, safety Developed in 1826 by John Walker (GB) at Stockton, Teeside.
microphone Invented by Alexander Graham Bell (US) in 1876. Prof. David Hughes, who coined the name, gives demonstration in London in Jan 1878.
micro-processor Invented 1971 by Marcian E. Hoff (US) and launched by US company Intel in December.
microscope Compound convex-concave lens invented c.1590 by Zacharias Janssen (Neth). Mounted concave focusing mirror, Leeuwenhoek microscope, developed c.1673.
microwave cooking Sir John Randall and Dr H. A. Boot (GB) develop magnetron that produces microwave energy in 1940. First cooker produced in late 1940s by Raytheon Inc. (US).
motorcycle Invented 1885 by Gottlieb Daimler, Cannstatt, Germany. Aug 29, patent granted. Nov 10, Paul Daimler first rider. 1888, Mrs Edward Butler first woman rider at Erith, Kent.
neon lamp Invented by Georges Claude (Fr) in 1910 and first installed at Paris Motor Show on Dec 3.
non-stick pan Plastic polytetrafluoroethylene discovered in 1938 by Dr Roy Plunkett of Du Pont company (US). Tefal company founded 1955.
nylon Developed in 1937 by Dr Wallace H. Carothers (US) at Du Pont Labs. First stockings produced in about 1937. Yarn production Dec 1939.

continued

Inventions continued

238

paper Mulberry-based fibre developed AD 105 in China. Introduced to West via Samarkand in the 14th century AD.
parchment Developed around 1300 BC in Egypt.
parking meter Invented on July 16, 1935, at Oklahoma City by Carlton C. Magee (US).
pasteurization The destruction of pathogenic microorganisms by heat was first developed in 1867 by Louis Pasteur.
photography In 1826, an eight-hour exposure on sensitized pewter plate was achieved by J. Nicéphore Niepce (Fr) at Chalon-sur-Saône, France. 1835, paper exposure by W. H. Fox Talbot (GB) at Lacock Abbey, Wiltshire. 1888, film exposure by John Carbutt (US).
piano Diagram and description of earliest piano published in 1709 by Bartolommeo Cristofori.
plastics Pyroxylin first discovered c. 1852 by Alexander Parkes.
porcelain First reported 851 in China, and in Baghdad in the ninth century.
printing Developed c. 1455 by Johann Gutenberg (Ger). Rotary printing developed 1846 by Richard Hoe (US).
propeller (ship) First developed in 1837 by Francis Smith (GB).
radar Radio reflection first discovered in 1922 by Dr Albert H. Taylor and Leo C. Young (US), and first put to use by Dr Rudolph Kuhnold, at Kiel, Germany on Mar 28, 1934. Name coined in 1940 by Cdr. S. M. Tucker USN.
radio telegraphy First broadcast, over 500 yards, by David Edward Hughes at Great Portland St, London. 1906, Dec 24, first public radio broadcast by Prof. R. A. Fessenden (US) at Brant Rock, Massachusetts, USA. 1901, Dec 12, Morse signals sent by Guglielmo Marconi (It) from Poldhu, Cornwall to St John's, Newfoundland.
rayon Invented in 1883 by Sir Joseph Swan (GB) and produced at Courtauld's Ltd, Coventry, England in Nov 1905. Name adopted in 1924.
razor First throw-away safety blades invented by King C. Gillette (US) in 1895. Electric model invented 1931 by Col. Jacob Schick (US).
record (long playing) Micro-groove developed in 1948 by Dr Peter Goldmark (US) in CBS Research Labs. Launched by Columbia on June 21.
refrigerator Simultaneous development in 1850 by James Harrison (GB) in Victoria, Australia, and Alexander Catlin Twining (US) in Cleveland, Ohio. 1913, first domestic model developed in Chicago.
rocket First liquid-fueled model tested by Robert Goddard (US) on Mar 16,1926. V-2 (Ger) first launched in 1942.
rubber Latex foam invented 1928 by E. A. Murphy and team at Fort Dunlop, Birmingham. Tire developed in 1846 by Thomas Hancock (GB). Following year, solid rubber models for vehicles. Vulcanized material developed in 1841 by Charles Goodyear (US); waterproof material by Charles Macintosh (GB) in 1823.
sewing machine Invented in 1829 by Barthélemy Thimmonier (Fr). 1851, first practical domestic machine by Issac M. Singer, Pittstown, NY, USA.
ship Journey from Indonesia to northern Australia c. 50,000 BC, possibly using double dug-out canoes. 1775, first steam ship, built by J. C. Périer (Fr) sails on Seine, near Paris. 1801-2, *Charlotte Dundas*, built by Hon. Sir Charles Parsons (GB) at Heaton, Tyne and Wear, attains 34.5 knots on first trial.
silk manufacture Reeling machines devised c. 50 BC in China. Silk mills, world's earliest factories, in Italy c. AD 1250.
skyscraper 10-storey Home Insurance Co. Building, Chicago, Ill., built in 1882 by William Le Baron Jenny (US).
slide rule Devised in 1621 by William Oughtred (GB).
spectacles Convex lens invented c. 1286 at Pisa, Italy. Concave lens for myopia developed by Nicholas of Cusa (It) c. 1450.
spinning frame Invented in 1769 by Sir Richard Arkwright (GB).
spinning jenny Textile spinning machine invented in 1764 by James Hargreaves (GB).
spinning mule Textile spinning machine invented in 1779 by Samuel Crompton (GB).
spray gun Devised in 1803 by Alan de Vilbiss (US).
steam engine Invented in 1698 by Thomas Savery (GB). Condenser model developed in 1769 by James Watt (Scot). Piston model developed in 1712 by Thomas Newcomen (GB).
steel production Achieved by Henry Bessemer (GB) at St Pancras, London, in 1855. Stainless steel first cast by Harry Brearly (GB) at Sheffield, on Aug 20, 1913.
stopwatch Invented by Edward Daniel Johnson in 1855.
submarine Model with hand-propelled screw and one-man crew devised by David Bushnell (US) and used off New York, 1776.
superconductivity 4 K level achieved in 1911 by Heike Kamerlingh Onnes (Neth) at Leiden. In Dec 1985 in Zürich, Karl Muller and Georg Bednorz discover barium-copper-lanthanum compound that is superconductive at 35 K. Paul Chu (US) adds yttrium and achieves 98 K in Houston in Feb 1987.
telegraph (mechanical) In Paris in 1787, M. Lammond (Fr) demonstrates first working model.
telegraph code Developed in 1837 by Samuel F. B. Morse (US). First transmitted at Morristown, NJ on Jan 8, 1838 by his assistant Alfred Vail (US), to whom the real credit for the invention belongs.
telephone First imperfect model, using electrical impulses, developed in 1849 by Antonio Meucci (It) in Havana, Cuba. First reliable model devised by Alexander Graham Bell in 1876. First telephone exchange at Boston, Massachusetts,1878.
telescope (refractor) Discovered by Hans Lipperschey (Neth), on Oct 2, 1608, at Middelburg in Holland.
television Mechanical model invented in 1926 by John Logie Baird (GB) and demonstrated to the public on Jan 27. Electronic model developed in 1927 by Philo Taylor Farnsworth (US). First color transmission on July 3, 1928, at 133 Long Acre, London.
terylene Developed in 1941 by J. R. Whinfield and J. T. Dickson (GB) at Accrington, Lancashire.
thermometer Gas thermoscope built at Royal Institute, London, by Michael Faraday, on Aug 29, 1831.
typewriter First practical 27-character keyed machine using carbon paper built in Reggio Emila, Italy, in 1907, by Pellegrine Tarri (It).
vacuum cleaner First workable model developed in 1901 by Hubert Booth.
washing machine (electric) First built in 1907 by Hurley Machine Co (US).
watch Earliest named watchmaker is Bartholomew Manfredi (It) in Nov 1462.
weather satellite Developed by NASA (US) in 1960.
wheel Developed c. 3580 BC by Sumerian civilization, Uruk, Iraq. Four-wheeled waggons depicted on pottery cup from Poland, c. 3500 BC.
windmill Used c. 600 in Persia for corn grinding. Oldest English post mill dates from 1191.
writing Earliest evidence of pictographs produced by Sumerian civilization c. 3500 BC
X-ray Developed by Wilhelm Konrad Röntgen (Ger) at University of Wurzburg on Nov 8, 1895.
zip fastener First developed by Whitcombe L. Judson (US) in 1891. 1913, Gideon Sundback (Sweden) invents first practical fastener.

Inventors

2381 **Alexanderson, Ernst Frederick Werner** 1878–1975, Swedish-born American electrical engineer and inventor (with 300 patents to his credit) of antenna structures, radio receiving and transmitting systems, a complete television system, and (by 1955) the color television receiver.

Archimedes c. 287–212 BC, Greek mathematician and inventor who founded science of hydrostatics (**1**). Popularly remembered for building siege-engines against Romans, for Archimedean Screw – still used in some parts of the world for raising water – and for his cry of "Eureka" on discovering the Archimedes Principle – that a body in a fluid "loses" weight equivalent to the weight of the liquid it displaces.

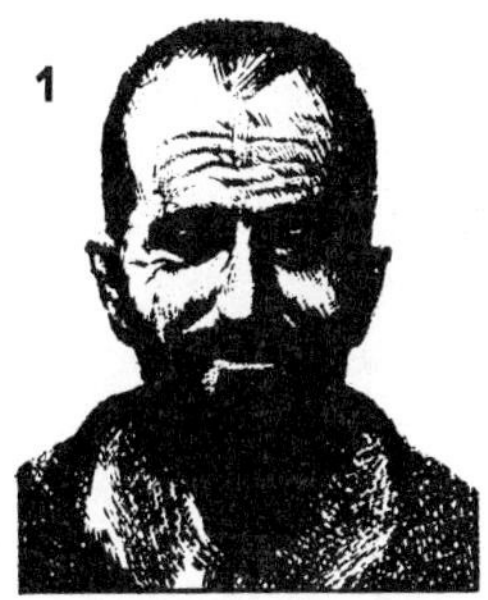

Armstrong, Edwin Howard 1890–1954, American electrical engineer and inventor. He devised the superheterodyne radio receiver, and, by 1939, had perfected the frequency-modulator system of radio transmission, which virtually eliminated the problem of interference from static.

Baekeland, Leo Hendrik 1863–1944, Belgian-born American chemist and inventor who emigrated to the USA in 1889. Invented photographic printing paper usable with artificial light, discovered first synthetic phenolic resin (Bakelite), and was a founder of the plastics industry.

Baird, John Logie 1888–1946, Scottish electrical engineer and television pioneer. In 1926, he gave the first demonstration of a television image. Other lines of research in the 1920s included radar and infrared television. Succeeded (1944) in producing three-dimensional and colored images.

Bell, Alexander Graham 1847–1922, Scots-born American inventor. After experimenting with various acoustical devices, Bell produced the first intelligible telephonic transmission when he sent a message to his assistant on 5 June 1875; he patented the telephone in 1876.

Benz, Karl Friedrich 1844–1929, German engineer and car manufacturer who developed the two-stroke engine 1877-9. In 1885, he completed his first car, one of the earliest petrol-driven vehicles. In 1926, after merger, Daimler-Benz and Co. was established.

Blériot, Louis 1872–1936, French aviator and inventor. Made first flight across English Channel on July 25, 1909, from Baraques to Dover in small, 24-horsepower monoplane. Invented auto lights.

Braun, Wernher von 1912–77, German and naturalized American rocket pioneer. Perfected and launched V-2 rockets against Britain in September 1944. Later developed Explorer I satellite (1958) and Saturn rocket for Apollo 8 Moon landing (1969).

Cayley, George 1771–1857, English engineer and pioneer of aviation who built and flew what was probably the first heavier-than-air machine, and, in 1853, built the first successful man-carrying glider. Invented new telescope, artificial limb and caterpillar tractor.

Daguerre, Louis Jacques Mandé 1789–1851, French photographic pioneer. From 1826 onwards, partly in conjunction with Niepce, he perfected his 'daguerrotype' process in which a photographic image is obtained on copper plate that has been coated with metallic silver and sensitized to light by iodine vapor.

Diesel, Rudolph (Christian Karl) 1858–1913, German engineer. Began work in 1885 on internal combustion engines. Constructed "rational heat motor," demonstrating first practical compression-ignition engine (which was about twice as efficient as the steam engine) in 1897.

Edison, Thomas Alva 1847–1931, American inventor – perhaps the most prolific the world has ever seen. Took out more than 1,000 patents in all, including gramophone (1877), incandescent light bulb (1879), electric valve (1883), and kinematoscope (1891). Produced first talking motion-pictures in 1912.

Fuller, (Richard) Buckminster 1895–1983, American engineer. Discovered energetic/synergetic geometry in 1917, and, later, "Tensegrity Structures". His structural designs were designed to provide economical, efficient, trouble-free living. After 1945, he developed his famous series of geodesic domes.

Geissler, Heinrich 1814–79, German inventor and glass-blower who devised a pump that could produce the most thorough vacuum possible in "Geissler tubes," in which the passage of electricity through rarefied gases can be seen. Also devised the Geissler mercury pump.

Goethals, George Washington 1858–1928, American engineer. Chief engineer for and administrator of Panama Canal project (1907–14), and civil governor of Canal Zone (1914–16).

Goldmark, Peter Carl 1906–77, Hungarian-born American engineer and inventor who developed the first practical color television system. Also, led team that invented long-playing microgroove record (1948), and later built special camera for lunar-orbiting space vehicle.

Gutenberg, Johannes 1400–68, German printer. Regarded as inventor of printing. At Mainz, Gutenberg entered into partnership with Johannes Fust, who financed a printing press. The latter completed famous 42-line Bible begun by Gutenberg, who is also credited with *Fragment of the Last Judgment* c. 1445.

Howe, Elias 1819–67, American inventor. By placing the eye near the needle's point and by using two threads, he constructed the first practical sewing machine. The first modern invention to lighten the load of household chores, this was patented in 1846.

Land, Edwin Herbert 1909–91, American inventor and physicist known especially for discoveries relating to light polarization, and for building the first successful helicopter – the VS-300.

Sperry, Elmer Ambrose 1860–1930, American inventor and electrical engineer who devised the gyroscopic compass (1911), and stabilizers for ships and aeroplanes. Also invented new types of dynamo, arc-light and searchlight, as well as an electrolytic process for obtaining pure caustic soda from salt.

Stanley, Francis Edgar 1849–1918, American inventor of "Stanley Steamer," a steam-powered automobile, 1897.

Stanley, William 1858–1916, American electrical engineer and inventor of transformer (1885). Work also included long-range transmission system for alternating current.

Steinmetz, Charles Proteus originally Karl August Rudolph, 1865–1923, German-born American electrical engineer. Discovered magnetic hysteresis, simple notation for calculating alternating current circuits, and lightning arresters for high-power transmission lines.

Taylor, Frederick Winslow 1856–1915, American engineer. Father of "scientific management," who applied its principles successfully to both small and large-scale business.

Tesla, Nikola 1856–1943, Yugoslav-born American physicist and electrical engineer. Left Edison Works at Menlo Park and concentrated on his own inventions, including improved dynamos, transformers, electric bulbs, and high-frequency coil which bears his name.

Trevithick, Richard 1771–1833, English engineer and inventor who devoted his life to improvement of steam engine, favouring higher steam pressures giving greater power from smaller cylinders. From 1800 to 1815, he built several steam "road carriages" and the first railway locomotives.

Tsai Lun c. 50–118, Chinese inventor of paper AD 105) made from tree bark and rags.

Watt, James 1736–1819, Scottish engineer and inventor who improved the Newcomen steam engine, devising the new rotary or "sun and planet" motion, expansion principle, double engine, parallel motion, smokeless furnace, and governor. The watt, a unit of electric power, is named after him.

Westinghouse, George 1846–1914, American engineer who gave his name, in 1863, to the air-brake for locomotives which he invented. He also pioneered the use of alternating current for distributing electric power.

Whitney, Eli 1765–1825, American inventor. In 1793, he devised the cotton gin for separating cotton fiber from seeds, which made cotton-growing highly profitable. In 1801 he devised precision-machining methods that made musket parts interchangeable.

239 TECHNOLOGY GLOSSARY

absolute zero Lowest temperature theoretically possible, called 0° kelvin and equal to approximately -273.15° C. Impossible to attain, though temperature of 0.000001° K has been achieved.
achromatic Without color, as when a lens transmits white light without breaking it up into component colors.
acoustics Branch of science concerned with sound and hearing.
air Envelope of gases surrounding Earth. Dry air at sea level consists of approximately 78% nitrogen, 21% oxygen and 1% carbon dioxide and inert gases, plus water vapor, hydrocarbons, sulfur compounds and dust particles in small, variable amounts.
alloy Metallic substance composed of two or more chemical elements, e.g. brass, steel.
alternating current Electric current that changes direction at regular intervals.
altitude Distance above ground or sea level.
ampere Unit for measuring amount of electric current flowing through a circuit.
amplifier A device used to increase strength of electrical signal.
angle of incidence Angle between ray of light (incident ray) meeting a surface, and a line perpendicular to the surface at that point.
angle of reflection Angle between ray of light (reflected ray) that is reflected from a surface, and a line perpendicular to the surface at that point.
atmosphere 1 Layer of gas or gases surrounding Earth or other heavenly body.
2 Unit of measurement equal to pressure that, at sea level and temperature of 33.8° F (0° C), will support a column of mercury in a barometer to a height of 29.92 in (766 mm).
automation Substitution of self-regulating, electronic devices for certain human skills in industry.
axis Real or imaginary straight line around which an object rotates.
barometer Instrument for measuring atmospheric pressure. Mercury type consists of a column of mercury inside a glass tube with the top sealed, and bottom open and resting in a well of mercury. Changing atmospheric pressure causes the mercury in the column to rise and fall. The aneroid type consists of metal bellows, with a vacuum inside, which expand and contract to operate a pointer.
battery Number of electric cells used together to produce a current. Dry battery (e.g. in flashlight) uses up its chemicals and has to be replaced. Storage battery has chemical action that can be reversed by passing current through it in the opposite direction to that in which it discharges, and can hence be alternately charged and discharged.
bell, electric Device using electric current to operate an electromagnet which attracts an iron striker toward a bell. When the electric circuit is broken, the striker springs back, and the process is repeated..
binocular Describes any optical device that allows both eyes to be used at once.
biosphere This term encompasses all Earth's living things and their environment.
boiling point Temperature at which liquid boils at standard atmospheric pressure.
British thermal unit (BTU) Amount of heat needed to raise temperature of 1 lb of water by 1° F.
cam Moving machine part which is not circular and which, while rotating about an axis not exactly at its center, transmits intermittent or back-and-forth motion to another part.
catalyst Substance which speeds up or slows down chemical reaction but which is not itself chemically changed as a result of the reaction.
cathode A negative electrode.
cathode ray tube Electrical device consisting of tube containing gases at very low pressure, in which a stream of electrons emitted from the cathode strike a fluorescent screen.
cell, electric Device in which a chemical reaction produces an electric current.
celluloid Inflammable plastic material manufactured from cellulose nitrate and camphor.
Celsius, or centigrade, thermometer Device using scale where freezing point of water is 0° C and boiling point (at standard atmospheric pressure) is 100° C.
centrifugal force Force with which orbiting body pulls against the restraint that holds it in a revolving path.
centripetal force Force preventing revolving object from flying off at tangent to its orbit. This force is necessarily equal and opposite to the centrifugal force which it counteracts.
circuit 1 Complete path of electric current.
2 One full orbital movement (revolution) by a heavenly body.
color Phenomenon depending on wavelength or frequency of light waves. Color red (red light), for instance, is produced by light waves of longer wavelength than color blue (blue light).
compact disk Plastic disk, coated in reflective material (usually aluminum), which either scatters or reflects back into a photoelectric detector a laser beam that is used to read (play) the encoded sound when the disk is rotated at high constant and linear speed.
compound engine Steam engine in which steam expands first in a high-pressure cylinder, and then still more in cylinders at lower pressures.
compound lens Lens made up of two or more separate lenses cemented together. Reduces distortion and color fringes.
computer Machine for performing rapid calculations. Digital models deal only with numbers (*see* binary system); analog models measure rather than count, and imitate physical or chemical processes by means of electrical circuits.
concave Curving inward; being thinner at the center than at the edges.
conductor Substance allowing heat or electric current to flow through it. Copper is a good conductor.
convex Curving outward; being thicker at the center than at the edges.
crank Bent shaft which, when rotating, can change direction or timing of movements of other parts of machine.
current Amount of electron flow, measured in units called amperes.
cybernetics Study of control mechanisms in living things and in machines.
direct current Electric current flowing in one direction only.
double-acting engine Engine in which steam pushes first on one, then on other side, of piston.
drag In aeronautics, the resistance to the forward movement of the wing caused by air friction. A well-designed wing has a minimum drag but gives a maximum lift.
efficiency Percentage of work obtained from a machine compared with the work put into it.
electricity Form of energy believed to be due to the movement of electrons. Can heat substances, produce magnetic effects, and cause chemical changes. The dynamic kind is electricity moving through a conductor; the static kind is a charge that can be built up on a nonconductor by friction.
electromagnetic waves Vibrations traveling through a wide range of materials, or through space at the speed of light. Include ultraviolet rays, visible light rays, infrared rays, radio waves and X-rays.
electron Smallest negatively charged particle. The number of electrons in an atom in its normal state is equal to the number of protons in the nucleus.
electron microscope Instrument that uses a beam of electrons instead of light to illuminate an object.
energy Capacity for doing work. *See also* heat energy, kinetic energy, and potential energy.
fahrenheit scale Scale on which freezing-point of water is 32° F and its boiling point at standard atmospheric pressure is 212° F.
fatigue Weakening of metals caused by repeated stresses. The amount of each stress may be very much less than a single breaking force, but, if it is repeated numerous times, fatigue may still develop.
fiber optics Devices that send images or light signals along glass fibers (optical fibers).
filament Fine thread or fiber. In electricity, fine wires which can be heated to relatively high temperatures by the passage of electric current without melting.
film, photographic Film is made of a transparent plastic material coated with silver salts: the salts are chemically affected by the light they receive when the film is exposed.
fluorescence Ability of certain substances to absorb light of one wavelength (i.e. color, when in a visible region of the spectrum) and emit light of another wavelength (or color).
focus Point at which rays of light are brought together after being reflected or refracted.
force A force tends to impart motion to a body at rest, or change the direction or speed of a body already in motion.
four-stroke engine Internal combustion engine involving the repetition of a cycle in which the piston first moves outward, drawing in a mixture of air and fuel, then thrusts inward, compressing the mixture, and is then pushed

continued

Technology glossary continued

239 out by the explosion of the mixture, and finally moves in to expel the burnt gases.

freezing point In general, temperature at which a liquid freezes at standard atmospheric pressure.

friction Resistance to relative motion between two surfaces in direct contact.

fuse Short length of wire made of an alloy that melts at low temperature. Electric circuits are always provided with a fuse so that if too much current flows, the fuse melts and the circuit is broken.

generator (dynamo) Device that generates direct or alternating electric current by rotating a coil of wire in a magnetic field.

geodimeter Device that uses the known velocity of light to measure distances. The time taken for a beam of light to be sent over the distance and reflected back to the point of its origin is computed electronically and then converted into distance. Effective up to 10 mi (about 16 km) in clear weather.

gravitation Force of attraction existing between all bodies and particles of matter. The Moon is kept in orbit by the mutual attraction of Moon and Earth. The attraction of the Moon exerts on the Earth's oceans is mainly responsible for the rise and fall of the tides. Newton's law of gravitation states that all bodies attract one another with a force directly proportional to the product of the masses and inversely proportional to the square of the distance between them.

gravity Force of attraction that one mass exercises on other masses.

gyrocompass Device containing high-speed gyroscope whose axle can be made to point in the same direction as the Earth's axis of rotation, i.e. true north and south. *See also* magnetic compass.

gyroscope Spinning wheel mounted so that it is free to rotate about any axis. Turning the wheel's support in any direction does not alter the position of the spinning wheel in space. If force is applied to the axle, it will turn slowly in a direction that is at right angles to the direction of the force.

heat energy Energy generated in a substance due to the movement of its molecules. The hotter the substance is, the greater the movement of molecules.

hologram Recording on film of two-dimensional interference pattern caused by two laser beams, one falling directly onto the film, the other reflected onto the film via the object that is being recorded.

horsepower Working rate needed to raise 1 lb weight 550 ft in 1 sec, measured in watts.

hovercraft Vehicle that supports itself on a cushion of air.

hydraulic machinery Machines operated by pressure transmitted through a pipe by a liquid.

incandescence State of glowing while at high temperature, e.g. red-hot poker.

insulator Nonconductor of heat or electricity.

internal combustion engine Engine that turns heat energy into power by burning fuel directly inside itself, e.g. car engine or gas turbine.

kinetic energy Energy that a body possesses because it is in motion, e.g. water pouring down a slope.

laser **L**ight **A**mplification by **S**timulated **E**mission of **R**adiation. Device producing narrow beam of very bright light or infrared rays, in which all the waves have exactly the same frequency, and are in phase.

lens Device capable of bending light rays to form an image.

lift Upward force produced by aircraft wing, helicopter rotor, and foils of hydrofoil.

light Electromagnetic waves, with lengths greater than those of ultraviolet rays and shorter than those of infrared rays, which stimulate sense of sight and serve to convey visual impression of objects.

liquid crystals Organic materials, which are crystalline when solid, that form partially ordered state when melted (liquid crystal state), becoming true liquids only after the temperature is raised further.

magnetic compass Device used to determine horizontal direction. Comprises magnetic needle, mounted on pivot and free to move horizontally, that comes to rest pointing toward Earth's magnetic poles.

magnetic field The force exerted by a magnet on electrically charged things or other magnets.

mass This may be defined either as the inertia of a given body, or as the gravitational force produced by a given body.

matter Anything that has mass.

metal Substance answering to all or most of following descriptions: ductile, malleable, lustrous, good conductor of heat and electricity, able to replace the hydrogen of certain acids and thus form salts.

metric system System of weights and measures of French origin, now adopted by many countries and used universally in science. The basic unit is the meter.

microscope Optical or electronic instrument giving greatly magnified images of objects usually too small to be clearly visible to the naked eye.

microwaves Electromagnetic radiation of a wavelength of between 1 mm and 10 cm (less than radio waves and more than infrared). Produced by klystrons and magnetrons.

molecule Smallest quantity of a substance that can exist independently with all the properties of that substance.

monochromatic light Light formed of electromagnetic vibrations of the same frequency, i.e. one color.

ohm Unit of electrical resistance. Defined as the mount of resistance in a circuit that will allow a source of electricity with the electromotive force or "pressure" of one volt to pass a current of one ampere.

ozone layer Layer of Earth's upper atmosphere in which a high proportion of oxygen exists in the form of ozone, i.e. oxygen with three, instead of two, atoms in each molecule.

particles, subatomic Particles with mass less than 1/16 that of a single atom of the most common isotope of oxygen, e.g. electron, meson, neutrino, neutron, photon, positron, proton. Also, composite, heavier particles such as alpha particles and deuterons.

petroleum Crude oil. Consists of a complex mixture of compounds, mostly hydrocarbons. Believed to have been formed by the decomposition of microscopic marine organisms in the absence of air.

photoelectric cell Device for detecting and measuring light. A photographer's photoelectric meter uses the element selenium, which generates a small electric current under influence of light. This current then used to deflect a pointer, thus measuring strength of the light.

photography Process of obtaining the permanent image of an object on a transparent film or glass plate that has been coated with an emulsion containing silver salts sensitive to light. Light from the object is briefly focused onto film or plate by temporarily removing the shutter over the lens.

piston Solid cylinder capable of moving back and forth, under pressure, within a close-fitting hollow cylinder.

polarization of light The process of arranging light waves so that they fall onto a single plane.

potential energy Stored-up capacity for doing work.

power Rate of output of work. Often used loosely to mean energy, or capacity for doing work.

pressure Force acting upon surface, measured as weight per unit area, e.g. 50 lb per sq in.

pyrometer Instrument used for measuring high temperature.

radar **RA**dio **D**etection **A**nd **R**anging. System of detecting distance, direction, and possibly the shape of distant objects by means of short electromagnetic waves transmitted to and reflected back from those objects.

radio Device used in broadcasting to convert sound impulses into electrical impulses affecting variations in electromagnetic waves; and also to convert such varying waves back into sound impulses.

reciprocating engine Engine in which pistons move up and down or to and fro.

refraction of light Change in direction of ray of light at point where it passes from one transparent medium (e.g. air) to another (e.g. water), whose surface it strikes at a slanting angle.

resolving power Ability of optical system (such as the eye, lens, or microscope) to separate images of objects lying very close together.

rotor System of rotating blades in turbine engine.

semiconductors Materials that are neither good conductors nor good insulators but somewhere between the two. The metals silicon and germanium are semiconductors.

single-acting engine Steam engine in which the force of the steam pushes on only one side of the piston.

solar cell Arrangement of metals capable of converting the energy in sunlight into electric energy. A photoelectric cell is a kind of solar battery.

sound Typical sense impression received by the ear when the ear drum is set in vibration by compression and rarefaction waves of a certain

continued

Technology glossary continued

239 limited range of wavelength and frequency. The waves may travel through air, and through many liquids and solids.

sound barrier Sudden increase of air resistance which a moving object must overcome as it accelerates from a speed less than that of sound to a speed greater than that of sound.

sound waves Longitudinal waves, within a limited range of wavelength, which travel outward in all directions from the vibrating source that has given rise to them. They may travel through air or other gases, or through many liquids or solids, but not through a vacuum.

spectrum Series of color bands obtained when a ray of light is passed through a triangular glass prism, or other device, which separates the light into rays of different wavelength.

stress Force acting on a given unit of area.

superconductors Materials which, at certain low temperatures, offer virtually no resistance to an electric current.

superheated steam Steam at a temperature of above 212° F (100° C), obtained by heating water under a pressure greater than atmospheric pressure.

supersonic Supersonic speed is speed greater than the speed of sound.

tensile strength Resistance of a given body to breakage due to stretching.

thermodynamics Study of processes that involve the transformation of heat into mechanical work, or of mechanical work into heat, or the flow of heat from a hotter to a colder body.

thermograph Graph that is drawn on a paper roll that is moving at a fixed speed, and recording temperature changes over a period of time.

thermometer Any instrument used to measure temperature.

thermostat Instrument used for automatically regulating temperature.

transformer Device consisting of two coils of wire, one with many more turns than the other; it is used to change a large alternating current of low voltage into a small one of high voltage.

turbine engine Engine with no pistons or cranks, that produces rotary motion directly.

two-stroke engine Internal combustion engine in which the explosion or power stroke occurs once for every two strokes of the piston.

ultrasonic Sound waves with frequencies above the range audible to the human ear.

vacuum Strictly, space occupied by no matter; commonly, one occupied by highly rarefied gases.

volt Unit measuring the difference in electric potential or electromotive force. One volt has the electromotive force required to produce a current of one amp through resistance of one ohm.

watt Unit of electrical power; product of amperes multiplied by volts.

weight Force which a given mass exerts at a given rate of acceleration.

wind power Energy in wind that may be exploited by windmills to generate electricity.

241 NUMBERS

Names for numbers

2411 Many numbers have names. Some of these names are in everyday use, others apply in more specialized areas.

Everyday use
1/10 Tithe
2 Pair, couple, brace
6 Half dozen
12 Dozen
13 Baker's dozen
20 Score
50 Half century
100 Century
144 Gross

Musicians
1 Soloist
2 Duet
3 Trio
4 Quartet
5 Quintet
6 Sextet
7 Septet
8 Octet

Multiple births
2 Twins
3 Triplets
4 Quadruplets (quads)
5 Quintuplets (quins)
6 Sextuplets

Prefixes

2412 Some names for specialized numbers have the same first part (prefix). These prefixes indicate the number to which they belong.

Semi-, hemi-, demi-	**1/2**
Uni-	**1**
Bi-, di-	**2**
Tri-, ter-	**3**
Tetra-, tetr-, tessera-	**4**
Quadri-, quadr-	**4**
Pent-, penta-, quinqu-, Quinque-, quint-	**5**
Sex-, sexi-, hex-, hexa	**6**
Hept-, hepta-, sept-, septi,	**7**
Septam-	**7**
Oct-, octa-, octo-	**8**
Non-, nona-, ennea-	**9**
Dec-, deca	**10**
Hendeca-, undec-, undeca-	**11**
Dodeca-	**12**
Quindeca-	**15**
Icos-, icosa-, icosi-	**20**

Prefixes in alphabetical order

Bi-	**2**
Dec-, deca-	**10**
Demi-	**1/2**
Di-	**2**
Dodeca-	**12**
Ennea-	**9**
Hemi-	**1/2**
Hendeca-	**11**
Hept-, Hepta-	**7**
Hex-, hexa-	**6**
Icos-, icosa-, icosi-	**20**
Non-, nona-	**9**
Oct-, octa-, octo-	**8**
Pent-, penta-	**5**
Quadr-, quadri-	**4**
Quindeca-	**15**
Quinqu-, quinque-	**5**
Quint-	**5**
Semi-	**1/2**
Sept-, septem-, septi-	**7**
Sex-, sexi-	**6**
Ter-	**3**
Tessera-	**4**
Tetr, tetra	**4**
Tri-	**3**
Undec-, undeca-	**11**
Uni-	**1**

Prefixes for power of 10
Listed are the internationallly agreed prefixes used to show multiples of the number 10. These prefixes are used with units of measurement. For example, a kilogram is 1,000 grams; a centimeter is 1/10 of a meter; and so on.

Prefix	Symbol	Value
Atto	a	0.000,000,000,000,000,001
Femto	f	0.000,000,000,000,001
Pico	p	0.000,000,000,001
Nano	n	0.000,000,001
Micro	μ	0.000,001
Milli	m	0.001
Centi	c	0.01

Prefix	Symbol	Value
Deci	d	0.1
Dec-, deca	da	10
Hect-, hecto	h	100
Kilo	k	1,000
Mega	M	1,000,000
Giga	G	1,000,000,000
Tera	T	1,000,000,000,000

Millions and billions

2413 **Millions and billions**
Listed are the names given to 10 when it is raised to various powers, these are numbers to the right of a figure e.g.10^8, indicating how many times it is to be multiplied by itself.

Power	Number in full	Name
10^2	100	Hundred
10^3	1000	Thousand
10^6	1,000,000	Million
10^9	1,000,000,000	Billion
10^{12}	1,000,000,000,000	Trillion
10^{15}	1,000,000,000,000,000	Quadrillion
10^{18}	1,000,000,000,000,000,000	Quintrillion
10^{100}	1 followed by 100 zeroes	Googol

Historic number systems

2414

	Roman	Arabic	Chinese	Hindu	Babylonian	Egyptian	Hebrew	Japanese
1	I	١	一	१	𒁹	𓏺	א	一
2	II	٢	二	२	𒈫	𓏻	ב	二
3	III	٣	三	३	𒐈	𓏼	ג	三
4	IV	٤	四	४	𒐉	𓏽	ד	四
5	V	٥	五	५	𒐊	𓏾	ה	五
6	VI	٦	六	६	𒐋	𓏿	ו	六
7	VII	٧	七	७	𒑂	𓐀	ז	七
8	VIII	٨	八	८	𒑄	𓐁	ח	八
9	IX	٩	九	९	𒑆	𓐂	ט	九
10	X	١٠	十	१०	𒌋	𓎆	י	十
50	L	٥٠	五十	५०	𒐐	𓎊	נ	五十
100	C	١٠٠	百	१००	𒁹𒐏	𓍢	ק	百
500	D	٥٠٠	五百	५००	𒑄𒎙	𓍦	ך	五百
1000	M	١٠٠٠	千	१०००	[illegible]	𓆼	'א	千

Roman number system

2415 The Roman numeral system is a method of notation in which the capitals are modeled on ancient Roman inscriptions. The numerals are represented by seven capital letters of the alphabet: I, V, X, L, C, D, and M. These letters are the foundation of the system; they are combined in order to form all numbers. If a letter is preceded by another of lesser value (e.g., IX), the value of the combined form is the difference between the values of each letter (e.g. IX = X (10) – I (1) = 9). Otherwise, they are added. To determine the value of a string of Roman numerals, find the pairs in the string. These begin with a lower value. Determine their values, then add these to the values of the other letters in the string:

MCMXCI equals
M+CM+XC+I equals
1000+900+90+1 equals
1991

A dash over a letter multiplies the value by 1,000 (e.g. $\overline{V}$ equals 5,000).

I	one
V	five
X	ten
L	fifty
C	one hundred
D	five hundred
M	one thousand

1 I	12 XII	35 XXXV	100 C
2 II	13 XIII	40 XL	200 CC
3 III	14 XIV	45 XLV	300 CCC
4 IV or IIII	15 XV	50 L	400 CD
5 V	16 XVI	55 LV	500 D
6 VI	17 XVII	60 LX	600 DC
7 VII	18 XVIII	65 LXV	700 DCC
8 VIII	19 XIX	70 LXX	800 DCCC
9 IX	20 XX	75 LXXV	900 CM
10 X	25 XXV	80 LXXX	1000 M
11 XI	30 XXX	90 XC	2000 MM

Computer coding systems

2416 ASCII (American Standard Code for Information Interchange) is an international coding system of character representation. Its 256 codes represent computer commands and letters of the alphabet. Hexadecimal is a system of numbering based on 16 digits (as opposed to 10 in the decimal system): 1 to 9 and A to F.
Binary, ASCII and hexadecimal systems are used in computer programming. The table below shows character equivalents in decimal, hexadecimal, and ASCII systems.

continued

Computer coding systems continued

2416

Dec	Hex	ASCII	Dec	Hex	ASCII	Dec	Hex	ASCII	Dec	Hex	ASCII	Dec	Hex	ASCII	Dec	Hex	ASCII
000	00	NUL	022	16	SYN	044	2C	,	066	42	B	088	58	X	110	6E	n
001	01	SOH	023	17	ETB	045	2D	-	067	43	C	089	59	Y	111	6F	o
002	02	STX	024	18	CAN	046	2E	.	068	44	D	090	5A	Z	112	70	p
003	03	SETX	025	19	EM	047	2F	/	069	45	E	091	5B	[	113	71	q
004	04	EOT	026	1A	SUB	048	30	0	070	46	F	092	5C	\	114	72	r
005	05	ENQ	027	1B	ESCAPE	049	31	1	071	47	G	093	5D	]	115	73	s
006	06	ACK	028	1C	FS	050	32	2	072	48	H	094	5E	^	116	74	t
007	07	BEL	029	1D	GS	051	33	3	073	49	I	095	5F	_	117	75	u
008	08	BS	030	1E	RS	052	34	4	074	4A	J	096	60	'	118	76	v
009	09	HT	031	1F	US	053	35	5	075	4B	K	097	61	a	119	77	w
010	0A	LF	032	20	SPACE	054	36	6	076	4C	L	098	62	b	120	78	x
011	0B	VT	033	21	!	055	37	7	077	4D	M	099	63	c	121	79	y
012	0C	FF	034	22	"	056	38	8	078	4E	N	100	64	d	122	7A	z
013	0D	CR	035	23	#	057	39	9	079	4F	O	101	65	e	123	7B	{
014	0E	SO	036	24	$	058	3A	:	080	50	P	102	66	f	124	7C	|
015	0F	SI	037	25	%	059	3B	;	081	51	Q	103	67	g	125	7D	}
016	10	DLE	038	26	&	060	3C	<	082	52	R	104	68	h	126	7E	~
017	11	DC1	039	27	'	061	3D	=	083	53	S	105	69	i	127	7F	DEL
018	12	DC2	040	28	(	062	3E	>	084	54	T	106	6A	j			
019	13	DC3	041	29	)	063	3F	?	085	55	U	107	6B	k			
020	14	DC4	042	2A	*	064	40	@	086	56	V	108	6C	l			
021	15	NAK	043	2B	+	065	41	A	087	57	W	109	6D	m			

Fractions, decimals, and percentages

2417 The following are representations of fractional quantities as fractions, decimals, and, percentages.

SIXTEENTHS

Fraction	Decimal	Percentage
1/16	0.0625	6.25 %
1/8	0.125	12.5 %
3/16	0.1875	18.75 %
1/4	0.25	25 %
5/16	0.3125	31.25 %
3/8	0.375	37.5 %
7/16	0.4375	43.75 %
1/2	0.5	50 %
9/16	0.5625	56.25 %
5/8	0.625	62.50 %
11/16	0.6875	68.75 %
3/4	0.75	75 %
13/16	0.8125	81.25 %
7/8	0.875	87.50 %
15/16	0.9375	93.75 %

NINTHS, SIXTHS

Fraction	Decimal	Percentage
1/9	0.111 111	11.11 %
1/6	0.166 667	16.67 %
1/3	0.333 333	33.33 %
3/6	0.5	50 %
2/3	0.666 666	66.67 %
5/6	0.833 333	83.33 %

SEVENTHS, FIFTHS

Fraction	Decimal	Percentage
1/7	0.142857	14.29%
1/5	0.2	20 %
2/5	0.4	40 %
3/5	0.6	60 %
4/5	0.8	80 %

PERCENTAGES

Percent	Fraction	Decimal
5 %	1/20	0.05
10 %	1/10	0.1
15 %	3/20	0.15
20 %	1/5	0.2
25 %	1/4	0.25
30 %	3/10	0.3
35 %	7/20	0.35
40 %	2/5	0.4
45 %	9/20	0.45
50 %	1/2	0.5
55 %	11/20	0.55
60 %	3/5	0.6
65 %	13/20	0.65
70 %	7/10	0.7
75 %	3/4	0.75
80 %	4/5	0.8
85 %	17/20	0.85
90 %	9/10	0.9
95 %	19/20	0.95

Prime numbers

2418 These are whole numbers that have only two factors – numbers by which it is divisible. These are the number itself and the number 1. The only even prime number is 2: all other prime numbers are odd.
There is an infinite number of prime numbers. The first 126 are given. The number below is the largest prime number known in 1952. The largest prime known has thousands of digits.

170,141,183,460,469,231,731,687,303,715,884,105,727

2	3	5	7	11	13	17	19	23	29	31	37	41	43
47	53	59	61	67	71	73	79	83	89	97	101	103	107
109	113	127	131	137	139	149	151	157	163	167	173	179	181
191	193	197	199	211	223	227	229	233	239	241	251	257	263
269	271	277	281	283	293	307	311	313	317	331	337	347	349
353	359	367	373	379	383	389	397	401	409	419	421	431	433
439	443	449	457	461	463	467	479	487	491	499	503	509	521
523	541	547	557	563	569	571	577	587	593	599	601	607	613
617	619	631	641	643	647	653	659	661	673	677	683	691	701

Composite numbers

2419 Composite numbers are all the whole numbers greater than one which are not primes. Here we look at quick ways to check if a composite number is exactly divisible by numbers from 2 to 13.

2
A number is divisible by 2 if its last digit is even, e.g. the last digit of 256 is 6, which is even, so 256 is exactly divisible by 2.

3
A number is divisible by 3 if the sum of its digits is a multiple of 3, e.g. 531 is exactly divisible by 3 because 5 + 3 + 1 = 9 = 3 x 3.

4
A number is divisible by 4 if its last two digits are a multiple of 4, e.g. 1932 is exactly divisible by 4 because 32 = 4 x 8.

5
A number is exactly divisible by 5 if its last digit is 5 or 0.

6
A number is exactly divisible by 6 if it is divisible by both 2 and 3.

7
To check for divisibility by 7, start at the right and separate the digits into groups of three. Beginning at the right with a +, write + and - alternately in front of each group. Do the sum. If the answer is a multiple of 7, then the original number can be divided by 7. For example, 14294863492 is exactly divisible by 7 because - 14 + 294 - 863 + 492 = - 91 = 7 x -13.

8
A number is exactly divisible by 8 if its last three digits are a multiple of 8.

9
A number is exactly divisible by 9 if the sum of its digits is a multiple of 9.

10
A number is exactly divisible by 10 if its last digit is 0.

11
To check for divisibility by 11, start at the left and add together the first, third, fifth, etc. digits. Then add the second, fourth, sixth, etc. digits. Subtract the second sum from the first. If the answer is 0 or 11, the original number can be divided by 11. For example, 1254649 is exactly divisible by 11 because 1+5+6+9 = 21, 2+4+4 = 10, and 21-10 = 11.

12
A number is exactly divisible by 12 if it is divisible by both 3 and 4.

13
To check for divisibility by 13, group the digits as if testing for divisibility by 7 and do the sum. If the answer is a multiple of 13, then the original number can be divided exactly by 13.

242 COUNTING SYSTEMS AND OPERATIONS

Mathematical symbols

2421

$+$	plus or positive
$-$	minus or negative
$\pm$	plus or minus, positive or negative
$\times$	multiplied by
$\div$	divided by
$=$	equal to
$\equiv$	identically equal to
$\neq$	not equal to
$\not\equiv$	not identically equal to
$\approx$	approximately equal to
$\sim$	of the order of or similar to
$>$	greater than
$<$	less than
$\not>$	not greater than
$\not<$	not less than
$\geqslant$	greater than or equal to
$\leqslant$	less than or equal to
$\gg$	much greater than
$\ll$	much less than
$\surd$	square root
∞	infinity
$\propto$	proportional to
Σ	sum of
Π	product of
Δ	difference
$\therefore$	therefore
$\angle$	angle
$\parallel$	parallel to
$\perp$	perpendicular to
$:$	is to

Decimal systems

2422 **Counting in powers of 10**
When a number is written in base 10 (the decimal system), the value of a digit in the number increases 10 times whenever it moves one place to the left. For example, 2 indicates 2 x 1; 20 indicates 2 x 10; 200 indicates 2 x 10 x 10 (i.e. 2 x 10^2); and so on. A number in base 10 can therefore be set out in columns, with each column representing a power (multiple) of 10. These powers of 10 are called the "place values" of the digits.

After the decimal point
In base 10, the decimal point separates those numbers 1 and greater than 1 (on left side of the point), from those numbers less than 1 (right side of the point). Each column to the right of the decimal point has one-tenth the value of the preceding column (to its left).

1980

1				10^3	thousands	1000
	9			10^2	hundreds	900
		8		10	tens	80
			0	1	ones	0

0.0891

0				10^{-1}	tenths	0.0
	8			10^{-2}	hundredths	0.08
		9		10^{-3}	thousandths	0.009
			1	10^{-4}	ten thousandths	0.0001

Arithmetic operations

2423

Addition		Subtraction		Multiplication		Division	
29	Addend	74	Minuend	46	Multiplicand	3	Quotient
+6	Addend	-16	Subtrahend	x9	Multiplier	Divisor 13) 44	Dividend
35	Sum	58	Difference	414	Product	39	
						5	Remainder

The four basic arithmetic operations are addition, subtraction, multiplication, and division. Each part of an arithmetic operation has a specific name. In a fraction the denominator is the number of parts to divide by and the numerator is the number to be divided.

Fraction

5/8 $\frac{5}{8}$ — 5 Numerator, 8 Denominator

Simple (or vulgar) fraction

9/7 $\frac{9}{7}$ — 9 Numerator, 7 Denominator

Binary numbers

2424 The binary system is formulated on a base of 2, or on a sum of powers of 2. For example, the number 101011 is equal to 40 (101000) + 3 (11); in the decimal system, this number equals 43. The system is used frequently in computer applications.

In describing computer storage, 1 bit = 1 binary digit; 1 byte = 8 bits in most systems; 1 megabyte (MB) = 1,048,576 bytes. The table shows other decimal/binary equivalents.

Binary	Decimal
1	**1**
10	**2**
11	**3**
100	**4**
101	**5**
110	**6**
111	**7**
1000	**8**
1001	**9**
1010	**10**
1011	**11**
1100	**12**
1101	**13**
1110	**14**
1111	**15**
10000	**16**
10001	**17**
10010	**18**
10011	**19**
10100	**20**

Binary	Decimal
10101	**21**
11110	**30**
101000	**40**
110010	**50**
111100	**60**
1011010	**90**
1100100	**100**
11001000	**200**
100101100	**300**
110010000	**400**
111110100	**500**
1001011000	**600**
1110000100	**900**
1111101000	**1000**
11111010000	**2000**
111110100000	**4000**
1001110001000	**5000**
10011100010000	**10000**
100111000100000	**20000**
11000011010100000	**100000**

Fibonacci sequence

2425 Each number in a Fibonacci sequence is the sum of the two numbers preceding it. The sequence can therefore be built up using simple addition. Below is an example of a Fibonacci sequence.

0+1	=	**1**
1+1	=	**2**
2+1	=	**3**
3+2	=	**5**
5+3	=	**8**
8+5	=	**13**
13+8	=	**21**
21+13	=	**34**
34+21	=	**55**
55+34	=	**89**
89+55	=	**144**
144+89	=	**233**
233+144	=	**377**
377+233	=	**610**
610+377	=	**987**
987+610	=	**1597**
1597+987	=	**2584**
2584+1597	=	**4181**
4181+2584	=	**6765**
6765+4181	=	**10946**
10946+6765	=	**17711**
17711+10946	=	**28657**
28657+17 711	=	**46368**
46368+28657	=	**75025**
75025+46368	=	**121393**
121393+75 025	=	**196418**
196 418+121393	=	**317811**
317811+196418	=	**514229**
514229+317811	=	**832040**
832040+514299	=	**1346339**

Multiplication table

2426 Right is a quick-reference table giving products and quotients. It can be used for either multiplication or division.

Multiplication
To multiply 6 by 9, for example, scan down column six until you reach row nine. The number in the square where column six intersects row nine is the product, 54.

Division
To divide 56 by 8, scan down column eight to find 56 (the dividend) then scan across to find the row number. This is the quotient, 7.

	Column											
Row	**1**	**2**	**3**	**4**	**5**	**6**	**7**	**8**	**9**	**10**	**11**	**12**
1	1	2	3	4	5	6	7	8	9	10	11	12
2	2	4	6	8	10	12	14	16	18	20	22	24
3	3	6	9	12	15	18	21	24	27	30	33	36
4	4	8	12	16	20	24	28	32	36	40	44	48
5	5	10	15	20	25	30	35	40	45	50	55	60
6	6	12	18	24	30	36	42	48	54	60	66	72
7	7	14	21	28	35	42	49	56	63	70	77	84
8	8	16	24	32	40	48	56	64	72	80	88	96
9	9	18	27	36	45	54	63	72	81	90	99	108
10	10	20	30	40	50	60	70	80	90	100	110	120
11	11	22	33	44	55	66	77	88	99	110	121	132
12	12	24	36	48	60	72	84	96	108	120	132	144

Interest

2427 Interest refers to the charge made for borrowing money. It is usually expressed in terms of percentage rates. There are two types of interest: simple interest and compound interest.

Simple interest
This type of interest is calculated on the amount of money originally loaned (the principal). The formula used to calculate simple interest is:

$$I = \frac{P \times R \times T}{100}$$

I is interest, P is principal, R is the percentage rate per unit time, and T is the length of time (measured in units) over which the money is invested or loaned.
The final sum – or amount of money to which the principal will grow – is figured using the formula:

$$S\ (\text{sum}) = P\left(1 + \frac{RxT}{100}\right)$$

Compound interest
Unlike simple interest, which is paid only on the principal, compound interest is paid also on the previous interest earned. Thus the sum – or amount to which the principal will grow – increases at a much faster rate than with simple interest. Compound interest is figured using the formula:

$$S = P(1 + i)^n$$

The 'i' represents the periodic interest; 'n' is the number of periods.
The table shows the compound interest paid (in dollars) on a principal of $100. The interest rate is in % per annum.

Comparing the two
Money grows much more quickly with compound interest than with simple interest. Compare, for example, the amount of time required for an amount of money to double itself with simple interest and with compound interest.

SIMPLE

Simple interest (in dollars) to add to $1000 (percent per annum)

Period	**2.5%**	**3%**	**3.5%**	**4%**	**4.5%**	**5%**	**5.5%**	**6%**	**6.5%**	**7%**
1 day	0.069	0.083	0.097	0.111	0.125	0.139	0.153	0.167	0.185	0.194
2 days	0.139	0.167	0.194	0.222	0.250	0.278	0.306	0.333	0.361	0.389
3 days	0.208	0.250	0.292	0.333	0.375	0.417	0.458	0.500	0.545	0.583
4 days	0.278	0.333	0.389	0.444	0.500	0.556	0.611	0.667	0.722	0.778
5 days	0.347	0.417	0.486	0.556	0.625	0.694	0.764	0.833	0.903	0.972
6 days	0.417	0.500	0.583	0.667	0.750	0.833	0.917	1.000	1.083	1.167
30 days	2.083	2.500	2.917	3.333	03.750	4.167	4.583	5.000	5.417	5.833
60 days	4.167	5.000	5.833	6.667	7.500	8.333	9.167	10.000	10.833	11.667
90 days	6.250	7.500	8.750	10.000	11.250	12.500	13.750	15.000	16.250	17.500
180 days	12.500	15.000	17.500	20.000	22.500	25.000	27.500	30.000	32.500	35.000
360 days	25.000	30.000	35.000	40.000	45.000	50.000	55.000	60.000	65.000	70.000

SIMPLE

Simple interest (in dollars) added on to $100 (percent per annum)

Period	**7%**	**8%**	**9%**	**10%**	**11%**	**12%**	**13%**	**14%**	**15%**
1 year	107.00	108.00	109.00	110.00	111.00	112.00	113.00	114.00	115.00
5 years	135.00	140.00	145.00	150.00	155.00	160.00	165.00	170.00	175.00
10 years	170.00	180.00	190.00	200.00	210.00	220.00	230.00	240.00	250.00
20 years	240.00	260.00	280.00	300.00	320.00	340.00	360.00	380.00	400.00
30 years	310.00	340.00	370.00	400.00	430.00	460.00	490.00	520.00	550.00
40 years	380.00	420.00	460.00	500.00	540.00	580.00	620.00	660.00	700.00
50 years	450.00	500.00	550.00	600.00	650.00	700.00	750.00	800.00	850.00

COMPOUND

Compound interest paid (in dollars) on a principal of $100 (percent per annum)

Period	**4%**	**5%**	**6%**	**7%**	**8%**	**9%**	**10%**	**12%**	**14%**	**16%**
1 day	0.11	0.014	0.016	0.019	0.022	0.025	0.027	0.033	0.038	0.044
1 week	0.077	1.096	0.115	0.134	0.153	0.173	0.192	0.230	0.268	0.307
6 months	2.00	2.50	3.00	3.504	4.00	4.50	5.00	6.00	7.00	8.00
1 year	4.00	5.00	6.00	7.00	8.00	9.00	10.00	12.00	14.00	16.00
2 years	8.16	10.25	12.36	14.49	16.64	18.81	21.00	25.44	29.96	34.56
3 years	12.49	15.76	19.10	22.50	25.97	29.50	33.10	40.49	48.15	56.09
4 years	16.99	21.55	26.25	31.08	36.05	41.16	46.41	57.35	68.90	81.06
5 years	21.67	27.63	33.82	40.26	46.93	53.86	61.05	76.23	92.54	110.03
6 years	26.53	34.01	41.85	50.07	58.69	67.71	77.16	97.38	119.50	143.64
7 years	31.59	40.71	50.36	60.58	71.38	82.80	94.87	121.071	150.23	182.62
8 years	36.86	47.75	59.38	71.82	85.09	99.26	114.36	147.60	185.26	227.84
9 years	42.33	55.13	68.95	83.85	99.90	117.19	135.79	177.31	225.19	280.30
10 years	48.02	62.89	79.08	96.72	115.89	136.74	159.37	210.58	270.72	341.14

243 AREA AND VOLUME

Calculating dimension

2431 **Perimeter** of a plane figure is the distance around its edge or boundary. It is measured in linear units.
Area of a figure is a measure of the size of its surface. Areas are measured in square units.
Volume of a solid figure is a measure of the amount of space it occupies. Volume is measured in cubic units.

Pi
Whatever the size of a circle, the ratio of its circumference to its diameter is always the same The Greek letter π (pi) is used as a symbol for its ratio: π = circumference ÷ diameter.
The value of π has been calculated to 160 million places of decimals but the value usually used in calculations is 3.1416. π is used in calculating the perimeters, areas, and volume of circular figures and solids.

$$\pi = 3.1416$$

Abbreviations
a = length of top
b = breadth of base
h = perpendicular height
l = length of base
r = length of radius
p = perimeter
d = diameter

Formulas for perimeters

2432

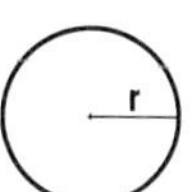

Circle

$$p = 2 \times \pi \times r$$
$$p = \pi \times d$$

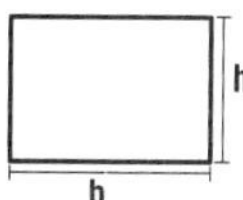

Rectangle

$$p = 2(h + b)$$

Formulas for area

2433

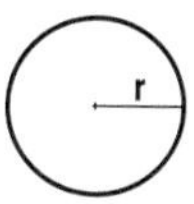

Circle

$$\pi \times r^2$$

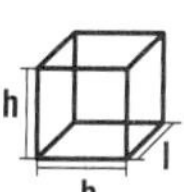

Cube (or cuboid)

$$h \times b \times 6$$

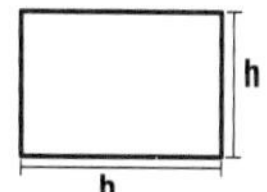

Rectangle

$$b \times h$$

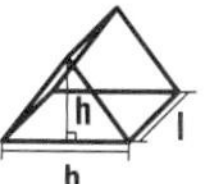

Prism

$$(b \times h) + (3 \times l \times b)$$

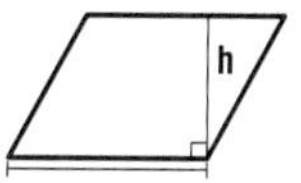

Parallelogram

$$b \times h$$

Cylinder

$$(2 \times \pi \times r \times l) + (2 \times \pi \times r^2)$$

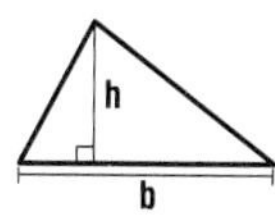

Triangle

$$\tfrac{1}{2} \times b \times h$$

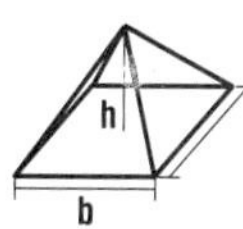

Pyramid

$$(2 \times b \times h) + (b^2)$$

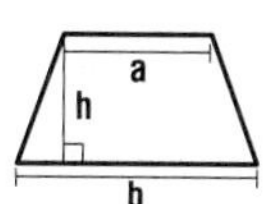

Trapezium

$$\frac{(a + b)\,h}{2}$$

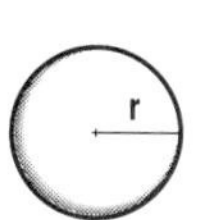

Sphere

$$4 \times \pi \times r^2$$

Formulas for volume

2434

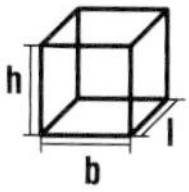

Cube or cuboid

$$b \times h \times l$$

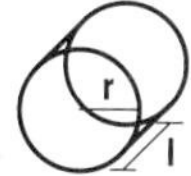

Cylinder

$$\pi \times r^2 \times l$$

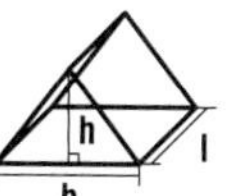

Prism

$$\frac{b \times h \times l}{2}$$

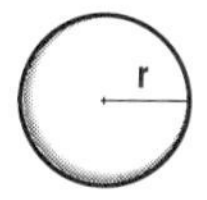

Sphere

$$\frac{4 \times \pi \times r^3}{3}$$

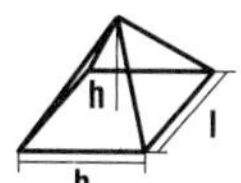

Pyramid

$$\frac{b \times h \times l}{3}$$

Cone

$$\frac{\pi \times r^2 \times h}{3}$$

Measuring angles

2435 Here we look at two units used for measuring angles, both of which are based on divisions of a circle. The degree is the more widely used of the two units, but the radian is preferred for some forms of mathematics.

Names for angles
Angles are named according to their size.
1 An acute angle measures more than 0° but less than 90°
2 A right angle measures 90°. Two lines at right angles are said to be perpendicular to one another
3 An obtuse angle measures more than 90° but less than 180°
4 A straight angle measures 180°
5 A reflex angle measures more than 180° but less than 360°
6 Complementary angles are two angles whose sum is 90° (a + b = 90°)
7 Supplementary angles are two angles whose sum is 180° (a + b = 180°)
8 Conjugate angles are two angles whose sum is 360° (a + b = 360°)

1
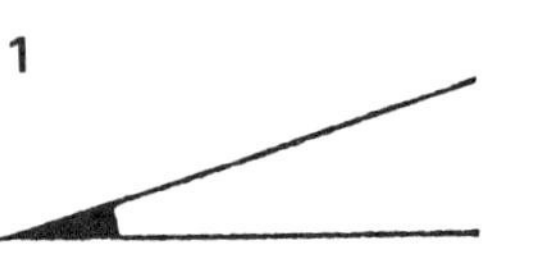
2
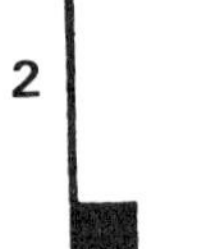
3

4

5

6

7

8

1 Degrees The degree system divides a circle into 360 equal parts. One degree (written 1°) is the angle at the center of a circle that cuts off an arc that is 1/360th of the circumference. There are 360 degrees in a circle. Here we show a quarter of a circle divided into 90 degrees.
2 Radians One radian (abbreviated to 1 rad) is the angle at the centre of a circle that cuts off an arc on the circumference which is equal in length to the radius. One radian equals 57.2958°, and there are 2π (approximately 6.28) radians in a circle.

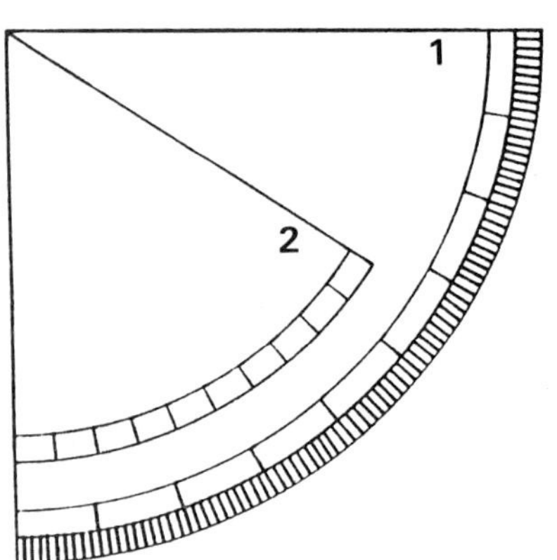

Subdivisions
60 minutes (written 60') = 1°
60 seconds (written 60") = 1'
100 centirads = 1 rad
1000 millirads = 1 rad

Polygons

2436 A plane figure enclosed by straight lines is called a polygon, from the Greek word *poly*, meaning many, and *gonia*, meaning angles. Here we are looking at the names, shapes, and angles of regular polygons with from 3 to 12 sides.

Regular and irregular polygons
All the sides of a regular polygon are the same length and all its angles are the same size. A regular polygon will fit into a circle with all its vertices (i.e. the points where two sides of the polygon meet) touching the circumference of the circle. The sides of an irregular polygon are of different lengths and its angles are of different sizes.

Names and angles
The table gives the names and numbers of sides of the first 10 regular polygons. Also listed are the sizes of the internal angles made by the sides where they join around the edges of the polygon, and the sum of all the internal angles in the polygon.

	Name of polygon	Number of sides	Each internal angle	Sum of internal angles
A	Triangle	3	60°	180°
B	Square	4	90°	360°
C	Pentagon	5	108°	540°
D	Hexagon	6	120°	720°
E	Heptagon	7	128.6°	900°
F	Octagon	8	135°	1080°
G	Nonagon	9	140°	1260°
H	Decagon	10	144°	1440°
I	Undecagon	11	147.3°	1620°
J	Dodecagon	12	150°	1800°

Quadrilaterals

2437

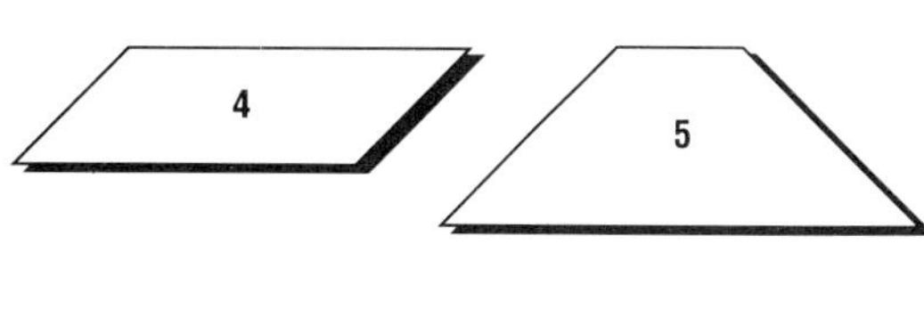

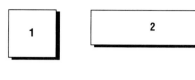

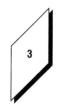

A quadrilateral is a four-sided polygon. There are five different-shaped quadrilaterals. They are:
1 Square: all the sides are the same length and all the angles are right angles
2 Rectangle: opposite sides are the same length and all the angles are right angles
3 Rhombus: all the sides are the same length but none of the angles are right angles
4 Parallelogram: opposite sides are parallel to each other and of the same length
5 Trapezoid: one pair of the opposite sides is parallel

Triangles

2438

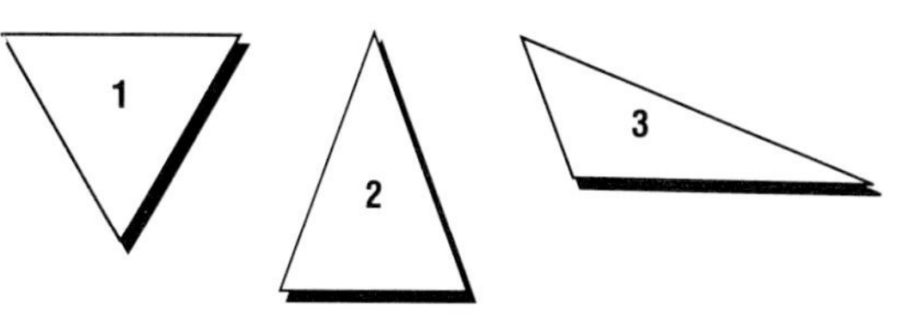

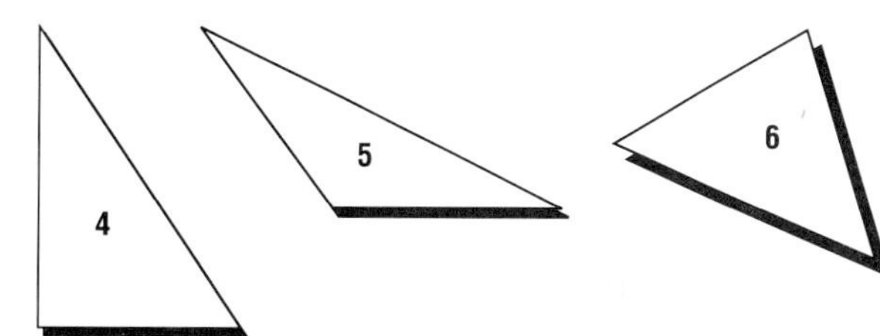

1 Equilateral: all the sides are the same length and all the angles are equal
2 Isosceles: two sides are of the same length and two angles are of equal size
3 Scalene: all the sides are of different length and all the angles are of different sizes
4 Right triangle: a triangle that contains one right angle
5 Obtuse angle: a triangle that contains one obtuse angle
6 Acute angle: a triangle with three acute angles

Solids

2439

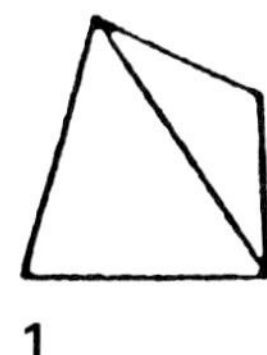

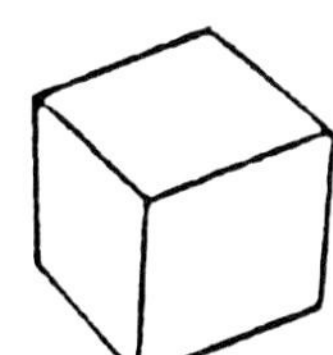

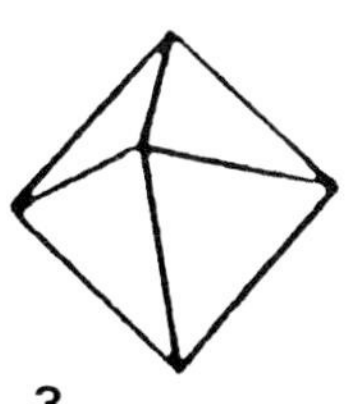

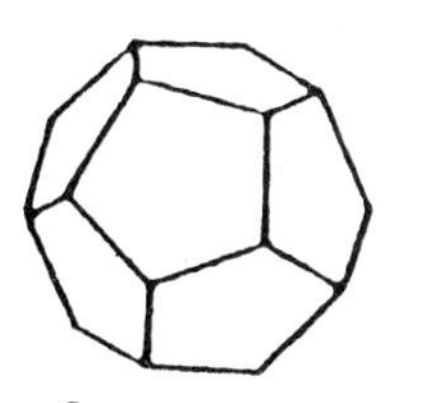

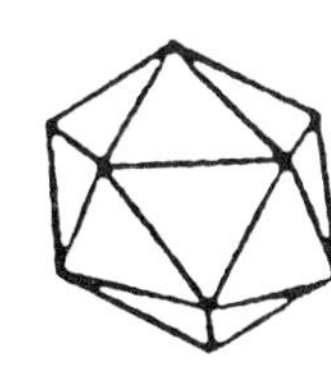

1 2 3 4 5

Regular solids
All the faces of a regular solid are identical regular polygons of equal size. A regular polyhedron will fit into a sphere with all its vertices touching the surface of the sphere.

There are only five regular solids. The names of these solids and the numbers of sides are listed.
1 Tetrahedron, 4 sides
2 Cube, 6 sides
3 Octahedron, 8 sides
4 Dodecahedron, 12 sides
5 Icosahedron, 20 sides

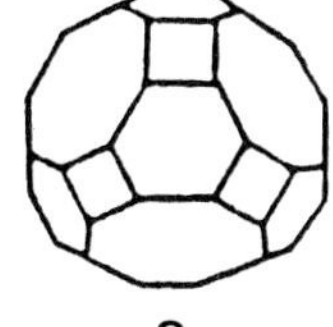

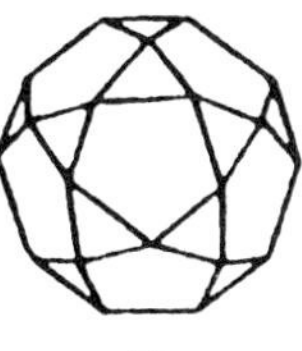

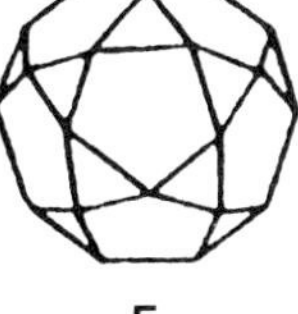

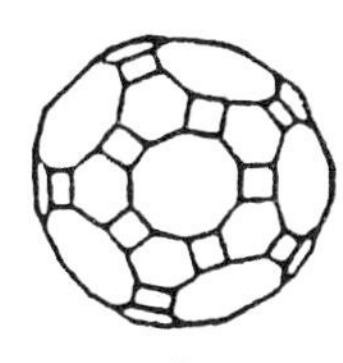

1 2 3 4 5 6

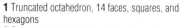

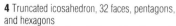

Semi-regular solids
These have two or more types of polygons as faces. Like regular solids, they will fit into a sphere with all their vertices touching the sphere's surface. Here we show six semi-regular solids. The names of these solids and the numbers and shapes of their faces are listed.

1 Truncated octahedron, 14 faces, squares, and hexagons
2 Cuboctahedron, 14 faces, triangles, and squares
3 Truncated cuboctahedron, 26 faces, squares, hexagons, and octagons
4 Truncated icosahedron, 32 faces, pentagons, and hexagons
5 Icosidodecahedron, 32 faces, triangles, and pentagons
6 Truncated icosidodecahedron, 62 faces, squares, hexagons, and decagons

244 UNIT SYSTEMS

The international system

2441

The International System of Units (or *Système International d'Unités* – SI) is the form of the metric system that has been in use since 1960.

Base units
There are seven base units in SI:

Unit	Symbol	Quantity
meter	m	length/distance
kilogram	kg	mass
ampere	A	electric current
kelvin	K	temperature
candela	cd	luminosity
second	s/sec	time
mole	mol	amount of substance

Supplementary units
There are also two supplementary units:

Unit	Symbol	Quantity
radian	rad	plane angle
steradian	sr	solid angle

Derived units
In addition, the system uses derived units, which are expressed in terms of the seven base units above. For example, velocity is given in meters per second (m/s). Other derived units in SI are referred to by special names. For example, the watt (W) is a unit of power; the joule (J) is a unit of energy.

The Imperial system

2442

Length

1 inch (in or ")						
1 foot (ft or ')	=	12 in				
1 yard (yd)	=	36 in	=	3 ft		
1 fathom (fm)	=	72 in	=	6 ft	=	2 yd
1 chain (ch)				66 ft	=	22 yd
1 furlong					=	220 yd
1 mile (mi)			=	5, 280 ft	=	1,760 yd

Volume

1 cubic in (in^3)					
1 fluid ounce (fl oz)					
1 pint (pt)	=	16 fl oz			
1 quart (qt)	=	32 fl oz	=	2 pt	
1 gallon (gal)			=	8 pt	= 4 qt
1 cubic foot (ft^3)	=	1,728 in^3			
1 cubic yard (yd^3)	=	46,656 in^3	=	27 ft^3	

Area

1 square inch (in^2)					
1 square foot (ft^2)	=	144 in^2			
1 square yard (yd^2)			=	9 ft^2	
1 square chain (ch^2)					= 484 yd^2
1 acre					= 4,840 yd^2
1 square mile (mi^2)	=	640 acres			

Weight

1 grain (gr)					
1 ounce (oz)	=	437.5 gr			
1 pound (lb)			=	16 oz	
1 stone (st)					= 14 lb
1 ton			=	35,840 oz	= 2,240 lb

245 CONVERSION FORMULAS

2451 Listed here are the multiplication/division factors necessary for converting units of length from imperial to metric, and vice versa, and from one unit to another in the same system. Note that two kinds of factors are given: approximate, for an quick conversion that can be made without a calculator; and accurate, for an exact conversion.

Milli-inches (mils) Micrometers (µm)		Approx	Accurate
mils	→ µm	× 25	× 25.4
µm	→ mils	÷ 25	× 0.0394

Inches (in) Millimeters (mm)		Approx	Accurate
in	→ mm	× 25	× 25.4
mm	→ in	÷ 25	× 0.0394

Inches (in) Centimeters (cm)		Approx	Accurate
in	→ cm	× 2.5	× 2.54
cm	→ in	÷ 2.5	× 0.394

Feet (ft) Meters (m)		Approx	Accurate
m	→ ft	× 3.3	× 3.281
ft	→ m	÷ 3.3	× 0.305

Yards (yd) Meters (m)		Approx	Accurate
m	→ yd	× 1	× 1.094
yd	→ m	÷ 1	× 0.914

Fathoms (fm) Meters (m)		Approx	Accurate
fm	→ m	× 2	× 1.83
m	→ fm	÷ 2	× 0.547

Chains (ch) Meters (m)		Approx	Accurate
ch	→ m	× 20	× 20.108
m	→ ch	÷ 20	× 0.0497

Furlongs (fur) Meters (m)		Approx	Accurate
fur	→ yd	× 200	× 201.17
m	→ km	÷ 200	× 0.005

Yards (yd) Kilometers (km)		Approx	Accurate
km	→ m	× 1000	× 1093.6
yd	→ fur	÷ 1000	× 0.0009

Miles (mi) Kilometers (km)		Approx	Accurate
mi	→ km	× 1.5	× 1.609
km	→ mi	÷ 1.5	× 0.621

Nautical miles (n mi) Miles (mi)		Approx	Accurate
n mi	→ mi	× 1.2	× 1.151
mi	→ n mi	÷ 1.2	× 0.869

Nautical miles (n mi) Kilometers (km)		Approx	Accurate
n mi	→ km	× 2	× 1.852
km	→ n mi	÷ 2	× 0.54

Areas

2452 Listed are the multiplication/division factors for converting units of area from imperial to metric, and vice versa. Note that two kinds of factors are given: approximate, for a quick conversion that can be made without a calculator; and accurate, for an exact conversion.

Circular mils (cmil) Square micrometers (μm^2)		Approx	Accurate
cmil	→ μm^2	x 500	x 506.7
μm^2	→ cmil	÷ 500	x 0.002

continued

Areas continued

2452

Square inches (in^2) / Square millimeters (mm^2)	Approx	Accurate
in^2 → mm^2	x 650	x 645.2
mm^2 → in^2	÷650	x 0.0015

Square inches (in^2) / Square centimeters (cm^2)	Approx	Accurate
in^2 → cm^2	x 6.5	x 6.452
cm^2 → in^2	÷ 6.5	x 0.15

Square chains (ch^2) / Square meters (m^2)	Approx	Accurate
ch^2 → m^2	x 400	x 404.686
m^2 → ch^2	÷400	x 0.0025

Square miles (mi^2) / Square kilometers (km^2)	Approx	Accurate
mi^2 → km^2	x 2.5	x 2.590
km^2 → mi^2	÷ 2.5	x 0.386

Square miles (mi^2) / Hectares (ha)	Approx	Accurate
mi^2 → ha^2	x 250	x 258.999
ha^2 → mi^2	÷250	x 0.0039

Hectares (ha) / Acres (cm)	Approx	Accurate
ha → acre	x 2.5	x 2.471
acre → ha	÷2.5	x 0.405

Square meters (m^2) / Square yards (yd^2)	Approx	Accurate
m^2 → yd^2	x 1	x 1.196
yd^2 → m^2	÷1	x 0.836

Square meters (m^2) / Square feet (ft^2)	Approx	Accurate
m^2 → ft^2	x 11	x 0.764
ft^2 → m^2	÷11	x 0.093

Volume

2453 Listed here are the multiplication/division factors for converting units of volume from one measuring system to another. Note that two kinds of factors are given: approximate, for a quick conversion that can be made without a calculator; and accurate, for an exact conversion.

1 : 1

UK gallons (gal) / US fluid gallons (fl gal)	Approx	Accurate
UK gal → US fl gal	x 1	x 1.201
US fl gal → UK gal	÷1	x 0.833

1 : 1

UK quarts (qt) / US fluid quarts (fl qt)	Approx	Accurate
UK qt → US fl qt	x 1	x 1.201
US fl qt → UK qt	÷1	x 0.833

1 : 1

UK pints (pt) / US fluid pints (fl pt)	Approx	Accurate
UK pt → US fl pt	x 1	x 1.201
US fl pt → UK pt	÷1	x 0.833

1 : 1

UK fluid ounces (fl oz) / US fluid ounces (fl oz)	Approx	Accurate
UK fl oz → US fl oz	x 1	x 0.961
US fl oz → UK fl oz	÷1	x 1.041

1 : 16

Cubic inches (cu in) / Cubic centimeters (cu cm)	Approx	Accurate
cu in → cu cm	x 16	x 16.387
cu cm → cu in	÷16	x 0.061

1 : 220

Cubic meters (cu m) / UK gallons (gal)	Approx	Accurate
cu m → UK gal	x 220	x 219.970
UK gal → cu m	÷220	x 0.005

1 : 30

US fluid ounces (fl oz) / Milliliters (ml)	Approx	Accurate
US fl oz → ml	x 30	x 29.572
ml → US fl oz	÷30	x 0.034

1 : 4

US fluid gallons (fl gal) / Liters (l)	Approx	Accurate
US fl gal → l	x 4	x 3.78
l → US fl gal	÷4	x 0.264

1 : 2

Liters (l) / UK pints (pt)	Approx	Accurate
l → UK pt	x 2	x 1.76
UK pt → l	÷2	x 0.568

1 : 35

Cubic meters (cu m) / Cubic feet (cu ft)	Approx	Accurate
cu m → cu ft	x 35	x 35.315
cu ft → cu m	÷35	x 0.028

1 : 1

Cubic meters (cu m) / Cubic yards (cu yd)	Approx	Accurate
cu m → cu yd	x 1	x 1.308
cu yd → cu m	÷1	x 0.765

1 : 1

Liters (l) / US fluid quarts (fl qt)	Approx	Accurate
l → US fl qt	x 1	x 1.056
US fl qt → l	÷1	x 0.947

1 : 264

Cubic meters (cu m) / US fluid gallons (fl gal)	Approx	Accurate
cu m → US fl gal	x 264	x 264.173
US fl gal → cu m	÷264	x 0.004

1 : 227

Cubic meters (cu m) / US dry gallons (dry gal)	Approx	Accurate
cu m → dry gal	x 227	x 227.02
dry gal → cu m	÷227	x 0.004

Weight

2454

Listed here are the multiplication/division factors for converting units of weight from imperial to metric, and vice versa, and from one unit to another in the same system. Note that two kinds of factors are given: approximate, for a quick conversion that can be made without a calculator; and accurate, for an exact conversion.

The term "weight" differs in everyday use than in scientific use. In everyday terms, we use weight to describe how much substance an object has. In science, the term "mass" is used to describe this quantity of matter. Weight in science is used to describe the gravitational force on an object and is equal to its mass multiplied by the gravitational field strength. In scientific terms, mass remains constant but weight varies according to the strength of gravity. All units that follow are strictly units of mass rather than weight, apart from the pressure units kg/cm² and PSI.

Grains (gr) Grams (g)		Approx	Accurate
g →	gr	x 15	x 15.432
gr →	g	÷ 15	x 0.065

Ounces (oz) Grams (g)			
oz →	g	x 28	x 28.349
g →	oz	÷ 28	x 0.035

Ounces troy (oz tr) Grams (g)			
oz tr →	g	x 31	x 31.103
g →	oz tr	÷ 31	x 0.032

Long tons (l t) Tonnes (t)			
l t →	t	x 1	x 1.016
t →	l t	÷ 1	x 0.984

Kilograms (kg) Pounds (lb)		Approx	Accurate
kg →	lb	x 2	x 2.205
lb →	kg	÷ 2	x 0.454

Kilograms per square centimetre (kg/cm²) Pounds per square inch (PSI)			
kg/cm² →	PSI	x 14	x 14.223
PSI →	kg/cm²	÷ 14	x 0.070

Tonnes (t) Short tons (sh t)			
t →	sh t	x 1	x 1.102
sh t →	t	÷ 1	x 0.907

Ounces troy (oz tr) Ounces (oz)			
oz tr →	oz	x 1	x 1.097
oz →	oz tr	÷ 1	x 0.911

Time

2455

Units of time

Listed here are some widely used names for periods of time.

Name	Period	Name	Period
millennium	1000 yrs	leap yr	366 days
half-millennium	500 yrs	yr	365 days
century	100 yrs	yr	12 months
half-century	50 yrs	yr	52 weeks
decade	10 yrs	month	28-31days
half-decade	5 yrs	week	7 days

Days, hours, minutes

Listed are the basic subdivisions of a day and their equivalents.

	Day	Hours	Minutes	Seconds
1 Day	1	24	1,440	86,400
1 Hour	1/24	1	60	3,600
1 Minute	1/1440	1/60	1	60
1 Second	1/86,400	1/3,600	1/60	1

Seconds

Greater precision in measuring time has required seconds (sec) to be broken down into smaller units, using standard metric prefixes.

1terasec (Ts)	10^{12}s	31 689 yrs
1gigasec (Gs)	10^{9}s	31.7 yrs
1megasec (Ms)	10^{6}s	11.6 days
1kilosec (ks)	10^{3}s	16.67 min
1millisec (ms)	10^{-3}s	0.001s
1microsec (µs)	10^{-6}s	0.000001s
1nanosec (ns)	10^{-9}s	0.000000001s
1picosec (ps)	10^{-12}s	0.000000000001s
1femtosec (fs)	10^{-15}s	0.000000000000001s
1attosec (as)	10^{-18}s	0.000000000000000001s

Astronomical time

In some fields, time is measured by motion; in fact, the motion of the Earth, Sun, Moon, and stars provided humans with the first means of measuring time.

Years, months, days

Sidereal times are calculated by the Earth's position according to fixed stars. The anomalistic year is measured according to the Earth's orbit in relation to the perihelion (Earth's minimum distance to the Sun). Tropical times refer to the apparent passage of the Sun and the actual passage of the Moon across the Earth's equatorial plane. The synodic month is based on the phases of the Moon. Solar time (as in a mean solar day) refers to periods of darkness and light averaged over a year.

Time	Days	Hours	Minutes	Seconds
sidereal year	365	6	9	10
anomalistic year	365	6	13	53
tropical year	365	5	48	45
sidereal month	27	7	43	11
tropical month	27	7	43	5
synodic month	29	12	44	3
mean solar day	0	24	0	0
sidereal day	0	23	56	4

Temperature

2456

Systems of measurement

Here, the different systems of temperature measurement are compared: Fahrenheit (° F), Celsius (° C), Réaumur (° r), Rankine (° R), and Kelvin (K).

1 boiling point of water
2 freezing point of water
3 absolute zero

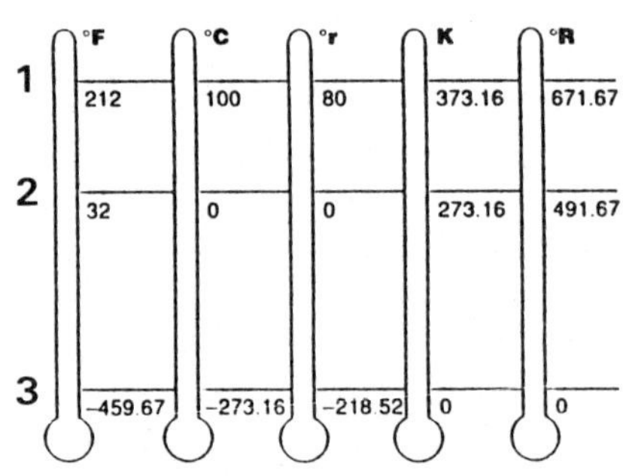

Formulas

°F → °C	(°F–32) ÷ 1.8
°C → °F	(°C x 1.8) + 32
°F → K	(°F–459.67) ÷ 1.8
°C → K	°C + 273.16
°r → K	(°r x 1.25) + 273.16
°R → K	°R ÷ 1.8
K → °F	(K x 1.8) – 459.67
K → °C	K – 273.16

Speed

2457 Listed here are the multiplication/division factors for converting units of speed from imperial to metric, and vice versa; and, also, for converting from one unit to another within the same system. Note that two kinds of factors are given: quick, for an approximate conversion that can be made without a calculator; and accurate, for an exact conversion.

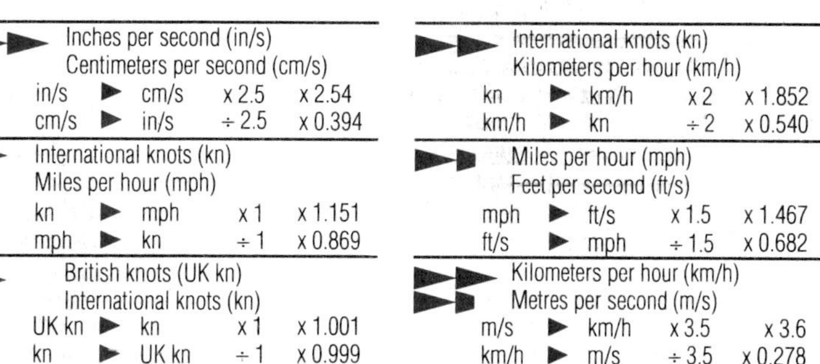

Miles per hour (mph) / Kilometers per hour (km/h)

	Approx	Accurate
mph ► km/h	x 1.5	x 1.609
km/h ► mph	÷ 1.5	x 0.621

Yards per minute (ypm) / Meters per minute (m/min)

	Approx	Accurate
m/min ► ypm	x 1	x 1.094
ypm ► m/min	÷ 1	x 0.914

Feet per minute (ft/min) / Metres per minute (m/min)

	Approx	Accurate
m/min ► ft/min	x 3	x 3.281
ft/min ► m/min	÷ 3	x 0.305

Inches per second (in/s) / Centimeters per second (cm/s)

	Approx	Accurate
in/s ► cm/s	x 2.5	x 2.54
cm/s ► in/s	÷ 2.5	x 0.394

International knots (kn) / Miles per hour (mph)

	Approx	Accurate
kn ► mph	x 1	x 1.151
mph ► kn	÷ 1	x 0.869

British knots (UK kn) / International knots (kn)

	Approx	Accurate
UK kn ► kn	x 1	x 1.001
kn ► UK kn	÷ 1	x 0.999

International knots (kn) / Kilometers per hour (km/h)

	Approx	Accurate
kn ► km/h	x 2	x 1.852
km/h ► kn	÷ 2	x 0.540

Miles per hour (mph) / Feet per second (ft/s)

	Approx	Accurate
mph ► ft/s	x 1.5	x 1.467
ft/s ► mph	÷ 1.5	x 0.682

Kilometers per hour (km/h) / Metres per second (m/s)

	Approx	Accurate
m/s ► km/h	x 3.5	x 3.6
km/h ► m/s	÷ 3.5	x 0.278

Energy

2458 Listed are the multiplication/division factors for converting units of energy from imperial to metric, and vice versa. Note that two kinds of factors are given: approximate, for a quick conversion that can be made without a calculator; and accurate, for an exact conversion.

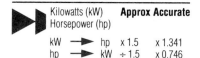

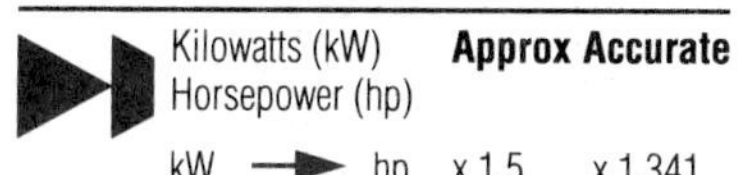

Kilowatts (kW) / Horsepower (hp)

	Approx	Accurate
kW → hp	x 1.5	x 1.341
hp → kW	÷ 1.5	x 0.746

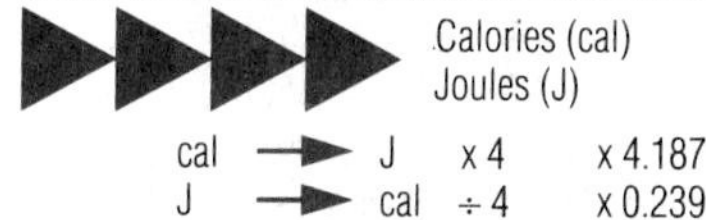

Calories (cal) / Joules (J)

	Approx	Accurate
cal → J	x 4	x 4.187
J → cal	÷ 4	x 0.239

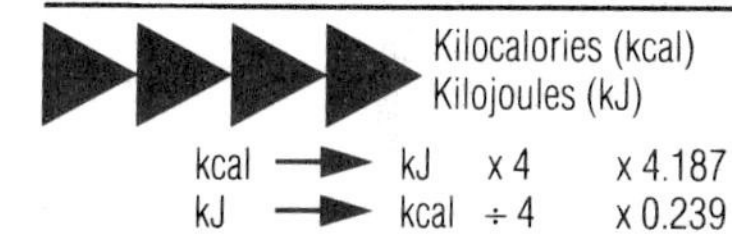

Kilocalories (kcal) / Kilojoules (kJ)

	Approx	Accurate
kcal → kJ	x 4	x 4.187
kJ → kcal	÷ 4	x 0.239

246 MEASUREMENTS GLOSSARY

acre A measure of land: originally the amount of land that a yoke of oxen could plough in a day. Equal to 4,840 yd².

amu *see* atomic mass unit

ampere (A) The unit for measuring electric current.

ångström (Å) A unit of length, used mainly to measure the wavelength of light. Named after the Swedish physicist A.J. Ångström (1814–74). Equal to 10^{-10} m (10^{-8} cm).

apothecaries' system A system of weights used especially by pharmacists.

are (a) A unit of measure equal to an area of 100 m² (1 are = 100 m²). *See also* hectare (ha): 100 are = 1 ha.

astronomical unit (au or AU) A unit of measure based on the distance between the Earth and the Sun. Approximately equal to 1.5 x 10^8 km.

atomic mass unit (amu)

chemical A unit of mass equal to $1/16$ of the weighted mass of the three naturally occurring neutral oxygen isotopes. 1 amu chemical = (1.660 ±0.000 05) x 10^{-27} kg. Formerly called the atomic weight unit.

international A unit of mass equal to half of the mass of a neutral carbon-12 atom. 1 amu international = (1.660 33 ±0.000 05) x 10^{-27} kg.

physical A unit of mass equal to $1/16$ of the mass of an oxygen atom. 1 amu physical = 1.660 x 10^{-27} kg.

atto- A prefix meaning a quintillionth (10^{-18}). For example, 1 attometer = 1 quintillionth of a meter.

avoirdupois system A system of weights based on the 16-ounce pound and the 16-dram ounce.

baker's dozen A counting unit equal to 13.

billion (bil) A number equal to 10^9.

bolt A measure of length, usually for fabric. A bolt of wallpaper equals 16 yd and a bolt of cloth equals 40 yd.

British thermal unit (Btu) Measure of heat needed to raise the temperature of one pound of water by 1° F. Equal to 252 calories.

bushel (bu) A measure of dry volume. In the ; US, 1 bu = 8 gal (64 US pt); in the UK, 1 bu = 8 gal (64 UK pt). The measures are not to be confused: 1.03 US bu = 1 UK bu.

caliber A unit of length used to measure the diameter of a tube or the bore of a firearm, in increments of $1/100$ in or $1/1000$.

calorie (cal) A measure of heat energy representing the amount of heat needed to raise the temperature 1 g of water by 1° C. Also called "small calorie": 1,000 cal = 1 kcal or Cal. *See also* joule, kilocalorie.

centi- Prefix meaning a 100th or $1/100$ in the metric system; e.g., a centiliter (cl) is a unit of volume equal to $1/100$ (0.01) liter.

centrad A measure of a plane angle, especially used to measure the angular deviation of light through a prism. 1 centrad = $1/100$ (0.01) radian.

century A measure of time equal to 100 years.

chain A measure of length equal to 22 yd. Also known as Gunter's chain.

engineer's chain A measure of length equal to 100 ft.

nautical chain A measure of length equal to 15 ft.

square chain A measure of area equal to 484 yd².

chaldron A measure of volume. 1 chaldron = 36 bu.

cord A unit of dry volume, especially used for timber. Equal to 128 ft³.

cubic units (cu or ³) These signify that three quantities measured in the same units have been multiplied together. For example, with a three-dimensional rectangular object, the height, breadth, and length may be multiplied togther to give its volume, which is then measured in cubic units.

cubit A unit of length approximately equal to 18 in. Originally based on the distance from the tip of the middle finger to the elbow.

cup A measure of volume (either liquid or solid) used especially in cooking. 1 cup = ½ pt (16 tbsp).

day

mean solar day A measure of time representing the interval between consecutive passages of the Sun across the meridian, averaged over one year. 1 day = 24 hr (86,400 sec).

sidereal day A measure of time approximately equal to 23 hr, 56 min, 4.09 sec. A sidereal day represents the time needed for one complete rotation of the Earth on its axis.

deca- Prefix meaning ten in the metric system; e.g., a decameter is a measure of length equal to 10 m.

decade A measure of time equal to 10 years.

deci- Prefix meaning $1/10$ in the metric system;

continued

Measurements glossary continued

246

e.g., a deciliter (dl) is a measure of liquid volume equal to 1/10 (0.01) litre.
decibel (dB) A measure of relative sound intensity.
degree (°)
  geometrical A unit of measure of plane angle equal to 1/360 of the circumference of a circle (1 circle = 360°).
  temperature A measure of temperature difference representing a single division on a temperature scale.
digit One of ten Arabic symbols representing the numbers 0 to 9. Also used in astronomy as a unit of measure equal to half the diameter of the Sun or Moon. Used in ancient Egypt as a measure of length: 1 digit = 1 finger width.
dozen A counting unit equal to 12.
drachm A unit of weight in the apothecaries' system. 1 drachm = 1/8 apothecaries' ounce (60 grains).
dram (dr) A unit of mass equal to 1/16 oz.
  fluid dram A unit of liquid volume. 1 dr = 1/8 fl oz.
dry Used to distinguish measures of dry (solid) volume as opposed to liquid (fluid) volume.
dyne A unit of force equal to that needed to produce an acceleration of 1 centimeter per second in a mass of one gram. Replaced in the international system by the newton (N): 1 dyne = 10^{-5} N.
electronvolt (eV) A unit of energy representing the energy acquired by an electron in passing through a potential difference of 1 volt. 1 eV = $(1.6 \pm 0.000\,07) \times 10^{-19}$ J.
erg A unit of energy equal to the energy produced by a force of 1 dyne acting through a distance of 1 cm. Replaced in the inernational system by the joule (J): 1 erg = 10^{-7} J.
fathom (fm) Unit of length, especially used to measure marine depth. 1 fm = 6 ft. Originally based on the span of two outstretched arms.
feet per minute A unit of speed representing the number of feet traveled in 1 min.
femto- A prefix meaning 1 quadrillionth (10^{-15}).
firkin A unit of volume, used especially to measure beer or ale. 1 firkin = 9.8 US gal.
fluid Used to distinguish units of liquid (fluid) volume as opposed to dry (solid) volume.
fluid dram see dram
fluid ounce see ounce
foot (ft) A unit of length equal to 12 inches.
furlong (fur) A unit of length equal to 1/8 mile (660 ft).
gallon (gal) A unit of liquid volume equal to eight pints. The US and UK gallons should not be confused: 1UK gal = 1.2 US gal.
gauge A unit of length used to measure the diameter of a shotgun bore; e.g., six-gauge equals 23.34 mm. Originally based on the number of balls, of certain size, contained in one pound of shot.
giga- A prefix meaning one billion (10^9). For example, 1 gigameter = 1 billion meters.
gill A unit of liquid volume. In the UK, 1 gill = 1/4 UK pt; in US (gi), 1 gi = 1/4 US fl pt. The two should not be confused: 1 UK gill = 1/2 US gi.
grade (^{g}) A measure of plane angle in geometry. 1^g = 0.9°.
grain (gr) A unit of mass measurement, used especially in the apothecaries' system. 1 grain = 1/7000 lb (avoirdupois); 480 grains = 1 ounce troy;
24 grains = 1 pennyweight.
gram (g) A unit of mass or volume measurement. 1 g = 0.001 kg.
gross A counting measure equal to 144 (or 12 dozen).
hand A unit of length, used especially to measure horses' height. 1 hand = 4 in.
hectare (ha) A measure of area, usually of land, equal to 10,000 m².
hecto- Prefix meaning 100; e.g., a hectometer (hm) is a unit of length equal to 100 m.
hertz (Hz) A unit of frequency measurement equal to one cycle per second.
horsepower (hp) A unit of work representing the power needed to raise 550 lb by 1 ft in 1 s.
  metric horsepower A unit of power representing that needed to raise a 75-kg mass 1 meter in one second.
hour (hr) A unit of time measurement equal to 60 min (3,600 s).
hundredweight (cwt) A unit of mass equal to 112 lb; 1 hundredweight troy = 100 pounds troy; 1 hundredweight = 4 quarters.
  short hundredweight (sh cwt) Equal to 100 pounds.
inch (in) A unit of length equal to 1/12 ft.
inches per second A unit of speed representing the number of inches traveled in one second.
joule (J) A unit of energy equal to the work done when a force of one newton is applied through a distance of one meter. Used instead of calorie: 1 J = 0.239 cal. Named after J.P. Joule (1818–89).
karat A unit of weight equal to 200 mg (3.1 grains). Also used as a measure of gold purity (per 24 parts gold alloy).
keg A unit of volume, used especially for beer, equal to approximately 30 gal. Also used as a measure of weight for nails, equal to 100 lb.
kelvin (K) A scale of temperature measurement in which each degree is equal to 1/273.16 of the interval between 0 K (absolute zero) and the triple point of water. K = °C + 273.16. Named after William Thomson, Lord Kelvin (1824–1907).
kilo- A prefix meaning 1,000; e.g., a kilogram (kg) is a unit of mass equal to 1,000 grams.
kilocalorie (kcal or Cal) A unit of energy measurement representing the amount of heat required to raise the temperature of one kilogram of water by 1 °C. Also called the 'international calorie'. 1 kcal = 1000 cal. *See also* calorie.
kilometer (km) A unit of length equal to 1,000 m.
kiloparsec A unit of distance used to measure the distance between galactic bodies. 1 kiloparsec = 3,260 light years.
kilowatt (kW) A unit of power equal to 1,000 watts (W).
kilowatt-hour (kWh) A unit of energy equal to the energy expended when a power of 1 kW is used for one hour.
knot (kn) A nautical unit of speed equal to the velocity at which one nautical mile is traveled in one hour. 1 kn = 6,076 ft per hour.
lakh An Indian counting unit equal to 100,000.
lambda (λ) A unit of volume measurement. 1 λ = 1 microliter (10^{-6} litre).
league A unit of length equal to 3 miles.
light year A unit of length (distance) representing the distance traveled by electromagnetic waves (light) through space in one year. 1 light year = 9 trillion miles.
liter (l) A unit of volume measurement equal to the volume of one kilogram of water at its maximum density. 1 litre = 1,000 cm³.
magnum A measure of volume, used especially for wine or champagne.1 magnum = 2/5 US gal.
mega- A prefix meaning one million; e.g., a megaton is a unit of weight equal to one million tons.
megahertz (MHz) A unit of frequency equal to one million cycles per second.
meter (m) A unit of length equal to 100 cm.
meters per minute (m/min) A unit of speed measurement representing the number of meters traveled in one minute.
metric system A system of measurement based on the meter.
metric ton *see* tonne
micro- A prefix meaning one millionth; e.g., a microliter is a unit of volume equal to one millionth of a liter.
micron (μm) A unit of length equal to 1/1000 (0.001) mm. Also called the micrometer.
mile (mi) A unit of length equal to 1,760 yd.
  nautical mile (n mi) A unit of length used in navigation. In the metric system, one nautical mile (international) = 1,852 m.
  sea mile A unit of length distinguished from the nautical mile. 1 sea mile = 1,000 fathoms (6,000 ft).
miles per hour (mph) A unit of speed representing the number of miles traveled in one hour.
millennium A period of time equal to 1,000 years.
milli- Prefix meaning one thousandth or 1/1000; e.g., one millimeter (mm) is a unit of length equal to 1/1000 (0.001) of a meter.
minim A unit of volume, applied to liquids. 1 minim = 1/480 fl oz.
minute
  geometric (') A unit of measure for plane angles. 1' = 1/60°.
  time (min) A unit of time measurement equal to 60.seconds. 60 min = 1 hr
month
  lunar A unit of time equal to four weeks (2,419,200 sec).
  sidereal *see* year, sidereal
  tropical *see* year, tropical
nano- A prefix meaning one thousand millionth (10^{-9}). 1 nanometer = 1 billionth of a meter.
nautical mile *see* mile
newton (N) A unit of force which, when applied, accelerates a mass of one kilogram by one meter per second per second. This unit has replaced the dyne: 1 N = 10^5 dynes. Named after Isaac Newton (1642–1727).
ohm (Ω) A unit of electrical resistance. One ohm equals the resistance across which a

continued

Measurements glossary continued

potential difference of one volt produces a current flow of one ampere. Named after G.S. Ohm (1787–1854).
ounce (oz) A unit of mass equal to 1/16 lb.
fluid ounce A unit of liquid volume measurement. In the US, 1 fl oz = 1/16 US pt; in the UK, 1 fl oz = 1/20 UK pt;
metric ounce A unit of mass equal to 25 grams. Also called a Mounce.
ounce troy A unit of mass in the troy system. Equal to 1/12 pound troy.
pace A unit of length/distance equal to about three feet, used in ancient Rome.
palm A unit of length used in ancient Egypt, equal to the width of an average palm of the hand (4 digits).
parsec (pc) A unit of length used for measuring astronomical distances. 1 parsec = 3.26 light years.
pascal (Pa) A unit of pressure equal to the force of one newton acting over an area of one square meter.
peck (pk) A unit of dry volume. 1 peck = 2 gal.
pennyweight (dwt) A unit of weight in the troy system equal to 1/20 ounce troy (24 grains).
perch A unit of length equal to 5½ yd. Also called a pole or a rod.
pi (π) Symbol and name representing the ratio of a circle's circumference to its diameter. Its value is approximately 3.14.
pica A unit of length, used by printers, approximately equal to 1/6 in.
pico- A prefix meaning one trillionth (10^{-12}). For example, 1 picometer = 1 trillionth of a meter.
pint (pt) A unit of volume. Two kinds of pint are used: 1 fl pt = 1/8 gal; 1 dry pt = 1/64 gal.
point A unit of length, used especially by printers, approximately equal to 1/72 in.
pole Unit of length equal to 5½ yd. Also called a perch or a rod.
pound (lb) A unit of mass equal to 453.59 g.
pound force A unit of force equal to 32.174 poundals.
pound troy (lb tr) A unit of mass in the troy system. 1 pound troy = 12 ounces troy.
poundal A unit of force equal to that needed to give an acceleration of one foot per second to a mass of one pound.
PSI Pounds per square inch: a unit for measuring pressure. One PSI equals the pressure resulting from a force of one pound force acting over an area of one square inch. *See also* pound.
quart (qt) A unit of volume, usually for liquids. 1 qt = 2 fl pt.
dry quart (dry qt) A unit of measure for dry (solid) volume .
quarter (qr)
mass quarter A unit of mass. 1 quarter = ¼ US ton (500 lb).
quarter troy (qr tr) A unit of weight equal to 25 troy pounds.
rad A short form of radian, a unit of measure for plane angles. *See also* centrad.
ream A unit of volume, used to measure paper in bulk. One ream equals about 500 sheets.
rod
area rod A unit of area equal to 30¼ yd². Also called a square perch or a square pole.
length rod A unit of length equal to 5½ yd. Also called a perch or a pole.
rood A unit of area equal to ¼ acre (1210 yd²).
score A counting unit equal to 20.
scruple A unit of mass in apothecaries' system equal to 20 grains.
second A unit of time equal to 1/60 minute.
geometric (") A measure of plane angle equal to 1/360°.
sidereal A unit of time equal to 1/86 400 of the interval needed for one complete rotation of the Earth on its axis.
square units (sq or ²) These signify that two quantities measured in the same units have been multiplied together. For example, to find the area of a square or rectangle, length and breadth are multiplied together to give the area, which is measured in square units.
stere A unit of volume, especially used for measuring timber. 1 stere = 1 m³.
tablespoon (tbsp) A unit of volume used in cooking and equal to 1.5 centiliters (3 tsp). 16 tbsp = 1 cup.
teaspoon (tsp) A unit of volume used in cooking and equal to 0.5 centiliter. 3 tsp = 1 tbsp.
tera- A prefix meaning one trillion (10^{12}). For example, 1 terameter = 1 trillion meters.
ton A unit of mass. In the US, 1 ton = 2,000 lb. In the UK, 1 ton = 2,240 lb. Called a long ton in the US.
ton troy (ton tr) A unit of mass equal to 2,000 pounds troy.
tonne (t) A unit of mass equal to 1,000 kg. Also called a metric ton.
tonne of coal equivalent A measure of energy production/consumption based on the premise that one tonne of coal provides 8,000 kilowatt-hours (kWh) of energy.
trillion A number equal to 10^{12}.
troy system A system of mass measurement based on the 20-ounce pound and the 20-pennyweight ounce.
volt (V) A unit of electromotive force and potential difference. Equal to the difference in potential between two points of a conducting wire carrying a constant current of one ampere (A), when the power released between the points is one watt (W). Named after Alessandro Volta (1745–1827).
watt (W) A unit of power equal to that available when one joule of energy is expended in one second. 1 W = 1 volt-ampere; 746 W = 1 horsepower (hp). Named after James Watt (1736–1819).
X-unit (x or XU) A unit of length used especially for measuring wavelength. 1 x-unit ≈ 10^{-3} ångström (10^{-13} m).
yard (yd) A unit of length equal to three feet. 1 yard = 3 ft (36 in).
yards per minute (ypm) A unit of speed representing the number of yards traveled in one minute.
year A unit of time measurement determined by the revolution of the Earth around the Sun.
anomalistic year Equals the time interval between two consecutive passages of the Earth through its perihelion (365 days, 6 hr, 13 min, 53 s).
sidereal year Equals the time that it takes the Earth to revolve around the Sun from one fixed point (usually a star) back to the same point (365 days, 6 hr, 9 min, 9 sec).
tropical year Equals the time interval between two consecutive passages of the Sun, in one direction, through the Earth's equatorial plane (or from vernal equinox to vernal equinox; 365 days, 5 hr, 48 min, 46 sec).

247 MATHEMATICIANS

Archimedes c. 287–212 BC, Greek, most celebrated ancient mathematician. Discovered formulas for areas and volumes of spheres, cylinders, parabolas, and other plane and solid figures.

Babbage, Charles 1791–1871, English pioneer of modern computers, dedicated to building calculating machines. His "difference engine," designed to calculate logarithm tables etc. by repeated addition performed by trains of gear wheels, failed because at the time the parts could not be machined precisely enough.

Bernoulli, Daniel 1700–82, Swiss professor of mathematics at St Petersburg from 1725, then of anatomy, botany, and physics at Basel from 1732. Solved differential equations, now known as "Bernoulli's equations." Worked on trigonometric series.

Boole, George 1815–64, English mathematician and logician. Outstanding pioneer of modern symbolic logic who greatly influenced Frege and Russell. In his *Mathematical Analysis of Logic* (1847) and *Laws of Thought* (1854), he used mathematical symbols to express logical relations.

Cantor, Georg 1845–1918, German mathematician whose ideas on theory of sets helped lay foundation for topology and modern analysis. Worked out highly original arithmetic of the infinite, extending concept of cardinal and ordinal numbers to finite sets.

Cardano, Girolamo 1501–76, Italian scientific thinker. He wrote over 200 treatises on such areas as physics, mathematics, astronomy, astrology, philosophy, music, and medicine. In his famous treatise on algebra, *Ars Magna*, the formulas for solving cubic and quartic equations were published for the first time.

Euclid fl. 300 BC, Greek geometer. His *Elements of Geometry* is probably the most famous mathematical book of all time, and is a model of rigorous mathematical exposition. Its 13 books describe a good part of all we know, even today, about lines, points, circles, and elementary solid shapes.

Euler, Leonhard 1707–83, Swiss mathematician and pioneer of topology. Published over 800 different books and papers on pure and applied mathematics, physics, and astronomy. He had amazing technical skill with complicated formulas and created the calculus of variations. His notation is still used today.

Fermat, Pierre de 1601–65, French mathematician. With Descartes, one of the two leading mathematicians of the early 17th century. His correspondence with Pascal marks the foundation of probability theory. Best known for work in number theory. His "last theorem" is the most famous unsolved problem in mathematics.

Fibonacci, Leonardo c.1170–c.1250, Italian mathematician. First outstanding mathematician of Middle Ages, who popularized modern (originally Indian) decimal numerical system. Discoverer of the "Fibonacci sequence" in which each number is equal to the sum of preceding two.

Galois, Carl Friedrich 1777–1855, German mathematician, astronomer, and physicist. One of the greatest mathematicians of all time. His *Disquisitiones Arithmeticae* (1801) heralded new advances in number theory. Worked on celestial mechanics as well as many areas of pure mathematics.

Gödel, Kurt 1906–78, Austrian logician and mathematician. Responsible for wealth of significant research in mathematical logic. In one of the most important theorems in modern mathematics (1931), he proved existence of formally undecidable elements in any formal system of arithmetic.

Hamilton, William Rowan 1805–65, Irish mathematician. His quaternions, invented as a new algebraic approach to three-dimensional geometry, have influenced much of modern algebra; his novel approach to dynamics became of importance in the growth of quantum mechanics in the 20th century.

Hilbert, David 1862–1943, German mathematician. In 1890, he produced definitive work on invariant theory which paved the way for modern algebraic geometry. His 1897 report on algebraic number theory helped form the basis of later research. He presented a famous list of 23 unsolved problems to the International Congress in 1900.

Klein, Christian Felix 1849–1925, German mathematician. Inventor of imaginary "Klein bottle" with an outside but no inside. His Erlangen Program showed how different geometries could be classified in terms of group theory. Also worked on function theory and elliptic and modular functions.

Kolmogorov, Andrei Nikolaevich 1903–87, Russian mathematician. He worked on the theory of functions of a real variable, functional analysis, mathematical logic, and topology, but is best known for the creation of axiomatic theory of probability and his work on Mavlov processes with Khinchin.

Lagrange, Joseph Louis de 1736–1813, French scientist. His work on the theory of algebraic equations is of importance in the early development of group theory. Also wrote on celestial mechanics, calculus, and number theory. His *Traité de mécanique analytique* was published 1788.

Laplace, Pierre Simon, Marquis de 1749–1827, French mathematician and astronomer. In his study of gravitational attraction of spheroids, he formulated the fundamental differential equation in physics that bears his name. *Système du monde* (1796) details all his astronomical theories.

Leibnitz, Gottfried Wilhelm 1646–1716, German mathematician and philosopher. "Universal" genius, remarkable for his encyclopedic knowledge and breadth of accomplishment. Developed, with Newton, early differential calculus. Also helped develop statistics, logic, and probability theory.

Möbius, August Ferdinand 1790–1868, German mathematician. Discovered Möbius strip (one-sided surface formed by giving rectangular strip a half-twist and then joining ends together) and Möbius net of projective geometry, as well as barycentric coordinates.

Napier, John 1550–1617, Scottish inventor of logarithms, which he describes in *Mirifici Logarithmorum Canonis Descriptio* (1614). He invented a calculating apparatus called "Napier's bones" which appears in *Rabdologia* (1617). Strict Presbyterian who also believed in astrology and divination.

Neumann, John (Johann) von 1903–57, Hungarian-born American, best known for mathematical work on theory of linear operators. Chief architect of the programmable computer. Also contributed to game and set theory and to description of quantum theory.

Newton, Sir Isaac 1642–1727, English scientist and mathematician. Was supposedly led to law of gravitation by fall of an apple in his garden in 1665/6. Also studied nature of light (*Opticks*, published 1703) and developed, in parallel with Leibnitz, differential calculus.

Pascal, Blaise 1623–62, French mathematician, physicist, theologian, and literary figure. At 16, he published his celebrated essay on conics. His correspondence with Fermat in 1654 laid the foundation of probability theory, while his papers on area of cycloid (1669) heralded the invention of integral calculus.

Poincaré, Jules Henri 1854–1912, French mathematician. Created theory of automorphic functions as well as many of basic ideas of topology, such as triangulation, homology, Euler-Poincaré's formula, and the fundamental group. Also founded study of modern dynamical systems.

Pythagoras 6th century BC, Greek mathematician and philosopher who had a profound influence on Plato. Associated with mathematical discoveries involving chief musical intervals, relations of numbers, and theorem bearing his name. Pythagoras had a mystical belief in the power of whole numbers.

Riemann, Georg Friedrich Bernhard 1826–66, German mathematician. Introduced concept of "Riemann surface" for "multi-valued" functions, as well as non-Euclidean concept of *n*-dimensional curved space. His "zeta function" is central to study of prime-number distribution.

Venn, John 1834–1923, English logician. Developed Boole's symbolic logic and, in his *Logic of Chance* (1866), the frequency theory of probability. Best known for his "Venn diagrams," giving pictorial representations of relations between sets.

Vieta, Franciscus (François Viète) 1540–1603, French mathematician. Found method for solving algebraic equations up to fourth degree and obtained value of *pi* as an infinite product. His *In Artem Analyticam Isagogue* (1591) is probably the earliest work on symbolic algebra.

311 WHAT IS COMMUNICATION?

We probably take communication for granted but it is vital for all of us. The survival of social groups depends on good communications. It is a means by which animals or humans form relationships and share their experience and knowledge. Furthermore, it is a way of sharing information and providing entertainment. There is a common structure to all acts of communication whether through language, gesture, code, or electrical impulse. In simple terms it involves the transfer of information from a source to a receiver, which is usually referred to as being part of a "communication chain." It can be direct, as in face-to-face conversation, or indirect, through the medium of the telephone or a computer.

There are many things that can prevent good communication, distort the original message, or cause a breakdown of communication. Theorists use the term "noise" to refer to any interference or impediment to the accurate transmission of information, and "high fidelity" or "faithful reproduction" if the message gets through successfully. Communication begins and ends with animate beings.

There are many different types of communication, and all of the senses can be used to make it effective. The most commonly used are sight and sound, which provide the most advanced systems of communication, such as speech and writing. Touch is also common to humans, ranging from handshakes, hugs, and cuddles to fistfights. Animals use smell and taste much more than do humans to communicate. These senses, however, are important to chemists and doctors for identification and diagnosis. Signs and gestures play a significant part in human communication, and even though we have developed language to an advanced state, much of our communication is face to face and without words.

Some signs and gestures have the same understanding worldwide, like pointing a finger to signal direction or shaking a fist to indicate anger, while others may have different meanings in different countries. Gestures can be used to express emotions both consciously and unconsciously and "body language", as it is called, is studied by psychologists.

Studies of the modes of communication used by animals have revealed that although animals do not have the power of speech they utilize every other method of communication, such as visual display (facial expressions, gesture, and posturing), taste, smell, touch, and sound. An animal's mode of communication always relates to its biological needs, from survival to the attraction of a mate. There is extraordinary diversity of animal signals, but an individual species uses only a small number of signals. The monkey, for example, has fewer than 40 signals and certain types of fish have only ten.

Linguistics is the scientific study of language. It aims to establish the facts, nature, and use of the world's languages and to propose principles that explain unity and diversity. It has different branches, such as semantics, which focuses on meaning in language and the changes in meaning. Semiotics is the study of signs, symbols, and patterns in human communication. It is concerned especially with nonverbal communication. Kinesics, a branch of semiotics is concerned with body language, meanings conveyed by physical gestures, and facial expressions.

312 LANGUAGES – SPOKEN

Origins of language

3121 Speaking begins with breathing, and air released from the lungs through the windpipe provides the source of energy for speech. People learned to speak thousands of years before they could write. In some cultures, particularly in South America and Africa, language has never been written down.

We do not know just when humans first learned to talk, or who the first person was to use a sound to describe an object or an event and then make someone else realize that the sound was its name. Some scholars believe that language began as an imitation of sounds in nature, such as the barking of certain animals and the noise of the wind.

The origins of language are unknown, but it is believed to be of quite recent origin in evolutionary terms. Archeologists have discovered that people similar to ourselves turned up around 25,000 years ago. They were better craftsmen than their predecessors, they walked more upright, and were perhaps more talkative and better able to teach their young how to handle tools. We have more idea of these people because they created pictures on the walls of the caves they lived in. They had begun to communicate beyond the human voice.

Classification of languages

3122 There are three methods of classifying languages. The first is by continent or country, but this geographical grouping ignores differences between languages that evolved separately from each other. The second, by historical development, stresses common evolutionary origins – for example, it maps the relation between old English and modern English. The third method is by grammatical structure. This can be analytic, stressing word order; agglutinative, which is splitting words into components with different grammatical roles; or inflective, with words based on a root plus a variable component.

The Proto-Indo-European family of languages, the largest, is shown below.

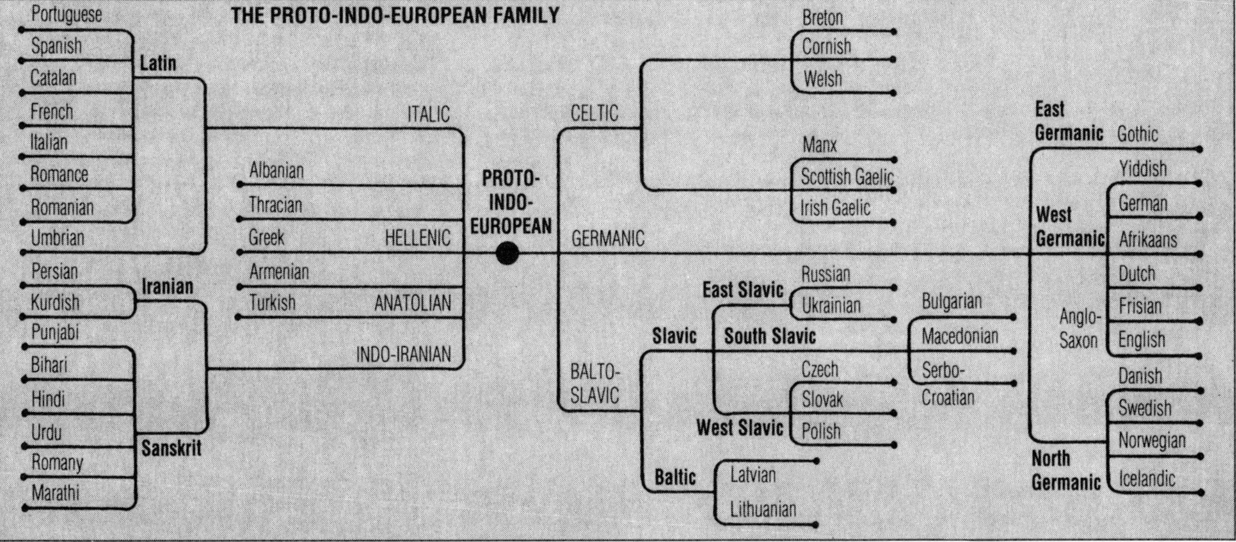

Language families

3123

Language families are groups of languages considered to be related because they all developed slowly from a single parent language. The majority of the world's population speaks one of the nine major languages, although there are other unclassified families spoken by small numbers of people.

The families

1 Indo-European The most important language family. It is represented worldwide and includes English, French, German, Hindi, Italian, Russian, Spanish, Swedish, and others. Some 2.24 billion persons speak languages in this family – about half the world's population.

2 Sino-Tibetan Second in numerical importance. It includes Chinese with its many dialects, Thai, Burmese, and Tibetan. Over 1 billion speakers.

3 Black African Three main families are Nilo-Saharan, Niger-Kordofanian, and Khoisan. About 330 million speakers.

4 Malayo-Polynesian This includes languages of Indonesia, the Philippines, Hawaii, New Zealand, Madagascar and most other islands of the Pacific and Indian oceans. About 233 million speakers.

5 Dravidian This family is spoken in southern India and parts of Sri Lanka. About 192 million people speak the languages in this family.

6 Afro-Asian This includes Arabic and Hebrew. Over 187 million persons speak languages in this family.

7 Japanese and Korean These form a family with over 181 million speakers.

8 Ural-Altaic This includes Finnish, Hungarian, Mongol, Manchu, and Turkish. More than 110 million persons speak the languages in this family.

9 Mon-Khmer Sometimes called Austro-Asiatic and found mostly in southeast Asia and parts of India. Over 70 million speakers.

10 All others There are well over 1,000 languages, many not classified, spoken by Amerindian peoples (north and south), Inuit people, Siberian tribes, Indo-Pacific islanders, and Australian aboriginals.

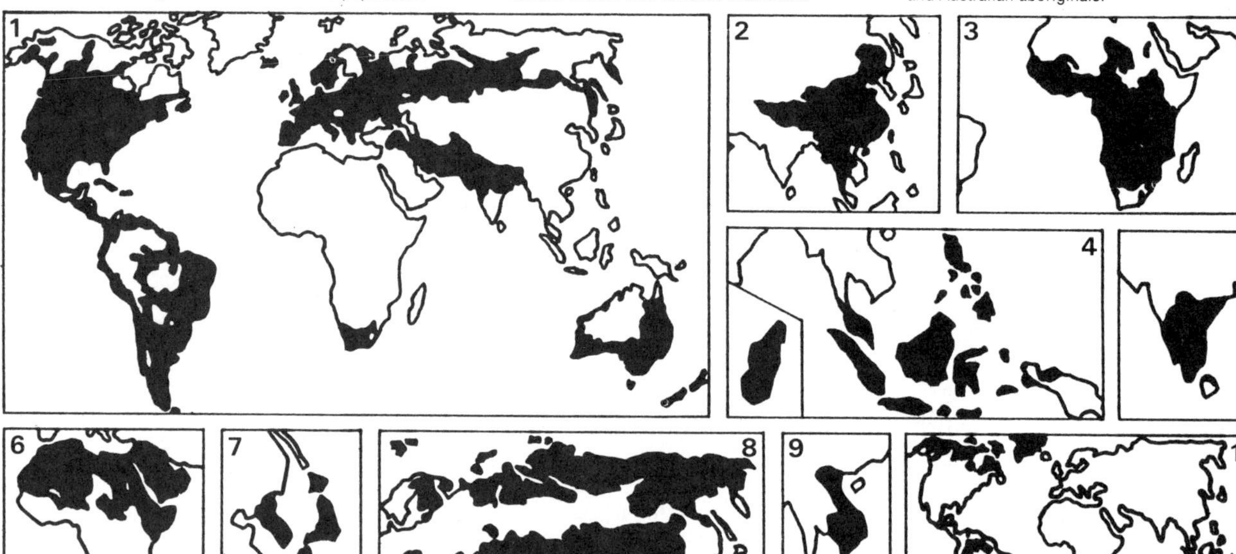

How languages evolve

3124

In order to understand the history of words etymologists study their origin, development, and the various changes in sound and meaning that have affected words since their first known appearance. For example, etymology shows that most English words are derived either from Proto-Germanic or from Latin and French languages, and that many learned English words were taken from Greek or made up of Greek elements. In the past 200 years English has borrowed words from languages in every part of the world, and it continues to do so.

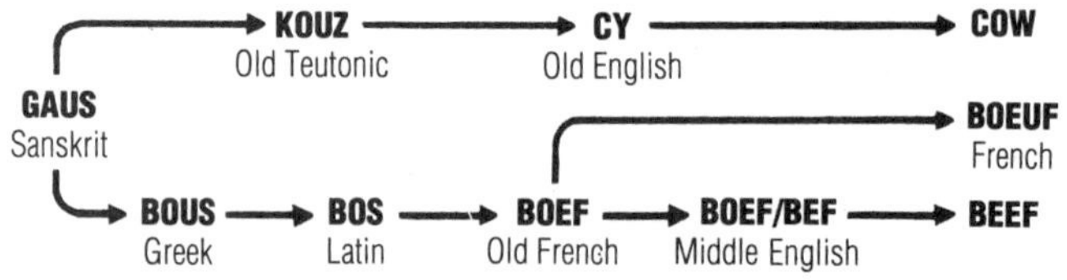

The world's major languages

3125

The total number of languages throughout the world is thought to be around 5,000. Chinese is spoken by the largest number of people but it has many dialects, such as Mandarin and Cantonese, that can be regarded almost as separate languages.

English is considered to be the most widely spoken language. Like French, Spanish, and Portuguese it has spread far beyond the land of its origin because of expansion, past colonization, and trade.

This list shows the top 20 most widely spoken languages (estimates of native-tongue speakers, in millions; percentage of world population in brackets). The bar chart below shows the relative proportions of the world's top ten languages.

1 Chinese 1,050 (21)
2 English 350 (7)
3 Spanish 250 (5)
4 Hindi 200 (4)
5 Arabic 150 (3)
6 Bengali 150 (3)
7 Russian 150 (3)
8 Portuguese 135 (2.7)
9 Japanese 120 (2.4)
10 German 100 (2)
11 French 70 (1.4)
12 Punjabi 70 (1.4)
13 Javanese 65 (1.3)
14 Bihari 65 (1.3)
15 Italian 60 (1.2)
16 Korean 60 (1.2)
17 Telugu 55 (1.1)
18 Tamil 55 (1.1)
19 Marathi 50 (1)
20 Vietnamese 50 (1)

Proportion of world population – top ten languages

1 2 3 4 5 6 7 8 9 10 All others

Where the major languages are spoken today

3126 These maps show where each of the languages listed below is spoken as a first (official) *and* a second or semi-official language, even though only a minority of people in those countries speak the second language fluently.

1 English
2 Italian
3 Portuguese
4 Spanish
5 French
6 German
7 Chinese
8 Russian
9 Arabic
10 Malay-Indonesian
11 Hindi
12 Bihari
13 Telugu
14 Punjabi
15 Bengali
16 Tamil
17 Urdu
18 Marathi

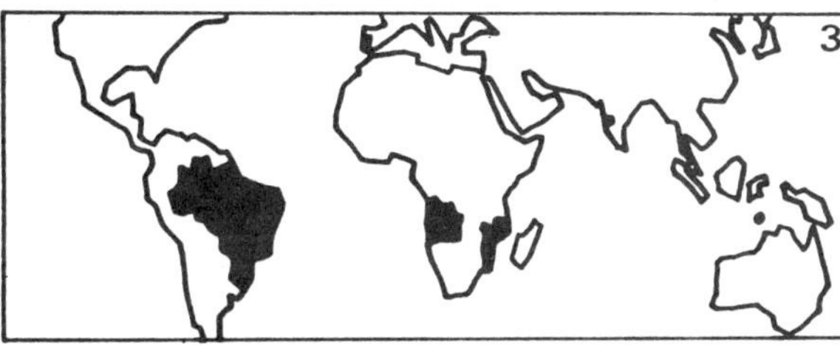

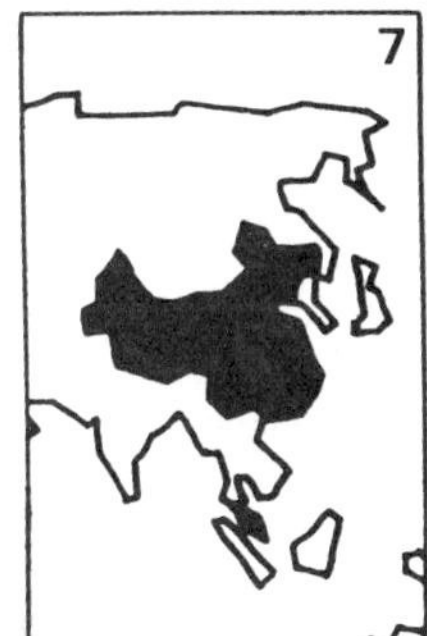

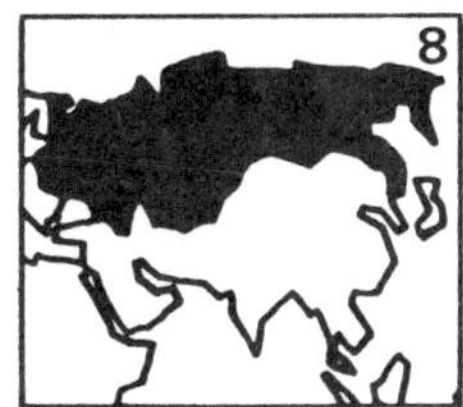

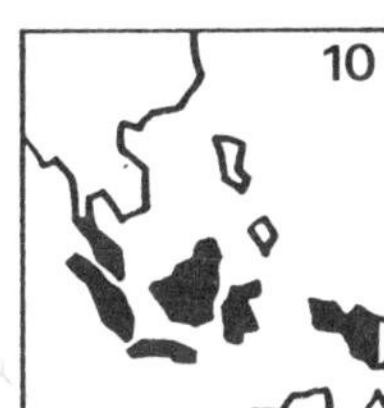

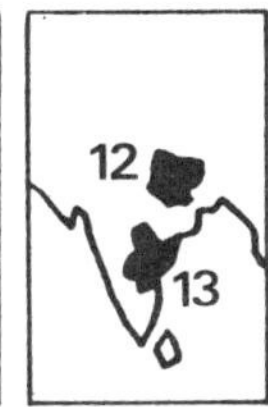

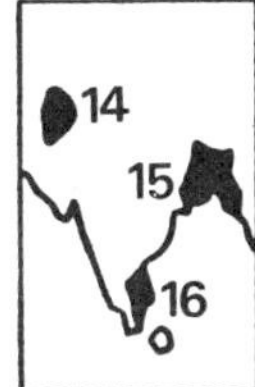

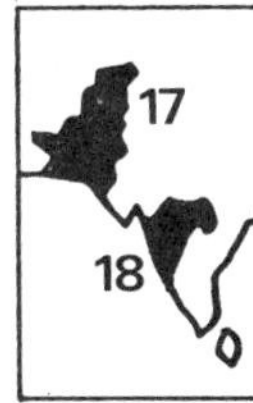

313 WRITING

Origins of writing

3131 Writing is a human invention. Its origins lie in the Middle East in the picture writing (pictograms) developed by the Sumerians about 3000 BC. It consisted of simplified pictures of objects or people. These were limited in what they could communicate so pictorial symbols were developed to represent more abstract meanings. These symbols, which stand for concepts, are known as ideograms. Eventually these symbols came to stand for a word in the language as opposed to an idea. They are called logograms. For example, instead of drawing pictures of five sheep to show a herd of five animals a person could draw one sign for the numeral "five" and one for "sheep." This system could require learning hundreds of symbols.

The writing system of the Chinese is based on the logogram and consists of more than 3,000 characters.

Gradually people learned to use a syllabic system (as in rebus writing) where a sign standing for one word also stands for any phonetic combination sounding like it. In English this rebus writing would express "belief" by a picture of a bee followed by a picture of a leaf. Finally, people developed alphabets in which individual signs stand for particular sounds.

1 Ancient Egyptian symbol for an ox's head
2 *Aleph:* the Phoenician letter meaning "ox"
3 *Alpha:* the first letter of the Greek alphabet
4 *A*: the first letter of the early Latin alphabet
5 *A*: the first letter of the Roman alphabet AD 114

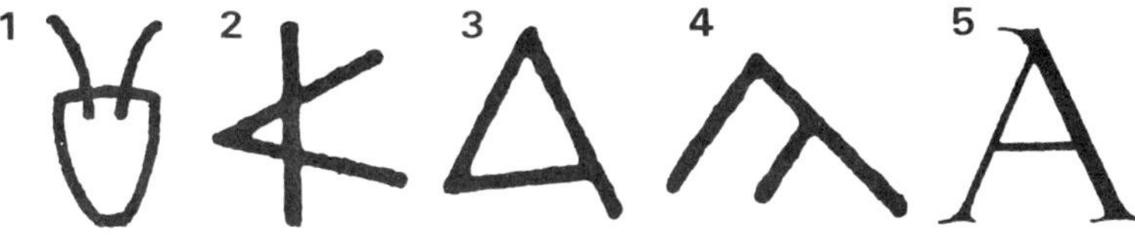

Landmarks in writing

3132 Early peoples used a variety of materials to write on, such as papyrus (used by the Egyptians to make paper), wax, stone, and wood. Various writing tools such as a quill, stylus, or chisel, were used.

A good example of the methods involved is evident in cuneiform – where wedge-shaped marks were made by the imprint of a stylus in soft clay, which was then hardened to preserve the tablet. In different regions, letters took on different shapes depending on what people used to write on or with.

The Chinese invented paper, and the Arabs learned the secret in AD 768 . From Arab manufacturing in the Middle East and Spain, paper spread to Byzantium in the 11th century and from there all over Europe.

The most important landmark in writing is the development of the alphabet. In early Syria and Palestine the Semites worked out an alphabet using signs to show the consonants of syllables, using their own set of characters. Around 1000 BC the Phoenicians developed an alphabet which the Greeks learned and modified. The Greeks standardized the direction of the written lines from left to right and they added symbols for vowels. All Western alphabets are derived from the Greek alphabet.

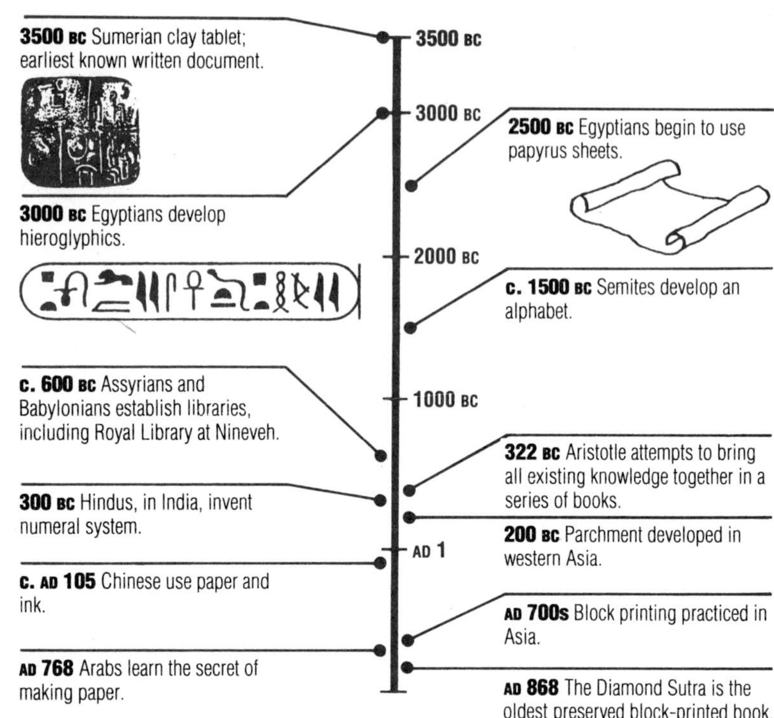
3500 BC Sumerian clay tablet; earliest known written document.
3000 BC Egyptians develop hieroglyphics.
c. 600 BC Assyrians and Babylonians establish libraries, including Royal Library at Nineveh.
300 BC Hindus, in India, invent numeral system.
c. AD 105 Chinese use paper and ink.
AD 768 Arabs learn the secret of making paper.
3500 BC
3000 BC
2000 BC
1000 BC
AD 1
2500 BC Egyptians begin to use papyrus sheets.
c. 1500 BC Semites develop an alphabet.
322 BC Aristotle attempts to bring all existing knowledge together in a series of books.
200 BC Parchment developed in western Asia.
AD 700s Block printing practiced in Asia.
AD 868 The Diamond Sutra is the oldest preserved block-printed book.

Early writing systems

3133 Throughout the ancient civilizations of the world writing systems of varying complexity arose as it became necessary to keep records and report significant events. The examples shown here give an idea of the variety and sophistication (or simplicity) of the systems and of their incredible diversity. Meanings or sound equivalents are given when known.

Hittite hieroglyphic pictograms

Assyrian cuneiform characters
1 Grain
2 Bird
3 Field
4 Fish

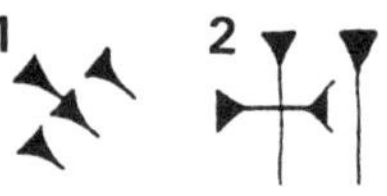
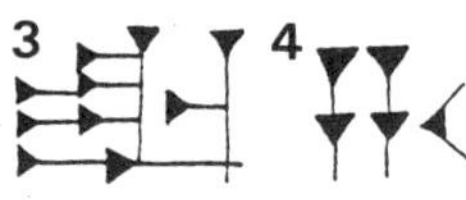

Early Chinese ideograms
1 Sun
2 Cloud
3 Moon
4 Hair

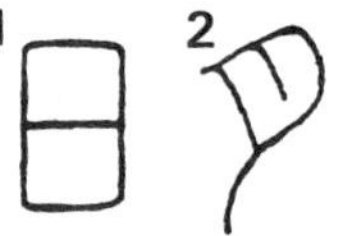
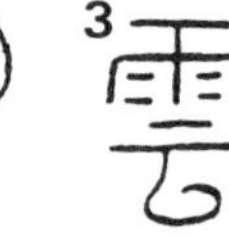

Cretan Linear B
1 Bull
2 Hand
3 Double axe
4 Dagger

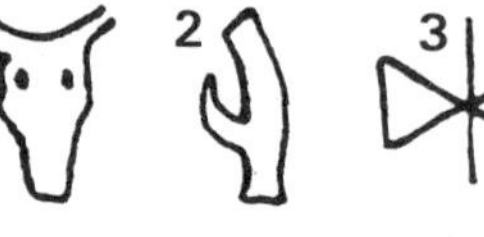
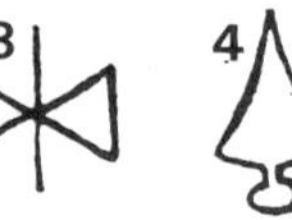

Cuneiform numerals

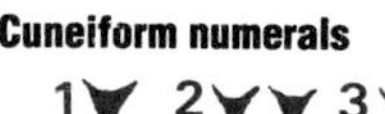
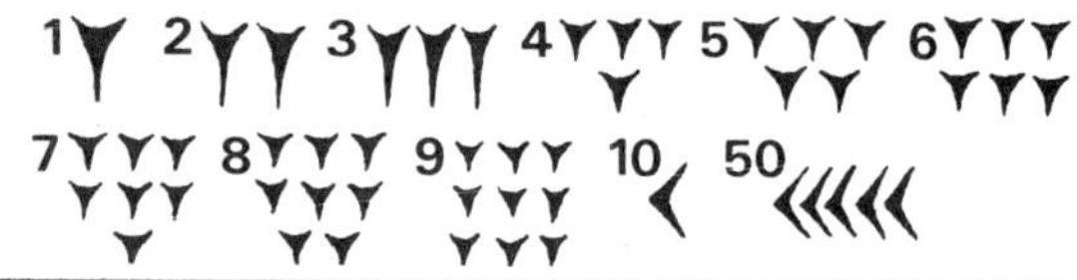
1 2 3 4 5 6
7 8 9 10 50

Mayan glyphs for numbers

1 2 3 4 5 10

Aztec pictograms
1 Market
2 Rain
3 Wall
4 Road

Egyptian hieroglyphic alphabet

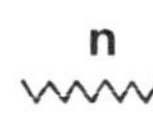

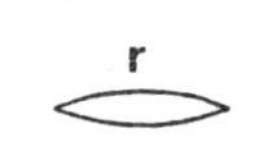
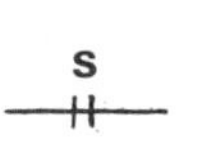

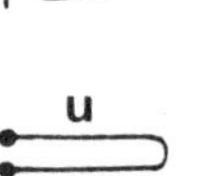

a b ch f g h k kh
l m n o p r s sh t u th z

Evolution of the Roman alphabet

3134 A majority of printed material uses the 26-letter alphabet called Roman. But the Romans did not invent it. They added the finishing touches to a system that had been developing for thousands of years.

The letters of the Roman alphabet have developed from the ancient Phoenician syllabary (a set of characters representing syllables), and this script in its Aramaic form was also the ultimate source of the Arabic alphabet. A strong likeness can be seen in the letters D, K, L, M, N, P, R and T. The Etruscans carried the Greek alphabet with them to central Italy. The Romans learned the alphabet from them and gave it much the same form that we use today.

The early Roman alphabet had about 20 letters and it gradually gained three more. The Romans gave most capital letters their modern form by AD 114. The letters J, U, and W were not added to the alphabet until the Middle Ages.

Phoenician

Old Hebrew

Early Greek

Classical Greek

Etruscan

Early Latin

Roman
A B C D E F G H I J K L M N O P Q R S T U V W X Y Z

Major alphabets of the world

3135 Apart from Roman, the other major alphabets in use today that had their origins in Europe and the Near East are Hebrew, Greek, and Russian. The parent alphabet of Russian, Cyrillic, was adapted from the Greek in the 9th century AD by St. Cyril and St. Methodius.

Hebrew

א	aleph	a	ל	lamed	l
בּ	beth	b	מ ם	mem	m
ב	veth	v	נ ן	nun	n
ג	gimel	g	ס	samekh	s
ד	daleth	d	ע	ayin	'
ה	heh	h	פּ	peh	p
ו	waw	w	פ ף	feh	f
ז	zayin	z	צ ץ	sadhe	ts
ח	heth	h	ק	qoph	q
ט	teth	t	ר	resh	r
י	yodh	y	שׁ	shin	sh
כּ	kaph	k	שׂ	sin	s
כ ך	khaph	kh	ת	tav	t

Greek

Αα	alpha	a	Ξξ	xi	x,ks
Ββ	beta	b	Οο	omicron	o
Γγ	gamma	g	Ππ	pi	p
Δδ	delta	d	Ρρ	rho	r
Εε	epsilon	e	Σσ	sigma	s
Ζζ	zeta	z	Ττ	tau	t
Ηη	eta	e	Υυ	upsilon	u,y
Θθ	theta	th	Φφ	phi	ph
Ιι	iota	i	Χχ	chi	kh,ch
Κκ	kappa	k	Ψψ	psi	ps
Λλ	lambda	l	Ωω	omega	o
Μμ	mu	m			
Νν	nu	n			

Russian (Cyrillic)

Аа	a	Сс	s
Бб	b	Тт	t
Вв	v	Уу	u
Гг	g	Фф	f
Дд	d	Хх	kh
Ее	e	Цц	ts
Жж	zh	Чч	ch
Зз	z	Шш	sh
Ии	i	Щщ	shch
Кк	k	Ъъ	*hard*
Лл	l	Ыы	y
Мм	m	Ьь	*soft*
Нн	n	Ээ	e
Оо	o	Юю	yu
Пп	p	Яя	ya
Рр	r		

continued

Major alphabets continued

3135 **Arabic**

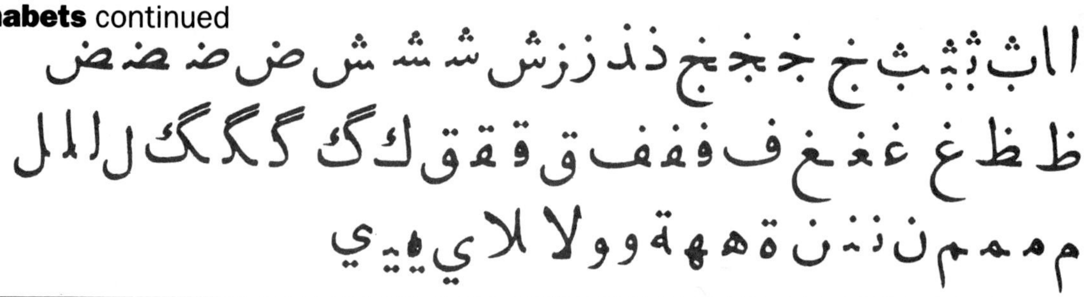

اا ث ثبث ج ججج ذ ذ ز زش ش ش ش ص ص ض ض ض

ظ ط غ غغغ ف ففف ق ققق ك ك گ گگگ ل ال ل

م ممم ن ننن ة ه هه ة وو لا لا ي ييي

Hindi
(example)

बाबतींत कोणालाहि कसलें भविष्य सांगतां येत नाहीं.
सरकारचे जे हवामानशास्त्रज्ञ अगदीं एकसारखे पावसाचा अभ्यास करीत
बसलेले असतात, त्यांनाहि कांहीं सांगतां येत नाहीं. त्यामुळें

Chinese
(selection of characters)

上帝憐愛世人，甚至將獨生子賜給他們，呌凡信他的不至滅亡，必得永生。

Japanese
(selection of characters)

Classical (Bugotai)

それ神はその獨子を賜ふほどに世を愛し給へり、すべて彼を信ずる者の亡びずして永遠の生命を得んためなり。

Colloquial (Kogotai)

神はそのひとり子を賜わったほどに、この世を愛して下さった。それは御子を信じる者がひとりも滅びないで、永遠の命を得るためである。

The written alphabet

3136 Since Roman times, the alphabet has been through a process of change and refinement to adapt it to the needs of scribes – those who kept written records and wrote out books before the days of printing. These "hands," the calligraphic interpretations that were used, owe their varying appearance to the needs of the period in which they were written. Criteria such as speed, legibility, beauty, space and size, and quality of writing materials, all had an effect on the subsequent appearance.

Rustica
Classical Roman was ideal for carving inscriptions but not ideal as a written hand. Rustica, evolved from Roman, was a flowing and compressed style suitable for writing on papyrus with square-ended reed pens.

ABCDEFGHIJKLMN
OPQRSTUVVWXYZ

Uncials
Improvements in writing implements, combined with the need to write quicker – but still legibly – because of the demand for Bibles and religious texts throughout Europe, led to the adoption of the uncial hand as the favored script of the main part of the first millennium AD.

AAAABCDEEFGh
IJKLMNOPQRRS
TTUVWWXYZ

continued

The written alphabet continued

3136 **Half uncials**
The forerunner of today's lowercase letters, half-uncials were a development of the uncial script, again probably because they were faster to write.

abcdefghijklmn
opqrstuvwxyz

Carolingian
Named after Charlemagne, the Frankish leader who recognized the power of the written word, Carolingian was the first true lowercase hand. Elegant, with long descenders and ascenders, it established itself as the formal book hand in Europe for around 300 years from about AD 800.

abcdefghijklmn
opqrstuvwxyz

Versals
Versal letters – essentially initial letters – were often used with Carolingian, uncial, and half-uncial letterforms when a decorated or large capital was needed at the beginning of a piece of text of an illuminated manuscript. They are purely decorative, with no lowercase form, and are built up from several careful pen strokes. A more rounded and decorative form, Lombardic, was also used.

ABCDEFGHIJKLM
NOPQRSTUVWXYZ

Gothic
In the Middle Ages, the increasing demands for documents for secular purposes led to a shortage of vellum to write upon and a consequent increase in its price. The need arose for a hand quick to write but dense and neat, to make economical use of the vellum. Gothic allows lines of text to be written closer together.

aabcdefghijklmn
oqprſsstuvwwxyz
ABEHJAORUX

Italic
The emerging Renaissance in Italy in the 15th century had a profound impact on calligraphic styles, as it did on everything else. Italic was the style that took over from Gothic, with flowing ascenders and descenders and decorative flourishes added. This elegant hand was adopted by the newly emerging printing houses for their typography, and it is still in use today.

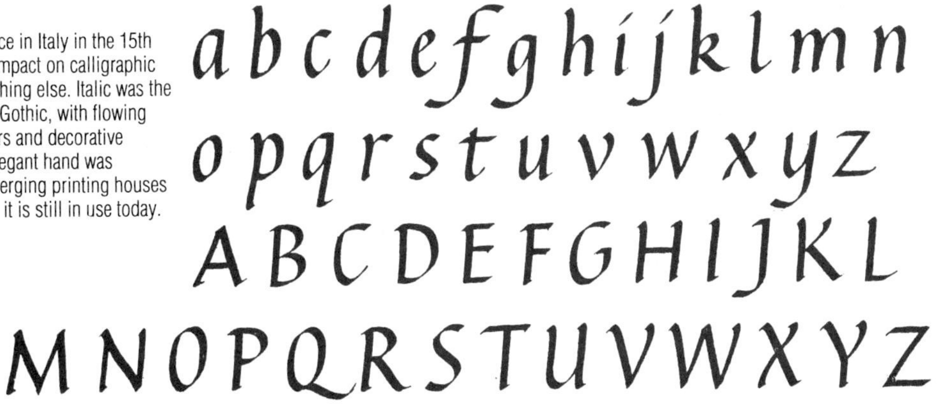

abcdefghijklmn
opqrstuvwxyz
ABCDEFGHIJKL
MNOPQRSTUVWXYZ

Copperplate/roundhand
The arrival of the quill pen, with its flexibility and ability to make thick and thin lines in the same stroke, allowed the calligraphers of the day to imitate what was the writing style of copper engravers of that period, who used a fine-pointed burin to cut into the copper, a method called intaglio. This fine, flowing hand became the accepted written hand, especially in the 19th century, when the introduction of mass-produced steel nibs meant all schoolchildren could learn to write.

abcdefghijkl

Diacritical marks

3137 Accents or diacritical marks are marks written usually over or beneath letters to indicate how the letter is to be pronounced. There are no true accents in English, although they survive in certain imported words, such as naïve. The accents most commonly used in European languages are illustrated here.

Some languages also use special characters, such as å and ø in Norwegian and Danish, and ß in German, in addition to the letters of the Roman alphabet.

à	grave	â	circumflex	ç	cedilla	ğ	breve
á	acute	ä	dieresis	ñ	tilde	ā	macron

314 ALTERNATIVE LANGUAGES

New languages

3141 Artificial or constructed languages, of which there are several hundred, have been devised by linguists to try to improve communication between peoples of different native tongues. The use of an easily learned common language bypasses the problems of translation or of learning several other languages. All constructed languages have in common a logical system of words and grammar, based mostly on the well-known European languages but avoiding the irregular spelling and idiosyncrasies that many of them have. The most successful is Esperanto, invented by Ludwig Zamenhof of Poland in 1887. Others are Volapuk, Interlingua, Ido, and Novial. None, though, has won general acceptance among the world's people.

English: Our father, which art in heaven, hallowed be thy name

Esperanto: Patro nia, kiu estas en la cielo, sankta estuvia nomo

Volapuk: O Fat obas, kel binol in suls, paisaludomoz nem ola

New forms of alphabet

3142 SHORTHAND
Shorthand is any system that allows speech to be written down rapidly, using symbols and abbreviations to represent sounds and words. Its main use is now in business and administration for rapid dictation. The most widely used written shorthands are the Gregg and Pitman methods. Speeds of over 200 words a minute can be attained by some users of shorthand, usually called stenographers.

Gregg:

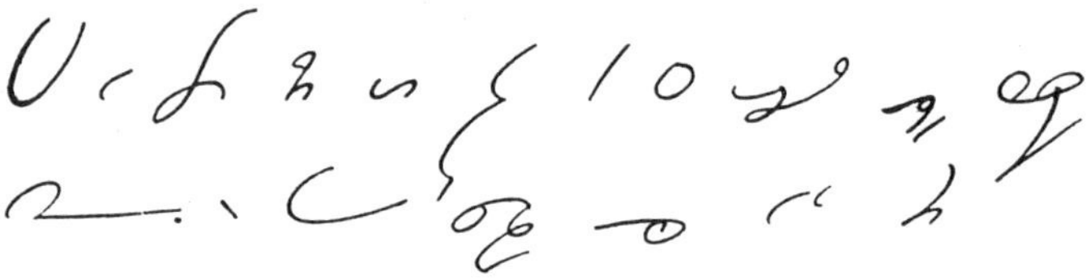

Pitman:

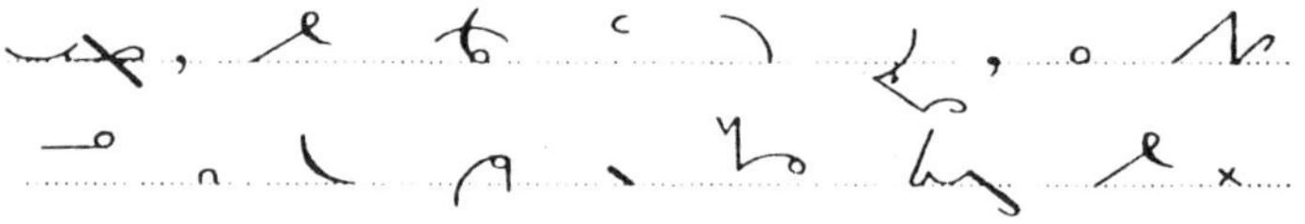

INTERNATIONAL PHONETIC ALPHABET
This alphabet, made up of letters from the Roman alphabet supplemented by letters from the Greek and other symbols, was devised to allow the accurate transcription of speech sounds, covering every sound from every language. Special marks are used to indicate length and quality of sounds. The alphabet is used mostly in dictionaries to aid pronunciation, and by specialists in the study of language.

The letters b, d, f, g, h, k, l, m, n, p, r, s, t, v, w, and z all have their usual values. The symbols for all the other sounds are shown at right.

ɑː	far	eɪ	day	əʊ	note	ɜː	burn	ð	these
æ	act	ɛə	dare	ɔː	thaw	ʌ	cut	ŋ	sing
aɪ	dive	ɪ	sit	ɔɪ	void	ʃ	ship	x	loch Scottish
aɪə	fire	iː	see	ʊ	pull	ʒ	treasure	əɪ	aye Scottish
aʊ	out	ɪə	fear	uː	zoo	tʃ	chew	ə	indicates the following consonant is syllabic – e.g. l in bundle
aʊə	flour	j	yes	ʊə	poor	dʒ	jaw		
ɛ	set	ɒ	pot	ə	the	θ	thin		

INTERNATIONAL TEACHING ALPHABET (ITA)
This alphabet was devised by Sir James Pitman to make the learning of English easier. Similar to the phonetic alphabet but simpler, it uses the Roman alphabet plus other symbols. Each of its 44 characters represents a sound that may be made up from several letters of the ordinary Roman alphabet, and may be spelled differently in each case. The ITA makes a consistent relationship between sounds and characters.

a	apple	ee	eel	k	kitten	ω	food	ʒ	treasure	wh	whee
ɑ	arm	e	egg	l	lion	ou	out	t	tree	y	yellow
æ	angel	f	finger	m	man	oi	oil	th	three	z	zoo
au	author	g	girl	n	nest	p	pig	th	mother	ʐ	is
b	bed	h	hat	ng	king	r	red	ue	due		
c	cat	ie	tie	œ	toe	ɹ	bird	u	up		
ch	chair	i	ink	o	on	s	soap	v	van		
d	doll	j	jam	ω	book	sh	ship	w	window		

315 LANGUAGE BY SIGNALS

There are in use today many language systems that do not involve the use of a "written" language as we generally know it. These have mainly been devised to act as a means of communication between people in very specific situations, where "normal" spoken or written language is not possible. Languages for the blind, deaf, and mute are obvious examples. Before the advent of telephone and two-way radio, visual and aural systems were devised to improve medium- and long-distance communication.

Braille

3151 This system was devised to make it possible for blind people to read. It is a code in which each of the letters of the Roman alphabet, numbers, and punctuation marks is represented by an arrangement of between one and six dots embossed into paper. The blind person "reads" by passing his or her finger along the rows of dots. It was invented by the Frenchman Louis Braille (1809–52), who was blind from the age of three.

a b c d e f g h i j k l m n o

p q r s t u v w x y z 1 2 3 4

5 6 7 8 9 0 , ; : . ! ( ) "? – Capital sign

Sign language

3152 There are several forms of language that use parts of the body – usually the hands – to communicate. By far the most widely used are those for the deaf and mute. The simplest of the methods is finger spelling, in which the hands and fingers indicate individual letters, one after the other, to spell out words. There are several different codes for finger positions, as shown below. More complex systems, such as American Sign Language, use movement of the fingers, hands, and body to convey entire concepts.

Finger spelling systems

North American manual alphabet

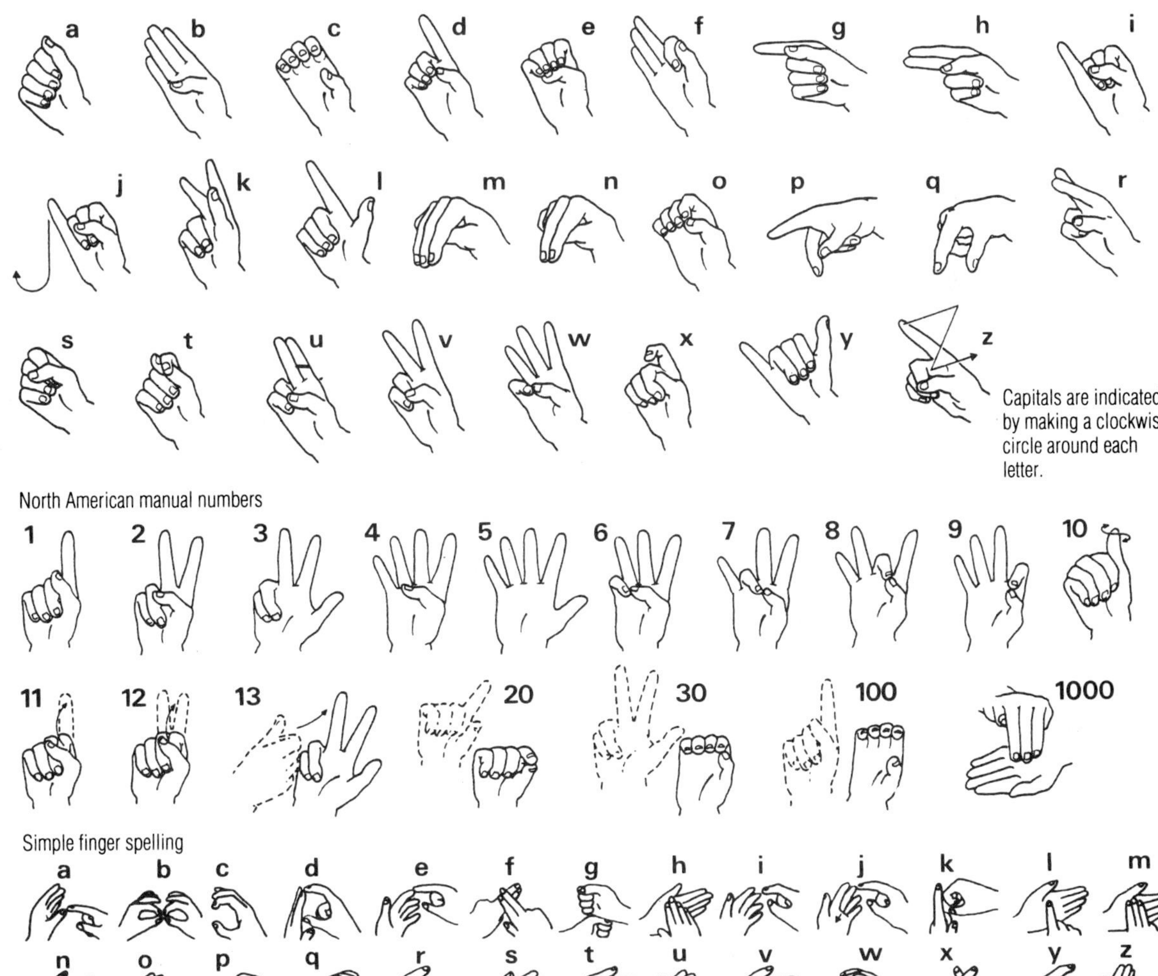

3153 Morse code
3154 Semaphore
3155 International flag code
316 **Modern communications**
3161 Time frame of modern communications

Morse Code

3153 Invented in 1838 by Samuel Morse for use in newly invented wire telegraphy, Morse Code is a signaling system that uses dots and dashes of sound in combinations to make letters, numbers, and punctuation. These are sent down a wire telegraph and decoded at the other end. It was the first really successful system devised for long-distance communication.

Alphabet

A	•—	H	••••	O	———	V	•••—
B	—•••	I	••	P	•——•	W	•——
C	—•—•	J	•———	Q	——•—	X	—••—
D	—••	K	—•—	R	•—•	Y	—•——
E	•	L	•—••	S	•••	Z	——••
F	••—•	M	——	T	—		
G	——•	N	—•	U	••—		

Numerals

1	•————	6	—••••
2	••———	7	——•••
3	•••——	8	———••
4	••••—	9	————•
5	•••••	10	—————

Punctuation

Comma	——••——	Question mark	••——••	Error	••••••••
Semicolon	—•—•—•	Quotation marks	•—••—•	Understand	•—•
Colon	———•••	Wait	•—•••	Hyphen	—••••—
Period	•—•—•—	End of message	•—•—•	Apostrophe	•————•

Semaphore

3154 Any visual signaling code system using movable arms, flags, or other devices can be called a semaphore system. Originally invented by Claude Chappe in France in 1794, semaphore is known by most people today as the movable flag system. A person holding a flag in each hand moves his or her arms to positions indicating letters and numbers. It is used mostly in ship-to-ship communication and at airports.

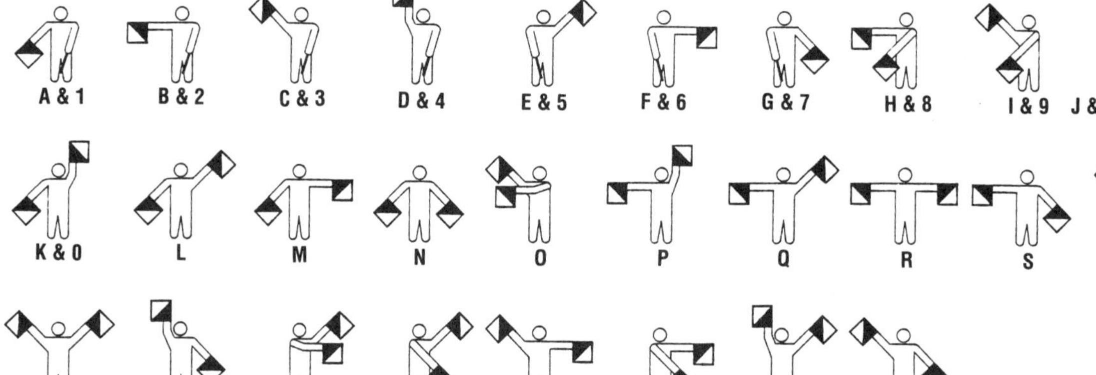

International flag code

3155 The International Flag Code has for a long time been used at sea to convey messages between ships. Flags of different colors and designs form an internationally accepted code for the letters of the alphabet and each also has a meaning of its own when flown individually.

A I am undergoing speed trials.
B I have explosives on board.
C Yes
D Keep clear.
E I am altering course to starboard.
F I am disabled.
G I require a pilot.
H Pilot is on board.
I I am altering course to port.
J I am sending a message by semaphore.
K Stop at once.
L Stop, I wish to communicate with you.
M A doctor is on board
N No
O Person overboard.
P (The Blue Peter) I am about to sail.
Q Quarantine flag.
R I have stopped.
S I am going astern.
T Do not pass ahead of me.
U You are in danger.
V I need help.
W Send a doctor.
X Stop, and watch for my signals.
Y I am carrying mail.
Z I am calling a shore station.

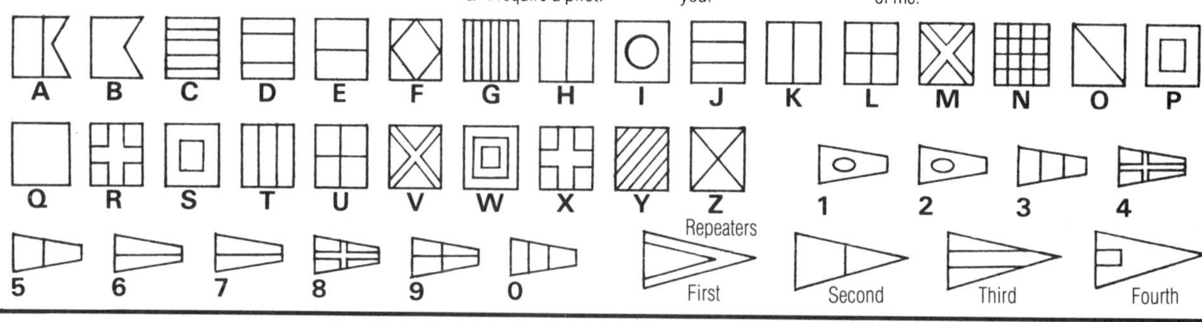

316 MODERN COMMUNICATIONS

Over the past 500 years, methods of communication have developed considerably. Mass communication, the sending of messages to large audiences, has grown with developments in printing since 1400, and with the inventions of telegraphy in the 19th century, the telephone in 1876, and television and radio in the 20th century. We can now communicate with each other from city to city, across oceans, and into space. Communication can be instant, bringing live images into people's homes from all over the world. It is vital to business, finance, and commerce.

Since World War II, mass communications have developed rapidly, making the world a much smaller place and nations and peoples dependent on them for information, entertainment, and education. They are also used to persuade people, as in political broadcasts or advertising.

Great advances in technology have enabled this to take place. Machines produce books, magazines, radio programs, television broadcasts, and films. Cameras and microphones serve as our eyes and ears, telling us about wars, events, and new discoveries. The three basic means, or media, of mass communication are the printed word, sound, and a combination of sound and image, such as television, film, and videotape. In business, machines such as the facsimile transmitter (fax), telex, mobile telephone, viewdata, and teletext, linking word processors through a telephone line, have made communication more instant and information more accessible. Satellites in space have made it possible to relay TV signals across oceans. They can also transmit radio, telephone, and other forms of communication.

There are new developments in fiber optics making it possible to use light to send more messages faster than could be done with electricity or radio waves. Advances in laser technology mean that holography may be used to produce films, photographs, and television programs consisting of three-dimensional images that float in space.

Time frame of modern communications

3161

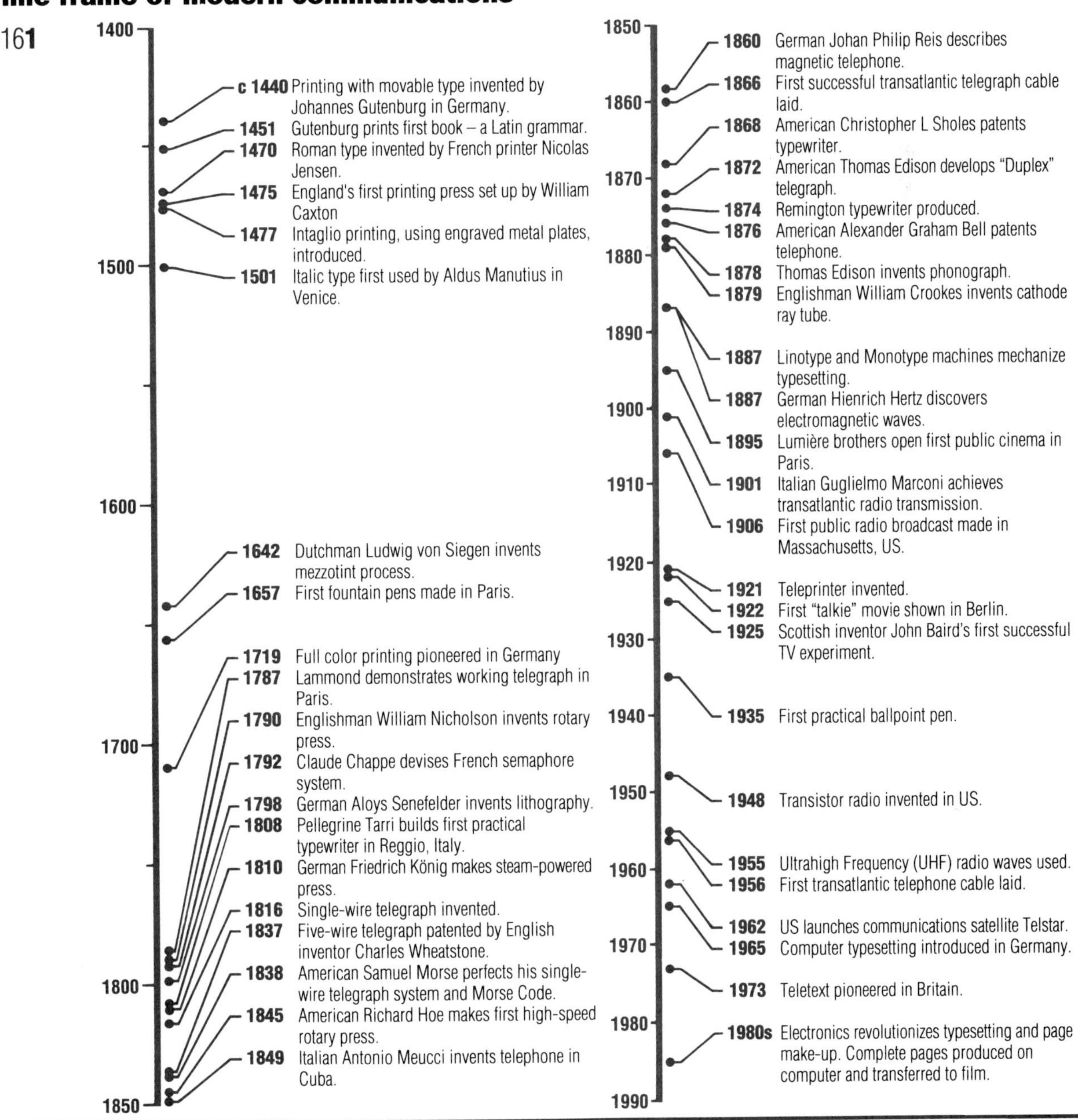

1400
c 1440 Printing with movable type invented by Johannes Gutenburg in Germany.
1451 Gutenburg prints first book – a Latin grammar.
1470 Roman type invented by French printer Nicolas Jensen.
1475 England's first printing press set up by William Caxton
1477 Intaglio printing, using engraved metal plates, introduced.
1500
1501 Italic type first used by Aldus Manutius in Venice.
1600
1642 Dutchman Ludwig von Siegen invents mezzotint process.
1657 First fountain pens made in Paris.
1719 Full color printing pioneered in Germany
1787 Lammond demonstrates working telegraph in Paris.
1790 Englishman William Nicholson invents rotary press.
1700
1792 Claude Chappe devises French semaphore system.
1798 German Aloys Senefelder invents lithography.
1808 Pellegrine Tarri builds first practical typewriter in Reggio, Italy.
1810 German Friedrich König makes steam-powered press.
1816 Single-wire telegraph invented.
1837 Five-wire telegraph patented by English inventor Charles Wheatstone.
1800
1838 American Samuel Morse perfects his single-wire telegraph system and Morse Code.
1845 American Richard Hoe makes first high-speed rotary press.
1849 Italian Antonio Meucci invents telephone in Cuba.
1850
1850
1860 German Johan Philip Reis describes magnetic telephone.
1860
1866 First successful transatlantic telegraph cable laid.
1868 American Christopher L Sholes patents typewriter.
1870
1872 American Thomas Edison develops "Duplex" telegraph.
1874 Remington typewriter produced.
1876 American Alexander Graham Bell patents telephone.
1880
1878 Thomas Edison invents phonograph.
1879 Englishman William Crookes invents cathode ray tube.
1890
1887 Linotype and Monotype machines mechanize typesetting.
1887 German Hienrich Hertz discovers electromagnetic waves.
1900
1895 Lumière brothers open first public cinema in Paris.
1910
1901 Italian Guglielmo Marconi achieves transatlantic radio transmission.
1906 First public radio broadcast made in Massachusetts, US.
1920
1921 Teleprinter invented.
1922 First "talkie" movie shown in Berlin.
1925 Scottish inventor John Baird's first successful TV experiment.
1930
1940
1935 First practical ballpoint pen.
1950
1948 Transistor radio invented in US.
1960
1955 Ultrahigh Frequency (UHF) radio waves used.
1956 First transatlantic telephone cable laid.
1970
1962 US launches communications satellite Telstar.
1965 Computer typesetting introduced in Germany.
1973 Teletext pioneered in Britain.
1980
1980s Electronics revolutionizes typesetting and page make-up. Complete pages produced on computer and transferred to film.
1990

Glossary of communications

3162

alphabet Normally a set of graphic symbols which, either singly or in combinations, represent the sounds of a language. Alphabetic writing appears to have begun around 1700 BC. Its inventors are thought to have been the Egyptians, Phoenicians, or Hittites. The word comes from the first two letters of the Greek alphabet, alpha and beta.

Baird, John Logie 1888–1946. Pioneer of early television with a mechanical system that produced flickering images.

ballpoint pen Original invention attributed to John Loud in the US in 1888. The first practical ballpoint pen was invented by Georg Biro in Hungary in 1938.

Bell, Alexander Graham 1847–1922. His pioneering work in telegraphy and telephony led to the invention of the telephone.

Braille, Louis 1809–52. Blind French teacher who published a system of writing allowing the blind to read by touch. Braille consists of a system of reading by feeling raised dots on a page.

British Broadcasting Corporation (BBC) Established under royal charter in 1927, it transmitted the world's first open-circuit TV broadcasts. It runs two national television stations, five national radio stations, and a number of local radio stations, and provides external services in 38 languages.

Caxton, William 1422–91. The first English printer. He set up a press in 1474 which produced the first printed book in English.

computer A device for processing information at high speeds by electronic methods.

cuneiform A non alphabetic system of writing used throughout the ancient world for over 2,000 years. It was probably invented by the Sumerians. A symbol was constructed out of sets of wedge-shaped strokes made in soft clay with pieces of reed.

Cyrillic Form of alphabet used in Russian, Bulgarian, and other languages which is derived from the Greek alphabet.

electrotype A copy of engravings and type made by an electroplating process.

engraving A plate engraved for printing, or a printed illustration.

etymology The study of the history of words, tracing them back to their earliest recorded forms.

fax Short for facsimile, machines that enable people to send copies of documents or pictures over telephone lines or radio links.

full color printing Process by which all colors can be produced from combinations of three primary colors – yellow, cyan (blue), and magenta (red) – and black.

Gutenberg, Johannes c .1400–68. German printer who invented the method of printing with movable metal type.

heliograph A system of sending signals by flashing sunlight from a mirror, used in the 1800s.

Hertz, Heinrich Rudolph 1857–94. German physicist who first produced and detected radio waves in 1888.

hieroglyphics Writing system which uses picture-characters to represent words, ideas, or sounds developed by the ancient Egyptians and early American Indians, such as the Aztecs.

ideogram A pictorial system used in a writing system to represent an entity or an idea. Ideograms are also called ideographs.

International Phonetic Alphabet A system developed during the late 19th century to symbolize every sound used in human language accurately. Used in the scientific study of pronunciation.

Italic type Style of letterforms developed for printing in Italy by Francesco Griffo in 1501.

kinesics The study of the way in which facial expressions and body movements are used for the purposes of communication. This is also known as body language, as is proxemics.

linguistics The scientific study of language. It has produced many specialized fields of study such as phonetics, grammar, and semantics.

linotype Machine invented in 1884 that speeded up typesetting, which had been a manual process.

lithography A form of planographic printing invented in 1798.

logogram A symbol used to represent a complete word or phrase. For example, the sign $, for dollar, is a logogram.

Marconi, Guglielmo 1874–1937. Italian electrical engineer who invented communication by radio by converting radio waves into electrical signals.

Morse Code Code invented by Samuel Morse for transmitting telegraph messages.

Morse, Samuel 1791–1872. US inventor who erected the first telegraph line between Washington and Baltimore in 1844.

papyrus A reedlike plant cultivated in Egypt and used by the ancient Egyptians to make paper.

photocopier A device that prints copies of documents and drawings from an optical image.

phototypesetting Machines that have revolutionized printing. They do not cast type from hot metal as in the old system. Instead they create images of characters on photographic paper or film, which is then used for platemaking. Some can set 20,000 or more characters per second.

pictograms Pictures of objects used widely in the ancient Middle East and by the Aztec and Maya of Central America.

printing The production of multiple copies of text or pictures, normally on paper. Printing has advanced rapidly with new technology over the centuries from its beginnings in China, where prints were made from a carved wood block. It was developed in Europe in the 14th century when Gutenberg invented a system of casting type and a printing press in c. 1440. Today complete pages can be produced by computers, transferred to paper by laser, and then photographed onto a printing plate.

radio The transmission of sound or other information by radio-frequency electromagnetic waves pioneered by Marconi. Like television, radio plays an important part in people's lives broadcasting news, drama, entertainment, the arts, and educational programs.

radio telephone Used for communicating with ships at sea from 1903 onward, before permanent cables were laid.

rays Particularly electromagnetic waves, which travel through space as fast as light. There are several kinds of electromagnetic waves, including radio waves (the longest), infrared rays, visible light, ultraviolet light, Xrays, and gamma rays (the shortest). Radio and television both use radio waves.

rebus A system using a mixture of words and pictures, the pictures representing syllables or words.

runes Letters of an alphabet used by the Teutonic peoples of northern Europe before AD 1000.

satellite A spacecraft launched into orbit around the Earth or entering an orbit around some other body in the solar system. Satellites are used for gathering information, intelligence, and increasingly for communication. They transmit radio, telephone, and television signals. Constant radio links became possible in 1963.

satellite TV Began in Europe in 1989 with signals beamed via the Astra satellite to home receivers.

semantics The study of the relationships between words and meanings that includes two distinct traditions of enquiry: the philosophical and the linguistic.

semaphore Signalling by means of two flags or mechanical arms, held in various positions to represent letters.

semiotics The study of signs and/or symbols; sometimes known as semiology.

syllabary A set of symbols used for representing syllables which can be seen in Japanese writing.

telecommunications The transfer of information by any electromagnetic means such as wire or radio waves. It includes telephones, telegraphy, radio, and television. It relies on a transmitter, a transmission channel, and a receiver.

telegram A message transmitted by telegraph.

telegraphy The invention of the electric telegraph, perfected in 1838 by Morse, saw the beginning of modern electronic communications. In simple terms it is the transmission of written or printed messages by electrical signals.

telephone Invented in 1876, the telephone has become a vital source of communication between people in business and everyday life. It carries sounds in the form of electrical signals along a wire. Mobile telephones are a more recent invention, allowing people to be contacted and to communicate while travelling in a car, train, and even aircraft.

teletext A fast form of telex that links word processors through a telephone line. Developed in Europe in the 1980s as a fast information service.

television Along with radio, one of the quickest forms of communication. It is the broadcasting of pictures and sound by radio waves or electric cable. It was invented by John Logie Baird in 1926.

telex A quick form of communication and an advance on simple telegraph systems.

continued

Glossary of communications continued

3162 It transmits a message from one machine to a similar one anywhere in the world at about 100 words per minute.
typesetting The process by which type is assembled for printing.
typewriter The first machine was invented in the US in 1867, but the commercial success of the typewriter began in 1874, when the Remington company produced its own machines.
videotape recorders These record pictures as well as sound on magnetic tape. They developed during the 1970s when video cassette recorders became cheap enough for home use.
viewdata A system by which information can be stored at a central point and retrieved by the use of a telephone line linked to word processors. It enables the user to call up thousands of pages of information.

321 SIGNALING SYSTEMS

Hundreds of signaling systems exist for a huge range of activities covering many aspects of human life. Each is specific to its own field, and usually meaningless out of context. Most can only work if some prearrangement takes place – fire and smoke signals, for example, will work only if someone is there looking for them, and understands what they mean. A sports field is full of codes – little signals from one team member to another, which together convey an idea, such as a strategy. Divers cannot use spoken language when underwater, so they use a system of internationally recognized signals to communicate. Each of these systems works because they are simple, each signal usually conveying an idea, such as an instruction.

Distress signals

3211 Used in situations of distress or emergency involving the need to communicate from land to air. These are some of the internationally recognized symbols that can be made on the ground – in snow, in soil, or with stones – to signal to overhead aircraft.

1 Aircraft badly damaged.
2 Serious injuries, need doctor.
3 Need medical supplies.
4 Need food and water.
5 Probably safe to land here.
6 Am proceeding in this direction.
7 Need fuel and oil.
8 All is well.
9 Send firearms and ammunition.
10 Need signal lamp on radio.
11 Show direction to proceed.
12 Need map and compass.
13 Will attempt to take off.
14 Send engineer.

Underwater signals

3212 Internationally recognized communication signals for use by divers operating underwater.
1 I am out of breath. The diver moves hands from side to side at chest level.
2 I have no air. The diver touches his or her mouthpiece repeatedly with cupped fingers.
3 Go up, or I am going up. This is either an order given or a statement made at the end of a dive. The fingers are clenched and thumb pointed upward.
4 Go down, or I am going down. An order or a statement made at the beginning of a dive. The fingers are clenched and the thumb is pointed downward.
5 Something is wrong. This does not necessarily mean an emergency but merely indicates that things are not right. The hand is held outward, palm down, and is moved gently up and down.
6 Stop, stay where you are. For this command the hand is held up, palm outward.
7 I am on reserve/I have very little air left in my cylinder. The fist is clenched, thumb over the fingers, and held at eye level.
8 I cannot pull my reserve. This indicates that the diver needs help to pull his or her reserve level. The fist is clenched and is rotated from side to side.
9 Danger. The diver draws a finger across his or her throat and points to the source of danger.
10 I am OK. The diver holds one hand up, thumb and index finger touching.
11 I need assistance. This signal is given on the surface. The diver holds one arm up, fist clenched, and waves it slowly from side to side indicating that he or she wants to be picked up.

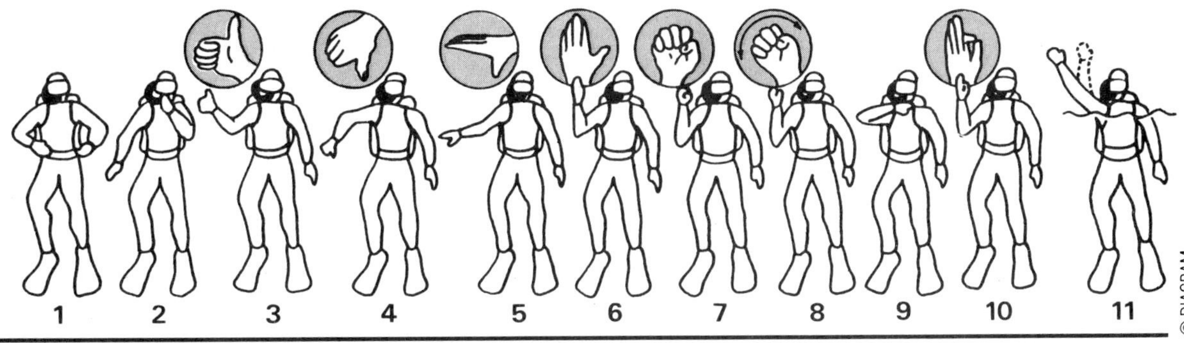

3213 International NATO alphabet
322 **Symbol systems**
3221 Astronomy symbols
3222 Electronic symbols
3223 Zodiac (astrological) symbols
3224 Heraldic devices

International NATO alphabet

3213 This is an internationally recognized system, by which each letter of the alphabet is given a name. It is of particular importance to people such as airline pilots, where there is no room for error in instructions that are being tranmitted by radio. With poor reception, the word "dog" might be difficult to understand, wheras "DELTA - OSCAR - GOLF" is quite clear.

A Alpha
B Bravo
C Charlie
D Delta
E Echo
F Foxtrot
G Golf
H Hotel
I India
J Juliet
K Kilo
L Lima
M Mike
N November
O Oscar
P Papa
Q Quebec
R Romeo
S Sierra
T Tango
U Uniform
V Victor
W Whiskey
X X-ray
Y Yankee
Z Zulu

322 SYMBOL SYSTEMS

Visual symbols communicate a concept, meaning, instruction, object, or part of a system. Unlike alphabetical characters, which have no meaning in themselves and only function when brought together to form words and sentences, symbols, like signals, convey a concept in themselves. Some symbols are general – directional symbols at airports, for example – and can usually be understood by anyone who sees them. These are usually semifigurative, little pictograms that we can recognize or that contain universally accepted shapes like arrows. Some symbols, on the other hand, are specific to one field of knowledge and are usually meaningless to those outside that field – for example, in electronics, astronomy, and biology. Only prior knowledge, or training in that field, will allow the "reader" to understand the "language" that the symbols speak.

Astronomy symbols

3221
1 Sun
2 New moon
3 First quarter moon
4 Full moon
5 Last quarter moon
6 Mercury
7 Venus
8 Earth; globular cluster
9 Mars
10 Jupiter
11 Saturn
12 Uranus
13 Neptune
14 Pluto
15 Star
16 Comet
17 Galactic cluster
18 Planetary nebula
19 Galaxy
20 Conjunction
21 Opposition
22 Ascending node
23 Descending node
24 Aries; vernal equinox
25 Libra; autumnal equinox
26 Right ascension
27 Declination
28 Astronomical unit
29 Proper motion
30 Annual parallax
31 Apparent magnitude
32 Absolute magnitude

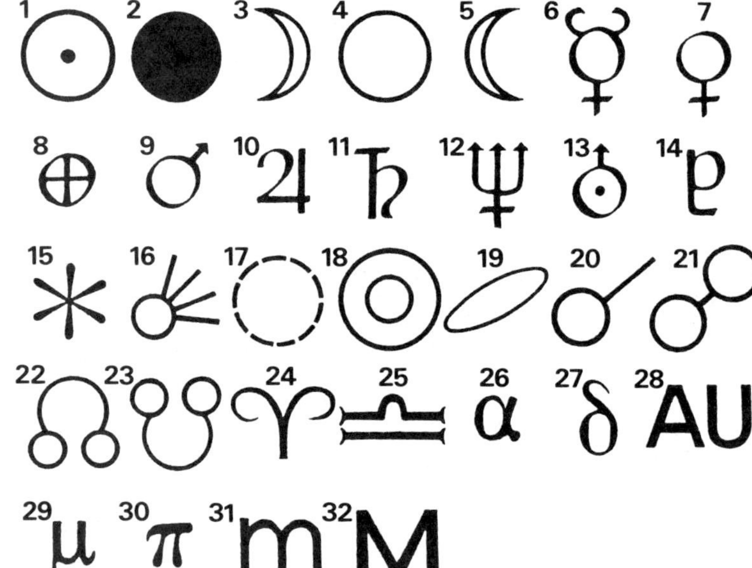

Electronic symbols

3222
1 Conducting path
2 Diode
3 Tunnel diode
4 u-p-n transistor
5 p-u-p transistor
6 Amplifier
7 Fuse
8 Resistor (fixed)
9 Resistor (variable)
10 Capacitor (fixed)
11 Capacitor (electrolytic)
12 Inductor (fixed)
13 Inductor (magnetic core)
14 Inductor (variable)
15 Simple switch
16 Cell
17 AC source
18 Ammeter
19 Voltmeter
20 Wattmeter
21 Transformer
22 Transformer (magnetic core)
23 Light emitting diode
24 Loudspeaker
25 Microphone
26 Chassil connection
27 Earth
28 Aerial
29 Neon lamp
30 No connection
31 Connector junction
32 Spark gap
33 Incandescent lamp
34 Cathode – directly heated
35 Cathode – indirectly heated

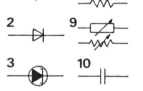

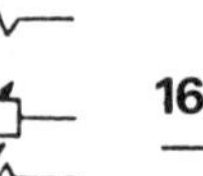
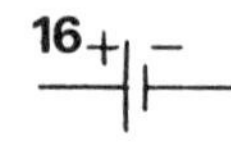
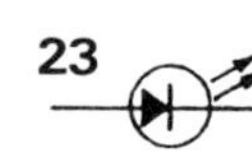
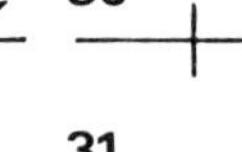
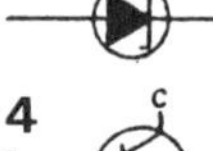
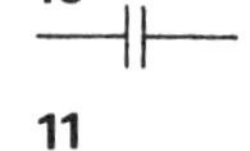
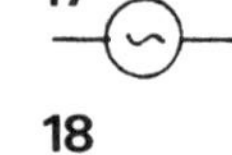
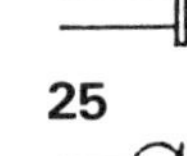
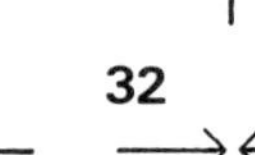
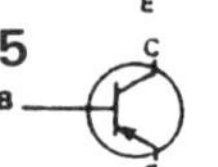

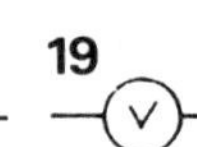

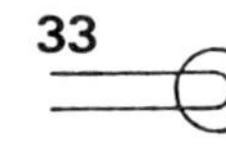
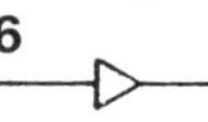
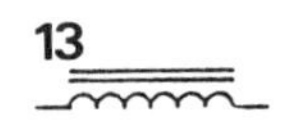
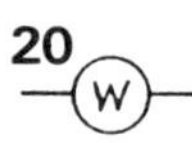
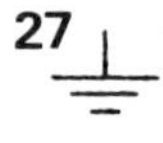
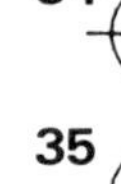
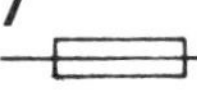

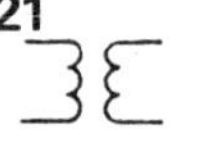

Zodiac (astrological) symbols

3223 Each of the 12 signs of the zodiac has its own identifying symbol (somtimes called a glyph), used to show its position on a birth chart.

1 Aries
2 Taurus
3 Gemini
4 Cancer
5 Leo
6 Virgo
7 Libra
8 Scorpio
9 Sagittarius
10 Capricorn
11 Aquarius
12 Pisces

Heraldic devices

3224 Heraldry began in Europe in the 12th century. Knights in armour began to wear identifying badges so that their identity would be clear to their followers and opponents, since the armour covered their faces and bodies in tournaments and in battles. These badges were known as the knight's coat-of-arms. In order to describe a coat of arms it is necessary to refer to the colors of the field (i.e. the background color), the charge color (the color of any item placed on the shield), plus any subsidury charges.

DIVISIONS OF FIELD

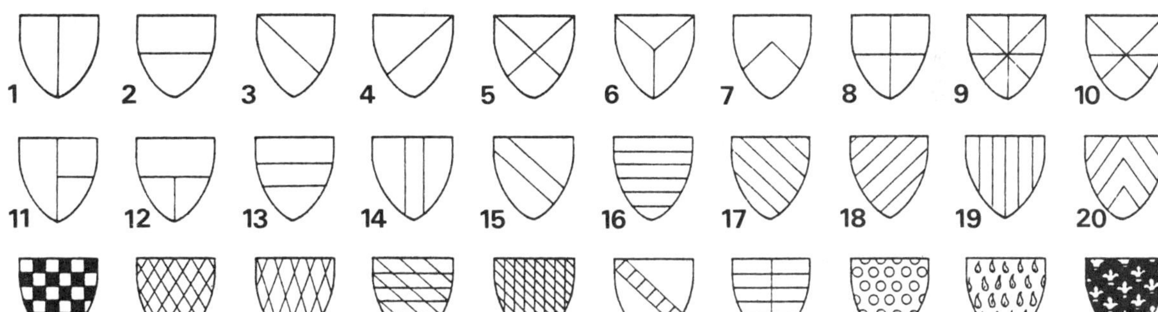

1 Per pale
2 Per fess
3 Per bend
4 Per bend sinister
5 Per saltire
6 Per pall
7 Per chevron
8 Per cross
9 Gyronny (8 piece)
10 Gyronny (6 piece)
11 Per pale sinister half per fess
12 Per fess per pale
13 Bar in fess
14 Bar in pale
15 Bar in bend
16 Barry
17 Bendy
18 Bendy sinister
19 Paly
20 Chevronny
21 Checky
22 Lozengy
23 Fusily
24 Barry bendy
25 Paly bendy
26 Company
27 Per pale and barry
28 Bezanty
29 Goutty
30 Semy de lys

CHARGES

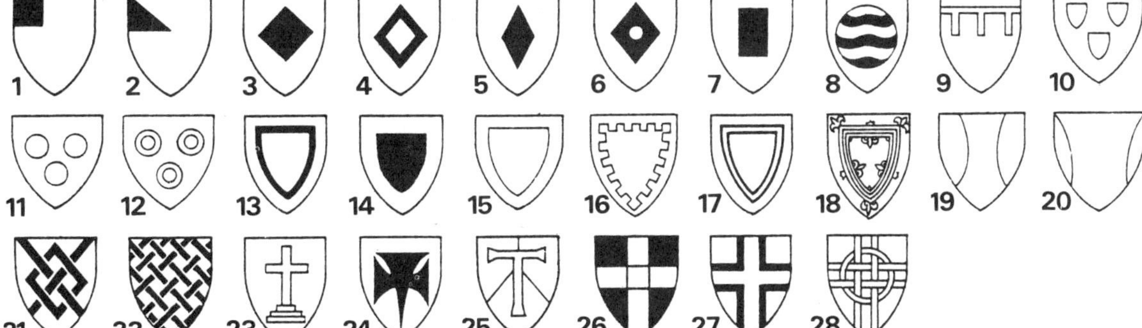

1 Canton
2 Gyron
3 Lozenge
4 Mascle
5 Fusil
6 Rustre
7 Billet
8 Rounded barry wavy
9 Label
10 Inescutcheon
11 Roundel
12 Annulet
13 Orle
14 Escutcheon
15 Bordure
16 Bordure embattled
17 Double treasure
18 Double treasure flory and counter flory
19 Flaunches
20 Flasques
21 Fret
22 Fretty
23 Calvary cross
24 Formy fitchy cross
25 Tau or St Anthony cross
26 Quarter pierced cross
27 Voided cross
28 Parted or Fretty cross

Ornamental devices

3225

Heraldic devices, originally marks of identification, became classic decorative features on architecture, furniture, pottery, silverware, cutlery, linen, and other personal items. Illustrated here are some of the more common devices and their names.

FIGURES

1 Lion rampant
2 Lion statant
3 Lion rampant guardant
4 Lion passant
5 Lion statant
6 Lion passant guardant
7 Lion sejant
8 Lion sejant rampant
9 Lion couchant
10 Lion salient
11 Lion coward
12 Lion queue fourchée
13 Demi-lion
14 Lion's head
15 Lion's face
16 Lion's paw couped
17 Stag at aze
18 Stag trippant
19 Stag at speed
20 Stag's head cabossed
21 Leopard's face
22 Boar rampant
23 Boar's head couped
24 Horse rampant
25 Bear's head couped
26 Dog rampant
27 Martlet
28 Pelican
29 Eagle displayed
30 Two headed eagle
31 Vol
32 Griffin
33 Wyvern
34 Dragon
35 Serpent nowed
36 Serpent vorant
37 Cockatrice
38 Fish hauriant
39 Dolphin
40 Two dolphins
41 Escallop
42 Garb
43 Fir trees eradicated
44 Oak tree on mount
45 Seiren
46 Mermaid
47 Triquetra
48 Appaumée
49 Patera
50 Bacranium

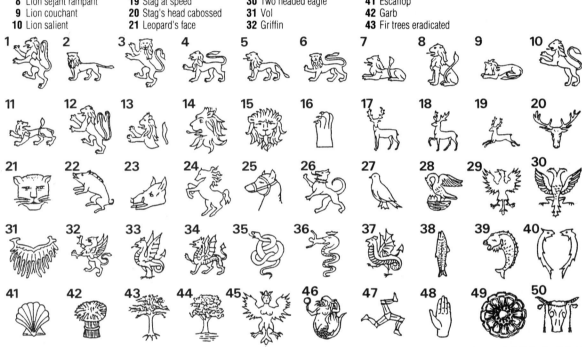

CROSSES AND OTHER SYMBOLS

1 Greek cross
2 Latin cross
3 Tau cross
4 Quadrate cross
5 Patriarchal cross/ Cross of Lorraine
6 Pointed cross
7 Fourchée cross
8 St Andrew's cross
9 Double cross
10 Forked cross
11 Papal cross
12 Cross crosslet
13 Cross moline
14 Cross recercellée
15 Cross fleuretteé
16 Cross pommée
17 Cross patée
18 Maltese cross
19 Cross cramponée
20 Cross botonée
21 Fylfot
22 Cross avellane
23 Cross potent
24 Cross fimbriated
25 Fivefold cross
26 Crescent
27 Increscent
28 Decrescent
29 Mullet
30 Star
31 Mullet pierced
32 Estoile
33 Trefoil slipped
34 Quatrefoil
35 Cinquefoil
36 Rose-en-soleil
37 Fleur-de-lis
38 Catherine wheel
39 Caltrap
40 Bowen knot
41 Bourchier knot
42 Stafford knot
43 Heneage knot
44 Wake knot
45 Acanthus

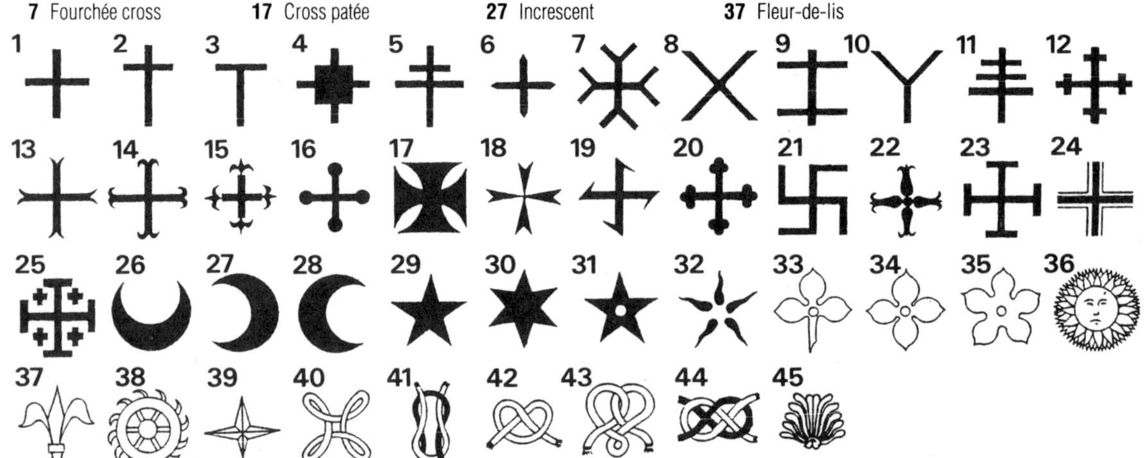

331 TIME

Measuring time

3311 The earliest measurements of time were based on the regular cycles of objects in the sky – the cyclical changes from light to darkness caused by the rising and setting of the sun; the observed changes in the phases of the Moon, and the positions of the stars in the night sky.

Early devices for measuring time included the sundial, which uses the shadows thrown by the Sun, and candles marked with lines spaced at regular intervals. The first clocks, mechanical devices for measuring time, appeared in early medieval times. By the 18th century clocks had been devised that could tell the time to the minute. Modern quartz-based clocks are accurate to within 60 seconds in a year.

How time is divided

3312 The 24-hour clock in worldwide use today is based on the rotation of the Earth, which divides time into regular, roughlty 12-hour cycles of light and dark. The Babylonians first divided thses cycles into days, recording a 24-hour day.

Early peoples also observed the successive changes in the phases of the Moon in a cycle lasting approximately $29^1/2$ days, or a month. By observing the changes in position of the Sun relative to the stars at sunset and just before dawn, they deduced that the Sun moves eastward around the sky in a cycle of seasons lasting $365^1/4$ days, or a year.

Divisions of time

Second	
Minute	60 seconds
Hour	60 minutes
Day	24 hours
Week	7 days
Fortnight	2 weeks
Month	varies between 28 and 31 days
Year	$365^1/4$ days; 52 weeks; 12 months
Decade	10 years
Century	100 years
Millennium	1,000 years

Exact divisions of time

hr=hour; min=minute; sec=second

1 mean solar day: 24 hr 3 min 56.555 sec
1 sidereal day: 23 hr 56 min 4.091 sec
1 solar, tropical, or equinoctial year: 365.2422 days
1 sidereal year: 365.2564 days
1 synodic (lunar) month: 29.5306 days
1 sidereal month: 27.3217 days
1 lunar year: 354.3672 days (12 synodic months)

Periods of time

Semidiurnal	twice a day
Diurnal	daily
Semiweekly	twice a week
Biweekly	twice a week; every two weeks
Triweekly	three times a week; every three weeks
Bimonthly	twice a month; every two months
Trimonthly	every three months
Semiannual	every six months
Biannual	twice a year (not necessarily at exactly half-year intervals)
Annual	yearly
Perennial	occurring year after year
Biennial	every two years
Triennial	every three years
Quadrennial	every four years
Quinquennial	every five years
Sexennial	every six years
Septennial	every seven years
Octennial	every eight years
Novennial	every nine years
Decennial	every ten years
Undecennial	every 11 years
Duodecennial	every 12 years
Quindecennial	every 15 years
Vicennial	every 20 years
Tricennial	every 30 years
Semicentennial	every 50 years
Centennial	every 100 years
Sesquicentennial	every 150 years
Bicentennial	every 200 years
Quadricentennial	every 400 years
Quincentennial	every 500 years
Millennial	every 1,000 years

Time around the world

3313 Each day – that is, one rotation of the Earth – lasts 24 hours, but it does not begin or end everywhere together. As the Earth spins, different places around the world are at different points in the day–night cycle. For convenience, in 1884, the world was divided into international time zones. The zones are based on 15-degree divisions of longitude, but the zones are not all equal in size, as political and geographical divisions are accommodated.

Greenwich Mean Time is the standard on which times in the zones are based. In the 19th century the British government decreed that standardization of time throughout the British Isles was necessary because of problems arising from the use of local time. So today, Standard Time, as it is called, is measured in zones that run north-south, starting from the Prime Meridian that runs through Greenwich in London.

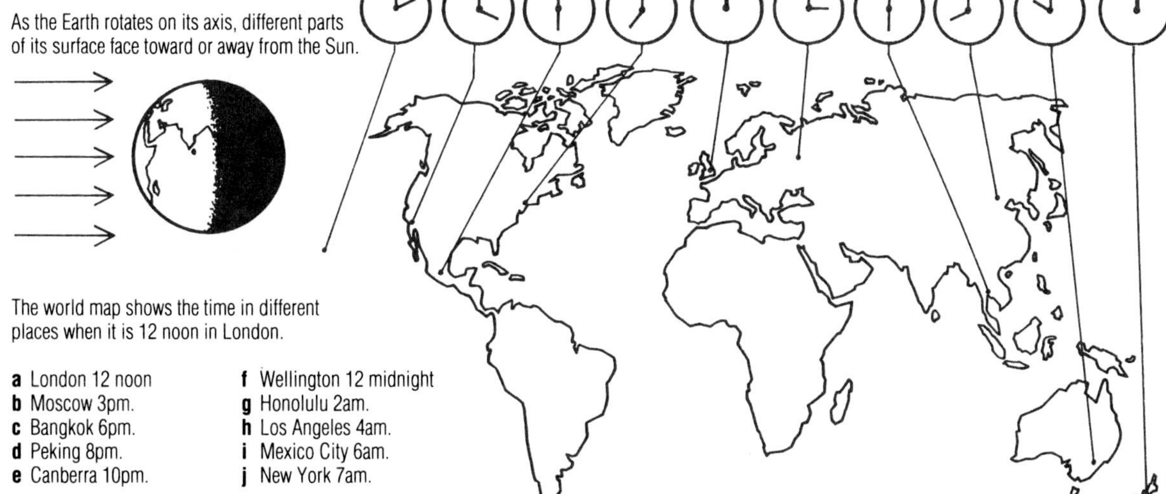

As the Earth rotates on its axis, different parts of its surface face toward or away from the Sun.

The world map shows the time in different places when it is 12 noon in London.

a London 12 noon
b Moscow 3pm.
c Bangkok 6pm.
d Peking 8pm.
e Canberra 10pm.
f Wellington 12 midnight
g Honolulu 2am.
h Los Angeles 4am.
i Mexico City 6am.
j New York 7am.

World time zones

3314 Times around the world are fixed in time zones one hour, and somtimes one half hour apart. These time zones are centered on the Prime Meridian running through Greenwich in London. Times can be said to be so many hours behind or ahead of Greenwich Mean Time (GMT). For example California's time zone is eight hours behind GMT (behind as the Earth rotates eastward). Therefore, when it is midnight in London, it is still 4 p.m. in California. On the line of longitude running 180 degrees from Greenwich on the other side of the Earth, the GMT -12 hours zone meets the GMT +12 hours zone, creating the International Date Line. At midnight on this line, both the hour and the date change. When you cross this line you go forward, or back, a day.

International Date Line

Prime Meridian

+5 hours +6 +7 +8 +9 +10 +11 ∓12 -11 -10 -9 -8 -7 -6 -5 -4 -3 -2 -1 0 +1 +2 +3 +4 +5 hours

US time zones

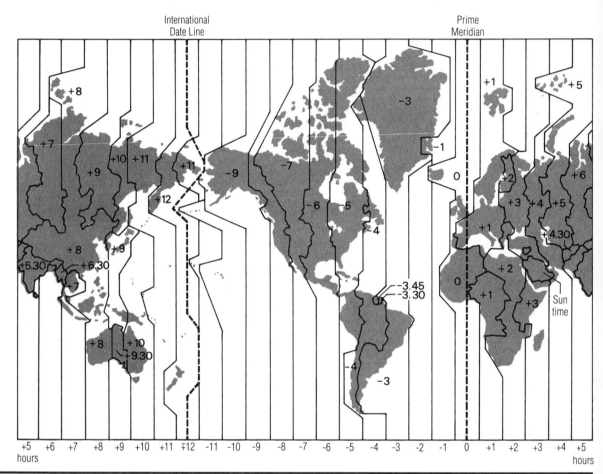

3315 The contiguous states of the US straddles four time zones.
1 Pacific time
2 Mountain time
3 Central time
4 Eastern time

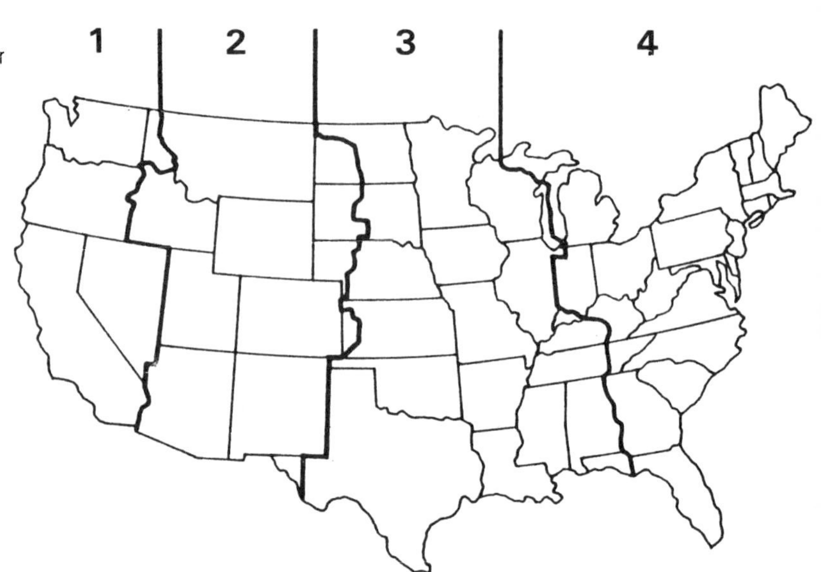

332 DISTANCE

World city distances

3321 Given in this table are the shortest surface distances between some of the world's major cities. These distances – called "Great Circle" distances – are measured on a globe and are shorter than actual journey distances using land, sea, or air routes.

Distance in miles

	Berlin	Bombay	Cape Town	Darwin	London	Los Angeles	Mexico City	Moscow	New York	Beijing	Quebec	Rio de Janeiro	Rome	Tokyo	Wellington
Berlin	—														
Bombay	3 910														
Cape Town	5 977	5 134													
Darwin	8 036	4 503	6 947												
London	574	4 462	6 005	8 598											
Los Angeles	5 782	8 701	9 969	7 835	5 439										
Mexico City	6 037	9 722	8 511	9 081	5 541	1 542									
Moscow	996	3 131	6 294	7 046	1 549	6 068	6 688								
New York	3 961	7 794	7 081	9 959	3 459	2 451	2 085	4 662							
Beijing	4 567	2 964	8 045	3 728	5 054	6 250	7 733	3 597	6 823						
Quebec	3 583	7 371	7 857	9 724	3 101	2 579	2 454	4 242	439	6 423					
Rio de Janeiro	6 114	8 257	3 769	9 960	5 772	6 296	4 770	7 179	4 820	10 768	5 125				
Rome	734	3 843	5 249	8 190	887	6 326	6 353	1 474	4 273	5 047	3 943	5 684			
Tokyo	5 538	4 188	9 071	3 367	5 938	5 470	7 035	4 650	6 735	1 307	6 417	11 535	6 124		
Wellington	11 265	7 677	7 019	3 310	11 682	6 714	6 899	10 279	8 946	6 698	9 228	7 349	11 524	5 760	—

US city distances

3322

Distance in miles

	Atlanta	Baltimore	Birmingham	Boston	Buffalo	Chicago	Cleveland	Dallas	Detroit	El Paso	Houston	Indianapolis	Kansas City	Las Vegas	Los Angeles	Louisville	Memphis	Miami	Milwaukee	Nashville	New Orleans	New York	Oklahoma City	Philadelphia	Phoenix	Pittsburgh	Reno	San Francisco	Santa Fe	Washington, DC
Washington, DC	650	40	755	435	380	705	365	1400	525	2045	1430	565	1050	2440	2725	600	905	1115	785	685	1115	230	1375	135	2340	230	2640	2875	1870	—
San Francisco	2595	2870	2425	3190	2740	2195	2550	1785	2475	1210	1950	2325	1890	580	400	2430	2175	3160	2190	2400	2295	3020	1690	2940	790	2645	220	—	1200	2875
New York	880	185	985	210	360	845	475	1625	650	2205	1655	720	1205	2580	2875	755	1130	1340	935	910	1340	—	1525	90	2500	365	2785	3020	2035	230
New Orleans	510	1150	355	1550	1245	945	1075	505	1070	1115	360	825	830	1745	1920	710	395	875	1000	530	—	1340	680	1225	1520	1080	2195	2295	1140	1115
Miami	665	1140	780	1565	1485	1400	1335	1370	1380	2005	1220	1220	1530	2555	2820	1080	1030	—	1460	930	875	1340	1555	1250	2410	1240	3000	3160	2010	1115
Los Angeles	2260	2720	2085	3085	2640	2120	2415	1425	2400	805	1545	2150	1610	285	—	2175	1835	2820	2175	2025	1920	2875	1350	2795	385	2510	475	400	860	2725
Dallas	820	1435	665	1805	1395	960	1210	—	1180	625	245	900	495	1240	1425	840	470	1370	1050	680	505	1625	210	1510	1020	1255	1690	1785	640	1400
Chicago	725	690	680	990	530	—	345	960	275	1530	1100	190	510	1790	2120	305	545	1400	90	460	945	845	840	770	1785	470	1940	2195	1315	705
Boston	1100	400	1195	—	455	990	630	1805	700	2410	1895	915	1420	2790	3085	960	1335	1565	1060	1115	1550	210	1655	300	2655	575	2960	3190	2235	435
Atlanta	—	670	155	1100	955	725	700	820	730	1455	840	550	815	2025	2260	410	420	665	805	250	510	880	905	790	1875	710	2475	2595	1445	650

341 COMPUTERS

(In order to fully understand computers, the reader should also consult the MATH section within which the BINARY SYSTEM is explained.)

A computer is an electronic device that processes information.
1 Information is fed in (input).
2 Information is processed by the computer.
3 Information is fed out again (output).

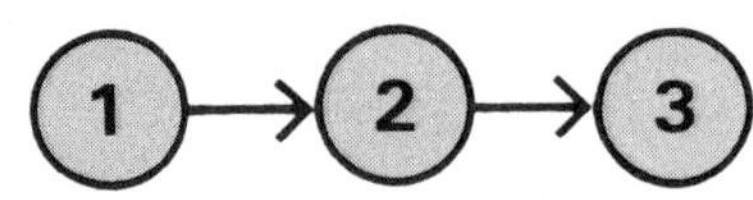

In mathematics, the system of binary notation uses only two digits. For this reason, it is used to operate computers, as the standard "0" and "1" digits are interpreted by the computer as "on" and "off" switches, and these are used to control electrical signals.

Types of computer

3411

Computers are classified according to their size and capacity.
Supercomputers These are used in research laboratories. They are very fast with large memories.
Mainframe computers These are large, powerful, and require special air-conditioned rooms. They can handle hundreds of users at a time.
Minicomputers These are about the size of a filing cabinet. They can handle a number of tasks at once.
Microcomputers (personal computers) These are small computers based on a single microprocessor chip. Most can only be used by one person at a time.
Word processors These are small computers designed specifically to handle words. They cannot do as much as microcomputers.

Hardware

3412

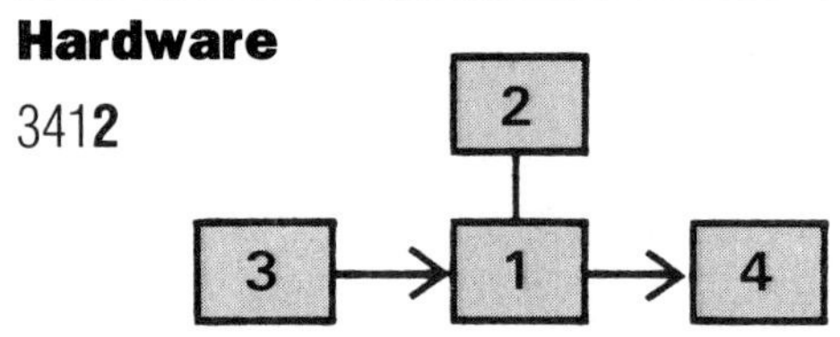

The tangible components of a computer system are referred to as "hardware". Normally there are four components to a computer: a central processing unit (**1**), a memory bank (**2**), equipment to feed information into the machine (**3**), and equipment to receive the output (**4**).

A common office computer set-up
1 Computer (the central processing unit housing the memory). This also has a video screen called a visual display unit (VDU).
2 The keyboard, for inputting information.
3 A printer.

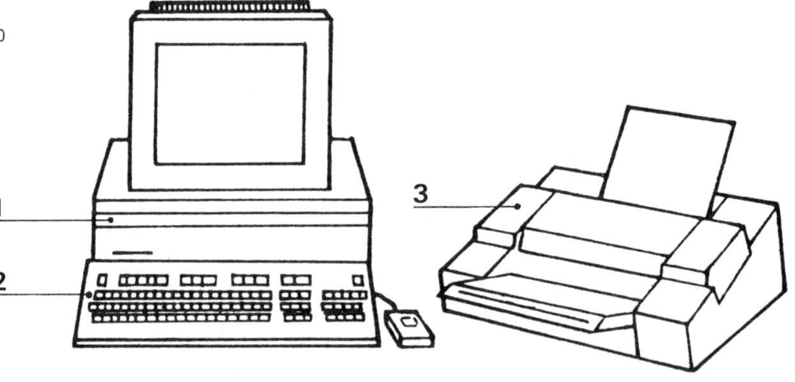

The central processing unit (CPU)
This is the control center of the computer and contains computer chips. Each chip (**1**) is like a tiny powerhouse: it houses a piece of silicon in which electrical circuits are embedded.
Inside a computer chip
1 Each computer chip is printed with a circuit. Different circuits control different operations within the computer.
2 Within each circuit there are microscopic switches. These turn electric currents on and off and convert them into a series of electrical pulses (bytes). It is these pulses that the computer uses to carry out its work.

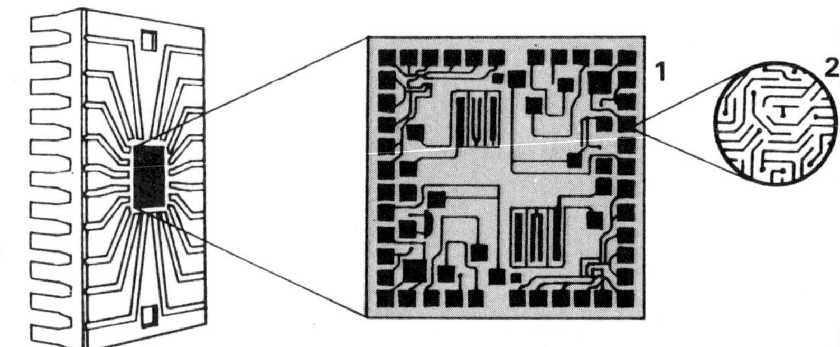

Memory
Computers have two memories: a temporary memory (called RAM, meaning Random Access Memory) and a permanent memory (called ROM, meaning Read Only Memory). The computer can read information in its permanent ROM memory, but cannot store information there. The computer can store information in the temporary RAM memory, but this is wiped clear when the computer is turned off.

continued

Hardware continued

3412 **Putting information into the machine**

1 Early computers read punched holes in a piece of paper or card, converting their information into binary code. Although punched cards are still used today, most office and home computers use a variety of other methods to input their information.
2 Keyboard. This is a typewriter keyboard, but instead of printing directly onto a sheet of paper, the computer sends electrical signals from the keys to the central processing unit.
3 A "Mouse". These are hand-held devices that can be moved about to operate a cursor on the VDU.
4 Electronic pad and pencil. These are used to draw images the computer can read.
5 Microphone for inputting sounds.
6 Joystick. Often used in computer games to input information about the direction a player wants to move.
7 Laser pen. Used to touch sensitive areas of the VDU.
8 Scanner. A device like a photocopier, but instead of producing a duplicated image on paper, it sends the image to the computer's central processing unit and then the VDU.

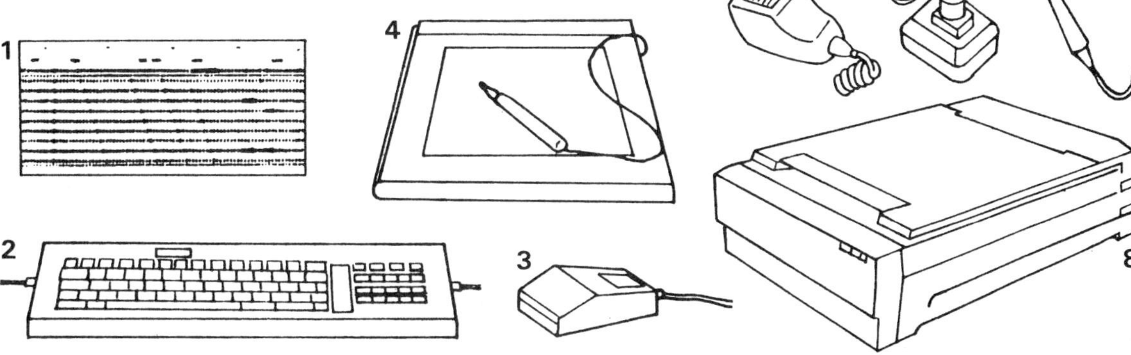

Storing information
Computer information can be stored in a variety of ways.
a In the memory of the machine.
b On a cassette disk.
c On hard disk (for large amounts of information).
d On a soft "floppy" disk (for smaller amounts of information).
e On reams of paper or punched cards.
f When disks are used, they are inserted into a disk drive, from which the computer can read it.

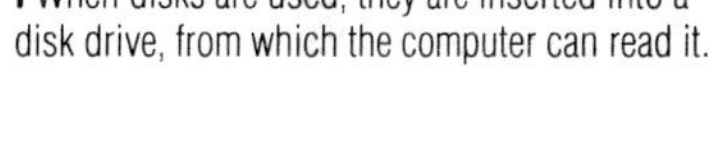

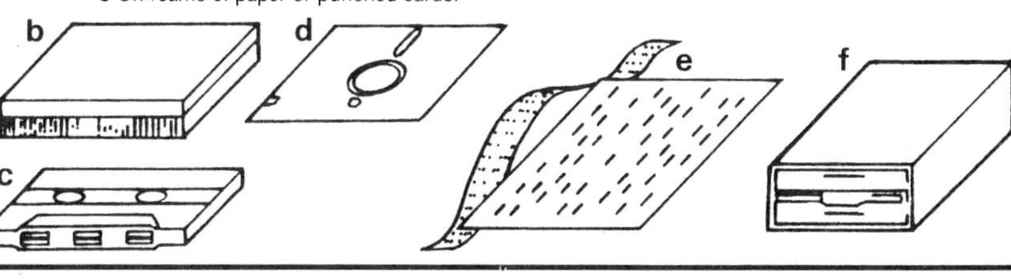

Software

3413 Computers work by following instructions. The set of instructions that tells a computer what to do is called a program (**1**). Just as some people can speak and understand more than one language, so can computers. Programs can be written in a variety of languages, such as COBOL, BASIC, and PASCAL.

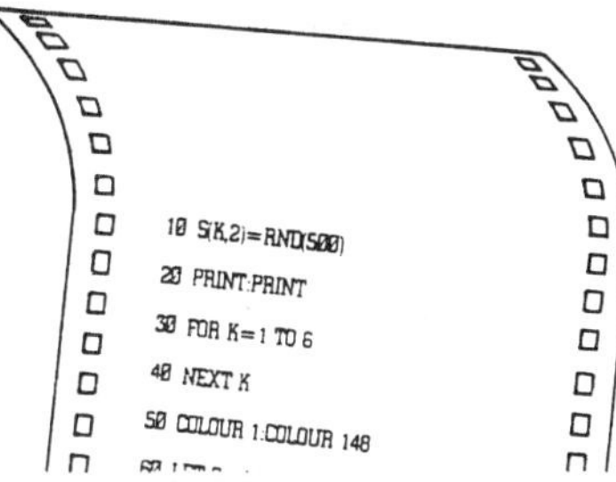

10 S(K,2)=RND(500)
20 PRINT:PRINT
30 FOR K=1 TO 6
40 NEXT K
50 COLOUR 1:COLOUR 148

"Software" refers to all the programs that can be run on one computer.
Sometimes, programs often contain errors – the computer does not follow the rules of the program, or the program does not perform the desired task. These errors are called bugs.

Printers

3414 Information from a computer can be printed to produce what is called a hard copy. There are many types of printer. Some print only text (**1**); others are designed to print images, such as charts, drawings, and diagrams (**2**). Printers that print charts and diagrams are often called plotters.

342 **COMPUTER GLOSSARY**

ALU (Arithmetic and Logic Unit) Circuits in CPU where calculations and comparisons carried out.
analog computer Machine that works on data represented by some physical quantity which varies continuously.
ASCII American Standard Code for Information Interchange. Eight-bit binary representation of letters and numbers.
backing store Programs or data saved outside computer on tape or disk.
bar code Code of black and white stripes that store information and are scanned by laser beams.
BASIC Beginners' All Purpose Symbolic Instruction Code.
baud rate Speed at which a bit goes from one part of computer to another. One baud is one bit

continued

Computer glossary continued

342

per second.
binary Numeration system based on digits 0 and 1.
bit Short for binary digit, either 1 or 0.
bug Mistake in a program.
bus Tracks along which data is moved about the computer.
byte Equal to eight bits. Computer memories are measured in terms of thousands of bytes.
cassette Cheap and popular way of storing programs.
character A number, letter, or symbol.
chip Tiny bit of silicon on which electronic circuits are printed.
COBOL Common Business Oriented Language.
command Instruction to computer, usually typed at a keyboard, that the computer obeys immediately.
compatibility Computers are compatible with one another if they can understand the same program.
computer Versatile electronic data-processing device with at least three components. Input and output is digital or analog, and processing involves storage, control, and arithmetical operations.
computer language Language in which operator "talks" to computer.
CPU Central processing unit. Circuits controlling all parts of computer where calculations occur.
data Information for computer to work on. Also, information and results from computer.
database A collection of related data specially organized to be retrieved quickly.
dialect Any of several versions of BASIC using slightly different commands.
digit Any of figures 0 to 9.
digital computer Computer working with data represented in digital form, usually binary 0s and 1s.
disk Flat plate, covered in magnetic material, which stores data on concentric tracks. Hard disks are internal and have greater storage capacity than floppy disks, which are external.
disk drive Machine that puts data on to, or reads it from, floppy disk.
error message Message flashed up on screen to tell the operator an error has occurred, and, sometimes, what and where it is.
flowchart Boxes or shapes drawn on paper and linked by lines to show order of a set of events.
Fortran High-level programming language used mainly by scientists and mathematicians.
gate Arrangement of transistors that works on pulses traveling through computer's circuits.
graphics Pictures made with a computer.
graphics tablet Input device which, by sensing pressure, translates position of pen or pointer on a pad into digital signal for computer, allowing user to draw shapes onto the screen and into memory.
hard copy Programs or data printed out by computer using printer.
hardware Computer and its internal mechanism, or piece of related equipment, such as disk drive or printer.
hexadecimal system Counting system, based on 16 digits (0 to 9 and A to F), useful for low-level programming.
input Any information or instructions that are fed into computer.
input device Machine with which to give information to a computer.
integrated circuit Minute electrical circuits containing thousands of electronic components on tiny chip of silicon.
interface Circuits converting computer signals into a form other electronic equipment can read.
interpreter Program checking, translating, and carrying out a written program one statement at a time.
joysticks Sticks for moving lights or shapes around screens.
keyboard Arrangement of keys used for putting instructions or information into computer.
kilobyte (k) 1 kilobyte =1,024 bytes.
light pen Light-sensitive input device with which one can "draw" on a VDU.
list Program written, typed, or printed out on paper.
load To put program into computer's memory from cassette tape or disk.
LOGO Simple computer language useful for drawing shapes.
machine code Pattern of electronic pulse signals which computer uses to do all its work.
magnetic tape Used to store data and programs.
mainframe computer Large computer with many terminals.
memory Store for data or program instructions, made up of main store and its backing store.
microcomputer Computer that uses microprocessor chip for its central processor.
microprocessor Computer held on a single chip.
minicomputer Small-sized computer with limited memory and a few peripheral devices.
mnemonics Code consisting of abbreviated instructions.
modem Short for modulator/demodulator. Converts computer signals into form that can travel down telephone lines.
monitor Part of ROM which holds instructions telling CPU how to operate.
motherboard Circuit board into which you can slot other PCBs.
mouse Moveable desktop device with ball underneath which relays speed and direction, thus guiding cursor across screen.
network System of computers, sometimes with other peripherals, linked together to share information.
output Any information the computer displays or prints.
output device Machine showing information processed by computer.
PASCAL Named after Blaise Pascal. High-level, general-purpose programming language.
PCB Printed circuit board. Board inside computer holding all chips and other components.
peripherals Equipment you can attach to computer, such as extra screens, printers, or plotters.
pixels Tiny areas (dots) making up computer graphic picture.
plotter Device for drawing two-dimensional graphic output from computer on paper.
port Socket on micro where you plug in lead linking it to another device.
printer Output device which prints results on paper.
program List of instructions telling computer what to do.
programmer Person who writes computer programs.
programming language Language, such as BASIC, in which program is written so that computer will understand it.
prompt Message that computer gives to its operator. May be symbol, sentence, or colored light.
RAM Random access memory. Temporary memory holding material lost if computer switched off.
robot Computer-controlled device performing fine, sophisticated movements depending on program.
ROM Read only memory. Permanent store of data and programs.
run Command to tell computer to carry out program. Can also imply loading, execution and output of whole package.
save Store a program outside computer, usually on tape or disk.
scanner Input device collecting data by recording brightness values for small areas as it moves across a surface.
screen resolution Number of pixel groups on screen which computer can control. Determines how sharp an image is produced on VDU.
sensor Device for sensing and measuring light, pressure, or temperature, and sending information back to computer.
silicon Chemical element from which chips are made.
software Computer programs.
supercomputer Fast computer with large memory, as used in research laboratories.
string Set of characters.
syntax error Mistake in programming language.
synthesizer Equipment or circuitry producing musical notes or sounds through loudspeakers.
terminal Device connected to computer allowing input and output of data.
transistor Semiconductor used as amplifier or switching device.
VDU Visual display unit. Screen, similar to TV screen, designed specially for a computer.
word processor Computer system designed to handle text. Faster, more flexible than typewriter.

411 THE FIRST HUMANS

Classification

4111 Increasing brain size, remodeled teeth, and hips and lower limbs redesigned for walking are major hallmarks of the human tribe, *Hominini.* This tribe holds at least two genera: the extinct *Australopithecus* ("southern ape"), and *Homo* ("man"). Some scientists add *Ramapithecus* (an early ape).

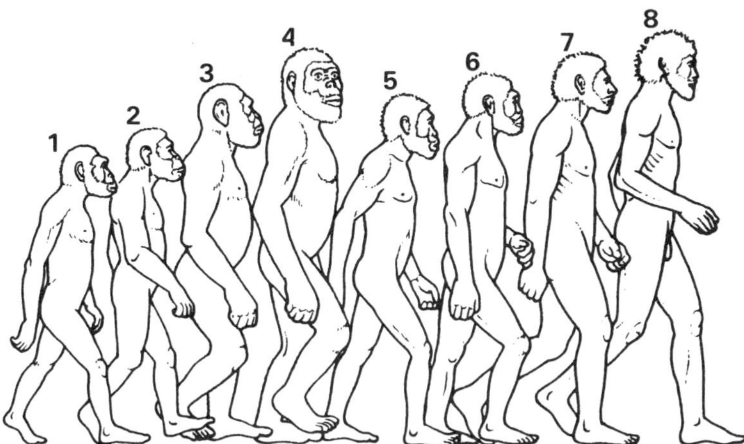

AUSTRALOPITHECUS
Australopithecines – the so-called "ape men" – evolved in Africa 4 million years ago, or even earlier. They evidently came from a dryopithecine ape ancestor, yet to be identified. There arose three or four species (experts disagree). By 2 million years ago one probably gave rise to the first species of our own genus, *Homo.* Both genera endured side by side for another million years before the last australopithecines died out, possibly exterminated in competition with its more intelligent ancestor.

1 *Australopithecus afarensis* ("the southern ape of Afar"), the first known "ape man" probably evolved from a late dryopithecine (an extinct ape), perhaps 4 million years ago. Its name came from sites in Ethiopia's northern Afar Triangle.
2 *Australopithecus africanus* ("the southern ape of Africa") lived perhaps from 3 to 1 million years ago. It probably evolved from *Australopithecus afarensis.*
3 *Australopithecus robustus* Once called *Parenthropus* ("beside man") this was a "robust southern ape" larger and more strongly built than *Australopithecus africanus.* Some have argued that "robust" fossils were just males and *africanus* fossils were females of a single species, but most experts reject that notion.
4 *Australopithecus boisei* ("the boise southern ape") was reputedly the biggest, burliest australopithecine, named after British businessman Charles Boise who helped fund fossil hunts that led to its discovery in East Africa in 1959. Its former name, *Zinjanthropus,* means "East African man," and it inhabited that region from 2.5 million to 1 million years ago.

HOMO
Homo features a relatively bigger brain than *Australopithecus,* thus a bigger brain case, but smaller, less projecting face, and relatively smaller cheek teeth but larger front teeth, with an open U-shaped tooth row. Arms are shorter in relation to legs, and hip bones permit both bipedal walking and giving birth to babies with large heads.
5 *Homo habilis* Known as "handy man" this was reputedly the first known species of our genus, *Homo.* This species lived about 2 million and 1.5 million years ago, perhaps longer. Possibly it evolved from *Australopithecus afarensis* or *africanus.* Artifacts found near its bones suggest it made basic bone tools, built simple shelters, gathered plant foods, scavenged big meaty limbs from carcasses or creatures killed by carnivores, and hunted small and maybe larger game. It probably gave rise to *Homo erectus.*
6 *Homo erectus* This was "upright man." It had a bigger brain and body than *Homo habilis,* its likely ancestor, and in many ways resembled a strongly-built version of its direct descendant, modern man. They lived about 1.6 million to 200,000 years ago, arguably longer. Improved technology including standard toolkits, big game hunting, use of fire, and improved building methods put *erectus* far ahead of other hominids.
7 *Homo sapiens neanderthalensis* This takes its name from fossils found in the Neander Valley, near Dusseldorf, Germany. The Neanderthal subspecies evolved from an archaic form of *Homo sapiens* perhaps as much as 200,000 years ago. Their physique and improved technology made some of these people probably the first hominids to endure the rigors of winter in a cold climate. Also, Neanderthal rituals seem to show a new level of sensibility and human self awareness.
8 *Homo sapiens sapiens* This is a subspecies known as fully modern man. It crops up widely in fossil record in 40,000-year-old sites as far apart as Borneo and Europe.

Evolution

4112 **1** Humans from australopithecines
2 Humans not from australopithecines

Alternatives of family trees show australopithecine, human, and African ape lineages and also how humans may have developed from australopithecines (**1**) or not from australopithecines (**2**). Estimates of some species' durability vary widely. Dots show unknown ancestors. Numerals represent time in millions of years ago.

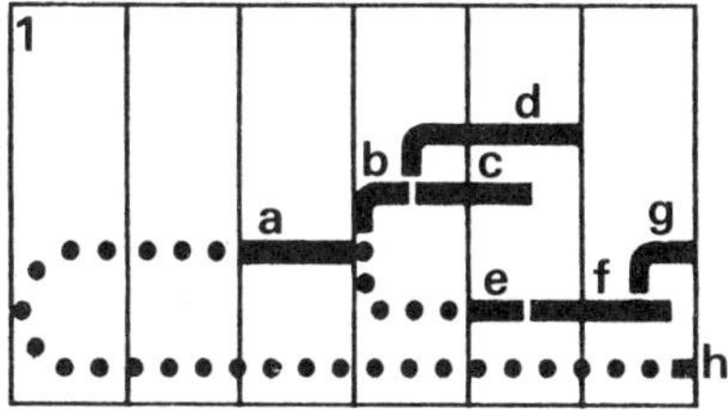

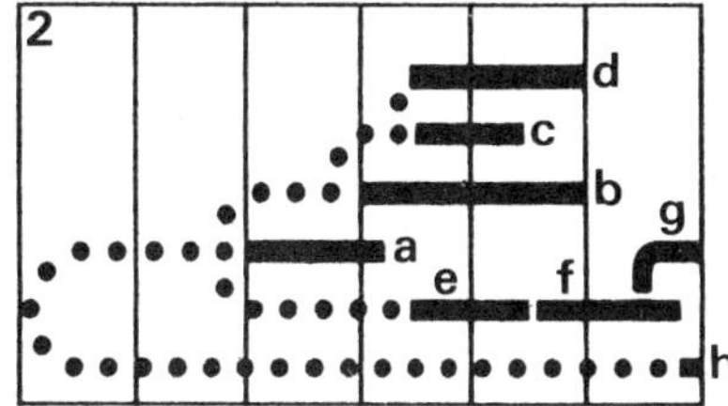

a *Australopithecus afarensis*
b *Australopithecus africanus*
c *Australopithecus robustus*
d *Australopithecus boisei*
e *Homo habilis*
f *Homo erectus*
g *Homo sapiens*
h African ape

412 THE FIRST TECHNOLOGIES

LOWER PALEOLITHIC
(3 million years BC–70,000 BC)
Abbevillian culture Rudimentary stone hand axes.
Acheulian culture Hand axes of stone, bone, wood (**1**), simple clothing.

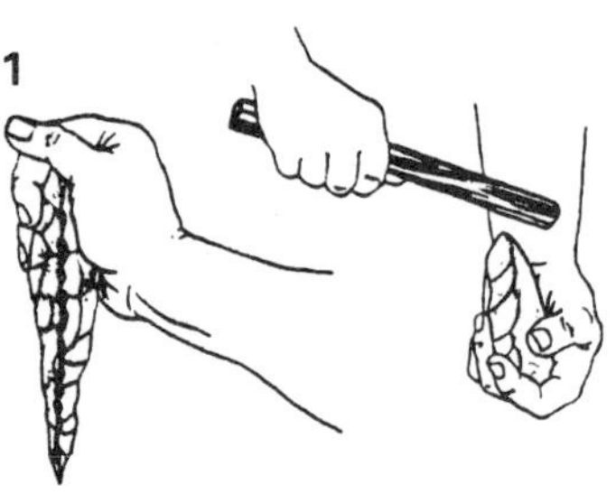

MIDDLE PALEOLITHIC
(100,000 BC–35,000 BC)
Mousterian culture Flaked stone tools (**2**), stone-tipped spears, clothing.

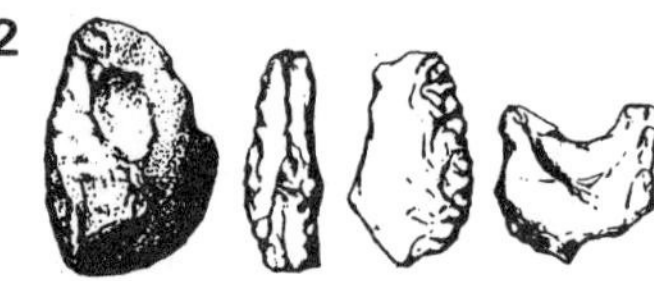

UPPER PALEOLITHIC (40,000 BC–12,000 BC)
Lower Perigordian culture Wooden hammer and punch, fine flint blades.
Aurignacian culture Beveled flint tool (burin), carved bone tools, and weapons.
Upper Perigordian culture Straight-backed flint knife, carved spearheads (**3**).

Solutrean culture Pressure-flaked flint tools, fine-pointed weapons.
Magdalenian Eyed needles (**4**), barbed spearheads (**5**), saw, awl, ornamented, and sewn leather clothing (**6**).

MESOLITHIC (12,000 BC–8000 BC)
Mesolithic culture Bow and arrow, nets, fishhooks and fish traps, coracle, raft, canoe (**7**), mattok, textiles , adz (**8**). Domestication of animals, beginnings of agriculture, development of walled settlements.

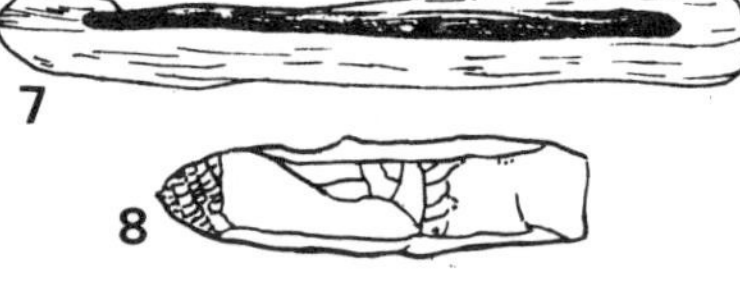

NEOLITHIC (9000–6000)
Plough, irrigation, improved farming implements (**9**), domestication of horses, baskets (**10**), vaulted bread ovens, coil-built pottery, and early copper smelting.

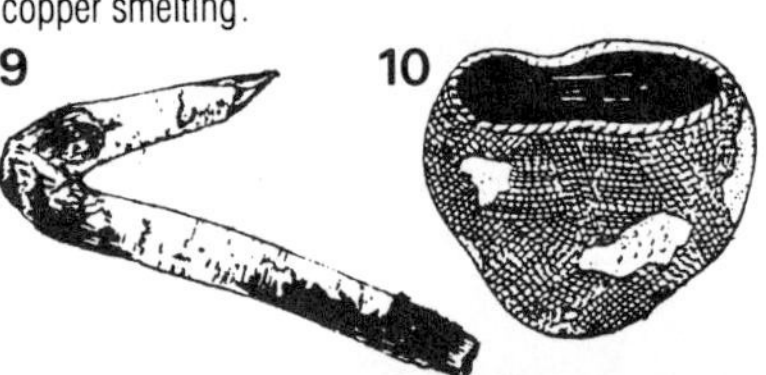

BRONZE AGE (4500 BC–1200 BC)
Sumerian civilization Invention of wheel (**11**), oars, making of bricks, smelting of copper, making of bronze, cuneiform (wedge-shaped) writing (**12**), invention of the arch and vault in construction.
Egyptian civilization Invention of calendar.

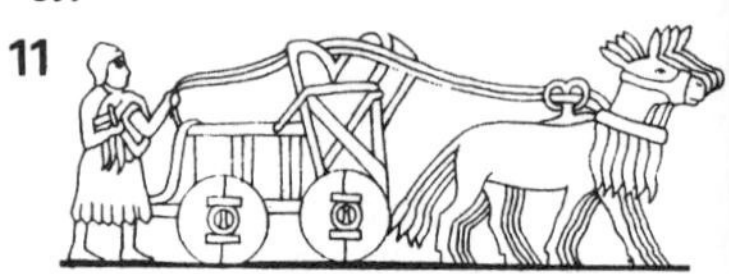

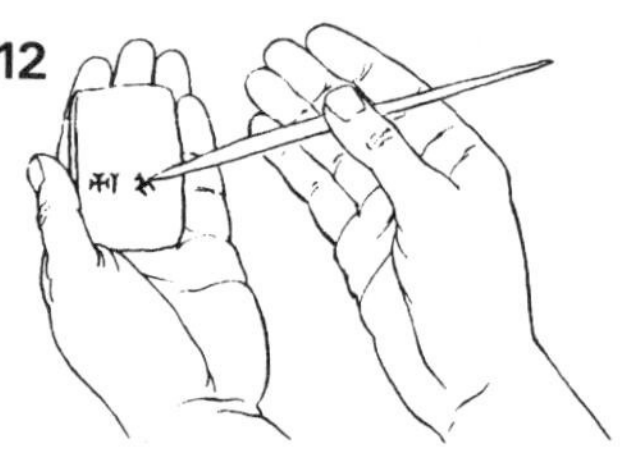

IRON AGE (1200 BC forward)
Hittite civilization Smelting and carbonizing iron supercede bronze for farming tools and weapons (**13**).

413 THE FIRST CIVILIZATIONS

1 Sumerian 4000–2000 BC
2 Egyptian 3500 BC–AD 1
3 Minoan 3000–1100 BC
4 Indus Valley civilization 3000–1500 BC
5 Babylonian 2200–550 BC
6 Yang-Shau Dynasty 2000–1500 BC
7 Assyrian 2000–600 BC
8 Shang dynasty c. 1766–c. 1122 BC
9 Greek 1200 BC
10 Etruscan 1200–200 BC
11 Olmec (S. American) 1200–100 BC
12 Zhou Dynasty c. 1122–256 BC
13 Teotihuacán (S. American) c. 100 BC

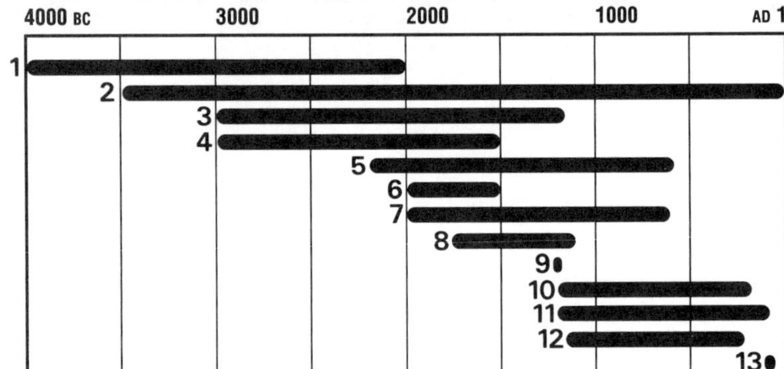

414 WORLD HISTORY CHART

Key dates

3000 BC – AD 1
1 Sumerian cities flourish
2 Egyptians build Great Pyramid
3 Minoan civilization
4 Hammurabi
5 Fall of Troy
6 Birth of Christ

AD 1–1000
7 Roman empire at maximum extent AD 117
8 End of Roman Empire in west AD 476
9 Traditional start of Islam AD 622
10 Emperor Charlemagne AD 771–814
11 Important Viking expeditions AD 840–885

1000–1500
12 Norman Conquest of England 1066
13 Third Crusade 1189–92
14 Genghis Khan 1206–27
15 Black Death in Europe 1348–50
16 Lorenzo de' Medici (of Florence) 1478–92
17 Columbus crosses the Atlantic 1492

1500–1800
18 Reformation started by Luther 1517
19 Queen Elizabeth of England 1558–1603
20 Pilgrims arrive at Cape Cod 1620
21 Thirty Years' War 1618–48
22 Louis XIV of France 1643–1715
23 Frederick the Great of Prussia 1740–86
24 American Independence 1776
25 French Revolution 1789
26 Napoleon, ruler of France 1799–1815

1800–1900
27 Latin American Revolutions 1806–25
28 American Civil War 1861–5

1900–1950
29 World War I 1914–18
30 World War II 1939–45

1950–1990
31 First men on the Moon 1969
32 End of Vietnam War 1973
33 Chernobyl nuclear reactor meltdown 1986
34 Disintegration of USSR 1991

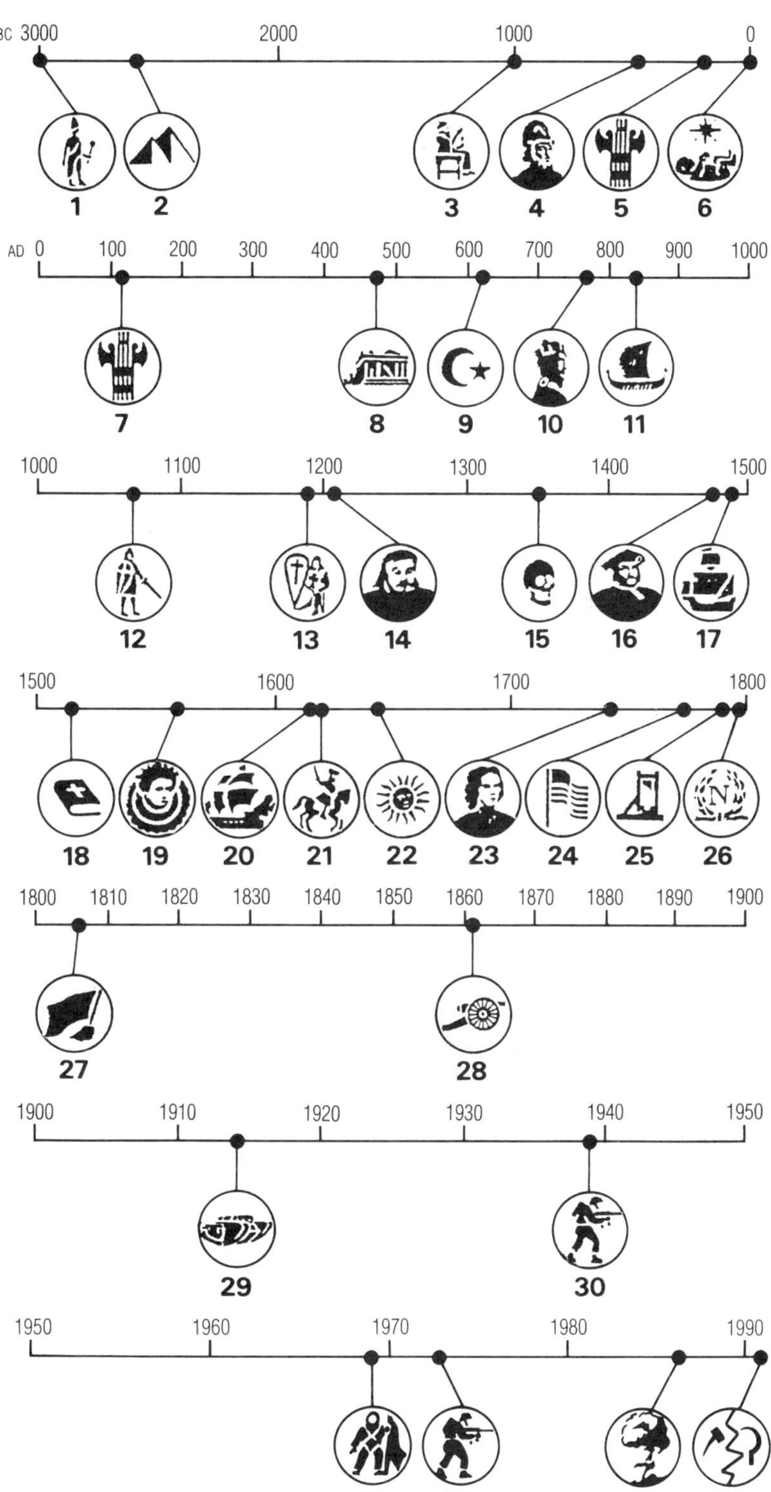

421 EASTERN ANCIENT CIVILIZATIONS

Places

4211

Major sites of early civilizations
1 Nile Valley
2 Mesopotamia
3 Indus Valley
4 Yellow River Valley

Great Wall of China This runs for nearly 1,400 mi (over 10,000 km) and is at least 20 ft (7 m) high. It was built around 215 BC and was constantly repaired, revised, and reconstructed. Six horsemen could ride abreast along it. 25,000 watchtowers kept its garrison in contact.

Silk Road 4,000 mi (6,400 km) trade route between China and the Roman empire.

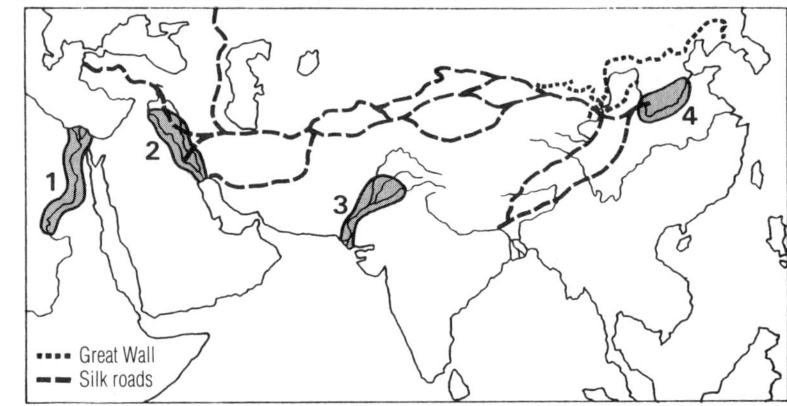

China

4212

c. 2600–1766 BC Yang-Shao and Lungshan cultures. Painted and fired pottery. Silkworm domesticated. Jade mined and carved.
c. 1766–1122 BC Shang dynasty. Bronze weapons, implements, and other objects, including cast vessels. Written documents. Astronomical observations. Mathematics developed.
c. 1122–256 BC Zhou dynasties. Rise of feudal warlords. Partition of country.
c. 400–200 BC Qin dynasty. Empire unified. Great Wall built. Golden Age of philosophy. Irrigation through canals invented. Cast iron weapons and tools.
c. 200 BC–AD 220 Han, Hsin, and later Han dynasties. Military conquests. Power struggles within court. Trade with west, especially Roman empire. Paper invented. Wheelbarrow invented. Power passes to competing warlords.

Major civilizations

1	Shang	c.1766–1122 BC
2	Zhou	1122–256 BC
3	Qin	221–206 BC
4	Han	200 BC–AD 220
5	Tang	618–960
6	Song	960–1279
7	Ming	1368–1644
8	Manchu	1644–1912

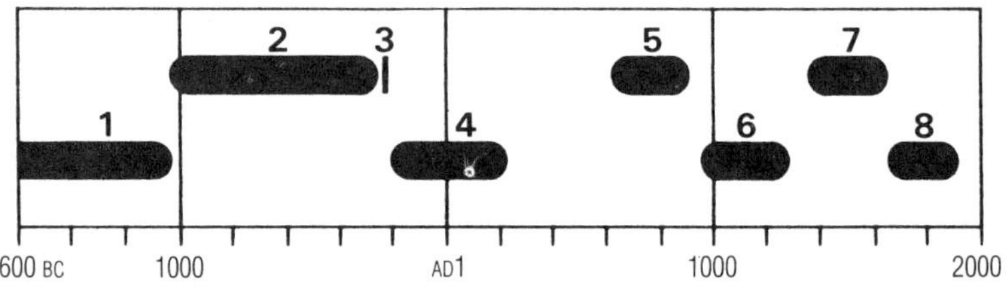

AD 220–589 Empire divided into three kingdoms, then into 16. Barbarian dynasties established in north, absorbed into Chinese culture. Political divisions retard cultural progress.

AD 589–618 Empire reunited. Great Wall reconstructed. Glazed stoneware. Cave temples. Representational paintings and sculptures
AD 618–960 Tang dynasty. Trade expansion. Golden age in arts.

India and Ceylon

4213

c. 2000–1200 BC Aryan people invade and absorb earlier Dravidian and Munda populations. Indus valley (Harrapa) civilization
c. 1200–800 BC Vedic era. Worship of nature gods. Religious and literary culture base with oral rather than written tradition. Agricultural and patriarchal society. Some Aryan inter tribal conflict.
c. 800–550 BC Transitional period. Society divided into three, later four classes, or castes. Doctrinal developments. Numerous petty states in north.
c. 550–320 BC Persian invasion. Invasion by Alexander the Great reaches Punjab. First Sanskrit grammar. Buddhism founded.
c. 320–100 BC Maurya dynasty unites north, extends conquest to most of peninsula. Buddhism developed and exported. Syrian and Greek conquests short-lived.
c. 100 BC–AD 200 Saka, Kushan, and Kanishka invasions. Sunga and Saka rulers. North-western area conquests.
c. AD 200–600 Southern (Pallava) dynasties develop codes for municipal and corporate life. Gupta empire subdues entire area, then succumbs to Hun invasions.

Japan and Korea

4214

c. 4500–1000 BC Early and middle Jomonshiki cultures. Pottery developed.
c. 1000–250 BC Late Jomon culture. First emperor. Chinese culture influential.
c. 250 BC–AD 200 Yaiyoi culture. Development of bronze, then iron weapons and implements. Massive stone monuments. Wet cultivation of rice. Urn burials.
c. AD 200–600 Yamoto (tomb) culture. Wide variety of iron implements. Numerous burial mounds. Buddhism introduced. Embassies to China. Rapid territorial expansion. Tenth emperor. Conquest of Korea leads to Korean settlements in Japan. Social organization on clan basis.
c. AD 600–645 Soga dynasty. Political centralization. China attempts several times to take over Korea.
AD 645–865 Power struggles. Chinese government imitated. Classic era of culture. Gradual shift toward a feudal, more strictly Japanese society. Dominance of Fujiwara clan.

Words

4215

Buddhism Religious and philosophical system founded c. 520–530 BC.
burning of the books (255–210 BC) Qin dynasty attempt to destroy all literature in private hands except official records and some practical works.
caste system Derives from Aryan hereditary division of population into priests (*Brahmins*), warriors and rulers (*Kshatriya*), farmers and merchants (*Vaisya*), and labourers, artisans, and domestic servants (*Sudra*).
Hindu beliefs Grew from post-2000 BC fusion of Aryan, Dravadian, and Munda cultures. Probably world's oldest surviving faith.
Sanskrit Oldest member of the Indo-European family of languages. Grammar fixed before c. 400 BC
Veda Oldest Hindu writings dating from c. 1000 BC incorporated in four collections
warlord Military commander wielding civil power. Sometimes in nominal allegiance to the king or emperor, usually defying such control.

People

4216 **Asoka** c. 274–c. 236 BC, Indian emperor of Maurya dynasty. Convert to Buddhism who organized it as state religion. Extended territory of empire by conquest of Kalinga (Orissa with the Circars, c. 262 BC).
Buddha "the enlightened". Title of Prince Gautama Siddartha, c. 563–c. 483 BC. Founder of Buddhism who abandoned life of wealth and luxury for life of ascetic. Taught that life is full of suffering, and that to attain *Nirvana* is only way to escape cycle of death and rebirth.
Chandragupta or Sandracottus, c. 350–c. 250 BC, Hindu emperor. Founder of Maurya dynasty c. 321–c. 184 BC who first united northern India from Herat to Ganges delta, and who defended it against Seleucus Nicator (c. 300 BC). Developed major public works program and elaborate administrative structure.
Confucius Latin for K'ung Fu-tzu, the Master K'ung, 551–479 BC, Chinese philosopher, writer, and statesman. Great moral teacher who tried to replace old religious observances with moral values as basis of social and political order. Advocated a golden rule of paternalism.
Fu Hsi Legendary Chinese emperor (c. 3000 BC) to whom is attributed invention of writing.
Jimmu Legendary first emperor of Japan who acceded c. 660 BC.
Sujin From c. AD 230, tenth Japanese emperor. Inaugurated period of rapid territorial expansion.

422 EARLY AMERICAN CIVILIZATIONS

North America

4221 **Major cultural areas established by AD 1500**
1 Arctic: (Inuit) hunters
2 Sub-arctic: hunters
3 North-west coast: fishers and hunter-gatherers
4 Interior plateau: fishers and hunter-gatherers
5 Great Plains: bison hunters and farmers
6 Eastern woodlands: hunter-fisher-gatherers, and farmers
7 Ohio and Mississippi valleys: farmers
8 California: hunters, fishers, and gatherers

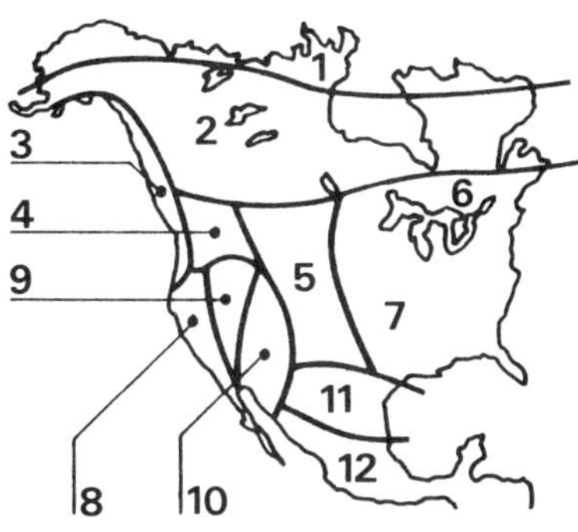

9 Great Basin: desert gatherers
10 South-west: farmers and gatherers
11 South-west deserts: gatherers
12 Mesoamerica: farmers and town and city dwellers

Central and South American cultures

4222 **Aztec** AD 1325–1521 Invading Aztec tribes ended the ruling Toltec power and in 1325 founded Tenochtitlán (now Mexico City). Aztecs were Indians rich with gold and silver, and medicinal skills. They composed poetry and music. Their state was militaristic, with a large, well-equipped army. Human sacrifice was the basis for faith according to Aztec religion. Between 1519 and 1521 Hernando Cortés and 400 Spanish troops invaded and defeated this Central American civilization.
Chibcha Advanced Indian civilization AD 1200–1538, conquered by the Spanish in the 1500s. They used gold, emeralds, and made textiles, baskets, and pots. They lived in small villages and farmed the lowlands of the high plains of the central Colombian Andes where they lived.
Mayan AD 100–1542 Indian civilization based on agriculture. Mayans built their homes and pyramidal temples from limestone. They carved important dates on stone using picture writing which has recently been deciphered. Cities centered around royal houses and religious structures. Mayan culture is noted for its advances in architecture, the arts, astronomy, and mathematics.
Incas AD. 1200–1535 The Incas built an extensive empire, the hub of which was the city of Cuzco. Their ruler was known asthe "Only Inca," and was regarded as a god. The Inca were sun-worshippers, and practiced human sacrifice. Their last king, Atahualpa, was captured by the Spanish expedition led by Pizzaro.
Olmecs Olmecs flourished between 800 BC and AD 200. They developed a counting system and a calendar, carved stone statues (**1**), and wrote using heiroglyphics. La Venta, the site ruins in Tabasco, was a major Olmec settlement.
Zapotec and Mixtec AD 300–1524

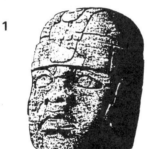

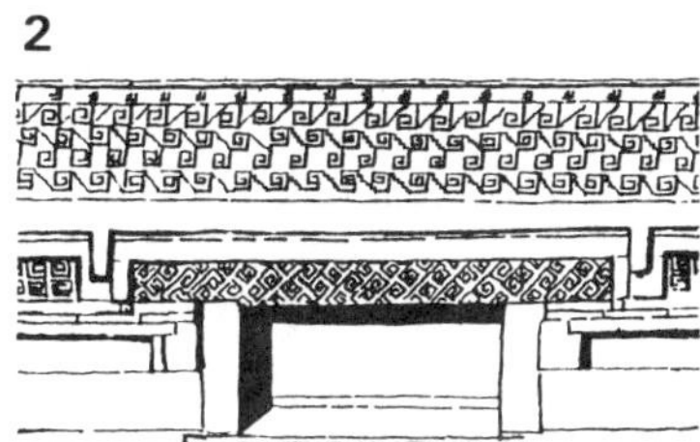

Indians who built their religious center of Monte Alban 1000–500 BC on a mountain top which they flattened themselves. They farmed, used a calendar, and wrote using heiroglyphics. Elaborate Zapotec tombs suggest that they believed in an afterlife. Mixtec Indians from western Oaxaca occupied the Zapotec "city" of Monte Alban before AD 1 and after 900. Among the many magnificent structures built at Monte Alban is the Hall of the Monoliths (**2**).

Teotihuacán 100 BC–AD 750

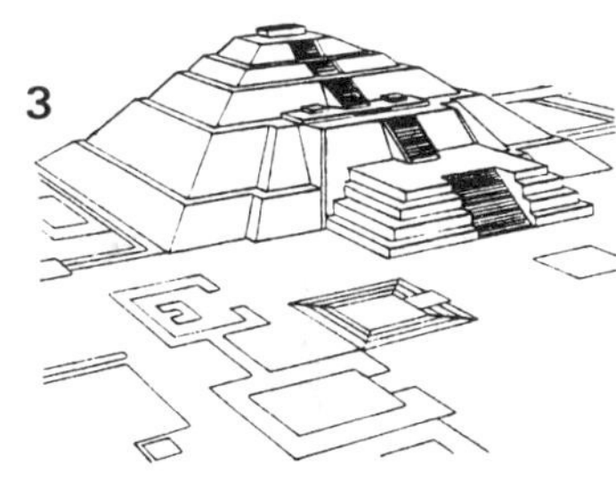

Teotihuacáns built an enormous city inhabited from about 400 AD and organized as a metropolis from about the beginning of the Christian era. The city included two outstanding temple-pyramids, dedicated to the Sun and the Moon (**3**) respctively. Little is known about Teotihuacán culture. They farmed and irrigated the land and set up trading posts with Mayans. The city was sacked and burned by invading Toltecs in about AD 650.
Toltec AD 900–1200
During the 900s Toltec Indians established an empire, making Tula (north of Mexico City) their capital. They controlled the Valley of Mexico until 1200. A fierce people, they invaded the Yucatán Peninsula then rebuilt an old Mayan religious center, Chichén Itzá. They worshiped the feathered serpent Quetzalcoatl and also believed in human sacrifice. This figure of a warrior (**4**) supported the roof of a temple at Tula.

continued

Central and South American cultures continued

4222

Period and location of Central and South American civilizations
1 Aztec AD 1325–1521
2 Chibcha AD 1200–1538
3 Mayan AD 100–1542
4 Inca AD 1200–1535
5 Olmec 800 BC–AD 200
6 Toltec AD 900–1200
7 Teothihuacán 100 BC–AD 750
8 Zapotecs AD 300–1524

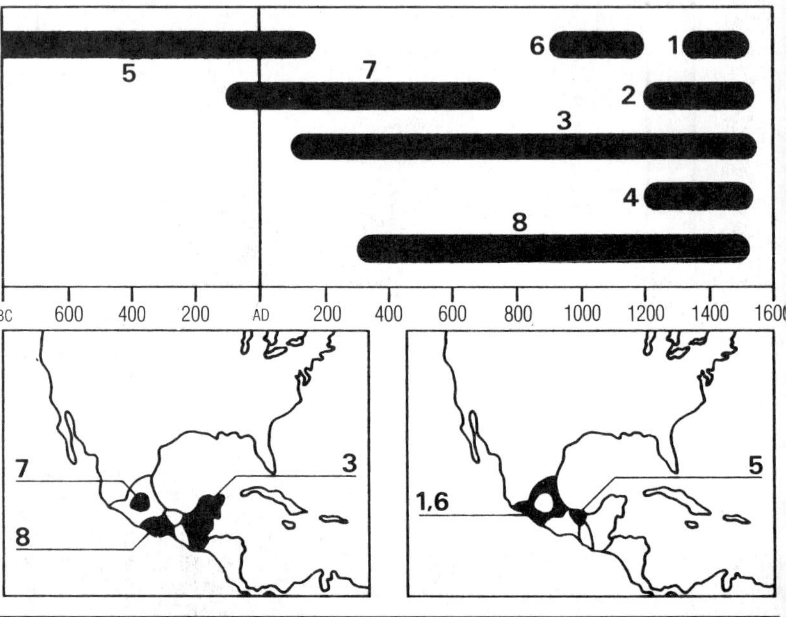

423 THE CIVILIZATIONS AND EMPIRES OF THE MIDDLE EAST

Places

4231

8 4 6

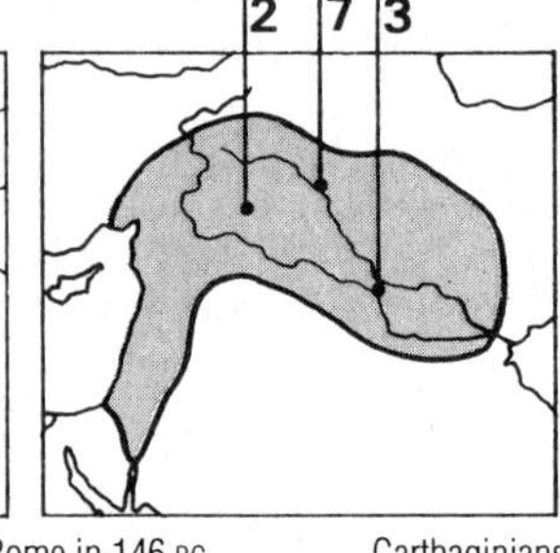

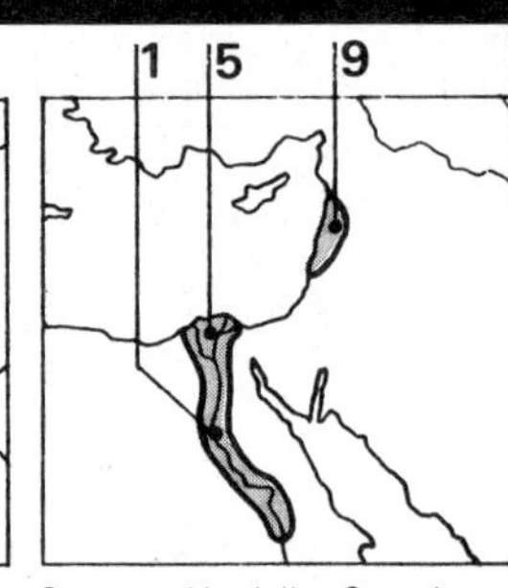

1 Amarna Egypt. City founded by "heretic" pharoah Akhenaton c. 1375 BC and abandoned after his death c. 1360 BC. Revolutionary in styles of art, architecture, and theology.
2 Assyria Mesopotamia. Dependency of Babylon which emerged as major independent state. Assyrian rulers were renowned for their buildings, and their troops for fighting prowess.
3 Babylon Mesopotamia. Capital of southern region. It became the capital for a succession of kingdoms and empires. Noted for culture and architectural splendour.
4 Carthage Phoenicia. Reputedly founded by Tyrian princess Dido. Center for trade and exploration. Destroyed by Rome in 146 BC.
5 Fertile crescent Area bordering Mediterranean and including Nile valley where western civilization and its derivations began. Farmed with settled communities from c. 8000 BC.
6 Hittites Indo-European people dominating area west of Euphrates river between 2000 and 1000 BC. Frequently at war with Egypt.
7 Nineveh Assyria. Capital of Assyrian empire from c. 700–600 BC. Famous for public buildings and complex canal system.
8 Numidia Roman name for area approximating to modern Algeria. Often occupied by Carthaginians. Conquered by Julius Cesar in 46 BC.
9 Phoenicia Region settled from 3000 BC corresponding to modern Lebanon. Sea traders and colonizers, the Phoenicians extended their empire to Carthage and Cyprus. First Persia then Alexander the Great conquered the eastern part. Carthage fell to Rome.

Events

4232

3000–2000 BC Egypt – Old Kingdom: Upper and Lower Egypt unified. Pyramids built. Centralized state administration. Mesopotamia: Sumerians settle in southern Mesopotamia. Gradual Semite infiltration. Walled cities. Ziggurats constructed. Royal tombs at Ur.
2000-1500 BC Egypt – Middle Kingdom: sphinxes built. Invasion of Upper Egypt by Semitic tribes dispossessed by Indo-European advance. Mesopotamia: Old Assyrian and first Babylonian empires. Semitic tribes advance to Euphrates. Canaanites invade. Settlement by Assyrian people. Supremacy of Babylon. Laws codified.
1500–715 BC Egypt – New Kingdom. Successful military campaigns into Asia and Nubia. Religious crisis during reign of Akhenaton (Amarna period). Campaigns in Palestine and Syria; Jerusalem plundered. Mesopotamia: Middle and New Assyrian empires. Babylon sacked by Hittites. Short-term regional domination from Ninevah. Attempted invasion by Medes and Persians rebuffed. Persia: Achaemenid dynasty. Median suzerainty. Phoenicia: client city-states established in Palestine through policy of exploration and trading. Carthage founded.
715–330 BC Egypt: Ethiopian, Assyrian, and

continued

Events continued

4232 Persian domination. Conquest by Alexander the Great. Mesopotamia: new Assyrian and Babylonian empires. Chaldean advances repulsed. Enlargement of Babylon. Jerusalem occupied and sacked. Persian occupation. Conquest by Alexander the Great. Persia: Achaemenid dynasty. Median rule supplanted. Conquest of entire Fertile Crescent area. Attempted revolts. Wars against Greece. Conquest by Alexander the Great. Phoenicia: domination first by Persia then by Greece. Series of trade and sphere-of-influence treaties with Rome.
330–30 BC Egypt: Ptolemaic dynasty descended from one of Alexander's generals. Incorporated as Roman province after defeat and suicide of Cleopatra and Mark Antony. Phoenician wars with Rome leading to destruction of Carthage.

People

4233 **Akhenaton** "heretic Pharaoh." Name assumed by Amenhotep IV, king of Egypt of 18th dynasty who ruled 1379–62 BC. Introduced purified and monotheistic solar cult of sun-disk (Aton), and built new capital at Amarna (Akhetatron). Married to Nefertiti.
Cleopatra VII 69–30 BC, queen of Egypt (**1**). Last and most famous of Macedonian dynasty of Ptolemies. Mistress of Julius Caesar, later married Mark Antony 37 BC, with whom she fled to Egypt after they were defeated by Roman forces. Committed suicide.
Cyrus II the Great 553–529 BC, founder of Persian empire. Fourth king of royal dynasty of Achaemenids. Acquired Babylon in 536 BC, becoming master of all Asia, from Mediterranean to Hindu Kush.
Darius III surnamed Codomannus. Ruled from 336–30 BC. Last Achaemenid ruler. Defeated by Alexander the Great at the Granicus 334 BC, at Issus 333 BC, and at Gaugamela or Arbela 331 BC. During flight, murdered by a satrap, Artaterxes (Ardashir).

1

Rameses I-XI 1320-1085 BC, 19th and 20th dynasty kings of Egypt (**2**) responsible for territorial gains, administrative successes, and much monumental building and sculpture.
Zoroaster Greek form of Zarathustra, c. 630–c. 553 BC, Iranian. Religious leader and prophet, founder or reformer of ancient Parsee religion as Zoroastrianism. Struggled to defend holy agricultural state against Turanian amd Vedic aggressors.

2

424 ANCIENT GREECE

Places

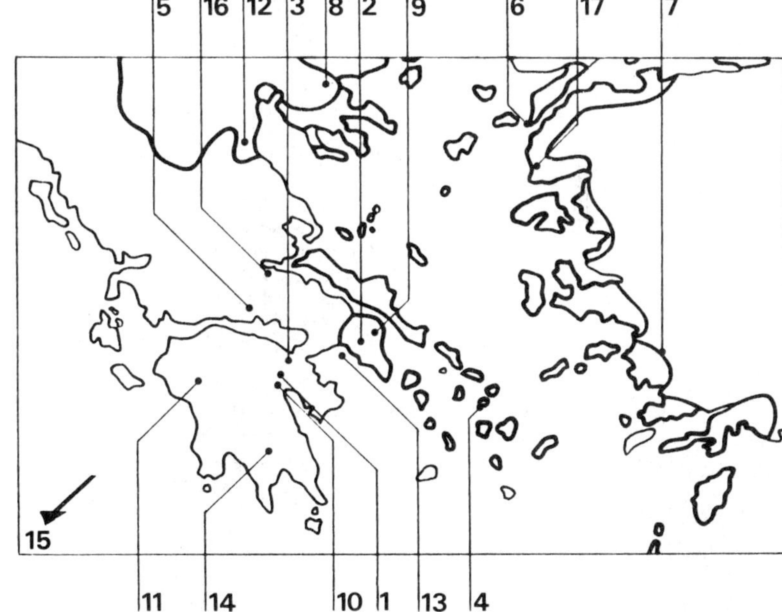

4241 **1 Argos** Greece. City-state allied with Athens against Sparta. In legend associated with Jason and the Argonauts and with Agamemnon's expedition against Troy.
2 Athens Greece. Leading ancient city-state considered cradle of western civilization
3 Corinth Greek city, founded by Sisyphus, according to legend, the chief trading center between east and west in the ancient world.
4 Delos Greece. Island shrine ranking with Delphi and Olympia.
5 Delphi Greece. Temple to and oracle of Apollo. The most important temple for all the ancient Greek people.
6 Hellespont A narrow strait separating the Aegean from the Sea of Marmara. In legend, Leander swam across it every night to be with Hero.
7 Ionia Area bordering Hittite empire whose Grecian people colonized widely in the 8th century BC but succumbed to Persia in the 6th century BC.
8 Macedonia Semi-Greek, semi-barbarian kingdom to the north of Greece, from which Philip II conquered the entire mainland, and Alexander the Great launched his conquests.
9 Marathon Scene of battle between Athens and Persia in 490 BC. The name attached itself to a long-distance footrace in commemoration of a soldier's epic journey with news.
10 Mycenae Greek city and capital of Achaean Greeks. Legendary home of Agamemnon.
11 Olympia Greece. Religious sanctuary and site of Olympic Games in which athletes from most city-states took part from 776 BC.
12 Olympus The highest mountain of Greece, situated in the north-east, between Thessaly and Macedonia. The legendary home of the chief Greek gods.
13 Salamis A Greek island, scene of a naval battle in 480 BC in which the Greeks defeated the Persians.
14 Sparta Greece. City-state challenging Athens for supremacy. Noted for military dedication and neglect of arts and philosophy.
15 Syracuse Sicily. Greek colony settled c. 734 BC. Achieved cultural eminence. Defeated Athens 415–413 BC. Conquered by Rome 211 BC.
16 Thermopylae A narrow pass between sea and mountains joining Thessaly with Locris. Scene of a battle in 480 BC in which the planned Persian invasion of Greece was halted.
17 Troy City on plain of Troas successively colonized, sacked, and abandoned. Commanded trade and strategic routes linking Europe with Asia. The legend of its ten-year siege by the Greeks and eventual sack is now thought to be based on a trade war. Ilium was another name for Troy.

Words

4242

Achaeans Greek people whom Homer identifies as the besiegers of Troy. Their capital was Mycenae.
acropolis Central, fortified administrative and religious district in Greek cities. The best-known is that of Athens, which was also a sanctuary.
agora Open meeting-place in Greek cities. The Roman forum was based on it.
Delian League confederacy of Greek city-states led by Athens against Persia.
demos Greek word denoting common people who held citizenship and therefore had rights.
Epicureanism Greek philosophy identifying good with pleasure but advocating a withdrawn and quiet life.
hoplite Greek heavily armed foot soldier who largely replaced the more aristocratic cavalry and chariot fighter.
Minos Legendary ruler of Crete. The name is probably a dynastic title. The Bronze Age Minoan civilization reached a high artistic level.
oligarchy Government by small faction or group of families, from Greek words meaning "a few" and "chief" or "principal."
Parthenon Temple of goddess Athena on Acropolis hill in Athens. Constructed on Pericles's direction.
Parthia Bactrian Short-lived Greek empire resisting Roman expansion. Parthian archers were famous for shooting backward at full gallop – the Parthian shot.
Peloponnese wars Series of conflicts between Athens and Sparta between 431 and 404 BC. They ended in Sparta capturing Athens.
phalanx Greek military tactic which ranked armored hoplites in close formation.
polis Greek term for a city-state – an area dominated by and administered from a central fortifiable town
pyrrhic victory One which proves more costly than defeat. Named for the Greek ruler who defeated a Roman army in 280 BC.
stoicism Greek philosophy adopted by Rome stressing private rectitude and involvement in public affairs.
tyrant Greek synonym for king or ruler, not necessarily denoting one who has seized power unconstitutionally or who rules oppressively.

Events

4243

3000–2000 BC Island civilizations in the Aegean sea, notably that of Crete.
2000–1000 BC Mainland Greece colonized by Indo-European people. Development of decorated pottery. First cities with individual rulers, as at Mycenae. Military expeditions aided by use of horses and of bronze weapons. Crete devastated by earthquakes, subsequent decline.
1000–650 BC Iron age begins. City-states with codified laws, in particular Athens. Stone temples and public buildings. Colonization of Sicily, lower Italy, and southern Gaul. Greek alphabet developed.
650–300 BC Literary and theatrical culture develops. Golden age of Athens; Parthenon completed. Rise of Sparta. Alexander of Macedon conquers Persia, Mesopotamia, Syria, and Palestine and reaches India.
300–146 BC Inter-state squabbles make Greece vulnerable to expansionist Rome. Independence lost. Defeated city-states incorporated into Roman province of Macedonia.

People

4244

Alexander III (the Great) 356–23 BC. Shown here, Alexander's empire 323 BC.

Son of Philip II, king of Macedonia. Conquered Egypt, Palestine, and Phoenicia, and ruled Armenia. Invaded India 327–25 BC. Held mass marriage of himself and Macedonian leaders with women of Persia.

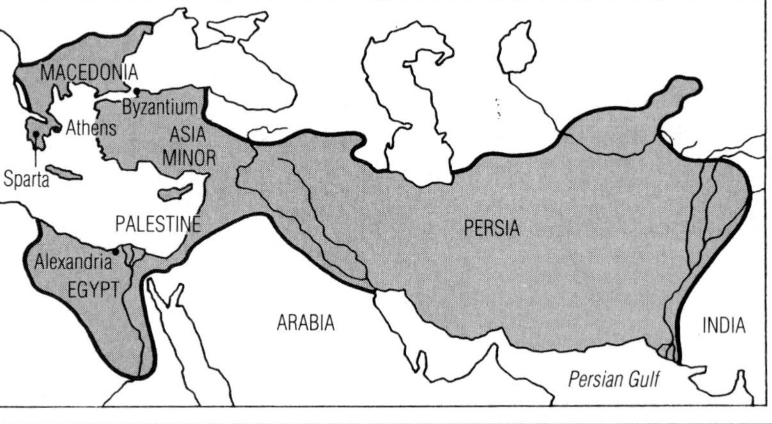

Aeschylus c. 525–c. 456 BC, Greek. Known as father of Greek tragedy. Distinguished by grandeur of conceptions in theology, in providential ruling of world, inheritance of sin, and conflict of rude with purer religion. Author of *Prometheus Bound* and *Oresteia* trilogy.
Aristophanes c. 448–c. 388 BC, Greek. Playwright whose *Acharnians*, *Knights*, *Clouds*, and *Wasps*, dating from period ending 425 BC, are masterpieces of political satire. In later comedies *Ecclesiazusae* and *Plutus*, political allusions and the chorus addressing the audience of old comedy style disappear.
Aristotle 384–22 BC, Greek philosopher and scientist (**1**), one of most important and influential figures in history of western thought. Book of works remarkable for its range, originality, systematization, and sophistication. Tutor of Alexander the Great.
Euripides 480 or 484–406 BC, Greek. Athenian dramatist and tragedian. Highly skilful playwright, with unerring instinct for "situation." Eighteen of his 80-odd dramas survive in complete form.
Homer 8th century BC, Greek epic poet, traditionally blind, to whom are attributed the *Iliad* (telling of seize and sack of Troy) and *Odyssey* (telling of wanderings of Odysseus on his adventurous return to Ithaca).
Pericles c. 490–29 BC, Greek. Statesman, leader of dominant democracy. Increased naval supremacy of Athens. Under his patronage, Greek architecture and sculpture reached perfection. Encouraged music and drama, as well as industry and commerce.

1

Phidias (Pheidias) born c. 500 BC, Greek. Sculptor and superintendent of all public works of art in Athens under Pericles. Constructed Propylaea and the Parthenon, and is believed to have made gold and ivory *Athena*, as well as the *Zeus* at Olympia, himself.
Plato c. 428–c. 348, Greek. One of most important philosophers of all time. Pupil (or associate) of Socrates and teacher of Aristotle. *Dialogues* and *Republic* contain such famous doctrines as theory of knowledge as recollection, immortality of soul, and theory of forms (or "ideas").
Socrates 469–399 BC, Greek. Along with Plato and Aristotle, one of three great figures in ancient philosophy. "Socratic method" of questioning involved deeper and more honest analysis of concepts such as justice, courage, and piety.

continued

People continued

4244 **Solon** 640 or 638–559 BC, Greek. Athenian lawgiver, merchant, and poet. Released debtors, reformed currency, and admitted new class (*thetes*) to the *ecclesia* (for election of magistrates) and to the *heliaea* (for judgment of magistrates), thus laying foundations for Athenian democracy.
Sophocles c. 496–405 BC, Greek. Athenian tragedian. One of great figures of Greek drama whose masterpiece is *Oedipus Tyrannus*, on which Aristotle based aesthetic theory of drama in the *Poetica*, and from which Freud derived the name and function of the "Oedipus complex."
Thucydides c. 460–c. 400 BC, Greek. Commanded Athenian squadron of seven ships at Thasos 424, and took refuge in exile after being condemned for failing to relieve Amphipolis. Wrote an eight-volume *History of the Peloponnesian War*.
Xenophon c. 435–354 BC, Greek. Athenian-born historian, essayist, military commander, and disciple of Socrates. Exiled for commanding as mercenary with Sparta. Wrote the *Memorials of Socrates*.

425 ANCIENT ROME

Events

4251 **1000–750 BC** Iron age migration of Italic people. Etruscan people from Asia Minor subjugate Tuscany area. Rome founded.
750–500 BC Rome under seven successive kings assumes dominance over other middle Italy cities. Etruscan power decays following Celtic invasions.
500–250 BC Roman republic. Celtic advance culminates in sack of Rome. City rebuilt. Defensive coalitions. Treaties with Carthage. Samnite wars lead to Roman domination of all lower Italy.
250–150 BC Series of wars against Carthage end with Roman victory. Conquest of Greece.
150–60 BC Political and social reform movements. Conquest of Numidia. Civil wars and power struggles. Conquest of Pontus, Sicily, and parts of north Africa. Dictatorship of Sulla.
60–44 BC Slave revolts. Further power struggles lead to new civil wars. Julius Caesar conquers Gaul and Spain; invasion of Britain; annexation of Egypt. Dictatorship leads to murder of Caesar.
45 BC–AD 70 Civil war. Senate then awards title of Augustus to Caesar's nephew Octavian. Gaul reorganized. Roman troops reach Danube and Elbe rivers. Uprising in Britain suppressed, southern Britain conquered. Augustus succeeded in turn by Tiberius, Caligula, Claudius, and Nero. Fire destroys much of Rome. End of Julian dynasty.
AD 70–100 Flavian dynasty of Vespasian, Titus, and Domitian. Spasmodic revolts throughout empire. Jerusalem sacked. Mount Vesuvius erupts, Pompeii and Herculaneum buried. British conquest expanded northward.
AD 100–305 Emperors succeed through adoption or by military acclamation. Trajan extends empire to east. Hadrian builds frontier fortifications. Second conquest of Jerusalem. Mounted people on eastern and northern borders of empire start to close in; provinces surrendered. Moves towards decentralization, including co-rulers. Inflation.
AD 305–340 Constantine (the Great) consolidates Empire of West. Byzantium renamed Constantinople and created Christian capital, the second Rome.
AD 340–410 Christianity becomes official state religion. Waves of invasion threaten emperors of both east and west Roman Empires. Western capital moved to Ravenna. Rome sacked by Visigoths.

Roman Empire at greatest extent AD 117

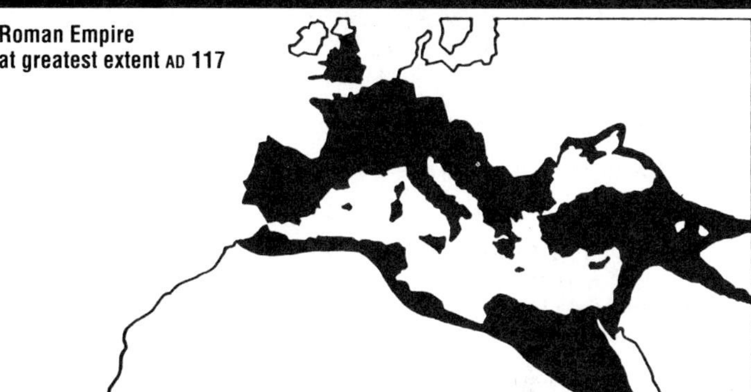

People

4252 **Agrippina, the Younger** AD 15–59, Roman. Mother of emperor Nero, whose third husband was her own uncle emperor Claudius, whom she is suspected of poisoning. Her ascendancy proving intolerable, Nero put her to death in AD 59.
Antonius, Marcus (Mark Antony) c. 83-30 BC, Roman. General and politician responsible for defeat of republic movement after death of Julius Cesar. Attempt to establish personal empire in Egypt with Cleopatra ended in defeat and suicide.
Attila c. 406–53, king of the Huns, called the "Scourge of God," who attacked both east and west Roman Empires. After defeat on the Catalaunian Plains, retreated to Hungary, but later invaded parts of Italy.
Boudicca incorrectly called Boadicea, 1st century AD, British. Warrior-queen of Iceni tribe, who led great uprising against Romans. Denied kingdom at husband's death, she sacked Roman Colchester and London. Committed suicide when defeated.
Caesar, Gaius Julius 100 or 102–44 BC, Roman (**1**). As general, if not as statesman, ranks among greatest in history. Conquered Gaul and parts of Germany and Egypt, and invaded Britain. Assassinated on assuming dictatorial powers.
Catullus, Gaius Valerius c. 84–c. 54 BC, Roman. Lyric poet. In Rome, met Lesbia, married woman to whom he sang in verses unequaled in lyric poetry of passion. Wrote strange, wild, imaginative *Attis*.
Crassus, Marcus Licinius c. 115–53 BC, Roman. Financier and politician, known as "Dives," "The Rich." Patron of young Julius Caesar who crushed revolt of Spartacus in 71 BC. As ruler of Syria, defeated by Parthians.
Hannibal "the grace of Baal," 247–182 BC. Carthaginian soldier (**2**), son of Hamilcar. Commander in chief at 26. Crossed Pyrenees into Gaul 219 BC and Alps into Italy 217 BC, with elephants. Eventually defeated by Rome, committed suicide.

1
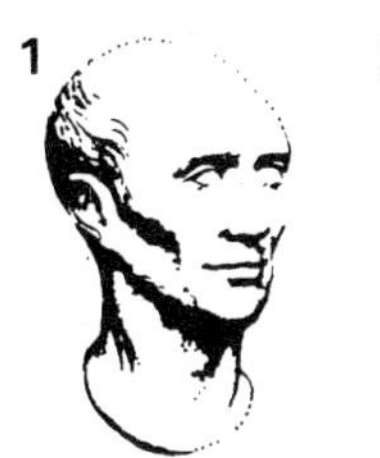

2

Horace, Quintus Horatius Flaccus 65–8 BC, Roman. Poet and satirist, who has enjoyed popularity unequaled in literature. In 19 BC, produced his greatest work, three books of *Odes*.
Livia, Drusilla later Julia Augusta, 58 BC–AD 29, Roman. Empress, third wife of emperor Augustus. Mother of Tiberius by first marriage. Believed to have exerted considerable power and influence over Augustus.
Livy properly Titus Livius 59 BC–AD 17, Roman. Historian whose impartiality figures as largely in his work as does his veneration for the good, the generous, and the heroic in man. Regarded history as fine art rather than as science.
Marius, Gaius 157–86 BC, Roman soldier. After annihilating invading hordes of Cimbri and Teutons in Gaul, declared savior of state. Main rival was Sulla. Died fighting after revenge attack with Cinna on aristocracy at Rome.
Messalina, Valeria c. 25–c. 48, Roman. Matron, third wife of emperor Claudius, and mother of Octavia (Nero's wife), whose name has become byword for avarice, lust, and cruelty. Love affairs and court intrigue led to her execution.
Pompey the Great, Gnaeus Pompeius Magnus 106–48 BC, Roman. Soldier and

continued

People continued

4252 statesman who reorganized eastern provinces. After final defeat at Pharsalia by Caesar in 48 BC, fled to Egypt, where he was murdered.
Poppaea Sabina d. AD 65, Roman. Beauty who discarded her first husband Otho to marry Nero, at whose hands she died. For three months in AD 69, Otho himself was emperor.
Sallust Latin Gaius Sallustius Crispus, 86–34 BC, Roman. Historian and politician, credited with development of monograph. His administration sullied by oppression and extortion, but charges against him failed after intervention of Caesar.
St Helena c. 255–330 AD, Roman empress. Mother of Constantine the Great. In AD 312, when toleration was extended to Christianity, was baptized. According to tradition, founded basilicas at Bethlehem and Golgotha.
Seneca, Lucius Annaeus called "the Younger," c. 4 BC–c. AD 65, Roman. Stoic philosopher, statesman, and tragedian. As Nero's tutor, virtually ruled Rome AD 54–62. Eventually lost favour with Nero, however, and was ordered to commit suicide.
Spartacus d. 71 BC, Thracian. Led slave revolt 73–71 BC, but was defeated by Crassus, and executed with his followers by crucifixion.
Suetonius, Gaius Suetonius Tranquillus AD 75–160, Roman biographer and antiquarian, whose best known work is *The Lives of the First Twelve Caesars*, remarkable for its terseness, elegance, and impartiality.
Sulla, Lucius Cornelius nicknamed by himself Felix the Fortunate, 138–78 BC, Roman. General and statesman, and cold-blooded, ruthless dictator 82–79 BC. Reformer of administration and constitution who was bitterly opposed by Marius.
Tacitus, Publius or Gaius Cornelius c. AD 55–120, Roman. Historian, administrator, and orator who married Agricola. Conqueror of Britain. Copied much from earlier historians, and was biased in his republican ideals and hatreds.
Virgil, Publius Vergilius Maro 70–19 BC, Roman. Poet whose epic work the *Aeneid is* based on story of Aeneas the Trojan, legendary founder of Roman nation and of Julian family. Writings established as classics even in his own lifetime.

Emperors

4253 **Augustus, Gaius Julius Octavianus** 63 BC-AD 14, first emperor of Rome, nephew of Julius Caesar. Reformed administration, and vastly enlarged territory of Roman empire in central and northern Europe.
Caligula Gaius Caesar Augustus Germanicus AD 12–41, nicknamed Caligula from his soldier's boots *caligae.* Infamous for financial, sexual, military, and administrative caprices. Brief but traumatic reign ended by assassination.
Claudius I full name Tiberius Claudius Drusus Nero Germanicus, 10 BC–AD 54, fourth Roman emperor whose supposed imbecility saved him from cruelty of Caligula. Inaugurated conquest of Britain. Poisoned by wife and niece Agrippina.
Constantine I called the Great, properly Flavius Valerius Aurelius Constantinus c. 274–337. In AD 323, became sole governor of Roman world. Chose Byzantium for capital, and in AD 330 renamed it Constantinople.
Hadrian, Publius Aelius Hadrianus 76–138, emperor from AD 117. From AD 120, began long tour of empire, visiting Gaul, Germany, Britain (where he built Hadrian's Wall), Spain, Mauritania, Egypt, Asia Minor, and Greece.
Marcus Aurelius Antoninus originally Marcus Annius Verus, AD 121–80. One of most respected emperors in Roman history, whose *Meditations* survive, and are a unique document of innermost thoughts. Also legislator and stoic philosopher.
Nero AD 37–68, emperor from AD 54 through 68 (**1**). Ruler of unstable though artistic temperament. Tutored by Seneca. Responsible for deaths of mother and wife. Financial extravagance caused unrest. Condemned to death by Senate, fled and committed suicide.
Titus, Flavius Sabinus Vespasianus AD 39-81, son of Vespasian. Commanded in Britain and Germany. Captured and destroyed Jerusalem AD 70. Completed Colosseum, built triumphal arch, and rebuilt much of Rome.
Trajan Marcus Ulpius Trajanus c. AD 53–117, successful general and administrator (**2**) who made Dacia, Armenia, and Mesopotamia into Roman provinces, and built new military routes, canals, bridges, harbors, and towns to cover empire.
Vespasian Titus Flavius Vespasianus AD 9–79, emperor of plebian provincial origin (**3**). Founder of Flavian dynasty. Restored government and finances to order, and extended and consolidated Roman conquests in Britain and Germany.

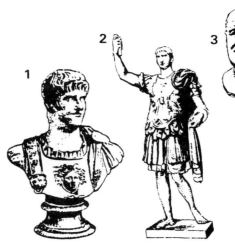

Rulers of Rome
1 Julius Caesar
2 Mark Antony
3 Nero
4 Trajan
5 Hadrian

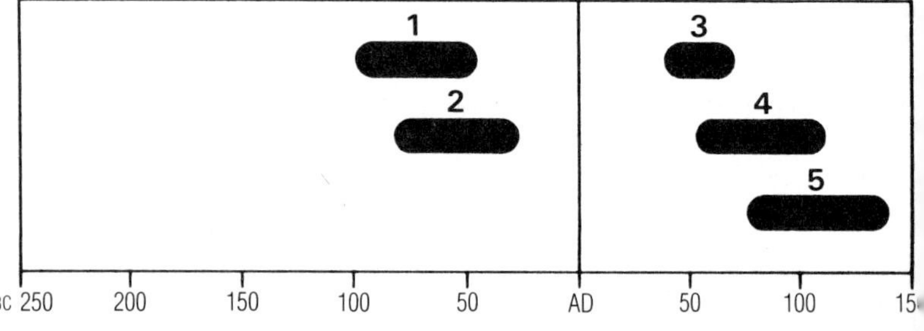

Words

4254 **Augustus** Roman title of honor awarded to Octavian and subsequently adopted as name as well as title.
Caesar Aristocratic Roman family name which became an imperial title.
Capitol Triple religious shrine on Rome's Capitoline Hill.
Celts People dominating western and central Europe from Bronze Age to the middle of the first century BC.
centurion Roman officer commanding an army unit of 100 men.
dictator Roman magistrate with temporary extraordinary powers, such as in time of national crisis. By the time of Sulla and Julius Caesar it had come to mean an extraconstitutional office with unlimited powers for an unspecified duration.
Etruscans Italic people who invaded from Asia

continued

Words continued

4254 Minor and settled between the Arno and Tiber rivers. By the 6th century BC they had achieved a high cultural level. By the 5th century BC they had been absorbed by Rome, who took over many aspects of their art and religious practices.
forum Roman central open area surrounded by temples and other public buildings and suitable for public meetings. It was derived from the Greek *agora*.
Gaul Western European area corresponding to modern France, Belgium, western Germany, and northern Italy. Inhabited by Celtic people who sacked Rome in 390 BC. Conquered primarily by Julius Caesar 58–50 BC.
gladiator Armed fighter for arena contests. Up to 5,000 pairs could perform in one spectacle.
Goths Germanic people who constantly attacked the Roman empire from the 3rd–5th century AD.
Huns Nomadic people invading south-eastern Europe in 4th century AD and building up empire won through cavalry and archery tactics. Conquerors of Visigoths. Power disintegrated after death of Attila.
legion Roman military unit, originally a citizen army, later comprising 4,000 to 6,000 heavy infantry soldiers with cavalry support.
Ostrogoths Eastern Gothic people who established empire bordering Black Sea. Conquered by Huns c. AD 370.
patricians Roman privileged citizen class for whom certain high state and priestly offices were reserved.
plebians Roman central citizen class with self-administrative rights.
Punic Wars Series of conflicts between Carthage and Rome 264–146 BC.
pyrrhic victory One which proves more costly than defeat. Named for the Greek ruler who defeated a Roman army in 280 BC.
Rubicon Stream between Gaul and Italy. Crossing it with his legions from his assigned command, Julius Caesar broke the law and committed himself to his bid for supreme power.
Sabines Italic tribe east of Tiber river conquered by Rome. Legend recounts that Roman settlers kidnapped their young women to provide brides.
Samnite Wars Conflicts between southern Italian mountain tribes, possibly of Sabine descent, and Rome between 343 and 290 BC.
senate Roman assembly of heads of patrician families. Supreme administrative authority, even under the empire
visigoths Gothic people who spread from Spain through Gaul then drove south to Rome, which they sacked in AD 410.

426 THE DARK AGES AD 400–800

Events

4261 **AD 400–450** Vandals and other Germanic tribes cross Rhine, enter Gaul, invade Spain. Visigoths enter Italy, capture Rome, settle in Aquitaine. Vandals cross to north Africa, capture Carthage. Western Roman Empire moves from Rome to Ravenna. Eastern Roman Empire cedes territory and tribute to Huns.
AD 450–500 Roman-Gothic army repels Huns from Gaul. Hunnish empire disintegrates. Vandals sack Rome. Visigoths enter Spain. Franks conquer north-west Gaul, king accepts Christianity. Ostrogoths conquer Italy. Saxons settle in England, advance checked at Mount Badon.
AD 500–600 Visigoths driven from France, Burgundy, Provence, Bavaria and east Switzerland conquered by Franks. Eastern Roman Empire attempts recovery of Western Empire, conquers Vandals in north Africa. Roman law codified. Roman victories reconquer Italy, south-east Spain. Slavs cross Danube. Irish tribes settle in Scotland. Christian missionaries.
AD 600–650 Slavs conquer Romans, counter-offensives attempted. Persians conquer Mesopotamia, Syria, Palestine, and Egypt. United Frankish kingdom. Muhammed converts Arabia. Arabs conquer Syria, Palestine, Iraq, Egypt, Persia.
AD 650–700 Northumbrian kingdom founded in England, invaded by Picts. Celtic Church loses separate identity. Arabs besiege Constantinople, conquer Carthage.
AD 700–800 Arabs invade Turkestan, India, Spain, and south-western France, defeated at Poitiers. Christian conversion of Germany begins. Byzantine empire splits with papacy. Mercian boundary creates Anglo-Welsh boundary, Viking raids. Frankish conquests, court established at Aix-la-Chapelle.

People

4262 **Alaric I** c. AD 370–410, king of Visigoths from AD 395, who invaded Greece and, in AD 410, Rome. Later that year, set off to invade Sicily and extend dominion over all Italy, but died at Cosenza.
Arthur (Artorius) 6th century, died c. AD 537, British. Semi-legendary king of Britons and national hero, represented as having united British tribes against invading Saxons. Said to have been defeated at "Camlan," and buried at Glastonbury.
Belisarius AD 505–65, Byzantine general who defeated Vandals AD 534–35, conquered Sicily AD 536, and occupied Rome, which he defended for a year AD 537–8. In AD 540, captured Ostrogoth capital of Ravenna.
Charles Martel "the Hammer," c. AD 688–741. Ruler of Franks from AD 719, progenitor of Carolingian dynasty, and grandfather of Charlemagne. Defeated Moors at Tours, near Poitiers, in AD 732, thus turning back tide of Arab conquest of Europe, then drove Saracens out of Burgundy and Languedoc AD 737.
Clovis (Old German Chlodwig), AD 465–511, Merovingian. Ruler of Franks. In AD 493, married St Clotilda of Burgundy, and was later converted to Christianity. In AD 507, defeated Visigoths. United northern Gaul.

Charlemagne, Carolus Magnus, Charles the Great, AD 742–814. King of Franks, and Christian emperor of west, who consolidated empire (from the Ebro to the Elbe). Promoted education and arts,and created stable administration.

Charlemagne's Empire

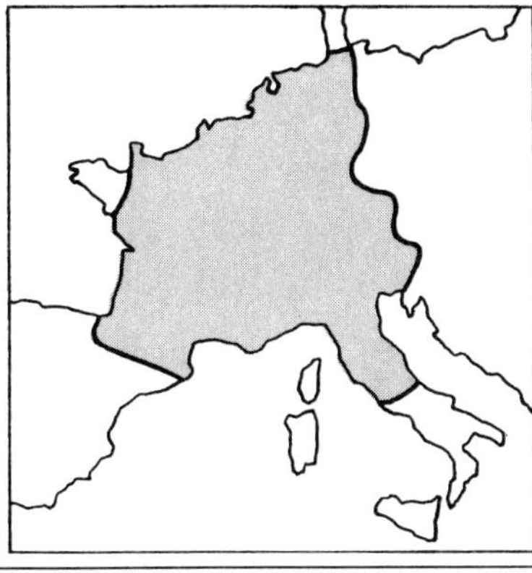

Gregory I the Great, c. 540–604. Pope from AD 590, saint, and father of Church, responsible for complete organization of public services, ritual, and sacred chants of Roman Church. Also organized mission to convert England.
Justinian I Flavius Petrus Sabbatius Justinianus, c. 482–565.

1

Byzantine emperor from AD 527 (**1**). Held eastern frontier against Persians, and reconquered former Roman territories in north Africa, Italy, and Spain. Attempted to unite Eastern and Western Churches.
Muhammed or Mohammed, c. AD 570–c. AD 632, Arab. Prophet and founder of Islam, born in Mecca. Soon after AD 600, received revelation of word of Allah known as Qur'an or Koran "reading." Migration of Muhammed and his followers to Medina, marks Hegira, the beginning of Muslim era.
Offa d. AD 96, king of Mercia from 757,

People continued

4262 overlord of all England south of Humber, who extended dominion over Kent, Sussex, Wessex,and East Anglia, and built great border earthwork, Offa's Dyke, to repel Welsh. Probably most powerful English monarch before 10th century (**2**).

2

St Augustine d. AD 604, Italian. Churchman, first archbishop of Canterbury. In 597, brought Christianity to Anglo-Saxons in southern Britain. Efforts to extend his authority over native British (Welsh) Church were less successful.
St Augustine St Aurelius Augustus, also known as Augustine of Hippo, AD 354–430. Theologian, greatest of Latin Church fathers. Author of the Confessions AD 400, classic of world literature, and monumental *The City of God* 412–27.
St Benedict of Nursia c. AD 480–c. 547, Italian. Founder of western monasticism. Retreated to cavern near Subiaco at 14 to practice religious exercises and escape evils of world. Declared patron saint of all Europe by Pope Paul VI in 1964.
St Columba also known as Colmcille ("Colm of the Churches"), AD 521–97, Irish. Apostle of Christianity in Scotland who founded monastery, at Iona, that became Mother Church of Celtic Christianity in Scotland. Renowned as man of letters.
Theodoric or Theoderic, surnamed the Great, AD 455–526. King of Ostrogoths, and founder of Ostrogoth monarchy. After five years' war, wrested Italy from Odacer, and brought tranquility and prosperity to the country. German figure of legend who features in *Nibelungenlied.*

Places

4263

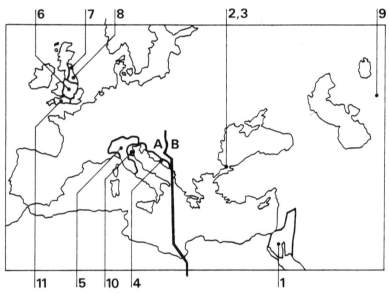

A Western Roman Empire
B Eastern Roman Empire

1 Arabia Roman province covering modern Jordan and Sinai.
2 Byzantium Eastern Roman Empire AD 320–1453 with capital at Byzantium (Constantinople, modern Istanbul).
3 Constantinople *see* Byzantium
4 Dalmatia Part of modern Croatia. Dominated by Rome AD 155–481. Battleground between Goths and Byzantine empire. Under Venetian domination 1420–1797.
5 Lombardy Northern Italian kingdom of Germanic tribes AD 568. Incorporated in Frankish empire AD 774.
6 Mercia Area between Wales, Humber, and Thames. Independent kingdom c. 650–877
7 Northumbria Anglo-Saxon kingdom stretching from Scotland to south and east Yorkshire c. AD 593–944.
8 Synod of Whitby 663–4 It decided on Roman rather than Celtic Christian usages.
9 Turkestan Central Asian region acting as trade and conquest crossroads c. AD 227–1220.
10 Venice Italian city state and dominant naval power from c. AD 450–1797.
11 Wessex West Saxon kingdom stretching from Devon to Sussex and north to Thames AD 494–927.

Peoples

4264 **Anglo-Saxons** West Germanic peoples who settled in Britain and dominated from AD 500 until the Norman conquest.
Celts Western and central European farming people declining under German and Roman expansion.
Franks Germanic tribe of Rhine region conquering Gaul from c. AD 500 and establishing empire.
Goths East Germanic people from Scandinavia who invaded parts of the Roman empire from the 3rd to the 5th centuries AD.
Huns Nomadic people invading south-eastern Europe in 4th century AD and building up empire won through cavalry and archery tactics. Conquerors of Visigoths. Power disintegrated after death of Attila.
Moors Muslims of mixed Berber and Arab descent conquering Spain 711–1492.
Ostrogoths The eastern group of Goths, who established a kingdom in Italy betwen AD 490 and 550.
Picts Warlike Scottish people with independent kingdom AD 297–843.
Saxons Germanic peoples from Baltic coast raiding and settling through Germany to Gaul and Britain. European areas eventually incorporated into Frankish empire.
Scots Celtic people from north of Ireland colonizing Argyll area in 5th century.
Vandals Germanic people invading Gaul and Spain c. AD 400. Sacked Rome AD 455. North African kingdom AD 429–534.
Vikings Scandinavian sea-warriors expanding into Britain, Gaul, and Russia AD 786–1066.
Visigoths Gothic people who spread from Spain through Gaul then drove south to Rome, which they sacked in AD 410.

427 CHARLEMAGNE'S LEGACY 800–1050

Events

4271 **AD 800–900** Charlemagne crowned emperor of Western Roman Empire, takes Barcelona. Muslims conquer Crete and Sicily. Wessex supreme over Anglo-Saxons. Norse base at Dublin, raids on France and Spain. Carolingian empire disintegrates. Union of Picts and Scots. Viking raids into Germany, France, England, and Mediterranean joined by Danes and Norsemen. Danes conquer north-east England, fail to take Wessex, cultural flowering under Alfred. Bulgars and Serbs convert to Christianity. Doctrinal rupture (schism) between Roman Catholic and Orthodox Churches.
AD 900–1000 Russians attack Constantinople. Normandy becomes Viking dukedom. Wessex defeats Scots, Norse, and Welsh. Vikings renew raids on England, settle in Iceland and Greenland. Ukraine converted to Christianity. Byzantines recover Crete, conquer southern Bulgaria.
1000–1050 Venetians conquer Istria, defeat Muslim raiders. Poland and Hungary convert to

continued

Events continued

4271 Christianity. Norsemen reach North America. Danes devastate England, exact tribute. Jerusalem shrine of Holy Sepulchre destroyed. Irish victory over Norse. Scots defeat Northumbrians, Lothian conquered and annexed, dynastic upheavals. Canute rules Denmark, England, and Norway, empire fragments on death. Muslim Spain fragments. Burgundy absorbed into German empire. Normans take Lombardy. Seljuk migration, Persia, Armenia overrun.

People

4272 **Aethelred II** wrongly referred to as "the Unready," 968–1016, English. King of England from AD 978, whose ineffective rule marked by half-hearted attempts to buy off Viking invaders, hence Anglo-Saxon nickname Unroed, which actually means "lack of counsel." Father of Edward the Confessor.

Alfred the Great 849–99, Anglo-Saxon king of Wessex (**1**). Conquered Danes at battle of Edington, Wiltshire. Built navy, promoted education and learning, fostered all arts, and, as legislator, compiled best among enactments of earlier kings.

1
2

Canute "the Great" c. 994–1035, king of England from 1016, Denmark from 1018, and Norway from 1030 (**2**). In England, brought firm government, justice, and security from external threat, and showed generosity to church. Anglo-Scandinavian empire collapsed after his death.

Edward "the Confessor" c. 1003–66, Anglo-Saxon, king of England from 1042. Elder son of Aethelred "the Unready." History of reign is in part story of struggle of Norman party, who held great influence over Edward, against national party led by Harold Godwin. Founded Westminster Abbey.

Erik the Red 10th century, Norwegian sailor who explored Greenland coast and founded Norse colonies there in AD 985. His son, Leif Eriksson, landed in "Vinland," often identified as America. Both men are subject of Icelandic sagas.

Frederick I Barbarossa (Redbeard), c.1123–90, German (**3**). Holy Roman Emperor, of the Hohenstaufen family, whose reign was one long struggle against refractory vassals at home and turbulent civic republics of Lombardy and pope in Italy.

3

Genghis Khan "Universal Ruler," real name Temujin, c. 1162–1227, Mongol who united Mongol tribes, and conquered empires stretching from Black Sea to Pacific. Skilful administrator and ruler.

Harold Godwinsson c. 1022–66, last Anglo-Saxon king of English. Brother-in-law of Edward the Confessor. Claimed throne at Edward's death, defeated Norwegian invasion, but was defeated in turn by William, Duke of Normandy. Died in battle.

Henry II 1133–89, English. From 1154, first Plantagenet king of England. Extended domains through marriage, diplomacy, and conquest. Administrative and judicial reformer. Quarrel with Becket over extent of clerical and royal powers led to archbishop's murder.

Henry IV 1050–1106. Holy Roman Emperor from 1056, king of Germans from 1053. Attempted to unite Germany under centralized monarchy, and to control appointment of senior clerics. This led to excommunication and eventual submission.

Macbeth c. 1005–57, king of Scotland from 1040, having defeated and killed King Duncan and driven his sons, Malcolm and Donald, into exile. Later defeated and killed at Lumphanan in 1057 by Duncan's son Malcolm III. Subject of famous play by Shakespeare.

William I "the Conqueror," 1027–87, duke of Normandy from 1035, king of England from 1066. Claimed English throne on death of Edward the Confessor. Defeated Harold at Hastings. Subdued revolts. Instituted feudal rule.

Words

4273 **Anglo-Saxon Chronicle** AD 891–1154. Historical account begun during reign of Alfred the Great.

Danegeld Tax levied on Anglo-Saxon population of England to buy off Danish invaders.

Genoa Italian naval city-state rivalling Venice 10th through 15th centuries.

Norsemen Western Scandinavian people raiding, exploring, and colonizing south to France, west to Britain, north to Labrador and Greenland.

Seljuks Turkoman tribes invading western Asia and dominating Palestine and Persia from 10th to 13th centuries.

428 CRUSADES AND CONQUESTS 1050–1400

Events

4281 **1050–1100** Muslims expelled from Sardinia. Normans retain Lombardy. Roman Catholic-Orthodox schism confirmed. Pope to be elected only by College of Cardinals. Normans conquer all southern Italy, take Sicily from Muslims. Duke William of Normandy invades England, takes throne, crushes rebellions. Venetians conquer Dalmatia. German emperor submits to pope. Seljuks take Antioch. Christian-Almoravid clashes in Spain. First Crusade proclaimed; crusaders capture Jerusalem.

1100–1150 Crusader states established in Levant. European cities establish identities. University in Paris. Almoravid gains in Spain, Aragon counterattacks. Knights Templar founded. Dynastic disputes in England. Polish and Russian principalities. Decline of Seljuk power. Saracen gains in Levant, Second Crusade. Portuguese gains from Muslims. Anjou conquers Normandy.

1150–1200 Anjou and Aquitaine united by marriage of Henry Plantagenet to Duchess Eleanor, Henry acceeds to English throne. Leon secedes from Castille. German empire controls northern Italy, defied by Lombard League. University at Bologna. Saxony and Bavaria conquer Lower Elbe, later reabsorbed into empire. Egypt under Saracen control. Anglo-Norman invasion of Ireland. Swedes settle Finland. Seljuks defeat Byzantine forces. Jews banished from France. Third Crusade. Kingdom of Bohemia.

1200–1250 Fourth Crusade. Byzantium sacked. France, England under papal interdict, call for Albigensian crusade. Mongolia united, empire stretches from Persia to Mongolia, invasions of Russia, Poland, and Hungary. Christian victories in Spain; Castile and Leon reunited, Majorca captured, Almoravid empire declines. Children's crusade. French victories over English and Germans. Barons revolt in England, Magna Carta, first Oxford University college. Fifth Crusade recovers Jerusalem, loses it to Turks. Byzantines recover Salonika.

1250–1300 Anarchy in German empire. Mongol victories. Baronial rebellion in England. Angevin successes in Italy, Sicilian revolt. England conquers Wales, annexes Scotland. Last crusader kingdom falls. Swiss confederation.

1300–1350 Flemish rise against French. Papal court forcibly moved to Avignon. Scots regain independence, thwarted in attempted invasion of England. Knights Templar abolished. Further expulsion of Jews from France. Aragon captures Sardinia, Granada Moors recapture Gibraltar, Castillian territorial gains. Mongol recognition of independent north-east Russia. English king

continued

Events continued

4281 claims French crown; start of Hundred Years War. Populist revolt in Rome. Plague sweeps Europe, 25 million die.
1350–1400 Ottoman Turks invade Europe. French and English peasant revolts. Venetians cede Dalmatia to Hungary, war with Genoa. Temporary peace between England and France, breaks down, French territorial gains. War in Castile. Papacy returns to Rome. Mongols invade Persia, Turkey, Russia, and India. Byzantine emperor acknowledges Ottoman suzerainty, Serbia and Anatolia annexed. Further Flemish revolts. Burgundian political and economic power. Swiss victory over Austrians.

The Crusades

4282 From 1095–1291 eight military expeditions to recapture Jerusalem from Muslims. Initially successful but eventually failed through international squabbling, military ineptitude, and greed.

1st Crusade 1096–99
Began by popular feeling to free the Holy Land from Muslim occupation. Within three years developed into military expedition.

2nd Crusade 1147–1149
King Louis VII of France and Emperor Conrad III of Germany led armies to recapture territory lost to Muslims.

3rd Crusade 1189–1192
Muslims recapture Jerusalem in 1187. Third crusade lead by Frederick I of Germany (Barbarossa), Philip II of France, and Richard 1st of England. Several successes against Muslim leader Saladin but Jerusalem remained in Muslim occupation.

4th Crusade 1201–1204
A crusade by Venetians and French to gain economic and political control of eastern Mediterranean.

Child's Crusade 1212
French and German youths under the age of 12 attempted to walk to the Holy Land. Few returned. Most were killed or became slaves.

5th–8th crusades
Subsequent crusades in the following years failed to establish permanent control in the Holy Land: 5th Crusade, 1218–21; 6th Crusade, 1228–29; 7th Crusade, 1248–51; 8th Crusade, 1270.

1st Crusade ———
2nd Crusade – – – –
3rd Crusade ··········
4th Crusade –•–•–

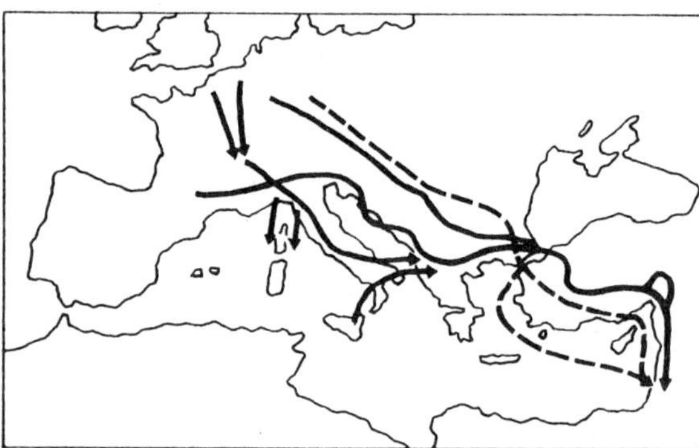

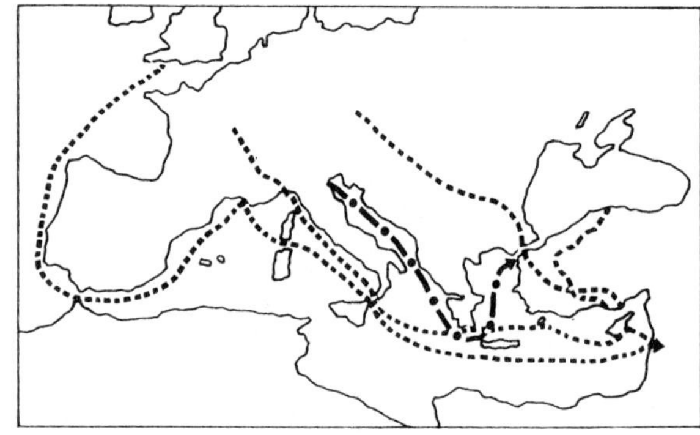

Places

4283 **1 Anjou** Independent feudal state in western France ruled by Plantagents 1109–1246.
2 Aquitaine Independent duchy in south-west France c. 900–1137. Possession disputed by France and England.
3 Aragon North-east Spain. Independent kingdom 1035. United with Castile 1479
4 Avignon French town on Rhône, seat of Papacy 1309–77.
5 Burgundy Duchy in eastern France including much of modern Belgium, Luxembourg, and Netherlands. Powerful and influential 1364–1477.
6 Canossa Italian castle in which German emperor Henry IV made submission to Pope Gregory VII.
7 Castile Central Spain. Autonomous from c. 960–1029. United with Leon 1072–1157. Dominant Spanish power 1188–1512.
8 Leon North-eastern and central Spanish kingdom c. 912–1230.

BATTLES
a Battle of Crécy 1346 in which English forces defeated French
b Battle of Hastings 1066 in which William Duke of Normandy defeated Harold to become king of England
c Battle of Lewes 1264 in which Simon de Montfort defeated Henry III.

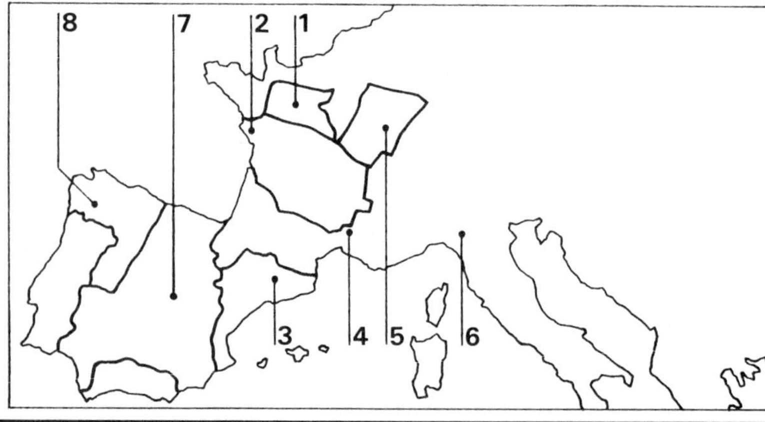

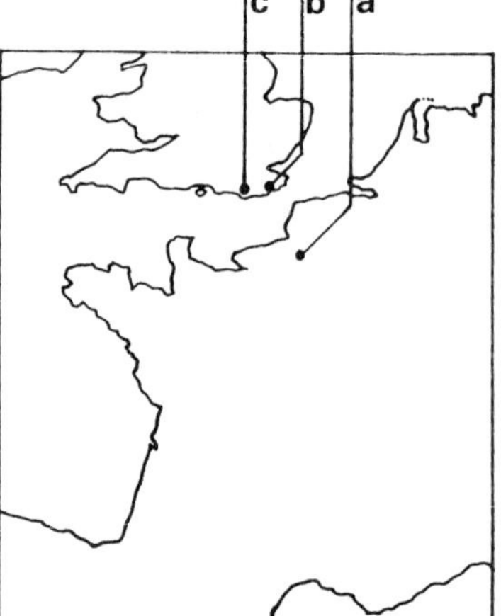

People

4284 **Alexander Nevski** 1218–63, Russian. Hero and saint, prince of Novgorod. In 1240, defeated Swedes in famous battle on Neva River, near modern St Petersburg, and in 1242 defeated Teutonic knights on frozen Lake Peipus.

Abelard, Pierre 1079–1142, French. Philosopher and scholar whose works include *Sic et Non*, a compilation of apparently contradictory biblical and patristic citations resolved according to rule of logic. Famous for passionate love affair with Héloise, niece of Canon Fulbert.

Becket, Thomas à 1118–70, English. Saint and martyr. Archbishop of Canterbury from 1162, fell out with Henry II, who voiced wish to be "rid of this turbulent priest" who championed rights of Church against king and state. Murdered in 1170.

Black Prince *see* Edward the Black Prince

El Cid, properly Rodrigo Diaz de Vivar, c. 1043–99, Spanish. Warrior hero immortalized as "El Cid" (The Lord) or "El Campeador" (The Champion). From 1081, began long career as soldier of fortune, serving Spaniards and Moors. Captured and ruled Valencia.

Eleanor of Aquitaine c. 1122–1204. Queen of France and England, daughter of Duke of Aquitaine. Married Louis VIII of France 1137, went on Second Crusade 1147–9, marriage annulled 1152, married Henry II of England 1152. Mother of kings Richard I and John.

Edward I 1239–1307, king of England, known as "Hammer of the Scots." Elder son of Henry III and Eleanor of Provence. Won great renown as knight on Eighth (and last) Crusade of 1270. Defeated Prince LLewelyn in 1282, and took over principality of Wales.

Edward III 1312–77, king of England from 1327, son of Edward II. In 1346, invaded France, conquered great deal of Normandy, and defeated French at Crécy. Ultimately failed to realize ambitions in France and Scotland, and faced financial ruin at home.

Edward the Black Prince 1330–76, English. Nobleman, eldest son of Edward III. Father of Richard II. In 1346, at 16, commanded right wing at Battle of Crécy, France, and later earned great victory at Poitiers. Made Prince of Aquitaine in 1362.

Louis IX (St Louis), 1215–70, king of France (**1**). Set off on Sixth Crusade 1248-54, but was held captive in Palestine until 1252, when he returned to France to continue long and peaceful reign. Died during Seventh Crusade.

1

Montfort, Simon IV de, Earl of Leicester, c. 1160–1218, Norman. Took part in Fourth Crusade 1202–04, and also undertook in 1208 crusade against Albigenses and fell at siege of Toulouse.

Montfort, Simon V de, Earl of Leicester, c. 1208–65, English. Statesman and soldier, son of Simon IV de Montfort. Led baronial revolt against Henry III. However, Barons soon grew dissatisfied with rule of "Simon the Righteous". Defeated by Prince at Evesham.

Philip II known as Philip-Augustus, 1165–1223.

2

First great Capetian king of France (**2**). Set out with Richard I on Third Crusade, 1190-91. In 1204, acquired dominions of Normandy, Maine, Anjou, Touraine, and overlordship of Brittany. Also built Notre Dames.

Richard I *coeur de Lion* "the Lionheart," 1157–99. King of England, third son of Henry II. In 1190, embarked on Third Crusade with Philip II Augustus. Captured by Austrians on way home in 1192, ransomed 1194. Killed during French skirmish.

Rienzo, Cola di c. 1313–54, Italian. Patriot, born of humble parentage, who incited citizens to rise against rule of nobles in Rome. Senators driven out and Rienzo took power, but forced to flee after seven months when papal authority turned against him.

Rollo (Hrolf), c. 860–c. 932, Viking. As leader of band of mercenary Vikings foraging in France in 911, was offered large tract of land on lower Seine (nucleus of future duchy of Normandy) by King Charles III "the Simple." Was such a huge man, no horse could carry him.

Saladin, properly Salah al-Din al-Ayyubi, 1137-93 (**3**).

3

Sultan of Egypt and Syria who was later defeated by crusader Richard I. Wise administrator who built citadels, roads, and canals. Opponents recognized his chivalry, good faith, justice, and greatness of soul.

Tamerlane Anglicized form of Timur-i-Lang, "lame Timur," 1336–1404. Mongol conqueror of Persia 1392–96, Turkey, Russia, and northern India 1398. Patron of visual arts and architecture. Died during expedition to conquer China.

Tell, William died c. 1310. Legendary Swiss patriot of Burglen in Uri, reputedly the savior of his native district from tyranny of Austria. *History of Switzerland* 1786 relates how Gessler, steward of Albert II of Austria, forced Tell, after his noncompliance, to shoot apple off son's head.

Timur *see* Tamerlane

Words

4285 **Albigenses** Cathar sect in southern France professing Manichaean dualism (good and evil of equal power, therefore denying God's supremacy over Satan). Savagely suppressed 1209–44.

Almoravids Berber Islamic tribesmen conquering Morocco and Algeria 1054–1147 and southern Spain 1085–1118. Succumbed to Christian reconquest.

Assassins Politico-religious Islamic sect sponsoring murder of opponents c. 1094–c. 1256.

Cathars *see* Albigenses

Concordat of Worms 1122 compromise agreement between Pope Calixtus II and Holy Roman Emperor Henry V over control of Church offices. Distinguished between secular and spiritual obligations of prelates.

Dance of Death *Danse Macabre* allegorical concept of power of death over all mankind, even the most powerful. Probably inspired by carnage of Black Death 1346–52 and Hundred Years' War 1337–1453.

Dauphiné Dauphinate area of south-eastern France. Acquired by French crown 1349 for heir to throne, henceforward known as the Dauphin.

Domesday Book 1086 survey of land holdings in England initiated by William the Conqueror.

Holy Sepulchre Tomb in Jerusalem reputed to be that of Jesus Christ. The Crusades sought to recover it from Muslim rule.

Hundred Years War 1337–1453 English Plantagenet kings' claim to French throne ended in expulsion of English from most of France.

Jacquerie 1358 French peasant revolt against nobility.

Knights, Teutonic *see* Teutonic Knights

Knights Templar 1119–1314 Military religious order founded to protect pilgrims to Holy Land and to gain territorial and political influence.

Lombard League Alliance of city-states resisting attempts at domination by Holy Roman Empire 1167–1250.

Magna Carta 1215 charter of English liberties granted by King John under threat of baronial civil war.

Manichaeism *see* Albigenses

Model Parliament 1295 first full English parliament.

Mongols Nomadic central Asian people whose empire under Genghis Khan stretched from China to Danube.

Saracens Arab peoples adopting Islam and opposing crusaders.

Schism 1054 Formal separation between Orthodox (eastern) and Roman Catholic (western) Churches.

Sicilian Vespers 1282 massacre of Angevins in and around Palermo precipitating Spanish-aided revolt against French rule.

Templars *see* Knights Templar

Teutonic Knights Religious and military order 1190–1525 establishing feudal state covering Prussia and east Baltic.

43 **America and Europe 1400–1850**
431 **European Exploration and Discovery 1400–1600**
4311 Events
4312 People
432 **The Renaissance**
4321 Events
4322 People
4323 Places in Italy
4324 Monarchs and rulers

431 EUROPEAN EXPLORATION AND DISCOVERY 1400–1600

Events

4311 **1400–50** Portuguese exploration on the West Coast of Africa. The Azores and Cape Verde are claimed for Portugal.
1450–90 Diego Cam pushes the Portuguese exploration of Africa to the tropic of Capricorn. Bartolomeu Dias rounds Cape of Good Hope.
1490–1500 First three voyages of Christopher Columbus, during which he discovers Cuba, Hispaniola (Dominican Republic and Haiti), and the Orinoco Delta on South American mainland. Vasco da Gama rounds Cape of Good Hope and finds route to India. John Cabot discovers Newfoundland.
1500–20 Pedro Cabral discovers Brazil for the Portuguese. Amerigo Vespucci establishes continental size of South America, and has the entire continent named after him. Vasco Nuñez de Balboa crosses the Isthmus of Panama and claims the Pacific for Spain. Hernando Cortés conquers Mexico for Spain. Ferdinand Magellan discovers westward route to the Pacific and circumnavigates the globe. Juan Ponce de León discovers Florida.
1520–40 Diego Lopez de Sequeira circumnavigates Africa. Pizarro conquers the Incas in Peru. Spanish exploration of New Mexico and California. Jacques Cartier explores the St Lawrence River as far as Montreal.
1540–60 Pedro de Valdívia explores in Chile, and south of the Bío Bío River. Hugh Willoughby and Richard Chancellor explore Canada in seach of the North East passage.
1560–80 Francis Drake sails to the Spice Islands and circumnavigates the globe. Martin Frobisher discovers Baffin Island and explores Hudson Bay. Andres de Urdaneta discovers northern route from the Philippines to Mexico. Alvaro de Mendaña, the first Spaniard to explore South Pacific, discovers Solomon Islands.
1580–1600 Walter Raleigh explores the Orinoco. Establishes British colony in North America, called Virginia. Mendaña and Pedro de Quiros discover the first of the Polynesian Islands. Willem Barents surveys Spitzbergen.

People

4312 **Cabot, John** (Giovanni Caboto) 1451–98, Italian navigator sent by Henry VII of England to explore the North American coast from Nova Scotia to Newfoundland.
Cabral, Pedro Alvares 1467–1520, Portuguese navigator who discovered Brazil in 1500 while sailing to India, claiming it for the Portuguese. Visited Calcutta and Sri Lanka.
Cartier, Jacques 1491–1557, French navigator who explored the St Lawrence waterway in Canada in two voyages, penetrating as far as Mount Royal (Montreal) in 1535.
Columbus, Christopher 1451–1506, Italian explorer, and discoverer of New World 1492, 1493-6 (West Indies), 1498–1500 (South American mainland), and 1502–4 (south side of Gulf of Mexico).
Copernicus, Nicolaus 1473–1543, Polish astronomer, founder of modern astronomy. Through observation, developed theory, propounded in *De Revolutionibus* (completed 1530, published 1543), that Earth revolves daily on axis and annually around Sun.
Da Gama, Vasco c. 1469–1524, Portuguese. The first European to navigate the Cape of Good Hope, on a journey which had also taken him within 600 miles of the South American mainland.
Drake, Sir Francis 1540–96 see section 4334
Diaz, or Dias, Bartolomeu c. 1450–1500, Portuguese navigator. Driven by violent storm, sailed round southern extremity of Africa, Cape of Good Hope, and discovered southernmost point of Africa, so opening route to India.
Frobisher, Sir Martin c. 1535–94, British explorer whose three attempts to discover the North West passage to India failed, but carried out coastal explorations of the north east of Canada.
Magellan, Ferdinand c. 1480–1521, Portuguese navigator, leader of first expedition, financed by Charles V, to circumnavigate globe. Crossed Atlantic 1519, and entered Pacific (named by him) in 1520. Magellan killed, but ship Victoria taken safely back to Spain by Sebastian del Cano.
Medici House of Tuscan banking family ruling Florence 1434–1737. Provided two queens consort for France, and three popes. Patron of arts and new learning, especially Cosimo (1389–1464), and Lorenzo (1449-92).
Vespucci, Amerigo 1451–1512, Italian-born Spanish explorer after whom continent of America is named. In 1499, promoted expedition to New World by Alonso de Hojeda, and sailed there in his own ship, exploring coast of Venezuela.

432 THE RENAISSANCE

Events

4321 **1400–20** Scholars migrating from Byzantium teach Greek and tenets of neo-Platonism in Italian universities. Timur the Lame invades Syria and China. Welsh rebellion against English rule. Lollards suppressed. Duke of Orléans killed by adherents of Duke of Burgundy, leads to civil war. English king captures Scottish king, claims French throne, allies with Burgundy. Papal schism ends.
1420–40 French government divided between English (from Paris) and French (from Poitiers). Ottoman attempt on Constantinople fails. Revival of French fortunes, Burgundy abandons English alliance. Medici dynasty established in Florence, Platonic Academy founded. Bohemian independence guaranteed. Portuguese voyages of exploration.
1440–80 Classical manuscripts collected in England. Printing invented in Mainz, spreads across Europe. Studies of New Testament based on original rather than medieval texts in northern Europe. Many universities founded. Constantinople falls, England loses all French possessions except Calais, civil war between rival claimants to succession to throne breaks out. Inquisition established in Spain. Aragon claims Naples.
1480–1515 Tudor dynasty succeeds Plantagenets in England. Muskovy adds territory. Venice acquires Cyprus. Americas discovered. India reached by Horn of Africa route. Rome replaces Florence as cultural centre. Castile conquers last Muslim enclave. French conquests in Italy. Jews expelled from Spain and Portugal.

People

4322 **Erasmus, Desiderius** c.1466–1536, Dutch humanist and scholar. One of most influential Renaissance figures. Traveled widely, writing, teaching, and meeting Europe's foremost intellectuals. Famous, satirical *Encomium Moriae* (*In Praise of Folly*) published 1509.
Galilei, Galileo, known as **Galileo** 1564–1642, Italian astronomer, mathematician, and natural philosopher (**1**) whose series of astronomical investigations convinced him of truth of Copernican heliocentric theory, and of illumination of Moon by reflection.

1

2

Gutenberg, Johannes Gensfleisch 1400–68, German. Regarded as inventor of printing. At Mainz, entered into partnership with Johannes Fust, who financed printing press. Began famous 42-line Bible, and is also credited with *Fragment of the Last Judgment*, c. 1455.
Joan of Arc, St, Jeanne d'Arc known as the Maid of Orléans, c. 1412–31 (**2**), French peasant girl and patriot, who led resistance against English 1429–30. Eventually sold to English, put on trial for heresy and sorcery, and burnt at stake as witch. Canonized in 1920.

continued

People continued

4322 **Julius II** born Giuliano della Rovere in Albizuola, 1443–1513, Pope from 1503. Career mainly devoted to re-establishing papal sovereignty in its ancient territory, and preventing foreign domination in Italy. Patron of arts and artists - especially Michelangelo and Raphael.

Machiavelli, Niccolò 1469–1527, Italian statesman, writer, and political philosopher (**3**). During diplomatic career, met Louis XII of France, Cesare Borgia, Pope Julius II, and Emperor Maximilian I. In *The Prince* (published 1532), described how ruler should acquire and retain power.

3

Petrarch, Francesco Petrarca 1307–74, Italian poet and scholar. One of earliest and greatest of modern lyric poets, and great humanist of Renaissance. Collected ancient Greek and Roman manuscripts. Great works include *Africa* and *De Viris Illustribus.*

Places in Italy

4323

Cities in Italy
1 Milan
2 Mantua
3 Verona
4 Venice
5 Ferrara
6 Rimini
7 Urbini
8 Genoa
9 Pisa
10 Florence
11 Siena
12 Rome

States in Renaissance Italy 1500
1 Duchy of Milan
2 Republic of Venice
3 Mantua
4 Ferrara
5 Republic of Genoa
6 Duchy of Modena
7 Republic of Florence
8 Republic of Siena
9 The Papal States
10 Kingdom of Naples

Monarchs and rulers

4324 **Borgia** House of Spanish–Italian family producing two popes, Calixtus III and Alexander VI, and Saint Francis. Cesare, Alexander's son, was able military and political commander. Lucrezia, the daughter, married thrice to augment family's power, and was patroness of arts and humanist learning.

1

Charles VII 1403–61 (**1**). King of France from 1422. During reign, Hundred Years' War came to an end, and English lost all land in France. First victory in 1426 at Montargis; Charles entered Paris 1436; fall of Bayonne 1451; death of Sir John Talbot at Castillon 1453.

Ferdinand II of Aragon and Sicily, Ferdinand V of Castile, Ferdinand III of Naples 1452–1516. First monarch of all Spain. Married Isabella of Castile in 1469. In 1492, took Granada from Moors, expelled Jews from kingdom, financed Columbus's expedition to New World.

Francis I 1494–1547. King of France from 1515 to 1547, and notable patron of Renaissance learning and arts, who created palace of Fontainebleu. Met Henry VIII of England at Field of Cloth of Gold in 1520. Asserted military power in Italy and against Spain.

Glendower, or Glyndwr, Owen c. 1350–c. 1416, Welsh rebel who claimed descent from Llywelyn ap Gruffydd. Engaged in guerrilla warfare against English lords of Marches which became national war of independence. Subsequently defeated, and died as fugitive.

Henry V 1387–1422. King of England from 1413. Great effort of reign was attempted conquest of France. At Agincourt, 1415, achieved victory against overwhelming odds, and two years later, again invaded France. 1420 Peace of Troyes recognized Henry as regent and heir of France.

Henry, known as **the Navigator** 1394–1460 (**2**), Portuguese son of John I of Portugal. Voyages of pupils resulted in discovery of Madeira Islands (in 1418), the Azores, and the Cape Verde Islands. His pupils also explored west coast of Africa, and established many trading posts.

2

Isabella of Castile 1451–1504, Spanish queen of Spain from 1474. In 1469, married Ferdinand "the Catholic" of Aragon, and became joint sovereign with him. With Ferdinand, in 1492, achieved conquest of Granada (ending Moorish power in peninsula). Patron of Columbus.

continued

Monarchs and rulers continued

4324 **Lancaster, House of** 1399–1471. One of two English dynastic houses formed when the royal Plantagenet family split in 1399.
Louis XI 1423–83. King of France from 1461, With mixture of force and diplomatic cunning, broke power of nobility led by Charles the Bold of Burgundy, who was killed in 1477. By 1483, had united most of France, and laid foundations for absolute monarchy.
Plantagenet, House of Surname applied to Angevin family which in 1154 succeeded to throne of England in the person of Henry II, and lasted until 1485.
Richard III 1452–85. King of England from 1483. Last Plantagenet monarch. As Duke of Gloucester, able soldier and administrator. Accused of murder of nephew and rightful king Edward. Killed at Battle of Bosworth, 1485.
Torquemada, Tomas de 1420–98, Spanish. Dominican monk, and first inquisitor-general of Spain from 1483. In this "Holy Office," sanctioned by pope, displayed pitiless cruelty. Was responsible for expulsion of Jews from Spain in 1492.
Tudor, House of 1485–1603. Kings of England of Lancastrian and Welsh descent.
Valois, House of, 1328–1589. French royal dynasty.
Warwick, Richard Neville, Earl of 1428–71, "the Kingmaker," English. Soldier and statesman who, during Wars of the Roses, held balance between Yorkist and Lancastrian factions, and masterminded transference of throne from Lancaster to York. Killed in battle after changing sides.
York, House of 1461–85. One of two English dynastic houses formed when the royal Plantagenet family split in 1399.

Places

4325

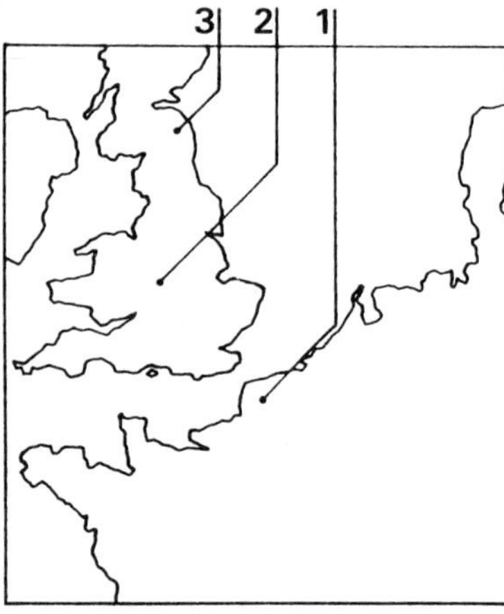

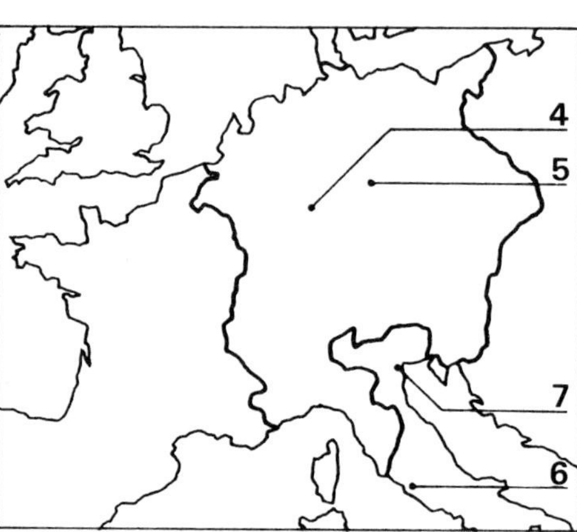

Holy Roman Empire at the time of Henry VIII
4 Frankfurt
5 Schmalkalden
6 Rome
7 Venice

1 Battle of Agincourt 1415, in which English under Henry V defeated French.
2 Battle of Bosworth 1485, last battle of Wars of Roses. Henry VII (Tudor) defeated and killed Richard III (Yorkist).
3 Battle of Flodden 1513, in which the English defeated the Scots under James IV, who died in the conflict.
Battle of the Oka 1480, in which Muscovites defeated Turks.
Battle of Tannenberg 1410, in which Poles defeated Teutonic knights.
Granada Muslim state 1238–1492 in southern Spain.
Holy Roman Empire Stretched from Netherlands through Germany, Switzerland, Austria, Hungary to Czechoslovakia. Reformation split Protestant princes and free cities from Catholic ones. Further weakened by Thirty Years' War.
Muscovy Principality of Moscow between 12th and 16th centuries which came to dominate Russia.

Words

4326 **Great Schism** 1378–1417 Period in which rival popes claimed office. Led to calls for church reform.
Hundred Years' War 1337–1453 Anglo-French conflict ending with expulsion of English from Normandy and Acquitaine.
Knights of St John Military religious order originally responsible for welfare of pilgrims to Holy Land. Installed at Rhodes 1310, forced by Turkish conquest to move to Malta 1522–30.
neo-Platonism Revival of philosophical system developed in third century.
new learning Study of biblical and classical texts in original languages.
Ottoman empire 1300–1922 Replaced Byzantine empire and dominated eastern Mediterranean throughout 16th and 17th centuries.
Siege of Malta see Knights of St John.
Siege of Rhodes see Knights of St John.
Tudor, House of 1485–1603 Kings of England of Lancastrian and Welsh descent.
Wars of the Roses 1455–85 Dynastic conflict for English throne between Lancastrian and Yorkist branches of House of Plantagenet.
Universal Man Renaissance concept of individual respected for skills in many fields of knowledge rather than for high birth.

433 THE REFORMATION AND RELIGIOUS WARS 1515–1688

Events

4331 **1515–20** Luther attacks sale of indulgences, defies excommunication, appeals to German nobility for support. Independence movement in Sweden crushed by Danish king. Ottoman sultan conquers Syria and Egypt. Portuguese bases in Ceylon. Spanish expeditions to Mexico. German gunsmiths develop wheel-lock weapons.
1520–30 Luther encourages suppression of peasants' revolt by German princes. Holy Roman Empire forces sack Rome, drive French from north Italy. Ottoman troops take Belgrade, invade Hungary, fail to take Vienna.
1530–55 Calvin develops Luther's ideas from Geneva. Calvinism spreads in France, Netherlands, and Scotland. England breaks with Rome, monastic property taken over by crown. German princes wage war against emperor for control of church lands. Lutherism spreads throughout north Germany and into Scandinavia. Muscovite ruler becomes tsar of Russia. Portuguese colonize Brazil.
1540–60 Counter-Reformation launched. Council of Trent held at Trento, in north Italy. Jesuit order founded, missions abroad. Russian territorial gains. England opens trade route to Moscow, returns to Protestant camp when Elizabeth I succeeds half-sister Mary. Spanish colonize Chile. Portuguese trade with China. Scottish reformers make first covenant, gain political control.
1560–1600 Wars of Religion in France. Protestants massacred, reprisals. Equal political rights confirmed through Edict of Nantes. Valois dynasty replaced by Bourbons. England launches voyages of discovery, beats off Spanish invasion. Scottish queen flees to

continued

Events continued

4331 England after defeat by Calvinist opponents, and is imprisoned, tried, executed. Netherlands revolt against Spanish rule eventually unites Catholics and Protestants.
1600–20 Stuart dynasty replaces Tudors in England, attempts absolutist rule, anti-Catholic legislation, Ireland submits, Authorized version of Bible, dissenting Protestants settle in America (New England). France weakened during minority of Louis XIII. Holy Roman Empire troops recover Bohemia, start of Thirty Years' War.
1620–50 Thirty Years' War devastates Germany, divides Holy Roman Empire, weakens Spain, strengthens France. Civil War in England, Scotland and Ireland in protest against Charles I's attempts to govern without Parliament. King eventually captured, tried and executed.
1650–60 Commonwealth in England, Irish revolts crushed, wars against Dutch. French nobility opposes centralized royal rule but eventually submits.
1660–88 Stuart dynasty restored to English throne. France at war first with Dutch, then with Britain. Absolute monarchy ends in Britain with "Glorious Revolution."

People: Religious leaders

4332 **Calvin, John** 1509–64, French theologian and reformer who systematized Protestant doctrines, and organized its ecclesiastical discipline. At Geneva, Switzerland, founded theocracy which was virtually to direct all affairs of city, and to control social and individual life of citizen.
Cranmer, Thomas 1489–1556, English Prelate and first Protestant archbishop of Canterbury. Assisted dissolution of Henry VIII's second, fourth and fifth marriages. 1547–53, tried to purge Church of England further. Burned as heretic.
Cromwell, Thomas, Earl of Essex c. 1485–1540, English statesman. Lord Privy Seal 1536–40. Facilitated English religious autonomy, and expedited confiscation of monastic property by Henry VIII. Tried to create Lutheran alliance through king's (fifth) marriage to Anne of Cleves. Executed.
Huss, or Hus, John c. 1369–1415, Bohemian religious reformer whose writings, such as *De Ecclesia*, vaunted state supremacy over church. Popular riots followed his excommunication in 1411. Writings condemned 1415. Burned 1415, his death provoked bloody Hussite wars.
Knox, John c. 1513–72, Scottish. Calvinist. Author of *History of the Reformation in Scotland.* Served as French galley slave 1548-9. After spells in Geneva, returned to Scotland in 1559. Led opposition to Mary Queen of Scots.
Laud, William 1573–1645, English Prelate and archbishop of Canterbury who opposed Puritanism and Presbyterianism. As result of riots and "Bishop's war" caused by his attempt to Anglicize church in Scotland, arrested by Parliament, tried for treason (1644) and beheaded.
Loyola, Ignatius St properly Iñigo de Oñaz y Loyola, 1491–1556, Spanish soldier and founder of Jesuits who wrote *Spiritual Exercises.* Convalescing from battle wound, turned to religious exercises, and in 1534, with St Francis Xavier, founded Society of Jesus. Canonized in 1622.
Luther, Martin 1483–1546, German religious reformer, and founder of Protestant Reformation, who preached doctrine of salvation by faith rather than works (**1**). Famous 95 theses, attacking ecclesiastical abuses, nailed to church door at Wittenberg in 1517. Translated Bible into German 1522–34.
More, St Thomas 1478–1535, English statesman and scholar who, by his *Utopia* (1516), takes his place with most eminent humanists of Renaissance. Refused to acknowledge King Henry VIII as head of church, was tried for high treason, and executed. Canonized 1935.

1

People: Monarchs

4333 **Bourbon, House of** 1589–1789, 1814–30. French royal dynasty which took name from castle of Bourbon, near Moulins in Allier, France.
Charles I 1600–49. King of Great Britain and Ireland from 1625, second son of James VI and I and Anne of Denmark (**1**). Belief in absolute monarchy, desire to rule without Parliament (which he did for 11 years) and adherence to Anglicanism led to Civil War. Defeated, he was imprisoned in 1646, tried for treason, and beheaded.
Charles II, 1630–85, King of Scotland and England from 1660, eldest son of Charles I and Henrietta Maria. Spent nine years in exile in France and Netherlands after defeat by Cromwell in 1651. Restored to throne after latter's death, he survived political mistrust through judicial alliances (**2**).
Charles V 1500–58. Holy Roman Emperor 1519–58, king of Spain (Charles I) 1516-56, nephew of Catherine of Aragon (Henry VIII's first wife). Founder of Habsburg dynasty who rejected Luther's doctrines, and struggled to maintain empire and Catholicism. Reign saw Spanish conquest of Mexico and Peru.
Charles IX 1550–74. King of France from 1559, second son of Henri II and Catherine de' Medici. Reign dominated by religious wars between Protestants and Catholics. Government effectively in hands of his mother, who was responsible (with his brother Henri) for St Bartholomew's Day Massacre of Huguenots in Paris in 1572.

1 2 3 4 5

Elizabeth I 1533–1603, "Virgin Queen" of England and Ireland from 1558, daughter of Henry VIII and Anne Boleyn, whose long reign coincided with emergence of England as world power, and flowering of English Renaissance (**3**). Allied herself with Protestants, and held off Spanish Armada (1588), French and Scottish threats.
Guise, House of Prominent ducal family of Lorraine, France, whose power challenged royal authority 1550–1650. Ferociously active against Huguenots 1562–88.
Gustav II Adolf (Gustavus Adolphus) 1594–1632 (**4**). Protestant king of Sweden from 1611, known as "the Lion of the North." Compelling leader of exceptional ability and military achievement who left Sweden the strongest power in Europe. Fought Poland (1621–29) and Holy Roman Empire (1630–2). Killed in battle.
Henri IV, known as **Henri of Navarre,** 1553–1610. King of France from 1589, first of Bourbon monarchy, who renounced Protestantism and became Catholic in 1593. 1598 Edict of Nantes, recognizing rights of Huguenot minority, brought end to more than 40 years of French religious wars. Conciliator, who also restored economy.
Henry VIII 1491–1547 (**5**). King of England from 1509, second son of Henry VII. Attracted

continued

People: Monarchs continued

4333 by humanism. Desire for heir led to six marriages, two daughters, and one sickly son. Thwarted in attempt to divorce first wife, Catherine of Aragon, asserted independence from Rome and assumed full authority over church in England.

Ivan IV, known as **"Ivan the Terrible"** (**6**) 1530–84. Grandson of Ivan III "the Great." Grand Duke from 1553, Tsar of Russia from 1547. Established new code of law and system of local self-government. Captured Kazan (1552), and Astrakhan (1552), invaded Livonia 1558, and ravaged Novgorod 1570.

James VI 1566–1625. King of Scotland from 1567, James I of England from 1603, son of Mary Queen of Scots (**7**). "Wisest fool in Christendom" was in fact tough-minded, talented ruler who transformed Scottish politics and society. Endeavoured to promote peace with Spain. As "absolute monarchist," clashed with Parliament.

James VII of Scotland, II of England (both 1685-88), 1633–1701. Second son of Charles I, brother of Charles II, whose conversion to Catholicism led to attempts to exclude him from succession. Eventually deposed by William (later III, of Orange), died in exile in France.

Louis XIV, known as the **"Sun King"** (Le Roi Soleil) 1638–1715. King of France from 1643 (**8**). Son of Louis XIII and Anne of Austria, came to throne aged five. Nobles rebelled during regency of mother, and Cardinal Mazarin. Ruled as absolute monarch, warring with Netherlands and Spain. Persecuted Huguenots.

Mary, Queen of Scots 1542–87. Daughter of James V of Scotland by Mary of Guise. Queen of France through marriage to François II 1558–60. Returned to Reformation Scotland 1561, deposed 1567, fled to England. Imprisoned 1569 by Elizabeth I. As Catholic heir to English throne, center of conspiracies. Tried and executed.

Mary I, Tudor 1516–58. Queen of England from 1553, daughter of Henry VIII by Catherine of Aragon. Attempted to restore Catholicism. In period of persecution which gave her name "Bloody Mary," Ridley, Latimer, and Cranmer all went to the stake. Married to Philip II, King of Spain. Died childless.

Philip II 1527–98 (**9**). King of Spain from 1556, only son of emperor Charles V. Husband of Mary I of England. Devout Catholic whose violent campaign against Protestants destroyed all harmony within his dominions. Revolt of Netherlands 1576. Wars against Turkey from 1571, and England 1588–1604.

Stuart, House of Scottish family from whom came royal line of (Stuart) sovereigns of Scotland (1371–1707), England (1603–1707), and Great Britain and Ireland (1707–14).

Rupert, Prince 1619–82, English Cavalry officer, third son of Frederick V of Bohemia and Elizabeth, daughter of James VI of Scotland and I of England. Brilliant cavalry tactician whose Civil War victories were halted by superior Parliamentary military discipline. After Restoration, experimented with science and printmaking.

Suleyman, "the Magnificent," 1494–1566, Ottoman emperor from 1520, son of Selim I, greatest of Ottoman sultans (**10**). Known to his own people as "Law Giver." Program of internal reform aimed at improving justice and administration, and ensuring freedom of religion. Captured Belgrade (1521) and Rhodes (1522).

William the Silent 1533–84. Count of Nassau and Prince of Orange from 1544. Roman Catholic, but moderate, tolerant man who led group of nobles calling for relaxation of heresy laws, and suspension of Inquisition. As Protestant convert, invaded Netherlands 1572 to try and oust Duke of Alva. Killed 1584.

People

4334 **Alva, or Alba, Ferdinand Alvarez de Toledo, Duke of** 1508–82, Spanish general and statesman, and brilliant scholar and tactician. On revolt of Netherlands, was sent in 1567 to enforce Spanish control there, and set up "Bloody Council," forcing emigration of thousands of Huguenot artisans.

Coligny, Gaspard II de 1519–72, French Huguenot leader who gained ascendancy over Charles IX, son of ambitious queen regent Catherine de' Medici, and as a result was one of first victims of Massacre of Huguenots on St Bartholomew's Day, 1572.

Cortés, Hernando 1485–1547, Spanish Conquistador and conqueror of Mexico (**1**). Acquired Tenochtitlan, capital of Mexico, in 1519, but had to recapture it in 1521 after Mexican revolt ("Night of Sorrows"). Returned to Spain 1528, and 1540. Died during expedition with Charles V to Algiers.

Cromwell, Oliver 1599–1685, English soldier and statesman, State Council chairman 1649–53, Lord Protector of England 1653–8. Became staunch opponent of Charles I during stormy parliament of 1628–9, and successfully led Parliamentarian forces in Civil War.

Drake, Sir Francis c. 1540–96, English navigator and pirate. First Englishman to see Pacific Ocean (after plundering on Isthmus of Panama in 1572), and to circumnavigate world (1577–80). In 1587, sacked Cadiz, and in 1588 fought Spanish Armada. Died during voyage to West Indies.

John of Austria, known as **Don John** 1547–78, Spanish soldier, illegitimate son of Emperor Charles V and Barbara Blomberg of Ratisbon. In October 1571, defeated Turks in great sea fight of Lepanto. Viceroy to Spanish Netherlands from 1576, defeated William the Silent at Gembloux in 1577.

Marlborough, John Churchill 1st Duke of 1650–1722, English soldier who transferred allegiance from James II to William III, who never thereafter entirely trusted him. Defeated French at Blenheim (1704), Ramillies (1706), Oudenarde (1708), and Bouchain (1711).

Pizarro, Francisco c. 1478–1541, Spanish conqueror of Peru who, with rival Almagro (conqueror of Chile), subdued Inca empire 1532–5, and was made marquis by Emperor Charles V. Founded number of coastal cities. Assassinated at Lima after retaking Cuzco from Almagro.

Pius V, St named Michele Ghislieri, 1504–72. Pope from 1566. Dominican friar and ascetic who labored to restore discipline and morality. As inquisitor general for Lombardy, rigorously repressed Reformed doctrines. Excommunicated Queen Elizabeth I of England in 1570.

Richelieu, Armand Jean Duplessis, Cardinal, Duc de 1585–1642, French Prelate and chief minister (from 1624) who took France into Thirty Years' War on Protestant side. Greatly increased power of French throne. Fought Huguenots as political rather than religious rebels.

Strafford, Thomas Wentworth, 1st Earl of 1593–1641, English statesman. Lord deputy of Ireland from 1632, then chief advisor to Charles I from 1639. Impeached by Pym and Puritans after failure to quell Scottish revolt 1640.

Tilly, Jan Tserklaes, Count of 1559–1632, Flemish soldier who, as commander of Catholic army at start of Thiry Years' War, was victorious at Weisser Berg and Prague (1620), thus destroying hopes of Elector Palatine. Sacked Magdeburg 1631. Killed in battle.

Wallenstein, or **Waldstein, Albrecht Wenzel Eusebius von** 1583–1634, Austrian soldier. Commander-in-chief of all imperial forces 1625–30, and 1632–34. Intrigued with Protestants and Catholics in hope of becoming ruler of united Germany, but was assassinated.

Places

4335 **1 Armada (Enterprise of England)** 1588, massive Spanish fleet sent to assist military invasion of England from Netherlands. Defeated and dispersed.
2 Sack of Antwerp 1576, by Spanish forces. Led to rise of Amsterdam as mercantile and cultural centre.
3 Battle of Edgehill 1642, first and indecisive Civil War battle.
4 Battle of Pavia 1525, in which Spanish under Charles V defeated and captured French king Francis I.
5 Siege of La Rochelle See Huguenots
6 Battle of Lepanto 1571, naval engagement between Turks and allied Spanish and Venetian fleets, who won.
7 Battle of Lutzen 1632, Swedish victory over imperial forces.
8 Battle of Marston Moor 1644, gave control of north of England to Parliamentarians.
9 Sack of Magdeberg 1631, by imperial forces under Tilly.
10 Battle of Naseby 1645, decisive encounter sealing ruin of Royalist cause.
11 St Bartholomew's Massacre 1572, sought to eliminate all Huguenots in Paris as well as in provinces, especially leaders.
12 Battle of Worcester 1651, final conflict of Civil War. Cromwell defeated Charles II's attempt to regain father's throne.

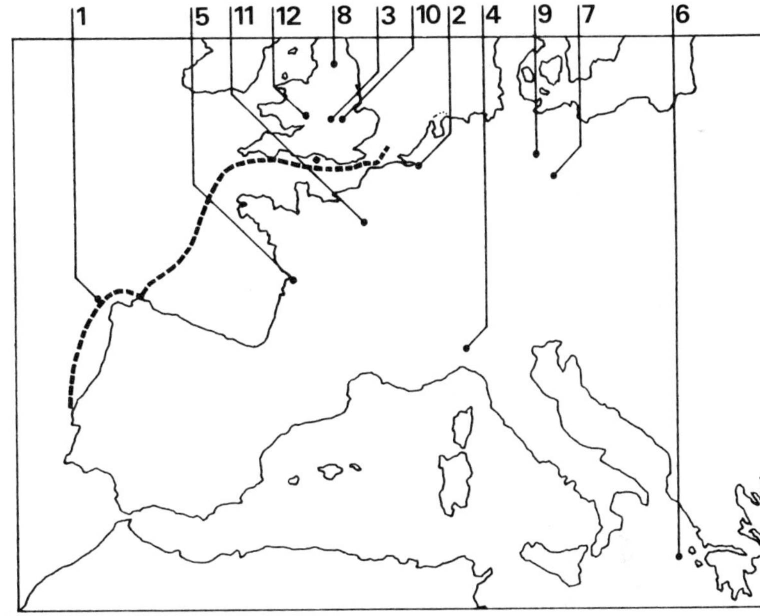

Words

4336 **Acts of Supremacy** 1534, 1559 Declared sovereign supreme head of church in England.
Anabaptists Radical Protestant movement founded 1525 and first based in Zurich. Communistic, polygamous theocracy established Munster 1534, suppressed 1535.
Anglican Church Reformed church of England first established 1534 but retaining elements of Roman Catholic dogma and ritual.
Augsburg Declaration 1555 Gave individual German princes freedom of religion. Subjects were required to follow ruler's faith.
Babington Conspiracy 1586 Catholic plot to assassinate Elizabeth I and put Mary Queen of Scots on English throne.
Bohemia Slav kingdom attempting to maintain independence of Holy Roman Empire. Rival claims to throne led to Thirty Years' War.
Catholic League 1609–48 Alliance of princes on imperial side during Thirty Years' War and preliminary engagements.
Cavaliers see Royalists.
Commonwealth 1649–60 Republican state in England between execution of Charles I and restoration of Charles II.
Council of Blood (Council of Troubles) 1567–74 Spanish instrument for suppression of religious and political revolt.
Council of Trent 1545–63 Ecumenical Catholic assembly which instituted major reforms and paved way for Counter Reformation.
covenanters Scottish Presbyterians opposed to Catholicism, episcopacy, and monarchical absolutism.
Diet of Worms 1521 Holy Roman Empire assembly attended by Luther under safe-conduct from Charles V. Its edict subsequently outlawed Luther.
dissenters Those who disassociated themselves from Church of England.
Dissolution of monasteries 1536–9 Suppression of religious houses and confiscation of their property, masterminded by Thomas Cromwell. Wolsey had earlier suppressed about 30 to finance the construction of Oxford college.
divine right (of kings to be absolute rulers) Doctrine adhered to by James I that caused downfall of Charles I.
Edict of Nantes 1598 Secured political rights and some freedom of worship for French Huguenots. Revoked 1685, leading to persecutions, emigration.
Fronde 1648–53 French civil disturbances led by royal princes and members of aristocracy during minority of Louis XIV. Failure paved way for king's subsequent absolutism.
Glorious Revolution 1688 Almost bloodless coup d'état which replaced Catholic authoritarian James II with Protestant William III and Mary II.
Gunpowder Plot 1605 Catholic conspiracy to blow up James I at opening of Parliament.
Holy Office see Inquisition
Huguenots French Protestants, mainly Calvinist. Powerful political and military challengers of royal power. Military base at La Rochelle captured after siege by Richelieu (1628).
Hussite Wars 1420–36 Wars between followers of Huss rejecting imperial claims to Bohemian throne and requiring freedom of conscience, and imperial forces backed by Papacy.
indulgences Catholic doctrine of remission of temporal punishment for confessed sins through penance, good works or almsgiving. Abuse of plenary (full) indulgences led to Luther's repudiation of doctrine. Pecuniary aspect abolished 1562.
Inquisition (Holy Office) Roman Catholic tribunal concerned with investigating and punishing heresy.
Jesuits see Society of Jesus.
Justification Doctrines of man moving from state of sin to state of grace through faith and good deeds. Catholicism accepted both concepts, Protestants upheld faith as sole validation.
Knights' War 1522–3 German uprising attempting to assert united national reformed religion.
Levellers 1645–9 English radical republican party.
Lollards English reforming sect following teachings of John Wycliffe.
Nonconformists Dissenters from Church of England.
Nonjurors Anglican clergymen refusing to take oath of allegiance to William III and Mary II.
Parliamentarians Supporters of Parliament rather than king during Civil War.
Peasants' Revolts 1524–5 Uprisings in Germany against feudal as well as church malpractices. Condemned by Luther.
Pilgrim Fathers English Puritans who founded colony of Plymouth in New England 1620.
Pilgrimage of Grace 1536 Northern English rebellion against dissolution of monasteries. Savagely suppressed.
Popish Plot 1678 Fictitious allegations against Catholics fabricated by Titus Oates and others. At least 35 innocent people were executed.
predestination Doctrine of Calvinist and other belief that God has determined from eternity those to be saved or damned regardless of merit or actions.
Presbyterians Reformers advocating elected church government without bishops or interference by secular rulers.

continued

Words continued

4336 **Protestants** Description of Lutherans after protest during Diet of Speyer (1527).
Puritanism Church of England reform movement in late 16th and 17th centuries seeking to exterminate all remnants of Catholic doctrine and ritual.
Quakers see Society of Friends.
Restoration 1660 Return of Stuart dynasty after Commonwealth. Also social and artistic fashions introduced during period 1660–1714.
Roundheads see Parliamentarians.
Royalists Supporters of Charles I and II during Civil War.
Rump 1648–60 Parliament purged of members unacceptable to army.
Santa Maria Ship in which Columbus sailed 1492.
Sicilies, Kingdom of the Two 1443–58, 1504–1713, 1759–1860 Joint rule of former independent kingdoms of Naples and of Sicily.
Society of Friends (Quakers) Christian sect without ritual, creed or priesthood, founded 1650 by George Fox.
Society of Jesus (Jesuits) Catholic missionary and teaching order founded 1534 by Ignatius Loyola, a Spanish soldier, military in discipline and often controversial.
Treaties of Westphalia 1648 Ended Thirty Years' War. Territorial gains for France and Sweden at imperial expense.
Thirty Years' War 1618–48 Central and western European conflict originally fought on Catholic versus Protestant issues but becoming increasingly secularized. France and Sweden both entered on Protestant side.
Wittenburg Declaration 1517 Luther's 95 "Theses" initiating Reformation.

434 THE AGE OF REASON 1688–1789

Events

4341 **1688–1707** Stuart Catholic king James II superseded by daughter Mary II and son-in-law William III of Orange. France and Holy Roman Empire at war. James II attempts to regain throne through Irish invasion, defeated. French settlers massacred in Canada, witch trials in New England, North Carolina divided from South.
1702–7 War of Spanish Succession. Spain joins coalition against France, naval engagements. Bank of England founded 1694. Russo-Turkish war 1695. France acquires Nice. William III succeeded by sister-in-law Anne. Dispute over succession to Spanish throne leads to war. Sweden invades Poland, challenges Russia. Hungary ceded to Austria by Turkey, later revolts against Austrian rule. British military successes against France. England and Scotland united as Great Britain.
1708–14 Sweden invades Russia, Cossack uprising, administration centralized. Coalitions against Sweden. Russian, Danish military successes. British military successes in Europe. France cedes north American territory to Britain. Indian Mogul empire disintegrates. Stuart dynasty ends in Britain, elector of Hanover succeeds as George I.
1715–39 Death of Louis XIV. Second attempt to restore Stuart monarchy in Britain fails. Russia dominates Finland, invades Sweden. Austro-Hungarian empire at war with Turkey. English Parliament legislates for Ireland. Prussian government centralized. Russia and Turkey ally against Persia. Britain and Spain at war. France expands influence in India and Canada. Wars of Polish Succession and Jenkins's Ear.
1740–9 Death of Charles VI, succeeded by daughter Maria Theresa, War of Austrian Succession. Attempt to restore Stuart monarchy in Britain fails. Prussian military successes. France and Britain at war in North America. Afghan state founded. France cedes territorial gains in India.
1750–63 Britain joins Austro-Russian alliance against Prussia. British territorial gains in India. *Encyclopédie* launched in France, judiciary asserts rights. Ministerial crisis in England. French and Indian war against Britain in North America. New alignments in Europe. Prussia repulses Russian invasion, aided by British subsidies. Britain establishes control over Canada, dominates West Indies. George II succeeded by George III, Catherine II takes power in Russia. Seven Years' War ends.
1764–75 American colonies oppose English-imposed taxes. Bengali administration reformed. Parliament declares general warrants (not naming individuals) illegal. Russia and Turkey at war. Proposals for partition of Poland between Austria, Prussia and Russia implemented. Swedish constitution. Austrian financial reforms. War of American Independence.
1776–89 French financial reforms fail. Spain and Portugal settle disputes over South American colonies, Spain acquires Florida. French territorial gains in West Indies. Dutch settlers clash with Bantu people in south Africa. Home Rule for Ireland demanded, Irish Parliament granted. Russia annexes Crimea. Loyalists settle in Canada at end of War of American Independence. Pitt the Younger becomes prime minister aged 24. League of German princes formed against Austria. Russia and Austria at war with Turkey and Sweden. Holland and Austrian Netherlands demand greater political autonomy. French king convenes Estates-General, Revolution begins.

People

4342 **Burke, Edmund** 1729–97, Irish statesman and philosopher. Developed Whig liberal policies. Supported American colonists' desire for independence. Instigated impeachment proceedings against Warren Hastings. Denounced French Revolution.
Bute, John Stuart, 3rd Earl of 1713–92, Scottish statesman who exercised strong influence over George III. Became main instrument for breaking power of Whigs, and establishing personal rule of monarch through parliament. Prime minister 1762–5.
Chatham, William Pitt, 1st Earl of known as "the elder Pitt," 1708–78, English statesman and orator. Secretary of State 1756–61, and Prime minister 1766–8. War policy characterized by unusual vigor, sagacity, and success.
Clive of Plassey, Robert, Baron 1725–74, English soldier and colonial administrator. Captured in 1746 by French at Madras in India, but escaped and later held Arcot against French-Indian army. In 1757, retook Calcutta. Committed suicide following Parliamentary inquiry.
Cumberland, William Augustus, Duke of 1721–65, English military commander, second son of George II, who, by violent suppression of Jacobite rebellion at Culloden, Scotland, in 1746, earned title "Butcher." Retired after surrendering at Kloster-Zeven (1757) during Seven Years' War.
Diderot, Denis 1713–84, French writer. One of most prolific and versatile: novelist, dramatist, satirist, philosopher, pioneering arts critic, and brilliant letter writer (**1**). Chief editor of *Encyclopédie* . *Pensées Philosophiques* burned in 1746.

Eugène of Savoy, Prince, properly **François Eugène de Savoie-Carignan** 1663–1736, Austrian soldier, and renowned military strategist. Under Emperor Leopold I, slaughtered Turks at Zenta in 1697, and later ended French campaign in Italy. Defeated by Villars at Denain, 1712.
Fleury, André Hercule de 1653–1743, French Prelate. Chief minister 1726–43, during minority and early manhood of Louis XV. Able administrator and diplomat, who minimized French involvement in external conflicts in order to recover her finances.
Hastings, Warren 1732–1818, English administrator. From 1773, first governor-general of India. Opposed in council by Sir Philip Francis. In 1777, Supreme Court frustrated attempt to oust him. Returned to England 1784, faced impeachment, but was acquitted 1788–95.
Hume, David 1711–76, Scottish philosopher and historian. First and most important work, *A Treatise of Human Nature,* continuing empiricist tradition of Locke and Berkeley, published 1739–40, but real fame came with *Political Discourses* (1752) and *History of England* (1754-62).

continued

People continued

4342 **Kaunitz-Rietberg, Wenzel Anton, Prince von** 1711–94, Austrian statesman, who opposed rise of Prussian power. As ambassador to French court, 1750–2, converted old enmity into friendship, and from 1753, as chancellor, directed Austrian politics for nearly 40 years.

Law, John, of Lauriston 1671–1729, Scottish financier who escaped from prison, fled to Europe, and made fortune in Genoa and Venice. Success of his private bank, set up in Paris, led to regent Philippe's (Duc d'Orléans) adopting Law's scheme for national bank in 1716. Died at Venice.

Locke, John 1632–1704, English philosopher. Major work, *Essay Concerning Human Understanding* (1690), regarded as first and probably most important statement of empiricist theory of knowledge. *Two Treatises of Government* (1690) had powerful influence on American and French revolutions.

Montesquieu, Charles de Secondat, Baron de la Bréde et de 1689-1755, French philosopher and jurist, member of French Academy from 1728. Traveled for three years to study political and social institutions. Monumental *De L'esprit des Lois* published 1748.

Necker, Jacques 1732–1804, French statesman and financier. From 1777, director general of finance, whose most ambitious scheme – establishment of provincial assemblies whose functions included levying taxes – was disastrous failure. Famous *Administration des Finances* published 1784.

Pitt, William "the Younger" 1759–1806, English statesman, second son of Earl of Chatham (**2**), who, in 1783, at 24, became Britain's youngest prime minister. Governed until 1801, then 1804–6. Laid foundation of colonial
administration in India and Canada.

Pompadour, Jeanne Antoinette Poisson, Marquise de 1721–64, mistress of Louis XV of France who assumed control of public affairs. In disastrous policy, engineered alliance with Austria which led to Seven Years' War. Lavish patroness of arts.

Rousseau, Jean-Jacques 1712–78, French political philosopher, educationist, and author (**3**). Masterpiece *The Social Contract* (1762), which proposed that individual should surrender his rights totally to collective "general will," became bible of French Revolution.

3

Saint Véran Gezan de 1712–59, French soldier. At start of Seven Years' War (1756), commanded French troops in Canada, and took Oswego, Fort William Henry, Luisburg, and Fort Duquesne from British. Died after defeat by General Wolfe.

Stuart, Prince Charles Edward Louis Philip Casimir, known variously as the **"Young Pretender," "Young Chevalier,"** and **"Bonnie Prince Charlie"** 1720–88, grandson of James II. Attempted to regain British throne for father 1745–6. Escaped to France after defeat at Culloden.

2

Stuart, Prince James Edward, known as **"Old Pretender"** 1688–1766. Claimant to throne of Great Britain, only son of James VII and II by Mary of Modena. Unsuccessfully attempted to recover British throne 1708, 1715. Died at Rome.

Turgot, Anne Robert Jacques 1727–81, French economist and statesman. Appointed comptroller general of finance after accession of Louis XVI (1774). Increased public revenue without imposing new taxes, and removed trade barriers between provinces. Writings anticipated Adam Smith.

Voltaire, François Marie Arouet de 1694–1778, French writer and philosopher (**4**). Embodiment of 18th century "enlightenment." Frequently imprisoned and exiled. Attacked social pretensions, political and social injustices, and religious intolerance.

4

Walpole, Sir Robert, Earl of Orford 1676-1745, English statesman, first Lord of Treasury and chancellor of Exchequer by 1721. As first prime minister (1721–42), chaired small group of ministers which was forerunner of present-day cabinet. Able but venal politician.

Wilkes, John 1727–97, English politician and journalist who became symbol of free speech and earned self-styled epitaph "friend of liberty." Champion of freedom of Press, and of sovereign rights of electorate. Became Lord Mayor of London in 1774.

Wolfe, James 1727–59, English soldier. Under General Amherst, captured Louisburg (1758). In 1759, following Pitt's plan to expel French from Canada, succeeded in routing French army, killing Montcalm, and capturing Quebec. Died in hour of victory.

Monarchs

4343 **Anne I** 1665–1714, Queen of Great Britain and Ireland from 1702, last Stuart monarch, daughter of James II, who achieved union of parliaments of Scotland and England in 1707. Reign also saw victories over French at Blenheim (1704), Ramillies (1706), Oudenarde (1708), and Malplaquet (1709).

Catherine II "the Great" 1729–96, Empress of Russia from 1762 (**1**), who greatly increased dominions and power of her country through three partitions of Poland, two Turkish wars (1774, 1792), and war with Sweden (1790). Promoted education, public health, and religious toleration.

1

Frederick II, "the Great" 1712–86, King of Prussia. Able administrator, and courageous, resourceful soldier who set country on road to political and military supremacy. By time of his death, area of Prussia had doubled. For much of reign, campaigned against Austrian aggrandizement.

George I 1660–1727, Elector of Hanover from 1698, and first Hanoverian king of Great Britain and Ireland from 1714. Held military command in War of Succession against Louis XIV of France. Reign saw unprecedented dominance of court party over parliament.

George II 1683–1760, King of Great Britain and Ireland and Elector of Hanover 1727-60, son of George I. Took field as commander of British army at battle of Dettingen (1743), which he won - last British monarch to take part in a battle.

George III 1738–1820, King of Great Britain and Ireland from 1760 (Elector of Hanover from 1815), grandson of George II. First Hanoverian king to gain general popularity. Attempts to tax American colonies led to 1776 proclamation of independence. Insane from c. 1790.

Gustav III 1746–92, King of Sweden from 1771, son and successor of King Adolf Frederick. Figure of enlightenment, at home with celebrated thinkers and artists of his day. Attempted to reform bureaucracy and break power of nobles. Killed by discontented noble during masked ball.

Joseph II 1741–90, Emperor of Germany from 1765, son of Francis I and Maria Theresa, who abolished serfdom, reorganized taxation, and curtailed feudal privileges of nobles. At first partition of Poland, acquired Galicia, Lodomeria, and Zips, and, in 1780, large part of Passau and Salzburg.

Karl XII (Charles XII) 1682–1718, King of Sweden from 1697, one of Sweden's greatest warrior kings. Achievements included invasion

continued

Monarchs continued

4343 of Denmark (1700), defeat of Saxons (1702), and surprise invasion of Russia (1707). Killed in battle during invasion of Norway.
Louis XV 1710–74. King of France, who succeeded great-grandfather Louis XIV in 1715 at age of five. Well-intentioned, but lacked great-grandfather's application and industry, and was dominated by mistresses. Involved France in overseas conflicts which led to colonial losses.
Maria Theresa 1717–80. Holy Roman Empress (**2**). Archduchess of Austria, and queen of Hungary and Bohemia from 1740. Majestic, spirited ruler who raised Austria from an impoverished condition to position of assured power. Reformed government, and boosted trade.
Mary II 1662–94. Stuart queen of Great Britain and Ireland from 1689, daughter of James VII of Scotland and II of England by Anne Hyde. Shared throne with husband King William III. More popular in kingdom than William, and largely responsible for raising moral standard of court life.

2

Peter I the Great, 1672–1725. Tsar of Russia from 1682, fourth son of Tsar Alexei I Mihailovitch by second wife (**3**). Campaigned successfully against Turks, Persians, and Swedes. Extended Baltic territory. Founded navy. Reformed administration, and westernized nation.

3

William III, 1650–1702. King of Great Britain and Ireland from 1689, with Mary II. Wife's claim to throne bolstered his own as grandson of Charles I. Stadtholder of Netherlands 1672. Organized opposition to French aggression 1672–8. Reconquered Ireland 1690. Renewed conflict with France 1691–7.

Places

4344 **1 Battle of Blenheim** 1704, in which English troops defeated French and Bavarians.
2 Battle of the Boyne 1690, in which Protestant forces led by William III defeated Catholic troops in Ireland led by James II.
3 Battle of Culloden 1746, in which English forces defeated Scots supporters of Young Pretender.
4 Battle of La Hogue 1692, in which Anglo-Dutch fleet annihilated French navy.
5 Battle of Malplaquet 1709, in which Allied troops defeated French but with heavy losses.
6 Battle of Minden 1759, in which Austrians and Russians defeated Prussians.
7 Battle of Plessey 1757, in which English troops defeated Bengalese to establish British ascendancy in India.
8 Battle of Ramillies 1706, in which English troops routed French to occupy Spanish Netherlands.
9 Massacre of Glencoe 1692, in which members of Macdonald clan were killed for allegedly failing to register allegiance to William III.
10 Sieges of Gibraltar 1727–28, 1779–82. Britain captured Gibraltar from Spain 1704. Spanish consistently tried to recover it.
11 Battle of Quebec 1759, in which British forces defeated French on Plains of Abraham to gain Canada.
12 Black Hole of Calcutta 1756, in which Bengalese ruler imprisoned British surrendered captives, most of whom died.

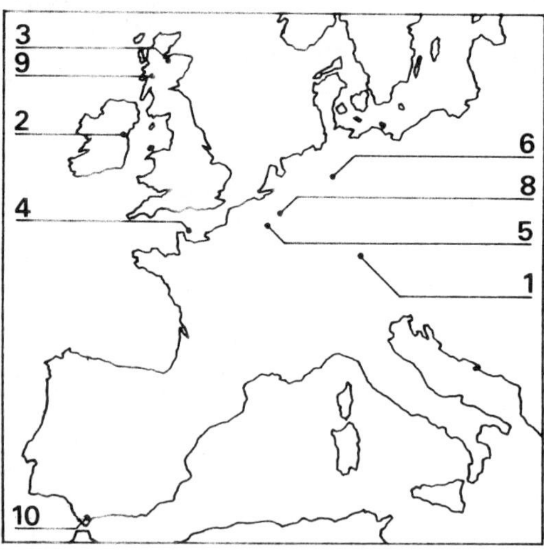

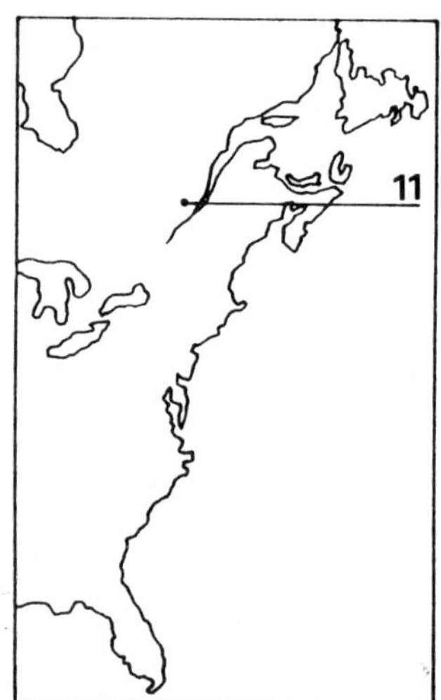

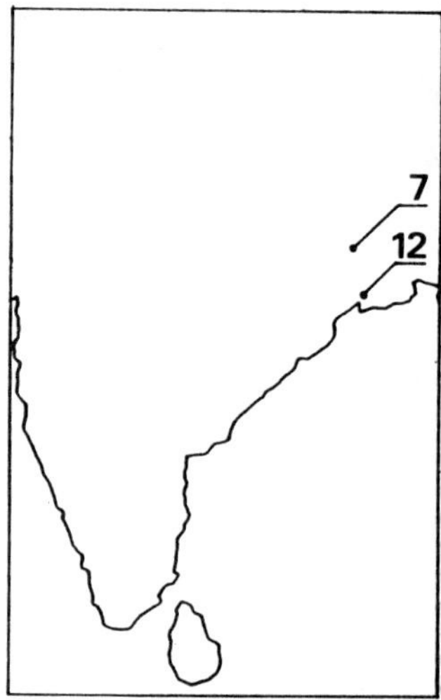

Words

4345 **Act of Settlement** 1701 Established Protestant succession in England of House of Hanover.
Act of Union 1707 United England and Scotland as Great Britain.
Bill of Rights 1689 Established constitutional and Protestant monarchy in Britain.
Catholic emancipation see Penal laws.
despotism, enlightened see Enlightened.
East India Company Trading company which effectively ruled British India from 1708–1857.
Encyclopédie 1751–80, 35-volume showcase for radical views on science, politics, religion, and economics.
enlightened despotism Rule by absolute monarch intended to ensure economic, intellectual and social comfort of subjects.
Gordon Riots 1780 Anti-Catholic emancipation agitation in London provoking street violence and property damage.
Jacobite rebellions 1715, 1745–6 Stuart Pretenders with French support landed in Scotland to recapture British throne but were defeated.
Jansenism Catholic sect, latterly centered on Port Royal lay convent in Paris, which denied free will and promoted austerity and church reform. Condemned by Pope in 1713, ensuing controversy split French church.
Home Rule Irish agitation for complete self-government from 1770s to 1920s.
India Act 1784 Established government control over East India Company.
North Briton Political periodical prosecuted for attacks on George III and Bute ministry from 1762, leading to political freedom of Press and illegality of general arrest warrants.
penal laws Anti-Catholic legislation in England, Ireland and Scotland denying land inheritance and voting rights and restricting access to legal, military, political, and scholastic professions. Pressure for their repeal lasted from 1700s to 1920s.

continued

Words continued

4345 **Perpetual Alliance** 1777 Pact between Spain and Portugal.
philosophes French intellectuals advocating changes in political and social structure as well as in religion and philosophy.
Port Royal see Jansenism.
Porteous Riots 1736 Edinburgh disturbances following death of 16 protestors against execution of convicted smugglers.
Pragmatic Sanction 1713 Attempt to guarantee succession to Austro-Hungarian throne of Maria Theresa.
Quadruple Alliance 1718 Pact between Britain, France, Holland, and Austro-Hungarian empire.
Quebec Act 1774 Guaranteed Roman Catholicism to French Canadians, opposed by New England Puritans.
Salem witch trials 1692 At least 19 men and women were executed and many more died in prison.
Seven Years' War 1756–63 War between Britain allied to Prussia, and France allied to Austria and Sweden.
South Sea Bubble Company formed 1711 to trade with Spanish American colonies. Share value soared from 120 in 1718 to 1,000 in August 1720. In December stock slumped, ruining investors and Government reputation.
Treaty of Versailles 1756 Diplomatically revolutionary alliance between France and Austria.
Treaty of Westminster 1756 Diplomatically revolutionary alliance between Britain and Prussia.
War of the Austrian Succession 1740–8 Death of Holy Roman Emperor led to France backing Spanish, Saxon and Bavarian candidates while Britain and Prussia supported emperor's daughter Maria Theresa.
War of Jenkins' Ear 1739–41 War between Britain and Spain occasioned by Spanish attacks on English ships.
War of the Polish Succession 1733–35 France and Spain supported rival candidate, for vacant Polish throne, to Austrian and Russian choice.
War of the Spanish Succession 1701–14 French king's grandson's claim to Spanish throne was opposed by England, Holland, the Empire, Prussia, Hanover, and Portugal.
Whigs Landed gentry and merchants who were against aristocracy. Word originally denoted a Scottish horse thief. Mercantile and dissenting interests represented.

435 THE AMERICAS 1491–1763

People

4351 **Baltimore, Lord First Baron** c. 1580–1632. Founded Maryland (named for Queen Henrietta Maria) for both Catholic and Protestant settlers. Second baron (1605–75) was governor from 1634. Both were Catholic.
Oglethorpe, James E 1696–1785. General who founded Georgia 1732. Invaded Florida 1740. Repelled attempted Spanish invasion of Georgia 1742.
Penn, William 1644–1718. Quaker (**1**). Champion of religious tolerance. Came to Delaware from England with coreligionists in 1682. Founder of Pennsylvania, which attracted German colonists through its constitution of political and religious toleration. Slave owner but concerned to mitigate worst aspects of slavery.
Pocahontas, Princess 1595–1617. Indian princess who saved life of Englishman John Smith (1580–1631), was converted to Christianity and in 1614 married Englishman John Rolfe (1585–1622). Came to England 1616. Died of smallpox on return journey.

1

Events

4352 **1492–1509** Columbus claims territory for Spain; Cabral for Portugal; Cabot for England; Spain and Portugal divide New World on 40°W longitude.
1501 First African slaves imported.
1504 French begin fishing off Newfoundland.
1513–43 Spanish cross Isthmus of Panama, enter Florida.
1517–50 Mexico taken by Spain; Spain controls most of South America and south of North America.
1521–5 Portuguese seek to found colonies in Newfoundland.
1530–8 Spanish take Peru and Colombia from Inca rulers.
1534–43 French settlements in Canada.
1550–80 Cattle introduced into South America.
1562 Slave trade starts between Africa and America.
1576–83 English colonies in north; Newfoundland claimed.
1583–7 English colonies in Newfoundland and Virginia; fail.
1600–14 French colonies in Canada; Dutch settlements on east coast.
1620 Pilgrim Fathers leave England, found New Plymouth.
1621–4 English and Dutch rivalry over east coast colonies.
1627–9 Further French colonization of Canada leads to English takeover.
1628–30 English settlements in Massachusetts.
1629–42 English Puritans emigrate in great numbers.
1632 French return to Canadian settlements.
1638–55 Swedish attempts to colonize fail.
1641–4 Full-scale war between French and Iroquois.
1642–60 English Royalists emigrate; Montreal founded.
1643–98 Confederation of New England colonies.
1646–50 Iroquois resume attacks on French settlements.
1650 English settlement of Carolina and Georgia begins.
1664 Dutch New Amsterdam taken by English; renamed New York.
1665–75 French defeat Mohawks; increased French colonization.
1673–4 Dutch retake New York.
1675–86 English in New England war with Indian tribes.
1676 Landless classes revolt in Virginia; Jamestown burnt.
1680–1726 Massive importation of African slaves.
1682–4 Pennsylvania founded; attracts German colonists.
1685–6 English and French at war over Hudson's Bay.
1690–6 French at war with Mohawks and Iroquois.
1692–4 Witchcraft trials in Salem; 20 die.
1699 French found Louisiana.
1701 Peace treaty between French and Indians.
1702–13 War between British and French ends with French losses.
1709 Mass German emigration to Pennsylvania.
1713 Britain dominant in most of North America
1714–17 French conflict with Fox tribe.
1722–4 Indians helped by French fight British in New England.
1726–53 French and British both build forts in north.
1730 First paper money issued by British colonies.
1733–4 Georgia founded; many Austrian Protestants arrive.
1736–44 Renewed French wars with Indian tribes.
1744–8 Franco-British war in Europe spills over into North America.
1756–63 War in Europe involves American, French, and British forces.
1759–60 British end French rule in Canada.

Words

4353 **Fox Wars** 1714–16, 1717–18. Fox tribe (of the Algonquin people) attempted to prevent French trading directly with Sioux.
House of Burgesses 1619 Virginia. First elected colonial legislature.
Iroquois Native North American people originally living between the Hudson and St Lawrence rivers.
Mayflower Compact Self-government agreement with equality under law made by

continued

Words continued

4353 Pilgrim Fathers while still at sea.
Mohawks Native North American people, a tribe of the Iroquois, originally living along the Mohawk River.
Orders of Connecticut 1639, first written constitution providing for male franchise and self-government.
Pilgrim Fathers 1620 English nonconformists (dissenters from Church of England) who sailed in the Mayflower from Plymouth to arrive in New England.
Sioux Native North American people originally ranging across Plains from Lake Michigan to Rocky Mountains.
Zenger Case 1735 New York libel action which established freedom of the Press.

Places

4354

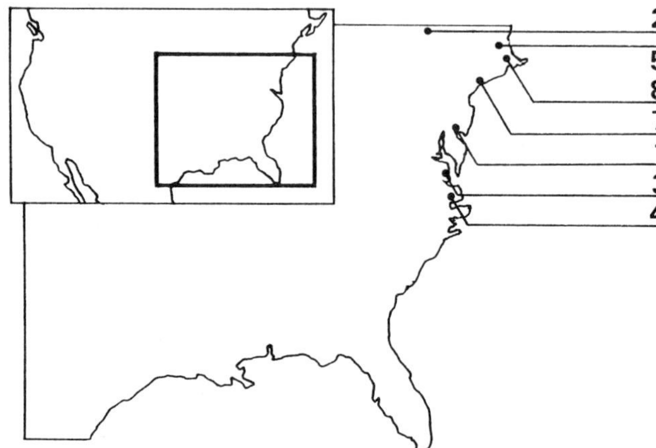

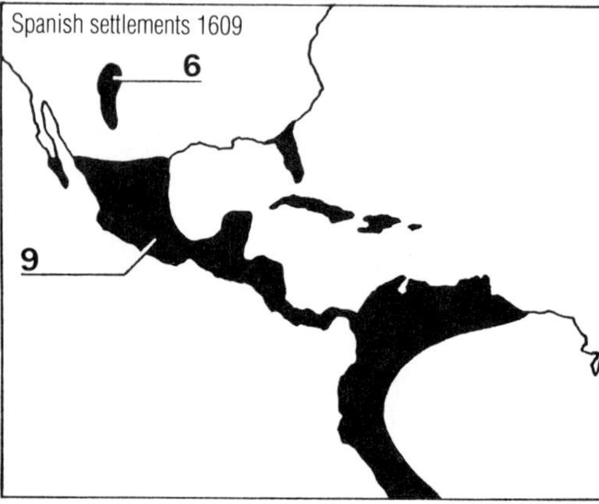

1 Edge Pillock Site of the first Indian reservation set up by New Jersey colonial assembly and settled by about 100 Unami Indians.
2 Heights of Abraham Plateau near Quebec; scene of battle between British forces under general James Wolfe (1727–59) and French under Marquis de Montcalm (1712–59). British victory. Both commanders were killed.
3 Jamestown First permanent English settlement, founded 1607.
4 Roanoke Island North Carolina site of first English attempted settlements in 1585 and 1587–88; both failed.
5 Salem Massachusetts town where unsubstantiated allegations of witchcraft by Anne Putnam and clergyman Samuel Parris in 1692 led to dozens of arrests, 19 people being hanged and one pressed to death (for refusing to plead either guilty or innocent).
6 Santa Fe Spanish settlement, site of North America's oldest surviving European building.
7 Stonington, Conn. Site where the first Indian war ended when the British virtually eliminated the Pequot in 1637.
8 Strawberry Hill, Plymouth Place where the first recorded treaty between whites and Indians was concluded
9 Tenochtitlan Capital of the Aztec empire, renamed Mexico City by Cortés.

436 THE AMERICAN WAR OF INDEPENDENCE 1763–89

Words

4361 **Articles of Confederation** Constitution which created the United States of America by a meeting of Congress in 1777. Effective 1781.
colonists Americans born in and living on the American continent.
Continental Congress National legislative body born of the struggle for independence. Earlier regional assemblies.
Conventions Constitutional assemblies.
Declaration of Independence Document asserting that "these united colonies are and of right ought to be free and independent states" 1775–6.
Hessians German mercenary soldiers hired by the British.
Loyalists Americans loyal to British Crown.
Patriots Americans demanding independence from Britain.
Tory Alternative term for loyalist.
Treaties of Alliance 1778 Agreements between France and the United States.
Treaty of Paris 1783 Definitive treaty of peace between Great Britain and the United States.

Places

4362 **Kinderhook, NY** Birthplace of Martin Van Buren, the first president of the United States to have been born a US citizen. He was born Dec 5, 1782.
Philadelphia Place where the Declaration of Independence received its first public reading, by John Nixon on Jul 8, 1776.
Portsmouth, NH Scene of the first military encounter of the Revolution in Dec 1774, when a band of militia seized arms from Fort William and Mary, after reports that the British were to station a garrison there.
St Pierre et Miquelon The last French possession in North America, after France had ceded her Canadian possessions to England in the Treaty of Paris (1763).
Valley Forge, Pennsylvannia Winter camp of George Washington and the Revolutionary Army in 1777–8.

1 The Thirteen Colonies
a Massachusetts territory
b New Hampshire
c Massachusetts
d Rhode Island
e Connecticut
f New Jersey
g Pennsylvania
h Delaware
i Maryland
j Virginia
k North Carolina
l South Carolina
m Georgia

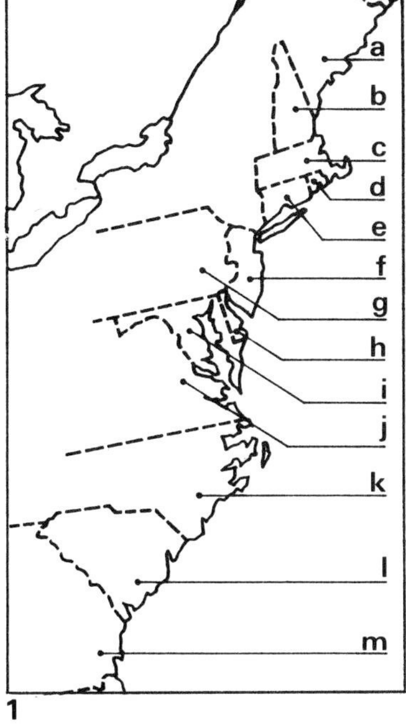

1

a b c d e f g h i j k l m n o p q
2

2 Battles
a Quebec
b Montreal
c Crown point
d Ticonderoga
e Oviskany
f Falmouth
g Lexington
h Bunker Hill
i Concord
j New York
k Princeton
l Trenton
m Philadelphia
n Brandywine
o Ohio River
p Norfolk
q Wilmington

Cornwallis's march →

Events

4363 **PRELIMINARIES**
1754–63 Seven Years' War between Britain and France involves American forces.
1764 American Revenue Act (Sugar Act) (Apr). New England protests (May-Sep). Currency Act (Sep). New York protests (Dec).
1765 Quartering and Stamp Acts (Mar). Congress called (Oct).
1766 British merchants petition for repeal (Jan). Stamp Act repealed. Declaratory Act states Parliament's overall authority (Mar). Sugar Act modified (Nov). New York Assembly refuses Army appropriations; suspended (Dec).
1767 Townshend Acts (Jun). Non-importation policies by Boston (Oct) and New York (Dec).
1768 Massachusetts denounces taxation without representation (Feb). Customs officials seize Liberty sloop; Boston riot (Jun). British troops quartered in Boston (Oct).
1770 Boston citizens killed in brawl with British troops (Mar). Import duties except on tea lifted.
1772 Revenue boat burnt at Rhode Island (Jun). Committees of correspondence formed (Nov-Feb 1774)
1773 Boston Tea Party (tea dumped in harbour by citizens). (Dec).
1774 Virginia calls for Congress of the Colonies (May). Coercive Acts (Jun). Suffolk Resolves in protest (Massachusetts) (Aug-Sep). First Continental Congress (Sep).
1775 Lord Chatham attempts conciliation; rejected by Parliament (Feb).

WAR FOR INDEPENDENCE
1775 Skirmishes at Lexington and Concord (Apr). British victory at Battle of Bunker's Hill (Jun). Washington assumes command of Continental Army (Jun). Montreal taken from British (Nov). Attempts to capture Quebec fail (Dec-May 1776).
1776 British defeated near Wilmington (North Carolina) (Feb). Continental fleet captures New Providence (Bahamas). British evacuate Boston. Congress authorizes privateering (Mar). Declaration of Independence (Jul). British victory at Long Island (Aug). British occupy New York (Sep). American defeat at Lake Champlain; retreat (Oct). American victory at Battle of Trenton (Dec).
1777 American victory at Princeton (Jan). La Fayette joins Washington (Jul). American victories at Oriskany and Bennington (Aug). British win Battle of Brandywine; British checked at Saratoga but occupy Philadelphia (Sep). British victory at Battle of Germantown; American victory at Saratoga (Oct). Articles of Confederation (Nov). Washington winters at Valley Forge (Dec).
1778 France signs treaty with of alliance with Americans (Feb). British peace commission; American naval raid on Whitehaven (England) (Apr). British evacuate Philadelphia; drawn Battle of Monmouth (Jun). French fleet arrives (Jul). Franco-American attack on Newport repulsed (Jul-Aug). British capture Savannah (Dec).
1779 American victory at Vincennes (Feb). Spain declares war on Britain (Jun). Congressional peace terms (Aug); American naval victories in North Sea (Sep). Franco-American attempt to retake Savannah fails (Oct).
1780 Russia suggests league of armed neutrality (Feb). British besiege Charleston (Feb-May). Mutiny in Washington's army averted (May). French reinforcements land (Jul). British victory at Battle of Camden (Aug). West Point surrender plot by Arnold discovered (Sep). American victory at Battle of King's Mountain (Oct). Dutch declare waron Britain (Dec).
1781 Mutiny in Pennsylvania crushed; American victory at Cowpers (Jan). Articles of Confederation ratified; costly British victory in Battle of Guilford Courthouse (Mar). British campaign in Virginia (May-Aug). Congressional peace commission (Jun). Yorktown campaign (Aug-Oct). French victory in naval Battle of Chesapeake Bay (Sep). British capitulation at Yorktown (Oct).
1782 British Government defeated in vote on war; resigns (Mar). Paris peace talks (Apr). British evacuate Savannah (Jul). Formal peace treaty signed (Nov). British evacuate Charleston (Dec).

continued

Events continued

4363 **1783** Cessation of hostilities (Feb). Congress ratifies peace treaty; 7,000 loyalists sail from New York (Apr). American Army deisbanded (Jun). Treaty of Paris signed by Britain, United States, France, and Spain (Sep). British leave New York City (Nov).

AFTERMATH
1784 Jefferson's first Territorial Ordinance (Apr). Dispute over title to Wyoming Valley (May-Jul). Congress session (Trenton) (Nov). New York as temporary capital city (Dec).
1785 Mount Vernon conference (Mar). Land Ordinance (May). Dispute with Spain over 31st Parallel (Jul-Aug 1786).
1786 Virginia Statute for Religious Freedom adopted (Jan). Economic depression (Jun-Sep). Proposed reorganization of Articles of Confederation (Aug). Massachusetts insurection (Shay's Rebellion) (Aug-Feb1787). Annapolis commerce convention (Sep).
1787 Constitutional Convention opens (Philadelphia) (May). Northwest Ordinance (Jul). Constitution signed (Sep).
1788 Constitution operational (Jul).
1789 George Washington inaugurated as first president of the United States of America (Apr).

Personalities

4364 **BRITISH**
John André Major Adjutant to Gen Clinton. Sent to negotiate with Arnold. Captured and hanged as spy (1780).
John Burgoyne General sharing command at Bunker's Hill (1775). Surrenders at Saratoga (1777).
Lord Chatham (William Pitt the Elder) Statesman seeking accommodation with American colonies (1775).
Sir Henry Clinton General sharing command at Bunker's Hill. Commander-in-chief 1778–81. Captor of Charleston (1780).
Lord Cornwallis General. Victor at Brandywine (1777) and Guilford (1781). Surrenders at Yorktown (1781).
Thomas Gage Colonial governor 1763–74. Military governor of Massachusetts 1774–75.
George III King of Great Britain and Ireland. 1760–1820.
Lord Howe (Richard) Admiral commanding naval forces 1776–8.
Lord Howe (William) General commanding in North America during Seven Years' War (1754–63). Commander in chief 1776–8.
Lord North Prime minister 1770–82. Firm for power of Crown and Parliament over colonies.
Thomas Paine Radical philosopher. Author of *Common Sense* (1776) and *Rights of Man* (1791).
Lord Rockingham Prime minister 1765–76, 1782. Opponent of war against colonists.
Charles Townshend Chancellor of Exchequer 1766. Designer of tax laws affecting America 1767.

AMERICAN AND ALLIES
Benedict Arnold General victorious in capture of Montreal (1775) and Saratoga (1777). Attempted to sell West Point to British for $20,000 (1780). Led British raids into Virginia and Connecticut (1780–81).
Pierre Caron de Beaumarchais French clock-maker, dramatist, and secret agent. Organized French funds for American munitions
Benjamin Franklin Inventor, publisher, diplomat (**1**). Framed Declaration of Independence (1776). Minister to France (1776–85). Served on Federal Constitutional Convention (1787).
Horatio Gates General. Victor at Saratoga (1777). Defeated at Camden and relieved of command (1780).
Marquis de Grasse-Tilly French admiral. Victor in Battle of Chesapeake Bay (1781).
Nathaniel Greene General. Second in command to Washington. Led southern campaign 1780-1.
Thomas Jefferson Lawyer, architect, legislator (**2**). Author of Declaration of Independence.
John Paul Jones Naval officer. Victor over British navy in several engagements 1775–81.
Baron de Kalb French officer. Volunteer serving with La Fayette 1777. Killed at Battle of Camden (1780).
Marquis de La Fayette French officer. Volunteer to serve with Washington 1777. Negotiated French military support for Americans 1779. Shared command at Yorktown 1781.
Louis XVI King of France 1774–93.
Paul Revere Silversmith. Helped organize Boston Tea Party 1773 (**3**). Rode to warn of British advance on Concord 1775. Commander of Boston 1778–79. Designed and printed first Continental currency.
Comte de Rochambeau Commander of French forces assisting Americans 1780–1.
Daniel Shays Soldier. Served at Bunker's Hill and Saratoga. Ringleader in 1786–7 insurrection at Springfield.
Baron von Steuben Volunteer officer appointed inspector-general 1778. Commanded with La Fayette in Virginia 1781.
George Washington Lieutenant colonel 1755–59 (**4**). Delegate to First and Second Continental Congresses. Commander of Continental Army 1775–83. Delegate to Annapolis Convention 1786. President of Federal Convention 1787. Elected first president of the United States in 1789.

1

2

3

4

437 THE FRENCH REVOLUTION

Words

4371 **Ancien régime** The name given to the social system in force in France before 1789.
assignats Paper currency issued during the Revolution which depreciated rapidly.
Bastille Royal prison in Paris used exclusively for state prisoners.
citoyen/ne abolition of titles required all French men and women to be addressed simply as "citizen."
Emigré/e Nobles fleeing revolution; they forfeited estates and were liable to summary execution if they returned.
Girondin Left-of-center political group that opposes Jacobin National Assembly.
guillotine Execution machine named for inventor and first used in April 1792. Also called "the national razor."
Jacobin Club patronised by radicals, hence catch-all term for extreme Revolutionaries. Opposed Girondins in National Assembly, gained control.
Liberté, Egalité, Fraternité – ou Mort! Battle slogan of Republicans.
Montagne Extreme left grouping in National Convention.
National Assembly The legislative body which succeeded the Estates-General, and which was dominated by the Third Estate, representing the people.
parlements Pre-revolutionary judicial assemblies with no legislative powers.
Quatorze Juillet Bastille fell on July 14, 1789.
Reign of Terror Period after Louis XVI's execution from October 1793 to July 1794 when the Jacobins ruled and during which thousands of people were executed for political reasons.
sans-culottes A name for republicans, originally meant as an insult, referring to the trousers worn by common people rather than courtly breeches.
tricolore Cockade or flag adding revolutionary blue and red to signify willingness to die to Bourbon dynasty's white.
tumbril Two-wheeled cart used to take condemned to guillotine.

Events

4372 **PRELIMINARIES**

1778–83 France intervenes in American War of Independence in support of the colonists. Senior Army officers influenced by American philosophical and political ideals. French financial deficit increased by costs of war.
1783–87 Financial crisis deepens with privileged classes refusing to yield tax-free status. 1785 diamond necklace scandal damages reputation of monarchy with all classes. Assembly of Notables (consultative body) called (February 1787); dissolved (May).

REVOLUTION

1788 Necker reappointed as finance minister with brief to reduce deficit and call meeting of Estates-General (first since 1614) (Aug).
1789 Estates-General meet at Versailles (May). Third Estate (middle classes) urged by Mirabeau assumes title of National Assembly; takes oath (Tennis Court Oath) not to disband until constitution created (Jun). Necker dismissed, then recalled; Bastille stormed; provincial peasant uprisings; emigration of nobles begins (Jul). Nobles yield feudal privileges; titles abolished; trade guilds dissolved; sale of offices under Crown prohibited; Bill of Rights (Aug). Paris mob marches on Versailles; royal family brought to Paris; National Assembly moves to Paris; liberal monarchic constitution; paper money (assignats) issued (Oct).
1790 *Dé partements* replace provinces; civil organization of clergy; king accepts constitution (Jul). Growth of radical political clubs (Aug). Necker dismissed; court makes accommodation with Mirabeau (Sep). 1791 Mirabeau dies (Apr). Royal family attempts flight; captured at Varennes and brought back to Paris (June). Pillnitz Declaration by Austrian emperor and Prussian king appears to threaten intervention in French affairs (Aug). National Assembly dissolved (Sep). Legislative Assembly elected (Oct).
1792 Formal Austro-Prussian alliance against France (Feb). Roland heads ministry (Mar). French declare war on Austria (Apr). Roland dismissed; mob attacks Tuilleries (Jun). National voluntary army formed (Jul). Tuilleries stormed; royal guard (Swiss Guard) massacred; royal family confined in Temple; Danton heads provisional government; Lafayette impeached and flees; Prussians take Verdun (Aug), 1,200 prisoners, mainly political or ecclesiastical, taken from Paris jails and killed (September Massacres); National Convention elected; monarchy abolished (Sep); French military successes (Sep-Oct.)
1793 Louis XVI tried and executed (Jan). War declared against Britain, Holland and Spain (Feb). Royalist uprising in Vendée (Biscay) (Mar). Committee of Public Safety headed by Danton; further issue of assignats (Apr). Marat assassinated by Charlotte Corday; Robespierre dominates Committee of Public Safety (Jul). Reign of Terror begins (Sep). Marie Antoinette tried and executed (Oct). Revolutionary calendar (Nov). French advance across Rhine; British fleet evacuates Toulon after artillery commanded by Napoleon Bonaparte effects capture of forts (Dec).
1794 Danton executed (Apr). Robespierre impeached and executed; end of Reign of Terror in which over 40,000 people were executed (Jul). Depreciation of currency follows new issue of assignats (Dec)

VICTORY AND CONQUESTS

1795 Bread riots; military successes (Apr-May). Abortive royalist invasion of Brittany (Jun-Jul). New constitution invests executive power in five-member Directory (Aug). Opposition crushed by Bonaparte's "whiff of grapeshot;" Convention dissolved (Oct).
1796 Bonaparte marries Josephine de Beauharnais (Mar) then successfully campaigns in Italy (Apr-Jul 1797). French advance into southern Germany repelled (Aug-Sep).
1797 Peace of Loeben (Apr). Reactionary members of Directory defeated in coup d'état (Sep). Treaty of Campo Formio (Oct).
1798 French troops occupy Rome, republic established (Feb). France invades Switzerland (Apr). Bonaparte sails for Egypt (May). In Battle of the Nile Nelson destroys French fleet (Aug). Second Coalition (principally Britain, Austria and Russia) against French (Dec).
1799 Campaigns against Austria (Mar-Oct). Roman republic overthrown (Jun). Russia withraws from coalition; Bonaparte returns from Egypt (Oct). Brumaire coup d'état by Bonaparte overthrows Directory (Nov). New constitution appoints Bonaparte as First Consul for ten years (Dec).

People

4373 **ROYALIST**

Charles X 1757–1836. King of France 1824-30, successor to brothers Louis XVI and Louis XVII, who tried to restore absolutism of old French monarchy. Known as Comte d'Artois before accession, led Ultraroyalists against constitutionalists. Overthrown in Revolution of July 27–29, 1830.
Fersen, Frederick Axel, Count von 1719–94, Swedish soldier and statesman. Initially served successively in French and Swedish armies, and was made field marshal 1770. Later became leader of anti-Royalist opposition, and was assassinated in Stockholm.
Louis XVI 1754–93 King of France from 1774, only son of Louis XV (**1**). Married in 1770 to Marie Antoinette. Resistance to demands of Constituent Assembly for equal rights and universal freedom led to Revolution. Republic proclaimed, and Louis guillotined for treason.
Marie Antoinette, 1755–93 Queen of France from 1774, fourth daughter of Empress Maria Theresa and Emperor Francis I. Opponent of new, liberal ideas behind Revolution. Miseries of France became identified with her extravagance. Died by guillotine.

1

REPUBLIC

Danton, Georges Jacques 1759–94, revolutionary leader who, in 1792, became minister of justice in new republic following fall of monarchy, and was one of nine original members of Committee of Public Safety. Lost power to Robespierre, and eventually guillotined on charge of conspiracy.
David, Jacques Louis 1748–1825, Neoclassical painter who entered with enthusiasm into Revolution. As member of Committee of Public Safety, voted for death of Louis XVI. After Bourbon restoration, banished as regicide in 1816. Died in Brussels.
Desmoulins, Camille 1760–94, Revolutionary and journalist who played dramatic part in destruction of Bastille. His witty, cruelly sarcastic *Révolutions de France et de Brabant* appeared weekly 1789–92. Later fell out with Robespierre, and was guillotined.
Fouquier-Tinville, Antoine Quentin 1746–95, politician. Public prosecutor to revolutionary Tribunal from 1793, who superintended all political executions (including those of friends Robespierre and Danton) during Reign of Terror until 1794. Died himself at guillotine.
Marat, Jean Paul 1743–93, revolutionary, physician and journalist. Radical paper, *L'ami du Peuple,* started 1789. Largely responsible for September massacres. With Robespierre and Danton, overthrew Girondins. Assassinated by Corday, member of Girondins.
Robespierre, Maximilian Marie Isidore de 1758–94, revolutionary, who brought in Reign of Terror. From 1793, member of Committee of Public Safety, and one of actual rulers of France. Popularity waned as power increased. Died by guillotine.
Roland de la Platière, Jean Marie 1734–93, statesman, leader of Girondists, Minister of Interior 1792–3, protested against September massacres, and took part in last struggle of Girondists. Committed suicide two days after wife, Madame Roland, had been guillotined.

continued

People continued

4373 **FENCE-SITTERS**

Fouché, Joseph, Duke of Otranto 1763–1820 Revolutionary and statesman. Member of National Convention from 1792, expelled as terrorist 1794, but made minister of police 1799 (until 1815). Made terms with Bourbons. Banished as regicide 1816–20.

La Fayette, Marie Joseph Paul Yves Roch Gilbert du Motier, Marquis de 1757–1834 Reformer who sailed to America on three occasions to help colonists. Sat in National Assembly of 1789. In 1830, took part in revolution, and commanded National Guard.

Mirabeau, Honoré Gabriel Riquetti, Comte de 1749–91 Revolutionary politician and orator. Author of *Essai sur les Lettres de Cachet* (1782), who advocated constitutional monarchy on English model. Though distrusted by court and extremists, elected president of National Assembly 1791.

Orléans, Louis Philippe Joseph, Duc d' 1747–93 Succeeded to title 1785. Dreamed of becoming constitutional king of France, or at least regent, but lost influence, and faith in Revolution. In 1792, adopted name Philippe Egalité, and became Paris deputy to Convention. Guillotined for conspiracy.

Talleyrand-Périgord, Charles Maurice de, Prince of Benevento 1754–1838 French statesman. Bishop from 1789. One of Assembly members (President from 1790) who drew up Declaration of Rights. Supported, then deserted, Napoleon. Louis-Philippe's advisor at July revolution.

Places

4374

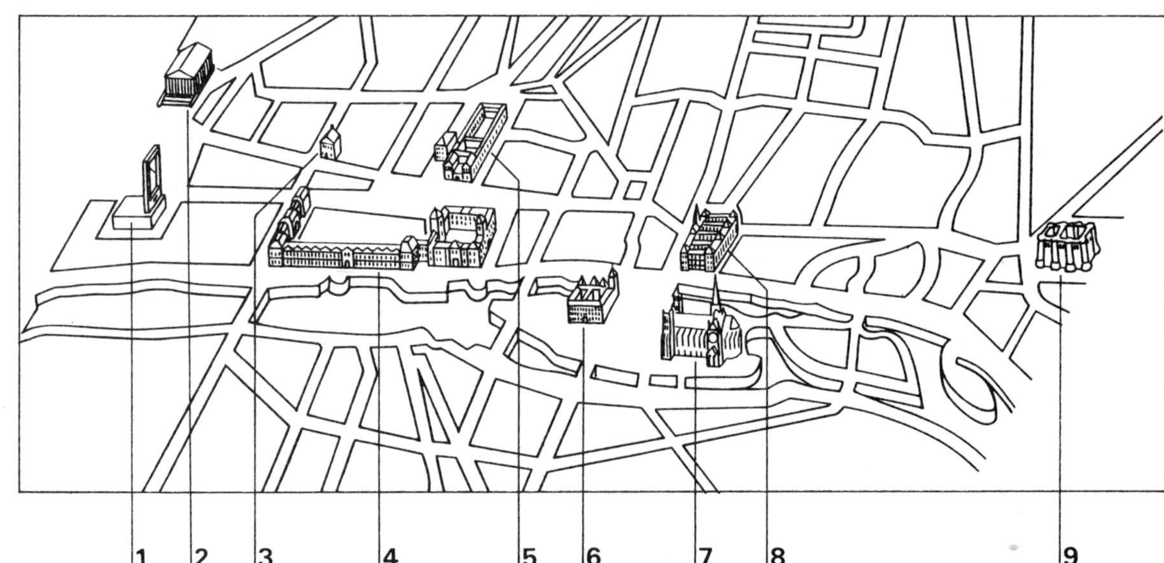

1 Site of guillotine
2 Madelaine
3 Jacobin Club
4 Louvre
5 Palais Royale
6 Palais Royale
7 Nôtre Dame
8 Hôtel de Ville
9 Bastille

Bastille A fortress in Paris, used as a prison until its storming on July 14, 1789, which marked the beginning of the Revolution.

Hôtel de Ville The seat of municipal authority in Paris, taken by the Revolutionary mob in July 1789.

Louvre Royal palace in Paris, begun in 1546, and used as the national museum and art gallery since 1793.

Tennis Court In the grounds of Versailles. The members of the Third Estate met there when Louis XVI locked them out of their meeting place, after they had proclaimed themselves the National Assembly.

Tuileries A royal residence in Paris, close to the Louvre. Louis XVI was brought there from Versailles in October 1789. It was destroyed in 1871 and is now the site of the Tuileries Gardens.

Valmy North of Paris, scene of a battle in which the Revolutionary Army halted the advance of Prussian invaders, securing the future of the Revolution. One observer commented that it marked "a new era in the history of the world."

Varennes Near Montargis, where Louis XVI was arrested after his escape from the Tuileries. This event was a turning-point in the Revolution, marking the end of the experiment with constitutional monarchy.

Versailles South-west of Paris, seat of the French monarchy 1682–1789. Louis XVI was forced to leave it in October 1789 and take up residence in the Tuileries.

The Three Estates

4375 **Estates-General** In 1789 nearly 1,200 representatives were elected, each by his own order.

First Estate (Clergy) About 80 prelates of whom about half were of political liberal tendencies and over 200 *curés* (parish priests)

Second Estate (Nobility) 270 representatives (noblesse de l'épée) of whom at least 90 were known to favour reform.

Third Estate (Bourgeoisie) About 650 deputies drawn mainly from the upper echelons of national and regional administration and the legal profession (*noblesse de la robe*). All income tax-paying male citizens were eligible to vote. This excluded the peasantry and the urban working class in the procession which preceeded the formal opening of the Estates-General by Louis XVI on May 4, 1789. As a political gesture, some nobles marched with the curés and the magistrates.

438 NAPOLEONIC TIMES

Events

4381 **THE CONSULATE**

1799 Napoleon Bonaparte appointed First Consul. Constitution reorganizes regional government and tax collection (Dec).
1800 Military campaign against Austria renewed (Apr-Dec).
1801 Treaty of Luneville effectively dismembers Holy Roman Empire; Spain cedes Louisiana to France (Feb). Treaty of Florence closes Naples to Britain; Elba ceded to France; Prussia allies with France (Mar); Concordat with Papacy (autumn).
1802 Treaty of Amiens between Britain and France (Mar). Legion of Honour created (May). Napoleon declared consul for life; new constitution (Aug).
1803 Dissensions with Britain; army encampment at Boulogne threatens English invasion (Oct).
1804 Assassination conspiracy against Napoleon discovered (Feb). Duc d'Enghien summarily executed (Mar). Napoleon proclaimed emperor (May) and crowned (Dec).

THE EMPIRE

1805 French fleet evades British blockage (Mar). Third Coalition against France (Aug). French naval power broken (Oct). France defeats Austria and Russia; Treaty of Pressburg (Dec).
1806 Napoleon makes elder brother Joseph king of Naples and younger brother Louis king of Holland. Confederation of Rhine set up by France (Jul). War against Prussia ends in Prussian surrender and French occupation of Berlin (Oct). France proclaims closure of continent to British trade; Poland invaded (Nov). Saxony and Turkey join Confederation of Rhine (Dec).
1807 British naval successes in Near East (spring). French advance into Russia (May-June). Treaties of Tilsit ally Russia with France against Britain and create grand duchy of Warsaw (Poland) (Jul). British bombard Copenhagen and arrest Danish fleet (Sep). Portugal occupied by France (Nov).
1808 France invades Spain (Mar). Joseph made king of Spain (May). Spanish people wage guerrilla war against French occupation (May-Nov 1814). Congress of Erfurt reinforces Franco-Russian alliance (Sep); capitulates to France; British invade Spain from Portugal (Dec).
1809 French defeat British army at La Coruña (Jan). British forestall further French invasion of Portugal (Feb-Jul). Napoleon drives Austrians back across Danube (Apr and Jul).Papal states annexed (May). Pope taken prisoner (Jul). Treaty of Schonbrunn weakens Austria (Oct). Tyrolean insurrection suppressed (November). Napoleon divorces Josephine (Dec).
1810 Napoleon marries Austrian archduchess Marie Louise (Apr). Louis abdicates as king of Holland (Jul). Sweden elects Bernadotte as heir to throne (Nov).
1811 Birth of Napoleon's son (Mar). Russia advances on Turkey.

DECLINE OF THE EMPIRE

1812 Treaty of St Petersburg between Sweden and Russia (Apr). Treaty of Bucharest between Russia and Turkey (May). Britain makes peace with Russia and Sweden; French invade Russia (June). Russians evacuate Moscow and fire city (Sep). French retreat from Moscow (Oct-Dec).
1813 Treaty of Kalisch between Russia and Prussia (Feb). Britain agrees to subsidize Swedish war effort (Mar). France forces Allied retreat through Germany (Mar-May). Britain agrees to subsidize Russian and Prussian war effort; British drive French north through Spain (Jun). Austria declares war on France (Aug). Treaty of Teplitz between Austria, Russia and Prussia (Sep); French defeats in and retreat from Germany (Oct). Allied peace offer rejected by Napoleon; Swedish invasion of Denmark (Nov). Allied armies cross Rhine (Dec).
1814 Treaty of Kiel between Denmark and Sweden; Denmark and Britain sign peace (Jan). Napoleon defeats Allied advance on Paris; refuses further peace negotiations (Feb). Treaties of Chaumont between Allies; Allies advance and take Paris (Mar). Napoleon abdicates; granted sovereignty of Elba (Apr). First Treaty of Paris restores Louis XVIII to French throne (May). Congress of Vienna (Sep-Jun 1815). Act of Congres of Vienna restores Austrian and Prussian monarchies, creates kingdoms of the Netherlands and of Poland, restores independence of Switzerland and reinstates Papal states, Spanish and some Italian dynasties (Jun).
1815 Napoleon escapes from Elba and lands at Cannes; Louis XVIII flees Paris; new alliance between Britain, Austria, Russia and Prussia (March). Napoleon crosses into Belgium; defeated at Waterloo; abdicates; exiled to St Helena (Jun). Louis XVIII returns (Jul). Holy Alliance between Russia, Austria and Prussia (Sep). Quadruple Alliance between Britain, Austria, Russia and Prussia renewed; Second Peace of Paris (Nov).

People

4382 **ALLIES**

Alexander I 1777–1825. Tsar of Russia from 1801, son of emperor Paul. Administrative and educational reformer. Initial ally (1807), but later opponent of Napoleon. Destroyed Napoleon's retreating army at Dresden and Leipzig 1813, and entered Paris 1814. Acquired Poland 1815.
Blücher, Gebhard Leberecht von, Prince of Wahlstadt, 1742–1819, Prussian soldier, known as "Marshal Forward." Distinguished himself against French at Lutzen, Bantzen, Haynau, and Leipzig (1813). Entered Paris 1814. With Wellington, completed 1815 victory at Waterloo.
Castlereagh, Robert Stewart, Viscount 1769–1822, British statesman, who, in 1812, achieved recognition as foreign secretary under Lord Liverpool. Highly unpopular figure, despite having engineered 40 years of peace that succeeded Napoleon's downfall. Committed suicide.
Charles, (Karl Ludwig Johann) 1771–1847. Archduke of Austria, third son of emperor Leopold II, and brother of emperor Francis II. As commmander of Austrian army, defeated Moreau and, on three occasions, Jourdan. Also won 1809 battle of Aspern. Governor of Mainz from 1815.
Francis II, of the Holy Roman Empire, I of Austria 1768–1835. Succeeded father, Leopold II, as Holy Roman Emperor 1792. Despite anti-liberal policy, was urbane and popular ruler. Emperor of Austria from 1804. Defeated Napoleon at Leipzig (1813), and won back Lombardy, Venetia, and Galacia.
Hofer, Andreas 1767–1810s Tyrolese patriot leader and innkeeper who called Tyrolese to arms to expel French and Bavarians. In 1809, defeated Bavarians at Iussel Berg, and later French, but was forced to disband when they reinvaded. Betrayed, tried by court martial, and executed.
Kutuzov, Mikhail Harionovich, Prince of Smolensk 1745–1813, Russian soldier, who commanded against French 1805–12. In 1812, as commander-in-chief, fought Napoleon obstinately at Borodino, but defeated. His army pursued retreating French out of Russia into Prussia, where he died.
Louis XVIII (Stanislaw Xavier) 1755–1824. King of France from 1795, whose harsh treatment of Imperialists, Republicans, and Protestants allowed Napoleon's return in 1815. Despite later moderation, unable to prevent slaughter of hundreds of Protestants and Republicans in "White Terror."
Metternich, Prince Clemens Lothar Wenzel 1773–1859, Austrian statesman. Foreign minister from 1809. Active representative of reaction, at home and abroad, who strove to repress all popular and constitutional aspirations, and as such was unwitting catalyst for French Revolution of 1848.
Moore, Sir John 1761–1809, Scottish soldier who served in American War of Independence, and Revolutionary war in France. Commander in chief of English army in Peninsula 1808. Allied with Spanish to expel France from Spain, but forced to retreat to La Coruña, where he was killed.

continued

People continued

4382

1

Nelson, Horatio, Viscount 1758–1806, English naval commander (**1**). Returned to hero's welcome after inflicting massive defeat on French fleet at battle of Nile, 1798. Vice admiral from 1801. In 1805, caught, and defeated, French fleet off Cape Trafalgar. Died in hour of victory.
Pius VII, named **Luigi Barnaba Chiaramonti** 1742–1823 Italian Pope from 1800. In 1801, concluded concordat with Napoleon. Later forced to sign new concordat and sanction annexation of papal states to French empire. Returned to Rome after fall of Napoleon in 1814.
Wellington, Arthur Wellesley, 1st Duke of, known as **"Iron Duke"** 1769–1852. Anglo-Irish soldier, and statesman (**2**). Created Duke of Wellington after driving French out of Spain and defeating them at Toulouse 1814. Defeated Napoleon at Waterloo 1815. Prime minister of England from 1828.

2

FRENCH
Bonaparte, Joseph 1768–1844. King of Naples and Sicily (1806–8), and King of Spain (1808–13), eldest surviving son of Charles and Marie Bonaparte and brother of Napoleon. Faced constant rebellion as ruler in Spain, and was decisively defeated by Wellington at Vitoria, 1813.
Bonaparte, Louis, 1778–184. King of Holland (1806–10), son of Charles and Marie Bonaparte, and brother of Napoleon. Married Napoleon's step-daughter, Hortense de Beauharnais (1783–1837, mother of future Napoleon III). Abdicated because Napoleon complained he supported Dutch interests.
Beauharnais, Eugène Rose de 1781–1824. soldier, son of Alexandre de Beauharnais and Josephine. Served with Napoleon in Italy and Egypt, and soon rose to highest military rank. Honorable and sagacious, showed great military skill in campaigns in Italy, Austria, and Russia.
Josephine de Beauharnais, née Marie Josephine Rose Tascher de la Pagerie 1763–1814. Wife of Napoleon and French empress, who attracted most brilliant society of France, and contributed greatly to establishing husband's power. Marriage, being childless, dissolved 1809.
Karl XIV Johan, originally **Jean Baptiste Jules Bernadotte** 1763–1844. King of Sweden and Norway from 1818. Brigadier-general (1794), then marshal (1804) in French army. Later, with Russia, defeated Napoleon in 1813. Secured union with Norway lasting until 1905.
Marie Louise, 1791–1847. Empress, daughter of Francis I of Austria. Married Napoleon 1810, and bore him future Napoleon II (1811–32), king of Rome 1811–14, duke of Reichstadt 1818–32. Returned to Austria after Napoleon's abdication.
Marmont, Auguste Frédéric Louis Viesse de 1774–1852 Soldier. Defeated Russians at Dalmatia (1805). Made marshal 1809. In 1814, forced to surrender Paris to Allies, which in turn compelled Napoleon to abdicate. Honored by Bourbons. Died at Venice.
Murat, Joachim 1767–1815 . Soldier and king of Naples from 1808. Served with Napoleon in Italy and Egypt, and married his sister Caroline 1800. Contributed to victories at Austerlitz (1805), Jena, and Eylau, crushed Austrians at Dresden (1813). Eventually executed.
Ney, Michel 1769–1815. Soldier. Marshal 1804. Hero of retreat from Moscow 1812. In 1813, present at Lutzen and Bautzen, but defeated by von Bülow at Dennewitz. Having enforced Napoleon's abdication in 1814, rejoined him to fight at Waterloo. Executed for high treason.
Soult, Nicolas Jean de Dieu 1769–1851. Marshal 1804. Served at Austerlitz, and in Prussian and Russian campaigns. Conquered and governed Portugal, and in 1809–10 overran Andalusia in Spain. Banished after Waterloo, but later made war minister (1830–4).

Bonaparte, Napoleon 1769-1821, Corsican. French Emperor who seized power in a coup in 1799. A brilliant general, he conquered a vast empire, failing only after a disastrous strategic error in trying to conquer Moscow. After defeat at the Battle of Leipzig, he went into exile on the island of Elba. He escaped in 1815 and returned to power in the period known as the Hundred Days, before final defeat at Waterloo. He died in exile on the island of St Helena. He laid the basis for modern French law in the "Code of Napoleon."

Places

4383

1 Trafalgar
2 Spain
3 Paris
4 Waterloo
5 Ulm
6 Jena
7 Lutzen
8 Leipzig
9 Confederation of the Rhine
10 Hohenlinden
11 Eyla
12 Tilsit
13 Friedland
14 Grand Duchy of Warsaw
15 Austerlitz
16 Wagram
17 Gmolensk
18 Borodino
19 Moscow
20 Marengo
21 Corsica
22 Elba
23 Kingdom of Italy
24 Kingdom of Naples
25 Illyrian Provinces

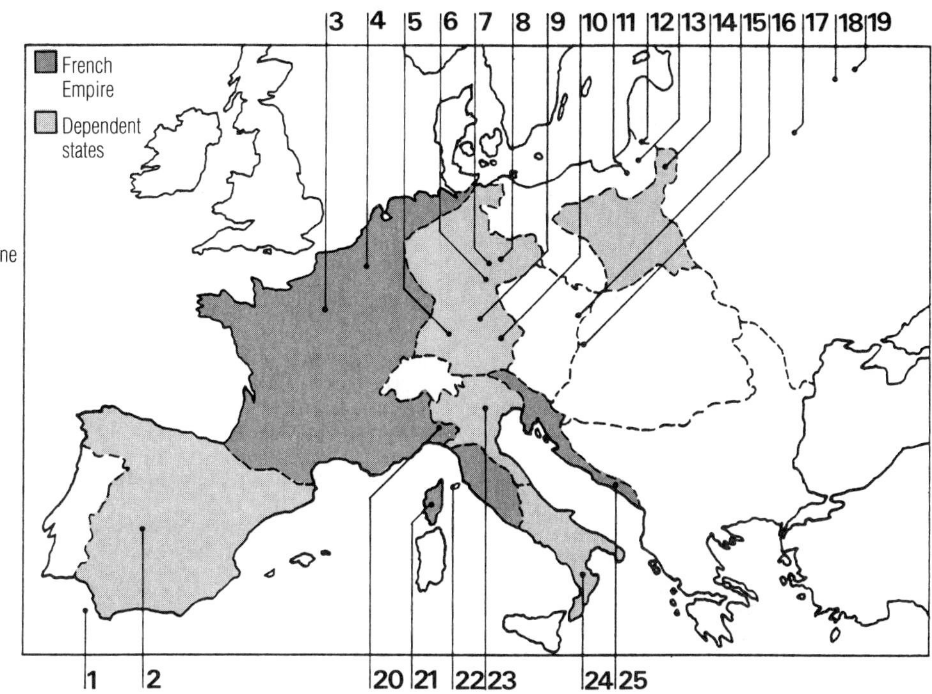

Austerlitz Scene of a battle in Austrian Empire in which Napoleon defeated the armies of Russia and Austria. It marked the defeat of the coalition between Russia, Austria, and Sweden.
Elba A rocky island off the western coast of Italy, to which Napoleon was exiled in 1814, after being defeated by the Prussians and their allies.
Leipzig Scene of a battle (also known as the Battle of the Nations) in Germany in which Napoleon was defeated by the coalition partners of Prussia, Britain, Russia, Spain, and Sweden and which marked the end of the Grand Empire. Invasion of France by the allies followed swiftly
Moscow Napoleon's occupation of Moscow, from September 14 to October 19, 1812 marked the peak of his conquests. He was forced to retreat after the city was fired by the Russians. This defeat marked the turning-point in his military career.
St Helena Island in the south-east Atlantic, scene of Napoleon's second exile, where he died on May 5, 1821.
Trafalgar Sea battle off southern Spain in which the British, under Horatio Nelson, defeated the French and Spanish fleets, and established British naval superiority for a century.
Waterloo A village in Belgium, site of the battle at which Napoleon was defeated for the last time after escaping from Elba.

439 NORTH AMERICA 1780–1860

Events

4391

1779–82 Spanish forces conquer Florida from British.
1781 American Revolution ends (Oct 19) with surrender of British general Lord Cornwallis; war continues until 1783.
1782 Virginia authorizes manumission of slaves.
1783 Maryland prohibits import of slaves; English Quaker association formed to fight slave trade, and free slaves.
1784 American ships begin trade with China; US consul at Canton.
1785–8 Dollar established as official US currency; economic crisis; interstate tariff barriers.
1787–9 Constitution debated, agreed, and signed; first president (George Washington) inaugurated.
1788 New Englanders settle in Ohio Valley; French Canadians settle in Illinois.
1790 Agreement for national capital on Potomac banks.
1791 Bill of Rights becomes law; Canada divided into Upper (mainly British) and Lower (mainly French).
1792–1803 Increased cotton planting and milling fuels demand for more slave labor in southern states; decimal coins minted.
1793 US neutral in French revolutionary conflict; Toronto founded.
1795 First Milwaukee trading post; Spain grants Mississippi free navigation rights.
1796 Settlements in Cleveland and Oklahoma; first US ship enters Monterey Bay (California).
1798 Disputes in Congress over potential enemy aliens; Georgia prohibits further import of slaves.
1799–1800 German Americans rebel against federal property tax.
1800 Washington DC replaces New York as capital.
1802 Military academy founded at West Point, New York.
1803 Louisiana bought from France, doubling size of US; slave imports resumed by South Carolina.
1804–6 Missouri river explored; first cattle drives.
1807–9 US ports closed to British naval vessels after incident; territorial waters extended
1808 Importation of slaves banned; illegal imports continue.
1809 Hudson's Bay Company traders begin to map Canada.
1810–11 Creole rebellion in Mexico defeated.
1811 Russian colony and trading post established in California.
1812–15 War between US and Britain; US troops invade Canada, repulsed; naval engagements; Capitol (Washington) burnt.
1813 Mexico declares independence from Spain.
1814 US and Britain cooperate in suppressing slave trade.
1817 Indians cede territory in Ohio; clashes in Georgia.
1818 US border with Canada established by convention (Oct).
1819 Spain concedes Florida to US.
1820 Land law leads farmers into debt to buy public land.
1821 Mexico claims freedom from Spain for California and Texas.
1822 Slave codes tightened in southern states following attempted slave and freedmen's rebellion in South Carolina.
1823–6 Tension builds between Indian tribes and frontier settlers.
1825 Ottawa, Canada, founded.

continued

Events continued

4391 **1826** Pennsylvania makes kidnapping (including runaway slaves) a felony; first overland journey to southern California.
1828 Import tariffs raised.
1829 Mexico abolishes slavery except in Texas.
1830–3 Southern states threaten secession over tariffs.
1831 Indian tribes denied access to federal courts; slave revolt in Virginia.
1832 Supreme Court rules that US has exclusive authority over tribal Indians and their lands.
1833 Trades union movement in New York; calls for total abolition of slavery increase.
1834 Department of Indian Affairs created; clashes between abolitionists and anti-abolitionists.
1835–6 Renewed clashes with Indians in Florida; conflict with Mexicans; republic of Texas founded; first Canadian railway.
1837 French Canadian rebellion against British rule.
1839–40 Union of Upper and Lower Canada.
1840–8 Split in anti-slavery movement over women's right to participate.
1841 Russian territory in California reclaimed.
1842 Legality of trades unions upheld; child labor law; recovery of fugitive slaves now permitted; border dispute with Canada.
1844 Texas Rangers gun down Comanche Indians; treaty with China.
1845 Canadian border dispute; Texas annexed, Mexican protests.
1846 War with Mexico; Californians proclaim independent republic. Irish immigrants following failure of potato harvest.
1847 Mexican military defeats; first Chinese immigrants.
1848 First women's rights convention; Mexican war ends, territory lost to US includes California; gold discovered.
1849 Economic depression in Canada; annexation to US sought.
1850 Attempts to reduce growing polarity between southern and northern states through legislation; many new railroads.
1851 Fugitive slaves rescued by freedmen and abolitionists in Boston and New York; fire destroys much of Library of Congress; mass emigration from Ireland to US following four years of famine.
1854 Attempts to rescue fugitive slaves leads to clashes; attacks on Roman Catholics by extremist Protestants; Indians granted equal fishing rights with Whites but settlers encroach on western reservations; Japan open to US trade.
1856 Clashes between abolitionists and pro-slavery proponents in Kansas.
1857 Arguments against slavery on economic grounds increase; Arkansas emigrants bound for California massacred by Indians in Utah.
1859 Indian reservation granted in New Mexico; Fugitive Slave Act upheld in Wisconsin; raid on Virginia arsenal thwarted; gold found in Rockies.

People

4392 **Burr, Aaron** 1756–1836. Vice-president 1800–04. Killed Hamilton in duel (1804). Wanted independent Mexico and Texas incorporating part of Louisiana. Tried for treason 1807 but acquitted. Unscrupulous in business and political dealings.
Hamilton, Alexander c. 1757–1804. As Treasury Secretary 1789-95 established federal bank. Federalist leader. Killed in duel with Burr.
Iturbide, Agustin de 1783–1824, Mexican independence leader. Crowned emperor (1822). Deposed and exiled (1823). Shot on return.
Jackson, Andrew 1767–1845 Seventh president (1828–36). Defended New Orleans from British (1815). Won victories over Indian tribes 1814, 1818.
Jefferson, Thomas 1743–1826. Third president (1801–9). Drafted Declaration of Independence (1776). Opposed centralization. Effected Louisiana Purchase (1803).
Santa Anna, Antonio de 1796–1876, Mexican revolutionary general, president and dictator, ruled for most of the period between 1824 and 1855. Took Alamo (1836).
Tubman, Harriet c. 1820–1913. Escaped Maryland slave, instrumental in bringing over 300 slaves to north via Underground Railroad.
Turner, Nat 1800–31. Slave who killed master and family in 1831 and led short-lived Virginia rebellion.
Webster, Daniel 1782–1852. Lawyer, politician and great orator. Opposed slavery but unwilling to break up Union to abolish it.

Places

4393

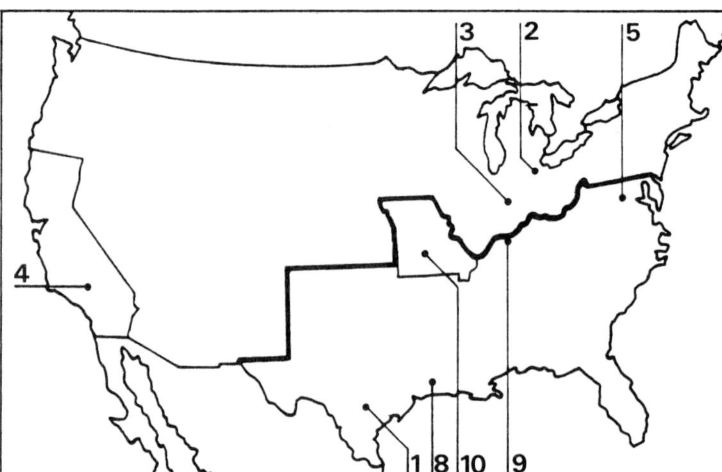

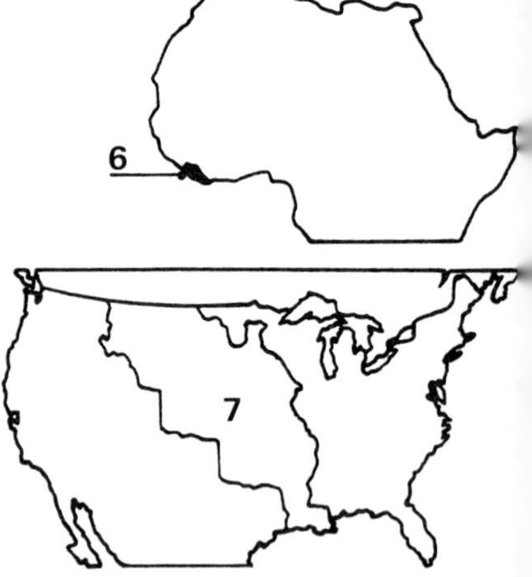

1 Alamo Siege (1836) Franciscan mission in Texas occupied by US troops and families beseiged by Mexican forces and taken after 11 days. Entire male US garrison, including James Bowie and David ("Davy") Crockett, killed.
2 Battle of Fallen Timbers (1794) Indian tribesmen in Ohio and Kentucky region defeated by US troops
3 Battle of Tippecanoe (1811) Shawnee nation defeated by US forces at Wabash.
4 Bear Republic (1846) Californian attempt to create republic independent of Mexico.
5 Harper's Ferry Virginia town with arsenal raided 1859 by Kansas abolitionist John Brown (1800–59) in hope that this would spark off a general slave insurrection. Brown was defeated by federal forces, tried for treason and hanged.
6 Liberia US freedmen's colony in Africa (since 1821) which became independent republic (1847)
7 Kansas-Nebraska Act (1854) Legislation opening reserved Indian lands in west to White settlers.
8 Louisiana Purchase 1803 $15 million paid by US to France for 828,000 square miles of territory.
9 Mason-Dixon Line Boundary as surveyed 1763–7 between Maryland and Pennsylvania regarded as dividing slave from free states.
10 Missouri Compromise 1820 Missouri admitted as slave state in return for entry of Maine as free state.

Words

4394 **"Cotton is king"** Book title quoted by South Carolina senator James H Hammond in 1858 speech taunting critics of South.
Democratic-Republicans Post-Revolutionary political grouping mainly of small farmers and workers advocating states' rights (led by Jefferson). Became Democratic Party in 1828.
Elgin Treaty 1854 Agreement establishing reciprocity between US and Canada.
Federalists Post-Revolutionary political grouping mainly of propertied and commercial classes advocating central government (led by Hamilton).
Forty-Niners 77,000 men who rushed to California in 1849 at news of gold discovery
Freeman's Journal 1827, New York. First Black newspaper.
Fugitive Slave Act 1793 Legislation criminalizing help to escaping slaves.
Gabriel's Insurrection 1800 Slave revolt in Virginia which led to plans for Black emigration to Africa.
Gadsden Purchase 1853.Territory acquired from Mexico permitting easy rail connections to be built between Texas and California.
gerrymandering Redrawing election district boundaries for political purposes (possibly because of Massachusetts governor Elbridge Gerry, 1812).
Jay's Treaty 1794 Settlement between Britain and US of outstanding territorial and trade disputes.
"Jim Crow" Blackface song and dance act based on deformed livery stable slave (c. 1833) which came to symbolize racial prejudice.
Lynch's Law Summary justice meted out by Virginia planter Charles Lynch in 1780 as head of extralegal court.

Monroe Doctrine 1823 Declaration closing Western hemisphere to European colonization and interference while accepting existing European colonies (**1**).
Republican Party formed originally in 1854 by disaffected Democrats opposed to extension of slavery and remnants of old Whig party.
Scott (Dred) Decision 1857 Legal ruling that fugitive slave Scott could not claim freedom by living in free territory nor had right to bring law suit in federal court.
sectionalism Tendency to favor or oppose territorial expansion, tariffs and other economic measures according to state rather than national interests.
Seminole Wars 1817–18, 1835–42 Conflicts with Indians in Florida and Georgia.
Shays' Rebellion 1786 Massachusetts farmers' uprising led by war veteran Daniel Shays.
Trail of Tears 1838–39, 14,000 Cherokee Indians forcibly relocated; 4,000 died on six-month journey.
"***Uncle Tom's Cabin***" Novel by Harriet Beecher Stowe (1811–96) about slavery in the South first serialized in 1851 and published in book form the following year.
Underground Railroad Escape route for southern slaves to Canada frequently opposed by White workers fearful for their own jobs.
Whiskey Rebellion 1794 Frontier farmers resisted excise duty; Federal militia suppressed revolt without bloodshed.
XYZ Affair 1797–8 France and US on brink of war over unnamed French Directory (government) members' attempt to extort money from US diplomats.

Joining the Union 1787–1959

4395

1800–49

1787–1799
1787 Delaware
1787 Pennsylvania
1787 New Jersey
1788 Georgia
1788 Connecticut
1788 Massachusetts
1788 Maryland
1788 South Carolina
1788 New Hampshire
1788 Virginia
1788 New York
1789 North Carolina
1790 Rhode Island
1791 Vermont
1792 Kentucky
1796 Tennessee

1800–1849
1803 Ohio
1812 Louisiana
1816 Indiana
1817 Mississippi
1818 Illinois
1819 Alabama
1820 Maine
1821 Missouri
1836 Arkansas
1837 Michigan
1845 Florida
1845 Texas
1846 Iowa
1848 Wisconsin

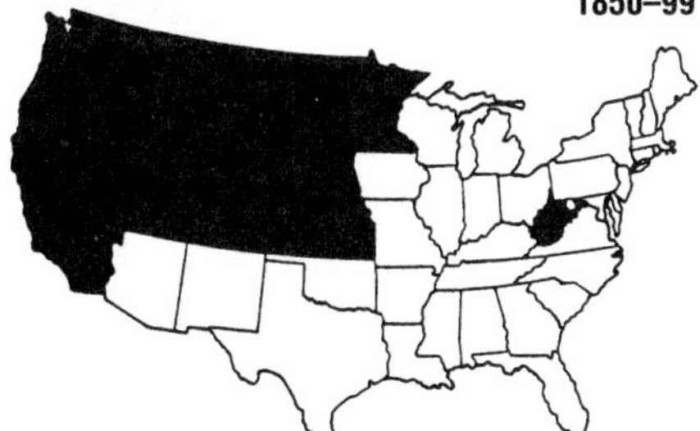

1900–59

1850–1899
1850 California
1858 Minnesota
1859 Oregon
1861 Kansas
1863 West Virginia
1864 Nevada
1867 Nebraska
1876 Colorado
1889 North Dakota
1889 South Dakota
1889 Montana
1889 Washington
1890 Idaho
1890 Wyoming
1896 Utah

1900–1959
1907 Oklahoma
1912 New Mexico
1912 Arizona
1959 Alaska
1959 Hawaii

441 American Civil War
4411 Events
4412 People
4413 Places
4414 Words

441 AMERICAN CIVIL WAR

Events

4411 **PRIOR TO THE WAR**

1857 Dred Scott Supreme Court decision that a slave was not free if taken to a free state. Congress therefore unable to bar slavery from a territory (Mar).
1859 Abolitionist John Brown's raid on armory at Harper's Ferry (Oct).
1860 Jefferson Davis calls for federal code to protect owners' rights to slaves as property (Feb). Lincoln elected president on a Republican platform opposing extension of slavery (Nov). South Carolina secedes (Dec).
1861 The seven Lower South states secede. The four Upper South states warn against Federal coercion. Texas, Virginia and Tennessee hold referenda with secession majority votes (Jan). Montgomery Convention frames Confederate constitution and sets up provisional government. Davis elected president (Feb). Davis calls for volunteers. Lincoln inaugurated (Mar).

THE WAR; 1861–5

1861 Confederate batteries open fire on Fort Sumter. Lincoln calls for volunteers (Apr). Union naval forces begin blockade of Confederate ports and coastline (May). Confederate victory at first battle of Bull Run (Jul). Missouri remains in Union after battle of Wilson's Creek. Confederate forces driven out of West Virginia (Aug). Confederacy fail in re-capture attempt (Sep). Confederate commissioners seized from British ship by Union patrol (Nov). War between Union and Great Britain averted by their release (Dec).
1862 Lincoln orders general offensive (Jan). Union victories in Tennessee and Kentucky culminating in Battle of Shiloh (Jan, Feb, Apr). Confederate forces pin down Union troops in Shenandoah Valley (Mar-Jun). New Orleans taken by Union. Confederacy adopts conscription (Apr). Battle for Richmond at Chickahominy River indecisive (Seven Pines) (May-Jun). Seven Days' battles end with Confederate withdrawal toward Richmond (Jun-Jul). Union forces defeated in second battle of Bull Run (Aug). Confederacy invades Maryland. Drawn battle near Sharpsburg. Lincoln issues preliminary emancipation proclamation (Sep). Confederate victory at Fredericksburg. Lincoln weathers cabinet crisis (Dec).
1863 Emancipation proclamation (Jan). Congress establishes National Banking System. French attempt at mediation (Feb). Union forces besiege and take Vicksburg to split Confederacy geographically (May-Jul). West Virginia admitted as a state (Jun). Union victory at battle of Gettysburg. Anti-conscription riots in New York (Jul). British and French governments deny shipbuilding facilities to Confederacy. Indecisive battle of Chickamauga (Sept). Gettysburg war cemetery inaugurated with address by Lincoln. Union victory at battle of Chattanooga reinforces geographical split of Confederacy (Nov).
1864 Union forces advance south and west (Mar-May). Indecisive battles with heavy casualties in The Wilderness and at Spotsylvania (May). Union advance through Georgia (May-Sept). Battles at Chickahominy and Cold Harbour and siege of Petersburg cause heavy Confederate losses without total Union victory. Confederate naval losses. Union presidential election campaign begins (Jun). Confederate advance towards Washington rebuffed (Jul). Second Shenandoah Valley campaign (Jul-Oct). Atlanta falls to Union forces (Sep). Lincoln re-elected (Nov). Union advance toward Savannah (Nov-Dec). Union victory at Battle of Nashville. Savannah falls (Dec).
1865 Union advance through North and South Carolina (Jan-Mar). Hampton Roads conference fails to agree terms. Union forces capture Charleston (Feb). Confederacy agrees to arm slaves for military duties (Mar). Confederate forces evacuate Petersburg and Richmond. Lincoln inaugurated for second term. Confederate forces surrender at Appomattox. Lincoln assassinated (Apr). Confederate capitulation (May).

Aftermath and Reconstruction

1865 Reconstruction proclamation (May). Abolition of slavery (Dec).
1866 Civil Rights Act grants citizenship to "Negroes" (Apr).

People

4412 **UNION LEADERS**

Grant, Ulysses Simpson (1) 1822–85. Soldier, and 18th president of US. Returned to army in 1861 on outbreak of Civil War. Defeated General Lee in decisive battle at Richmond in 1865. General 1866, Republican president 1868. Guaranteed universal right of suffrage.
Johnson, Andrew (2) 1808–75. 17th president of US, 1865–9. Moderate Democrat, who was alone among Southern senators in standing by Union during Civil War. Conciliatory policy of urging readmission of Southern representatives opposed by radical majority in congress.
Lincoln, Abraham 1809–65, 16th president of US from 1860 (**3**), famous for Gettysburg Address of 1863, including words "government of the people, by the people, for the people." Great achievement of administration was emancipation of slaves in all American states. Assassinated at Washington.
McClellan, George Brinton 1826–85. Soldier. In Civil War in 1861, as major-general in US army, drove enemy out of West Virginia. Later forced to retreat, fought disastrous battle of Bull Run, 1862. Defeated by Lincoln in 1864 presidential elections.

1

2

3

Seward, William Henry 1801–72. Statesman. Opposed proslavery policy of President Fillmore. Lincoln's secretary of state 1861–9. In "Trent Affair" during Civil War, advised that Confederate envoys should be given up to England. Supported Johnson's reconstruction policy.
Sherman, William Tecumseh 1820–91. Soldier. At Bull Run, 1861, won promotion to Brigadier-general of volunteers. Major-general 1862. Drove General Johnston back to Atlanta in 1864. 1865, General Lee surrendered, and Johnston made terms with Sherman.
Stanton, Edwin McMasters 1814–69. Lawyer and statesman. Secretary of war under Lincoln from 1862, was suspended by Johnson (1867), and reinstated by Senate. When Johnson's impeachment failed, Stanton resigned (1868).

CONFEDERATE LEADERS

4

Beauregard, Pierre Gustave Toutant 1818–93. Confederate soldier. General who opened hostilities by attack on Fort Sumter (1861). In virtual command at battle of Bull Run (1861). After defeat in 1862, retreated to Corinth, Mississippi. Defeated Butler 1864.
Booth, John Wilkes 1838–65. Assassin. Unsuccessful actor who, in 1865, entered into conspiracy to avenge defeat of Confederates, and shot President Lincoln at Ford's Theater, Washington. Tracked down in Virginia and, refusing to surrender, shot.
Davis, Jefferson 1808–89. President of Confederate States. History of tenure is that of War of 1861–5. In May 1865, after collapse of government, imprisoned by Union Cavalry for two years, then released on bail. Included in amnesty of 1868.
Jackson, Thomas Jonathan, "Stonewall Jackson" 1824–63. Soldier and Confederate general . Commanded brigade at Bull Run, where firm stand gained him title "Stonewall." Major-general 1861. Died after accidental shooting by own troops.
Lee, Robert E (Edward) 1807–70 (**4**). One of greatest Confederate generals of Civil War. Battle against General Pope, invasion of Maryland and Pennsylvania, and other achievements were cardinal to history of war. Surrendered to General Grant 1865.

Places

4413

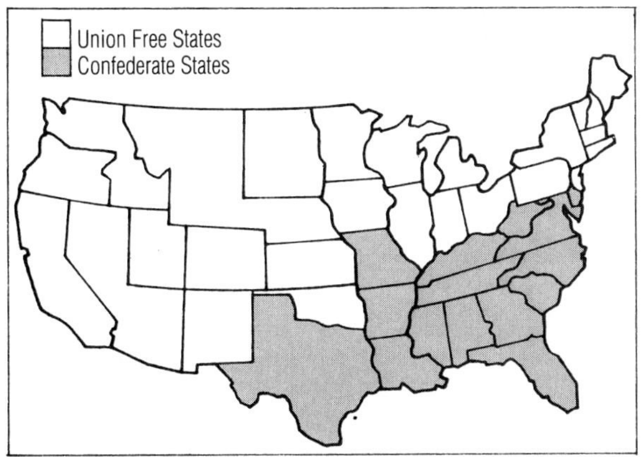

Union Free States
California
Colorado (Territory)
Connecticut
Dakota (Territory)
Delaware
Illinois
Indiana
Indian Territory (slavery abolished 1862; now Oklahoma)
Iowa
Kansas
Kentucky
Maine
Maryland
Massachusetts
Michigan
Minnesota
Missouri
Nebraska (Territory)
Nevada (Territory)
New Hampshire
New Jersey
New Mexico (Territory)
New York
Ohio
Oregon
Pennsylvania
Utah (Territory)
Vermont
Virginia - West (statehood 1863)
Washington (Territory)
Wisconsin

Confederate States
Alabama
Arkansas
Carolina - North
Carolina - South
Florida
Georgia
Louisiana
Mississippi
Texas
Tennessee
Virginia

1861–2
1 Bombardment of Fort Sumter Apr 12–14
2 Battle of Bull Run Jul 21
3 Battle of Wilson's Creek Aug 10
4 Forts Henry and Donelson taken by Grant Feb 6–16
5 Jackson's Shenandoah Valley Campaign Mar 23–Jun 9
6 Battle of Shiloh Apr 6–7
7 New Orleans Bombardment Apr 25
8 Battle of Seven Pines (Fair Oaks) May 31–June 1
9 Seven Days' battles before Richmond June 26–July 2
10 Second Battle of Bull Run (Manassas) Aug 29–30
11 Battle of Antietam (Sharpsburg) Sep 17
12 Battle of Fredericksburg Dec 13
13 Battle of Murfreesboro (Stones River) Dec 31–2 Jan 1863

Area under Union control by end of 1862

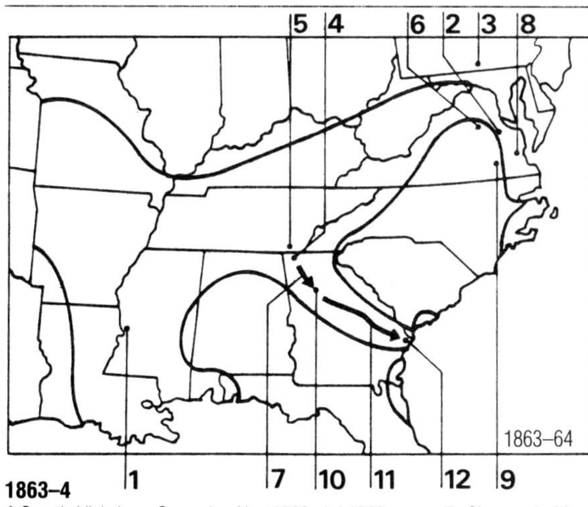

1863–4
1 Grant's Vicksburg Campaign Nov 1862–Jul 1863
2 Battle of Chancellorsville May 1–6
3 Battle of Gettysburg Jul 1–3
4 Battle of Chickamauga Sept 19–20
5 Battle of Chattanooga Nov 23–25
6 Battle of the Wilderness May 5–6
7 Sherman's March to Atlanta May 5– Sep 2
8 Battle of Cold Harbor Jun 1–12
9 Battle of Petersburg Jun 15–18
10 Capture of Atlanta Sept 2
11 March to the Sea Nov 14–Dec 22
12 Savannah occupied by Union Dec 22

Area under Union control by end of 1864

1865
1 Sherman's drive through the Carolinas Jan 16–Mar 21
2 Lee's surrender at Appomattox Courthouse Apr 9

Area under Union control by end of 1865

Words

4414

butternut Light brown dye used for Confederate uniforms. Obtained from a solution of acorns or walnut hulls.
carbet-bagger Northern adventurer in South during Reconstruction for pecuniary or political gains.
emancipation Abolition of slavery.
free state One where slaves have been freed or where slavery has not been permitted.
Fugitive Slave Law 1851 Legislation authorizing special commissioners to arrest actual or presumed fugitive slaves and return them to their putative owners.
Ku Klux Klan Postwar secret society dedicated to re-assert White supremacy through violence.

continued

Words continued

4414 **mule and five acres** The politicians' promise to newly franchised "Negroes" if they would vote for them.
Reb Contraction of Rebel, that is, a Confederate supporter.
Rebel yell The shrill and chilling shout given by Confederate troops as they advanced.
Reconstruction The political process by which the southern states were restored to the Union.
Secession The act of leaving the Union by any state.
state Internally autonomous territorial and political unit.
stonewalling Defensive rather than offensive tactics as displayed by Jackson at Bull Run in 1861.
Territory A part of the US with its own legislature but a governor appointed by the president and not admitted as a full state.
Trent Affair 1861 Diplomatic crisis with Britain over seizure of Confederate commissioners from the British steamer Trent.
Underground Railroad Clandestine organization for assisting slaves to escape from the South involving over 3,000 active workers.

442 AMERICA 1860–1917

Events

4421 **1860** Navajo Indians attack New Mexico fort; Lincoln elected president; South Carolina secedes from United States.
1861 Mississippi, Florida, Alabama, Georgia, Louisiana, Texas, Virginia, Tennessee, Arkansas and North Carolina secede; Confederate States of America proclaimed; Civil War begins.
1862 First Union military successes; other indecisive engagements; slavery abolished in US territories; Apache raids against California settlers.
1863 Forced resettlement of Navajo and Apache tribes; Union defeats; Confederate advance halted; draft riots in northern cities; bread riots in blockaded southern cities; French intervention in Mexico; throne offered to Austrian prince.
1864 Union troops advance through Missouri and Georgia; Lincoln reelected; Cheyenne Indians on warpath in Colorado.
1865 Civil war ends with Confederate surrender; Lincoln assassinated; Colorado Indian Reservation established.
1866 US government demands removal of French troops from Mexico; Civil Rights legislation passed.
1867 Dominion of Canada created; US buys Alaska from Russia for $7.2 million; Mexican emperor surrenders to insurgents and is shot.
1868 Former Confederate states readmitted to Union; Navajo Indians restricted to small area.
1870 First Black members of Senate and House of Representatives.
1872 First consumer protection law.
1873 Financial crisis.
1875 Comanche Indians cede Texan territory; Civil Rights legislation; anti-Black laws in Tennessee.
1876 Coup d'état in Mexico; US presidential election stalemate; racial conflict in South Carolina; Cheyenne and Sioux Indians oppose White settlers; Battle of Little Bighorn.
1881 President Garfield assassinated; further anti-Black legislation in Tennessee; rise of anti-Semitism.
1885 Riots by disaffected west Canadians; anti-Chinese riots in Washington Territory.
1886 Strikers killed by police in Chicago; anti-Chinese riots spread to Seattle; US troops defeat Apache Indians; Florida passes anti-Black legislation.
1888 Further anti-Chinese riots in Seattle; immigration from Britain peaks.
1889 Oklahoma Territory and South Dakota former Indian lands made available to White homesteaders; Pan-American conference in Washington; disputes between cattle and sheep farmers escalate.
1891–3 Anti-Black legislation in Alabama, Arkansas, Georgia, Louisiana and Tennessee; series of workers' strikes.
1894 Economic depression as income tax levied and tariffs reduced.
1896 Racial segregation upheld by Supreme Court decision; Canadian gold rush after Klondike discovery.
1898 Spanish-American war lasts 112 days; Puerto Rico, Guam, and Philippines ceded by Spain to US; Louisiana disenfranchises Blacks; race riots and lynchings.
1901 President McKinley assassinated; New York Stock Exchange panic; Alabama legislation disenfranchises Blacks.
1902 Coal miners strike across country.
1903 Panama isthmus leased from Colombia by US; Panama declares independence from Colombia; US recognizes new republic; coal miners win hours cut and wage rise.
1905 US mediates in Russo-Japanese conflict; moves to ban Japanese immigration.
1906 Earthquake in San Francisco, over 450 die; race riots in Texas; San Francisco attempt to segregate oriental schoolchildren fails.
1907–8 Economic crisis.
1910 Mexican social revolution; clothing workers strike; Blacks begin move from south to north.
1911–12 US marines sent to Nicaragua and Honduras after coup; homesteaders' residence requirement reduced.
1913 Import duties reduced; liability for income tax increased; new coup in Mexico.
1914 US forces enter Mexico; civil war in Mexico; voting rights demanded by women; Panama Canal opened.
1915 German sinking of Lusitania fuels call for US intervention in World War I.
1916 US forces intervene in Mexico and Santo Domingo; volunteer flyers join French forces.
1917 US enters World War I on Allied side.

Words

4422 **Chinese Exclusion Act 1882** Legislation prohibiting return of Chinese workers who had left the US.
Emancipation Proclamation Lincoln's statement affirming abolition of slavery as a war aim (1862). 4 million slaves automatically freed (1863).
Homestead Act 1862 Legislation offering federal land to settlers and farmers.
IWW ("Wobblies") 1905 Cross-industry grouping of workers.
"Jim Crow" laws Legislation enacted in southern states after emancipation to restrict Black rights and enforce segregation.
"Molly Maguires" 1860s to 1880s Secret Irish-American society especially active in mining areas.
NAACP Crusading National Association for the Advancement of Colored People, founded 1909.
Scallywags (alternatively "scalawags") White Southerners who supported Black emancipation and Republican Party.

People

4423 **Booth, John Wilkes** 1838–65. Actor who shot Lincoln. Shot to death as he escaped from a hiding place.
Carson, Kit 1809–68. Former trapper and Indian expert, officer in charge of Indian resettlement 1863–6.
Cochise d. 1874, Apache chief leading raids in California 1861–71 but eventually accepting resettlement.
Diaz, Porfiro 1830–1915, Mexican president 1877–80, 1884–1911 (**1**). Originally associate of Juarez he opposed the latter from 1868. Pursued policies of modernization and reconciliation.

1

continued

People continued

4423 **Geronimo** 1829–1909, (**2**) Chiricahua Apache leader (real name Goyathalay) raiding into Mexico 1872–6 and opposing White settlers in South West 1876–86.

Juarez, Benito 1806–72. Mexican leader of Indian stock opposing emperor Maximilian. President 1861–5, 1867–72, with policies emphasizing republican principles and confiscating church property.

Maximilian, Archduke 1832–67. Brother of Austrian emperor Franz Josef. Emperor of Mexico under French auspices 1864–7. Defeated, tried, and shot.

Roosevelt, Theodore 1858–1919. (**3**) President 1901–9. Extended US military and diplomatic influence with expansionist policies and regulation of trusts, monopolies and the civil service.

Sherman, William T 1820–91. Union general gaining Atlanta (1864) and marching across Georgia to Charleston harbor (1864–65). Army commander 1869.

Villa, Francisco c.1877–1923. Popularly called Pancho Villa. Mexican revolutionary and guerrilla leader.

Wilson, Woodrow 1856–1924. President 1913–21. Took US into World War I in 1917; proposed 14-point peace plan 1918 (**4**).

443 EUROPE IN THE 19TH CENTURY

New Nations

4431

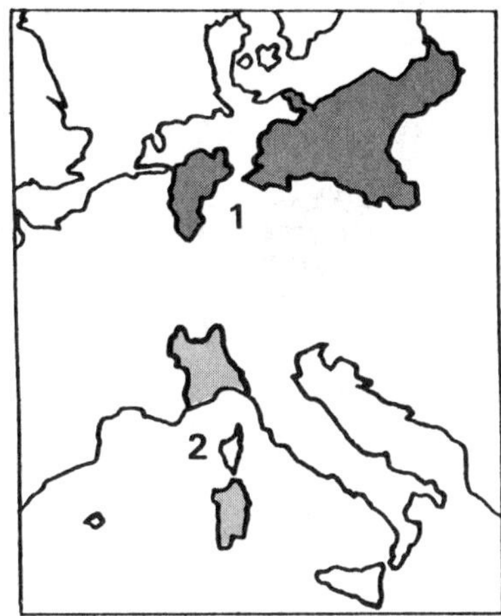

1 Prussia to 1866
2 Kingdom of Sardinia 1859

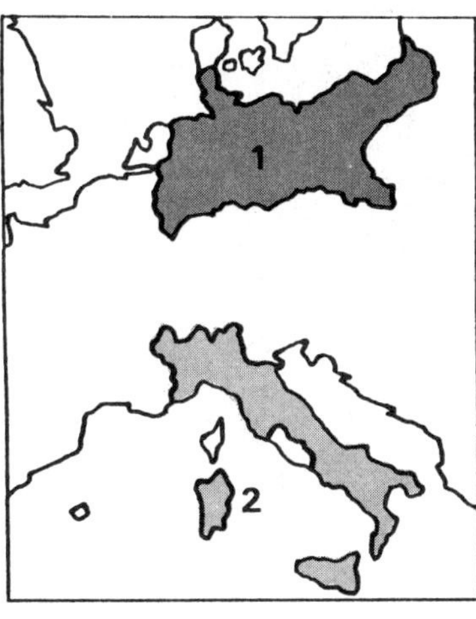

1 Prussia (North German Federation) 1867
2 Kingdom of Sardinia 1860

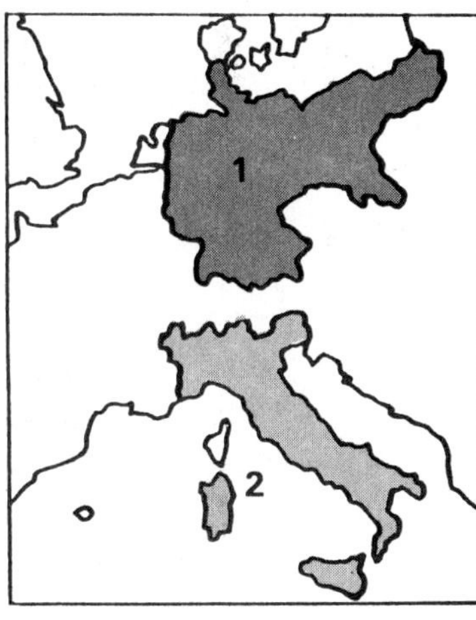

1 The new German Empire 1871
2 The new unified Italy 1870

Events

4432 **1815** Napoleonic Wars end; Bourbon monarchy restored in France and overall status quo; Russia rules Poland.
1817-19 Famine in Ireland; risings in Catalonia, Portugal; British laws on child labor; troops mutiny in Spain demanding constitution.
1820 Revolutions in Spain, Portugal and Naples; George III of Britain dies, succeeded by George IV; troops mutiny in Russia.
1821 Napoleon I dies; revolts in Italy against Austrian rule.
1822 Greece proclaims independence from Turkey, massacres; uprisings in Spain; Portuguese constitution; famine in Ireland; Russia sets up protective tariffs.
1823-6 Turkey fails to defeat Greeks, troops purged; British legal reforms, economic crisis (to 1827); unrest in Russia; French troops in Spain (to 1828).
1827-8 Turkish fleet defeated by alliance of British, French and Russian fleets; Russia and Turkey at war; customs union between Prussia and Hesse.
1829 Legal disabilities of Roman Catholics end in Britain; Russo-Turkish war ends with Russian territorial gains; Greek independence recognized; liberal uprisings in Portugal (to 1831).
1830 George IV dies, succeeded by brother William IV; revolution in France ousts Bourbon dynasty, duc d'Orléans succeeds as Louis Philippe; risings in Poland; Belgium proclaims independence.
1831 Holland invades Belgium; regional risings in France and Russia; Polish constitution abolished; French expedition against Portugal.
1832–3 Parliamentary reform in Britain; abortive royalist rising in France; French troops in Belgium; civil war in Portugal; rival claimants to Spanish throne.
1834 Slavery ended in British possessions; civil war in Spain (to 1839).
1835–6 English local government reformed; Portuguese constitution again restored.
1837 William IV dies, succeeded by niece Victoria, English industrial depression (to 1842); liberal constitution agreed in Spain; Hanover constitution suppressed.
1838–9 Riots in France; German states' monetary union; Turkish constitution; free trade and electoral reform agitation in England and Ireland.
1841–3 Basque uprising; Turkish independence guaranteed; independence demanded for Ireland; unrest in Serbia; revolution in Greece.
1844–6 New constitution in Spain and controversy over royal marriages; famine in Ireland; Poles rise; coup in Portugal; anti-Austrian demonstrations in Italy.
1847–8 Industrial depression and political rallies in England; civil war in Switzerland; revolutions in France, Austria, papal states, Naples and Sicily; Venice declares independence, joins Piedmont; constitutions in Hungary, Prussia.
1849–50 New constitution in Denmark; Prussia

continued

Events continued

4432 proposes German union omitting Austria; short-lived republic in Rome; Hungary proclaims short-lived independence; unrest in Ireland; anti-Prussian grouping includes Austria and Russia.
1852 New constitution in France; commercial treaty between Hanover and Prussia; Austria proposes customs union with south German states, abolishes constitution, makes commercial treaty with Prussia; Danish independence guaranteed.
1853 Second Empire proclaimed in France; political reforms in Portugal; Crimean War.
1854–5 Allied troops suffer losses in series of sieges and battles; rebellion in Spain; epidemics in Portugal; liberal institutions abolished in Hanover.
1856 Crimean War ends with Russian territorial losses; plans to abolish serfdom in Russia and other interior reforms, amnesty for Poles; reforms in Turkey; commercial legislation in Britain and France; unrest in Spain; liberalization in Portugal.
1857–60 Economic crisis in Britain; Spanish situation stabilizes; independence of Montenegro recognized; legal disabilities for Jews end in England; France at war with Austria over Italian independence; renewed calls for German unity.
1861 Serfdom abolished in Russia, constitution granted to Finland, troops fire on Polish demonstrators; centralized constitution in Austria; Italy proclaimed united monarchy; Romania an independent monarchy uniting Moldavia and Wallachia.
1862–4 French commercial treaties with Prussia and Italy, troops withdraw from Italy; nationalists fail to capture Rome; new king of Greece elected; new constitution in Denmark, territorial dispute leading to war with German confederation; Poland rebels, Prussia and Russia crush rising; riots in Ireland.

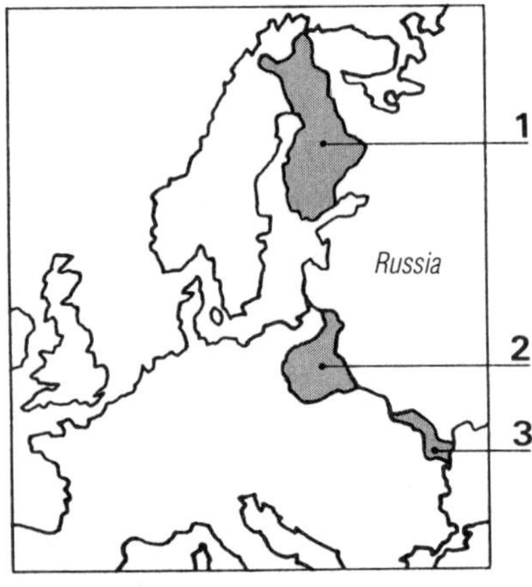

Expansion of the Russian Empire in the 19th century

Territory acquired

1 Finland and Lapland
2 Poland
3 Bessarabia (Moldavia)

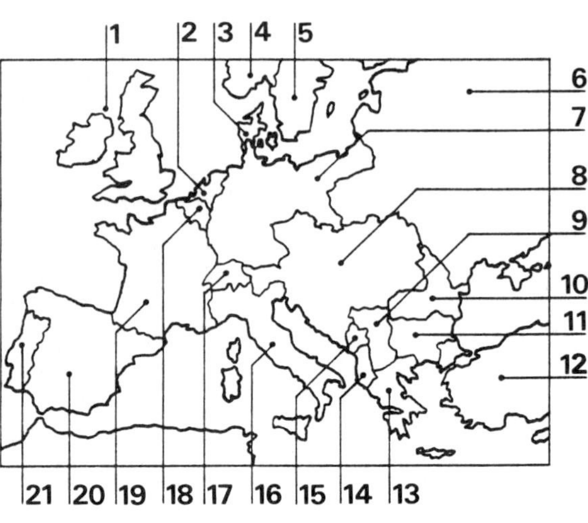

Countries of Europe 1913 – post Balkan war

1 United Kingdom
2 Holland
3 Denmark
4 Norway
5 Sweden
6 Russia
7 German Empire
8 Austro-Hungary
9 Serbia
10 Romania
11 Bulgaria
12 Turkey
13 Greece
14 Albania
15 Montenegro
16 Italy
17 Switzerland
18 Belgium
19 France
20 Spain
21 Portugal

1865–7 Arrests of nationalists in Ireland lead to terrorist attacks; new constitutions in Denmark and Sweden; Austrian constitution annulled, Transylvania incorporated into Hungary, dual monarchy of Austria-Hungary; France territorial claims; alliance between Italy and Prussia, Prussia annexes Hanover, Hesse, Holstein, and Saxony; Crete unites with Greece; war between Austria and Italy.
1868–9 Spanish army and navy revolts; Greece evacuates Crete; Portugal abolishes slavery; freedom of Parliament, Press and assembly in France.
1870–1 Municipal government reformed in Russia; Rome taken, becomes national capital, pope retains Vatican; war between France and Prussia ends with French defeat yielding Alsace-Lorraine, Second Empire falls, Paris besieged; Germany proclaimes empire at Versailles; Britain legalizes trades unions and abolishes purchase of military commissions.
1872–75 Constitutional dispute in Denmark (to 1894); civil war in Spain; local government reform in Germany; administrative and industrial laws reformed in Britain; alliance between Austria, Germany, and Russia; military reforms in Russia; risings against Turkey in Bosnia and Herzogovina; Swiss constitution.
1876–78 New constitution in Spain; Bulgarians massacred by Turks, Turkey at war with Serbia, Russia and Greece, new Turkish constitution, peace treaty recognizes Montenegrin, Romanian, and Serbian independence, Bulgaria autonomous under Turkish suzerainty, Bosnia and Herzegovina awarded to Austria, Cyprus to Britain.
1880–83 Russian terrorist attacks, tsar murdered, anti-Semitic outrages, student unrest; renewed agitation in Ireland, murders; electoral law reformed in Italy; monarchies in Romania and Serbia; alliance between Austria and Serbia; new constitution in Bulgaria; alliance between Austria, Germany, and Romania.
1884–86 Male suffrage in Britain and Ireland, attempts to secure home rule for Ireland fail, agitation for home rule in Scotland; strikes in Russia suppressed by troops; Serbia invades Bulgaria, defeated; German settlements in Poland proposed.
1887–1889 Agreements between Britain, Italy, Austria, and Spain on Mediterranean; dock strike in London, local government reform, navy increased; political scandals in France; students hanged in Russia, repressive measures in Poland; military agreement between Germany and Italy; coup in Bulgaria; German army increased.
1890–3 Bismarck dismissed as German chancellor; entente between France and Russia; first Labor Party members elected to British Parliament; German declared official language in Alsace-Lorraine.
1894–1900 Armenians massacred by Kurds; military secrets scandal in France (to 1906); Queen Victoria celebrates 60 years of reign; Zionist congress in Basle; Russian political party founded to press for representative government.
1901–06 Start of armaments race between Britain and Germany; growth of agitation for reform in Russia, Jews massacred, workers' demonstration fired on, tsar's powers limited; Queen Victoria dies, succeeded by son Edward VII, program for tariff reform in Britain; secret treaty between France and Italy; accord between France and Britain; Norway independent from Sweden.
1907–10 Germany refuses to limit armaments; Russian alliance with Britain and France, secret pact with Bulgaria against Austria and Germany; Austria annexes Bosnia and Herzogovina; Crete proclaims union with Greece; revolt in Turkey leads to deposition of sultan; male suffrage in Sweden; constitutional crisis in Britain over plan for welfare benefits to be financed by tax increases.
1911–14 Crisis over proposals for Irish home rule; Anglo-French naval agreement; Balkan War; Albania becomes independent; Austria declares war on Serbia when heir to empire is assassinated in Bosnia by Serbian nationalist.

People

4433 **Albert of Saxe-Coburg-Gotha, Prince** 1819–61. Cousin and husband of Queen Victoria. Patron of arts, interested in social and industrial reform.
Alexander II b. 1818, r. 1855–81. Tsar of Russia. Reformer. Abolished serfdom 1861. Assassinated.
Alexander III b. 1845 r. 1881–94. Tsar of Russia. Reactionary, persecuted Jews, liberals and intellectuals.
Ataturk, Kemal 1881–1938. Original name Mustafa Kemal. Turkish general and statesman. Founder of Turkish republic. President 1923–38. Responsible for westernization and secularization of nation.
Bismarck, Prince Otto von 1815–98, Prussian statesman nicknamed "The Iron Chancellor" (**1**) Premier of Prussia 1862–90, chancellor of Germany 1871–90. Architect of German empire. Concerned for foreign alliances. Hoped to stem socialism through social reforms.

1

Boycott, Captain 1832–97. Land agent in Ireland who refused to accept rents at level requested by tenants in 1880; tenants then refused to harvest crops. Name now used to denote method by which community ignores an individual.
Cavour, Count Camillo 1810–61, Italian statesman. Premier of Piedmont-Sardinia 1852–9, 1860–1. Architect of Italian unity.
Disraeli, Benjamin, Earl of Beaconsfield 1804–81, English statesman and novelist of Jewish descent. Chancellor of Exchequer 1852, 1858, 1865. Prime minister 1868, 1874–80. Responsible for extending franchise, acquiring Suez Canal and Cyprus, and making Victoria empress of India.
Dreyfus, Captain Alfred 1859–1935, French Jewish military officer falsely accused of and sentenced for treason 1894–1908, but eventually exonerated in 1906.
Franz Josef b. 1830, r. 1848–1916. Ruler of Austro-Hungarian empire. Inflexible politically but popular. Personal life marred by suicide of son and heir Rudolf (1889), and assassination of wife Elizabeth (1898). Ultimatum to Serbia in 1914 led to World War I.
Garibaldi, Giuseppe 1807–82 (**2**).

2

Italian nationalist and revolutionary leader and soldier. In 1860 he led 1,000 volunteers to capture Naples and Sicily.
Gladstone, William E 1809–98. English statesman nicknamed "The Grand Old Man." Prime Minister 1868–74, 1880–5, 1886, 1892–4. Achieved educational and electoral reform but failed to accomplish Irish home rule.
Hardie, Keir, 1856–1915, Scottish socialist and politician. Elected to Parliament 1892. Founded Independent Labor Party 1893, began Labor Party 1900 and formally founded it 1906.
Hill, Sir Rowland 1795–1879, English schoolmaster who in 1840 instituted first postal service paid for in advance and based on weight rather than distance.
Kossuth, Lajos 1802–94, Hungarian statesman leading revolt against Austrian rule 1848. Provisional governor 1849 but forced into exile same year.

3

Marx, Karl 1818–83, German philosopher and economist (**3**) who laid the foundations of Communism. His writings include *The Communist Manifesto* and *Das Kapital.*
Metternich, Prince Clemens Lothar Wenzel 1773–1859, Austrian statesman. Foreign minister from 1809, chancellor from 1821–48. Champion of autocracy at home and throughout Europe. Ousted in 1848 revolution.
Napoleon III b. 1808, r. 1852–70, d.1873, French emperor, nephew of Napoleon I. After abortive coup attempts elected president 1848, proclaimed Second Empire 1852. Pragmatic politician with liberal leanings. Initial success in foreign affairs but forced to surrender army and abdicate after defeat in Franco-Prussian war.
Nicholas II b. 1868, r. 1894–1917, d. 1918. Tsar of Russia. Autocratic but incompetent. Forced to grant constitution in 1905. Military reverses in World War I precipitated revolution. Abdicated, but imprisoned and shot with family.
Nightingale, Florence 1820–1910, English nurse who raised quality of profession, organized hospitals in Crimea 1855–6, founded training school for nurses 1860.
O'Connell, Daniel 1775–1847, Irish nationalist orator and leader. Election to Parliament in 1828, forced RC emancipation. Failed to achieve Irish independence.
Parnell, Charles S 1846–91, Irish Protestant nationalist leader. Led home rule movement 1880–90 in Parliament but scandal over affair with agent's wife Kitty O'Shea lost him support.
Peel, Sir Robert 1788–1850, English statesman. Secretary for Ireland 1812–18. Home Secretary 1822–27, 1828–30. Prime Minister 1834–5, 1841–6. Organized London police, assisted Catholic emancipation, campaigned for free trade. Founder of modern Conservative Party.
Pius IX, Pope b. 1792, r. 1846–78, (Pio Nono). Originally considered liberal, he fled 1848 Rome uprising and refused to accept incorporation of Rome and papal states into kingdom of Italy 1870.
Rasputin, Grigori c. 1871–1916, Russian peasant mystic who came to dominate Alexandra, wife of Nicholas II, through apparent ability to cure their son Alexei who was haemophiliac. Murdered by members of tsar's family.
Talleyrand-Périgord, Prince Charles Maurice de 1754–1838, French statesman. Wily survivor. Having served the Revolution and Napoleon, he regained office under the restored Bourbon kings and then under Louis Philippe.
Victor Emmanuel b.1820. King of Sardinia-Piedmont 1849–78. Proclaimed first king of Italy 1861, king of entire united country 1870–8.
Victoria, Queen b. 1819, r. 1837–1901.

4

Queen of Great Britain and empress of India (**4**). Raised prestige of monarchy and worked constitutionally with ministers, even those she personally disliked. Mourned her husband excessively.
Wilberforce, William 1759–1833, English politician and philanthropist. Abolitionist campaigner, securing end of slave trade in 1807 and of slavery itself throughout Britain and her colonies in 1833.

Words

4434 **Bloody Sunday** 1905 Day on which Russian troops fired on peaceful workers' deputation to tsar in St Petersburg.
Cato Street Conspiracy 1820 Inefficient plot to assassinate British cabinet.
Charge of the Light Brigade 1854 Heroic but ill-advised British cavalry charge to overrun Russian gun positions during battle for Balaclava; 505 out of 700 died.
Chartism 1838–48 English popular movement demanding male suffrage, annual Parliaments, reform of electoral boundaries, and voting by secret ballot.
Commune 1871 Radical Paris government opposed to peace terms for end of Franco-Prussian war and right-wing composition of newly elected National Assembly. Suppressed with atrocities on both sides.
Conservative Party British right-of-center political party developed from 1832 electoral reforms and heir to Tory Party. Originally pragmatic rather than ideological in motivation.
Corn Laws 1815–46 British legislation regulating grain imports. Beneficial to farmers but cause of staple food shortages in larger, particularly industrial, towns and in impoverished rural areas.
Duma Russian elected legislative assembly unwillingly convened by Nicholas II in 1905 and finally overthrown in 1917 Bolshevik revolution.
Entente cordiale Alliance between Britain and France in 1904 largely due to behind-the-scenes diplomacy of Edward VII.
Fenians Agitators for Irish independence, members of secret organization prepared to use violence if constitutional means failed.
Holy Alliance 1815 Agreement by rulers of Austria, Prussia, and Russia advocating government by Christian principles, which effectively bound their countries to maintaining pre-French revolution constitutions and laws.
Janissaries Elite but turbulent Turkish troops eventually suppressed with loss of between 6,000 and 10,000 lives in 1826 by sultan Mahmud II.
Jingoism Excessively chauvinistic patriotism, derived from music-hall song "*we don't want to fight but by jingo if we do....the Russians shall not have Constantinople.*"
Labor Party British left-of-center political party evolving from 1893 socialist Independent Labor Party incorporating trades unions and socialist organizations.
League of Three Kings 1849 Alliance between rulers of Hanover, Prussia, and Saxony in opposition to agitation for constitutional reforms.
Liberal Party British centrist political party evolving from 1830s and containing radical elements as well as remnants of old Whig Party.
Pacifico Affair 1849–50 confrontation between Britain and Greece over arrest of Jewish British subject serving as Portuguese consul in Athens. Occasioned famous speech in Parliament by British foreign secretary Lord Palmerston quoting St Paul "*civis Romanus sum*" ("I am a Roman citizen").
Pogrom Deliberate organized persecution of ethnic group, especially Jews in Russia. Name comes from Russian and Yiddish words for thunder and destruction.
Protocol of Elders of Zion Faked memorandum of alleged agreement at 1897 Zionist Congress for world domination. Classic anti-Semitic propaganda
Social Democratic Party Russian political group agitating for parliamentary government. Founded 1898. Split into Bolsheviks (meaning majority, more radical wing) and Mensheviks (meaning minority, more moderate) in 1903.
Tolpuddle Martyrs 1834 English farm workers who had formed trades union sentenced to transportation for seven years. Public outcry led to return in 1836.
Young Europe/Ireland/Italy/Russia/Turks Sequence of radical and constitutional movements between 1830 and 1913 mainly involving young intellectuals.

Places

4435 **1 Crimean War** 1853–6 Russia and Turkey originally at odds over custody of Christian holy places in Palestine. French and British drawn into conflict through alliance with Turkey. Russia eventually ceded territory after high allied casualties due partly to military incompetence.
2 London Great Exhibition 1851 World fair in specially constructed Crystal Palace in Hyde Park. First such event leading to similar fairs in Paris 1855 and elsewhere.
3 Mayerling Austrian hunting lodge where crown prince Rudolf and mistress Marie Vetsera committed suicide 1889.
4 Missolonghi Greek town where Lord Byron died 1824; site of battles during war of independence against Turkey 1824, 1826.
5 Peterloo Massacre 1819 British soldiers ordered to fire on crowd at rally in support of parliamentary reform and repeal of the Corn Laws.
6 Phoenix Park Murders 1882 British Chief Secretary for Ireland (Lord Frederick Cavendish) and Under-Secretary (Thomas H Burke) murdered while walking in Dublin park. Led to suspension of trial by jury and reciprocal violence.
7 Sarajevo Bosnian capital where 1918 assassination of Archduke Franz Ferdinand, heir to Austro-Hungarian throne, by Serb nationalist sparked off World War I.
8 Schleswig-Holstein Dispute 1844–1920 Exceptionally complicated wrangle between Denmark and Germany over formerly independent duchies. War between 1863 and 1865 gave Holstein to Austria and Schleswig to Prussia. North part (Schleswig) returned to Denmark in 1920, south (Schleswig Holstein) remained German.
9 Suez Canal between Mediterranean and Red Sea constructed 1858–69 by French diplomat and engineer Ferdinand de Lesseps. Britain bought control in 1875.
a Port Said
b Great Bitter Lake
c Gulf of Suez (Red Sea)

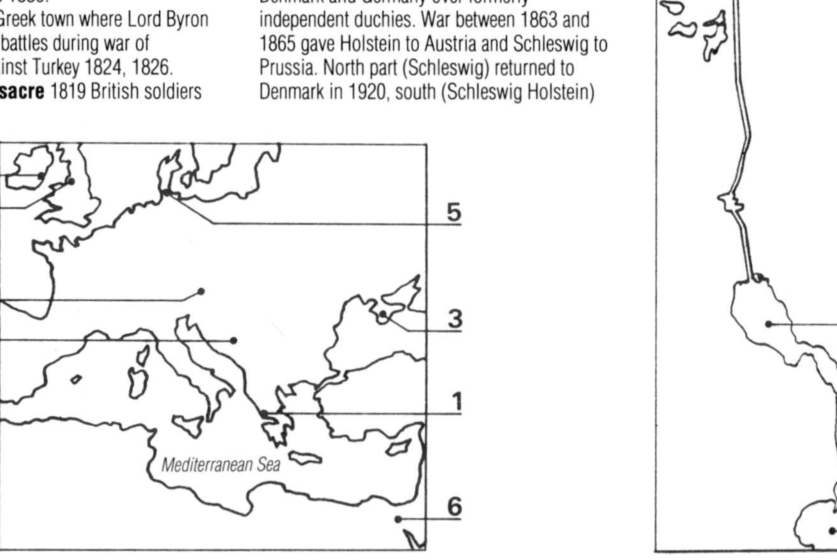

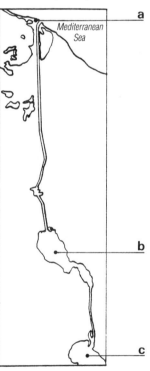

444 THE WORLD 1814–1914

Events

4441 **1815–16** Brazil proclaimed empire equal with Portugal; Venezuela and Argentina gain independence; Britain acquires Ceylon, influence in India expanded; Java returns to Dutch ownership; Anglo-Dutch fleet destroys Algiers port; first free immigrants to Tasmania.
1817–19 Chile invaded from Argentina, independence proclaimed; Venezuela, Ecuador, and New Granada declare joint republic; Morocco prohibits privateering; French influence extended into Senegal; Zulu empire in southern Africa; military actions in India; power struggle in Afghanistan.
1820–2 Brazil declares independence from Portugal; Liberian Republic founded in Africa for freed slaves; African Gold Coast becomes British colony; Arab slave ships restricted to Arabia and east Africa.
1823–6 Portugal recognizes Brazilian independence; Bolivia, Columbia, and Peru break apart; Argentina at war with Brazil; Britain recognizes newly independent South American states, begins annexation of Burma, fights in East Africa.
1827–30 Anglo-Brazil trade treaty; Uruguay becomes independent; colonization of western Australia; Mysore incorporated into British India; French conquer Algeria.
1831–5 Syria invaded by Egypt; Britain abolishes slavery; Falkland Islands occupied by Britain; civil service in India opened to Indians; African tribes oppose increasing British and Dutch settlements.
1836–40 South Australia becomes British province; New Zealand becomes British colony; clashes between Dutch settlers and African tribes; Britain at war with Afghanistan and China; slavery abolished in India; France annexes Gabon; Turks attempt invasion of Syria.
1841–5 Egypt granted hereditary ruler; British massacred during retreat from Afghanistan; China opens ports to foreign trade; Britain takes Hong Kong, annexes Sind, Punjab, and Natal; Orange Free State established in southern Africa; New Zealand settlers fight with Maoris; French occupy Tahiti; Japan relaxes embargo against foreign ships.
1846–50 Racial segregation begins in southern Africa as Zulu reservations set up in Natal; rebellion in China.
1851–6 Transvaal independence recognized by Britain, Britain annexes Kaffraria, gives freedom of government to Cape Colony, Natal becomes separate colony; renewed fighting in Burma, British territorial gains; Oudh annexed; independence of Afghanistan recognized by Persia.
1857–9 Indian troops rebel against British, massacre at Cawnpore, Lucknow besieged, British military victory, but control of India passes from East India Company to British Parliament; France completes conquest of Algeria; France, Russia, and Britain gain territorial concessions from China.
1860–5 Anglo-French forces occupy Peking (Beijing); Maoris fight settlers in New Zealand; Britain annexes Lagos; joint US, British, French, and Dutch fleet shells Japanese ports; Black insurrection in Jamaica; British moves toward colonial self-government.
1866–72 Cuba attempts breakaway from Spain; British military operation in Ethiopia after diplomats kidnapped; Basutoland annexed by Britain; French rights over Cambodia recognized by Siam; Japanese emperor regains political power.
1873–9 Britain secures end of Zanzibar slave trade, troops defeat Ashantis; French protectorate over Annam; Japanese expelled from Korea, Korean independence recognized; Britain and France control Egypt; Britain annexes Transvaal, defeats Zulus.
1880–5 Britain forces settlement with Afghanistan; nationalist revolt in Egypt; French protectorate over Tunis; Sudan revolts against Egyptian rule; French capture Hanoi; Chinese assert sovereignty over Annam; Germany claims south-west African territory, occupies Togoland and Cameroons; Britain and Germany annex New Guinea; British protectorate over southern Nigeria and Bechuanaland; French attempt to annex Madagascar; Belgian king personally owns Congo (now Zaire); Transvaal becomes independent republic.
1886–9 German development plans for Zanzibar; Mashonaland and Matabeleland become British spheres of influence; Sarawak and Brunei under British protection; British troops defeated in Sudan; Ethopia becomes Italian protectorate; Brazil becomes republic.
1890–5 Rhodesia established, involved in war with Matabele people; Nyasaland, Uganda become British protectorates; France occupies Ivory Coast and Dahomey; China and Japan at war over Korea, Japan keeps Formosa, Port Arthur, Korean independence recognized ; revolutionary movement begins in China; failed raid by British from Bechuanaland into Transvaal; Anglo-Venezuelan border dispute; Cuban revolt against Spain.
1896–1902 British forces attempt to recapture Sudan; France annexes Madagascar; Ethiopians defeat Italians, Italy relinquishes claim; Spain and US at war over Cuba, Cuba gains independence; Britain at war with Boers, annexes Orange Free State and Transvaal, extends territories in Nigeria; nationalist rebellion against foreigners in China; Australia becomes self-governing dominion; Russia occupies Manchuria; Anglo-Japanese mutual defence treaty; Anglo-German fleet seizes Venezuelan fleet.
1903–8 Russia and Japan at war, Russian defeat, fleet destroyed; British expeditionary force sent to Tibet; New Zealand granted dominion status; revolt against German rule in south-west Africa; rise of nationalism in India following partition of Bengal; France and Germany at odds over interests in Morocco; calls for republic in China; Belgian government acts on forced labor scandal in Congo.
1909–14 South Africa granted united independent dominion status; liberal revolution in Persia; Japan annexes Korea; French protectorate over Morocco recognized; Italy invades Libya, at war with Turkey, Turkey cedes Tripoli to Italy; republic declared in China; insurrection in British Somalia.

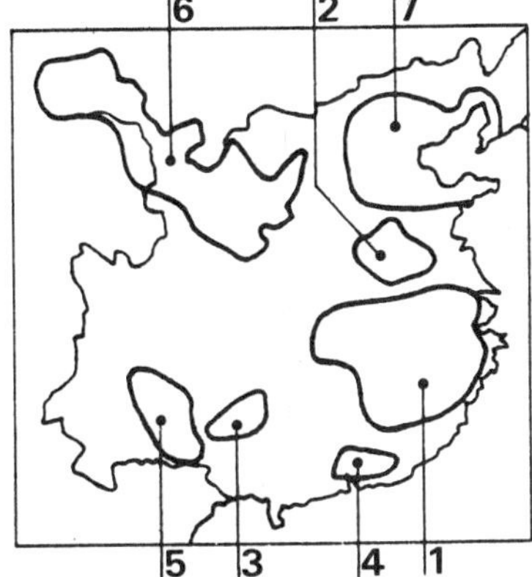

Rebellions in China 1850–1901
1 T'ai ping rebellion 1850–64 (showing area of T'ai ping control)
2 Nien rebellion 1853–68
3 Kweichow Miao tribal rising 1854–72
4 Hakka-Cantonese war 1855–7
5 Yunnan Muslim rebellion 1855–73
6 North western Muslim rising 1863–73
7 Boxer Rebellion 1900–1

Growth of British India

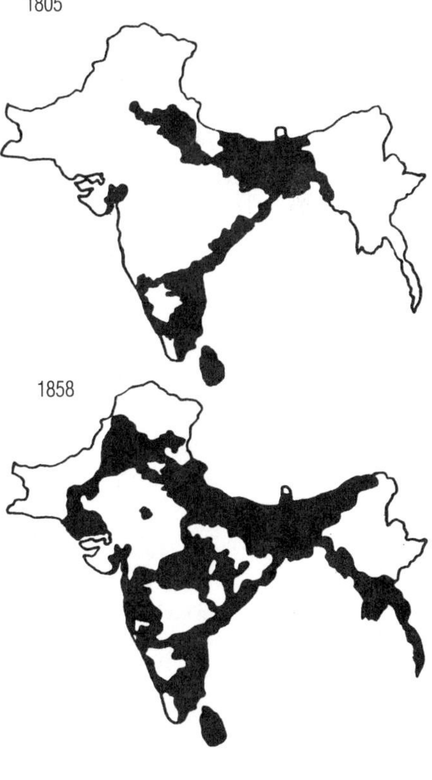

Places

4442 **1 Afghan Wars** 1838–42, 1878–81 British attempts to establish political and military ascendancy in Afghanistan fiercely resisted with many British casualties, notably in retreat in 1842 evacuation through Khyber Pass, when only one man survives out of army of 16,000.
2 Agadir Crisis 1911 Germany sends gunboat to protect its Moroccan interests. War with Britain averted through French intervention.
3 Ashanti Wars 1824–31, 1873–4, 1893–4, 1895–6 African kingdom in central Ghana eventually suppressed to become British protectorate after bitter fighting.
4 Greater Colombia 1819–26 Attempt by Simón Bolivar to weld newly independent Latin American states into republican confederation. "Latin America is ungovernable" he sighs on his deathbed.
5 Fashoda Incident 1898–9 Anglo-French confrontation in Sudan over French military actions, which nearly leads to war.
6 Indian Mutiny 1857–8 Indian soldiers rebels against British officers and civilians (see also below, Sepoys) and kills military and civilian personnel, including women and children. British atrocities in reprisal, notably for massacre at Cawnpore 1857 and after relief of Lucknow 1858.
7 Kandyan Wars 1803, 1815 British armed intervention in kingdom of Kandy (Ceylon, now Sri Lanka) ending in abolition of kingdom and British rule.
8 Mahratta Wars 1803, 1817–19 British armed intervention in kingdom of Mahratta (India) ending in incorporation of kingdom into Bombay.
9 Orange Free State Central southern African province settled by Boers 1836, annexed by Britain 1848, incorporated into South Africa 1910.
10 Transvaal North-east southern Africa province settled by Boers 1836, becomes British colony 1902, joins South Africa 1910.

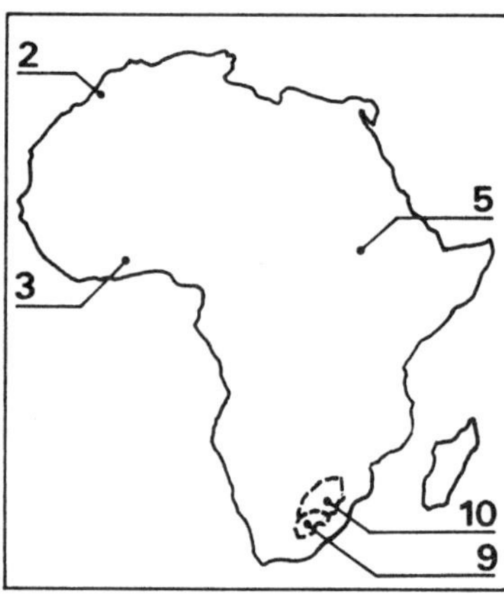

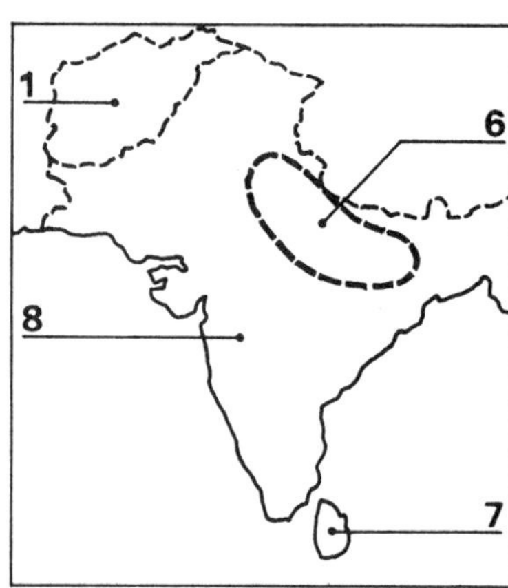

Peoples

4443 **Bantus** Native African people inhabiting southern, eastern, and central parts of the continent.
Boers Descendants of Dutch and French Huguenot settlers in southern Africa. At war with Britain over claims to independence 1842–3, 1891, 1899–1902. The Boer republic lasted from 1880 to 1902.

Bolivar, Simón 1783–1830 , South American military and political leader. Liberated his native Venezuela, also Ecuador and Peru from colonial rule but failed to achieve ultimate goal of Latin American unity. Bolivia, originally Upper Peru, was named for him (**1**).
Gordon, Charles G 1833–85, British general nicknamed "Chinese Gordon" who assisted in crushing T'ai Ping rebellion 1863–4. Governor of Sudan 1877–80. Returned to assist Egyptians to crush revolt but was trapped in Khartoum and killed when besieged city fell.
Gurkhas Hindu people living mainly in Nepal. Famous for tradition of military service in British army.
Jameson, Sir Leander S 1853–1917, British colonial administrator who led unsuccessful raid from Bechuanaland to recapture Transvaal in 1895. Prime Minister of Cape Colony 1904–8.
Kruger, S J Paulus 1825–1904, Boer statesman and opponent of British colonial adventurism. President of Transvaal 1883–1900.
Manchus Mongolian people from Manchuria who conquered China in 1644 and ruled (Ch'ing dynasty) until 1912.
Maoris Native New Zealand people descended from Polynesian voyagers and opposing British settlers by force 1842–5, 1860–70.
Matabele Warlike southern African people driven out of Transvaal by Boers 1837 and fighting against White settlers and forces in Rhodesia 1893.
Muhammad Ahmed c. 1843–85. Known as the Mahdi. Sudanese religious and nationalist leader of revolt against Egyptian rule 1881. Captured Khartoum 1885.
Muhammad Ali 1769–1849, Turkish military leader who became viceroy of Egypt 1805–48 and ruled virtually as independent sovereign.
O'Higgins, Bernardo 1778–1842, Chilean patriot of Irish descent. Leader in struggle for independence from Spain; president 1817–23.
Raffles, Sir Thomas S 1781–1826, English colonial administrator who founded Singapore in 1819.
Rhodes, Cecil J 1853–1902, English colonial administrator and financier (**2**). Made fortune out of South African gold and diamond mines. Prime Minister of Cape Colony 1890-6. Rhodesia (now Zimbabwe and Zambia) named for him.
Shaka d. 1828 Zulu chief and military leader who founded empire.
Sikhs Monotheistic Hindu sect founded in 16th century. Britain annexed their Punjab territory after bitter fighting 1844–9.
Sun Yat-sen 1866–1925, Chinese statesman instrumental in overthrow of Manchu dynasty. First president of republic 1911–12.
Tz'u-hsi 1834–1909, Chinese dowager empress and effective ruler, though officially only regent, from 1862 until death.
Zulus Native south-east African people who developed powerful warrior clan system during 19th century and opposed encroachment of White settlers.

The British Empire 1939

4444 After the loss of its American colonies during the early 1700s, the British Empire continued to expand through the 1800s and early 1900s. The map shows the extent of its empire during the inter-war period. After World War II, many former British colonies became independent countries. The British Empire evolved into the Commonwealth of Nations, an association of states that won independent status, plus those that still retain dependent status. Many of the countries shown on the map are still British dependencies.

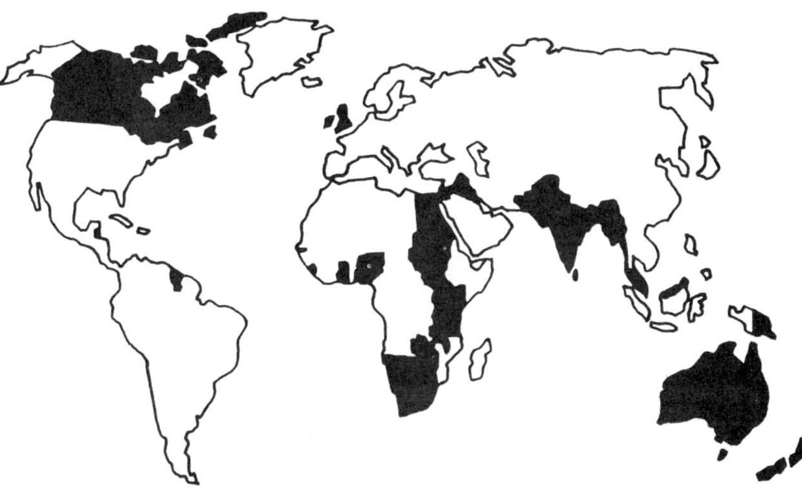

Words

4445 **Boxers** Chinese nationalist secret society which unsuccessfully attempted rebellion to overthrow foreign interests 1900–1.
East India Company 1600–1874 British trading company which became effectual military and civil ruler of Indian sub-continent until 1857. Also known as "EIC" or "John Company." There were similar Dutch and French operations within those countries' Asian spheres of influence.
Great Trek 1834–8 Migration with ox wagons by Boer farmers from Cape Colony to north and east of Orange River after Britain abolished slavery.
Kuomintang Chinese political party founded in 1912, dominant from 1928 to 1949.
Opium Wars 1839–42, 1856–60 British military action in China to force Chinese to buy vast quantities of opium produced in India in spite of Chinese efforts to ban the drug and stop drain of silver.
privateering Activities by armed but privately owned vessels commissioned for war service by a government. Really a species of legalized piracy.
sepoys Native Indian soldiers recruited into British service. Hindus lost caste if required to cross seas to fight, as happened during Crimean War (1853–6), or use anything made from cattle (sacred animal). Muslims were contaminated by touching pig products. New uniform cockades allegedly made from cow and pig skin and cartridges allegedly greased with cow and pig fat probably triggered off the 1857 mutiny.
shogunate 1192–1867 Japanese rule by sequence of hereditary military dictators paying only nominal allegiance to emperor.
suttee Hindu practice by which a widow immolated herself on husband's funeral pyre. British tried to stamp out custom from 1829 with limited success.
T'ai Ping Rebellion 1850–64 Southern China revolt against Manchu rule led by Christian convert Hung Hsiu-ch'uan (1812–64) in which probably between 20 and 30 million died.

European Empires in Africa 1914

4446

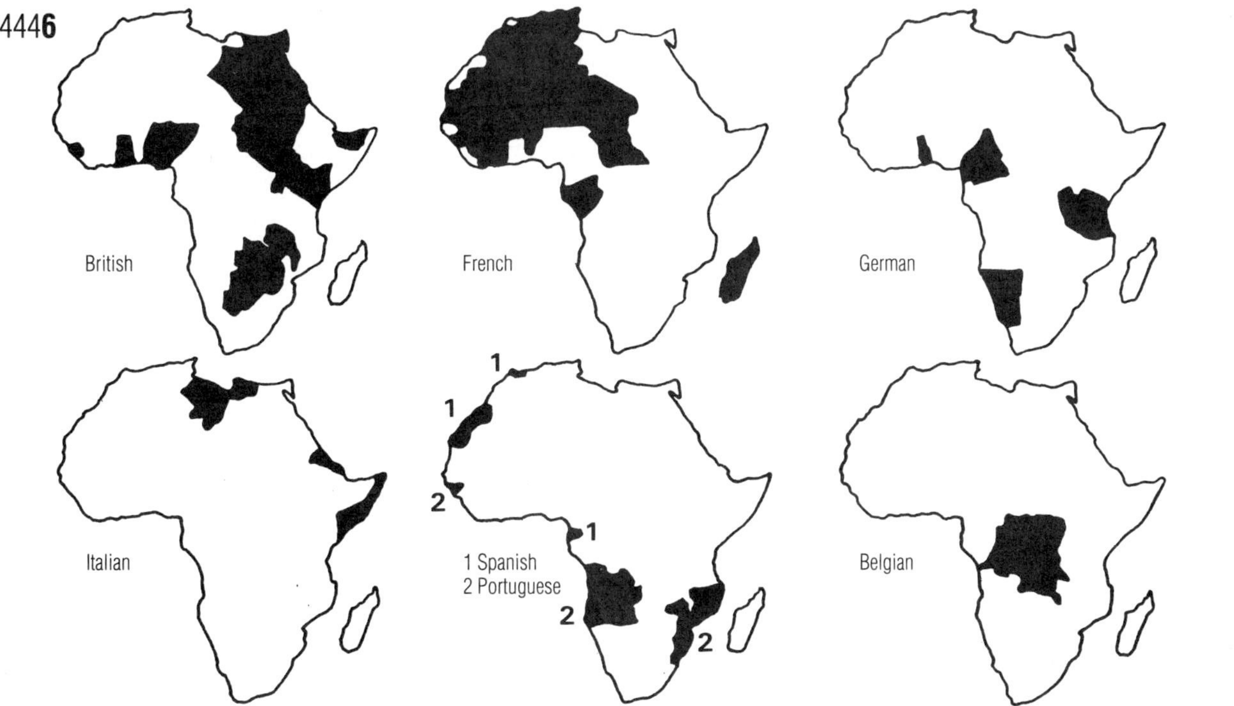

451 WORLD WAR I

The Opposing sides

4511 CENTRAL POWERS
1914 Austria, Germany, Hungary, Ottoman Empire.
1915 Bulgaria.
ALLIES
1914 Belgium, British Empire, France, Japan, Montenegro, Russia, Serbia.
1915 Italy, San Marino.
1916 Portugal, Romania.
1917 Brazil, China, Cuba, Greece, Liberia, Siam, USA.
1918 Costa Rica, Guatemala, Honduras, Nicaragua.

Places

4512

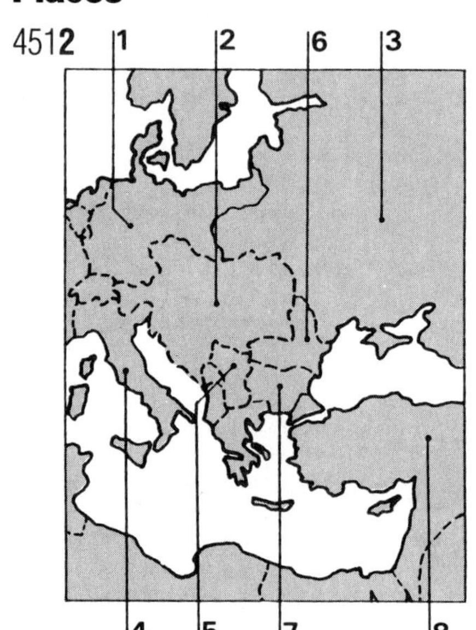

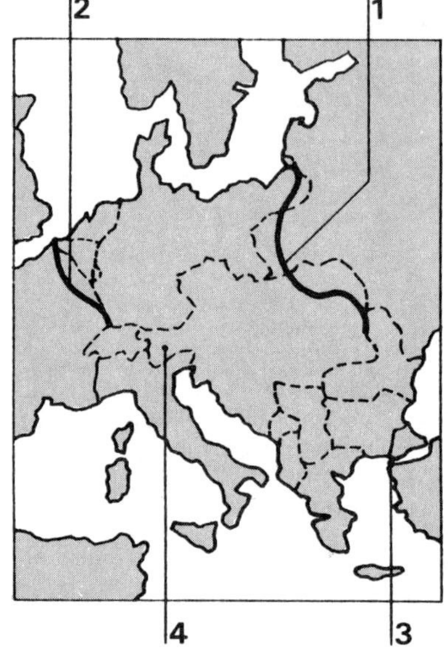

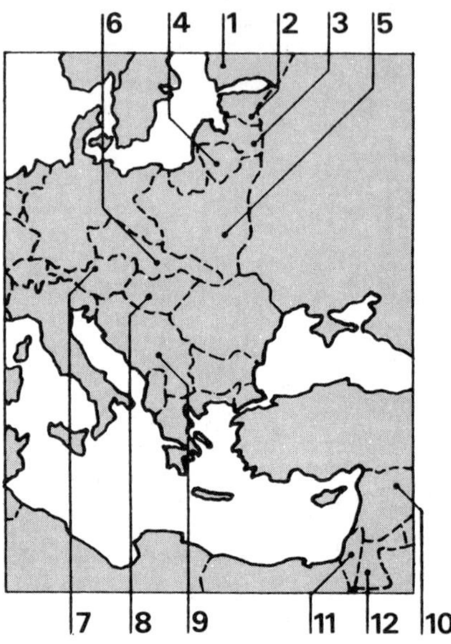

National boundaries in Europe 1914
1 German Empire
2 Austria-Hungary
3 Russia
4 Italy
5 Serbia
6 Romania
7 Bulgaria
8 Ottoman Empire

Battle fronts in Europe
1 Eastern front Land currently Poland, Russia, Ukraine, Hungary, Romania, over which Germany and Russia fought
2 Western front Land currently Belgium and north-east France, over which the Allies defended attacks by the Central Powers
3 The Dardanelles Allied invasion of the north-east coast of Turkey
4 Italian-Austrian front Area north of Venice over which Italy fought Austria
Atlantic German blockade of Great Britain by use of submarines

New countries created 1918–21
1 Finland
2 Estonia
3 Latvia
4 Lithuania
5 Poland
6 Czechoslovakia
7 Austria
8 Hungary
9 Yugoslavia
10 Syria
11 Palestine
12 Trans-Jordan

Events

4513 **1914** June 28 Archduke Francis Ferdinand assassinated.
Jul 28 Austria-Hungary declares war on Serbia.
Aug 1,2,3,4 Germany declared war on Russia, France, and invades Belgium.
Aug 4 Great Britain declares war on Germany.
Sept 6–9 Battle of the Marne.
Oct 19–Nov 22 Battle of Ypres.
1915 Feb 18 Blockade of Great Britain.
Apr 22–May 25 2nd Battle of Ypres.
Apr 25 Gallipoli (Dardanelles) attacked by Allies.
May 7 Germans sink *Lusitania*.
1916 Feb 21–Dec 18 Battle of Verdun.
May 31–Jun 1 Naval Battle of Jutland.
July 1–Nov 18 Battle of the Somme.
Sept 15 British use tanks.
1917 Mar 14 Germans retreat to Hindenburg Line (**7**).
Jun 26 American troops arrive in France.
Jul 31–Nov 18 3rd Battle of Ypres.
Nov 7 Bolsheviks gain power in Russia.
Dec 9 Allies enter Jerusalem.
Dec 15 German-Russian armistice.
1918 Jan 8 Woodrow Wilson announces peace plans called "Fourteen Points"
Mar 21 Further Battle of the Somme.
Apr 9 German offensive at Lys.
May 27 German offensive at Aisne.
Jul 15 German offensive at Marne.
Jul 18 2nd Battle of the Marne.
Aug 8 German lines broken at Amiens.
Sept 30 Bulgaria-Allies armistice.
Oct 30 Ottoman-Allies armistice.
Nov 3 Austria-Allies armistice.
Nov 9 Kaiser Wilhelm abdicates.
Nov 11 German-Allies armistice.

People

4514 **Ferdinand I** 1861–1948, youngest son of Prince Augustus of Saxe-Coburg and Princess Clementine of Orléans. Prince of Bulgaria from 1887, but in 1908 proclaimed Bulgaria independent and took title of king or tsar. Abdicated 1918 after unsuccessful invasion of Serbia.
Francis Joseph properly Franz Joseph I 1830–1916, Emperor of Austria (1848), king of Hungary (1867). Subdued Hungarian revolt, lost Lombardy, and reasserted claim to rule as absolute sovereign. Attack on Serbia sparked off World War I.
Hindenburg, Paul von Beneckendorff und von 1847–1934, German soldier and president (1925–34). Recalled as general at start

continued

People continued

4514 of war. Defeated Russians at Tannenburg (1914), and Masurian Lakes (1915), but later forced to retreat from western front (1918).
Mata Hari Stage name of Gertrude Margarete Zelle 1876–1917, Dutch spy. Became dancer in France (1903), had many lovers, several in high military and governmental positions (on both sides). Found guilty of espionage for Germans and was shot in Paris.
Wilhelm II 1859–1941, 3rd German emperor 1888–1918, and 9th King of Prussia, whose speeches had as their constant theme German imperialism. Developed navy, and encouraged economic penetration of Middle East. Failed to prevent World War I. Forced to abdicate 1918.

RUSSIA
Lenin, (formerly Ulyanov), Vladimir Ilyich 1820–1924, revolutionary. Converted to Marxism in 1889, exiled to Siberia 1895, refugee in Western Europe 1900–17. Founder of Bolsheviks, inspirer of November 1917 revolution, and head of new Soviet state.
Nicholas II 1868–1918, last tsar of Russia from 1894. Initiated 1898 Hague Peace Conference. Reign marked by alliance with France, and disastrous war with Japan (1904–05). Forced to abdicate at revolution (1917), shot with family by Bolshevik revolutionaries.

FRANCE
Clemenceau, Georges 1841–1929, known as "The Tiger." Entered French National Assembly in 1876, became leader of extreme left. Premier 1906–09, 1917–20. Founded *L'Aurore*, and from 1918 was an Academician.
Foch, Ferdinand 1851–1929, soldier, who proved himself great strategist at the Marne (1914). and 1st Battle of Ypres (Oct–Nov 1914). As generalissimo of Allies from 1918, directed offensives which drove back Germans and won War.
Pétain, Henri Philippe Omer 1856–1951, soldier and statesman. By 1916, in charge of an army corps. Defence of Verdun ("They shall not pass") made him national hero. Commmander-in-chief 1917, then marshal of France from 1918.

GREAT BRITAIN
Asquith, Herbert Henry 1st Earl of Oxford and Asquith, 1852–1928, Liberal statesman. chancellor of Exchequer (1905–08), then prime minister from April 1908. Confronted by series of international crises that led to war. War policy criticized for lack of vigor.
Beatty, David Beatty 1st Earl, 1871–1936, naval commander. During war, destroyed three German cruisers at Heligoland Bight, and sank the *Blucher* near Dogger Bank. At battle of Jutland (May 1916), badly mauled opponents. commander-in-chief 1916 after Jellicoe, First Sea Lord 1919.
Cavell, Edith Louisa 1865–1915, nurse. From 1907, first matron of Berkendael Medical Institute in Brussels – later Red Cross hospital during war. Arrested 1915, charged by Germans with having helped about 200 Allied soldiers escape to neutral Holland, and executed.
Haig, Douglas 1st Earl 1861–1928, soldier and field marshal. In Aug 1914, took 1st Corps of British Expeditionary Force to France, and became commander-in-chief in 1915. Successful offensive against Germany in 1918 ended war.
Jellicoe, John Rushworth 1st Earl, 1859–1935, naval commander. After minor engagement at Heligoland Bight (1914) and off Dogger Bank (1915), repelled German fleet at sea off Jutland, 1916. Admiral of Fleet from 1919.
Kitchener, Horatio Herbert 1st Earl Kitchener of Khartoum 1850–1916, soldier and statesman. In 1898, won back Sudan for Egypt. As chief of staff, then commander-in-chief in South Africa (1900–02), ended 2nd Boer War. Secretary for war from 1914. Lost with *HMS Hampshire* off Orkney.
Lawrence, Thomas Edward known as "Lawrence of Arabia," (**1**) 1888–1935, soldier and Arabist. During war, worked for army intelligence in North Africa 1914–16. In 1916, joined Arab revolt against Turks. Entered Damascus with General Allenby in 1918.

1

Lloyd George, David 1st Earl 1863–1945. Liberal statesman. By his forceful policy as coalition prime minister, 1916—922, was, as was later said of him, "the man who won the war." One of "big three" at peace negotiations.

UNITED STATES
Pershing, John Joseph known as "Black Jack" 1860–1948, soldier. Served in Cuban War (1898), with Japanese army during Russo-Japanese War (1904–5), and in Mexico (1916). Commander-in-chief of American Expeditionary Force in Europe from 1917, US army chief-of-staff 1921–4.
Wilson, Thomas Woodrow 1856–1924 28th president of USA (elected 1912, 1916) (**2**). His administration was memorable for prohibition, women's suffrage amendments of constitution, America's participation in World War I, his part in peace conference, and championing of League of Nations.

2

452 AMERICA 1918–1941

Words

4521 **bootlegging** Making, carrying, and selling illegal goods, notably alcohol during Prohibition.
Declaration of Lima 1938 Agreement reached at Pan-American conference to safeguard countries' security in event of attempted Fascist European takeovers.
Depression, The Worldwide economic crisis of early 1930s characterized by mass unemployment and galloping deflation.
Dust Bowl, The Farming areas impoverished between 1934 and 1936 by topsoil erosion caused by drought, winds, and unsuitable crop selection.
"Monkey Trial" 1925 Tennessee schoolteacher John Scopes fined for teaching Darwin's theory of evolution.
Moral Rearmament Christian movement (1921), originally called First Century Christian Fellowship, founded in 1938 by German-American evangelist, Frank Buchman.
New Deal Roosevelt's 1932 pledge for people while accepting Democratic presidential nomination; also the legislative program of his administration.
Prohibition 1920–33 legislation prohibiting sale of alcohol which led to illicit sales and gangsterism.
St Valentine's day massacre 1929 incident in Chicago in which seven gangsters were killed by members of rival gang, probably ordered by Al Capone.
"Scottsboro Boys" 1931–7 Alabama case involving nine Black youths accused of raping two young White women.
un-American Activities, Committee to Investigate Set up in 1938 to enquire into Nazi activities but then changed to devote itself almost entirely to exposing alleged Communist subversion.

Events

4522 **1918** World War I ends; president Wilson proposes 14-point peace plan; influenza epidemic; fuel crisis.
1919 Senate rejects World War I peace treaty, rejects US membership of League of Nations; strikes; riots.
1920 Mexican president assassinated; sale of alcoholic beverages prohibited throughout US; women's suffrage amendment.
1921–23 Business failures; unemployment rises.
1924 US imposes immigration restrictions.
1929 New York (Wall Street) stock exchange crashes; lynchings in Mississipi; gang warfare in Chicago.
1930 Fresh Wall Street share crash; unemployment rises again; farmers' increasing mortage debt.
1931 Canada raises tariffs; US bank failures rise; over 8 million unemployed; record wheat crop drives down prices; banks foreclose on farm mortgages; industrial production falls.
1933 US abandons gold standard; sharp decrease in national income; Blacks lynched in south.
1934 Mexico resumes land redistribution; US begins tariff cuts; dust storms denude farm topsoil; drought reduces corn crop.
1935 Emergency relief measures to help unemployed; old age pensions and unemployment benefits voted.
1939 German Jewish refugees refused admission to US; World War II begins.
1940 US exchanges destroyers for Britian for right to build air and naval bases in Canada; budget includes increased defence appropriation.
1941 Japanese bomb US fleet at Pearl Harbour (Hawaii); Japan and US declare war; Germany and US declare war.

People

4523 **Capone, Alphons** (Al) 1899–1947, Italian-American Chicago racketeer (**1**).

1

Coolidge, Calvin 1872–1933, president 1923–29. Favored domestic and foreign policies of non-intervention (**2**).
Hoover, Herbert 1874–64, president 1929–33. Organized relief for Europe during and after World War I. Failed to alieviate effects of Depression (**3**).
Lindbergh Case 1932 The baby son of aviator Charles Lindbergh 1902–74 (**4**), was kidnapped and murdered; a ransom was demanded; German American BR Hauptmann was charged 1934 and executed 1936.

2

3

4

Roosevelt, Eleanor 1984–62 (**5**). Wife of president Roosevelt. Supporter of liberal causes through speeches and writings.

5

Roosevelt, Franklin Delano 1882–1945, president 1933–45. Instituted major economic and social reforms. Forceful leader of country during World War II although confined to wheel-chair by paralysis.
Sacco, Nicola (1892–1927) and **Vanzetti, Bartolomeo** (1888–1927), Italian-American anarchists executed 1927 for alleged part in 1920 Massachusetts payroll robbery and murders.

453 EUROPE 1918–1940

Events

4531 **1918** World War I ends with revolution in Germany, republic declared; civil war in Russia, tsar and family shot; civil war in Ireland, women over 30 given vote in Britain.
1919–22 Austria becomes republic, Czechoslovakia, Hungary, Poland and Yugoslavia independent; attempted uprisings in Germany, Hungary squashed; Northern Ireland accepts home rule, southern Ireland declared free state; Poland at war with Russia, defeated; Greece at war with Turkey, defeated; Turkish sultan deposed, republic established; coalition government falls in Britain; inflation rises rapidly in Germany.
1923–5 France and Belgium occupy Ruhr as Germany fails to pay war reparations; attempted German coup as currency collapses; Italian elections result in Fascist majority, dictatorship established, judiciary and trade unions restricted; short-lived Labor government in Britain.
1926–9 Strikes in Britain; power struggle in Russia; German economy collapses; continued modernization in Turkey; women over 21 given vote in Britain; Portugal becomes dictatorship; international economic slump.
1930–2 French troops leave Rhineland, France begins anti-German defense works; German elections indecisive; collective farms in Russia; coalition government in Britain, free trade abandoned.
1933–5 Germany becomes one-party state as Hitler takes power, anti-Semitic legislation; political purges and treason trials in Russia; pacifist movement in Britain; Austrian chancellor assassinated; Saar votes for reunion with Germany.
1936–8 Abdication crisis in Britain as George V dies, succeeded by son Edward VIII and then by second son George VI; Germany forms alliances with Italy and Japan, Rhineland re-militarized; plot to overthrow French republic fails; civil war in Spain until 1939; Germany annexes Austria, part of Czechoslovakia, intensifies anti-Jewish laws; anti-Semitic legislation in Italy.
1939–40 Spanish civil war ends with Nationalist government recognized abroad; Germany annexes remainder of Czechoslovakia, Makes new alliances with Italy and Japan and non-aggression pact with USSR; Italy invades Albania; Britian and France declare war on Germany after Germany invades Poland; World War II begins.

People

4532 **Casement, Sir Roger** 1864–1916, British diplomat and Irish nationalist. Hanged for treason for attempting to gain German support for Irish independence. Allegations of homosexuality contributed to general consensus for execution.

Chamberlain, Neville 1869–1940, British Conservative prime minister 1937–40. After successful career, including being chancellor of Exchequer 1923–4, 1931–7, incurred increasing criticism for policy of attempting to appease dictatorial regimes of Germany and Italy, especially in signing Munich Pact.

Clemenceau, Georges 1841–1929, French statesman, prime minster 1906–09, 1917–20. Much admired for leadership during World War I and firm but non-vindictive attitude afterwards.

Daladier, Edouard 1884–1970, French statesman of radical socialist persuasion. Prime minister 1933, 1934, 1938–40. Signed Munich Pact.

de Valera, Eamon 1882–1975, Irish statesman. Leader of nationalist movement, suffering imprisonment by Britain. Leader of Sinn Fein 1917–26. Leader of Fianna Fail from 1927. Maintained Irish neutrality during World War II. Prime minister 1932–48, 1951–54, 1957–59; President 1959–73.

Dollfuss, Engelbert 1892–1934, Austrian politician, leader of Christian Socialist Party. Opposed by both Nazis and Socialists. Used political violence to suspend parliamentary rule and govern dictatorially. Murdered during attempted Nazi coup.

Franco, Francisco 1892–1975, Spanish soldier and military dictator. When civil war broke out in 1936 amalgamated legionnaires commanded in Morocco 1935–6, into nationalist force. Ruled Spain as *caudillo* (absolutist leader) from 1939.

Goebbels, Josef 1897–1945, German Nazi propagandist attracted to more radical elements of National Socialist ideology. Brilliant manipulator of "set piece" occasions, such as rallies. Committed suicide with wife and children.

Goering, Hermann 1893–1946, German Nazi military and political leader. Joined Nazi Party 1922, Reichstag president 1932, 1933, created Gestapo 1933. Hitler's deputy during World War II but with declining influence. Tried and convicted as war criminal 1945–6, but committed suicide before execution.

Himmler, Heinrich 1900–45, German Nazi leader and chief of police 1934–45. Major responsibility for racial policies and for enforcement of totalitarian state. Attempted to negotiate German surrender 1945, captured by British but committed suicide.

Hindenberg, Paul von 1847–1934, German field marshal and statesman. Directed German military strategy during World War I. President 1925–34. Appointed Hitler as chancellor 1933.

Hitler, Adolf 1889–1945, German dictator born in Austria (**1**). Created Nazi Party 1919–25. Imprisoned after attempted coup 1923, wrote political testament, *Mein Kampf.* Chancellor 1933, president 1934 with title of *führer* (leader). Suppressed opposition ruthlessly and instituted ferocious anti-Semitic measures. Invasion of Poland in 1939 precipitated World War II. Committed suicide in Berlin with mistress Eva Braun as Germany faced defeat.

Kerensky, Alexander 1881–1970, Russian moderate revolutionary leader. Prime minister July-November 1917. Overthrown by Bolshevik coup but managed to leave country. Spent rest of life in exile.

Laval, Pierre 1883–1945, French politcian. Deputy 1914–19, 1924–7. Senator from 1927. Foreign minister 1934–6, prime minister 1931–2, 1935–6, 1942–4. Proposed ties with Nazi Germany and Fascist Italy. Led collaborative Vichy government. Tried for treason and executed.

Lenin, Vladimir Ilyich 1870–1924, Russian revolutionary and Marxist leader, architect of Soviet state (**2**). In exile 1897–1917, led Bolshevik wing of Social Democratic Party. Returned to Russia 1917, overthrew provisional government and defeated counter-revolutionary forces. Creator of Communist International.

1

Lloyd George, David 1863–1945, British Liberal statesman. Chancellor of Exchequer 1908–15, prime minister 1916–22, party leader 1926–31. Efficient leader during World War I. Concerned to fund social reform through taxes.

Luxemburg, Rosa 1871–1919, Polish-born German revolutionary leader. Opposed World War I, imprisoned 1915–18. Founded German Communist Party 1918. Sought to restrain more militant colleagues but was brutally murdered by counter-revolutionary forces.

2

Mosley, Sir Oswald 1896–1980, British politician. Formerly Labor Party member, he founded British Union of Fascists 1932. Led anti-Jewish demonstration in London's East End 1936. Imprisoned 1940.

Mussolini, Benito 1883–1945, Italian dictator (**3**). Former socialist who organized *fasci* (workers' groups). Became premier 1922, established dictatorship 1925 as *duce* (leader). Invaded Abysinnia (Ethiopia) 1935, Albania 1939, Greece 1940. Entered World War II as Hitler's ally, ousted 1943 following military defeats, captured by partisans 1945 and shot with mistress Clara Petacci.

3

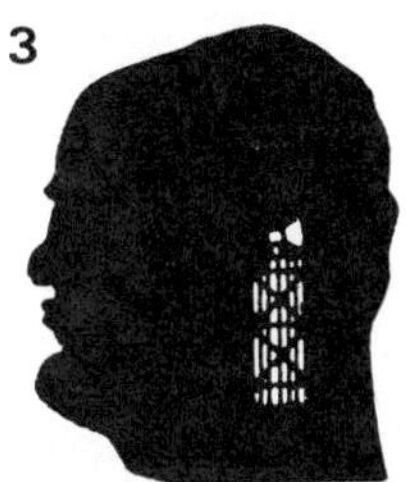

Ribbentrop, Joachim von 1893–1946, German Nazi diplomat. Ambassador in London 1936-8. Foreign minister 1938–45. Tried as war criminal 1945–6 and hanged.

Salazar, Antonio de 1889–1970, Portuguese dictator. Prime minister 1932–68, architect of 1933 authoritarian constitution. Maintained neutrality during World War II. Stifled opposition but modernized public works and finances.

Stalin, Josef 1879–1953, Russian leader. Successor to Lenin and virtual dictator from 1929. Achieved economic development, repressed opposition through terror, purges and show trials. After World War II controlled eastern European "satellite" countries by backing Communist revolutions and governments.

Trotsky, Leon 1879–1940, Russian revolutionary leader and theorist (**4**). After Lenin's death defeated in power struggle with Stalin and banished 1929. Continued writing against Stalin during exile and murdered in Mexico by Stalinist agents.

4

Places

4533 **1 Guernica** Basque town bombed, with many civilian casualties, by German aircraft in fighting against Franco's Nationalist forces 1937. Inspired major Picasso painting of same name.
2 Munich German town where Nazi Party had headquarters and where Hitler attempted coup in 1923. 1938 Munich Agreement between Britain, France, Germany and Italy ceded part of Czechoslovakia to Germany.
3 Nuremberg German town where massive Nazi rallies were staged 1933–8. Nuremberg Laws 1935 legitimized anti-semitism and began full-scale persecution of Jews. Trials of German war criminals held under Allied auspices 1945–6.
4 Rhineland Debatable territory on German border with France and Belgium. Demilitarized 1919 but not completely evacuated until 1934 (see also Ruhr and Saarland.) Remilitarized by Hitler 1936.
5 Ruhr German coal-mining and industrial region occupied by Belgian and French forces 1923–5 when Germany defaulted on war reparations payments.
6 Saarland German coal-mining and industrial region under international administration 1920–35. Rejoined Germany as result of plebiscite 1935.
7 Sudetenland Czechoslovak northern region with largely German-speaking population. Annexed by Germany 1938, annexation ratified by Munich Agreement.
8 Ulster The Six Counties of Northern Ireland. Originally settled largely by Protestants from Scotland in 17th century, partitioned from Republic of Ireland 1921 and focus of political and religious conflict ever since.
9 Weimar German cultural center in 18th and 19th centuries, scene of adoption of 1919 constitution, hence term Weimar Republic (1919–1933).

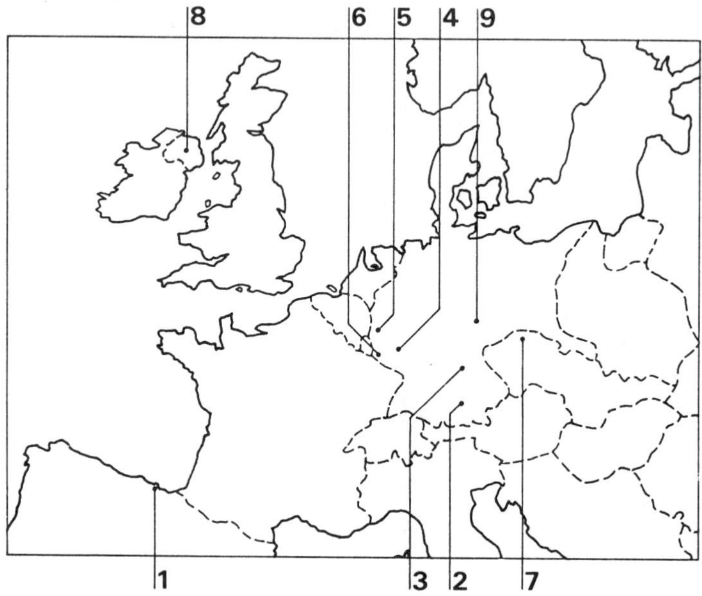

Terms

4534 **abdication crisis** 1936 Edward VIII wished to marry US divorcee Wallis Simpson, met with opposition from royal family, the Church of England, and political leaders. Abdicated with title Duke of Windsor, married Mrs. Simpson 1937 and thereafter lived in exile.
appeasement Policy of agreeing to demands of potentially hostile nation in order to maintain peace, specificaly British government's attitude to Hitler's Germany 1937–8.
axis National alliances to co-ordinate foreign policy, specifically pact between Hitler and Mussolini 1937.
Black and Tans 1919–21, British force sent to Ireland to combat Sinn Fein and using very similar terror tactics. Nicknamed for color of uniforms.
Comintern 1919–43, international Communist organization to promote revolutionary Marxism, also called Communist International and Third International. Founded by Lenin and used by Stalin as political instrument.
Communist Party Formally constituted in Russia March 1918 from Bolshevik Party and became ruling party. Similar, minority parties created elsewhere. In all countries within Soviet sphere of influence, the Communist Party was ruling party, usually only one permitted, until 1990s.
concentration camps For detention of political and other opponents first set up by British in South Africa during Boer War 1899–1902. German camps established in Nazi Germany first in 1933 at Dachau and Oranienburg to use Jews, other ethnic minorities, and political or religious opponents as forced labor. Later camps, such as Auschwitz and Belsen, were just extermination centers claiming millions of lives.
Easter Rising 1916, week-long Irish rebellion against British rule, notably in Dublin where republic was proclaimed. The rising was suppressed, and leaders hanged for treason, thereby becoming martyrs.
Falange Right-wing Spanish political party founded by José Primo de Rivera (1903–36) in 1933 and taken over by Franco as ruling and legislative body.
fascism Right-wing militarist, nationalist and authoritarian regime, such as that founded by Mussolini 1919 and inspiring, among others, the German Nazi Party.
Five-Year Plans 1928, 1933, 1938, Soviet system of economic planning aimed at development of heavy industry (latterly armaments) and collectivization of agriculture. Never really fulfilled targets and usually either quietly abandoned or run into next of sequence.
General Strike 1926, week-long 3–million strong strike by most sectors of British labor with slogan "Not a penny off pay! Not a minute on day!" triggered by private coal-mine owners attempting to cut pay rates and increase working day. Essential services during strike were run by volunteers, including students.
Gestapo *Geheime Staatspolizei* German secret state police, established by Goering in 1933 to arrest and murder opponents of Nazi Party. Enlarged under Himmler 1934. Became part of SS 1936.
gulag Russian administration of forced labor camps, acronym for State (or Main) Administration of Corrective Labor Camps, from 1930s. Used for detention of political opponents, especially intellectuals.
Kristalnacht 9–10 Nov 1938, Nazi-led riots triggered by assassination of Nazi diplomat in Paris by Polish Jew, in which German Jewish shops, homes, and synagogues were looted and demolished, and up to 30,000 Jews deported to concentration camps.
kulak Russian term meaning a tight-fisted person; used of peasant farmers who gained land after 1906. After 1917 they opposed collectivization of agricultural land and in 1929 Stalin began their liquidation.
Lateran Treaty 1929, agreement between Mussolini and pope Pius XI establishing concordat between Italy and Church, recognizing sovereignty of Vatican City State and compensating for territories confiscated in 1870.
Maginot Line 1929–34, French defensive fortifications south of Belgium to Swiss border. Belgians refused to extend line along their German frontier, so strategy was useless, as proved by German advance in 1940.
Marxism-Leninism Karl Marx 1818–83, promulgated that human actions and institutions are economically determined, that class struggle is basic agency of historical change, and that communism will eventually supercede capitalism. Lenin adopted the ideological basis but modified and interpreted it to stress that capitalism survived through imperialism. Developed idea of the Communist Party as professional elite leading the struggle against capitalism, and thereby eventually exercising post-revolutionary dictatorship of proletariat.

continued

Terms continued

4534 **Nazi Party** *Nationalsozialistische deutsche Arbeiterpartei*. Right-wing, authoritarian, and nationalist party founded in 1919 and led from 1921 by Hitler. Achieved limited electoral success but took power when Hitler was offered post of chancellor in 1933. Dominated German life until collapse at end of World War II. Spawned various look-alike parties elsewhere. Illegal since 1945 but neo-Nazi groups have surfaced in Germany and other countries attracting disaffected young men of post- World War II generation.
Night of the Long Knives 1934 Nazi purge of radical, social revolutionary elements in party led by Ernst Roehm 1887–1934, who was among the 80 or so who were killed.
putsch German word for thrust, meaning attempt to overthrow government, such as that led by Hitler from a Munich beer-hall in 1923, which failed ignominiously.
Reichstag Parliament building of German empire in Berlin; burned down in February 1933 almost certainly with Nazi assistance though Communists blamed.
SA *Sturmabteilung* Nazi brownshirted storm-troopers founded in 1921, led by Ernst Roehm and eliminated as power force in 1934.
SS *Schutzstaffel*. Nazi blackshirted bodyguard for Hitler founded in 1923 and commanded by Himmler from 1929. Carried out liquidation of SA leadership in 1934. Acquired executive and military functions including elite *Waffen-SS* regiments who were exempt from normal army control and *SS-Totenkopfverbande* who provided concentration camp guards.
Sinn Féin Gaelic for "Ourselves Alone" Irish nationalist party founded 1902 and absorbing other groups 1907–8. Prominent in 1913–14 Irish home rule crisis and 1916 Easter Rising. Now political wing of Irish Republican Army (IRA).
Soviet Russian term for local, regional or national elected government council which grew out of pre-Revolutionary workers' councils. These initially democratic bodies were dominated by Bolsheviks (later Communists) after 1917.
Spartacists *Spartakusbund* 1916–19 German revolutionary socialist group led by Rosa Luxemburg and Karl Liebknecht 1871–1919, and named for leader of 73 BC slave revolt against Rome. Nucleus of German Communist Party. Bloodily suppressed in 1919 with leaders killed.
swastika Hooked cross; ancient religious symbol associated in late 19th century with revival of interest in German legends and mythology. Adopted as symbol by extreme right-wing groups in Germany from 1919 and made Germany's national emblem in 1935.

454 WORLD 1918–1940

Places

4541 **1 Afghan War 1919** Conflict between Britain and Afghanistan leading to Afghan independence.
2 Amritsar 1919 Indian town in Punjab where British troops under General Dyer fired on meeting for independence; 379 died, 1,200 were wounded. Dyer was forced to resign after commission of inquiry censured his conduct.
3 Gran Chaco War 1932–5 Territorial dispute in border area between Bolivia and Paraguay. Dispute had flared into intermittent violence since 1928, defying international mediation. Paraguay gained most by 1938 settlement.
4 Manchukuo Chinese province of Manchuria occupied by Japanese in 1931. Puppet regime under former Chinese emperor Pu Yi installed as president, called emperor from 1934. Overthrown by Chinese Communists and USSR in 1945.
5 Rif War 1920–6 Berber people's revolt in Atlas Mountains area of Morocco against French rule.

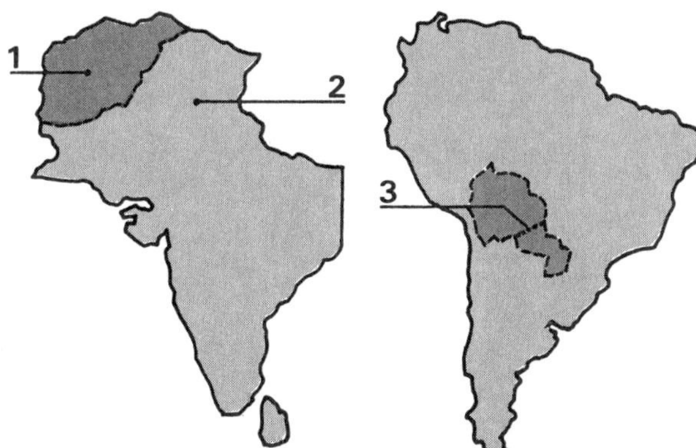

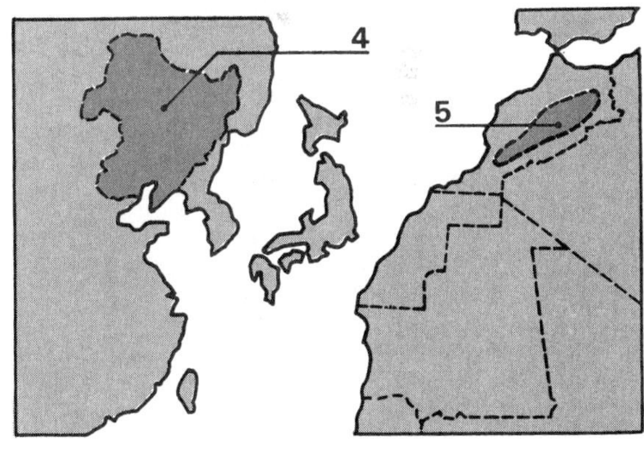

Events

4542 **1918** British, Dutch, and US companies exploit Venezuelan oil; nationalists demand independence for Egypt; administrative devolution in India; Japan takes territory from Russia and China.
1919–22 Constitution in Chile, Communist Party formed; petroleum regulatory laws in Venezuela; riots in Egypt leading to end of British protectorate; Armenia, Tunisia, seek independence; rebellion in Morocco; Britain and France partition Togo; campaign for responsible government in Rhodesia; British East Africa becomes Kenya, German East Africa becomes Tanganyika; legislative council in Uganda; series of coups in Afghanistan; martial law in India after British troops kill demonstrators, nationalists' demands grow; New Zealand governs West Samoa; Communist Party formed in China, independence of country guaranteed.
1923–6 New constitution and kingdom proclaimed in Egypt; Moroccan rebellion ends; Britain refuses to evacuate from Sudan; coup in Persia; Lebanon proclaims republic; anti-Bantu laws in South Africa, sexual relations between races banned, repatriation of Indians sought; South and North Rhodesia formally annexed by Britain, demands for union with Nyasaland; Cameroons administered as part of Nigeria; strikes in Ceylon, Hindu-Muslim riots in India; anti-foreign riots in China.
1927–30 Coups in Ethiopia, Egypt, Persia; Iraq independent; new constitution in Syria; domestic slavery abolished in Sierra Leone; South African Communist Party reorganized, increased Bantu membership, White women given vote, Jewish immigration reduced; agitation on Kenyan land and social issues; demonstrations and boycotts in India, proposals for federation of Muslim provinces; rebellion in lower Burma; Communist agitation in Malaya and Dutch East Indies; political situation stabilizes in China, Japan and USSR invade then withdraw.

continued

Events continued

4542 **1931–3** Uprisings in Brazil, Cuba; Bolivia at war with Uruguay until 1935; Egypt allies with Iraq; workers demonstrate in Morocco; slavery abolished in Ethiopia; Saudi Arabia becomes independent kingdom; Africans' residential rights limited in South Africa; Japan invades China, occupies Manchuria 1945; controversy in Burma over proposals to separate from India.
1934–7 New constitutions in Brazil, Uruguay; war between Bolivia and Paraguay ends; military coup in Venezuela; constitutional reform in Leeward and Windward Islands; Haitians killed in Dominica; hostilities begin between Italy and Ethiopia leading to annexation 1941; Britain evacuates Egypt except for Suez Canal zone; attempts to regularize British presence in Aden through treaty with India and Yemen; six-week war between Saudi Arabia and Yemen; Persia becomes Iran; Arab revolt in Palestine (until 1939), partition plans; Syria signs Convention with France; Chinese Communists march north, set up new state, Nationalists attempt to unite country, declare war on Japan until 1945; Burma separates from India, nationalists score election success in India.
1938–40 Abortive Nazi plots in Brazil, Chile; West Indies agitate for reform; civil disobedience campaign in Tunisia; French fleet destroyed by Britain off Algeria; South Africa divided over German aggression in lead-up to World War II; partition and independence proposed by Britain for Palestine; fighting between USSR and Japan on Chinese border, Japan occupies most of China, sets up puppet regimes, signs treaty with Siam; pacifist movement in India; Gandhi declares that independence should not come out of British ruin, and Britain promises dominion status at end of war.

People

4543 **Balfour, Arthur** 1848–1930, British Conservative statesman. Prime minister 1902–5. Foreign secretary 1916–19. In 1917 the Balfour Declaration stated British support for a national Jewish homeland in Palestine while safeguarding civil and religious rights for non-Jewish communities in area.
Chiang Kai-shek 1887–1975, Chinese military and political leader. President 1928 until 1931 and again from 1943 to 1949, fighting local war lords, the Japanese and Chinese Communists except between 1937 and 1945. Led non-Communist Nationalists to Formosa (Taiwan) in 1949 and headed government there until death.
Chou En-Lai 1898–1976, Chinese Communist political leader. Organized 1927 Shanghai revolt and took prominent part in "Long March" of 1934–5. Prime minister and foreign minister from 1949. Used influence to restrain extremists.
Gandhi, Mohandas Called *Mahatma* "Great Soul" 1869–1948 (**1**), Indian patriot, social reformer, and moral teacher. Lived in South Africa 1893–1914. On return to India led independence movement and was frequently arrested. Campaign was one of non-violent civil disobedience. Attempted to rid India of caste system and worked to unite Hindus and Muslims. Assassinated in 1948 by Hindu extremist.
Haile Selassie 1892–1975, Emperor of Ethiopia from 1930–74. Rigorously opposed attempted Italian annexation, spent exile in Britain gaining public support for independence 1936–41. Supported African unity and mediated in civil wars but overthrown by army coup and died in exile.
Hirohito 1901–89, Emperor of Japan. Regent 1926-89. Discarded traditional divine status 1946. Role in Japan's militarism and territorial aggression leading to World War II still disputed, though he evaded trial as war criminal through Allied need to stabilize Japan politically.
Jinnah, Mohammed Ali 1876–1948, Indian Muslim statesman and creator of modern Pakistan. Joined Muslim League 1916, reorganized it 1934 and became president. Wished for peaceful co-operation between Hindus and Muslims but by 1940 convinced of need for partition. First governor-general of Pakistan 1947–8.
Mao Tse-tung (Mao Zedong) 1893–1976, Chinese Communist leader. Revolutionary activities from 1921. Led "Long March" 1934–5. Victor in civil war 1949. Radical ideological differences with USSR led to emphasis on role of peasantry rather than urban working class or party bureaucracy.
Nehru, Jawaharlal 1889–1964, Indian Hindu nationalist leader and statesman. Leading member of Congress from 1919, president from 1929, repeatedly imprisoned by British during 1930s and 1940s. First prime minister of independent India 1947–64. Used influence for peace. Daughter Indira Gandhi and grandson Rajiv both became prime ministers, both were assassinated.
Pahlavi dynasty ruled Persia, now Iran from 1925 to 1978, usurping power from Qajar dynasty. Reza 1877–1944 and ruled 1925–41, was army officer who gained power by coup in 1921 and was chosen shah four years later. His son Mohammed Reza 1919–80, ruled 1941–78, had insecure early reign, attempted modernization while maintaining absolute rule 1962 and was overthrown and forced into exile partly through pro-US policies 1978–9.
Pu Yi, Henry 1906–67, last (Manchu) emperor of China. Ruled 1908–12. Installed by Japanese as ruler of puppet Manchurian state 1934–45. Accepted "re-education" by Communists and ended days as gardener.
Smuts, Jan Christiaan 1870–1950, South African soldier and statesman. Fought British on Boer side 1899–1902. Prime minister 1919–24, 1939–48. Tried to heal racial and political rifts within country and was considered too pro-British by many Afrikaners, leading to political defeat in 1948.
Strijdom, Johannes 1893–1958, South African politician. Uncompromizing Afrikaner stance. Nationalist MP 1929, party leader 1934, prime minister 1954–8. Extreme advocate of apartheid.

1

Terms

4544 **Afrikaans** South African language closely related to Dutch and Flemish. Afrikaners are descendants of original Dutch and French Huguenot settlers.
aliyah Hebrew word meaning migration of Jews to Palestine, mainly from eastern Europe but eventually from throughout the Diaspora.
apartheid Afrikaans word meaning state of being apart. Afrikaner doctrine of racial segregation which made people of mixed race or African descent into second-class citizens, restricted geographically, educationally, socially, and professionally.
civil disobedience Policy of non-violent non-cooperation initially propagated in India by Mahatma Gandhi in 1920 as a means to independence.
Congress Abbreviated name of Indian National Congress Party. Formed in 1885 as educational association to encourage political development and developed into principal vehicle for opposition to British rule. Led by Gandhi from 1920.
Haganah Secret society formed by Jews in Palestine in 1920 to defend themselves against attacks by Arabs. Formed nucleus of eventual Israeli army.
Long March 1934–5, 6,000 mile (9,700 km) journey to northern China by 100,000 Communist forces and civilians fleeing Kuomintang in south. Only 4,000 survived.
mahatma Sanskrit word meaning "great of soul", given as title to Gandhi by Hindu followers.
mandates Given at end of World War I to victorious colonial powers to administer colonies and other dependencies of Germany and former Turkish (Ottoman) empire.
Mapai *Miphlegeth Poalei Israel* Workers' party formed by Jewish immigrants in Palestine in 1930 and serving in Israeli coalition governments 1948–77. In 1968 combined with smaller socialist parties to form modern Israeli Labor Party.

continued

Terms continued

4544 **Muslim Brethren** Islamic revival movement founded in Egypt in 1928. Powerful force in nationalist movement with mass support by 1939. Syrian branches established 1937. Dissolved in 1948 because of use of violence and assassination to gain ends, and went underground, but temporarily reconstituted in 1951.
Muslim League Indian political movement active from 1906 and prominent from 1934, aiming at independent state. This was achieved in 1947 with partition and creation of Pakistan.
Twenty-one Demands Initially made by Japan upon China in 1915 with the aim of making China a Japanese protectorate through forced appointment of "advisers." Partly controlled through British pressure.
unequal treaties Chinese term for agreements reached in 19th and 20th centuries to permit equal trading opportunities and unrestricted admission forced on China by Belgium, Britain, France, Holland, Italy, Japan, Portugal, and US.
Wafd Arabic word meaning delegation that came to be name of leading Egyptian nationalist party governing 1936-8. Dissolved in 1953.
war lords Chinese generals commanding private armies who dominated various provinces politically as well as militarily between 1916 and 1928.

455 WORLD WAR II

The opposing sides

4551 **Axis powers**
1939 Germany
1940 Italy, Hungary, Romania, Japan
1941 Bulgaria

Principal allies
1939 Great Britain, British Commonwealth of Nations, France
1941 USA, USSR

The war in Europe

4552

Battles
1 Dunkirk evacuation May–Jun 1940
2 Battle of Britain Aug–Sept 1940
3 Normandy landings Jun 1944
4 Battle of the Bulge Dec 1944
5 El Alamein Oct–Nov 194
6 Siege of Leningrad Nov 1942–Feb 1943
7 Battle of Anzio Jan 1944

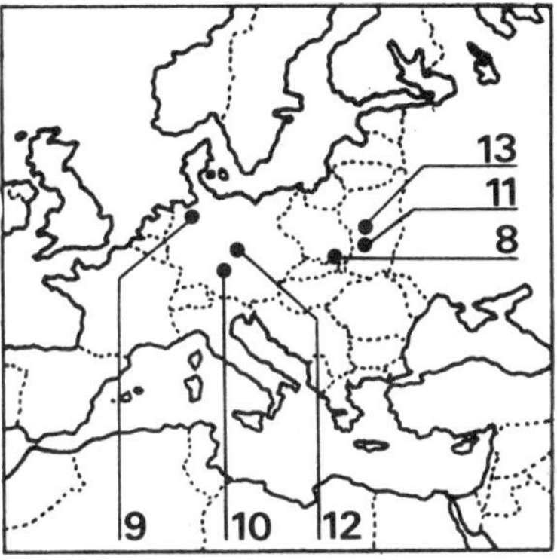

Concentration camps
8 Auschwitz
9 Belsen
10 Dachau
11 Sobibor
12 Theresienstadt
13 Treblinka

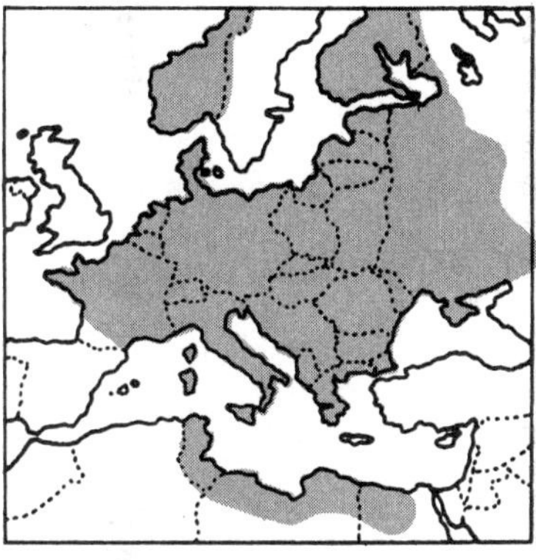

Greatest extent of Axis territory June 1944

Events

4553 **1936** Germany and Italy declare Berlin–Rome axis (Oct).
1938 Germany annexes Austria (Mar). Germany annexes German-speaking areas of Czechoslovakia (Sept–Oct). Japan in control of most of mainland China (Oct).
1939 Germany annexes rest of Czechoslovakia (Mar). Germany and USSR sign non-aggression pact (Aug). Germany invades Poland. Great Britain and France declare war (Sept).
1940 Germany invades Denmark and Norway (Apr). Germany invades Netherlands, Belgium, and France (May to Jun). Italy declares war on Great Britain and France (Jun). Battle of Britain air offensive (July to Oct). Germany, Italy, and Japan sign alliance (Sept). Italy invades Greece (Oct).
1941 USA and Great Britain sign Lend-Lease Agreement for war materials and foodstuffs (Mar). USSR and Japan sign non-aggression pact (Apr). Germany invades USSR (Jun). Germany begins systematic elimination of Jews from occupied territories (Jul). USA, USSR and Great Britain sign Lend-Lease Agreement (Oct). Japan bombs US fleet at Pearl Harbor in Hawaii. USA declares war on Japan. Germany and Italy declare war on USA (Dec).
1942 Japan conquers Philippines (Jan). Japan conquers Malaya, Indonesia, and Singapore (Feb). Japan occupies Burma (Mar). Great Britain drives Germany and Italy out of North Africa (May to Nov).
1943 USSR forces German retreat from Stalingrad after 17-month siege (Feb). Allies invade Sicily (Italy). Mussolini resigns (Jul). Mussolini rescued by Germans (Sept). Allied leaders' Teheran conference agrees on plans for invasion of German-occupied Europe (Nov).
1944 Allied forces land in France (D-Day, Normandy) (Jun). USSR forces reach German frontier (Aug). USSR declares war on and invades Bulgaria (Sept).
1945 Allied leaders plan invasion of Germany (Yalta) (Feb). Allied forces encircle Berlin. Hitler commits suicide. Mussolini shot by partisans (Apr). Germany surrenders (May). Allied conference to settle future of Germany (Potsdam) (Jul and Aug). USA drops atomic bombs on Japan (Aug). Japan surrenders (Sept). United Nations Organization formally constituted (Oct). Trial of German leaders accused of war crimes (Nuremburg) (Nov).
1946 Formal peace conference (Paris) (Jul to Oct). Verdicts in Nuremburg trials (Sept).
1947 Formal signing of peace treaties (Feb).

The war in the Pacific

4554 **Battles, bombings, and landings**

1 Burma Jan–May 1942
2 Singapore Dec 1941–Feb 1942
3 Manila Dec 1941–Jan 1942
4 Pearl Harbor Dec 1941
5 Midway Jun 1942
6 Iwo Jima Feb 1945
7 Leyte Oct 1944
8 Okinawa Apr 1945
9 Hiroshima Aug 1945
10 Nagasaki Aug 1945

 **Japanese empire 1942**

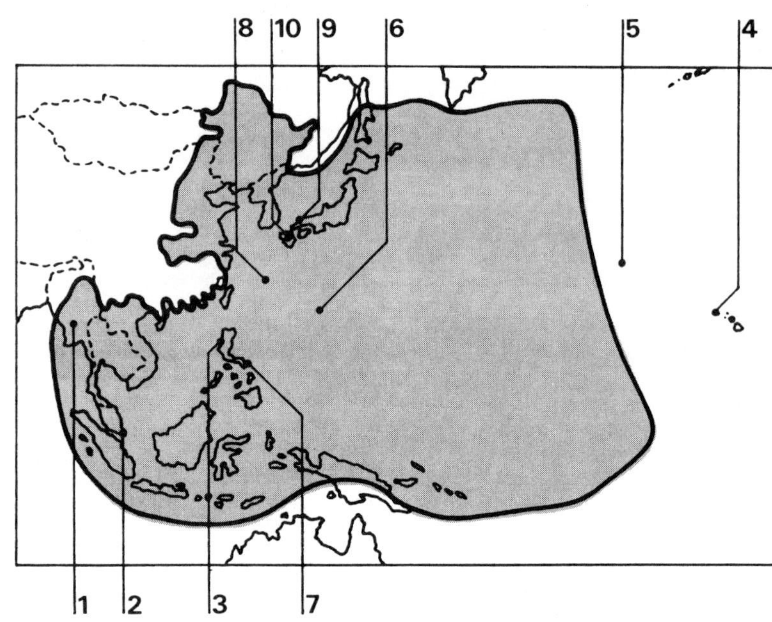

People

4555

ALLIES

Churchill, Winston Leonard Spencer 1874–1965, English statesman (**1**). Brilliant orator and courageous war leader. As prime minister 1940–5, led Britain alone against Germany and Italy, mobilizing national spirit of resistance.

Eisenhower, Dwight David 1890–1969, American general and 34th US president (**2**) whose relative inexperience balanced by sincerity, integrity, and talent for conciliation. Supreme commander Allied Expeditionary Forces 1943–5. Oversaw successful North African (1942) and Continental (1944) invasions.

De Gaulle, Charles André Joseph Marie 1890–1970, French general and first president of Fifth Republic. Popular and successful, if somewhat authoritarian, statesman. Leader of French government in exile during German occupation. Returned to Paris in 1944 at head of early liberation force.

MacArthur, Douglas 1880–1964, American general. Supreme commander Allied Forces in Pacific. Brilliant military strategist who, in 1945, completed liberation of Philippines and accepted final surrender of Japan.

Montgomery, Bernard Law 1st Viscount Montgomery of Alamein 1887–1976, English soldier. General commanding in North Africa, Italy, and northern Europe. Following 1942 Battle of Alamein, succeeded, after series of hard-fought, tenacious campaigns, in driving Axis forces back to Tunis.

Patton, George Smith 1885–1945, American soldier (**3**), known as "Old Blood and Guts." In 1943 commanded US 7th Army in Sicilian campaign. At head of 3rd Army, swept across France and Germany 1944–5 and reached Czech frontier.

Roosevelt, Franklin Delano 1882–1945, American and 32nd US president (**4**). After success of "New Deal" program, re-elected in landslide election. When World War II began, modified US neutrality to favor allies. Produced Atlantic peace charter with Churchill.

Stalin, Joseph Properly Iosif Vissarionovich Dzhugashvili, 1879–1953, Russian marshal and premier 1941–53. Ruthless dictator. Praised for resourcefulness as war leader but criticized for 1939 "friendship pact" with Nazi Germany.

Tito Properly Josip Broz, 1892–1980, Yugoslav Communist resistance leader, later marshal 1941–5. In mid-1941, organized partisan forces against Axis conquerors of his country, and by 1943 established provisional government in Bosnia. President for life from 1974.

Truman, Harry S 1884–1972, American and 33rd US president 1945–53. Elected to US senate in 1934 and 1940. Special committee, of which he was chairman, said to have saved US more than $15 billion in defence budget. Responsible for decision to drop first atom bombs on Japan.

continued

People continued

4555 **AXIS**

Hitler, Adolf 1889–1945, German *Führer* (chancellor) 1933–45. Leader of Nazi party and chief architect of Third Reich, finally brought down by Allied Forces after 12 years of unparalleled barbarity in which 30 million people lost their lives.
Hirohito 1901–89 Japanese 124th emperor reigned 1926–89. First Japanese prince to visit the West in 1921. Reign marked by rapid militarization and by aggressive wars against China 1931–2 and 1937–5, and USA 1941–5, latter ending with two atomic bombsopped by Allied powers on Hiroshima and Nagasaki.
Laval, Pierre 1883–1945, French politician. Premier 1931–2 and 1935–6. From socialism moved to right, and in Vichy government was Pétain's deputy 1940. As prime minister 1942–4, openly collaborated with Germans. After liberation, fled country, but was brought back and executed.
Mussolini, Benito 1883–1945, Italian *Duce* (leader) 1922–43. After World War I, organized *Fascisti* as militant nationalists to defeat socialism and in 1922 established himself as dictator. Entered World War II in 1940, but met with disaster everywhere. Executed 1945 after failed comeback.
Pétain, Henri Philippe Omer 1856–1951, French soldier and marshal. National hero after his defence of Verdun during World War I. With French collapse in 1940, became head of Vichy administration which collaborated with Germans. Imprisoned for life after liberation.
Quisling, Vidkun 1887–1945, Norwegian diplomat and fascist leader. In 1933, founded *Nasjonal Samling* (National Party) in imitation of German National Socialist party, and was puppet Prime Minister in German-occupied Norway. Tried and executed as traitor in May 1945.
Rommel, Erwin 1891–1944, German general. Commanded Hitler's headquarters guard during Austrian, Sudetenland, and Czech occupations and throughout Polish campaign. Brilliant commander in North Africa campaign. Later, commander of Channel defenses in France. Died by self-poisoning after having supported failed plot against Hitler.

Terms

4556 ***Anschluss*** Germany's annexation of Austria in 1938.
blitz/blitzkrieg Aerial campaign with heavy bombardment. Applied particularly to German bombings of Warsaw and London.
Final solution German attempt to exterminate all Jews through deportation to forced labor concentration camps, mass gassings, and other executions.
Gestapo *Geheime Staatspolizei* Nazi secret police from 1933.
kamikaze Japanese planes loaded with explosives flown by pilots trained to make suicidal crash attacks on targets.
Luftwaffe German air force.
Maginot Line French fortifications which failed to halt German advance in 1940.
Nazi Fascist National Socialist Workers' Party of Germany, founded in 1919 and led by Hitler.
Panzer Small, armored, four-wheel drive military personnel vehicle used by German army.
partisans French, Italian, Greek, Yugoslav, and other resistance fighters against German occupation.
Phony war September 1939 to April 1940 during which Britain was officially at war with Germany but not involved in the fighting.
swastika Nazi symbol of a cross with the arms bent at right angles in a clockwise direction.
Sudetenland German-speaking area of Czechoslovakia and formerly part of the Austro-Hungarian empire annexed by Germany in 1938.
U-boat or *Unterseeboot* A German submarine.
V-1 and V-2 *Vergeltungswaffe eins/zwei* German flying bombs and rockets used principally in raids against British towns.
Vichy French town which was the center for the puppet regime installed during the German occupation 1940–5.
war bonds Government debt certificates, guaranteeing payment with interest, sold to help the war effort.
Wehrmacht German armed forces.

Aftermath of World War II

4557

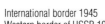

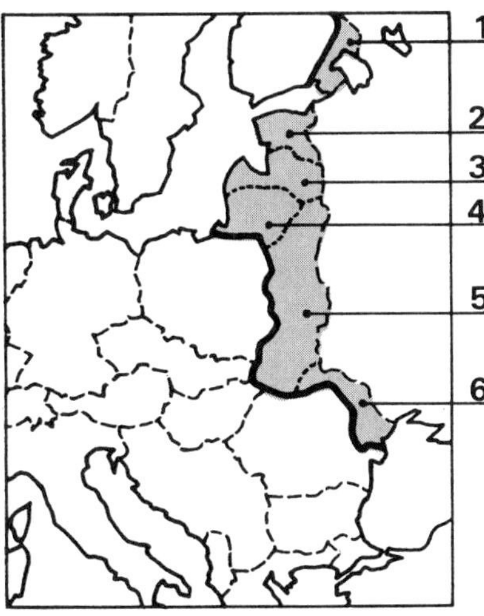

Areas annexed by USSR between 1939–45

1 Southeast Finland
2 Estonia
3 Latvia
4 Lithuania
5 East Poland
6 Northeast Romania

------ International border 1945
—— Western border of USSR 1945

1 2 3 4 5

6 7 8

East European states which, after WWII, became communist and dominated by USSR

1 East Germany 1949
2 Czechoslovakia 1948
3 Poland 1947
4 Hungary 1949
5 Romania 1947
6 Yugoslavia 1945
7 Albania 1946
8 Bulgaria 1947
—— "Iron Curtain" 1955
(Yugoslavia expelled from Eastern Bloc in 1948)

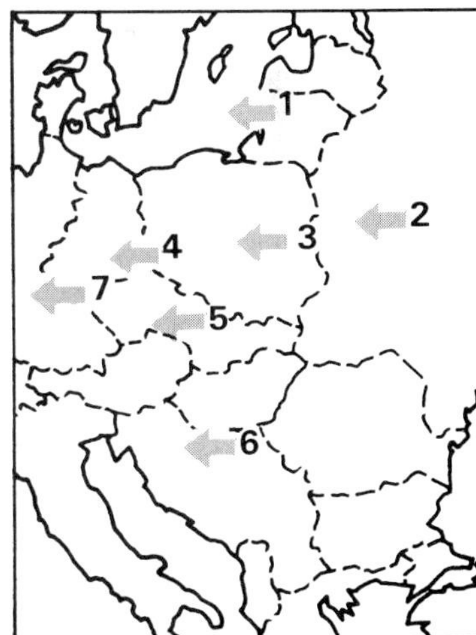

Movements of peoples westward due to expansion, resettlement and forced migration after World War II from:

1 Baltic states: 200,000
2 Russia: 2,300,000
3 Poland: 4,500,000
4 Germany: 11,850,000
5 Czechoslovakia: 1,950,000
6 South East Europe: 500,000
7 Peoples settled beyond Eastern Europe by refugee organizations: 1,000,000

461 AMERICA 1945–1990s

Places

4611 **Bay of Pigs** 1961 unsuccessful invasion attempt by Cuban exiles with CIA backing with aim of ousting Castro.

Little Rock Arkansas town scene of violent confrontation in 1957 and 1958 over integration of schools.

My Lai Vietnamese village where villagers were massacred in 1968 by US troops under Lt William Calley.

Events

4612 **1945** Death of president Roosevelt; World War II ends after US drops two atomic bombs on Japan; alleged Soviet spies arrested in Canada.

1946 Philippines gain independence from US; commission to settle Indian claims; flour shortage due to exports to Europe; birthrate soars as servicemen return.

1948 Men between 18 and 25 registered for military service; energy crisis; strikes as cost of living rises; Newfoundland votes for federation with Canada.

1950 US intervenes against Communist North Korean forces invading South Korea; US recognizes independence of Vietnam.

1951 Peace treaty signed with Japan, formally ending hostilities of World War II; mutual defence pacts signed with Philippines and with Japan; floods devastate Kansas and Missouri.

1952 Coup in Cuba; Puerto Rico becomes self-governing commonwealth.

1954 Racial segregation in public schools ruled unconstitutional.

1955 Black leaders killed; segregation in public parks, pools, playgrounds and on interstate buses and trains ruled unconstitutional.

1956 Further anti-segregation rulings; counter measures in Alabama.

1957–58 School integration struggles; civil rights legislation; Mafia killings in New York; unemployment rises.

1959–60 Cuban leader Batista ousted by Marxist Fidel Castro; USSR offers military support as US imposes trade embargo; Black demonstrations in South.

1963 Civil rights marches; riots; president Kennedy assassinated; alleged assassin shot while under arrest.

1964 US intervention in Vietnam; race riots; civil rights legislation; discontent between English- and French-speaking Canadians.

1965–67 US bombing raids in North Vietnam; opposition to war grows; escalation of civil rights demonstrations; French Canadian separatist movement.

1968 Civil rights leader Martin Luther King assassinated; urban riots; brother of late president Kennedy assassinated; increased rallies and demonstrations against Vietnam War.

1969–70 US begins troop withdrawal from Vietnam; environmental movement; racial violence in South.

1972 President Nixon visits China; US resumes bombing of North Vietnam.

1973 Ceasefire in Vietnam; US troops leave; vice-president Agnew resigns over tax evasion disclosure; dollar devalued; oil supplies to US banned by Arab states.

1974 President Nixon resigns when threatened with impeachment; amnesty for draft evaders.

1975 US signs treaty with USSR recognizing post World War II European boundaries and human rights.

1976 Stronger control over and greater accountability by intelligence services urged following concern over activities.

1977 US agrees to evacuate Panama Canal Zone by year 2000.

1978 National campaign to reduce federal and state taxation; president Carter mediates between Egypt and Israel; withdraws support for Iranian imperial regime.

1979 World oil crisis triggers plans for US gasoline rationing; full diplomatic relations established with China and East Germany (German Democratic Republic); US withdraws support for Nicaraguan regime; US hostages seized in Iran.

1980 Unsuccessful attempt to rescue hostages in Iran; huge ransom demanded.

1981 Newly inaugurated president Reagan wounded in assassination attempt; income tax reductions projected; US hostages released by Iran.

1982 Canada formally gains complete national sovereignty.

1983 US marines killed in Lebanon; US troops invade Grenada.

1985 US bans trade with Nicaragua; US and USSR presidents fail to agree over arms control.

1986 US citizens ordered to leave Libya, trade banned, Libyan ships and towns bombed after Libyan missiles attack fleet; military and economic aid for anti-Marxist rebels in Angola and Nicaragua; US troops deployed in Bolivia; scandal over sale of arms to Iran.

1987 Wall Street stock exchange slump; US and USSR agree on arms limitations; Iran arms scandal escalates.

1988 Iranian aircraft shot down; free trade agreement between US and Canada.

1989 US shoots down Libyan aircraft; extra troops ordered into Panama; earthquake in San Francisco; US rejects Iranian offer to assist in freeing hostages held by pro-Iranian groups in return for unfreezing of blocked assets; plan to solve increasing drugs problem; financial aid package for Poland and Hungary; invasion of Panama ousts dictator.

1990 Economic sanctions against Nicaragua lifted; Canadian Mohawk Indians in land rights dispute; US joins UN military action following Iraqi invasion of Kuwait; temporary government bankruptcy.

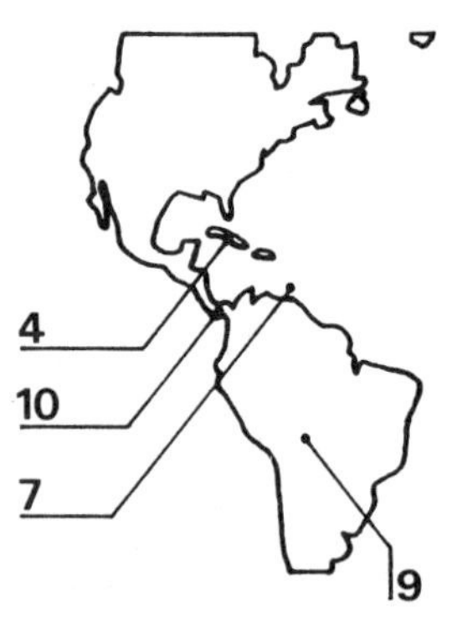

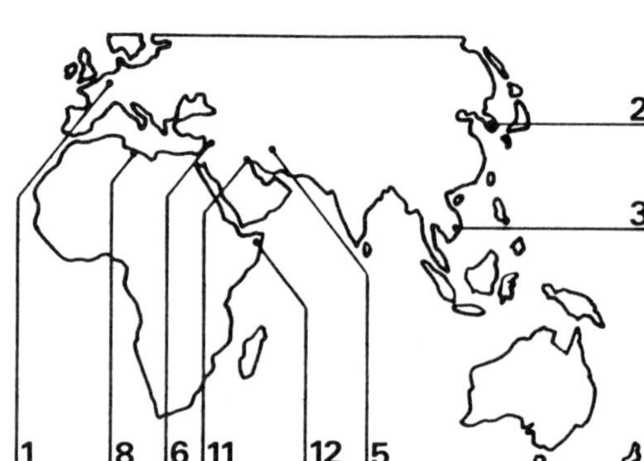

US military involvement worldwide since 1945
1 Germany: US Berlin airlift 1948–49
2 Korea 1950–53
3 Vietnam, Cambodia, Laos 1959–73
4 Dominican Republic: 1965
5 Iran 1980: hostage rescue fiasco
6 Lebanon 1982–3
7 Grenada 1983
8 Libya: towns bombed 1986
9 Bolivia 1986
10 Panama 1989
11 Persian Gulf War 1991
12 Somalia 1993

Words

4613 **Alliance for Progress** 1961 economic and social co-operation between US and Latin American countries.

Black Muslims Political movement of Black people adapting Islamic religious practices and seeking to establish Black nation.

CIA Central Intelligence Agency set up in 1947 to counter Communist activities outside USA but increasingly after 1967 undertaking internal surveillance activities.

"Cold War" Phrase coined by Bernard Baruch to describe ideological conflict between western countries and Soviet bloc.

Gray Panthers Organization fighting for rights of older and retired people founded in 1972.

"Hot Line" Emergency communications link between US and USSR presidents from 1963 to reduce risk of accidental war, especially nuclear strikes.

continued

Words continued

4613 **"I have a dream"** Key phrase in speech by Martin Luther King in 1963 during civil rights march to Washington.
"Ich bin ein Berliner" Key phrase in speech by president Kennedy in 1963 during visit to West Germany.
Iran-Contra Affair Scandal from 1986 over secret deals to sell arms to Iran and divert proceeds to fund Contra rebel forces in Nicaragua.
Medicare Act 1965 Provision for health insurance program for elderly.
"Pentagon Papers" Classified documents detailing US involvement in Vietnam from 1945 to 1968 'leaked' to Press in 1971.
Radio Free Europe Radio broadcasts to Soviet bloc from 1949 funded by CIA.
Siege of Wounded Knee 1973 Indian protest against treatment lasted ten weeks; two died.
Voice of America Radio broadcasts emphasizing US policies and values to foreign countries from 1942 funded by Congress.
Watergate Affair "Bugging" of Democratic headquarters during 1972 election campaign exposed by campaigning journalists over which president Nixon is forced to resign in 1974 after admitting false denial of knowledge (1974).

People

4614 **Birch (John) Society** Extreme right-wing political society founded 1958.
Carter, James b.1924, president 1977–81. Failed in attempts to free US nationals held hostage in Iran.
Castro, Fidel b.1927, Marxist leader of Cuban revolution. President since 1959.
Dulles, John F 1888–1959, secretary of state 1953–59 . Concerned with moral dimension in international affairs. Believer in personal diplomacy.

1

Eisenhower, Dwight David 1890–1969, Allied commander 1943–45, NATO commander 1950–52, president 1953–61 (**1**) . Politically inexperienced but with flair for conciliation and maintenance of international stability.
Hiss Case Allegations that Alger Hiss, a State Department employee and Communist Party member, supplied classified documents to USSR agents.
Hoover, J Edgar 1895–1972, FBI director from 1924. Controversial for attitude to alleged Communist subversion in 1950s and anti-Vietnam war and Black civil rights activists in 1960s.

2

Kennedy, John F 1917–63, first RC and youngest president 1961–63. Implemented civil rights legislation and endeavored to assist other economically deprived social minorities with firm but moderate foreign policies. Assassinated, probably by Lee Harvey Oswald.
Kennedy, Robert 1925–68, brother of president Kennedy, attorney general 1961–64 (**2**). Energetic campaigner for civil rights. Assassinated while campaigning for presidential nomination.

3

King, Martin Luther, Jr. 1929–68, Black Baptist minister and civil rights leader with brilliant powers of oratory and charismatic presence (**3**). He consistently advocated a non-violent campaign. Assassinated.

4

Kissinger, Henry b.1923, German-born White House national security adviser 1969–73. Secretary of state 1973–77 (**4**). Conducted many diplomatic missions abroad.

5

MacArthur, Douglas 1880–1964, General commanding Pacific forces 1942–45, Allied occupation of Japan 1945–51, and UN forces in Korea 1950–51 (**5**). Dismissed for wanting to extend war into China and failed to win presidential nomination.

6

McCarthy, Joseph 1909–57, Senator leading "witch-hunt" against suspected Communists and sympathizers (**6**), especially in the government and entertainment industry during 1950s. Censured when extended attacks to army personnel.

Marshall Plan US aid for European countries to aid post-war recovery from 1947. Named for proposer, secretary of state General George Marshall (1880–1959).

7

Nixon, Richard b.1913, president 1969–74 (**7**). Ended involvement in Vietnam, eased US-Soviet relations and established diplomatic relations with China. Lost credibility over denials of involvement in Watergate scandal and resigned under threat of impeachment. Granted full pardon.
Reagan, Ronald b.1911, president 1981–89. Former film actor. "Reaganomics" policy involved cuts in taxation and public spending and increased military expenditure. Intensely anti-Soviet. Lost popularity over Iran-Contra Affair.
Rosenberg Case Ethel and Julius Rosenberg executed in 1953 after being convicted of selling US atomic secrets to USSR.

8

Truman, Harry S 1884–1972, president 1945–53 (**8**). Approved atomic bombing of Japan and involved US in Korean War. Attempted social reform and civil rights legislation. 1947 Truman Doctrine was proposal for economic and military aid to European and other countries apparently threatened by Communist takeover.

462 EUROPE 1945–1990s

Events

4621 **1945–47** Second World War ends; peace terms and post-war settlements; trials and executions of war criminals; civil war in Greece; Germany and Austria under four-power Allied rule; Allied forces evacuate Italy; British Labor government nationalizes aviation and coal; US provides funds for Greece and Turkey.
1948–51 USSR tightens control over eastern Europe; Communist takeover in Albania, Bulgaria, Czechoslovakia, Hungary, Poland, and Romania; Germany divided into East (Communist controlled) and West (federal democracy); Ireland leaves British Commonwealth; Britain celebrates end of wartime austerity measures.
1952–55 George VI dies, succeeded by daughter Elizabeth II; continuing political and military unrest in Cyprus; Britain, France, and US end occupation of West Germany, attempted rising in East foiled by Soviet troops; power struggle in USSR as Stalin dies; military occupation ends in Austria.
1956–59 Stalin's personality cult denounced by Khrushchev, triggers de-Stalinisation policies across eastern Europe; riots in Poland; attempted Hungarian uprising crushed by Soviet troops; terrorist attacks in Cyprus; economic agreements create Common Market and Free Trade Area; France exchanges Fourth for Fifth Republic as General de Gaulle takes power.
1960–64 Cyprus achieves independence, fighting breaks out between Greeks and Turkish Cypriots, UN intervenes; East Germany builds wall across Berlin; Britain's application to join EEC vetoed by France.
1965–69 Military coup in Greece; Britain reduces armed forces, civil disturbances in Ulster lead to deployment of British troops; strikes and demonstrations in Paris; attempted liberal reforms in Czechoslovakia lead to Soviet troops invading; new German chancellor seeks better relations with eastern Europe.
1970–74 rioting in Poland, Communist Party leader resigns; women gain vote in Switzerland; Britain imposes direct rule in northern Ireland; East and West Germany establish diplomatic relations; Turkish invasion of Cyprus as conflict escalates leads to partition of the island; army coup in Portugal.
1975–79 Britain holds first referendum, votes to remain in EEC, fishing dispute with Iceland, rise in unemployment, sectarian murders in Northern Ireland; Polish cardinal elected pope; direct elections to European parliament.
1980–84 Yugoslav president Tito dies; major industrial unrest in Poland leads to USSR being warned against invasion by EEC, NATO and US, free trades union banned; hunger striker dies in northern Ireland, riots; attempted assassination of pope, Britain and Vatican establish full diplomatic relations, pope visits Britain and Ireland; attempted assassination by IRA of British prime minister and cabinet.
1985–88 Coal miners strike in Britain, continued IRA bomb attacks in Northern Ireland; leadership changes in USSR bring Gorbachev to power; shift in power after Irish elections.
1989–90 Political parties permitted in Hungary by new constitution; free parliamentary elections in Poland; East German border opened by Hungary permitting East Germans to flee to West, mass demonstrations lead to removal of travel restrictions, free elections, reunification; Bulgarian president resigns, free elections promised; Czech government resigns following massive demonstrations, free elections; Romanian demonstrations brutally suppressed leading to army revolt, trial and execution of president and wife, free elections; Lithuania declares independence, USSR begins to fragment, mass resignations from Communist Party; Albanian leadership reluctant to yield to change; continuing violence in Northern Ireland and bombings in Britain, prime minister Thatcher defeated in Conservative Party leadership ballot, resigns, and is succeeded by John Major; British and French farmers clash over meat imports; Serbs seize Croatian territory in Yugoslavia, Slovenia votes for independence.

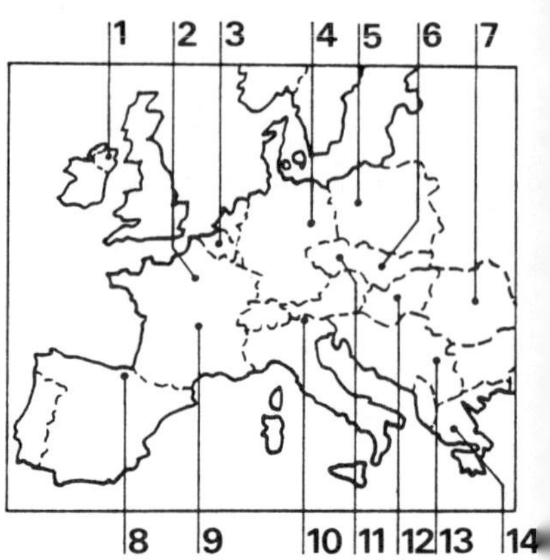

Trouble spots and areas of conflict in Europe since 1945
1 Northern Ireland: Protestant and Catholic conflict
2 Paris: student riots 1968
3 Belgium: Flemish – Walloon conflict
4 East Germany: uprising 1953
5 Poznan, Poland: riots 1956; labor unrest 1976–82
6 Czechoslovakia: Soviet invasion 1968
7 East Europe: anti-Communism uprising 1989–90
8 Spain: Basque separatist movement
9 France: OAS and right-wing terrorism
10 South Tirol: disputed status and terrorism
11 Prague: communist coup 1948
12 Hungary: nationalist uprising 1956
13 Yugoslavia: civil wars and fragmentation 1991–93
14 Greece: civil war 1944–49; military coup 1967

People

4622 **Adenauer, Konrad** 1876–1967 German statesman. Imprisoned by Nazis, founded Christian Democratic Union. Chancellor of West Germany 1949–63, foreign minister 1951–55. Negotiated German entry to EEC, NATO. Established diplomatic relations with USSR in 1955.
Attlee, Clement 1883–1967 British Labour Party leader, prime minister 1945–51. Presided over nationalization of utilities, independence of former colonies, and introduction of comprehensive social welfare programs.
Brandt, Willy 1913–93 German statesman. Opposed Hitler. Mayor of West Berlin 1957–66. Chairman of Social Democratic Party from 1964. Chancellor of West Germany 1969–74. Nobel Peace Prize 1971. Consistently advocated improved relations with East Europe.
Ceausescu, Nicolae 1918–89 Romanian dictator. Communist Party member from 1933. Head of state 1967–89. Ruled with repression of any opposition. Fostered personality cult. Corruption and exactions of regime provoked riots which were savagely suppressed, leading to revolution. Executed with wife Elena.
De Gaulle, Charles 1890–1970 French general and statesman (**1**). Attempted to modernize French army 1930s. Left France and founded Free French movement from London 1940–4. Returned to Paris as head of provisional government 1944–6. First president of Fifth Republic 1959–69. Restored political and economic stablity in France, granted independence to African colonies and Algeria. Fostered ties with West Germany while vetoing Britain's entrance to EEC in 1962–3 and 1967
Dubcek, Alexander 1921–89 Czech politician. As Communist Party leader attempted political reform 1968–9. Demoted and expelled from party by invading Soviet troops but became symbol of reasoning opposition. Chairman of federal assembly 1989.
Elizabeth II b.1926 r1952– queen of Great Britain, head of British Commonwealth (**2**). Succeeded father George VI. Much traveled, especially throughout British Commonwealth, with concern for individual countries and constitutional government in general. Has tried to bring British monarchy in line with 20th century, not always with complete success.

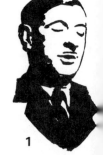

Gomulka, Wladyslaw 1905–82 Polish statesman. Imprisoned 1951 even though general secretary of Communist Party 1943–8, 1956–70, for resisting Soviet domination. Forced into retirement 1970.

continued

People continued

4622 **Gorbachev, Mikhail** b.1931, Soviet president. As Communist Party general secretary 1985–88 began social and political reform programmes, including *glasnost*and *perestroika*. Policy of non-interference led directly to 1989 revolutions throughout eastern Europe. President 1988–91, leaving office after attempted coup by military hard-liners.

Havel, Vaclav b.1936, Czech playwright and reluctant politician. As political dissident and co-founder of Charter 77 suffered smear campaign, banning of plays and two periods of imprisonment. Elected president of Czechoslovakia after overthrow of Communist regime 1989.

Heath, Sir Edward b.1916, British statesman and music-lover. Elected leader of Conservative Party 1965–75. Prime minister 1970–74 negotiating British entry into EEC 1973 and improving relations with China. Fervent advocate of Britain taking full European role and therefore opposing and opposed by Margaret Thatcher, who succeeded him as party leader 1975.

Jaruzelski, Wojciecek b.1923, Polish general and politician. Chief of general staff 1965, minister of defence 1968, Communist Party first secretary from 1981, prime minister 1981–85. Lifted martial law 1983. Elected president 1985.

John Paul II (Karol Wojtyla) b. 1920 r1978– Polish pope, first non-Italian since 1522.
Worked in quarries during German occupation. Ordained 1946, archbishop of Cracow 1964, cardinal 1967. Doctrinally conservative but massive popular appeal with extensive world tours, including many to non-RC countries. Survived assassination attempts in 1981 and 1982.

Juan Carlos b. 1938 r 1975– Spanish king. Groomed for throne by Franco but has reversed late dictator's policies to reign as constitutional monarch, despite two failed right-wing coups.

Kadar, Janos 1912–89 Hungarian politician. Imprisoned by Communist regime 1951–54, joined 1956 revolutionary government but formed puppet pro-Soviet ministry after Soviet invasion 1956–58, 1961–65. First secretary Communist Party 1956–88, party president briefly 1988 but dismissed in 1989.

Khrushchev, Nikita Sergeyevich 1894–1971, Soviet politician (**3**). Joined Communist Party 1918, fought in civil war, organized guerrilla operations during World War II. Became party first secretary 1953, denounced Stalinism 1956, relegated potential rivals 1957 Prime minister 1958–64 initiating policy of peaceful coexistence with west but became involved in increasingly bitter struggle with China. Attempted reform of agriculture and industry, failure led to removal from office.

3

Kohl, Helmut b.1930, German statesman and leader of Christian Democratic Party. Chancellor of West Germany 1982–90, chancellor of reunited Germany 1990. Committed to European unity and improvement of relations with France.

Macmillan, Harold 1894–1986 British statesman, supporter of paternalist Conservative Party traditions but aware of necessity of political changes. Prime minister 1957–63. Telling phrases in speeches: "you've never had it so good" epitomized 1950s–60s prosperity; "wind of change" accepted decolonization of Africa at same period; "selling family silver" criticised Thatcher government's privatization of nationalized industries in 1980s.

Makarios (Mikhail Khristodolou Mouskos) 1913–77 Greek Cypriot leader and patriarch of Orthodox Church. Supported movement for union with Greece but negotiated with British 1950s leading to deportation 1956–59. President of Cyprus 1960–74, 1974–77. Failed to prevent partition of island 1974.

Masaryk, Jan 1886–1948, Czech statesman, son of country's first president. Vice-president of government in exile 1940–45, foreign minister 1941–8. Died in suspicious circumstances after Communist takeover.

Mindszenti, Josef 1892–1975 Hungarian cardinal. Accused of treason by Communist regime 1949 and sentenced to life imprisonment. Escaped during 1956 revolution to take sanctuary in US embassy.

Molotov, Vyacheslav 1890–1986 Soviet politician. Member of Politburo 1926–57 and loyal colleague of Stalin. Foreign minister 1939–49, 1953–6, deputy prime minister 1943–56, ambassador to Mongolia 1957–60 as influence declined with rise of Khrushchev and forced into retirement 1961–62.

Monnet, Jean 1888–1979 French economist and diplomat. Deputy secretary general of League of Nations 1919–23, chairman Franco-British Economic Co-Ordination Committee 1939–40. Architect of EEC 1952–75.

Nagy, Imre 1896–1958 Hungarian politician. Lived in USSR 1930–44. Agriculture minister promoting reform 1945–6. Prime minister 1953–5, 1956. Attempts at liberalization led to dismissal from Communist Party 1955. Briefly reappointed during 1956 Hungarian rising but arrested on Soviet intervention. Secretly executed 1958. Rehabilitated and remains honourably reburied 1988–9.

Shevardnadze, Eduard b.1928, Soviet politician. Foreign minister 1985–90. Concerned that countries should formulate own foreign policy. Resigned over fears of presidential dictatorial powers and likelihood of backlash reactionary coup. Defied coup leaders when this happened 1991.

Spaak, Paul 1899–1972, Belgian statesman. Premier 1938–39, 1946, 1947–49, foreign minister 1954–57, 1961–66. First UN General Assembly president 1946, NATO secretary general 1957–61. Instrumental in setting up EEC .

Thatcher, Margaret b.1925, British politician. Conservative MP 1959–92. Education minister 1970–74, elected party leader 1975, prime minister (first British woman) 1979–90. Opposed to closer British involvement in Europe and centrist policies in general. Promoted links with US, privatization of nationalized industries and utilities and monetarist stance on economic matters.

Tito (Josip Broz) 1892–1980, Yugoslav statesman. Communist Party member early 1920s, secretary general 1937. Led partisan opposition to Germans from 1941, marshal 1943, prime minister 1946–53, president 1953–80. Creator of unified Yugoslav state which fragmented from 1991. Defied attempted Soviet control from 1948, worked for co-operation among non-aligned nations while developing relations with Western states.

Togliatti, Palmiro 1893–1964 Italian politician. Co-founder of Communist Party, secretary 1926–64. Exile in USSR during Second World War. Returned to Italy 1944 and rebuilt party into largest in western Europe.

Walesa, Lech b.1943, Polish trade unionist. Shipyard worker who became leader of free trade union Solidarity 1980. Forced government concessions but imprisoned 1981–82. 1983 Nobel peace prize. Head of Solidarity governmemt 1989. President of Poland 1990.

Wilson, Harold b.1916, British politician. Labour Party MP 1945–1983, party leader 1963–83. Prime minister 1964–70, 1974–76. Defender of US policy in Vietnam. Imposed statutory incomes policy to deal with balance of payments crisis 1964–66.

Yeltsin, Boris b.1931, Russian politician. Communist Party member 1960–1988, attempting to restore efficiency and combat corruption. Elected to parliament 1989, won presidential election 1990, resisted hard-liners' attempted coup 1991. Initially supported by Gorbachev later became opponent.

Places

4623 **Berlin Blockade** 1948–9 USSR imposed restrictions on traffic between western zones and Berlin. When this became absolute, supplies were airlifted into west Berlin by Britain and US. Blockade lifted after negotiations.

Berlin Wall 1961–89. Concrete barrier built by East Germany across border between East and West Berlin to stem flood of over 2 million refugees fleeing west. Over 200 people were killed by border guards attempting to cross mine-strewn and barbed-wire hedged area.

Bruges Belgian city where British prime minister Margaret Thatcher in 1988 denounced European Economic Community for allegedly introducing socialism "through the back door."

Gdansk (formerly Danzig) Polish town with important shipyards. Strikes in 1980 led to establishment of free trades union Solidarity led by shipyard electrician Lech Walesa and so ultimately to restoration of democracy.

Helsinki Agreement 1975. Pact between 35 nations concerned with European security and economic collaboration between eastern and western blocs. Its provisions reaffirming human rights proved a catalyst for 1989–90 break-up of eastern Europe, though not before many supporting those provisions had suffered.

Prague Spring 1968–69 Attempt to present "socialism with a human face" as initiated by Dubcek . Suppressed by Soviet invasion.

Timisoara Romanian city where troops fired on demonstrators in December 1989. About 670 died, 1,200 were injured. Set off further popular uprisings. Troops surrendered and switched sides leading to overthrow of Ceausescu regime.

Words

4624 **Brezhnev Doctrine** 1968–89 Justification for intervention by Warsaw Pact countries in affairs of member states. Promulgated by Soviet Communist leader Leonid Brezhnev (1906–1982) to explain why five countries under Soviet control invaded Czechoslovakia in 1968 to quash Prague Spring.

Bundestag One of two houses of West German federal parliament 1949–90.

CAP (Common Agricultural Policy) Subsidies from central fund to farmers of countries belonging to EC. Controversial, leading to so-called butter mountains and wine lakes through over-production in these areas.

Charter 77 Czech group of civil rights activists formed 1977 to monitor abuses by authorities. Members were harassed and imprisoned.

Cod War 1972–76 Fishing dispute between Britain and Iceland.

Cold War 1945–90 tension over considerable period of time between individual countries or power blocs falling short of formal armed conflict. Term first used in 1947 US Congress debate.

COMECON 1949 Association of Soviet-dominated nations, originally those of East Europe but later including Mongolia (1962), Cuba (1972), and Vietnam (1978) intended to co-ordinate economic development. Used by Stalin to put pressure on Yugoslavia and to counter growing western economic interdependence.

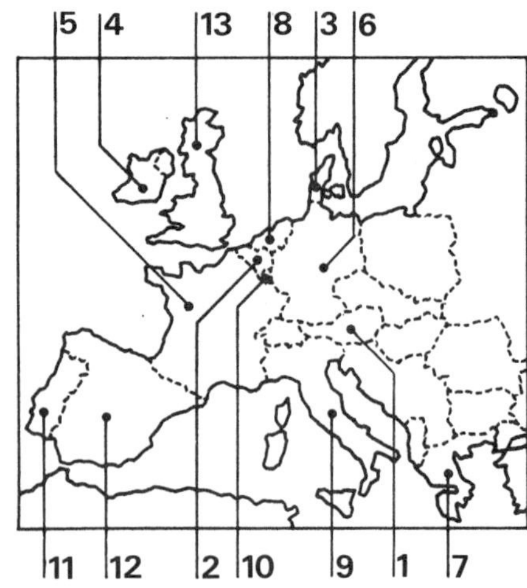

EC member states 1993

1 Austria
2 Belgium
3 Denmark
4 Ireland
5 France
6 Germany
7 Greece
8 The Netherlands
9 Italy
10 Luxembourg
11 Portugal
12 Spain
13 United Kingdom

Common Market: see *EC*, below.

Council of Europe Organization established in 1949 to achieve greater European unity, matters of national defence being excluded. Belgium, Denmark, France, Ireland, Italy, the Netherlands, Norway and Sweden were original members. Greece, Iceland and Turkey joined later in 1949, then West Germany (1951), Austria (1956), Cyprus (1961), Switzerland (1963), and Malta (1965). (Greece withdrew in 1969.) Not to be confused with Council of EC.

Democratic Republic 1949–1990 East German nation state created during Allied military occupation of Germany when east of country was under USSR control.

detente French diplomatic term meaning reduction of tension between two countries with opposing policies. Used especially in reference to US – USSR relations 1968 onward.

dissidents Term applied to those individuals, particularly in eastern Europe and USSR, refusing conformity with politics and beliefs of society in which they live. Often persecuted, imprisoned, exiled or executed.

EC (European Community) European grouping from 1958, consisting of the European coal and steel community (ECSC), the European Economic Community (EEC), and the European Atomic Energy Commission (Euratom). The aim of the original member countries: Belgium, France, Italy, Luxembourg, the Netherlands, and West Germany, was to work together for economic and political union. Now also includes Denmark (1973), Greece (1981), Ireland (1973), Portugal (1986), Spain (1986), and UK (1973). and reunited Germany (1990). Nationalistic cracks have begun to shatter façade of harmonious agreement.

EFTA (European Free Trade Area) European economic grouping from 1960, originally of Austria, Denmark, Norway, Portugal, Sweden, Switzerland, and UK. Finland joined 1961, Iceland 1970. Denmark, Portugal, and UK subsequently left to join EC .

EOKA Anti-British Greek Cypriot terrorist group led by colonel Grivas and designed to obtain independence for island from direct British rule 1955–59. Staged coup 1974 which led to Turkish invasion and forced partition.

ETA Initials of militant Basque terrorist group seeking to create independent republic. Responsible for many acts of sabotage, murder, and intimidation.

Eastern Bloc Communist states of eastern Europe, including those of Balkans. Strength through cohesion weakened politically and economically since 1989.

enosis Greek term meaning unity, describing Greek Cypriot movement for political union with Greece. Turkish Cypriot minority bitterly opposed this and it led directly to 1974 invasion and partition.

Federal Republic of Germany 1949–90 West German nation state created at end of Allied military occupation.

Festival of Britain 1951 celebration of the end of rationing and other wartime and postwar austerity measures. Mainly focussed on London with new public buildings and display of industrial and cultural achievements.

Fifth Republic 1958– French republic established with election of De Gaulle to presidency. Characterized by powerful constitutional position of president.

Fourth Republic 1945–58 French republic established at end of World War II. Characterized by excessive number of short-lived ministries and colonial agitation for independence.

glasnost Russian word meaning openness. Set in motion 1985 by Gorbachev. Meant that intellectual atmosphere lightened and both contemporary social matters, politics, and history of Stalinist era could be discussed.

greens Ecology parties which first contested West German elections 1979. While in most European countries, few parliamentary seats have been gained, successful grass roots lobbying and use of media have forced other parties to acknowledge and promote environmental issues.

IRA (Irish Republican Army) Militant nationalist organization striving for united independent Ireland through increasingly terrorist means. Responsible for many civilian deaths both in Britain and Northern Ireland. Considered military wing of Sinn Fein. Also called Provisional IRA.

Iron Curtain "From Stettin in the Baltic to Trieste in the Adriatic, an iron curtain has descended across the Continent" was Sir Winston Churchill's description of Soviet domination of East Europe made in a speech at Westminster College, Missouri, in 1946.

Marshall Plan 1948 Crucial financing by US of European postwar economic recovery conceived by Secretary of State George Marshall (1880–1959). USSR rejection meant that

continued

Words continued

4624 $17,000 million mainly went to West European countries.
Monnet Plan 1947 Program for French economic recovery and development named for economist Jean Monnet .
NATO (North Atlantic Treaty Organization) Organization created in 1949 committing US to peacetime European defence. Initial signatory states were Belgium, Canada, Denmark, France (withdrew 1966), Iceland, Italy, Luxembourg, the Netherlands, Norway, Portugal, UK, US. Greece and Turkey signed 1952 and West Germany 1955.
ostpolitik German term for policy of improving relations with East Europe begun in 1969 by West German Chancellor, Willy Brandt.
perestroika Russian word meaning restructuring. Attempt by Gorbachev to regenerate Soviet economy by encouraging market forces, decentralizing factory management, and generally democratizing Communist Party and government.
Politburo (contraction of politicheskoe buro) Russian name for supreme executive and policy-making Communist Party committee.
Profumo Affair 1963. Scandal involving British war minister John Profumo (1915–), his relationship with Christine Keeler and her concurrent affair with Soviet naval attaché. Profumo resigned, Keeler drew prison term.
Schuman Plan 1950. Proposal by former French prime minister Robert Schuman (1896–1963) to pool West Europe's coal and steel resources. It was the nucleus of EC.
Solidarity Polish trade union and reform movement formed in late 1970s in Gdansk shipyards and officially registered 1980. It demanded liberalization of Communist regime and formation of free trade unions. Won short-lived concessions before being banned and leader Lech Walesa detained. Clandestine through rest of decade until part of first non-Communist government since 1948 in 1989.
Truman Doctrine 1947 Provision by president Harry Truman (1884–1972) of US aid to Greece and Turkey as part of anti-Communist foreign policy which signalled start of Cold War containment policy.
Velvet Revolution 1989–90 peaceful end to Communist rule in Czechoslovakia. So named for quiet resignation of Communist government following massive but peaceful demonstrations.
Warsaw Pact 1955 East European defence treaty under Soviet leadership as response to NATO. Signatory states were Albania (ceased to participate 1961, withdrew 1968), Bulgaria, Czechoslovakia, East Germany, Hungary, Poland, Romania, and USSR.
Winter of Discontent 1978–79 widespread strikes in Britain against Labour government's wage restraint policy leading to uncollected refuse, unburied bodies, and electoral defeat.

463 WORLD 1945–1990s

Events

4631 **1945** World War II in East ends as US drops atomic bombs on Hiroshima and Nagasaki, Japan surrenders. Military coups in Brazil and Venezuela.
1946 Civil war in China between Communists and Nationalists. Civil war in Indo-China against French (until 1954). Perón elected president in Argentina.
1947 Arabs reject UN proposal to partition Palestine between Arabs and Jews. India partitioned between Hindus (India) and Muslims (Pakistan), many die during mass exodus. Coup in Venezuela.
1948 Gandhi murdered by Hindu extremist. State of Israel sanctioned by UN, recognized by US, Arab-Israeli conflict follows, Jordan seizes West Bank and part of Jerusalem, Egypt takes Gaza Strip. Korea divided into People's Republic (North, Communist) and South. State of emergency in Malaya. Ceylon independent. Afrikaaners in power in South Africa, pledged to apartheid. Civil war in Colombia. Burma independent.
1949 Indonesian Republic becomes independent of Netherlands. Communists control Chinese mainland as People's Republic under Mao Zedong, Nationalists under Chiang Kai-shek escape to Taiwan (Formosa).
1950 War between North and South Korea, China supports North, UN forces support South (to 1953). Treaty of Friendship between China and USSR. China invades Tibet. India republic within British Commonwealth. Anglo-Iranian dispute over nationalization of oilfields and refineries.
1951 US signs Pacific security treaties. Japan signs peace treaties. King of Jordan assassinated in Jerusalem. Egypt abrogates 1936 treaty with Britain. Libya independent. Military coup in Bolivia.
1952 Morocco rebels against French rule (to 1956). Anti-British riots in Egypt. State of emergency in Kenya (to 1956). Women given vote in Mexico.
1953 Egyptian monarchy overthrown, republican one-party state. French occupy northern Vietnam, Cambodia proclaims independence. Federation of Nyasaland with Northern and Southern Rhodesia. End of Korean War. Coup in Colombia.
1954 French defeated in northern Vietnam, Vietnam divided into Communist North, and South. French troops sent to Algeria, war for independence follows (to 1962). New dictatorship in Paraguay. Coup in Guatemala.
1955 Strikes and rebellion in Argentina lead to ousting of Perón by military junta. Power struggle in Brazil.
1956 Suez Canal nationalized by Egypt, Anglo-French-Israeli military intervention. Morocco, Sudan, and Tunisia independent. Civil war in

Major wars and conflicts of the world 1945–93
1 Cuba: civil war 1956–59; missile crisis 1962
2 Central America: civil war in El Salvador 1979–92
3 Algeria: independence struggle 1954–62
4 Near East: Arab-Israeli wars 1948–49. 1956, 1967, 1973; Lebanese civil war 1975–6
5 Armenia-Azerbaijan war 1988
6 Middle East: Iran-Iraq war 1980–90; Iraq invasion of Kuwait 1990; Persian Gulf war 1991
7 Sino-Indian war 1962
8 Tibet: Chinese invasion 1959
9 Korean war 1950–53
10 China: civil war 1946–49; Sino-Soviet border conflicts 1969, 1972
11 Vietnam: civil war 1946–54; N-S war 1963–75; invades Cambodia 1978; invaded by China 1979
12 Malaya emergency 1948–60
13 Falklands war 1982
14 Nigeria: Biafran war 1967–70
15 Egypt: Suez crisis 1956
16 Angola: civil war 1975–
17 South Africa: state of emergency imposed 1985
18 Kenya: Mau Mau emergency 1952–60
19 Somalia–Ethiopia war 1977
20 Afghanistan occupied by Russia 1979–88
21 India: partition 1947; Indo Pakistan wars 1947–9, 1965, 1971 (Bangladesh independence)

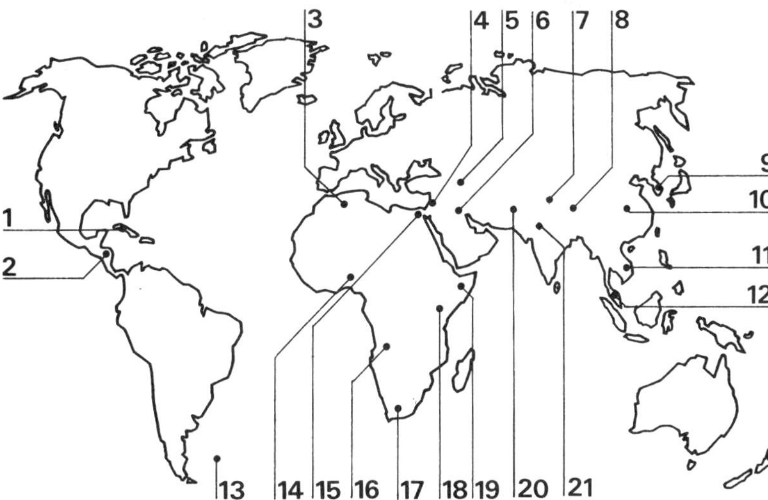

continued

Events continued

4631 Cuba. Islamic constitution in Pakistan. Nicaraguan president assassinated.
1957 Gold Coast becomes independent Ghana. Malay states independent. Coup in Colombia. Dictatorship in Haiti.
1958 Egypt, Syria, Iraq, and Jordan form federations. Anti-western riots in Lebanon. Revolution in Iraq, king killed. Coup in Venezuela. Argentina returns to civilian rule.
1959 West Indian Federation established. Tibet rising against China crushed, border clashes between China and India. Revolution in Cuba brings Castro to power.
1960 Seventeen Belgian, British, and French African colonies gain independence, secession movement follows in Congo (to 1964). Cuba nationalizes US property, allies with Communist powers. Blacks killed during anti-apartheid demonstration in Johannesburg. End of state of emergency in Malaya. Ideological dispute between China and USSR.
1961 South Africa becomes republic, leaves British Commonwealth. US-backed invasion of Cuba fails. Dominican Republic dictator assassinated. Jamaica withdraws from West Indies Federation. Kuwait independent, claimed by Iraq.
1962 Confrontation between US and USSR over USSR missile bases in Cuba. US military command in South Vietnam. Border clashes between China and India. Algeria gains independence. Australian Aborigines given vote. Military coup in Peru. Jamaica, Trinidad and Tobago independent.
1963 Kenya, Zanzibar independent. Military coup in Syria. South Vietnam government overthrown. Federation of Malaysia established, confrontation between Malaysia and Indonesia. Coup in Dominican Republic.
1964 Indonesia invades Malaysia. US escalates support for South Vietnam. Nyasaland becomes independent Malawi. Northern Rhodesia becomes independent Zambia, Tanganyika and Zanzibar unite as Tanzania. Military coup in Brazil.
1965 US begins bombing raids on North Vietnam, South Vietnamese army supported by US marines. Military coup in Dominican Republic, US intervenes. China launches cultural revolution. India and Pakistan at war over Kashmir. Singapore secedes from Malaysia. White minority Rhodesian government declares independence from Britain. Military coup in Algeria.
1966 UN imposes trade sanctions on Rhodesia. Military coup in Nigeria. Revisionists purged in China. International protests against US involvement in Vietnam. South African premier assassinated. British Guiana independent within British Commonwealth as Guyana. Military coup in Argentina.
1967 Israel occupies Sinai desert, Arab Jerusalem, west bank of Jordan, Syrian Golan Heights. Eastern Nigeria attemps to secede, civil war follows. Argentine Marxist revolutionary Che Guevara killed in Bolivia. Brazil constitution suspended. Britain reduces military commitments in Far East.
1968 Britain withdraws all military commitments east of Suez, restricts Commonwealth

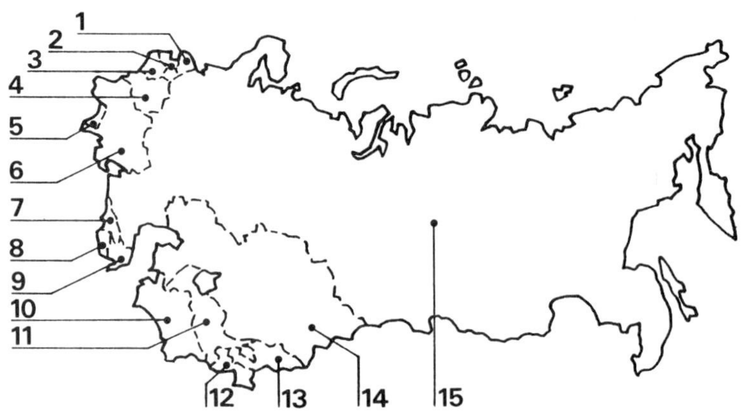

The independent republics of the former Soviet Union, from 1990

1 Estonia
2 Latvia
3 Lithuania
4 Belorus
5 Moldova
6 Ukraine
7 Georgia
8 Armenia
9 Azerbaijan
10 Turkmenistan
11 Uzbekistan
12 Tadjikstan
13 Kazakhstan
14 Kirghizia
15 Russia

immigration. Massive North Vietnam offensive against South. Military coup in Peru.
1969 Agitation by Palestinians in Israeli-occupied territory. New military coup in Libya overthrows monarchy, establishes republic. Laos requests US aid against Communists. Border clashes between USSR and China. Riots in Argentina.
1970 Civil war in Jordan. Coup in Syria. Nigerian civil war ends. Khmer Republic established in Cambodia, US troops invade, withdraw. Presidential elections in Mexico and Chile.
1971 Vietnam fighting spills over into Cambodia and Laos. Coup in Uganda. Civil war between East and West Pakistan, India intervenes, independent Bengali state of Bangaladesh formed. State of emergency in Ceylon. China admitted to UN, Taiwan expelled. Haiti dictator dies, son succeeds.
1972 Civil war in Lebanon. Israeli Olympic Games athletes killed by Palestinian terrorists. Ceylon becomes Republic of Sri Lanka. Pakistan leaves British Commonwealth. Uganda expels Asians. Nationalization policy in Chile. US president visits China.
1973 US withdraws from Vietnam. Military coup in Chile, president killed. Arab-Israeli war, Arabs impose oil embargo on Western nations supporting Israel.
1974 Portuguese African colonies of Angola, Guinea-Bissau, and Mozambique independent. Revolution in Ethiopia.
1975 South Vietnam surrenders to North, ending war. Communist victories in Cambodia. Laos becomes Communist state. State of emergency in India. Coup in Bangladesh. Suez Canal reopened. Civil war in Angola, South Africa intervenes. Fighting between factions in Lebanon. Papua New Guinea independent.
1976 Nigerian leader assassinated. Major riots in South African townships, so-called independent homelands created. Spain withdraws from Western Sahara, partition between Morocco and Mauretania resisted. Chinese leader Mao Zedong dies. Syrian troops enter Lebanon. Coup in Thailand. Reign of terror in Cambodia (Kampuchea). Military coup in Argentina.
1977 Conflict between Ethiopia and Somalia. Crack-down on anti-apartheid organizations in South Africa, leading to UN arms embargo. Egyptian president visits Israel. Massacres of political opponents in Uganda revealed. Pakistan constitution suspended. Riots in Sri Lanka.
1978 Israeli-Lebanese border incidents, UN force sent. Secession movement in Ethiopia. Uganda invades Tanzania. Diplomatic relations established between US and China, US links with Taiwan severed. China and Japan sign treaty of friendship. Scandal over use of political funds in South Africa.
1979 Islamic republic in Iran, Islamic fundamentalists riot in Mecca. Coups in Uganda, Central African Republic, and Ghana. Egypt and Israel sign peace treaty in US. Britain resumes control of Rhodesia pending elections. Coup in Afghanistan backed by USSR. China invades Vietnam. Vietnam invades Kampuchea. Former Pakistan prime minister executed. Grenada regime ousted. Reformist coups in Nicaragua and El Salvador. US embassy personnel taken hostage in Iran.
1980 Islamic states condemn USSR invasion of Afghanistan. Rhodesia becomes independent Zimbabwe. US attempt to rescue US embassy personnel in Iran fails. War between Iran and Iraq (to 1988). Radical Communist leaders tried in China. Civil war in El Salvador after archbishop murdered. Maoist insurgents in Peru. Chile bans political parties. Violence during Jamaica elections.
1981 Iran frees US hostages. Israel annexes Golan Heights. Coup in Ghana. Egyptian president assassinated. State of emergency in Sri Lanka. Attempted coup fails in Thailand. Philippines lifts martial law.
1982 Civil war in El Salvador. Argentina seizes Falkland Islands, surrenders after defeat by British expeditionary force. Joint US and Honduran military exercises put pressure on Nicaragua. Civilians massacred in Guatemala, military coup. Iran invades Iraq. Israel invades

continued

Events continued

4631 southern Lebanon, refugee Palestinians in camps massacred by Lebanese Christian militia. Coups in Kenya and Uganda foiled. New constitution in China.
1983 US embassy, French, and US military headquarters bombed in Lebanon, civil war intensifies. Iran recaptures territory lost to Iraq. Drought and famine in Ethiopia, international response. Philippines opposition leader returns from exile, assassinated. Korean airliner shot down by USSR. Violent clashes in Sri Lanka. Sikh terrorism in Punjab area of India. US troops invade Grenada. Military rule in Argentina ends. Coup in Guatemala.
1984 Iran-Iraq war again escalates, Iran attacks foreign oil tankers in Persian Gulf. Tri-racial parliament in South Africa. Agreement between Britain and China on future of Hong Kong. Indian troops storm Sikh temple, prime minister assassinated. Border clashes between India and Pakistan. Conflict escalates in Sri Lanka. Attempted coup in Thailand.
1985 Israel withdraws forces from Lebanon. Middle East peace process halted by hijackings. Coups in Nigeria, Sudan, and Uganda. US air attack on Libya. Further border clashes between India and Pakistan. US trade embargo against Nicaragua. Opposition to military rule in Chile grows.
1986 New coup in Uganda. South African raids into Botswana, Zambia, Zimbabwe. State of emergency in South Africa, US trade sanctions. Campaign for greater democracy in China, student demonstrations. Terrorist attacks in Sri Lanka. Calls for end of military regime in Pakistan. Presidential elections in Philippines, coup attempts follow. Haiti dictator flees. Political prisoners killed in Peru. Guerrilla groups and death-squads in Colombia.
1987 Palestinians on West Bank and in Gaza rise against Israeli occupation. Britain and US increase naval activity in Persian Gulf. Iranian Islamic fundamentalists again riot in Mecca. Coup in Tunisia. Backlash against reform in China, agreement with Portugal on future of Macao. India imposes emergency rule in Punjab. Indian troops invited into Sri Lanka. New constitution in Philippines, attempted coup suppressed. US suspends aid to Nicaraguan opposition groups, puts pressure on Panama military leader.
1988 US warship shoots down Iranian airliner. UN sponsors peace plan for Afghanistan, USSR troops begin withdrawal. Palestinian leader calls for independence, with Israel's right to exist, and recognition. Iran-Iraq war ends. Kurds massacred in Iraq. Pakistan election following death of president. Riots in Burma, elections promised. Military rule in Haiti. Military coup fails in Argentina. US charges Panama military leader with drug offences.
1989 USSR troops complete withdrawal from Afghanistan, fighting continues between Marxist government and Muslim opponents. Iranian spiritual leader dies. Coup in Sudan. Death of Japanese emperor, political scandals topple ministry. Student pro-democracy demonstrations in China suppressed, many die. Vietnam forces begin to leave Cambodia. Indian forces withdraw from Sri Lanka. Pakistan rejoins British Commonwealth. Coup in Paraguay. Death squads increase in El Salvador. Peace negotiations in Nicaragua. Colombia attempts anti-drug mafia measures. US invades Panama, military leader seized and extradited to US.
1990 South Africa frees Black leaders, discussions on political future. South West Africa independent as Namibia. Riots in Kenya. Sudan clashes. Nigeria coup fails. South Africa legalizes Communist Party. Iraq invades, annexes Kuwait, Arab and Western nations send in troops (to 1991). Strikes in Nepal lead to promise of liberalization. Pakistan government overthrown. Attempted coups foiled in Afghanistan and Philippines. China lifts martial law in Tibet. Western hostages freed in Lebanon. Riots in Jerusalem. Elections in Nicaragua, ceasefire, US lifts sanctions. Chile dictatorship ends. State of siege in Haiti. Former Panamanian military leader on trial in US. Widow of former Philippines president on trial.

People

4632 **Allende, Salvador** 1908–73 Chilean politician. Socialist Party secretary 1943, senator 1945. President 1970. Died during US-backed military coup.
Amin, Idi b.1925, Ugandan dictator. Came to power 1971, rule marked by brutality and massacres. Ordered mass expulsion of Asians 1972. Overthrown 1979 and fled to Libya.
Aquino, Corazón b.1933, Philippine politician. Entered politics 1985 following assassination of husband Benigno 1983. Elected president 1986, survived six attempted coups. Presidency confirmed by referendum 1987.

1

Arafat, Yasser b.1929, Palestinian leader. Founded al-Fatah 1956, chairman of PLO 1969 (**1**). Policies more moderate since 1973. Backed 1990 Iraqi invasion of Kuwait.
Assad, Hafez Ali b.1928, Syrian ruler. Defence minister 1966. Mounted coup 1970. President since 1971.
Banda, Hastings b.1906, African nationalist. President of Nyasaland African National Congress 1958. Imprisoned 1959–60. Prime Minister of Malawi 1963. President 1966.
Bandaranaike, Sirimavo b.1916, Sri Lankan politician. Prime minister 1960–5, 1970–7. Created republican constitution of 1972. World's first woman prime minister.
Batista, Fulgencio 1901–73, Cuban dictator. Led 1933 military coup, developed fascist state. President 1940–4, 1954–9. Fled as Castro gained support.
Begin, Menachem 1913–1992, Polish-born Israeli politician (**2**). Headed Betar 1939, imprisoned by USSR 1940–1. Led Irgun 1943–8. Founded Herut movement 1948. Joint chairman Likud Party from 1973. Prime minister 1977–83. Nobel Peace Prize 1978.
Ben Bella, Ahmed b.1919, Algerian revolutionary leader. President FLN 1952–62. Prime minister 1962–5. Deposed by military coup 1965, under house arrest 1965–80.
Ben-Gurion, David 1886–1973 Polish-born Zionist leader and Israeli statesman. Settled in Palestine 1906. Chairman Jewish Agency 1935–48. Prime minister 1949–53, 1955–63.
Bhutto, Benezir b.1953, Pakistani politician, daughter of Zulifar Bhutto. Prime minister 1988–90.
Bhutto, Zulfikar Ali 1928–79, Pakistani politician. Foreign minister 1963–6. President 1971–3. Prime minister 1973–7. Ousted by military coup 1977, executed 1979.
Biko, Steve 1946–77, South African Black nationalist radical leader. Co-founder South African Students' Organization, Black People's Convention 1968. Arrested 1977, died in police custody.
Botha, Pieter (Pik) b.1916, South African politician. Entered National Party government 1935, party leader 1978–89. Prime minister 1978–84. President 1984–9. Resigned from National Party 1989.
Bourguiba, Habib b.1903, Tunisian nationalist leader. Formed Neo-Destour Party 1934, imprisoned by French. President 1957–87. Deposed 1987.
Castro, Fidel b.1926, Cuban revolutionary Marxist leader (**3**). Imprisoned 1953, led abortive revolts against Batista regime 1956, 1958, successful coup 1959. Prime minister 1959–76. President 1976–
Dalai Lama (Tenzin Gyatso) b.1935, Tibetan spiritual leader (**4**), 14th holder of office 1940. Left Tibet 1959 following Chinese invasion. Nobel Peace Prize 1989.

2

3

4

continued

People continued

4632

5

6

7

Dayan, Moshe 1915–81, Israeli general and politician (**5**). Chief of staff 1953–8, led Sinai assault 1956. Agriculture minister 1959–64, defence minister 1967–4, led forces 1967 in Six Days War. Foreign minister 1977-9.
Deng Xiao Ping b.1904, Chinese Communist leader. Purged 1966, reinstated 1969, vice-premier 1975. Ordered Tiananmen Square attack, retired 1989. Purged 1976–7.
Duvalier, François (Papa Doc) 1907–71, Haitian dictator 1957–71 ruling by terror.
Duvalier, Jean-Claude (Baby Doc) b.1951, Haitian dictator 1971–86. Succeeded father 1971. Forced into exile by popular unrest and military coup.
Faisal, King b. 1906, r1964–75 Saudi Arabian monarch. Crown Prince 1953, prime minister 1953. Competed for power with King Saud 1958–64. Proclaimed king 1964. Conservative in policy, he built up country's oil revenue. Assassinated.
Farouk, King b.1920 r1936–52 d1965 Egyptian monarch increasingly anti-British 1944–52. Personal extravagence and military failure to defeat Israel led to overthrow by military coup 1952.
Galtieri, Leopoldo b.1927, Argentine president and dictator 1981–2. Ordered invasion of Falkland Islands 1982, military failure led to removal from power.
Gandhi, Indira 1917–84 Indian politician, daughter of Jawaharlal Nehru (**6**). Joined Congress Party 1955, leader 1959–69, 1971–84. Prime minister 1966–77, 1980–4. Assassinated by Sikh bodyguards.
Gandhi, Rajiv 1944–91 Indian politician, son of Indira Gandhi, grandson of Nehru. Entered politics on death of elder brother Sanjay 1980. Prime minister 1984–9. Assassinated by Tamil separatist.
Guevara, Ernesto (Che) 1928–67, Argentinian Communist revolutionary leader. Joined Castro 1956. Cuban minister for industry 1959–65. Led guerrilla group into Bolivia 1966–67, killed by government troops.
Hammarskjold, Dag 1905–61, Swedish statesman. Secretary-General of United Nations 1953–61. Greatly assisted resolution of Suez crisis 1956, mediated in Congo crisis 1960–1. Killed in plane crash. Posthumous Nobel Peace Prize 1961.
Hawke, Robert b.1929, Australian politician and trade unionist. MP 1980, prime minister 1983–91.
Ho Chi Minh (Nguyen That Thanh) 1890–1969, Vietnamese revolutionary nationalist leader (**7**). Founded Communist Party of Indo-China 1930, organised Vietminh opposition to Japan during Second World War. President of Vietnam 1945–54, president of North Vietnam 1954–69.
Hussein, King b.1935 r1952, Jordanian monarch. Western-educated with policies at divergence with those of most of neighboring Arab states. One of the region's great survivors.
Hussein, Saddam b.1937, Iraqi dictator. President from 1979, pursuing extermination policies against Kurd and Shi'ite minorities. At war with Iran 1980–8. Invaded and annexed Kuwait 1990 but forced to withdraw 1991.
Kaunda, Kenneth b.1924, Zambian leader. Leader of African National Congress 1949–58, imprisoned. Founder of United National Independence Party 1960. Elected president 1964, assumed autocratic powers 1972, reaffirmed as president under new constitution 1973. In 1980 he survived an attempted coup, but in 1990 he was forced to accept a multiparty political system after widespread demonstrations. In 1991 he was replaced by Frederick Chiluba.
Kenyatta, Jomo 1893–1978 Kenyan nationalist leader (**8**). Imprisoned 1952–61 on suspicion of organizing Mau Mau rebellion. Negotiated Kenyan independence 1963. Prime minister 1963. President 1964–78.
Khomeini, Ayatollah 1900–89 Iranian fundamentalist Islamic leader. Exiled 1964 for opposition to Shah's westernization and modernization policies. Returned to Iran 1979. Severed relations with West, enforced Shi'ite fundamentalism and waged 1980–8 war with Iraq.
Kim Il Sung b.1912, North Korean soldier and politician. Prime minister 1948–72, instituting Korean War 1950–3. President from 1972. Stalinist policies, cultivating personality cult and proclaiming son Kim Jong as successor.
Klerk, F W de b.1936, South African politician. Leader of National Party and country's president 1989. Policy of dismantling apartheid criticized as too little and too slow by many Black activists and too much and too fast by White right-wing extremists. Legalized ANC 1990.
Lee Kuan Yew b.1923, Singapore statesman. Founded Socialist People's Action Party 1954. Prime minister from 1959. Authoritative regime but considerable economic achievements.
Lin Biao 1907–1, Chinese Communist military leader. Communist Party member from 1925, army leader on Long March, against Japanese, against Kuomintang. Led Chinese armies in Korean War 1950–52. Marshal 1955, defence minister 1959. Nominated as successor to Mao Zedong 1966. Allegedly died in plane crash after attempting coup 1971.
Liu Shaoqi 1898–1974, Chinese Communist leader. Elected to party central committee 1927, vice-chairman 1949. Chairman of republic 1959–68. Position weakened during Cultural Revolution through emphasis on workers rather than peasantry. Stripped of all offices 1968.
Lumumba, Patrice 1925–61, Zairean politician. Prime minister and defence minister 1960, favoring central government rather than federation. Arrested and allegedly captured and shot by Katangan rebels.
Malan, Daniel 1874–1959, South African politician. Preacher in Dutch Reformed Church 1905–15. Nationalist MP 1918. Prime minister 1948–54. Intensely Afrikaner nationalist, opposing South African involvement in World War II. Instituted apartheid 1948–50.
Mandela, Nelson b.1918, South African Black nationalist leader and lawyer. Member of ANC executive from 1948 advocating multi-racial democracy and non-terrorist violent action. Arrested, imprisoned 1963, sentenced to life imprisonment 1964. Refused pardon in return for renunciation of political violence 1986. Released 1990. Second wife Winnie controversial for political activities.
Manley, Michael b.1924, Jamaican statesman. Leader of People's National Party 1969. Prime minister 1972–80, 1989–. Radical policies gradually moderated. Third World(qv) spokesman.
Marcos, Ferdinand 1917–89, Philippines politician. President 1965–86, prime minister 1973–86. Declared martial law 1972. Corrupt and oppressive regime. Overthrown by Corazón Aquino in peaceful coup after rigged elections 1986, and exiled. Wife Imelda renowned for influence and extravagant lifestyle.
Meir, Golda 1898–1978 Russian-born, US-educated Israeli stateswoman (**9**). Labor Party activist 1921–48. Minister to USSR 1948. Labor

8

9

continued

People continued

4632 minister 1949–56, foreign minister 1956–65. Prime minister 1969–74. Attempted to maintain peace with Arab nations through diplomacy, support eroded through 1973 war.

Mobutu, Sese Seko (formerly Joseph Désiré) b.1930, Zairean dictator. Chief of staff 1960–1. Commander 1961–5. President 1965, assuming additional olffices of prime minister and defence minister 1966. Regime notoriously corrupt.

Mugabe, Robert b.1924, Zimbabwean Marxist politician. Joined ZAPU 1961, arrested 1962, fled to Tanzania, formed ZANU 1963. Imprisoned 1964–74. Led guerrilla campaign 1976–9. Prime minister from 1980. President from 1987. Merged ZANU with ZAPU 1988 to create one-party state

Mujibur Rahman, Sheikh 1920–75, Bangladeshi politician. Led Awami League to electoral victory 1970. Proclaimed independence from Pakistan 1971. Prime minister 1972–5 following war of independence. President 1975 but assassinated with family during military coup.

Mussadeq, Mohammed 1880–1967, Iranian politician. Foreign minister 1922–4. Returned to parliament 1942, prime minister 1951–3. Violently nationalist, promoting nationalization of oil industry. Overthrown by coup encouraged by Shah and with western aid 1953.

10

Nasser, Gamal 1918–70, Egyptian nationalist leader (**10**). Fought in 1948 Arab-Israeli War. Founded officers' group which overthrew king Farouk 1952. Ousted Neguib 1954. Prime minister 1954–6, president 1956–70. Nationalization policies led to Suez crisis of 1956. Fostered Arab unity, instigated Aswan Dam and other civic projects.

Neguib, Mohammed 1901–84, Egyptian nationalist leader. Leader in officers' group which overthrew King Farouk 1952. President 1952–54 until ousted by Nasser and placed under house arrest.

Ne Win, U b.1911, Burmese military and political leader. Chief of staff with collaborationist army during Japanese occupation 1942–4, led guerrillas supporting Allies 1944–5. Army commander 1948–58. Prime minister 1958–60. Seized power in 1962 coup to create one-party state. President 1974–81. Resigned from politics following demonstrations and violent suppression 1988.

Ngo Dinh Diem 1901–63. Vietnamese politician. Provincial governor 1929–32, becoming increasingly anti-French. Founded anti-colonial anti-Communist National Union Front 1947, banned and exiled. Prime minister 1954–5. President of South Vietnam 1955–63. Assassinated in engineered coup.

Nkomo, Joshua b.1917, Zimbabwean politician. ANC president 1957–9, exiled 1959–60. National Democratic Party president 1960–2, president of ZAPU 1961–87. Imprisoned 1963–74. Joint leader with Mugabe of Patriotic Front guerrilla movement 1976–9. Minister for home affairs 1980–1. Tribal differences ended cooperation with Mugabe 1982. Vice-president merged ZANU/ZAPU 1987.

Nkrumah, Kwame 1909–72, Ghanaian nationalist leader. Prime minister 1952–60. President 1960–6. Overthrown by military coup while in China 1966, in exile until death. Lenin Peace Prize 1962.

Noriega, Manuel b.1934, Panamanian dictator. Chief of intelligence agency 1969, chief of armed forces 1981, virtual dictator 1983–9. Indicted in US on drugs racketeering charges 1988. Survived coup attempt, fled US invasion mission 1989. Surrendered to US, extradited and charged 1990.

Nyerere, Julius b.1922, Tanzanian statesman. Founder member Tanganyika African National Union. Prime minister 1961–2, president 1962–4. Negotiated union with Zanzibar to form Tanzania. President 1964-85. Ended Amin's Ugandan dictatorship through invasion 1978.reform Tanzania. President 1965–85. Ended Amin's Ugandan dictatorship through invasion 1978.

Obote, Milton b.1924, Ugandan politician. Prime minister 1962–6. President 1966–71. Overthrown by Amin while in Singapore 1971. Returned with dissidents aided by Tanzanian army 1979. President 1980–5. Overthrown and exiled 1985.

Ortega Saavedra, Daniel b.1945, Nicaraguan politician. Underground activist against Somoza regime 1959–66. Imprisoned 1969–74. Fought successful guerrilla campaign 1977–9. Member of reconciliation junta 1979. President 1989–90.

Perón, Eva 1919–52, Argentine actress, married Juan Perón 1945. Politically astute, co-governed with husband 1946–52, built up immense popular following. Died of cancer.

Perón, Isabel b.1931, Argentine dancer, second wife of Juan Perón. Vice-president 1973–4, president 1974–6, ousted by military coup.

11

Perón, Juan 1895–1974, Argentine politician. Nationalist and self-sufficiency policies (**11**). President 1946–55. In exile following increasingly repressive regime. Reelected 1973. Died in office.

Pinochet Ugarte, Augusto b.1915, Chilean military leader. Army chief of staff 1972. Led right-wing military coup 1973. President of government 1973–4. Commander-in-chief 1973–80. President of country 1974–89. Repressive political regime. Rule rejected by 1988 referendum but retained control of armed forces.

Pol Pot (Saloth Sar) b.1928, Cambodian Communist leader. Communist Party member 1946, secretary 1963. Organized Kampuchea Khmer Rouge guerrillas, captured capital Phnom Penh 1975. Prime minister 1976–9 as Maoist dictator, millions died. Overthrown by Vietnamese invasion 1979. Resumed guerrilla war with Chinese support 1982–5. Renewed attempts to regain power 1989.

Qaddafi, Muammar al- b.1942, Libyan dictator. Came to power through 1969 coup, president from 1977. Open supporter of terrorist groups, leading to 1986 air attacks by US.

Sadat, Anwar 1919–81 Egyptian military leader. Member of officers' group which overthrew monarchy 1952, served under Nasser 1954–70. President 1970–81. Dismissed USSR advisers 1972. After 1973 sought peaceful solution to Arab-Israeli problem, visiting Israel 1977, signing peace 1979. Assassinated by Islamic fundamentalist soldiers 1981. Nobel Peace Prize 1978.

Senghor, Leopold b.1906, Senegalese poet and politician. Developed concept of Black culture in Paris 1930s. President of Senegal 1960–80. Conciliated Muslims, kept French support through anti-Marxist pronouncements.

Shamir, Yitzhak b.1915, Israeli politician. Prime minister 1983–4, foreign minister 1984–6, prime minister 1986–8. Hard line policies against Palestinians in Israeli-occupied territories.

Sihanouk, Prince Norodom b.1922, Cambodian leader. Head of state 1960–70. Deposed 1970, organized resistance from exile 1970–5. Returned to power 1975–6. Renewed claim to be country's legitimate leader 1982.

Smith, Ian b.1919, Rhodesian politician. Elected to assembly 1948, founded right-wing White Rhodesia Front 1962. Prime minister 1964–79. Declared country's unilateral independence 1965. Forced to negotiate settlement giving Black majority rule 1976–9. Minister in Zimbabwe government 1979–80.

Somoza, Anastasio 1925–80 Nicaraguan dictator. Succeeded assassinated father as president 1967–72, 1974–9. Imposed martial law 1972. Overthrown by guerrilla forces 1979, having lost US support through human rights violations. Assassinated in exile 1980.

Sukarno, Ahmed 1901–70 Indonesian nationalist leader. Founded Nationalist Party 1928, exiled by Dutch 1933–42, led independence struggle 1945–9. President 1949–67 but power reduced by 1966 military coup.

Syngman Rhee 1875–1965 South Korean politician. President 1948–60 with corrupt and oppressive regime. Forced into exile 1960 by popular uprising.

Trujillo Molina, Rafael 1891–1961 Dominican military dictator. Led coup 1930. President 1930–61 with family in state offices. Assassinated by army officers.

continued

People continued

4632 **Tshombe, Moise** 1919–69, Congolese political leader. Worked towards loose federation within country after 1960 independence. Led Katangan separatists 1960–3. Prime minister and president 1964–5. Died in exile after treason charges.
Verwoerd, Hendrik 1901–66, South African politician. Put apartheid into practice 1950–7. Prime minister 1958–66. Took South Africa out of British Commonwealth 1961. Assassinated by White opponent 1966.
Vo Nguyen Giap 1912–86, North Vietnam general. Led forces against French 1951–4, against US 1965–75. Commander-in-chief and deputy prime minister 1976–86.
Vorster, Balthazar 1915–83, South African politician. Opposed Allies in World War II, imprisoned 1942–4. Minister of justice 1961–6, implementing apartheid. Prime minister 1966–78, president 1978–9, adapting more conciliatory approach. Forced to resign following political scandal.
Weizmann, Chaim 1874–1952, Russian-born Zionist and Israeli statesman. Adviser for Balfour Declaration 1917. President World Zionist Organization 1920–9, 1939–46. First president of Israel 1949–52.
Whitlam, Gough b.1916, Australian politician. Labor Party prime minister 1972–4, 1974–5. Dismissed by governor-general Sir John Kerr for refusing to call election. retired from parliament 1978.

Zia ul-Haq, Mohammed 1924–88, Pakistani general and politician. Led 1977 military coup overthrowing Bhutto. President 1978–88. Ordered Bhutto's execution 1979. Presidency confirmed by referendum 1984. Killed in air crash (**12**).

Places

4633 **Amritsar city** In Punjab, Golden Temple centre of Sikh religion. Storming of temple by Indian army in 1985 to flush out separatists led to assassination of prime minister Indira Gandhi.
Biafra Eastern Nigerian region which attempted secession 1967–70. Devastated by famine 1968–70.
Chatila Lebanon refugee camp for Palestinian refugees from Israeli-occupied territories. Scene, with Sabra, of 1982 massacre by Lebanese militia with tacit Israeli support.
Dien Bien Phu Vietnamese village. Site of 1954 battle in which French troops were routed by Viet Minh under Vo Nyguyen Giap leading to loss of Indo China empire.
Entebbe Ugandan airport. Scene of Israeli commando raid after Palestinian terrorists hijacked French aircraft 1976.
Eritrea North Ethiopian province federated 1952, secessionist movements since 1974 violently suppressed. Famines 1973, 1983–5, 1987.
Gaza Strip Israeli-occupied Egyptian territory. Many refugees following creation of Israel 1948, harsh Egyptian rule 1948–67. Captured by Israel 1967, under military rule. Many subsequent Jewish settlements, much Arab unrest.
Golan Heights Israeli-occupied Syrian territory. Strategically important. Captured by Israel 1967.
Kashmir Land disputed by India and Pakistan since 1947. North-west under Pakistani control as Azad Kashmir, rest incorporated into India as Jammu and Kashmir 1956.
Katanga Congo province rich in minerals attempting to secede from newly independent Zaire 1960–2. Violence continued to 1967.
Kurdistan Mountainous area of east Turkey, north Iraq, north-west Iran, and south-east Armenia claimed as autonomous homeland by nomadic Kurdish people, a persecuted minority in all these countries.
Namibia Formerly South West Africa. Guerrilla campaign for independence led by SWAPO from bases in Angola and Zambia. UN-supervized ceasefire 1989 leading to independence 1990.
Sabra: see Chatila, above.
Sharpeville South African township where police fired on demonstration 1960. Many died, leading to state of emergency.
Sinai Egyptian mountainous area occupied by Israel 1967, partly returned 1975.
Soweto South African township where riots occurred 1976 following attempt to make Afrikaans compulsory in schools.
Suez Canal Egyptian nationalization 1956 led to British, French, and Israeli intervention. UN organized ceasefire and reopening, British and French withdrew, Israelis kept Sinai.
Tiananmen Square Beijing main square where students' pro-democracy demonstrations in 1989 were brutally suppressed by government troops, many died.
Transkei South African province nominally independent Bantu homeland 1963, 1976. Not recognized internationally.
West Bank of River Jordan, including Jerusalem. Annexed by Jordan 1948, captured by Israel 1967. Scene of increasing unrest as extremist Jewish settlements set up and Arab demonstrations proliferate.

Words

4634 **ANC** African National Congress. Political pressure group, especially in South Africa. Banned and leaders imprisoned 1964–90.
ANZUS Australia, New Zealand, and US Pacific security treaty signed 1951. New Zealand withdrew 1985.
Arab League Organization of independent Arab states formed 1945 to promote military, economic, political, and cultural cooperation.
Azania Black nationalist name for South Africa.
Baghdad Pact Defence agreement between Turkey and Iraq 1955, joined by Britain, Pakistan, and Iran. US joined, Iraq withdrew 1959.
Bandung Conference Afro-Asian solidarity conferences 1955, 1965.
Central African Federation of Nyasaland, Northern and Southern Rhodesia 1953–63.
Contras Nicaraguan right-wing exiles conducting guerrilla campaign 1979–90 with covert arms supplies from US.
Cultural Revolution 1965–8 Chinese youth-led mass movement inspired by Mao Zedong to change popular ideology. Wrecked many lives and cultural institutions.
Dirty War Argentine military campaign against left-wing guerrilla groups and other opponents of regime 1976–82.
Eisenhower Doctrine 1957 US initiative to limit USSR influence in Middle East by economic and military aid.
FLN Front de Liberation Nationale Algerian nationalist political and military movement 1954–62.
Fatah, al- Syrian branch of PLO increasingly powerful after 1967.
Fatwa 1989 death sentence pronounced by fundamentalist Iranian leader on British writer Salman Rushdie for novel *The Satanic Verses* deemed blasphemous by devout Muslims.
Front Line States Black African presidents of Angola, Botswana, Mozambique, Tanzania, Zambia, and Zimbabwe seeking peace settlement in South Africa.
Gang of Four Radical Chinese Communist leaders, including widow of Mao Zedong, advocating revolutionary rather than economically pragmatic policies in power 1974–6. Tried and condemned 1980.
Great Leap Forward Chinese Communist attempt to accelerate agricultural collectivization 1958–61.
Intifada Arab name for uprising against Israeli occupation in Gaza Strip and West Bank.
Irgun Jewish terrorist organization 1931–48 active against British Mandate.
Khmer Rouge Cambodian Communist guerrilla forces 1970–89 led by Pol Pot.
Likud Israeli right-wing political alliance winning elections in 1977, 1988.
Maoism Marxist ideology emphasizing peasantry rather than proletariat as main force for revolutionary change propounded by Mao Zedong (1893–1976).
Mau Mau Kenyan Black militant and terrorist movement 1952–60.
Mujaheddin Afghan Islamic guerrillas 1979–90 fighting USSR invasion in support of Marxist government.
Muldergate South African 1978 scandal over alleged misuse of state funds by information minister Mulder leading to 1979 resignation of president Vorster.

continued

Words continued

4634 **OAU** Organization of African Unity set up 1963 accepting inherited colonial borders and mediating successfully in many disputes.
PLO Palestine Liberation Organization founded 1964 in Jordan and dominated by Syria. Led by Arafat. Has mounted attacks on Israeli-occupied territory. Involved in international terrorism. Not recognized by Israel.
Pathet Lao Laotian rebel movement established 1949. Aided Viet Minh 1953. Fought against government forces 1959–75. Effective government since 1975.
Red Guards Chinese students, wearing red armbands, who took a prominent role in 1965–9 Cultural Revolution.
SEATO South-East Asia Treaty Organization set up in 1954 by Australia, Britain, France, New Zealand, Pakistan, Philippines, Thailand, and US to combat Communist expansion. Dissolved 1977.
SWAPO South West Africa People's Organization. Black independence movement founded 1959. Guerrilla activities from 1966. Banned 1978 but continued activities from across border to 1989.
Sandinistas Nicaraguan opposition group waging guerrilla war against Somoza regime and achieving political power 1979. Defeated in 1990 elections.
Shining Path Maoist guerrilla group in Peru 1980–2, active and still in existence.
Six Day War 1967 conflict between Israel and Arab states. Egypt blockaded Gulf of Aqaba, Israel bombed Egypt, Iraq, Jordan, and Syria, reached Suez Canal and captured West Bank and Golan Heights.
Tamil Tigers Sri Lankan separatist guerrillas 1981–90, leading terrorist raids and opposing intervention by Indian troops.
Tet Offensive Communist North Vietnamese attacks on South Vietnam capital during 1968 lunar festival.
Third World Underdeveloped and poorer nations of Africa, Asia, and Latin America neither part of capitalist West nor Communist East, but often regarded as a proving ground and sphere of influence by both.
UAR United Arab Republic 1958–1961 short-lived union of Egypt with Syria.
UDI Unilateral Declaration of Independence by White Southern Rhodesian government in 1965 to avoid moves towards Black majority rule.
Vietcong Communist guerrilla forces in South Vietnam 1954–73, 1975–6.
Viet Minh North Vietnam Communist political group formed 1941 by Ho Chi-minh. Forces entered Hanoi to form government 1945. Became part of Vietnam Workers' Party 1951.
Yom Kippur War 1973 Egyptian and Syrian attack on Israel during religious festival. Israel counter-attacked and UN mediated ceasefire.
ZANU Zimbabwe African National Union formed 1963 by Mugabe. Incorporated ZAPU (below) 1989.
ZAPU Zimbabwe African People's Union formed 1962 by Nkomo. Defeated in 1980 elections and merged with ZANU (above) 1989.

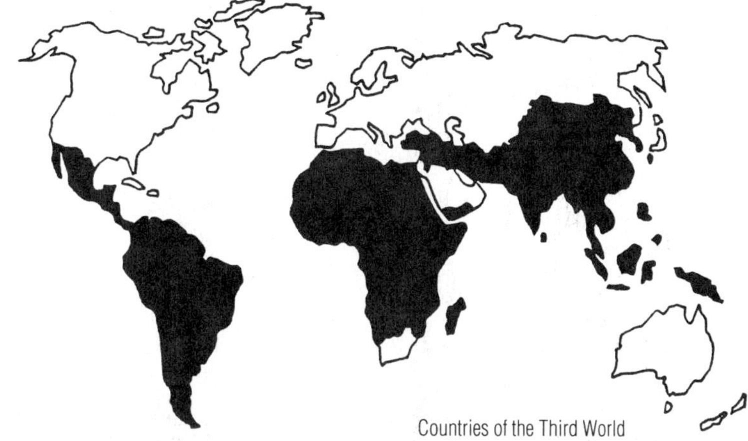
Countries of the Third World

464 AFRICA 1945–1990s

Mediterranean and arid north

4641

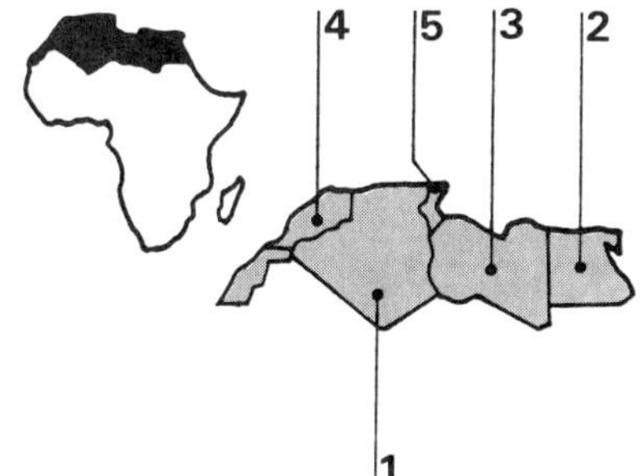

1 ALGERIA
French colony from 1842 to 1962
1954 War for independence led by Moslem Front de Liberation Nationale (FLN).
1962 Jul 3 Independence day. FLN in power.
1963 Sep Ben Bella elected first president of Republic.
1965 Jun Military coup by Colonel Houari Boumédienne.
1976 Nov Referendum establishes new constitution.
1978 Dec Boumédienne dies.
1979 Jan M. Bendjedid Chadli elected President. Ben Bella released from house arrest. FLN take on new party structure.
1981 Algeria helps secure release of US prisoners in Iran.
1983 Dec Chadli re-elected.
1988 Government policies provoke riots; 170 killed. Reform program introduced.
1990 Fundamentalist Islamic Salvation Front (FIS) wins elections.
1991 State of emergency declared after clashes between government and FIS.
1992 Jan Military government seizes power. Feb Riots. Emergency rule imposed.

2 EGYPT
British protectorate from 1914 to 1936.
1936 Independence. King Fuad succeeded by son Farouk.
1946 British troops remain in Suez Canal Zone. Rest withdrawn.
1952 Jul Military coup. Farouk ousted by army.
1953 General Muhammad Naguib becomes president. Egypt becomes republic.
1954 Naguib replaced by Colonel Gamal Nasser. Egypt attacked by Israel, Britain, and France. UN negotiates ceasefire and Anglo-France withdrawal.
1970 Colonel Anwar Sadat becomes President.
1973 Failed attempt to regain Sinai and Gaza Strip from Israel leads to renewed fighting. Henry Kissinger (US) arranges ceasefire.
1978–1979 USA Camp David talks. Egypt and Israel agree end to 31-year old hostilities.
1981 Oct Sadat assassinated. Hosni Mubarak succeeds him.
1987 Apr Mubarak re-elected.
1991 Military support to US in Persian Gulf War.

3 LIBYA
1911 Conquered by Italy.
1912 Sovereignty passed to Italy by Turkey
1929 Colony named Libya.
1942 Divided into three provinces: Fezzar (under French), Cyrenaica and Tripolitania (under British).
1951 Dec 24 Independence day. Declared United Kingdom of Libya by UN. King Idris in power.
1969 Sep Revolution: monarchy overthrown. Country declared republic. Revolutionary Command Council, under Colonel Muammar Qaddafi, in office. Arab Socialist Union (ASU) proclaimed only legal party.

continued

Mediterranean and arid north continued

4641

3 LIBYA
1972 Proposed federation of Libya, Syria, and Egypt dropped.
1980 Proposed merger with Syria falls through. Libyan troops begin fighting in Chad.
1986 US bombs Qaddafi's HQ after he is suspected of complicity in terrorist activities.
1988 Oct Libya and Chad resume diplomatic relations.
1989 Jan US shoots down two Libyan aircraft.
1992 Jan UN demands that Libya turn over suspected terrorists. Mar UN imposes sanctions against Libya.

4 MOROCCO
1912 Morocco divided into French and Spanish protectorates.
1956 Mar Sultanate of Morocco created after declarations made with France on Mar 2 and with Spain on Apr 7.
1957 Aug Sultan adopts title King Mohammad V.
1961 Feb Hassan II comes to throne.
1972 Mar New constitution: king gains executive power.
1975 Nov Spain gives up control of Western Sahara; Morocco, Mauretania, and Algeria fight for control.
1976 Guerrilla war in Western Sahara with Polisario Front. Diplomatic relations with Algeria broken.
1983 Morocco agrees to peace formula for Western Sahara, but refuses to negotiate with Polisario.
1988 May Diplomatic relations with Algeria restored.
1993 Mar Opposition parties boycott preparations for general elections.

5 TUNISIA
Colonized by the French from 1881 to 1956
1956 Mar 20 Tunisia becomes independent sovereign state.
1956 Apr Habib Bourguiba prime minister, Neo-Destour Party in office.
1957 Jul Constituent Assembly abolishes monarchy and elects Bourguiba first president of Republic.
1958 Feb French forces from Algeria attack Tunisian border.
1958 Oct Nearly all French troops withdrawn.
1969 Sep Ben Salah, unpopular minister, stripped of office.
1974–6 Hundreds of students jailed for plotting against state.
1975 Mar Bourguiba made president for life.
1985 Sep Diplomatic relations broken with Libya, after 90,000 Tunisians expelled from Libya.
1987 Sep Dispute resolved and diplomatic relations restored with Libya.
1987 Nov Ben Ali takes over as President.
1988 Jan 405 political prisoners released.
1988 Apr Multi-party system introduced.
1992 Islamic fundamentalist group (Nahda) banned.

Sudano-Sahel

4642

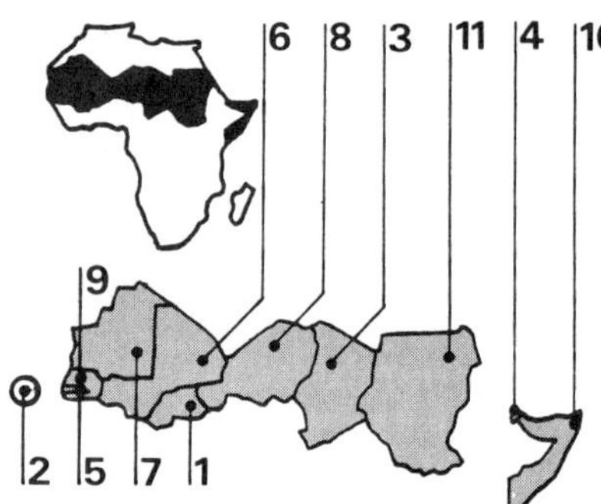

1 BURKINA FASO
French colony from 1896 to 1960. Formerly called Upper Volta.
1960 Aug 5 Independence day.
1960 Dec Maurice YamQogo becomes president.
1966 Jan Popular uprising topples YamQogò. Sangoula Lamizana takes over.
1974 Feb Military coup creates single-party government.
1975 Dec National strike sparked off by border dispute with Mali.
1978 Jul Joseph Conombo elected as prime minister.
1980 Nov Colonel Saye Zerbo overthrows Lamizana's government.
1982 Nov Successful military coup. Jean-Baptiste Ouédrago new head of government.
1983 Aug Prime Minister Sankara overthrows Ouédrago.
1984 Aug Country renamed Burkina Faso.
1987 Oct Blaise Compaore's Front Populaire seizes power.
1991 Jan Referendum approves new constitution.
1991–92 Compaore becomes president and Ouédrago prime minister.

2 CAPE VERDE
Portuguese colony from 1462 to 1975
1951 Cape Verde made an overseas province of Portugal.
1956 Amilcar Cabral founds the African Party for the Independence of Guinea and Cape Verde (PAIGC).
1974 Apr Downfall of Salazarist regime in Lisbon leads to mass support for PAIGC.
1975 Jul 5 Independence day. PAIGC in power.
1979 Apr PAIGC expels dissenting Trotskyists.
1980 Nov Jo]o Vieira takes power in Guinea-Bissau, putting an end to attempted unification with Cape Verde.
1981 Jan PAIGC renamed Partido Africano da Independencia de Cabo Verde (PAICV).
1991 Jan Transitional government formed, headed by opposition leader Carlos Veiga.

3 CHAD
Colonised by the French from 1890 to 1960
1958 The Union Nationale Tchadienne (UNT) formed.
1960 Aug 11 Independence day. Parti Progréssiste Tchadien (PPT) in office François Tombalbaye head of state.
1966 Jun The Chad National Liberation Front (FROLINAT) formed against Tombalbaye's military administration.
1975 Apr Tombalbaye toppled by Odingar.
1979 Apr Formation of Government of National Union.
1979 Nov New government set up, with Goukouni as President.
1980 Dec Habré's troops defeated by Libya.
1982 Jun Habré captures N'djamena.
1982 Oct Habré sworn in as President.
1984 Jun Habré forms the National Movement for Independence and Revolution (UNIR).
1987 Habré's forces liberate the whole of the north from Libya.
1990 Dec Government ousted by rebel forces. Idriss Deby new leader.

4 DJIBOUTI
French colony from 1862 to 1977
1949 First anti-colonial demonstration held by Somali nationalists.
1957 Territorial assembly set up.
1967 Mar Referendum in favor of unity with France leads to violent riots.
1970s Growth of African People's League for Independence (LPAI), first inter-ethnic party.
1976 Jul Resignation of Ali Aref, symbol of French domination.
1977 Jun 26 Independence day. Hassan Gouled and new inter-ethnic government in power.
1978 Sep Hassan Gouled heads new government.
1979 Mar New party, Rassemblement Populaire pour le Progrés (RPP), takes over role of LPAI.
1981 Jun First Presidential elections since independence. President Gouled stays in office.
1991 Violence quelled after guerrillas demand multiparty elections.
1992 Hassan Gouled wins first multiparty elections.

continued

Sudano-Sahel continued

4642 **5 GAMBIA, THE**
1783 British gain control of area.
1888 The Gambia becomes Crown Colony.
1948 First Gambian in Parliament.
1959 Formation of People's Progressive Party (PPP).
1961 Feb End of all-party government.
1963 Oct Self-government achieved. Head of PPP, Dawda K. Jawara, becomes prime minister.
1965 Feb 18 Independence day.
1970 Apr Gambia becomes republic. Sir Jawara made president.
1977 Severe drought.
1979 May PPP National Congress. Jawara remains secretary general.
1981 Jul Failed coup by low-ranking soldiers.
1982 May PPP win majority in free election.
1987 Mar Jawara wins election against The Gambia People's Party (GPP).
1992 Mar Government announces defeat of mercenary invasion.

6 MALI
1883 French capture Bamako and start colonization.
1946 Formation of Rassemblement Démocratique Africain (RDA).
1958 Creation of the Republique Soudanaise.
1960 Sep 22 The Soudan achieves independence and is renamed Mali. Modibo Keita President at head of Soudanese Union.
1968 Nov Peaceful coup. Keita falls and Lieutenant Moussa Traoré becomes head of state.
1974 New party: Democratic Union of the Malian People.
1979-80 Students go on strike.
1981 Sep Traoré pardons more than 40 prisoners.
1981 Dec Failed coup by 15 junior officers of gendarmerie.
1985 Dec Burkina Faso troops occupy Malian villages.
1986 Dec Mali and Burkina Faso agree to keep the peace at summit.
1991 Mar Traoré overthrown in coup.
1992 Jan Malians vote for multiparty constitution.

7 MAURITANIA
1903–1960 Ruled as a French protectorate.
1948 Founding of Union Progressiste Mauritanienne (UPM).
1960 Nov 28 Independence granted by French. Ould Daddah becomes president.
1961 Dec Daddah creates single Parti du Peuple Mauritanien (PPM).
1978 17,000 men in action against Polisario Front.
1978 Jul Comité Militaire de Redréssement National (CMRN) takes power, led by Ould Salek.
1979 Jun Salek resigns and is succeeded by Ould Louly.
1979 Aug Peace agreement with Polisaro Front.
1980 Jan Heydalla ousts Louly.
1984 Dec Heydalla overthrown by Taya.
1986 Jul Democratically elected councils.
1992 Violence mars presidential elections, the military claim victory.

8 NIGER
1890 French begin colonization.
1906 Present boundaries fixed.
1926 Niamey becomes new capital.
1946 Emergence of Niger Progressive Party (PPN), led by Hamani Diori.
1960 Aug 3 Independence day. Diori becomes president.
1964 Sawaba opposition attack frontiers.
1965 Attempted assassination of Diori.
1970 Great drought.
1974 Military coup by Lieutenant-Colonel Seyni Kountche.
1980 Uranium boom. Revenue shoots up.
1983 Oct Second attempted coup against Kountche.
1987 Nov Kountche dies. Ali Saibou takes over.
1988 Aug Saibou sets up Mouvement National pour une Societé de Developement (MNSD).
1991 Sep Government dissolved, transitional administration set up.

9 SENEGAL
1814 Britain turns over its territories in Senegal to France.
1892 French troops conquer most of Senegal's independent kingdoms.
1960 Aug 20 Independence day. Léopold Senghor is president.
1968 Strikes by students and workers union.
1978 Elections confirm power of Senghor and his Parti Socialiste.
1980 Senghor retires.
1981 Jan Abdou Diouf takes over as president.
1981 Apr Limit removed on number of political parties.
1982 Feb Formation of Senegambian Confederation.
1983 Electoral triumph for Diouf.
1986 Feb Death of Cheikh Anta Diop.
1988 Uprisings during elections. Diouf wins.
1991 National Assembly adopts constitutional amendments.

10 SOMALIA
Colonized by Britain, France, Italy, and Ethiopia from late 19th century.
1940 Italy occupies Somali Protectorate.
1941–2 Britain defeats Italy and takes over government.
1942 Birth of Somali Youth League, freedom movement.
1954-5 Ethiopia acquires the Haud and Reserved Areas. Violent response throughout Somali lands.
1960 Jul 1 Independence day. Civilian government.
1969 Oct Peaceful coup by Major-General Mohamed Siyad Barre. Supreme Revolutionary Council established.
1974 Famine precipitates collapse of Ethiopian administration.
1974 Feb Somali Democratic Republic joins Arab League.
1980 Stepping up of war (begun in 1977) between Ethiopian troops and pro-Somali guerrillas in the Ogaden.
1986 Barre and Ethiopia's Mengistu agree to try to resolve "areas of basic differences" between two countries.
1987 Unprovoked attack by Ethiopia during further peace talks.
1991 Barre flees from rebel factions. Ali Mahdi Mohammed interim president. North East Somalia recedes and forms Somalian Republic. Mohammed ousted by members of rival clan.
1992 Ceasefire. US organizes emergency famine relief.
1993 Jan Disease devastates refugee population.

11 SUDAN
British colony from 1898 to 1956
1877 Charles Gordon made governor general by Egypt.
1898 "Condominium" agreement with Egypt gives Britain political domination of Sudan.
1925 Birth of Gezira, huge-scale irrigated farming project.
1945 Formation of Umma (People's) Party by Mahdists.
1950 Formation of Sudan Workers' Trade Union Federation.
1956 Jan 1 Independence day. Umma Party in power.
1966 Reformist wing of Umma Party puts Sadiq al-Mahdi in power.
1969 Mar Colonel Jaafar el-Nimeiry seizes power in coup. He is supported by Sudanese Communist Party.
1983 Sep Nimeiry introduces Sharia Islamic law banning all alcohol and severely penalizing theft and adultery.
1985 Apr Army, under General Abdul Rahman Swaredahab, takes power and declares martial law.
1986 Apr Umma elected back into power. Al-Mahdi prime minister.
1989 Jul Bloodless military coup. Brigadier Omar El-Beshir becomes head of state.
1990 Oct US and other countries, outraged by Sudan's warring factions and support of Iraq, withhold food relief until spring 1991.
1991 Peace talks postponed.

Humid and subhumid west

4643

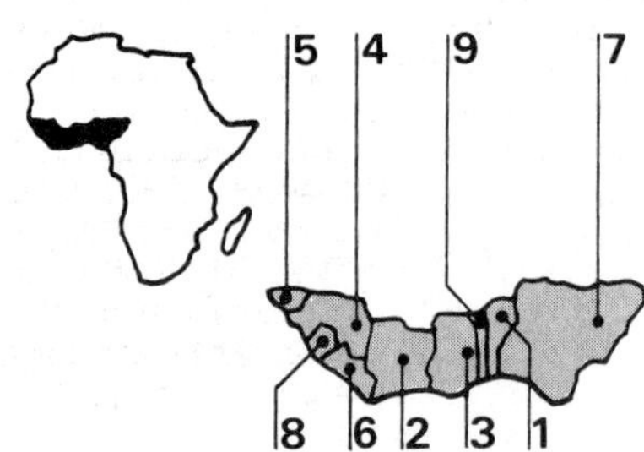

1 BENIN
French colony from 1894 to 1960. Formerly called Dahomey.
1960 Aug 1 Independence day. Hubert Maga becomes president.
1963 Oct Regime overthrown by Colonel Christophe Seglo.
1967 Seglo toppled by Lieutenant-Colonel Alphonse Alley.
1968 Emile Zinsou forms civilian government.
1969 Dec Kouandété's coup removes new civilian government.
1972 Oct Mathieu Kerekou takes power.
1972 Nov Kerekou establishes National Council of the Revolution.
1975 Nov Dahomey becomes People's Republic of Benin.
1977 Jan Failed military coup by Bob Denard.
1979 Nov First general election since 1972.
1980 Feb Kerekou made first president by new Assembly.
1982 Oil production starts.
1990 Aug New constitution proposed in national referendum.
1991 Mar First popularly elected president.

2 COTE D'IVOIRE
French colony from 1893 to 1960
1950-60 Parti Democratique de la Côte d'Ivoire (PDCI), led by Félix Houphouet-Boigny, moves to forefront of political arena.
1960 Aug 7 Independence day. Houphouet in power.
1968 Violent student protests.
1977 Major cabinet overhaul.
1980 Apr Failed coup. Oulai Zoumana arrested.
1980 Sep PDCI Congress lays down new democracy.
1985 Dec Diplomatic relations with Israel restored.
1986 Apr Jacques Chirac visits country.
1986 Oct Five Arab countries break diplomatic ties with Côte d'Ivoire.
1990 Jan Pope John Paul II dedicates controversial new Catholic basilica.
1990 May Pressure to remove Houphouet leads to hijacking of airport.
1991 First multiparty elections. Opposition accuses victorious ruling party of fraud.

3 GHANA
British colony from 1874 to 1957
1947 Kwame Nkrumah formed the Convention People's Party (CPP).
1950 Nkrumah sentenced for sedition.
1951 Nkrumah released from jail.
1957 Mar 6 Gold Coast gains independence. Renamed Ghana, with Nkrumah elected prime minister.
1960 Ghana becomes a republic. Nkrumah becomes president.
1966 Feb Nkrumah overthrown by coup. National Liberation Council (NIC) in power.
1969 Oct Return to civilian rule, Dr K A Busia's Progress Party in power.
1972 Jan Successful coup d'etat, Colonel I Acheampong rules with National Redemption Council.
1978 July Achaempong replaced by Lieutenant General F Akuffo.
1979 Flight Lieutenant JJ Rawlings seizes power and calls for elections in July.
1979 Sep Rawlings steps down. H Limann becomes president.
1981 Dec Rawlings is returned to power.
1983 1.2 million Ghanians expelled from Nigeria.
1992 Nov 3 Presidential elections, boycotted by the opposition, won by J J Rawlings.
1993 Jan 7 Civilian rule under Rawlings, leader of the National Democratic Congress (NDC).

4 GUINEA
French colony from 1893 to 1958
1958 Oct 2 Independence day. Sékou Touré president, Parti Démocratique de Guinea (PDG) in office.
1970 Nov 22 Portuguese troops and Guinean opponents fail in invasion attempt.
1978 Over 1,500 Russian experts working in the country.
1980 May Failed assassination attempt on Touré.
1984 Mar Death of President Touré.
1984 Apr Military coup. Colonel Lansana Conté becomes president.
1985 Jul Failed political coup by Diarra Traoré.
1986 Sep Cooperation treaty between neighboring countries Sierra Leone and Liberia.
1991 Oct Court agrees to multiparty politics.

5 GUINEA-BISSAU
1879 Portugal declares country a colony.
1973 Three-fourths of country now free from Portuguese rule.
1973 Sep 23 Independence unilaterally proclaimed.
1974 Sep Portugal recognizes independence. African Party for Independence for Guinea and Cape Verde (PAIGC) in power.
1978 Nov Small guerrilla uprising is thwarted.
1980 Nov João Bernardo Vieira (alias Commander Nino) seizes power from president Luiz Cabral and sets up all-African government.
1983 Jul Relations restored with Cape Verde.
1985 Nov Fourth failed coup against Vieira.
1986 Jul Six executed for part in Nov coup.
1991 May Single party formally abolished.

6 LIBERIA
1847 Jul 26 Independence day.
1869 First rulers, mulattoes, ousted by True Whigs.
1930 Slavery trade causes GB and USA to break off diplomatic relations for five years.
1942 Mutual defence pact signed with US.
1944 William Tubman becomes president. True Whigs remain in power.
1971 Jul William Tolbert succeeds Tubman.
1976 Government ends Firestone's control over rubber profits.
1979 Apr Violent protests against rise in price of rice.
1979 Independent candidate Amos Sawyer gains support.
1980 Apr Military coup. Master Sergeant Samuel Doe takes power.
1980s Series of failed coups.
1985 Oct Doe wins majority in rigged elections.
1990 Doe under siege from Charles Taylor and National Patriotic Front of Liberia (NPFL).
1991 Doe assassinated. Nov Ceasefire negotiated by peacekeeping forces of five West African nations.

7 NIGERIA
1883 British military conquest begins.
1960 Oct 1 Independence day. Alliance government: Northern People's Congress (NPC) and National Council for Nigeria and the Cameroons (NCNC).
1966 Jan General Ironsi thwarts coup attempt and takes power.
1967 May Ojukwu declares secession of Eastern region from Nigeria.
1970-5 General Gowon in power after civil war.
1974 Oil boom.
1975 Jul Peaceful coup by General Murtala Muhammad.
1979 Oct Civilian rule. President Shagari sworn into office.
1983 Jan Unskilled foreigners ordered out of country.
1983 Dec Military coup by Muhammadu Buhari.
1984 Feb Second wave of religious riots.
1985 Aug Palace coup. Ibrahim Babangida takes over.
1992 May Transfer to civilian rule postponed. Opposition leaders arrested.

continued

Humid and subhumid west continued

4643 **8 SIERRA LEONE**
British colony from 1808 to 1961
1850 Over 100 different languages spoken.
1898 Imposition of hut tax leads to war between settlers and indigenous rebels.
1952 First general elections. Milton Margai of Sierra Leone People's Party (SLPP) becomes prime minister.
1957 Siaka Stevens leaves (SLPP) to form All People's Congress (APC).
1961 Apr 27 Independence day. SLPP in power under Margai.
1967 APC wins elections. Military coup by force commander. Two days later, second coup. National Reformation Committee, led by Brigadier Juxon-Smith, takes power.
1968 Re-establishment of civilian rule under Stevens and APC.
1977 Stevens declares State of Emergency after student demonstrations over the economy.
1978 Bill establishes one-party state and outlaws opposition parties.
1980 Jul Hosting of Organization of African Unity (OAU) summit.
1982 May Violent elections: internal APC factions in conflict. Most ministers re-elected.
1985 Oct Major-General Joseph Momoh elected new president.
1992 Military coup. Leaders promise democratic elections.

9 TOGO
German colony from 1902 to 1914. Country divided between French and British after World War I by League of Nations.
1946 Comité de l'Unité Togolaise (CUT) wins territorial elections. Sylvanus Olympio made president.
1958 Apr Elections. CUT wins 33 seats, and Olympio becomes prime minister.
1960 Apr 27 Independence day. Olympio becomes president of Republic. CUT in power.
1963 Jan Olympio assassinated in military coup. Nicolas Grunitzky, leader of Parti Togolais du Progrés (PTP), takes over.
1967 Jan Military coup. General Eyadema ousts Grunitzky.
1969 Rassemblement du Peuple Togolais (RPT) formed.
1985 Mar Elections for Parliament, open to all RPT members.
1985 Aug Bomb explosions before and after Pope's visit.
1987 Jan Eyadema celebrates 20 years in power.
1991 Aug Elections. Prime minister temporarily abducted. Coalition government formed, including rebel forces.

Humid central

4644

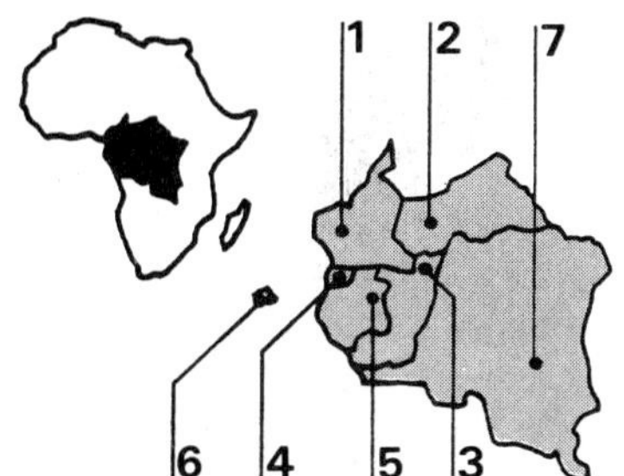

1 CAMEROON
German colony from 1884 until after World War I when west of country is taken over by British and east by French.
1955 Demonstrations by Union des Populations du Cameroun (UPC) harshly suppressed.
1958 Feb Ahidjo replaces Mbida as prime minister.
1958 Sep 300 UPC rebels killed during uprising.
1960 Jan 1 East Cameroon achieves independence under prime minister Ahmadou Ahidjo and the Union Camerounaise.
1961 Oct 1 Federal Republic formed with West Cameroon.
1982 Nov Ahidjo resigns. Paul Biya takes over.
1984 Apr Failed coup by supporters of Ahidjo.
1986 Aug Volcanic eruption kills 2,000 and poisons 20,000.
1992 Oct Biya as president: clampdown on press and opposition.
1993 Students occupy London embassy, elections planned.

2 CENTRAL AFRICAN REPUBLIC
French colony from 1894 to 1960
1894 Boundaries laid down by France and Belgium.
1908–11 French military conquests.
1959 Mar Boganda, founder of Mouvement l'Evolution Sociale de l'Afrique Noire (MESAN), dies and is succeeded by David Dacko.
1960 Aug 13 Independence day. MESAN in power, under Dacko.
1965 Dec General strike in response to ailing economy.
1966 Jan Jean-Bodel Bokassa removes Dacko from power.
1976 Bokassa declares himself "Emperor."
1979 Jan Increasing civil unrest leads to riots.
1979 Sep French government puts Dacko back in power.
1981 Feb Referendum introduces multiparty democracy.
1981 Sep André Kolingba displaces Dacko.
1985 Sep Kolingba brings civilians into new government.
1986 Nov Democratic constitution approved by referendum.
1993 Feb Kolingba sacks prime minister and constitutional government for blocking democracy.

3 CONGO
1880 French begin colonization.
1924 Real domination begins as French start work on Congo Ocean Railway.
1957 Oil discovered at Pointe Indienne.
1960 Aug 15 Independence day. Fulbert Youlou and Democratic Union for the Defence of African Interests (UDDIA) in power.
1964 Creation of National Movement of the Revolution (MNR).
1963 Aug Youlou regime falls. Old guard and new militia in conflict.
1968 Aug Alphonse Massamba-Débat, ruler since 1963, is ousted by Marien Ngouabi.
1972 Failed "leftist" coup by Ange Diawara.
1977 Mar Ngouabi assassinated. Army chief Yhombi-Opango takes over power and declares martial law.
1979 Feb Yhombi thrown out after popular opposition.
1979 Feb Sassou Nguesso takes over.
1979 Mar Yhombi expelled from PCT (Congolese Worker's Party).
1984 Aug Ange Edouard replaces Sylvian Goma as prime minister.
1991 Oppositional political parties legalized.
1992 Claude Antoine Dallosld becomes prime minister.

4 EQUATORIAL GUINEA
Colonized by several European countries during 19th century
1900 Treaty of Paris fixes boundaries of Spanish enclave on mainland.
1968 Sep Macías Nguema elected president.
1968 Oct 12 Independence day. Macías Nguema in power.
1970 Nguema sets up one-party, repressive dictatorship lasting ten years.
1979 Aug Successful coup. Lieutenant-Colonel Teodoro Obiang Nguema Mbasogo seizes power.
1981 Apr Failed coup attempt.
1982 Aug New constitution given strong support.
1982 Oct Nguema inaugurated as president.
1983 May Failed coup attempt.
1983 Parliamentary elections held.
1986 Jan Obiang reshuffles cabinet and takes over defence portfolio in response to rumours of military coup.
1986 Jul Government claims to have defused assassination plot.
1992 Jan Legislation for multiparty transitional party passed.

continued

Humid central continued

4644 **5 GABON**

French colony from 1910 to 1960
1940 Free French take Gabon from pro-Vichy government.
1946 Gabon made "overseas territory" of France.
1960 Aug 17 Independence granted. Bloc Démocratique Gabonais (BDG) in power.
1961 Feb Leon M'Ba, founder of Mouvement Mixte Gabonais (MMB), elected president.
1964 M'Ba overthrown by military coup but restored by French.
1967 Nov M'Ba dies. Omar Bongo becomes second president.
1968 Mar Bongo sets up one-party state.
1974 May Work starts on Trans-Gabon railway.
1977-8 Collapse of economy.
1979 Dec Bongo re-elected.
1985 1,800 prisoners released in act of clemency.
1986 Nov Bongo starts another seven-year term.
1990 May Several members of oppositon party killed or detained. After anti-government protests, elections end one-party rule.

6 SÃO TOMÉ AND PRINCÍPE

1530 Slave revolt begins centuries of struggle against Portuguese rule.
1552 Portugal formally annexes São Tomé.
1573 Portugal formally annexes Princípe.
1960 Formation of Committee for the Liberation of São Tomé and Principe (CLSTP).
1963 CLSTP leads powerful general strike.
1972 CLSTP becomes Movement for the Liberation of São Tomé and Princípe (MLSTP).
1974 Mass strikes and demonstrations by pro-MLSTP Civic Association.
1975 July 12 Manuel Pinto da Costa leads country into independence at head of MLSTP.
1979 Mar Former minister Da Graza jailed for part in coup plot.
1983–4 Acute drought.
1991 Mar First presidential elections.

7 ZAIRE

Belgian colony from 1908 to 1960. Formerly "the Congo."
1959 Lumumba forms Mouvement National Congolais (MNC).
1960 Jun 30 Independence day. Lumumba prime minister. Nationalist alliance in office.
1960 Sep Military coup by Colonel Joseph-Désiré (later General Sese Seko) Mobutu.
1961 Feb Lumumba murdered.
1961 Aug Reconciliation of opposition Moderates and Nationalists.
1963 Nationalist parties form Comité National de Libération (CNL) and take control of eastern half of country.
1964 CNL declares "People's Republic of Congo," which collapses a few months later at hands of Belgian troops.
1965 Nov Second coup by General Mobutu.
1970 May Mobutu's Mouvement Populaire de la Revolution is only legal party.
1971 The Congo renamed Zaire.
1984 Zaire rejoins Organisation of Africa Unity (OAU).
1991 Failed military coup.
1992 National conference set up to draft multi-party constitution.
1993 Rioting and French Ambassador killed.

Subhumid and mountainous east

4645

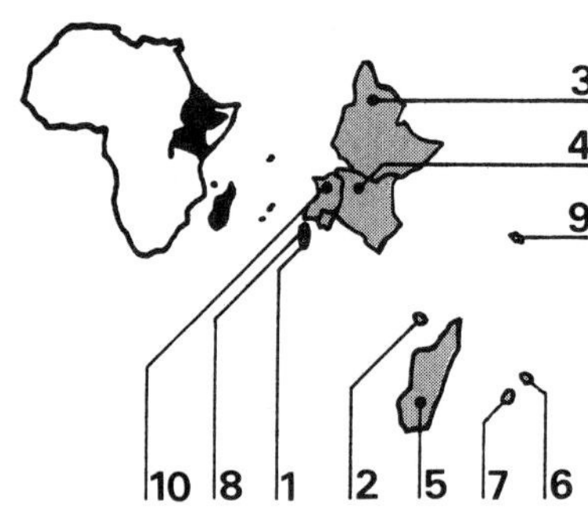

1 BURUNDI

Germany colony from late 19th century to World War I. Under Belgian rule until 1962.
1961 Oct Assassination of Rwagasore, the first major nationalist.
1962 Jul 1 Independence day. Mwami Mwambutsa becomes king and head of state.
1965 Oct An abortive coup led by the Hutu. The Mwami flee, and the Tutsi Elite remove the Hutu threat.
1966 Jul Michel Micombero becomes Tutsi president.
1966 Nov Ntare V, king since July, is deposed and remains in exile.
1972 Apr Hutu uprising. Government dismissed and Ntare executed.
1976 Nov Colonel Bagaza takes over power in "palace revolution."
1980 Bagaza replaces junta with a central committee and politburo.
1981 Nov First national referendum since independence approves new constitution.
1987 Sep Bagaza overthrown by Major Pierre Buyoya in military coup. Constitution suspended. Ethnic clashes between Tulse and Mutu.
1992 Draft constitution for military state.

2 COMOROS

French colony from 1912 to 1976
1975 Jun French National Assembly proposes island-by-island referendum on independence.
1975 Jul 6 Ahmed Abdallah announces unilateral declaration of independence.
1975 Aug Abdallah deposed by Ali Soilih. Socialist Revolution begins.
1976 Jan Soilih becomes head of state.
1978 May Soilih ousted by Bob Denard in military coup.
1978 Oct Abdallah re-elected head of state.
1981 Nov UN General Assembly, in 115-to-1 vote, persuades France to consider returning island of Mayotte, held by the French since 1841, to the Comoros.
1984 Dec Further resolution by UN over Mayotte, which France again rejects.
1985 Mar Failed coup by members of presidential guard.
1989 Nov Abdallah assassinated by members of armed forces. Denard remains effective ruler.
1990 Mar Said Mohammed Djohar begins six-year term as president. Union Comorienne pour le Progrés (Udzima) in power.
1992 Jan New transitional coalition government formed, headed by opposition leader Taki.

3 ETHIOPIA

1889–1913 Emperor Menelik expands country's territory through conquest.
1960s Introduction of commercial agriculture. Somali resists Ethiopian rule.
1974 Final collapse of imperial regime due to decline of military power, grass-roots discontent over unemployment, inflation, and increasing poverty. Sep Haile Selassie, emperor since 1941, removed. Military dictatorship.
1977 Feb Mengistu Haile Mariam becomes chairman of Provisional Military Council (PMAC), and consolidates personal dictatorship.
1978 Massive Soviet intervention allows military regime to regain power in the Ogaden. Cuban aid decisive in causing Somali's forces to withdraw. Eritreans give up all towns captured.
1984 Sep Formation of Worker's Party of Ethiopia (WPE), headed by Mengistu.
1985 Major drought. Resettlement program set up.
1985 Mar CIA airlift of Falashas causes Muslim protest.
1987 Drought recurs: foreign aid averts disaster.
1991 Eriteans capture Assab. Mengistu flees. Tigeran rebels capture capital and form provisional government. Eritrean independent referendum set for 1993.

continued

Subhumid and mountainous east continued

4645 **4 KENYA**
British colony from 1920 to 1963
1954–60 Political concessions granted to Africans.
1963 Dec 12 Independence day. Kenyan African National Union (KANU) in power, led by Jomo Kenyatta.
1978 Aug Death of Kenyatta. Daniel Arap Moi becomes president.
1978 Oct Assassination plot uncovered.
1982 Jun Creation of one-party state.
1982 Aug Failed coup attempt.
1983 Jun Moi suspends Charles Njonjo, Minister of Constitutional Affairs, from cabinet.
1984 Dec Njonjo found guilty of illegal activities.
1986 Student protests over staff salary increases.
1988 Long-serving vice-president demoted.
1989 May George Saitoti becomes vice-president.
1990 Jul Worst rioting since independence.
1991 Moi introduces multiparty politics.
1992 Dec 29 Elections. Moi as president.

5 MADAGASCAR
French colony from 1882 to 1960
1947–8 Mass insurrection against French rule fails.
1960 Jun 26 Independence day. First Malagasy Republic led by Philibert Tsiranana.
1972 May Unrest in major towns. General Ramanantosa takes over power.
1975 Jun Didier Ratsiraka voted into office by Military Directorate. Ratsiraka appoints Supreme Revolutionary Council (CSR).
1982 Fourth coup plot against Ratsiraka uncovered.
1985 Aug Leader of Kung Fu cult killed by security forces.
1990 May Second "radio coup" is quelled.
1991 Major protests against socialist government. Transitional government formed.
1993 Feb. Albert Zafy wins elections ending 13 years of dictatorship.

6 MAURITIUS
1715 Arrival of French colonists.
1810 British conquer the island.
1936 Dr Maurice Cure founds Labor Party (LP).
1953 Under Seewoosagur Ramgoolam, LP wins general elections.
1968 Mar 12 Independence day. Ramgoolam and LP in office.
1979 Aug Strike by plantation and dock workers.
1982 Jun Elections. Mouvement Militant Mauricien (MMM) and Parti Socialist Mauricien (PSM) alliance topples Ramgoolam.
1984 Dec Ramgoolam dies at 85.
1985 Veeraswamy Ringadoo made new governor-general.
1985 Dec Four alliance MPs caught smuggling heroin at Amsterdam.
1992 Jun. Cassam Uleem elected as president. Mauritius officially a republic.

7 RÉUNION
1810–14 English occupation.
1814 May Island restored to French.
1936 May Comité d'Action Démocratique et Sociale formed.
1959 Réunion Communist Party (PCR) launches campaign for autonomy within French Republic.
1976 Oct Visit by French President Giscard d'Estaing.
1977 Apr Meeting of PCR and other progressive parties.
1978 Jun Formation of Anticolonialist Front for the Self-Determination of Réunion (FRACPAR).
1979 May Meeting of Permanent Liaison Committee.
1979 Cyclone Claudette hits Réunion.
1990 Mar France allows TEIE FREEDOM to broadcast legally after protests.
1992 Camille Sud reelected president of regional council.

8 RWANDA
German colony from 1890 to 1916
Belgian colony from 1916 to 1962
1957 Hutu peasantry calls for end to Tutsi monopoly.
1959 Death of Mwami Matari III. Tutsi coup leads to Hutu uprising. Mwami Kigeri V flees country.
1961 Sep Parmehutu, Hutu majority party, elected into power.
1962 Jul 1 Independence day. Gregoire Kayibanda becomes first president.
1963–4 Tutsi raids lead to brutal Hutu reprisal.
1973 Jul General Habyarimana ousts Kayibanda.
1984 Apr Program of "rigor and austerity."
1989 Torrential rain and hailstorms cause famine.
1990 Failed coup by Rwanda refugees from Uganda. Nov. Multiparty political system introduced.

9 SEYCHELLES
1770s French settlement by planters and slaves.
1814 Treaty of Paris confirms British sovereignty.
1903 Seychelles becomes crown colony.
1964 Birth of Seychelles People's United Party (SPUP), led by France-Albert René, and Democratic Party (SDP), led by James Mancham.
1967 First full election. SPUP and SDP in stalemate.
1970 Second election. SDP wins.
1971 Mahe International Airport opens. Boom in tourism.
1976 Jun 29 Independence day. SDP-SPUP coalition in power.
1977 Jun Military coup. René ousts Mancham as president.
1978 Jun René's party renamed Seychelles People's Progressive Front (SPPF).
1979 Jun One-party constitution established. René reelected.
1981 Major coup attempt by South African mercenaries.
1984 Nov Exiled opposition leaders form Seychelles National Movement (SNM).
1991 Dec. Government surrenders monopoly of power.

10 UGANDA
British colony from 1894 to 1962
1902 Apr Large part of eastern Uganda handed over to Kenya.
1960 Milton Obote forms Ugandan People's Congress (UPC).
1962 Oct 9 Independence day. Obote becomes prime minister, Kabaka of Buganda head of state. UPC-Kabaka Yekka coalition government.
1967 Apr New constitution. Socialist reforms.
1971 Jan Military coup by Major-General Idi Amin.
1978 Oct Amin invades Tanzania.
1979 Mar Birth of Ugandan National Liberation Front (UNLF).

continued

Subhumid and mountainous east continued

4645 **10 UGANDA**
1979 Apr UNLF ousts Amin. Yusufu Lule in power.
1979 Jun National Consultative Council (NCC) votes Godfrey Binaisa into power.
1980 May Binaisa arrested by UNLF military faction.
1980 Dec Elections restore Obote and UPC to power.
1985 Jul Military coup. Obote ousted by Brigadier General Okello.
1986 Jan Military coup by Yoweri Museveni and National Resistance Movement (NRM).
1992 Jan Plans for reformed constitution and elections announced.

Subhumid and semiarid south

4646

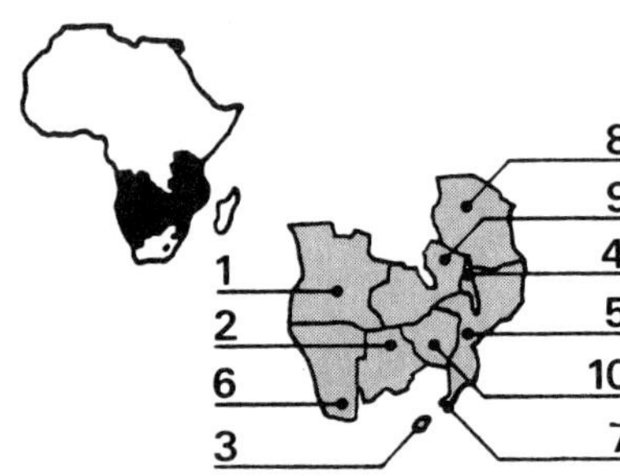

1 ANGOLA
Portuguese colony from 1838 to 1961
1961 Feb and Mar Revolts launched against colonial rule.
1966 Mar Formation of National Union for the Total Independence of Angola (UNITA).
1975 Nov Independence day. Popular Movement for the Liberation of Angola (MPLA) in power.
1976 MPLA's Agostinho Neto becomes first president.
1979 South Africa and Rhodesia step up post-independence military action against Angola. Sep Neto dies and Dos Santos becomes president.
1988 Dec After talks, South Africa agrees to withdraw 2,000 troops from Southern Angola while Cuba agrees to withdraw all its troops (around 60,000) in the north.
1989 Jun Dos Santos and UNITA's Savimbi sign historic Gbadolite Declaration calling for a ceasefire.
1993 Jan UNITA versus NPA (the government) civil war, heavy casualties.

2 BOTSWANA
British colony from 1885 to 1966
1961 Jan Seretse Khama forms Botswana Democratic Party (BDP).
1966 Sep 30 Independence day. Khama and BDP in power.
1971 Mining of diamonds begins at Orapa.
1976 Aug National currency, the pula, established.
1975 Jul Strike action by unskilled workers at Selebi-Phikwe.
1980 Jul Khama dies at age of 51. Dr Quett Masire elected president by BDP.
1984 Sep First elections since death of Khama.
1985 Jun In internationally condemned action, South African commandos carry out pre-dawn raids in Gaborone.
1986 Feb Botswana agrees not to harbor guerrillas of the African National Congress.
1986 May Further raids by South Africa fail to hit ANC members.
1987 Sept Referendum results in favor of electoral and constitutional reform.
1991 Oct Botswana Peoples Progressive Front formed by opposition alliance.

3 LESOTHO
1868 Mar British Protectorate conferred.
1952 Founding of Basutoland African Congress (later BCP), led by Ntsu Mokhele.
1965 May Self-government under Basutoland National Party (BNP).
1966 Oct 4 Independence day.
1967 Jan King Moshoeshoe II loses all political power.
1979 Jan Chief Jonathan (BNP) bans opposition parties and arrests their leaders. Cabinet minister murdered.
1980 Aug First meeting between Jonathan and South African Premier Botha.
1980 Sep Jonathan's brother seriously injured.
1982 Dec South Africa carries out raid on Maseru.
1986 Jan Major General Lekhanya takes power.
1986 Mar Security pact signed with South Africa.
1991 Apr. Coup led by Col Ramaema ousts Lekhanya.
1993 Mar General elections return country to civilian rule.

4 MALAWI
Colonized by British missionaries
1959 Mar Colonial powers declare state of emergency.
1961 Aug Malawi Congress Party elected into power, led by Hastings Banda.
1964 Jul 6 Independence day.
1977 Feb Two party members sentenced to death for treason.
1978 Jun First general election since 1961. Reports of rigging leads to rebanning of foreign journalists.
1980 Jan Expulsion from party of Aleke Banda.
1981 Mar Gwanda Chakuamba, Youth and Culture Minister, imprisoned for sedition.
1983 Mar Attati Mpakati, leader of Socialist League, is murdered in Harare.
1986 Dec Joint defence and security agreement between Malawi and Mozambique.
1992 Anti-government demonstrations. Calls for democratic reform.
1993 Planned referendum on multi-party system.

5 MOZAMBIQUE
First colonized by Portugal
1963 Formation of Frelimo, the Mozambican Liberation Front.
1974 Portuguese government ousted.
1975 Jun 25 Independence day. Frelimo in power.
1977-8 Floods cause havoc in valleys.
1979 Sep Rhodesian forces attack Mozambique.
1980 President Machel carries out government and administration overhaul.
1984 Mar Nkomati Accord: Mozambique to keep out ANC, South Africa to stop supporting National Resistance Movement (MNR).
1986 Oct Machel killed in plane crash.
1986 Nov Joaquim Chissano elected new head of party.
1990 Apr & May New constitution opened to public debate.
1991 Partial ceasefire agreement with guerrillas.
1993 Elections planned.

continued

Subhumid and semiarid south continued

4646 **6 NAMIBIA**
1890 Present boundaries laid down by imperial powers.
1915 Portugal conquers the Ovambo territory.
1915 Treaty of Versailles confirms South African rule.
1950s Growth of nationalist over tribal forces.
1960 Apr Birth of South Western African People's Organization (SWAPO).
1966 Oct UN vetoes South African occupation.
1966 Aug First military action by SWAPO.
1977 Parts of Ovamboland under SWAPO rule.
1978 May South Africa bombs SWAPO refugee camp.
1980 Ceasefire attempts.
1981–2 Peace initiatives continue.
1988 Aug All parties agree to UN independence plan.
1990 Mar 21 Independence day. Sam Nujoma President, SWAPO in power.
1991 Jul South African government admits to funding opposition parties.

7 SWAZILAND
British colony from 1902 to 1968
1902 Country placed under British High Commissioner for South Africa.
1963 Formation of Ngwane National Liberatory Congress (NNLC), led by Dr Ambrose Zwane.
1966 British transfer powers over communal land and mineral rights to the monarchy.
1968 Sep 6 Independence day. King Sobhuza II in power.
1973 Apr Sobhuza dissolves all political parties after constitutional crisis in which NNLC member is denied parliamentary seat.
1977 Mar Democratic system abolished by monarchy.
1979 Jan New parliament opens. King retains power to veto resolutions and to dismiss ministers.
1982 Aug Sobhuza dies. Dzeliwe becomes Queen Regent.
1983 Ntombi takes over as Queen Regent.
1984 Jun Prime Minister Prince Bhekimpi dismisses finance and foreign ministers and police and army chiefs, accusing them of plotting to take over power.
1986 Apr Coronation of new king Makhosetive Dlamini.
1991 King agrees to review electoral system.

8 TANZANIA
Originally two separate states, Tanganyika and Zanzibar. Tanganyika, held by Germany from late 19th century, is restored to Britain by League of Nations after World War I.
1890 Zanzibar made British protectorate.
1954 Jul Birth of Tanganyika African National Union (TANU). Julius Nyerere president.
1961 Dec 9 Independence day. TANU in power. Nyerere prime minister.
1962 Tanganyika declared Republic within Commonwealth and Nyerere becomes first president.
1964 Apr 27 United Republic of Tanzania formed by merger of Tanganyika and Zanzibar.
1965 Jul Creation of one-party state after attempted military mutiny.
1977 Feb Establishment of new party, Chama Cha Mapinduzi (CCM), with Nyerere as chairman.
1978 Ugandan invasion. Counter-invasion by Tanzanian and anti-Amin forces.
1983 Mar Anti-corruption campaign. Over 1,000 charged.
1985 Nov Ali Hassan Mwinyi elected new president by CCM.
1991 Multiparty politics introduced.

9 ZAMBIA
British colony from 1924 to 1964
1951 Formation of African National Congress.
1953 Federation with South Rhodesia leads to growth of African nationalist groups.
1958 ANC splits. Militant wing forms United National Independence Party (UNIP).
1964 Oct 24 Independence day. UNIP in power under president Kenneth Kaunda.
1969 Elections. ANC reduces UNIP's majority.
1972 One-party constitution established.
1975 Zambia supports Savimbi's UNITA (also backed by USA and South Africa) in Angolan civil war.
1979 Jul Zambia hosts Commonwealth Conference.
1980 Oct Curfew imposed in response to strikes led by Zambia Congress of Trades Unions (ZCTU).
1985 Recession provokes further wave of strikes, Mar. In response, Kaunda bans all strikes in essential sectors.
1991 Multiparty election landslide , victory for democratic forces and sound rejection of socialism.

10 ZIMBABWE
Self-governing colony from 1923 to 1980. Formerly called Rhodesia.
1890 British invasion. Capital at Salisbury (now Harare).
1922 Referendum. Southern white population chooses "responsible self-government."
1923 Southern Rhodesia made self-governing colony.
1953 Creation of Federation of Rhodesia and Nyasaland.
1963 Federation dissolved. Ian Smith becomes new prime minister of Southern Rhodesia.
1970 Rhodesia declares itself republic.
1976 Joshua Nkomo's Zimbabwe African People's Union (ZAPU – formed 1961) and Robert Mugabe's Zimbabwe African National Union (ZANU – formed 1963) merge as Patriotic Front (PF).
1980 Apr 18 Independence day. Rhodesia renamed Zimbabwe. ZANU-PF in office under Mugabe.
1986 Elections. ZANU-PF increases large majority.
1987 ZAPU party disbanded.
1991 Single party state abandoned.

South Africa

4647 **1652** Colonized by the Dutch East India Company.
1806 Company goes bankrupt. Colony handed over to the British.
1899–1902 Destruction of independent Boer republics by British.
1910 Formation of Union of South Africa. White minority rule.
1912 Birth of African National Congress (ANC). Increasing resistance by black workers to proletarianization.
1948 National party comes to power under D F Malan.
1955 ANC proclaims Freedom Charter for just and democratic country.
1961 South Africa declared a republic.
1975 Inkatha, Zulu tribal group formed in 1928, reconvened by Chief Buthelezi.
1976 Uprising in Soweto, fueled by workers growing discontent.
1983 Aug Launch of United Democratic Front (UDF), in league with ANC and led by Albertina Sisulu.
1984 Sep Botha elected South Africa's first executive state president.
1986 Government declares State of Emergency.
1989 De Klerk suceeds Botha. Walter Sisulu and five other ANC members, who were jailed for life in 1964, are set free.
1990 De Klerk legalises 33 opposition groups and releases Nelson Mandela, ANC member imprisoned for 26 years. Government begins talks with ANC. State of emergency lifted. ANC ends armed struggle.
1991 End of apartheid legislation.
1992 Voters approve plan to move toward majority rule. Massacre at Boipatong, ANC drop out of talks.

511 EARLY THEATER c. 3000 BC–AD 600

Theater everywhere had its beginnings in religious ritual. In ancient Greece theater originated in the songs and dances to honor Dionysus, god of fertility and wine.

When one performer interacted with the group, drama was born. Later two more actors, always men, were added, playing all the parts in masks and costumes indicating character. Tragedies, comedies reflecting current politics and manners, and satyr plays, which made fun of the love-life of the gods, competed in day-long festivals, performed first in market places, then in theaters with a circular level area for the chorus, and later with a narrow raised platform added, which the actors could sometimes use.

The Romans built similarly shaped, but often more elaborate theaters and tended to a taste for sensational and scabrous plays.

Oriental theater forms developed independently but also had their origins in religious dance.

Events

5111 **c. 534 BC** First tragedy in Athens by Thespis of Icaria.
c. 525–456 BC Aeschylus, Athenian tragic playwright (82 plays, 5 survive).
c. 510–post 423 BC Cratinus, Athenian comic playwright (28 plays)
c. 496–406 BC Sophocles, Athenian tragic playwright (123 plays, 7 survive).
c. 490 BC Actors in Greek theater use cothurnus, mask and choir.
485/80–407/6 BC Euripides, Athenian tragic playwright (90 plays, 19 survive).
484 BC Aeschylus first wins playwright competition in Athens.
472 BC *The Persians* by Aeschylus.
c. 471 BC Aeschylus introduces second actor.
c. 466 BC Sophocles introduces third actor.
458 bc *Oresteia* by Aeschylus.
457/45-c. 385 BC Aristophanes, Athenian comic playwright (44 plays,11 survive).
c. 441 BC *Antigone* by Sophocles.
431 BC *Medea* by Euripides.
c. 430 BC Euripides introduces "Deus ex machina."
427 BC *Oedipus the King* by Sophocles.
423 BC *The Clouds* by Aristophanes.
415 BC *The Trojan Women* by Euripides.
414 BC *Birds* by Aristophanes.
414–412 *Iphigenia in Tauris* by Euripides.
413 BC *Electra* by Euripedes.
411 BC *Lysistrata* by Aristophanes.
408 BC *Orestes* by Euripides.
405 BC *The Frogs* by Aristophanes.
364 BC First theatrical performance in Rome.
365/60–264/3 BC Philemon of Syracuse, founder of Athenian New Comedy.
c. 342–c. 292 BC Menander, Athenian comic playwright (100+ plays).
c. 328 BC Dionysus theater in Athens built.
c. 317 BC Menander's probable first play *Dyskolos (Bad-tempered Man).*
c. 254–c. 194 BC Plautus, Roman comic playwright (40-130 plays, 21 survive).
c. 250 BC Atellan farce reaches Rome.
c. 240 BC Greek drama imported to Rome.
c. 195–159 BC Terence, Roman comic playwright (6 plays survive).
c. 186 BC *Pot of Gold* by Plautus.
166 BC *The Girl from Andros* by Terence.
160 BC *Brothers* by Terence.
55 BC Pompey opens first permanent theater in Rome.
c. 22 BC Pantomimes established in Rome.
c. 13 BC Theater of Marcellus, Rome.
c. AD 25–65 Seneca the Younger writes nine Athenian-modeled tragedies.
AD 197 or 203 *De spectaculis* by Tertullian attacks all theatrical displays.
c. AD 290 Roman theater in Verona.
c. AD 300 Beginnings of Indian theater.
c. AD 300 Bhasa, Indian dramatist.
5th century AD Kalidasa, Indian dramatist.
6th century AD *Vasantesena* by Chudraka, India.

Greek and Roman dramatists

5112 GREEK DRAMATISTS

Aeschylus c. 525–456 BC, greatest of dramatic poets before Shakespeare. Of his 90 plus plays few survive, among them *The Persians* (he fought against them at Marathon) and the *Oresteia* (*Agamemnon, The Libation Bearers, The Eumenides*). Only fragments survive of his masterly satyr dramas. He introduced the second actor and so almost invented drama.
Aristophanes c. 450–385 BC (**1**), Wrote 40 comedies on local topics. *The Clouds, The Wasps, The Birds* and, especially, *Lysistrata* can still delight modern audiences.
Euripides 484–406 BC (**2**), *Medea, Hippolytus, The Trojan Women, Electra, The Bacchae* are among the 92 plays he is said to have written.
Sophocles 496–406 BC, introduced a third actor and reduced the role of the chorus. *Ajax, Antigone, Oedipus the King* and fragments of a satyr play, *The Trackers,* are among his surviving plays. His characters are much more developed than in earlier tragedies. He introduced a prologue to outline preceding events.
Menander c. 342–292 BC, Greek dramatist of "New Comedy" who devoted more importance to plot. Later imitated by Plautus and Terence.

1

2

ROMAN DRAMATISTS

Plautus, Titus Maccius c. 254–181 BC, wrote complicated, riotously bawdy plays with strong characterization, often reworking earlier Greek comedies, including *Menaechmi, Amphitryon.*
Seneca, Lucius Annaeus c. 4 BC–AD 65. Tragedies such as *Medea, Pheadra,* and *Oedipus* place emphasis more on emotion than on plots, which echo the horrors of life in Nero's Rome.
Terence c.190–159 BC. His elegant and urbane plays, more original and less farcical than Plautus, though also plundering Greek sources, include *The Brothers* and *The Eunuch.*

512 MEDIEVAL THEATER AD 600–1500

In the 6th century official Christian disapproval led to theaters being closed, but drama was reborn in dramatizations of Biblical episodes within Church ritual. These were performed for particular Church festivals on stages with multiple settings, or, In Britain, presented on wagons (pageants), which traveled from place to place. These pageants were usually presented by a particular craft guild. Plays became increasingly secular, some with comic episodes, or dealt with general ethical ideas rather than Bible stories.

TYPES OF PLAY

Miracle plays Dealt with incidents from the life of a saint or Biblical episode, performed on the appropriate festival.
Mystery plays Religious drama originally presented by members of a craft guild, the mysteries being craft secrets, no plot elements. Often presented in cycles of short plays, each by a different guild, on the same day.
Morality plays Secular plays, but dealing with moral issues, often with characters representing vices and virtues.

Events

5121 **600–1200**
c. AD 700 Bharavabhuti, Indian dramatist.
c. AD 900–1000 Miracle plays flourish in England, France and Germany.
c. AD 966 *Abraham* by Roswitha von Gandersheim.
c. AD 975–980 *Visitatio Sepulchri* performed at St Gall, Switzerland.
c. 1150 Hilarius in Paris writes Latin plays.

1200–1400
c. 1200 *Jeu d'Adam*, Anglo-Norman play.
c. 1200 *Play of Holy Nicolaus* by Jean Bodel, France.
1298 Passion play performed in Latin at Cividale, north Italy.
1320 *Play of the Wife and Foolish Virgins* performed in Eisenach, Germany.
1325 Adam de la Halle's farces performed in Arras, France.
c. 1350 *The Chalk Circle* a Chinese drama by Li Hsing Tao.
c. 1375 *Piers the Plowman*, English verse play by William Langland.
c. 1377 *The Conquest of Jerusalem* performed at Paris banquet.
c. 1388 *The Fall of Troy* performed at Paris banquet.

1400–1500
c. 1400 Clerical theater at its height in Italy.
1404 *Pi Pa Ki (Story of the Lute)*, Chinese play in final edition.
c. 1400–1500 Morality plays develop in France.
c. 1460 *Rheinisches* sacred German Easter play.
c. 1460–1529 John Skelton, English playwright.
c. 1469–1529 Juan del Encina, Spanish playwright.
1470–1520 Bernando Dovizi da Bibbiena, Italian comic playwright.
c. 1470–1536 Gil Vicente, founder of Portuguese theater.
1486 *Menaechmi* by Plautus performed in Ferrara, Italy.
c. 1495 *Mankind* and *Everyman* written and performed in England.
1497 *Fulgens and Lucres* by Henry Medwell performed in London.
c. 1497–c. 1586 John Heywood, English playwright.
1499 *Celestina*, Spanish drama, probably by Fernando de Rojas.

513 RENAISSANCE THEATER 1500–1650

Religious and morality plays developed into secular narratives. Interest in classical texts led to revival of ancient plays in schools and universities. In London and in Spain playhouses were built based on the inn yards in which traveling troupes performed. In Italy roofed versions of the ancient theaters at several courts. Indoor theaters developed where greater scenic illusion could be presented.

In royal and ducal palaces lavish spectacles were devised, the beginnings of opera and ballet. In the public theaters of England and Spain playwriting much freer than that of ancient times began to flourish while in Italy an improvised drama using stock characters developed: the *commedia dell'arte.*

Events

5131

1

1500–1550
1508 *The Little Treasure Casket* by Ludovico Ariosto, Italian comedy.
1511 *Morality of the Four Seasons* by Gil Vicente, Spanish/Portuguese *auto sacramental* or sacred play.
1512 First use of word *masque* in English to denote a poetic form of dramatic art.
1514 *Faras y eglogas* by Lucas Fernández, collection of six Spanish plays.
c. 1515–20 *Magnyfycene* by John Skelton.
1517 *Propalladia* by Bartolomé Torres Naharro, collection of seven plays in Spanish.
1524 *La Sofonisba* by Giangiorgio Trissino, Italian tragedy in blank verse.
1529 *Imber aureus* by Antonia Telesia, a mythological tragedy.
1533 *Johan Johan* by English dramatist John Heywood.
1536 *King Johan*, first English historical play, by John Bale performed.
1539 *Gentse Spelen* Flemish allegorical plays performed at Ghent.
1540 *Ane Satyre of the Thrie Estaits* by Sir David Lyndsay, Scottish morality play.
1541 *Orbecche* by Giambattista Chinzo Giraldi, Italian tragedy.
1545 *The Four P's* by John Heywood, English interlude.
1546 *Lisabetha* by Hans Sachs (**1**), German tragedy.
1548 First Paris theater, Hotel de Bourgogne, opens.
1549 Foundation of permanent theater in Rome.

1550–1600
1550 *Tobie Commedia* by Olaus Petri, earliest extant Swedish drama.
1550 *Ralph Roister* by Nicholas Udall, earliest known English comedy.
1552 *Cléopâtre Captive* by Etienne Jodelle, first classical tragedy in French.
1554–70 Formation of the first *commedia dell'arte.*
1562–1635 Félix Lope de Vega (**2**), Spanish dramatist (431 plays survive).
1564–1593 Christopher Marlowe, English dramatist (6 plays).
1564–1616 William Shakespeare, English dramatist (37 plays).
1566 *The Supposes* by George Gascoigne, earliest English prose comedy, acted at Gray's Inn, London.
1568 *Corral*, Spanish "yard play."
1576 Burbage's the Theatre opens in London.
1577 The Curtain Theatre, London, opens.
1579 Public playhouses established in Madrid.
1584 *Alexander and Campaspe* by John Lyly, Blackfriars Theatre, London.

2

1585 Teatro Olimpico, Vicenza, opens.
c. 1586 *Kabuki* theater established in Japan.
1589–92 *Henry VI*, three parts, by William Shakespeare
1590 *Tamburlaine the Great* by Christopher Marlowe.
1592 *Midas* by John Lyly.
1592–93 *Richard III*; *The Comedy of Errors* by William Shakespeare.
1593–94 *Titus Andronicus*; *The Taming of the Shrew* by William Shakespeare.
1594–95 *The Two Gentlemen of Verona*; *Love's Labor's Lost*; *Romeo and Juliet* by William Shakespeare.
1595 *Richard I*; *A Midsummer Night's Dream* by William Shakespeare.
1596–97 *King John*; *The Merchant of Venice* by William Shakespeare.

continued

Events continued

5131 **1597–98** *Henry IV parts I and 2* by William Shakespeare.
1598–99 *Much Ado About Nothing*; *Henry V* by William Shakespeare.
1599–1600 *Julius Caesar*, *As You Like It* by William Shakespeare.
1599 The Globe Theatre, London, built in Southwark.

1600–1650
1600 *Summer's Last Will and Testament* by English playwright Thomas Nashe.
1600–81 Pedro Calderón de la Bàrca, Spanish dramatist (120 plays).
1600–01 *Hamlet*, *The Merry Wives of Windsor* by William Shakespeare.
1601–02 *Twelfth Night*, *Troilus and Cressida* by William Shakespeare.
1602–03 *All's Well That Ends Well* by William Shakespeare.
1604–07 *Comedias* by Spanish playwright Félix Lope de Vega.
1604–05 *King Lear*, *Macbeth* by William Shakespeare.
1606–07 *Antony and Cleopatra* by William Shakespeare.
1606 *Volpone, or the Fox* by English playwright Ben Jonson.
1606–1684 Pierre Corneille, French dramatist (34 plays).
1607–08 *Coriolanus*; *Timon of Athens* by William Shakespeare.
1608–09 *Pericles* by William Shakespeare.
1609–10 *Cymbeline* by William Shakespeare.
1610–11 *Winter's Tale* by William Shakespeare.
1611–12 *The Tempest* by William Shakespeare.
1612–13 *Henry VIII*; *The Two Nobel Kinsmen* by William Shakespeare.
1612 *The White Devil* by English dramatist John Webster.
1616 *Works of Benjamin Jonson* by Ben Jonson.
1617 *Pyramé et Thisbé* by French dramatist Théophile de Viau.
1618 Teatro Farnese, Parma, opens.
1621 *Andromeda* by Félix Lope de Vega.
1622 *A New Way to Pay Old Debts* by English dramatist Philip Massinger.
1623 *The Duchess of Malfi* by John Webster.
c. 1632 *The Oberammergau Passion Play* inaugurated, Bavaria.
1616 *Le Cid* by Pierre Corneille.
1636–91 *Comedias*, Vol 1 by Pedro Calderoón de la Barca.
1641 *The Cardinal* by English dramatist James Shirley.
1641 Theatres in England closed by order.
c. 1643 Illustre Théâtre founded in Paris by Jean-Baptiste Molière.
1645 *The Great World Theater* by Pedro Calderón de la Barca.
c. 1649 *Carolus Stuardus* by German writer Andreas Gryphins.

Renaissance dramatists

5132 **Jonson, Ben** 1572–1637. Friend of Shakespeare. The social and political satire of his plays twice landed him in jail. As well as *Volpone*, *The Alchemist*, *Bartholomew Fair* and other plays for London's public theaters, he wrote masques for the Jacobean court.
Marlowe, Christopher 1564–93. Author of dramas in rich verse for London's public theaters which strongly influenced Shakespeare. Openly atheist and homosexual, he was killed in a tavern brawl (probably assassinated in connection with secret-service activities) after writing only *Dr Faustus*, *Tamberlaine*, *The Jew of Malta*, *Edward II*.
Vega, Félix Lope de 1562–1635. A prolific Spanish writer of *Fuenteovejuna* and, he claimed, over 1,500 other plays for the open air theaters of Madrid and the royal court which reflect the contemporary code of honor.
Webster, John c. 1580 –1634. *The Duchess of Malfi* and *The White Devil*, dramas of passion, intrigue and fine English poetry. He collaborated on other plays and may have been an actor.
Calderoón de la Barca, Pedro 1600–81. Spanish author of secular comedies, elaborate court entertainments and, especially after becoming a priest, of religious plays, best known for *The Mayor of Zalamea* and *The Constant Prince* but author of more than 200 plays.

Shakespeare, William 1564–1616. Poet and playwright (**1**) for London theater companies of which he was a member. He wrote 37 plays:

Histories
King Henry VI, Parts I, II and III (1592)
King Richard III (1593)
King Richard II (1594)
King John (1594)
King Henry IV, Part I (1597?)
King Henry IV, Part II (1598)
King Henry V (1599)
King Henry VIII (1611)
Timon of Athens

Comedies
Love's Labour's Lost (1590)
The Comedy of Errors (1591)
Two Gentlemen of Verona (1592)
A Midsummer Night's Dream (1594)
The Merchant of Venice (1595)
The Taming of the Shrew (1596)
The Merry Wives of Windsor (1599)
Much Ado About Nothing (1599)
As You Like It (1600)
Twelfth Night (1600)
All's Well That Ends Well (1602)
Measure for Measure (1604)

Romances
Pericles (1608)
Cymbeline (1610?)
The Winter's Tale (1610?)
The Tempest (1611)

Tragedies
Romeo and Juliet (1593)
Titus Andronicus (1594)
Julius Caesar (1599)
Troilus and Cressida (1602)
Hamlet (1602)
Othello (1604)
King Lear (1605)
Macbeth (1606)
Antony and Cleopatra (1607?)
Coriolanus (1608)

1

Famous Renaissance actors

5133 **Alleyn, Edward** 1566–1626. Rival of Burbage and lead actor with the Admiral's Men who appeared in Marlowe's plays.
Burbage, Richard 1567–1619. Leading actor of the Admiral's Men and the Chamberlain's Men - the companies to which Shakespeare belonged and who first played such roles as Hamlet, Othello, Lear, and Richard III.
Kempe, Will ?–1603. Clown with the Chamberlain's Men.
Rueda, Lope de c. 1505–65, Spanish actor-manager who also wrote popular plays.
Tarleton, Richard ?–1588. Clown, popular with Elizabeth I until he offended her. The probable target of Shakespeare's criticism in *Hamlet*.

5144 POST SHAKESPEAREAN THEATER 1650–1800

Puritan administrations closed English playhouses from 1642 and when theaters opened again 20 years later they were like those which had developed in France – platform stages with doors to provide access at the sides and an arch behind which scenery could be set. In the following centuries the arch moved forward to form a picture frame for the whole action.

French drama developed witty plays satirizing society influenced by the Italian *commedia* and ancient comedy and tragedies following classical forms, both of which were reflected in English and other drama.

In the late 18th and in the 19th centuries German dramatists led a move toward romanticism followed by Gothic-style melodramas.

5141 Events
5142 Post Shakespearean dramatists
5143 Post Shakespearean actors
515 **Naturalism in the theater 1800 – 1900**
5151 Events
5152 Dramatists

Events

5141 **1650–1700**
1651 *The Mayor of Zalamea* by Pierre Calderón de la Barca.
1654 *Lucifer* by Joost van den Vondel.
1660 *Sganarelle* by Jean-Baptiste Molière (**2**).
1664 *The Rival Ladies* by John Dryden.
1664 *La Tartuffe* by Jean-Baptiste Molière.
1666 *Ludi Theatrales Sacri* by Jakob Bidermann (posthumous).
1667 *Andromaque* by Jean Racine (**1**).

1668 *Amphitryon* by Jean-Baptiste Molière.
1669 *The Wild Gallant* by John Dryden.
1670 *Le Bourgeois Gentilhomme* by Jean-Baptiste Molière.
1673 *La vida es sueño* by Pedro Calderón de la Barca.
1677 *All for Love* by John Dryden.
1677 *Phèdre* by Jean Racine.
1680 *La Comédie Française* theater founded in Paris.
1691 *Athalie* by Jean Racine.
1694 *Love for Love* by William Congreve.

1700–1750
1700 *The Way of the World* by English writer William Congreve.
1703 *The Love Suicides at Sonezaki* by Chikamatsu Monzamonz, Japan.
1713 *Cato* by English writer Joseph Addison.
1716 First American theater in Williamsburg, Virginia.
1718 *Oedipus* by French philosopher François-Marie Voltaire.
1722 *The Conscious Lover* by Irish dramatist Richard Steele.
1727 Caronile Neuber made director of the Court Theater in Saxony.
1727 *Le Philosophe Marie* by French dramatist Philippe Destouches.
1728 *Love in Several Masques* by English comic playwright Henry Fielding.
1732 Covent Garden Theatre opens in London.
1736 A theater built in Charleston, South Carolina.
1740–45 *Die deutsche Schaubühne* 6 vols by German writer Johann Gottsched.
1741 *Merope* by François-Marie Voltaire.
1748 *The Treasure of Royal Retainers*, Japanese *kabuki* theater.
1749 *Irene* by English writer Samuel Johnson.

1750–1800
1752 Nassau Street Playhouse in New York.
1753 *Mirandolina* by Carlo Goldoni (**3**).
1755 *Miss Sara Sampson* by German playwright Gotthold Ephraim Lessing.
1758 *Le Père de Famille* by French writer Denis Diderot.
1759 *The Prince of Parthia* by Thomas Godfrey, first American dramatist.
1761 *The Jealous Wife* by English dramatist George Colman.
1767 *Minna von Barnhelm* by Gotthold Ephraim Lessing.
1773 *Goetz von Berlichingen* by Johann Wolfgang von Goethe.
1775 *Philip II* by Italian dramatist Vittorio Alfieri.
1776 The Burgtheater opens in Vienna.
1779 *The Critic* by Richard Sheridan.
1781 *The Robbers* by Friedrich von Schiller.
1784 *Le Mariage de Figaro* by Caron de Beaumarchais.
1789 *Torquato Tasso* by Johann Wolfgang von Goethe.

Post Shakespearean dramatists

5142 **Beaumarchais, Pierre-Augustin Caron de** 1732–99, French satirist of upper class behavior in *The Barber of Seville*, *The Marriage of Figaro*. Founder of the *Société des Auteurs* (Society of Authors), he established the principle of paying royalties to dramatists.
Congreve, William 1670–1707, English Restoration writer, unequalled for his comedies of manners such as *Love for Love*, *The Way of the World*. He wrote one tragedy, *The Mourning Bride*.
Corneille, Pierre 1606–84. The "father" of French tragedy, first wrote comedies achieving success with the tragi-comic *Le Cid*. His plays on historical and mythological themes include *Medea*, *Oedipus*, *Cinna* and the spectacle play *Andromeda*.
Farquhar, George 1678–1707. An actor turned to playwright whose work marks a transition from Restoration to later English drama in *The Constant Couple*, *The Recruiting Officer*, *The Beaux Stratagem*.
Goethe, Johann Wolfgang von (1749–1832), German poet, novelist, actor, theater director, best known for *Egmont*, *Torquato Tasso* and *Faust*, a drama huge in every sense and rarely staged because of the difficulties it presents.
Goldoni, Carlo 1707–93, Venetian who changed the Italian theater of improvised *Commedia dell'arte* to scripted comedies with lively characterization such as *The Servant of Two Masters*, *The Fan*. From 1761 he lived in Paris writing mainly in French.
Lessing, Gotthold Ephraim (1720–81). The first major German playwright and drama critic of the literary Enlightenment. His reputation was founded on *Miss Sara Sampson*, *Minna von Barnhelm*, or *Soldier's Luck*, and *Emilia Galotti*.
Marivaux, Pierre 1688–1763. In comedies such as *The Game of Love* and *Chance* with precise social settings, crediting even servants with feelings which are subtly analyzed, brought more realism to French drama.
Molière, Jean-Baptiste Poquelin 1622–73, France's greatest actor and dramatist, leader of his own company, often appearing before Louis XIV. Plays ridiculing pretension and hypocrisy range from high comedy to farce, including *Le Bourgeois Gentilhomme*, *School for Wives*, *The Miser*, *Tartuffe*, *The Misanthrope*.
Racine, Jean 1639–99, French writer of stark and simply plotted tragedies (and one comedy) strictly adhering to the classical unities, including *Andromaque*, *Phèdre*, *Brittanicus*.
Schiller, Friedrich von 1759–1805. Poet, who first achieved success with the *Sturm und Drang* play *The Robbers*, and for a time co-director with Goethe of the Weimar court theater. Historical plays such as *Mary Stuart* earned him a leading place in German drama.
Sheridan, Richard Brinsley 1751–1816, Irish author of comedies of fashion and society such as *The Rivals*, *The School for Scandal*, *The Critic*. Became manager of Drury Lane Theater and then a politician. *Pizzaro*, a great contemporary success was his version of an Historical play by German dramatist August Kotzebue.
Vanbrugh, John 1664–1726, English architect as well as playwright. Author of *The Relapse*, *The Provoked Wife*.
Wycherley, William 1641–1715, English Restoration dramatist of often indecent comedies with a moral core, including *The Country Wife*, *The Plain Dealer*.

Post Shakespearean actors

5143 **Aldridge, Ira** 1806–72. Black American actor. Unable to make a career in the USA, he had some success in Britain (becoming a naturalized Englishman) and especially in Germany and Russia, where he played King Lear.
Baron, Michel 1653–1729. Theater family orphan whom Molière gave boy roles. Later became chief actor of the *Comédie -Française*, the French National Theater established by Louis XIV.
Betterton, Thomas 1635?–1710. Leading actor of the English Restoration period.
Booth, Junius 1796–1852, English tragic

continued

Post Shakespreaean actors continued

5143 actor, a rival of Kean, to whose Othello he played Iago, before transferring to the American stage. John Wilkes Booth, one of three actor sons, was the assassin of President Lincoln.
Bracegirdle, Anne 1673?–1748, English actress, known for her Millamant in *The Way of the World* and other Congreve roles.
Cibber, Colley 1671–1757, English actor-manager, successful in roles such as Lord Foppington in Vanbrugh's T*he Relapse*. He also wrote plays.
Ekhof, Konrad 1720–78. Beginning in the old declamatory school, the first German actor to adopt a more natural style. For a time worked with Goethe at Weimar.
Forrest, Edwin 1806–72. First American born star actor, described as a "ranter" at first but later outstanding as Shakespeare's tragic heroes and as a Native American chief in Stone's *Metamora*. His rivalry with Macready led to New York riot in 1849.
Garrick, David 1717–79, English actor equally admired in comedy and tragedy. He replaced the formal declamation of Quin's day with more natural delivery, introduced concealed stage lighting at Drury Lane and banned spectators from the stage itself.
Grimaldi, Joseph 1778–1837, British clown and acrobat who added the clown character to the harlequinade. Great inventor of pantomime tricks.
Gwynn, Nell 1650–87, Actress mistress of English king Charles II.
James 1692–1766, English tragedian, last of the school of declamatory performance.
Kean, Edmund 1787?–1833.,English tragic actor, acclaimed in villanous roles such as Richard III. Coleridge wrote that to see Kean act "is like reading Shakespeare by flashes of lightning."
Kemble, John Philip 1757–1823. Brother of Sarah Siddons, a handsome but rather formal actor famous for his Hamlet and other tragic roles.
Macklin, Charles 1699–1797, Irish actor famous for his Macbeth and Shylock (1741), which he played as tragic parts after 90 years of being interpreted by comedians.
Macready, William 1793–1873, English tragedian and rival of Kean and later of Edwin Forrest.
Molière, Jean Baptiste Poquelin 1622-73. Greatest French actor, as well as playwright, of his time.
Oldfield, Anne 1673?–1730, English actress much admired in Farquhar's plays. Buried in Westminster Abbey.
Phelps, Samuel 1804–78, English actor who excelled as Shakespeare's Lear, Othello, and Bottom (in *A Midsummer Night's Dream*).
Schroder, Friedrich Ludwig 1744–1816, German actor who ousted Ekhof from his leading position and introduced Shakespeare to the German stage.
Siddons, Sarah 1755–1831, English tragic actress, noted for her Lady Macbeth. Dignified on stage and off, she brought respectability to the profession.
Talma, François Joseph 1763–1826. Declamatory French actor who made his style less exaggerated, emphasizing sense rather than meter, and began, under the influence of the painter David, to dress plays according to the period of their action.
Woffington, Peg 1718?– 60, Irish actress of great beauty, excellent in comedy and sometimes appearing in travesties.

515 NATURALISM IN THE THEATER 1800 – 1900

The use of gas and then electric lighting and the ability to darken the auditorium made for more effective stage illusion and this was matched by increasing naturalismin both scenery and acting. Eugene Scribe 1791–1861, established the pattern of the "well-made play" with clear exposition of character and plot, usually in three acts with dramatic endings. After a period when most theater was conceived purely as entertainment, toward the end of the 19th century a number of dramatists began to deal with social and political ideologies.

Events

5151 **1800–1850**
1800 *Mary Stuart* by Friedrich von Schiller.
1804 *Wilhelm Tell* by Friedrich von Schiller.
1808 *Faust* Part I by Johann Wolfgang von Goethe.
1808 *The Broken Pitcher* by German playwright Heinrich von Kleist.
1810 *Kätchen von Heilbronn* by Heinrich von Kleist.
1820 Edmund Kean acts Richard III in New York.

1

1825 *Boris Godunov* by Russian writer Alexander Pushkin (**1**).
1831 *School for Coquettes* by English dranatist Catherine Gore.
1832 *Faust* Part II by Johann Wolfgang von Goethe.
1836 *The Revisor* by Russian dramatist Nikolai R. Gogol.
1838 First fully professional theater opens in Chicago.
1841 *Cecil or the Adventures of a Coxcomb* by Catherine Gore.
1845 *King Rene's Daughter* by Henrik Hertz.

1850–1900
1850 P.T. Barnum persuades Jenny Lind to tour USA.
1852 First fully professional theater opens in San Francisco.
1862 Italian actress Eleanora Duse's debut aged four in *Les Misérables*.
1867 *Peer Gynt* by Norwegian playwright Henrik Ibsen.
1869 Booth's Theater opens in New York.
1878 Henry Irving starts managing the Lyceum Theatre, London.

2

1881 *Ghosts* by Henrik Ibsen.
1888 *Miss Julie* by Swedish playwright August Strindberg.
1890 *Hedda Gabler* by Henrik Ibsen.
1892 *Widowers' Houses* by Irish playwright George Bernard Shaw (**2**).
1894 *Arms and the Man* by George Bernard Shaw.
1895 *The Importance of Being Earnest* by Oscar Wilde.
1896 *The Seagull* by Russian dramatist Anton Chekhov.

Dramatists

5152 **Boucicault, Dionysus Larner** 1820–96, English actor and prolific dramatist (150 plays, though some - *The Streets of New York*, *The Streets of London* - differed in little more than a change of location) of *London Assurance*, *The Corsican Brothers*, *The Shaugraun*, and the first serious drama about black Americans, *The Octoroon*.
Dumas, Alexandre 1824–95, French novelist/dramatist - he wrote *The Lady of the Camellias* as a novel and as a play, also realistic comedies of manners.
Wilde, Oscar 1855–1900. Witty Anglo-critic of social mores in *Lady Windermere's Fan*, *A Woman of No Importance*, *An Ideal Husband*, *The Importance of Being Earnest*. Author of a verse drama (originally in French), *Salomé*. He was imprisoned for his homosexuality.

516 NEW STAGES 1900–1990s

Naturalistic plays and picture-frame theaters dominated the first half of the 20th century but increasingly both plays and playhouses have exploited the theatrical experience rather than imitative naturalism which is readily available through film and television. Arrangements where stages thrust out into the audience or the audience surrounds the acting area increase actor-spectator contact and performance spaces are sometimes convertible to different forms.

Events

5161 **1900–1950**

1903 *Reigen* by Austrian dramatist Arthur Schnitzler.
1904 *The Cherry orchard* by Anton Chekhov
1915 Provincetown Players led by Eugene O'Neill founded in Massachusetts.
1920 *Beyond the Horizon* by Eugene O'Neill.
1921 *Six Characters in Search of an Author* by Luigi Pirandello produced in Rome.
1924 *St Joan* by George Bernard Shaw.
1925 *Hay Fever* by Noel Coward.
1920 Spanish playwright Federico Garcia Lorca directed Madrid's La Barca Theater.
1933 *Blood Wedding* by Federico Garcia Lorca.
1935 *Murder in the Cathedral* by T.S. Eliot performed in Canterbury Cathedral.
1938 *Our Town* by Ameican dramatist Thornton Wilder.
1941 *Mother Courage and her Children* by Bertolt Brecht.
1946 *A Streetcar Named Desire* by Tennessee Williams.
1949 *Death of a Salesman* by Arthur Miller.

1950–1990s

1953 *The Chairs* by Eugene Ionesco (produced in Paris).
1953 *Waiting for Godot* by Samuel Beckett (produced in Paris).
1954 *Cat on a Hot Tin Roof* by Tennessee Williams.
1956 *Long Day's Journey into Night* by Eugene O'Neill.
1956 *Look Back in Anger* by John Osborne.
1957 *Endgame* by Samuel Beckett.
1960 *Rhinoceros* by Eugene Ionesco.
1962 *Who's Afraid of Virginia Woolf* by Edward Albee.
1962 La Mama Experimental Theater Club founded in New York.
1964 *Rosencrantz and Guildenstern Are Dead* by Tom Stoppard.
1965 *The Odd Couple* by Neil Simon
1971 *Macbeth* by Eugene Ionesco.
1974 *Short Eyes* by Miguel Pinero.
1980 *The Fifth of July* by US dramatistLandford Wilson.
1982 *The Real Thing* by Tom Stoppard.
1985 *A Lie of the Mind* by Sam Shepard.

Dramatists

5162 **Albee, Edward** b. 1928, American, beneath the realistic surface of whose plays lurk many allegories. *Who's Afraid of Virginia Woolf?, Tiny Alice, A Delicate Balance.*

Anouilh, Jean 1910–87, French dramatist whose plays often deal with loss of innocence, sometimes with humor. *Thieves' Carnival, Antigone, Ardele, Ring Round the Moon.*

Artaud, Antonin 1896–1948, French actor, director and theoretician of the "Theater of Cruelty". He gave emphasis to non-linguistic elements but wrote *The Cenci.*

Ayckbourne, Alan b. 1939. Prolific and popular British writer mainly of comedies of middle-class life. *Relatively Speaking, Bedroom Farce, Norman Conquests, Women in Mind.*

Barker, Howard b. 1946, Brecht-influenced British dramatist. *Victory, The Castle.*

Beckett, Samuel 1905-89. Irish writer (who often wrote in French), His plays ignore conventional theatrical considerations and often deal with the difficulty of communication and the individual's powerlessness to control destiny. *Waiting for Godot, Endgame, Happy Days.*

Bennett, Alan b. 1934. A perceptive and compassionate recorder of English character and an accomplished farceur, he also has a keen political sense in *Forty Years On, Habeas Corpus, Enjoy, The Old Country, Kafka's Dick.*

Bond, Edward b. 1934. A politically committed British writer who often gives a radical rereading of the historical subjects of his plays. *Saved, Narrow Road to the Deep North, Lear, Bingo, Restoration.*

Brecht, Bertolt 1898–1956, German exponent of "epic theatre" intended to make audiences critically examine characters and incident. Founded the Berliner Ensemble, placing emphasis on group playing. *The Threepenny Opera, Galileo, Mother Courage and her Children, The Caucasian Chalk Circle.*

Brenton, Howard b. 1942, British dramatist on strong political themes. *Hitler Dances, Epsom Downs, Romans in Britain, Pravda* (with David Hare).

Chekhov, Anton 1860–1904 (**1**), Russian doctor and writer whose careful character plays of frustration and waste in provincial life are touched with humor and show Russia ripe for revolution. *The Seagull, Uncle Vanya, Three Sisters, The Cherry Orchard.*

1

Churchill, Caryl b. 1938, British dramatist who tackles feminist and wider political issues. *Cloud Nine, Top Girls, Serious Money.*

Coward, Noel 1899–1973, English actor, composer and playwright of wit and sophistication. Beneath the surface humor there is often a serious critique of social mores as in *The Vortex, Hay Fever, Private Lives.*

Eliot, T.S. (Thomas Stearns) 1888–1965 (**2**). American-born poet, dramatist and critic who became a British citizen. He was the central force in the development of modern English poetry, and revived verse plays his religious dramas, *The Rock, Murder in the Cathedral.*

2

Fo, Dario b. 1926, Italian performer and writer of left-wing political farces such as *Accidental Death of an Anarchist, Can't Pay Won't Pay.*

Fugard, Athol b. 1932. Has made a major contribution to understanding of his native South African under apartheid in *Sizwe Banzi is Dead, "Master Harold" ... and the Boys.*

Genet, Jean 1910–86, French existentialist, whose powerful, often stylized plays sometimes draw on his long incarceration in prison and his homosexuality in making powerful statements on personal and public politics. *The Balcony, Deathwatch, The Blacks.*

Gorki, Maxim 1868–1936. Successful before the Russian revolution in which he became important with *The Lower Depths,* a picture of the Moscow underworld, and *Summerfolk.* He established the socialist realist style.

Griffiths, Trevor b. 1935, English writer whose socialism informs his plays. *Comedians, The Party.*

Hampton, Christopher b. 1946, British dramatist and adaptor. *Total Eclipse, The Philanthropist, Tales From Hollywood, Dangerous Liaisons.*

Hare, David b. 1947, British dramatist and director whose plays offer a critique of contemporary society. *Fanshen, Plenty, Map of the World, Pravda* (with Howard Brenton).

Ibsen, Henrik 1828–1906, Norwegian whose realistic plays concerned with social problems and psychological conflict led a radical change in style and content. *Peer Gynt, A Doll's House, Ghosts, An Enemy of the People, The Wild Duck, Hedda Gabler, The Master Builder.*

Ionesco, Eugene b. 1912, French dramatist who inaugurated the "Theater of the Absurd" with *The Bald Primadonna,* followed by *The Chairs,* Rhinoceros, *Exit the King.*

Mamet, David b. 1947, American streetwise dissector of the contemporary scene. *American Buffalo, Glengarry Glen Ross.*

Miller, Arthur b. 1915, American dramatist mainly of social and political issues. *All My Sons, Death of a Salesman, The Crucible, After the Fall.*

continued

Dramatists continued

5162 **O'Casey, Sean** 1880–1964, Irish writer, established through Dublin's Abbey Theater with realistic dramas reflecting ordinary life and Irish politics in *Juno and the Paycock, Plough and the Stars.*

O'Neill, Eugene 1888–1953, American of Irish theatrical stock, Nobel Prize winner. His dramas, often of American immigrant life, have classic weight, among them *Moon for the Misbegotten, Long Day's Journey into Night.* In *Mourning Becomes Electra* he transfers the *Oresteia* to a New England setting.

Orton, Joe 1933–67, English writer of black farces which often set out to shock the bourgeoisie. His career was cut short when he was murdered by his male lover. *Entertaining Mr. Sloane, Loot, What the Butler Saw.*

Osborne, John b. 1929, English former actor whose *Look Back in Anger*, the first "kitchen-sink" drama led radical changes in British theater in the 1950s. *The Entertainer, Luther, Hotel in Amsterdam.*

Pinter, Harold b. 1930, English writer whose ambiguous dialogue and frequent silence define a personal style. Some hidden menace seems to lie behind the situation in most of his plays. *The Birthday Party, The Caretaker, The Homecoming, No Man's Land.*

Pirandello, Luigi 1867–1936, Italian winner of a Nobel Prize for literature, from 1925 director of his own theater company, whose plays often emphasize the theatrical event as metaphor, as in *Six Characters in Search of an Author.*

Rattigan, Terence 1911–77, English writer of light comedies who also tackled more serious topics within the format of the "well-made play." *French Without Tears, The Deep Blue Sea, Separate Tables.*

Rostand, Edmund 1868–1918, French dramatist whose colorful romantic plays were a reaction to the somber naturalistic school. *L'Aiglon*, a vehicle for Sarah Bernhardt as Napoleon's son, and *Cyrano de Bergerac* are the best known.

Russell, Willy b. 1947, British dramatist and song-writer who combines lively popular entertainment with a strong subtext. *Educating Rita, Shirley Valentine.*

Shaffer, Peter b. 1927, English dramatist ranging from light comedy to historical and psychological drama. *Royal Hunt of the Sun, Equus, Amadeus.*

Shaw, George Bernard 1856–1950, Irish critic, political pamphleteer and Nobel Prize winner. A champion of Ibsen's plays, which influenced his own, he leavened dramas of ideas with humor and often gave the best speeches to his devil's advocate. Plays include *Widower's Houses, Pygmalion, Man and Superman, Major Barbara, St Joan, Back to Methuselah.*

Shepard, Sam b. 1943, American, whose plays explore the American myth. *Fool for Love, True West.*

Simon, Neil b. 1927, American writer of popular Broadway comedies, several autobiographical, including *Barefoot in the Park, The Odd Couple, The Sunshine Boys, Brighton Beach Memoirs.*

Stoppard, Tom b. 1937,Czech born, English dramatist noted for verbal wit and intellectual games. *Rozencrantz and Guildenstern are Dead, Jumpers, The Real Thing.*

Strindberg, August 1849–1912. A Swede, at first followed the lead of Ibsen but increasingly reflected the conflict between the sexes evident in his own life. *The Father, Miss Julie, The Dance of Death, The Ghost Sonata.*

Wesker, Arnold 1932– , English socialist writer of the 1950s "new wave" who has since moved away from his early naturalistic style. *Chicken Soup with Barley, Chips with Everything, Roots.*

Wilder, Thornton Niven 1897–1975, American playwright and novelist. His earlier plays were short literary dramas written for university theaters. *Our Town* (1938), a view of American provincial life, and *The Skin of our Teeth* (1942), in which he dealt with the theme of survival,were profound works which won the Pullitzer prize.

Williams, Tennessee 1914–83. American whose plays, often with Southern settings, strong female roles, exploited their own theatricality often tackle problems of sexual orientation and other once taboo topics. *The Glass Menagerie, A Streetcar Named Desire.*

Actors

5163 **Ashcroft, Peggy** 1907–93 English actress who ranged from a delightful Juliet to Hedda Gabler and a fierce Queen Margaret in *Henry VI* and was as at home in Brecht, Albee, Rattigan or Pinter. She made a vital contribution to the Royal Shakespeare Company and was made a Dame in 1956.

Barrymore, Ethel 1878–1959, American actress who after early success in New York played opposite Irving in London. She succeeded in Ibsen as well as in popular dramas, appeared in vaudeville and in many movies.

Barrymore, John 1882–1942, American matinee idol and light comedian who also succeeded as Hamlet but disappointed in his later career, spent largely in movies. Brother of Ethel Barrymore.

Bernhardt, Sarah 1844–1923. Eccentric French actress with a beautiful voice who scored international success in plays by Sardou, Dumas and Rostand and in roles from Phèdre to Hamlet (in travesti). She continued to perform even after the amputation of a leg.

Booth, Edwin 1833–93. First American actor to achieve a European reputation, mainly in tragic roles.

Campbell, Mrs Patrick 1865–1940, English actress who succeeded in Shakespeare and Ibsen as well as lesser work. She captivated Bernard Shaw who wrote the part of Eliza in *Pygmalion* for her.

Cornell, Katherine 1893–1974, American actress, particularly associated with the role of Elizabeth in *The Barretts of Wimpole Street*, but as successful in Shakespeare and Shaw.

Coquelin, Constant-Benoit 1841–1909, French actor outstanding in Molière's comic roles and as Rostand's Cyrano de Bergerac.

Cushmann, Charlotte 1816–76, American actress known for her Lady Macbeth and Gay Spanker in *London Assurance* who also played in travesti as Hamlet, Romeo (opposite sister Susan's Juliet) and Oberon.

Dullin, Charles 1885–1949, French actor and director who founded his own experimental theater.

Duse, Eleanora 1858–1924, Italian actress, rival of Bernhardt. Outstanding in Ibsen and a wide range of emotional roles, she was noted for not using makeup and could blush or pale at will.

Evans, Edith 1888–1976), English actress outstanding as Millamant (*The Way of the World*), Rosalind (*As You Like It*), Lady Bracknell (*Importance of Being Earnest*), Nurse (*Romeo and Juliet*) and many other classic and modern roles. Made a Dame in 1946.

Fontanne, Lyn 1887–1983, English-born actress who, already established, from 1924 became wife and professional partner of Alfred Lunt.

Gielgud, John b. 1904, English actor, known for his mellifluous verse-speaking, and acclaimed in many Shakespearean roles, Restoration comedy, Chekhov, Wilde's *The Importance of Being Earnest* and modern roles from Albee to Pinter, in later years showing new skills as a fine character actor. Knighted 1953.

Hayes, Helen 1900–93, American actress, who became famous for her performances in *Pollyanna* (1917-18), *Dear Brutus* (1919) and *The Wisteria Trees* (1951). She appeared in many films, including *The Sin of Madelon Claudet* (1931).

Irving, Henry 1838–1905, English actor-manager who dominated the London stage from 1870 and the first to receive a knighthood. Successful in many roles but especially as Hamlet, Shylock and in the melodramatic *The Bells.*

Jouvet, Louis 1887–1951, French actor and director especially associated with the works of Jean Giraudoux and Molière.

Knipper, Olga 1868–1959, Russian actress who appeared in all Chekhov's plays and became his wife. In 1943 she was still playing Ranevskaya in *The Cherry Orchard*, a role she created in 1904.

Lunt, Alfred 1892–1977, American actor who, with his wife (Lyn Fontanne) became celebrated for their teamwork in intimate modern comedies.

MacLiammoir, Micheal 1899–1978. Charismatic Irish actor and director, co-founder (with Hilton Edwards) of the Dublin Gate Theatre. His career was capped by a series of virtuoso one-man shows.

Magnani, Anna 1908–73, Italian actress of great emotional power, best known overseas for her movies.

Mei Lan-fang 1894–1961, Chinese actor, excelled in female roles in Beijing Opera. Touring the world in the 1920s and 30s he influenced the theories of Brecht and became a friend of Stanislavsky and Nemirovich-Danchenko.

continued

Actors continued

5163 **Moissi, Alexander** 1880–1935, German actor of Italian origin who played in Shakespeare and Shaw. Remembered for his Orestes and Oedipus in Max Reinhardt productions of Sophocles' plays.
Olivier, Laurence 1907–89, English actor and director whose early career ranged from Coward's *Private Lives* to Shakespeare at the Old Vic. Knighted in 1947 and director of National Theatre 1961–72, he gained acclaim for parts as diverse as Oedipus, Richard III, Justice Shallow (Shakespeare's *Henry IV*) and Archie Rice (Osborne's *The Entertainer*).
Paxinou, Katina 1900–73, Greek actress, playing many roles in the Greek classics, often directed by her husband Alexis Minotis, but also impressive as Mrs Alving in *Ghosts* and in modern movie roles.
Redgrave, Michael 1908–85, English actor, a fine comedian but more often seen in heroic roles and as Shakespeare's Prospero and Shylock and as Uncle Vanya. Knighted in 1959.
Richardson, Ralph 1902–83, English actor, equally successful in Shakespeare (especially with London's Old Vic) and modern plays - one of his later successes was in Pinter's *No Man's Land.* Knighted in 1947.
Terry, Ellen 1847–1928, English leading lady to Henry Irving. Better in comedy than tragedy (though many acclaimed her Lady Macbeth) she was made a Dame in 1925.
Thorndike, Sybil 1882–1976, English actress celebrated for her roles in many modern plays, in Chekhov, Shakespeare, Ibsen and Euripides. Shaw wrote *St Joan* for her. Made a Dame in 1931.
Tree, Herbert Beerbohm 1853-1917, English actor-manager famous for his elaborately-mounted productions which ranged from Shakespeare to new plays, including Shaw's *Pygmalion* in which he was the first Professor Higgins.
Weigel, Helene 1900-72, German actress, wife of Bertolt Brecht and director of the Berliner Ensemble after his death. Her most famous role was Mother Courage.

CONTEMPORARY ACTORS
Although there is no lack of fine actors in theater today, less emphasis is given to "stars," and individual popular fame now comes through films and television which reach much wider audiences. While reputations made in other media give some names great drawing power, it would be invidious to single out a few names from the many fine contemporary performers.

517 DIRECTORS

The role of the play director has grown in importance through the 20th century. Previously lead actor, author or stage manager devised the production, though George II, Duke of S'achsen Meiningen directed the plays in his court theater establishing an overall style, his stage groupings seeking a more natural, though still dramatic effect. He was greatly influenced by the historicism of Charles Kean who had shown great care in the mounting of productions.
Actor-managers such as Irving, Tree and especially David Belasco 1853-1931, in America gave great attention to scenic effect but were not great innovators or theorists. The development of naturalistic drama with more everyday settings made illusionistic staging easier, its high priest was André Antoine 1858–1943, at his Théâtre Libre in Paris where he also revolutionized French acting.

Abbott, George (1887–) American director and playwright, who made his name as an actor in fast moving farce. As a playwright, he achieved great success with *The Fall Guy* (1925) and *Three Men on a Horse* (1935). He directed many musical comodies on Broadway during the 1930s, 1940s, and 1950s, notably *Pal Joey* (1940), and *The Pajama Game* (1954).
Appia, Adolphe 1862–1928, Swiss artist and theorist who rejected painted scenery in favour of sculptural forms and lighting which he saw as the visual counterpart of music, while throwing emphasis on the actor.
Beck, Julian 1925–85, American creator with his wife Judith Malina of the Living Theater, a collective which developed confrontational performances that often invaded audience space.
Brecht, Bertolt 1898–1956, German dramatist and director who sought to counter "suspension of disbelief" by abandoning illusionist theater, though not the use of theatrical effect.
Brook, Peter b. 1925, Innovative British director. He directed the Royal Shakespeare company's Theater of Cruelty season based on the ideas of Artaud; the wild and intense Weiss *Marat/Sade;* and *A Midsummer Night's Dream* set in a white box and using circus and juggling skills. Set up the International Center for Theater Research in Paris where he has drawn actors with skills from Western, Asian and African traditions to create complex productions from apparently simple devices.
Craig, Gordon 1872–1966, English actor-designer, son of Ellen Terry, who devised systems of screens and moveable cubes for settings with strong lighting. Though few of his projects became actual productions, his influence was widespread.
Grotowski, Jerzy b. 1933, Polish director of an experimental laboratory theater based on psychophysical principles, apparently spontaneous but rigorously controlled, often using unusual spacial relationships with the audience.
Guthrie, Tyrone 1900–71, Irish director always experimenting with style, for example staging Shakespeare out of period. Especially associated with the Old Vic. After staging arena productions at the Edinburgh Festival he was an advocate of the open stage, first at Stratford Ontario then at the theater in Minneapolis named after him.
Hall, Peter b. 1930, English director of the Royal Shakespeare Company 1960-73 and the National Theatre 1973-88. Particularly associated with Shakespeare, Pinter, and Beckett.
Kazan, Elia b. 1909, American actor-director, one of the founders of the Actors' Studio in New York which taught "Method" acting developed from the ideas of Stanislavsky.
Meyerhold, Vsevolod 1874–1940, Russian director who worked with Stanislavsky and developed ideas borrowed from Craig using the actor like a marionette under his control in constructivist settings.
Mnouchkine, Ariane b. 1938, French director, founder-member of the Théâtre du Soleil with whom she has developed, improvised and devised productions which have drawn on the techniques of widely different cultures and experimented with audience-actor relationships.
Papp, Joseph 1921–93, American director who created the open-air semi-arena stage in New York's Central Park and the New York Public Theater.
Piscator, Erwin 1893–1966, German director, follower of Rheinhardt, who initiated "epic" theater, later developed by Brecht, and the use of documentary material.
Planchon, Roger b. 1931, French director, influenced by Vilar and Brecht who has drawn from every possible source to enlarge the range of stagecraft.
Reinhardt, Max 1873–1943, Austrian director. Adept at handling crowds and spectacle, from outdoor performances of morality plays and *Faust*, to Greek tragedy in vast auditoria. And, most famously, *The Miracle* converting theaters and exhibition halls into huge medieval environments but also staging intimate drama in intimate locations. He saw theater as a communal event and in Berlin had built a theater seating 3,000 with a huge thrust stage.
Stanislavsky, Konstantin 1863–1938), Russian director (with Vladimir Nemirovich-Danchenko) of the Moscow Arts Theater, where naturalistic staging and acting concentrating on psychological understanding illuminated productions, especially of Chekhov. His principles developed into a system of actor training called "Method."
Vilar, Jean 1912–71, French director, head 1951–62 of the Théâtre National Populaire, the directness and simplicity of whose productions had considerable influence on others.

518 THEATER (GENERAL)

Parts of a theater

5181

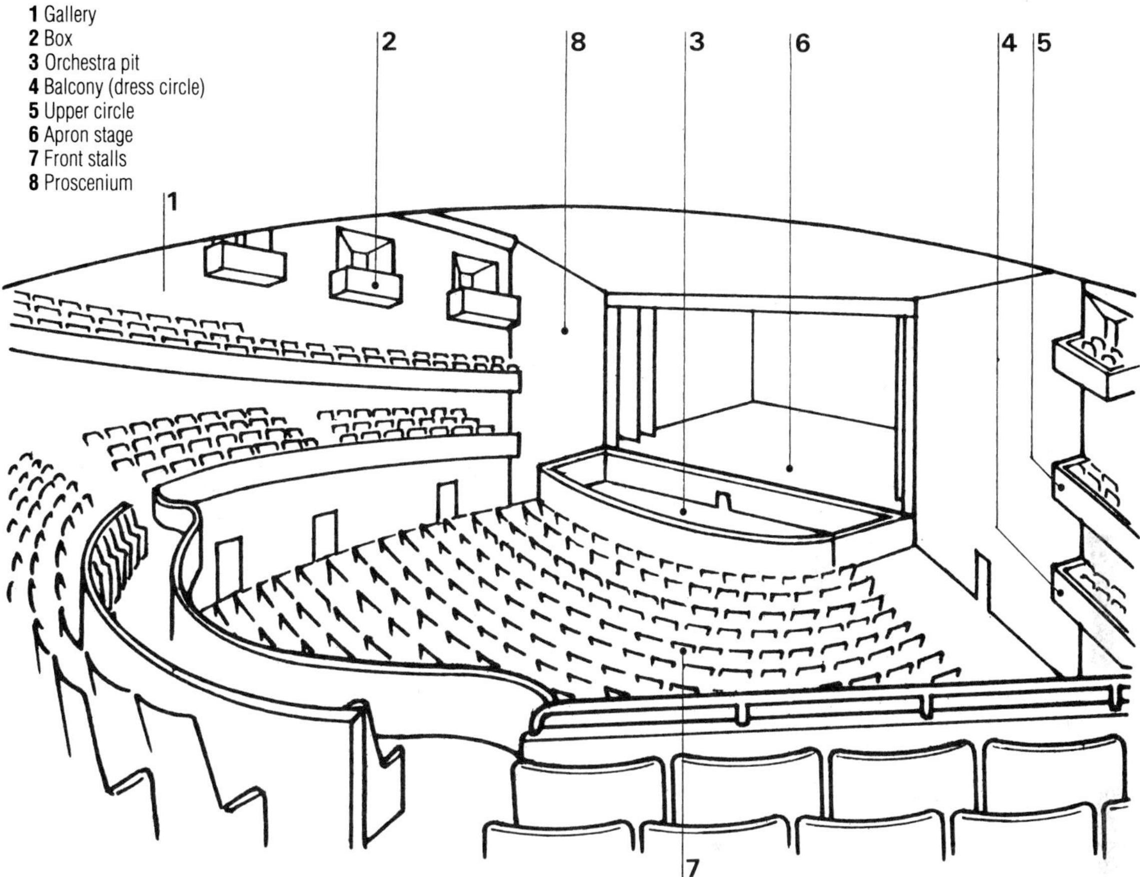

apron Extension of stage in front of proscenium arch.
auditorium The area where the audience sits.
box Separate compartment in auditorium seating small group of people. Usually on sides near stage but in some old theaters a whole tier may be divided.
box office Place where tickets are bought. At one time only boxes were reserved.
box set Stage scene made up of enclosing walls, like a room.
circle A balcony or tier in the auditorium; dress circle, usually most expensive seats where spectators used to dress formally, is the first tier.
dimmer A rheostat, apparatus to lower intensity of lamps.
dips Sockets in the stage for plugging lamps or electrical effects.
foh Front-of-House, the audience part of the theater, including foyers, bars etc.
forestage Part of stage in front of curtain in proscenium theaters.
gallery The highest of the tiers of audience seating.
op (opposite prompt) The left hand side of the stage when facing the audience (right in UK).
pit The seating area on the lower level of the auditorium (now more frequently called the stalls); orchestra pit, lowered area in front of proscenium for musicians.
stalls Separate seats, usually with arm rests, originally front of the lower level of the auditorium, now usually all that level.
thrust stage A stage projecting into the audience area.
wings areas Beyond the acting area to the side of the stage.

TERMS FOR SCENERY AND PROPS
batten Wooden bar or metal pipe from which scenery or lights are suspended.
border Horizontal scenic cloth or curtain masking lights and space above stage.
brace Support set at an angle to hold scenery upright and secured by a weight on a projecting foot.
cloth Canvas scenery suspended from above; a backcloth at the rear of the stage, a cloth with shapes cut from it so that the audience can see beyond.
cyclorama A curved and stretched cloth around the rear of the stage which gives the impression of sky or extensive space.
flat Scenic unit of canvas stretched on a frame.
flies Space above the stage where scenery and lighting can hang out of audience view.
floats Footlights, because originally wicks floating in bowls of oil.
flood A lamp giving a broad spread of light, not focusable.
follow spot One which can be moved to keep an actor lit as he moves about the stage.
footlights A row of lights at the front of the stage, necessary in the past to counter the heavy shadows cast by overhead lighting on actors' faces.
gauze A fine mesh cloth, often painted, visible when lit from the front but disappearing when only lit from behind.
spot A focusable lamp.
tabs Tableau curtains, originally used to disclose a tableau, now usually as house tabs for a front curtain.
trap Opening in the stage, covered by hinged or sliding panels, as in a grave trap, a rectangular opening for obvious purposes. A star trap has triangular hinged panels filling a circular hole through which an actor can pop up suddenly.
traverse Curtains which are drawn across the stage.

People

5182

director Person who controls artistic aspects of a production and directs and rehearses actors; formerly called the producer, but this now more usually the person who presents the show and organizes finance.
stage manager Person responsible for organizing rehearsals, coordinating technical elements and ensuring performances run smoothly, usually helped by Assistant Stage Managers (ASMs). Sometimes with a Stage Director as the head of the team and in theaters with a large repertoire a Production Manager responsible for future planning and overall control.

Technical stage terms

5183

alienation effect Use of techniques to interrupt emotional involvement and encourage audience to make a critical appraisal of the situation.
arena theater Theater-in-the-round, also originally used to describe open stage.
blocking Deciding actors' movements about the stage.
call Announcement or signal to actor or technician that he or she is needed.
catharsis Purification of emotions by showing pity and fear.
chorus The group of performers representing ordinary people in Greek drama, commenting on the action; in modern times a group of singers and dancers, distinct from the principal players.
corpse To be unable, when performing, to hide a laugh at some distraction or error.
cue Words or action to which an effect must be made; also a lighting or sound effect.
deus ex machina Originally a god lowered from above who might change or resolve a Greek drama to provide its closure; now a sudden introduction of a character or other device to untangle a situation and (usually) bring about a happy ending.
dress rehearsal Rehearsal in costume with scenery and effects, as though it were a performance.
dry To forget the words of one's part.
effects Sounds and lighting changes to simulate real incident or create dramatic circumstances required by play.
fade in/out Increase or decrease of strength of light or sound from zero level.
get in/out Unloading and setting up/dismantling and unloading scenery into a theater.
repertory The range of plays a company performs in a season; often with the same core of actors.
soliloquy A speech in which a character reveals his of her thoughts to the audience.
stock company American term for a company in which the same actors perform in several plays in a season, especially "Summer Stock."
tableau Moment when the action is frozen and actors hold a pose, most frequently at the beginning or end of a scene.
theater-in-the-round Acting space with audience on all sides, not necessarily in a circle.

Theater genres

5184

WESTERN THEATER GENRES
absurd, theatre of the 1950s drama of Ionesco and others which presented the absurdity of the human condition and used irrational forms to do so.
burlesque A parody of a particular play or genre; in America from 1866 a variety show with comedy, acrobats and, from 1920s, strippers such as Gypsy Rose Lee.
comedy Drama that ends happily, an amusing play.
comedy of manners Witty drama satirizing social convention and behavior as in Wycherley and Wilde.
commedia dell'arte 16th-17th century improvised Italian drama based on stock characters such as Harlequin and Pulchinello.
cruelty, theater of Drama inspired by theories of Antonin Artaud aiming to release awareness of repressed feelings in the audience.
farce Broad comedy depending on situation and the exposure of hypocrisy especially in conventional figures.
grand guignol Short plays based on escalating shock-horror and violence, named for a Paris theater which specialized in them
harlequinade A development from French dumbshow versions of the *commedia dell'arte*, featuring Harlequin, Pantaloon, Columbine and Pierrot, an essential element of early British pantomimes.
masque Spectacle with scenery, music and dance, usually on a mythological theme, developed in Renaissance courts.
melodrama Originally a play with music, but popularly a play using heightened effects including transformations, contrasting innocence and evil and often given a "Gothic" setting.
miracle play Medieval religious drama.
mime Communication by gesture, usually without words.
morality play Development from mystery play presenting allegories of life with personification of vices and virtues.
musical comedy Play in which songs and frequently dance are introduced, with music in a popular vein. Since the use of more serious plots and the greater integration of the musical elements the word "comedy" is now rarely used.
mystery play Medieval religious drama originally performed by craft guilds.
pageant Spectacle usually in the form of recreation of historic episodes or processions, often with a sequence of tableaux on floats, taking the name from the pageant wagons on which mystery plays were often performed.
pantomime A Roman dumbshow, performed by a masked actor, or any mime performance, but more usually the British Christmas entertainment, usually built around a fairytale plot, which developed from the harlequinade. It traditionally features transvestite performers in the leading male romantic role and as the comic "dame."
puppet theatre There are many forms of puppets, usually controlled by unseen operators, although in *Bunraku* the black clothed puppeteers are visible. Marionettes are operated by strings on which they are suspended, rod puppets by sticks usually controlled from below, glove puppets worn on the hand, and there are huge figures moved by operators inside them as in some Spanish fiestas and the work of companies such as Welfare State and the Bread and Puppet Theater. Other forms, which throw shadows onto a screen, are found in Greece and Indonesia.
promenade performance A production in which the audience is able to move about changing its relation to scenes which may take place anywhere among them, or in a succession of different locations.
revue A show made up of a series of monologues or sketches, musical and dance numbers and satirical items.
tragedy Serious drama in which the protagonist is overcome, usually because of some personal failure or fatal destiny.

ORIENTAL THEATER GENRES
bunraku Japanese puppet theater, performed in full stage settings by almost life-size puppets held by black clothed and masked operators, also known as *joruri* it predates the *kabuki* theater and the plays of Chikamatsu Monzaemon, the "Japanese Shakespeare." His plays were written for these puppets. Only one company survives.
Chinese opera Indigenous theater form making considerable use of dance, acrobatic, and martial arts with stylized costume and gesture.
joruri A more correct name for *bunraku.*
kabuki Japanese popular drama developed in 16th century, usually with legendary or historic plots. Highly stylized, though less ritualized than *no*, all roles played by men.
kathakali Indian dramatic form acted by men and boys using stylized makeup and gesture.
no (or noh) Japanese classical theater, highly stylized and masked, with mythological plots. The court form as opposed to the "popular" *kabuki* drama.

521 MAKING MUSIC

Musical instruments

5211 Musical instruments are grouped into five categories according to the way sound is produced. These categories are aerophones, idiophones, membranophones, chordophones, and mechanical and electrical instruments.

Aerophones
Aerophones are instruments in which the sound is produced by the vibration of air. They are classified according to how the vibration is generated. In instruments with a blow hole (**1**) or whistle mouthpiece (**2**) the air vibrates after being directed against a sharp edge. Vibrations in a tube may also be produced by reeds – single (**3**), double (**4**), or free (**5**). In cup mouthpiece instruments (**6**), air is made to vibrate by the action of the player's lips. In a free aerophone (**7**) there is no enclosed column – the air vibrates around the instrument as it travels through the air.

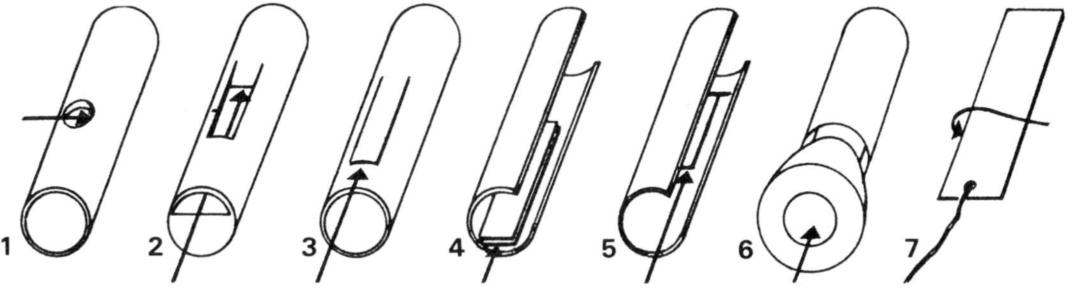

Idiophones
Idiophones are instruments made of naturally sonorous material classified according to the ways in which they are used to make sound. The eight sounding methods are stamping (**1**), stamped (**2**), shaken (**3**), percussion (**4**), concussion (**5**), friction (**6**), scraped (**7**), and plucked (**8**).

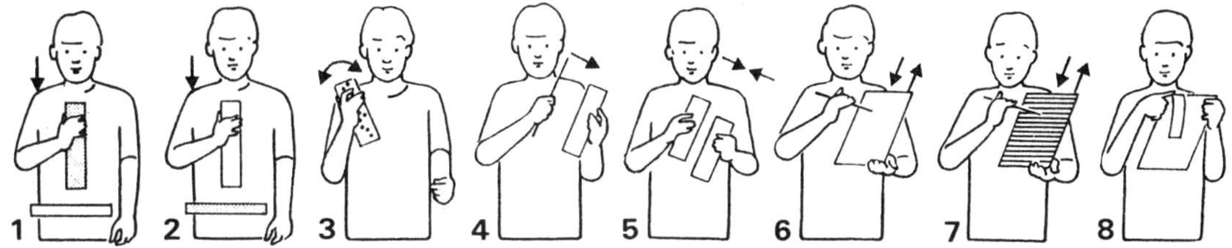

Membranophones

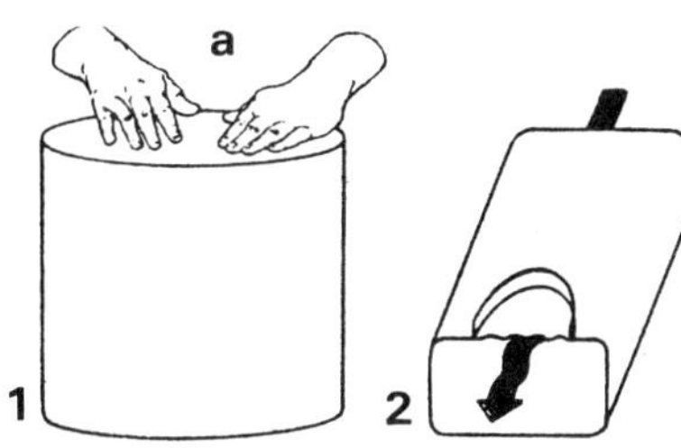

Membranophones are instruments in which the sound is made by the vibration of a stretched membrane, or skin. There are two basic types – drums (**1**) and mirlitons (**2**). A mirliton is sounded by blowing or humming into the instrument. The skin of a drum may be made to vibrate by beating with the hands (**a**), sticks (**b**), padded beaters (**c**), or wire brushes (**d**). The skins of the clapper drum (**e**) are struck with small beads as the drum is shaken. Most friction drums are sounded by a stick piercing the skin (**f**).

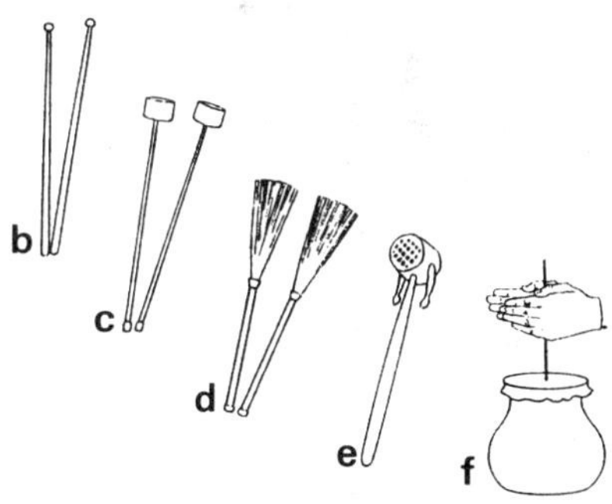

Chordophones
Chordophones are instruments in which the sound is made by the vibration of strings. There are five basic types: bows, lyres, harps, lutes, and zithers. The musical bow (**1**) has one or more strings attached to each end of a curved stick. The strings of the lyre (**2**) run from the resonator to a crossbar supported by two arms. Harp strings run at an oblique angle from the resonator to the neck (**3**). Instruments of the lute family have strings running from near the base of the body, over a bridge, to the end of the neck (**4**). Zither strings (**5**), raised by bridges, run along the instrument's entire length parallel to the body.

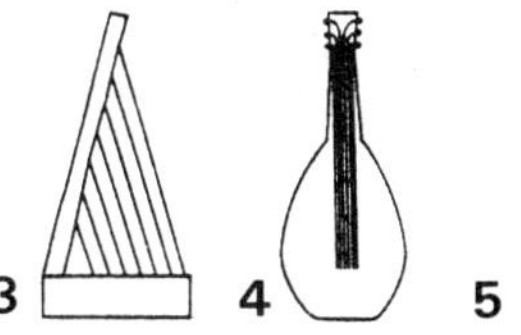

Mechanical and electrical
There are many mechanical and electrical instruments. These include radio-electric instruments, electric organs, electro-mechanical instruments, electric guitars, mechanical instruments, automatic pianos, carillons and chimes, and music boxes.

Famous instrumentalists

5212 The musicians who become most famous are those who have the opportunity to display their virtuosity as soloists in works for their instruments. There are not many concertos for drums or double-bass, for instance. Most of the best known soloists play the piano, violin or cello. Many composers, such as child prodigy Mozart, Chopin, Paganini, and Liszt gained equal fame as performers.

Armstrong, Louis 1900–71 (**1**).

Widely known by his nickname "Satchmo," short for "Satchel Mouth." He was one of the world's best known trumpet players. First learned to play the trumpet at reform school then in 1922 went to Chicago to play the cornet in King Oliver's Creole Jazz Band.
Ashkenazy, Vladimir b. 1937, Russian-born Icelandic pianist, a child prodigy at 15, music director with Royal Philharmonic Orchestra from 1987.
Brain, Dennis 1921–57, English horn player for whom Britten wrote his *Serenade*.
Bream, Julian b. 1933, British guitarist and lutanist, almost alone revived the lute and encouraged new writing for the guitar.
Brendel, Alfred b. 1931, Austrian pianist pre-eminent in the Haydn to Schubert repertoire.
Casadesus, Robert 1899–1972, French pianist associated with the work of his friend Ravel.
Casals, Pablo 1876–1973, Spanish cellist who revived Bach's unaccompanied works.
Du Pré, Jacqueline 1945–87, British cellist, especially associated with the Elgar cello concerto. Her career was cut short by multiple sclerosis in 1972.
Galway, James b. 1939, Irish flautist with a classical and near pop repertoire.
Goossens, Leon 1896–1988, English oboist, Vaughan Williams and others wrote works specially for him.
Gould, Glenn 1932–82, Canadian concert pianist specializing in Bach.
Grappelli, Stephane b. 1908, French violinist, after classical training turned to jazz; peformed and recorded with Menuhin.
Heifetz, Jascha 1901–87, Russian-born American, a child prodigy who became the finest of modern violinists. Transcribed many works for solo violin as well as playing the concerto repertoire.
Hess, Myra 1890–1965, British concert pianist, especially remembered for her London wartime concerts.
Horowitz, Vladimir 1904–89, Russian-born American pianist who excelled in interpreting the romantic composers.
Kennedy, Nigel b. 1956, British classical and jazz violinist.
Kreisler, Fritz 1875–1962, Austrian violin virtuoso who employed extensive vibrato.
Landowska, Wanda 1879–1959, Polish-born harpsichordist, moved to France in 1900 and later to US in 1940.
Larrocha, Alicia de b. 1923, Spanish concert pianist specializing in Spanish music and acclaimed for her Mozart interpretations.
Marsalis, Wynton b. 1961, American trumpeter in both jazz and classical repertoire.
Menuhin, Yehudi b. 1916, American-born British violinist. A boyhood recording of Elgar's violin concerto with the composer in 1932 began his deserved life-long celebrity.
Paganini, Niccolò 1782–1840. The greatest violin virtuoso of the 19th century. Born in Italy, Paganini exploited new fingering and tuning techniques and made extensive use of pizzicato and harmonics (**2**).

Rampal, Jean-Pierre b. 1922, French flautist, especially associated with the Baroque repertoire.
Rostropovich, Mstislav b. 1927, Russian cellist, pianist, and conductor, premiered cello concertos by Prokofiev, Shostakovitch, and Britten, and many other works written for him.
Rubinstein, Artur 1887–82, Polish-born American pianist noted for his interpretations of Mozart and Spanish music and, in his later years, Chopin.
Schnabel, Artur 1882–1951, Austrian-born American pianist and composer, first to record all the Beethoven sonatas. Also revived Schubert's sonatas.
Segovia, Andrés 1893–1987, Spanish classical guitar virtuoso in part responsible for establishing this as a modern classical solo and concerto instrument (**3**).

Shankar, Ravi b. 1920. Born in Benares (Varanasi), India, a famous seat of Hindu culture, Shankar is the world's best known exponent and popularizer of the Indian sitar. He founded India's National Orchestra of Chamber Music and made an impact in the West when he appeared in the 1960s as The Beatles' guest star (**4**).

Stern, Isaac b. 1920, Russian-born American violinist. His New York debut in 1937 began a distinguished solo career in concertos and chamber works.
Zimbalist, Efrem 1889–1985, Russian-born American violinist and composer.

Music notation

5213 **Key Signature**

1 G major
E minor
2 D major
B minor
3 A major
F sharp minor
4 E major
C sharp minor
5 B major
G sharp minor
6 F sharp major
D sharp minor
7 C sharp major
A sharp minor

1 
2 
3 
4 
5 
6 
7 

continued

Music notation continued

5213

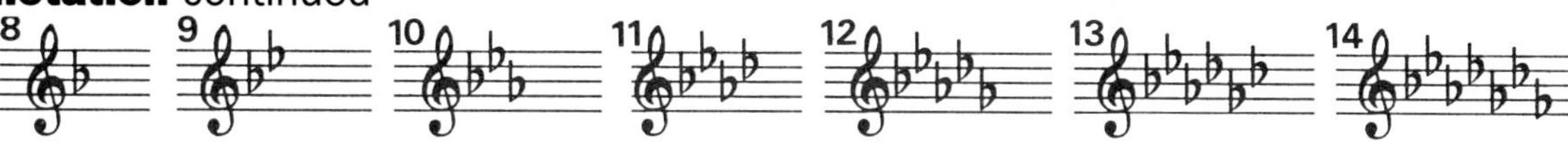

8 F major
D minor
9 B flat major
G minor
10 E flat major
C minor
11 A flat major
F minor
12 D flat major
B flat minor
13 G flat major
E flat minor
14 C flat major
A flat minor

The diatonic scale

Symbols used in writing music

1 Staff
2 Treble (G) clef
3 Bass (F) clef
4 Alto (C) clef
5 Bar line
6 Measure
7 Final bar
8 Whole note (semibreve)
9 Half note (minim)
10 Quarter note (crotchet)
11 Eighth note (quaver)
12 Sixteenth note (semiquaver)
13 Whole rest
14 Half rest
15 Quarter rest
16 Eighth rest
17 Sixteenth rest
18 Measure's rest
19 Triplet
20 3/4 time
21 4/4 time
22 2/2 time
23 6/8 time
24 5/8 time
25 Triad (3 note chord)
26 Arpeggio (rolled chord)
27 Sharp
28 Flat
29 Natural
30 Double sharp
31 Double flat
32 Dissonance
33 Tie
34 Slur
35 Glissando
36 Legato
37 Non legato
38 Repeat
39 Tremolo
40 Piano (soft)
41 Pianissimo (very soft)
42 Forte (loud)
43 Fortissimo (very loud)
44 Sforzando (with sudden force)
45 Crescendo
46 Decrescendo
47 Swell
48 Repeat from beginning
49 Turn
50 Trill
51 Staccato
52 Pause

Chamber groups

5214

Chamber groups have from two to ten performers, each playing a different part.
1 Baroque sonatas for solo instruments such as the oboe or flute have a cello and harpsichord accompaniment. (Similar in style are trio sonatas featuring two treble instruments – oboes, flutes, recorders, or violins – with cello or keyboard continuo).

Chamber groups continued

5214

2

3

2, 3 String trios and **string quartets** were particularly popular in the classical period. String trios used a violin, viola, and cello and string quartets two violins, viola, and cello.

4 A piano trio replaces one of the instruments of a string trio with a piano.

5 Solo sonatas of the classical period usually feature one melody instrument with piano accompaniment.

6 The wind quintet, a common grouping of wind and brass consists of a flute, oboe, clarinet, bassoon, and horn.

4

5

6

Orchestra seating plan

5215 **Usual orchestral seating plan**
Instruments of the four "families"– woodwind, brass, percussion and strings – are positioned in groups. This arrangement helps blend the tone colors of individual instruments, and helps the musicians play together in their groups.

Woodwind
1 Piccolo
2 Flutes
3 Oboes
4 Cor anglais
5 Clarinets
6 Bass clarinet
7 Bassoons
8 Contrabassoon

Brass
9 Horns
10 Trumpets
11 Tenor trombones
12 Tuba

Percussion
13 Tam-tam
14 Cymbals
15 Xylophone
16 Glockenspiel
17 Tubular bells
18 Side drum
19 Bass drum
20 Timpani

Strings
21 Harp
22 1st violins
23 2nd violins
24 Violas
25 Cellos
26 Double basses

Famous orchestras

5216 **BBC Symphony Orchestra** UK, chief conductor Andrew Davis.
Berlin Philharmonic Orchestra Germany, founded 1882, principal conductor Claudio Abbado.
Boston Symphony Orchestra US, founded 1881, music director Seiji Ozawa.
Chicago Symphony Orchestra US, founded 1891, music director Daniel Barenboim.
City of Birmingham Symphony Orchestra UK, music director Simon Rattle.
The Cleveland Orchestra US founded 1918, conductor Christoph von Dohnányi.
Czech Philharmonic Orchestra Prague. Established in 1896, became independent in 1901.
Detroit Symphony Orchestra US, founded 1914, principal conductor Günther Herbig.
Gewandhaus Orchestra of Leipzig Germany, founded 1781, conductor Kurt Masur.
Hallé Orchestra, Manchester UK, founded 1858. Principal conductor Stanislaw Skrowaczewski.
Houston Symphony Orchestra US, founded 1913, principal conductor Christoph Eschenbach.
Israel Philharmonic Orchestra Tel Aviv, founded 1936, music director Zubin Mehta.
London Philharmonic Orchestra UK, founded 1932, music director Franz Welser-Möst, conductor laureate Klaus Tennstedt.
London Symphony Orchestra Founded 1904, principal conductor Michael Tilson Thomas.
Los Angeles Philharmonic Orchestra US, founded 1919, principal conductor Esa-Pekka Salonen.
Montreal Symphony Orchestra Title dates from 1953, principal conductor Charles Dutoit.
Moscow Philharmonic Orchestra Russia, principal conductor Vassili Sinaiski.
New York Philharmonic Orchestra US, founded 1842, principal conductor Kurt Masur.
Orchestre de la Suisse Romande Geneva, Switzerland, founded 1918, principal conductor Armin Jordan.
Oslo Philharmonic Orchestra Norway, founded 1871, chief conductor Mariss Jansons.
Philadelphia Orchestra US, founded 1900, music director (from 1993) Wolfgang Swallisch.
The Philharmonia UK, founded 1945, music director Giuseppe Sinopoli.
Pittsburgh Symphony Orchestra US, founded 1895, principal conductor Lorin Maazel
Royal Concertgebouw Orchestra Amsterdam, Netherlands, founded 1888, principal conductor Riccardo Chailly.
Royal Philharmonic Orchestra UK, founded 1946, music director Vladimir Ashkenazy.
St Louis Symphony Orchestra US, founded 1880, music director Leonard Slatkin.

continued

Famous orchestras continued

5216 **St Petersburg Philharmonic Orchestra** (formerly Leningrad PO), Russia, founded 1921, music director Yuri Temirkanov.
San Francisco Symphony Orchestra US, founded 1911, principal conductor Herbert Blomstedt
Tokyo Philharmonic Orchestra Japan, founded 1940 (as the Central Symphony Orchestra).
Vienna Philharmonic Orchestra Austria, founded 1842.

Musical forms

5217 **anthem** Choral piece for use in church services.
arabesque Ornate musical passage.
ballad Narrative song, or piece in similar style.
can can Composition in 2/4 time in which one part is repeated by and overlaps another. In vogue in Paris in 1830s.
cantata Sung work, now usually accompanied by an orchestra, shorter than an oratorio.
capriccio Short, lively instrumental piece, often humorous.
chamber music Music for a small group of musicians, suitable for playing in small halls.
chorale Stately hymn, especially of Lutheran Church.
coda Passage bringing a work or movement to a conclusion.
concerto Work for a solo instrument, with orchestral accompaniment.
counterpoint Two or more melodic lines combined harmoniously.
divertimento Entertaining chamber suite or miniature symphony.
divertissement Fantasia on well known tunes.
étude Study, exercise to display technique.
fugue A composition of many parts on a short theme and using counterpoint.
Gregorian chant Unaccompanied church vocal music without definite rythm.
impromptu Improvised composition or piece suggesting spontaneity.
intermezzo Play with music between acts of an opera, later any interlude or a short movement in a symphony.
lieder German song style (*lied* = song), especially as used by Romantic composers.
madrigal Unaccompanied song for several voices.
Mass Liturgy of the Eucharist and a setting of it to music.
minuet A graceful 17th-century court dance in triple time, used as third movement in many classical symphonies.
motet Polyphonic sacred music for unaccompanied voices.
movement Section of a large work, especially a symphony, usually complete in itself.
music theater Theatrical work with music and drama integrated, as opposed to opera where music tends to be the most important component.
nocturne Lyrical serenade, especially in Chopin's works for piano.
opera Extended drama, its text sung, often with bravura solo and multiple voice passages.
operetta Light opera, often with spoken dialogue.
oratorio Work for solo voices, chorus, and orchestra, usually of a religious or contemplative nature.
overture Orchestral introduction to an opera or ballet, sometimes to a symphony, or an independent and usually programmatic concert work.
plainsong Nonmetrical church chant.
polyphony Music with independent melodies interwoven.
program music Piece depicting elements of a story, scene, or philosophical ideas.
recitative Singing style like declaimed speech, used for essential narration in some operas and oratorios.
requiem Funeral mass and musical setting of it.
rhapsody Instrumental fantasia, often based on folk song.
rondo Instrumental music with a recurring main theme.
scherzo Lively piece, often humorous, in triplet time and used for the third movement of symphonies and sonatas.
serenade or **serenata** Piece appropriate for evening; a composition in several movements for a small group.
sinfonietta A short, light form of symphony.
sonata Instrumental work in three or four movements for soloist or with piano accompaniment.
suite Group of dances; a set of instrumental pieces drawn from a longer opera, ballet, or similar work.
symphonic poem Narrative orchestral piece, usually in one movement.
symphony Extended orchestral work, usually in four movements.
toccata Keyboard work to display virtuosity.
variations Development of a single theme through a variety of forms.

Musical instructions

5218 **accelerando** Getting gradually faster.
adagio Slower pace.
affettuoso With warmth.
agitato Restlessly.
alla breve Twice the speed notes show.
allegretto Moderately fast.
allegro Fast pace.
andante Gently, flowing.
apassionato Passionately.
arpeggio Notes in rapid succession.
coll'arco With the bow.
con bravura Boldly.
crescendo Increase volume gradually.
da capo Repeat from beginning.
decrescendo Decrease volume.
diminuendo Getting softer.
dolce Sweetly.
dolente Sadly.
doppio movimento Twice as fast.
estinto So soft you can hardly hear.
falsetto Singing above normal range.
forte Loudly.
fortissimo Very loudly.
forzando With strong accents.
giocoso Merrily.
glissando Sliding through notes.
grazioso Gracefully.
grave Slowly and heavily.
largo Broadly, and slower than adagio and lento.
legato Smoothly.
lento Slower than adagio.
maestoso Grandly.
mezzo forte Moderately loud.
obbligato Essential.
pianissimo Very softly.
piano Softy.
pizzicato Plucked not bowed.
poco a poco Little by little.
preciso Precisely.
rallentando Slowing down.
rinforzando Reinforcing.
sostenuto Sustained.
sottovoce In a low voice.
staccato Sharp and separated, not flowing.
tremolo Rapidly repeating one note.
tutti All, the whole orchestra or chorus.
unison All singing same notes.
vivace Lively.

522 COMPOSERS

Early Renaissance

5221 Although surviving examples and representations show us some of the instruments of ancient times and by reconstructing and playing them we can discover what kinds of sound they produced, we can only guess what music they made. The Greeks invented a system of notation of which fragments survive, but experts differ as to how they should be read.

We can imagine the rhythms of work songs and tribal music as they are reflected in relic cultures, but the earliest western music of which we have full knowledge is that which the Christian Churches developed into hymns and liturgical chants. The earlier forms in triple time, based on plainsong and organum, and known as *ars antiqua*, became much freer in the 14th century, with triple time and independent part writing and the development of polyphony: *ars nova*.

During the Renaissance, increasingly complex polyphonic styles developed, with liturgical

continued

Early Renaissance continued

5221 differences creating the chorale in Lutheran Germany, and the anthem in Protestant England. In Venice, the two balconies of St Mark's encouraged the use of antiphonal effects. More instrumental music began to be written for the organ and the virginals, and for consorts, small groups of instruments such as recorders and viols.

EARLY RENAISSANCE COMPOSERS

Binchois, Gilles c. 1400–60. Prominent Franco-Flemish 15th century composer, also an organist.

Bull, John 1563–1628, English composer and organist, probably wrote the original version of *God Save the Queen* as a piece for virginals.

Byrd, William 1543–1623, English composer, with Tallis joint organist at the Chapel Royal and shared a national monopoly of music printing. He wrote in all the styles of his day, including madrigals and pieces for virginals, but excelled in religious music, for both Catholic and Protestant churches.

Dowland, John 1562–1626, English composer (possibly born in Ireland), especially of songs accompanied by the lute, of which he published several books. He was famous as a lutanist.

Dufay, Guillaume before 1400–74, Franco-Flemish cleric, composer of songs and masses, sometimes with accompanying instruments.

Dunstable, John c. 1390–1453, English mathematician and composer of church and lay music displaying melodic invention in counterpoint: one melody combining with another.

Gabrielli, Andreas c. 1510–86, Italian composer, organist at St Mark's, Venice who, with his nephew and pupil Giovanni 1557–1612, who succeeded him there, pioneered the writing of instrumental music. They wrote some concertos together. Giovanni often used several choirs and orchestral groups, each placed in its own gallery.

Gesualdo, Carlo 1560–1613, Italian prince who wrote madrigals adventurous in their harmonies.

Gibbons, Orlando 1583–1625, English composer, organist, and virginal player known for his anthems, madrigals, and keyboard pieces.

Josquin des Prés c. 1440–1521, Flemish pupil of Ockeghem, composer of expressive chansons, masses and motets (including one on the Stabat Mater) in a style then known as musica reservata.

Lassus, Roland de c. 1532–94, Flemish composer of some 2,000 works, religious and secular. From 1556 composer to the king of Bavaria.

Machaut, Guillaume de c. 1300–77, French priest, wrote religious and secular vocal music, chief exponent of ars nova. The earliest extant polyphonic mass is his for four voices.

Marenzio, Luca 1553–99, Italian composer of madrigals and some church music.

Morley, Thomas 1557–1602, English composer of songs, instrumental and church music, often of a light and sprightly character.

Ockeghem, Jean de c. 1425–95, Flemish composer of masses, motets, and songs who often chose a secular tune as *cantus firmus*, the fixed melody to which a descant was added.

Palestrina, Giovanni c. 1525–94, Italian composer of church music with long flowing melodies for unaccompanied choir and of a few madrigals. He perfected the polyphonic style begun in the Netherlands.

Perotin c. 1160–1240, French composer of well-structured liturgical music, choirmaster at Nôtre Dame in Paris.

Tallis, Thomas c. 1505–1585, English composer and organist with a solemn style of great contrapuntal ingenuity.

Taverner, John c. 1495–1545, English composer and organist, chiefly of church music. He abandoned music after being imprisoned for heresy.

Victoria, Luis de c. 1548–1611, Spanish composer who worked in Rome for 20 years and is stylistically linked with Palestrina. His rich textures may have up to 12 vocal lines.

Baroque

5222 This is the period in which the major and minor scales replaced the old church modes and music began to portray more complex emotions. It saw the beginning of opera, ballet, and oratorio. This was also the period of rising importance of instrumental music, and forms such as sonata and concerto with the regular use of ensembles. These were the nucleus for what became the modern orchestra. Initially this was the orchestra for the opera house, which added more instruments as it abandoned the use of harpsichord continuo.

BAROQUE COMPOSERS

Albinoni, Tomasso 1671–1750, Italian violinist and composer especially of concerti grossi and more then 50 operas.

Bach, Johann Sebastian 1685–1750 (**1**).

German organist and composer of oratorio, cantata, organ and other keyboard music demonstrating great contrapuntal skill. In the 19th century he was given a standing he never enjoyed in his life and hailed as the greatest of musicians. Three of his sons also achieved distinction as composers.

Buxtehude, Diderik c. 1637–1707, German-Danish composer of brilliant contrapuntal music, a model for Bach, whose own music came to overshadow it.

Corelli, Arcangelo 1653–1713, Italian violinist and composer mainly for the violin, who established the form of the concerto grosso.

Couperin, François 1668–1733, French court composer, especially of music for the harpsichord.

Handel, George Friederic 1685–1759, German composer who established himself in London where he wrote Italian style operas, oratorios and concerti and occasional pieces for the court such as the *Water Music* and *Music for the Royal Fireworks*. He was a noted harpsichord and organ player.

Lully, Jean-Baptiste 1632–87, Italian, became a violinist for the teenage Louis XIV of France, danced in court ballets and became the king's composer, creating the French form of opera.

Monteverdi, Claudio 1567–1643, Italian, violinist, singer, writer of madrigals, a priest from 1632. He was the first composer to use instruments for dramatic effect, employing new rhythms. After eight books of madrigals which became increasingly like cantatas and operas, he wrote the first really effective operas, including *Orfeo* and *The Coronation of Poppea*.

Purcell, Henry 1659–95, English composer best known for his opera *Dido and Aeneas* and his theater music, including *The Faery Queen*.

Scarlatti, Alessandro 1660–1725, Sicilian composer of hundreds of cantatas and operas. In Naples he developed the style of opera with numerous arias which became the Italian style.

Scarlatti, Domenico 1685–1757, Italian composer of operas in the style of his father, and of sonatas for the harpsichord, on which he was a virtuoso.

Schütz, Heinrich 1585–1672, Considered the greatest German composer of the 17th century. A pupil of Gabrielli, he wrote the first German opera. His work combined Gabrielli's polychoral style and the influence of Monteverdi opera with German native musical traditions.

Telemann, Georg Philipp 1681–1767. Prolific German composer of operas, cantatas, suites, and concertos which reflect all the musical styles of his day.

Vivaldi, Antonio 1678–1741 (**2**).

Italian virtuoso violinist and composer, nicknamed the "red priest" for his red hair. Wrote operas, church music, and oratorios but best known for his concerti, including *The Four Seasons*.

Classical and Romantic

5223 Though classical music is often used to refer to "serious" or art music of any period, as distinct from popular or folk music, it is particularly applied to music of the period between 1750 and the early 1800s. At that time, the symphony and concerto became important forms, and contrast of every kind began to replace the harmonic unity of the Baroque, with emphasis on melody and color. This gave way to music very expressive of personal feeling, as in the more dramatic work of Beethoven.

The 19th century saw the emergence of very individual styles – the free, personal, and expressive forms of the Romantic period, in which music reflected the spread of the romantic idea prevalent in all the arts. From depicting episodes, of a storm or country scene, for instance, whole works might have a descriptive and evocative intention – the tone poem or the symphonic poem, often scenic or dramatic but by the end of the century often brooding and nostalgic, reflecting, perhaps, the course that history was taking.

CLASSICAL AND ROMANTIC COMPOSERS

Beethoven, Ludwig van 1770–1827. Masterly German composer, who greatly extended the scope of the symphony, the piano concerto and sonata, but also wrote for a wide range of instruments. His works include an opera, ballet, and two masses. For the last decade of his life he was completely deaf but still composed magnificent works (**1**).

Bellini, Vicenzo 1801–35, Italian composer of operas *Norma* and *La Somnambula.*

Berlioz, Hector 1803–69 (**2**).

French composer, an innovator in orchestration, whose works were usually inspired by some litery association or non-musical allusion as in his *Fantastic Symphony* and his operas.

Brahms, Johannes 1833–97, German composer with a distinctive romantic style. His piano writing exploits his own dramatic keyboard playing. His orchestral work keeps close to classical form – contemporaries thought him old fashioned. From 1887 he concentrated on chamber music and songs.

Bruckner, Anton 1824–96, Austrian composer of epic symphonies and choral works, often reflecting his deep religious feeling.

Chopin, Frédéric François 1810–49, Polish composer and pianist, wrote mainly for the piano with remarkable harmonic imagination and to display piano technique.

Franck, César 1822–90, Belgian composer of a symphony, symphonic variations and poems, choral, organ, and piano works with rich chromatic harmonies. He devoted much of his life to teaching, which limited his output.

Glinka, Mikhail 1804–57, Russian composer best known for his two operas: *A Life for the Tsar* uses Russian and Polish folk music alongside typical Italian arias and gives the chorus a major role, *Ruslan and Lyudmila,* which is based on a narrative poem by Pushkin, shows his brilliant orchestration.

Gluck, Christoph Willibald von 1714–87, Bavarian composer best known for his operas and ballet scores, which reflect ballet master Noverre's belief that music and dance should contribute to the drama, not just be decorative. He often uses instruments in a particularly imaginative way.

Grieg, Edvard 1843–1907 (**3**).

Norwegian composer of tuneful and harmonic songs, sonatas and orchestral works often imbued with the spirit of Norwegian national song and dance.

Haydn, Franz Joseph 1732–1809, Austrian composer who established the classical form of the sonata, symphony, and string quartet.

Lehár, Franz 1870–1948, Hungarian composer of operettas, including *The Merry Widow.*

Liszt, Franz 1811–86, Hungarian piano virtuoso and composer (**4**) of piano works, concertos, vocal works, the first symphonic poems, and many piano transcriptions of songs and operas. After joining a minor religious order in 1865 he was known as Abbé Liszt.

Mahler, Gustav 1860–1911 (**5**). Austrian (Bohemian born) composer and conductor best known for his long symphonies which use large forces and very personal orchestration. Several using a chorus and soprano soloist, while his *Song of the Earth* is a song cycle in symphonic form.

Mendelssohn-Bartholdy, Felix 1809–47, German composer of passionately lyrical music combined with classical form from concert overtures such as *Fingal's Cave* to oratorios, concertos, symphonies, and lieder.

Mozart, Wolfgang Amadeus 1756–91, Austrian child prodigy as harpsichordist and composer, often considered the most complete musical genius ever. Writing often at prodigious speed he turned out keyboard, vocal, orchestral, and chamber works, but opera was his favorite form.

Offenbach, Jacques 1819–80, German born composer who created the French operetta with *Orpheus in the Underworld* and *La Vie parisienne.*

Paganini, Niccolò 1782–1840. Virtuoso Italian violinist and guitar player who wrote works for these instruments.

Puccini, Giacomo 1858–1924, Italian composer, mostly of operas with strong melodies and dramatic plots such as *Tosca, Madama Butterfly,* and *Turando,* which now form an important part of the international operatic repertoire.

Rimsky-Korsakov, Nikolay 1844–1908, Russian composer of operas and colorful orchestral works which usually have a literary or thematic program and draw on Russian folk tunes and ancient and oriental modal scales. He also revised and reorchestrated the work of friends such as Borodin and Mussorgsky and it is often his versions that have made them famous.

Rossini, Gioacchino 1792–1868, Italian composer, mainly of operas but also of church music, songs, and piano pieces. His contemporaries thought he used a lot of "noisy" effects – he liked orchestral crescendos.

Sammartini, Giovanni Battista c. 1700–75, Italian composer of symphonies and string quartets which pioneer the style developed by Haydn and Mozart.

continued

Classical and Romantic continued

5223 **Schubert, Franz** 1797–1828. Austrian composer (**6**) best known for his hundreds of song settings and for his piano works. He also wrote symphonies, church music, and operas.
Schumann, Robert 1810–56, German composer, pianist and conductor, wrote piano works, songs, string quartets, concertos, symphonies, and an opera. In his 40s he became mentally unstable and threw himself into the Rhine. He spent the rest of his life in an asylum.
Smetana, Bedrich 1824–84, Czech composer of operas and symphonic poems, whose work draws on Czech folk rhythms and became the foundation of a patriotic Czech school.
Sousa, John Philip 1854–1932, American band-conductor, composer of operettas and marches, including *The Stars and Stripes for Ever.*
Strauss, Johann 1825–99. Austrian violinist and composer (**7**) of operettas, polkas, and waltzes, including *The Blue Danube.* Known as the Viennese "Waltz King". Also composer of *Die Fledermaus.* His father (also Johann) and other relations were also musicians and composers.
Tchaikovsky, Pyotyr Ilyich 1840–93, Russian composer of symphonies, operas, ballet scores, concertos, and other works in a distinctly Russian style, full of melody and emotionally direct and powerful, whether melancholic or romantically exuberant.
Verdi, Guiseppi 1813–1901, Italian composer, mainly of operas and an operatic Requiem Mass. His earlier operas follow the Italian pattern of arias and ensembles but in *Aida* (1869) and later works (*Otello, Falstaff*) there are identifiable character themes and the big set pieces grow out of the action.
Wagner, Richard 1813–83, German composer, particularly of operas, for which he wrote his own libretti, developing them into serious music dramas without Italian-style arias. He made use of *leitmotifs*, themes to represent each character or force within the work, especially in his four opera cycle *The Ring of the Nibelungs.* He saw opera as a combination of all the arts and created his own Festival Theater at Bayreuth, opened in 1876, where he could supervise all aspects of their performance.

Twentieth century

5224 While a number of composers have continued to write in a romantic vein and others have looked back and drawn on early styles, the present century has seen a searching for new forms and a mixing of old ones in new ways. Folk music, of composers' own and other lands, jazz, new ways of producing sound either with traditional instruments or electronically have all had their influence. Schoenberg and his followers abandoned old concepts of tonality, rhythm, melody, and harmony and devised a scale of 12 notes, the serial technique used by many modern composers, which can often sound disturbing and unusual to those not accustomed to it. Recently a trend toward minimalism has been heard in music as in other arts, finding an enthusiastic response not only from the concert goer but also from pop music fans bridging the divide which has often separated "classical" from popular music.

TWENTIETH CENTURY COMPOSERS
Babbitt, Milton b. 1916, American composer influenced by the serial compositional techniques of Schoenberg and Webern. Later work uses tapes and synthesizers. Works include *Ensembles for Synthesizers* and *Tape With Voice.*
Barber, Samuel 1910–81, American composer of operas, ballet, songs, and concertos, is best known for his *Adagio for Strings.* Often melodic and romantic in style but also incorporating folk, jazz and 12-tone techniques.
Bartók, Béla 1881–1945, Hungarian composer who developed a national style, though his later work was often atonal with extreme dissonance. He wrote an opera, ballets and instrumental works sometimes for unusual combinations, such as *Music for Strings, Percussion and Celesta.*
Berg, Alban 1885–1935, Austrian composer, pupil of Schoenberg whose atonal idiom he developed in the operas *Wozzeck* and *Lulu,* and in other works.
Berio, Luciano b. 1925, Italian-American composer of experimental instrumental and dramatic works.
Bernstein, Leonard 1918–1990, American composer and conductor best known for his Broadway musicals, such as *West Side Story*, and ballets, but his eclectic range encompasses a modern mass and other sacred music, symphonies and chamber works. See also 5225.
Boulez, Pierre b. 1925, French composer using 12-tone techniques and electronic sounds. He has written less in recent years but as a conductor still champions new music.
Britten, Benjamin 1913–76, English composer of operas, chamber music, and choral works, including the *War Requiem*, often writing for boys' voices or for the tenor voice of his friend Peter Pears.
Cage, John 1912–92, American composer experimenting with chance sounds, "prepared" pianos (changed by placing objects on the strings) and even a work consisting of silence.
Carter, Elliott b. 1908, American composer tending toward a neoclassical style.
Copland, Aaron 1900–92, American composer, much of whose work, especially his ballet scores, grows from American subjects. His work offers strong tunes and is easy to follow, though some of his chamber and symphonic music make much greater demands on the listener.
Davies, Peter Maxwell b. 1934, British composer of experimental music theater pieces and a wide range of other work, recently much influenced by the land and seascapes of the Scottish island of Orkney where he lives part of the year.
Debussy, Claude 1862–1918, French composer who used free rhythms and short melodic fragments to create evocations of mood, landscape, and emotion such as *The Sea* or *The Afternoon of a Faun* but also challenged pianists with his keyboard studies.
Delius, Frederick 1862–1934, English composer of operas, concertos, and large scale orchestral works, but best known for his orchestral tone poems such as *On Hearing the First Cuckoo in Spring.*
Elgar, Edward 1857–1934, English composer of strongly melodic symphonic and choral work. The adoption of his coronation ode *Land of Hope and Glory* as an anthem of empire does not reflect his own attitudes, though his music is full of feeling for the English countryside and people.
Fauré, Gabriel 1845–1924, French composer of piano works, a Requiem, many songs, chamber music and music for the theater.
Gershwin, George (**1**) 1898–1937, American composer of popular songs, musicals, and jazz-inspired orchestral compositions including *Rhapsody in Blue* and the opera *Porgy and Bess.*

continue

Twentieth century continued

5224 **Glass, Philip** b. 1937, American composer in minimalist style, who has written theater works together with director Robert Wilson, several operas including *Akhnaten,* and film scores. He has gained a wide audience among pop music fans as well as concert goers.

Górecki, Henryk b. 1933, Polish composer who studied with Messiaen. Has deep affinities with Penderecki. Best known for his Third Symphony.

2

Henze, Hans Werner b. 1926, German composer of operas and orchestral works, his early work was often neo-romantic but is now increasingly experimental.

Holst, Gustav 1874–1934, English composer influenced by folk music and Hinduism (resulting in settings of Hindu scripture). An experimenter with harmonics, writer of operas, choral works and music for military bands, but best known for his orchestral suite *The Planets.*

Ives, Charles 1874–1945, American composer drawing deeply on American folk, church, and vaudeville sources, using chords and dissonances in his own way, quite different from European contemporaries.

Janácek, Leos 1854–1928, Czech composer of concertos, operas, and other vocal works drawn on national subjects and influenced by Czech folk song and speech rhythms.

Lutoslawksi, Witold b. 1916, Polish composer using experimental techniques in symphonic and chamber works.

Messiaen, Olivier 1908–92, French composer drawing on Gregorian chant, unusual percussion, and electronic instruments to create works often of deep religious feeling.

Milhaud, Darius 1892–1974, French composer, one of *Les Six* with Poulenc, whose work ranges from conventional chamber music to the highly rhythmic ballet *The Creation of the World* and colossal operas.

Nielsen, Carl 1865–1931, Danish composer of symphonies, concertos, and opera. His *First Symphony* begins in one key and ends in another, a progressive tonality evident in other works.

Nono, Luigi b. 1924, Italian composer of avant-garde opera.

Penderecki, Krzysztof b. 1933, Polish composer in an avant-garde style of large scale orchestral works.

Poulenc, François 1899–1963, French composer (**2**), disciple of Satie and one of *Les Six*, whose work ranges from short piano pieces to opera, and includes much chamber music.

Prokofiev, Sergey 1891–1953, Russian composer (**3**) of operas, ballets, film scores, and concert works. Though early work is often dissonant it is always full of orchestral color, melody, and rhythm.

Rakhmaninov, Sergey 1873–1943, Russian pianist and composer (**4**) in an emotional romantic style, best known for his *Rhapsody on a Theme of Paganini.*

3

4

Ravel, Maurice 1875–1937, French composer, at first of piano works but later a master of orchestral sound from the strong rhythms of *Bolero* to the lyrical impressionism of *Daphnis and Chloë.*

Reich, Steve b. 1936, American minimalist composer.

Riley, Terry b. 1935, American composer and saxophonist. Best known for such minimalist pieces as *In C* and his keyboard studies.

Satie, Erik 1866–1925, French composer of often witty music, especially piano works. A defiant modernist, he is famed for the whimsical titles – for example *Gymnopédies* – he attached to his works.

Schoenberg, Arnold 1874–1951, Austrian composer who radically changed western music with atonal writing (as in *Pierrot Lunaire*) which he developed into his 12-tone technique of composition.

Scriabin, Alexander 1872–1915, Russian composer and virtuoso pianist whose piano works make great demands on keyboard coverage and rhythmic complexity. He invented new ways of building chords.

Shostakovich, Dmitry 1906–75, Russian composer of opera, ballet, film music, and magnificent symphonies which celebrate both the glories and the agonies of Soviet life.

Sibelius, Jean 1865–1957, Finnish composer whose music often has national associations linked to national sagas. His *Finlandia* was banned by the Russian Tsar because of its association with the Finnish independence movement.

Stockhausen, Karlheinz b. 1928, German composer (**5**) of wide experimentation using electronic and conventional instruments, sometimes introducing random elements.

Strauss, Richard 1864–1949, German composer of songs, symphonic poems, operas, and ballets which move from the grand and dramatic such as *Salome* to more intimate works in his later years.

Stravinsky, Igor 1882–1971, Russian composer (**6**) famous for his ballets for Diaghilev's *Ballet Russe*. The *Rite of Spring,* now a well-loved classic, caused uproar at its premier, its savagery showing how much Stravinsky had changed musical taste. He adopted 12-tone techniques for some later works but still projected his unmistakable style.

5 6

Thompson, Virgil b. 1896, American composer of sophisticatedly simple works, many of which reflect his admiration for Satie, including film scores, operas, and chamber music.

Tippett, Michael b. 1905, British composer of operas (to his own librettos), oratorios, chamber and symphonic works.

Vaughan Williams, Ralph 1872–1958, English composer whose music, often imbued with feeling for his native countryside and its folksongs, which he collected, includes operas, symphonies, choral works, and orchestral pieces with solo instruments, such as the lyrical *The Lark Ascending.*

Walton, William 1902–83, British composer of opera and orchestral music from the witty setting of poems by Edith Sitwell, such as *Façade* and the oratorio *Belshazzar's Feast,* to scores for Olivier's Shakespeare movies.

Webern, Anton 1883–1945, Austrian composer who adopted the 12-tone technique.

Weill, Kurt 1900–50, German composer whose orchestral work was influenced by jazz. Best known for *The Threepenny Opera* and other theater pieces with texts by Brecht, but he also wrote musical shows for Broadway. See also 5225.

Xenakis, Iannis b. 1922. Romanian-born Greek composer. Is also a mathematician and although he mainly writes for conventional instruments this has an important role in his composition.

Composers of musicals

5225 Popular musical theater has developed from the operettas which flourished in Europe from the mid-19th century, gradually giving way to the musical comedy after World War I, especially in America where *Show Boat* – based on Edna Ferber's novel (Jerome Kern and Oscar Hammerstein II) introduced a more real-life subject matter. From the 1940s musicals more frequently began to tackle serious topics, such as the racial conflicts of *West Side Story* (Leonard Bernstein and Arthur Laurents), and, more recently, with the works of Stephen Sondheim or Andrew Lloyd Webber have becoming increasingly like operas.

continued

Composers of musicals continued

5225 **Berlin, Irving** 1888–1989, American composer of hits from *Alexander's Ragtime Band* to *God Bless America.* Best known musicals, *Annie Get Your Gun* and *Call Me Madam.*

Bernstein, Leonard 1918–19920, American composer, conductor, pianist bridging classical and Broadway. Shows include *On the Town, West Side Story, Candide.*

Cohan, George M 1878–1942, American composer and lyricist who set the pace for musical comedy with *Little Johnny Jones* (1904). His tunes include *Give My Regards to Broadway.*

Coward, Noel 1899–1954, English playwright, actor, and composer of musical comedies, including *Bitter Sweet.*

Gay, Noel 1898–1954, English composer of musicals including *Me and My Girl.*

Gershwin, George 1898–1937, American composer of witty hits, with lyrics usually by his brother, Ira, and of musical comedies including *Lady Be Good, Funny Face, Strike Up the Band* and the more operatic *Porgy and Bess.*

Herbert, Victor 1859–1924, Irish-born composer of 41 American operettas, including *Naughty Marietta.*

Kern, Jerome 1885–1945, American composer of well-loved hits such as *Smoke Gets in Your Eyes.* Beginning with a series of operetta-type shows with words by P G Wodehouse, he brought the idea of shows based on believable people rather than fairytale romance to Broadway, especially in *Show Boat* (1927 with book by Oscar Hammerstein II). Also composed movie musicals as vehicles for Fred Astaire.

Loesser, Frank 1910–69, American composer and lyricist of *Guys and Dolls, The Most Happy Fella.*

Loewe, Frederick 1901–88. Born in Berlin, he moved to the US in 1924. Pianist and composer of American musicals *Brigadoon, Paint Your Wagon* and *My Fair Lady* (with Alan Jay Lerner).

Lloyd-Webber, Andrew b. 1948, English composer whose staging of musicals (with words by Tim Rice) *Joseph and the Amazing Technicolor Dreamcoat, Jesus Christ Superstar* and *Evita* launched a new style of musical. These, plus *Cats* and *Phantom of the Opera,* have brought worldwide success.

Porter, Cole 1891–1964, American composer and lyricist of sophisticated songs and musicals including *Anything Goes, Kiss Me Kate.*

Romberg, Sigmund 1887–1951, Hungarian born composer of American operettas such as *The Student Prince* and *The Desert Song.*

Schonberg, Claude-Michel b. 1944, French composer of *Les Misérables* and *Miss Saigon* which challenged the dominance of musical theater by Lloyd Webber and the Americans in the 1980s.

Sondheim, Stephen b. 1930, American composer and lyricist, first noted for his lyrics for *West Side Story* but since established as the composer-writer of through composed musicals including *A Little Night Music, Sweeney Todd,* and *Sunday in the Park with George.*

Sullivan, Arthur 1842–1900, English composer, conductor best known for the many satiric light operas written with texts by W S Gilbert, including *The Pirates of Penzance, The Mikado, Iolanthe, The Yeoman of the Guard.*

Suppe, Franz von 1819–95, Dalmatian composer of light orchestral music and operettas.

Weill, Kurt 1900–50, German composer of theater pieces with Bertolt Brecht, such as *The Threepenny Opera,* and after fleeing to the United States before World War II, of Broadway musicals including *Knickerbocker Holiday* (which includes *September Song*) and *Lady in the Dark.*

Wilson, Sandy b. 1924, British dramatist and composer best known for his parody of the 1920s musical, *The Boy Friend,* and the witty *Valmouth,* based on a Ronald Firbank novel.

523 CONDUCTORS

The conductor of an orchestra, choir or opera guides the musical interpretation, rehearses the musicians and directs the performance, beating the pulse of the music with a baton or his hands, cueing in instruments and voices, and controlling volume.

Small groups of musicians could play together without a conductor but as ensembles became bigger and scores more complex one member, usually a keyboard player, would direct the others, until conducting became a separate role, often carried out by the composer.

Lully conducted by pounding a big stick on the floor – and died from an abscess which developed after he hit his foot. Some conductors waved a violin bow or a roll of paper so that players could see their "beat" and in the 19th century they began to use a baton. Von Bülow and Mahler established the importance of the conductor as orchestra trainer and since their time conductors have become as famous as any other musicians.

The many conductors who are primarily composers are not included in the list that follows.

Abbado, Claudio b. 1933, Italian conductor of opera (including La Scala, Milan, 1968–86) and associated with the Berlin Philharmonic, London and Chicago Symphony Orchestras.

Ansermet, Ernest 1883–1969, Swiss conductor associated with *Ballet Russe* and founder of the Orchestre de la Swisse Romande.

Barbirolli, John 1899–1970, British conductor, especially associated with the Hallé Orchestra.

Beecham, Thomas 1879–1961, British conductor, founder of Royal Philharmonic Orchestra and British National Opera Company, introducing Richard Strauss to Britain.

Boult, Adrian 1889–1983, English conductor especially associated with the BBC Symphony Orchestra.

Bülow, Hans von 1830–94, German pianist and conductor of some Wagner first performances; said to be first to conduct from memory.

Davis, Colin b. 1927, British conductor associated with the BBC Symphony Orchestra and the Royal Opera.

Fiedler, Arthur 1894–1979. American conductor associated with the Boston Symphony ("Boston Pops") Orchestra.

Karajan, Herbert von 1908–89, Austrian conductor particularly associated with the Vienna Opera and Salzburg Festival.

Klemperer, Otto 1885–1973, German conductor known for his interpretations of Beethoven and Mahler.

Maazel, Lorin b. 1930, American conductor, the youngest and the first American to conduct at Bayreuth.

Koussevitzky, Serge 1874–1951, Russian-American conductor for many years with the Boston Symphony and a great champion of 20th century music.

Levine, James b. 1943, American conductor associated with the Cleveland Orchestra and the Metropolitan Opera.

Mehta, Zubin b.1936 Indian conductor associated with several orchestras in Canada, Israel, and the US.

Monteaux, Pierre 1875–1964, French conductor, especially with *Ballet Russe* and Boston Symphony, conducted premieres of Stravinsky's *Petrouchka* and *Rite of Spring.*

Ozawa, Seiji b 1935. Japanese conductor associated with several American orchestras.

Previn, Andre b 1929. American composer-conductor associated with the London and Pittsburgh Symphony Orchestras.

Rattle, Simon b. 1955, British conductor who has turned the City of Birmingham Symphony Orchestra into one of international rank.

Reiner, Fritz 1888–1963, Hungarian-American conductor known for his intepretation of Wagner and Richard Strauss.

Rozhdestvensky, Gennadi b. 1931, Russian symphonic and opera conductor.

Sargent, Malcolm 1895–1967, British conductor, long associated with the BBC Promenade Concerts.

Solti, Georg b. 1912, Hungarian conductor, especially of opera, associated with the Chicago Symphony and the Royal Opera.

Szell, George 1897–1970, Hungarian pianist and conductor most associated with the Metropolitan Opera and Cleveland Orchestra.

Toscanini, Arturo 1867–1957, Italian conductor associated with La Scala Milan, New York Philharmonic and NBC Symphony Orchestra, a lively interpreter of Verdi, Wagner and Beethoven.

524 VOCAL MUSIC

Types of singing voice

5241 **1** Bass
2 Baritone
3 Tenor
4 Contralto
5 Mezzo-soprano
6 Soprano

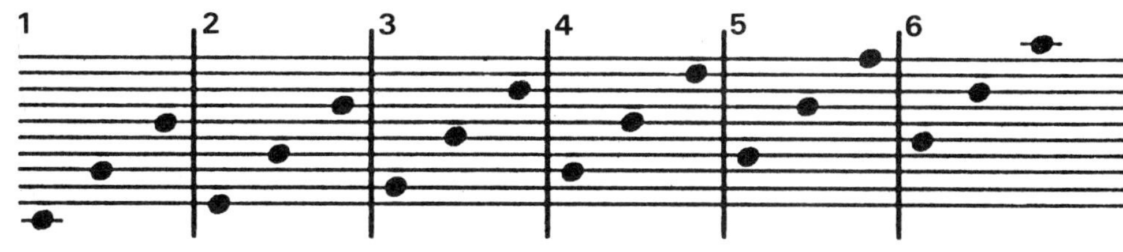

Adult male and female voices are divided into three vocal ranges: tenor, baritone, and bass; and soprano, mezzo-soprano, and alto, respectively. Other terms are, however, also used.

alto High in Italian. The lower type of female voice, but originally in church music the male high voice above the melody sung by tenors. Term now mainly used of boys' and female voices in choirs.
baritone Man's voice of intermediate range, the usual range in which most men speak and sing.
bass The lowest male voice, a true bass not only reaches low notes but also has a deep quality. Although often given long low notes, the bass can be as vocally agile as any other singer.
basso profundo A bass voice of unusually low range.
castrato Adult male voice in soprano or contralto range achieved by castration to prevent voice deepening. Found in European church choirs in 17th and 18th century and a popular voice for operatic composers such as Handel.
coloratura soprano A soprano with an agile, florid style.
contralto Lowest range of any female voice.
counter tenor The term now more usually used for an adult male alto soloist.
falsetto A male voice pushed above the normal range, as in the adult alto, now usually used for a tone lacking the fullness of the counter tenor.
heldentenore Hero tenor in German. A tenor with the power to sing above the sound of a large orchestra.
mezzo-soprano Female vocal range almost as high as a soprano and almost as low as an alto, usually rich and ideal for dramatic roles in opera which are frequently written for this range, for example Carmen.
soprano The highest type of female voice, approximately from middle C upward for two octaves, or the same range for a boy or castrato. They may be either light and sweet or richly dramatic.
tenor The highest natural adult male voice which may be either light and agile or rich and sonorous.

Great singers

5242 **Battle, Kathleen** b. 1948, American soprano opera and concert artiste.
Björling, Jussi 1911–1960, Swedish operatic tenor.
Bumbry, Grace b. 1937, American mezzo-soprano, international opera singer.
Caballé, Montserrat b. 1933, Spanish operatic soprano, the leading singer in bell canto style.
Callas, Maria 1923–77, Greek-American operatic soprano of great vocal and dramatic versatility.
Carerras, José b. 1946, Spanish tenor acclaimed for his Alfredo (*Traviata*) and Rodolfo (*Bohème*).
Caruso, Enrico 1873–1921, Italian operatic tenor of lyrical quality in all the French and Italian repertoire.
Chaliapin, Fyodor 1873–1938, Great Russian bass of powerful voice and great acting skill, especially remembered for his *Boris Godunov*.
Cristoff, Boris 1914–93, Bulgarian bass-baritone famous for his *Boris Godunov*.
Domingo, Placido b. 1941, Spanish operatic tenor internationally acclaimed in Verdi and Puccini roles.
Fishcher-Dieskau, Dietrich b. 1925, German operatic baritone and lieder singer.
Flagstad, Kirsten 1895–1962, Norwegian operatic soprano especially remembered for her Wagner performances.
Gedda, Nicolai b. 1925, Swedish operatic tenor.
Gigli, Benjamino 1890–1957, Italian tenor prominent in opera and as a recitalist.
Gobbi, Tito 1915–1984, Italian operatic baritone, acclaimed for his Scarpia in *Tosca*.
Hampson, Thomas b 1955, American baritone with wide international following. He made his NY Metropolitan debut as Count Almaviva in 1986.
Hendricks, Barbara b. 1948, American soprano, who studied at the Juillard School. Has appeared at the Paris Opéra, Covent Garden, London, La Scala (Milan), and NY Metropolitan.
Horne, Marilyn b. 1934, American mezzo-soprano best known for coloratura roles in opera.
Lehmann, Lilli 1848–1929, German operatic soprano and lieder singer, mostly known for her Mozart and Wagnerian roles. For her debut in *The Ring* she was coached by Richard Wagner himself.
Lind, Jenny 1820–1887, The "Swedish nightingale" with a voice of great vocal purity. She toured the world in opera and oratorio.
Ludwig, Christa b. 1924, German operatic mezzo-soprano who also sings lieder.
Melba, Nellie 1861–1931, Australian operatic soprano of pure and effortless tone, best known for her roles in *La Traviata* and Delibes's *Lakmé*.
McCormack, John 1884–1945. Irish operatic tenor, also sang lieder and Irish folksong.
Melchior, Lauritz 1890–1973, Danish operatic tenor, specialised in Wagnerian roles.
Merrill, Robert b. 1917, American operatic baritone.
Milnes, Sherrill b. 1935, American operatic baritone.
Moffo, Anna b. 1934, American operatic soprano.
Nilsson, Birgit b. 1918, Swedish operatic soprano known for her Wagnerian roles, *Elektra* and *Salome* (Richard Strauss), *Tosca* and *Turandot*.
Norman, Jessye b. 1945, American soprano; well known on opera and concert circuits. Particularly noted for breadth of image and beauty of tone.
Pavarotti, Luciano b. 1935, Italian tenor best known for his performances in the main Italian operatic repertoire (Bellini, Verdi, Puccini).
Pons, Lily 1898–1976, French-born American coloratura soprano.
Pears, Peter 1910–86. English tenor created many roles in operas by Britten, which were written for his voice. Also remembered for his work in oratorio and lieder.
Price, Leontyne b. 1927, American operatic soprano, especially known as *Aida*.
Robeson, Paul 1898-1976. American dramatic bass-baritone and actor.
Schwarzkopf, Elisabeth b. 1915, German operatic soprano and lieder singer known for her *Traviata*, *Butterfly*, and Mimi in *La Bohème*.
Scotto, Renata b. 1934, Italian operatic soprano.
Sills, Beverly b. 1929, American coloratura soprano, director of New York City Opera from 1979.
Söderström, Elizabeth b. 1927, Swedish soprano with wide concert and opera repertoire, especially Mozart and Strauss.

continued

Great singers continued

5242

Stade, Frederica von b.1945, American operatic mezzo-soprano.
Sutherland, Joan b. 1926, Australian coloratura soprano best known for her Bellini and Donizetti heroines.
Tebaldi, Renata b. 1922, Italian lyric soprano especially known for her Puccini operatic roles.
Te Kanawa, Kiri b. 1944, New Zealand soprano acclaimed as the countess in *The Marriage of Figaro,* and many other roles.
Tetrazzini, Luisa 1871–1940, Italian coloratura operatic soprano.
Teyte, Maggie 1888–1976, English operatic soprano linked with Covent Garden and French song, especially Debussy.
Tucker, Richard 1914–1975, American operatic tenor and cantor.
Vickers, Jon b. 1926. Canadian operatic tenor ranging from Wagner to operas by Britten and Tippett.
Visnevskaya, Galina b. 1926. Russian soprano star at Bolshoi and in the West. Britten wrote soprano part in *War Requiem* for her.
White, Willard b. 1946. Jamaican bass, a great Porgy in *Porgy and Bess.* His roles include Wotan in Wagner's *The Ring,* and he has acted in Shakespeare's O*thello.*

Famous operas

5243

Some operas are popularly known by their English titles, but for many their foreign names are better known and are used here. The composer is named first, followed by librettist(s).

Aida (Verdi/A. Ghislanzoni, 1871. Originally written to celebrate the opening of the Suez Canal. Story of an Ethiopian princess, captured by an Egyptian general, and their fatal love.
La Bohème (Puccini/G Giacosa, L Illica, from a novel by Burger, 1896). Bohemian artists and poets in Paris and the love of one of them for the consumptive and dying Mimi. Leoncavallo wrote an opera on the same story premiered in 1897.
Carmen (Bizet/H Meilhac, L Halévy, from a story by Prosper Mérimée, 1875). A soldier deserts after falling in love with a gypsy girl, she leaves him for a bullfighter and he kills her outside the Seville bullring.
Così fan Tutte Mozart/ L da Ponte, 1790). Young men pretend to go away to war, returning disguised, they court their own lovers to test their fidelity.
Don Giovanni (Mozart/L da Ponte, 1787). Episodes from the love-life of Don Juan who is finally dragged down to hell by the statue of a man he killed.
Eugene Onegin (Tchaikovsky/after Pushkin, 1879). Onegin flirts with a young woman then spurns her. Later when she is a settled noblewoman, he returns, rekindles her love, but is himself rejected.
Fidelio (Beethoven/J Sonnleithner, 1805). The composer's only opera. A young woman seeking her imprisoned husband disguises herself as a man to gain access to his prison, eventually freeing him and other innocent prisoners while the wicked governor is punished.
Lady Macbeth of Mtensk (Shostakovitch/ with L Preis, 1934). In the Russian provinces a woman murders her merchant husband and brings disaster upon herself and her lover.
Madama Butterfly (Puccini/G Giacosa, L Illica from a David Belasco play, 1904). American naval officer "marries" a Japanese girl in a fake ceremony, deserts her and returns with his real wife to collect his child, the mother killing herself as soon as they have gone.
The Magic Flute (Mozart/E Schikaneder, 1791). A magic flute secures the hero a path through danger to enlightenment, echoing Masonic and humanist symbolism.
The Marriage of Figaro (Mozart/ L da Ponte from comedy by Beaumarchais, 1786). Count Almaviva, whose servant Figaro intrigued to secure his marriage, now seeks to seduce Figaro's own intended, his wife's attendant. His wife has an innocent romance with a young man, arousing the suspicion and jealousy of Almaviva, who in turn is exposed in his infidelity.
The Midsummer Marriage (Tippett 1955). Combines ancient mythologies and modern characters in a parable of the search for truth and enlightenment through ritual purification.
Otello (Verdi/A Boito after Shakespeare, 1887). Moorish general in the service of Venice marries a Venetian against her father's wishes, is trapped by his aide into believing her unfaithful and in his jealousy kills her. Rossini wrote an earlier opera version, 1816.
Peter Grimes (Britten/M Slater from poem by Crabbe, 1945). English East Anglian town turns against misanthropic fisherman accused of causing death of boy assistant.
The Rake's Progress (Stravinsky/ W H Auden, C Kallman suggested by Hogarth's paintings, 1951). Scenes from the life of a decadent man-about-town until he ends up dying in a madhouse.
The Ring of the Niebelungs (Wagner 1869–76). Sequence of four operas based on Nordic myth: The Rhinegold, The Valkyrie, Siegfried, The Twilight of the Gods; treachery among gods and their human offspring to obtain the ring which symbolizes power and for which love must be relinquished leading to the destruction of Valhalla.
Rosenkavalier, Der (R Strauss/H von Hofmannstlah, 1911). A young man asked to present a rose from a nobleman to his betrothed falls in love with her himself. The older woman in love with him resigns herself and helps the young lovers to happiness.
Tosca (Puccini/G Giacosa , L Illica, from Sardou's play, 1900). A painter helps hide a revolutionary, is himself arrested and his opera singer mistress bargains for his life. Though she kills the villain, her lover is shot and she flings herself into the Tiber.
Traviata, La (Verdi/F M Piave from Dumas's The Lady of the Camellias, 1853). A courtesan gives up the man who really loves her on his father's insistence but they are reunited before her death from consumption.
Turandot (Puccini/G Adami, P Simoine from a play by Gozzi, 1926). Chinese princess unwilling to marry demands suitors to answer trick questions or lose their lives, but is won over by love.
The Turn of the Screw (Britten/M Piper, 1953 after Henry James story). Two children are controlled and corrupted by ghosts.
Wozzeck (Berg/from Büchner's play, 1925). Army orderly, abused by everyone, murders his lover. Filled with remorse, he drowns himself.

525 DANCE

Ballet terms

5251

Ballet developed in Italy and France from court entertainments of music, dance, and spectacle, usually based on a mythological subject. Performers were originally the nobility, including Louis XIV of France, who set up a royal dancing school which became the Paris Opera. When the king stopped dancing and greater skill became demanded, performers were increasingly professionals.

Theater performers wore masks, partly in imitation of their idea of classical style, partly because at first the professionals were all men – even in female roles until 1681.

Ballet became a dramatic form instead of a sequence of songs and dances. Noverre dispensed with heavy clothes, wigs, and masks, and introduced more natural gestures.

Romanticism affected both story and style in ballet and other arts during the 19th century. In the 20th century, the dazzling theatricality of Diaghilev's *Ballet Russe* brought new vitality, followed by a move to abstraction on the part of many choreographers. Later, there developed modern forms of dance not based on the classic steps and, in Martha Graham's system, based on contact with the ground rather than seeking to leave it.

BALLET TERMS
Because classical ballet had its origins in France, its technical vocabulary is in French.
air, en l' (in the air) A succession of movements is executed in the air. The opposite is par terre.
arabesque (**1**) Pose as though poised for flight, supported on one leg, the other extended backward and the arms disposed harmoniously usually with the greatest reach.
attitude Pose on one leg with corresponding arm open to side or back, other leg extended to

continue

Ballet terms continued

5251 back at 90° with knee bent, corresponding arm raised above head – *en greque*. The raised leg has heel touching supporting leg and the same arm as the supporting leg raised above head (**2**).
ballerina, Female dancer of chief classical roles in a company; **prima ballerina assoluta** Title bestowed on only a few occasions on outstanding leading dancer of Russian Imperial Ballet.
barre Wooden bar just above hip height to give hand support for ballet class exercises.
battement (beating) Leg exercises of various kinds executed with a beating motion.
batterie (succession of beats) Movements in which the feet beat together during jumps, grand batterie when jump is high, **petite batterie** when elevation is slight.
battu A beaten step
bourrée Series of small even staccato steps; the pas de bourrée involves three transfers of weight from foot to foot and has over 20 different variations.
brisé (broken) A leap with the legs lightly beaten before landing on both feet.
chasse Step from a plié in fifth sliding one foot out, heel down, before transferring weight to it, also done as a jumping step.
choreography The art of composing dance, the steps; choreographer, the dance maker.
ciseaux (scissors) Jump from and ending in fifth with legs apart like open scissors.
closed position With feet in first, third or fifth.
corps de ballet Usually the dancers in the company not classed as soloists who dance together. In Paris Opera whole company are known as the corps, lower ranks being called *les quadrilles*.
coryphée A leading member of the corps de ballet. In classical French and Russian ballet, it is a term used for a minor soloist.
coupe Step with weight on right foot, left is drawn up in front in fifth, cutting away the right foot which is raised, or similar executed as a jump; **coupe dessou** is with the foot behind.
couru A running step, see bourrée.
dégagé Freeing the working foot in preparation for a step. Shifting of weight from one foot to the other.
demi (half) As in demi plié (half bent knees), demi-pointe (half on toes)
divertissement Originally a danced interlude in an opera, a self-contained series of dances inserted in the main ballet – such as when the main characters sit to watch an entertainment, usually designed to show off techique.

elevation Term applied to all aerial movements.
enchainement (linking) Sequence of steps making a continuous phrase.
entrechat A jump in fifth in which the legs are crossed and uncrossed at the lower calf. Entrechats are numbered not by the beats but by the number of positions taken by the legs, even numbers land in fifth, odd on one foot. Nijinsky reportedly reached entrechat dix (ten).
étoile (star). Premier Danseur Etoile, highest title given to leading dancers of Paris Opera.
fermé (closed). In positions first, third and fifth
fish dive Position in which dancer is caught and supported by partner with head and shoulders just clear of the floor.
fouette (**3**) (a whipped movement). Step executed on pointe, the working leg whipped out to the side and in to the knee with a slight circular movement, frequently combined with turns as fouette en tournant, to which it gives momentum.
jeté (thrown step). A spring forward, backward or sideways; **grand jeté** aleap from one foot to the other.
ouverte Open position of the feet.
pas (step) A complete leg movement walking or dancing, also solo or a dance for a certain number as pas de seul (one), de deux (two) (**4**), de trois (three), de quatre (four).
petit tours (little turns) Short fast turns progressing in a line.
piqué Stepping directly onto pointe without bending knee.
pirouette Turn on one foot propelled by swing of the arm (**5**).
plié (bend). Bending of the knees while erect with the feet turned out, heels on the ground; **demi plié** becomes so low that heels must be raised, **grand plié** lower with the buttocks as near the heels (still kept as close to the ground as possible).
pointe shoes Shoes with reinforced toes, originally padded with cotton but since 1860s stiffened with glue and darned to give support when dancing on toe tips.
pointe The extremity of the toe, a point on the toe. A trois quarts (3/4) raised on flexed toes, a demi-point on the ball of the foot.
premier danseur (male), danseuse (female). The leading dancer or, for women, the rank below *étoile*.
promenade A slow turn on one foot with the body held in a set pose.
régisseur Stage manager responsible for mounting and rehearsing ballets in repertoire.
relevé (lifted step) Raising on full or part point.
repetition Rehearsal.
révérence A bow or curtsy.
rivoltade Jump and turn with one leg passing in front of the other landing in reverse direction.
sur les pointes (on the pointes) à pointe, see pointe.
terre à terre (ground to ground. Steps which leave the ground only sufficiently to be pointed
toe shoes US. term for pointe shoes.
tour A turn.
tutu Originally a short petticoat sewn together between the legs at each performance for concealment; now short classical ballet skirt made of knickers trimmed with several layers of superimposed frills.
variation A solo dance, especially a solo section of a pas de deux.

Famous ballets

5252 Composers' names are given first, then the choreographers'. Many scores have been used by more than one choreographer.

Afternoon of a Faun (Debussy/Nijinsky 1912). Erotic games between a faun and nymphs, original choreography like a two-dimensional vase painting. Robbins' 1953 version used two dancers in a ballet studio.
Apollo (Apollon-Musagete, Stravinksy/ Balanchine, 1928). The god Apollo with the muses. (Adolphe Bolm had created different choreography a few weeks earlier.)
Appalachian Spring (Copeland/Graham 1944). Farm, church and homestead scenes as a young pioneer couple move into their new home.
Dances at a Gathering (Chopin/Robbins 1969). Though it has a strong ambience and many changes of mood, Robbins said "there are no stories to any of these dances ... the dancers are themselves dancing ..."
Dark Elegies (Mahler/Tudor 1937). An intimate portrayal of grief as pairs of parents mourn the death of their children in an accident.
La Fille mal gardée (Herold/Ashton, 1964). Bucolic comedy of love on a farm with a strong "dame" role. Among other versions, some to different music: Arthur St-Leon 1786, Aumer 1828, Petipa and Ivanov 1882.
The Firebird (Stravinsky/Fokine 1910). A Russian prince captures a miraculous bird and with the help of a magic feather frees princesses from an evil magician's spell.
The Green Table (Cohen/Jooss 1932). Inspired by World War I. While ordinary people suffer, politicians and racketeers meet around

continued

Famous ballets continued

5252 green table to decide their fate.
Napoli (various/Bournonville 1842). A tale of a fisherman and his bride, inspired by a visit to Italy.
Les Noces (The Wedding, Stravinsky/Nijinska 1923). The preparations and celebration of a wedding in old Russia.
The Nutcracker (Tchaikovsky/Ivanon 1892). At a Christmas party little Clara is given a nutcracker. It is repaired after her brother breaks it, but she comes downstairs at night to find it and sees toys come to life and the nutcracker turn into a prince who takes her on a journey to the Land of Sweets.
Petrouchka (Stravinksy/Fokine 1911). At a fairground in St Petersburg puppets come to life, Petrouchka is brokenhearted because his beloved loves the Moor.
The Rite of Spring (Stravinksky/Nijinsky 1913). Primitive ritual in which a maiden is chosen and sacrficed as a fertility offering. There are later versions by Macmillan, Béjart, Graha, and others.
Rodeo (Copland/de Mille 1942). A square dance caller leads courting and rodeo competition at Burnt Ranch.
Romeo and Juliet (Prokofiev/Lavrovsky 1940). Shakespeare's tale of ill-starred love. This was the original version in which Ulanova danced Juliet. Lifar, Ashton, Nureyev also produced choreography to this score.
The Sleeping Beauty (Tchaikovsky/Petipa 1890). Fairytale story of the princess asleep for 100 years and wakened with a kiss.
Swan Lake (Tchaikovsky/Petipa-Ivanov 1893). Two earlier choreographers produced flops. A prince falls in love with Odette, under a spell which makes her a swan. It has been given both sad and happy endings.
La Sylphide (Schneitzhoffer/F. Taglioni 1832). The first "romantic" ballet, replacing former classical themes. A supernatural being falls in love with a young Scotsman.
Les Sylphides (Chopin/Fokine 1909). Plotless ballet of a poet and group dressed like La Sylphide consisting of ensemble dances and variations.

The five positions in ballet

5253

The five positions of the feet and the ports de bras, the matching arm positions, from which ballet steps begin and to which they return, ensure balance in any position of the body. They are said to have first been laid down by Charles Beauchamp, but he probably codified already accepted 17th-century practice.
There are also false or revised positions with feet and knees turned in which were formerly used for the entrances of comic characters but are now rarely seen.

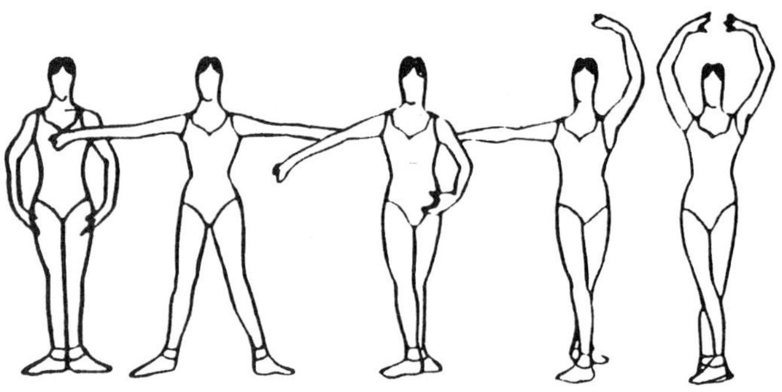

Dancers and choreographers

5254 With one or two exceptions most choreographers have themselves begun as dancers. This listing gives only a selection of the world's great dance-makers and includes only a few outside the field of classical ballet.

Ailey, Alvin 1931–89, American dancer/choreographer of mixed dance styles with his own dance company.
Alonso, Alicia b. 1921, Cuban ballerina and choreographer, director of National Ballet of Cuba.
Ashton, Frederick 1904–88, British choreographer (began as a dancer), director of the Sadler's Wells and Royal Ballet; he played a large part in developing British ballet style.
Astaire, Fred 1899–1987, American dancer in shows and movies, noted for his fine tap dancing; originally in partnership with his sister Adèle, on the screen frequently partnered by Ginger Rogers.
Balanchine, George 1904–83, Russian choreographer and dancer with Ballet Russe and other companies becoming director of New York City Ballet in 1948, the most influential classical dance-maker of his time in America, his ballets often abstract.
Baryshnikov, Mikhail b. 1948, Russian dancer and occasional choreographer. After leaving the Kirov Ballet he joined American Ballet Theatre, later becoming its director.
Beauchamp, Charles 1636–1705, French dancer/choreographer, credited by Rameau with inventing the five positions. First director of Louis XIV's Dance Academy.
Béjart, Maurice b. 1927, French choreographer of radical and dramatic works blending classical and modern styles; director of his own Ballet of the XX Century and Ballet Béjart.
Bournonville, August 1805–79, Danish dancer/choreographer, established the style and teaching of the Danish romantic ballet.
Bruhn, Erik b. 1928, Danish dancer, soloist with major American companies and director of Royal Danish Ballet.
Camargo, Marie Anne 1710–70, French dancer who made dance history by shortening her skirt to a few inches above the instep.
Castle, Vernon 1887–1918, British dancer, and his American wife Irene (1893-1969) were sensational exhibition ballroom dancers.
Charisse, Cyd b. 1923, American dancer, long-legged star of many musicals.
Cranko, John 1927–73, South African choreographer important for his contribution to British ballet and as director of the Stuttgart Ballet.
Cunningham, Merce b. 1919, American dancer/choreographer formed his own company after working with Martha Graham, creating abstract work, with steps often created independently of any musical accompaniment.
d'Amboise, Jacques b. 1934, American dancer with New York City Ballet and in movie musicals. Has also choreographed.
de Valois, Ninette b. 1898, British dancer and choreographer but chiefly important for the development of Sadler's Wells Ballet, which became the Royal Ballet.
de Mille, Agnes b. 1908, American choreographer, drawing on traditional American sources. Created dance for several great musicals of the 1940s.
Diaghilev, Sergei 1872–1929, Russian impresario, neither dancer nor choreographer but his Ballets Russes revolutionized ballet.
Duncan, Isadora 1878–1927, American dancer whose original free-flowing, barefoot style of expressive and dramatifc dance has had great influence.
Eissler, Fanny 1810–84, Austrian dancer, popular romantic ballerina in London and Paris, also performed folk dances.
Fokine, Michel 1880–1942, Russian leading dancer but remembered for his choreography especially for Diaghilev (including *Petrouchka* and *Firebird*) which changed balletic style.
Fonteyn, Margot 1919-91, British dancer of incomparable character and technique who led the Sadler's Wells and Royal Ballets.
Franca, Celia b. 1921, English dancer/choreographer, founder of National Ballet of Canada.
Graham, Martha 1893–91, American dancer, choreographer, teacher and a leader of the modern dance movement who evolved her own austere and dramatic dance forms.
Fuller, Loie 1862–1928, American dancer famous as much for her use of scarves and

continued

Dancers and choreographers continued

5254 lighting to achieve effects as for her dance.

Hayden, Melissa b. 1923, Canadian ballerina with Ballet Theatre and New York City Ballet.

Helpmann, Robert 1909–86, Australian dancer/choreographer played an important role in the development of British ballet.

Jooss, Kurt 1901–79, German choreographer of expressionist works, especially the anti-war *Green Table.*

Karsavina, Tamara 1885–1978, Russian ballerina with Diaghilev, partnering Nijinksy and creating Firebird and other roles.

Kelly, Gene b. 1912, American dancer/choreographer and actor especially in Hollywood musicals.

Kirstein, Lincoln b. 1907, American co-founder (with Balanchine) of the American School of Ballet and director of the New York City Ballet. Neither dancer nor choreographer, he was a prime-mover in the creation of American ballet.

Lifar, Serge 1905–86, Russian dancer and choreographer, soloist with Diaghilev, for a time director of Paris Opera Ballet.

Macmillan, Kenneth 1929–92, British dancer and choreographer and a Director of the Royal Ballet.

Makarova, Natalia b. 1940, Russian ballerina with Kirov Ballet and with American Ballet Theatre.

Markova, Alicia b. 1910, English dancer, joined Diaghilev, then a star of British ballet. She founded: the Markova-Dolin Ballet and Festival Ballet.

Massine, Leonide 1899–1975, Russian dancer and choreographer for Diaghilev and Ballet Russe de Monte Carlo.

Mitchell, Arthur b. 1934, American dancer with New York City Ballet and founder of the Dance Theater of Harlem. Instrumental in bringing more black dancers into classical ballets.

Nijinska, Bronislava 1891–1972, Polish-Russian dancer and choreographer with Diaghilev and companies, including her own Théâtre de Danse in Paris; sister of Vaslav Nijinsky.

Nijinsky, Vaslav 1890–1950, Russian premier dancer with Diaghilev and idiosyncratic original choreographer of *The Afternoon of a Faun* and *The Rite of Spring.* Considered the greatest dancer of his time but mental illness forced retirement in his twenties.

Noverre, Jean Georges 1727–1810, French dancer/choreographer who advocated many reforms set out in his *Letters on Dancing* (1760). Advocated that dance relate to the tone and tempi of the music and more naturally expressive movement which could be understood by more than a narrow cognscenti.

Nureyev, Rudolf 1938–93, Russian dancer at the Kirov. Defected to the West and soon joined the Royal Ballet, partnering Margot Fonteyn; a star guest with many companies, then director of Paris Opera Ballet. A dramatic and technical virtuoso, ranked with Nijinsky as the most charismatic of dancers.

Pavlova, Anna 1881–1931, Russian dancer with Diaghilev and touring the world with her own company. Ranked the greatest ballerina of her time and noted for her Dying Swan solo.

Petipa, Marius 1818–1910, French choreographer who developed the Russian ballet in St Petersburg.

Petit, Roland b. 1924, French dancer and choreographer. Founded his own company and later became director of Ballets de Marseilles.

Robbins, Jerome b. 1918, American dancer and choreographer of musicals and ballets, director of New York City Ballet.

Robinson, Bill ("Bojangles" 1878–1949) American dancer, king of tap.

Rogers, Ginger b. 1911, American dancer and movie actress, partner of Fred Astaire.

St Denis, Ruth 1877–1968, American choreographer and dancer, founder with her husband Ted Shawn of the Denishawn School, influential in the development of American dance.

Taglione, Maria 1804–84, Swedish-Italian dancer of ethereal style who popularized the pointe shoe; leading ballerina of the romantic period.

Tharp, Twyla b. 1941, American dancer and choreographer blending personal and classical techniques; director of Netherlands Dance Theatre, Stuttgart Ballet, and of her own company.

Tudor, Antony 1908–87, English dancer and choreographer, especially of psychological ballets for Ballet Rambert and American Ballet Theatre.

Tune, Tommy b. 1939, American show dancer and choreographer.

Vestris, Auguste 1760–1842, French dancer, son of Gaetano, one of the greatest dancers of all time with a phenomenally long career – 36 years as premier dancer of the Paris Opera and age 75 danced partnering Marie Taglioni.

Vestris, Gaetano 1729–1808, Italian dancer, star, and later ballet master of the Paris Opera.

526 MAJOR EVENTS IN POPULAR MUSIC 1877 – 1991

1870s

1877 Thomas Alva Edison successfully demonstates phonograph.

1880s

1882 "Tin Pan Alley" founded around 28th & Broadway, New York.
1884 Emile Berliner records *The Lord's Prayer* on cylinder, now preserved in BBC archives – world's oldest surviving record.
1886 Patent for "Gramophone" wax cylinder system granted to Bell. American Gramophone Company formed at Bridgeport, Connecticut.
1888 Emile Berliner invents flat recording disc of zinc. First popular artist recording made by pianist Josef Hoffman for Edison.
1889 Columbia Phonograph Company formed.

1 Early cylinder recording machine, 1880s

1890s

1890 First recording studios opened—5th Avenue, New York. Edison markets "speaking dolls" with mini-discs inside.
1892 First million-selling song on sheet music – *After The Ball.*
1893 Tchaikovsky dies in St. Petersburg, Russia.
1896 Clockwork speed-controlled gramophone introduced.
1898 Eldridge Johnson patents sound amplifying horn. Gramophone Company (later HMV) makes first discs in UK.
1899 Francis Barraud's painting of the dog Nipper is named "His Master's Voice." First factory exclusively making gramophone records opens in Hanover, Germany.

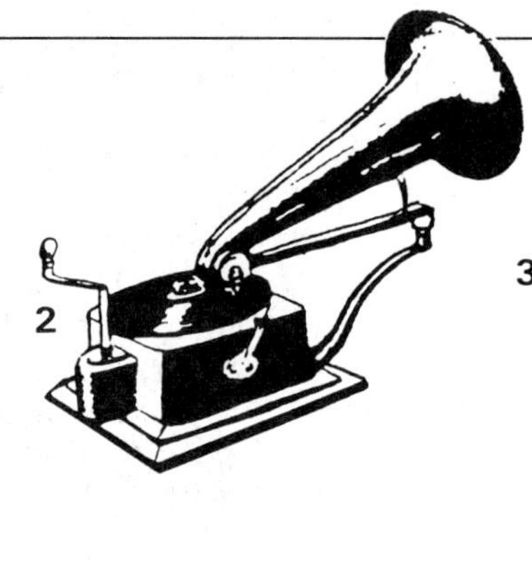

1 Advertisement from *Sear's Catalog* of 1898
2 Improved Berliner Phonograph, 1899
3 Sheet-music cover from Scott Joplin's ragtime composition, *Maple Leaf Rag*, 1899
4 Columbia "Eagle" gramophone, 1899

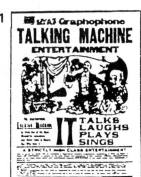

1900s

1900 Paper labels first introduced on records (**1**).
1901 Marconi's first wireless signal. Emile Berliner and Eldridge Johnson forms Victor Talking Machine Co.
1902 Caruso makes London debut in *Rigoletto* at Covent Garden. First known black vocal group – Dinwoodie Colored Quartet.
1903 Caruso made first million-selling record – *On With The Motley*. Introduction of first royalty system for recording artist payment. Caruso makes US debut in *Rigoletto* at Metropolitan Opera House, New York. First "unbreakable" records – cardboard discs covered with shellac.
1906 First console gramophone with internal horn – Victor Victrola (**2**).

1 Two early record company labels
2 Victrola IV gramophone with enclosed horn, 1907

continue

Major events in popular music 1877–1993 continued

1910s

1911 Archibald Joyce forms first British big band.
1912 First recordings of ragtime tunes. Cylinder recording ceases; double-sided discs become standard.
1913 Decca introduces portable gramaphone in UK.
1914 W C Handy records The *St Louis Blues* (**2**). ASCAP formed in US to collect perfoming rights due on recordings. Irving Berlin's first musical, *Watch Your Step*, produced in New York.
1915 Cylinder recordings replaced by RPM.
1917 First jazz recording—*Darktown Strutters Ball* by Original Dixieland Jazz Band.
1919 First UK jazz release – *At The Jazz Band Ball* by original Dixieland Jazz Band. Radio corporation of America (RCA) is founded.

1 Drum with logo of Original Dixieland Jazz Band, 1917
2 Original cover of W.C. Handy's first and greatest song hit – *The St Louis Blues* – 1914

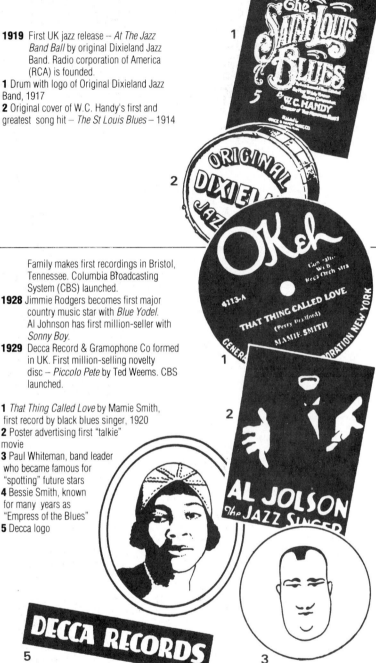

1920s

1920 *Dardanella* by Ben Selvin's orchestra is first million-selling dance record. First blues vocal recorded by a black artist – *That Thing Called Love* by Mamie Smith. First commercial radio broadcast in US – Station WEAF, New York. Paul Whiteman finds orchestra fame with *Whispering*.
1922 Marconi's first regular enytertainment broadcasts on radio, from 2MT in Essex, UK.
1923 Record sales slump due to new craze for radio sets. Fiddlin' John Carson makes first country music recordings. Bessie Smith's *Down Heartland Blues* was Columbia Record's first pop hit.
1924 Electronic recording technique perfected by Bell Company. First country music million-seller – Vernon Dalhart's *The Prisoner's Song*. First live performance of Gershwin's *Rhapsody In Blue* by Paul Whiteman's Orchestra at Aeolian Hall, New York.
1925 Electric recording introduced commercially; microphone replaces acoustic horn.
1926 John Logie Baird demonstrates television. *The Grand Ole Opry* launched on US radio.
1927 First auto-change record player to take 12 stacked discs. Al Johnson stars in first talkie, a musical film, *The Jazz Singer*. Country music pioneers Carter Family makes first recordings in Bristol, Tennessee. Columbia Broadcasting System (CBS) launched.
1928 Jimmie Rodgers becomes first major country music star with *Blue Yodel*. Al Johnson has first million-seller with *Sonny Boy*.
1929 Decca Record & Gramophone Co formed in UK. First million-selling novelty disc – *Piccolo Pete* by Ted Weems. CBS launched.

1 *That Thing Called Love* by Mamie Smith, first record by black blues singer, 1920
2 Poster advertising first "talkie" movie
3 Paul Whiteman, band leader who became famous for "spotting" future stars
4 Bessie Smith, known for many years as "Empress of the Blues"
5 Decca logo

1930s

1930 Mills Brothers' *Tiger Rag* was first black vocal group million-seller.
1931 EMI Records formed in UK by merger of HMV with Columbia.
1934 Decca label formed in America. First Academy Award-winning film song – *The Continental* from *Gay Divorce*.
1935 Swing music comes to prominence on record. *Lullaby Of Broadway*, from *Gold Diggers of 1935*, was second Oscar-winning song. First production of Gershwin's *Porgy and Bess*, in New York. First "chart" show on US radio – *Your Lucky Strike Hit Parade* – featuring week's 15 most popular songs on disc and sheet music.
1936 First million-selling musical show disc – Jeanette MacDonald/Nelson Eddy's *Indian Love Call*.
1937 First million-seller by a female group – Andrews Sisters' *Bei Mir Bist Du Schön*. Bing Crosby's first million-seller – *Sweet Leilani*. Bluesman Robert Johnson makes last recordings in Dallas. Tommy Dorsey's first million-seller swing arrangement of *Marie*. George Gershwin dies in California. Bessie Smith dies in Mississippi.
1938 First light orchestral million-selling single – *Jealousy* by Fiedler/Boston Pops. Ella Fitzgerald's first million-seller – *A-Tisket, A-Tasket*. Benny Goodman plays first ever jazz concert to

continued

Major events in popular music 1877–1993 continued

526

1930s

be held at Carnegie Hall, New York.

1939 Lale Anderson records *Lily Marlene*, biggest hit of World War II. Glenn Miller records his signature tune – *In The Mood.*

1940s

1940 *Billboard* publishes first US singles chart – Tommy Dorsey at number one. Bob Wills and Bing Crosby both have million-sellers with *San Antonio Rose.*

1941 Glenn Miller has first million-seller with *Chattanooga Choo-Choo.*

1942 Bing Crosby records *White Christmas*, biggest-selling single ever. Tommy Dorsey's *There Are Such Things*, with Frank Sinatra on vocals, sells a million. First war-inspired million-seller – *Praise The Lord & Pass The Ammunition* by Kay Kyse. Capitol Records scores first blg hit with Ella Mae Morse's *Cow-Cow Boogie.*

1943 Frank Sinatra has first million-seller with *All Or Nothing At All.*

1944 Glenn Miller disappears in plane over English Channel. Louis Jordan has first million-seller with *Is You Is Or Is You Ain't My Baby.* US Musicians Union lifts two year three month recording ban.

1945 Arthur Smith records *Guitar Boogie*, future instrumental pop standard. Speciality Records' first million-seller with Roy Milton's *R.M. Blues.*

1946 Ink Spots sell a million apiece of *To Each His Own* and *The Gypsy.* Al Jolson's *The Jolson Story* is first "album" to sell a million – though issued as collection of 78s. Post-war boom puts US record sales 100% up on 1945 figures. RCA presses its hundred millionth disc.

1947 Frankie Laine's first million-seller with *That's My Desire.*

1948 Microgroove long-playing record introduced by Columbia, and 45rpm single by RCA. Elvis Presley's family moves to Memphis in search of more opportunity. Nat "King" Cole has first million-seller with *Nature Boy.* Fats Domino's first million-seller with *The Fat Man.* Bluesman John Lee Hooker finds name with *Boogie Chillun* and *I'm In The Mood.* Jazz guitarist Lonnie Johnson sells a million of *Tomorrow Night.* US annual record sales top 250 million for first time.

1949 Columbia achieve 3.5 million LP sales within 12 months of first release. Capitol and Decca launch their first LPs and 45s in the US. *Oklahoma* original stage cast album was first 33 rpm LP to sell a million. Gene Autry records *Rudolph The Red-Nosed Reindeer* – second all-time biggest Christmas hit. Hank William' first million-seller with *Lovesick Blues.*

1 Glenn Miller, bandleader whose dance music became popular during World War II
2 Capitol Records pop logo
3 Louis Jordan, rythm and blues singer
4 Fats Domino, keyboard player and vocalist
5 Johnnie Ray, who was more famous for crying on stage than for his musical performance
6 Bing Crosby, whose career began in swing era
7 Frank Sinatra – "Old Blue Eyes"
8 Nat "King" Cole, who played in small combos at the beginning of his career and sang solo later on
9 Hank Williams, country singer

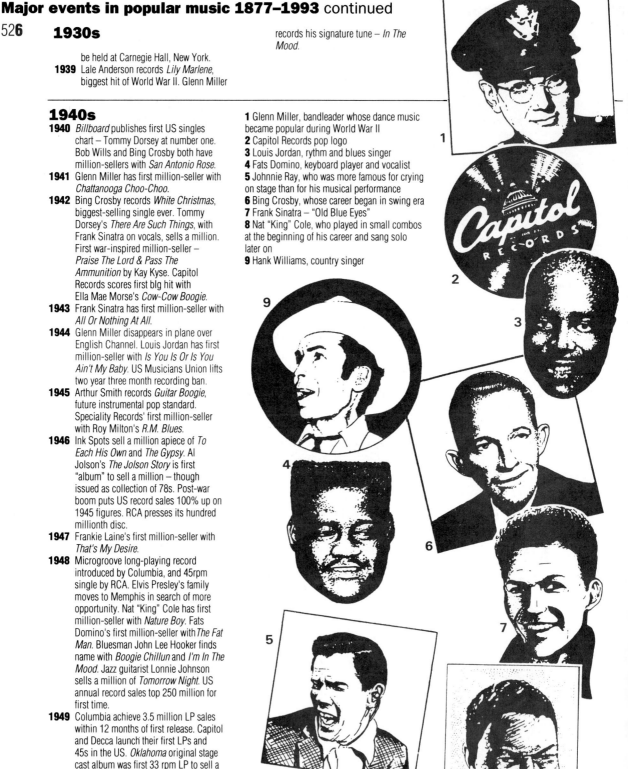

continued

Major events in popular music 1877–1993 continued

526

1950s

1950 Decca introduces LP in the UK. Roy Brown has early R&B million-seller with *Hard Luck Blues.* Zitherist Anton Karas has instrumental million-seller with *Third Man Theme.* Al Jolson dies in San Francisco.
1951 Johnnie Ray has double-sided million-seller with *Cry/Little White Cloud That Cried.*
1952 First 45 rpm singles issued in UK. RCA makes first three-speed record player for 78s, 45s, and 33s. Vera Lynn is first UK artist to top US singles chart, with *Auf Wiedersehen Sweetheart.* Earl Bostic's *Flamingo* is first R&B instrumental million-seller. Fats Domino scores second million-seller with *Goin' Home. New Musical Express* (*NME*) introduces first UK singles chart – Al Martino's *Here In My Heart* at number one. Lloyd Price has first million-seller with *Lawdy Miss Clawdy.* American Bandstand premiere.
1953 Trumpeter Eddie Calvert has million-seller with *Oh Mein Papa.* Stan Freberg has first parody hit with *St George & The Dragonet.* Orioles have first Doo-wop group million seller with *Crying In The Chapel.* Drifters, featuring Clyde McPhatter, have their first smash with *Money Honey.* Hank Williams dies in a car crash.

1

1954 Hillbilly singer and guitarist Bill Haley records a new version of the old Sonny Dae and the Knights' recording *Rock Around The Clock.* It becomes the first major world-wide rock 'n' roll hit.
1955 RCA Victor Records buy 20-year-old Elvis Presley's contract from the small Memphis label Sun Records, for total fees of $40, 000. In the 22 years to Elvis's death, and ever since, RCA have recovered their investment several thousand times over.
1956 Despite a backlash from many American citizens, rock 'n' roll continues to boom with the emergence of artists like Little Richard, Buddy Holly (**1**), Gene Vincent, Chuck Berry, and the Johnny Burnette rock 'n' roll Trio.
1957 American Bandstand, the most influential and long-running pop music programme in the world, makes its national debut on ABC-TV.
1958 Elvis Presley gains favor with American citizens when he is enrolled in the US army as Private 53310761. RCA make sure that a wealth of material already recorded is released during his two-year stint in the forces.
1959 The first major tragedy to hit rock 'n' roll occurs on February 3rd when a plane carrying Buddy Holly, Ritchie Valens, and Big Bopper crashes in Iowa killing all on board. Grammy Awards first presented by National Academy of Recording Arts and Science.

1960s

1960 The rebellious image of rock 'n' roll is giving way to a new brand of clean-cut pop singers, such as Mark Dinning, Bobby Darin, Connie Francis, Fabian, and Bobby Vinton.
1961 Tamla Records gain their first US chart-topper with the Marvelettes' *Please Mr Postman.* The Label thrives throughout the sixties and seventies, and is still providing hit music today.
1962 The Beach Boys make the US hot 100 with their first single, *Surfin'.* The Californians sprearhead a brief music trend before becoming one of the biggest selling bands in the history of rock music.
1963 A group of four young Liverpudlians calling themselves The Beatles have recyled American R&B music and are topping the British charts with every single they release.
1964 Beatlemania arrives in America when the band fly into JFK airport to start their first American tour. The Beatles dominate the charts. The Beatles (**1**) are joined in the so-called British Invasion by The Rolling Stones, The Dave Clark Five, Herman's Hermits, and dozens of others.
1965 The folk rock movement, which is gaining momentum both in the US and Britain, is divided by the decision of Bob Dylan (**2**) to add electric guitar to his previously acoustic act. The Byrds, the Lovin' Spoonful, and Joan Baez are the other leading lights in the folk boom.

1

2

1966 The Beatles play their last ever live concert, at Candlestick Park, SF. Tired of touring, they settle down to concentrate on their studio recordings.
1967 The first result of the Beatles new regime is the milestone LP *Sergeant Pepper's Lonely Hearts Club Band.* Sixteen days after its release, the world's first major pop festival takes place at Monterey, California, USA, featuring dozens of major acts over its three days of performance.
1968 The heavy metal era starts to take shape as the Yardbirds metamorphose into Led Zeppelin, Deep Purple make their live debut, and the MC 5 record the live LP *Kick Out The Jams.*
1969 On August 15 some 400, 000 people descend on Max Yasgur's farm at Woodstock NY, US, to watch Jimi Hendrix, The Who, Creedence Clearwater Revival, Santana, Jefferson Airplane, Janis Joplin, and many others take part in the massive Woodstock Festival.

continued

Major events in popular music 1877–1993 continued

526 1970s

1970 A bleak year for rock 'n' roll that sees Jimi Hendrix (**1**) and Janis Joplin die, the Beatles divide, and Josie and the Pussycats start a two-year run on CBS-TV.

1971 Jim Morrison joins the casualty list (permanent) – as does Duane Allman – while Led Zeppelin release their fourth album containing the classic *Stairway To Heaven.*

1972 David Bowie's LP *The Rise And Fall Of Ziggy Stardust And The Spiders From Mars* is released in the UK, turning him from a cult success to a million-selilng megastar.

1973 Bruce Springsteen releases his debut LP, *Greetings From Asbury Park, NJ.* Although slow to take off, by 1975 he will appear on the cover of *Time* and *Newsweek.*

1974 While bands like Yes, Jefferson Starship, The Rolling Stones, Mott The Hoople, Wings, and Wishbone Ash all undergo personnel changes, a little-known group called the Ramones make their live debut at CBGB's on the Bowery, New York City.

1975 A growing disenchantment with the current pop scene leads to a band called the Sex Pistols making their live debut as a support act at a college gig. They are pulled off the stage after just ten minutes.

1976 American "poetess" Patti Smith takes her act across to England closely followed by the Ramones. By the end of the year the new punk rock sound led by The Sex Pistols and The Damned is becoming popular in England.

1977 Dozens of groups spring up in the wake of The Sex Pistols. In America, groups such as Talking Heads, Blondie, and The Heartbreakers make their mark on the cult. Elvis Presley dies suddenly, aged 42.

1978 Disco has sudden worldwide success as the film *Saturday Night Fever* breaks box-office records. The soundtrack album and various singles top their respective charts and sell in massive numbers.

1979 *Sex Pistol* Sid Vicious, awaiting trial for the murder of his girlfriend, Nancy Spungen, overdoses on heroin.

1980s

1980 In December John Lennon is shot dead outside his New York apartment by fanatic, Mark Chapman. The mourning that follows is usually bestowed upon presidents and monarchs.

1981 Simon and Garfunkel reunite for the first time in 11 years to play a concert in New York's Central Park, followed by a tour. Simon continus his hugely successful solo career, producing the masterpiece *Gracelands*, while Garfunkel concentrates on acting. MTV – "Music Television" – premieres on cable, featuring videos of popular music.

1982 Michael Jackson's *Thriller* LP is released. It spends 37 weeks at the top of the US album chart and sells over 40 million copies worldwide.

1983 Kiss appear on MTV without their faces painted. This massively successful heavy rock group previously hid behind garish comic book makeup.

1984 Soul singer Marvin Gaye, responsible for some of Motown's greatest records, is shot dead by his father during a family row.

1985 Following the British Band Aid charity record *Do They Know It's Christmas?* at Christmas 1984, and USA For

1 Michael Jackson

Africa's *We Are The World*, the world's biggest pop festival for 15 years takes place as artists at the JFK Stadium in Philadelphia and Wembly Stadium in London combine for a massive televised charity show benefiting the hunger-stricken Ethiopians.

1986 The long awaited Bruce Springsteen box-set is finally released by CBS. A five album package entitled *Bruce Springsteen And The E-Street Band Live 1975–85.* It fulfills its sales expectations.

1987 Former Wham! vocalist George Michael, releases his debut solo LP *Faith.* It reaches number one in both the US and his native UK, remaining on the charts for over a year. The songs featured include the controversial *I Want Your Sex*, which reaches number two on the US singles chart, and the title track, which goes to number one after heavy exposure on MTV.

1988 The latest manufactured pop sensation to make it big are New Kids On The Block. The New Kids dominate the Top Ten on both sides of the Atlantic making huge profits.

1989 The pop trend in the UK is for Australian soap stars like Kylie Minogue and Jason Donovan to turn their talent to singing, with bestselling results.

1990s

1990 The New Kids On The Block rapidly give way to the Teenage Mutant Ninja Turtles, a cartoon creation who move into film and music. The first movie is a massive success and a second is quickly made, also featuring Vanilla Ice, a white rap artist who is also becoming popular.

1991 The controversial singer, Madonna (**1**) causes a storm when the behind-the-scenes tour film *Truth Or Dare (In Bed With Madonna)* is released in the UK featuring sexually provocative scenes.

1992 Madonna publishes book of photographs, *Sex*, which receives massive publicity. A revival of 1970s music leads to the development of "rave" music and 1970s fashions.

1993 Grunge is the major trend in music, with the group Nirvana its chief exponent.

531 PREHISTORIC ART

Paleolithic and other "primitive" art

5311 **Development**
There are probably four stages of development in art between 35,000 and 10,000 years ago.
Period I (32,000–25,000 years ago) featured animals mostly drawn on small, portable objects.
Period II (25,000–19,000 years ago) produced early cave art including hand prints and engraved and painted silhouettes of animals with sinuous curved backs.
Period III (19,000-15,000 years ago) included lively, well-drawn horses and cattle.
Period IV (15,000–10,000 years ago) stressed portable art, symbolic, and lifelike creatures.
Location of cave paintings
Paleolithic art (from 24,000 BC) includes cave painting of the Perigordian and later Solutrean and Magdalenian periods (18,000–10,000 BC) first discovered at Vienne, France in 1834. Lascaux, also in France (c. 15,000 BC) was discovered in 1940. Other notable sites are in northern Spain, western North America, the Urals, India, and North and southwest Africa. Much of the prehistoric cave art is of remarkable quality, bold, direct, and lively

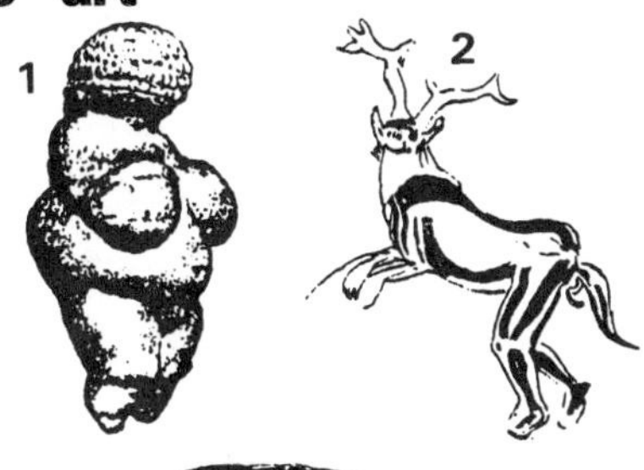
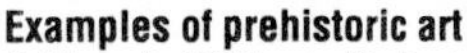
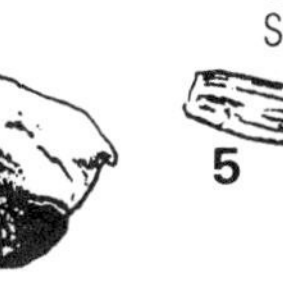

Examples of prehistoric art
1 "Venus" of Willendorf in Austria, a figurine with exaggerated female features.
2 "Sorcerer" from Les Trois Frères cave in France – painting of a figure that seems half stag, half man.
3 Bison licking its back, a reindeer-antler carving.
4 Painted horse outline with dots and hand prints added, on a wall in Pech-Merle cave (France).
5 Seals engraved on an antler baton, from Montagaudier (France).
6 Mesolithic bowman featured on cave walls in Spain from Epipaleolithic times.

Mesopotamian art

5312 Mesopotamian art (6000–539 BC) covering the Sumerian, Babylonian, and Assyrian periods. This art is epitomized by many styles which incorporate figures, animals, plants, and mythical animals. Notable examples include the jewelry from Ur, the tiles from the gates of Babylon, and the sculptural works from the palaces of the Assyrian kings (Nineveh).

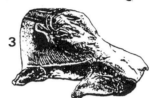

1 Tomb decoration from Ur
2 Sumerian head of a woman carved from sandstone, height 2.5 in (about 6 cm).

532 EGYPTIAN AND CLASSICAL ART 3100 BC–AD 400

Styles and movements

5321 **Egyptian art** (3100–341 BC) Like all ancient art Egyptian art fulfilled a religious function based on the notion of immortality. Monumental sculptures were made to grace tombs and temples. Pictures of the deceased were often included among the material possessions entombed with him or her. During the Hellenistic period (34–27 BC), mummies often incorporated realistic portraits of the deceased.

1 Egyptian papyrus showing the soul of Ani
2 Greek vase, showing a drinking party
3 Statue of Artemis, Greek fertility goddess

Ancient Greek–Hellenistic period (2800–27 BC) Minoan and Mycenean art (2800–1100 BC) consists mainly of sculptured engravings, decorated pottery and some frescoes. The archaic period (800–500 BC) saw developments in sculpture, especially human figures. This was carried forward during the classical period (500–323 BC) in which the body was idealized and movement was introduced both in pose and drapery. During the Hellenistic period (323–27 BC) a more dramatic and realistic approach was established. Throughout the entire period pottery was decorated with figures and scenes from story and legend.

Roman art (100 BC – AD 400) The Romans excelled in copies of Greek sculpture and relief carving, such as in frescoes at Pompeii Unlike the Greeks, the Romans had a highly developed realistic portrait art, in which people's faces were portrayed rather than idealized. Mosaic floors were also highly decorative.

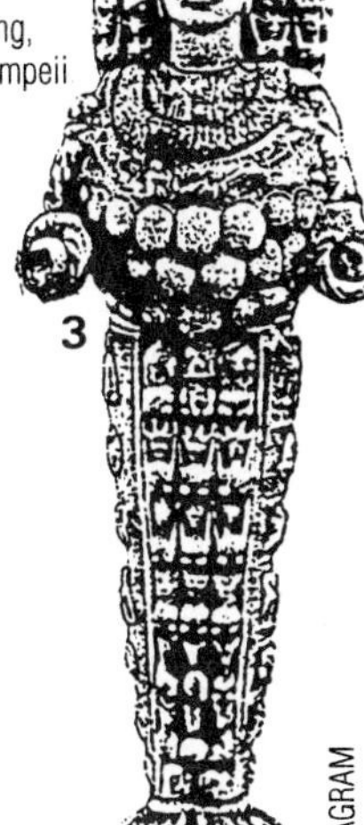

Events: sculpture

5322 **c. 3100 BC** Ceremonial palette of King Narmer, Egypt (**1**).

c. 2900 Cylinder seals, Mesopotamia.
c. 2800 Clay sculpture, monkey with a young one, India.
c. 2740 *Lady of Warka*, Mesopotamia.

c. 2500 Sphinx of Giza (Pharoah Chephren's head with lion's body), Egypt (**2**). Seated figure of a scribe, Egypt.
c. 2300 Bronze head of Sargon the Great, Mesopotamia (**3**).
c. 2000 Animal miniatures (faience), Egypt.
c. 1890 Portrait of Queen Nofret, Egypt.
c. 1850 Crouched figures in Egypt.
c. 1700 Statue of Hammurabi the Great, Mesopotamia.
c. 1470 Snake Goddess of Knossos, Crete.
c. 1385 Colossi of Memnon (65 ft [20 m] statues of Amenhotep III), Thebes, Egypt.
c. 1365 Painted limestone head of Queen Nefertiti (Ägyptisches Museum, Berlin) (**4**). Bek, Egyptian sculptor and painter.

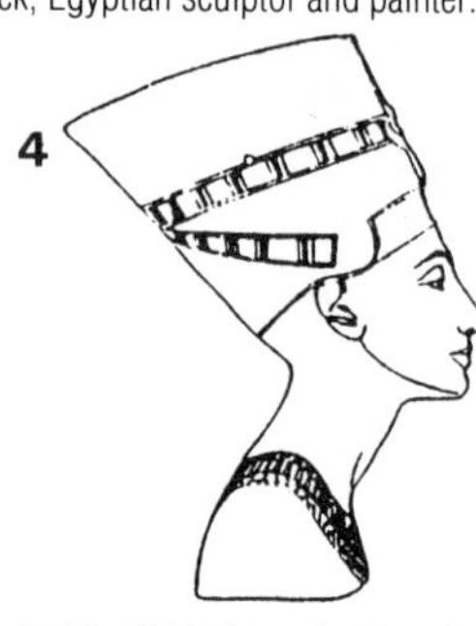

c. 1345–1340 Tutmosis, Egyptian sculptor, creates heads of Akhenaten and Nefertiti.
c. 880 Gold statue of King Assurnasirhpali, Mesopotamia.
c. 747 Statue of Arnernidis, Egypt.
c. 600 *Kouros* statue from Sunium, Greece.
c. 570 *The Calf-Bearer*, votive offering (Acropolis Museum, Athens).
c. 560 Statue dedicated to Hera by Cheramyes, from Samos (Louvre, Paris).
c. 550 *Perseus Beheading the Gorgon* from Temple C at Selinus (National Museum, Palermo, Sicily).
c. 500–480 *Apollo* from Portnaccio Temple at Veii (Villa Giulia, Rome). Bronze *She-wolf* (Palazzo dei Conservatori, Rome).
480 BC *The Kritios Boy* (Acropolis Museum Athens).
c. 460–450 *Discobolus* Myron of Athens (copy in Therme Museum, Rome).
c. 442–438 *Parthenon* frieze, Athens.
c. 440 *Doryphorus* Polyclitus of Samos or Sicyon (copy in National Museum, Naples).
c. 435 *Zeus*, colossal statue at Olympia, by Phidias.
c. 432 *Parthenon* pediments (British Museum).
c. 375–370 *Irene and Plutus* Cephisodotus of Athens (copy in Glyptothek, Munich).
c. 350–330 *Aphrodite of Cnidus* Praxiteles of Athens (copy in Vatican Museum). *Hermes and the Infant Dionysus* Praxiteles (Olympia Museum, Greece).
c. 300–290 *Tyche of Antioch* Eutychides (copy in Vatican Museum).
c. 280 Portrait of Demosthenes (copy in Ny Carlsberg Glyptothek, Copenhagen).
c. 230-220 Statues of Gauls, set up in Pergamum (W Asia Minor) (copies in Rome).
c. 200 *Winged Victory of Samothrace* (Louvre, Paris).
c. 197–180 *Battle of Gods and Giants*, frieze of Great Altar at Pergamum (State Museum, Berlin).
c. 167 Frieze of monument of Aemilius Paullus, Delphi, Greece.
c. 150 *Brutus* (so designated) (Palazzo dei Conservatori, Rome).
c. 125–100 *Venus de Milo* (Louvre, Paris).
c. 75–65 Head of a Priest (Vatican Museum).
AD 13–9 *Ara pacis*, Rome.
c. 14–27 Statue of Augustus (Vatican Museum).
69–79 Portraits of Vespasian, Rome.
c. 81 BC Reliefs on Arch of Titus, Rome (**5**).

AD 106–13 Column of Trajan, Rome .
c. 117 Tomb of Ho Ch'uping, Han Dynasty, China.
161-80 Bronze equestrian statue of Marcus Aurelius, Piazza del Campidoglio, Rome.
c. 180 Column of Marcus Aurelius, Rome.
203 Arch of Septimus Severus, Rome.
211–17 Bust of Caracalla (Museo Capitolino, Rome).
242–73 Rock carvings of Shapur I the Great, Naqsh-i-Rustam, Persia.
312–15 Reliefs of arch of Constantine, Rome.
c. 313 Colossal head of Constantine, Rome.
c. 390 Base of the obelisk of Theodosius, Constantinople.

Events: painting

5323 **c. 3000 BC** Murals in Egypt
c. 2500 Painted black and red Yangshoa culture pottery in China (**1**).
c. 2400 Ni-Auch-Pta, Egyptian painter and sculptor

c. 1712 BC Painting, *Lion-hunt* in Mesopotamia.
c. 1700 Mural, *Family of Lord Chui*, in Egypt.
c. 1500 *Bull-Games*, murals in Crete.
c. 1365 Bek, Egyptian painter and sculptor.
c. 530–520 *Apollo and Heracles Struggling for the Tripod* (vase) by the Andocines painter.
c. 510 *Heracles and Antaeus* (calyxcrater vase) Euphronius.
c. 500-490 *Dionysus ampnora* the Cleophrades painter.
c. 480 *Tomb of the Diver* (banqueting scenes), Paestum, S Italy.
c. 450–440 *Achilles* (vase) the Achilles painter (Vatican Museum).
c. 350 *Ajax and Cassandra* (vase) Asteas, Paestum school (Villa Giulia Museum, Rome).
c. 300 *Battle of Issus*, mosaic (copy in National Museum, Naples).
c. 250 *Tomb of Orcus*, Tarquinia, Italy.
c. 200 *Stele of Hediste* from Demetrias (Volvos Museum, Greece).
c. 150 *Scenes from the new Comedy* (mosaic panels) Dioscurides of Samos.
c. 100 *Dionysus Riding a Cheetah*, mosaic in Delos, Greece.
c. 80–40 *Dionysiac frieze*, Pompeii.
c. 50–40 *Odyssey* landscapes, Esquiline Hill house, Rome (Vatican Museum).
c. AD 1–10 Boscoreale Villa paintings, near Pompeii (National Museum, Naples).
c. 63–69 *House of the Vetii*, Pompeii.
AD 64–68 Paintings of Nero's Golden House, Rome, by Faulbus.
c. 250–300 *Return of Persephone from Hades*, Rome.
c. 305 Great hunt mosaic, imperial villa at Piazza Armerina, Sicily.
c. 337–50 Vault mosaics of S Constanza Church, Rome.

533 CHRISTIANITY AND THE DARK AGES AD 400 – 1200

Styles and movements

5331 **Early Christian art** Christian symbolism in art spread rapidly throughout the Roman world by the end of the first Christian century, from the Roman catacombs to mosiac floors in British villas, and crosses, e.g. High King Sinna's *Cross of the Scriptures* at Clonmacnoise, County Offlay, Ireland (**1**).
Migration period (AD 150–1000) A term covering the art of the Huns, post-Roman Celtic art in Britain and Ireland, and pre-Carolingian Frankish and Viking art.
Byzantine art (c. AD 330–1450) Centered on Constantinople, the eastern capital of the Roman Empire. A formal, stylized art drew on the traditions of Hellenic, Roman, and Middle Eastern styles. The First Golden Age was in the 6th century, when S Sophia was built. The Second Golden Age (1051–1185) dominated, like the first by mosaic work, was the period of its greatest influence in the West. The Third Age (1261–1450) saw the rise of fresco painting.
Carolingian art (AD 800–70) Schools of Illuminated manuscripts, mainly in France.
Ottonian art (AD 870–1050) Schools of Illuminated manuscripts, mainly in Germany.
Romanesque art (1050–1200) This widespread and mainly architectural style is distinguished by its use of rounded arches and powerful use of religious symbolism. Illuminated manuscripts of high quality include the *Winchester Bible.*

Islamic art (7th century–17th century) Highly decorative and proscribing representational work, Islamic art was based on Koranic calligraphy and reached its greatest development in the fields of miniature painting, ceramic tiles, and carpet weaving, in which floral and geometric patterns became highly intricate.
Abu Ali Ibn Muqlah (died 940 CE) established rules for writing so that the Islamic letters would be beautiful and in proportion. Standard phrases, such as "In the name of God," "The Mercy-Giving," were used to decorate mosques.

Events: sculpture

5332 **SCULPTURE**
c. AD 300–625 Japanese *haniwa*: a hollow pottery figure. This figurine is from the Yamato period (**1**).
c. 422–32 Doors of S Sabina, Rome.
c. 527 *Justinian (?) on Horseback*, ivory, probably from Constantinople (Louvre, Paris).
531–79 Palace of Chosroes the Great, Ctseophon (barrel vaulted hall), Iraq.
545–53 Throne of Archbishop Maximian, Ravenna.
610–29 The Marriage of David, silver plate, Cyprus (Nicosia Museum).
c. 675–85 Celtic *Ruthwell Cross*, Scotland.
717 Buddha with the God of the Sun and Moon (above life-sized bronze), Nara, Japan.
749 AD *The Neighing Stallion*, China.
c. 775–800 AD *Pinecone*, Chapel of Charlemagne, Aachen, Germany.
c. 840 *Golden Altar* Volvinio, S Ambrogio, Milan.
c. 950–1000 *Christ Pantocrator*, enamel miniature, Mount Athos, Greece.
c. 980–1000 *Europa and the Bull*, Byzantine Veroli Casket (V&A, London).
1015 Bronze Doors, mounted, Hildesheim Cathedral, Germany (**2**).
c. 1090–95 *Capitals depicting the tones of plainsong*, Cluny (Musée de Farin).
c. 1090–1100 Bronze Doors of S Zeno, Verona, Italy.
c. 1100–6 *Creation* Wiligelmo, façade of Modena Cathedral, Italy.
c. 1100–1200 *Virgin and Child*, ivory statuette (V&A, London).
c. 1150–55 Royal Portal, west front of Chartres Cathedral, France.
c. 1178 *Descent from the Cross* Antelami, Parma Cathedral, Italy.
1181 Klosterneuburg Altar, Stiftkirche, Austria, Nicolas of Verdun.

2

Events: painting

5333 **c. AD 400–50** Vatican Vergil, book illustrations (Bibliotecca Apostolica, Rome). *The Good Shepherd* mosaic from Tomb of Galla Placida, Ravenna.
c. 500–600 *Book of Genesis*, book illustrations, Vienna. *St Peter*, Monastery of S Catherine, Mount Sinai.
c. 547 *Justinian and his Suite*, mosaic, S Vitale, Ravenna.
c. 640 *S Demetrius and Suppliants* mosaic, St Demetrius, Salonika.
c. 700 *Lindisfarne Gospels*, book illustrations (British Museum, London).
c. 705 *Enthroned Virgin and Child*, Byzantine icon, Rome.
c. 762 *Annunciation* fresco (S Sofia, Benevento, Italy).
c. 781 *Godescal Sacramentary*, book illustrations (Bibliothèque Nationale, Paris).

1 Bayeux Tapestry. France c. 1077

continued

Events: painting continued

5333 **c. 790–800** *Harley Gospels,* book illustrations (British Museum, London).
817–24 *S Prassade,* mosaics, Rome.
c. 900–1000 *Paris Psalter,* book illustrations (Bibliothèque Nationale, Paris).
924 *Concert at the Palace,* China.
961 Chinese Academy of Painting founded by Emperor Lin Yu of Nanking.
977–93 *Egbert Codex,* book illustrations, Trier, Germany.
1047 *Beatus,* book illustrations (Biblioteca Nacional, Madrid).
AD 1068 *Shotoku Taishi Eden* (**2**) Yamato-style painting, Japan.
c. 1077 *Bayeux Tapestry,* France.

2

c. 1100 *Christ Pantocrator,* dome mosaic, Church of Daphni, Greece.
c. 1120 *Albani Psalter,* book illustrations (British Museum, London).
c. 1125 *Our Lady of Vladimir,* icon (Tretyakov Gallery, Moscow).
c. 1125–50 *Pantheon Bible* book illustrations, Rome.
1148 *Christ Pantocrator,* mosaic, apse of Cefalù Cathedral, Sicily.
c. 1175–1200 *St Paul and the Viper,* mural, Canterbury Cathedral.

534 MIDDLE AGES 1200 - 1450

Styles and movements

5341 **Gothic art** The successor to Romanesque art throughout Europe. The first great Gothic building was the abbey church of S Denis, outside Paris, which differed from Romanesque mainly by ribbed vaulting, pointed arches, and with flying buttresses which allowed large expances of wall to be replaced by stained glass windows. Sculpture became more narrative in content and realistic in style.

Events: sculpture

5342 **c. 1210–15** South Portal, Chartres Cathedral.
c. 1225-55 West Front, Wells Cathedral, England.
c. 1235 *Portada del Sarmental,* Burgos Cathedral, Spain.
1248–50 *Uta,* Naumburg Cathedral, Germany.
1260 Pulpit by Nicolò Pisano, Pisa Baptistery.
1265 Pulpit of Siena Cathedral, Nicola Pisano.
c. 1275–1300 *Descent from the Cross* (Louvre, Paris).
1284–98 Sculptures on façade, Siena Cathedral, by Giovanni Pisano, including the sculptured head of the prophet Isaiah (**1**).
1291–3 *Queen Eleanor,* Westminster Abbey, London, by William Torel.
c. 1299 *Virgin and Child,* Cathedral Treasury, Pisa, by Giovanni Pisano.
1302 Pulpit, Pisa Cathedral by Giovanni Pisano.
c. 1320 *Milan Madonna,* Cologne Cathedral
1325–51 North Choir Screen, Nôtre-Dame, Paris.
1330-36 Bronze doors, south side of baptistery, Florence Cathedral, by Andrea Pisano.
1339 *Madonna of Jeanne d'Évreux,* gilt statue (Louvre, Paris).
c. 1360–70 *Madonna della Rosa,* S Maria della Spina, Pisa, by Giovanni Pisano.
1365–7 *Queen Philippa of Hainault,* Westminster Abbey, London, by Jean of Liège.
c. 1375 Monument of Cansignorio della Scala, S Maria Antica, Verona.
1384 Tomb of Philippe le Hardi, Dijon, by Jean de Marville, Sluter and Werve.
1391–7 Statues of Main Portal, Chartreuse de Champmol nr Dijon, by Claus Sluter.
1401–2 *Sacrifice of Isaac* Ghiberti and Brunelleschi (Bargello, Florence).
c. 1410 Golden Table from S Michael's Church, Lüneburg, Hanover.
c. 1411 Stone Choir Screen, Canterbury Cathedral.
1425–36 Alabaster Altarpiece Pedro Johan, Tarragona Cathedral, Spain.
1425–52 *Gates of Paradise* Ghiberti, baptistery of Florence Cathedral.
1428 *Angel of the Annunciation* Delemer, Ste Marie-Madeleine, Tournai, Belgium.
1430–42 *David* Donatello (Bargello, Florence).
c. 1435 Doors of S Peter's, Rome, begun by Filarete.
c. 1443 Gattamelata Monument, Piazza del Santo, Padua, begun by Donatello.

1

Events: painting

5343 **c. 1210–20** Painted Cross, Berlinghiero, Lucca, Italy.
c. 1220 *Story of Charlemagne,* Chartres Cathedral, France.
c. 1260 *Madonna della Trinità* Cimabue (Uffizi, Florence).
c. 1275–1300 Westminster retable, Westminster Abbey, London.
1285 Gospel book by Theophilus the Monk (British Museum, London). *Rucellai Madonna* Duccio di Buoninsegna (Uffizi, Florence).
c. 1290 *Last Judgement* Pietro Cavallini, S Cecilia, Rome.
c. 1296 *Life of S Francis,* Assisi, probably begun by Giotto.
1304–05 Fresco cycle in Arena Chapel by Giotto (Padua, Italy).
1308 *Maestà,* Opera del Duomo by Duccio di Buoninsegna, Siena (Italy).
c. 1320 *Manesse Codex,* book illustrations, Heidelberg, (Germany).
c. 1320-25 Annunciation altarpiece by Simone Martini (Uffizi, Florence).
1344 *Falconry,* Palace of the Popes, Avignon.
c. 1349 *Great East Window,* Gloucester Cathedral.
c. 1350 *Triumph of Death* Francesco Traini, Campo Santo, Pisa.
c. 1365 S *Guy* Master Theoderik of Prague (National Gallery, Prague).
1373–78 *Le Parlement de Narbonne* (Louvre, Paris).
c. 1380 *Nativity* Giusto de Menabuoi, (Padua Baptistery, Italy).
1385-1402 *Brussels Hours* Jacquemart de Hesdin (Bibliotèque Royale, Brussels).
c. 1400 S *Veronica,* panel (Alte Pinakothek, Munich).
c. 1410-20 *Icon of the Old Trinity* Andrei Rublev (Tretyakov Gallery, Moscow).
1413 *Coronation of the Virgin* Lorenzo Monaco (Uffizi, Florence).
c. 1416 *Très Riches Heures de Duc de Berry* book illustrations, Paris, begun by the Limbourg brothers (Musée Condé, Chantilly).
c. 1420–30 *Mérode Annunciation* Robert Campin (Metropolitan Museum, New York).

continued

Events: painting continued

5343 **1426–28** *The Tribute Money* Masaccio, S Maria del Carmine, Florence.
1432 *G*hent Altarpiece by van Eyck brothers (S. Bravo, Ghent)
c. 1438 *Descent from the Cross* Rogier van der Weyden (Prado, Madrid).
c. 1440–47 *Annunciation* Fra Angelico, S Marco, Florence.
1443–45 *Virgin of the Councillors* Louis Dalmau, Barcelona.
1444 *Miraculous Draught of Fishes* Konrad Witz (musée d'Art et d'Histoire, Geneva).

People

5344 **Pisano, Nicola** c. 1225– 1280, Italian sculptor. Revived and fused classical forms with traditional Gothic style. His sculpted panels in the Pisa Baptistery marked a new, strongly dramatic style of composition. He later collaborated with his son Giovanni.

535 RENAISSANCE AND EARLY 18TH CENTURY 1450 - 1750

Styles and movements

5351 **Renaissance** (c. 1300–1545) Meaning "rebirth," the term describes the revival of classical learning and art. Centered at first in Florence, it marked the end of the Middle Ages and was the outstanding creative period in western art. Architecture, painting, and sculpture, deriving from Greek and Roman models, developed with an unparalleled vigor and prominence, and the artist gained a role in society hitherto unknown, mainly due to the rival city states that employed them. Artistic innovation included perspective and painting with oil.

Mannerism (c. 1520–1700) A mainly Italian style deriving from the all-pervasive influence of Michelangelo and Raphael (i.e. in their "manner") that exaggerated their styles into extravagant contortions for an emotional effect.

Baroque art (c 1600–1720) Drawing on the exuberance of mannerism and on the resurgence of Roman Catholic doctrine, the aim of baroque art was to unite the main parts of building, sculpture, and painting into an overall dramatic effect that is mainly "frontal," i.e. it is best seen from one, rather than many viewpoints. Its exuberance and monumentality make it one of the most robust movements in art history.

Events: sculpture

5352 1450–1500
1457–60 *Judith and Holofernes* Donatello, Piazza della Signoria, Florence.
1458 *Alonso de Velasco* Egas Cueman, Guadalupe Abbey, Spain.
1465–71 Sculpture of Triumphal Arch, Naples, completed by Pietro da Milano.
1469–74 Choir stalls, Ulm Minster, by Syrlin the Elder (Germany).
1471–81 *Coronation of the Virgin* by Pacher, S Wolfgang, Salzkammergut, Austria.
1475–7 *Altar of the Virgin* Wesel (Rijkmuseum, Amsterdam).
1477–89 High Altar by Veit Stoss, S Mary, Cracow (Poland).
c. 1485 *Lamentation* Nicolo dell' Arca, S Maria della Vita, Bologna.
1491–93 *Adam and Eve* Riemenschneider, Würzburg.
1493 Tabernacle by Adam Krafft, S Lorenz, Nuremberg.
c. 1498–1500 *Pietà* Michelangelo, S Peter's, Rome.

1500–1600
1501–04 *David* Michelangelo, Florence.
1505 Tomb of Julius II, S Peter's, Rome, Michelangelo.
1507–19 *Shrine of Sebaldus*, Nuremburg, by Vischer family.
1508–33 Family mausoleum of Emperor Maximilian, Hofkirche, Innsbruck, Austria.
1512–18 Henry VII's tomb by Pietro Torrigiano, Westminster Abbey, London.
1515–16 Statue of Moses by Michelangelo S Pietro in Vincoli, Rome.
1515–31 Funeral monument of Louis XII by Giovanni Giusti, S Denis, Paris.
1520–3 *Bamberg Altar*, Bamberg Cathedral, by Veit Stoss (Germany).
1520–34 Tomb of Lorenzo de' Medici (**1**), by Michelangelo (S Lorenzo, Florence).
1521 Altar for the Royal Chapel, Felipe Vigarny, Granada.
1525-30 *Virgin and Child*, Konrad Meit Brussels.
1526-31 Tomb of Philibert le Beau of Savoy, Brou, supervised by Conrad Meit.
1532 Bronze *Apollo Fountain*, Peter Flötner Pel!erhau, Nuremberg.
1534 *Hercules and Cacus* Baccio Bandinelli, Piazza della Signoria, Florence.
1536 *Fountain of Hercules and Antaeus* Niccolò Tribolo, Florence,
1537 *Great Portal of S Michel*, Dijon.
1539 *The Royal Salt*, Cellini (Kunsthistorisches Museum, Vienna.
1545–54 *Perseus*, Loggia dei Lanzi, by Cellini, Florence.
1548–59 Tomb of Francis I, S Denis, by Pierre Bontemps, Paris.
1550–51 *Carytadis* Jean Goujon (Louvre, Paris).
1554–67 *Mars and Neptune* Jacopo Sansovino (Doge's Palace, Venice).

1

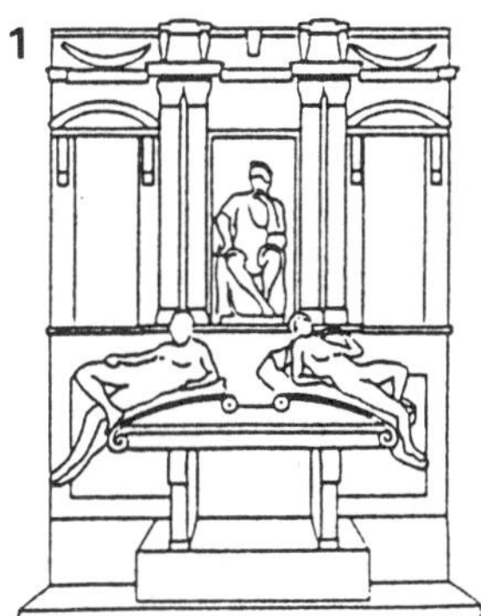

1560–3 Tomb of Gian Giacomo de' Medici by Leone Leoni, Milan Cathedral.
1560–3 *Three Graces* Pilon, Louvre, Paris.
c. 1561 Marble reliefs for Tomb of Maximilian, Alexander Colin, Innsbruck, Austria.
1564 *Rondanini Pietà* Michelangelo, Castello Sforzesco, Milan.
1567 *Neptune Fountain* Giambologna, Bologna.
1569 S *Jerome* Alessandro Vittoria, Chiesa dei Frari, Venice.
1575 *Fountain of Neptune* Bartolomeo Ammanati, Piazza della Signoria, Florence.
c. 1579 *Mercury* Van der Schardt, (National Museum, Stockholm).
1580 *The Medici Mercury* Giambologna (Museo Nazionale, Florence).
1581–85 *The Tortoise Fountain* Landini, Piazza Mattei, Rome.
1583 *The Meleager Group* Bandini Urbino (Prado, Madrid).
1584 Tomb of Valentine Balbiani by Pilon, Louvre, Paris.
1598 *Philip II and his Family* Pompeo Leoni, Escorial, Great Chapel.

continued

Events: sculpture continued

5352 1600–1700

1600 *Statue of S Cecilia* Stephano Madernao, S Cecilia, Rome.
1609 *Annunciation Group*, Francesco Mochi, Orvieto Cathedral, Italy.
1609–14 *Philip III* Pietro Tacca, bronze equestrian statue, Plaza Mayor, Madrid.
1610–11 *Spring* Hans Krumper (National Museum, Munich).
1617 *Pietà* Gregorio Fernandez (Museo Provincal, Valladollid).
1622 Monument to Francis Holles by Nicholas Stone, Westminster Abbey, London.
1622–4 *Apollo and Daphne* Bernini, Galleria Borghese, Rome.
1624 *Baldacchino* Bernini (**2**), above tomb of S Peter, S Peter's, Rome.
1630 *Mannekin-Pis* J Duquesnoy the Elder (Musée Communal, Brussels).
1630–1 *Ecce Homo* Georg Petel, Augsburg Cathedral.
1640 S *Philip Neri* Alessandro Algardi (S Maria in Vallicella, Rome).
1642 *The Four Corners of the World* Gilles Guérin (Palais de Chaillot, Paris).
1645 *Ecstasy of S Theresa* Bernini, S Maria della Vittoria, Rome.
1646 *Meeting of Leo I and Attila* Algardi (Vatican Museum, Rome).
1647 Statue of Queen Anne of Austria by Simon Guillain (Louvre, Paris).
1648 *Fountain of the Four Rivers* Bernini, Piazza Navona, Rome.
1648–65 *Justice and Prudence* Artus Quellin the Elder, Amsterdam Town Hall.
1656 *Cathedra Petri*, Bernini, S Peter's, Rome.
c. 1658 S *Peter* Rombout Verhulst, S André, Antwerp.
1661–5 Stucco decoration by Antonio Raggi , Granada Cathedral.
1664 *The Virgin of Bethlehem* Alonso Cano, Granada Cathedral.

1667 *The Ecstasy of S Catherine* Melchiorre Cafà, S Caterina da Siena, Rome.
1667–82 *Milo of Crotona* Pierre Puget (Louvre, Paris).
1668 *Apollo and the Nymphs* François Girardon, Versailles.
1669 Pulpit in S Gudule, by H F Verbruggen, Brussels.
1667–82 *Milo de Crotona* by Pierre Puget (Louvre, Paris).
1673 Bust of Sir Christopher Wren by Edward Pierce (Ashmolean Museum, Oxford).
1675 Tomb of Cardinal Richelieu begun by Girardon, Chapel of the Sorbonne, Paris.
1677–81 Monument to de Ruyter, Admiral of the Dutch Fleet by Verhulst, New Church, Amsterdam.
1682 *The Cosimo Panel* Grinling Gibbons, Florence.
1689 *The Seine and the Marne* Etienne Le Hongre, Versailles.
1689–94 *Reliquary* Parodi, S Antonio, Padua.
1690–6 *Charity* Giacomo Serpotta, Oratorio di S Lorenzo, Palermo, Sicily.
1693 High Altar of San Esteban by José de Churriguera, Salamanca.
1697 Equestrian statue of the Great Elector by Andreas Schlüter, Schloss Charlottenburg, Berlin.

1700–1750

1700 Heads by Andreas Schlüter, (22) Hof des Zeughauses, Berlin.
1708–13 *S John* Camillo Rusconi, S Giovanni in Laterano, Rome.
1710 Statue of Marie-Adalaïde of Savoy as Diana by Antoine Coysevox (Louvre, Paris).
1716 *The Flaying of Marsyas* G B Foggini (private collection, Britain).
c. 1717–18 *Three Satyrs* Balthasar Permoser, Zwinger Palace, Dresden.
1721 High Altar, Weltenburg church, by Aegid Asam, Bavaria. *The Apotheosis of Prince Eugene* Permoser, Venice.
1721–32 *Altar Trasparente* Narciso Tomé, Toledo Cathedral.
1727 High Altar Monastery of Melk designed by Lorenzo Mattielli, Austria.
1731 Monument to Isaac Newton by John Rysbrack, Westminster Abbey, London.
1732 *The Trevi Fountain* designed by Nicola Salvi, executed by Pietro Bracci, Rome.
1739 Monument to Pope Benedict XIII by Carlo Marchionni and Bracci, S Maria Sopra Minerva, Rome.
1743–6 Pulpit in Onze Lieve Vrouwe Kerke van Hanswijk by Verhaegen, Malines, Belgium.
c. 1745 *An Angel in Flight* Ignaz Günther, Nuremburg. *Virgin and Child and Little S John* Francisco Salzillo, Murcia Cathederal, Spain.
1747–50 *Cupid with his Bow* Edmé Bouchardon (Louvre, Paris).

Events: painting

5353 1450–1500

1452 *Bartolini Tonso* Fra Filippo Lippi, (Palazzo Pitti, Florence).
c. 1465 Portraits of the Duke and Duchess of Urbino by Piero della Francesca (Uffizi, Florence).
1467–9 S Vincent panels by Nuño Gonçalves (Museum, Lisbon).
1467–9 Crucifixion Triptych by J van Ghent, S Bavon, Ghent, Belgium.
1470 *Ecce Homo* Antonello da Messina.
1474 *Arrival of Cardinal Francesco Gonzaga* Andrea Mantegna (Palazzo Ducale, Mantua).
c. 1475 *Madonna of the Rosebower* Martin Schongauer, S Martin, Colmar, Alsace, France.
1481–3 Sistine Chapel frescoes, Botticelli, Ghirlandaio, Perugino, and others, Rome.
1485 *Garden of Earthly Delights* Hieronymous Bosch (Prado, Madrid).
1490 *Pietà of Canon Luis Despla* Bartolomé Bermejo, Barcelona Cathedral.
1494 *Calumny of Apelles* Sandro Botticelli
1495–7 *Last Supper* Leonardo da Vinci, S Maria delle Grazie, Milan.
1498 *Self-Portrait* Albrecht Dürer (Prado, Madrid).

1500–1600

c. 1501 *The Doge Loredano* Giovanni Bellini (National Gallery, London).
c. 1503 *Mona Lisa* Leonardo da Vinci (Louvre, Paris).
1504 *Adam and Eve*, engraving by Albrecht Dürer.
1507 Giorgione and Titian paint Fondaco dei Tedeschi, Venice.
1508 *Hours of Anne of Brittany*, book illustrations by Bourdichon (Bibliothèque Nationale, Paris). *Disputa, School of Athens, Parnassus,* and *Law*, frescoes by Raphael, Vatican.
c. 1509 *Isenheim Triptych* Matthias Grünewald, Colmar Alsace, France.
1511 *Adoration of the Trinity* Dürer (Vienna).
1514 *Henry the Pius of Saxony* Cranach the Elder (Germäldegalerie, Dresden).
1514 *Melancholia*, engraving by Drürer, Nuremberg.
1515 *Virgin with S Francis* Antonio Correggio (Dresden).
1516 *Sistine Madonna* Raphael (Dresden).
1517 *Madonna of the Harpies* Andrea del Sarto (Uffizi, Florence).
1518 *Assunta* Titian, Church of the Frari, Venice.
1519 *Pesaro Madonna*, Titian, Frari, Venice.
1525 *S Mary with Burgomaster Meier* Hans

continued

Events: painting continued

5353 Holbein, Darmstadt Germany.
1526–30 *The Assumption*, Parma Cathedral, dome fresco, by Correggio.
1528 *Descent from the Cross* Jacopo Pontormo (S Felicità, Florence).
1529 *Battle of Alexander the Great* Albrecht Altodorfer (Munich).
1530 *Adoration of the Shepherds* Correggio.
1533 *The Ambassadors* Hans Holbein (National Gallery, London).
1534–41 *Last Judgement* Michelangelo (Sistine Chapel, Vatican).
c. 1535 *La Madonna del Colle Lungo* Parmigianino (Uffizi, Florence).
1545 *Venus, Cupid, Time, and Folly* Agnolo Bronzino (National Gallery, London).
1548 *The Miracle of the Slave* Jacopo Tintoretto, Scuola di S Marco, Venice.
1549 *Cardinal Granvella* Antonio Moro.
1550 *Feast of the Gods* Frans Floris (Musée des Beaux-Arts, Antwerp). Portrait of Sir John Luttrell by Hans Eworth (Courtauld Institute, London).
1553 *Venus and Adonis* Titian (Prado, Madrid).
1554 *Queen Mary Tudor* Antonio Moro, (Prado, Madrid, and Fenway Court, Boston).
1559 *Battle of Carnival* Pieter Bruegel the Elder (Vienna).
1560 *Eurydice and Aristaeus* Niccolò dell' Abbate (National Gallery, London).
1561 *Pierre Quthe* François Clouet (Louvre, Paris).
1563 *The Tower of Babel* Bruegel the Elder (Kunsthistoriches Museum, Vienna).
1564–87 *Life of Christ* series begun by Tintoretto for Scuola di San Rocco, Venice.
1565 *Alexander and the Family of Darius* Paolo Veronese (National Gallery, London).
c. 1567–8 *The Wedding Feast* Bruegel the Elder (Kunsthistoriches Museum, Vienna).
1570 *Leda* Tintoretto, Venice.
Anne of Austria Sánchez Coello.
1573 *The Feast in the House of Levi* by Paolo Veronese (Accademia Venice).
1575 *Moses saved from the Waters* Paolo Veronese.
1577 *El Espolio* by El Greco (Toledo Cathedral).
1579 Drawings of the Three Coligny Brothers by Marc Duval (Cabinet des Estampes, Paris). *Martyrdom of S Lawrence*, by Juan Navarrete (El Escorial, Spain).
1581 Portrait of Drake (miniature) by Nicholas Hilliard (National Maritime Museum, Greenwich).
1586 *Burial of Count Orgaz* El Greco, S Tomé, Toledo.
1588 *Paradise* Tintoretto, Doge's Palace, Venice.
1589 *Bacchus* Caravaggio, Rome.
1595 Frescoes for the Farnese Gallery by Annibale Carracci, Rome.
1595–8 *The Risen Christ*, El Greco (Hospital of S John, Toledo).
1597–1601 *The Calling of S Matthew* Caravaggio, S Luigi dei Francesi, Rome.

1600–1700
1600–8 *Conversion of S Paul* and *Crucifixion of S Peter* Caravaggio (S Maria del Popolo, Rome).
1609 *Flight into Egypt* Adam Elsheimer (Alte Pinakothek, Munich).
1611–14 *Descent from the Cross* and *Raising of the Cross* Rubens (Antwerp Cathedral).
c. 1613 *The Immaculate Conception* El Greco.
1614 *Communion of S Jerome* Domenichino (Vatican Museum, Rome).
1616 *Richard Sackville, Earl of Dorset*, miniature by Isaac Oliver (V & A, London). *The Company of S George* Frans Hals, Haarlem (Netherlands).
1617 *The Rape of the Daughters of Leucippus* Rubens (Alte Pinakothek, Munich).
c. 1619 *The Water seller* Valázquez (Wellington House, London).
c. 1620–5 *Medici Cycle* Rubens (Louvre, Paris).
1624 *The Laughing Cavalier* Frans Hals (Wallace Collection, London).
c. 1628 *Time Conquered* Simon Vouet (Prado, Madrid).
c. 1629 *The Rape of the Sabines* Pietro de Cortona (Capitoline Gallery, Rome).
1631 *The Realm of Flora* Nicolas Poussin, (Rijksmuseum, Amsterdam).
1632 *The Anatomy Lesson* Rembrandt.
1634–5 *The Surrender of Breda* Velázquez (Prado, Madrid).
1635 Ceiling of the Whitehall Banqueting House, London, by Rubens.
c. 1638 *Charles I on Horseback* Van Dyck (National Gallery, London).
1639 *Seaport at Sunset* Claude Lorraine, (Louvre, Paris).
c.1640 S *John the Baptist* Guido Reni (Dulwich Picture Gallery, London).
1642 *The Night Watch* Rembrandt, (Rijksmuseum, Amsterdam).
1646 *The Miracle of San Diego* Esteaban Murillo (Prado, Madrid).
c. 1650 *The Rokeby Venus* Diego Velázquez (National Gallery, London).
1650 *Nativity* Carlo Maratta (S Giuseppe dei Falegnami, Rome).
1652 *Clubfooted Boy* José Ribera (Louvre, Paris).
1654 *Bathsheba with King David's letter* Rembrandt (Louvre, Paris). *Las Meninas* Velázquez (Prado, Madrid).
c. 1660 *Immaculate Conception* Esteban Murillo (Prado, Madrid).
1661 *Landscape with a Watermill* Jacob van Ruisdael (Rijksmuseum, Amsterdam).
1665 *The Gallant* Ter Borch, Deventer (Holland).
c. 1665–8 *The Lacemaker* Jan Vermeer (Louvre, Paris).
1667 *The Four Hours of the Day* Claude Lorraine (Rome).
1669 *Self-Portrait* Rembrandt (National Gallery, London) (**1**).
1672 *Autumn Landscape* Kao-ts'en, China.
1675 *Beggar Boys Throwing Dice* Murillo (Alte Pinakothek, Munich).
c. 1677 *Duke of Monmouth* Godfrey Kneller (Goodwood, Sussex).
1679–84 *Scenes from the Life of Louis XIV*, Le Brun (Hall of Mirrors, Versailles).
1680 *Parnassus* Claude Lorraine, Rome.
1682–3 *Apotheosis of the Medici* Luca Giordano (Medici-Riccadi Palace, Florence).
1685 *Charles II adoring the Blessed Sacrament* Claudio Coello (Sacristry of El Escorial, Spain).
1686 *The Port of Amsterdam* Van de Velde the Younger (Rijkmuseum Amsterdam).
1689 *The Avenue, Middelharnis* Meindert Hobbema (National Gallery, London).
c. 1693–5 *Madonna* Maratta (Vatican Gallery, Rome).

1700–1750
1701 *Louis XIV* Hyacinthe Rigaud (Louvre, Paris).
1702 Ogota Korin unites Kano and Yamato schools of painting, Japan. Portrait of Newton by Godfrey Kneller (National Gallery, London).
1703–11 *The Tame Raven* Alessandro Magnasco (Uffizi, Florence).
1704–07 Ceiling of Salon in the Summer Palace by Andrea Pozzo (Liechtenstein).
c. 1712 *The Sacraments* Giuseppe Crespi Bologna (Dresden).
1714 *The Marriage of Elector William* Giovanni Pellegrini (Schlessheim Palace, Düsseldorf).
1715 *Mezzetin* Antoine Watteau (Metropolitan Museum, New York).
1715–17 *Scenes of the Life of S Paul* James Thornhill (Dome of S Paul's, London).
1717 *The Embarkation for Cythera* Watteau (Louvre, Paris).
1720 *Martyrdom of S Bartholomew* Giambattista Tiepolo (S Stae, Venice).
1725 *Scene in Venice, the Piazza* Antonio Canaletto (Metropolitan Museum, New York).
1726–30 Ceiling in the Karlskirche by Johann Rottmayr (Vienna).
1728–30 *The Bucintoro returning to the Molo*, Canaletto (H.M. The Queen, Windsor).
c. 1730 *Faustina Bordoni* Rosalba Carriera (Venice).
1735–40 Frescoes in Verolanvora Church by Tiepolo.
1740 *The Triumph of Venus* François Boucher (National Museum, Stockholm). *Benediction* Jean-Baptiste Chardin (Louvre, Paris).

continued

Events: painting continued

5353 **1742** *Diana resting after her Bath* Boucher (Louvre, Paris).
1745 *Shortly after the Marriage* William Hogarth (National Gallery, London).
c. 1745 *The Banquet, Antony and Cleopatra* fresco begun by Tiepolo (Palazzo Labia, Venice).
1748 *Calais Gate* Hogarth (National Gallery, London).

People

5354 EARLY ITALIAN RENAISSANCE

Cimabue, Giovanni (Cenni di Peppi) c. 1240–1302, Italian painter. He departed from the austere conventions of Byzantine art, thus laying down the foundation for his pupil Giotto's humanistic naturalism. Recorded as having worked on the *S John* mosaic in Pisa Cathedral in 1302.
Duccio di Buoninsegna c. 1260–1320, Italian painter. Founder of Sienese school. In his works, the Byzantine tradition in Italian art attains its highest level of sophistication. His masterpiece is the two–sided *Maestà* for the altar of Siena Cathedral (1308).
Giotto di Bondone c. 1266–1337, Italian painter and architect. Regarded as forerunner of Renaissance style of art. Under Cimabue's influence, he broke with Byzantine convention, producing simple and accessible narratives with realistic figures. Major works include frescoes in the Arena Chapel, Padua, and in S Croce, Florence.
Lorenzetti, Ambrogio c 1300–48, Italian painter. Younger brother of Pietro Lorenzetti. Painted in Cortona and Florence, but mainly in Siena, where he painted an *Annunciation* and, in the Palazzo Publico, his well-known allegorical frescoes (including realistic landscapes) depicting good and bad government.
Lorenzetti, Pietro c 1280–1348, Italian painter. Elder brother of Ambrogio Lorenzetti. An early Sienese painter, he produced the polyptych in S Maria at Arezzo, and frescoes of the *Passion* in the Lower Church of S Francis, Assisi. His *Madonna* (1340) is in the Uffizi Gallery, Florence.
Martini, Simone c. 1284–1344, Italian painter. Foremost artist of 14th-century Sienese school, distinguished by elegant lines and exquisite colors. Worked first in Assisi (1333–39), then at the papal court in Avignon (1339–44). His *Annunciation* is in Florence's Uffizi Gallery.
Pisano, Andrea c 1270–1349, Italian sculptor. Probably born in Pisa, he settled in Florence, working in bronze and marble, and completed the bronze doors of the baptistery there in 1336. Succeeded Giotto as chief artist at Florence Cathedral in 1337, and produced reliefs and statues at Orvieto Cathedral from 1347.

15TH CENTURY RENAISSANCE

Angelico, Fra (Guido di Pietro) c. 1400–55, Italian painter. A Dominican monk, all his work is religious in character. His early works, influenced by Masaccio, include an *Annunciation* (c. 1440). His great series of frescoes in the San Marco monastery, Florence (now a museum), was designed for pious meditation.
Antonello da Messina c. 1430–79, Italian painter. Sicily's only major 15th century artist, his style is a subtle combination of northern and Italian influences. He popularized oil painting, and worked in Venice in 1475. His works include *S Sebastian* (1475–7).
Bosch, Hieronymous (Jerome van Aeken) c. 1450–1516, Flemish painter. His apparently chaotic. and nightmarish works such as. *The Garden of Earthly Delights* (c. 1485) are actually highly complex allegorical paintings drawing on Christian and folk symbolism. Bosch's works gradually slipped into obscurity, until their "rediscovery" by the surrealists.
Botticelli, Sandro (Alessandro Filipepi) 1444–1510, Italian painter. He was a student of Filippo Lippi, whose linear style influenced his earlier work. His works include two of the best-known of all paintings, *Primavera* and the *Birth of Venus* (1482–4), both in the Uffizi Gallery. Botticelli's later work reflects a deepening and highly emotional spirituality, notably in the *Mystic Nativity* (1500).
della Francesca, Piero c. 1416–92, Italian painter, scientist, and mathematician. Influenced by Masaccio. His precise, geometric compositions have a cool passionate intensity, and often a monumental grandeur. His works include the *History of the True Cross* frescos (c. 1452–64) at Urbino.
della Robbia, Luca c. 1400–82, Italian sculptor. Established a glazed terracotta business at Florence, and produced ten superb panels of angels and dancing boys for the cathedral. Noted also for terracotta works such

1

as *The Resurrection* (c. 1445).
Donatello (Donato di Niccolò) c. 1386–1466, Italian (**1**). Regarded as the greatest Renaissance sculptor and the first since classical times to produce work not dependent on an architectural setting. His masterpiece is the noble, classical *David* (1430s) in Florence. Later works, such as *Judith and Holofernes* (1457–60) have a powerful emotional intensity.
Eyck, Jan van c. 1370–1440, Greatest Flemish painter of the 15th century. His style is characterized by meticulous attention to detail, strong awareness of texture, and very realistic. light effects. His works include the Ghent altarpiece (1432), upon which his little-known brother Hubert (died c. 1426) is recorded as having worked, and the *Arnolfini Marriage* (1434).
Fouquet, Jean c. 1420–80, French painter. Louis XI's painter at Tours from 1475, his miniatures show a combination of Italian detail and perspective with northern realisms. His works include the Melun dyptich (c. 1450) and a *Book of Hours* (1460).
Ghiberti, Lorenzo 1378–1455, Italian goldsmith, bronze-caster, sculptor, and scholar. Much of his life was spent on a set of bronze doors for the Florence Baptistery. A second set, *Gates of Paradise*, was completed 1452. A humanist and scholar, he wrote on the history of art.
Lippi, Fra Filippo c. 1406–69, Italian painter. A pupil of Masaccio, he began his greatest work, on the walls of Prato Cathedral, in 1452. Other works include *Madonna with Child* and *Angels* (c. 1465) and later nativities. His wife was the model for many of his madonnas.
Mantegna, Andrea 1431–1506, Italian painter. Influenced by Donatello, his sculptural style makes great use of foreshortening for illusionistic effect. Classical motifs figure largely in his work, which anticipates the Baroque era.
Masaccio (Tomasso di Ser Giovanni di Mone) 1401– c. 1428, Italian painter. Leading figure of the early Renaissance, his dramatic, life–like portrayal of Biblical events greatly influenced Michelangelo. His works include the Pisa polyptych (1426) and the Brancacci Chapel frescoes in Florence's S Maria del Carmine (1427).
Memlinc, Hans, c. 1440–94, Flemish, the pupil of Rogier van der Weyden, he was a painter of religious works, as well as an innovative and creative portraitist. Important works include the triptych of the *Madonna Enthroned* (1468) and the *Shrine of S Ursula* (1489).
Pollaiuolo, Antonio c. 1432–98, Italian goldsmith, medallist, metal-caster, and painter. One of the first artists to bring anatomical expertise to his work, he produced lively and vigorous pictures with skillful suggestion of movement. His works include *Hercules and Deinera* (c. 1470).
Quercia, Jacopo della c. 1374–1438, Italian sculptor. Born and died in Siena, where *Fonte Gaia* was produced. The *Tomb of Ilario del Carretto* (1406) at Lucca contrasts, in style, with his dramatic portals for S Petronio in Bologna, which Michelangelo admired.
Uccello, Paolo c. 1396–1475, Italian painter. Renowned for his use of the new science of perspective, he worked in Venice as a mosaicist (1425–31) before moving to Florence. His *Battle of San Romano* (1454–7) in the Palazzo

continued

People continued

5354 **van der Weyden, Rogier** (Rogier de la Pasture) 1400–64, Flemish painter. Worked at Brussels as painter to the city. His fine attention to detail and skillful depiction of nature is typical of the early Flemish school. He is noted for his dramatic and emotional style. His masterpiece is *The Last Judgement* (1444–48).
Verrochio, Andrea del c. 1435–88 Italian sculptor, painter, and goldsmith. A key figure of the early Renaissance. He ran a busy workshop. Leonardo da Vinci was his pupil, and contributed to his *Baptism of Christ* (c. 1472). His sculptures include *David* (1476) and the bronze equestrian statue *Bartolemeo Colleoni* (c. 1483–8).

16TH CENTURY RENAISSANCE
Altdorfer, Albrecht c. 1480–1538, German painter, engraver, and architect. The pioneer of copperplate etching, and key figure of the Danube School of artists who developed landscape painting. His works, e.g. *The Battle of Alexander* and *Darius on the Issus* (1529), often portray religious or historical subjects against evocative landscape backgrounds.
Andrea del Sarto 1486–1531, Italian painter. A talented draughtsman with a strong feeling for color harmony. His works include the fresco cycles in Florence's S Annunziata and the famous altarpiece *The Madonna of the Harpies* (1517), now in the Uffizi.
Bellini, Giovanni c. 1430–1516, Italian painter. The greatest Venetian painter of his period, he progressed from an early severe, Gothic manner to a more sensuous and naturalistic style, painting figures against landscape backgrounds. He is particularly noted for his Madonna and Child paintings.
Bramante, Donato 1444–1514, Italian architect and painter. He first established himself as a painter, his *Men at Arms* frescoes (c 1480–5) being of particular note. He designed S Peter's (started 1506) and was the tutor of Raphael (who portrayed him as Euclid in *The School of Athens*).
Breughel, Pieter the Elder c. 1515–69 (**2**), Flemish painter, influenced by Bosch. He is noted for his realistic scenes of peasant life, often on proverbial themes, and his occasionally haunting and beautiful depiction of landscape e.g. *The Hunters in the Snow* (c. 1565),

Dürer, Albrecht 1471–1528, German painter and engraver. Renowned for his great skill in exploiting the artistic potential of his materials. His albums of engravings (some shown here from *Vier Bücher von menschlicher Proportion*, 1528) had an enormous influence on other artists. His later works; such as *Four Apostles* (1526), display a strong sympathy with the Lutheran Reformation.

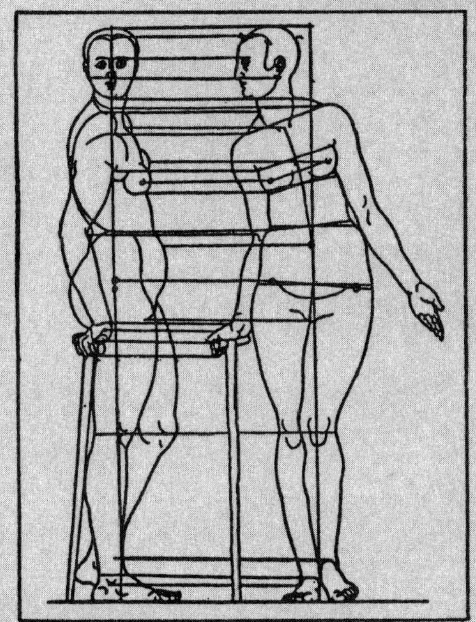

Bronzino, Il (Agnolo di Cosimo di Mariano) 1500–71, Italian mannerist painter, the pupil (and adopted son) of Pontormo. His unemotional works include portraits and frescoes.
Cellini, Benvenuto 1500–71, Italian sculptor, engraver, and goldsmith. Best known now for his highly colorful autobiography (first published 1728). His works include the bronze mannerist sculpture *Perseus* (1545–54) and gold and enamel salt cellar with figures of Neptune and Ceres (1539).
Correggio, Antonio Allegri da c. 1494–1534, Italian painter. His frescoes and paintings such as *Jupiter and Io* (c 1530) had great influence on the later Baroque and Rococo movements. His work on cupolas in Parma shows the influence of Mantegna, whose techniques of foreshortening he imagimatively extended.
Cranach, Lucas ("the Elder") 1472–1553, German painter. His works include religious and classical subjects, hunting scenes and portraits. He also created woodcut prints supporting the Reformation and several portraits of Martin Luther.
Giambologna (Giovanni Bologna) 1529–1608, Flemish-born Italian sculptor. His mannerist works include the bronze *Fountain of Neptune* (1563–7) and *The Rape of the Sabines* (1583).
Giorgione del Castelfranco c. 1475–1510, Venetian painter. One of the first artists to paint for private collectors. His work is rich, colorful, poetic, and "romantic" in atmosphere. Works include *Enthroned Madonna* (1505) and *The Tempest* (1505–10) (**3**).

Giulio Romano c. 1492–1546, Italian painter and architect. The pupil of Raphael, and a leading exponent of mannerism. He broke with

continued

People continued

5354 classical conventions in designing the Palazzo del Tè (begun 1526) in Mantua, one of the first mannerist buildings. He is the only contemporary artist mentioned by Shakespeare, in *The Winter's Tale.*

Goujon, Jean c. 1510–68, French sculptor. Influenced by Parmigianino, he is noted for his development of mannerist traditions in sculpture, and for his caryatids (1550–1) for the Louvre. He is thought to have fled France as a Protestant exile and to have died in Bologna.

Grunewald, Matthias (Mathis Nithadt) c. 1460–1528, German painter, architect, and engineer. The nine paintings of his great Isenheim Monastery altarpiece (1509) demonstrate his use of unusually vivid colors and of distortion to convey great emotional intensity.

Hilliard, Nicholas 1547–1619, English court miniaturist and goldsmith. The finest English painter of the 16th century, he worked for both Queen Elizabeth I and James I. His best-known works are his beautifully detailed miniatures of gentlemen, e.g. *A Young Man Among Roses* (1588).

Holbein, Hans the Younger c. 1497–1543, German painter. He was noted particularly for his realistic and often moving portraits and religious paintings, e.g. *The Death of Christ* (1521) and *Sir Thomas More and his Family* (1527), the latter being regarded as the first true domestic group portrait. He was also a highly skilled miniaturist, and achieved great fame for his *Portrait of Henry VIII* (1537).

Michelangelo (Michelangelo di Lodovico Buonarroti) 1475–1564, Italian sculptor, painter, and poet. His monumental works, characterized by their grandeur and sublimity, include the great ceiling paintings for the Sistine Chapel (1508–12) and the marble statue of *David* (1501–4) in Florence. He was recognized as one of the greatest artists of all time by his contemporaries.

Leonardo da Vinci 1452–1519, Italian painter, sculptor, draughtsman, philosopher, architect, and engineer (**1**). He was a pupil of Verrocchio, and the outstanding genius of the Renaissance. His mastery of the arts and sciences (**2**) was fully recognized by his contemporaries. His many great works include *The Last Supper* mural (c. 1495), the *Mona Lisa* (c. 1503) and the cartoon of the *Virgin and S Anne* (1504–06).

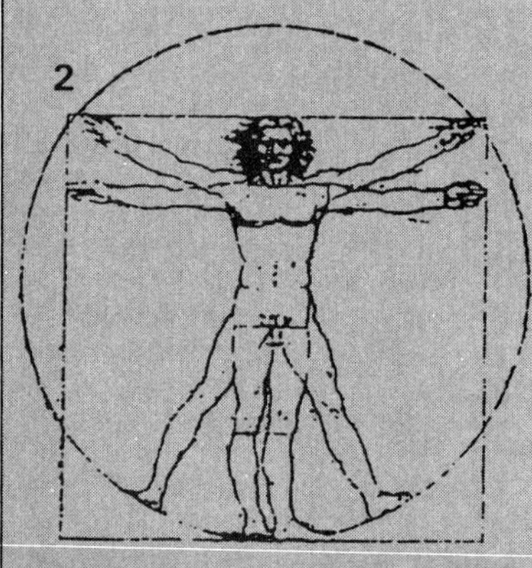

Parmigianino (Girolamo Francesca Maria Mazzola) 1503–40, Italian mannerist painter and etcher, influenced by Correggio and Raphael. His works include the well-known *Madonna del Colle Lungo* (c. 1535). He was very influential on French mannerist painting.

Raphael (Raffaello Sanzio) 1483–1520, Italian painter. A prominent figure of the High Renaissance, he was strongly influenced by Leonardo and Michelangelo, combining the boldness of the latter with the delicacy of the former. His works include the *School of Athens* fresco (c 1509) and humanistic depictions of the *Madonna and the Holy Family.*

Tintoretto, Jacopo (Jacopo Robusti) 1518–94, Venetian painter. Influenced by Titian and Michelangelo. His work displays a transition from classical to the baroque. His mastery of perspective and light effects is evident in *The Finding* and the *Removal of the Body of S Mark* (1562).

Titian (Tiziano Vecellio) c. 1487–1576, Venetian painter, influenced in his early stages by Bellini and Giorgione. After 1516 his works took on a more colorful, dynamic character. His radical techniques are demonstrated in his *Assumption of the Virgin* (1516–18).

Veronese, Paolo (Paolo Caliari) 1528–88, Italian painter, influenced by Titian. He became the key decorative artist of the Venetian school with his great technical mastery and abundance of costume and architectural detail. His works include *The Triumph of Venice* (1585).

17TH CENTURY

Bernini, Giovanni Lorenzo 1598–1680, Italian sculptor, architect, stage designer, and dramatist. A leading artist of the baroque, noted especially for his dynamic portrait sculptures in Rome in the 1630s, where he also designed fountains and other buildings. His masterpiece is *The Ecstasy of S Theresa* (1645–52).

Caravaggio, Michelangelo Merisi da c. 1573–1610, Italian painter. A highly original artist, his mastery of *chiaroscuro* in such works as the *Crucifixion of S Peter* (1600–8) has been particularly admired. His masterpiece is *The Beheading of John the Baptist* (1608), painted after fleeing Rome in 1606, following his murder of a racqets opponent.

Claude Lorraine (Claude Gellée) 1600–82, French painter. Claude settled in Rome in 1627, and was influenced early on by mannerism. His style later became more classical, and he produced several famous landscapes on pastoral or classical themes, e.g. *Landscape at Sunset* (1639). His work became so popular that he issued a book of etchings, *Liber Veritatis* (1635) to guard against forgeries.

Dyck, Sir Anthony van 1599–1641, Flemish painter. Influenced by Rubens, for whom he trained, he gained an international reputation for his extraordinary skills as a portrait painter of nobility, and became court painter in 1632 to Charles I, who knighted him.

El Greco (Domenikos Theotocopoulos) 1541–1614, Cretan-born Spanish painter, architect, and sculptor (**1**). Influenced by Tintoretto and Michelangelo, he may also have been a pupil of Titian. Notable particularly for his portraits and his elongated, strongly spiritual religious paintings and landscapes, using a pallet of cold blues and grays, e.g. *The Assumption* (1613).

Gibbons, Grinling 1648–1721, Dutch woodcarver and sculptor. He came to England in 1671, where he soon became established as the leading woodcarver of his day, specializing in interior limewood carvings of natural subjects for wealthy patrons. Petworth House and S Paul's Cathedral have examples of his work.

Girardon, François 1628–1715, French. Sculptor. One of the leading sculptors of his day, he is best-known for his tomb (1675–7) in Paris for Cardinal Richelieu.

Hals, Frans c. 1581–1666, Dutch painter. His first important work is *The Banquet of the S George Civic Guard* (1616), a group portrait whose informal approach was very influential. His most famous work is the *Laughing Cavalier* (1624), a work wholly typical of his exuberant approach to both art and life.

continued

People continued

5354 **Hobbema, Meindert** 1638–1709, Dutch painter. The pupil of van Ruisdael, he concentrated on less dramatic subjects such as woodland scenes. His masterpiece is *Avenue at Middelharnis* (1689).
Hooch (Hoogh), Pieter de c. 1629–84, Dutch painter. His quiet, Vermeer-like calm domestic interiors and gardens, e.g. the *Courtyard of a House in Delft* (1658), are among the finest examples of the Dutch school of painting.
Murillo, Bartolomeo Esteban 1618–82, Spanish painter. Influenced by Zurbaran, he gained a reputation as a popular painter of rather sentimental genre and religious scenes in a style dubbed "vaporous" for his use of soft colors and draperies.
Poussin, Nicolas 1594–1655, French painter. Influenced by Titian and Veronese, he developed a more classical style in the 1630s, characterized by careful figure composition within landscapes. His works include *The Holy Family on the Steps* (1648).
Rembrandt, Harmensz van Rijn 1607–69, Dutch painter, draughtsman, and etcher. One of the very greatest painters, his early work, e.g. *The Blinding of Samson* (1636), is baroque and remarkably confident in style. Later works on religious themes attain a level of still-unsurpassed spiritual intensity. Other works include the group portrait *The Night Watch* (1642), and many remarkable self-portraits.
Rubens, Sir Peter Paul 1577–1640, Flemish painter and diplomat. He began copying Italian paintings during his diplomatic service for the Duke of Mantua, and was a renowned painter by the time he produced his masterpiece, the *Descent from the Cross* (1611–14). He was knighted by Charles I for service in diplomatic missions.
Ruisdael, Jacob van c 1628–82, Dutch painter. He was the outstanding Dutch landscape painter of the 17th century, with a rare gift for capturing the light and atmosphere of sea and land. His masterpiece is *The Jewish Cemetery* (c. 1660).
Velàzquez, Diego Roderiguez de Silva y 1599–1660, Spanish painter (**1**). His earliest paintings belonging to the "bodegone " genre (peculiar to Spain) were of domestic scenes, e.g. *An Old Woman Cooking Eggs* (1618). He later painted some remarkable portraits, e.g. *Pope Innocent X* (1650) and the superb *Las Meninas* (1654).
Vermeer, Jan 1632–75, Dutch painter. His works – small-scale, carefully composed interior scenes (like those of Hooch) – are typical of Dutch art of the period, but go far beyond anything else of their kind in artistic merit due to Vermeer's technical mastery of daylight and shadow. His paintings of the town of Delft, particularly *A View of Delft*, have also been highly praised.
Zurbaran, Francisco 1598–1664, Spanish painter. He lived and worked in Seville virtually all his life, his work consisting mostly of religious paintings in an austere, spiritually intense style. His works include several portraits of S Francis and some still lifes.

536 LATE 18TH CENTURY AND EARLY 19TH CENTURY

Styles and movements

5361 **Rococo art** (c 1735–65) A mainly French style, rococo is characterized by elaborate and superficial decoration. Elegance was the keynote and the style mirrored the extravagance and brilliance of court life.
Neo-classicism (c 1750–1850) A movement that developed in revolutionary France, the style expressed the qualities of harmony, order and clarity associated with Greek and Roman art. Classical subjects were used as allegories for the present political situation. The antithesis of romanticism, it espoused accepted notions of beauty and tended to reject individual inspiration.
Romanticism (c 1780–1850) A mainly literary movement, romanticism was a reaction against neo-classical principles and the Industrial Revolution. Deriving inspiration from untamed nature, Romanticism centered on the importance of individual feeling towards the natural world.
Realism (c 1830–80) A largely French movement that developed in reaction to idealized and mythical/historical subjects. Courbet is by far the most notable practitioner of the form.
The Pre-Raphaelite Brotherhood (1848–56) Founded by William Holman Hunt, John Everett Millais, and Dante Gabriel Rossetti, this group sought to recapture the innocence and beauty of Italian forms, pre-Raphael in protest against what they saw as the prevailing "frivolity" of art of their day.

Events: sculpture

5362 **1750–60** Statue of Emperor Francis I by Balthasar Moll, Vienna.
1750–62 *Allegory of Disenchantment* by Queirolo, Naples.
1753 Tomb of the Maréchal de Saxe by Jean–Baptise Pigalle, S Thomas, Strasbourg.
1754 *The Agony in the Garden* by Francisco Salzillo, Murcia, Spain.
1761 *The Nightingale Monument,* Louis Roubiliac, Westminster Abbey, London.
1763 *Tobias and the Angel,* Ignaz Günther, Bürgesaal, Munich.
1766 ***S** Bruno*, Jean-Antoine Houdon, S Maria degli Angeli, Rome.
1767 *Venus Bathing,* Christophe Allegrain (Louvre, Paris).
1770–80 *Diana and the Nymphs,* Luigi Vanvitelli, Caserta.
1778 *Thetis and her Nymphs,* Thomas banks (V & A, London). Seated Statue of Voltaire, Houdon, Comédie-Françaís, Paris.
1782–90 *Psyche Abandoned,* Augustin Pajou (Louvre, Paris).
1787–93 *Cupid and Psyche,* Antonio Canova (Louvre, Paris).
1790–93 Monument to Graf von der Marck, Berlin, by Johann Scadow.
1791–92 *The Fury of Athamas,* John Flaxman, Ickworth House, Suffolk, England. Monument to Lord Chief Justice Mansfield by Flaxman, Westminster Abbey, London.
1795–1806 *Emperor Joseph II,* Franz Zauner, Vienna.
1802 Bust of Napoleon by Corbet, Versailles
1808 *Venus Victrix* (Pauline Bonaparte), Antonio Canova (Museo Borghese, Rome).
1810–23 *Fox Monument,* Richard Westmacott, Westminster Abbey, London.
1817 Bust of Giuseppe Bossi by Pacetti. (Brera, Milan).
1817–19 *Three Graces and Cupid,* Bertel Thorvaldsen, Copenhagen.
1821 Bust of Goethe by Christian Rauch, Weimar.
1831 Tomb of Pope Pius VII, Rome, completed by Thorvaldsen.
1832 *Lion Crushing a Serpent,* Antoine-Louis Barye (Walters Art Gallery, Baltimore).
1833–6 *La Marseillaise,* François Rude, Arc de Triomphe, Paris.
1834 *Massacre,* bronze bas-relief, by Auguste Préault (Chartres Museum).
1836 *Scott Monument* designed by Kemp, Edinburgh.
1837 Monument to Countess Zamoyski by Lorenzo Bartolini, S Croce, Florence.
1839–52 Monument to Frederick the Great by Rauch, Unter den Linden, Berlin.

1 This 18th century drawing shows the proportions that artists must follow when constucting images of Buddha.

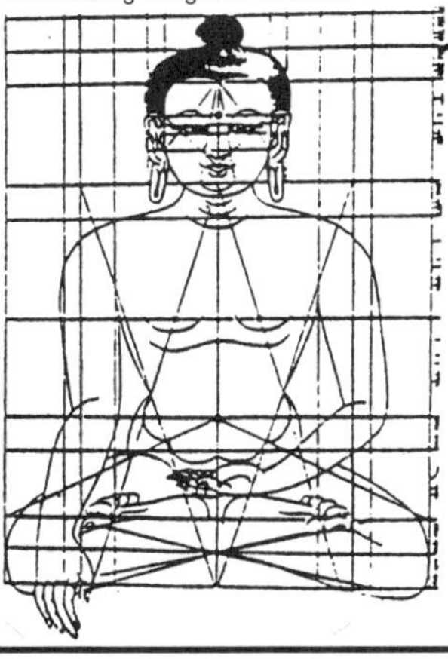

Events: painting

5363 **1750** *Robert Andrews and his Wife* Thomas Gainsborough (National Gallery, London).
1751 *The Rhinoceros* Pietro Longhi (Ca' Rezzonico, Venice).
1752 *Young Girl Resting* François Boucher. *Madam de Pompadour* Maurice de la Tour (Louvre, Paris)
1753 *Europe* Giambattista Tiepolo, Residenz, Würzburg
c. 1755 *The Painter's Wife* Allan Ramsay (National Gallery of Scotland).
1757 *Ancient Rome and Renaissance Rome* Giovanni Panini (Metropolitan Museum, New York).
1764–6 *Apotheosis of the Spanish Monarchy* Tiepolo, Royal Palace, Madrid.
1766 *The Swing* Jean Fragonard (Wallace Collection, London).
c. 1772 *Self-Portrait* Joshua Reynolds (Royal Academy, London).
1775 *Self-Portrait* Jean-Baptiste Chardin (**1**) (Louvre, Paris).
c. 1780 *View of S Maria della Salute and the Dogana* Francesco Guardi (Wallace Collection, London).
1781 *Sir Brooke Booth* Joseph Wright of Derby (National Gallery, London).
1784 *The Oath of the Horatii* Jacques-Louis David, (Louvre, Paris).
c. 1785 *The Morning Walk* Gainsborough (National Gallery, London).
1787 *Goethe in the Campagna* Johann Tischbein (Städel, Frankfurt).
1792 *The Sleeping Endymion* Anne-Louis Girodet (Louvre, Paris).
1793 *The Murdered Marat in his Bath* David (Musée des Beaux-Arts, Brussels).
1795 *Elohim Creating Adam* William Blake (Tate Gallery, London).
c. 1797–1800 *Maja Nude* Francisco de Lucients (Prado, Madrid).
1800 *Napoleon Crossing the Alps* David (Versailles).
1802 *Ossian Receiving the Generals of the Republic* Anne-Louis Girodet (Malmaison).
1804 *Plague at Jaffa* Antoine Gros (Louvre).
1807 *Sun Rising in a Mist* J M W Turner.
1808 *Grande Baigneuse* Jean-Auguste Dominique Ingres (Louvre, Paris). *Rape of Psyche* Pierre-Paul Prud'hon.
1812 *Hannibal crossing the Alps* Turner (Tate Gallery, London).

1812–20 *Head of Princess Lieven* Thomas Lawrence (Tate Gallery, London).
1814 *The Third of May 1808* Goya (Prado, Madrid).
1819 *The Raft of the Medusa* Théodore Géricault (Louvre, Paris).
1820 *Belshazzar's Feast* John Martin (Mellon Collection).
c. 1820–23 *Saturn Devouring One of his Children* Goya, (Prado, Madrid).
1821 *The Haywain* Constable (National Gallery, London).
1824 *Arctic Shipwreck* Caspar David Friedrich (Kunsthalle, Hamburg).
c. 1825 *Satan Smitting Job* William Blake (Tate Gallery, London).
1827 *The Death of Sardanpoulus* Eugène Delacroix (Louvre, Paris).
1829 *The Leaping Horse* John Constable (Tate Gallery, London).
1830 *Liberty Leading the People* Delacroix (Louvre, Paris). *Coming from Evening Church* Samuel Palmer (Tate Gallery, London).
1832 *Fifty-three Stages of the Tokaido* Ando Hiroshige (color print series, Japan).
1834 *Rue Transnonain, April 14, 1834* Honoré Daumier.
1837 *The Old Shepherd's Chief Mourner* Edwin Landseer (V & A, London). *Avenue of the Chestnut Trees* Théodore Rousseau (Louvre, Paris).
1838 *The Fighting Temeraire* Turner (National Gallery, London).
1844 *Rain, Steam, and Speed* Turner (National Gallery, London).
1845 *Room with an Open Window* Adolf Menzel.

People

5364 **Boucher, François** 1703–70, French painter. A rococo artist, he was an associate of Watteau and trained as an engraver. His works include *The Triumph of Venus* (1740) and the *Reclining Girl* (1751). He was also an interior designer, and worked on Versailles Palace and designed sets for the Paris Opera.
Canaletto, Giovanni Antonio 1697–1768, Venetian painter. One of the finest architectural painters, with superb compositional skills, his works include views of Venice, e.g. *The Stonemason's Yard* (c. 1730). Prolific and commercially successful, he issued large numbers of etchings.
Chardin, Jean-Baptiste Simeon 1699–1779, French painter. Unlike most rococo art, his works are realistic and feature small-scale genre paintings and still lifes, e.g. *Rayfish, Cat, and Kitchen Utensils* (1728). Fragonard was his pupil.
Fragonard, Jean-Honoré 1732–1806, French painter. A leading rococo painter, his early works were usually on historical subjects, e.g. *Coreseus Sacrificing Himself to Save Callierhoe* (1765). He became especially noted for such picturesque, slightly erotic works as *The Swing* (1766). His patrons included Madame du Barry and Madame Pompadour.
Gainsborough, Thomas 1727–88, English painter. Influenced by Watteau in his early work, he developed a light, very individual style in his portraits, many of which portray sitters in a delicately observed landscape setting, e.g. *Mr and Mrs Andrews* (1750). He later created "fancy" paintings of imaginary subjects, e.g. *Peasant Girl Gathering Sticks* (1782).
Guardi, Francesco 1712–93, Venetian painter. Known mainly for his views of Venice, which were freer in style than those of Canaletto, he was a highly prolific artist who also produced still lifes, portraits, and historical and religious subjects.
Hogarth, William 1697–1764, English painter and engraver. Noted especially for his series of moralistic narrative paintings such as *Marriage à la Mode* (1742–5) and many fine portraits, e.g. *Captain Coram* (1740). His keen sense of satire and outrage at hypocrisy and injustice made him one of the leading social critics, as well as a leading artist, of the age.
Stubbs, George 1724–1806, English painter and engraver. His keen interest in anatomy and great skill in drawing and composition, as demonstrated in his book *Anatomy of the Horse* (1766), established him as one of the best painters of animals of all time. His works include *Mares and Foals by a River* (1763–8) and the extraordinary imaginary work *Horses Attacked by a Lion* (1770).
Tiepolo, Giambattista 1696–1770, Italian painter. Regarded as the finest Italian artist of the 18th century and the main fresco painter of the rococo period, his works, characterized by a delicate use of *chiaroscuro*, include the *Antony and Cleopatra* series (1750s).
Watteau, Jean-Antoine 1684–1721, French painter. A leading rococo painter, he is especially noted for his delicate use of color and sensitive composition. His works include *Embarkation for Cythera* (1717) and *Enseigne de Gersaint* (1721), the latter indicating a development towards realism.

18th CENTURY NEO-CLASSICAL ARTISTS
Canova, Antonio 1757–1822, Italian sculptor. He progressed from an early naturalistic style to the calm mastery of neo-classical principles displayed in such works as his tomb (1783–7) for Clement XIV. He made several portrait sculptures of Napoleon.
David, Jacques-Louis 1748–1825, French painter. He began as a rococo painter and became the leading neo-classical artist of his day, with works such as *The Oath of the Horatii* (1784) and the *Death of Socrates* (1787). He strongly sympathized with the French Revolution and survived various purges to become Napoleon's court painter. His work, e.g.

continued

People continued

5364 *The Coronation of Napoleon* (1805–7), is seen by some as prefiguring modern totalitarian art.
Flaxman, John 1755–1826, English sculptor, designer, and illustrator. A highly skilled artist in low-relief design, his clients included Josiah Wedgwood. His illustrations for the *Iliad* and *Odyssey* were influential on artists such as Ingres. He became Professor of Sculpture at the Royal Academy in 1810.
Gibson, John 1790–1866, English sculptor. One of Flaxman's protégés, he acquired an international reputation with works such as his polychromatic *Tinted Venus* (1851–2).
Houdon, Jean-Antoine, 1741–1828, French sculptor. Noted for his realism rather than for adherence to neo-classical principles, he became the greatest French sculptor of his day with portrait busts such as those of Voltaire and Benjamin Franklin (1778).
Ingres, Jean Auguste Dominique, 1780–1867, French painter. An excellent draughtsman, he won the *Prix de Rome* in 1801 with *The Ambassadors of Agamemnon* after studying with David. Other works include *The Vow of King Louis VIII* (1824) and *The Turkish Bath* (1859–62).
Reynolds, Joshua 1723–92, English painter and writer on art. He developed a style, expounded in his *Discourses*, which he dubbed the "Grand Manner," a fundamentalist neo-classical approach in which noble, legendary, or historical figures are portayed in idealized settings. His many portraits include *Commodore Keppel* (1753). He was the first president of the Royal Academy.

AMERICAN 18TH–EARLY 19TH CENTURY PAINTERS AND SCULPTORS
Hicks, Edward 1780–1849, American painter. An outstanding "primitive" painter, he trained as a sign painter. A devout Quaker, he painted over 100 versions of his best-known work, the *Peaceable Kingdom*, which depicts fierce and domestic animals, and children, co-existing in harmony.
Trumbull, John 1756–1843, American painter. He worked in West's studio in London in the 1780s and specialized in works depicting events during the American War of Independence, in which he served. His works include *The Death of General Warren at the Battle of Bunker Hill* (1786).
West, Benjamin 1738–1820, American painter. He settled in London in 1763, where many American artists came to work at his studio. His greatly innovative *The Death of General Wolfe* (1770) broke with tradition in its depiction of the figures in contemporary clothes. A neo-classicist at first, his style gradually became more romantic in spirit, e.g. *Death on a Pale Horse* (1802).

ROMANTIC ART
Barye, Antoine-Louis 1796–1875. French sculptor and painter. Renowned for his exotic and often violent subject matter, he achieved great popularity with his works depicting animals, e.g. his bronze *Tiger Devouring a Crocodile* (1831).
Blake, William 1757–1827, English painter, engraver and poet (**1**). While serving his apprenticeship as an engraver, he became a devotee of "gothic" church art, which inspired his love of detailed line. His works include beautiful watercolors replete with private symbolism, and several extraordinary illustrated books such as *Songs of Innocence* (1789). Fuseli described him as "damned good to steal from."
Constable, John 1776–1837, English painter Inspired by a deep love for the English countryside, his works, including *Cloud Studies* (1816–22) and *The Haywain* (1821) were initially more popular in France than in England. He eventually became recognized as one of the greatest and most innovative landscape artists, and influenced the Impressionist movement.
Delacroix, Eugène 1798–1863, French painter. Influenced by Constable and Gericault, he became one of the greatest romantic artists with works such as *Women of Algiers* (1834) and several great portraits, e.g. *Chopin and George Sand* (1838).
Fuseli, Henry 1741–1825, Swiss painter. He settled in England in 1765, and became professor of painting at the Royal Academy. Not easily classifiable, his works exhibit a strong fascination for the macabre, e.g. *The Nightmare* (1781), and he had a strong revival in the 20th century.
Géricault, Théodore, 1791–1824, French painter. Regarded as the major founder of romantic painting, the stark, powerful realism of works such as his *Raft of the Medusa* (1819) caused much outrage when first exhibited, and were hugely influential upon later artists. Other works include *The Derby at Epsom* (1820).
Goya y Lucientes, Francisco de 1746–1828, Spanish painter and printmaker (**2**). Influenced by Tiepolo and Velàzquez, Goya developed a powerful, free-flowing style all his own. His works include several innovative and startlingly honest court portraits, and a horrific series of etchings, such as *The Disasters of War* (1810– 20) depicting the carnage in Spain following invasion by the French, also portrayed in the highly dramatic *May 2nd, 1808* and *May 3rd, 1808.*
Rodin, Auguste 1840–1917, French sculptor. His *Age of Bronze* (1875–7) , a male nude figure, attracted much controversy when exhibited. He was subsequently commissioned by the state to create a bronze door for a planned museum, and spent much of the rest of his life working on this unfinished project, though elements from the design were used to create his most famous works, *The Thinker* and *The Kiss.* He was enormously influential on following sculptors.
Turner, Joseph Mallord William 1775–1851, English painter. He exhibited his first work at the Royal Academy aged 15, and soon became recognized as a prodigious talent, with a rare gift for depicting gradations of light and color. His works include *The Shipwreck* (1805), *The Fighting Temeraire* (1838), and *Rain, Steam, and Speed* (1844). Constable described his works as "airy visions painted with tinted steam."

1

2

537 LATE 19TH CENTURY AND EARLY 20TH CENTURY 1850–1950

Styles and movements

5371 **Art Nouveau** (c. 1890–1915) A development of the Arts and Crafts movement, with two main strands: one of fluid symmetry and flowing linear rhythms (**1**), one of geometrical austerity.

1

continued

Styles and movements continued

5371 **Arts and Crafts movement** (c 1870–1900) Based on the revival of interest in the medieval craft system and led by William Morris, its aims were to fuse the functional and the decorative, and to restore the values of handmade crafts in the face of the growing mass-produced wares of the late 19th century.
Symbolism (c 1880–1905) Influenced by the Pre-Raphaelites and by romanticism, Symbolism originated in France as an intellectual alternative to the straight visual work of the Impressionists. There were two main strands: those, e.g. Redon, influenced by literature, and those, e.g. van Gogh, who explored the symbolic use of color and line to express emotion.
Impressionism (1874–1886) Centering on a diverse group of eight artists, including Cézanne, Renoir, Manet, and Monet, who held eight exhibitions between 1874 and 1886, the movement derives its name from a painting by Monet, *Impression: Sunrise.* Impressionists were concerned with light and its effects, and the use of "broken" color.
Pointillism (or "Divisionism")(c. 1880–1915) Based on the color theories of Chevreul, its aim was to achieve greater pictorial luminosity by placing small marks of pure primary color on the surface, allowing them to merge at a viewing distance to create an optical mixture.
Post–Impressionism (c. 1880–1910) A term loosely applied to a diverse group of artists whose paintings developed from Impressionism and who worked in widely divergent styles, e.g. Gauguin and Matisse.

Events: sculpture

5372 **c. 1850** *Tinted Venus* John Gibson, (P J Dearden Collection).
1851 *The Greek Slave* Hiram Powers, Washington (Yale University Art Gallery).
1852–3 *Le Maréchel Ney* François Rude, Paris.
1853 *Andrew Jackson* Clark Mills, Washington.
1864–76 *Albert Memorial* George Gilbert Scott, London (**1**).
1865 *Freedman* John Ward, Boston.
1865–7 *Ugolino and his Sons* Jean-Baptiste Carpeaux (Louvre, Paris).
1869 *The Fugitive's Story* John Rogers (Historical Society, New York).
1871 *The Dying Centaur* William Rimmer, Boston.
1874 *Mercury and Psyche* Begas, Berlin.
1875 Equestrian statue of Joan of Arc Emmanuel Frémiet, Paris. *Minute Man* Daniel C French, Concord, Mass.
1877 *Age of Bronze* Auguste Rodin (Tate Gallery, London).
1880 *Gates of Hell*, unfinished bronze Rodin, Paris.
1881 *Fourteen–Year–Old Dancer* Edgar Degas (Mellon Collection).
1884 *The Burghers of Calais* Rodin, Paris.
1886 *Statue of Liberty*, Frédéric Bartholdi New York (**2**).

1

2

1886–1902 *Beethoven* Max Klinger, Leipzig.
1887 Memorial to Lincoln Augustus Saint-Gaudens, Chicago.
1891 *Wittelsbach Fountain* Adolf von Hildebrand, Munich.
1892 The Eros Fountain Alfred Gilbert, Piccadilly Circus, London.

Events: painting

5373 **1850** *Raftsmen Playing Cards* George Bingham (City Art Museum, St. Louis). *Round Table of Sanssouci* Adolf Menzel.
1855 *The Studio of the Painter* Gustave Courbet (Louvre, Paris).
1856 *Mme Moitessier* Jean-Auguste Dominique Ingres (Louvre, Paris).
1859 *Thunderstorm with Rocky Mountains* Albert Bierstadt (Museum of Fine Arts, Boston).
c. 1860 *Young Spartans* Edgar Degas (National Gallery, London).
1863 *Le Déjeuner sur l'Herbe* Edouard Manet (Louvre, Paris). *The White Girl I* James Whistler (National Gallery, Washington).
1865 *Olympia* Edouard Manet (Louvre, Paris).
1866 *Prisoners from the Front* Winslow Homer (Metropolitan Museum, New York).
1872 *Impression: Sunrise* Claude Monet (Musée Marmotton, Paris).
1872–3 *The House of the Hanged Man* Paul Cézanne (Louvre, Paris).
1874 *The Dancing Class* Degas (Musée de L'Impressionnisme, Paris).
1875 *The Gross Clinic* Thomas Eakins (Jefferson Medical College, Philadelphia).
1876 *The Swing* Auguste Renoir (Musée de L'Impressionnism, Paris).
1877 *Nocturne in Black and Gold* Whistler (Institute of Art, Detroit).
1884 *Toilers of the Sea* Albert Pinkham Ryder. *Mme Gautreau* John Singer Sargent (Metropolitan Museum, New York).
c. 1884 *Les Parapluies* Auguste Renoir (National Gallery, London).
1888 *Severed Ear* Vincent Van Gogh (Courtauld Institute, London).
1893 *The Cry* Edvard Munch (Oslo).
1897 *Boulevard Montmartre* Camille Pissarro (Hermitage, St Petersburg).

People

5374 REALISM
Bartholdi, Frédéric Auguste 1834–1904, French sculptor. Best known for his monumental sculpture *Liberty Enlightening the World*, i.e. the Statue of Liberty.
Corot, Jean-Baptiste Camille 1796–1875, French painter (**1**). His highly popular and influential landscapes, e.g. *The Farnese Gardens* (1826), led to him being awarded the *Légion d'Honneur* in 1846.

1

Courbet, Gustave 1819–77, French painter. His early work was romantic in style, but in the 1850s he began producing innovative works such as *The Stonebreakers* (1851) which were attacked by critics and public for their gritty, down-to-earth realism.
Homer, Winslow 1836–1910, American painter. Influenced by both photography and Manet, he is particularly noted for the clarity and brightness of his paintings, e.g. *Breezing Up* (1876). The sea was a favorite subject.

continued

People continued

5374 IMPRESSIONISM

Cézanne, Paul 1839–1906, French painter. Influenced by Delacroix and Pissarro, he began painting from nature from the late 1860s. His strong interest in form and structure led to works such as *Bathers* (1906), which were to be very influential on the Cubists.

Dégas, Edgar 1834–1917, French painter. Influenced by the old masters of the Renaissance and Japanese woodcuts, he met Monet in the 1860s and began exhibiting with the Impressionists. His pastels of racehorses and dancers are particularly well regarded.

Manet, Edouard 1832–83, French painter. His *Spanish Guitar Player* was well-received at the 1861 Salon, but his much more controversial *Déjeuner sur l'Herbe* was rejected in 1863, outrage being expressed at the nude female figure. Several of his pupils, e.g. Degas, became Impressionists, and though he never exhibited with painters of the group, their works influenced his later paintings.

Monet, Claude 1840–1926, French painter. His *Impression: Sunrise* (1872) gave its name to the Impressionist movement. He worked with Sisley and Renoir and was influenced by Manet, but was drawn more to experimenting with light and color, e.g. *Women in a Garden* (1867) and *Haystacks* (1891). In his later work, notably the *Waterlilies* series (1899–1926), the subject is often eclipsed by the vibrant lighting.

Pissarro, Camille 1830–1903, French painter. He studied under Corot, was influenced by Constable, and became a leading Impressionist with works such as *Red Roofs* (1887). He later experimented with pointillism and developed a freer style of brushwork.

Renoir, Pierre Auguste 1841–1919, French painter. He exhibited in the first three Impressionist exhibitions and developed his own style, giving emphasis to perspective, solidity of form and careful preliminary sketching in works such as *The Bathers* (c. 1884–87).

Sisley, Alfred 1839–99, French (of English extraction). Painter. An admirer of Corot, he came under the influence of Renoir and Monet while studying in Paris. Noted especially for his peaceful landscapes, e.g. *Floods at Marly* (1876).

Whistler, James Abbot McNeill 1834–1903, American (**2**). Influenced by Courbet, he settled in London in 1859 and became famous as a portraitist with works such as his portrait of his mother, titled *Arrangement in Gray and Black*. His experiments in color and tone resulted in works with titles such as *Chelsea: Nocturn in Blue and Green* (c. 1870).

2

PRE-RAPHAELITE MOVEMENT

Hunt, William Holman 1827–1910, English painter. With Millais and Rossetti, he founded the Pre-Raphaelite Brotherhood, and was opposed to frivolous subjects, and sought inspiration in nature and natural composition. A devout Christian, his works are often allegorical, e.g. *The Scapegoat* (1854), or moralistic, e.g. *The Awakening Conscience* (1854).

Millais, John Everett 1829–96, English painter. A child prodigy, he founded the Pre-Raphaelite Brotherhood with Hunt and Rossetti. He later became president of the Royal Academy and produced official portraits and cloyingly sentimental works such as *Bubbles* (1886).

Rossetti, Dante Gabriel 1828–82, English painter and poet (**3**). A founding member of the Pre–Raphaelite Brotherhood, he drew on medieval literature and legend for inspiration. His models included his wife, Elizabeth Siddal, e.g. in *Beata Beatrix* (1864). His works influenced the Symbolists.

3

NEO-IMPRESSIONISM

Seurat, Georges 1859–91, French painter. The founder of neo-Impressionism, he invented pointillism, a system in which the picture is made up of minute blocks of color that blend together when seen from a distance, as in *Le Cirque* (1891).

Signac, Paul 1863–1935, French painter. He exhibited with the Impressionists in 1886, and joined Seurat in experimenting with pointillism. His theories are set in his book *From Delacroix to Neo-Impressionism* (1899). His free style and bright palette influenced Matisse.

POST–IMPRESSIONISM

Gauguin, Paul 1848–1903, French painter, printmaker and sculptor. He worked as a stockbroker before becoming a painter in 1873, and developed his own simplisitic, richly colored style after exhibiting with the Impressionists. His interest in primitive art led him to the South Sea Islands, where he painted his masterpieces, including *Where do we come from? What are we? Where are we going?* (1897).

Munch, Edvard 1863–1944, Norwegian painter. Gauguin was a strong influence upon the development of his emotional expressionism. Much of his painting is obsessed with sickness and isolation to a rather morbid degree, characterized by distortion of line and strong contrasts, as in his best-known work *The Scream* (1893).

Rousseau, Henri Julien ("Le Douanier") 1844–1910, French naive painter. He enjoyed early commercial and critical success with landscapes such as *Forest of Compiègne* (1834), but later suffered so many rejections from the Salon that he was dubbed "Le Grand Refuse." He later became leader of the Barbizon school and was an influence upon the surrealists.

Sargent, John Singer 1856–1925, American painter. He trained in Paris, where his portrait of *Mme X* (1884) caused outrage for its eroticism. He became a prominent society painter in London from 1885, and also painted watercolor landscapes and murals.

Toulouse-Lautrec, Henri (Marie Raymond) de 1864–1901, French painter and lithographer. Of aristocratic lineage, his growth was stunted in youth due to ill health and an accident. Influenced by Degas, his chosen subjects were drawn from café and cabaret society and prostitution. He is best known for his lithographs advertising cafés and entertainers.

Van Gogh, Vincent 1853–90, Dutch painter (**4**). A lay preacher before taking up painting in 1880, his highly distinctive work combined realistic subject matter with a bold, expressionist style and impasto surface, e.g. *The Potato Eaters* (1885). His late works, e.g. *The Cornfield* (1889), display the turbulent mental imbalance that led him to take his own life. His art has had a profound influence on many 20th-century artists.

4

continued

People continued

5374

EXPRESSIONISM
Kandinsky, Wassily 1866–1944, Russian painter. He founded the school of abstract expressionism c. 1910, with his non-figurative paintings whose significance depended upon the interrelation of colors and forms. He formed the "Blue Rider" group with Franz Marc, and taught at the Bauhaus in Germany (1922–33). He also wrote a treatise *On the Spiritual in Art* and experimented with the correlation of musical notes with color and painting.

ART NOUVEAU
Beardsley, Aubrey Vincent 1872–98, English illustrator. Beardsley's work, in the sinuous Art Nouveau style, is representative of the so-called decadent 1890s. His sensuous, flowing black and white illustrations for Oscar Wilde's *Salome* are characteristic of his work.

538 20TH CENTURY 1950 – TODAY

Styles and movements

5381

Naive art (20th century and earlier) Works by self-taught artists whose fresh, untutored style is noted for its simplicity and innocence. Notable naive artists include Grandma Moses and "Douanier" Rousseau.
Fauvism (c. 1905–7) A shortlived but influential movement of artists surrounding Matisse, characterized by daring, spontaneous handling of paint in bold, brilliant, often non-representational color. "Fauve" means "wild beast," a critic's response to a 1905 exhibition of works by Matisse and others.
Die Brücke (The Bridge) (c. 1905–13) A group of German expressionists, including Kirchner, whose manifesto was to overthrow the concept of art as an end in itself, and to integrate art and life by using art as a means of communication. Influenced by tribal art and van Gogh, the founders lived and worked communally, using clashing colors and aggressive distortions in their intense works.
Expressionism (c. 1905–25) An emphasis on pictorial distortion or chromatic exaggeration within any art of any period. The movement emphasizing heightened emotion and the artist's subjective vision, and characterized by bold brushwork and stylized forms. Influenced by Gauguin, van Gogh, Munch, and Fauvism, the movement includes the more specific groups of Die Brücke and Der Blaue Reiter.
Cubism (c 1907–23) The style developed by Picasso and Braque in response to Cézanne's late works, and to African tribal art. The first major painting in this style was Picasso's *Les Demoiselles d'Avignon* (1906), and the term itself was coined by a critic after seeing Braque's 1908 work. "Analytic" (early) cubism presented the work from a variety of viewpoints. "Synthetic" (late) cubism introduced decorative elements such as lettering and applied materials such as newspaper (collage) to achieve a balance between the depiction of reality and the picture as an object of reality in its own right. Cubism has been enormously influential on modern art.
Futurism (c. 1909–19) A movement of writers and artists founded by the poet Filippo Marinetti (who described speed as "a new form of beauty"), its manifesto advocated incorporating the thrust of modern technology into art in order to express the movement and dynamism of modern life.
School of Paris (c 1910–50) The large international group of Paris-based artists which made the city the center of the art world until the emergence of the New York School.
Der Blaue Reiter "The Blue Rider" (c. 1911–14) A loose-knit group of expressionist painters including Kandinsky, Klee, and Marc, united by Kandinsky's dictum that "the creative spirit is hidden within matter."
Dada (c. 1915–23) An art movement originating in Zurich 1915, dada (the name chosen at random) rejected accepted aesthetic values and advocated an irrational form of non-art or anti-art. Leading figures included the poet Tristan Tzara and the sculptor Jean Arp.
Bauhaus School (c. 1919–33) A German school of architecture and applied arts founded by the architect Walter Gropius. The aim was to integrate the disparate arts and crafts under the principle of function dictating form. The influence of the bauhaus masters on modern architecture has been deep and long-lasting.
Surrealism (c. 1924–) A French avant-garde movement which drew on dadaist principles in art and on the psychoanalytic theories of Freud. Irrational association, spontaneous techniques and an elimination of premeditation to free the workings of the unconscious mind, and an interest in dreams, inspired its practitioners.
Kinetic art (c. 1930–) An art form in which light and balance create a work that moves – or appears to move air currents, electric motors, artificial lighting, etc, to create such effects.
Abstract Expressionism (c. 1940–) A movement that developed in New York in the 1940s which broke away from the realism hitherto dominant in American art, and which became the first American movement to have a significant influence on European art. Notable pracitioners included Jackson Pollock (the main exponent of action painting) and De Kooning.
New York School (c. 1945–60) A loosely associated group of mainly abstract expressionist painters, such as Pollock and De Kooning, who attempted to build a uniquely American non-representational mode of artistic expression.
Op art (c. 1950–) A form of abstract art that bases itself on creating static two-dimensional objects which appear to move on a flat surface.
Pop art (c. 1955–) A reaction against abstract expressionism, the movement started almost simultaneously in the UK and USA and used the images of mass media, advertising, and pop culture, presenting common, everyday object as art.
Minimal art (c. 1960–) A rejection of the aesthetic qualities of art in favor of the physical reality of the art object. Materials used are usually non-traditional and often in geometrically arranged units, as in the sculptor Carl Andre's notorious *Equivalent VIII* (1966), which consisted of 120 fired bricks arranged in a solid rectangle on London's Tate Gallery floor.

Events: sculpture

5382

1901 *Madelaine I* Henri Matisse (Baltimore Museum of Art).
1905 Sculptures, Frogner Park, Oslo, Gustav Vigeland.
1906 *Ecce Puer* Medardo Rosso (Winston Collection, Paris).
1912 *Head* Pablo Picasso (Kunsthaus, Zurich). *Standing Woman* Gaston Lachaise (Whitney Museum, New York)
1914 *Horse* Marcel Duchamp (Modern Art Museum, Paris).
1915 *Glass of Absinthe* Picasso (Collection Kahnweiler, Paris).
1919 *Veiled Beggar Woman* Ernst Barlach (Lisa Arnold Collection, NY).
1921 *The Gift* Man Ray (unknown collection).
1923 *Column* Naum Gabo (Museum of Modern Art, New York).
1928 *Design for a Monument* Picasso (bronze, formerly in artist's collection).
1929 *Reclining Figure* Henry Moore (City Art Gallery, Leeds).
1932 *Woman with her Throat Cut* Alberto Giacometti (Museum of Modern Art, NY).
1933 *Calderberry Bush* Alexander Stirling Calder (Sweeney Collection, NY).
1936–37 *Montserrat* Julio Gonzales (Stedelijk Museum, Amsterdam).
1938 *The Complaint* Kathe Kollwitz (Munich).
1939 *Bird Basket* Henry Moore (Mrs Moore Collection).
1942 *Horizontal Spines* Alexander Calder (Phillips Academy, Mass).
1944–6 *Bird* Joan Miró.
1949 *Horse and Rider* Marino Marini (Walker Art Museum, Minneapolis).
1951 *Ivor Stravinsky* Marino Marini (Minneapolis Institute of Arts). *Baboon and Young* Pablo Picasso (Museum of Modern Art, NY).
1951–3 *The Ruined City* Ossip Zadkine, (Rotterdam).
1953–6 *Variations within a Sphere No.10: The*

continued

Events: sculpture continued

5382 *Sun* Richard Lippold (Metropolitan Museum, New York).
1956–7 *Falling Warrior* Henry Moore (Joseph H. Hirshhorn Collection, New York).
1958–9 *Metamachine* Jean Tinguely (Private Collection).
1959 *The Yellow Buick* César (Museum of Modern Art, New York).
1960 *Monumental Head* Alberto Giacometti (Joseph H. Hirshhorn Collection, New York).
1962 *Lock* Anthony Caro (Kasmin Collection, London).
1963 *Signe* Brauner (Alexander Iolas Gallery, New York). *Hamburger with Pickle and Tomato attached* Claes Oldenburg (Carroll Janis Collection, New York). *Cubi XVIII* David Smith (Tate Gallery, London).
1965 *Space Modulation IV* Eduardo Chillida (Maeght Collection, Paris).
1966 *Fat Chair* Joseph Beuys.
1968 *Portrait of Mies van der Rohe* Marino Marini.
1969 *Lipstick, Yale,* Oldenburg.
1970 *Spiral Jetty* at Great Salt Lake, Utah, Robert Smithson.
1976 *Running Fence*, 24 mi (38 km) across California, Christo.
1977 *Stone Field*, Hartford, Conn. Carl Andre. *Batcolumn Chicago*, Oldenburg. *Honigpumpe am Arbeisplatz* Beuys.
1979 *Meta-harmony 2* Jean Tinguely.
1981 *Tilted Arc* Serra. *With Life* Braslow.
1983 *The End of the 20th Century* Beuys.
1985 *Man Asleep* Gormley.

Events: painting

5383 **1903** *The Old Guitarist* Pablo Picasso, (Art Institute, Chicago).
1905 *Portrait with a Green Stripe* Henri Matisse (Art Museum, Copenhagen).
1906–7 *Les Demoiselles d'Avignon* Pablo Picasso (Museum of Modern Art, New York).
1907 *The Wake of the Ferry* John Sloan (Phillips Collection, Washington).
1909 *The Kiss* Gustav Klimt (Museé des Beaux-Arts, Strasbourg).
1911 *Composition No. 4* Wassily Kandinsky (Düsseldorf). *I and the Village* Marc Chagall. *Large Blue Horse* Franz Marc (Walker Art Gallery, Minneapolis).
1914 *The Tempest* Otto Kokoschka (Kunstmuseum, Basle).
1916–26 *Nyphéas* Claude Monet (Orangerie, Paris).
c. 1917 *Seated Nude* Amadeo Modigliani (Courtauld Institute, London).
c. 1918 *White Square on a White Ground* Kasimir Malevich (Museum of Modern Art, New York).
1920 *The Mechanic* Ferdinand Léger (Gallerie Louis Carré, Paris).
1921 *Composition in Red, Yellow, and Blue* Piet Mondrian (Gemeente Museum, The Hague).
1923–4 *The Tilled Field* Joan Miró (Clifford Collection, Radnor, PA).
1925 *Fish Magic* Paul Klee (Museum of Art, Philadelphia).**1926** *Black Iris* Georgia O'Keefe (Metropolitan Museum, New York).
1929 *Sailing Boats* Lyonel Feininger, (Tannahill Collection, Detroit).
1931 *The Persistence of Memory* Salvador Dali (Museum of Modern Art, New York).
1933 *The Human Condition* René Magritte (France).
1937 *Guernica* Picasso (Prado, Madrid).
1940 *Gas* Edward Hopper (Museum of Modern Art, New York).
1942–43 *Broadway Boogie-Woogie* Piet Mondrian (Museum of Modern Art, New York).
1948 *Cry of Liberty* Karel Appel (Stedelijk Museum, Amsterdam).
1948 *Full Fathom Five* Jackson Pollock
1951 *Crucifixion* Salvador Dali (Glasgow Art Gallery).
1951–2 *T-50 Painting 8* Hans Hartung (Museum of Modern Art, New York).
1952 *Woman I* Willem de Kooning (Museum of Modern Art, New York).
1953 *The Snail* Henri Matisse (Tate Gallery, London).
1954 *Flag* Jasper Johns (Collection Philip Johnson, NY).
1958 *Two Openings in Black over Wine* Mark Rothko (Tate Gallery, London).
1962 *Marilyn Monroe* Andy Warhol (Jasper Johns Collection, NY).
1962–3 *Picture Emphasising Stillness* David Hockney (Glazebrook Collection, London).
1963 *Whaam!* Roy Lichtenstein (Tate Gallery, London).
1965 *Weatherside* Andrew Wyeth (Laughlin Collection, NY).
1967–8 *Arny* Victor Vasarély (Gallery Denise René, Paris).
1968 *White, Black, Yellow* Nay.
1970 *Piazza d'Italia* Giorgio de Chirico.
1971 *Circus with Jugglers* Marc Chagall.
1973 *Rainy Days* Hundertwasser.
1976 *Adam masstäblich* Rudolf Hausner.
1979 *Earthcycle* Nagaoka.
1979–85 *Sad Flowers* Hodgkin.
1981 *Leda* Fuchs.
1984 *Forbidden to Awaken the Gods* Mariani.
1985 *Electric Painting* Jorg Immendorff.

People

5384 **Bacon, Francis** 1909–92, Irish-born British painter. He became famous overnight in 1945 when he exhibited *Figure in a Landscape* and the triptych *Three Studies for Figures at the Base of the Crucifixion.* His best-known works are his disturbing series of paintings based on Velàzquez's *Portrait of Pope Innocent X.*
Brancusi, Constantin 1876–1957, Romanian-born French sculptor. Based in Paris from 1904, he began working in marble and limestone, then progressed to wood and metal, always allowing the material to dictate the flow of his organic style, as in *Sleeping Muse* (1910) and *The Seal* (1936).
Butler, Reg 1913–81, English sculptor. An assistant to Henry Moore from 1947, he experimented with welding techniques and became famous with his *Unknown Political Prisoner* (1953).
Chagall, Marc 1887–1985, Russian-born French painter. He moved to Paris in 1910, where he began his dreamlike works inspired by his Russian childhood, e.g. *I and the Village* (1911). He was also a noted illustrator and stage and stained glass designer.
Epstein, Sir Jacob 1880–1959, American-born British sculptor. Much of his work, e.g. *The Monument to Oscar Wilde* (1912), attracted much controversy because of alleged indecency. His portrait busts were much admired. Notable works include *Christ* (1919) and *Adam* (1939).
Giacometti, Alberto 1901–66, Swiss painter and sculptor. A member of the surrealists from 1930–35, he developed his own distinctive style of thin, elongated figures. *Four Women on a Base* (1950) is a representative work.
Hepworth, Barbara 1903–75 English sculptor. Shown here (**1**) with one of her sculptures (**2**) *Mother and Child.* Many of Hepworth's later sculptures are in bronze; earlier works were created using stone and wood. Hepworth developed an abstract style and often incorporated wires and string into her sculptures.
Hockney, David b 1937, English painter, printmaker, and designer. A prolific and wide-ranging artist, Hockney's best-known works, which reflect his homosexuality and fascination with water, are paintings such as *Peter getting out of Nick's Pool* (1966). Other works include the etchings *Rake's Progress* (1963) and many imaginative stage designs.
John, Augustus 1878–1961, English painter. An outstanding and innovative draughtsman, he had 38 paintings displayed at the New York Armory show of 1913. His portraits, e.g, *The Smiling Woman* (1908), were highly influential. His elder sister, Gwen John (1876–1939), was also a fine painter.

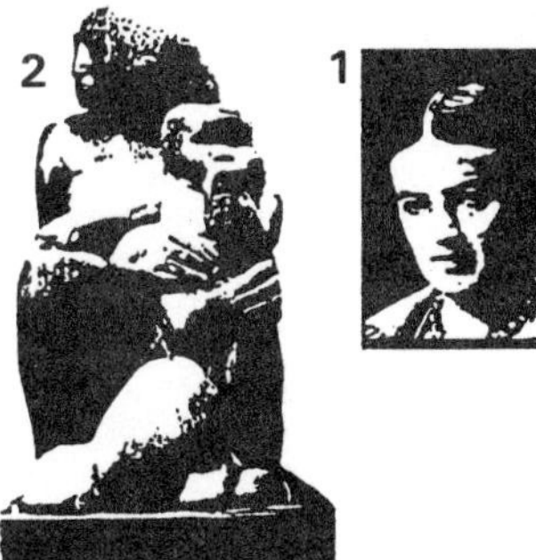

continued

People continued

5384 **Klee, Paul,** 1879–1940, Swiss painter. He exhibited with the Blue Rider group in 1912, and was inspired by a trip to Tunisia in 1914 to progress towards his highly individual work, characterized by light, bright, delicately colored abstract works. His work was banned by the Nazis in the 30s, and his later work is darker in tone.
Matisse, Henri 1869–1954, French painter. Influenced by the neo-impressionists, he went on to exhibit vivid and colorful works in 1905 that were dubbed "fauves" (wild animals). His work includes *Bathers by a River* (1916–17).
Mondrian, Piet 1872–1944, Dutch painter. Influenced initially by symbolism and expressionism his work became cubist after he moved to Paris in 1911. His paintings gradually became more abstract and geometrical, including such canvases as *Composition in Yellow and Blue* (1929).
Moore, Henry 1898–1987, English (**3**). Sculptor. Influenced by African and Mexican art, his sculptures revived direct carving methods as against moulding and casting. His innovative, highly influential near–abstract sculptures include *Reclining Figure* (1929) and *Two Forms* (1934).

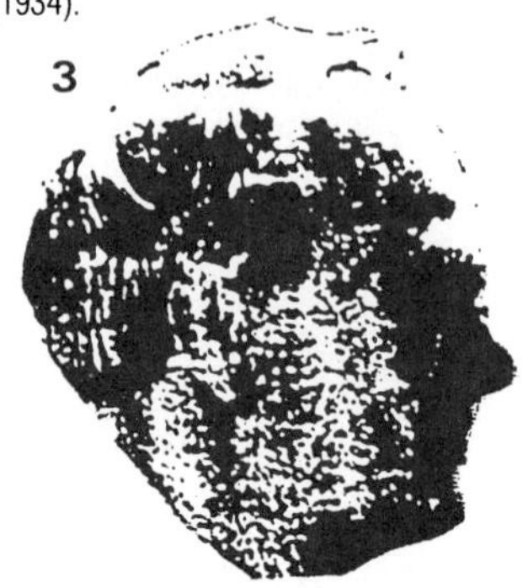

Nolan, Sir Sidney b. 1917, Australian painter. Self-taught, he established his reputation with surreal figurative works based on themes from Australian history and legend. Notable works include the Ned Kelly series began in 1946, e.g. *Kelly at Glenrowan* (1955).
Spencer, Stanley 1891–1959, English painter. Uninfluenced by contemporary trends, his works are based upon a highly personal visionary approach to both life and art, as in *The Resurrection, Cookham* (1923–7). He also painted some notoriously explicit self-portraits and more orthodox landscapes.
Utrillo, Maurice 1883–1955, French painter. Largely self-taught, he was encouraged to paint by his mother, the painter Suzanne Valadon (1867–1938). He is especially noted for his Montmartre scenes, e.g. *La Place du Tertre* (c. 1910), in rich yet subtle colors and thick impasto.

CUBISM
Braque, Georges (1882–1963,) French painter. Developed cubism with Picasso. They were concerned with showing a three-dimensional world on a two-dimensional surface. Much of Braque's early work is inspired by Cézanne, e.g. *Houses at L' Estaque* (1908), and some is very similar to Picasso's work at this time, e.g. *The Portuguese* (1911).
Picasso, Pablo 1881–1973, Spanish painter, Land sculptor (**4**). Regarded by many as the greatest artist of the 20th century, his superb draughtsmanship was evident early on, in works such as *The Girl with Bare Feet* (1895). Influenced by African art from 1907, he painted *Les Demoiselles d'Avignon* in 1906–7, the work which heralded Cubism and a new development in art. He never ceased experimenting, and in 1937 painted *Guernica*, a profoundly emotional anti–war protest.

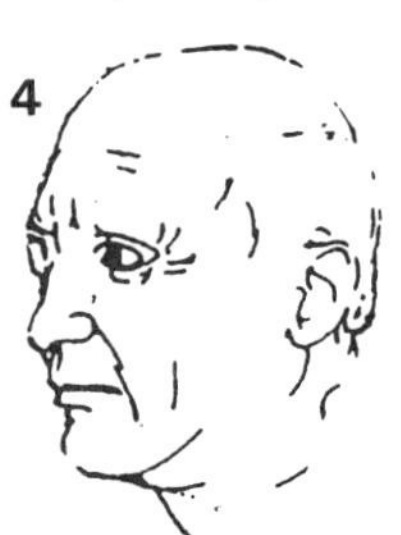

SURREALISM
Dali, Salvador 1904–89, Spanish painter (**5**). His early work was cubist in style, and he joined the surrealists in 1928. His style is immediately recognizable precise in execution gives hallucinatory detail to his (often peculiar) neuroses. Works include *The Persistence of Memory* (1931) and *The Last Supper* (1955).

Miró, Joan 1893–1983, Spanish painter, sculptor, and designer. Influenced by cubism and dada, *Catalan Landscape* (1923) marks the beginning of his surrealist style. His works are characterized by bright, free-flowing, and floating forms in a dream-like world.

ACTION PAINTING
Pollock, Jackson 1912–56, American psainter. Initially nfluenced by surrealism and American Indian art, he went on in the 1940s to produce his mosr famous works: abstract, "action paintings," in which the paint is poured or splattered over the floor, e.g. *Echo, Number 25* (1951).

KINETIC ART
Calder, Alexander 1898–1976, American sculptor notable for his moving, kinetic sculptures or "mobiles" (he called non-moving sculptures "stabiles.") His works include *The Brass Family* (1929) and *Mobile* (1958,)

539 ART TERMS AND TECHNIQUES

General art terms and techniques

5391 **abstract art** An art form that represents ideas (by means of geometric and other designs) instead of natural forms. Compare representational art.
brush drawing Generally an Oriental technique of painting that relies on varieties of brushwork, usually executed over a wash of diluted watercolor.
caricature A picture ludicrously exaggerating the qualities, defects, or peculiarities of a person or idea.
cartoon (a) A humorous sketch or drawing usually telling a story or caricaturing some person or action. (b) In fine arts, a preparatory sketch or design for a picture or ornamental motif to be transferred to a fresco or tapestry.

continued

General art terms and techniques continued

5391 ***chiaroscuro*** (Italian, "light-dark") 1 The rendering of light and shade in a painting. 2 The subtle gradations and marked variations of light and shade for dramatic effect. 3 A woodcut print produced from two blocks.
colors, complementary Two colors at opposite points on the color scale, for example, orange and blue, green and red.
colors, primary Red, yellow, and blue, the mixture of which will yield all other colors in the spectrum but which themselves cannot be produced through a mixture of other colors.
colors, secondary Orange, green, and purple, colors produced by mixing two primary colors.
composition The organization of the parts of a work into a unified whole.
coulisse Objects and figures arranged at the sides of a painting in order to focus the eye onto the central piece of the work.
diptych A work of art with two panels, as in a two-panelled altarpiece.
distemper Cheap and impermanent method of painting in which powdered colors are mixed with glue.
dragging A technique of applying paint lightly over a textured surface to gain the effect of both light and dark "broken" color.
easel picture or **cabinet picture** (in the Renaissance) A small painting meant to be displayed on an easel rather than hung.
egg and dart (in classical art) A decorative technique that alternated arrowlike shapes with oval forms.
etching A process in which a special needle is used to draw a design on a metal plate overlaid with wax. The plate is then treated with acid, inked, and finally used to print reproductions of the design.
figurative A representation of a human or an animal form.
finger painting Chinese watercolor technique using a finger instead of a brush.
foreshortening Reducing or distorting in order to represent three-dimensional space as perceived by the eye, according to the rules of perspective.
foxing A brown spotting that discolors prints, caused by dampness.
fresco The technique of painting on moist lime plaster with colors ground in water or a limewater mixture.
fugitive pigments Inferior pigments that tend to fade when exposed to the sun or disintegrate in a polluted atmosphere.
genre painting A realistic style of painting in which everyday life forms the subject matter, as distinguished from religious or historical painting.
hard-edge painting A painting executed in long and thick flat color areas, all of which have sharply defined edges.
highlight The lightest point or tone in a painting.
icon Religious painting (usually on wood or ivory) associated with Eastern churches.
impasto 1 In painting, the thick application of paint. 2 In ceramics, the application of enamel or slip to a ceramic object to form a decoration in low relief.
isocephaly (in classical Greek art) A technique which poses groups of figures at the same height, regardless of the action or purpose of each figure.
landscape A painting whose main subject is pure landscape without human figures; rare in western art before 17th century.
lay figure A wooden model of the human body that is jointed so that it can be posed and arranged in clothing; used by artists and sculptors.
letterism Letters, symbols, and words placed in artistic juxtaposition; an art form popular in the 1950s.
macalature A "thin" or partially obscured print made from a plate that needs re-inking.
makemono A painting (generally Oriental) on a long scroll.
middle distance or **middle ground** The represented space in a picture between background and foreground.
miniature Tiny painting (less than 6 in or 15 cm across), usually a portrait.
mural Painting or decoration applied to a wall, usually executed in oil, fresco, or tempera.
narrative painting One that tells a story; very popular in Victorian England.
oiling out Process of rubbing oil into a painting to brighten up colors. Although a luster is restored for a while, the ultimate effect is to further darken the shades.
optical mixting The visual mixing of colors performed by the eye from a distance, i.e. dabs of blue and yellow paint combine to give the sensation of green.
palette 1 A flat surface used by a painter to mix colors, traditionally oblong with a hole for the thumb. 2 The range of colors available to a painter.
papiers collés (Fr. "pasted papers") Pictures made from bits of paper, tissue, cardboard, etc., that have been glued together in artistic color or form.
passage 1 A particular part of a painting. 2 The transition from one shade to another. 3 A special technique. 4 An area in a painting that has been painted over by someone other than the artist.
paste 1 A soft, subdued color. 2 A dry paste made up of ground pigments, chalk and gum water formed into a stick. 3 A drawing made with such a stick.
pellicle The fine "skin" that forms when oil paint dries.
perspective A method of representing three-dimensional volumes and spatial relationships on a flat surface.
petard An artwork produced to draw attention to itself through unusual composition, subject matter, etc.
pigments Dry paints or dyes that are mixed with oil, water, or other material.
plastic (in a painting) Conveying a three-dimensional impression through the modelling and movement of the figures.
polychrome Of many or various colors.
polyptych A work of art involving two or more panels, most frequently denoting more than three panels, since diptych (two panels) and triptych (three panels) are more commonly used.
portrait painting Representation of a human being. The first portraits were usually of kings or leaders.
primary colors *See* colors, primary.
priming The application of a coat of white paint (usually zinc or lead) to a sized canvas in order to prepare it for painting.
psychedelic art Pseudo-visionary works created by artists under (or claiming to be under) the influence of drugs (**1**).

1

quadratura Painting on a ceiling or a wall to create the illusion of limitless space.
relief 1 The projection of an image from its background. 2 (painting and drawing) The apparent projection of parts conveying the illusion of three dimensions. 3 (printing) Any process in which ink impressions are produced from the high areas of prepared printing blocks.
representational art An art form that endeavors to show figures and objects exactly as they appear to the eye. Compare abstract art.
retreating color Shades of green or blue used to suggest distance.
scumbling A painting technique in which parts are overlayed with opaque or semi-opaque color applied lightly with an almost dry brush.
secondary colors *See* colors, secondary.
squaring The transferral of a small sketch to a larger space by dividing the sketch into numbered squares and copying the design in each square onto the larger surface.
stenciling A method of producing images or letters from sheets of cardboard, metal, or other materials from which images or letters have been cut away.
still life Study of an arrangement of inanimate objects, such as fruit or flowers; favorite form of the Dutch School.
tactile values Those elements in art that convey an illusion of the tangible, so that the viewer's senses react to temperature, motion, texture, etc.
texture 1 The visual and tactile quality of a work effected through the particular way the materials are worked. 2 The distribution of tones or shades of a partcicular color.
tinsel painting or **oriental** or **crystal painting** A painting on glass that has been backed by tinfoil; a popular fad in the 19th century.
tone The quality or value of color, e.g. warm or cold tones.
triptych Series of three painted panels or doors that are hinged or folded.
trompe l'oeil (in painting) The fine, detailed

continued

General art terms and techniques continued

5391

rendering of objects to convey the illusion of spatial and tactile qualities.
underpainting The initial painting of a picture in one color to lay out the composition.
values (in painting) The degree of lightness or darkness in a color.
vanitas A still life art form developed in the 17th century to reflect the transience of life. Usually depictions of such objects as dead flowers, skulls, hourglasses, etc.
veduta A painting of a city or town lucid and faithful enough the location is easily identified.

Sculpture terms and techniques

5392

alabaster Marble-like stone, usually white.
anaglyph Carving or ornament in bas-relief.
armature Metal or wood framework used to support a sculptor's clay, plaster, or wax model.
assemblage Sculpture creation by constructing the work from diverse objects. Compare carving.
atlas, Telemon Male statue used as a column, as in an ancient Greek temple.
banker Sculptor's workbench.
bronze Alloy of copper or tin used by sculptors in ancient Greece, Rome, China, and Africa; revived in modern times.
bust Sculpture of the upper part of the human body.
calvary Representation of the crucifixion.
cameo Small bas-relief carving in stone, glass, or shell, the design in relief being a different color from the background.
candlemaking Now regarded as a skilled decorative sculptural process; liquid candle wax can be colored, perfumed, and whipped to make it frothy; when set it can be carved like clay.
carving Sculpture creation by "subtracting" or removing extraneous material to create the finished work. Compare assemblage.
caryatid Female statue used as a column, as in an ancient Greek temple.
cast Figure made from the mold of original model. See *cire perdue*, plaster cast, sand cast.
chryselephantine Made or decorated with gold or ivory, in the manner of ancient Greek statues.
cire perdue (French, "lost wax") Traditional method for casting bronze sculptures. The model with waxed surface is enclosed in the mould; the wax is melted and runs through holes at the bottom; molten metal is then poured through holes at the top, filling up the space left by the wax.
corbeil Sculpture of a basket of fruit or flowers, used as an architectural ornament.
diaglyph Carving or ornament in intaglio.
figurine Miniature figure.
free-stone An easily worked fine-grained limestone or sandstone.
genre sculpture Style that reflects everyday or rustic life; hallmark of Etruscan art and of Biblical subjects in the Middle Ages.
gesso Mixture of plaster of Paris or gypsum and glue, used as a base for bas-relief or to prepare a painting surface.
gisant A figure that is recumbent on the stone lid of a tomb.
heroic sculpture Figure or group of figures carved larger than life.
intaglio Carving in which the design is cut into the surface. Compare relief.
kore A female draped statue found in Archaic Greek art as a votive offering or placed on a grave. Similar male statues are called *kouros.*
kouros Ancient Greek male statue, usually nude, placed on graves or as votive offerings.
light sculpture A form of sculpture that utilizes light bulbs, the sun, and laser beams as the primary medium of expression.
mantle Clay mold around a wax model.
maquette (French, "small model") Small wax or clay model made by a sculptor in preparation for larger work.
marble Popular stone for sculpture because of its extreme durability; found in all colors rangng from nearly pure white to nearly pure black.
mobile Movable sculpture of shapes cut out of wood or sheet metal, linked by wires or rods in order to revolve easily or move up and down; invented by American sculptor, Alexander Calder (1932). Compare stabile.
modeling Building up of forms in three dimensions by means of plastic material such as clay or wax.
obelisk (primarily Egyptian) A monumental pillar that tapers in the shape of a pyramid.
origami The art (originating in Japan) of folding paper.
papier mâché (French, "Chewed paper"). A fine paper pulp that has been cast and moulded into strong structures. Easily absorbent paper, such as newsprint, is best.
pietà Representation of Mary with the body of Jesus.
plaster cast Intermediate stage in bronze sculpture from which the final mold is made.
polychromatic sculpture Sculpture painted in naturalistic colors to make it more lifelike, mostly pre-1500s.
putto or ***amorino*** Figure of a small child or cherub.
relief sculpture not free-standing from background; various degrees, from bas-relief (low relief) to *alto-relievo* (high relief). Compare *intaglio.*
restrike Impression taken from a sculptor's mold at some time after the original edition.
sand cast Mold of special sand made from plaster model and from which bronze cast is produced.
sculpture-in-the-round Sculpture that can be seen from all sides.
spall Chip broken from a stone carving.
stabile Sculpture resembling a mobile, but which does not move. Compare mobile.
synthetic sculpture Sculptures made from man-made materials. Expanded polystyrene blocks or sheets are excellent for ephemeral sculptures. Fiberglass sculpture is generally a mixture of polyester resin and shredded glass fibers.

Art media

5393

acrylic paint A synthetic, quick-drying paint that can be used in thick, heavy layers or thin washes on most surfaces. Additives can be used to provide matt or gloss finishes.
airbrush A compressed-air powered atomizer which is used to spray paint. Shaped like a large fountain pen, it produces a fine mist of color giving a smooth finish with subtle tonal gradations. The instrument is commonly used in advertising and graphic design.
chalk A soft stone, similar to a very soft limestone, used for drawing. Crayon is powdered chalk mixed with wax or oil.
encaustic The process of burning-in colors, particularly through inlaying colored clays, and by fusing or burning wax colors into the surface of ceramics.
fresco A painting directly painted onto a wall that has previously been covered with a damp freshly laid layer of lime plaster, the paint and plaster bonding chemically to become permanent.
gouache or **poster paint** An opaque mixture of watercolor paint and white pigment, as opposed to pure watercolor which employs transparent colors.
inks Liquids for drawing or painting; generally the colors are a suspension or present as a dye. Sometimes, as with Indian ink or white ink, there may be opaque pigments in suspension. Inks may be applied with different types of pen or soft hairbrushes.
oil paint A paint made by mixing color pigments with oil (usually linseed oil) to produce a malleable, slow-drying substance. The technique evolved gradually during the latter Middle Ages. The van Eyck brothers did much to perfect the medium.
pastel A paint medium of powdered color mixed with gum arabic to form a hard stick. When applied to paper, the color adheres to the surface and can be made permanent by fixing with spray varnish.
pencil A mixture of graphite and clay in stick form covered by a hard casing. The greater the clay element, the harder the pencil.
tempera A paint medium made by mixing color pigments with substances such as egg white, egg yolk, glue, gelatine, or casein. True tempera is when the colors are ground with egg yolk only. The medium was largely supplanted in the 15th century by oil paint.
watercolor A paint medium of color pigments mixed with water-soluble gum arabic. When moistened with water, a watercolor paint produces a transparent color that is applied to paper, usually white, the paper showing through the paint.

541 CLASSICAL LITERATURE c. 2345 BC – AD 600

People were recounting stories and making poems long before they began to write them down. The ancient epics and sagas would have been told or sung by bards who learned them from their predecessors in a way that still continues with the Hindu epics in India's illiterate communities.

No one knows who first told the stories of the Mesopotamian *Epic of Gilgamesh* and the long Hindu epics of the *Ramayana* and the *Mahabharata,* or who composed the early Confucian texts such as the *I Ching* or *Book of Changes.* Even the great Greek epics of the *Iliad* and the *Odyssey,* which may be considered the beginning of western literature, draw on a long tradition of oral poetry.

In Mesopotamian legend, Gilgamesh, king of Uruk, defeats and then befriends the wild man Enkidu, resists the erotic blandishments of the goddess Ishtar, and sets off on a quest to find the secret of eternal life. Such tales with many episodes and incidents are a common literary form. The Indian epics explore moral and spiritual dilemmas as they tell of dynastic battles controlled and aided by the gods. The earliest extant tales of other lands are similarly concerned with gods and heroes, while other texts record laws or religious rituals. Later writers have often drawn heavily on the myths of the ancient world, reshaping them to contemporary ends.

Events

5411

c. 2345 BC Earliest pyramid texts.
2000–1500 BC *The Story of Sinuke,* oldest Egyptian "novel."
pre-1200 BC Sumerian *Epic of Gilgamesh* retold in Babylonia and recorded.
c. 800 BC *Iliad* and *Odyssey* by Homer. The scene (**1**) from the *Iliad* appears on a 5th century Greek vase.

1

c. 800 BC *Book of Songs,* oldest Chinese poem.
c. 700 BC *Works and Days* by Hesiod.
c. 694 BC *Theogony* by Hesiod.
c. 660 BC *Warsongs* by Callinus of Ephesus.
c. 650 BC *Fables* by Archilochus of Paros. Clay tablet library of 25,000 tablets founded at Nineveh, Mesopotamia.
c. 600 BC *'Veda'* literature in India completed.
c. 590 BC Sappho of Lesbos's poems.
c. 565 BC Alcaeus of Lesbos's poems.
c. 530 BC Poems of Ibycus of Rhegium.
c. 520 BC Anacreon of Teos's poems.
c. 500 BC Aesop's *Fables* extant.
c. 490–47 BC Pindar's poems.
c. 444–25 BC *History of the Persian Wars* by Herodotus in nine volumes.
c. 403 BC *History of the Peloponnesian War* by Thucydides.
c. 393 BC *Persica* by Ctesias of Cnidus (history, summary survives).
c. 386–77 BC *Anabasis (March up Country)* – a history of a military expedition – by Xenophon.
c. 335 BC Aristotle founds Peripatetic School library, Athens.
c. 310 BC *Bhagavad Gita* written, India.
c. 305 BC Library of Alexandria founded by Ptolemy I (grows to over 4 million volumes).
c. 300 BC Novels and short stories in China.
c. 280–40 BC Alexandrian *Hymns, Epigrams, and Causes* by Callimachus of Cyrenne.
240 BC Work of Livius Andronicus – first translation of Greek drama – performed in Rome; translates *Odyssey.*
c. 201 BC *The Punic War* by Gnaeus Naevius (epic poem).
c. 200 BC *De agricultura* by Cat the Elder.
c. 175 BC *Annales* by Quintus Ennius (epic poem).
c. 146 BC *Satires* by Gaius Lucilius.
c. 140 BC *Histories* by Polybius.
c. 60 BC *Lovesongs to Lesbia* by Catullus.
c. 55 BC *On Oratory* (*De oratore*) by Cicero.
c. 50 BC *Solomon's Psalms* written in Jerusalem. *On the Gallic War (De bello Gallico)* by Julius Caesar.
c. 47 BC *On the Civil War (De bello civili)* by Julius Caesar.
c. 42–37 BC *Bucolia* by Virgil.
c. 38 BC Historian Asinius Pollio founds first public library in Rome.
37–30 BC *Georgics* by Virgil.
c. 36–32 BC *On Famous Men (De viris illustribus)* by Cornelius Nepos.
37–30 BC *Georgics* by Virgil.
33 BC Augustus founds Octavian and Palatine public libraries in Rome.
30 BC *Aeneid* begun by Virgil.
c. 29 BC *History of Rome* begun by Livy
c. 28–16 BC *Elegies* by Properitus.
c. 23–13 BC *Odes* by Horace.
c. 20 BC *Loves (Amores)* by Ovid.
c. 20–15 BC *Epistles* by Horace.
c. 19–18 BC *Poetic Art (Arts Poetica)* by Horace.
c. 1 BC *Art of Love* by Ovid.
c. AD 9 *Metamorphosis* by Ovid.
c. AD 59 *Satyricon* by Petronius (novel).
c. AD 65 *Pharsalia* by Lucan (epic poem).
AD 77–8 *History of the Jewish War* by Flavius Josephus.
c. AD 94–5 *History of the Jewish People* by Josephus.
AD 98 *Germania and Agricola* by Tacitus.
c. AD 100 Trajan founds the Ulpian Library at Rome. *Buddhacharita* by Asvogoshus, India.
c. AD 100–27 *Satires* by Juvenal.
c. AD 105–15 *Lives* by Plutarch.
c. AD 117 *Annals* by Tacitus.
c. AD 120 *Lives of the Caesars* by Suetonius.
c. AD 180–90 *The Golden Ass* or *Metamorphoses* by Apuleius.
c. AD 235 *History of Rome* by Dio Cassius.
c. AD 248 *Daphnis and Chloe* by Longus of Lesbos (pastoral romance).
c. AD 250 Earliest known Christian library (at Jerusalem).
c. AD 280 *Instructiones* by Commodianus (Christian poet).
c. AD 332 *Ecclesiastical History* by Eusebius.
c. AD 337–95 Constantinople Library expands from 6,900 to 100,000 volumes.
c. AD 350 Gothic Bible translation by Ulfilias.
c. AD 371 *Mosella* poem by Ausonius.
c. AD 390 *Roman History* by Ammianus Marcellinus.
c. AD 398 *Saturnalia* by Macrobius (prose compendium).
c. AD 400 *Psychomachia* by Prudentius (Christian epic poem).
c. AD 450 *Carmen paschale* by Sedulius (gospel poem).
c. AD 490 *De Laudibus Dei* by Dracontius of Carthage (Christian poem).
c. AD 529 Benedictine Monte Cassino has first western monastic library.
c. AD 535 *Diwan* by Al Kais (Arab poetry).
c. AD 550 *Hero and Leander* by Musaeus (epic poem).
c. AD 554 *History of the Wars* by Procopius.
c. AD 560 *Secret History* by Procopius.

Classical authors

5412

For 2,000 years the literature of Greece and Rome formed the bedrock of European culture. Latin was the international language of the educated throughout Christendom. Classical styles had considerable influence on later forms and surviving dramatic texts continue to be performed (see THEATRE for writers mainly known for their plays).

Apuleius active AD 155, North African Latin author of *The Golden Ass,* a bawdy picaresque satire told by a man turned into a donkey.
Aristotle 384–322 BC, Greek philosopher whose *Poetics* established many of the concepts of literary theory. He also wrote about political theory and natural history.
Catullus c. 87–54 BC, Roman lyric poet, noted for his short love poems.
Herodotus c. 484–420 BC, Greek historian of the wars with Persia. Known as the "father of history."
Hesiod 7th century BC, Greek poet. First to write didactic verse including an account of a farmer's life and *Theogony,* a genealogy of the gods.

continued

Classical authors continued

5412 **Homer** 8th century BC, Greek poet, reputedly blind though nothing certain is known about him. Credited with composing the *Iliad*, the story of the war between Greeks and Trojans, and the *Odyssey*, the adventures of Odysseus (Latin Ulysses) on his interrupted ten-year voyage home from that war.
Horace 65–8 BC, Sardonic and realistic Roman lyric poet and satirist. Works include *Ars Poetica* and *Satires*.
Juvenal c. AD 60–140, Roman satirical poet who denounced the vices of Imperial Rome.
Lao Tzu c. 570 BC, Chinese philosopher reputed to be the author of the *I Ching*, though this *Book of Changes* contains traditional knowledge dating back several centuries earlier.
Livy 59 BC – AD 17, Roman historian and important prose writer of Augustinian period.
Martial c. AD 43–120, Roman poet and epigrammatist; sharp and often obscene.
Ovid 43 BC – AD 17, Roman poet of witty, sensual, amorous verse. Wrote the long narrative *Metamorphoses* – recounting myths in which people change their form – which provided material for many Renaissance writers.
Petronius died AD 66 (ordered by Nero to commit suicide). Roman satirist, author of the salacious and picaresque *Satyricon*.
Pindar c. 520–440 BC, Greek lyric poet, who wrote odes celebrating victorious athletes.
Plato c. 427–347 BC, Greek philosopher, pupil of Socrates, whose teaching he records, and tutor of Aristotle. His works on love and government are often cast in the form of dialogues.
Plutarch c. AD 46–120, Greek philosopher and biographer, noted for his *Parallel Lives of distinguished Greeks and Romans* (much used as a source by Shakespeare).
Sappho born c. 650 BC, Greek poet whose passionate love songs placed her among the greatest lyric poets. Only short fragments of her work have survived.
Socrates c. 469–399 BC, Greek philosopher whose central theme was the quest for truth and who frequently answered a question with another question. No texts are extant and he is largely known through his pupil Plato.
St Augustine of Hippo AD 315–430, North African Christian convert who interpreted Christian doctrine in the light of Platonic philosophy. Works include *Confessions*, *City of God*.
Tacitus AD 56–117, Roman historian, a great prose stylist. His works include *Historiae*.
Theocritus c. 310–250 BC, Greek poet who established the pastoral form with the herdsman symbolizing the tensions between city and countryside, art and life. Shepherds and shepherdesses singing to each other in a world of peace. Works include *Idylls*.
Thucydides c. 470–404 BC, Greek historian of the Peloponnesian War.
Virgil 70–19 BC, Roman poet of pastoral poems and of the *Aeneid*, an epic following the Trojan hero Aeneas from the fall of Troy – via Carthage and his affair with Dido – to the founding of the Roman state.

542 MEDIEVAL LITERATURE 600–1500

While eminent churchmen produced tomes of philosophy and moral teaching, and monks recorded history in Latin, most storytellers of Europe used their vernacular tongues.

The bards of northern Europe sang tales of their own gods and epics of human heroes, such as the alliterative Icelandic *Eddas* and the Anglo-Saxon poem *Beowolf*, while in France and Spain the exploits of the knights of Charlemagne were told by minstrels in the *Song of Roland* and the story of The Cid.

The troubadours, the lyric poets of Provence, developed tales of courtly love which placed the woman on a pedestal, untouchable; while *Minnesingers* (love singers) flourished in Germany. Epic and romance on both sides of the English Channel were merged in tales of King Arthur and the knights of his Round Table.

Events

5421 **c. AD 632** *The Six Days (Hexameron)* by George the Pisidian (Byzantine poem).
c. AD 650 *Kadambari* by Bana (Sanskrit poetical novel), India.
c. AD 671 *Hymn to the Creator* by Caedmon (earliest English Christian poet).
AD 712 *Kojiki* compiled (first history of Japan).
c. AD 730 Anglo-Saxon heroic poem Beowulf written. The display (**1**) is of an 11th century manuscript.
AD 731–2 *Ecclesiastical History of the English People* by the Venerable Bede.
c. AD 737 Textbook of poetics by Sanskrit author Bandin, India.
c. AD 795 *Helena* by Cynewulf (Anglo-Saxon poem).
c. AD 814 *Wessobrunn* prayer written.
c. AD 831 *Life of Charlemagne (Vita Caroli Magni)* by Einhard.
c. AD 858 *Library (Biblotheca)* of lost books by Patriarch Photius of Constantinople.
AD 883 *Gesta Caroli* by Notker Balbulus (epic poem on Charlemagne).
AD 890 *Taketori Mongatari*, earliest Japanese narrative work.
c. AD 940 *Ecbasis captivi (The Flight of the Prisoner)* written.
c. AD 948 *Egill Skallagrimsson*, Icelandic autobiographical saga.
c. AD 961 *Eyvind Skaldaspillar* by Hakonarmal (Norwegian epic poem).
c. AD 1000 *Diary of a May-Fly* by Japanese poetess.
c. 1008 *Genji monogatari*, love novel by Japanese poetess.

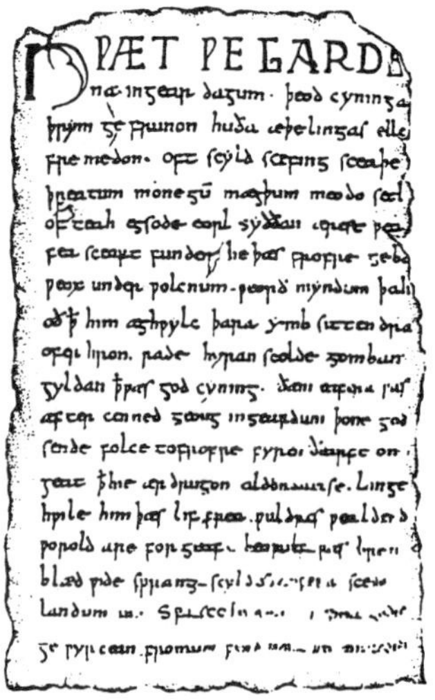

1

c. 1020 *Homiliae catholicae (Lives of Saints)* by Aelfric.
c. 1100 *Song of Roland* written in France (heroic poem).
c. 1130 *Le Bestiaire* by Philippe de Thaon.
c. 1136 *Historia calmitatum mearum* by Abelard (Heloise love story).
1168 *Artus* by Chrétien de Troyes (court romance).
1171 *Lancelot* by Chrétien de Troyes.
c. 1172 *Roman de Troie* (Troy novel) by Benoit de Sainte-More (Old French poem).
1176 First Welsh eisteddford held at Cardigan Castle.
1180 *Legend of the Holy Grail* by Chrétien de Troyes.
c. 1190 *Erek* by Hartman von Aue (Arthurian romance).
c. 1196 *Igor Song* written in Russia.
c. 1200 *Roman de Merlin (Merlin novel)* by Robert de Borron.
c. 1203 *Parzival* by Wolfram von Eschenbach (epic poem).
c. 1205 *Nibelungenlied* written in present shape.
c. 1210 *Tristan und Isolt* by Gottfried of Strasburg.
c. 1220 *Flore and Blancheflor* by Konrad Fleck.
c. 1225 *Edda* by Snorri Sturluson (Icelandic Norse mythology).
1226 *Cantico del Sole* by St Francis of Assisi. *Roman de la Rose* (story of courtly love) by Guillaume de Lorris.
1250 *Furor amoris* by Sister Hadewijch.
1257 *Fruit Garden*, by Saadi, Persian poems.
1267 *The Treasure Book* by Brunetto Latini.
c. 1270 *Cronica General* written in Spain.
1290 *La gran conquista de Ultramar* written in Spain. *The New Life* by Dante Alighieri.
1307–21 *The Divine Comedy* by Dante Alighieri.
1309 *History of St Louis* by Jean de Joinville.
1314 *The Novel of the Fauvel* by Gervais du Bus.
c. 1337 *The History of England* by Robert Mannying.
c. 1340 *Africa* by Francesco Petrarch (epic poem).
1343 *Fiametta* by Giovanni Boccaccio (elegiac

continued

Events continued

5421 **1350–60** *Der meide Kranz* by Heinrich von Mugeln.
1351 *Epistle to Posterity* by Petrarch (autobiography).
1353 *Decamerone* completed by Boccaccio.
1360 *Sir Gawain and the Green Knight* (Anon).
c. 1362 *Der Seuse* by Henrich Seuse.
1362–92 *Piers Plowman*, attributed to William Langland (Middle English poem).
1364 *Book of the True Poetry* by Guillaume de Machaut.
1366 *Canzoniere* by Petrarch.
c. 1370–1400 *Chronicles* by Jean Froissart.
1375 *The Bruce* by John Barbour (Scottish national epic poem, printed 1570).
1381 *Vox clamantis* by John Gower.
1383 *Bible Translation* by John Wycliffe.
1384 *The Parlement of Foules* by Geoffrey Chaucer.
c. 1385 *Troilus and Criseyde* by Chaucer.
1387 *L'histoire de Lusignan* by Jean d'Arras.
1387–1400 *Canterbury Tales* by Chaucer (23 tales).
c. 1390 *The Book of the Hundred Ballades* by Jean de Senechal.
c. 1391 Manuscript of the Innsbruck passion play.
c. 1392 *The Book of Troie* by Hans Mair.
1403 *Rimaldo del Palacio* by Pedro Lopez de Ayala (satirical poem). *Der Minnenlop* by Dirc Potter.
1421 *The Siege of Thebes* by John Lydgate.
1425 *Hermaphroditus* by Antonio Beccadelii.
1426 *La Belle Dame sans Merci* by Alain Chartier (poem).
c. 1430 *Corbacho* by Alfonso Marinez de Toledo.
1435 *Della pittura (On Painting)* by Leon Battista Alberti.
c. 1440 *Hymn to Liberty* by Thomas von Stangnas.
1444 *Alexander* by Johannes Hartlieb. *Euryalus and Lucretia* by Aeneas Silvio Piccolomini (Pope Pius II). *Elegantiarum* by Lorenzo Vall.
c. 1445 *Cancionero de Baena* by J A de Baena.
c.1450 *Robin Hood and the Monk* written. Vatican Library founded.
1456 *Le Petit Testament* by François Villon (poem).
1459 *Petit Jehan de Saintré* by Antoine de la Sale.
1461 *La Grand Testament* by Francois Villon.
c. 1469 *William Tell* legend written.
1470 *Morte D'Arthur* by Thomas Malory.
1472 *Orlando Innamorato* by Matteo Maria. Boiardo (romantic epic).
1476 *Copolas de Manrique* by Jorge Manrique (Spanish poetry). *Novellino* by Tommaso Masuccios (50 Neapolitan stories).
1480 *Stylpho* by Jakob Wimpfeling.
1481 *Morgante* by Luigi Pulci (chivalric epic poem).
1482–87 *Sylvae* by Angelo Poliziano (four lectures in verse).
1492 *La Carcel de Amor (The Prison of Love)* by Duego de San Pedro (early Spanish novel).
1498 *Reinke de Vos* by Heinrek van Alkamar.
1498–99 *The Bowge of Court*, by John Skelton (satirical poem).
1499 *La Celestina*, probably by Fernando de Rojas.

Medieval authors

5422 **Aelfric** c. AD 955–1020, English monk. Wrote lives of the saints in Old English.
Alfred the Great AD 849–99, King of Wessex who himself translated texts by Bede and others into Anglo-Saxon and supervised the production of the *Anglo-Saxon Chronicle*.
Boccaccio, Giovanni 1313–75, Italian poet known for his *Decameron*, 100 stories, often spicey, some based on the Arabic *Thousand and One Nights*, and presented as told by ten Florentines escaping plague, each telling a tale every ten days.
Caedmon 7th century Anglo-Saxon monk, the earliest English poet whose name is known. A single hymn survives in a manuscript of Bede.
Chaucer, Geoffrey c. 1343–1400 English poet (**1**), who introduced rhyming verse to English poetry. Best known for his *Canterbury Tales*, a story sequence told by well-characterized pilgrims traveling to the shrine of St Thomas.
Chrétien de Troyes active 1170–90, French poet of the Arthurian tales.

1

Dante, Alighieri 1265–1321, Italian poet (**2**), writing in Tuscan of lovepoems addressed to the idealized Beatrice, andthe *Divine Comedy*, describing a journeythrough Hell, purgatory and paradise written in *terza rima*.

2

Froissart, Jean c. 1337–1410, French poet and chronicler of his own time.
Geoffrey of Monmouth died 1155, English historian and teller of the tales of King Arthur (first recorded in Welsh poetry and in Latin histories by Welsh monks).
Gower, John c. 1330–1408, English poet, especially of love stories such as *Confessio Amantis (Lover's Confession)*, a set of exemplary tales related to the seven deadly sins.
Khayyam, Omar c. 1048–1122, Persian mathematician, astronomer, philosopher, and poet, best known in the west for the collection of his quatrains assembled and translated into English by Edward Fitzgerald as *The Rubaiyat*.
Langland, William c. 1330–86, English poet of *The Vision of Piers Plowman*, an allegory, in alliterative verse, of life in England as an ordinary farmer searches for a truly Christian life.
Lo Kuan-Chung active 14th century, Chinese novelist, supposed author of *The Romance of the Three Kingdoms*, on the exploits and stratagems of generals and statesmen of the 3rd century – a popular handbook of chivalry and strategy in later times.
Lorris, Guillaume de died 1237, French poet of the first part of *The Romance of the Rose*, a dream allegory of courtly love.
Mallory, Thomas c. 1408–71, English author of a prose collection of Arthurian romances known under the title of its last book, *Morte d'Arthur (The Death of Arthur)*. Printed by William Caxton it was a source for later Arthurian tales.
Meun, Jean de c. 1250–1305, French poet who wrote the second part of *The Romance of the Rose*.
Murasaki, Shikibu AD 978–1001, Japanese court lady, author of *The Tale of the Genji*; often considered the greatest masterpiece of Japanese prose and the first true novel, it unites the styles of earlier romance and traditional tales, setting a pattern for later court story-telling.
Petrarch, Francesco 1304–74, Italian poet (**3**) known for his sonnets to an idealized love.

3

St Bede (the Venerable) c. AD 673–735, English monk, author (in Latin) of the *Ecclesiastical History of the English People*.
Tu Fu AD 712–70, Chinese poet, greatest of the Tang period; his concise and evocative verse, originally nature-based, increasingly reflected his humanism and critical view of authority.
Villon, François c. 1431–63, French poet and balladeer, his impassioned verse often skillfully combines exalted ideas with the commonplace.

543 RENAISSANCE LITERATURE 1500–1700

The development of the printing press made much wider dissemination of books possible. The reawakening of interest in classical culture and learning, with its modification of the medieval world picture, saw both a continuation of the tradition of courtly and platonic love, and eroticism following the models of Ovid and Catullus. But, despite the influence of classical concepts, most western poetry was still deeply Christian. Although learned books might still be written in Latin, most writers used their native tongue. Among prose works in English, the translation of the Bible by a team of scholars ordered by James I ranks among the finest, while in Spain Cervantes' *Don Quixote*, though echoing the chivalric romance, is often regarded as the first true novel.

The development of theater during the Renaissance brought a flowering of drama in Spain and Elizabethan England and an attempt to imitate classical forms, especially in 17th century France. For dramatists see THEATER.

Events

5431**1**

1502 *Quattuor libri amorum* by Konrad Celtis.
1503 *The Thrissill and the Rois* by William Dunbar (Scottish poetic allegory).
1504 *L'Arcadia* by Jacopo Sannazzaro (pastoral romance).
1508 *Amadis de Guala* by Garci Rodriguez de Montalvo (narrative chivalry). *Lament for Makaris* by William Dunbar (poem).
1514 *Herodian* by Eobanus Hessus (poems).
1515 *Till Eulenspiegel (Master Tyll Owlglass)* published at Strasbourg.
1516 *Orlando Furioso* by Ludovico Ariosto (romantic epic). *Utopia* by Sir Thomas More. *Cancioneiro Geral* by Garcia de Resende (anthology of Iberian poems).
1517 *Liber Macaronices* by Teofilo Folengo (satirical poem on romantic epics).
1520 Francis I founds Royal Library of France.
1521 Bible translation begun by Martin Luther.
1522 *De partu Virginis* by Sannazzaro (religious poem).
1523 *A Goodly Garland* or *Chapelet of Laurell* by John Skelton (poem).
1525 *Prose della volgar lingua* by Pietro Bembo (earliest popular Italian writing).
1527 *De arte poetica* by Marco Girolamo Vida. *Cortegiano (The Courtier)* by Baldassare Castiglione (guide to manners).
1528 *Arminius* by Ulrich von Hutten (romantic dialogue).
1529 *El Relos de principes* by Antonio de Guevara (Spanish guide for princes).
1531 *Adolescence Clementine* by Clement Marot (poems).
1534 *Gargantua* by François Rabelais (satirical novel).
1538 *De anima et vita* by Juan Luis Vives (psychology).
1543 *History of Richard III* by Sir Thomas More.
1544 *Il Canzoniere* by Matteo Bandello (lyric poetry). *Délie Objet de Plus Haute Vertu* by Maurice Sceve (poem).
1545 *Toxophilus* by Roger Ascham (treatise on archery).
1547 *L'Italia Liberata da' Goti* by Giovanni Giorgio Trissino (epic poem).
1548 *Esopus* by Burkhard Waldis (German revision of Aesop's *Fables*).
1549 *L'Olive* by Joachim Du Bellay (first French sonnet sequence).
1551 *Amours de Cassandre* volume 1 by Pierre de Ronsard (poem).
1553 *The Palyse of Honor* by Gavin Douglas (allegorical poem). *Les Folastries* by Pierre de Ronsard (poem).
1554 *Le Novelle* by Matteo Bandello (214 short stories).

1

1555 *Arthur of Lytell Brytayne* by John Bourchier, Lord Berners.
1557 *Tottel's Miscellany* (songs and sonnets), compiled by Richard Tottel and Nicholas Grimald. *Der Goldfaden* by Jorg Wickram (first German romance novel).
1558 *Heptamaron* by Margaret of Navarre (novel). *Les Antiquités de Rome* and *Les Regrets* by Joachim du Bellay (sonnet sequences).
1559 *La Diana* by Jorge de Montemayor (Spanish pastoral romance).
1560 *Ching P'Ing Mei* by Hsü Wei (first classic Chinese novel). *Les Discours* by Pierrede Ronsard (poems on wars of religion).
1561 *A Marvellous Hystory* intitled *Beware of the Cat* by William Baldwin (early fiction).
1562 *Rinaldo* by Torquato Tasso (epic poem).
1565 *Ecatommiti* by Giambattista Cinzio Giraldi (moral and love stories).
1567 *Epitaphs, Epigrams, Songs, and Sonnets* by George Turberville.
1568 *Works*...newly collected by John Skelton.
1569 *La Araucana* by Alonso de Ercilla y Zuñiga (Spanish epic on Chile's conquest).
1572 *Os Lusiados* by Luis Vaz de Camoens (Portugal's national epic poem). *La Franciade* by Pierre de Ronsard (unfinished epic poem on French kings).
1573 *Aminta* by Torquato Tasso (pastoral poem). *Der Flöhatz* by Johann Fischart (satire on women).
1576 *A Voyage by River from Zurich to Strasbourg* by Johann Fischart (satire).
1577 *History of Travel in East and West Indies* by Richard Eden. *Chronicles of England, Scotland, and Ireland* (two volumes) by Raphael Holinshed.
1578 *Euphues, the Anatomy of Wit* by John Lyly. *Sonnets pour Hélène* by Pierre de Ronsard.
1579 *The Shepheard's Calendar* by Edmund Spenser (12 eclogues), from which a scene is shown here (**1**).
1580 *Threny* by Jan Kochanowski (Polish laments).
1580 & 1588 *Essais* by Michel de Montaigne (3 volumes).
1581 *Gerusalemme Liberata* by Torquato Tasso, published in Ferrara.
1583 *Pegasides Pleyn Amorosity* (*The Palace of the Maidens*) by Baptisa Honwaerd (Dutch poem).
1585 *Galatea* by Miguel de Cervantes (pastoral romance).
1586 *Discourse of English Poetrie* by William Webbe.
1588 *Pandosto of Dorastus and Fawina* and *Perimedes the Blacksmith* by Robert Greene (romances).
1590 *The Countess of Pembroke's Arcadia* by Sir Philip Sidney. *Polythmnia* by George Peele (verses for tournament).
1590–6 *The Faerie Queene* by Edmund Spencer.
1591 *Astrophel and Stella* by Philip Sidney.
1592 *Diana* by Henry Constable (sonnet sequence). *A Quip for an Upstart Courtier* by Robert Greene (pamphlet). *Pierce Penniless, his Supplication to the Devil* by Thomas Nashe (prose satire).
1594 *The Unfortunate Traveler* by Thomas Nashe (early pictaresque novel).
1595 *Amoretti* by Edmund Spencer. *St Peter's Complaint* by Robert Southwell (Catholic poem)
1598 Bodleian Library founded at Oxford. *Hero and Leander* by Christopher Marlowe and George Chapman (poem).
1599 *Guzman de Alfarche* by Mateo Aleman.
1602–14 *La Lira* by Giambattista Marino (poetry).

continued

Events continued

5431 **1603** *The Sharper's Life* by Francisco Gomez de Quevedo (picaresque novel).
1605 *Don Quixote* part 1, by Miguel de Cervantes (picaresque novel; part 2, 1615) of which a scene is shown here (**2**). *Poems Lyric and Pastoral* by Michael Drayton.

2

1607 *Astrée* part 1, by Honoré d'Urfé (pastoral romance).
1609 *Sonnets* by William Shakespeare (original quarto).
1610 Academy of Poetry founded at Padua. *The Muses Garden of Delights* by Robert Jones. *The Civil Wars of Granada* by Perez de Hita (Spanish novel).
1611 *Crudities* by Thomas Coryate (travel stories).
1612 *Polyolbion* part 1, by Michael Drayton (verse description of England; part 2, 1622).
1613–14 *Soledades* by Don Luis de Gongora (lyric poems).
1616 *Les tragiques* by Abbé d'Aubigné (verse satire).
1617 James I makes Ben Johnson first English poet laureate.
1619 *Oden and Gesange* by Georg Rudolf Weckherlin (poems).
1621 *Argenis* by John Barclay (allegorical political novel).
1622 *Histoire Comique de Francion* by Charles Sorel (French burlesque novel). *Secchia Rapita (The Rape of the Bucket)* by Alessandro Tassoni (mock-heroic poem).
1623 *Flowres of Sion* by William Drummond (Scottish religious poems). "Polish Horace" Maciej Sarbiewski crowned poet laureate by Pope at Rome. *Adone* by Giambattista Marino (45,000-line poem).
1624 *On German Poetry* by Martin Opitz.
1625 *Essays: Counsels Civil and Moral* by Sir Francis Bacon (final edition of 58 essays).
1626 George Sandys translates Ovid's *Metamorphosis* in America.
1627 *Nimphidia* by Michael Drayton (and other poems). *Dafne* by Martin Opitz. *Los Suenos* by Francisco Gomez de Quevedo (burlesques of hell, judgment day, and the world). *Osman* by Ivan Gundulic (Croat epic).
1630 *Hexaemeron* by Andres Arrabo (religious poem) initiates modern Danish literature. *Oeuvres poétiques* by François Malherbe.
1633 *The Temple* or *Sacred Poems* by George Herbert. *Poems* by John Donne (posthumous).
1635 *La Vida es sueno (Life is a Dream)* by Pedro Calderon de la Barca.
1637 *The Gentle Craft* by Thomas Deloney (in praise of shoemakers). *Lycidas* by John Milton.
1640 *Poems* by Thomas Carew.
1641 John Evelyn begins his *Diary*. *El Diabolo cojuelo* by Luis Vélez de Guevara (picaresque novel).
1642 *Cooper's Hill* by Sir John Denham (first pastoral poem in English). *Brieven der Heiligh Maeghden* by Joost van den Vondel (early Dutch fiction). *Teutsche Poemata* by Paul Fleming.
1643 *Davideis* by Abraham Cowley.
1644 German poetry society, *Pegnitzischer Blumenorden*, founded at Nuremberg.
1645 *L'Allegro; Il Penseroso; Sonnets* by John Milton. *Rotokritos* by Vitzentzos Kornaros (Cretan epic poem). *Die adriatische Rosemund* by Philip von Zesen (autobiographical novel). *Poems* by Edmund Waller.
1646 *Poems* by James Shirley. *Poems* by Henry Vaughan.
1647 *Philosophical Poems* by Henry More.
1648 *Le grand Cyrus* begun by Madeleine de Scudéry (ten volumes of romances).
1649 *Trutznachtigall* by Friedrich von Langlenfield (posthumous lyrical religious poems).
1650 *Manual of Dutch Poetry* by Joost den Vondel.
1651 *Poems* by John Cleveland.
1652 *Veer Schertz-Gedichte* by Johann Lauremberg (comic poems in Low German).
1653 Chetham's Library, Manchester, founded.
1654 *Epigrams* by Friedrich von Logau.
1654–60 *Clélie: Histoire Romaine* by Madeleine de Scudéry (10 volumes).
1656 *La Pucelle* by Jean Chapelain (12 cantos). *Poems* by Abraham Cowley.
1657 *Histoire Comique des États et Empires de la Lune* by Cyrano de Bergerac.
1658 *Hercules* by George Stiernheilm (Swedish epic poem).
1660 *Astraea Redux* by John Dryden (poem). Samuel Pepys begins his *Diary*.
1661–70 *Pharamond* by Gauthier de Costes de La Calprenede (12 volumes).
1662 *Poor Robin's Almanac* started.
1663 *Helden Briefe* by von Hofmann von Hofmannswaldau.
1665 First literary periodical, *Journal des Savants*, Paris. *The Life of Richard Hooker* by Izaak Walton. *The English Rogue* by Richard Head (picaresque novel).
1665–74 *Contes et Nouvelles en verse* by Jean de la Fontaine (part satirical poem).
1666–7 *Annus Mirabilis* by John Dryden (poem).
1667–74 *Paradise Lost* by John Milton (epic poem).
1668 First Italian magazine, *Giornale de Letterati*. *Oroonoko* by Mrs Aphra Behn (novel).
1668–93 *Fables choisies mises en vers* by La Fontaine (3 volumes).
1669 *Simplicius Simplicissimus (Description of the Life of a Strange Vagabond)* by Hans Jakob Christoph von Grimmelshausen.
1670 John Dryden made English poet laureate and historiographer royal.
1671 *Paradise Regained* and *Samson Agonistes* by John Milton (epic poems).
1672 Oxford Clarendon Press founded.
1673 *Poems Upon Various Occasions* by John Milton.
1674 *L'Art Poétique* by Nicholas Boileau-Despréaux. *Il Pentamerone* by Giambattista Basile (stories). Japanese haiku poetry by Matsuo Munefusa.
1678 *La Princesse de Clèves* by Marie-Madeleine, Comtesse de La Fayette (novel).
1679 *Liao Chai P'u-Sungling* (Chinese short stories).
1681 *Miscellaneous Poems* by Andrew Marvell (posthumous).
1681–2 *Absalom and Achitophel* by John Dryden (two-part satirical poem).
1682 *Poezy of Verscheide gedichten* by Joost van den Vondel (posthumous).
1684 *Letters Written by a Turkish Spy* by Giovanni Paolo Marana (early spy story). *History of the Buccaneers of America* by Dutchman Alexander Olivier Esquemeling. Dutch literary review, *Nouvelles de la République des Lettres.*
1685 *Divine Poems* by Edmund Waller.
1687 *The Hind and the Panther* by John Dryden. *Lives of the English Poets* by William Winstanley.
1689 *Die asiatische Banise* by Anselm von Ziegler (baroque novel).
1692 *Incognita* by William Congreve (novel).
1695 *Den Vermakelijkten Avonturier* by Nicolaas Heinsius (picaresque novel).
1696 *Schelmuffsky* by Christian Reuter (comic novel).
1697 *Contes de ma mere l'Oye* by Charles Perrault (fairy tale).
1699 *Télémaque* by François de Salignac de la Mothe-Fénelon (satire).

Renaissance authors

5432 **Ariosto, Ludovico** 1474–1533, Italian poet of the epic romance *Orlando Furioso.*
Bacon, Francis 1561–1626, English statesman, philosopher, and essayist.
Basho, Matsuo 1644–94, Japanese poet – whose verse echos the tranquility he found in nature – developed the *haiku* into a distinct poetic form. He is also remembered for his travel book *The Narrow Road to the Deep North.*
Bellay, Joachim du 1525–60, French poet influenced by neoplatonism.
Bunyan, John 1628–88, English puritan, author of *The Pilgrim's Progress,* a moral allegory following the medieval quest form, in which the pilgrim Christian (**1**) passes through a variety of tests in search of the Celestial City.

1

Buonarotti, Michelangelo 1475–1564, Famous as a painter and sculptor, he also wrote accomplished sonnets.
Burton, Robert 1577–1640, English clergyman and fine prose stylist whose *Anatomy of Melancholy* – a treatise on "the disorder of philosophers" – ranges from ribald stories to science and theology.
Camoens, Luis de 1524–80, Portuguese poet of a pseudo-classical epic *The Lusiads,* based on Vasco da Gama's voyages of discovery.
Cervantes, Miguel de 1547–1616, Spanish poet, dramatist and author (**2**) of *Don Quixote de la Mancha* and other tales.

2

Descartes, René 1596–1650, French philosopher whose theory of knowledge, Cartesianism, underlies modern science and philosophy.
Donne, John 1572–1631, English divine and poet (**3**), foremost of a group – which included George Herbert, 1593–1633, and Richard Crashaw, 1612–95 – later dubbed "Metaphysical" for their use of abstract ideas and paradoxes to express feelings. His impassioned love poems contrast with the questioning and spirituality of his religious verse.

3

Erasmus, Desiderius c. 1466–1536, Dutch humanist and leading scholar whose books and tracts spread Renaissance ideas through northern Europe.
Herrick, Robert 1591–1674, English priest and poet of sacred and delicately sensual secular verse.
Hobbes, Thomas 1588–1679, English philosopher and political theorist. His *Leviathan* concludes that people need strong leadership and that outside the "civilized" world life is "brutish and short."
Locke, John 1632–1704, English philosopher whose *Two Treatises on Government* sanctioned the right to revolt, while his *Essay concerning Human Understanding* argued that all ideas are derived from experience.
Machiavelli, Niccolo 1469–1527, Italian political theorist best known for *The Prince,* a treatise on the devious art of government. Other works include the licentious comedy *The Mandrake.*
Marvell, Andrew 1621–78, English poet and parliamentarian who wrote verse and prose satires (often attacking vice and corruption) and lyrical poems strong in metaphysical symbolism.
Milton, John 1608–74, English poet (**4**)

4

steeped in the humanist tradition. His *Paradise Lost,* the story of Satan's rebellion against God and of the fall of man, is perhaps the last great poem in epic style, and sonnets such as *On His Blindness* are among the finest. Among his political tracts *Areopagitica* remains the definitive attack on censorship in defense of freedom of speech.
Montaigne, Michel Eyquem de 1553–92, French writer mainly responsible for establishing the essay form.
More, Thomas 1478–1535, English statesman and humanist (**5**), author of *Utopia,* a fantasy of an idealized state. Executed for his opposition to Henry VIII's supremacy over the English church. He was canonized by the Catholic Church in 1935.

5

Newton, Isaac 1642–1727, English scientist, mathematician, and philosopher. Best known for his laws of gravity and motion, his *Principia Mathematica* and *Opticks* were his most influential works.
Pepys, Samuel 1633–1703, English admiralty official and diarist. His diary, giving a lively picture of his time, was written in code and not published until 1825.
Rabelais, François c. 1460–1553, French doctor and satirist known for his rambling, bawdy, prose fantasies *Gargantua* and *Pantagruel.*
Ronsard, Pierre de 1525–85, French poet, one of a group, known as the *Pleiade,* associated with Catholicism.
Shakespeare, William 1564–1616, English poet, actor, and dramatist whose sonnets and poems would have earned his place in literature even without his many plays. (See Theater).
Sidney, Philip 1554–86, English poet, diplomat and soldier, an all-round "Renaissance man" remembered for his pastoral *Arcadia,* his sonnets, and *A Defence of Poetry* which championed English as a language for poetry.
Spenser, Edmund 1552–99, English poet celebrated for his allegorical romance *The Faerie Queene* and eclogue collection *The Shepheard's Calendar.*

544 18TH CENTURY LITERATURE

The 17th century writers were greatly influenced by classical models, especially French dramatists, and this continued in the 18th century with poets such as Alexander Pope. At the same time more realistic story telling was developing into the novel form, framed as sequences or exchanges of letters in Richardson, Laclos, and Burney.

In France a school of practical philosophy was led by Voltaire and Diderot, while Rousseau pleaded for naturalism of feeling and freedom from constraint. This was followed by the *Sturm und Drang* (Storm and Stress) movement in Germany and the development of a romanticism which can also find its roots in Rousseau. In England, romanticism – more apparent in verse than in the novel – also took the genre of macabre and fantastic tales.

Events

5441

1

1700 *Carmen Saeculare* by Matthew Pryor. *Advice to a Daughter of a Trimmer* by 1st Marquess of Halifax.
1701 *The True-Born Englishman* by Daniel Defoe (satire).
1702 *The Art of English Poetry* by Edward Busshe.
1704 *Miscellany Poems* by William Wycherley. *The Tale of a Tub* and *The Battle of the Books* by Jonathan Swift (satires).
1706 *The Apparition of One Mrs Veal* by Daniel Defoe.
1707 *The Devil Upon Two Sticks* by Alain-René Lesage.
1709 *Pastorals* by Alexander Pope.
1710 *The Whig Examiner* literary magazine started by Joseph Addison. *Collected Works* by William Congreve (three volumes).
1711 *The Spectator* magazine started by Joseph Addison and Richard Steele. *Essay on Criticism* by Alexander Pope. *The Conduct of the Allies* by Jonathan Swift (political satire).
1712 *The History of John Bull* by John Arbuthnot. *The Rape of the Lock* by Alexander Pope (mock-heroic poem); a scene is shown here (**1**).
1713 Scriblerus Club formed in London by Swift, Pope, Congreve et al.
1714 *The Shepherd's Week* by John Gay (satirical eclogues).
1716 *Fénix Renascida*, ed Matias Pereira de Silva (Portuguese poetry anthology). *Ori-Taku-Shiba* by Hakuseki (autobiography).
1719 *Robinson Crusoe* by Daniel Defoe. *Pedar Paars* by Baron Ludvig Holberg (Danish comic heroic poem).
1720 *Memoirs of a Cavalier* by Daniel Defoe. *Collected Poems* by John Gay. First newspaper serialization of fiction, England.
1721 *Collected Works* by Joseph Addison. *Lettres Persanes* by Montesquieu (novel in the form of correspondence).
1722 *A Journal of the Plague Year* and *Moll Flanders* by Daniel Defoe.
1723 *La Henriade* by François-Marie Voltaire (history).
1724 *Roxana, The Fortunate Mistress* by Daniel Defoe. Longman founded, England's oldest non-university publisher.
1725 Alexander Pope's translation of *The Odyssey*.
1726 *Gulliver's Travels* by Jonathan Swift.
1727 *Poems on Various Occasions* by William Shenstone.
1728 *The Dunciad* by Alexander Pope (lampoon). *Poems* by Allan Ramsay.
1729 *The Alps* by Albrecht von Haller (Swiss pastoral poem).
1730 *The Season* by James Thomson (collected edition).
1732 *The London Magazine* founded.
1732–57 *Poor Richard's Almanack* by Benjamin Franklin.
1733 *Essay on Man* by Alexander Pope. *English Letters* by François-Marie Voltaire. *Manon Lescaut* by Antoine François Prévost (novel).
1734 *The Lives and Adventures of the Most Famous Highwaymen* by Charles Johnson.
1738 *London* by Samuel Johnson (epic poem after Juvenal).
1739 *Verses on the Death of Dr Swift* (satire).
1740 *Pamela; or Virtue rewarded* by Samuel Richardson.
1741 *Familiar Letters* by Samuel Richardson.
1742 *Persian Eclogues* by William Collins. *Joseph Andrews* by Henry Fielding.
1743 *The Grave* by Robert Blair (poem, later illustrated by William Blake).
1744 *Life of Mr Richard Savage* by Samuel Johnson. *The Little Pretty Pocket-Book* by John Newbury (children's book).
1745 *Directions to Servants in General* by Jonathan Swift (satire).
1746 *Tales and Fables* by Christian Fürchtegott Gellert.
1747 *Ode on Eton College* by Thomas Gray.
1748 *Clarissa* by Samuel Richardson (novel). *The Adventures of Roderick Random* by Tobias Smollet.
1749 *The History of Tom Jones, A Foundling* by Henry Fielding. *Der Frühling (The Spring)* by Ewald von Kleist (poem).
1750 *The Memoirs of a Woman of Pleasure* by John Cleland. *Poems of Several Occasions* and *Works* by James Thomson.
1751 *An Elegy Written in a Country Church Yard* by Thomas Gray. *The Adventures of Peregrine Pickle* by Tobias Smollett.
1752 *The Female Quixote* by Charlotte Lennox.
1753 *Sir Charles Grandison* by Samuel Richardson.
1753–4 *Ferdinand Count Fathom* by Tobias Smollett (prototype horror story).
1754 *Collected Works* by Henry St John, Viscount Bolingbroke (posthumous).
1756 *Idyls and Unkel und Yariko* by Solomon Gessner. *Désastre de Lisbonne* by François-Marie Voltaire.
1757 *The Fleece* by John Dyer (poem).
1758–60 *The Idler* by Samuel Johnson (weekly periodical).
1759 *Rasselas* by Samuel Johnson (moral tale). *Candide* by François-Marie Voltaire (philosophical novel).
1760 *Fragments of Ancient Poetry* by "Ossian" alias James Macpherson (famous fraud).
1760–7 *Tristram Shandy* by Laurence Sterne.
1761–5 *The New Heloise* by Jean-Jacques Rousseau.
1762 *Emile, ou traité de l'Education* by Jean-Jacques Rousseau.
1763 *Il Mattino* by Giuseppi Parini (poem).
1764 Literary Club, London, founded (by Johnson, Goldsmith, Gibbon et al.
1765 *The Castle of Otranto* by Horace Goldsmith (early medieval horror or Gothic novel). *The Vicar of Wakefield* by Oliver Goldsmith (novel).
1766 *The Story of Agathon* by Christoph Martin Wienland (German psychological poem).
1768 *A Sentimental Journey* by Thomas Sterne.
1770 *The Deserted Village* by Oliver Goldsmith (poem).
1771 *Odes* by Friedrich Klopstock.
1772 *Gottinger Haribund* of young patriotic German poets formed.
1774 *Sorrows of Werther* by Johann Wolfgang von Goethe. *Letters to His Son* by Lord Chesterfield (gentleman's manners).
1775 *A Journey to the Western Islands of Scotland* by Samuel Johnson.
1776–88 *Decline and Fall of the Roman Empire* by Edward Gibbon.
1778 *Evelina* by Fanny Burney (novel).
1779–81 *Lives of the Poets* by Samuel Johnson.
1780 *On German Literature* by Frederick the Great.
1781 *Confessions* by Jean-Jacques Rousseau (autobiography).
1782 *Poems* by William Cowper. *Les Liaisons Dangereuses* by Pierre de Laclos (novel).
1782–3 *The Spirit of Hebrew Poetry* by Johann von Herder.
1783 *Poetical Sketches* by William Blake, of which an illustration is seen here (**2**).

2

1785 *The Task* and *John Gilpin* by William Cowper.
1786 *An Arabian Tale* by William Beckford. *Poems chiefly in the Scottish Dialect* by Robert Burns. *Volksmärchen der Deutschen* by Johann Masäus (fairy tales published since 1782).
1788 *Paul et Virginie* by J H B de Saint-Pierre. *Songs of Innocence* by William Blake.
1790 *Anton Reiser* by Karl Moritz (four-volume autobiographical novel completed). Royal Literary Fund founded by David Williams.
1791 *Life of Johnson* by James Boswell. *Justine* by Marquis de Sade.
1792 *The Pleasures of Memory* by Samuel Rogers.
1793 *Poor Lisa* and *Natalia* by N M Karamzin (Russian short stories).
1794 *The Mysteries of Udolpho* by Anne Radcliffe.

continued

Events continued

5441 **1795** *Wilhelm Meister* by Johann Wolfgang von Goethe. *Letters Concerning the Aesthetic Education of Mankind* by Friedrich Schiller.
1797–9 *Hyperion* by Friedrich Hölderlin (romantic novel in letters).
1798 *Lyrical Ballads* by Samuel Taylor Coleridge and William Wordsworth.
1799 *The Pleasures of Hope* by Thomas Campbell (didactic poem).

18th century authors

5442 **Blake, William** 1757–1827, English poet and artist whose anti-materialist poems (**1**), *Songs of Innocence,* were charged with personal experience illustrated with his own hand-colored drawings.

1

Boswell, James 1740–95, Scottish lawyer and writer known mainly for his *Life of Samuel Johnson* whom he often accompanied.
Burney, Fanny 1752–1840, English author of *Evelina* (written in letter form) and other novels.
Burns, Robert 1759–96, Scottish poet (**2**), initially a farm laborer but the success of his verse, the best of which is written in Scottish dialect, gained him a place in fashionable society.

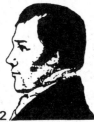

Cao Xueqin died 1763, Chinese novelist, author of the great novel of manners of Chinese literature *The Story of the Red Chamber* (also known as *The Story of the Stone*) which mixes humor, poetry, and an affirmation of Buddhist belief as it recounts the changing fortunes of one family.
Cleland, John 1709–89, English novelist and hack journalist known for his scabrous *Memoirs of a Woman of Pleasure,* better known as *Fanny Hill.*
Defoe, Daniel 1660–1731, English pamphleteer and novelist, a clever propagandist for whoever employed him. Author of *The Journal of the Plague Year* and the novels *Moll Flanders* and *Robinson Crusoe.*
Diderot, Denis 1713–84, French philosopher and novelist best known for his *Encyclopedia.*
Fielding, Henry 1707–54, English novelist and dramatist whose stage satires led to stricter state censorship. His innovative novels include *Joseph Andrews* (with hero rather than heroine the seat of virtue), *Jonathan Wilde* (presenting the criminal world as an allegory of contemporay political life), and the uproarious *Tom Jones.*
Franklin, Benjamin 1706–90, American statesman, scientist and author of philosophical satires and an autobiography. He helped draft the *Declaration of Independence.*
Gibbon, Edward 1737–94, English historian known for his massive *History of the Decline and Fall of the Roman Empire.*
Goethe, Johann Wolfgang von 1749–1832, German writer and poet (**3**) influential in many spheres including science, politics, and especially theater. His short epistolary novel *The Sorrows of Young Werther,* a story of unrequited passion ending in suicide, helped set the style of *Sturm und Drang,* while *Wilhelm Meister* shows a hero accepting his place in society
Goldsmith, Oliver 1730–74, Irish poet, dramatist, and reviewer whose *Vicar of Wakefield* was one of the most popular novels of its time.
Gray, Thomas 1716–71, English poet known for his *Elegy Written in a Country Churchyard.*
Johnson, Samuel 1709–84, Dr Johnson was a critic, essayist, poet, editor of Shakespeare, and novelist (**4**), but was best known as lexicographer for his *Dictionary of the English Language.*

4

Laclos, Choderlos de 1741–1803, French author of *Dangerous Liasons,* both a satire on aristocratic corruption and an investigation of sexual psychology.
Lennox, Charlotte 1720–1804, American-born English novelist and dramatist best known for *The Female Quixote* modeled on Cervantes.
Paine, Thomas 1737–1809, English-born American political theorist and pamphleteer, best known for his *Rights of Man* and his attack on Christian revelation *The Age of Reason.*
Pope, Alexander 1688–1744, English poet and accomplished satirist, translator of Homer and in his *Essay on Criticism* the arbiter of neoclassical style.
Radcliffe, Anne 1764–1823, English writer of popular gothic novels, the most successful being *The Mysteries of Udolpho.*
Richardson, Samuel 1689–1761, English novelist whose morally ambiguous *Pamela* and *Clarissa* reveal new levels of emotional and psychological characterization.
Rousseau, Jean-Jacques 1712–78, French philosopher, author of rather didactic novels, of *The Social Contract* which famously began "Man is born free, and is everywhere in chains," and of an autobiography which set a fashion for frank confession.
Sade, Marquis de 1740–1814, French soldier and writer (**5**) of several novels whose dominant theme is the urge to derive pleasure from inflicting pain (hence the term "sadism").
Schiller, Friedrich 1759–1805, see THEATER
Sterne, Laurence 1713–68, Irish-born preacher and author of the idiosyncratic novels *Tristram Shandy* and *Sentimental Journey*
St Pierre, Bernardin de 1737–1814, French author of *Paul et Virginie,* a tale of innocent children maturing on an idyllic island, which gave a foretaste of romanticism.
Swift, Jonathan 1667–1745, Anglo-Irish churchman, poet, and satirist whose masterpiece, *Gulliver's Travels,* is mainly known in bowdlerized juvenile versions restricted to its Lilliput episode, which does not reflect its quality.
Voltaire François, Marie Arouet 1694–1778, French philosopher, dramatist, and scientist (**6**) who preached humanity, truth and moderation, though *Candide,* the novel for which he is now best known, pessimistically rejects excessive trust and idealism.

6

Walpole, Horace 1717–97, English author, patron of neo-gothic architecture and author of the first major gothic novel, *The Castle of Otranto.*

545 19TH CENTURY LITERATURE

The romantic tradition continued into the next century, especially in English verse.
Wordsworth and Coleridge, whose joint collection *Lyrical Ballads* was published in 1798, were followed by Byron, Shelley, Keats, Wordsworth, and Browning, and by novelists Austen and the Brontë sisters. English fiction had already aimed to produce a picture of real life, as reflected in Dickens's sense of social concern, and this concept of realism in literature evolved internationally in France through Balzac and other French writers, in Russia and in Germany.
This in turn led on to the naturalism which Zola espoused, characterized by close observation and documentation of everyday life, with an emphasis on individual behavior, and often motivated by a wish to reform society.

Events

5451 **1800** *The Farmer's Boy* by Robert Bloomfield (poetry illustrated by Bewick woodcuts). *Hymn to the Night* by Novalis, alias Friedrich von Hardenberg (prose lyrics).
1801 *Atala* by René de Chateaubriand (novel).
1802 *Minstrels of the Scottish Border* by Walter Scott. Literary journal the *Edinburgh Review* founded.
1803 *Thaddeus of Warsaw* by Jane Porter (historical novel).
1804 *Flegeljahre* by Jean Paul Richter (novel).
1806 *Rhymes for the Nursery* by Jane and Ann Taylor.
1807 *Hours of Idleness* by Lord Byron. *Corinne* by Madame de Stael. *Ode on Imitations of Immorality* by William Wordsworth.
1808 *Marmion* by Walter Scott (epic poem).
1809 *Elective Affinities* by Johann Wolfgang von Goethe (novel). *Knickerbocker's History of New York* by Washington Irving.
1810 *The Lady of the Lake* by Walter Scott.
1811 *Sense and Sensibility* by Jane Austen. *Udine* by Friedrich Fouqué.
1812 *Fairy Tales* by Jacob and Wilhelm Grimm.
1812–18 *Childe Harold's Pilgrimage* by Lord Byron
1813 *Pride and Prejudice* by Jane Austen. *Queen Mab* by Percy Bysshe Shelley (anti-religious poem).
1814 *Waverly* by Walter Scott (historical novel). *The Corsair* by Lord Byron.
1815 *Die Elixiere des Teufels (The Devil's Elixir)* by Earnest Hoffmann (novel).
1816 *Emma* by Jane Austen. *Kubla Khan* by Samuel Taylor Coleridge (written 1797).
1817 *Manfred* by Lord Byron.
1818–23 *Don Juan* by John Keats. *Frankenstein* by Mary Shelley.
1819 *Odes* by Victor Hugo.
1820 *Ivanhoe* by Walter Scott (historical novel). *Prometheus Unbound* by Percy Bysshe Shelley.
1821 *Poems* by Heinrich Heine.
1822 *Poemes* by Alfred de Vigny.
1824 *Canzoni e Versi* by Giacomo Leopardi.
1825 *Boris Gudunov* by Aleksander Pushkin (published 1831).
1826 *The Last of the Mohicans* by James Fenimore Cooper.
1828 *The Three Musketeers* by Alexander Dumas Sr.
1829–48 *Les Chouans* and *La Comédie Humaine* by Honoré de Balzac.
1830 *Le Rouge et Noir* by Stendhal.
1831 *Notre-Dame de Paris* by Victor Hugo. *Crochet Castle* by Thomas Love Peacock (satirical novel).
1832 Book jackets first introduced by British publishers.
1834 *The Last Days of Pompeii* by Edward Bulwer-Lytton.
1835–72 *Fairy Tales* by Hans Christian Andersen (first four of 168).
1836 *Nature* by Ralph Waldo Emerson. *Mr Midshipman Easy* by Frederick Marryat.
1838 *Oliver Twist* by Charles Dickens.
1839 *The Charterhouse of Parma* by Stendhal.
1840 *Tales of the Grotesque and Arabesque* by Edgar Allen Poe.
1842 *Dead Souls* by Nikolai Gogol. *Ballads and Other Poems* by Henry Wadsworth Longfellow.
1843 William Wordsworth made poet laureate on Southey's death.
1844 *The Count of Monte Christo* by Alexander Dumas Sr.
1845 *Sybil, or the Two Nations* by Benjamin Disraeli (political novel).
1846 *Book of Nonsense* by Edward Lear, a drawing from one of the limericks, *There was an old man of Aosta*, is shown here (**1**).
1847 *Wuthering Heights* by Emily Brontë. *Jane Eyre* by Charlotte Brontë.
1848 *Vanity Fair* by William Thackeray. *The Biglow Papers* by James Russell Lowell.
1849 *David Copperfield* by Charles Dickens.
1850 Alfred Lord Tennyson succeeds Wordsworth as poet laureate.
1851 *The Golden Legend* by Henry W. Longfellow (poem).
1852 *The History of Henry Esmond* by William Thackeray. *Bleak House* by Charles Dickens.
1853 *Tanglewood Tales* by Nathaniel Hawthorne.
1854 *Westward Ho!* by Charles Kinsley. *Der Trompeter von Säcgingen* by Josef von Scheffel (verse romance).
1855 *The Song of Hiawatha* by Henry W. Longfellow (epic poem). *Maud and Other Poems* by Alfred Tennyson. *The Warden* by Anthony Trollope.
1856 *Die Leute von Seldwyla (The People of Seldwyla)* by Gottfried Keller (Swiss short stories).
1856–7 *Madame Bovary* by Gustave Flaubert.
1857 *Les Fleurs de Mal* by Charles Baudelaire. *Tom Brown's Schooldays* by Thomas Hughes.
1858 *The Defence of Guinevere* by William Morris (poems).
1859 *Oblomov* by Ivan Goncharov. *A Tale of Two Cities* by Charles Dickens.
1860 *The Woman in White* by Wilkie Collins. *On the Eve* by Ivan Turgenev.
1861 *Silas Marner* by George Eliot.
1862 *Les Misérables* by Victor Hugo. *Fathers and Sons* by Ivan Turgenev.
1863 *Man without a Country* by Edward E Hale (short story).
1864-9 *War and Peace* by Leo Tolstoy.
1865 *Alice's Adventures in Wonderland* by Lewis Carroll. An illustration from this story is shown here (**2**). *Drum Taps* by Walt Whitman.
1866 *Crime and Punishment* by Fyodor Dostoyevsky.
1867 *Sea Spray and Smoke Drift* by Adam Lindsay Gordon (first famous Australian poet).
1868 *The Moonstone* by Wilkie Collins (early detective story).

1

2

continued

Events continued

5451 **1869** *Fêtes Galantes* by Paul Verlaine.
1870 *Twenty Thousand Leagues Under the Sea* by Jules Verne.
1871 *Democratic Vistas* by Walt Whitman.
1873–6 *Anna Karenina* by Leo Tolstoy.
1874 *Far from the Madding Crowd* by Thomas Hardy.
1876 *L'Aprés-Midi d'une Faune* by Stephane Mallarmé (poem).
1879 *Daisy Miller* by Henry James. *Der grüne Heinrich* by Gottfried Keller (Swiss novel).
1880 *Ben Hur* by Lewis Wallace. *Nana* by Emile Zola.
1881 *Ballads and Sonnets* by Daniel Rossetti.
1883 *Treasure Island* by Robert Louis Stevenson. *Beyond Human Endurance* by Björnstjerne Björnson (Norwegian novel).
1884 *With Fire and Sword* by Henryk Sienkiewicz (Polish historical novel).
1885 *Bel Ami* by Guy de Maupassant. *Germinal* by Emile Zola.
1885–8 *The Arabian Nights* translated by Richard Burton (16 volumes).
1886 *Les Illuminations* by Arthur Rimbaud. *The Son of a Servant* by August Strindberg (Swedish autobiography).
1887 *A Study in Scarlet* by Arthur Conan Doyle (first Sherlock Holmes story).
1888 *Plain Tales from the Hills* by Rudyard Kipling.
1889 *Three Men in a Boat* by Jerome K. Jerome.
1890 *Hunger* by Knut Hamsun. *The Kreutzer Sonata* by LeoTolstoy. *The Picture of Dorian Gray* by Oscar Wilde.
1891 *Tess of the d'Urbervilles* by Thomas Hardy.
1894 *The Jungle Book* by Rudyard Kipling.
1897 *From the Four Winds* by John Galsworthy.

19th century authors

5452 **Alcott, Louisa May** 1832–88, American novelist and social reformer (**1**). Author of *Little Women* and its sequels.

Anderson, Hans Christian 1805–75, Danish author (**2**), now largely remembered for his fairy tales.
Arnold, Matthew 1822–88, English poet and critic, important as a commentator on Victorian society.
Austen, Jane 1775–1817, English novelist (**3**), who provides a sometimes satirical record of middle-class life in Regency England in books such as *Pride and Prejudice*.

Balzac, Honoré de 1799–1850, French novelist and short story writer describing people of all classes in a sequence of books which he called collectively *The Human Comedy*.
Baudelaire, Charles 1821–67, French poet (**4**) noted for his macabre imagery, as in *Les fleurs du mal*.

Brontë Three English sisters, all accomplished novelists: **Anne** 1820–49, best known for *Tenant of Wildfell Hall*, **Charlotte** 1816–55, author of *Jane Eyre*, and **Emily** 1818–48, *Wuthering Heights*. Their first publication was a joint book of verse under the names Ellis, Curer, and Acton Bell.
Browning, Elizabeth Barrett 1806-61, English poet, already well established when she married Robert, known especially for her *Sonnets from the Portuguese*. She was active on social issues.
Browning, Robert 1812–89, English poet, much of his work is narrative, sometimes in the form of monologue.
Butler, Samuel 1835–1902, English novelist best known for *Erewhon*, a satire on Victorian hypocrisy, and the autobiographical *The Way of All Flesh*.

Byron, Lord George Gordon 1788–1824, English romantic poet (**5**), champion of political liberty, supporter of Italian independence and Greek revolt against Turkey, now often remembered only for the sexual scandals for which he was ostracized by English society.
Carrol, Lewis (pen-name of Charles Lutwidge Dodgson) 1832–98, English mathematician and author of *Alice's Adventures in Wonderland* and its sequel, written for the little daughter of Oxford colleagues.
Clare, John 1793–18764, English poet, a farm laborer who wrote about rural life, much of his work produced in insane asylums after committal in 1837.
Coleridge, Samuel Taylor 1772–1834, English romantic poet, though poems such as the disturbing *Rime of the Ancient Mariner* intentionally contrast with his friend Wordsworth's poems drawn from everyday life.
Collins, Wilkie 1824–89, English novelist who introduced the detective to English fiction in *The Moonstone*.
Cooper, James Fenimore 1789–1851, American novelist of frontier life as in *The Last of the Mohicans*.
Crane, Stephen 1871–1900, American journalist, poet and novelist, best remembered for his study of a young soldier undergoing the strain of the Civil War in *The Red Badge of Courage*.
Dickens, Charles 1812–70. English novelist and journalist (**6**), creator of colorful characters in strong though sometimes sentimental tales, such as *Oliver Twist*, that were mainly written in weekly episodes. His journalism was a powerful weapon against social ills.

Dickinson, Emily 1830–86, American poet, a recluse whose idiosyncratic verse was largely published posthumously.
Disraeli, Benjamin 1804–81, British statesman, Jewish, though baptized Christian. He was twice prime minister. His novels depict the "two-nation" society created by the Industrial Revolution and promote his political ideas.
Dostoevski, Fyodor 1821–81, Russian novelist whose sensational and brilliantly expounded plots, as in *Crime and Punishment*, offer a frame for profound moral and religious discussion. Also wrote *The Brothers Karamazov*

continue

19th century authors continued

5452 **Doyle, Arthur Conan** 1859–1930, English doctor and writer who invented the character of Sherlock Holmes.
Dumas, Alexandre 1802–70, French novelist and dramatist, best known for the romantic *Three Musketeers* and *Count of Monte Cristo*. His son, also **Alexandre** 1824–95, is remembered for his novel and play *Camille* used by Verdi for *La Traviata*.
Eliot, George 1819–80, pen-name of Mary Ann Evans, English author (**7**) of novels of English life at a time of rural change, such as *Middlemarch*.

7

Emerson, Ralph Waldo 1803–82, American philosopher, poet, and essayist, exponent of transcendentalism, which insisted on the oneness of all forms of life.
Flaubert, Gustave 1821–88, French novelist, his masterpiece is *Madame Bovary*, the story of a provincial housewife's self-deception, adultery, and suicide.
Gaskell, Elizabeth 1810–65, English novelist, mainly of country life, as in *Cranford*. Often, like Disraeli, exploring the injustice of the "two-nation" society of contemporary Britain.
Gogol, Nikolai 1809–52, Russian novelist and dramatist, author of *Dead Souls* and fine short-stories.
Hardy, Thomas 1840–1928, English novelist and poet. His stories, mainly set in his native countryside of Dorset (Wessex) often show a deep empathy with the natural world. A concern for other creatures is evident in his stylistically very varied poems.
Hawthorne, Nathaniel 1804–64, American novelist (**8**) whose work often explores Protestant guilt, as in *The Scarlet Letter*. He also wrote children's stories, such as *Tanglewood Tales*.
Henry (pen-name of William Sidney Porter) 1862–1910, American short story writer (**11**) noted for his use of caricature and surprise endings.
Hugo, Victor 1805–85, French romantic novelist, dramatist, and poet, author of *Les Misérables* and *The Hunchback of Notre Dame*.
Irving, Washington 1783–1859, American essayist and author (**9**) of a long biography of George Washington, but best known for short stories such as *Rip Van Winkle*.

8

9

10

11

14

James, Henry 1843–1916, American-born British novelist (**10**) whose work often deals with the contrast between American and European cultures. A master of the short story as in the chilling *The Turn of the Screw*.
Keats, John 1795–1821, English romantic poet (**12**), responsive to the physical rather than the intellectual world in poems such as *Ode to a Nightingale*.

12

Kipling, Rudyard 1865–1936, English writer (**13**) born in India, which features in much of his journalism and fiction. Long lambasted for his supposed imperialist jingoism. Closer reading reveals a much more cynical and critical viewpoint. His poems of army life and children's books, such as *The Jungle Book*, were very popular.

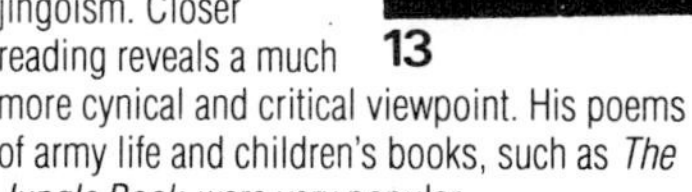
13

Longfellow, Henry Wadsworth 1807–82, American poet, one of the most popular of his time, especially *Excelsior* and his narrative poems on American legends such as *Evangeline* and especially the Native American tale *The Song of Hiawatha* with its pounding unrhymed rhythms (which resulted in many parodies).
Mallarmé, Stéphane 1842–98, French poet, one of the Symbolist group who aimed to present "not the thing, but the effect produced."
Maupassant, Guy de 1850–93, French short story writer who skillfully reconstructs reality rather than presenting a picture direct from life.
Melville, Herman 1819–91. American novelist who drew on his experiences at sea for his masterpieces: the allegorical *Moby Dick* and his short novel of the innocent seaman *Billy Budd*.
Morris, William 1834–96, English artist, poet, and author of the utopian romance *Nowhere* which embodied his socialist ideology.
Poe, Edgar Allan 1809–49, American poet and writer (**14**) best known for his macabre short-stories such as *The Fall of the House of Usher* and the detective story *Murders in the Rue Morgue*.
Pushkin, Aleksander 1799–1837, Russia's greatest poet, dramatist, and novelist, author of *Eugene Onegin* and *The Queen of Spades*.
Rimbaud, Arthur 1854–91, French poet who briefly experimented with vivid, sometimes hallucinatory verse, as in *Les Illuminations*, before abandoning poetry when 19 at the end of a passionate friendship with Verlaine (described in *A Season in Hell*).
Sand, George 1804–76, pen-name of Amandine-Aurore-Lucie Dupin, French writer of pastoral novels and agitator for women's independence. She had a long affair with the composer Chopin.
Shelley, Mary Wollstonecraft 1797–1851, English novelist, author of *Frankenstein, the Modern Prometheus*, a Gothic fantasy with much more profound meaning than distorted stage and film adaptations suggest. Second wife of Percy Bysshe Shelley, the posthumous publication of whose verse she supervised.
Shelley, Percy Bysshe 1792–1822, English romantic poet of *Ode to a Skylark* and poems which reflect his idealism and radical politics such as *Queen Mab*, *The Mask of Anarchy*, and *Prometheus Unbound*. He was expelled from Oxford University for co-authoring a tract called *The Necessity of Atheism*.
Stevenson, Robert Louis 1850–94, Scottish novelist, author of *Treasure Island* and other adventures, of the short story *The Strange Case of Dr Jekyll and Mr Hyde*, and many essays and poems.
Stoker, Bram 1847–1912, Irish novelist known primarily as the author of *Dracula*.
Stowe, Harriet Beecher 1811–96, American novelist and writer on domestic economy, best known for the anti-slavery novel *Uncle Tom's Cabin*. Patronizing in retrospect, it was effective in exposing the evils of slavery.
Swinburne, Algernon Charles 1837-1909, English poet and critic of sensuous verse which scandalized contemporaries with its hints of depravity and paganism.

continued

19th century authors continued

5452

15

16

17

18

19

20

Tennyson, Alfred 1809–92, English poet (**15**), well known for his retelling of the Arthurian legends, who balanced his romantic inheritance against a reflection of the conflicts and duties of Victorian life.
Thoreau, Henry David 1817–1862, American philosopher, a transcendentalist, like Emerson, who advocated passive resistance to tyrannical governments in civil disobedience. His *Walden* describes a two-year retreat in a woodland cabin.
Tolstoy, Leo 1828–1910, Russian philosopher and writer (**16**), in his greatest novels, *War and Peace* and *Anna Karenina*, his beautifully drawn characters often stand as universal types. His "Christian pacifism" influenced many, including Ghandi.
Trollope, Anthony 1815–82, English novelist, especially of a sequence of books showing provincial life in an imaginary country town and another sequence about a family in politics.
Twain, Mark 1835–1910, pen-name of Samuel Langhorne Clemens, American novelist, lecturer (**17**), and humorist most famous for *The Adventures of Tom Sawyer* and *The Adventures of Huckleberry Finn* and a satirical travel book *Innocents Abroad.*
Turgenev, Ivan 1818–83, Russian novelist (**18**) exploring the issues of serfdom and revolutionary change among the aristocrats and intelligentsia.
Verlaine, Paul 1844–96, French poet, a symbolist, although after the end of his friendship with Rimbaud he reverted to more conventional and sentimental verse.
Verne, Jules 1828–1905, French novelist whose fantasies such as *Journey to the Center of the Earth* helped establish the science fiction genre.
Wells, H G 1866–1946, English novelist, writer of social satires and of science fiction for which he is best remembered, such as *War of the Worlds* and *The Time Machine.*
Whitman, Walt 1819–92, American poet (**19**) who celebrated America (as a land of liberty and democracy), nature, and his own individuality and sexuality.
Wilde, Oscar 1854–1900, Irish dramatist (see Theater), poet, author (**20**) of *The Picture of Dorian Gray*, short stories and *The Ballad of Reading Gaol*, an account of his imprisonment for homosexuality as a result of his affair with poet Lord Alfred Douglas.
Wordsworth, William 1770–1850, English poet (**21**) whose work reflects both his initial support for the French Revolution, his response to the English countryside, and deep self-inquiry.

21

Zola, Emile 1840–1902, French novelist who considered the individual shaped by society and thought his job to be to reform society as well as describe it, as shown in novels such as *Germinal*, which portrays the brutalized lives of a mining community.

546 TWENTIETH CENTURY LITERATURE

Modern writing has seen considerable experiment in form in both novels and poetry. While a strong strain of realism has continued in fiction, together with popular romances, thrillers, spy, and detective stories, some writers have placed literary experiment before story-telling.

While some pursued formal devices, Borges linked realism with surrealist allegory to develop magic realism, and was followed in mixing the fantastic with the ordinary by several South and Central Americans, Pynchon, Grass, Rushdie and other writers.

Events

5461

1900 *Sister Carrie* by Theodore Dreiser. *Lord Jim* by Joseph Conrad.
1901 *Buddenbrooks* by Thomas Mann.
1902 *The Times Literary Supplement* first issued. *The Hound of the Baskervilles* by Arthur Conan Doyle.
1903 *The Riddle of the Sands* by Erskine Childers.
1904 *The Sea Wolf* by Jack London.
1904–12 *Jean-Christophe* by Romain Rolland.
1905 *The Scarlet Pimpernel* by Baroness Orczy.
1906 Everyman Library of cheap classic books begins in London.
1906–7 *Nils Holgerson* by Selma Lageröf.
1906–21 *The Forsyte Saga* by John Galsworthy.
1907 *The Mother* by Maxim Gorki.
1908 *A Room with a View* by E M Forster. *Metropolis* by Upton Sinclair.
1909 *Casper Hauser* by Jakob Wassermann.
1910 *Clayhanger* by Arnold Bennett.
1911 *Poems* by Rupert Brooke.
1912 *Gitanjali* by Rabindranath Tagore (poems).
1913–27 *Remembrance of Things Past* by Marcel Proust.
1914 *Dubliners* by James Joyce.
1915 *The Thirty-Nine Steps* by John Buchan.
1916–18 *Le Leda senza Cigno* by Gabriele D'Annunzio (poems).
1917 *Jew Süss* by Lion Feuchtwanger (English trans 1922).
1918 *Eminent Victorians* by Lytton Strachey.
1919 *Winesburg Ohio* by Sherwood Anderson (short stories).
1920 *Chéri* by Colette.
1922 *The Waste Land* by T S Eliot (poem). *Ulysses* by Joyce published in Paris. PEN (Poets, Essayists, Novelists) founded in London.
1924 *The Magic Mountain* by Thomas Mann. *A Passage to India* by E M Forster. *Carry on Jeeves* by P G Woodhouse.
1925 *Les Faux-monnayers* by André Gide. *The Trial* by Franz Kafka (posthumous). *Manhattan Transfer* by John Dos Passos.
1926 *Seven Pillars of Wisdom* by T E Lawrence.
1927 *To the Lighthouse* by Virginia Woolf.
1928 *Lady Chatterley's Lover* by D H Lawrence.
1929 *All Quiet on the Western Front* by Erich Maria Remarque.
1930 *As I Lay Dying* by William Faulkner. *Collected Poems* by Robert Frost.
1930–43 *The Man Without Qualities* by Robert Musil.
1931 *Den blakyst* by Kristmann Gudmundsson (Icelandic novel).
1932 *Brave New World* by Aldous Huxley.
1933 *La Condition Humaine* by André Malraux

continue

Events continued

5461 **1934** *And Quiet Flows the Don* by Mikhail Sholokhov.
1935 Penguin books founded.
1936 *Gone with the Wind* by Margaret Mitchell.
1937 *To Have and Have not* by Ernest Hemingway.
1939 *The Happy Return* by C S Forester (first Hornblower novel).
1940 *The Power and the Glory* by Graham Greene.
1942 *L'Etranger* by Albert Camus.
1944 *The Razor's Edge* by William Somerset Maugham. *Agustino* by Alberto Moravia.
1945 *Christ Stopped at Eboli* by Carlo Levi. *Animal Farm* by George Orwell.
1946 *All the King's Men* by Robert Penn Warren.
1949 *The Second Sex* by Simone de Beauvoir.
1950 *Seventy Cantos* by Ezra Pound (poems). *A Question of Upbringing* by Anthony Powell.
1951 *Complete Poems* by Robert Frost. *The Caine Mutiny* by Herman Wouk.
1951–75 *A Dance to the Music of Time* by Anthony Powell (12 volumes).
1952 *Men At Arms* by Evelyn Waugh.
1953 *Go Tell it on the Mountain* by James Baldwin.
1954 *Lucky Jim* by Kingsley Amis. *Lord of the Flies* by William Golding. *I'm Not Stiller* by Max Frisch. *Confessions of Felix Krull* by Thomas Mann.
1955 *The Quiet American* by Graham Greene. *The Diary of Anne Frank* by Anne Frank (posthumous). *Lolita* by Vladimir Nabokov.
1956 *Anglo-Saxon Attitudes* by Angus Wilson.
1957 *Room at the Top* by John Braine. *Doctor Zhivago* by Boris Pasternak (published in Italy). *Voss* by Patrick White.
1958 *Justine* by Lawrence Durrell. *The Tin Drum* by Günther Grass.
1959 *Billards at Half-Past Nine* by Heinrich Böll.
1960 *Summoned by Bells* by John Betjeman (poetic autobiography).
1961 *Babi Yar* by Yevgeny Yevtushenko.
1962 *One Day in the Life of Ivan Denisovich* by Alexander Solzhenitsyn.
1963 *The Spy Who Came in from the Cold* by John Le Carré.
1964 *The First Circle* by Alexander Solzhenitsyn.
1965 *The Rosy Crucifixion* by Henry Miller.
1966 *The Green House* by Mario Vargas Llasa.
1967 *One Hundred Years of Solitude* by Gabriel Garcia Marquez.
1968 *Les Fruits de l'Hiver* by Bernard Clavel (Prix Goncourt).
1969 *The French Lieutenant's Woman* by John Fowles. *The Gate of the World by* Henry Williamson (15th and last novel in *Chronicle of the Ancient Sunlight*).
1970 *Last Things* by C P Snow (11th and last novel in *Strangers and Brothers* series).
1971 *The Bell Jar* by Sylvia Plath (posthumous autobiographical novel).
1972 *Watership Down* by Richard Adams.
1973 *Group Portrait with Lady* by Heinrich Böll.
1974 *Something Happened* by Joseph Heller.
1975 *The Memoirs of a Survivor* by Doris Lessing.
1976 *Terra Nostra* by Carlos Fuentes. *Selected Stories* by Nadine Gordimer.
1977 *The Castle of Crossed Destinies* by Italo Calvino.
1978 *The World According to Garp* by John Irving.
1979 *A Bend in the River* by V S Naipaul. *Sophie's Choice* by William Styron.
1980 *Rites of Passage* by William Golding.
1981 *Midnight's Children* by Salman Rushdie.
1982 *Chronicle of a Death Foretold* by Gabriel Garcia Marquez.
1984 *Polomar* by Italo Calvino. *God Knows* by Joseph Heller.
1985 *Foreign Affairs* by Alison Lurie. *The Bone People* by Keri Hulme. *Lake Wobegon Days* by Garrison Keillor.
1986 *The Flying Change* by Henry Taylor (American poetry).

20th century authors

5462 **WRITERS IN ENGLISH**

Amis, Kingsley b. 1922, English novelist and poet of both comic satire and more profound explorations of the human condition. His son **Martin** b. 1949, has gained a reputation with somewhat violent novels.

Anderson, Sherwood 1876–1941, American novelist of small-town life as in the tragic *Winesburg, Ohio.*

Angelou, Maya b. 1928, American poet, dramatist whose work reflects her upbringing as a poor black in St Louis.

Asimov, Isaac b. 1920, Russian-born American science fiction author, a leader in the genre.

Atwood, Margaret Eleanor b 1939, Canadian poet and novelist whose work explores both the female identity and the cultural identity of Canada.

Auden, Wystan Hugh 1907–73, English-born American poet of the left in his youth, but a Christian liberal in later life. Often colloquial in style and technically inventive.

Baldwin, James (**1**) 1924–87, American novelist whose work explores both black and homosexual issues and whose essays challenge white supremacists.

Bellow, Saul b. 1915, Canadian-born American novelist exploring the self and the disintegration of urban life.

Bennett, Arnold 1867–1931, English novelist, known for his series of novels set in the pottery towns of central England.

Berryman, John 1914–72, American poet of introspection, idiosyncratic in style.

Bowles, Paul b. 1910, American novelist and composer, long domiciled in Morocco and best known for *The Sheltering Sky.* He is often thought of as the forerunner of Kerouac and other "beat" writers.

Bradbury, Ray b.1920, American author of imaginative and poetic science fiction.

Brooke, Rupert 1887–1915, English poet known for his patriotic war poems.

Buchan, John 1875–1940, English writer of adventure stories such as *The Thirty-Nine Steps.*

Burgess, Anthony b. 1917, English novelist and composer, author of numerous major novels, often satirical, from the nightmare fantasy of *A Clockwork Orange* to the witty *Earthly Powers.*

Burroughs, William b. 1914, American beat novelist whose work often features explicit violence and homosexuality.

Caldwell, Erskine 1903–1987, American novelist writing especially about poor whites in the southern states.

Capote, Truman 1924–84, American novelist with a light poetic touch – especially when drawing on his southern childhood – and of stories based on murder cases.

Cather, Willa 1876–1947, American novelist of immigrant life on the plains based on her own Nebraska childhood.

Chandler, Raymond 1888–1959, American writer (**2**) of thrillers and detective stories. Creator of Philip Marlowe.

Christie, Agatha 1890–1976, English detective story writer, creator of Hercule Poirot and Miss Marple.

Conrad, Joseph 1857–1924, Polish-born English novelist whose dark novels, often centered on an "outsider," draw on his previous experience at sea.

Cummings, e(dward) e(stin) 1894–1962, American poet, novelist, and artist, an experimenter in free-verse who preferred not to use capital letters.

Dos Passos, John 1896–1970, American novelist known for his trilogy of American life *The 42nd Parallel, 1919* and *The Big Money.*

Dreiser, Theodore 1871–1945, American novelist who saw human nature as trapped in a pattern of natural law and social conditioning, as in the doom-laden *An American Tragedy.*

Durrell, Lawrence 1912–90, English poet and novelist famous for his *Alexandria Quartet: Justine, Balthazar, Mountolive,* and *Clea.*

Eliot, T(homas) S(tearns) 1888–1965, American-born English poet (**3**). A giant among poets, his work is full of erudite allusions, but it was its reflection of topical concerns which gave it immediacy. His innovations have lasting influence.

continued

20th century authors continued

5462 **Faulkner, William** (**4**) 1897–1962, American novelist, especially of the social, sexual, and racial tensions of the Deep South.

4

Fitzgerald, F. Scott (**5**) 1896–1940, American novelist whose glamorous tales of high society are suprisingly moralistic, as in *The Great Gatsby*.

5

Fleming, Ian 1908–64, (**6**) English journalist and creator of spy 007 James Bond.

6

Forster, E(dward) M(organ) 1879–1970, English novelist of middle-class relationships and in *A Passage to India* of the conflict between Indians and the British Raj.

Frost, Robert 1874–1963, American poet exploiting the distinctive rhythms of American speech and drawing his inspiration mainly from the people and landscape of New England.

Galsworthy, John 1867–1933, English novelist and dramatist, known for his dynastic sequence *The Forsyte Saga*.

Ginsberg, Allen b. 1926, American "beat" poet who achieved notoriety with his poem *Howl* and often celebrates sexuality and explores anti-establishment themes.

Graves, Robert 1895–1985, English poet and novelist, received acclaim for his autobiographical account of World War I, *Goodbye to All That*, and his historical novels about Rome: *I, Claudius* and *Claudius the God*.

Greene, Graham 1904–91, English novelist, (**7**) who often explores broadly religious or political themes. He divided his work into "entertainments" and more serious work; though his writings often have a thriller or spy element, which appeals to the popular reader, he ranks among the best modern novelists.

7

Hemingway, Ernest 1899–1961, American novelist with a style shorn of decoration and based in apparent macho values, though perhaps his greatest work is a more spiritual novella *The Old Man and the Sea*.

Hughes, James Langston 1902–67, American poet, drawing his inspiration from Harlem and the plight of fellow urban blacks.

Hughes, Ted b. 1930, English poet, especially successful when writing about the natural world.

Huxley, Aldous 1894–1963, English novelist and essayist (**8**), mainly of sardonic satires on society and intellectual life. *Brave New World* was a picture of a rigid totalitarian system. He experimented with hallucinogens and claimed they gave him the insights he records in *The Doors of Perception*.

8

12

Joyce, James 1882–1941, Irish novelist and writer of short stories (**9**), some based on autobiographical material. *Ulysses* (recalling Homer's *Odyssey*) sometimes uses stream-of-consciousness narrative. Banned for its sexual explicitness, it is now recognized as a master work. Despite its many literary allusions it is not difficult to read, which cannot be said of *Finnegans Wake*, which carries linguistic experiment to the extreme.

9

Kerouac, Jack (**10**) 1922–69, foremost of the American "beat" writers, remembered mainly for the autobiographical *On the Road*.

10

Larkin, Philip 1922–85, English poet of a lyrical colloquialism.

Lawrence, D(avid) H(erbert) (**11**) 1885–1930, English poet, painter, and novelist, originally controversial for his frank treatment of sex and use of four-letter words. In his poetry, and in books such as *Sons and Lovers* and *Lady Chatterly's Lover*, he seeks a new gender balance and proposes renewing the relation between man and nature, damaged by dehumanizing industrialization.

11

Le Guin, Ursula b. 1929, American science-fantasy novelist, especially acclaimed for her *Earthsea* trilogy written mainly for younger readers.

Lewis, Sinclair 1885–1951, American (**12**) novelist who portrays small-town life in novels such as *Main Street*, describes an attempt to avoid conformity in *Babbitt*, and exposes evangelical hypocrisy in *Elmer Gantry*.

London, Jack 1876–1916, American novelist and short-story writer. Subjects range from *White Fang* (the life of a dog in the Yukon), to a documentary of London slum life in *People of the Abyss*.

Lowell, Robert 1917–77, American pacifist poet of very personal verse.

McCarthy, Mary 1912–89, American novelist, especially of academic life in *The Group*.

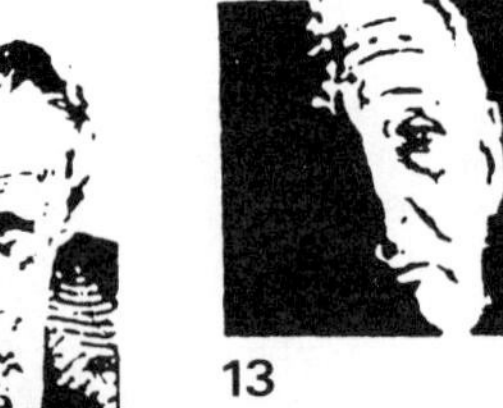
13

14

McCullers, Carson 1917–67, American novelist and writer of short stories often centered on misfits, as in *The Ballad of the Sad Café* and *Reflections in a Golden Eye*.

Mailer, Norman b. 1923., American novelist and essayist whose fiction often draws directly on his own experience, as in the World War II novel *The Naked and the Dead* (though *Ancient Evenings* is set in ancient Egypt). He has also written on the 1967 anti-Vietnam War demonstrations.

Miller, Henry 1891–1980, American novelist notorious for the recording of his sexual exploits in *Tropic of Cancer* and *Tropic of Capricorn*, though books such as *Colossus of Marousi* are of much higher quality.

Murdoch, Iris b. 1919, English academic and novelist of intellectual comedies sometimes spiced with offbeat sex, symbolism, and the macabre.

Nabokov, Vladimir 1899–1977, Russian-born American novelist (**13**) originally writing in Russian. Best known for *Lolita*, though this tale of an academic in love with a young girl is far from his finest.

Nash, Ogden 1902–71, America poet with his own brand of clever comic verse.

Orwell, George 1903–50, English novelist and essayist (**14**). Author of valuable studies of poverty and of the Spanish Civil War, and of two classic political allegories: *Animal Farm* and *1984*.

Owen, Wilfrid 1893–1918, English poet, the definitive poet of World War I, able to convey both its horror and its cathartic beauty in poems such as *Strange Meeting*.

Plath, Sylvia 1932–63, American poet of confessional verse using often bizarre images and expressing her sense of victimization by men, only two volumes of which were published before her suicide.

Pound, Ezra 1885–1972, American poet who advocated fragmentation and shifts of tone. His support for Italian fascism led to his committal to a mental asylum after World War II.

Proust, Marcel 1871–1922, French novelist and essayist (**15**), whose multi-volume work generally known in English as *Remembrance of Things Past*, presents a complex picture of his own relationships and the mores of French society.

15

continued

20th century authors continued

5462 **Pynchon, Thomas** b. 1937, American novelist who often uses black humor and elements of magic realism in portraying the mess in which he sees the modern world.
Runyon, Damon 1884–1946, American author of racy short stories about New York lowlife such as *Guys and Dolls* and *Pal Joey.*
Rushdie, Salman b. 1947, Indian-born British novelist using elements of magic realism. He scored a great success with *Midnight's Children*, but his use of Koranic parallels in *The Satanic Verses* led to charges of blasphemy and a *fatwah* (death sentence) from the Ayatollah Khomeini of Iran and forced him into hiding.
Salinger, J D 1919– American novelist and short-story writer, famous for his portrayal of an adolescent boy in *Catcher in the Rye.*
Sandburg, Carl 1878–1967, American poet, much influenced by Whitman. Also the author of a long biography of Lincoln.
Shaw, George Bernard 1856–1950, Irish critic, essayist, and playwright (**16**) he also wrote five excellent novels. (see Theater)
Singer, Isaac Bashevis b. 1904, Polish-born American novelist and short-story writer whose work is often based on traditional Jewish folk-tales and mysticism.
Steinbeck, John 1902–68, American novelist (**17**) especially of the Depression with *Grapes of Wrath* and *Of Mice and Men.*
Thomas, Dylan 1914–53, Welsh poet (**18**) whose boozy reputation belies his fine verse, best known through the radio verse drama *Under Milk Wood.*

Thurber, James 1894–1961, American cartoonist, essayist, and story-teller (**19**) who drew his humor from a banal everyday world full of dominating women and odd juxtapositions.
Tolkien, J R R 1892–1973, South African-born British scholar and writer of fantasies in the style of the Nordic sagas he studied (**20**).
Vidal, Gore b. 1925, American novelist, critic, and commentator his work includes historical fiction (from a non-establishment viewpoint), sexual comedy, and, in his earliest work, a study of the difficulties of a young upper-class homosexual.
Waugh, Evelyn 1903–66, English writer of satirical novels based on his own experiences, and of the more introspective *Brideshead Revisited* and latterly of the disturbing autobiographical *The Ordeal of Gilbert Penfold.*
White, Patrick 1912–90, Australian novelist, some of whose work is set in the Australian outback, often showing men reacting to extreme situations.
Williams, William Carlos 1883–1963, American poet and novelist whose later poems use everyday speech and often take everyday objects as their subject.
Wolfe, Thomas 1900–38, American novelist of rather formless novels, especially the four-volume sequence beginning with *Look Homeward Angel.*
Woolf, Virginia 1882–1941, English novelist (**21**), who with her husband Leonard was the center of the "Bloomsbury Group" of British artists and writers. 21 Initially realist, she increasingly uses a stream-of-consciousness narration to show reality as it passes through the mind of her characters in novels such as *To the Lighthouse.*
Yeats, William Butler 1865–1939, Irish poet, much influenced by Blake. Initially strongly linked to Irish myth and fairy-tale, his work becomes more pared and personal in his later life. He supported Irish nationalism and became a member of the Irish senate.

WRITERS IN OTHER LANGUAGES
Apollinaire, Guillaume 1880–1918, French poet who coined the term "surrealism" and explored the effect of irrational juxtapositions and visual, rather than literary, effects.
Aragon, Louis 1897–1982, French poet and novelist, a surrealist before embracing socialist realism.
Beauvoir, Simone de 1908–86, French novelist and essayist. Longtime companion of Sartre whose existentialist views she shared. Her analysis of woman's condition in *The Second Sex* became a cornerstone of the feminist movement.
Boll, Heinrich 1917–85, German novelist, his finest novel *The Lost Honor of Katharina Blum* reflects the attacks made on him by sections of the press for his "unpatriotic" criticism of German postwar society.
Borges, Jorge Louis 1899–1988, Argentinian poet and short-story writer who considered fantasy and dream no less real than social realism and mixed them in magic realist manner.
Calvino, Italo b. 1923, Cuban-born Italian novelist moving from early studies in harsh realism to more fantastical books in the magic realist style.
Camus, Albert 1913–60, Algerian-born French novelist and dramatist whose work often centers on the alienated individual with a rather nihilistic interpretation of existentialism, as can be seen in *The Stranger.*
Canetti, Elias b. 1905, Bulgarian-born German writer (British citizen) best known for *Auto da Fe*, an allegory of the collapse of civilized European thought before the onslaught of 20th century political forces.
Capek, Karel 1890–1938, Czech novelist and dramatist (see Theater).
Colette 1873–1954, French novelist (**22**), best known for books such as *Cheri* and *Gigi*, set in the demi-monde in which she herself moved.

Dinesen, Isak (pen-name of Karen Blixen) 1885–1962, Danish short-story writer of fantasies such as *Seven Gothic Tales,* though now more widely known for her autobiographical *Out of Africa* about colonial life in Kenya.
Eco, Umberto b. 1932, Italian semiologist and novelist who gained international attention with his medieval detective story *The Name of the Rose,* which applied a semiological approach to investigated murders in a medieval monastery.
Elytis, Odysseus b. 1911, Greek poet and essayist who celebrates human life even when evoking a vision of war and its aftermath. *The Axion Esti,* his major work, is part spiritual autobiography, part meditation on modern history.
Fuentes, Carlos b. 1928, Mexican diplomat, dramatist and novelist often writing in magic realist style as in his first collection of stories *The Masked Days.*
Genet, Jean 1910–86 (**23**) French dramatist (see Theater) and novelist whose novels draw on his own experience of prison and the criminal world, and, in *Our Lady of the Flowers* explores the life and fantasies of a homosexual woman. 23
Gide, André 1869–1951, French novelist, conventional in style but uncompromising in his concern for personal, sexual, and social awareness.
Grass, Günter b. 1927, German novelist, poet and dramatist. *The Tin Drum,* a satire on the rise and fall of the Third Reich, presented through the mind of a dumb child, is his best known work.
Hesse, Herman 1877–1962, German-born Swiss novelist and poet influenced by oriental mysticism and Jungian theory. *Steppenwolf* and *The Glass Bead Game* were popular in the "alternative culture" of the 1960s.

continued

20th century authors continued

5462 **Kafka, Franz** 1883–1924, Czech novelist (**24**). *The Trial* and *The Castle* show characters trapped in the coils of bureaucracy, as though prescient of later dictatorships. His short story of a man who wakes in insect form, *Metamorphosis*, is probably his best known work.
Kemal, Yashar b. 1923, Turkish novelist who draws on the feuds and banditry of his family background in novels such as *Memed, my Hawk*.
Lampedusa, Giuseppe Tomasi de 1896-1957. Sicilian aristocrat and author of *The Leopard* which charted the effect on a family like his own of the rising under Garibaldi and the annexation of Sicily.
Lorca, Federico Garcia 1898–1936, Spanish poet and dramatist (see Theater), his verse much influenced by surrealism.
Lu Hsiin 1881–1936, Chinese essayist and story teller, often regarded as the most important literary figure of modern China. Much concerned with the reform of Chinese society and literature, best known for his allegory of the country's ills, *The True Story of Ah Q*.
Mahfuz, Najib b. 1911, Egyptian novelist whose work has been controversial both for its treatment of Islam, for which the allegorical *Awlad Haritna* was banned in Egypt, and for his harsh picture of national politics, as in *Miramar*.
Mann, Thomas 1875–1955, German novelist who explores such themes as the alienation of the artist from contemporary values in massive novels like *The Magic Mountain* and brilliant short stories such as *Death in Venice*.
Marquez, Gabriel Garcia b. 1928, Colombian novelist, a leading magic realist as

24

in *One Hundred Years of Solitude*.
Mishima, Yukio 1925–70, Japanese novelist, fascinated by death and his own homosexuality in novels such as *Confessions of a Mask*; his work culminated in his own public suicide.
Moravia, Alberto b. 1907, Italian realist novelist at first critically portraying the preoccupations of Rome's decadent bourgeoisie but, in *Woman of Rome* and later work, broadening his range to include the problems of the working class.
Natsume, Soseki 1867–1916, Japanese writer, the outstanding novelist of the Meji period, known in the West mainly for a sequence of novels beginning with *I am a Cat* – narrated in a feline persona – which satirize intellectual pretensions.
Neruda, Pablo 1904–73, Chilean poet and diplomat whose verse can be both highly personal and reflect his strong left-wing beliefs. The impressive *Canto General*, which includes a section inspired by a visit to the Inca site of Macchu Picchu, traces the history of Latin America and evokes the grandeur of its landscapes.
Pasternak, Boris 1890–1960, Russian poet and novelist best known for *Dr Zhivago*, set in the immediate post-revolutionary period.
Paz, Octavio b. 1914, Mexican poet. In Spain at the time of the Civil War he strongly opposed both fascism and the totalitarian left. Much of his most important work is a reflection on Mexican cultural and national identity.
Rilke, Rainer Maria 1875–1926, German poet of mystical and religious verse.
Sartre, Jean-Paul 1905–80, French philosopher, dramatist, and novelist (**25**), both existentialist and Marxist. His three novels under the title *Roads to Freedom* chart life at the approach to, and during, World War II.

25

Seferis, Giorgos 1900–71, Greek diplomat and lyric poet whose work draws on the tradition of Greek ballad and folksong, especially that of Crete (though he adopted freer modes in later work); partly influenced by Eliot, whose *Waste Land* he translated.
Solzhenitsyn, Alexander b 1918, Russian historian and novelist whose work – such as *One Day in the Life of Ivan Denisovich* and *The Gulag Archipelago* – draws on his own experience in Stalin's labour camps.
Soyinka, Wele b. 1934, Nigerian poet, novelist and dramatist. His work reflects the concerns of African politics; *The Man Died* describes his imprisonment by his own government.
Tagore, Rabindranath 1861–1941, Indian poet and philosopher.

547 LITERARY AND POETRY TERMS

Literature terms

5471 **allegory** Form in which the action and other elements stand for similar real life circumstances.
alliteration Use of a sequence of words beginning with the same initial letter.
antithesis Placing ideas together to stress a contrast.
aphorism Brief, witty statement of a general truth.
assonance Use of words which repeat similar vowel sounds.
bathos Sudden change from the exalted to the ridiculous.
deconstruction Critical interpretation of a text by studying linguistic signs in isolation from other elements such as knowledge of its author and cultural background.
epigram A brief but memorable statement making a pithy observation.
epilogue A postscript outlining what happens to characters after the ending of the main story, or a final passage to point a moral or offer an apologia to the reader.
episode An incident or group of incidents forming a section of a story; one installment of a serialized story.
euphemism An inoffensive substitute for a distasteful word or phrase.
euphony A combination of pleasant sounding words.
euphuism A high-flown rhetorical literary style.
foreword Introduction, in which the author sets out his intentions, or written by another person giving their endorsement of the book or its author.
hyperbole Use of exaggeration for emphasis.
innuendo Subtle or indirect implication, usually of something discreditable.
irony Using expressions of which the opposite to the literal meaning is intended.
litotes Assertion of a positive by denying its negative, often in the form of a deliberate understatement for effect.
metaphor Use of an object or action to represent another. Mixed metaphor is the joining together of unmatched metaphors with ridiculous results.
metonymy Use of a suggestive or related word instead of naming the thing meant.
neologism A newly coined word or expression.
onomatopoeia Use of words which sound like the thing described.
oxymoron Statement combining two conflicting terms for effect.
palindrome A word or phrase that reads the same backwards.
parody Imitating another work or style with intention to ridicule.
pastiche An imitation of another's style.
periphrasis Round about way of expressing a point.
personification Giving objects or concepts a personal living form.
preface Introduction, often explaining the structure or purpose of what follows.
prologue An introductory section explaining what happens before the main action.
pun Comic play on words which sound the same but differ in meaning.
simile Likening one thing to another.
stream-of-consciousness Narrative using an uninterrupted sequence of thoughts, perceptions, and feelings.
structuralism Critical discipline which studies a text in relation to other known elements, including knowledge of the author, contemporaneous culture, literary convention, and facts not mentioned in the text but known to intended readers in addition to the text itself.
syllepsis Use of one word linked in different senses to two statements, usually used for its comic effect.
synecdoche A figure of speech where use of a part stands for the whole.
tautology Unnecessary repetition.
zeugma Another expression for syllepsis.

Poetry forms and terms

5472 **acrostic** A verse in which the initial letters of each line form a word or phrase reading downwards.
alexandrine A line of verse in iambic hexameter.
anapest A metrical foot with three syllables, two unstressed and one stressed.
antistrophe The second of two metrical systems used alternately within a poem.
aubade A poem appropriate to greeting the dawn.
ballad A narrative poem in short stanzas, often of folk origin and intended to be sung.
blank verse Unrhymed verse, often (especially in Shakespeare) in iambic pentameters.
caesura A pause in a line, usually for sense but forming part of the metrical foot.
couplet Two lines of rhymed verse in the same meter. In a closed couplet the meaning is complete.
dactyl A metrical foot of one stressed syllable followed by two unstressed ones.
elegy A serious reflective poem, especially one lamenting a death.
envoi A brief postscript in verse or prose.
foot A metrical unit of a group of syllables, a unit of rhythm.
free verse Unrhymed and following no strict metrical pattern, cadence often providing form.
haiku Epigrammatic Japanese verse form employing 17 syllables.
hexameter A metrical line of six feet.
iambic A metrical foot of two syllables with the second accented.
lay A short narrative poem, usually meant to be sung.
limerick A five-line comic verse, the third and fourth lines shorter and rhyming, the other lines sharing a different rhyme.
meter The rythmical structure of a line of verse.
octave A group of eight lines of verse.
ode A lyric poem, usually in elaborate form, typically addressed to and eulogizing a particular subject.
ottava rima Eight-line stanza form in iambic pentameter, the rhyme pattern abababcc.
pentameter A meter of five feet to the line.
prosody The principles and elements of versification: meter, rhyme, etc.
quatrain A group of four lines, usually rhymed.
refrain A phrase, line, or group of lines repeated through a poem, usually at the end of each stanza.
rhythm The pattern of stress through verse. Sprung rhythm has one stressed and several unstressed syllables to each foot.
rhyme Similarity in sound of endings of different words, especially vowels of the last stressed syllables (and any which follow them). Masculine rhymes stress the last syllable, feminine do not; imperfect rhymes have vowels which do not quite match; identical use the same word, often with different meaning; eye rhymes look but do not sound the same (though in old poems this may be due to a change in pronunciation); internal rhymes are when a word within a line rhymes with its last word.
scansion The metrical pattern of a line.
sestet Group of six lines.
sonnet A poem of 14 lines in iambic pentameter rhymed to a fixed scheme: Petrarchan — divided in both form and sense as an octave and a sestet (the rhyme scheme usually abbaabba, cdecde or cdcdcd); Miltonic — similar but without the break; English or Shakespearean — three quatrains and a couplet (abab, cdcd, efef, gg); Spencerian — three quatrains and a couplet (abab, bcbc, cdcd, ee).
spondee A metrical foot of two syllables, both accented.
stanza A group of lines forming a regular metrical division within a poem.
strophe The first of a set of metrical systems (usually repeated) in a poem.
tercet A group of three lines, often connected by rhyme.
terza rima A series of tercets rhyming aba, bcb, cdc, and so on.
tetrameter A meter of four feet to the line.
threnody A funeral song or dirge.
trimeter A meter of three feet to the line.
trochee A metrical foot of two syllables, the first accented the second not.
verse Technically is one metrical line of a poem, but more commonly used to mean a stanza and as a general description of poetry as distinct from prose.
verse libre (French) Free verse.
weak ending One that is unaccented.

Prose literary genres

5473 **autobiography** Recounting of the writer's own life.
biography Story of a person's life, recounted by another.
chronicle A chronological account of events.
crime story May be built around criminal activity where the identity of the criminal is known or unimportant.
detective story Story hinging on the solving of a crime, how it was committed and the identification of a murderer, thief, or other criminal.
epic A long narrative poem usually concerning a central character of heroic stature or incidents of national or tribal importance.
epistle A letter or a literary work imitating letter form.
epitaph A eulogy commemorating the dead.
essay A prose composition on a particular subject.
fable A short, allegorical story to point a moral, especially using animal characters.
faction A retelling of a story concerning real people and events but which imaginatively constructs dialogue and incident where no factual record exists.
fantasy A story having a large fantasy content, involving things or events not known in real life.
fiction Literature, especially stories, based on invented character and incidents — though fiction may often be set against a background of real events and draw on real-life experience.
gothic A style characterized by gloom, the grotesque and supernatural, popular in the late 18th century and revived in the 20th; often set in ruined castles, abbeys, or old houses.
graphic novels Stories in picture strips.
historical Set in a period earlier than the present.
horror story Tale intended to frighten, often involving the supernatural.
lampoon A satire ridiculing a person.
legend An unverifiable story handed down from earlier times, or a modern story that presents similar characteristics. In medieval times used when telling the life story of a saint.
magic realism Originally used in the 1920s to describe paintings which combined surreal fantasy with matter-of-fact representation; adapted for more recent literary work which combines documentary realism with imaginative fantasies.
memoir A biography or historical account based on personal knowledge; as "memoirs" usually indicates fragments of autobiography rather than a complete retelling.
myth A fictitious story, frequently intended to explain a phenomenon and generally concerning gods or beings from before written history; a story in which a theme or character embodies an idea in a similar way.
novel A fictitious narrative in which characters and action are usually a reflection of real life.
novelette A short novel, usually light and often sentimental in tone.
novella A short narrative tale (but longer than a short story,) often one with a moral or satirical point.
picaresque A genre in which a roguish hero or heroine goes through a series of adventures
roman á clef A story based on real characters and events known to the author but presented under fictitious names.
romance Originally a tale of chivalry or of characters remote from ordinary life (and written in one of the Romance languages,) popularly a story of love, usually somewhat idealized and with a happy ending.
satire A genre using irony or ridicule to hold contentious issues, folly, or evil in scorn.
science fiction (SF) A genre that makes imaginative use of scientific knowledge or conjecture of future scientific development. When this is pseudo-scientific with no grounding in real science it is often known as science fantasy.
short story A short but complete piece of prose fiction concentrating on a single theme.
thriller A tale of mystery, espionage, or crime of which the main purpose is to entertain with suspense and shock.
western A tale set in the western states of the USA, especially in the period of settlement and early development, usually involving gunmen, outlaws or settlers in conflict with Native Americans.

551 PHOTOGRAPHY

Photography consists of recording the pattern of light in the scene photographed onto a sensitive film so that it can later be faithfully reproduced.

Types of camera

5511

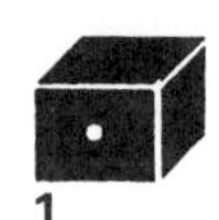
1

2

3

4

5

6

7

8

9

1 Camera obscura
2 Daguerreotype
3 Single lens reflex
4 Rangefinder/Viewfinder
5 Twin lens reflex
6 Pocket
7 Self-contained
8 Studio
9 Cine

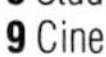

10

There are several types of camera, from the ancient camera obscura to the sophisticated and specialized cameras of today. The camera obscura, on which the photographic camera is based, was known to Aristotle; if an image in a strong light is placed in front of a darkened box with a pinhole in one wall, the rays of the light will shine through the pinhole and project the image, upside down and laterally reversed, onto the rear wall of the box. It was not until 1824 that it was discovered, by Nicephore Niepce, that if the wall was replaced by a light-sensitive plate the image could be made semi-permanent. His associate Daguerre (**10**) discovered how to produce positive images, and William Henry Fox Talbot worked on producing a latent image for later development. From this idea of negative/positive photography the modern cameras evolved; film is exposed in the camera and later developed to form a negative. The positive print is then processed and printed.

Major photographers

5512

In 1839 early daguerreotypes made French painter Paul Delaroche declare "From today painting is dead!" It was not, though as photographs challenged its recording role in art, new abstract forms developed, and photographers in turn produced surreal and altered images.

Painters from Delacroix to Hockney have used photographs as a reference aid and early photographers often arranged pictures to look like paintings – long exposures required careful posing and soft focus gave romantic effects – but the immediacy given to the photograph by improvements in cameras and film reinforced arguments that it was a technical skill, not an art. Today no-one would deny that the best photography requires an artist's eye in the selection and recording of an image, even in documentary reportage.

The studio, the camera, and the darkroom all give the photographer opportunities to control, alter and combine images and photography and can both capture the elusive revealing moment and offer created images that do not exist in life.

Adams, Ansel 1902–84 (**1**), American photographer, especially of the American western landscape and of natural spectacle, mostly using large-format cameras giving great tonal control to give his black and white prints.

1

Adamson, Robert 1821–48, Scottish photographer who set up an Edinburgh studio in 1842 and collaborated with David Octavius Hill in fine studies of local fisherfolk, military, and celebrities.
Arbus, Diane 1923–71, American photographer of street life, best known for her sympathetic and validating studies of human "freaks."
Atget, Eugene 1857–1927, French photographer of French countryside, urban scenes, and working people.
Avedon, Richard b. 1923, American portrait and fashion photographer. At age ten his first portrait was of pianist-composer Sergey Rachmaninoff. He became one of the highest paid of all photographers.
Bailey, David b. 1938, British photographer famous for 1960s fashion shots that broke the pattern of girls as clothes-horses. His fine nudes and reportage contrast with his fashion work.
Beaton, Cecil 1904–80, British designer, decorator and photographer of fashion and high society who also produced fine pictures of war.
Bourke-White, Margaret 1904–7, American, beginning as an industrial photographer, joined *Fortune* and *Life* magazines, and covered World War II in Europe. One of the first to bring the photo-essay to journalism.
Brady, Mathew B. 1823–96, American photographer, opened a "Gallery of Illustrious Americans" in New York of his own and other's pictures and recorded the Civil War, employing others to help, expecting the government to buy the pictures – he went bankrupt when they did not.
Brandt, Bill 1904–83, British photographer, assistant to Man Ray in his twenties, his diverse work ranges from formal abstractions and landscape to reportage but is especially known for images of working-class life in the 1930s and his outstanding treatment of the nude.
Brassai 1899–1984, Hungarian-born French photographer Gyula Halesz, documented Paris nightlife (mainly by flash) in the 1930s, before turning to more abstract work.
Cameron, Julia Margaret 1815–79, Indian-born Englishwoman, began photography at 50 taking beautifully posed and lit portraits of locals on the Isle of Wight, and later in Sri Lanka, and of famous contemporaries such as the poet Tennyson, whose *Idylls of the King* she illustrated with her photographs.
Capa, Robert 1913–54, Hungarian-born photojournalist, gained fame with Spanish Civil War pictures and covered World War II for *Life* magazine. Founding Magnum Photos with Cartier-Bresson in 1947, he concentrated on guiding younger members of the agency until going to cover war in Indo-China (now Vietnam)

continued

Major photographers continued

5512 where he was killed.

Cartier-Bresson, Henri b. 1908, French painter turned photographer, co-founder of Magnum Photos, famed for his ability to encapsulate a brief moment in time without contrivance, finding the most telling images.

Curtis, Edward 1868–1952, American photographer who documented the life, customs, and dignity of Native Americans.

Evans, Walker 1903–1975, American photographer who recorded the lives of the rural poor and a famous series shot on New York subways.

Fenton, Roger 1819–69, English founder of the (Royal) Photographic Society and the first war photographer – in the Crimea – though long exposures made action scenes impossible.

Fox Talbot, William 1800–77 (**2**), English pioneer photographer discovered the latent image and developed calotype. Also the first to use photographs as illustrations for a book.

2

Frank, Robert b. 1924, American photographer of the urban scene; and of the photo essay *The Americans*.

Gardner, Alexander 1821–82, American photographer, especially of the Civil War, as one of Brady's team.

Heartfield, John 1891–1968, German photographer using photomontage as a tool for political and social comment.

Hill, David Octavius 1802–70, Scottish artist who, with the help of Robert Adamson, used calotypes of 450 sitters to help him paint a huge group portrait of the Assembly of the Free Church of Scotland. He collaborated in later photography.

Jackson, William Henry 1843–1942, American photographer of landscape, Nebraskan tribes, and the Union Pacific railroad. His pictures of Yellowstone were influential in persuading Congress to create the National Park.

Kertész, André 1894–1985, Hungarian-born photographer of Paris street-life and artists bringing a surreal touch to documementary.

Lange, Dorothea 1895–1965, American photographer who attracted attention with studies of homeless migratory workers and joined the Farm Security Administration photographic team 1935–41.

Lartigue, Jacques-Henri 1894–1986, French painter and photographer who, rather than compose shots in a painterly way, took what are essentially snapshots, but ones which freeze passing moments in a fascinating way.

Lichfield, Lord (Patrick) b. 1939, English photographer noted for royal portraits and landscape photography.

McCullin, Donald b. 1935, English photojournalist, especially of war, though now concentrating on other subjects.

Mapplethorpe, Robert 1946–90, American photographer known especially for his male studies, often with erotic overtones, and portraits of flowers and people.

Muybridge, Eadweard 1830–1904, English-born photographer who made sequential shots to record movement in animals and people (initially to determine a bet by the Governor of California on how horses gallop).

Nagy, Laszlo Moholy 1895–1946, Hungarian photographer who led others in photographing objects from unusual angles, transforming the expected image.

O'Sullivan, Timothy c. 1840–82, American photographer for Brady during the Civil War, and of scenery, especially in Arizona and New Mexico.

Parkinson, Norman 1913–90, British fashion and portrait photographer, a leader in the field from 1930s, especially in his color work.

Penn, Irving b. 1917,–American photographer of fashion and celebrity portraits but also known for a series of photographs of Native Americans and one of laborers posed with their tools. He was an innovator in the use of large-grain in color photographs.

Ray, Man 1890–1976, American artist and photographer of witty and surreal studies.

Smith, Eugene 1918–78, American photographer for *Newsweek* and *Life*, badly wounded covering World War II. A moving study of the effects of pollution on a Japanese fishing community brought him a beating up by men from the company responsible.

Snowdon, Lord (Antony Armstrong-Jones) b. 1930, British portrait photographer, and social documentarian.

Steichen, Edward 1879–1973, American photographer. He trained as a painter and used chemicals to create impressionistic images, but after commanding the US Army photographic division in World War I he followed a more realistic style of clear-cut images.

Stieglitz, Alfred 1864–1946, American photographer, advocate of an aesthetic value for photography outside any descriptive or utilitarian role. He is noted for hand camera shots of New York in all kinds of weather, and made a remarkable "extended" portrait of his wife, Georgia O'Keeffe, covering 1917-33.

Strand, Paul 1890–1976, American photographer whose direct, objective pictures showed the beauty of simple objects and forms.

Weston, Edward 1886–1958, American photographer, originally very romantic using retouching and soft focus but, influenced by Stieglitz, changed to using precise photography to reveal subtle tone and detail.

Photo-art terms

5513 Lens, aperture, exposure time, filters, double exposure, lighting, enlargement to show grain, choice of film stock and printing paper all affect the photographic image. These are further ways in which it can be manipulated.

bas relief Effect of dimensional depth created by making a light-positive image on film and exposing this sandwiched with the negative but not quite in alignment when making a print.

chemical toning Converting a black and white image to color by the use of chemicals or dies.

collage Combining images from several photographs, usually rephotographing to provide a finished print.

combination printing Abutting images from more than one negative to create one image, as in creating a panoramic scene, usually by joining prints and rephotographing, or combining the same image repeated to form repetitive or kaleidoscopic effects.

contre jour Photographed into the sun or light source.

cropping Cutting or framing an image to improve the composition of the image.

image distortion Changing the spacial relationship between parts of the image, usually by printing with paper at an angle to the enlarger beam.

lith processing Making intermediate negatives exposed to different tonal values, used in posterization.

montage printing Combining two images so that they appear as one.

posterization Producing an image in which certain levels of grey tone are eliminated, using lith processing. This limits the range of tones for more graphic boldness.

pseudo-solarization The Sabattier effect.

Sabbatier effect Tonal reversal of parts of the image by exposing a negative to light half way through its development.

tone separation Another name for posterization.

552 CINEMA

Early cinema: silent films

5521 1895 saw the simultaneous introduction of a series of cameras and projectors in both Europe and the USA. Named Kinetoscope, Cinematographe, or Bioscope, they all did the same thing - they recorded and reproduced black and white images of people and places, which moved. The technical aspects of the cinema developed amazingly fast. Within three decades almost everything in use today had been demonstrated: color, 3-D, wide-screen, and sound.

The earliest films were of everyday scenes and actions, running only a minute or two. Soon one and two reel comedies and dramas were being made. But they were not the jerky, naïve productions sometimes seen on television today. Good prints, projected at correct speed, show us that they were well-mounted and photographed, their moods and motivations clarified by specially arranged or composed music played live in the cinemas.

Early US film production was centered on New York. From 1909 the independent film-makers moved to southern California to avoid the production ban which the American and French equipment companies tried to impose on them.

At the outbreak of the First World War in 1914 world cinema production was led by Europe - especially by Italy with its spectacles *Quo Vadis?* 1912, *Cabiria* 1913 and by France with Max Linder comedies, its Louis Feuillade serials with cliff-hanger endings and *film d'art* [Sara Bernhardt in *Queen Elizabeth* 1912].
The French Pathé company alone distributed more film in the US than all the American producers combined. The First World War reversed this situation. Disrupted European production gave the US industry an advantage which it never really lost.

American producers began combining into large companies to gain market advantage, increasing efficiency with the studio system and encouraging audience loyalty through the star system. They also exploited postwar economic conditions in Europe, financing production there, then importing its better talents, including directors whose styles created genres and stars who became legends. Since films had no recorded dialogue there were no language problems, so Hollywood movies were seen all over the world.

EVENTS
1900 *Cinderella* by Georges Mélies.
1902 *Le Voyage dans la Lune* by Georges Mélies (**1**).

1

1903 *The Great Train Robbery*, produced by Edwin Porter.
1905 Nickelodeon, early cinema, Pittsburgh.
1909 D. W. Griffith transforms child actress Gladys Smith into Mary Pickford.
1910 *Effecting a Cure* by D. W. Griffith.
1912 Sarah Bernhardt in *Queen Elizabeth.* Charles Pathé produces first news film.
1913 Hollywood becomes center of the film industry.
First Charles Chaplain motion picture.
1914 *A Versatile Villain* by Mack Sennet.
1915 *The Tramp* by Charles Chaplin.
The Birth of a Nation produced by D.W. Griffith.
1916 *Intolerance* by D. W. Griffith.
1919 *Blind Husbands* by Eric von Stroheim. *The Cabinet of Doctor Caligari* by Robert Wiene. United Artists Corporation formed. Mary Pickford marries Douglas Fairbanks.
1921 *The Kid* by Charles Chaplin.
1922 *Nanook of the North* by Robert Flaherty. *The Iron Horse* by John Ford. *Nosferatu* by F. W. Murnau.
1923 *A Woman of Paris* by Charles Chaplin. *The Covered Wagon* by James Cruse. *Safety Last* by Harold Lloyd. *Our Hospitality* by Buster Keaton. First Film Festival in Venice. Warner Brothers founded.
1924 *The Ten Commandments* by Cecil B. de Mille. *The Last Laugh* by Murnau. Metro-Goldwyn-Mayer founded.
1925 *The Gold Rush* by Charles Chaplain. *Battleship Potemkin* by Sergei Eisenstein.
1926 *Ben Hur* with Ramon Navarro.
Greta Garbo's first US motion picture.
Metropolis by Fritz Lang. *Napoleon* by Abel Gance.
1927 *The General* by Buster Keaton.

STARS AND DIRECTORS OF THE SILENT SCREENS
Arbuckle, Roscoe "Fatty" 1881–1932, American comedy fat-boy of early two-reelers. Career ended by involvement in a hotel bedroom scandal in which a girl died.
Barrymore, John 1882–1942, American star, talented, romantic leading man with the famous profile. Long career which tailed off due to alcoholism.
Brookes, Louise 1906–85, American flapper (**2**) who made an incredible impact in two German films directed by G.W. Pabst, *Pandora's Box* and *Diary of A Lost Girl* (1929). Her individuality lost her favor with the US studios.

2

Bow, Clara 1905–65. American, sexy "It" girl, vivaciously portrayed the typical 20s flapper (**2**).
Chaplin, Charles 1889–1977, British-born legendary and influential comedian, worked in America. Limited output. Most famous films built around a little-man, tramp with bowler hat and cane character as he is shown here – *City Lights, Gold Rush* etc.
Fairbanks, Douglas (Julius Ullman) 1883–1939, American swashbuckling, acrobatic star of adventure films, *Robin Hood, Thief of Bagdad,* etc. Married Mary Pickford.
Felix the Cat American cartoon character created about 1921.
Gilbert, John 1897–1936, American leading man. Achieved most fame partnering Garbo– *Flesh and the Devil* (1927), *Love* (1928). Career became a casualty of studio politics at the introduction of sound.
Gish, Dorothy (Dorothy de Guiche) 1898–1968, American actress popular in films of D. W. Griffith, *Hearts of the World,* (1918). Sister of Lillian Gish.
Griffith, D. W. 1874–1948, American pioneer producer-director. Developed and refined existing techniques. Noted for sentimental domestic subjects–*Broken Blossoms* (1919) –and epics–*Birth of a Nation* (1915), *Intolerance* (1916).
Hart, William Surrey 1870–1946, American, first cowboy star (as Rio Jim, "the good badman").
Ince, Thomas Harper 1882–1924, American pioneer director, worked with Sennett, Griffith, and Hart. Considered initiator of the studio system, died in mysterious circumstances.
Keaton, Buster (Joseph Francis) 1895–1966, great American silent film comedian (**3**). Usually portrayed a pale young man whose impassive, quiet determination brought both disaster and ultimate triumph – *The General* (1927), *Sherlock Jnr* (1924). Conflict with studio chief, Louis B. Mayer, shortened his career.

3

continued

Early Cinema: silent films continued

5521 **Linder, Max (Gabriel Leuvielle)** 1883–1925, French comedian of national celebrity, influenced Chaplin and others. His character was that of a well-off bachelor in pursuit of well-bred, pretty women.
Lloyd, Harold 1893–1971, American comedian with business acumen who successfully continued into sound films. Famous as a bespectacled, timid, clean-cut, young American, his films often featured thrilling stunts, notably hanging from a high building by the hands of a clock.
Lumière, Auguste 1862–1954, and **Louis** 1864-1948, French inventors and pioneer film-makers. The first Frenchmen, in 1895, to demonstrate moving pictures with their Cinematographe. Subsequently, as producers, they spent much time fighting their rivals Gaumont and Pathé.
Méliès, Georges 1861–1938, French conjuror who produced the cinema's first trick and fantasy films. Imaginative and humorous, some of his techniques remain a mystery.
Murnau, F. W. (F. W. Plumpe) 1888–1931, Imaginative German director, often worked with Emil Jannings–*Nosferatu* (1922), *The Last Laugh* (1924). Made some films in America including *Sunrise* (1927).
Negri, Pola (Applonia Chalupek) 1897–1987, Polish-born actress who also worked in Germany. In 1922 she became first European to be given the Hollywood star treatment. Exotic and vampish, her success barely outlasted the silent era.
Pickford, Mary (Gladys Mary Smith), 1893-1979, Canadian-born astute American actress (**4**), noted for her portrayals of ringletted adolescents, known as "the world's sweetheart." She co-founded United Artists and became very wealthy. First married to Douglas Fairbanks.
Porter, Edwin S. 1870–1941, Scots-born American director. Worked for the Edison Company in the first years of the century, introducing to America many innovations in cinematic technique: close-ups, cross-cutting, stop-action and double exposure – *The Great Train Robbery* (1903).

4

Sennett, Mack (Michael Sinnott) 1884–1960, Canadian-born American producer and director of wild irreverent slapstick comedies, the biggest, most original influence of his time. With the Keystone Company he developed the Keystone Kops, the Sennett Bathing Beauties and produced Arbuckle, Chaplin, Keaton, and Swanson.
Valentino, Rudolph (Rudolpho Guglielmi Di Valentino). 1895–1926, Italian-born American romantic idol (**5**), usually cast as elegant gigolo or exotic lover – *Four Horsemen of the Apocalypse* (1922), *The Sheikh* (1921).
White, Pearl 1889–1938, American actress, known as the queen of the silent serials, *The Perils of Pauline* (1914), the *Exploits of Elaine* (1914), etc.

5

The Talkies

5522 The first commercially successful sound films were made by Warner Brothers using synchronized gramophone discs. The first feature film with dialogue (*Don Juan*) was shown in 1926 but it was not until a year later that a sound film caught the public imagination, *The Jazz Singer.* Within two years Fox studios had a successful sound-on-film recording system. After that studios fell over themselves to find more new ideas that could fight the effects of the recession and keep audiences in the cinema.

Gradually they succeeded and in the pre-war period Hollywood produced three-fourths of the world's films, in 1937 alone it made 600 titles. At the end of World War II, just as Hollywood hoped for access to world markets lost by the conflict, those very countries decided to protect their own industries and imposed import taxes and quotas. American studio profits were further affected by labor disputes, Federal Court decisions under the Anti-Trust laws (divorcing the control of cinemas from production companies), the upheavals caused by Senator McCarthy and the un-American Activities Committee, as well as currency and tax restrictions - including the freezing of dollar funds abroad. Cinema attendances dropped as television became more popular.

Studios fought back with larger and clearer screen pictures through the inventions of Cinemascope, Cinerama, Todd A-O and 70 mm prints. Eastmancolor, cheaper and easier to use, replaced Technicolor. Sound improved with the use of stereo and the Dolby (noise reduction) system. The other novelties of 3-D and Aromarama proved short-lived. Technical innovations spurred producers to make more colorful and spectacular films, giving experiences which could not be imitated by television. It also encouraged subjects of sex and violence, thought of at the time as unsuitable for home viewing.

But bigger pictures meant much bigger initial investment and with the waning power of so many of the old style studio chiefs, through retirement or death, accountants and bankers assumed a more central place in the production process.

The audience decline was not arrested. Some studios merged or closed. Some, who had been in B-feature production, easily transferred their craft and low-budget know-how to television production. Today most American studio names are now international organizations (sometimes a division of a global enterprise) specializing in distribution and finance. No longer actively involved in production they are the heart of "The deal." Packages (script/director/star) devised by agents and artists may be financed, brokered or distributed by them, sometimes to or through other companies. Most producers are now "independents," needing to measure success by tie-ins with books, records and merchandise. And their film's international release may mean to a videocassette company or to a TV satellite, "footprinting" millions of homes in parts of the world previously counted in movie theaters. Cinema is no longer limited to being a picture on a strip of celluloid projected to groups of people. It is now a moving image recalled from many different storage methods, still seen by millions, sometimes simultaneously, or one by one.

EVENTS
1927 *The Jazz Singer,* with Al Jolson, first "talkie" (**1**).

1

2

1927 *King of Kings* by Cecil B. de Mille.
1928 *Plane Crazy,* the first Walt Disney cartoon, was released. *Diamond Lil,* with Mae West. *The Circus* by Charles Chaplin. *Un Chien Andalou* by Louis Buñuel. *October* by Eisenstein.
1929 *The Love Parade* by Ernst Lubitsch. Warner Bros announce they will make no more "black and white" films.
1930 *The Blue Angel* by Joseph von Sternberg *Murder* by Alfred Hitchcock. Advent of the wider screen.
1931 *M* by Fritz Lang.
1932 *A Nous la Liberté* by René Clair. *Trouble in Paradise* by Ernst Lubitsch. *Blonde Venus* by Josef von Sternberg. Gary Cooper in *A Farewell to Arms.* Shirley Temple's debut (**2**).
1933 Alexander Korda's *The Private Life of Henry VIII,* with Charles Laughton. *King Kong* by Merian C. Cooper and Ernest B. Schoedsack.
1934 *Twentieth Century* by Howard Hawks. *Merry Widow* by Ernst Lubitsch. *Toni* by Jean Renoir. *The Scarlet Empress* by Josef von Sternberg.

continued

The talkies continued

5522 *The Last Millionaire* by René Clair.
1935 Greta Garbo in *Anna Karenina*.
The Thirty-Nine Steps by Alfred Hitchcock.
1936 *Modern Times* by Charles Chaplin.
Triumph of the Will by Leni Riefenstahl.
1937 *Snow White and the Seven Dwarfs* by Walt Disney.
1937 *The Great Illusion* by Jean Renoir.
1938 *Alexander Nevsky* by Sergei Eisenstein.
Bringing Up Baby by Howard Hawks. *The Lady Vanishes* by Alfred Hitchcock.
1939 *Gone With the Wind* with Clark Gable (**3**) and Vivien Leigh. *Stage Coach* by John Ford.
Ninotchka by Ernst Lubitsch. *The Rules of the Game* by Jean Renoir.
1940 *The Great Dictator* by Charles Chaplin.
The Philadelphia Story by George Cukor.
1941 *Meet John Doe* by Frank Capra.
Citizen Kane by Orson Welles.
1942 *Battle of Midway* by John Ford.
To Be or Not to Be by Ernst Lubitsch.
1943 *Casablanca* by Michael Curtiz.
1944 *Hail the Conquering Hero* by Preston Sturges. *Going My Way* by Leo McCarey.
1945 *Rome, Open City* by Roberto Rossellini.
1946 *My Darling Clementine* by John Ford.
1947 *Monsieur Verdoux* by Charles Chaplin.
1948 *Red River* by Howard Hawks. *The Big Sleep*, with Humphrey Bogart. Warner Brothers-Pathé produce first color newsreel. *Bicycle Thieves* by Vittorio De Sica.
1949 *The Third Man* by Carol Reed with Orson Welles.

3

STUDIOS

Columbia Founded 1920 as C-B-C (Joe Brandt, Jack and Henry Cohn), named Columbia 1924. Produced low-budget and B-features, also serials *(Blondie* and *Batman*). Some success in the 30s with sophisticated comedies and in the 40s with single star vehicles. Still a major player.

MGM Biggest of the Hollywood studios, founded 1924 (Metro Pictures, the Goldwyn Co, and Louis B. Mayer Productions). Studio head Mayer made family-oriented subjects, from the modest *Andy Hardy* series to lavish color costume musicals. Postwar studio head, Dore Schary, shifted emphasis to westerns and serious dramas.

Paramount Adolph Zukor merged Famous Players company with Jessy Lasky's Co in 1916 then acquired Paramount Pictures distribution company. Noted for comedies with Mae West, the Marx Brothers, Bing Crosby, and Bob Hope. Other films were sophisticated, European style ones. Continues successfully as a Gulf & Western company.

RKO Started 1928. (Radio Corporation of America, distribution company Film Booking Offices of America, cinema chain the Keith-Orpheum Corporation.) Major company with some memorable films but unstable management. Sold 1955.

Twentieth Century-Fox Founded by William Fox, 1916. First company to succeed with sound-on-film recording,1927. Merged with Twentieth Century Productions,1935. Studio head Darryl F. Zanuck, later Spyros P. Skouras. Produced stories with American settings, then musicals and action pictures in color, postwar social dramas and location thrillers. Now owned by Rupert Murdoch.

Universal (Founded 1909 as the Independent Motion Picture Co. by Carl Laemmle). Made many routine features, serials, B-westerns, but most associated with horror films. Merged with International Pictures, 1946. Bought by Music Corporation of America 1962, now associated with Steven Spielberg films.

United Artists Differs from other companies, it never owned a studio. Started in 1919, by Chaplin, Fairbanks, Pickford, and Griffith, to distribute their work. From 1924 run by Joseph Schenck. At various times has handled the work of Sam Goldwyn, Walt Disney, David O. Selznick, and Alexander Korda. Sold to MGM in 1981.

Warner Brothers Pictures Founded 1923. First company to have commercial success with a sound feature (*The Jazz Singer*, 1927). Studio boss Jack Warner specialized in budget films made with gritty realism: gangster stories, comedies, even musicals.1950s ventures into new technologies were costly and the company now survives as film production arm of Warner Communications.

STARS AND DIRECTORS OF HOLLYWOOD MOVIES
[American unless stated otherwise]

Allen, Woody (Allen Stewart Konigsberg) b. 1935. Director of nostalgic, sophisticated comedies often stylistic spoofs (**4**) – *Annie Hall* (1977), *Hannah & Her Sisters* (1986), *Radio Days* (1987).

4

Astaire, Fred (Frederick Austerlitz) 1899–1987. Dancing star/actor – *Top Hat* (1935), *Easter Parade* (1948), *Funny Face* (1957), *Towering Inferno* (1975).

Beatty, Warren b. 1937. Actor/director – *Bonnie & Clyde* (1967), *Reds* (1981), *Dick Tracey* (1990).

Bergman, Ingrid 1915–82, Swedish-born actress – *Casablanca* (1943), *Spellbound* (1945), *Murder on the Orient Express* (1974).

Berkeley, Busby (William Berkeley Enos) 1895–1976. Director specializing in song and dance – *42nd Street* (1933), *Strike Up the Band* (1940), *For Me & My Girl* (1942).

Bogart, Humphrey 1899–1957. Actor of tough-guy roles (**5**) – *The Petrified Forest* (1936), *Casablanca* (1942), *The Big Sleep* (1946), *The African Queen* (1951), *The Caine Mutiny* (1954).

5

Burton, Richard (Richard Jenkins) 1925–84, Welsh-born British-American actor – *Look Back in Anger* (1959), *Cleopatra* (1962), *Who's Afraid of Virginia Woolf* (1966), *The Taming of the Shrew* (1967).

Coppola, Francis Ford b. 1939. Director (**6**) – *The Godfather* (1972), *Apocalypse Now* (1979), *The Cotton Club* (1984), *Gardens of Stone* (1987).

6

Crawford, Joan (Lucille le Sueur) 1908–77. Intense actress – *Rain* (1933), *Mildred Pierce*, (1945), *Whatever Happened to Baby Jane?* (1962).

Cronenberg, David b. 1943, Canadian-born cult sci-fi director – *Rabid* (1977), *Videodrome* (1982), *Dead Ringers* (1988).

Davis, Bette 1908–89. Actress of bitchy roles *Dangerous* (1935), *Little Foxes* (1941), *All*

continued

The talkies continued

5522 *About Eve* (1950), *Whatever Happened to Baby Jane?* (1962).

DeMille, Cecil Blount 1881–1959. Pioneer producer-director with long, active career. Most noted for early sex comedies, biblical epics, and action adventures – *Squaw Man* (1913), *The Cheat* (1915), *King of Kings* (1927), *The Ten Commandments* (1923 and 1956).

Dean, James 1931–55. Moody iconic actor. *East of Eden* (1955), *Rebel Without A Cause* (1955), *Giant* (1956).

Dietrich, Marlene (Maria Magdalena von Losch) 1901–92, German actress/cabaret style singer of smouldering glamour (**7**) – *Blue Angel* (1930), *Shanghai Express* (1932), *Scarlet Empress*, (1934), *Destry Rides Again* (1939), *Judgement at Nuremberg* (1961).

7

Eastwood, Clint 1930. Actor director (**8**). *A Fistfull of Dollars* (1964), *Play Misty for Me* (1971), *Bird* (1988).

8

Flaherty, Robert J. 1884–1951. Documentary film-maker, uncompromising, poetic. *Nanook of the North* (1922), *Man of Aran* (1934), *Louisiana Story* (1948).

Fonda, Henry 1905–82. Actor – *Young Mr Lincoln* (1939), *The Grapes of Wrath* (1939), *Twelve Angry Men* (1957), *On Golden Pond* (1981). Father of Jane.

Fonda, Jane b. 1937. Actress. *Cat Ballou* (1965), *Klute* (1971), *Coming Home* (1978), *On Golden Pond* (1981).

Ford, John (Sean Aloysius O'Feeney) 1895–1973. Legend-creating director with long career *Iron Horse* (1924), *Stagecoach* (1939), *The Grapes of Wrath* (1939), *The Quiet Man* (1952), *The Searchers* (1956), *Seven Women* (1966).

Ford, Harrison b. 1942. Actor. *Raiders of the Lost Ark* (1981), *Witness* (1985).

Garbo, Greta (Greta Gustafsson) 1905–90, Swedish actress who became a legendary Hollywood star. Despite skirmishes with studio bosses and a desire to keep a private life, her bankability ensured her survival. Retired 1941. *Flesh & the Devil* (1927), *Queen Christina* (1934), *Camille* (1936), *Ninotchka* (1939).

Gish, Lillian (Lillian de Guiche) 1899–1993. Actress of delicate beauty and resilient longevity. *Birth of A Nation* (1915), *Broken Blossoms* (1919), *The Wind* (1928), *Duel in the Sun* (1946), *Night of the Hunter* (1955), *The Whales of August* (1987).

Hitchcock, Sir Alfred 1899–1980. British director, from 1940 in Hollywood. *Blackmail* (1929), *39 Steps* (1935), *Rebecca* (1940), *Psycho* (1960), *The Birds* (1963).

Hoffman, Dustin b. 1937. Versatile actor. *Midnight Cowboy* (1969), *All the President's Men* (1976), *Kramer v Kramer* (1980), *Tootsie* (1983), *Rain Man* (1988).

Karloff, Boris 1887–1969, British-born US actor famous for role of monster in *Frankenstein* (1931), *Unconquered* (1947), *Targets* (1967).

Lang, Fritz 1890–1976. German director of distinction. *Metropolis* (1926), *M* (1931), *Testament of Dr Mabuse* (1932). Moved to Hollywood 1935. *Woman in the Window* (1944), *The Big Heat* (1953).

Laurel and Hardy Comedy team of Stan Laurel 1890–1965, real name Stanley Jefferson, and Oliver Hardy 1892–1957 (**9**). Hardy played an authoritative father-figure and Laurel was his opposite – irresponsible and childlike. *Our Relations* (1936), *Way Out West* (1937).

9

Leigh, Vivien (Vivien Hartley) 1913–67, British leading actress. *Gone With the Wind* (1939), *Caesar and Cleopatra* [UK] (1945), *Streetcar Named Desire* (1951).

Lubitsch, Ernst 1892–1947, German-born director of polished, witty, amoral comedy. Worked in Hollywood. *Forbidden Paradise* (1924), *Design for Living* (1933), *Ninotchka* (1939), *To Be or Not To Be* (1942).

Marx brothers Comedy team of brothers Chico (Leonard) 1891–1961, Harpo (Adolph) 1893-1964, Groucho (Julius) b. 1895, Zeppo (Herbert) b. 1900 (**10**). A fifth brother Gummo (Milton) b. 1901 was originally a part of their live act. *Animal Crackers* (1930), *Duck Soup* (1933), *A Night at the Opera* (1935).

10

Monroe, Marilyn (Norma Jean Baker) 1926–62. Actress whose sex appeal was exploited and not her other gifts (**11**). *Gentlemen Prefer Blondes* (1953), *Bus Stop* (1956), *Some Like It Hot* (1959), *The Misfits* (1961).

11

Nicholson, Jack b. 1937. Actor. *One Flew Over the Cuckoo's Nest* (1976), *Terms of Endearment* (1983).

Poitier, Sidney b. 1924. Black actor whose roles and persona have helped reduce race barriers. *No Way Out* (1950), *Blackboard Jungle* (1955), *Heat of the Night* (1967), *Guess Who's Coming to Dinner* (1967).

Streep, Meryl b. 1951. Versatile actress. *Kramer v Kramer* (1979), *Sophie's Choice* (1982), *Out of Africa* (1986).

Spielberg, Steven b. 1947. Director and producer. *Jaws* (1975), *Close Encounters of the Third Kind* (1977), *ET* (1982), *Indiana Jones and the Last Crusade* (1989), *Jurassic Park* (1993).

Stroheim, Erich von 1885–1957, Austrian-born director and actor. His costly passion for exactitude produced influential films of brilliance but ultimately curtailed his directing career. *Greed* (1923), *Wedding March* (1926–28), *Queen Kelly* (1928). Acted in *La Grande Illusion* [Fr] (1937), *Five Graves to Cairo* (1943), *Sunset Boulevard*, (1950).

Swanson, Gloria (Josephine Swenson) 1898–1983. Star actress and producer with long career. Started in Sennett comedies, graduating to roles of voluptuous luxury with DeMille. *Male and Female* (1919), *Queen Kelly* (1928), *Sunset Boulevard* (1950).

Taylor, Elizabeth b. 1932, British born star *Cleopatra* (1962), *Who's Afraid of Virginia Woolf?* (1962).

Welles, Orson 1915–85. Actor and director (**12**) whose unconventionality did not fit the studio system. *Citizen Kane* (1941), *The Magnificent Ambersons* (1942), *The Third Man* (1949), *Othello* (1952), *Touch of Evil* (1958), *The Trial* (1962), *Chimes at Midnight* (1966).

12

World cinema

5523 The Russian revolution of 1917 accorded film making a value in the nation's affairs, as a medium of information and also of propaganda. Nazi Germany realized this value too, and gradualy so did every country which could finance its own industry. Cinema was used throughout World War II to motivate the fight and soothe the battle-weary the world over. Afterwards cinema became an important symbol of national recovery and independence. Feature production, often undertaken in technically limited conditions, developed very differently in each country, depending on its politics, ideology, and economic conditions as well as local traditions and tastes.

In western Europe, Germany in the Nazi period was noted for its strong visuals. France developed an "alternative" and art cinema in the 30s, and postwar the "New Wave" directors found revitalizing approaches to both techniques and subjects. Italy re-emerged as a cinematic force in the 40s with neo-realism, then developed both a commercial sector for spectacular international co-productions and spaghetti westerns along with highly personal films from a range of talented directors.

British cinema evolved a non-commercial documentary movement in the 30s and immediately postwar a series of idiosyncratic anti-authoritarian productions known as the Ealing comedies.

Russian cinema produced some of the glories of early silent and sound film. It declined under Stalin but, along with other eastern European countries, produced individual films of note after his death.

Asia has three of the world's biggest industries in India, Hong Kong, and China. All produce many popular titles – lurid Indian melodramas, Cantonese Kung Fu adventures are mostly of interest to those sharing the appropriate local language. Main exceptions are the films of Satyajit Ray (India) and the work of one or two directors in the provincial studios in Communist China which reflect recent liberal trends.

Finally, Japan produces both popular monster and violent gangster titles for its home market but has a strong list of directors of international interest.

EVENTS
1950 *Rashomon* by Akira Kurosawa. *Sunset Boulevard* by Billy Wilder.
1951 *The African Queen* by John Huston. *Strangers on a Train* by Alfred Hitchcock.
1952 *High Noon* by Fred Zinnemann.
1953 *Monsieur Hulot's Holiday* by Jacques Tati. Cinemascope introduced by Twentieth Century-Fox in *The Robe.*
1954 *Seven Samurai* by Akiro Kurosawa. *La Strada* by Federico Fellini.
1955 *Rebel Without a Cause,* by Nicholas Ray. *French Can-Can* by Jean Renoir. *Rock Around the Clock* with Bill Haley.
1956 *The Seventh Seal* by Ingmar Bergman.
1959 *Ben-Hur* by William Wyler. *Some Like it Hot* by Billy Wilder.
1960 *La Dolce Vita* by Federico Fellini. *Breathless* by Jean-Luc Godard. *Psycho* by Alfred Hichcock (**1**).

1

1961 *Jules and Jim* by François Truffaut.
1966 *Blow-Up* by Michelangelo Antonioni.
1967 *2001: A Space Odyssey* by Stanley Kubrick.
1969 *Easy Rider* starring Peter Fonda and Denis Hopper. *Satyricon* by Federico Fellini.
1970 *Claire's Knee* by Eric Rohmer.
1971 *Death in Venice* by Luchino Visconti.
1972 *The Godfather* by Francis Ford Coppola.
1974 *Scenes from a Marriage* by Ingmar Bergman.
1975 *One Flew Over the Cuckoo's Nest* by Milos Forman.
1976 *Rocky* by John Avildsen.
1977 *Annie Hall* by Woody Allen. *Star Wars* by George Lucas.
1978 *Superman* by Richard Donner.
1979 *Manhattan* by Woody Allen. *The Marriage of Maria Braun* by Rainer Werner Fassbinder.
1981 *Mephisto* by Istvan Szabo.
1982 *Gandhi* by Richard Attenborough. *ET* by Steven Spielberg.
1983 *The Day After* by Milos Forman.
1985 *Out of Africa* by Sydney Pollack.
1986 *The Color Purple* by Steven Spielberg.
1987 *The Last Emperor* by Bernardo Bertolucci.

STARS AND DIRECTORS OF WORLD CINEMA

Bardot, Brigitte (Camille Javal) b. 1933, French (sex-kitten) actress – *God Created Woman* (1956).
Bergman, Ingmar b. 1918, Swedish director. *Smiles of a Summer Night* (1955), *Wild Strawberries,* (1957), *Fanny and Alexander* (1982).
Bogarde, Dirk (Derek Van Den Bogaerd) b. 1920, British actor. *Victim* (1961), *Death in Venice* (1971).
Buñuel, Luis 1900–83, Spanish director, worked in France and Mexico, surrealist, subversive. *Un Chien Andalou* (1928), *Viridiana,* (1961), *Belle de Jour* (1966).
Clair, René (Rene Chomette) 1898–81, French director. *Italian Straw Hat* (1927), *A Nous La Liberté* (1931), *I Married A Witch* [USA] (1942).
Depardieu, Gerard b. 1948, French actor. *Jean de Florette* (1985), *Cyrano de Bergerac* (1991). Some work in USA.
Eisenstein, Sergei 1898–1948, Russian director, influential theorist, particularly concerning montage. *Battleship Potemkin* (1925), *October* (1928), *Ivan the Terrible* (1 & 2) (1944–6).
Fassbinder, Rainer Werner 1946–82 (**2**), German director. *Fear Eats the Soul* (1974), *Lola* (1981).

2

Fellini, Federico b. 1920, Italian director. *La Strada* (1954), *Dolce Vita* (1960), *8½* (1963), *Casanova* (1976).
Gance, Abel 1889–1981, French producer-director, pioneer of new techniques, including wide-screen and stereo. *La Roué* (1922), *Napoleon* (1926).
Jancsó, Miklós b. 1921, Hungarian director *The Round-Up* (1975), *Red Psalm* (1971).
Jannings, Emil 1886–1950, German actor some work in USA. *The Last Laugh* (1924), *Blue Angel* (1930).
Kaige, Chen b. 1952, Chinese director. *Yellow Earth* (1984), *King of the Children* (1987).
Kurosawa, Akira b. 1910, Japanese director. *Rashomon* (1950), *Seven Samurai* (1954), *Ran* (1985).
Lean, Sir David 1908–91, British director. *Bridge on the River Kwai* (1957), *Passage to India* (1984).
Magnani, Anna 1907–73, Italian star. *Open City* (1945), *The Miracle* (1950), *Rose Tattoo* (1955).
Olivier, Laurence (Lord) 1907–89, British actor. *Rebecca* (1940), *Richard III* (1956), *Sleuth* (1972).
Paradjanov, Sergo b. 1924. Georgian director. *Colour of Pomegranites* (1969), *Legend of the Suram Fortress* (1985).
Powell, Michael 1905–90, British director. *Life and Death of Colonel Blimp* (1943), *Red Shoes* (1948).
Ray, Satyajit 1921–92, Indian Director. *Apu Trilogy* (1955-59), *Charulata* (1964), *Distant Thunder* (1973).
Renoir, Jean 1894–1979, French director. *La Grande Illusion* (1937), *Règle du Jeu* (1939),

continued

World cinema continued

5523

Resnais, Alain b. 1922, French director. *Hiroshima Mon Amour* (1959), *Last Year In Marienbad* (1961).
Tarkovsky, Andrei 1932–86, Russian director exiled in Paris at the end of his life. *Solaris* (1972), *Stalker* (1979), *Offret* (1986).
Truffaut, François 1932–84, French director. *Jules et Jim* (1961), *Day for Night* (1973).
Wajda, Andrzej b. 1926, Polish director. *Kanal* (1957), *Man of Marble* (1976), *Danton* (1982).

Movie terms

5524

animation Still paintings, drawings, or puppets filmed to give illusion of movement (cartoons). American Walt Disney, (1901–66), produced many, including the first full-length feature.
documentary Structured, factual film, sometimes part-dramatized with actors.
dubbing Replacing all or part of soundtrack with other sounds (French – *doubler*).
film noir Moody style of gangster or thriller film, often shot in dark contrasting images.
montage French for editing. Often means image developed by rapid cuts instead of in one shot.
new wave French 50s directors whose films revitalized techniques and subject matter.
reel A film spool, usually containing about 1,000 feet of film, approximate running times of 15 mins (silent) and 11 mins (sound). Early cinemas with one projector had to stop to change reels, thus a reel was a convenient production (or part) length and hired as a One (or Two)-Reeler.
star system Use of actors to attract and keep audiences, depends on actor constantly playing similar parts.
studio system Application of assembly-line manufacturing and cost control principles to film production. Emphasizes planning and management over creative process.
technicolor Three films, each sensitive to different colors, run simultaneously in a special camera. Superseded by Eastmancolor, single film which runs in standard camera.
western Stories of the white settlers in America and their conflicts with the Native Americans and each other. At first simplistic "cowboy and Indian" tales, they developed allegorical, mythical, and epic dimensions, rarely historically accurate. Usually made in USA, e.g. *Stagecoach, High Noon.* Italian 60s imitations known as Spaghetti Westerns.
widescreen Projection screen wider than the standard aspect ratio (proportion) of 4 ft high by 5 ft wide, usually 3 ft x 7 ft. Several patented systems: Cinemascope – uses standard proportion frame on 35 mm film but uses anamorphic lens to squeeze picture onto negative and again to correct it when projected from the print; Panavision – high quality system, uses double width (70 mm) film, either in camera and projection or for camera only and then squeezes the image onto 35 mm print for projection; Todd A-O uses 65 mm film; Vistavision – uses 35 mm film but run sidewise through the camera.

Technical terms in movies
close-up Holding the camera near the subject and taking the picture at close range (**1**).
cut Moving rapidly between scenes, to add pace and excitement to the narrative.
dubbing Can mean either replacing the soundtrack with a foreign language one, combining several soundtracks on a single one, or adding sounds such as music to the film.
fade in An effect in which the image appears on screen gradually out of darkness.
fade out The opposite of fade in, in which the image gradually fades away into darkness.
frames the individual still pictures which make up a film.
dissolve Moving from one scene to another by fading the first out and the second in so that the two merge imperceptibly.
long shot A shot in which the camera seems to be a long way from the subject, which appears in the distance (**2**).
panning Moving the camera to follow a moving object or person, or to create a panoramic view of a scene (**3**).
rough cut Preliminary edited footage.
rushes Unedited footage, usually screened at the end of a day's filming.
scene A series of shots that make up one single unit of the film's action. Also, the stage-setting and backcloths for a film.
sequence A single episode in a film which is uninterrupted.
take Each scene in a film is shot several times, to produce different versions for the director to choose from.
shot A series of frames concerned with a single event.
tracking Moving along with a camera to follow the action.

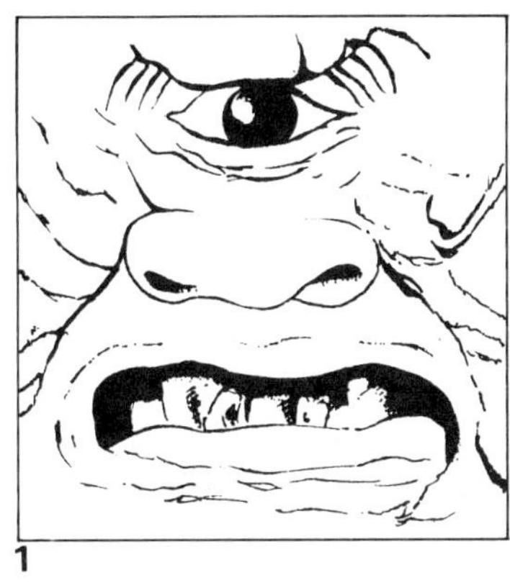
1

2

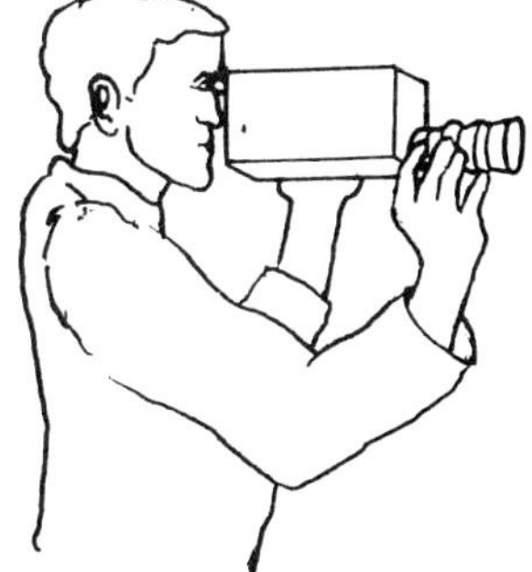

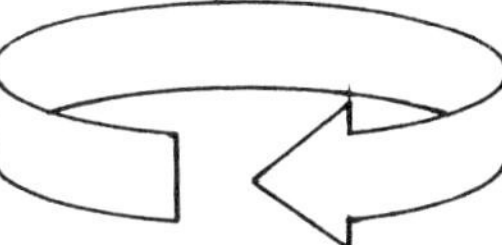
3

561 FURNITURE

Terms

5611

armoire Large ornate cabinet or wardrobe.
chaise longue Reclining chair with a long padded seat resembling a settee.
chesterfield Large padded sofa, often with button upholstery, with no woodwork showing.
cheval glass Long mirror mounted on swivels in a frame.
chiffonier Ornamental cabinet with drawers or shelves; high and narrow chest of drawers.
club chair Deep, thickly upholstered easy chair with heavy arms and sides, and often a low back.
commode Ornate, low cabinet or chest of drawers, usually on legs or short feet.
console table Table supported by decorative brackets fixed to a wall.
credenza Cupboard or sideboard, typically without legs.
davenport Small writing desk with side drawers and sloping top.
dos-à-dos Sofa that accommodates two people seated back to back.
escritoire Portable writing desk, typically with a hinged top closing over small drawers.
farthingale chair Armless chair with a high seat and low straight back.
fauteuil Upholstered armchair.
love seat Large chair or small sofa that seats two people.
morris chair Large easy chair with an adjustable back and big loose cushions.
ottoman Long upholstered seat, with or without back.
pier table Table designed to stand against a wall between two windows.
pouffe Large firm cushion used as a seat; low, soft, backless couch.
secrétaire Drop-front desk, sometimes with drawers below and a bookcase above.
tabouret Low stool or cabinet.
tallboy Double chest of drawers, with one section standing on top of the other.
teapoy Small tea table, typically with three legs.
tete-à-tete S-shaped sofa allowing two people to face each other when seated.
torchière Slender decorative candlestand, often with a tripod base.
triclinium Couch or set of couches surrounding three sides of a table.
whatnot or **étagère** Lightweight stand with three or more open shelves.
Windsor chair Comfortable wooden chair with arms, a spoked back, and splayed legs.

Styles

5612

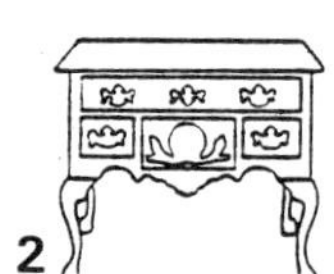

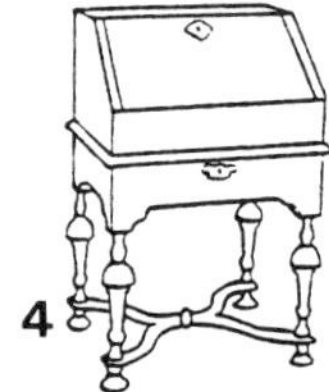

Abbotford period/baronial style monastic style Weighty Regency Gothic revival furniture of the 1820s and 1830s originally made for Sir Walter Scott's Abbotsford home (Scotland).
Adam Delicate 18th-century English neoclassical style developed by Robert Adam.
Adirondack furniture Simple American rural wood style (**1**) produced from the 1890s to the early 1940s. Named after the mountains in New York state.
American Chippendale Plainer and more Palladian version of the late 18th-century British domestic style (**2**). Used local woods, not just mahogany, and rural versions persisted beyond 1800. See country Chippendale.
American empire style Early 19th-century blending of French Empire and British Regency features in which mahogany was followed by rosewood and black walnut (1820s on). C H Lannuier and Duncan Phyfe were the outstanding makers.
American Jacobean furniture Predominant 17th-century colonial English form, also known as pilgrim due to most existing examples, especially oak chests, coming from New England. Rectangular, simply decorated, and a few basic types.
American moderne Loose description of a 1930s US style (**3**), derived from Art Deco and international modern, that often incorporated materials such as Bakelite and chrome.
American Queen Anne style Colonial style that started later and lasted longer than in Britain with more solid rather than veneered walnut being used.
American William and Mary style Longer lasting colonial version of the British style. Walnut and maple wood, together with new tables, desks (**4**), and cupboards, began to replace oak pieces in wealthy homes.
Art Deco Decorative arts and architectural style emanating from Paris in 1925 and common in both Europe and America. Stylized and modernist (**5**), it reconciled methods of mass-production and manufactured materials (such as Bakelite) as well as using luxury items. Furniture included metalwork designs.
art furniture movement British 1860s and 1870s design movement led by Eastlake and Godwin that favored simplicity but wanted fine design for mass production as well (**6**).
Art Nouveau Dominant style of decoration and of avant-garde design in Europe from the 1880s to World War I (**7**). Called *Le Modern Style* in France, *Jugendstil* in Germany, and *stile Liberty* in Italy. Art Nouveau creatively adapted sinuous natural forms in an attempt to avoid architectural and design styles based on archeological recreations of the past. Also influenced by Japanese art.
Arts and Crafts movement British late 19th-century crafts revival inspired by William Morris to return to individual craftsmanship in the tradition of medieval guilds, and thus non-industrial quality that included deliberately priming cottage furniture (**8**).
auricular style Dutch-devised sinuous early 17th-century variant on late mannerist ornamentation, originally developed in silverwork. The German description *Knorpelwerk* means "cartilage work" (**9**).

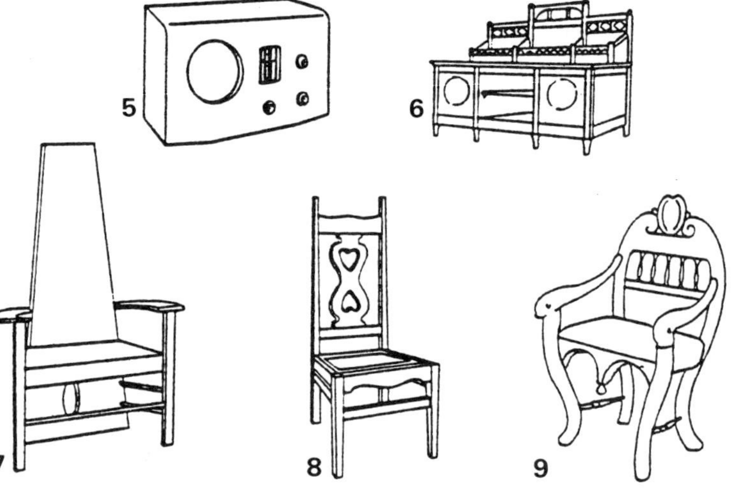

continued

Styles continued

561**2**

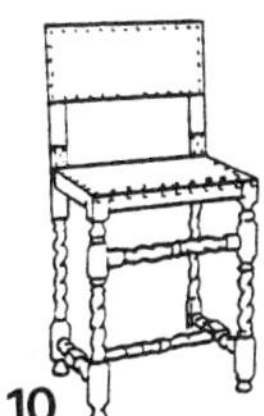
10

11

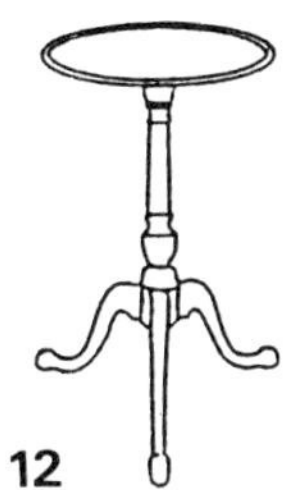
12

13

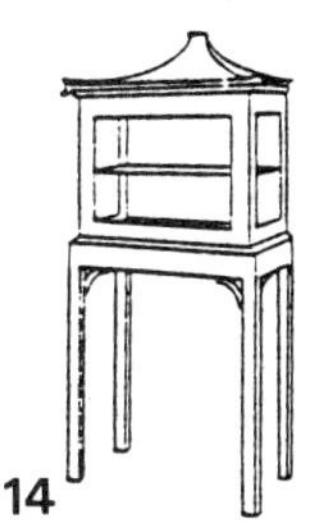
14

baroque 17th-century and early 18th-century European furniture (**10**) of elaborate ornamental character with sweeping S-curves an important feature.

Bauhaus German school of architecture and design 1919–33. Founded by the architect Walter Gropius, it epitomized the marriage of modern design, mass production, industrial design, and a Teutonic romantic approach to abstract art. Alfred Arndt (b. 1898) led the furniture workshop. Housed in Weimar until 1925 and in Dessau until 1932, it was finally closed down by the Nazis, though it continued to have a great influence on modern architecture and design.

Biedermeier sofa style Conventional 19th-century style developed in Germany and based on French Empire and English Regency neoclassical styles (**11**). Popular with the middle class, it spread to Scandinavia and Russia. Furniture came in light-colored woods with ebony ornamentation and horsehair upholstery. Named after a journal's figure of fun. See Danhauser Furniture makers and designers (561**3**).

Boston Chippendale Local American style produced c. 1755–90 featuring slender cabriole legs (**12**), sober ornamentation, and bombé chests.

Buhl or **Boule** or **Boulle** Style developed by the French cabinetmaker André C Boulle (1642–1732) using inlays of metal and tortoiseshell.

Byzantine chair furniture East Roman Empire furniture style based on Constantinople from the 5th to 15th centuries. Inherited and elaborated early Christian and Hellenistic forms, blending them with Persian, Islamic, and even Chinese influences (**13**). Featured elaborate turnings; metal X-frame chairs; foot stools; lecterns; round or semicircular dining tables; canopy beds; open and closed cupboards; separate bookcases in the late period; and elaborately decorated chests.

Chinese Chippendale Modern term for British 1750s and 1760s rococo fashion and oriental ornament, as popularized by Thomas  Chippendale, that featured pagodas and geometrical fretwork (**14**).

Chippendale Elegant and ornate mid 18th-century English style developed by Thomas Chippendale (**15, 16**).

Churrigueresque Lavishly exuberant Spanish baroque style named after three prolific architect brothers. Its chairs were usually leather upholstered and the decoration's abundant inlaid features influenced Spanish colonial patterns (**17**).

consulate style Brief French transitional period named after Napoleon's term as First Consul. More formal and rectangular than the preceding directoire pieces, it introduced many of the military and Egyptian motifs that became common under the Empire (**18**). New forms were the *lit droit* and the *lit en bateau.*

country Chippendale Late 18th-century rural English and American simplified version of the main style using local woods rather than mahogany (**19**).

desornamentado style Spanish late 16th-century reaction against excessive Renaissance decoration in architecture and furniture. The sparse furniture was allowed plain molding (**20**), turned legs, and panels. Lasted until the 19th century in Mexico and provincial Spain.

De Stijl Dutch purist modernist movement that published a magazine of this title 1917–31. At least four members, especially Gerrit Rietveld, designed furniture on a rigorous application of an ideology based on the right angle and use of primary colors.

directoire Revolutionary furniture that reduced in scale and simplified the preceding Louis XVI style, especially in its late Etruscan phase. New daybed forms it introduced were the *Méridienne* and the *Récamier.* The fasces and cape of liberty were important additions to the traditional classical ornaments.

directory/American regency Very early 19th-century transitional phase between early US federal and empire styles that drew on Sheraton's later output. Brought in paw feet, the federal eagle, classical flutings and Greek *klismos.*

Egyptian style/Egyptiennerie Although interest in ancient Egypt was apparent by the 1760s, it was Napoleon's Egyptian Expedition (1798–99) that inspired Dominique-Vivant Denon's *Voyage in Lower and Upper Egypt* (1802), a richly engraved style book that shaped Empire and Regency furniture on both sides of the Atlantic. The Egyptian style was revived in the US during the 1860s and 1870s (**21**).

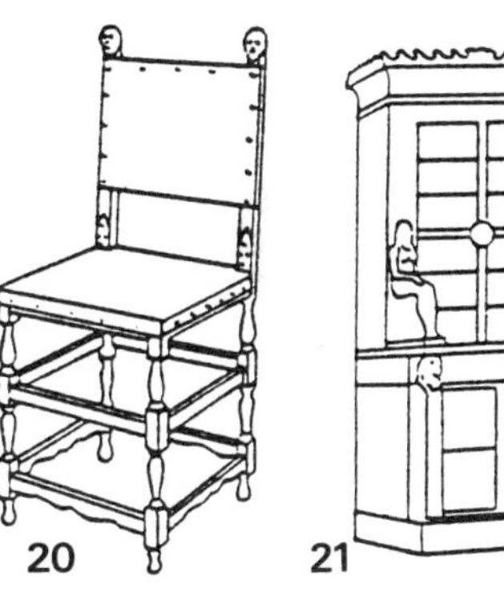
20 21

Empire style Virtually created by Napoleon's edict as First Consul (1799), it long outlasted Waterloo in Europe and America. Especially strong in furniture and furnishings (**22**), it emphasized martial glory, the letter N, Egyptiennerie, the swan (Josephine's favorite), gilt bronze, and mahogany. The *lit en bateau* and the *lit droit* were widely used, while the full-length Psyche mirror (cheval glass) gained widespread currency in what was the golden age of the military tailor.

22

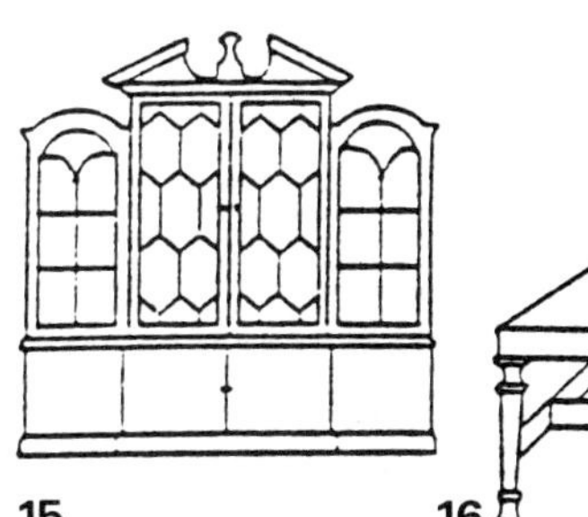
15

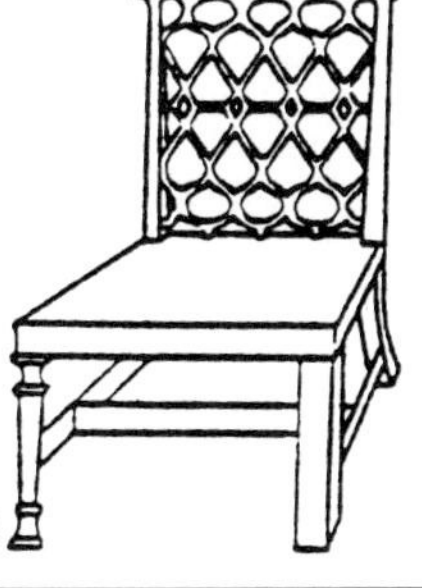
16

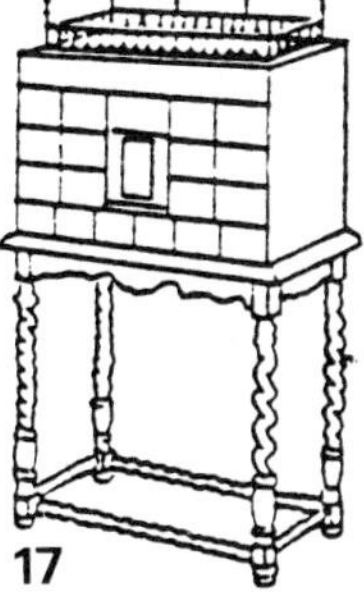
17

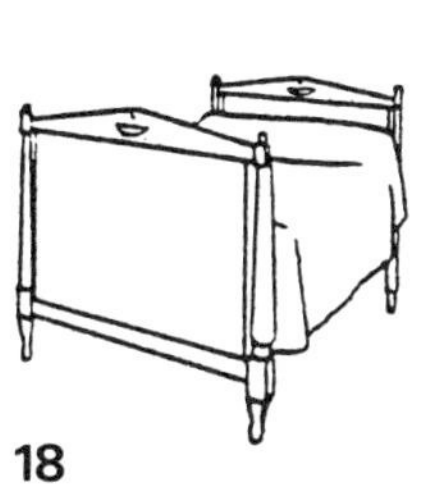
18

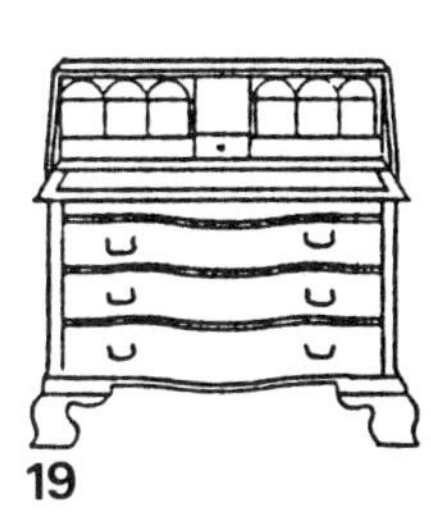
19

continued

Styles continued

5612

23

24

25

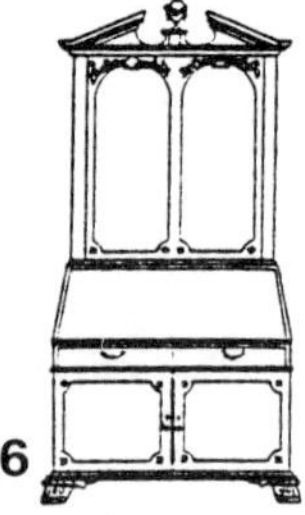

26

27

Etruscan furniture Inventive pieces by this ancient Greek-influenced people included the woven basket chair; the unique *cista,* round chest or casket; a solid tub-shaped armchair in bronze; bronze tripods and candelabra (**23**); and the placing of foot and head rests on the Greek *kline* (couch).

Federal style American neoclassical style coinciding with the first generation of the new republic. Blended Anglo-French influences in mainly mahogany or fruitwood pieces (**24**). The American eagle was the outstanding decorative feature.

Fernandino style Spanish Napoleonic Empire-derived style named after King Ferdinand VII (1820–33). Its somewhat clumsy products boasted bronze mounts, giltwood appliqué, and many classical symbols.

François I style French Italianate style that made furniture more colorful and elaborately carved. It incorporated architectural elements, arabesque, and mannerist motifs (**25**). Walnut was the most common wood employed.

Georgian style Term used in architecture to describe the range of late Renaissance English classical style, and in furniture for a variety of styles popular in England under the reigns of George I, II, and III (**26**). Its use reflects the fact that Britain's most famous designers (Chippendales, Adam brothers, Hepplewhite, and Sheraton) flourished in the greater part of this regal era.

Glasgow school A group of designers centered around the Glasgow School of Art, and led by Charles Rennie Mackintosh, his wife Margaret Macdonald, her sister Frances, and her husband Herbert MacNair. They were a major force in Art Nouveau handicrafts and architecture. The furniture was light, simple, and open, with Celtic motifs, and was marketed in London from 1898.

Gothic style European furniture from the 12th to 16th centuries revived in the 19th century. Massive oak pieces centered on the chest, stonemasonry-style carving, arcading, and vivid painting. Introduced the cupboard, wainscot chair, slab-ended stool/bench (15th century), and the linefold motif.

Greek ancient furniture Almost none survives, but there are artwork depictions from the 9th century BC to the Roman end of the Hellenistic era. The couch (*kline*) was the outstanding item. Seating types included the *diphros, diphros okladias*, and the *klismos*, a Greek invention. Tables were small three- or four-legged designs kept under the *kline*. The cupboard first appeared in Hellenistic times and the *kibotos* chest followed Egyptian precedent.

Hepplewhite style Furniture produced to or similar to the designs of the London shop-owner George Hepplewhite (active c. 1760–86), whose posthumous *Cabinet-maker and Upholster's Guide* (1788; revised editions 1789, 1794) contained almost 300 unsigned examples. Ten in a catalog of the same year are his only signed work. Hepplewhite reinterpreted Adam's neoclassical style into a simpler, gentler-curved elegance (**27**). Serpentine and bow fronts, the shield-back chair, window seats, and Prince of Wales feathers are all characteristic.

high-tech/industrial style International functional furniture design propagated in 1970s America that strives for novelty and ergonomic efficiency.

high Victorian style Another term for rococo revival in Britain and America.

Hispano-Moresque style Mudéjar ("Moorish inspiration") geometrically inlaid Spanish furniture of the late Gothic and Renaissance periods.

international style European interwar style, so-called in 1932, that spread to America and the rest of the world. Its functional, often standardized furniture is made today (**28**).

Isabellino style Neo-Gothic revival in mid 19th-century Spain named after Queen Isabella (1833–68) that surpassed others in both color and ornamentation.

Jacobean style General term for 17th-century English furniture (**29**). Initially differed little from Tudor work until continental-style arabesque carving and mannerist decorations grew in popularity. Upholstery and lightness became more general, as did the gateleg table. The Commonwealth (1649–60) reduced decorating to a minimum, typified by the Cromwell chair, and is sometimes treated as a separate period. From 1660 (see Restoration style) England rejoined the European baroque mainstream and began the Age of Walnut.

Japanese style (Japonism/Japonaiserie) Late 19th-century taste for Japanese art after trade resumed in 1853. Many major British designers, such as Godwin, adapted furniture to Japan's asymmetrical lightness and simplicity. Continental Art Nouveau makers took up the fashion in the 1890s, and America was influenced from the late 1870s, especially in bamboo work.

Liberty style See Art Nouveau.

Louis XIII style Early 17th-century French furniture in showy mannerist fashion and made of ebony or walnut wood, decorated with lavish semi-precious stones and veneering (**30**). Flemish-imported geometric panels are its most distinctive feature. The cabinet, the most important piece, sometimes had a fall front added, thus becoming the *secretaire à abattant.* Mainly oblong-shaped tables abounded and dining tables first had extensions. Upholstery included leather and became fixed for the first time.

Louis XIV style France's baroque period centered on the glorious reign of the Sun King, of which the vast new Palace of Versailles (1686 on) was the apotheosis. Furniture formed part of an integrated royal program of the decoration, in which magnificent but disciplined design enveloped the 20,000-member hierarchical court, where even the size of foot stools was graduated. New and enduring furniture forms were the canapé sofa; the confessional armchair; the *fauteuil* armchair; the console table, often marble topped; and the commode, which ousted the traditional chest. Chinoiserie joined the decorative repertoire from the 1670s. One that has now died out is the sedan chair (**31**).

Louis XV style The true Louis XV rococo style occupies the middle years of that king's reign and is arguably furniture's richest period. The finest aristocratic homes had winter and summer sets of curving furniture, elegantly made from up to 50 types of wood that were carved and ornamented to the highest standards with metalwork, chinoiserie, gilt, mirrors, porcelain plaques, and bright colors. The *bergère* easy chair, first made c. 1725, proliferated as did the cabriole chair, the *duchesse*-type rolltop model made for the king himself, and the mechanically ingenious dual-purpose *secretaire à Capuchin* or *à la Bourgogne*. Illustrated here is a wooden sleigh (**32**) from the period.

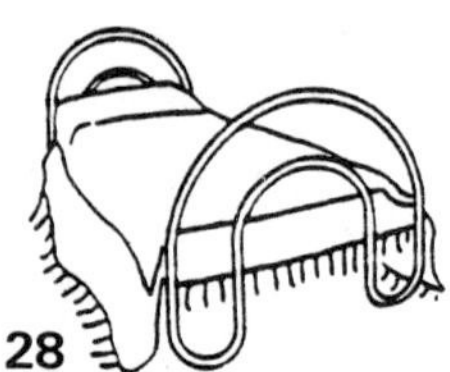

28

29

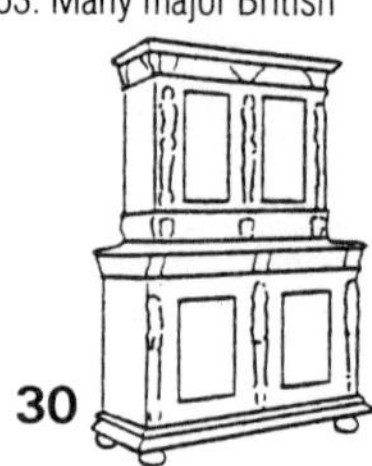

30

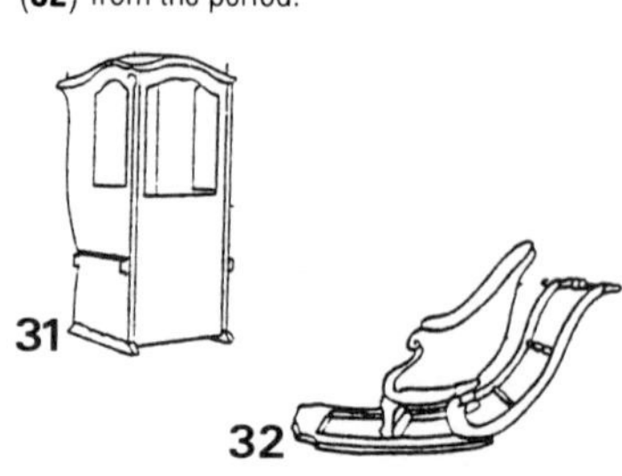

31

32

continued

Styles continued

5612

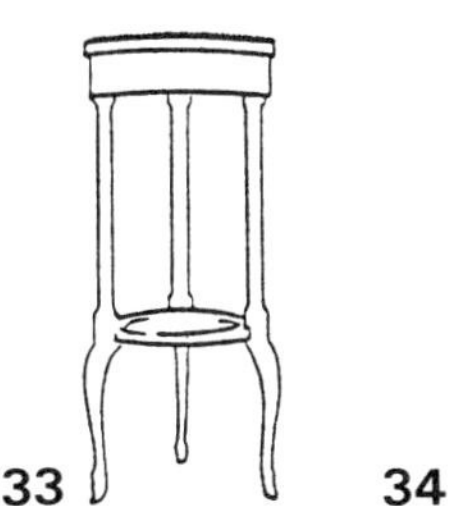
33

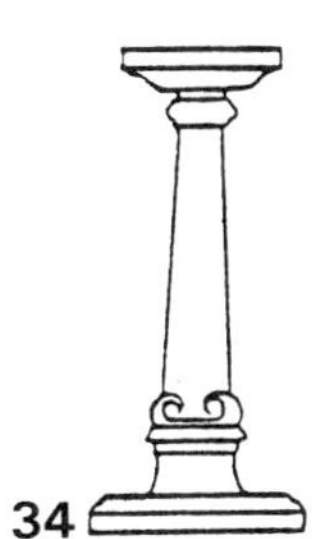
34

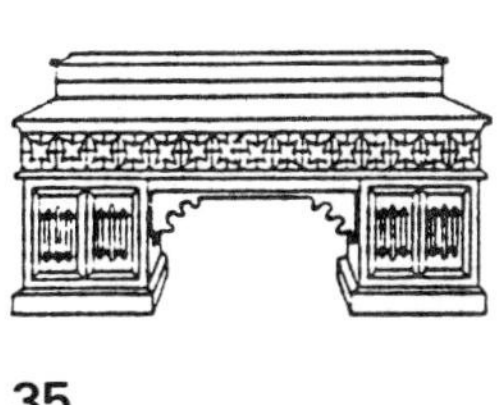
35

36

37

Louis XVI style This reaction to rococo flippancy predated and outlasted the king whose name describes it. Sparing neoclassical themes and straight lines returned (**33**). The cabriole leg was ousted by square or round-turned feet and then the saber leg. Breakfront case shapes replaced the flamboyant bombé. Plain or pale colors supplemented brighter ones. More numerous skilled cabinetmakers obtained wider patronage. Three specialized types of commode appeared in the 1770s followed c. 1775 by the *bonheur de jour*, a popular cabinet-surmounted small writing desk.
Louis XVI revival Mid 19th-century style that crossed the Atlantic from the court of Napoleon III and Empress Eugènie's Second Empire to Civil War-era America. More ostentatious than the original, especially in deep-button, coil-sprung upholstery. Widespread and prolonged use in burgeoning grand hotels across the world led to its description as "Louis the Hotel" style.
mannerist style European fashion of Italian origin in the late 16th and early 17th centuries. Emphasized arabesque and grotesque ornament. Special furniture forms were the French *table à l'Italienne* and the German *Kunstschrank*. The even more serpentine auricular phase prevailed until the coming of baroque.
mission furniture American style arising from the British Arts and Crafts movement, which inspired Gustav Stickley (1854–1942) to found his own *The New York Firm* (1898–1915). It made simple, massive oak pieces with cloth, canvas, or leather upholstery, as did the Royston Community (1895–1938). Stickley's magazine *The Craftsmen* (1901–15) spread the gospel of utility of design to the west coast.
Moorish style Long-lasting Islamic Iberian style created by the ruling Moors who invaded from North Africa and were brilliant woodcarvers and leatherworkers. Little furniture was used or survives from this era, in which richly covered cushions were important, but it was part of the Muslim world inspiration for a 1856–1907 revival. See Hispano-Moresque.
neoclassical style Furniture of Greco-Roman inspiration (**34**) (archeological discoveries from the 1740s) from the 1760s to the 1830s embracing many different national styles.
neo-Gothic style/Gothic revival Historicist, romantic, and catholic attempts to revive Gothic medieval art from the late 18th to the end of the 19th centuries (**35**). The first furniture designs were published in 1742, influenced Chippendale, and produced the Gothic Windsor chair, popular for two decades. Regency Gothic preceded the stronger 19th-century revival, which swept the continent during the 1830s and dominated American work 1830–80 ending with the Eastlake phase.
Palladian style First distinctive British Georgian style designed by the architect William Kent, who drew inspiration from the work of Andrea Palladio. His furniture combined lavishly sculpted Italian baroque models with symmetrical ornament to match the interior designs (**36**). Kent's work was published in 1744.
Pennsylvania German/"Dutch" 18th- and 19th-century softwood local style retaining European baroque features (**37**), especially the Schrank wardrobe and the softwood chest with their folk decoration.
Philadelphia Chippendale Pennsylvania's capital style of c. 1755–90, rich in rococo carving and fluted coronets on cabinets (**38**).
pillar and scroll/American restoration style Brief imitation of France's post-Napoleonic fashion, emphasizing pillar feet, scroll brackets, and arms. Documented by John Hall's 1840 pattern book.
plateresque style Early 16th-century Spanish Renaissance style derived from silversmith work decorating simple furniture shapes with geometric intricacy.
Queen Anne Early 18th-century English baroque style characterized by fine upholstery and wood inlays. Key elements included the cabriole leg; the drop handle; figured walnut veneering (**39**); fiddleback chair backs; and minimal carved decoration. Better joinery eliminated stretchers. New forms introduced were the china (display) cabinet, the spoonback chair for more comfort, and the card table, the tea table, and the kneehole desk.
Régence style Important transitional style between the main Louis XIV and XV periods. Cultural life returned from Versailles to Paris and this lighter atmosphere was reflected in more curvaceous furniture, the cabriole leg, and the removal of stretchers. Forms included new commodes, the *à la Règence*, and the *bergère* armchair. Ornamentation followed the lozenge shape, foliate scrolling, espagnolettes, and ormolu mounts. Slipcovers were an innovation for those not able to afford separate seasonal suites of furniture.
Regency Gothic Brief British fashion in the late 18th and early 19th centuries, inspired by Pugin's father, for Gothic church ornamentation that predated the fuller Gothic revival.
Regency style Decorative early 19th-century English style that drew on Greco-Roman, Egyptian, Chinese, and French Empire themes and hence at the time was called English Empire. Named after George IV's Regency and reign (1811–30), it extended either side through the pattern books of Sheraton, Hope, and George Smith (active 1804–28). "Grecian" arch-backed chairs of *klismos* pattern with scroll arms and saber legs best exemplify the style's elegance (**40**). The sofa table was a Regency innovation. Decoration included the acanthus, guilloche, dolphin, and brass inlay. See ornamentation.
Renaissance revival Mid- and late 19th-century European and American style initiated in Italy, massive and rectangular with a veritable orgy of nationalistic decoration from many sources. Remained particularly popular with the Italian and German public until 1914.
Renaissance style European classical and architecturally inspired furniture of the 15th to 17th centuries (**41**) with many phases and national variations. Walnut began to replace oak. New forms included the *cassone*, the mule chest, and the chest of drawers. Cupboards proliferated into the wardrobe, armoire and cabinet.
Restoration style Post-Waterloo French Bourbon taste that continued Empire work wholesale except that it removed Napoleonic devices and rejected mahogany for lighter-colored woods.

38

39

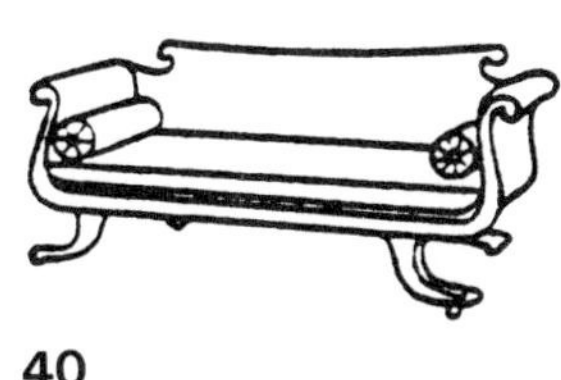
40

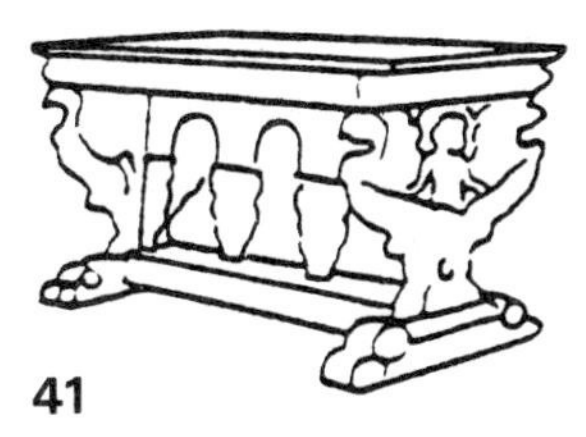
41

continued

Styles continued

5612**2**

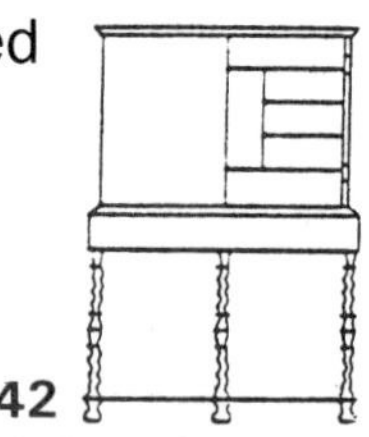
42

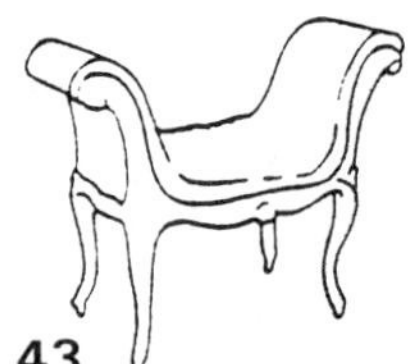
43

44

45

Restoration style Spirited English furniture (**42**) from the restoration of Charles II to the close of James II's reign in 1688. The first to adapt continental baroque. Walnut supplanted oak. Fertile ornamentation brought in spiral turning, scrollwork, deep carving, gesso decoration, and floral marquetry. Caning, lacquering, and japanning were all new techniques. Numerous new forms appeared, such as the wing chair, the daybed, the slant-front bureau, in c. 1670, the scritoire writing cabinet, and small occasional tables.
rococo Style of French asymetrical furniture, originating in the 18th century, emphasizing the S-shaped curve and comfort in reaction to baroque formality. It was characterized by improved plush upholstery, chinoiserie, bright colors, swirling carving, and extravagant marquetry, the style, which widely exported, represents the zenith of restless frivolity of Louis XV furniture (**43**).
rococo revival European and American middle-class reenactment of rococo, beginning only 60 years after its eclipse, but this often symmetrical version offered the added comfort of coil-sprung, button-backed upholstery (**44**), in new French seating forms such as the *indiscret*, *crapaud*, *borne*, and *pouf*. Dominated 1840s–70s US fashion despite other revivals.
Romanesque style Early medieval work that rarely survives. An exception is the famous and so-called Dagobert bronze throne, a monumental 8th-century Frankish continuation of the Roman X-frame folding chair. Chip carving on brightly painted oak timber (**45**) predominated in pieces resembling the era's Romanesque architecture.
Roman style Marble, iron, bronze, silver, wooden, and wicker furniture of Rome and its Empire that reinterpreted Etruscan, Greek, Hellenistic, and Egyptian precedents. The most common chair was the curule, derived from the Greek *diphros okladias*. There was the *bisellium* double seat (settee); pater familias' *sodium* (thronelike seat); an Etruscan tublike armchair; and the woman's *cathedra*. Among numerous stools, the folding *sella* was for campaign and administrative use. The *lectus* served as dining couch and bed, being a Greek *kline* with fulcrum headrest added, and in the 1st century AD backs and sides were also fitted. The late imperial *sigma* was a semicircular couch for six or more diners. The first console tables for sideboard use against a wall appeared, as did four-legged tables with stretchers. The cupboard was developed with *armaria* for weapons and the open buffet display board. The movable bronze bath became a 19th-century standard.
Scandinavian furniture A vanguard post–World War I modern furniture movement marrying fine design to industrial production and materials. Alvar Aalto in Finland spearheaded the movement, followed by Kaare Klint in Denmark. After 1945 Scandinavian designers, though still often home-based, were working for an appreciative and growing US-led world market.
Second Empire Ornate 19th-century French style.
Sheraton Late 18th-century English style developed by Thomas Sheraton, characterized by graceful proportions.
Spanish colonial style Spanish overseas imperial furniture of the 17th and 18th centuries made chiefly in Mexico City, Lima, Bogotá, and Quito though Cuba and the Philippines were also major producer colonies. European in form, but often with Indian carving and a more lavish use of silver, mother-of-pearl, and other ornament than at home. Mexico continued the desornamentado style, while Peru remained faithful to baroque.
transition style Two periods of French furniture a century apart. The first coincides with Louis XIV's first years on the throne: baroque features began to appear. The second, more significant, occupies Louis XV's final years: rococo furniture began to receive neoclassical ornamentation and more restrained curves.
Tudor style English, predominantly 16th-century furniture in a Renaissance, increasingly mannerist-influenced provincial style. It developed the draw-leaf table by 1550; the decorative nonesuch chest; and the Farthingale chair (the latter two being 19th-century names). Holly and ebony were new woods. The reign of Elizabeth I is sometimes separated from the four earlier Tudors, but in fact the ornate Italianate trend only became more pronounced.
William and Mary style Late 17th-century English baroque furniture much influenced by the Dutch and Huguenot designers in the royal couple's household. Made of walnut and with Dutch marquetry and oyster veneer. New forms were the 1690s bureau, the bookcase, the card table; and the tea table. Carved scroll supports and the baluster were popular details.

Furniture makers and designers

5613**3** **Aalto, Hugo Alvar Henrik** 1899–1976, Finnish architect who also designed much wooden furniture from the 1920s, transferring the new tubular steel cantilever to his laminated bent plywood chairs. Founded Artek of Helsinki (1933) to make and sell his furniture and furnishings.

1

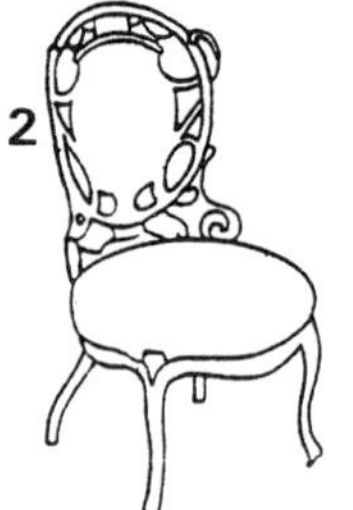
2

3

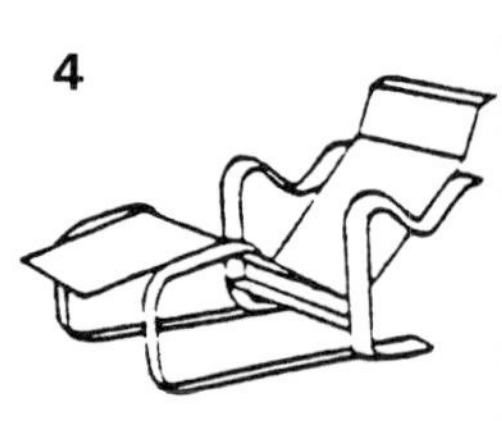
4

Adam, Robert 1728–92. Highly influential Scottish neoclassical architect and designer who, with his brothers, perfected the marriage of furniture and interior design. Ornate Adam furniture was made by Chippendale in the 1760s and 1770s. Introduced satinwood, the Etruscan style, and the sideboard flanked by pedestals (**1**).
Bellini, Mario b. 1935, Italian industrial and office designer whose work includes modular furniture for companies like Cassina. Best known pieces are Chair 932 (1967) and marble/glass Colonnato table (1977).
Belter, John Henry 1804–63, German-born New Yorker, who made his name synonymous with the New World rococo revival. Favored carving in rosewood and invented a form of bentwood lamination for it (**2**) together with a mechanical saw.
Bérain, Jean 1637–1711, French baroque stage and set designer who was Louis XIV's *dessinateur du roi* from 1674. His furniture designs were imitated across Europe. These lighter, fantastical pieces foreshadowed régence and rococo with their chinoiserie, *singerie*, arabesque, and marquetry ornamentation.
Bertoia, Harry 1915–78, Italian-American designer active c. 1937–55 who worked with Saarinen, Eames, and Knoll. For the latter he originated mass-produced, curved, light steel chairs including the classic 1952 Diamond model (**3**) adjustable to two different angles.
Breuer, Marcel Lajos 1902–81, Hungarian Bauhaus-trained architect who also came to head its furniture department and design stylish pieces such as the Wassily leather and tubular steel chair and a soon-to-be standard 1928 cantilevered chair. His work has been influential to the present day thanks to its functional elegance and wide use of materials. The English Isokon Company made his 1935–37 bent plywood designs (**4**).
Burton, Scott 1939–89, American designer and sculptor who began with bronze historical

continued

Furniture makers and designers continued

5613

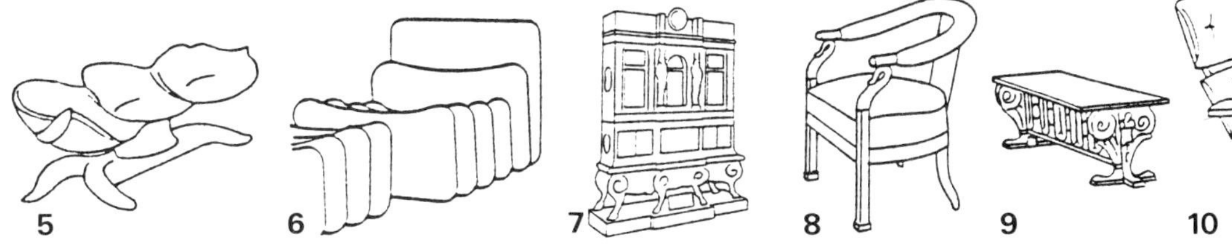

replicas before developing 1970s "vernacular" chair sculptures. He designed striking 1980s permanent outdoor seating in stone for public buildings in Boston, New York, and Liverpool.

Castle, Wendell b. 1932, American leader of the 1970s handicraft furniture revival with sculpted pieces of laminated wood (**5**).

Chippendale, Thomas 1718–79. The household name of English furniture design who published *The Gentleman and Cabinet-maker's Directory* (1754), the first exhaustive catalog (with 160 plates) devoted purely to furniture design. Chippendale's London business, carried on by his son Thomas (1749–1822), lasted over 70 years to produce Regency furniture. An organizer and master-designer, the elder Chippendale successfully adapted many styles, beginning with French rococo, though specific Chippendale-manufactured furniture is both rare and hard to identify.

Colombo, Joe Cesare 1930–71. Highly original Italian 1960s designer, famed for his multi-purpose Addition seating system (**6**) and the first plastic chair to be made by one-process injection molding.

Cressent, Charles 1685–1758. Leading French régence and Louis XV cabinetmaker. Specialized in curved design with gilt-bronze ormolu mounts. Devised the commode that bears his name and concentrated on floral marquetry after c. 1748.

Cucci, Domenico c. 1635–1704/5, Italian baroque furniture maker who lavishly furnished Louis XIV's palaces with extravagant pieces decorated by ebony, gilded, and precious-stone studded pieces (**7**).

Cuvilliés, François the Elder 1695–1768. Wallonia-born Bavarian rococo architect and designer who started as court dwarf to the Elector and went on to design Bavaria's finest rococo palace interiors. The furniture was of a transformed bubbling Louis XV pattern which Cuvilliés detailed in engravings from 1738.

Dagly, Gerhard Fl. 1687–1714. Best known European white lacquermaker of his time. Used his Flemish home town Spa's black and gold color scheme, as well as brighter ones and chinoiserie, while working for the Elector of Brandenburg.

Danhauser, Joseph 1780–1830. Leading Vienna workshop owner from 1804 who popularized the Biedermeier style. His company went on until 1838 (**8**).

Deutscher Werkbund German industrial design group of 1907–33 founded in Dresden. Its furniture practitioners included van de Velde, Josef Hoffman, Walter Gropius, Otto Wagner, and Bruno Paul. Immediately influential on the modern movement and for the resolution of the conflicts between art and industry.

Deutscher Werkstätte German reforming design movement stemming from an 1897 Munich workshop. The Dresden successor body, founded by a furniture maker, produced machine-made furniture in 1906.

du Cerceau, Jacques Androuet the Elder c. 1520–84, French designer who published a pattern book (c. 1550) of mannerist decoration and architectural furniture (**9**).

Dunand, Jean 1877–1942, Swiss Art Deco designer who founded a firm after 1918 to produce lacquered furniture, often decorated with precious metals or inlaid eggshell.

Eames, Charles 1907–78. Outstanding American modern designer renowned for his 1946 molded plywood chair, a 1956 laminated rosewood and aluminum swivel armchair (**10**), and modular storage units.

Eastlake, Charles Locke 1836–1906. British design writer whose *Hints on Household Taste in Furniture* (1868) enjoyed enormous influence on both sides of the Atlantic (**11**).

Ercolani, Lucien b. 1888, Anglo-Italian maker and designer who founded Furniture Industries Ltd in the 1920s to produce Ercol traditional rustic pieces, in particular the Windsor chair.

Gallé, Emile 1846–1904, French Art Nouveau glassmaker and founder of the School of Nancy, he also produced, with Louis Majorelle (1859–1926), a richly decorated furniture range after 1885 using many woods, natural ornamental themes, and carved quotations (**12**).

Gillow, Robert 1703–72. Founder of a famous English cabinetmaker's that traded in Lancaster and London. Their records date back to 1731, most pieces being name-stamped after the 1760s. The company (Waring and Gillow) only closed in 1974, having employed Hepplewhite, as well as inventing the original billiard table (1760–70) and the telescopic dining table (c. 1800). Shown here is a sloping clerk's desk (**13**).

Godwin, Edward William 1833–86. British designer and architect who initially produced neo-Jacobean furniture and c. 1862 switched to Japanese designs, creating a revolutionary Anglo-Japanese style (**14**) in the Art Furniture movement (Oscar Wilde was a client).

Gragg, Samuel 1722–1855. An early American user of the bentwood technique (**15**) who patented the "elastic" chair in Boston (1808–15).

Heal, Sir Ambrose 1872–1959, British maker and designer whose inherited London company was at the forefront of Arts and Crafts and Art Nouveau designs from 1893. Tubular steel was added to the range in the 1920s and Heal's son Christopher (b. 1911) became the leading international and contemporary style designer from 1934 (**16**).

Hope, Thomas 1769–1831. Wealthy Scottish collector, designer, and writer who pioneered Regency style and took Egyptiennerie to Britain. Published the influential *Household Furniture and Decoration* (1807) (**17**).

Hoppenhaupt, Johann Michael 1709–55 and **Johann Christian** 1719–86, German designer brothers who worked in Frederick the Great's palaces from 1740 and, with Johann August Nahl (1710–85), effectively brought rococo furniture to Prussia. Johann Michael succeeded Nahl as the king's Director of Ornaments in 1746. The brothers favored rich marquetry and plain veneer with chinoiserie. The elder Hoppenhaup published his designs (1751–55).

Hunzinger, George 1835–98, American chairmaker and designer who founded his own New York firm in 1866 and patented over 20 designs. His chairs were individualist creations in revival styles with much turnery.

Ince and Mayhew active 1758–1802. Successful London firm imitating and contemporary with Chippendale that published

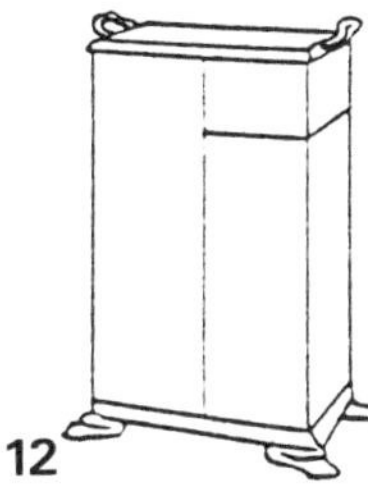

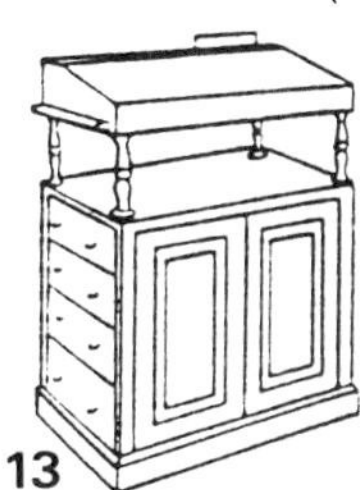

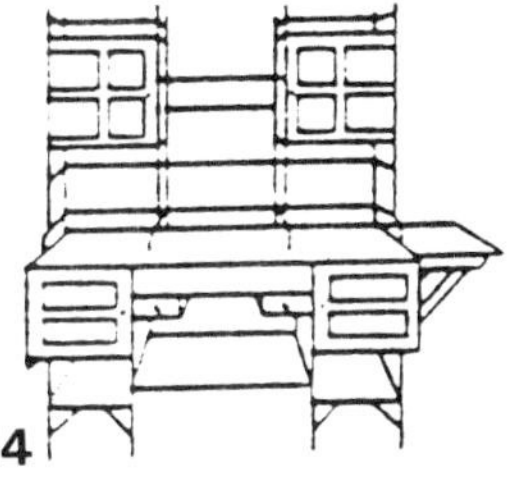

continued

Furniture makers and designers continued

5613

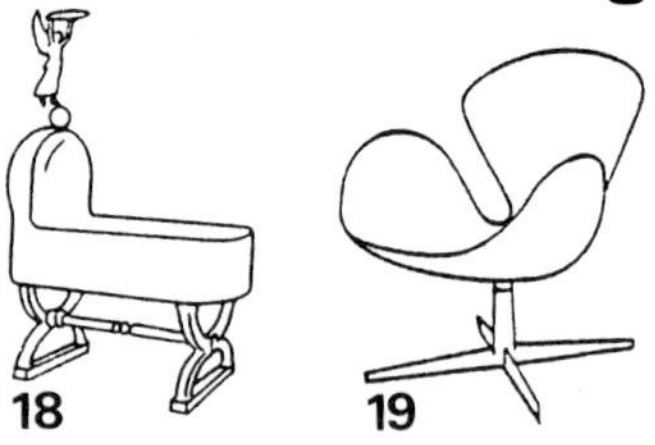

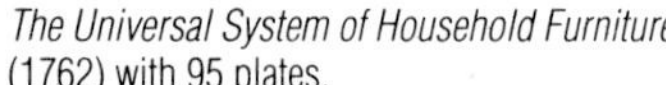

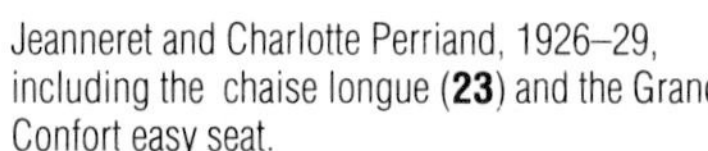

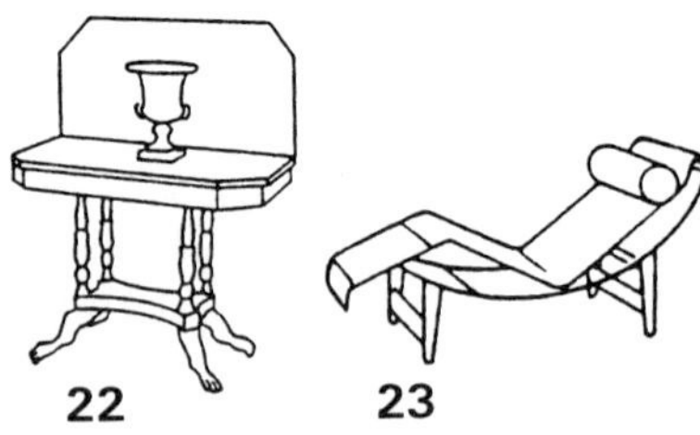

18 19 20 21 22 23

The Universal System of Household Furniture (1762) with 95 plates.

Jacob family active c. 1755–1847. Three-generation French furniture-making dynasty who span Louis XV to Gothic Revival styles. Georges (1739–1814), a *menuiser* from 1765, perfected the Louis XVI chair adding his personal marguerite symbol. He brought in English-style mahogany, the saber leg, and the English lyre-back chair (1780s). Produced furniture for the Revolutionary government (1792). Father and sons (Georges 1768–1802 and François 1771–1841) combined to become the leading producers of *directoire*, consulate, and Empire furniture, especially for Napoleon's palaces (**18**). His son Georges-Alphonse (1799–1870), took over the business, selling it in turn to Jeanselme.

Jacobsen, Ame 1902–71. Danish designer (also an architect) best known for a 1952 stacking chair range (still made), and the sculptured plastic "Swan" (**19**) and "Egg" chairs.

Juhl, Finn b. 1912. One of the first Danish modern designers in the late 1940s (**20**).

Juvarra, Filippo 1678–1736, Sicilian early rococo architect and stage designer, whose flamboyant furniture fills palaces he planned in Messina, Turin, Mafra (Portugal), and Madrid. He favored exquisite scrollwork legs, figure supports, and large pictorial inlays.

Klint, Kaare 1888–1954. Influential Danish Scandinavian modern designer who headed the Copenhagen Royal Academy of Arts' new furniture department from 1924. He sought biotechnological "tools for living" with plain woods, natural colors, and without pretentious decoration.

Knoll Associates/International New York company, active from 1938, that pioneered international modern style designs by top names and marketed them internationally (**21**).

Lannuier, Charles-Honoré 1779–1819. Parisian-trained American empire style cabinetmaker who emigrated to New York in 1803 and produced lighter empire pieces with imported materials (**22**). He and Phyfe embody this American style.

Le Corbusier (Charles Edouard Jeanneret) 1887–1965. Pivotal modern architect who also designed furniture with his brother Pierre Jeanneret and Charlotte Perriand, 1926–29, including the chaise longue (**23**) and the Grand Confort easy seat.

Legrain, Pierre 1889–1929. The most avant-garde French Art Deco designer, primarily a bookbinder, whose 1920s furniture included African-derived stools, a glass grand piano, and use of chromium, vellum, and velvet.

Mackintosh, Charles Rennie 1868–1928, Scottish Art Nouveau designer who made furniture (**24**) for his buildings in partnership with his wife Margaret Macdonald, notably for the Glasgow School of Art and for several Glasgow tea-rooms (c. 1897–1912). At 1890s Paris and Munich exhibitions he strongly influenced European design trends.

Marot, Daniel 1663–1752, Dutch baroque architect and designer, of French Hugeunot family, who translated Louis XIV baroque to William and Mary whose court architect he became. Visited England (Hampton Court Palace) 1694–98. May have originated the design of the standard William and Mary chair and his engraved designs (1702) influenced elaborate beds, tables, and *guéridons.* A Marot chair is shown here (**25**).

Mies van der Rohe, Ludwig 1886–1969, German-American international modern architect and designer who designed cantilevered tubular-steel furniture from 1926 (**26**), culminating in the revolutionary 1929 Barcelona chair. Knoll International reissued his elegant work in the 1950s.

Morris and Company 1861–1940. Craft co-operative founded by the writer and designer William Morris as the center of his Arts and Crafts movement. It produced simple streamlined furniture (**27**) which was sometimes painted with medieval scenes by Pre-Raphaelite artists. See Webb.

Oeben, Jean-François 1721–63, French Louis XV and transitional style maker trained by Charles Boulle and patronized by Madame de Pompadour from c. 1745. He succeeded Boulle as royal cabinetmaker in 1753 and specialized in mechanically fitted pieces, culminating in his novel rolltop desk (**28**) for the king (1760–69). See Riesener.

Phyfe, Duncan 1768–1854. Foremost American directory and empire cabinetmaker in New York after c. 1792. He simplified Sheraton's designs in particular, preferring veneering to carving (except fluting and reeding) and delighting in paw feet. Modified the curule chair. Switched his 1,000-strong workshop to pillar and scroll rosewood work after c. 1830, retiring in 1847 with a $500,000 fortune. A Phyfe card table is shown below (**29**)

29

Piffetti, Pietro 1700–77, Italian rococo maker who worked in Turin for the Piedmont royal court from 1731, producing luxuriously elaborate pieces (as seen below) with much ivory inlay and bronze mounting. The Quirinale Palace, Rome, also has his creations (**30**).

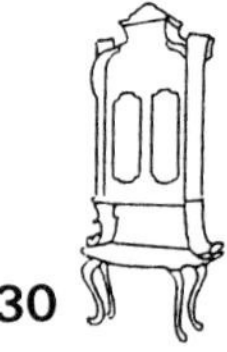

30

Pugin, Augustus Welby Northmore 1812–52. Seminal British designer who worked with his father on Regency Gothic furniture, (seen below), and published *Gothic Furniture in the style of the 15th Century* (1835). Produced 1,200 pieces for the Houses of Parliament from 1840 (**31**)

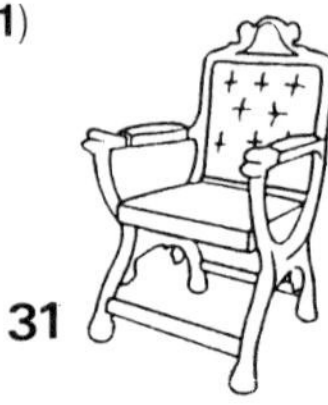

31

Race, Ernest 1913–63, British contemporary style designer whose demountable 1947 B A chair was the first to use cast aluminum. His 1951 Antelope chair was similarly innovatory,

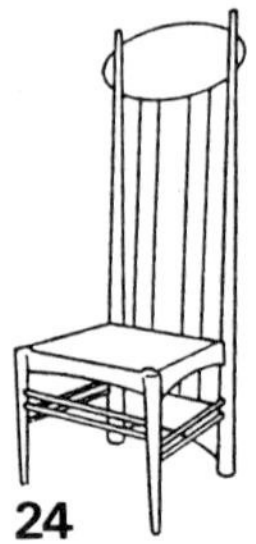

24

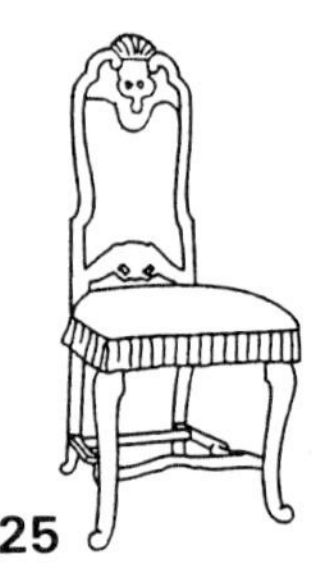

25

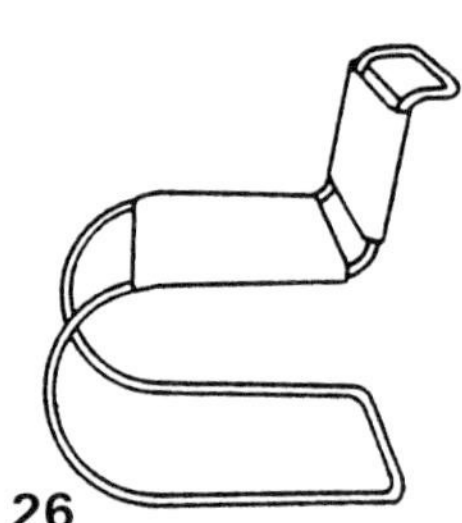

26

27

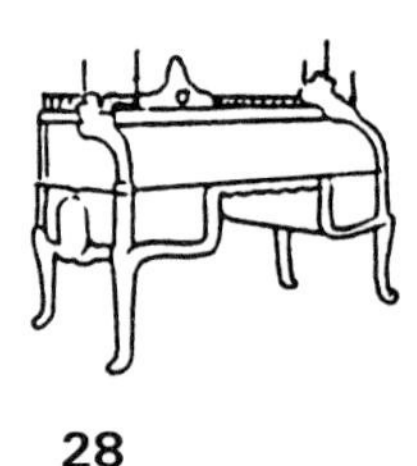

28

continued

Furniture makers and designers continued

5613

32

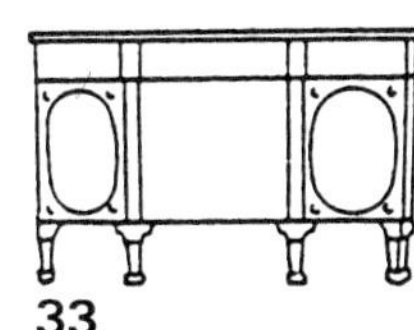
33

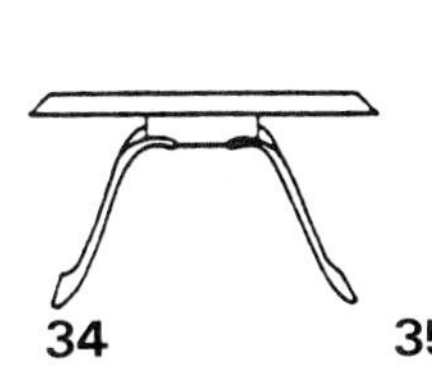
34

35

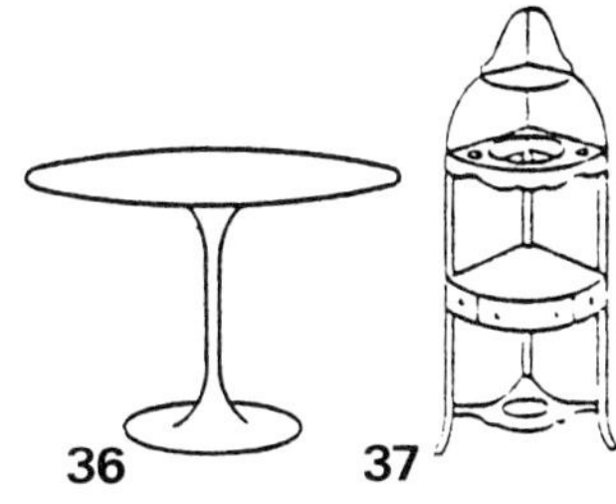
36 37

as his company, Race Furniture, remains.

Riesener, Jean Henri 1734–1806, French Louis XVI cabinetmaker who succeeded Oeben, his teacher, finishing the rolltop *bureau du roi*, and producing his own superlative marquetry-rich work with bronze mounts of his own casting. As king's cabinetmaker 1774–84 he received 900,000 livres' worth of commissions (**32**).

Rietveld, Gerrit Thomas 1888–1964, Dutch De Stijl furniture maker who led the movement in furniture with his Red-Blue armchair design of 1917, a Cubist brightly colored "spiritual" but nonfunctional creation. Influenced Breuer and the Bauhaus yet none of his work was mass produced.

Roentgen, Abraham 1711–93, and **David** 1743–1807, German Rhineland cabinetmakers with a workshop at Neuwied from 1750. Abraham retired in 1772. David made the business Europe's largest and finest, opening branches in Paris (1774), Vienna, Naples, and Prussia (1791). He became Marie Antoinette's cabinetmaker and sold pieces to Catherine the Great; pictorial marquetry was his neoclassical specialty (**33**). French Revolutionary troops sacked the Neuwied workshop.

Ruhlmann, Jacques-Emile 1879–1933. Foremost French Art Deco designer and maker, whose post-1918 workshop produced the style's highest quality work, in which the legs look integral with the carcass (**34**). From 1930 he shifted into international modern with pieces for the Palace of the Maharajah of Indore.

Russell, Sir Gordon 1892–1980, British international style and utility designer (**35**). From a craftsman's family, he began with Cotswold School Arts and Crafts movement work before designing 1930s radio cabinets. He manufactured international style furniture in London and Worcester, then headed Britain's 1942 wartime utility program. After the war he was the Industrial Design Council's first director and opened the Design Centre in 1956.

Saarinen, Eliel 1873–1950, and **Eero** 1910–61, Finnish-American father and son designers and architects. Eliel designed Art Nouveau furniture before 1900 and emigrated in 1923. He equipped Cranbrook Academy with modern furniture, nursing future designers there, starting with Eames. The latter worked with Eero on 1940 designs of storage units and molded plywood chairs that led on to Saarinen's fiberglass Womb (1948) and Tulip (1957) chairs for Knoll International. Shown is a table by Eero (**36**).

Schuster, Franz 1892–1976, Austrian unit furniture pioneer from 1927. His work strongly influenced Scandinavian developments.

Secession Movement Austrian Vienna-based artists who left the Academy in 1897, exhibited Mackintosh's furniture, and simulated Art Nouveau. Josef "Square" Hoffmann (1870–1956), was the outstanding designer, furnishing his buildings and working for Thonet.

Sheraton, Thomas 1751–1806, English neoclassical designer and transatlantic style setter. His *The Cabinet-Maker and Upholster's Drawing Book* in four parts 1791–94 (revised editions 1793, 1802), with 111 engravings, transformed Adam and Hepplewhite into a lighter, more delicate style. *The Cabinet Directory* (1803), with 88 engravings, first published Egyptiennerie in Britain and formulated Regency style, as did an unfinished 125-part encyclopedia (1805) that reached the letter C. Ironically, only a glass-fronted bookcase can definitely be attributed to this trained cabinetmaker. Shown is a corner basin stand (**37**).

Stickley, Gustav 1857–1942, Foremost American mission furniture designer from 1898 of simple settles, sideboards, tables, and a variant of the Morris chair. His brothers left the cooperative in 1901 to market similar revival items. Despite his bankruptcy in 1915, Stickley's ideas influenced Chicago and west coast designers.

Tatlin, Vladimir 1885–1953, Russian constructivist designer who made a curvilinear tubular-steel cantilevered chair in 1927 that was mass produced in Italy.

Thonet, Michael 1796–1871, German designer and mass-manufacturer who patented revolutionary bentwood (1841) for chair frames and lightened and curved them. In 1859 he designed the easy-to-assemble bentwood Thonet No 14 chair, furniture's all-time bestseller that is still being made. Other designs included hat stands, rockers, and café chairs. By 1871 Thonet was making 400,000 pieces a year for a worldwide market. Thonet brothers, having commissioned many 20th-century designers, remains in business.

van de Velde, Henri 1863–1957, Belgian Art Nouveau architect, designer, and propagator of modernism. He made geometric, abstract furniture for his 1894–95 home (**38**) and for the Paris gallery *L'Art Nouveau*. In Germany and Switzerland 1899–1924 he shifted toward Bauhaus functionalism.

Vile and Cobb active c. 1750–78. Famous London makers of expensive rococo mahogany work (**39**), especially case pieces for George III.

Vredeman de Vries, Hans c. 1527–post 1604 and **Paul** 1567–post 1630, Dutch designers who published much-imitated pattern books in 1560–88 and 1630 respectively. Their carving and ornamentation designs prevailed across northern Europe late in the 17th century. Hans was also an auricular style creator.

Webb, Philip Speakman 1831–1915. Late Victorian British architect and designer of the c. 1865 Morris chair as William Morris' firm's chief designer in the Arts and Crafts movement. From 1875 he concentrated on pieces integrated with his buildings (**40**).

Wegner, Hans b. 1914, Danish modern designer of handmade but functional wooden work since 1940, such as his Peacock chair (1947), which triumphantly married traditional cabinetmaking skills to streamlined design.

Wright, Frank Lloyd 1867–1959, American architect and designer who started furniture making in 1895 to exaggerated linear designs (**41**). His Larkin Administration Building (Buffalo, New York, until 1950) contained the world's first purpose-built steel office furniture. The same year saw his geometric cube wooden chair, and Japonisme became a powerful influence from 1905. After 1915 sculptural and architectural qualities prevailed at the expense of comfort.

38

39

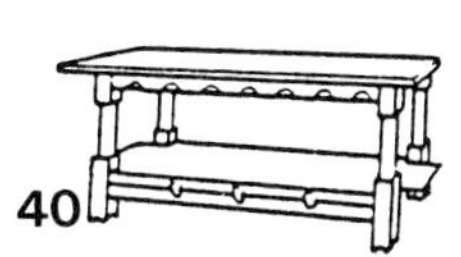
40

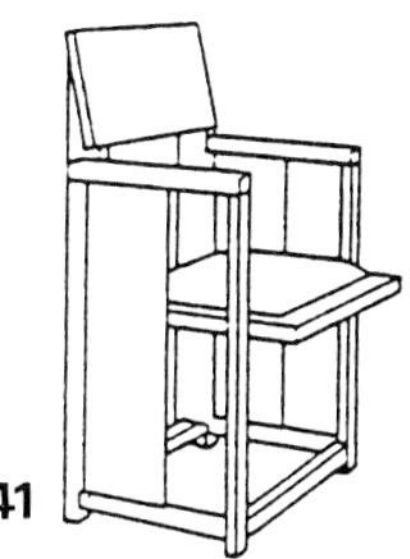
41

562 FASHION AND CLOTHING

Women's fashions

562**1**

1 Ancient Egyptian
2 Ancient Greek
3 Ancient Roman
4 French c. 1250
5 Italian c. 1300
6 French c. 1430
7 English c. 1540
8 Spanish c. 1550
9 German c. 1550
10 English c. 1600
11 Puritan c. 1650
12 French c. 1780
13 French c. 1805
14 English c. 1817
15 American c. 1870
16 American c. 1870
17 French c. 1906
18 French c. 1927
19 French c. 1950
20 Modern blue jeans

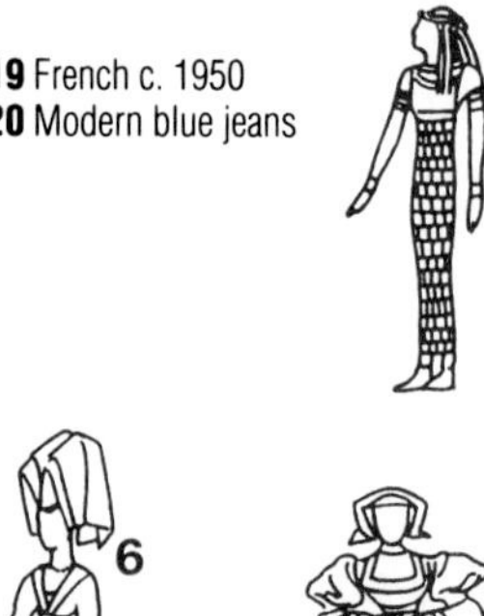

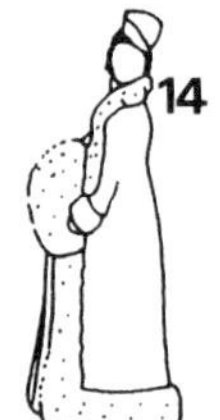

Men's fashions

562**2**

1 Ancient Egyptian
2 Ancient Greek
3 Ancient Roman
4 1st century Frankish
5 French c. 1260
6 English c. 1350
7 German c. 1350
8 Italian c. 1450
9 French c. 1550
10 French c. 1550
11 French knight c. 1630
12 French c. 1680
13 English c. 1680
14 French c. 1780
15 French c. 1795
16 English c. 1795
17 French c. 1830
18 English c. 1870
19 English hunting 1950s
20 Business suit 1950s

International clothing sizes

562**3** UK clothing sizes are the same as US sizes for some items – children's shoes, for example; for other items, sizes vary. Listed here are the European equivalents of UK and US clothing sizes. Also listed are US and UK shoe sizes.

Women' clothing

USA	UK	Europe
6	8	36
8	10	38
10	12	40
12	14	42
14	16	44
16	18	46
18	20	48
20	22	50

Men's shirts

USA / UK	Europe
12	31-31
12½	32
13	33
13½	34-35
14	36
14½	37
15	38
15½	39-40

continued

International clothing sizes continued

5623 **Men's shirts** continued

USA / UK	Europe
16	41
16½	42
17	43
17½	44-45

Men's suits and overcoats

USA / UK	Europe
36	46
38	48
40	50
42	52
44	54
46	56

Children's clothing

USA	UK	Europe
2	16-18	40-45
4	20-22	50-55
6	24-26	60-65
7	28-30	70-75
8	32-34	80-85
9	36-38	90-95

Women's shoes

USA	UK	Europe
5	3½	36
6	4½	37
7	5½	38
8	6½	39
9	7½	40

Men's shoes

USA	UK	Europe
7	6½	39
7½	7	40
8	7½	41
8½	8	42
9	8½	43
9½	9	43
10	9½	44
10½	10	44
11	10½	45

Men's socks

USA / UK	Europe
9	38-39
10	39-40
10½	40-41
11	41-42
11½	42-43

Children's shoes

USA / UK	Europe
0	15
1	17
2	18
3	19
4	20
4½	21
5	22
6	23
7	24
8	25
8½	26
9	27
10	28
11	29
12	30
12½	31
13	32

563 PRINTING

Methods of production

5631 There are four major methods of duplicating images by printing:
1 The relief process, in which raised surfaces are inked and pressed onto paper.
2 The intaglio process, in which incised (lowered surfaces) are inked and pressed onto paper.
3 The surface process, in which flat areas are inked and pressed onto paper.
4 The stencil process, in which holes allow ink to pass through a surface onto paper.

1 The relief process
The most common materials from which you can cut away areas, which will appear white when the raised ink surfaces will print black, are: linoleum (linocuts); wood (woodcuts, when using the side surface; wood engraving, when using the end surface); and metal (either by phototransfer of the image, which is then etched to produce a raised gradation of dots called a halftone, or by pressing the shapes into metal, the method originally used to produce type fonts).

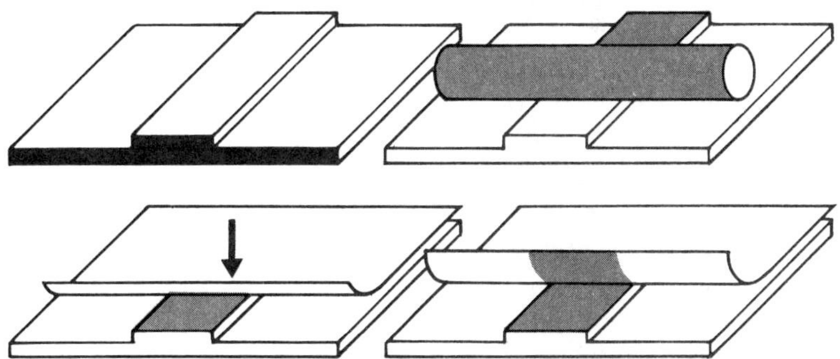

2 The intaglio process
The most common material into which incised lines are cut is metal, usually copper, zinc, or steel. The grooves may be scratched (drypoint), cut (engraving), or bitten into the surface with acid (etching). Tonal areas can be obtained by etching into porous granulated covering (aquatint) or engraving with multipointed tools (mezzotint). Commercial printing techniques transfer the image by photography, then the details are etched into the plate. This method (photogravure) is most often used for four-color magazines.

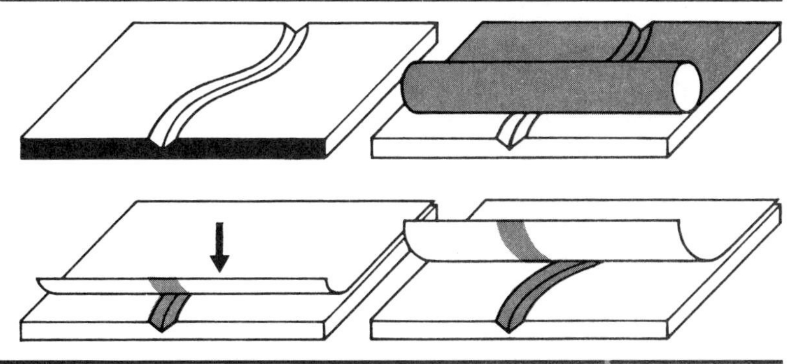

continued

Methods of production continued

5631 **3 The surface process**
This method, the planographic technique, uses the principle of water-resistant marks retaining printing ink. Originally developed from drawing onto smooth-surfaced stones (lithography), it is now used on prepared metal plates. Depending on the surface of the plate and the tools used to produce the drawing, great detail of tone, texture, and line can be achieved.

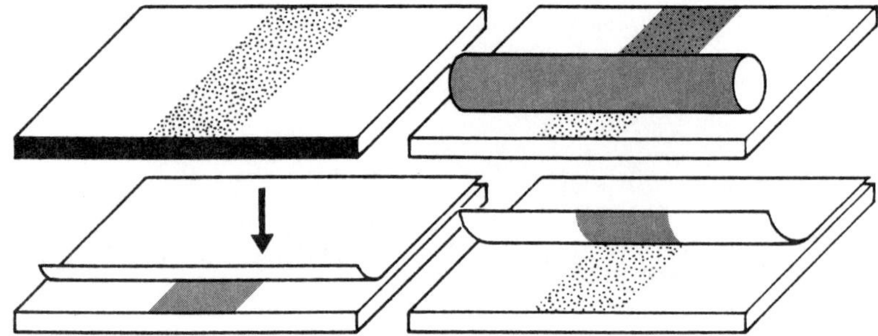

4 The stencil process
Images are cut into a strong, thin material, and ink pushed through onto paper, using brushes, rollers, or a squeegee (a rubber blade). Fine details are difficult to achieve. Rather than cut completely through a surface, the intended areas may be left clear on a stretched material, and the areas not being printed protected by a filler (silkscreen printing).

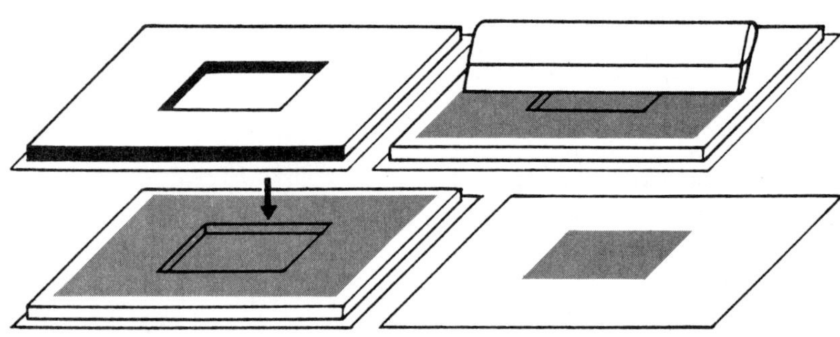

Terms and techniques

5632 **aquatint** Engraving method producing fine-grain tonal areas rather than lines. Invented mid-18th century and popular in the next century for reproducing watercolors. The tone ground is first etched on the plate, then acid-resistant designs drawn on before further etching.
burin Short steel engraving tool, usually lozenge-shaped in section, cut obliquely to a point. The round handle is pushed by the palm while the fingers guide the point.
burr Rough, upturned edge made by an engraver's burin or needle. Gives a soft, rich line to drypoint, but is removed when sharp line is required as in line engraving.
drypoint Engraving technique dating from 15th century. The design is scratched directly onto a copper plate with a sharp tool held like a pen, often producing a "burred" edge, giving a soft, rich texture, but this only survives for small editions.
edition Copies printed at one time.
engraving Any method of cutting into metal or wood to make a surface to receive ink for printmaking, but frequently used for what is technically called line engraving.
etching Developed in 16th century. Engraving on a wax-covered metal plate which is scratched with a needle to expose surface then placed in acid, which cuts into the plate where scratched. Longer exposure to acid makes a darker print line.
intaglio Carving in small scale, as on a gemstone, the design cut into the surface. Hence any such form of printmaking process such as etching (as opposed to a cameo gem or relief etching, and a woodcut in which the ground is cut away leaving a projecting design).
limited edition Fixed number of copies printed, usually individually numbered and signed by the artist, e.g. 3/25, indicating that this is the third impression from an edition of 25 copies. Plates are often defaced or destroyed when the edition is complete to prevent later printing. The size of the edition affects market value.
line engraving Engraving directly onto a metal plate with cutting tools, producing precise lines and shading added by hatching dots. Probably began in 15th-century Italy, flowering in the work of Dürer.
linocut Soft linoleum is cheaper and easier to work than wood, especially on a large sheet, but can make prints in a similar way. A 20th-century technique used by Matisse and Picasso.
lithography Printing from a design drawn in greasy crayon directly on a slab of stone or other smooth surface. Ink rolled over the stone adheres only to the drawing to create the printed image.
mezzotint Engraving using tonal areas. A rocking tool creates a burred surface on the plate, which is smoothed away to leave the desired strength of image. Invented in the 17th century but rarely used since photographic ways of reproduction were invented.
monotype Printmaking from an image printed (usually in oils) on a sheet of glass or metal. Only one sheet can be printed, though the color can then be reinforced and a few successive differing images made.
print Strictly any picture or design made from an inked surface, but now also art images made by stencil and other processes. Loosely used for all kinds of mechanically produced reproductions of paintings.
proof Trial image taken of a print.
relief etching Process in which the design is drawn in acid-resistant varnish and the non-printing surface etched away with acid, so that the printing surface stands out in relief (the opposite of the intaglio process).
serigraphy A form of silk screening which uses the more spontaneous tusche-washout method to prepare the stencil.
silkscreen printing Use of fine silk mesh mounted on a frame to support a stencil, so that "island" parts of the stencil (like the center of an "o") do not fall out. Alternatively, the use of a similar screen in which the cut stencil is replaced by painting the design directly on the screen with a glue or varnish. Ink is forced through unmasked parts of the screen by a squeegee. Andy Warhol was well known for his silkscreen pictures.
state Any of the images through which a print may pass as the artist alters the design, as frequently occurs in the work of Rembrandt. If no changes are made, this may be described as the "only state." Art historians may dispute whether differences are deliberate or merely caused by wear on the plate.
stencil A sheet of paper, metal or other material perforated with a design through which color can be applied to a surface beneath.
woodcut A form of relief printing in which a design is cut or gouged out of the surface of a block of hardwood. Ink or paint is then applied to

continued

Terms and techniques continued

5632 the surface to print out the design. Separate blocks can be used for multicolored images or, especially in 18th- and 19th-century Japan where the technique was perfected, different areas of a single block may also be inked differently.
wood engraving Like woodcut but using hardwood sawn across the grain and with a finer design, cut more shallowly using burins and similar engraving tools. Thomas Bewick excelled in this technique.

564 POTTERY AND PORCELAIN

Pottery and porcelain terms

5641 **argil** Clay used by potters.
basaltware Black, unglazed pottery.
biscuit ware Pottery fired but not glazed.
blunger Vessel in which pottery ingredients are mixed.
bone china Porcelain containing bone ash made in 20th-century UK, for high-quality tableware.
cameo ware Pottery with raised white designs on a contrasting background.
celadon ware Pottery originating in China, with a pale gray-green glaze.
ceramics (1) Anything made of baked clay. (2) The potter's art.
china (originally "Chinaware") Chinese porcelain of 16th century; now any Chinese porcelain or western version.
chinoiserie Decoration on 18th-century European porcelain, depicting Chinese scenes.
clair de lune Pale gray-blue glaze applied to certain Chinese porcelain.
clay The potter's basic material, found just below the topsoil, formed by decomposition of rock: kaolin or china clay, a pure white, coarse clay; ball clay, a highly plastic, fine pure clay; fireclay, a dark rough clay, able to stand high temperatures, but not plastic; buff or stoneware, a smooth plastic clay hardening at high temperatures.
coiling A simple method.of producing clay pots (**1**). Cylindrical strips of clay are formed from the clay body and then coiled on top of one another.

1

crackleware Pottery or porcelain with a network of fine cracks in the glaze.
creamware High-quality earthenware perfected by Josiah Wedgwood in the 18th century in Staffordshire, England.
delftware Tin-enameled earthenware, mostly blue and white, originally made in Delft (Holland) in 17th and 18th-centuries.
earthenware Pottery fired to relatively low temperature 2,012° F (about 1,100° C), easy to work, and having a dull finish.
enamel Colored glaze used to decorate pottery already glazed; popular in 15th and 16th centuries.
faience Fine pottery with a colorful glaze, named after Faenza, Italy, one of its sources.
fairing Pottery of a type sold or given as a prize at traveling fairs.
firing Process of hardening shaped clay by heating it. See pottery.
glazing Process for producing finish to pottery. Glaze is a coating of glass that gives the pottery a smooth surface color, and makes it waterproof.
glost firing A second firing for purpose of fusing glaze after initial biscuit firing.
imari Japanese porcelain with a decorated blue underglass over which the colors of red and gold are laid.
ironstone Hard, white pottery introduced by C J Mason in the 19th century.
jasperware Colored stoneware with raised designs in white, invented by Josiah Wedgwood.
kiln Chamber in which clay is fired.
lambrequin Scalloped edging decorating an item of porcelain.
majolica or **maiolica** Brightly decorated pottery in 16th-century Italian style.
molded ware Pottery formed by pressing the clay against or into some kind of mold.
muffle Kiln in which pottery is fired without direct exposure to the flames.
Nanking ware Chinese-style porcelain with a blue and white pattern, originally imported into Europe from Nanking.
pallet Spatula or paddlelike implement used for mixing or shaping clay.
Parian ware Fine white porcelain resembling marble, produced in Britain and the US.
paste Mixture from which porcelain is made; hard-paste porcelain made from kaolin (see clay) and petuntse, the true porcelain originating in China and rediscovered in Meissen (Germany) in 18th century, fired at very high temperatures; soft-paste porcelain made from white clay and fusible silicate, more translucent than hard paste but with softer whiteness.
porcelain The finest pottery, white all through and translucent. See paste.
potter's wheel A device with a flat rotating disk on a platform, usually powered by a treadle, on which clay is molded by hand.
pottery Strictly, all baked-clay ware except stoneware and porcelain. More generally, the art of shaping and molding all clays while soft and malleable and firing them in a kiln to render the created shapes firm and stable. Firing drives off the water combined with the constituent materials within clay and binds them together. Glazes are often added to make the ware waterproof.
saggar Casing of fine clay in which delicate ceramic ware is fired.
slab ware Made from slabs of clay that have been rolled out to an even thickness and cut into flat shapes.
slip Clay in liquid form, used for casting, joining, or decoration.
stoneware Hard, strong type of pottery fired at about 2,282° F (1,250° C) and able to hold liquid without glazing; used for items such as pots and heavy dishes.
terracotta Brownish-red burnt-clay pottery, baked in molds and used for architectural molding, sculpture, and decorative vessels.
throwing Shaping wet clay by hand on potter's wheel.
turning Final trimming of partially dried pottery on potter's wheel or lathe.
underglaze Pigment or decoration applied to pottery before it is glazed

Major pottery and porcelain factories

5642

English	
Bow	1744–1776
Bristol	1749–1781
Caughley	1772–1812
Chelsea	1745–1784
Coalport	1796
Derby	1750–1848
Derby, Royal Crown	1876
Liverpool	1710–c. 1800
Spode	1770
Wedgwood	1759
Worcester	1751

German	
Frankenthal	1755–1800
Höchst	1750–1796
Ludwigsburg	1758–1824
Meissen	1710
Nymphenburg	1753

French	
Chantilly	1725–1800
Limoges	1771
Mennecy	1734–1806
Sèvres	1756
Vincennes	1738–1756

Irish	
Belleek	1857

US	
Bennington	1793–1894
Greenpoint	1848
Tucker	1826–1838

Danish	
Copenhagen	1774

Chinese dynasties
Shang c. 1550–c. 1030 BC
Chou c. 1030–256 BC
Ch'in 221–207 BC
Han 202 BC–AD 220
Three Kingdoms 221–265
Southern & Northern dynasties 265–581
Sui 581–618
T'Ang 618–906
Five Dynasties 907–960
Sung 960–1279
Yüan 1260–1368
Ming 1368–1644
Qing 1644–1912

565 GLOSSARY OF DECORATIVE ARTS

appliqué An alien material applied to the surface of an art object or painting for ornamentation.

brass rubbing An impression made of a brass engraving by covering it with paper and rubbing the paper with graphite or chalk. The brass rubbing shown here was made from a brass of Sir Thomas Walsch and his wife. The brass is in Wanlip, Leicestershire, England, and was made in 1397; the two figures are in the traditional pose of effigies, with their hands in the position of prayer (**1**).

1

cameo A gem on which a design has been engraved in relief.

chasing Ornamentation on metal by embossing (carving or stamping a design) or engraving (cutting lines into wood, metal, etc).

collage A work of art created by attaching paper, wood, fabric, etc onto a flat surface.

découpage The decoration of a surface with shapes cut from paper or cardboard.

enamel Glass that has been heated to form a base of porcelain, which is then decorated with scenes or designs. Popular in the 15th and 16th centuries.

gilding Covering an object with gold.

inlaying The decoration of an object with fine materials set into its surface.

macramé Ornamental work created by weaving and knotting coarse thread into patterns (**2**).

marquetry Colored or varnished woods, ivory, or other materials that are inlaid flush with the surface of an object, especially in furniture.

millefiori A glassmaking technique in which flowerlike sections appear from sticks of colored glass that have been cut on the transverse. Sometimes used for beads in jewelry; also embedded in shapes of clear glass to form paperweights.

netsuke Small Japanese figures (predominantly animals) usually carved from ivory and used to decorate belts, purses, tobacco pouches, etc. Highly collectable, these miniature works of 16th-century art are said to acquire an "aura" the more they are handled.

ormolu Gilded bronze used to decorate furniture.

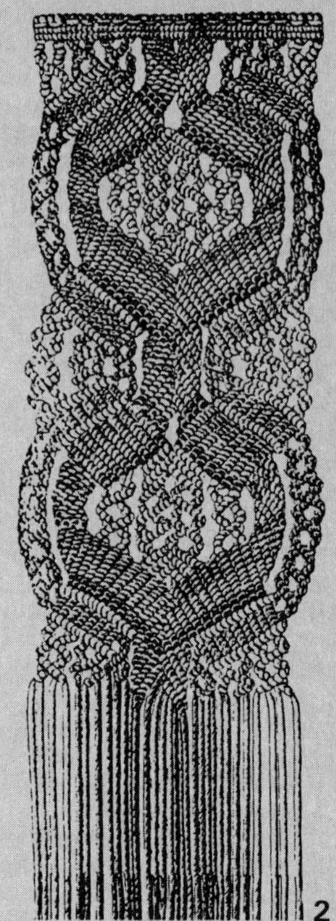
2

faceting A process of cutting regular planes on stone in a predetermined pattern that is related to the stone's crystalline structure. The first precious stones used for decorating jewelry were not faceted at all, but smoothed and rounded into the cabochon style; a cabochon is a stone with a flat back and a domed face. It was discovered, however, that some stones reflect more light if they are cut into facets, and so the face was cut into regular panes as in the rose cut. The backs of these early cut stones were still flat, but through experiment lapidaries learned to shape the bottom of a stone into a point (known as a pavilion) that further increased the gem's "fire." The cuts illustrated here are shown from the top and from the side.

1 Cabochon cut, with a flat back and domed face.

2 Baguette cut; this cut is particularly suitable for emeralds and sapphires. A true baguette cut has the same cuts on the back as on the face.

3 Rose cut, a cut that was particularly popular for early faceted stones.

4 Trap cut; the face is similar to a baguette, but the back is cut into a pointed pavilion.

5 Antique cushion, a fancy cut for rectangular stones.

6 Brilliant cut, often used for modern diamonds.

7 Fancy cuts used for pear-shaped stones.

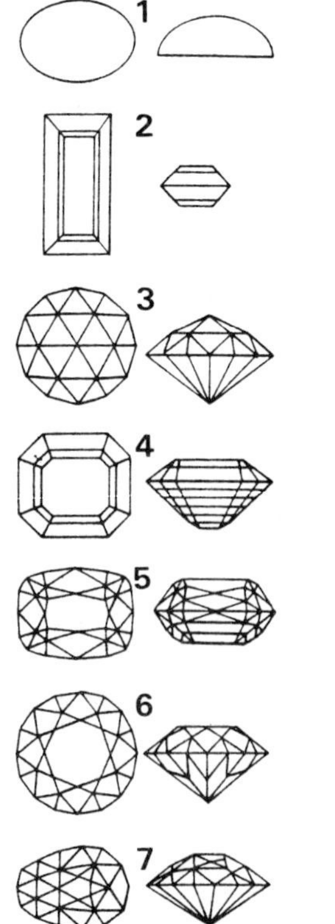

paper cuts Pictures cut into paper (**3**). The example shown here is a traditional Chinese paper cut of a fish shape called Fu Kkuei Yu Yü and is a charm meant to ensure that the recipient will have abundant wealth.

3

repoussé Decorative art worked in metal with the design hammererd into relief from the reverse side.

rosemaling Carved or painted decoration with floral motifs.

sgraffito Ceramic decoration in which the topmost layer (glaze, plaster, etc) is carved with a design to reveal selected areas of the ground.

silhouettes Pictures made by reproducing in one color, usually black, the outline of the model (**4**). The traditional outline for the silhouette is a profile likeness, although in the 19th century the clothing was often included so that the artist's skill could be shown in depicting the frill and flounces of contemporary fashion.

continued

Glossary of decorative arts continued

565

setting A method of mounting gemstones, holding them in place against unexpected blows that might otherwise dislodge them. Some settings are designed to be as unobtrusive as possible, but others are developed so that they become design elements in their own right. The styles in which gemstones have been mounted and set in the past have been determined by a number of factors. Fashion has played an important part; for instance, the widespread use of faceted stones in Elizabethan times led to the development of inconspicuous settings such as the claw setting (**2**), in which the minimum surface area of the stone is covered by the metal. The development of more complex techniques has also affected style; for example, pearls were generally set in the Middle Ages by driving a rivet right through the pearl, but as this spoiled the appearance of the stone a method was developed for fixing pearls invisibly.

Shown here are some of the variations in setting and mounting styles.
1 Bezel setting
2 Claw setting
3 Riveting
4 Graining
5 Flush setting
6 Invisible setting for pearls
7,8 Two modern settings for gemstones that have been cut into unusual shapes.

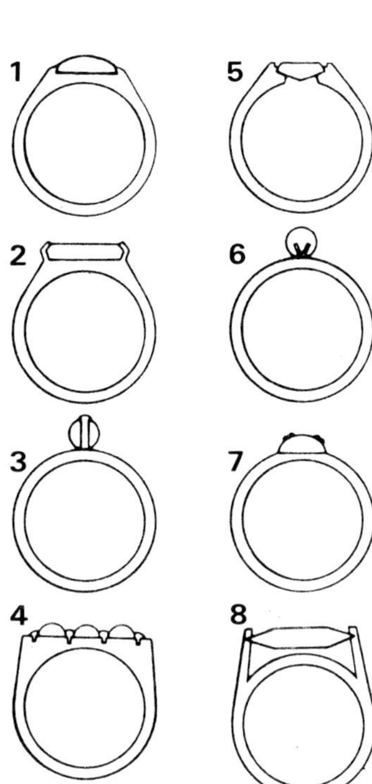

stenciling A method of transferring a design by painting through shapes cut in a thin sheet of metal, paper, or similar material (**5**). Stencils can be used for tiny designs, such as initials or small flower motifs, or for giant designs suitable for decorating an entire room.
tole Object made of tin and decorated with colorful designs.

566 SILVER MARKS

A hallmark is an impression that is stamped on gold or silver ware. In England, items of gold and silver must be stamped at an official Assay Office. The hallmark consists of four marks: the standard of finesse; the office where the item was marked; the year of the Assay; and the maker's initial.

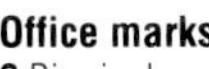

Standard hallmarks
1 22-carat gold
2 18-carat gold
3 14-carat gold
4 9-carat gold
5 Sterling silver

Office marks
6 Birmingham
7 London
8 Sheffield
9 Edinburgh

Date letters for 1933–34
10 Birmingham
11 London
12 Sheffield
13 Edinburgh

571 TYPES OF BUILDING

acropolis A hilltop citadel (**1**), especially in ancient Greece, and most notably in Athens, containing the most splendid temples and treasuries.

1

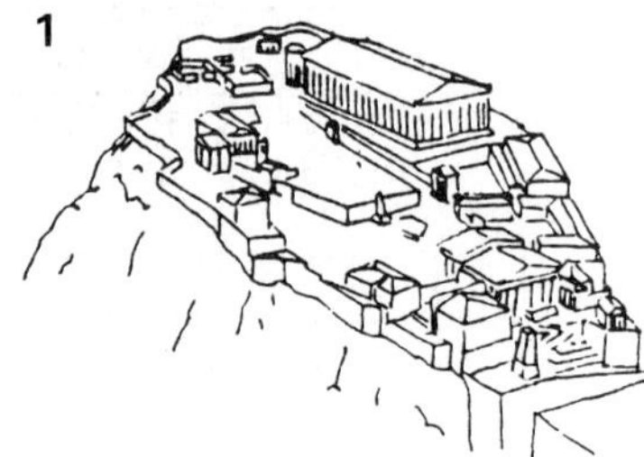

adobe Spanish word for a sun-dried brick, common in ancient cultures and especially in arid lands. Particularly associated with the house building of the Pueblo Indians in the southwest USA and Mexico (**2**).

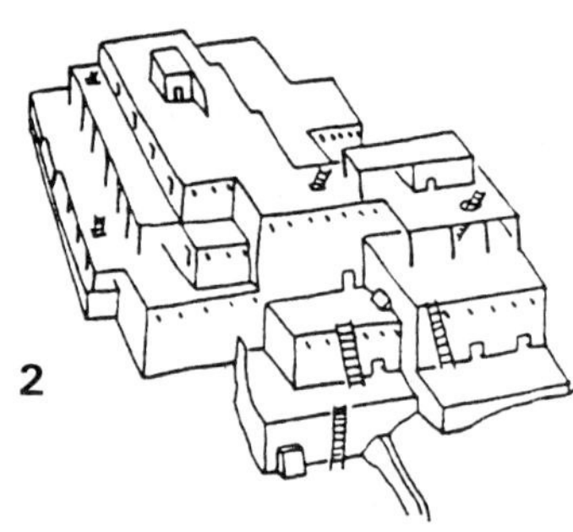

2

aedicule Small shrine or tabernacle of wood or stone, framed by columns and surmounted by an entablature and pediment.
almshouse Charitable housing.
amphiprostyle A temple with columns and a portico at each end.
amphitheater An open-air, round or oval theater with rising rows of seating.
apartment house Building containing multiple dwelling units with a common entrance and services.
aqueduct An elevated masonry or brick channel for carrying water, widely used by the Romans.
arsenal Building for manufacturing and storing armaments. Two historic examples are in Venice and Piraeus.
baptistery Either a separate building or the part of a church reserved for the performance of the rite of baptism.
barbican Fortifications protecting a draw-bridge, castle entrance, or fortified town gate.
barracks Block accommodation for the military since Roman times.
basilica In classical architecture, a large rectangular Roman hall with colonnades and a semi-circular apse, used primarily as a court of law. By the 4th century adapted as one of the basic plans for Christian churches in western architecture, as opposed to the cruciform plan adopted in Constantinople for the east.
bastion A pentagonal work projecting from the main rampart. Dominant feature of European military architecture from the 16th to 19th centuries.
belvedere An open-sided roofed terrace, usually at the top of a building, with a commanding or interesting view of a town square, formal garden, or landscape (**3**).

3

bunker Underground military installation for protection against air attack.
campanile Italian for a bell tower detached from the main body of a church.
castle A fortified building, set of buildings, or place.
catacomb Subterranean burial ground, best known as used by the early Christians outside the walls of Rome.
cathedral Christian church which is also the seat of a bishop and hence the center of a diocese.
cenotaph A monument to those buried elsewhere (**4**).

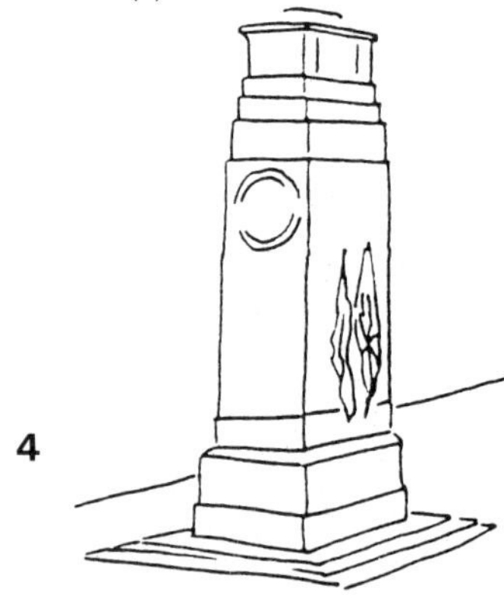

4

chalet A Swiss mountain hut.
chantry A small self-contained chapel, usually inside but sometimes outside a medieval church, financially endowed by the founder so that regular masses could be said for the repose of his or her soul.
chapel 1 A small church which is not a parish church. **2** A Nonconformist church.
chapter-house The administrative meeting place of a monastery or cathedral.
church Term for an ecclesiastical building used by any Christian denomination.
circus 1 A hippodrome for horse and chariot racing. **2** A circular arrangement of terraced houses, as in Bath, England.
citadel A fortified place attached to, or within, a city.
conservatory Glass greenhouse which can combine the function of growing and protecting plants and domestic use.
cottage A small country dwelling place usually originally built for a farm laborer and his family.
crescent A crescent-shaped row of terraced houses.
dolmen A megalithic burial mound.
duplex apartment A maisonette, a flat or apartment on more than one floor.
flat/apartment A single story unit of habitation in a multi-story building.
folly A sham building, sometimes a ruin, built to enhance a vista or a landscape.
fort A small stronghold with all-round defenses such as an Iron Age fort, American West log fort, or Roman garrison.
fortress A large, complex military stronghold with defense in depth and considerable perimeter. In the 19th century a whole city defended by a ring of forts might be so designated.
forum In Roman architecture an open space surrounded by public buildings and colonnades (**5**).

5

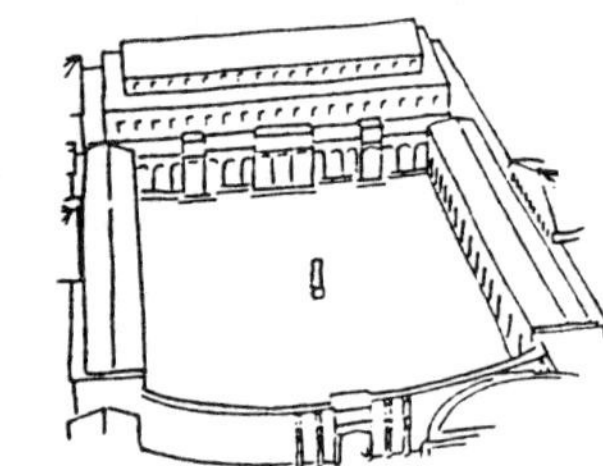

gatehouse The rooms or apartments above a fortified medieval gateway.
gazebo A small summerhouse or pavilion with a view, or a belvedere on the roof of a house (**6**).

6

hall church A type of church common in Germany in which the aisles are the same height as the nave, which is therefore lit from the aisle windows.
hôtel A large French town house.
hunting lodge Buildings usually located in forests to accommodate hunters.
hypostyle A thickly pillared hall, especially in ancient Egypt, in which the roof rests directly on the columns.
kiosk 1 A small pavilion or summer-house. **2** A small shop building on the street or inside a bigger building.

continued

Types of building continued

571**1** **library** Store house for books.
lighthouse Tall structure containing a light to warn approaching ships of coastal dangers.
loggia An open-sided gallery, usually with pillars, common in Renaissance Italy (**7**).

7

lych gate A covered wooden gate at the entrance to a churchyard.
manor house A medium-sized medieval house in the country or a village, the center of a manor.
manse A house attached to a church and provided for the minister in Scotland and northern England.
mansion house A grand residence.
martello tower English artillery coastal fortification copied from a tower captured in Corsica 1794; 74 were built on the east and south coasts of England against the French invasion threat 1805-12.
martyrium A Christian church sited over the grave(s) of martyr(s).
mausoleum A large, grand tomb comprising a separate structure or building (**8**).

8

mews A small terrace of stables and staff accommodation in a cobbled street behind a row of rich town (especially London) houses.
minaret Tower usually attached to a mosque from which the Muslim faithful are called to prayer.
minster A loose term given to a number of medieval English cathedrals and major churches. It originally implied a monastery and monastic church.
monastery A building complex, including a church or abbey, inhabited by monks or nuns.
mosque Islamic place of worship.
motte-and-bailey A mound or motte surmounted by a wooden (later stone) tower (bailey) and enclosed by a ditch and palisade. The earliest example of this primitive castle form is on the River Loire (France) and is dated 1010.
museum Building for the presentation of valuable or historical artifacts.
obelisk A monument of Ancient Egyptian origins, consisting of a tall tapering shaft of stone with a pyramidal top.
observatory Building housing a telescope.
odeion A small classical building for musical contests.
orangery A conservatory for growing oranges, glazed on the south side.
oratory A small private chapel.
outhouse A small building detached from a house, such as a garden shed or sometimes a toilet.
pagoda Buddhist Indian, Southeast Asian or Chinese temple in the form of a tower (**9**), copied as a decorative building in Europe from the 18th century P'ai Lou, a highly decorated Chinese gateway.

9

palace, palazzo A major royal or episcopal residence.
palisade A defensive fence of strong wooden stakes.
penthouse 1 An outhouse with a lean-to roof. **2** A separate structure on the roof of a high rise building.
pillbox Ferro-concrete machine gun (or small gun) emplacement first used in 1917.
refectory A communal dining hall.
skyscraper A very tall building of steel skeletal construction, developed in the USA from the 1880s.
stadium A sports ground for athletics.
stave church Scandinavian timber-framed and timber-walled church built from the 11th century onward.
stoa In Greek architecture a covered colonnade or hall (often with shops) open on the colonnaded side and sometimes two-storied (**10**).

10
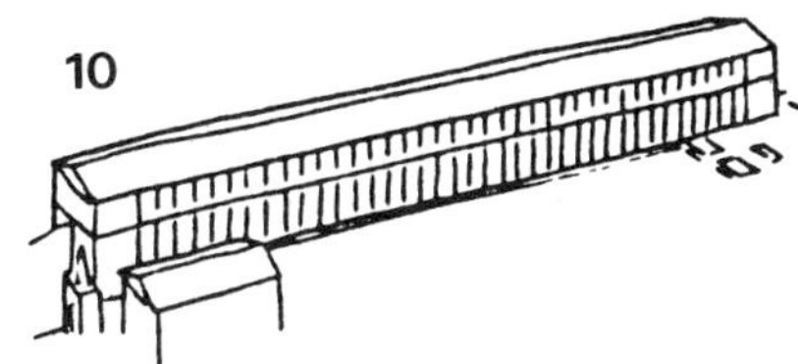

synagogue A Jewish place of worship.
tabernacle The portable sanctuary in which the ancient Israelites carried the Ark of the Covenant (**11**).

11

temple A place of worship particularly associated with classical Greek architecture.
theater A building designed for the performance of plays (**12**).

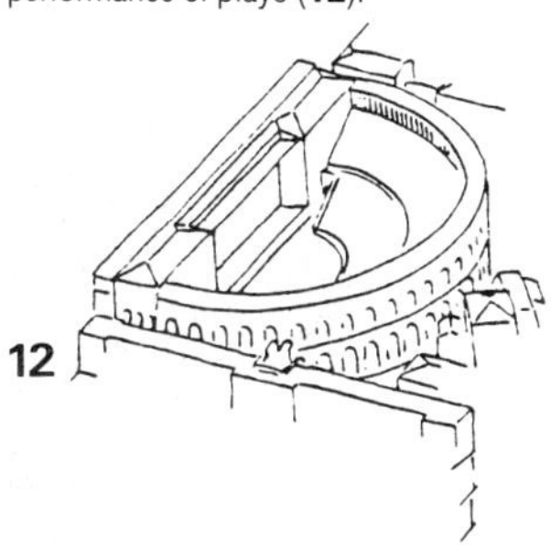
12

thermae Roman public baths.
tholos A circular domed building.
tomb A place for the burial of a corpse.
tower A very tall structure, usually square or circular, designed for observation, communication, and defense.
town hall Municipal buildings for the council and local administration.
tower block High rise apartment block.
triumphal arch A Roman monumental gateway, much imitated in the Renaissance and since, to celebrate military victory or prowess (**13**).

13

triumphal column A decorated column to celebrate a military victory.
viaduct A series of arches which carry a road, canal or railway over a valley, water, or low ground.
villa 1 A Roman or Renaissance country house. **2** A modern detached house.
watchtower A tall tower for military observation, often part of a castle.
ziggurat A stepped pyramid.

572 HISTORY OF WESTERN ARCHITECTURE

Classical

5721

Etruscan 750–100 BC
Greek 600–300 BC
Hellenistic 300–30 BC
Roman 300 BC–AD 365

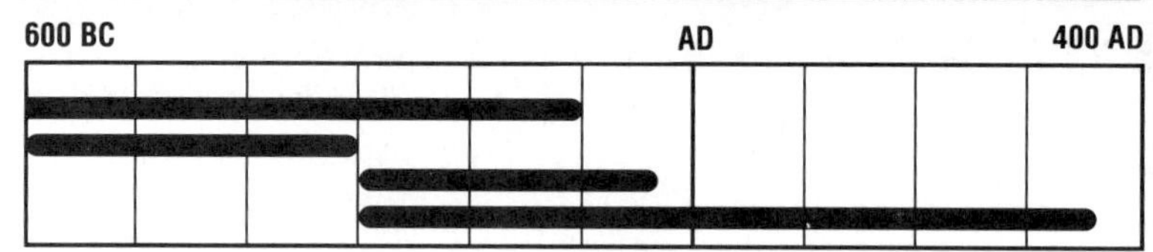

STYLES

Etruscan styles (750–100 BC) Building style of the Romans' predecessors in Italy. Only Etruscan city walls and elaborate tombs, rich in decoration, survive.

Greek styles (600–300 BC) The classical period of Greek architecture lasted from the 7th to the 4th century BC. The zenith was reached with the Parthenon at Athens (c. 447–44 BC) which exemplified a formal, proportional, traditional architectural style that has established an endlessly self-perpetuating canon of taste into the late 20th century.

Hellenistic styles (300–30 BC) Greek architecture's development in the east Mediterranean and Asian kingdoms founded after Alexander the Great and absorbed by Rome.

Roman styles (300 BC–AD 365) Ancient Rome emphasized the building of monumental public sites (baths, amphitheaters and aqueducts, etc), military engineering (Hadrian's wall) and rural villas. The Romans rediscovered brick and concrete to develop the first large vaults (groin variety invented) and domes by the first century BC. Relied on them and arches, more so than columns, unlike the Greeks.

ORDERS

In classical architecture the five standard arrangements and decorations of base, column, capital, and entablature: Doric, Ionic, Corinthian, Tuscan, and composite.

A Classical orders
1 Doric
2 Ionic
3 Corinthian

B Derived orders
4 Tuscan
5 Doric Roman
6 Composite

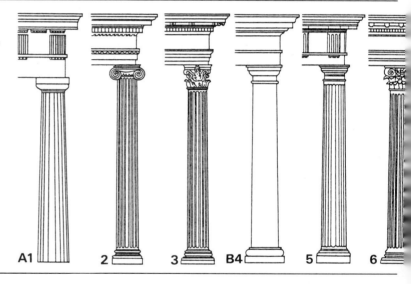

A1 2 3 B4 5 6

FEATURES OF A CLASSICAL BUILDING

architrave In classical architecture the lowest of the three divisions of a beam, or entablature.
atlanta Greek name for carved male figure (Latin: *telamon)* used as decorative support in classical and Baroque architecture.
base The lowest visible part of a building, or of an architectural or ornamental feature, e.g. attic base.
cap In joinery, part of a wood structure.
capital The architectural feature at the head of a column.
caryatid Sculpted female figure used as a column, most famously in the porch of the Erechtheum in Athens.
column An upright circular support.
cornice The upper and projecting part of an entablature in classical architecture.
entablature The upper part of an order of architecture, or visual beam, comprising the cornice, frieze, and architrave.
fluted column A column with a fluted shaft.
frieze The middle section of an entablature an ornamental band, either abstract, botanical or figurative, around the upper walls of a room below the cornice.
pedestal The supporting parts of a column.
pediment A low pitched triangular gable above a temple façade or a smaller version of same above a door or window.
plinth The base of a wall or a column pedestal.
rusticated column A ringed or banded column.
shaft The main body of a column or a small column attached to a pillar or pier.
volute The scroll on an Ionic column the same in motif.

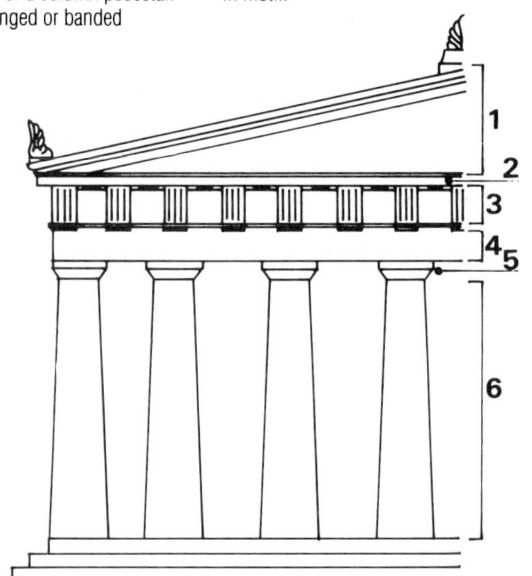

Façade features
1 Pediment
2 Cornice Entablature
3 Frieze Entablature
4 Architrave Entablature
5 Capital
6 Column

Early Christian

5722

Early Christian 313-800
Byzantine 330-1453
Carolingian 751-987
Romanesque 800-1270
Ottonian 919-1024
Cistercian 1098–1270
Gothic 1140-1534
Rayonnant 1194-1400
Flamboyant 1400-1500

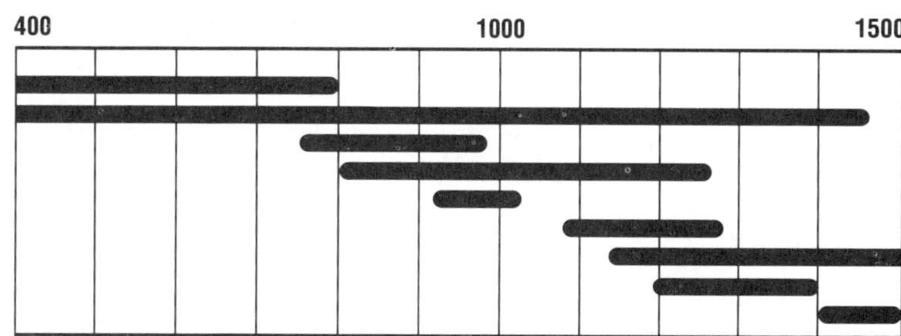

EUROPEAN

Early Christian (AD 313–c. 800) Christian buildings exist for the 3rd century such as meeting houses, catacombs, and martyr's shrines. From Constantine's Edict of Toleration (AD 313) onward, the Roman basillican form was adopted as the standard church ground plan until Byzantine centrally-planned churches appeared.

Byzantine (AD 330–1453) A Christian style developed after Constantinople's foundation as the new capital of the Roman Empire. It initially blended Hellenistic, Roman, and early Christian styles. In the west it gave way to Romanesque. In the east it developed a style of centrally-planned, highly decorated, domed church architecture that was exported to the Balkans, Russia, and throughout the Middle East.

Carolingian (c. AD 751–987) Attempt to recreate a Roman Imperial style in northern Europe by the Emperor Charlemagne (reigned 768–814) and his court at Aachen (**1**). It anticipated Romanesque.

Romanesque (AD 800–1270) Europe-wide architectural style that broadly embraced building from the age of Charlemagne (c. AD 800) to the beginning of the Gothic. Characterized by rounded arches, clearly articulated ground plans and elevations, basilican-plan churches, and both barrel vaults and early rib vaults (**2**).

Ottonian (AD 919–1024) Transnational period in German architecture between Carolingian and Romanesque (**3**).

Cistercian (1098–1270) Severe Romanesque style used by the Cistercian monastic order founded at Citeaux (France) in 1098 which rapidly founded 750 monasteries throughout Europe.

Gothic (1140–1534) Architectural style based on the structural introduction of the flying buttress, ribbed vault, and pointed arch which reduced walls to a minimum allowing for galleries and large stained glass panels such as the rose window.

Rayonnant (1194–1400) French mid-Gothic style relying on massive round stained-glass windows and a wholesale use of tracery (**4**).

Flamboyant (1400–1500) Late French Gothic tracery style, distinguished by sinuous wavy tracery (**5**).

Anglo-Saxon 650–1066
Norman 1045–1180
Early English 1175–1250
Decorated 1290s–1375
Perpendicular 1350–1530

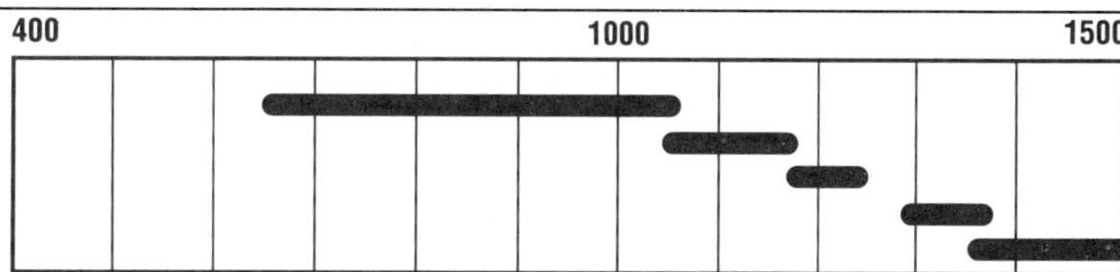

BRITISH

Anglo-Saxon (650–11th century) Style in Britain where most early buildings were of wood and have now disappeared. More developed church architecture with towers decorated with pilaster stripes still being produced after the Norman conquest.

Norman (1045–1180) The English name for Romanesque architecture (**1**), the first example of which was King Edward the Confessor's Westminster Abbey (1065) and which was further imported from Normandy by William the Conqueror the following year.

Gothic (1140–c. 1630) Term for three periods of English architecture.

Early English (c. 1175–c. 1250) The first style of English Gothic architecture (**2**), prevalent from the late 12th century to the late 13th century. Although French in origin, its ground plan, decoration, and elevation are from the outset specifically English in style.

Decorated style (1290s–c. 1375) The second distinct phase of English Gothic architecture, prevalent from the 1290s to the end of the 14th century. Simple geometrical forms, conventional yet fresh foliage, and the ogee arch are typical characteristics (**3**).

Perpendicular (c. 1350–c. 1530) Third and most English, of England's three Gothic architecture styles (**4**). Characterized by an emphasis on horizontals and verticals, by large windows, by lierne vaults and then fan vaults, it was common from the 1350s until the 16th century, and in some areas, even later. It reached its height with buildings such as King's College Chapel, Cambridge (1446–1515).

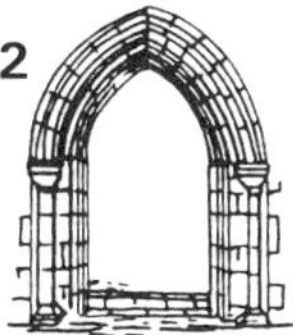

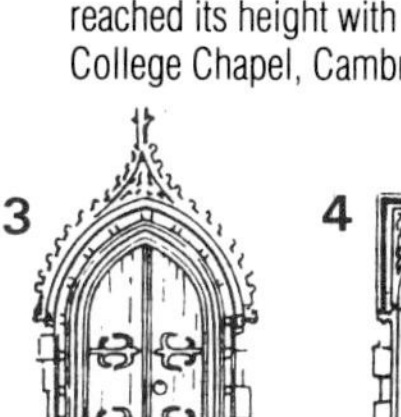

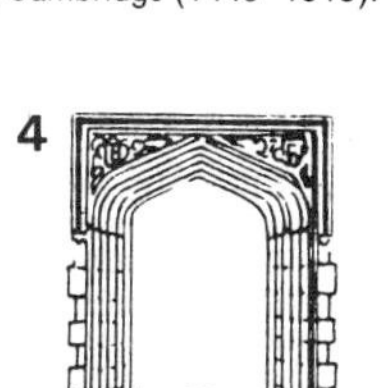

continued

Early Christian continued

5722

Asturian 700–900
Visigothic 711–914
Mozarabic 800–1140
Mudéjar 1110–1522
Manueline 1495–1522

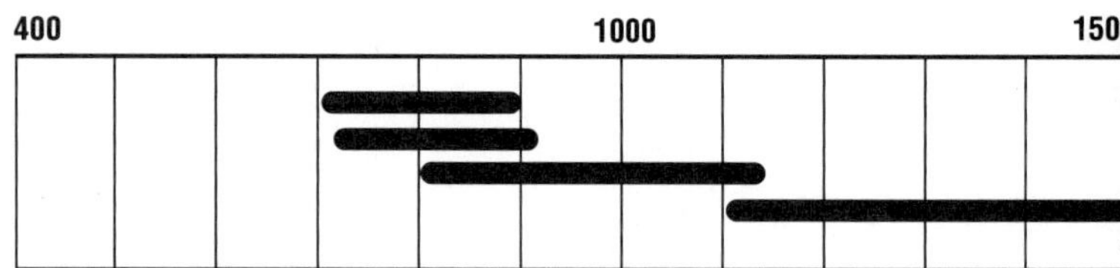

SPANISH AND PORTUGUESE

Asturian (700–900) Christian architecture of a relatively small region around Oviedo, northwest Spain, unconquered by the Moors at this time.

Visigothic (711–914) Style current in Portugal and Spain during the rule of the Visigoths, which borrowed elements from both Roman and Byzantine styles.

Mozarabic (800–1140) Christian architecture and design in Iberia from the 9th to the 11th centuries which demonstrates the influence of Moorish and Islamic building style, especially the horseshoe arch (**1**).

Mudéjar (1110–1500) Christian architecture in Spain that was entirely Muslim in style, as opposed to Mozarabic which only borrowed a number of features and elements (**2**).

Manueline style (1495–1521) Portuguese architecture during and just after the prosperous reign of King Manuel I the Fortunate (1495–1521), the culmination of the late Gothic style (**3**).

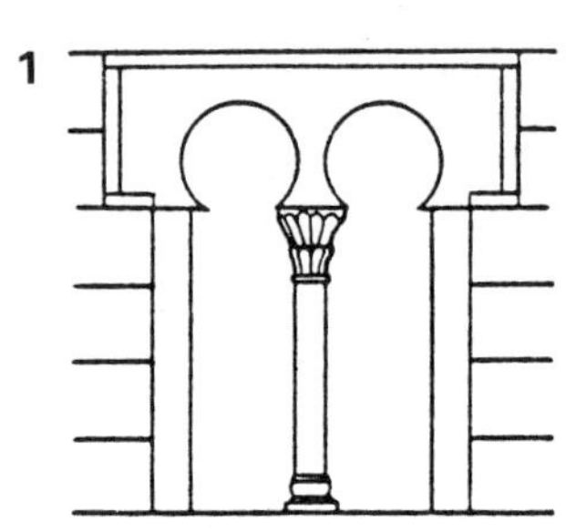

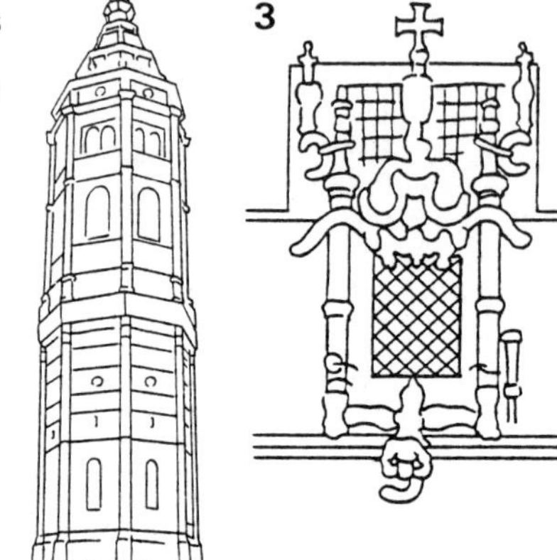

FEATURES OF A GOTHIC CHURCH

Gothic (1140–c. 1530) A European style of architecture predominant from the 12th to the 16th centuries characterized by the use of the pointed arch, the rib vault, and the flying buttress. It is a style most noted for its church architecture in which the religious aims are height and light, both achieved through a mixture of skeletal structures, ever increasing windows, vaulting and the transference of weight downward and sideways via rib and buttress.

1 Boss An ornamental stone or wood block usually decorating the crossing points of a vaulted ceiling.
2 Buttress Masonry support along the side of a wall.
3 Clerestory Row of windows above the roof of the side aisles.
4 Finial Carved ornamental foliage on the top of a pinnacle or spire.
5 Flying Buttress Masonry support buttress which is arched so that its base is away from the wall.
6 Gargoyle A water spout carved with a grotesque head.
7 Pier A masonry support in solid but not necessarily columnar form.
8 Pinnacle A turret,or a tall ornament.
9 Rib A structural device of a vault or roof.
10 Spandrel A triangular space formed by the arch and the walls.
11 Tracery Masonry designs within a window.
12 Triforium An arched passage above a nave.

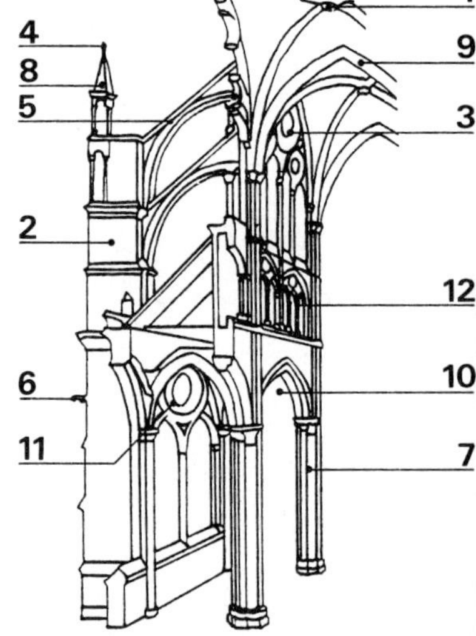

Renaissance

5723

ITALY
Renaissance Quattrocento 1420–1500
Cinquecento 1500–1530
Mannerist 1530–1600
BRITAIN
Tudor 1485–1558
Elizabethan 1558–1618
SPAIN
Plateresque 1480–1552

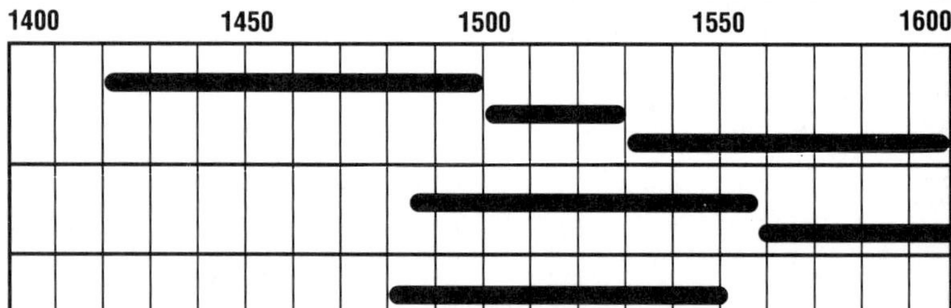

In the broadest architectural sense, the Renaissance was a period in Italy during which the motifs and principles of ancient classical architecture were reapplied and integrated with existing Italian architectural traditions. A ten-volume treatise, *De Architectura,* by the Roman architect Marcus Vitruvius Pollio (active 46–c. 13 BC), was rediscovered in the Renaissance and became an endless and fertile source of inspiration for architects and designers.

The Renaissance is historically divided into two periods: *Quattrocento* (early Renaissance, c. 1420–1500) and *Cinquecento* (high Renaissance c. 1500–30s).

English Tudor (1485–1558) English architecture during the reigns of the five Tudor monarchs, which saw the final flowering of English Perpendicular style and the introduction of Romanesque motifs.

English Elizabethan (1558–c. 1618) Early English Renaissance building during Elizabeth I's reign (1558–1603) and a little after.

Mannerist (c. 1530–c. 1600) Italian, and Italianate predominant style from Michelangelo until Baroque. A reaction against high Renaissance Classical perfection, mannerism either coldly and rigorously applied Classical rule and motif or deliberately flouted Classical convention.

continued

Renaissance continued

5723 RENAISSANCE ARCHITECTS

Alberti, Leon Battista 1404–72, Florentine poet, scholar, mathematician, and compiler of treatises on the arts. Leading Italian Renaissance architect and theorist, responsible for the façade (1456–70) of S Maria Novella, Florence (**1**).

Bramante, Donato 1444–1514, leading Italian high Renaissance architect. Born near Urbino, he was influenced by Alberti and Leonardo. His greatest work was in Milan and in Rome where, in 1506, he began the rebuilding of St Peter's on a Greek cross plan, until the death of his patron, Pope Julius II, in 1513.

Brunelleschi, Filippo 1377–1446, a Florentine, the first great architect of the Italian Renaissance. His most famous architectural work was the dome and lantern which completed the building of the cathedral in Florence (1420–38.)

Delorme, Philibert 1500/15–70, French classical who traveled and lived in Rome. Was very influential through writings. Most of his work has been destroyed, but one exception is tomb of St Francis I at St Denis (1547).

Jones, Inigo 1573–1652, English classical architect. Designed many major buildings for James I and Charles I. One of the first Englishmen to study architecture in Italy and to understand rules of classicism. Particularly influenced by Palladio. Two of his best-known

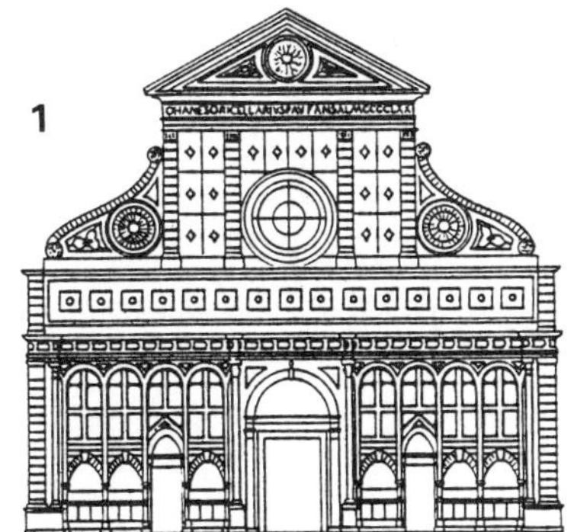
1

buildings include the Queen's House, Greenwich (1616–35) and the Banqueting Hall, London (1619–22).

Mansart, François 1598–1666, first great French classical architect, whose genius was early demonstrated in the Orleans wing of the Chateau du Blois (1635–8). His erratic nature, however, prevented many of his buildings from being completed. Brought the mansard roof into common use.

Palladio, Andrea 1508–80, Venetian architect and theorist whose all-pervasive influence created the style internationally known as Palladianism. Studied the Roman architect Vitruvius, and was fascinated by Roman symmetrical planning and laws of harmonic proportions. His villas, such as the Villa Capra, Vicenza (begun 1550) (**2**) were the inspiration for much early 18th-century English country house building.

Raphael (Raffaello Sanzio) 1483–1520, consummate high Renaissance painter and architect. His building style took over from Bramante's late work. It is seen to best effect in, for example, his last building, the Chigi Chapel in S Maria del Popolo, Rome (c. 1513–14).

Serlio, Sebastiano 1475–1554, Italian painter, architect, and theorist whose book *L'Architettura* (1537–51) codified the classical orders. It became a prime source of both classical motif and Renaissance Italian styles for British and French architects.

2

MANNERIST ARCHITECTS

Buonarotti, Michelangelo 1475–1564, Italian Renaissance sculptor, architect, painter, and poet, he overturned all the classical theories, preoccupations, structural considerations and decorative motifs of the early Renaissance. He sculpted rather than built his buildings, using mass, weight, and decorative motif to create an organic and dynamic whole, an example of which is the monument to Lorenzo de' Medici, Medici Chapel, Florence (1521–34) (**2**). He worked mainly in Florence, but also in Rome, where he finished St Peter's Cathedral (1546–64). Michelangelo not only created Mannerist architecture but also influenced, for better or worse, nearly all subsequent classical styles.

Romano, Giulio c. 1492–1546, Roman Mannerist painter and architect whose most famous work was at the court of Federigo Gonzaga in Mantua, especially the Palazzo del Tè (**1**) (c. 1525–31).

1

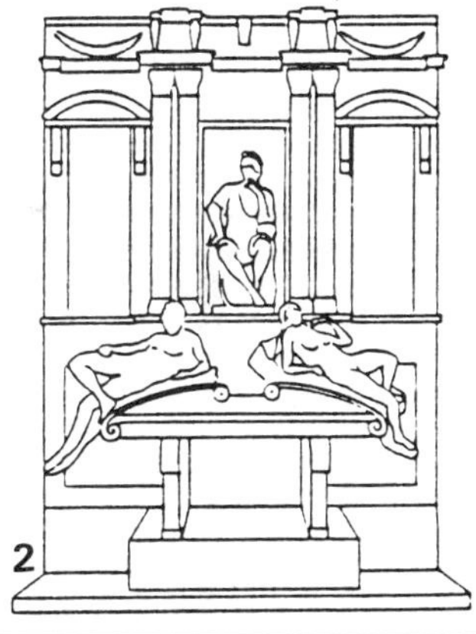
2

17th century

5724

Italy
Early Baroque 1585–1625
High Baroque 1625–75
Late Baroque 1675–1715
FRANCE
Louis XIV 1643–1715
ENGLAND
Stuart 1618–90
Jacobean 1618–25
AMERICA
English Colonial 1607–1700
Dutch Colonial 1614–64

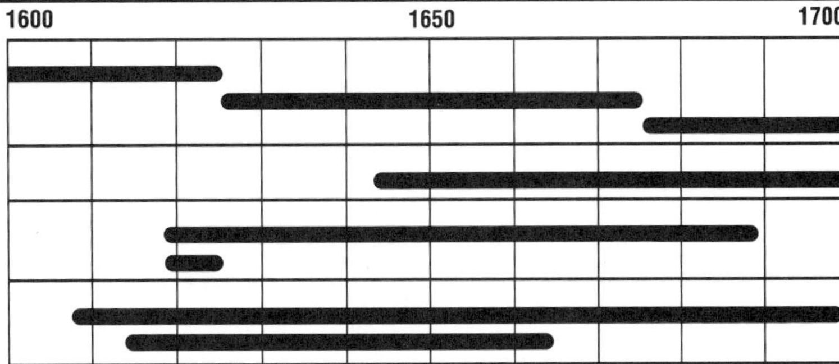

Baroque The dominant European style of architecture and decoration. Spanning 130 years in Italy, this period is subdivided as early Baroque (c. 1585–c. 1625); high Baroque (c. 1625–75); and late Baroque (c. 1675–c. 1715). The age of high Baroque in Germany and central Europe began c. 1680 and ended c. 1750. Its component parts comprised classical forms and motifs transformed by an exuberance and richness of decoration, spatial complexity, weight, and complex use of existing space and vista.

continued

17th century continued

5724

American Dutch Colonial 1614–64 Dutch architectural style transported to the American colonies, appearing in the form of narrow farmhouses with clapboard gables or step-gabled brick townhouses.
American English Colonial 1607–1700 English architectural style found in the English colonies of America, which was based on Tudor architecture, but with variations related to economic, social, and religious differences.
Jacobean (Britain) (c. 1618–25) Period named after King James I (reigned 1603–25) that incorporates the first precise rendering of Italian Renaissance style and motif in British architecture.

17th CENTURY ARCHITECTS
Asam, Cosmas Damian 1686–1739 and **Egid, Quirin** 1692–1750, brothers who were the leading late Baroque architects and decorators in Bavaria.
Bernini, Gianlorenzo 1598–1680, the Italian sculptor who dominated the history of Roman Baroque art. Also an architect of immense distinction, whose buildings (e.g. the Baldacchino in St Peter's, 1624–33, and Palazzo di Montecitorio, 1650 onward) have in many ways determined the architectural character of Rome.
Borromini, Francesco 1599–1667, the most original Roman Baroque architect, the rival of Bernini. His first great success was the tiny church of S. Carlo alle Quattro Fontane (1638–46), in which a truly original use of space triumphed over a very difficult and diminutive site.
Campen, Jacob van 1595–1667, Dutch Palladian architect mainly in The Hague and Amsterdam who combined classical motif with Dutch brick work and hipped roofs.
Cortona, Pietro Berrettini da 1596–1669, Roman Baroque architect and painter, especially famous for his theatrical use of concave and convex shapes, as with the church of S Maria della Pace (Rome 1656–57).
Fischer von Ehrlach, Johann Bernhard 1656–1723, Austrian Baroque architect who rose to become Imperial Court Architect (1704). His Salzburg churches and Prague and Vienna palaces constitute an impressive reminder of the grandiose but harmonious Habsburg Baroque style he evolved. Best-known are the Schönnbrunn Palace (1696–1711) and the Karlskirche (1716–37) (**1**). His *A Plan of Civil*

1

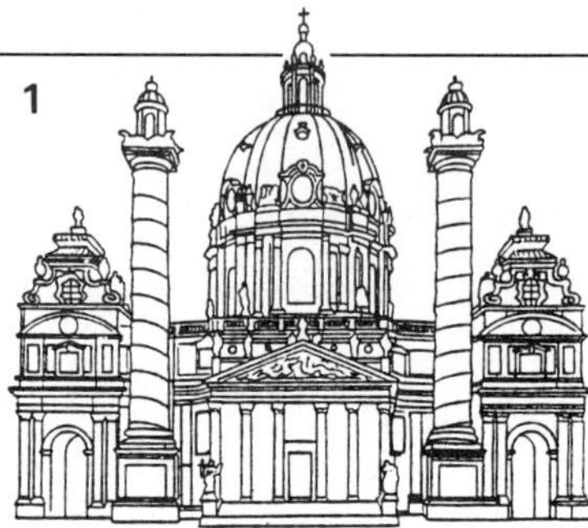

and Historical Architecture (1721) was the first treatise to analyze Chinese and Egyptian architecture.
Fontana, Carlo 1638–1714, Rome-based architect who worked for ten years under Bernini and influenced pupils throughout Europe, such as Pöppelmann (Germany), Gibbs (England), and Fischer von Ehrlach and Hildebrandt (Austria).
Guarini, Guarino 1624–83, leading Italian Baroque architect and mathematician, all of whose surviving buildings are in Turin, e.g. the Capella della S Sindone (1667–90).
Hardouin-Mansart, Jules 1646–1708, highly successful French Baroque architect to the court of Louis XIV. From 1678 he was in charge of the development of Versailles. His contributions to Paris include the Place Vendôme (1698) and the Invalides Chapel (1680–91).
Hildebrandt, Johann Lucas von 1668–1745, Austrian military engineer and Baroque architect whose Vienna and south German palaces were even more Italianate (*à la* Guarini) than Fischer von Ehrlach's. Prince Eugene's Belvedere summer palace (1714–24) is his masterpiece, containing characteristic octagonal and oval rooms off spectacular staircases.
Pöppelmann, Matthaeus Daniel 1662–1736, German Baroque architect appointed to the Elector of Saxony's court (1705). His most original building was the partially finished Zwinger pavilion or "Roman arena" (his own description) at Dresden (1711–22).
Wren, Sir Christopher 1632–1723, preeminent English architect, also a scientist of distinction in London and Oxford and a member of parliament. In 1667 he became a surveyor under the Rebuilding Act after the Great Fire of London (1666) and in 1669 was made Surveyor-General of the King's Works. His scholarly, refined, detailed, and inventive Baroque style was intensely English, the most notable example being St Paul's Cathedral, London. His grandest secular building was the Greenwich Hospital (1696 onward).
Vauben, Sebastien le Prestre de 1633–1701, French fortress builder, siege engineer and Marshall of France who is the greatest name in military architecture. Refortified or built from scratch 160 fortresses and directed over 50 successful sieges for Louis XIV. Devised the case mated bastion tower in 1687 and a powder magazine (standard until 1874). Founded France's engineering corps (1690), the modern world's first such permanent professional body.

18th century

5725

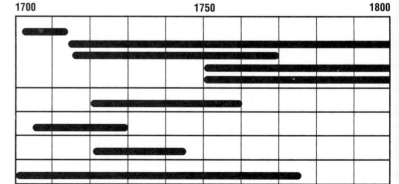

BRITAIN
Queen Anne 1702–14
Georgian 1714–1837
Palladian 1715–70
Gothic Revival 1750–1900
Neoclassical 1750–1840
GERMANY
Rococo 1720–60
FRANCE
Régence 1705–30
PORTUGAL
Pombaline 1721–45
AMERICA
Georgian 1700–76

STYLES
Churrigueresque (c. 1680–1780) Exuberant Spanish Baroque style epitomized by the three Churriguera brothers from Barcelona. They incorporated Latin American art and decorative elements.
Federal (1790-1820s) US east coast version of the European Adam neoclassical fashion.
Georgian (1714–1837, US c. 1700–76) Term loosely used (and much subdivided) to describe English late Renaissance classical architecture during the reigns of the first four Goerges.

continued

18th century continued

5725 **Jeffersonian** (1790s–1830s) Roman temple inspired design of the state capitals, universities, and private homes, which the third president pioneered
Neoclasssical (1750s–1840s) 18th-century classical movement based on a more correct archeological interpretation of Greco-Roman building. It supplanted Rococo.
Palladian (c. 1715–1770s) European and American classical design derived from buildings and treatises of Andrea Palladio.
Rococo (1720–60) A decorative anti-rational style of architecture that emerged c. 1720 and lasted until c. 1760. It was at once the child and antithesis of Baroque. In France it was associated with lightness, swirling forms, and the frippery of the court; in south Germany and Austria with almost ecstatic exuberance and spatial complexity. It denied structure and dwelt on line and emotion. A typical example is the Zwinger (**1**) built in 1718 in Dresden.

1

18TH CENTURY ARCHITECTS

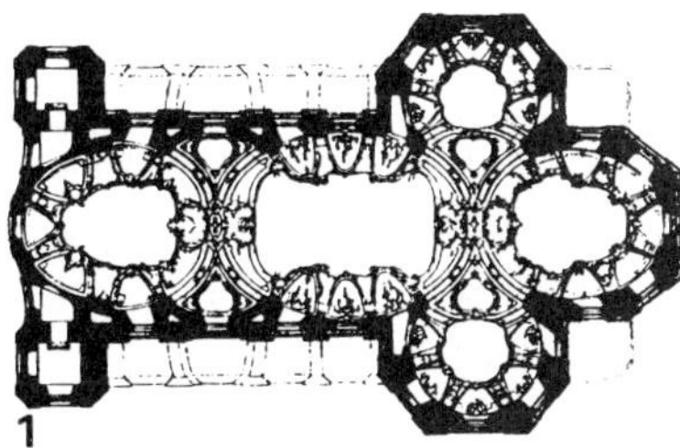
1

Fischer, Johann Michael 1692–1766, South German rococo architect who built 22 abbeys and 32 churches all richly decorated, frequently monumental, and spatially subtle.
Neumann, (Johann) Balthasar 1687–1753, the finest and most versatile German rococo architect began as a military engineer. His creations, such as the church at Vierzehnheiligen (1743/4–72) (**1**), were often oval-based in plan and sumptuously decorated, and are the apotheosis of this mobile and decorative style.
Boullée, Étienne-Louis 1728–99, influential French classical architect whose emotional approach to design led to a style that was romantic in scale and feeling.
Gabriel, Jacques-Ange 1698–1782. French neoclassical architect who in 1742 became *premièr architect* to Louis XV and Madame de Pompadour. His works were elegant and refined, avoiding the excesses of rococo, and imbued with good taste and beautiful proportions. Among his masterpieces are the Petit Trianon palace at Versailles (1762–8) and the Place de la Concorde, Paris (1755).
Jefferson, Thomas 1743–1826, third president of the US and influential architect in large part responsible for a stylistic mixture of Serlio, Palladio, and Gibbs that dominated American neoclassical architecture, especially in the new capital city of Washington and Jefferson's own Virginia home, Monticello.
Latrobe, Benjamin Henry 1764–1820, first American architect of international standing, born in England and trained there and in Germany. Emigrated to US (1796) where he introduced both the Greek and Gothic revival styles. Best-known for his 1803–17 work on the Washington Capitol and White House, but his masterpiece is Baltimore Cathedral (1805–18).
Ledoux, Claude-Nicolas 1736–1806, a highly imaginative and original French neoclassical architect, with geometrical simplicity and an almost expressionist use of form, typified by his saltworks at Arc-et-Senans (**2**) (1775-9). His career was ruined by the French Revolution and thereafter he only published the designs which have made him more highly considered in the 20th-century than in his own lifetime.

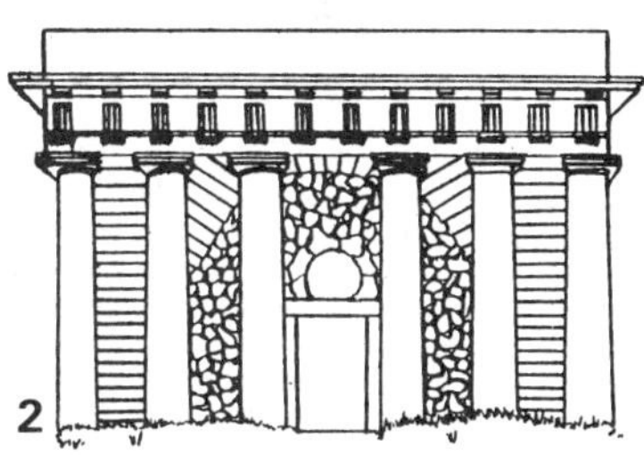
2

19th century

5726

BRITAIN
Gothic 1750–1900
Greek 1806–40
Regency 1810–30
Victorian 1830–1900
FRANCE
Empire 1800–30
Second Empire 1848–70
Beaux Arts 1865–1913
AMERICA
Greek 1798–1860
Gothic 1825–70
Italianate 1850–85
Beaux Arts 1865–1913
Queen Anne 1874–90
Classical 1890–1943

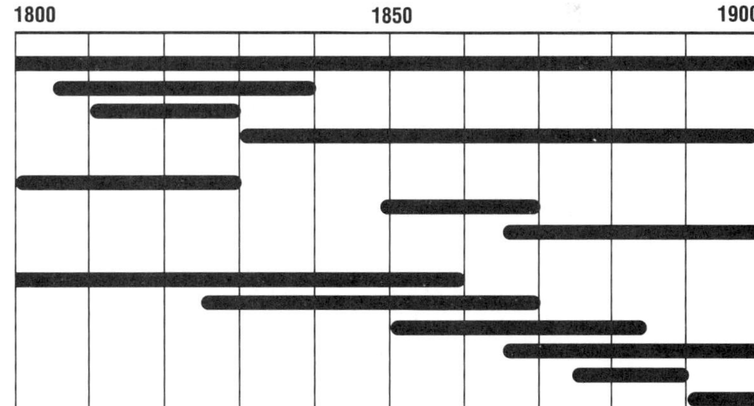

REVIVALIST STYLES
Beaux Arts (US c. 1865–c. 1913) Heavy, monumental detail by architects who attended the Paris École des Beaux Arts after the 1850s. An example is City Hall, Philadelphia (**1**, over).
Classical (US 1890s–c. 1943) Broadly based on the style of ancient Greece and Rome.
Egyptian An exotic style popular in the latter half of the 19th century using the new evidence of archeological excavation in Egypt.
Empire (1800–1830s) Decorative style common throughout Europe in the wake of Napoleon.
Exotic (1830s–c. 1920s) Collective term for several oriental 19th-century revival building styles, such as Egyptian, Turkish, and Moorish fashions.
Gothic (c. 1750–c. 1900) Historic, romantic and a catholic attempt to revive medieval Gothic architecture and ornament from the late 18th century to the end of the 19th century. It ranged from the picturesque love of ruins and Gothic follies, to state symbolism of the Houses of Parliament in London (1834) and the high seriousness of Victorian ecclesiastical building.
Greek (1798–c. 1860) The specifically Greek contribution to neoclassical architecture only became known about 1750. Such knowledge inspired Ledoux, Soane, and a host of Victorian followers. At its best the Greek revival stood for

continued

19th century continued

5726 a purity and simplicity of structure and form.
Italianate (US 1850s–c. 1885) Almost a pre-Civil War national style that adapted Tuscan villa and Renaissance palace features for houses and commercial buildings. Used cast iron for many decorative features. Also known as bracketed, American, Tuscan, or Lombard style.

19TH CENTURY ARCHITECTS
Brunel, Isambard Kingdom 1806-59, British Victorian engineer, designer of the Clifton suspension bridge, the Great Western Railway from London to Bristol, famous ships, such as *Great Western* and *Great Eastern* and the docks at Monkwearmouth, Bristol.
Morris, William 1834-96, English designer whose Arts and Craft Movement influenced every aspect of architectural and interior design in the early modern period. His insistence on craftsmanship provided the intellectual justification for rejecting slavish copying of the past, yet his parallel rejection of machinery and mass-productions potential was inconsistent in some ways both with his social and cultural message.
Schinkel, Karl Friedrich 1781-1841, versatile 19th-century Prussian architect who studied under Gilly in Berlin. Much of his work was in pure Grecian neoclassical style, culminating in Berlin's old museum (1823-30), but he also worked in the Gothic and Romanesque (Runbogenstil) styles and was interested in industrial developments.

20th century

5727

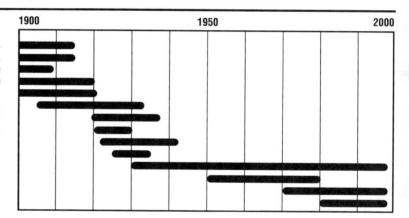

	1900 – 1950 – 2000
Arts and Crafts 1880–1914	
Art Nouveau 1880–1914	
Chicago School 1884–1909	
Jugendstijl 1889–1920	
De Stijl 1892–1921	
Expressionism 1905–33	
Bauhaus 1919–37	
Constructivism 1920–30	
Fascism 1922–43	
Art Deco 1925–35	
International Modern 1930–onward	
Brutalism 1950–onward	
Post Modern 1970–onward	
High Tech 1980–onward	

STYLES
Art Deco (1920s and 1930s) Style in the decorative arts and architecture emanating from Paris in 1925 and common in both Europe and America between the world wars. Stylized and modernist, it reconciled methods of mass production and man-made materials (such as Bakelite) with sophisticated design. (**1**) Cinema, Rayners Lane, London.

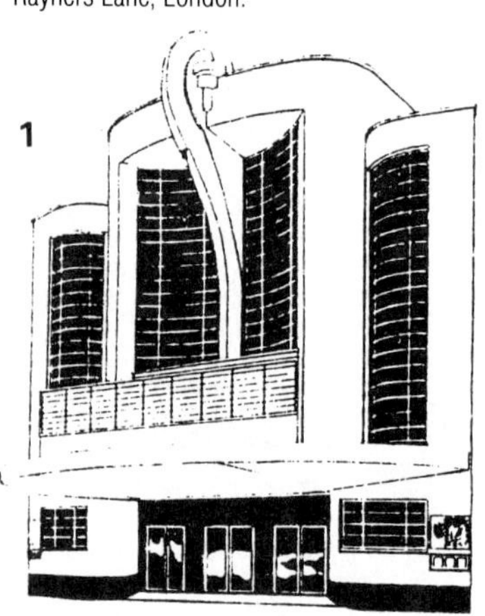

Art Nouveau (1880s–1914) The dominant style of decoration and of *avant garde* building in Europe from the 1880s to World War I. Called *Jugendstijl* in Germany and *stile liberty* in Italy, art nouveau creatively adapted sinuous natural forms in an attempt to avoid architectural and design styles based on the archeological re-creation of the past. (**2**) Entrance to Castel Beranger.
Bauhaus (1919–37) German school of architecture and design (1919–33) founded by the architect Walter Gropius. Epitomized the marriage of modern design, mass production, industrial design, and the teutonic romantic approach to abstract art. Housed in Wiemar until 1925 and at Essau until 1932, it was finally closed down by the Nazis. A style that ruled in modern architecture and design until the 1970s. (**3**) German exhibition pavillion, Barcelona.
Chicago School (1884–1909) Commercial style using the first complete iron and steel skeleton technology to build skyscrapers of 6–20 stories.
Expressionism (c. 1905–33) North European architectural style prevalent in the first quarter of the 20th century that did not treat buildings as

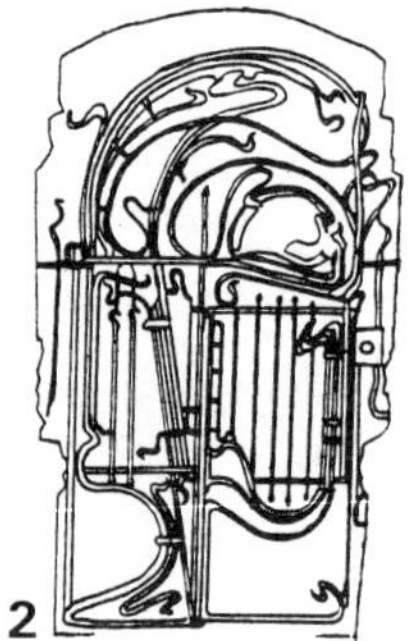

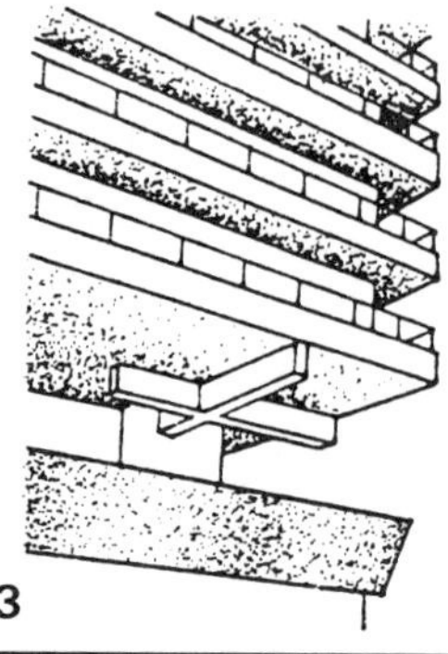

continued

20th century continued

5727 purely functional, but also as exciting sculptures in their own right, e.g. Gaudi in Spain, Klint in Denmark, Poelzig and Mendelsohn in Germany. (**4**) Einstein Tower, Potsdam.
Functionalism (1920s–70s) A building created by an architect whose only concern is that it functions correctly, without any decoration, symbolism, or apparent aesthetic consideration.
International/ International modern style (1920s–onward) The rational style in 20th century architecture, as pioneered by architects such as Frank Lloyd Wright and Walter Gropius, spread by the Bauhaus, and at its most influential in the 1930s. (**5**) Harvard Graduate Center, Cambridge, Massachusetts.
Post-Modernism (1970s–) Reaction against the austerity of the international modern styles and the commercialization of modern structural techniques. Basically it reintroduced ornament and decorative motif to building, often in garish colors and illogical juxtaposition. (**6**) AT&T offices, New York.
Prairie style (c. 1900–c. 20s) Midwest movement led by Frank Lloyd Wright that built geometric, low, and spacious houses with integrated interiors reflecting the spirit of the expansive landscape of the Midwest.

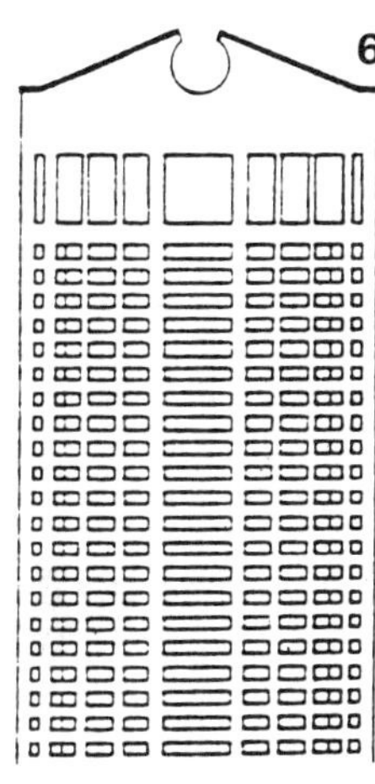

20TH CENTURY ARCHITECTS
Aalto, Hugo Alvar Henrik 1898–1976, Finnish architect, worked in the international modern style, with a real feeling for raw materials, especially wood and brick. Also invented bent plywood furniture.
Arup, Ove 1895–1988, Danish engineer and architect who pioneered methods of concrete construction in London in the 1930s. His own postwar output achieved a harmonic and creative working relationship between engineering and architectural design.
Behrens, Peter 1868–1940, designer and architect who moved from the Arts and Crafts Movement to design factories, shops, and industrial products in Germany. A father of modernism, Gropius, Mies van der Rohe, and Le Corbusier all worked in his AEG design office (1910).
Breuer, Marcel Lajos 1902–81, Hungarian architect, studied and worked at the Bauhaus and later practiced in the USA. He tempered a severe international style with an instructive feeling for raw materials.
Garnier, Tony 1869–1948, visionary modern French architect who designed a *cité industrielle* that heralded a new approach to town planning. He built a slaughterhouse and stadium (1901–16) at Lyons, both featuring his love of reinforced concrete and cantilevers.
Gaudi, I Cornet, Antonio 1852–1926, Catalan-Spanish architect, the most famous and extreme builder and designer in the art nouveau style. His best-known work, the cathedral of the Holy Family in Barcelona (**1**) was begun in 1883 and remains incomplete – in part due to the impossibility of reconciling an almost Baroque and very three-dimensional design with the realities of architecture.
Gropius, Walter 1883–1969, German Bauhaus architect who became the grand old man of international style modern architecture from his training under Peter Brehrens, through his foundation of Bauhaus, to his postwar years at Harvard, US.
Le Corbusier (Charles-Edward Jeannetre) 1887–1965, Swiss-born French modern architect of unrivalled brilliance, influence, and output. His early career as a cubist painter was reflected in the 1920s simple, almost cubist, white houses (e.g. Garches villa, (**2**). The rationalism of international modernism was apparent in his concern with city planning and the mass production of housing. His later work however became anti-rationalist and sculptural, such as the chapel at Notre Dame at Ronchamp, France (1950–54).
Lissitsky, Eleazar Markevich 1890–1941, Russian constructivist architect, painter, typographer, designer, and theorist. His concept of Proun involved the interaction between the pictorial and the structural. He influenced De Stijl while working in the west (1922–31).
Jacobsen, Arne 1902–71, Danish international architect (also a furniture and jewelry designer) who used the rationalism of the 1930s with a constant precision and elegance as seen in Denmark's houses and town halls.
Johnson, Philip Cortelyou b. 1906, American architect who coined the term international modern and was one of its

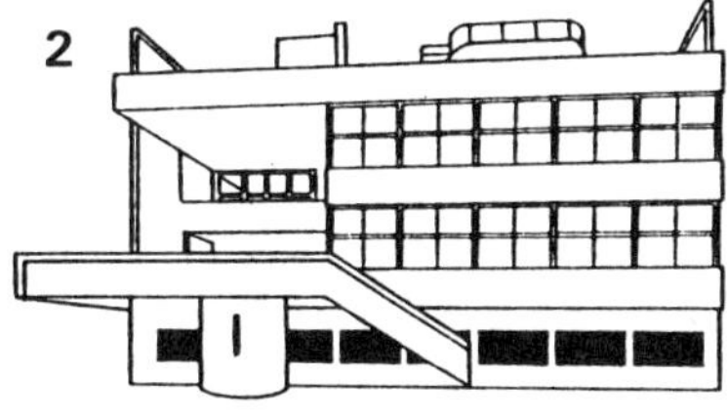

continued

20th century continued

5727 most famous protagonists, as in the New York State Theater in the Lincoln Center (1962–4). He later became the founding father of postmodernism.

Mackintosh, Charles Rennie 1862–1928, leading Scottish architect of the Glasgow School whose art nouveau design integrated all aspects of building, decoration, and furniture; especially at the school of art (library wing), Glasgow (1907–9) (**3**).

Mendelsohn, Erich 1887–1953, pioneer German expressionist architect whose extreme use of streamlined curves was only achieved once, in the Einstein Tower, Potsdam (1919–20). Although retaining an expressionist look in his building, Mendelsohn's later work in Germany, England, Israel (hospitals), and the US was sobered by the 1930s international modernism.

Mies van der Rohe, Ludwig 1886–1969, German modern architect who moved swiftly from a neoclassical to an ultra-expressionist style. Later, as director of the Bauhaus from 1930, became a pillar of international modernism. His enormously influential role continued as head of the Illinois Institute of Technology in Chicago, for whom he designed a new campus (1939). His modernism remained unswervingly rational and wedded to the rigid integrity of the 30s.

Nervi, Pier Luigi 1891–1979, Italian engineer, architect, and inspired designer in concrete. Built stadia, aircraft hangars, exhibition halls, and skyscrapers all with a mixture of elegance and technological daring, the hallmark of postwar Italian modern architecture. Famous examples are the Pirelli building at Milan (with Gio Ponti 1955–8) and the Palazzo dello Sport (Rome, 1960).

Niemeyer, Oscar b. 1907, Brazillian modern architect who worked during 1936 in Rio de Janiero with Le Corbusier. He developed his own anti-rational, expansive, sculptural style in the church of St Francis at Pampulha (1942-3). He was chief architect for the creation of the new capital city of Brasilia (1957 onward), full of breathtaking buildings, aesthetic contradictions, and severe practical and social problems.

Oud, Jacobus Johannes Pieter 1890–1963, Dutch architect and member of De Stijl, a movement which stood for severe cubistic approach to building, as opposed to the expressionistic. Specialized in public housing and estates, especially at Rotterdam (1918–27) and the Hook of Holland (1924–27) (**4**).

Perret, Auguste 1874–1954, French modern architect who was first in France consistently to use a concrete structure with its members deliberately exposed and integrated with the decorative design. Early examples, such as flats in Paris' Rue Franklin (1902–3) (**5**), combined concrete construction with art nouveau detailing. Later his work such as the rebuilding of Le Havre (1946 onward) was almost classical in its balance and austerity.

Rogers, Richard b. 1933, British post-modernist architect whose innovatory output includes the Paris Pompidou Center (1977) and London's high-tech Lloyds Building (1986).

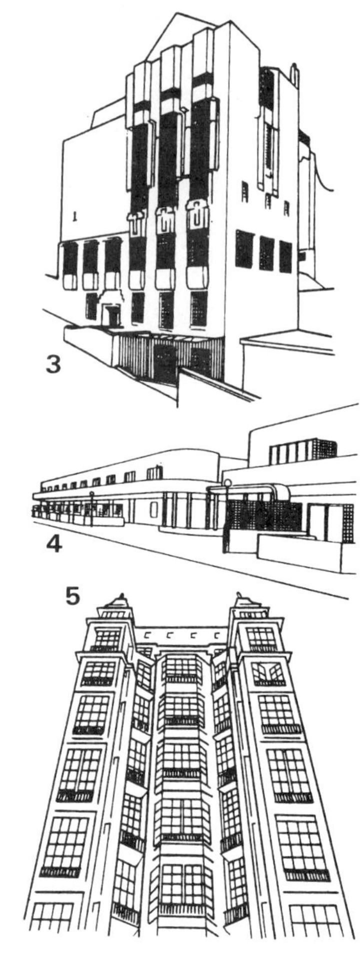

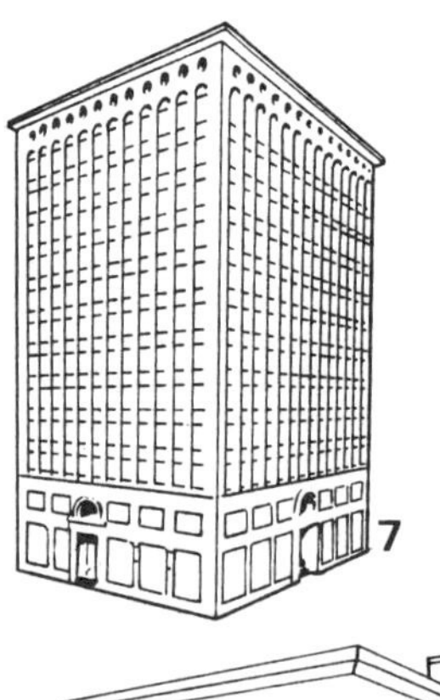

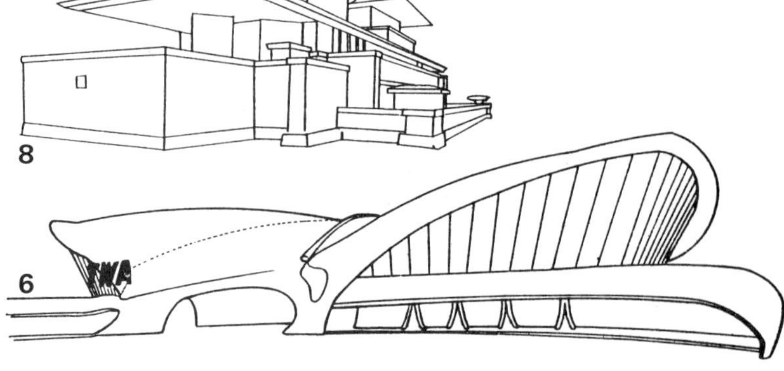

Saarinen, Eero b. 1910, American modern architect whose works ranged from the severe international modern style to the far more expressionistic work such as the TWA terminal at JFK Airport, New York, (1956–62) (**6**).

Sullivan, Louis Henry 1856–1924, Chicago-based architect and decorator who, with Dankmar Adler, designed over 100 buildings (1880–95) including the revolutionary early steel framed skyscrapers (**7**).

Stirling, James b.1926, internationally renowned postwar British architect whose uncompromising use of form and material has brought him close to Brutalism; as at the history faculty building, Cambridge (1965–8). His *Staatsgallerie*, Stuttgart, Germany is nonetheless a popular success.

Tange, Kenzo b. 1913, leading Japanese modern architect, engineer, town planner. Well-known for his work in Japan's major cities since 1950 and designing Nigeria's crescent shaped capital Abuja.

Tatlin, Vladimir 1885–1953, Russian abstract painter, sculptor, theater/industrial designer, and visionary architect whose grandiose project for a monument to the third international (1919) was a key architectural concept of constructivisim.

Velde, Henri van de 1883–1957, Belgian painter and art nouveau architect. In 1895 he designed for Bing's shop *L'art nouveau* in Paris, and settled at Berlin where his new style was instantly popular. Rebuilt the Art School (1904) and the School of Arts and Crafts (1907) in Weimar which developed into the Bauhaus.

Webb, Philip 1831–1955; English domestic architect and designer, friend of William Morris and leading figure of the Arts and Craft movement. For Morris he built the Red House, Bexeley, Kent (1859), the start of a vogue for rustic country houses until the 1890s in which Webb and Richard Norman Shaw (1831–1912) were foremost.

Wright, Frank Lloyd 1869–1959, constantly inventive and most famous American modern architect. His career spans the Sullivan era in Chicago and the postwar era. Early on he developed his trademark the 'prairie house' with low spreading rooms, projecting roofs and gardens, e.g. Robie House (1905). Later he worked on projects such as the office skyscrapers of Bartlesville, Oklahoma (1955) and the Guggenheim Museum in New York (1942) (**8**).He described his work as organic architecture and was very influential worldwide.

573 ARCHITECTURAL FEATURES

Parts of a building

5731 ROOF TYPES
1 Gabled (pitched, saddleback)
2 Hipped
3 Hipped gable (jerkin head)
4 Gambrel (US), Mansard (UK)
5 Mansard (UK and US) (double-pitch)
6 Lean to
7 Monitor
8 Skirt
9 Saw tooth
10 Valley (m-shaped)
11 Penthouse
12 Rainbow
13 Ogee
14 Barrel
15 Flat
16 Y-form
17 Hyperbolic paraboloid

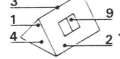

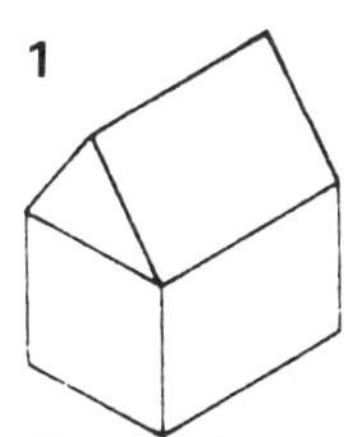
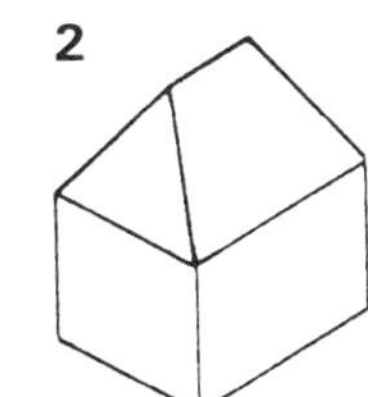
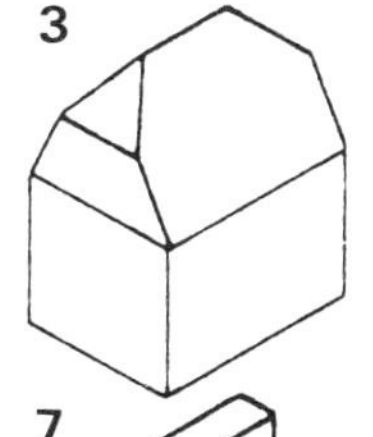
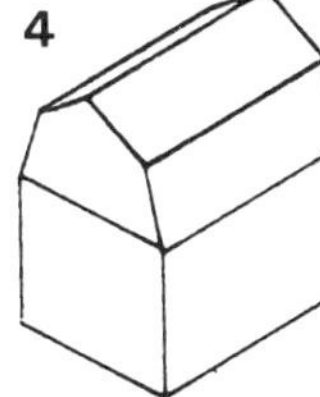
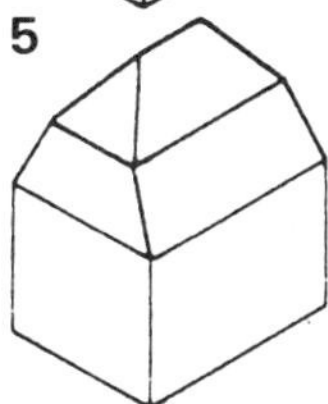
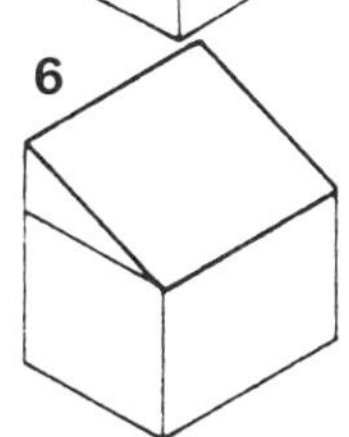
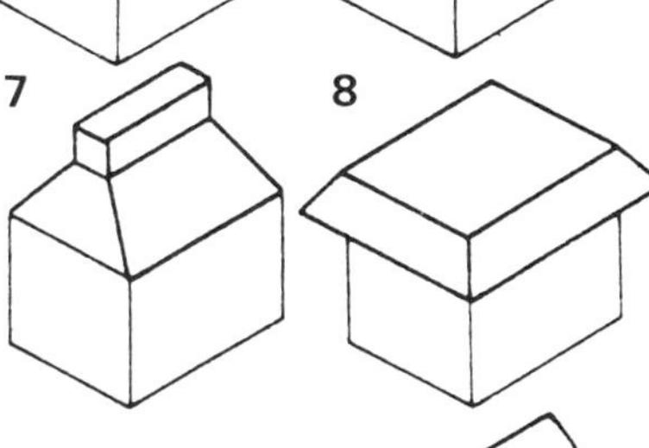
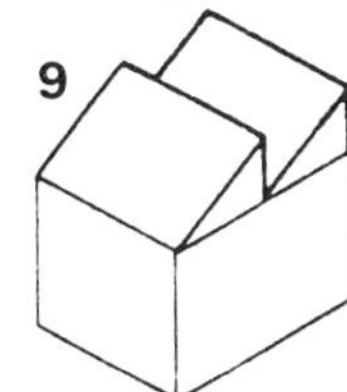
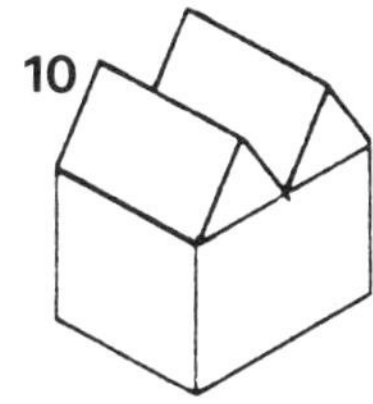
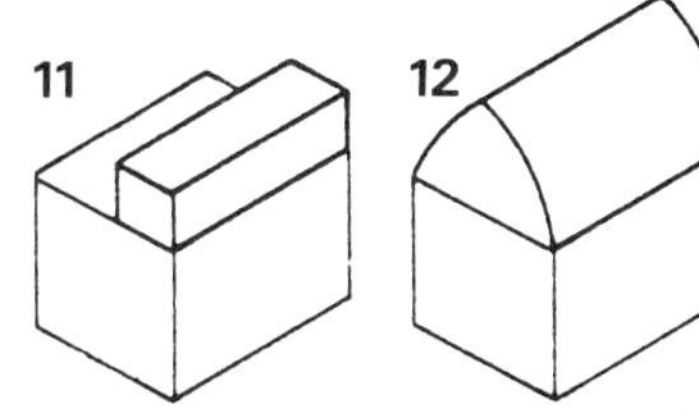
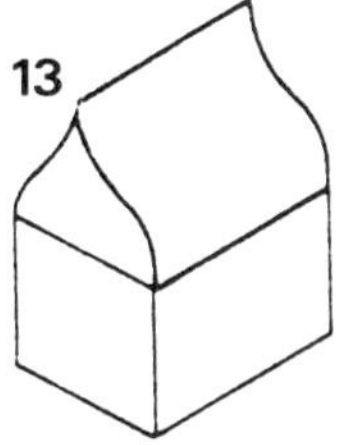
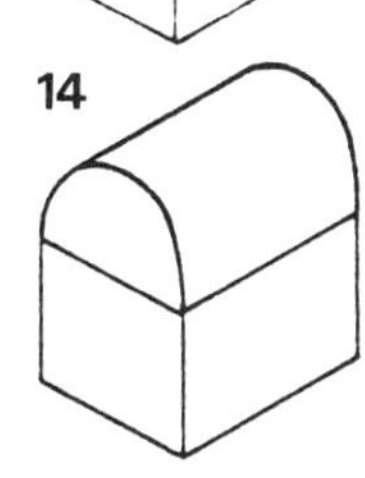
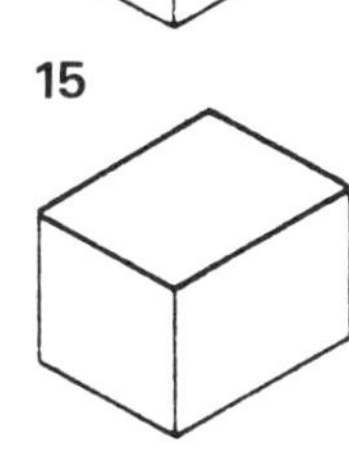
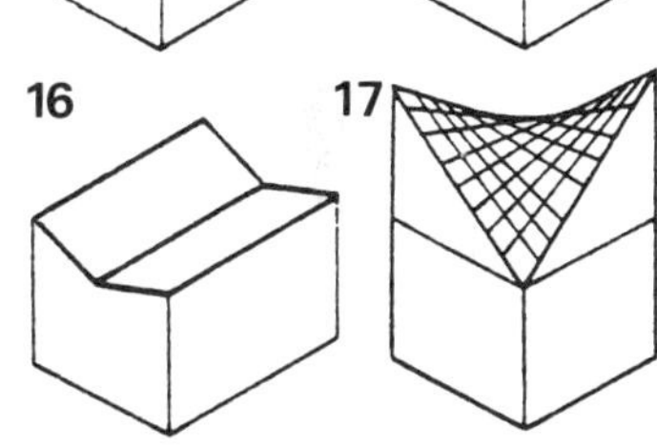

PARTS OF A ROOF
1 Verge
2 Eave
3 Ridge
4 Gable
5 Hip
6 Valley
7 Dormer
8 Gablet
9 Skylight

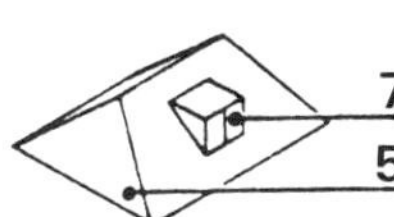
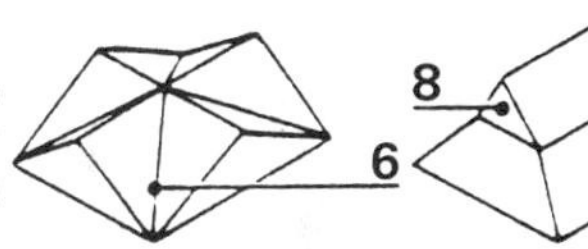

DOME TYPES
1 Dome (cupola)
2 Sail dome
3 Drum dome
4 Pendentive
5 Domical
6 Umbrella (parachute)

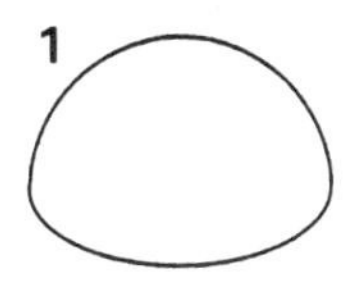

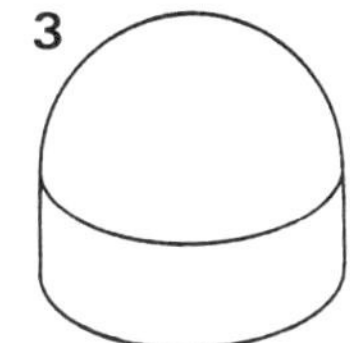
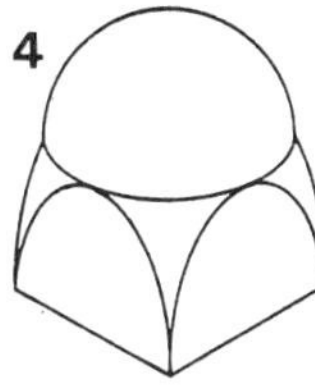
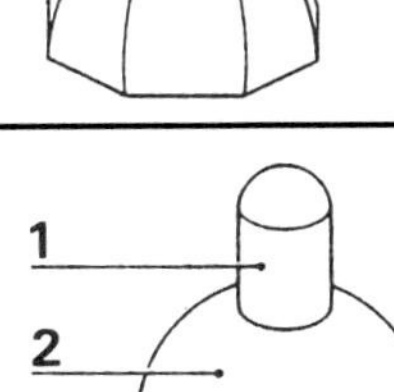

PARTS OF A DOME
1 Lantern
2 Dome (cupola)
3 Drum
4 Pendentive
5 Oculus
6 Attic tier/story

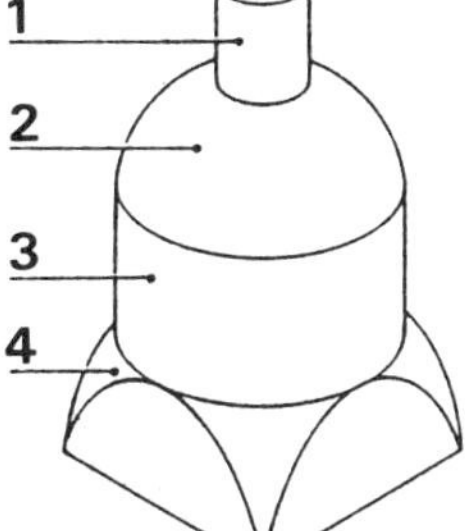

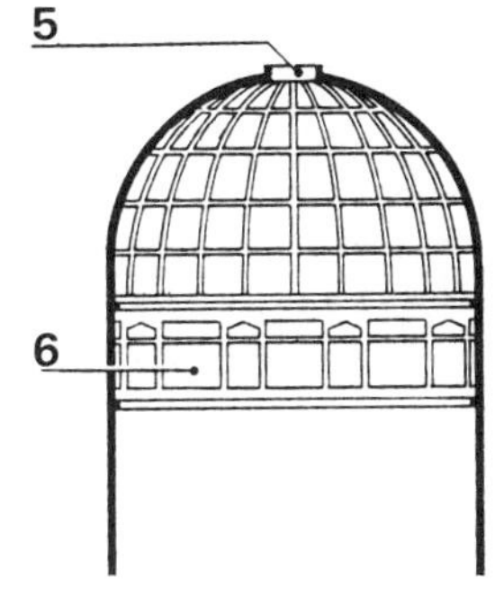

continued

Parts of a building continued

5731

TYPES OF VAULT
1 Barrel (wagon, tunnel)
2 Groin (cross)
3 Oblong
4 Rib
5 Squinch arch
6 Sexpartite
7 Lierne
8 Fan

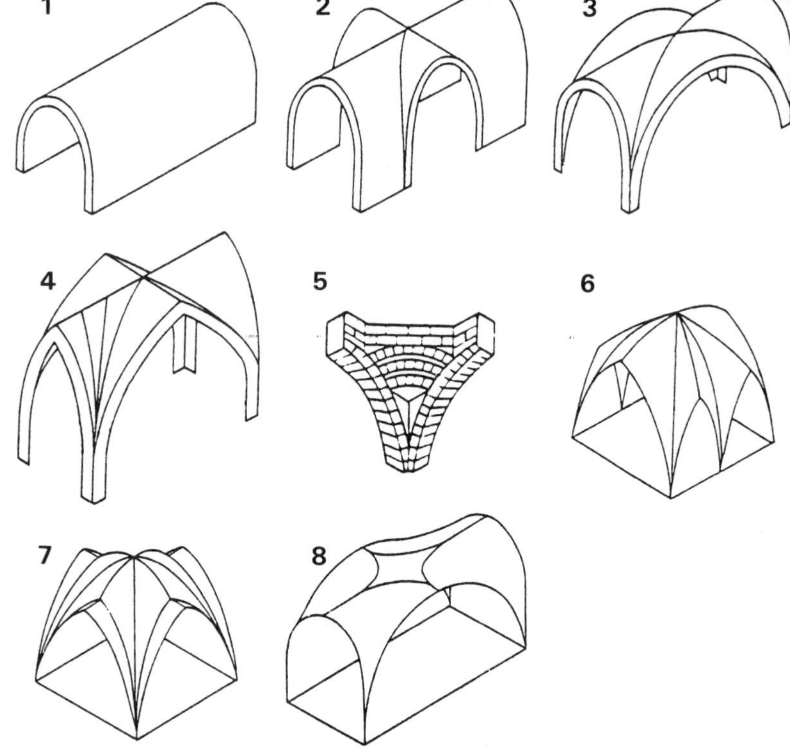

TYPES OF ARCH
1 Semicircular
2 Semicircular stilted
3 Segmental
4 Round horseshoe
5 Horseshoe
6 Three-centered
7 Depressed three-centered
8 Elliptical
9 Parabolic
10 Round trefoil
11 Round trifoliated
12 Pseudo three-centered
13 Shouldered
14 Venetian
15 Florentine
16 Stilted
17 Triangular
18 Corbelled
19 Pointed horseshoe
20 Pointed Saracenic
21 Lancet
22 Equilateral
23 Drop
24 Pointed segmental
25 Four-centered (Tudor)
26 Rampant
27 Pseudo four-centered
28 Pointed trefoil
29 Pointed trifoliated
30 Cinquefoil
31 Ogee
32 Flat arch

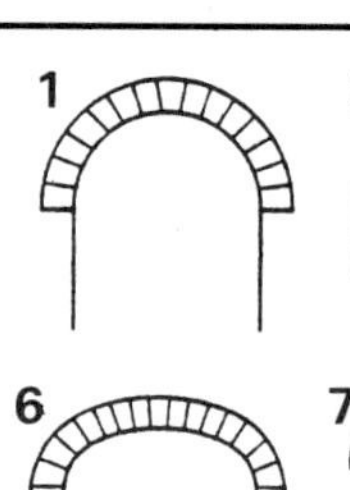
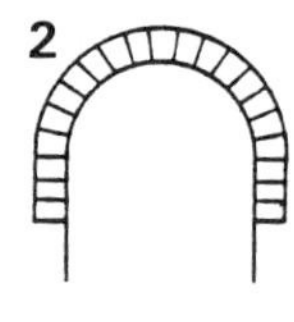
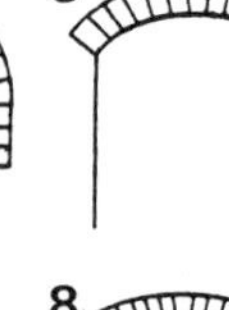

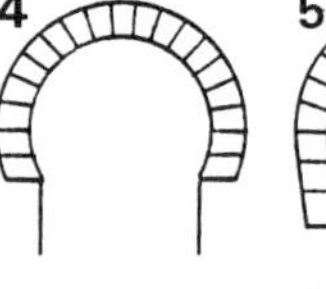
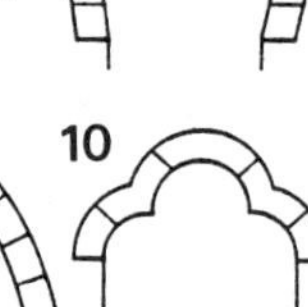

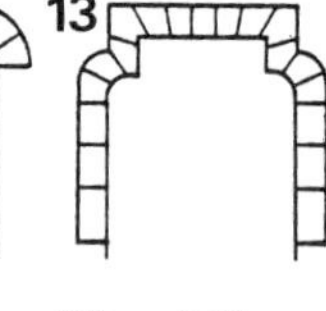

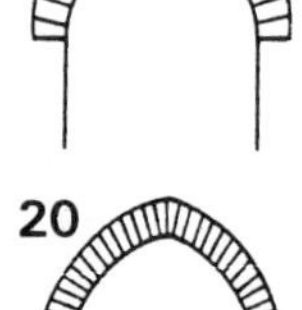
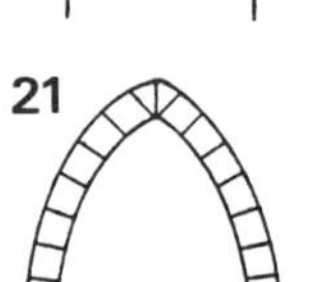
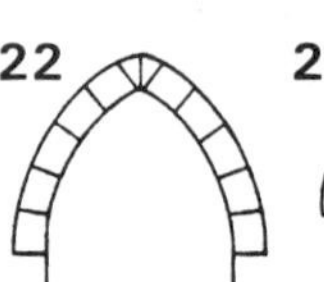
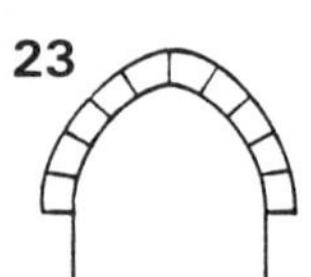
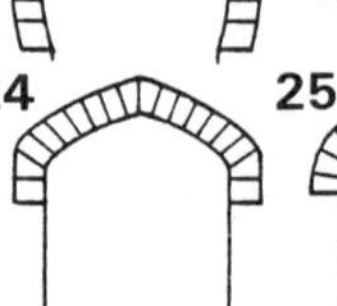
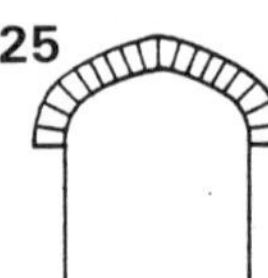
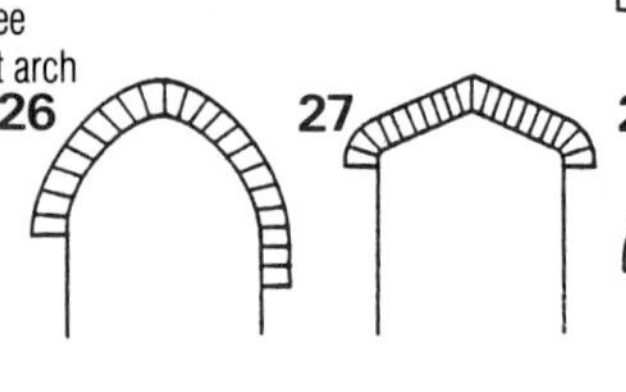

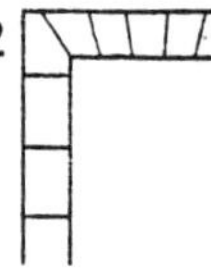

continued

Parts of a building continued

573**1** TYPES OF WINDOW

1 Protruding windows
a Box
b Bay
c Bow
d Barrel
2 Roof windows
a Rooflight
b Eyebrow
c Gabled dormer
d Hipped dormer
e Oriel

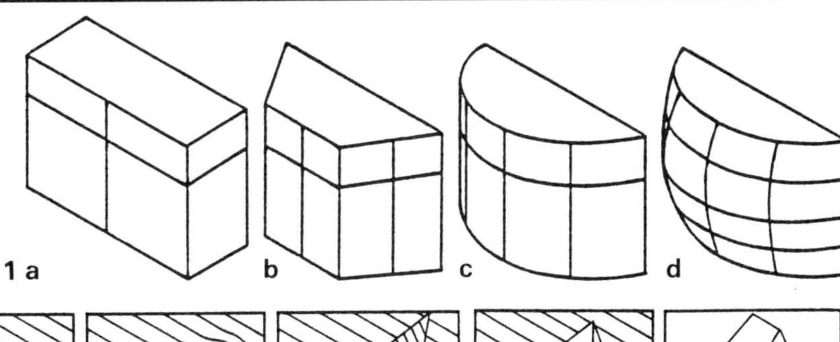

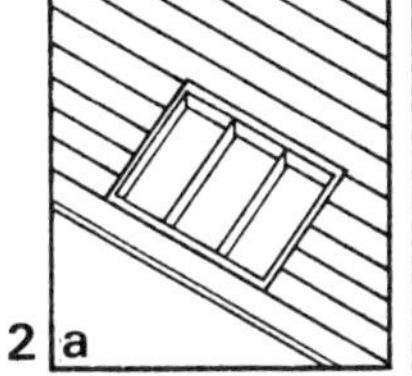

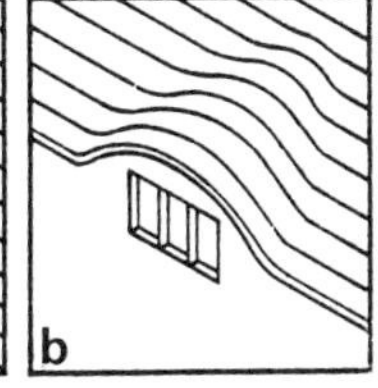

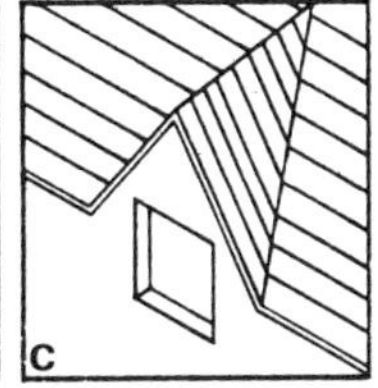

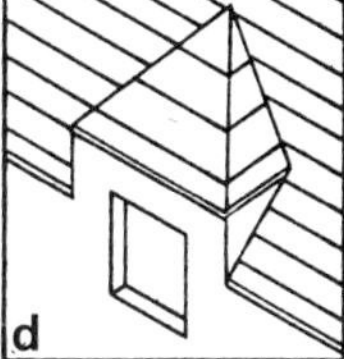

PARTS OF A WINDOW
1 Hood
2 Sill (apron)
3 Header (head frame)
4 Jamb
5 Hanging stile
6 Pane
7 Glazing bar
8 Weatherboard
9 Mullion (muntin)
10 Sash frame
11 Shutters (jalousie)
12 Transom

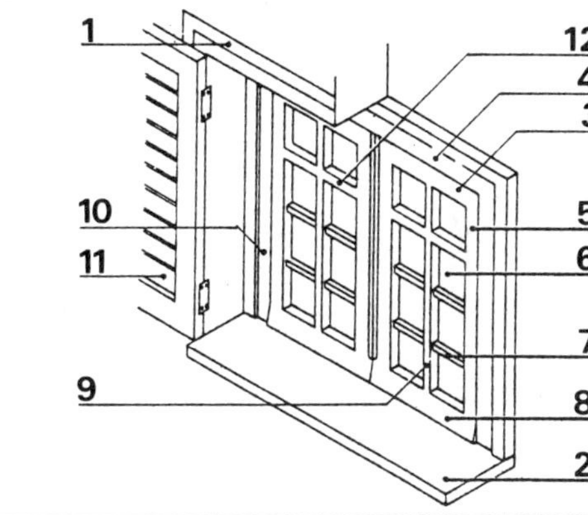

CHURCH WINDOWS
1 Window types
a Light
b Shaft
c Mullion
d Transom
e Lancet
f Tracery
g Plate tracery
h Cusp
i Foil
j Cusping
k Mouchette
l Dagger
m Trefoil
n Quatrefoil
o Multifoil
p Rose (catherine wheel, compass)

2 Tracery forms
a Geometrical
b Intersecting
c Panel
d Reticulated
e Curvilinear (flowing)

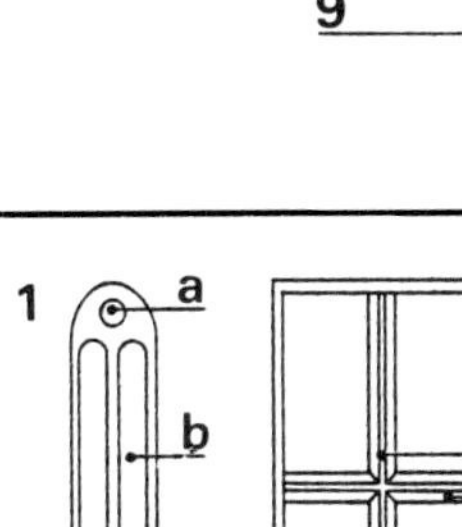

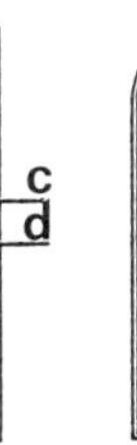

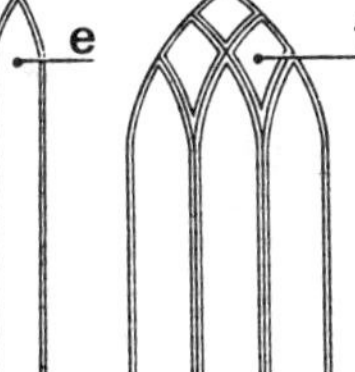

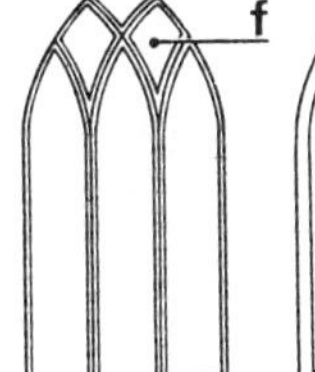

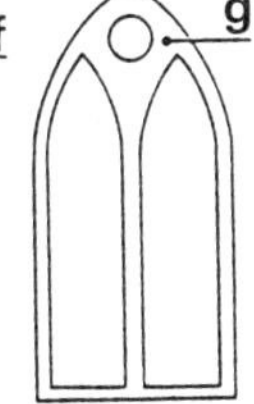

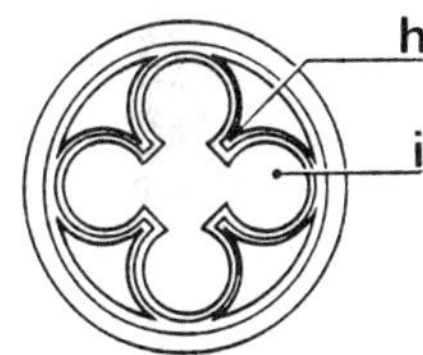

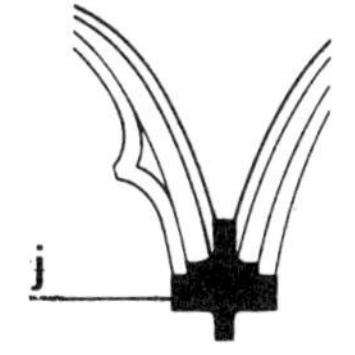

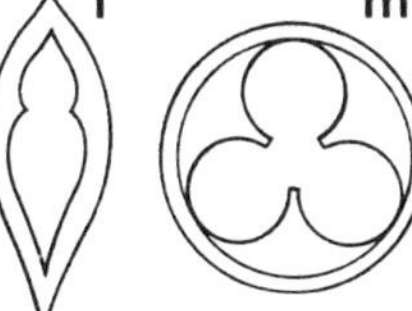

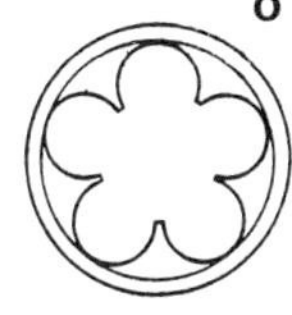

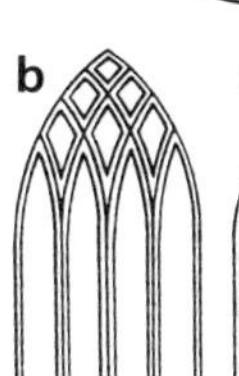

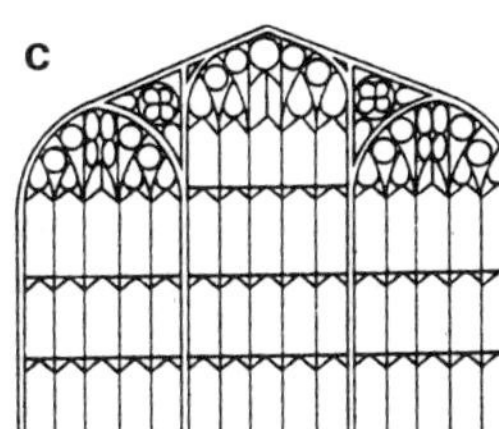

continued

Parts of a building continued

5731 WINDOWS - TYPES
1 Deadlight
2 Mullion
3 Sash (double hung)
4 Sliding
5 Casement
6 French
7 Pivoting (horizontal)
8 Pivoting (vertical)
9 Accordion
10 Folding
11 Hopper
12 Louvered
13 Combination
14 Projected
15 Leaded
16 Awning
17 Lattice window

DOORS - TYPES
1 Flush
2 Panel
3 Glass
4 Ledge and brace
5 Dutch (stable)
6 Screen
7 Louvered
8 French
9 Hanging
10 Revolving
11 Swing
12 Double swing
13 Sliding
14 Double slide
15 Accordion
16 Folding
17 Roll
18 Turnstile

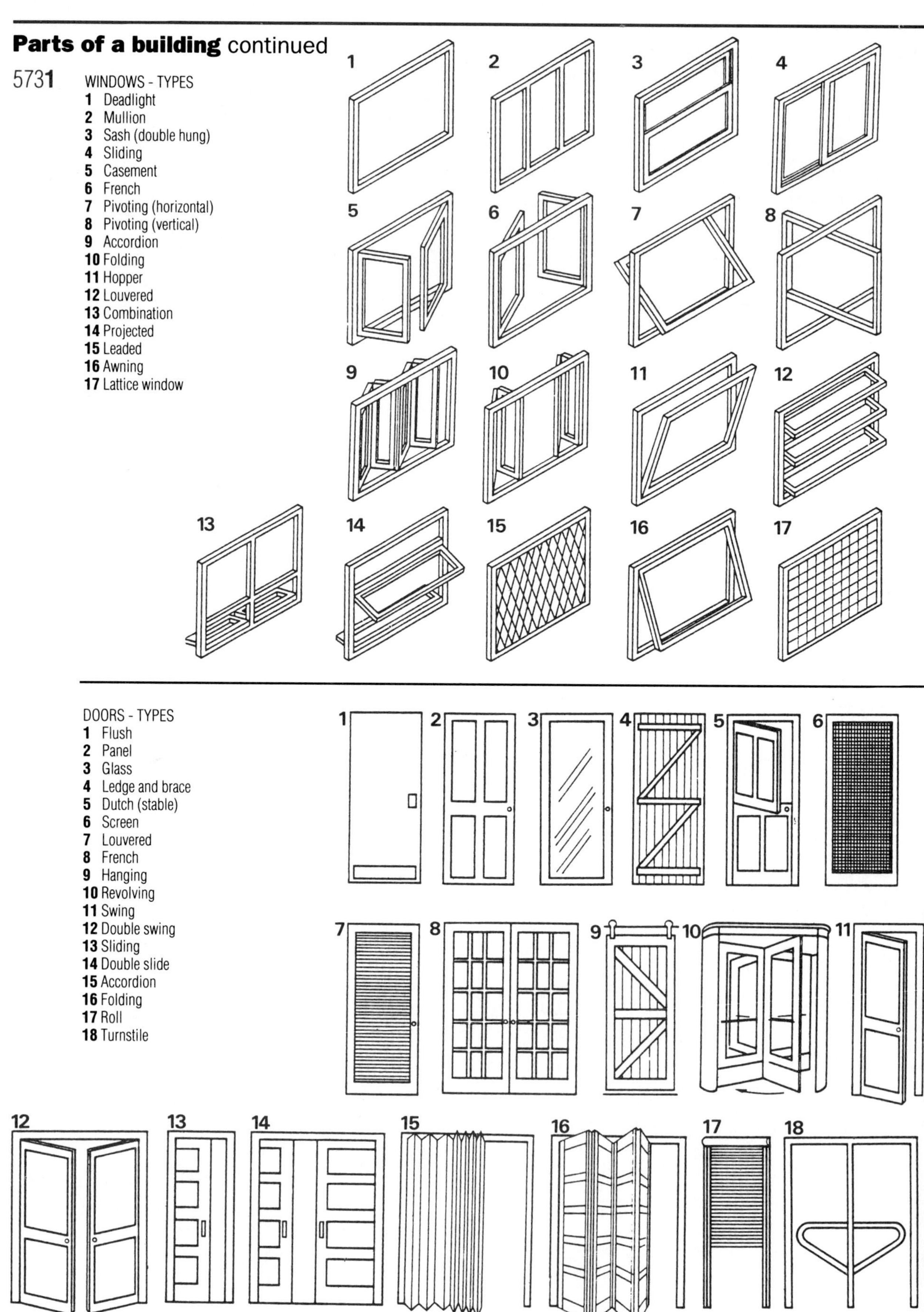

continued

Parts of a building continued

5731 PARTS OF A DOOR

1 Architrave
2 Top rail
3 Shutting stile
4 Hanging stile
5 Top panel
6 Muntin
7 Lock rail
8 Middle panel
9 Bottom panel
10 Bottom rail (plinth block)
11 Cornice
12 Lintel
13 Header
14 Jamb
15 Hinge
16 Weatherboard
17 Threshold

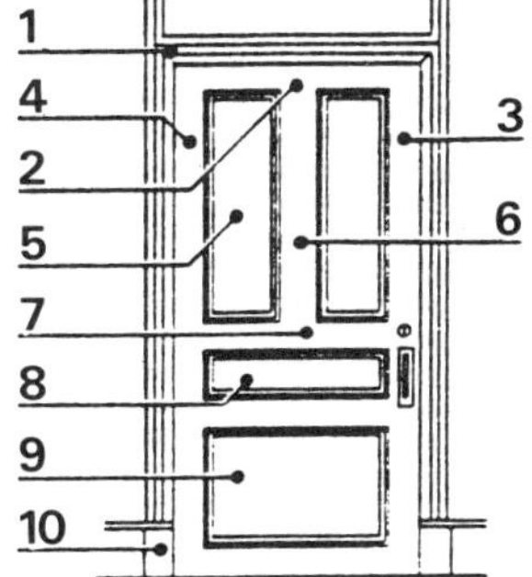

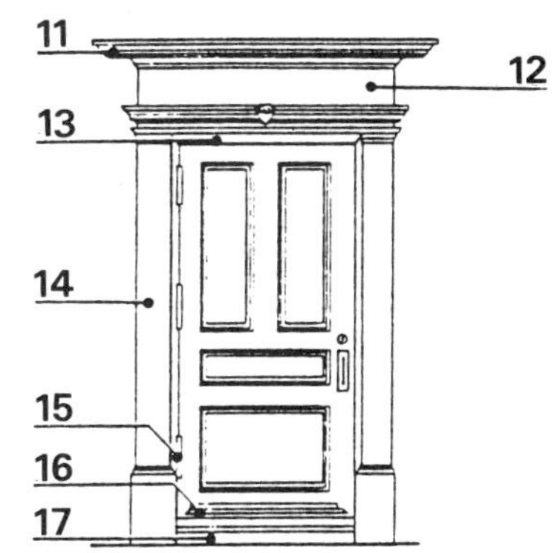

COLUMNS AND CAPITALS

1 Column parts
a Cap (capital)
b Abacus
c Shaft
d Base
e Banding
f Necking
g Apophyge

2 Column variants
a Caryatid
b Atlanta (telamon)
c Fluted column
d Spiral fluted
e Rusticated
f Solomonic (Salomónica column)

3 Capital forms
a Bud (lotus)
b Bell (papyrus)
c Volute
d Palm
e Bull
f Foliated
g Cushion
h Scalloped
i Waterleaf
j Crocket
k Stiff-leaf

4 Column and pier forms
a Clustered
b Octagonal
c Filleted
d Compound
e Base moulding
f Pilaster
g Engaged
h Shaft ring

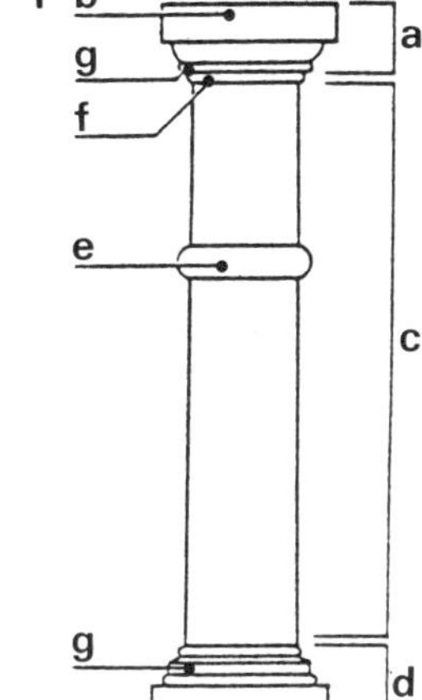

2 a b c

2d e f

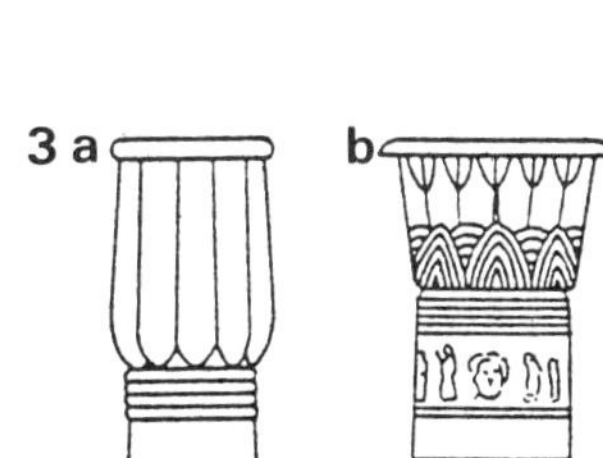

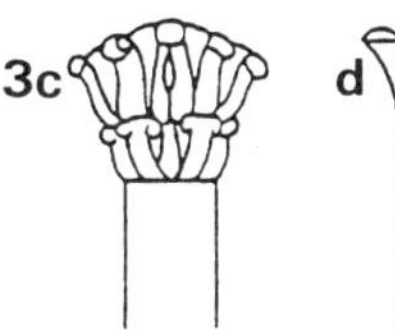

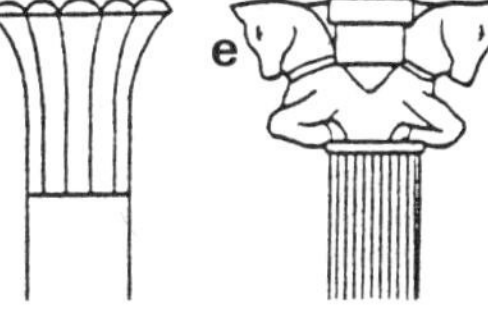

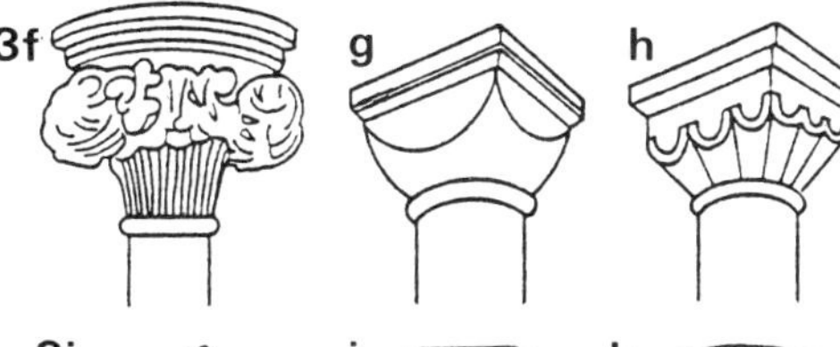

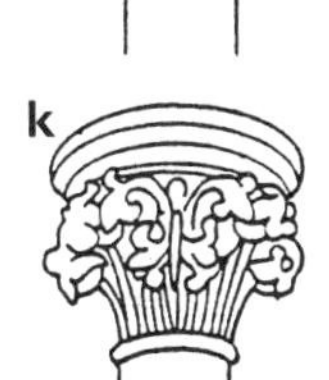

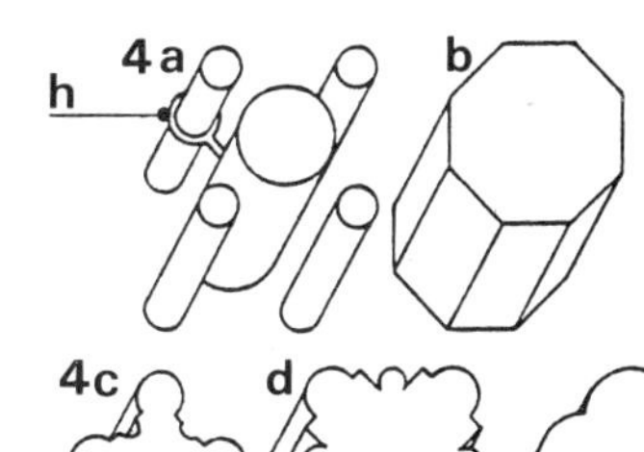

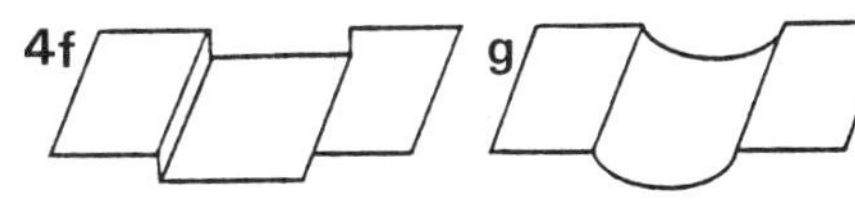

Parts of a church

5732 EXTERIOR

1 Bartizan A small turret which has a fortification style top called crenellation.
2 Bellcote A framework on the eves of a bell tower from which to hang bells.
3 Bell gable Same as bellcote.
4 Belvedere A tower with a viewing gallery.
5 Buttress A masonry support alongside a wall.
5a Flying buttress Buttress that is arched so that its base is away from the wall.
6 Campanile A bell tower usually separated from the main building.
7 Flèche A small wooden spire.
8 Gargoyle A spout carrying water from the roof, usually decorated with grotesque figures or a head.
9 Galilee At the west end of a church, an enclosed porch.
10 Lantern The topmost section of dome – usually with windows.
11 Loggia A gallery open on one or more sides.
12 Louvre A window opening, often in church towers, which is covered in overlapping boards.
13 Porch The covering of an entrance.
14 Portico A protecting porch consisting of columns and a pediment.
15 Sanctuary knocker Large ring affixed to door that can be struck by a fugitive from the law.

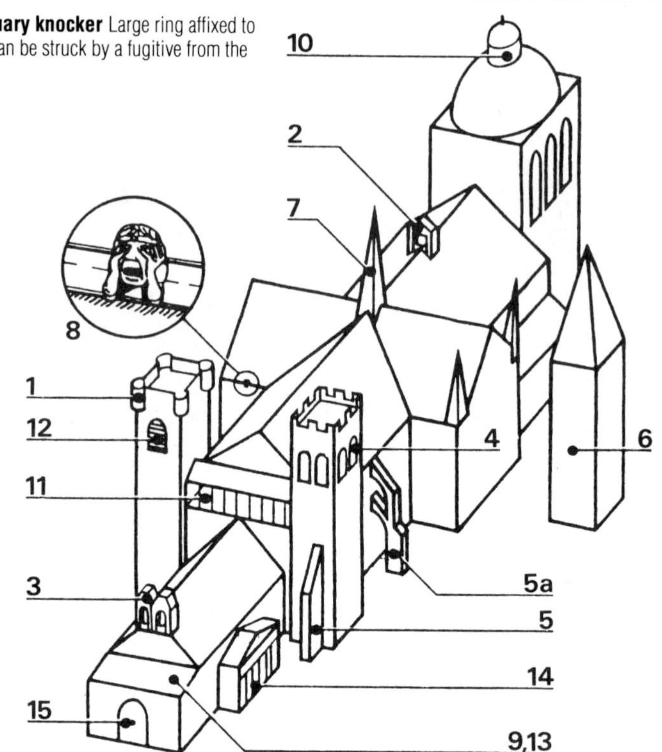

INTERIOR

1 Aisle The side corridors of the main church. The north aisle is on the left when facing the altar and the south aisle on the right.
2 Almonry A special room used for the distribution of alms.
3 Ambulatory The continuation of the aisle around the choir and behind the altar.
4 Chancel The area containing the choir and the altar, originally reserved for the clergy.
5 Chapel A small area set aside for private worship.
5a Chantry chapel A special endowed chapel in which prayers are said for the soul of the benefactor.
5b Lady chapel Set at the east end and dedicated to the Virgin Mary.
6 Chapterhouse The administrative meeting place.
7 Choir The area between the nave and the altar.
8 Cloister The covered walkway around a courtyard.
9 Crossing The central area between the nave, the chancel, and the transepts.
10 Crypt The area under the main church which contains graves or relics.
11 Presbytery The area around the main altar.
12 Sacristy A room for storing the priests vestments and sacred vessels.
13 Sanctuary The most sacred part of the chancel.
14 Nave The main area of the church used by the congregation. It usually has aisles on either side.
15 Slype A passageway from cloister to transept of chapter house.
16 Vestry A word for sacristy where vestments and sacred vessels are kept.
17 Transept The two areas on either side of the crossing which form the cross shaped plan of the church.

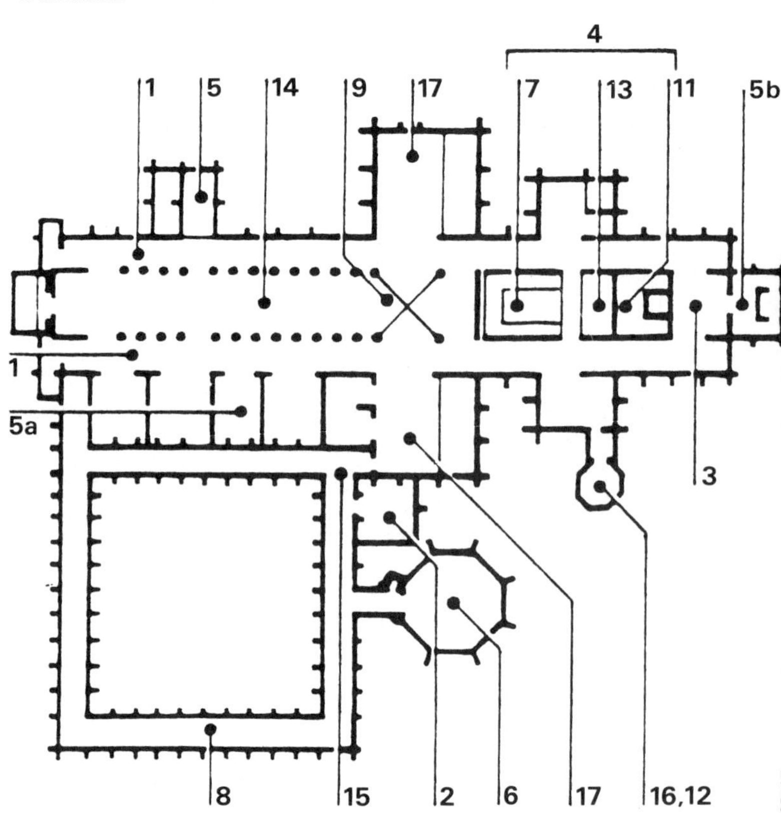

continued

Parts of a church continued

5732 FURNISHINGS OF A CHURCH

1 Altar The table at the east end of the church from which acts of worship are conducted.

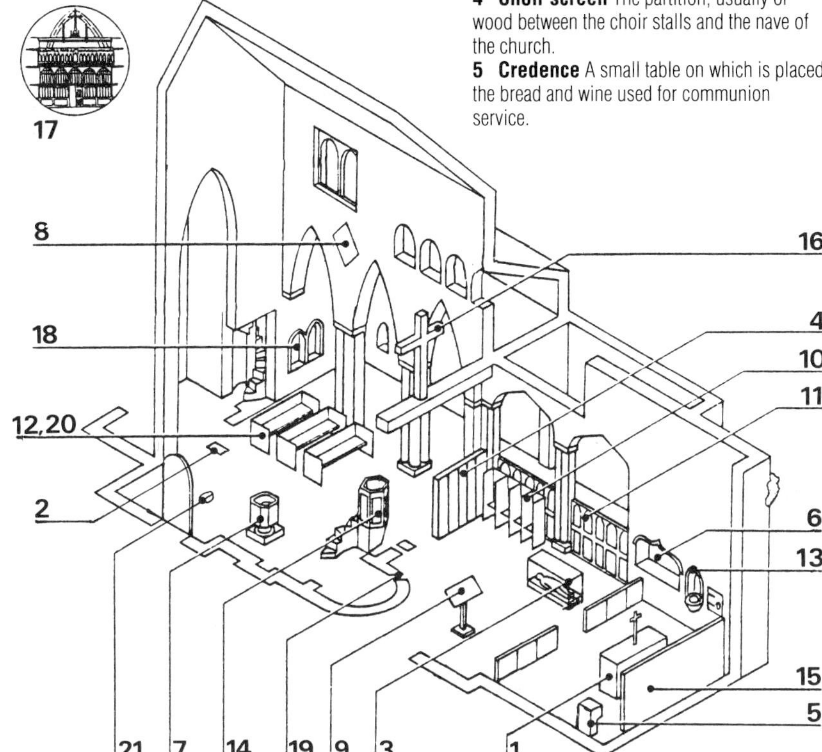

2 Brass plates Engraved with a memorial inscription or effigy, usually set in the floor of a church to mark a tomb.
3 Canopy A small protective hood usually over a pulpit or tomb.
4 Choir screen The partition, usually of wood between the choir stalls and the nave of the church.
5 Credence A small table on which is placed the bread and wine used for communion service.
6 Easter sepulcher A recess in the north chancel to hold the effigy of the risen Christ. Used during Easter celebrations.
7 Font A large, raised, fixed basin containing holy water used for baptisms.
8 Funeral shields Usually wooden painted shields bearing the arms of deceased local gentry.
9 Lectern A desk or stand to hold a Bible or large service book.
10 Misericorde A decorated ledge on the underside of a wooden hinged seat which folds up to provide some support for a choir singer or worshipper when standing.
11 Parclose screen A screen around an altar, shrine, or chapel to exclude non-worshippers.
12 Pew Wooden seating for the congregation.
13 Piscina A stone basin with a drain near the altar for washing sacred vessels.
14 Pulpit An elevated platform, often approached by a flight of steps, from which the church lessons are read and sermons preached.
15 Rederos A decorated screen behind the altar.
16 Rood A cross or crucifix at the east of the nave, in front of the choir stalls.
17 Roodscreen The support to the Rood, often elaborately carved in wood or stone.
18 Sedilia Seats for clergy on the south side of the choir aisle, often recessed into the wall.
19 Squint A small slit in the wall or pier to enable members of the congregation (usually in a separate room) to have sight of the altar.
20 Stall Another name for a pew. A series of similar seats carved in wood or stone.
21 Stoup Basin of Holy Water near entrance.

Parts of a castle

5733

1 Watchtower Usually the tallest turret on a keep or wall.
2 Keep The strongest building, the principal tower in the castle.
3 Flanking tower This protrudes from the wall to enable archers to fire back toward the castle.
4 Inner bailey The area closest to the keep, usually separated from the outer bailey by an inner ring of walls.
5 Angle tower This is positioned on a corner to enable archers to cover two sides of a castle.
6 Gatehouse Defenses over a gate.
7 Portcullis Heavy gate which can be lowered when the castle is under attack.
8 Drawbridge Bridge, that spans a ditch or moat, which can be raised to prevent access to a castle.
9 Ramparts The defense walls or castle battlements.
10 Palisade Wooden defense walls.
11 Outer bailey The area outside the inner defenses and protected by outer ramparts.
12 Scarp Sloping land at the foot of the battlement walls.
13 Moat Usually a man-made ditch filled with water which surrounds a castle.
14 Postern gate (sally port) A small entrance away from the main gate.
15 Arrow slit Openings in the wall through which archers could fire at attackers.
16 Outer curtain wall The outermost wall usually linking turrets (bastions).
17 Bastion An individual turret.
18 Garderobe A medieval toilet.
19 Crenellations Indentations through which archers could shoot.
20 Machicolation A projecting parapet high up on the outer side of castle walls and towers with floor openings from which defenders could pour oil or drop stones, etc. on their attackers.

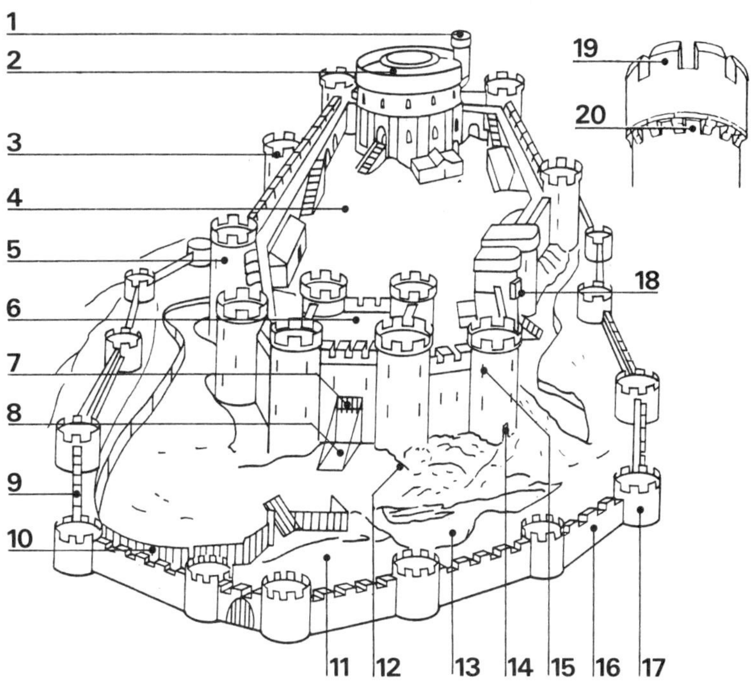

Parts of a monastery

5734 **Abbot's lodge (1)** Living quarters of the abbot (chief monk) of the monastery.
Almonry A special place for the distribution of alms to the poor.
Calefactory (2) A heated sitting room.
Cemetery (3) Burial ground.
Cellar (4) Storage area for food, wine, etc.
Cells (5) Single rooms for individual monks.
Chapter house (6) The building attached to the church in which meetings for the monks are held.
Church (7) A public place of worship.
Cloister (8) A covered walkway around a quadrangle, which has colonaded inner sides and solid outer walls.
Dormitory (9) Sleeping quarters.
Farm buildings
Gardens
Guest houses (10)
Hostelry Part of the monastery in which travelers and members of the public are entertained, fed, and accommodated.
Infirmary (11) Place for tending the sick. Some monasteries had separate infirmaries for lay brothers.
Kitchen
Latrines Toilets and washing facilities.
Refectory (12) Dining room.
Sacristy Room in the church serving as a repository for the sacred vessels and vestments.
Scriptorium A room for the writing and copying of manuscripts.
Scullery Small room for the preparation of vegetables and washing of dishes.
Slype (passageway) **(13)** A covered walkway joining the transept to the chapter house.
Undercroft (14) Vaulted chamber beneath the church.

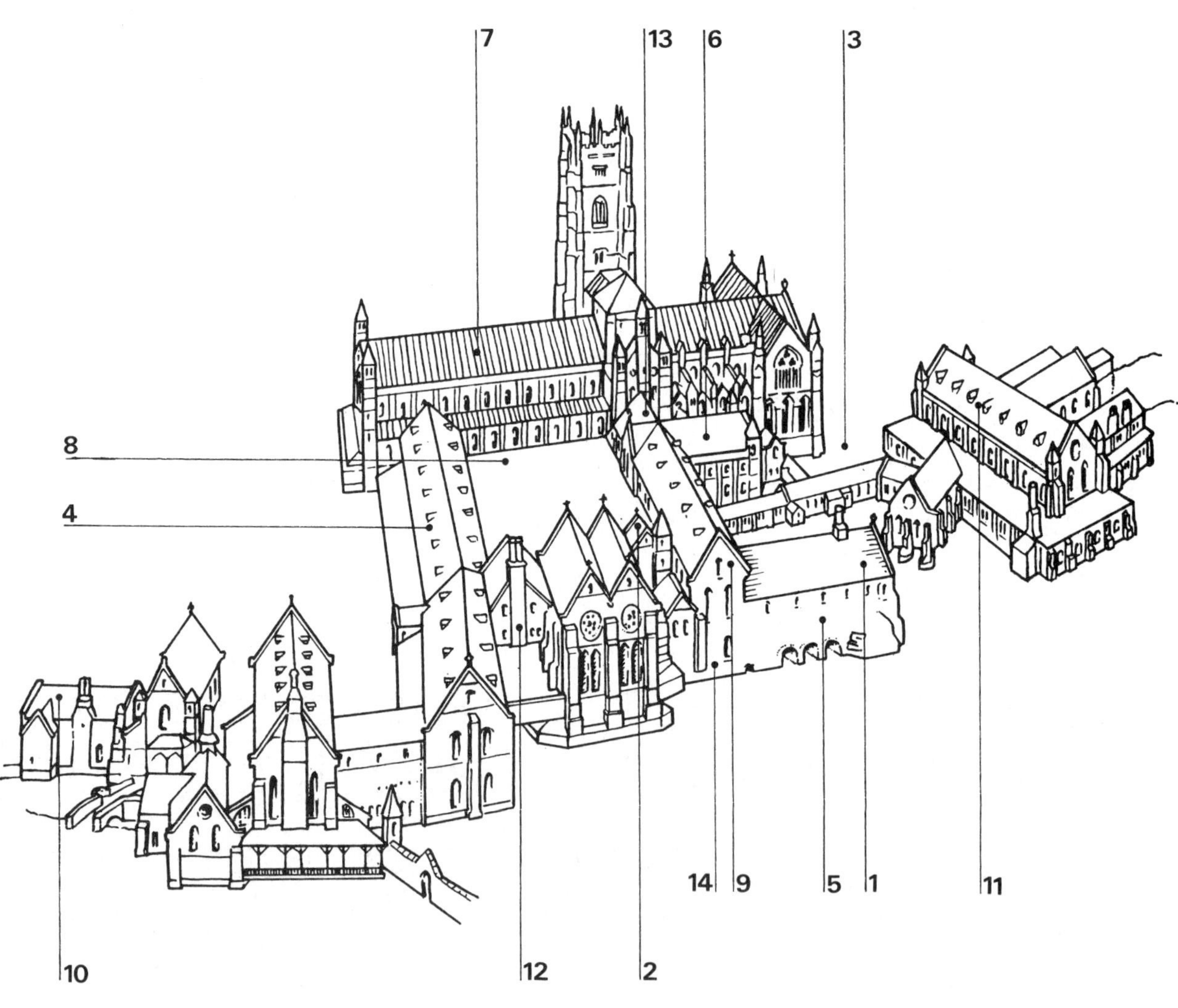

611 HISTORY

Timeline

6111 Judaism is probably the world's oldest monotheisitic religion, believing in One Almighty God. It was founded in Israel-Syria by Abraham. The early people called Hebrews were nomadic tribes. Judaism became a distinct religion after the Jews had been taken to Babylon in 586 BC. This made them aware of their traditions, writing them down and living by them. In AD 70 with the destruction of Jerusalem the Jews were scattered.

2000–1400 BC Abraham settles in Canaan, later called Palestine, from Mesopotamia. He is descended from Shem, Noah's son. Abraham's son was Isaac, whose son Jacob had 12 sons. One of these sons, Joseph, lived in Egypt. When famine broke out in Canaan, Jacob and his other sons went to live in Egypt.
1309–1291 Israelites enslaved in Egypt.
1275 Israelites escape from Egypt to Canaan, called the Exodus.
1275–1235 Israelites wandering in the desert. The Law of the Ten Commandments carved in stone is given to Moses on Mount Sinai.
1235–1020 Time of the Judges, rulers appointed by God to rescue the Israelites when they lapsed into worshipping other gods. This period covers Joshua conquering all of Canaan up to Saul and David ruling the Israelites.
1235–1200 After Moses' death Joshua led the Israelites across Jordan and split the Promised Land between the Twelve Tribes of Israel.
1100–1002 Phililstines invade Canaan. Saul becomes the first king of all the tribes of Israel
1000–961 David becomes king and is more successful than Saul at uniting all the tribes of Israel. Makes Jerusalem the capital of Israel.
961–722 David's son Solomon rules and builds a temple in Jerusalem. After his death in 922 BC the kingdom is split in two, forming Judah and Israel.
586 Nebuchadnezzar, ruler of Babylon, finally conquers the Israelites and destroys the Temple. Over the next six years he deports most of them to Babylon where they stay until the Persians conquer Babylon and send them back.
520–515 The Temple is rebuilt in Jerusalem.
332 Jerusalem captured by Egyptians.
323–198 Canaan ruled by Egypt.
AD 63 Romans enter Jerusalem and storm the Temple.
66 The Jews of Judea rebel against the Romans.
70 Romans destroy the Temple and exile Jews from Jerusalem.
73 Mass suicide at the fortress of Masada.
325 The Christian emperor Constantine stops Jews from entering Jerusalem.
527 Persecution of Jews by Emperor Justinian.
636 Muslim forces conquer much of Middle East.
1099 Massacre of Jews in Jerusalem by Crusaders.
1290 Jews expelled from England.
1306 Jews first expelled from France.
1348 Ghettos form in Germany after the Jews are blamed for the Black Death.
1349 Jews first expelled from Hungary
1355 Massacre of Jews by Christians in Toledo, Spain.
1391 Massacre of Jews in Spain.
1399 Persecution of Jews in Poland.
1492 Jews expelled from Spain.
1494 First Jewish ghetto in Poland.
1516 Turks conquer Palestine.
1654 Arrival of the first Jews in North America.
1656 Jews allowed to live in England again.
1727 Jews first expelled from Russia. Most flee to Poland.
1728 First synagogue built in North America.
1730 First public synagogue in New York.
1791 Civil rights and liberties granted to Jews in France. Pale of Settlement established in Russia.
1871–1906 Pogroms, or persecution of Jews in Russia.
1882 First major migration of Jews to Palestine.
1904 Second wave of migration to Palestine, large numbers also go to the USA.
1909 Tel Aviv founded.
1917 Balfour Declaration, document which declared the Jews' right to a national home.
1919–23 Third wave of migration to Palestine and also to the USA.
1920 Palestine under mandate to British government.
1924–32 Fourth wave of migration to Palestine.
1935 German government introduce Nuremburg laws against the Jews.
1938 Kristallnacht, night of violence, burning of Jewish synagogues and institutions and destruction of businesses.
1942–5 The Holocaust, Hitler's genocide of millions of Jews.
1948 Israel gains independence.
1967 Six-Day War with Arab states.
1973 Yom Kippur War.
1980 First wave of Ethiopian Jews airlifted to Israel.
1982–3 Israeli forces invade Lebanon.
1987 Beginning of Intifada, uprising in Israel by Palestinian Arabs.

The Twelve Tribes of Israel

6112 The Twelve Tribes of Israel were descended from the 12 sons of Jacob who was renamed Israel, "striver for God." The tribes are sometimes called the children of Israel. Before the Israelites became a unified nation in the Time of the Judges, they were a loosely connected group of tribes. They all had a common religion and ancestry.

Jacobs' sons (and the emblems of their tribes) were Reuben (**1**), Simeon (**2**), Levi, Judah (**3**), Issachar (**4**), Zebulun (**5**), Dan (**6**), Napthali (**7**), Gad (**8**), Asher (**9**), Joseph, and Benjamin (**10**). The tribe of Levi was not counted as it had been chosen for holy duties; to maintain the sacred number of 12 tribes, Joseph's sons, Manasseh (**11**) and Ephraim (**12**) formed two tribes.

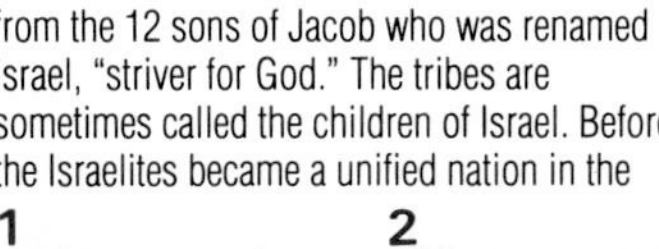

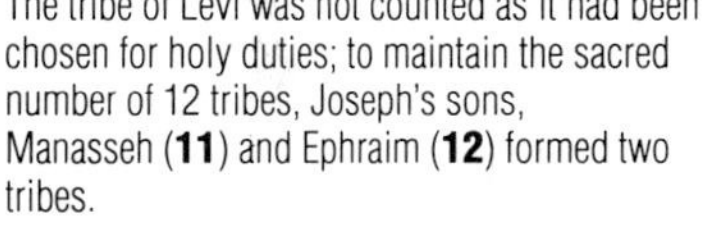

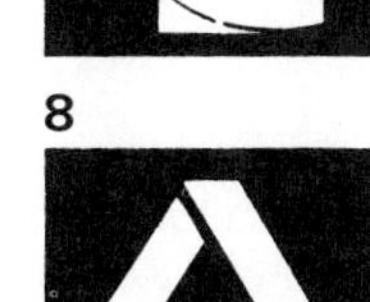

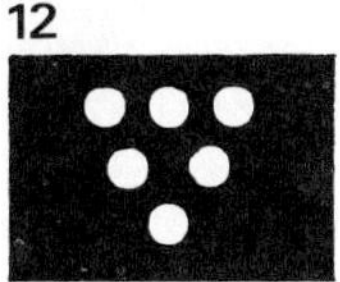

1 2 3 4 5 6 7 8 9 10 11 12

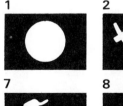

The Prophets

6113 The Hebrew prophets did more to increase the growth and strength of Judaism than historical events. They were teachers and thinkers who played an important role in the political and religious life of the ancient Hebrews. The prophets were led by God who allowed them to foresee events. They commented on the present, especially criticizing the religion of the time, denouncing evil and telling the people to be moral and good. Samuel, Nathan, Elijah, and Elisha insisted on the Twelve Tribes being united and on their God being unique. Later prophets Amos, Isaiah, Jeremiah, and Ezekiel gave Judaism a moral content. Other prophets are Amos, Hosea, Micah, Deborah, Haggai, Zechariah, and Obadiah. Moses is probably the greatest of the prophets.

612 ORGANIZATION

Branches of Judaism

6121 Outside the state of Israel there is very little formal religious organization. Congregations of synagogues are largely autonomous with no central authority. All congregations elect their own rabbi. Some communal organizations exist in North America to further Jewish ideas and ideals.

There are three major branches of Judaism today:

Orthodox Judaism
Followers of orthodox Judaism keep to all the traditional beliefs and ways of life. They believe that God revealed the laws of the *Torah* and the *Talmud* directly to Moses on Mount Sinai. All Jewish laws are strictly observed, including dietary rules and the keeping of the Sabbath. Prayer is conducted three times a day. All orthodox men wear caps, or *yarmulka,* all the time as a sign of respect to God.

Reform Judaism
Reform Judaism was started during the 1800s by some Jews who questioned the traditional teachings of how the sacred writings of Judaism came into being. The *Talmud* was considered to be a human creation and not the revelation of God, and its authority was therefore weakened for them. They claimed that Judaism is defined first by the Bible. Contemporary Reform Jews argue that moral and ethical teachings are the most important aspect of Judaism. Much of the ritual and tradition of Orthodox Judaism have no significance for them.

Conservative Judaism
Conservative Judaism was developed during the mid-1800s. Its followers believe the *Talmud* has as much authority as the Bible. But they stress that the scriptures should be interpreted with modern knowledge and culture in mind. The rituals of Judaism are de-emphasized. However, they follow more of the traditional practices than the reform Jews.

Other sects of Judaism include:

Hasidim
The Hasidic movement emphasizes vigorous observance of Jewish laws and God through enthusiastic power and mysticism. The Hasidim follow or gather around *tzaddik*, or charismatic leader (*rebbe.*) The movement emerged in 18th-century Europe.

Kabbalah
The Kabbalah is a form of Jewish mysticism which is set out in a treatise called the *Zohar.* This movement emerged in 13th-century Spain and is the basis of Jewish mysticism today.

Zionism
Zionism is a secular nationalist movement. It emphasizes Jewish nationhood and culminates in a return to the land of Israel, the Jewish spritual home.

Places of worship

6122 **The synagogue**
The synagogue is at the center of Jewish life as a house of worship, a center for community activity and Jewish education. All synagogues contain the ark, a chest in which the scrolls of the *Torah* are kept. In front of the ark hangs the eternal light, a lamp whose constant flame symbolizes God's eternal presence. In the sanctuary of a synagogue there will be a *menorah*, or branched candlestick and a tablet bearing the first two words of the Ten Commandments written in Hebrew.

The rabbi
The spiritual leader of the synagogue is the rabbi. He is a teacher and interpreter of the Jewish law. He delivers sermons, gives advice to people and performs many other functions in the Jewish community. Each synagogue elects its own rabbi.

The cantor
The cantor chants prayers during worship in the synagogue. He has a trained voice and special knowledge of Hebrew. Sometimes the cantor might direct a choir and conduct religious teaching.

Worship
Worship takes place in the synagogue and in the home. At home Jewish people might say daily prayers, light Sabbath candles, and bless the wine and bread at the Sabbath meal.

Bar mitzvah
At the age of 13, a Jewish boy becomes a full member of the community. The event, called *bar mitzvah*, is celebrated in the synagogue. Some reform and conservative synagogues perform a similar ceremony for girls called *bat mitzvah* or *bas mitzvah.* The young person reads from the *Torah* during the ceremony.

Plan of a typical orthodox synagogue
1 The holy ark
2 *Torah* scrolls of the law
3 *Bimah* (raised platform)
4 Reading desk
5 Seat for wardens
6 Men's seats
7 Women's seats in gallery
8 *Menorah* (7-branch candlestick)
9 Ten Commandments
10 *Ner Tamid* (eternal light)

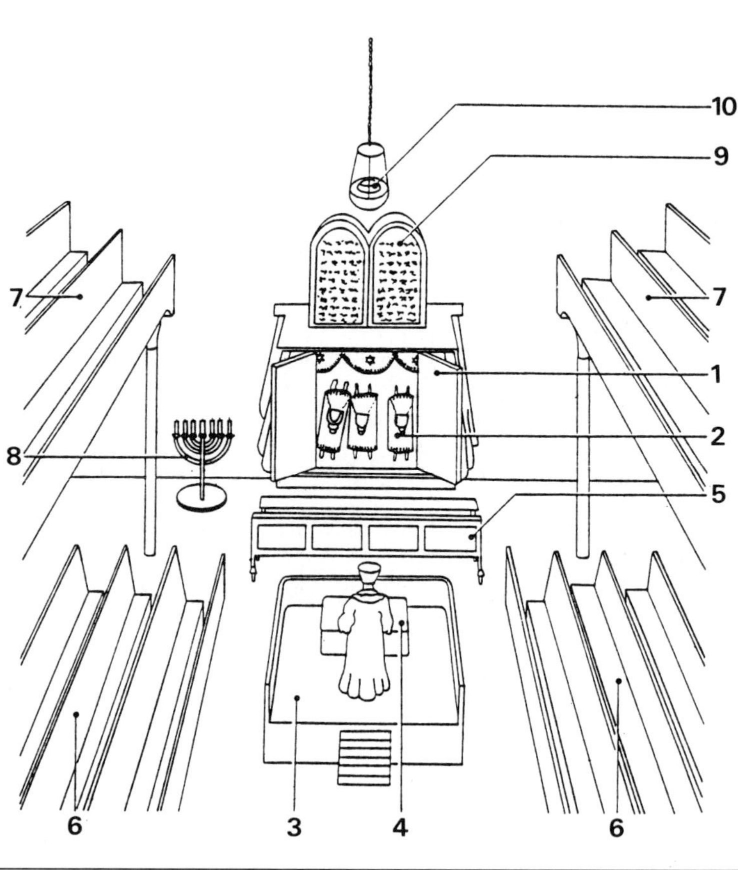

613 BELIEFS

The Covenant with God

6131 The most important teaching of the Jewish faith is that there is only one God.

Jews believe that God made a special agreement, or covenant, with Abraham to bless his descendants and give them land if they worshipped and remained faithful to God.

Jews are sometimes called the Chosen People, as God chose them for special duties. For example, they must be just and merciful and treat everyone with respect and serve only one God. This assures them of God's love and protection but it makes them especially accountable for any sins.

Judaism does not try to convert people to its beliefs but it accepts people who choose to convert to Judaism.

The Ten Commandments

6132 God gave the Israelites the Ten Commandments through their leader the prophet Moses. The Ten Commandments were carved on two stone slabs, or tablets by God when Moses climbed Mount Sinai to speak to God. These laws explained how the Israelites should live their lives and build their community.

1 I am the Lord thy God, who brought thee out of the land of Egypt – out of the house of bondage. Thou shalt have no other gods before me
2 Thou shalt not make unto thee any graven image...Thou shalt not bow down thyself to them nor serve them
3 Thou shalt not take the name of the Lord thy God in vain
4 Remember the Sabbath day, to keep it holy
5 Honor thy father and thy mother
6 Thou shalt not kill
7 Thou shalt not commit adultery
8 Thou shalt not steal
9 Thou shalt not bear false witness against thy neighbor
10 Thou shalt not covet they neighbor's house, thou shalt not covet they neighbor's wife, nor... any thing that is thy neighbor's

Thirteen principles of faith

6133 The medieval Jewish philosopher Moses Maimonides (1135–1204) drew up 13 points which are generally thought to sum up the most important beliefs of the Jewish religion.

1 That God exists
2 That God is One alone
3 That God has no corporeal presence
4 That God is outside the scope of time
5 That God alone is to be worshipped
6 That God informs his prophets
7 That Moses was the greatest of the prophets
8 That the *Torah* is the work of God
9 That the *Torah* cannot change
10 That God apprehends the thoughts and acts of all people
11 That those who do good will receive their reward, and those who do evil will receive retribution
12 That the Messiah will come
13 That there will be a bodily resurrection of the dead, although only the soul may be eternal

Dietary laws

6134 Many Jews follow rules based on Biblical laws about what they can eat. Jews can only eat meat from animals that graze and that have cloven, or split hoofs. This does not include pigs or horses. Jews can only eat fish with scales and fins, and not shellfish. Birds can be eaten but not birds of prey. Meat and dairy products are both kept and eaten separately, using separate utensils. Correctly prepared food is called *kosher* which means lawful and proper.

Acceptable foods

Foods refused by some Jews

Zionism

6135 Zionism was a movement to set up a Jewish homeland in the Holy Land. During the 15th and 16th century a few fundamentalist Jewish leaders attempted to establish movements with the aim of resettling Jews permanently in Palestine. It was not until the 19th century that politicians took up the idea especially following large numbers of Jews emigrating to Palestine from Russia and eastern Europe. Theodor Herzl, considered the father of modern Zionism, wrote his *Jewish State* in 1896. In 1948 the Zionists finally achieved their aim and the independent state of Israel was established as a Jewish state.

614 SACRED TEXTS

The Bible

6141 Judaism has two major collections of writings which are sacred, the Bible and the *Talmud*.

The Hebrew Bible, (the *Tanakh*) is also Christianity's Old Testament in which the Jewish *Torah* is known as the Pentateuch. It was written over a period of 1, 000 years.

The *Tanakh* is divided into three books:

1 The *Torah* (The Law) Contains five books: *Genesis*, *Exodus*, *Leviticus*, *Numbers*, and *Deuteronomy*. It represents God's covenant with his chosen people, the Jews and God's instructions on daily life.

2 *Nevi'im* (The Prophets) There are eight volumes including the Prophets: Joshua, Judges, Samuel, Kings, the later Prophets: Isaiah, Jeremiah, Ezekiel and the Twelve minor Prophets.

3 *Ketubim* (The Writings) There are 11 books. These are *Psalms*, *Proverbs*, *Job*, *Song of Songs*, *Ruth*, *Lamentations*, *Ecclesiastes*, *Esther*, *Daniel*, *Ezra, and Nehemiah*, *Chronicles*.

continued

The Bible continued

6141

TANAKH

TORAH

PENTATEUCH

Five books
- Genesis
- Exodus
- Leviticus
- Numbers
- Deuteronomy

NEVI'IM

PROPHETS

Eight Volumes

Former Prophets
- Joshua
- Judges
- Samuel
- Kings

Latter Prophets
- Isaiah
- Jeremiah
- Ezekiel
- 12 minor prophets

KETUBIM

WRITINGS

Eleven books
- Psalms
- Proverbs
- Job
- Song of Songs
- Ruth
- Lamentations
- Ecclesiastes
- Esther
- Daniel
- Ezra & Nehemiah
- Chronicles

The Talmud

6142 The *Talmud* includes the interpretations and commentaries of the *Torah* by rabbis and teachers of the Law which were written down in the *Mishnah*. This is an oral code of laws. The *Mishnah*'s six books cover agriculture, festivals, civil and criminal laws, marriage and divorce, temple sacrifice, dietary laws, and ritual purification. The *Gemara* contains commentaries and an elaboration of the *Mishnah* text. The *Midrash* is sermonic exposition and offers popular interpretation of the Bible (the Five Books of Moses).

615 PEOPLE

Abraham the first of the Patriarchs, the historical first father of the Israelites and believed to have lived between 2000 BC and 1500 BC. He is also revered by Muslims and Christians.

Adam according to the Bible, the first man. He was uniquely made and not born. He gave rise to the entire human race but by succumbing to temptation he degraded it.

Assyrians and Babylonians two principal empires in the Tigris and Euphrates valley.

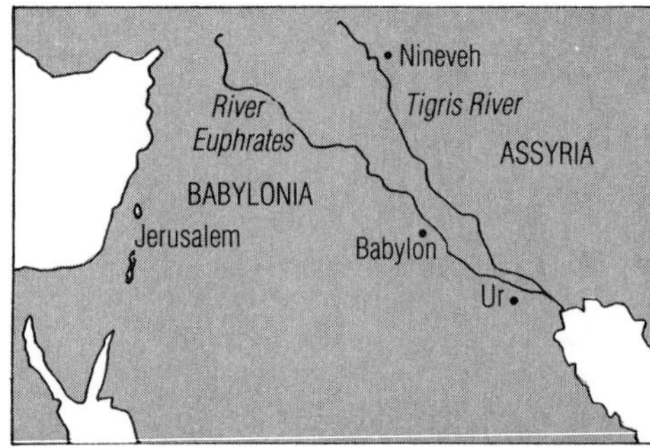

Ba'al Shem Tor 1700–60, the founder of the Hasidim in Poland.

Ben-Gurion, David 1886–1973, Israeli statesman and known as the father of the nation. He was born in Poland and became Israel's first prime minister from 1948–53, and held the post again from 1955–63.

David King of Israel c. 1001–968 BC, reigned for 33 years. The warrior king who at a young age killed the giant Goliath with his sling. He captured Jerusalem and made it a capital city, bringing to it the Ark of the Covenant. He was the first king of Judah and of Israel and was gifted musically and artistically.

Deborah prophetess and Judge. Wife of Lapidoth. With Barak she defeated the Canaanites at Mount Tabor. She sang a famous song of praise and triumph considered to be one of the most beautiful early Hebrew poems; found in Judges 5.

Dayan, Moshe 1915–81, Israeli general born in Palestine. Defense minister in 1967, 1969–74.

Elijah prophet of the 9th century BC. Champion of the Jews and their religion and rival of Ahab who brought the heathen cult of Baal into Israel. Elijah defeated and humiliated him on Mount Carmel.

Esther wife of Ahasuerus King of Persia. She was the niece and adopted daughter of Mordecai, a Jew. Esther saved the Jews from massacre by gaining the audience of the king to whom all were forbidden to approach without announcement.

Eve the first woman, created by God from Adam's rib. Eve means mother of all living, life, life giving. She gave in to temptation in the garden of Eden and God condemned her and all women to bear children in pain and to be dominated by men, and banished her and Adam from Eden.

Gideon one of the Judges of Israel. He delivered Israel from the Midianites who were ravaging the country. He won with an army of 300 men and the support of God. Famous for using trumpets on entering battle and scaring the enemy.

Hebrews name for the Jews. Hebrew is the name of a language, one of many within the Semite group.

Herod known as the Great. Governor of Galilee from 47 BC and king of Judea from 37 to 4 BC. He sided with the Romans to secure power and fortune. After his death Augustus divided Herod's kingdom between his three sons. Herod rebuilt the Temple in Jerusalem.

Isaiah statesman, counsellor of kings in Judah, and a prophet. He possessed great poetic eloquence and imagination. A righteous figure who spoke out against idolators, perverts, drink, sex, and overrich landowners. He prophesied that after the fall of Assyria God would restore peace, create a new beginning for the world, and a universal empire would be governed from Jerusalem.

Israelites the descendants of Israel, whose original name was Jacob.

Jacob the son of Issac and Rebecca. To escape the jealousy and wrath of his brother Esau, Jacob was sent away. On his journey he dreamt he saw a ladder set between Earth and heaven with angels going up and down it. He made the stone where he rested his head into a pillar, poured oil over it and called the place Bethel: "the Lord's house." Later named Israel, Jacob through his 12 sons was the forebear of all the Israelites: the 12 tribes and the Levites.

Jeremiah a prophet who witnessed the decline of the kingdom of Judah. Frequently in danger throughout his life he spent several years in hiding, was imprisoned as a traitor, and was physically assaulted by his own people. His name is now synonymous with pessimism, persecution, and despair.

Job a good man tested cruelly by God to see if misfortune would make him revile God and curse him. His flocks, herds, and his sons and daughters were destroyed and he himself was afflicted with horrible boils and pains but he only doubted his own righteousness and never cursed God. He eventually prospered and fathered a new family.

Jonah an unwilling prophet. He disobeyed God's command and ran away to sea. A terrible

continued

People continued

615 storm engulfed the ship he was traveling on and the shipmates, blaming Jonah for their misfortune, threw him overboard. He was swallowed by a huge fish and spent three days and three nights trapped inside its belly. When he eventually returned to land God repeated his command to go to Nineveh to denounce its vices, and Jonah obeyed.

Joseph the son of Jacob and great lord of Egypt. A great dreamer despised by his half-brothers who sold him for 20 pieces of silver. In Egypt he won the confidence of the Pharoah by interpreting his dreams and preventing a terrible famine. Eventually re-united with his family whom he saved from starvation. He died in Egypt.

Joshua after the death of Moses, God spoke to Joshua telling him to take possession of all the country between the "great sea" and the Euphrates. He led his people across the Jordan, conquered kings, peoples and cities, and divided the Promised Land between the 12 tribes of Israel and the Levites.

Judges rulers of ancient Israel appointed by God at various times during the period between the death of Joshua and the institution of monarchy in ancient Israel, to rescue the Israelites from their sins. They normally took power in a crisis.

Judith a widow who cut off the head of Nebuchadnezzar's general Holofernes to save her compatriots.

Lot nephew of Abraham. He was warned by God to leave Sodom before it was destroyed. He escaped but his wife stopped to look back at the destruction of Sodom and Gomorrah and was turned into a pillar of salt.

Meir, Golda 1898–1978, Israeli stateswoman who was born in Russia. She became prime minister of Israel in 1969 through 1974.

Moses an awesome figure in the Jewish religion and history. The most revered prophet and leader who led his people from slavery to the Promised Land. Chosen by God as his instrument of communication, Moses delivered the Ten Commandments and God's law.

Noah a righteous man told by God to build himself an ark, take his family, every kind of food, and a pair of each living creature on board. The Earth was flooded for 40 days and nights and everything destroyed. The ark grounded at Mount Ararat and God promised never again to curse the Earth and kill living creatures because of man.

Philistines ancient peoples who were at war sporadically with the Israelites. Thought to be from Asia Minor.

Prophets all the Hebrew prophets were inspired by God who gave them foresight and compelled them to proclaim what was coming.

Rachel one of Jacob's wives who bore two sons, Joseph and Benjamin.

Ruth an ancestress of the royal line of David.

Samson a character known for his great strength and vulnerability. A judge of Israel and son of Menoah who killed 1,000 Philistines with the jaw bone of an ass. He fell in love with Delilah, a Philistine woman who discovered the secret of his strength lay in his hair. The Philistines shaved his head and put out his eyes. He was humiliated and imprisoned but his hair grew and he died while pulling down the pillars of a house which crushed three thousand Philistines who were mocking him.

Samuel the last of the Judges of Israel. He defeated the Philistines, recovered the Israelite cities of the coast and championed Saul as king of the Israelites and later David.

Sodomites the people of Sodom, an ancient city on the west shore of the Dead Sea which was linked with Gomorrah.

Solomon son of David and King of Israel 968–928 BC. The name Solomon is synonymous with wisdom and opulence. He enjoyed a long and exceptionally prosperous reign, creating great wealth in preference to making war, is credited with the composition of thousands of sayings and hundreds of songs and the building of the first Temple in Jerusalem.

Zephaniah prophet who concentrated his attack on the ruling class of Judah in the later 7th century BC.

616 THE CALENDAR

Jewish calendar

6161 **Years**

The Hebrew year is calculated by lunar months each beginning with the New Moon which appears every 29-30 days. Seven times during every 19 years an extra month of 30 days is added to the calendar which makes up for short years. An ordinary year has 353, 354, or 355 days. A leap year with the extra month has 383 days, 384, or 385 days.

Months

The Jewish months (**1**) fall as shown in the table compared with the Christian calendar (**2**).

Time

Years are counted from the Creation of the Earth which is calculated to have been in 3761 BC. Years are labeled AM, or *Anno Mundi,* meaning in the year of the world. AD 2000 is therefore AM 5761.

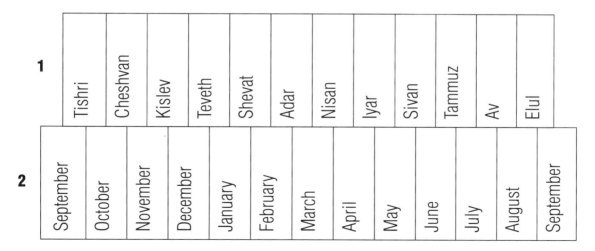

1	Tishri	Cheshvan	Kislev	Teveth	Shevat	Adar	Nisan	Iyar	Sivan	Tammuz	Av	Elul	
2	September	October	November	December	January	February	March	April	May	June	July	August	September

Festivals

6162

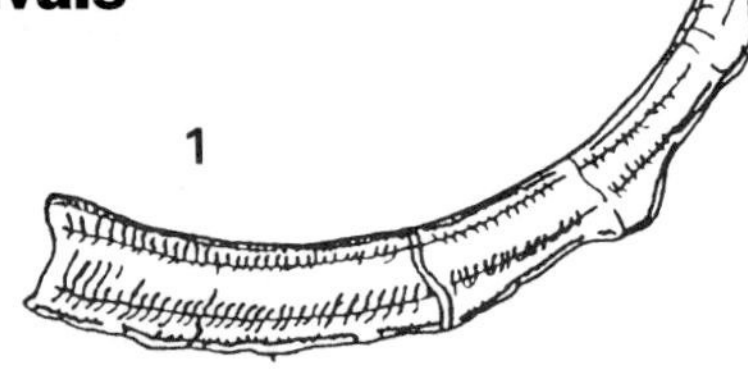

Rosh Hashanah (Jewish New Year) days 1–2 Tishri. Prayers are offered to the sovreignty of God. The Shofar (**1**) is blown during the synagogue service as a call to penitence.
Yom Kippur (Day of Atonement, the holiest day) day 10 Tishri

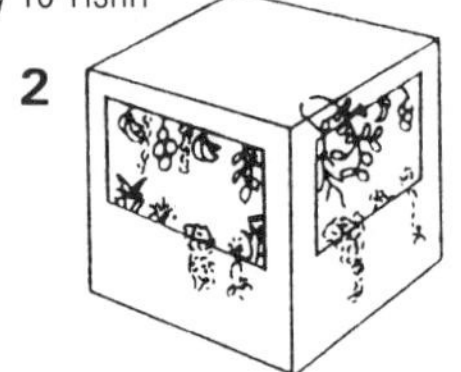

Sukkoth (Feast of the Tabernacles (**2**)) Days 15–21 Tishri. An ancient festival associated with harvest (Leviticus 23: 39–43)

Hanukkah (Feast of Lights) Day 25 Kislev
Festival of Lights commemorates Maccabean Revolt. It lasts eight days and symbolizes victory of God over evil. A nine-branched candlestick (**3**) is lit.
Purim Days 14–15 Adar
Recalls Queen Esther saving the Jews in Persia from massacre by Haman. Masks and *haman gregers* (rattles) give this festival a joyous feeling.
Shavuot (Feast of Weeks) Days 6–7 Sivan

Passover Days 15–22 Nisan
The Seder meal
1 *Haggadah* (Passover ritual book), one for each celebrant and visitor
2 Elijah's Cup kept for the prophet's return
3 The three *matzoth* (unleavened bread)
4 Candles for holiday
5 Cups of wine, each celebrant drinks four to recall God's four promises of redemption
6 *Betzah* (roasted egg) symbol of new life and hope
7 *Karpas* (spring green)
8 *Maror* (bitter herbs, usually horseradish), with 7 and 9 reminders of suffering
9 Salt water
10 *Haroset* (paste made with apple, nuts, cinnamon, and wine) symbolizes building mortar of captivity
11 *Z'roah* (roasted shankbone of lamb) recalls the Passover lamb
12 *Seder* dish, often ornate

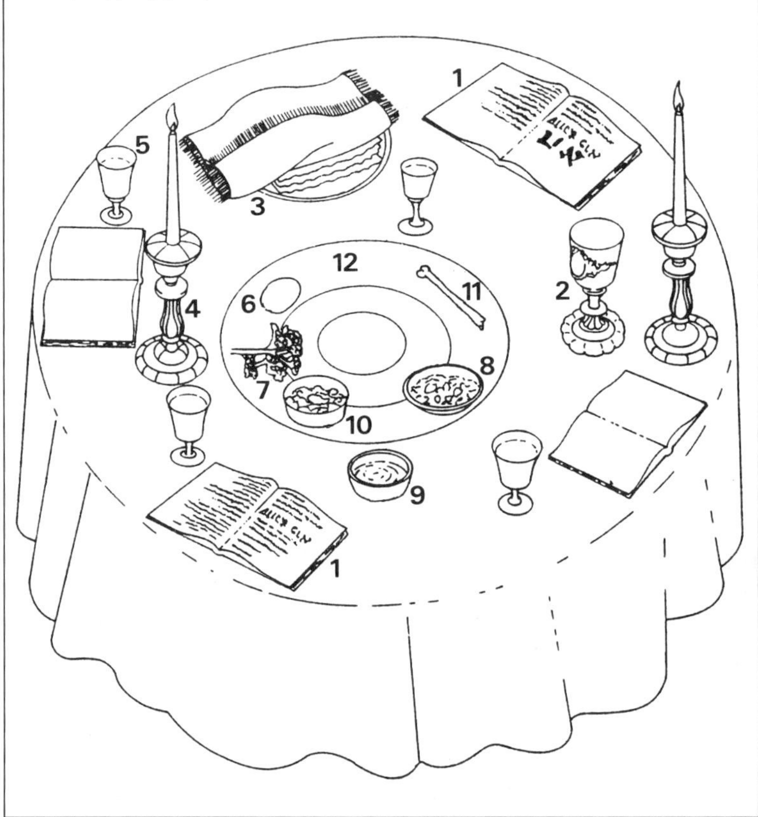

617 DISTRIBUTION

There are approximately 18 million Jews throughout the world. The largest group is in North America, which has 47.5% of Jews in the world. About 20.5% of all Jews live in Israel. 15.8% live in countries of the former Soviet Union. Europe only has 6.6% and South America only has 4.25% of the total. Another 4.55% are scattered throughout other parts of the world.

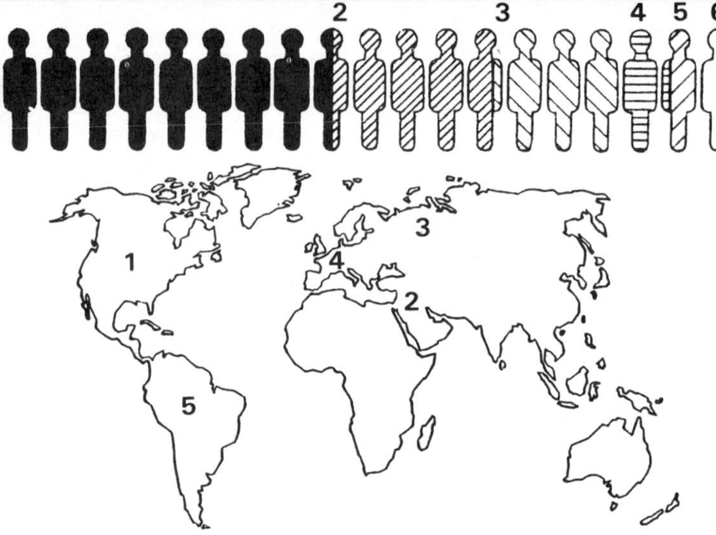

618 CEREMONIAL OBJECTS

The following is a list of objects important in the Jewish religion for purposes of worship either in the synagogue or in the home. Some are objects which are symbolic of the Jewish faith and which are worn or used for special occasions.

challah loaves The Sabbath meal begins with a blessing said over two loaves of bread. These are a reminder of the Jews wandering in the wilderness and collecting two portions of manna before the Sabbath.

chanukkiah A candle holder for nine candles lit on each of the eight days of Hanukkah with the servant candle or Shamash in the center.

kippah/ yarmulka

Skull caps (**1**) worn by men and boys over 13 years old. Kippah are worn during prayer or all the time as a sign of respect, a reminder that God looks down on man.

the Holy Ark This is a closet where the *Torah* is kept in the synogogue.

matzah Unleavened bread eaten at Passover as a reminder of the hurry in which the Jews left Egypt.

menorah Seven-branched candlestick representing the seven days of Creation; found in the synagogue and in the home.

mezuzah A wooden or metal case containing parchments inscribed with verses from the Bible. It is fixed to the right-hand side of a door to a Jewish building and is a reminder of god's presence everywhere.

Sabbath candles Candles are lit at the beginning of the Sabbath by the woman of the house while they recite a blessing.

seder plate A special plate used at the Passover meal to hold the six symbolic foods.

shofar Ram's horn blown in the synagogue at Rosh Hashanah.

Sefer Torah

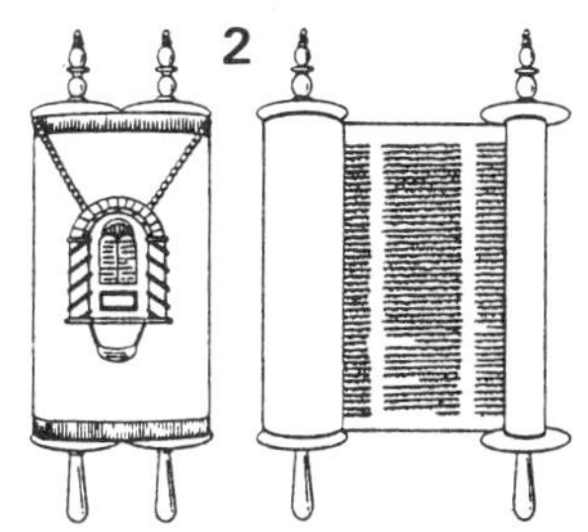

The *Torah* is hand-written on parchment scrolls and wound on wooden rollers (**2**). Western scrolls are covered with a velvet mantle and a silver breast plate is hung on the front.

tallith A four-cornered prayer shawl made of wool, linen, or silk (**3**). The fringes are counted and knotted. The tallith is worn by men over the shoulders for worship in the synogogue. A blessing is said before the tallith is worn.

Tefillin/ phylacteries

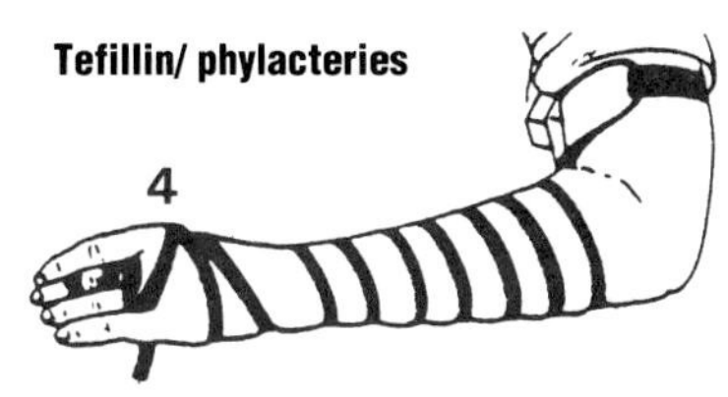

Two small black leather boxes worn on the head and on the left arm attached with long leather straps (**4**). They contain part of the *Shema* and passages from *Exodus*.

yad A hand pointer used for following the text of the *Torah* when reading. It is used to prevent hands touching the parchment.

619 GLOSSARY

Babylon The capital city of the ancient empire of Babylonia which conquered the Israelites in the 6th century BC and exiled them to Babylon.

bar mitzvah A ceremony undergone by a Jewish boy when he is 13 showing that he is now a full member of the Jewish community. The event is celebrated in the synagogue.

Canaan The land promised by God to Abraham. It became known as Palestine.

cantor The person who chants prayers during worship in the synagogue.

chosen people The Jews or ancient Hebrews or Israelites are the nation chosen by God. They have made a convenant with God.

covenant An agreement made between God and the Israelites in which God promises to love and protect them but requiring certain duties in return.

Creation God's Creation of the world as described in Genesis. The Creation took six days and on the seventh day God rested.

Day of Atonement The holiest day of the year, also called Yom Kippur, a day of fasting and prayer.

diaspora The dispersion and exile of Jews first by the destruction of the kingdom of Israel and of the kingdom of Judah and later by improved communications, commercial opportunities and especially the spread of the Roman Empire. Jews were scattered throughout Europe, Asia, and later North America. Term used for Jewish communities outside the land of Israel. This dispersion was sometimes forced, such as in the exile to Babylon in 586 BC and at the destruction of the Temple by the Romans in AD 70.

Exodus The flight of the Children of Israel from Egypt into the wilderness and eventually to Canaan.This map shows the traditional route of the Exodus.

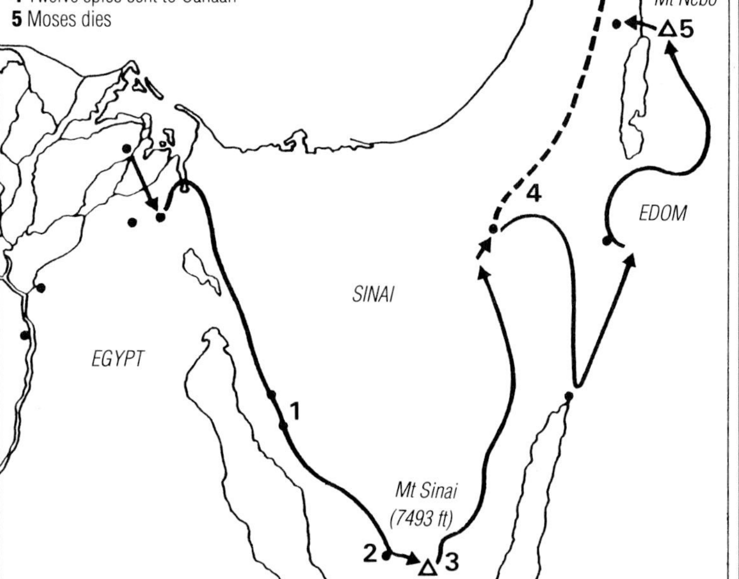

continued

Glossary continued

619

huppa A canopy under which a bride and bridegroom stand during a traditional Jewish wedding ceremony.

Israel The name of Jacob and of the Twelve Tribes which united to form the kingdom of Israel ruled by Saul, David, and Solomon. After Solomon's death the kingdom split into two kingdoms; Israel was the larger and was ruled by Solomon's son Jeroboam, Judah was the other kingdom. The kingdom of Israel came to an end when it was invaded by the Assyrians in 722 BC and its inhabitants scattered. A modern, independent state of Israel was established in 1948.

Holy places in Israel are:
1 Mount Carmel and the cave of Elijah
2 Sechem, site of a major shrine and meeting place during the tribal period of settlement c. 1200–1050 BC
3 Mount Zion, Jerusalem, alleged tomb of King David
4 Bethlehem, traditional site of Rachel's tomb and birth place of David
5 Hebron, site of cave of Machpelah, sacred burial place of Patriarchs and Matriarchs, Haifa

1
Sea of Galilee
R Jordan
2
Sechem
3
Jerusalem
4
Bethlehem
5
Hebron
Dead Sea

Israelites The descendants of Jacob who made up the Twelve Tribes.
Jerusalem

1

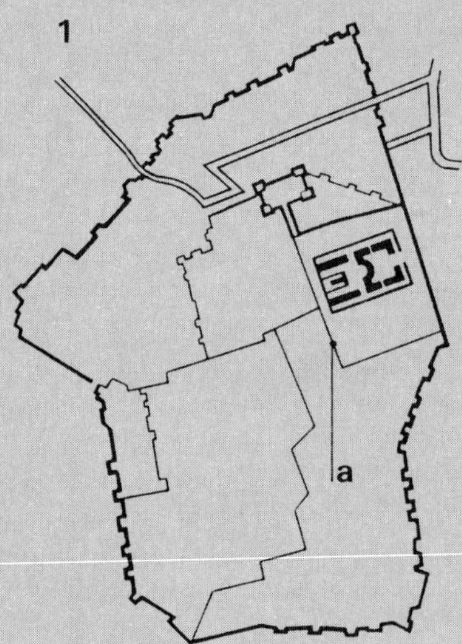

Holy city for Jews and the capital city of the ancient kingdom of Judah (**1**). The Western Wall (**a**), venerated as the only remaining part of the Temple.
Judah, or Judea One of the Twelve Tribes of Israel and a son of Jacob. Judah was one of two kingdoms into which Israel was split after the death of Solomon. Judah was ruled by Solomon's son, Rehoboam. The capital of Judah was Jerusalem. The kingdom was finally destroyed in 586 BC by Nebuchadnezzar but its people were not destroyed as were those of Israel.
Kosher This means ritually correct, proper and applies to food which has been prepared following Jewish dietary laws.
Manna Food that God gave the Israelites during their time in the wilderness after the food they had brought with them ran out. Manna appeared in the morning on the ground. It was small like hoar frost.
matzah Unleavened bread eaten at Passover.
menorah A candle holder with seven branches.
messiah The "promised" or "anointed one," a saviour who will deliver mankind from its sins. Jews believe that the messiah is yet to come.
Mount Sinai The mountain which Moses climbed to recieve the Ten Commandments from God.
Palestine The name given to the Holy Land. It was originally called Canaan. In 1948 Palestine was split between Israel and Jordan.
Passover The deliverance of the Israelites from Egypt, and the annual festival kept in memory of the event.
patriarchs The forefathers of the Israelites and founders of the Jewish religion: Abraham, Isaac, Jacob, and Jacob's sons.
Pentateuch The first five books of the Hebrew Bible, called the Five Books of Moses.
Philistine A people who were the enemies of the Israelites in their settlement of the Promised Land in the Old Testament.
Promised Land The land that God promised to give to the descendants of Abraham, Isaac, and Jacob which was known as Canaan, or Palestine.
prophet Someone who brings a message from God to the people. They most frequently spoke of true worship of God, upright living, and the coming of the Messiah.
rabbi This is the spiritual leader, teacher, and interpreter of Jewish law. They deliver sermons in the synagogue, give advice, and perform many other functions.
Sabbath The seventh day of the week in the Jewish religion, Saturday. It is a holy day and a day of rest.
shiva A seven-day period of mourning which the family enter into after a funeral.
siddur A prayer book used in the synagogue and for the chanting of prayers.
Star of David A symbol of Judaism and of

2

Israel (**2**). It consists of two triangles which interlace to form a six-pointed star. In Hebrew it is called the shield of David.

Tabernacle The dwelling place of the tent of the Lord was the portable sanctuary made by the Children of Israel during years of wandering in the wilderness.
tallith A shawl worn by men for prayer.
Talmud With the *Tenakh*, Judaism's two most sacred collections of writings. This is a collection of legal and ethical writings, history, and folkore.
tefillin

3

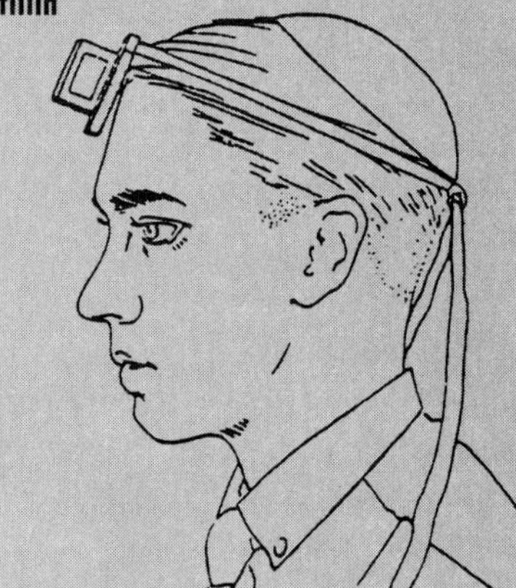

Small black boxes containing scriptures and worn on the forehead (**3**) and left arm.
Tenakh The Hebrew Bible which is also Christianity's Old Testament.

621 HISTORY

Timeline

6211 Christianity grew out of the life and teachings of Jesus Christ. Born a Jew, Jesus lived in Palestine which was then ruled by the Romans. It was the Romans who crucified Jesus around AD 30. The followers of Jesus believed he was the Messiah, the son of God, sent as a saviour who died to save mankind and that after his death he rose again and went to heaven. They spread the message of Christianity to major cities throughout the Roman Empire. Over the centuries Christianity divided into three major groups: Roman Catholics, Eastern Orthodox, and Protestants.

Major dates

6–4 BC Jesus born in Bethlehem.
AD 7–8 Jesus visits the temple at Jerusalem.
27 John the Baptist begins to preach. He baptizes Jesus who then begins his mission.
29–30 Jesus is crucified and resurrected. His disciples begin their preaching at Pentecost.
36 Paul, who until now had persecuted Christians, is converted. He begins his mission to spread the "word."
44 St James the apostle is martyred; beheaded by Herod Agrippa.
49–52 Paul's second missionary trip through Asia Minor (Turkey) and Greece.
53–57 Paul's third mission through Asia Minor and Greece.
67 Paul probably executed in Rome.
80 Gospels of Matthew, Mark, and Luke are complete.
90 St John's gospel.
177 Christians persecuted by Marcus Aurelius at Lyons, France.
202 Emperor Septimus Severus forbids Christians to preach their faith.
250 Emperor Decimus executes Christians who reject Roman gods.
257 Emperor Valerian punishes Christians for their religion.
313 Emperor Constantine actively champions the Christian cause.
325 Final clarification that Christians need not be Jewish. Council of Nicea.
330 Constantine founds Constantinople which becomes a religious administrative center.
405 Publication of the Bible in Latin by Jerome.
432 St Patrick reaches Ireland.
451 Council of Chalcedon divides power between Rome and Constantinople.
529 St Benedict founds the first Western monastic order.
867 Schism between Byzantium (Constantinople) and Rome.
869 Fourth Council of Constantinople heals division with Rome.
940 Monastic revival in Britain.
1018 Council of Pavia, papal decree reinforces celibacy of the clergy.
1054 Eastern and Western Christianity finally split.
1095 First Crusade announced by Pope Urban II.
1099 Crusaders take Jerusalem.
1304 Pope Clement V transfers the papacy to Avignon, France.
1378 Rival popes in Rome and Avignon.
1420 Papacy moved permanently to Rome.
1456 First printed Bible produced in Mainz, Germany.
1479 Establishment of the Spanish Inquisition.
1492 Jews and Muslims expelled from Spain.
1517 Martin Luther nails 95 theses on the church door at Wittenberg. The origins of Protestanism.
1521 Diet of Worms bans Luther.
1519–31 Zwingle, Swiss reformer begins work in Zurich.
1527–36 German Lutheranism spreads to Scandinavia.
1534 Luther's German Bible appears. Henry VIII of England breaks with Church of Rome and becomes head of the Church in England.
1536 Dissolution of the English monasteries.
1541–64 John Calvin's reform at Geneva spreads Protestantism to France, Netherlands, Scotland.
1542 Inquisition established in Italy.
1560 Protestantism established as national religion of Scotland.
1562 Beginning of religious wars in France between Catholics and Huguenots (Protestants).
1620 Pilgrim Fathers land in North America.
1685 Persecution of Protestants in France begins.
1688 James II, last Catholic monarch of Britain, is expelled.
1738 John Wesley begins his mission in England.
1784 Wesley ordains elders for mission in North America.
1790 Clergy and monastic orders persecuted in France during the Revolution.
1795 Methodist separate from Church of England.
1859 Charles Darwin's *Origin of Species* and theory of evolution attacked by Church authorities.
1865 William Booth begins ministry in England. This leads to the foundation of the Salvation Army.
1869 First Vatican Council in Rome declares the pope to be infallible.
1901 Pentecostal movement begins in America.
1948 First meeting of the World Council of Churches aimed at promoting understanding, tolerance and cooperation between all Christian Churches and denominations.

622 ORGANIZATION

Christian groups

6221 Most followers of Christianity belong to three major groups: Roman Catholic, Eastern Orthodox, and Protestant.

oikoumene

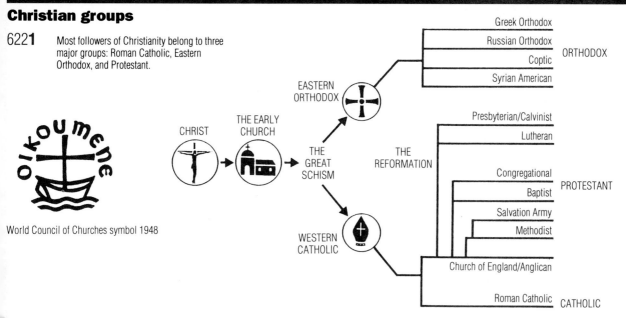

World Council of Churches symbol 1948

CHRIST
THE EARLY CHURCH
THE GREAT SCHISM
EASTERN ORTHODOX
WESTERN CATHOLIC
THE REFORMATION

Greek Orthodox
Russian Orthodox
Coptic
Syrian American
ORTHODOX

Presbyterian/Calvinist
Lutheran
Congregational
Baptist
Salvation Army
Methodist
PROTESTANT

Church of England/Anglican
Roman Catholic
CATHOLIC

6222 Roman Catholicism
6223 Eastern Orthodox Churches
6224 Protestant groups
6225 Clergy
6226 Places of worship
6227 Sacraments
6228 Holy orders

Roman Catholicism

6222 The Roman Catholic Church is the largest Christian Church in the world. It traces its origins to earliest Christianity in Palestine. The pope, who is the bishop of Rome, is the spiritual leader of the Roman Catholic Church. He is elected by the College of Cardinals. The pope is represented in the world by bishops, priests, and deacons. The center of the Roman Catholic Church is Vatican City, a tiny independent state over which the pope has complete control.

Roman Catholics believe the gospel of Jesus and the teachings of the Bible and their Church's interpretations of these. God's grace is conveyed through the sacraments, especially Communion. Roman Catholics believe that the only way of being saved and going to Heaven after death is to be absolved of all sin.

Eastern Orthodox Churches

6223 The Eastern Orthodox Churches are a federation of Churches united by common beliefs and traditions, which include the major Christian Churches in Russia, eastern Europe, and western Asia. Four Eastern Orthodox Churches hold special honor for historical reasons. They are the Churches of Antioch, Constantinople, Jerusalem, and Alexandria. Major Eastern Orthodox Churches include those of Greece, Russia, Romania, Bulgaria, and Cyprus.

The Eastern Orthodox Church's split from the Roman Catholic Church, or Western Church, began in the 5th century BC and the split became final in 1054. This split, or schism, still exists, although relations between the Roman Catholic Church and the Eastern Orthodox Churches have improved since 1962–65.

The Eastern Orthodox belief is based on the Bible and the holy traditions. It rejects the beliefs developed by Western Churches. Eastern Orthodox Churches give the greatest honor to the leader of the Church of Constantinople, he is known as the ecumenical patriarch, but he has power only over his own Church.

Protestant groups

6224 Protestantism is used to describe hundreds of Christian denominations and sects. It evolved mainly from the Reformation, a religious and political movement begun in Europe in 1517. The word Protestant means protester after early Protestants spoke out against Roman Catholics.

Protestantism differs from other Christian Churches in that it believes the Bible should be the only authority and does not include traditions. The nature of faith and grace differs for Protestants as they believe that humans are incapable of saving themselves because of their sins. They stress the importance of faith in God above doing good works. The main Protestant groups are :

Amish Mennonites
Founded in Switzerland in the 1500s, most emigrated to Pennsylvania, USA, in the 18th century. The Bible is the sole rule of faith. Mennonites shun worldly ways, modern innovation, and technology.

Baptists
The Baptist Church has about 31 million followers. Baptism was founded in England by John Smyth in 1609 and Roger Williams in Rhode Island in 1638. Authority stems from the Bible. Most Baptists are against alcohol and tobacco. Only when a person is old enough to consciously accept the Christian faith are they baptized, a total immersion in water.

Church of England
The Church of England was founded in 1534 when Henry VIII broke with the Roman Catholic Church and made himself head of the Church of England. The Bible is the most important document and emphasis is put on the essential Christian doctrines and beliefs.

Episcopal Church
This is an American offshoot of the Church of England, established in 1784. It has about 2.7 million followers in the USA.

Lutheran Church
The Lutheran Church bases its faith on the Bible and the writings of Martin Luther. Salvation comes through faith alone. Lutherans are conservative in religious and social ethics. There are around 8 million followers.

Methodist Church
This was founded by John Wesley in 1738. Worship varies by denomination within Methodism. The Church is highly organized and it is particularly concerned with pastoral and missionary work. There are about 13.5 million followers.

Presbyterian Church
The Presbyterian Church grew out of the Calvinist Churches of France and Switzerland. First church founded by John Knox in Scotland in 1557. Faith is in the Bible, the Church is organized as a system of courts. Services are simple with emphasis on the sermon.

Salvation Army
The international organization founded in 1865 by William Booth. It is run on military lines and members wear uniforms. Morality is highly esteemed. It rejects the sacraments. Well-known for its evangelistic and social work.

Unitarians
The Unitarians were founded as a sect in northern and eastern Europe in the 1560s. They believe that Jesus was an inspiring example of human goodness but that he was not divine. They do not believe in the Trinity.

Other Protestant groups include:
Adventists
Seventh-Day Adventists
Brethren
Christian Reformed Church
Christian Scientists
Church of God in Christ
Church of the Nazarene
Congregationalists
Moravian Church
Pentecostal Churches
Shakers

Clergy

6225 **The Roman Catholic Church** has three levels of clergy and the pope is responsible for the whole Church. A bishop is appointed by the pope and is responsible for a diocese which is a district of a Church. The priest or pastor is the leader of a parish which includes all Catholics living in an area, and the third level is a deacon.

The Eastern Orthodox Churches have the same three divisions and two minor orders, subdeacons and readers, who assist the priest during religious services.

Protestant Churches differ in their organization with some having no leader of the congregation and all the members being equal.

Places of worship

6226 Christians gather in buildings called churches because they believe God intended them to meet in groups for worship and because they feel it encourages members to be moral and upright. Roman Catholic and Eastern Orthodox churches are elaborate and richly decorated. Protestant churches vary from the elaborate buildings and ceremonies of certain Anglican churches to the simple and informal.

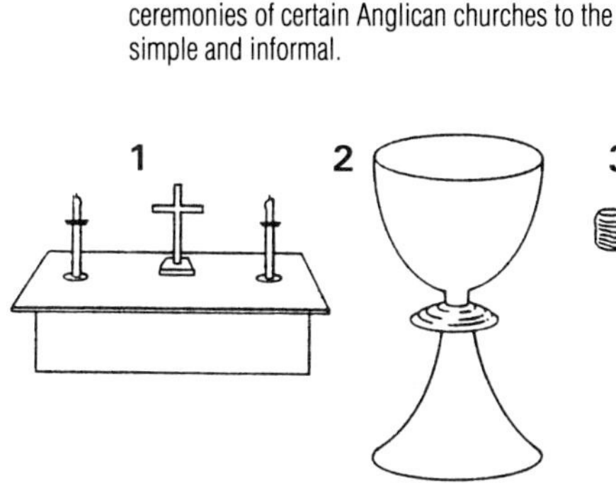

Church objects
1 Altar or altar table of the simple kind
2 Communion chalice for wine
3 Palm cross given to congregation in some churches on Palm Sunday
4 Sanctuary lamp, hung near the vestry (right of the altar), symbolizes the light which comes from God
5 Paschal (Easter) candle, lit from Holy Saturday to Ascension Day
6 Votive candle stand for lighting candles as a prayer is said (especially Catholic and Orthodox Churches)

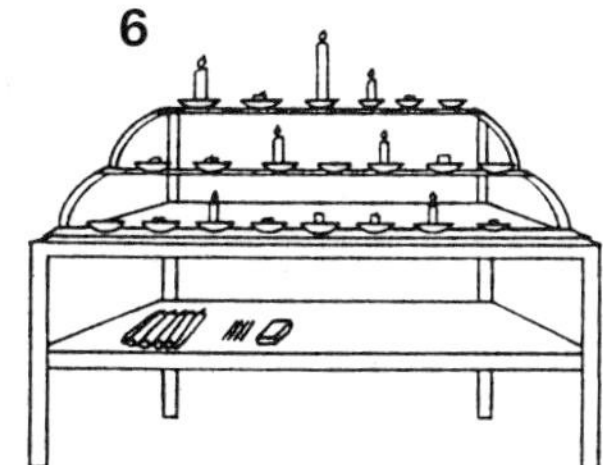

Sacraments

6227 The Seven Sacraments are ceremonial signs of God's action in people's lives. The signs take the form of words and gestures that are symbols of God's grace. The sacraments of both the Roman Catholic Church and the Eastern Orthodox Churches are the same, although the Eastern Church does not have a fixed number of sacraments. They believe in:
1 Baptism
2 Confirmation
3 Eucharist, which is mass or holy communion
4 Penance or confession
5 Marriage
6 Anointing of the sick, a sacrament given to the dangerously ill or the very old
7 Holy orders – the sacrament when people chosen by the Church become bishops, priests or deacons

The various Protestant denominations disagree about the nature and number of sacraments. Most denominations include at least two sacraments – baptism and communion.

Holy orders

6228 Religious societies of men and women exist who live together under a set of rules. They take vows of poverty, chastity, and obedience. Religious institutes are led by appointed leaders called superiors. Monks who live in austere solitude are hermits.

Orders of monks, friars, and hermits
The dates of their foundation are in parentheses.
Ambrosian monks (c. 1370-1850)
Augustinian hermits (1256)
Augustinian canons (c. 1060)
Augustinian monks (388)
Augustinian recollect friars (1588)
Basilian monks (c. 360)
Benedictine monks (529)
Camaldulian monks (c. 970)
Capuchin friars (1525)
Carmelite friars (c. 1155)
Carthusian monks (1080)
Celestine monks (c. 1260)
Cistercian monks (1098)
Cluniac monks (1090)
Constitutions of Theodore (c. 800)
Christian brothers (1802)
Discalced Carmelite friars (1562)
Dominican friars (1215)
Fontevrault monks (c. 1100)
Franciscan friars (1209)
Franciscan Observant friars (1415)
Hieronoymite friars (1374–1835)
Hospitaller friars of St John of God (1537)
Marist brothers (1817)
Mekhitarist monks (1702)
Minim brothers (1435)
Monks of Our Lady of Ransom (1223)
Olivetan monks (1319)
Order of St Gilbert of Sempringham (1148–1536)
Pachomian Monks (318)
Premonstratensian canons (1200)
Priests of the Sacred Heart (1878)
Servite monks(1233)
Silvestrine monks (1231)
Servite monks (1233)
Society of St John the Evangelist (1866)
The Taize Community (1948)
Trappist monks (1664)
Trinitarian order (1198)
Vallombrosan monks (c. 1038–1869)

Orders of nuns
Beguine nuns (c. 1180)
Benedictine nuns (529)
Bridgettine nuns (1344)
Carmelite nuns (1452)
Carthusian nuns (1229)
Discalced Carmelite nuns (1562)
Fontevrault nuns (c. 1100)
Little Sisters of the Poor (1840)
Nuns of the Community of St Mary (1865)
Passionist nuns (1770)
Poor Clare nuns (1214)
Poor Clares of Reparation (1922)
Redemptorist nuns (1750)
Servite nuns (1640)
Sisterhood of St John the Divine (1884)
Sisters of Charity of St Vincent de Paul (1629)
Sisters of Mercy (1827)
Sisters of the Institute of the Blessed Virgin Mary (1609)
Sisters of Our Lady of Charity of the Good Shepherd (1883)
Society of the Sacred Heart of Jesus (1880)
Theatine nuns (1583)
Ursuline nuns (1535)

Major missionary orders
Columban fathers (1917)
Divine World of Missionaries (1875)
Missionaries of the Sacred Heart of Jesus (1854)
Passionists (1725)
Redemptorists (1732)
Salesians of St John Bosco (1859)
Society of Jesus (better known as Jesuits) (1534)
Society of the Sacred Mission (1894)
Theatine brothers (1524)
Vincentian brothers (1625)

623 BELIEFS

Principal Christian beliefs

6231 The principal beliefs of all Christians are:

- That there is only one God
- That God sent his son Jesus into the world to help his people fulfil their religious duties
- Jesus spread God's message
- That Jesus was God incarnate (though some regard him as a great but human teacher,) that he was a divine being who took on a human appearance and the characteristics of man
- That Jesus was the Saviour, the Messiah, who died to save humanity from eternal sin
- That after Jesus' earthly life God's presence remained on earth in the form of the Holy Spirit. Most Christians accept this doctrine of the Holy Trinity as central to their faith
- That Jesus' life and death made salvation and eternal life possible for others
- Jesus rose from the dead and ascended into heaven.

The creeds

6232 These are statements of religious belief and faith. The most important are the Apostles' Creed which is officially recognized by some Churches, though not all, and the Nicene Creed, originally written in Greek and accepted by Roman Catholic, Eastern Orthodox, Anglican, and major Protestant Churches. There are differences in opinion; the Orthodox Church rejects the inclusion of the "father and son" in the section on the Holy Spirit. They argue that the Spirit proceeds from the Father alone. Alternative wording is given in parenthesis in the following text.

The Nicene Creed
I believe in One God,
the Father Almighty,
maker of heaven and Earth
and of all things visible and invisible.
And in one Lord Jesus Christ,
the only begotten Son of God,
begotten of the Father
before all worlds, (God of God)
Light of Light,
Very God of Very God,
begotten, not made,
being of one substance (essence)
with the Father;
by whom all things were made;
who for us men
and for our salvation, came down from heaven,
and was incarnate by the Holy Ghost of the
Virgin Mary,
and was made man;
and was crucified also for us
under Pontius Pilate:
he suffered and was buried;
and the third day he rose again,
according to the scriptures;
and ascended into heaven,
and sitteth on the right hand of the Father;
and he shall come again, with glory,
to judge both the quick and the dead;
whose kingdom shall have no end.
And (I believe) in the Holy Ghost,
the Lord and Giver of Life;
who proceedeth from the Father
(and the Son); who
with the Father and the Son together
is worshipped and glorified;
who spake by the prophets.
And (I believe) in one Holy Catholic
and Apostolic Church.
I acknowledge one baptism
for the remission of sins;
and I look for the resurrection of the dead,
and the life of the world to come.
Amen.

624 SACRED TEXTS

The Bible

6241 The most sacred book for all Christians is the Bible. There are many translations and versions of the Bible in existence. It is normally divided into two books: the Old and the New Testaments.

1 The Old Testament
The Old Testament is also the most sacred text of the Jewish religion. Written originally in the Hebrew language it covers the creation of the world, the struggles of the ancient Israelites, God's law revealed to Moses, and the journey from slavery in Egypt to the Promised Land, from around 1300 BC to the 100s BC.

The Jewish canon consists of 24 books. Protestant and Catholic editions adopt the Jewish canon but divide some of the books up, increasing the number to 39. There are four sections in the Christian Bible: the Pentateuch (**a**), the Historical books (**b**), the Wisdom books (**c**), and the Prophets (**d**).

2 The New Testament
This is not accepted by the Jews. It covers a period of about 100 years recording the life of Jesus Christ. It ends around AD 125. The New Testament also deals with the development of the early Church and the meaning of faith in Jesus. It was originally written in Greek which was widely spoken during Jesus' life. There are 27 books organized into four sections. The Gospels (**a**), the Acts of the Apostles (**b**), the Letters (**c**), and Revelation (**d**).

1 THE OLD TESTAMENT 39 books

LAW	a
	Leviticus
Genesis	Numbers
Exodus	Deuteronomy

HISTORY	b
Joshua	2 Kings
Judges	1 Chronicles
1 Samuel	2 Chronicles
2 Samuel	Ezra
1 Kings	Nehemiah

STORIES / POETRY / WISDOM	c
Ruth	Psalms
Esther	Song of Solomon
Daniel	Lamentations
Jonah	Proverbs
Job	Ecclesiastes

PROPHECY	d
	Hosea
Isaiah	Joel
Jeremiah	Amos
Ezekiel	Obadiah

PROPHECY	d
	Zephaniah
Micah	Haggai
Nahum	Zechariah
Habakkuk	Malachi

2 THE NEW TESTAMENT 27 books

GOSPELS	a
Matthew	Luke
Mark	John

HISTORY	b
Acts	

LETTERS (attributed to Paul)	c
Romans	Colossians
1 Corinthians	1 Thessalonians
2 Corinthians	2 Thessalonians
Galatians	1 Timothy
Ephesians	2 Timothy
Philippians	Titus

LETTERS	c
	2 Peter
Philemon	1 John
Hebrews	2 John
James	3 John
1 Peter	Jude

PROPHECY	d
Revelation	

625 PEOPLE

Andrew a fisherman. The first to be called of Jesus' 12 Apostles. He was the brother of Peter.

Apostles Jesus chose 12 Apostles to follow him and spread his teachings after his death. Shown here are some of their emblems.

1 Peter, the key to the Kingdom of Heaven (usually crossed keys but sometimes shown with only one key)
2 Andrew, decussate cross (he was crucified on a cross of this shape)
3 Thomas, spear or arrow. "Doubting Thomas" thrust his hand into the wound made by a spear in Christ's side
4 James the less, a fuller's bat, a sort of club used in the treatment of cloth
5 John, chalice and dragon (or serpent)
6 Jude, club, cross, or sometimes a carpenter's square or ship
7 Matthew, purse or money box, sometimes a spear or axe
8 Matthias, axe, halberd, lance or sometimes a book and stone
9 Bartholomew, butcher's flaying knife
10 Philip, cross, often loaves and fishes
11 James, scallop shells
12 Simon, a long saw, and sometimes one or two fish

Augustine 354–430, Bishop of Hippo. Theologian and philosopher, defender of the faith against various heresies.
Barnabas also called Joseph. One of the chief spreaders of Christianity with Paul. He was from Cyprus and fairly wealthy. He sold his lands and gave the money to the apostles.
Booth, William 1829–1912, British preacher and founder of the Salvation Army. He was born in Nottingham and became a traveling Methodist preacher. He left the Methodist Church to do evangelical work among the poor. He founded the Salvation Army when the established Churches refused to accept his slum converts.
Calvin, John 1509–64, French Protestant reformer and founder of Calvinism. Influenced by Luther, he traveled around Europe promoting Protestantism. He wrote an influential definition of the reformed faith. Churches founded on Calvinist principles include the Reformed Churches and the Presbyterian Churches.
disciple a pupil. As well as the 12 Apostles, Jesus also enlisted the help of 70 others to help with the work of spreading his teachings.
Henry VIII 1491–1547, King of England who split with the Roman Catholic Church and made himself head of the Church of England.
Hus, Jan c. 1370–1415, Bohemian religious reformer. His followers are known as Hussites. They began a religious and political reform of Bohemia which produced the Moravian Church.
Iscariot, Judas disciple of Jesus. He betrayed Jesus to the authorities for 30 pieces of silver. Judas hanged himself from guilt after betraying Jesus.
James Two of Jesus' Apostles were called James. One was James the Greater, brother of John, sometimes described as the brother of Christ. He was among the 12 Apostles.
James the Less son of Alphaeus. Became a highly respected figure in the early Christian Church of Jerusalem.

Jesus called Christ. He gave his name to the religion of Christianity. He is thought to have been born between 12 and 4 BC. Son of Mary and the foster son of carpenter Joseph of Nazareth. He taught by parables and performed miracles. His ideals are best explained in the Sermon on the Mount. Jesus is believed to have been the Messiah and to have risen from the dead. These became firmly established beliefs and formed a new religion.

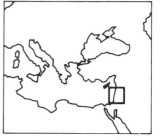

This map shows places in Jesus' life

1 Sidon
2 Tyre
3 Chorazin
4 Ptolemais (Acre)
5 Gennesaret
6 Magdala
7 Cana
8 Tiberias
9 Nazareth
10 Nain
11 Caesarea
12 Sebaste (Samaria)
13 Sychar
14 Joppa
15 Arimathea
16 Jericho
17 Emmaus
18 Jerusalem
19 Bethphage
20 Azotus
21 Caesarea Philippi
22 Capernaum
23 Bethsaida
24 Gadara
25 Gerasa
26 Bethany
27 Qumran
28 Bethlehem

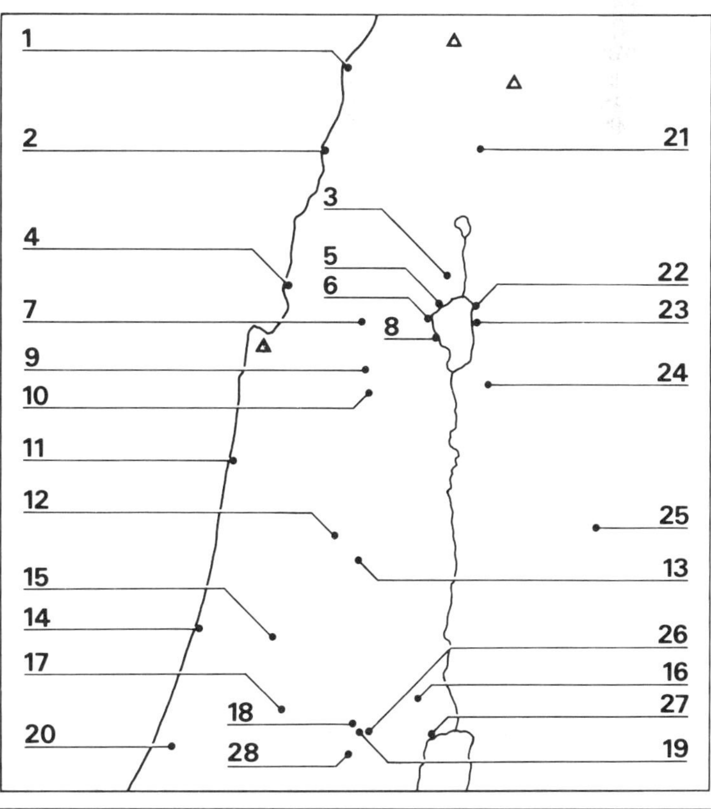

continued

People continued

625 **Jerome** c. 342–420, scholar and translator of the Bible into Latin (the Vulgate).

John author of last of the four gospels whose emblem is shown (**1**).

1

It is very different to the other gospels and many important events in Jesus' life are not mentioned. This gospel concentrates instead on the implications of Jesus' mission.

John the Baptist hermit and preacher. He was a relative of Jesus and known as the Baptist because he made his followers go through a ceremony of baptism to show they had repented of their sins. Jesus began his public life by being baptized. John was eventually imprisoned by Herod the ruler of Galilee and beheaded to keep a promise to his stepdaughter Salome.

Joseph husband of Mary, foster father of Jesus. He was a carpenter from Nazareth but also a descendant of the royal line of David (*see* Judaism.)

Knox, John c. 1514–72, a Scottish scholar and historian. A prominent preacher in Henry VIII's England. Established the Presbyterian Church in Scotland in 1557.

Luke Greek Gentile probably born in Antioch. His emblem is given below (**2**).

2

Author of one of the four gospels. It contains more material about the birth and early life of Jesus than the other three gospels.

Luther, Martin c. 1483–1546, German

3

theologian (**3**) who broke with the Catholic Church and led the Protestant Reformation. Luther translated the New Testament into German and produced a Reformed church service and liturgy also in German. Lutheran Churches today are the main ones in northern Europe.

magi wise men. Three kings who visited Jesus, Mary, and Joseph soon after the birth of Jesus. They were guided by a star and brought gifts of gold, frankincense, and myrrh.

Mark author of one of the four gospels which records the life of Jesus. His emblem is given below (**4**).

4

It is generally considered to be the earliest of the gospels.

Mary mother of Jesus. Christians refer to her as the Virgin Mary, as according to the New Testament Jesus was miraculously conceived while Mary was still a virgin. She is revered for her humility and motherly love. She is particularly honored by the Roman Catholic Church.

Mary Magdalene in the New Testament a woman follower of Jesus who witnessed his crucifixion and with two other women discovered his empty tomb and announced his resurrection.

Matthew one of the 12 Apostles and author of the first gospel. His emblem is given below (**5**).

5

messiah a person annointed. The Jews believe in a messiah, described in the Old Testament, who would come and save the Jews and who would unite and lead them. Christians and the New Testament give the title to Jesus.

Paul preacher and teacher. Along with Peter, one of the foremost leaders of the early Christian Church. Paul, originally called Saul, was an enemy of the Christians and persecuted them. As he rode to Damascus one day in order to suppress Christians there, he was blinded by a light and God spoke to him. After this Saul became a Christian and changed his name. He spent the rest of his life bringing the gospel to people. The New Testament includes many of Paul's letters to early Christian Churches.

Peter chief of Jesus' 12 Apostles. He was a fisherman originally called Simon. Peter showed great faith and great failings. He went on to become leader of the early Christians and founded the Church in Rome.

Pilate, Pontius 1st century AD, Roman governor. Procurator of Judaea and Samaria (26–36.) Condemned Christ to death but according to the New Testament he did so unwillingly.

Pharisees ancient Jewish religious and political party. An intellectually elite group. They were a strict religious group which held strongly to the *Torah* and additional laws. They regarded those who were unable to conform to their austere way of life as hopeless sinners. They were the enemies of the Sadducees. Pharisees are frequently criticized by Jesus in the Gospels.

Sadducees A political and religious Jewish sect mainly from the wealthy and priestly establishment. They were strongly associated with the Law.

St Benedict of Nursia during the 500s established monasteries where monks and nuns lived in separate communities. He set down rules for the monastic way of life. For about 500 years most monks belonged to the Benedictine order. The Benedictines helped to spread Christianity in western Europe.

St Francis of Assisi c. 1182–1226, founder of the Franciscan order in 1209. Renounced wealth to live in poverty and devote himself to prayer and charitable work.

Scribes ancient Jewish biblical scholars who continued the tradition of handwriting the *Torah* and who cultivated its study and interpretation. Frequently linked with the Pharisees.

Simons, Menno 1496–1561, Dutch ex-priest and leader of the Anabaptists who went to America and to Russia. He and his followers became founders of the Mennonite Church.

Smyth, John 1554–1612, founder of the Baptists in England.

Wesley, John 1703–91, founder of Methodism (**6**). He began his teaching within the Church of England in 1738. As a young priest he went to America with his brother where he was influenced by the Moravian Church. A separate Wesleyan Methodist Church was established in 1791.

6

Zwingli, Huldreich 1484–1531, Swiss theologian and preacher (**7**) who pioneered Reformist ideals in Switzerland. He founded the sect called Anabaptists.

7

626 THE CALENDAR

The Julian calendar was used in the Christian world until the 16th century when the Gregorian calendar was adopted by most Churches. Some Orthodox Churches still prefer to use the Julian calendar, which is why Christmas and Easter celebrations happen at different times. Advent, four Sundays before Christmas, marks the beginning of the Christian Year. Some festivals are celebrated on fixed days and happen at the same time every year, like Christmas and saint's days. Others, such as Easter, are worked out according to the Moon and are celebrated at different times each year.

This chart compares the Roman Catholic and Eastern Orthodox calendars.

	The Roman Catholic tradition	Eastern Orthodox tradition
December	**8** Immaculate Conception **25** Christmas Day	**25** Christmas Day
January	**1** Solemnity of Mary, Mother of God **6** Epiphany	**1** St Basil's Day; Circumcision of the Lord **6** Epiphany
February	Ash Wednesday	**2** Hypapante (Christ's meeting with Simeon)
March	**19** St Joseph's Day **25** The Annunciation Palm Sunday	**25** Annunciation Orthodox Sunday Palm Sunday
April	Holy Week Easter	Easter
May	Ascension Day Pentecost	Ascension Day Pentecost
June	Trinity Sunday Corpus Christi **29** St Peter and St Paul	
July		**17** St Marina's Day
August	**6** Transfiguration **15** Assumption of Blessed Virgin Mary	**6** Transfiguration **15** Assumption (falling asleep of Blessed Virgin)
September	**8** Nativity of the Virgin	**1** New Year **8** Nativity of Blessed Virgin **14** Exaltation of Holy Cross
October		**26** St Demetrius' Day
November	**1** All Saint's Day	**21** Presentation of Blessed Virgin Mary in Temple **30** St Andrew's Day

627 DISTRIBUTION

Christians make up the largest religious group in the world with an estimated one billion followers. It is the major religion of Europe, the Western Hemisphere, and Australia. Of these, 900 million people are Roman Catholics and about 140 million people belong to the Eastern Orthodox Churches. About 327 million people, or 6% of the world's population, belong to the various Protestant groups.

The number of Christians in millions (approximate)

1 Europe	310	**6** Central America	47	**11** Australia	9		
2 South America	153	**7** Britain	42	**12** New Zealand	2		
3 North America	131	**8** Pacific Islands	35	**13** Middle East	1.5		
4 Africa	69	**9** Caribbean Islands	18	**14** Japan	1		
5 Former Soviet Union	60	**10** India/Pakistan	13				

628 CEREMONIAL OBJECTS AND SYMBOLS

Ceremonial objects

6281 **advent candles** Candles marked into 24 sections and burned daily during Advent, the preparation period before Christmas which covers the four Sundays.
Bible The most holy book.
Christmas cards Greetings sent at the festival of Christmas. They contain secular and religious messages.
cross *see* following page.
crucifix The cross with a figure of the crucified Christ. Significant for Roman Catholics and Orthodox Christians.
decorated Easter eggs A symbol of new life given by Orthodox Christians on Easter Day when Jesus' resurrection from the dead is celebrated.
icon Associated with prayer in the Eastern Orthodox Church. Icons are special holy pictures of Jesus, Mary, or various Saints. They are used in worship at home or in a church and are regarded as a window onto heaven.
pictures and statues Usually of the young Jesus, saints, or nativity figures. They are reminders of those people who set examples in their closeness to God and their faith.
prayer books Used in some churches to follow and join in the services.
rosary beads Used by Catholics as an aid to prayer. A short phrase or prayer is said for each bead.
stole Hung around the necks of clergy as a sign of office.
vestments Robes worn by leaders of services in Catholic, Orthodox, and Anglican Churches.
votive Candle, bought in a church and offered to God with a prayer. A candle symbolizes light, truth, and the presence of God.

continued

Ceremonial objects continued

6281

the cross Probably the most important Christian symbol reminding followers of the sacrificial death of Jesus and his subsequent resurrection. Also symbolizes the victory of good over evil

Illustrated here are a variety of crosses relating to Christian worship.

1 Plain Latin
2 St George's or Greek cross
3 Russian Orthodox
4 St Peter's
5 St Antony's or Tav
6 St Andrew's
7 Patriarchal
8 Cross of Lorraine
9 Cardinal
10 Papal cross
11 Crosslet cross
12 Jerusalem or Crusader cross
13 Maltese cross
14 Celtic
15 Easter cross
16 Calvary cross (faith, hope, and charity)
17 Crucifix of dying Christ
18 Cross of Christ the King
19 Cross representing the Evangelists, one at each point
20 Ansate cross

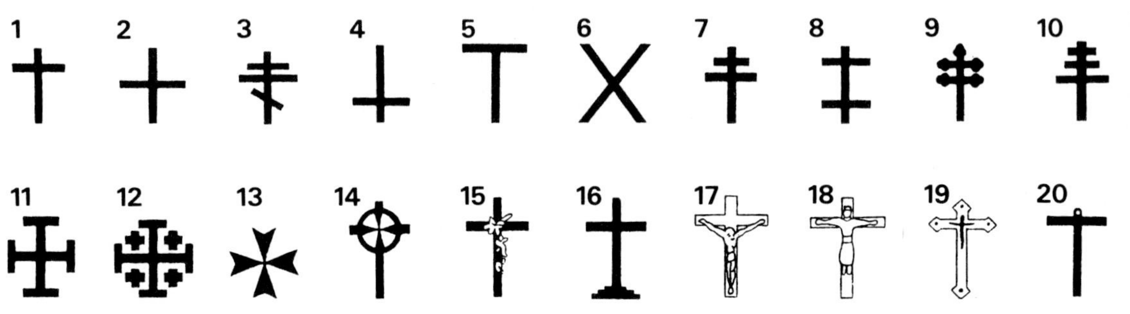

Religious symbols

6282

1 Three linked circles: the unity of God
2 The Lamb of God: John the Baptist's description of Jesus and Christ's redeeming death, recalling Jewish Passover lamb
3 The Dove of Peace: symbol of God's spirit at Jesus' baptism
4 The Crown of Thorns: Christ on the Cross
5 *Alpha omega*: Christ the beginning and the end (Greek alphabet)
6 Palm leaves (Palm Sunday): celebration of Christs's entry into Jerusalem
7 Cross keys of St Peter: the keys to Heaven
8 Flames of fire: Holy Spirit
9 *Chi Rio*: first two letters of Christ in Greek superimposed
10 Scallop shell: pilgrim symbol for St James of Compostella
11 INRI *Iesus Nazarenus Rex Iudaiorum*: Jesus of Nazareth King of the Jews: Latin inscription over cross
12 Fish symbol used from late 2nd century AD. The Greek word for fish *icthus* forms the initial Greek letters of Jesus Christ, God's Son, Savior

1

2

3

4

5

6

7

8
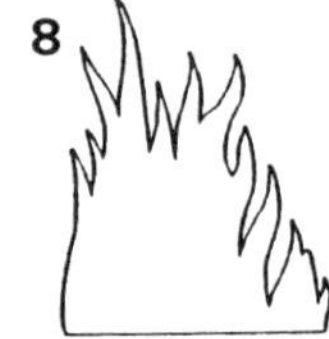
9
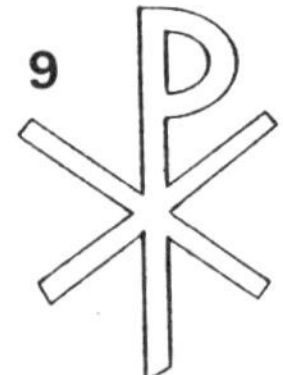
10
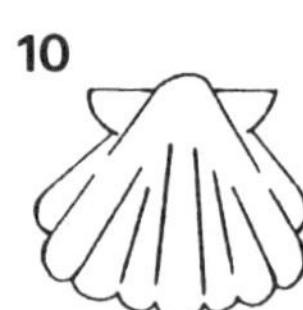
11

12
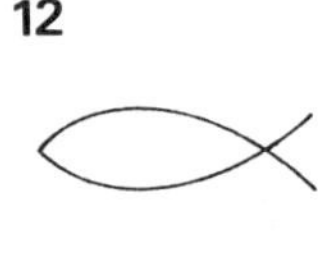

629 GLOSSARY

advent Preparation for the coming of Christ. Festival before Christmas.
ascension Celebration of Jesus' ascension into heaven. Forty days after Easter.
cardinals, College of A body of the highest authority next to the pope in the Roman Catholic Church. The pope is elected from one of the cardinals, and is elected by them. They assist the pope in religious and non-religious affairs.
Christmas This celebrates the birth of Christ. The festival is held on the 25 December. The Nativity (depicting the birth of Christ, **1**) is a common theme for Christmas theater plays and celebrations.
clergy Religious leaders; a member of the Church.
creeds Statements of Christian belief.
cross The main Christian symbol, reminds Christians of Jesus' sacrificial death and his resurrection. Symbol of good over evil.
crucifix Cross with the figure of crucified Jesus, especially important to Roman Catholics.

1

continued

Glossary continued

crusades During the Middle Ages Christian armies tried to recapture Jerusalem which had been conquered by Muslim Turks. These military expeditions were called crusades. They began before 1100 and ended in the late 1200s.

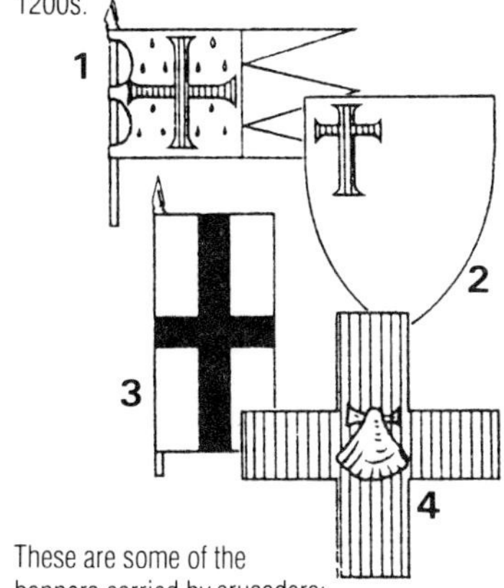

These are some of the banners carried by crusaders:
1 Early banner of the Knights of St John (red cross with holy blood drops)
2 Knights Templar shield with red cross (second crusade onward)
3 Banner of the Teutonic Knights (black Latin cross)
4 Hospitalers of St Thomas of Canterbury in Acre 1191-1291, a small English order which wore a red cross with a white scallop shell at the intersection

doctors (of the Roman Catholic Church) These are saints whose doctrinal writings have special authority either by papal decree or by the Church's universal agreement.
1 Gregory the Great
2 Augustine
3 Basil
4 John Chrysostom
5 Gregory of Nazianus
(from 1148 mosaic in Cefalu Cathedral, Sicily)

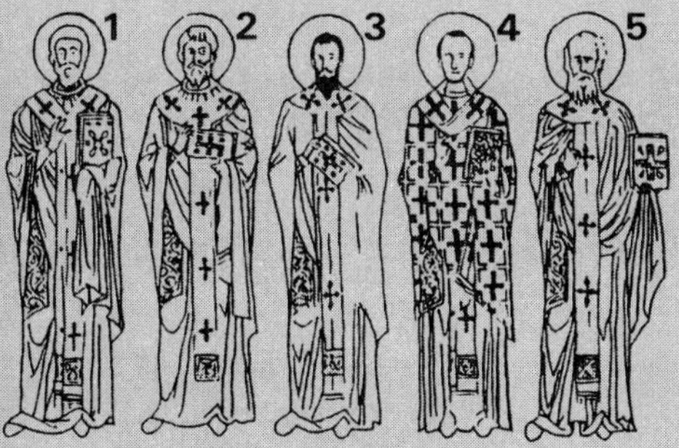

Easter Commemorates the death and resurrection of Jesus.
eucharist Also called communion, mass, or Lord's Supper. Church service which remembers the Last Supper. The wine and the bread or wafer, taken by the participants are symbols of Jesus' body and blood which he commanded that his followers eat and drink
evangelist A person who brings or announces good news; author of one of the gospels.
gentile A non-Jewish person.
gospel Means good news; good news of the coming of the Kingdom of God. There are four gospels included in the New Testament.
Last Supper The traditional Passover meal which Jesus shared with his Apostles the night before his death. Jesus is said to have blessed bread and told the Apostles to "Take eat, this is my body" and passed wine saying "This is my blood." These elements are part of the communion service.
lent A period of spiritual discipline, fasting, and penance leading up to Easter.
monasticism Withdrawing from everyday life to concentrate on prayer and meditation.
parable A story told by Jesus to convey his religious message.
Pentecost Marks the coming ofthe Holy Spirit.
resurrection Rising from the dead. Reports of Jesus' resurrection convinced many people that Jesus was the Son of God.
sacraments Outward and visible signs of an inward faith. Ceremonies in which a spiritual benefit is given to an individual.
saints People who have died for the faith or who have been thought worthy of special honor and remembrance by the Church as examples to Christians, and in the Roman Catholic Church as mediators with God.
stations of the cross Plaques or pictures (about 14) placed around the walls of a Catholic church marking the stages of Jesus' journey to his crucifixion and burial.

Trinity Three persons in one God. The belief that God is three persons - the father, the son who is Jesus, and the Holy Spirit which is the spirit of God's grace.

These symbols are often used by Christians to represent the Trinity.

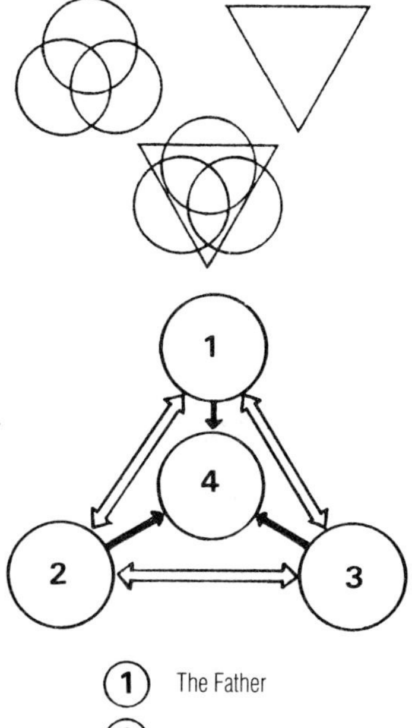

(1) The Father
(2) The Son
(3) The Holy Spirit
(4) God

Typical arrangement of the stations of the cross
The series of pictures of the Passion of Christ is used in Roman Catholic and Anglican worship during Lent or Holy Week. The priest leads the congregation to each station in the order given. This pilgrimage in spirit dates from the 13th century.
1 Pilate's condemnation
2 Christ receives his cross
3 Christ falls to the ground
4 Christ meets his mother
5 Symon of Cyrene takes the cross
6 Veronica wipes Christ's face
7 Christ falls a second time
8 Christ tells the women of Jerusalem not to weep for him
9 Christ falls a third time
10 Christ is stripped
11 Christ is nailed to the cross
12 Christ dies on the cross
13 Christ's body is placed in arms of his mother
14 Christ's body entombed

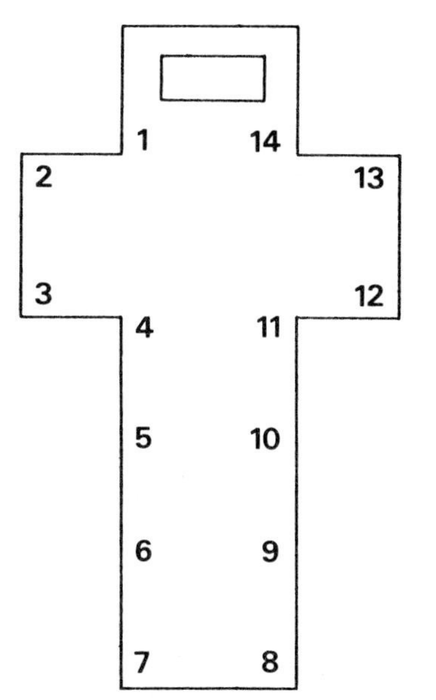

631 HISTORY

Timeline

6311 Islam is the name of the religion preached by the prophet Muhammad in the early AD 600s. Islam first began in Arabia in ancient times. The Arabs were pagan people divided into tribes which formed two groups. By 100 BC the southern tribes had established several kingdoms. One of the northern tribes, the Quraysh later gained control of the city of Mecca. The Arabs worshiped nature and idols. Arabia was a wild and lawless land where fierce desert tribes fought continually, but Jews and Christians lived freely among the Arabs.

AD 570 Birth of Muhammad. He belonged to the Quraysh tribe and grew up in Mecca. As he grew older he began to be incensed by injustice and by the worship of idols.
610 Muhammad has a vision on Mount Hira in which he is told to be one of God's prophets. He begins to preach that wrongdoers will be punished.
622 The Hegira. Muhammad's escape to the city of Medina after attacks for his teachings. People of Medina accept Muhammad's teachings.
First year of Muslim calendar.
Muhammad begins to attack travelers from Mecca.
630 Muhammad occupies Mecca. Destroys pagan idols in the Ka'aba, a famous shrine, and makes the Ka'aba a mosque.
632 Muhammad's death. Caliphs lead Muslims.
632–4 Abu Bakr becomes first caliph. Restores peace among tribes who revolted after Muhammad's death. Sends successful expeditions into Syria, Palestine, and Iraq.
634–61 Holy wars, or jihads continue. Syria, Palestine, Iraq, Egypt, and part of north Africa are gained.
634–44 Caliph Omar.
635–7 Capture of Damascus and Jerusalem.
644–56 Caliph Uthan.
656-61 Caliph Ali.
661–750 Umayyad caliphs rule. Muawiya first Umayyad caliph. Umayyads fight Turkish tribes in central Asia and send expedition to Sindh in India and reach borders of China. Also fight Byzantines in Turkey and around the Mediterranean Sea. Capture Cyprus, Rhodes, and Sicily. Complete conquest of north Africa. Attacks on Constantinople.
661 Umayyads establish Damascus as the capital.
691 Umayyads build Dome of the Rock and Al-Aqsa mosque in Jerusalem.
711 Umayyads invade Spain
732 After crossing Pyrenees into France the Muslim army is turned back by Charlemagne.
750 Beginning of conversion to Islam in conquered lands. Abbasid and Alids, two branches of Muhammad's family, overthrow Umayyads. One Umayyad prince escapes and establishes dynasty in Spain.
750–1258 Abbasids quarrel with Alids and win. Abbasids establish Caliphate of Baghdad where the new capital is built.
909–1171 One of the Alids, Ubaydullah, founds the Fatimid dynasy named after Muhammad's daughter from whom he claims descent. Fatimids rule north Africa, Egypt, Syria, Palestine, part of Saudi Arabia, and Yemen. Cairo becomes capital of their empire.
1000s Muslim Turks called Seljuks gain control of central Asia. They challenge Abbasids and gain control. Fatimid dynasty does not yield.
1092 Death of Malikshah, the last strong leader of Muslim Turks, who then split into rival groups.
1095 First of the crusades, or holy wars as Muslims threaten Christian Europe. Christians of Western and Eastern Churches unite to fight Muslims. Christians conquer Palestine and part of Syria.
1099 Christians capture Jerusalem.
1187 Great Muslim general Saladin recaptures Jerusalem.
1258 Abbasid empire falls to Mongols.
1291 Crusaders retreat.
1300s Ottoman Turks, a group under the Seljuks, capture part of Turkey and establish the Ottoman dynasty which ruled the greatest Muslim state of modern times.
1453 Ottomans capture Constantinople, a Christian city, making it the capital of the Ottoman Empire and rename it Istanbul
early 1500s Ottomans conquer Mameluke dynasty in Egypt. Ottoman empire expands rapidly into Europe and Asia.
1683 Ottomans stopped by Christians in Vienna.
1700 Existence of three great Muslim empires: Mogul empire in India, the Safavid empire in Persia (Iran) and the Ottoman empire in Turkey.
1900 European colonial powers control most of the Muslim world but throughout this century Muslim peoples have gained independence.
1922 End of Ottoman Empire. Atatürk establishes non-religious state of Turkey.
1948 Partitioning of the old state of Palestine and creation of Israel.
1956 Pakistan is established as the first Islamic republic.
1967 Six-Day War between Israel and the Arab states.
1979 Islamic Revolution in Iran.
1991 Aftermath of Gulf War and thousands of Shiites in Iraq are forced to take refuge in the marshes of the south after unsuccessfully rebelling against Saddam Hussein. War in Yugoslavia begins between Muslims and non-Muslim peoples.

Muhammad

6312 Muhammad was the founder of the Islamic religion. He is called a Prophet of Islam. Muhammad which means, "Praised One" is also spelt Mohammed, Mahomet, and Mohomed. Muslims believe that Muhammad was the last messenger of God and that he completed the sacred teachings of the early prophets Abraham, Moses, and Jesus.

Muhammad was born in Mecca. His father died before he was born and his mother died when he was a child. His grandfather and his uncle became his guardians. At the age of 25 Muhammad entered the service of a wealthy widow called Khadija. Muhammad later married her. One of their daughters, Fatima, married Ali, the son of Muhammad's uncle. One day when Muhammad was meditating on Mount Hira an angel, who Muslims believe to be the angel Gabriel, appeared telling him he was to serve as a prophet.

Muhammad began to preach publicly but was attacked for doing so and escaped to Medina. Here he became the leader of a religion and a community and he made his religious message into law. Muhammad seems to have expected Jews and Christians to accept him as a prophet. He chose Jerusalem as the direction to be faced for prayer like the Jews, but the Jews plotted against him with his enemies. Muhammad drove them out of the city and organized a solely Muslim community. Followers of Islam were now to face Mecca for prayer to show it was independent of all religions.

Muhammad died in AD 632 and his tomb is in the Prophet's Mosque in Medina.

632 ORGANIZATION

Muslim sects

6321 In AD 661 after a violent struggle resulting in the death of Ali, Muhammad's son-in-law, the Muslim world split into two major groups, Sunni and Shiah, resulting in differences of doctrine, ritual, and religious style. There are also a number of smaller sects.

Sunni Muslims

Sunni Muslims make up about 85-90% of all Muslims and are the more traditional group. They recognize that after Muhammad's death leadership passed to caliphs from his tribe. The *sunna* is a code of behavior based on Muhammad's example recorded in the *Hadith.* Shiite groups are guided more directly by the teachings of their religious teachers.

Shiite Muslims

Shiites are the largest minority. They regard only descendants of Muhammad's daughter Fatima and her husband Ali to be rightful leaders of the Muslim community. They are called Imams and are given great respect. Only

continued

Muslim sects continued

6321 an Imam can interpret Islam for the age in which he lives. Shiites believe in 12 Imams, they do not recognize the caliphs who were not descendants of Ali.

Shiism emphasizes sacrifice and martyrdom and believes in an inner hidden meaning of the Koran. Shiites give particular importance to the places associated with the deaths of Ali and his sons and also to the anniversary of their martyrdom. Only in Iran are Shiite Muslims a majority.

Baha'ism

The Baha'i faith grew out of the Shiite Muslim sect. There are approximately 4.5 million Baha'i followers worldwide. It was founded in what is now Iran in 1863 by Mirza Husaynali who was known as the Baha Allah. Baha'ism has no clergy or sacraments and has no formal organization. There are ceremonies for births, deaths, and marriages held in temples.

Followers of the Baha'i faith believe that God sent a series of prophets to teach moral truths. Their prophets include the Hebrew ones such as Abraham and Moses, Jesus, and Muhammad. They believe in the absolute oneness of God, as do Muslims. Baha'ism believes in the unification of all faiths, harmony and equality between all people, education for all, and obedience to government.

Wahhabis

Wahhabis make up another prominent sect. They are a puritanical sect who are dominant in Saudi Arabia. The movement was begun by Muhammad bin' Abd al-Wahhab (1703–87). He opposed customs such as honoring the tombs of holy men, the use of rosaries in prayer and other customs. He called for a return to the simplicity of early Islam. Continuing Wahhabi influence in Saudi Arabia means a resistance to Western ways, such as drinking alcohol.

Ismaili Muslims

Ismailis are a sub-group of Shiite Islam and they also believe that leadership of the Muslim community is passed on through Ali. They separated from other Shiites in giving allegiance to Ismail the successor of the sixth Imam. The Ismailis' greatest political success was the creation of the Fatimid caliphate. Ismailis believe that the Koran has a hidden meaning accessible only through the Imams. Ismailis have been split into sub-groups such as the Druzes, Bohoras, and Nizaris who are also called Khojas and are the largest Ismaili group. They recognize the Aga Khan as the 49th Imam.

Sufi Muslims

Sufis are Muslim mystics. Since the early days of Islam they have tried to draw even closer to God. They are named after their woollen garment (suf) which shows they do not care about material wealth. Many founded orders of organized followers who accepted the guidance of the founding member, or shaikh. Some of these orders have helped the spread of Islam beyond the Middle East. In some parts of the world even Muslims who are not Sufis greatly respect the shaikhs.

Black Muslims

The Black Muslims are an American movement officially called the Nation of Islam. It was founded by Elijah Muhammad and developed by him and Malcom X from the ideas of Wallace D. Fard as a protest against the inequalities suffered by black Americans. It rejects Chrisitianity as a white person's religion and takes Islam as a religion of power and prestige, rooted in their ancestral lands. It imposes high standards and stern discipline on its followers. The Black Muslims differ in regarding Wallace D. Fard as a prophet equal to Muhammad, ignoring an afterlife, and regarding black people as superior to any other race instead of taking all Muslims as brothers.

The movement now admits white people and has been renamed The American Muslim Mission. A small faction still calls itself "Nation of Islam", and is led by Louis Farrakham.

Places of worship

6322 The mosque is the place of worship for all Muslims and is their most important building. A typical mosque is bare and simple inside and has no furnishings. It does contain a pulpit for the preacher and a lecturn for the Koran. A *mihrab*, or niche, points in the direction of Mecca. It is empty but it may be richly decorated. Most mosques have at least one minaret, or tower from which the *muezzin* chants the call to prayer, and a walled courtyard with a fountain for ceremonial washing before prayer. Mosques may be decorated with patterns or verses from the Koran.

Many mosques also contain a religious school where young people learn to read and memorize the Koran. Some mosques also have a religious college, or *madrash,* where students can complete their religious studies. Graduates from these colleges may be called *mullahs* and can teach in a mosque, school, or college.

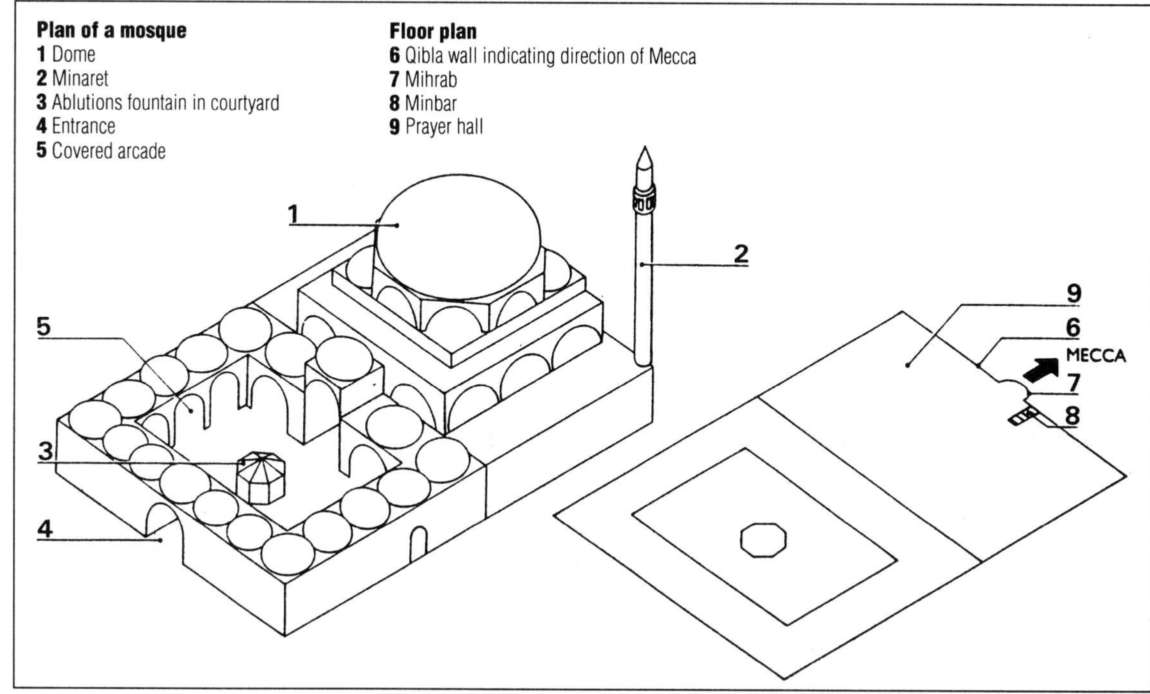

Islamic life

6323 **Holy men**
Islam does not have an organized priesthood. Any good and able Muslim can lead prayers. However, in the larger mosques it is usual to have a trained imam. The imam is the person who leads the prayers and preaches the sermon in the mosque at Friday prayers. The caliphs led the people in religious and political matters, so they were the chief imams.

The imam is usually an expert in Islamic law and may also teach Arabic and the Koran as part of his duties. An imam does not have the same role as a priest in a Christian church. There are no sacraments in Islam so the imam is not essential for ceremonies such as marriages to be carried out correctly.

Politics and religion
In the Western world it is usual to seperate religion from politics. Religion is considered to be a private matter while politics deals with public matters. In traditional Muslim countries, especially Saudi Arabia, politics and religion merge together as both are seen as doing the will of God. Muhammad was both a religious leader and a political leader as he led a community of believers. An Islamic state must have laws based on the Koran and only Muslims can hold important positions of power.

Women and Islam
The Koran states that women are spiritually equal to men but it also confirms the authority of husbands over wives. The Koran, however, did give women many rights they did not previously possess. Women were allowed property and given rights of inheritance. Special allowance is made for women in respect to certain religious duties. Women do not have to attend Friday prayers at the mosque. When they do they pray separately from the men. Women can only lead prayers if the other worshippers are all women.

Women and men should both dress modestly in accordance with the *Koran* and in some countries women still wear the veil or an all-enveloping garment. *Purdah* which hides women from men has been used until this century. Women are kept hidden in private apartments but they are not kept apart from one another. Purdah is still used in Pakistan, Saudi Arabia, Iran, and in countries concerned about Western influences.

633 BELIEFS

Essential Islamic beliefs

6331 The most basic and important of all Muslim beliefs is in the oneness of God. He is the creator of the whole universe. Absolute power and unity lie with God who is just and merciful. The Koran teaches that God wishes people to repent and purify themselves so that they can attain paradise after death.

Muslims believe that Muhammad was the last of the prophets. The Jewish prophets of the Old Testament and Jesus were his predecessors. The Koran forbids humans and animals to be shown in pictures, so Islamic art rarely depicts living beings. The Koran also denounces usury, or money lending, gambling, drinking alcohol, and eating pork.

Islam teaches that life on Earth is a period of testing and preparation for the afterlife. Muslims believe in a judgment day when everyone will receive a record of his or her deeds on Earth. The good will go to heaven and the wicked will go to a hell which resembles the Christian hell. The cardinal sin of man is pride.

The Five Pillars of Faith

6332 All Muslims accept the duties expected of them to show their belief in God. These are known as the Five Pillars of Faith. They are:

Shahadah
A declaration of faith: there is no god but Allah and that Muhammad is a prophet of Allah.

Salah
Muslims must pray five times a day: at dawn, at noon, in the afternoon, in the evening, and after nightfall. Before prayer, Muslims wash their face, hands and feet.

Zakat
An annual donation of a 2.5% of one's wealth each year is given for the poor, the disadvantaged or for religious purposes, such as building mosques or education. Zakat is a "purification" of wealth through sharing.

Sawm
Fasting takes place in the month of Ramadan. Muslims may not eat or drink from sunrise to sunset. Travelers, the sick, soldiers on active duty are exempt, but they must make up the lost days of fasting.

SHAHADAH Declaration of faith

SALAH Prayers five times a day

ZAKAT Welfare contribution

SAWM Fasting during Ramadan

HAJJ Pilgrimage to Mecca

Hajj
This is the pilgrimage to Mecca. All able Muslims are required to make the journey to Mecca at least once during their life. Many ceremonies are required during the pilgrimage. The most important are walking around the Ka'aba seven times and kissing or touching the Black Stone in its wall. Most Muslims also include a visit to the Mosque of Muhammad in Medina .

Some Muslim theologians added a sixth Pillar of Faith by including the *jihad*, or holy war.

Prayer

6333

Prayer, or *salah*, is the core of Muslim worship. The Koran constantly stresses the importance of prayer. An announcement of intention to make an act of worship, or *niya* should be made before prayer. This is to ensure the worshipper's total concentration, sincerity, and to stop it becoming an empty act.

Prayer positions in sequence
Each prayer position is given a name: *Niya* (**1**), *Fatihah* (**2**), *Ruku* (**3**), *Sujud* (**4**), *Jalsah* (**5**).

continued

Prayer continued

6333 Wherever they are in the world, Muslims always pray facing toward Mecca. This is indicated in mosques by a niche. Prayer can take place in any clean place but Muslims are encouraged to pray together rather than alone. Ceremonial washing takes place before prayer.

On Fridays, Muslims should attend noon prayers at the mosque. This is the day set aside by Muhammad for congregational prayer. The prayer leader faces Mecca. The men stand in rows behind him. Women pray separately from the men either behind or to the side of them. Prayers include reciting passages from the Koran and other phrases of praise to God.

A prayer mat

The head is usually covered for prayer which includes bowing and kneeling with the face down to the ground. Shoes are not allowed to be worn inside a mosque and must be removed before prayer. Prayer rugs are often used but are not essential. Prayers are said in Arabic no matter what language a person usually speaks.

634 SACRED TEXTS

The Koran and other texts

6341

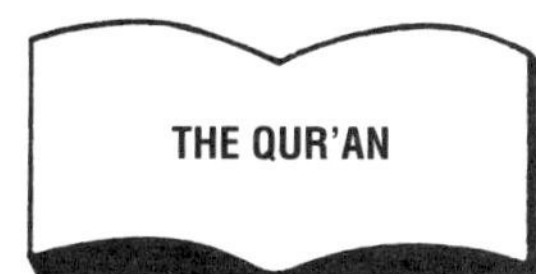

The message revealed to Muhammad from Allah through the angel Gabriel

Muslims believe in the revealed books mentioned in the Koran

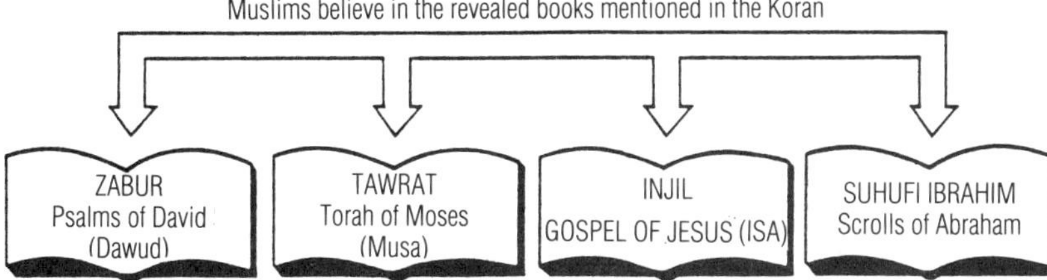

THE HADITH

What the Prophet Muhammad said and did

THE SUNNAH

The rules and regulations of Muslim life. The ways by which Islamic belief and practice are regulated.

The Koran (or Qur'an in Arabic) is the most sacred book for Muslims, who believe it to be the actual words of Allah (God) as revealed to Muhammed, the revered Prophet, by the Angel Gabriel. The Koran is divided into 114 chapters, known as *suras*, each of which has a name. The *suras* vary in length from two lines to over 700. They were collected together and written down on the orders of the Caliph Uthman (644-56.)

Pious Muslims recite the first chapter *al-Fatiha* (the opening) every day as part of their prayers. The Koran is the basic source of guidance for all Muslims living in the world and it is the inspiration for law and literature, manners and morals.

The Hadith, meaning "tradition", "speech" or "news" is what the Prophet Muhammed said and did. It provides, after the Koran itself, the most important source of Islamic law and custom.

The Sunnah are the rules and regulations of Muslim life and the ways by which Islamic belief and practice are regulated according to the example set by the prophet.

Baha'i texts
Baha'ism has five major sacred texts. The *Kitab al-Aqdas*, the Most Holy Book, contains Baha Allah's laws. The *Ketab e Iqan*, the Book of Certitude, has written down the teachings on the nature of God and religion. The *Hidden Words* is a collection of sayings for men's souls. The *Seven Valleys* is a mystic treatise. Both the *Hidden Words* and *Seven Valleys* are mystical treaties describing a spirit journey.

635 PEOPLE

Abu Bakr a rich merchant who believed Muhammad's preachings and became the first capliph after Muhammad's death.
Abu Talib Muhammad's uncle who became his guardian.
Aisha Muhammad's child bride and daughter of Abu Bakr.
Atatürk, Kemal 1881–1938, Turkish statesman and chief founder of the modern state of Turkey. In 1922 when the Ottoman sultan was desposed, Atatürk became the first president and continued as president from 1923 through 1938. He worked to make Turkey a modern secular state.
Fatima Muhammad's daughter. She married Ali, son of Abu Talib. Many Muslims trace their origins to this couple, including the Fatimid caliphs.
Ibrahim The first Muslim. According to the Koran, God revealed Islam to Ibrahim first. Ibrahim turned his back on pagan religions and put his belief in God. This is the Abraham of the Christian and Jewish tradition.
Ismail Ibrahim's son who is, according to Muslim tradition, the father of the Arab peoples. Tradition tells of his rebuilding the Ka'aba with Ibrahim after it had been destroyed by the great flood described in the Old Testament.
Khadija Muhammad's first wife who was 15 years older than him. Muhammad first entered into Khadija's service but later he married her. They had two sons and four daughters. The sons died young. Khadija was Muhammad's first disciple.
Mirza Husaynali 1817–92, founder of the Baha'i faith and known as the Baha Allah, or "Glory of God."
Muawiya founder of the Ummayyad caliphate.
Omar (Umar Ibn al-Khattab) A Meccan leader who persecuted Muhammad at first. He later accepted his teachings. He became the second caliph after Muhammad's death.
Seljuk founder of Seljuk Turks and first leader of the Muslim Turks of central Asia.

636 THE CALENDAR

The Muslim calendar (called *hijri*) is based on the lunar cycle, and a year consists of around 354 days. The Muslim calendar starts from the year AD 622, the year that Muhammad escaped from Mecca to Medina. Muslims do not recognize the term AD (*Anno Domini*) in Christian dating as they do not recognize Jesus as "Lord."

The chart shown here marks months and festivals during the Muslim year.

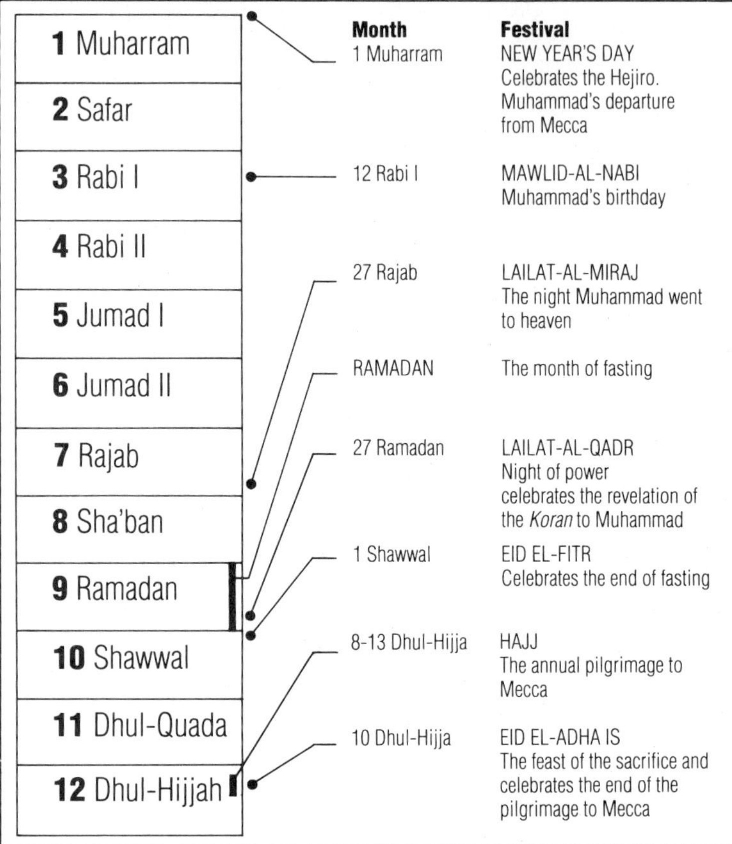

1 Muharram
2 Safar
3 Rabi I
4 Rabi II
5 Jumad I
6 Jumad II
7 Rajab
8 Sha'ban
9 Ramadan
10 Shawwal
11 Dhul-Quada
12 Dhul-Hijjah
Month
Festival
1 Muharram
NEW YEAR'S DAY
Celebrates the Hejiro.
Muhammad's departure from Mecca
12 Rabi I
MAWLID-AL-NABI
Muhammad's birthday
27 Rajab
LAILAT-AL-MIRAJ
The night Muhammad went to heaven
RAMADAN
The month of fasting
27 Ramadan
LAILAT-AL-QADR
Night of power
celebrates the revelation of the *Koran* to Muhammad
1 Shawwal
EID EL-FITR
Celebrates the end of fasting
8-13 Dhul-Hijja
HAJJ
The annual pilgrimage to Mecca
10 Dhul-Hijja
EID EL-ADHA IS
The feast of the sacrifice and celebrates the end of the pilgrimage to Mecca

Baha'i feasts and festivals

The Baha'i year is divided into 19 months of 19 days each. The calendar of the major feasts and festivals is as follows:

21 March	New Year
21, 29 April	Baha Allah's declaration of his mission
23 May	Declaration of the mission of the Bab
20 October	Birth of the Bab
12 November	Birth of the Baha Allah
29 May	Passing of the Baha Allah
9 July	Martyrdom of the Bab

Ramadan and Eid-el-Fitr festival

6361

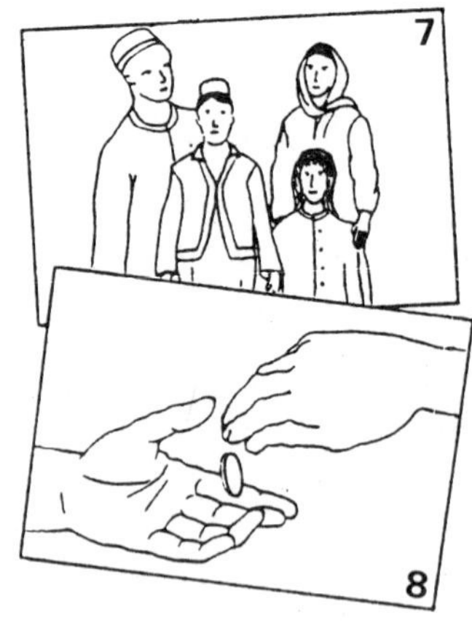

1 During the month of Ramadan Muslims fast
2 No food of drink is allowed between dawn and sunset
3 Small snacks and drinks are taken before dawn
4 29 or 30 days later, the festival of fast breaking, Eid-el-Fitr, is celebrated
5 All five daily prayers should be said at the mosque
6 Muslims exchange presents and cards
7 Friends and families get together to celebrate
8 Money (Zakat-el-Fitr) is given to the poor

637 DISTRIBUTION

There are an estimated one billion Muslims in the world. The largest groups are found in the Middle East, Pakistan, Bangladesh, Africa, Indonesia, Turkey, Albania, and Bosnia.

 Muslims over 50% of population

 Muslims over 10% of population

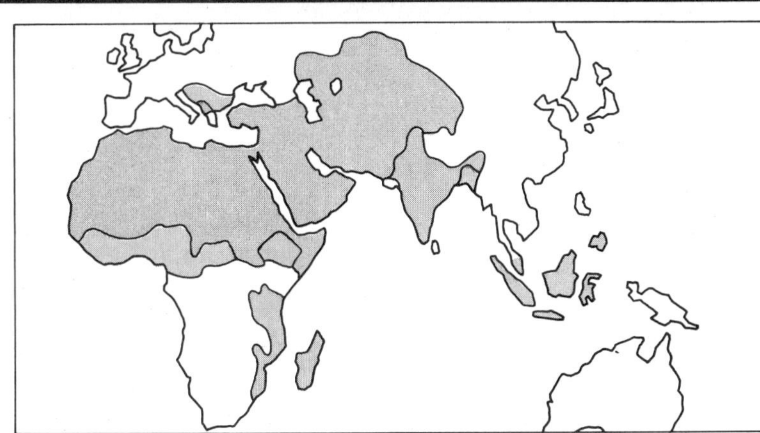

 Sunni Islam

 Shi'a Islam

638 CEREMONIAL AND HOLY OBJECTS

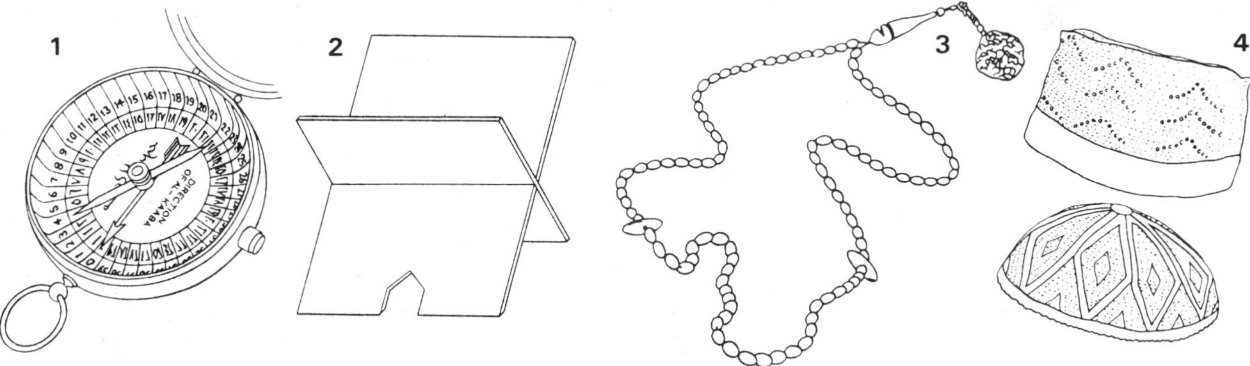

compass (**1**) Carried by Muslims so that they can discover in which direction Mecca lies.
crescent From early in Muslim history the crescent has been used as a decorative motif in Islamic art. It did not become a symbol of Muslim identity until the 18th century. It appears on the flag of Muslim countries. The Red Crescent is the Muslim equivalent of the Red Cross organization.
Eid cards Greetings cards sent at the festivals of Eid el-Fitr and Eid el-Adha. They may have "Happy Festival" written inside. Some have verses from the Koran inside and these must be treated with special respect.
ihram Garment worn by pilgrims performing the Hajj. It consists of two pieces of seamless white cloth which expresses equality before God.
Koran The Muslim holy book written in Arabic. It was revealed to Muhammad by God. Koran means "recitation" in Arabic.
Koran stand (**2**) Ornately carved and decorated wood bookstands used to hold the Koran and to make reading easier.
prayer counter Used by Muslims on the pilgrimage to count prayers.
prayer rug A mat used for daily prayers. Muslims must pray in a clean place. The mat is pointed toward Mecca. Mats are usually decorated with Islamic patterns and may show the Ka'aba or the Prophet's Mosque in Medina.
takiyah Prayer cap (**4**) crocheted or embroidered cap of any material worn by Muslims for prayer. They are worn inside the mosque and show respect and submission to God. Especially worn by south Asian Muslims.
tasbih/sebha (**3**) Beads used to count prayers or to recite the 99 names of Allah. There are either three sets of 33 or 99 beads.

The three most important Muslim holy places

6381

1 Mecca Ka'aba ("cube") the holiest place in the holiest city, reputedly built by Ibrahim. It contains the Black Stone that pilgrims come to kiss.

2 Medina Prophet's Mosque contains his tomb and is the site of the very first mosque.

3 Jerusalem Dome of the Rock built 685-91 on the place Muhammad ascended to heaven. Now a shrine for Muslim pilgrims.

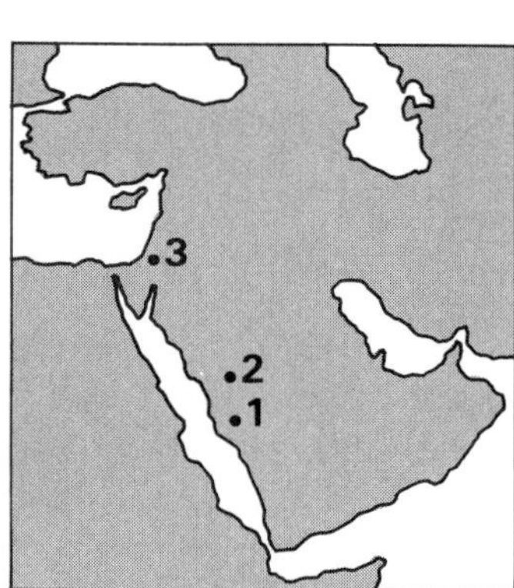

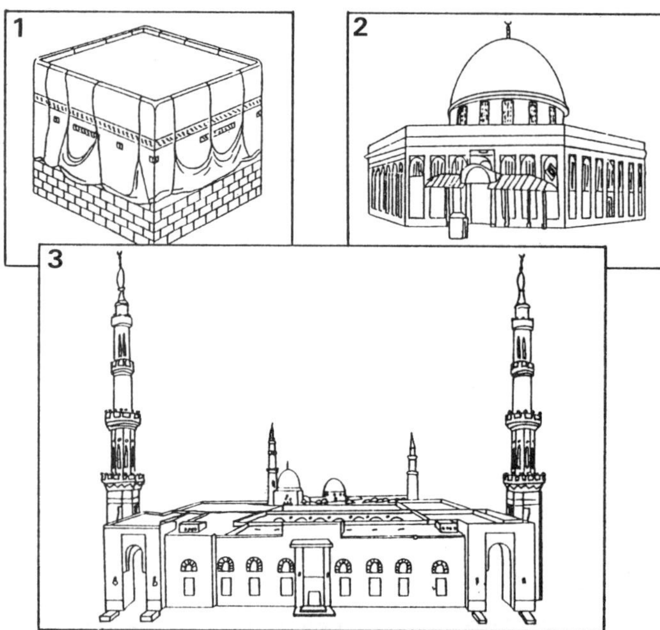

639 GLOSSARY

ayatollah This is a title held by the highest religious leaders of the Shiite sect. Ayatollahs guide Shiites in spiritual and worldly matters. An ayatollah can become the leader of the nation.

hajj The pilgrimage to Mecca which all Muslims must achieve at least once during their life.

hejira Muhammad's escape from Mecca to Medina in AD 622.

Islamic decoration Calligraphy or geometric patterns. Islamic art never has pictorial representations. Verses from the *Koran* and the *Shahada* or the *Bisamillah* are often used for decoration.

Ka'aba The most sacred shrine of Islam. It stands in a corner of the Grand Mosque in Mecca. It is the point to which all Muslims turn when they pray. Muslims believe that the Ka'aba was built by Adam, then rebuilt by Ibrahim and restored in Muhammad's time. It is thought to be the point where Creation began. The Ka'aba has a black stone in one corner which is thought to be especially sacred. The Ka'aba is empty. A black cloth usually covers the outside.

muezzin Crier or caller to prayer. Announces prayer times from the minaret of a mosque.

Muslim A follower of the religion of Islam. In Arabic Muslim means one who submits (to God).

The Hajj: the pilgrimage to Mecca

There are seven stages to this pilgrimage

1 Walk seven times counter-clockwise round the Ka'aba
2 Run seven times between As-Safa and Al-Marwah
3 Stay overnight at Mina
4 On the Plain of Arafat for prayer all day
5 Stay overnight at Muzdalifah
6 On to Mina to spend three nights there during which stones are thrown at the pillars and an animal is sacrificed
7 Return to Mecca, complete seven more circuits of Ka'aba

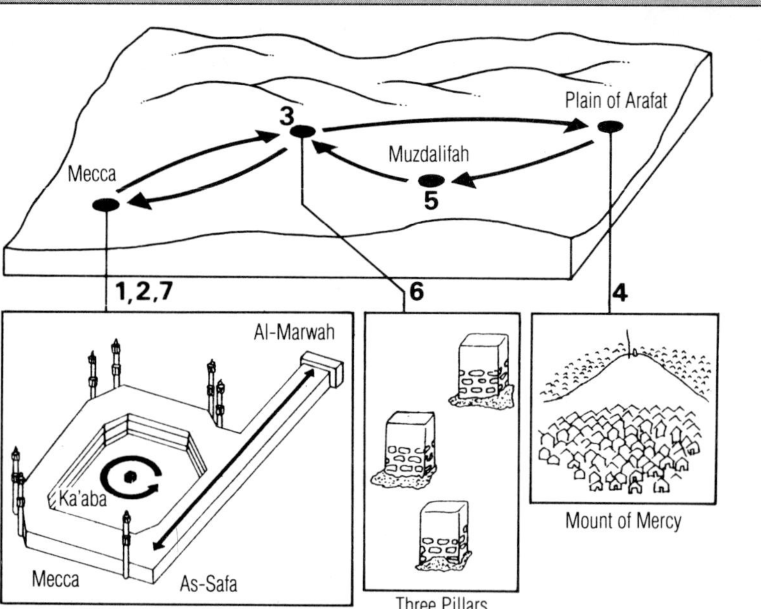

641 HISTORY

Hinduism: timeline

6411 Hinduism is one of the oldest religions in the world. The origins of Hinduism date back to prehistoric India.

2000 BC Indus Valley Civilization flourishes.
1500 BC A religion which is an early form of Hinduism develops in India among the Aryan invaders.
1000 BC *Rig Veda* written. It includes hymns of Aryan priests and shows Iranian influence.
1000–100 BC Spread of Brahmin religion, a forerunner to Hinduism.
800–400 BC Composition of the sacred texts the *Upanishads*.
650–450 BC Century of religious change in India including breakaway sects of ascetics.
c. 500 BC Teachings of Mahavira the Jain and Gautama the Buddha. Asceticism increasing as young men give up the world to search for release from transmigration. Orthodox Brahmin teachers react by devising the four *ashramas*. Hinduism now begins to center on the concept of four classes (*varna*) and four stages of life (*ashramas*). This forms the ideal that Hindus are encouraged to follow.
265–238 BC Ashoka in power. Although he is a Buddhist he supports non-violence and vegetarianism which are Hindu beliefs. Brahminic revival after Ashoka's death.
200 BC – AD 400 Rise of major sects: Vaishnavism, Saivism, and Saktism.
1–400 Spread of Hinduism in South-east Asia.
4th–6th century AD Rise of temple architecture using stone and brick. Wood previously used.
12th century Spread of Islam in India. Royal patronage of Hinduism is withdrawn.
1947 India gains independence from British rule.
1955–6 Rights given to widows and daughters.
1961 Giving of dowries forbidden although still widely practiced.

Sikhism: timeline

6412 Sikhism originated in India in the 15th century. Sikh means disciple and all Sikhs are disciples of their ten gurus. Sikhism took elements of Hinduism and Islamic Sufi practice and belief and fused them together forming a formidable religion.
1469 Birth of Guru Nanak.
1500 First Sikh, Guru Nanak, begins to preach. Tries to unite Islam and Hinduism. Adopts beliefs from both faiths.
1539 Angad becomes Guru; nominated by Nanak.
1552 Anar Das becomes Guru.
1574 Ram Das Sodhi becomes Guru.
1581 Ram Das' youngest son, Arjun Mal, becomes the fifth Guru.
1606 Arjun tortured to death in Lahore and Hargobind, his son, becomes Guru.
1645 Har Rai becomes the seventh Guru.
1661 Hari Krishen becomes the eighth Guru but dies aged eight.
1664 Tegh Bahadur beccomes the ninth Guru.
1675 Tegh Bahadur is executed in Delhi.
1675 Gobind Rai Singh becomes the tenth Guru.
1699 Persecution compels Sikhs to arm themselves. Gobind Rai baptizes five Sikhs into a new fraternity called the *Khalsa,* meaning "the pure." Adds Singh, meaning lion, to name.
1708 Gobind not a successful fighter and chased out of Punjab and assassinated. Before his death he announces the succession of the Gurus at an end. Banda Singh takes over as Sikh military leader.
1716 Banda Singh executed with 700 of his followers in Delhi.
1761 Sikhs establish themselves as rulers of the Punjab and take Lahore as their capital.
1799 Ranjit Singh crowned maharaja of the Punjab.
1818 Invades Multan and Kashmir regions.
1839 Ranjit Singh dies and kingdom begins to disintegrate.
1846 Khalsa army defeated by the British army.
1847 British take territory. Sikhs forced to reduce their army and to give up Jammu and Kashmir regions.
1848–9 Second Sikh War. All territory taken by British.
1857 Indian Mutiny begins. Sikhs stay loyal to British and are rewarded with land. Number of Sikhs in British army grows.
1914–18 Sikhs form more than one-fifth of the British Indian Army.
1919 Disturbances lead to 400 people being killed at Amritsar. Sikhs turn from British support to join Gandhi's freedom movement.
1947 India partitioned and Sikhs divided equally between India and Pakistan, but some 2,500,000 Sikhs leave Pakistan. Indian government abolishes privileges given to religious groups by British.
1966 Punjab created as a Sikh province.
1970s Sikhs begin to want more control of the Punjab. Growth of tension between Sikhs and Hindus. Sikh fundamentalism grows, led by Jarnail Singh Bhindranwale.
1980s Violence grows and Sikhs inflict reign of terror on Punjab. Thousands of Sikhs are arrested and imprisoned by the government.
1984 Sikh fundamentalists occupy Golden Temple at Amritsar. Indian army moves in and kills several hundred Sikhs. Indira Gandhi, the Indian prime minister, is assassinated by two Sikh bodyguards, provoking violence between Hindus and Sikhs. Sikh community demands a separate Sikh state.

642 ORGANIZATION

Hindu caste system

6421 The word *dharma* in Hinduism stresses not just the importance of beliefs but also a strict set of rules for a way of life. Books on *dharma* cover general moral laws like those of kindness, hospitality, and trustfulness. All Hindus are expected to follow these teachings. The books on *dharma* say that all human beings are not born equal mainly because of their previous incarnations. They divide the community into four great classes, or *varna.* This is commonly known as the caste system.

For centuries in India, one large group called untouchables, or pariahs, belonged to no caste and existed outside the four *varnas.* They were shunned and neglected. In 1947 discrimination on the basis of caste became illegal, although prejudice against them still exists.

The diagram shows the various castes with the brahmins at the top of the pyramid and the untouchables at the bottom.

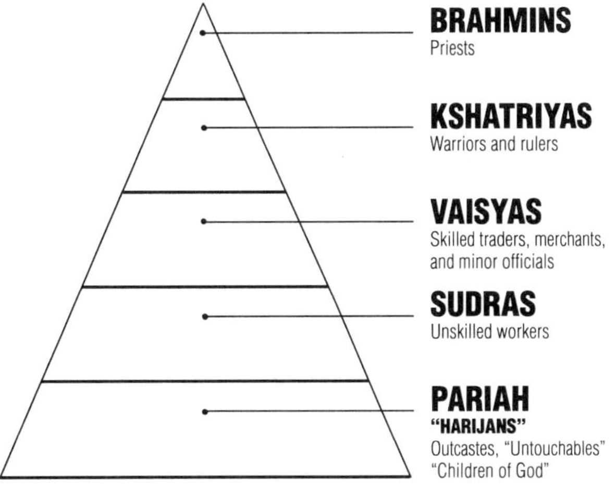

6422 Hindu worship
6423 Hindu religious rites
6424 Sikh religious structure
643 Beliefs
6431 Essential Hindu beliefs

Hindu worship

6442 There is no formal organization or structure for religious worship. In practice Hinduism varies in nature from village to village and region to region. The rituals of temple worship are complex and demanding and they are supervised by a brahman priest or teacher.

Hindus believe that their gods live in the temples like a house. Followers worship as individuals not as congregations. A visit to a temple may be made once a day, once a week, once a month, or once a year. Or perhaps even never. A Hindu does not fail in his religion if he never visits a temple.

A typical temple will have many shrines each devoted to a particular deity, and one principal shrine honoring a single important god or goddess. All deities are portrayed in sculptured images and they are considered to be living beings. Priests wash and dress the images and bring them food Ordinary Hindus perform *puja,* offering fresh flowers and food to the god. There are annual festivals to remember events in the lives of the gods, when people come to worship, pray for assistance, and enjoy the pagentry.

Brahman
Brahmans, or priests, receive offerings from worshippers who kneel in front of their god's image. A brahman says all prayers in Sanskrit. Much of a priest's time is taken up by looking after the images inside the temple. He washes, dresses, and decorates them. Worshippers give the priest gifts and offerings.

Hindu saints
Saints are very important to Hindus. They might be living men or dead men. Some saints may be yogis, men who practice yoga, and others may be spiritual leaders called gurus. There are many local and regional saints. Hindu monks and nuns join together in religious orders under the leadership of a saint.

Home worship
In practice many Hindu observances take place in the home. A majority of homes have a shrine which is devoted to a particular god chosen by the family. Some important religious ceremonies are performed in the home, including a Hindu boy officially joining the Hindu community. Other rituals include those connected with pregancy, childbirth, and marriage.

A Hindu family home shrine
1 Picture of Shiva Nataraja
2 Oil lamp and ghee holder
3 Book of scriptures
4 Bell
5 Offerings of fruit
6 Offerings of flowers
7 Frayer beads
8 Incense sticks
9 Photograph of guru
10 Om symbol
11 Bells

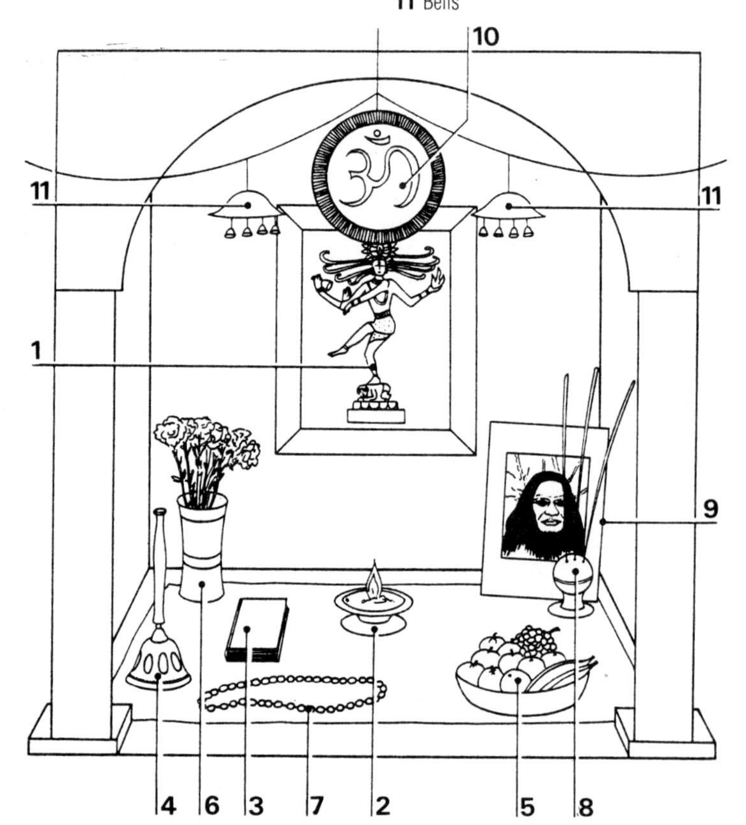

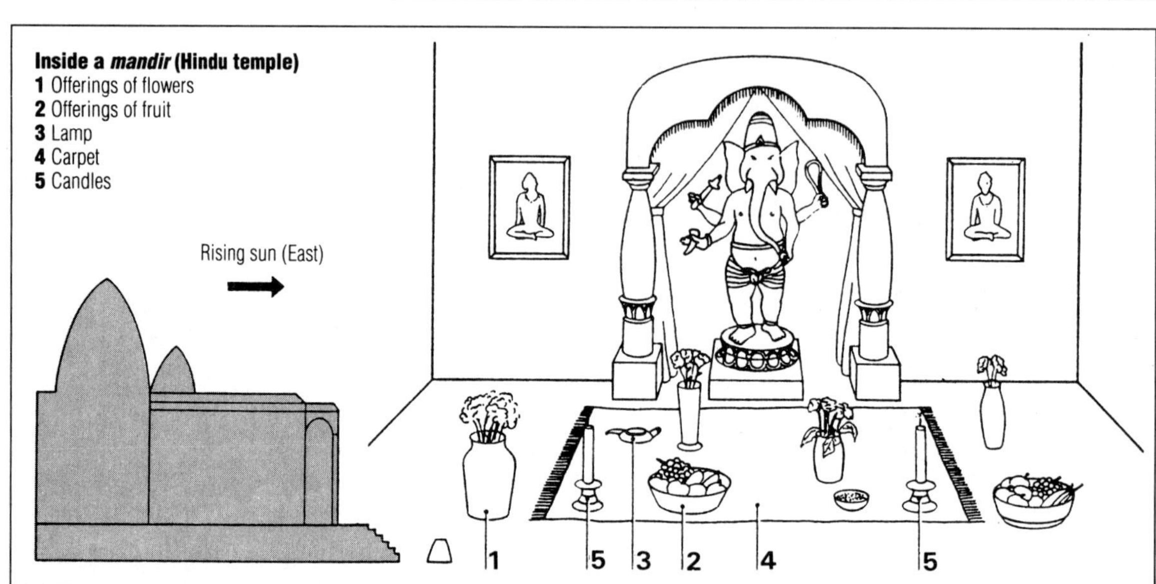

Inside a *mandir* (Hindu temple)
1 Offerings of flowers
2 Offerings of fruit
3 Lamp
4 Carpet
5 Candles

Hindu religious rites

6423 **Upanayana**
This is a traditional rite of initiation for a child born into a brahman family. It confirms the child as a full member of the Aryan community. Normally only boys of the three highest classes can perform this rite. Today this is not regularly performed except by brahmans.

Funeral rites
These are very important and if they are not observed properly Hindus believe the soul is liable to remain a ghost haunting the scenes of its past life and causing trouble to the living. Only a son can perform the funeral rites, which include cremation. The family are supposed to hide from society for ten days after the funeral while ceremonies are performed to provide the soul of the dead man with a new body for the next life.

Marriage
In orthodox Hinduism marriage is a religious rite. During the wedding ceremony the couple walk around a sacred fire holding hands, taking seven steps together. For the orthodox the marriage cannot be dissolved once the seven steps have been taken.

Sikh religious structure

6424 The ideal goal of all young Sikhs is to take *pahul*, or baptism and become *khalsa. Khalsa* is the idea of a chosen race of soldier saints committed to a strict code of conduct which includes devotion to a life of prayer and righteousness, abstention from alcohol, tobacco, and narcotics.

There is no priestly caste although the guidance of the guru towards *moksa*, or release from the cycle of rebirth, is essential. The guru is seen as being only slightly below God. He points the way to truth, explains reality and gives the disciple the gift of the divine word, *namadan.* Worship in temples includes hymns of praise and morning prayer. A Sikh temple is called a *gurdwara,* meaning "gateway to the guru." In affluent homes, a room will often be set apart for worship. Worship of images is forbidden and the only object of worship is the *Adi Granth* the Sikhs' most sacred book.

643 BELIEFS

Essential Hindu beliefs

6431 Hinduism has developed over thousands of years. Many cultures, races, and religions have contributed to its formation. Hinduism was not founded by one person and the faith is difficult to define briefly. Many sects arose within Hinduism and they all developed their own philosophy and ways of worship. However there are basic beliefs about divinity, life after death, personal conduct, and the acceptance of the caste system which ranks people from birth based on such things as religious practice, job, area.

Hinduism's sacred writings, the *Vedas,* have contributed to its essential beliefs. The *Vedas* are seen as the supreme authority of the faith, revealing unalterable truths.

Another common characteristic of Hinduism is the existence of the priestly class called brahmans. They are considered spiritually superior by birth and they represent ideal purity and social prestige.

Hindus believe in a sole reality, an ultimate cause, a source and goal of all existence, the ultimate reality. This is called Brahman. Brahman is all things and is in all things. Everything in the universe is made from Brahman.The belief in the religious search for ultimate reality has been central to India's beliefs throughout the history of Hinduism.

Reincarnation and karma
Hinduism teaches that the soul never dies. When the body dies the soul is reborn. This is called reincarnation. The soul may be reborn time and again, as another person, an animal, or even a plant, until it reaches its final goal. Hindus believe that all things have souls, unlike western religion which believes that only people have souls. A person's every action decides how the soul will be born in its next reincarnation. If the person is good the soul will be born into a higher state. If the person leads an evil life the soul will be born into a lower state. Reincarnation continues until the soul reaches spiritual perfection.

Hindu philosophy
Over the centuries many schools of thought have sprung up within Hinduism. Six of these schools have become important. They are:
1 Nyaya, this deals with logic
2 Vaisheska, which is concerned with the nature of the world
3 Sankhya, which examines the universe's origin and evolution
4 Yoga, which is a set of mental and physical exercises aimed to free the soul from relying on the body so that it can unite with Brahman, the most important and universal spirit
5 and **6** Purva-mimamsa and Vedanta interpret the holy writings

The sacred symbol **om** or **aum**

Swastika
symbol of good luck

Shri Yantra
used when meditating

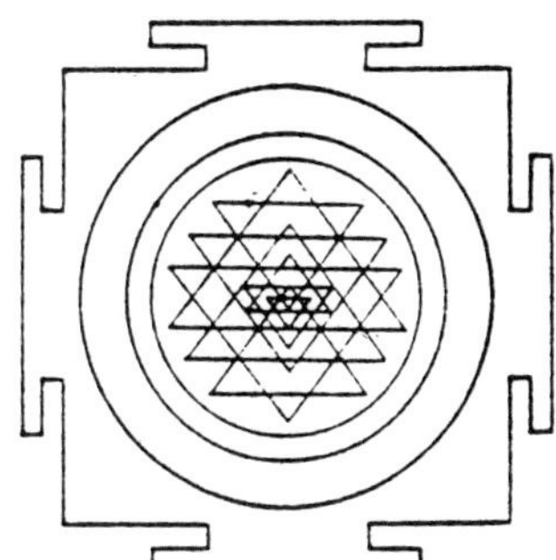

Hindu gods

6432 Hinduism believes in many gods. Early Hindus worshipped gods who represented powers in nature such as rain. Gradually a belief developed that the gods were all part of one universal spirit called Brahman. Therefore Brahman is made up of many gods. The most important of these are Brahma, Vishnu, and Shiva. Vishnu is often seen as the good aspect of Brahma, and Shiva as the destructive or bad side. Brahma, the other great diety remains in the background and has not had a major following since ancient times. Hindus may not worship either Vishnu or Shiva but one or more of the other Hindu gods.

Vishnu and his attributes
1 Disk
2 Mace
3 Conch shell
4 Lotus
5 Seven-headed cobra
6 Caste mark (placed by priest during worship)
7 Garland of forest flowers

The great god Vishnu appears on earth in various forms known as avatars – descents. Traditionally ten incarnations have been identified, though only two (Rama and Krishna) play a significant role in the lives of Hindu worshippers.

The ten incarnations of Vishnu
1 Matsya: fish
2 Kurma: tortoise
3 Varaha: boar
4 Narasimha: man-lion
5 Vamana: dwarf
6 Parashurama: Rama with the axe
7 Rama: prince
8 Krishna: young hero and lover
9 The Buddha
10 Kalki: incarnation yet to come

Brahma and his attributes
Although not from the earliest Vedic period, Brahma is the Hindu creator god, holding the balance in a "trinity" with Vishnu and Shiva by the late 1st century BCE.

1 Four faces standing for the four quarters of the universe
2 Sacrificial ladle
3 String beads for prayer
4 Four vedas (scriptures)
5 Jar of Ganges water
6 Lotus throne (all gods sit or stand on one)

Today he has only three temples dedicated to him, but his image is in all those for Vishnu and Shiva.

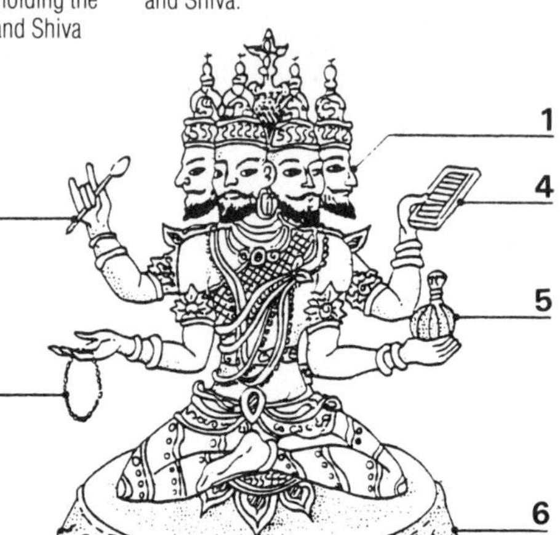

Shiva Nataraja, Lord of the Dance
One of the main Hindu deities. Shiva is also Nataraja, Lord of the Dance and is often represented in this form.
1 Crushing the dwarf demon (ignorance)
2 Drum in right hand for steady rhythm
3 Fire of destruction in left hand
4 Arc of flames represents the eternal life and death cycle
5 Cobra, the symbol of fertility
6 Leopard-skin loin cloth representing strength
7 Concentration
8 Many hands, raised in blessing or inviting refuge

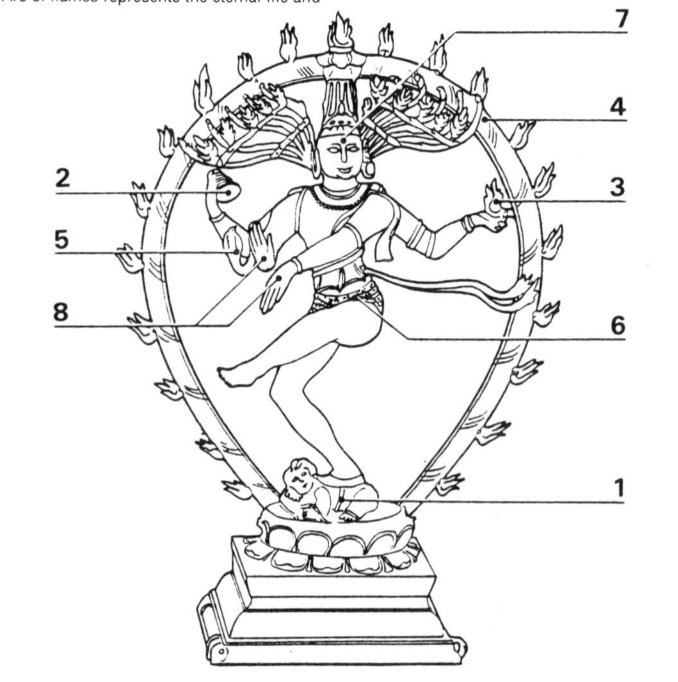

Sacred rivers and cities in India

6433

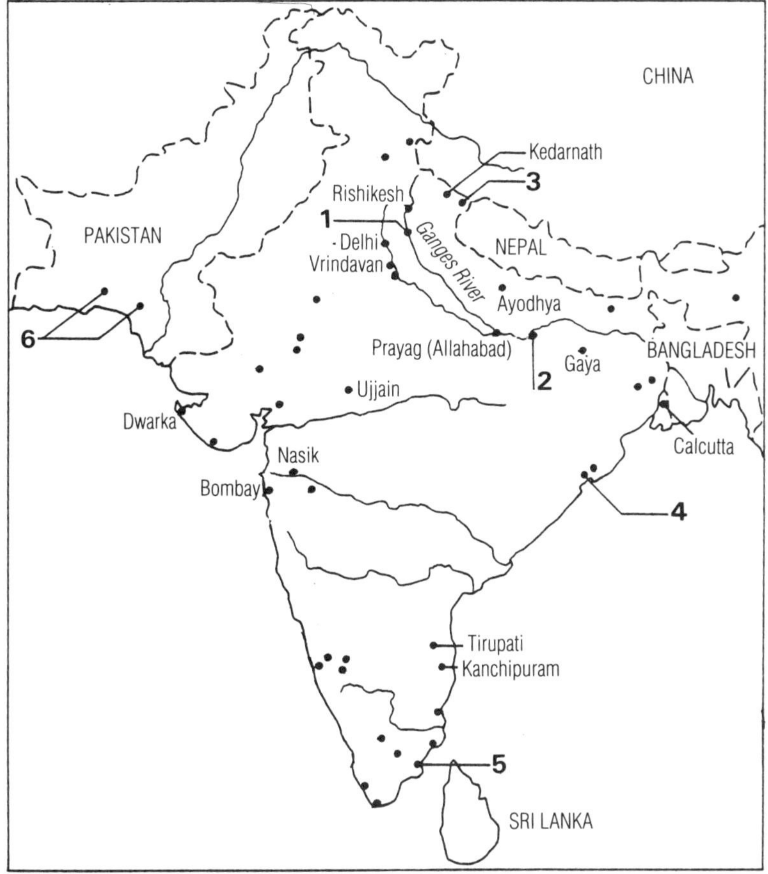

1 Hardwar means "Lord's Gate," a center where the ashes of the dead are committed to the Ganges
2 Benares on the Ganges river bank is a city of the god Shiva and an ancient center of Vedic scholarship
3 Badrinath has a shrine to Vishnu on a source of the Ganges
4 Purl is on the temple-rich Orissa coast.
5 Rameswaram is the most holy place after Benares, its island temple marks Rama's journey to rescue his wife Sita in Sri Lanka
6 Mohenjo-Daro and **Harappa** are cities of the Indus Valley civilization (c. 2500–1700 BC), which anticipated Hinduism in many ways

Pilgrimages

6434 Pilgrimage is an important feature of the Hindu faith and there are many holy and religious sites all over India such as Dwarka, Benares, and Badrinath. Pilgrimages are undertaken to show devotion to the faith, to perform ceremonial rites after a parent's death or as part of a religious festival. There are many sacred rivers and the Ganges River is considered to be the most sacred and the ideal place for funerals.

Principal pilgrimage sites in India

■ Place with religious significance for all Hindus in India, attracting many pilgrims

← A popular pilgrimage circuit lasting 10 weeks

The outlined shapes beside each place name denotes the principal deity or form of worship

□ Vishnu

△ Shiva

○ Sakta (Mother Goddess or Devi)

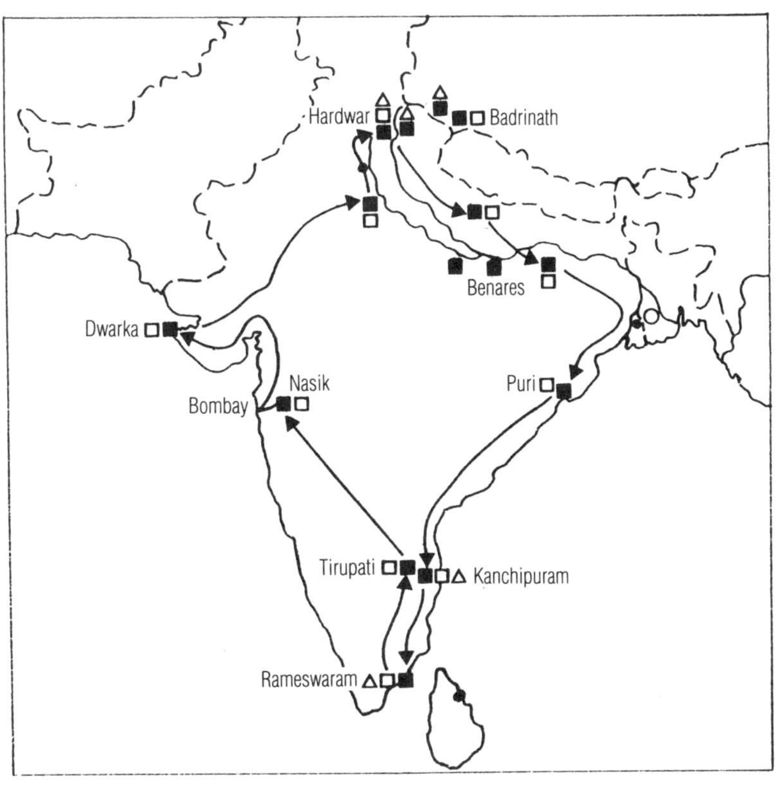

Modern Hinduism

6435 The 19th and 20th centuries produced changes and new religious movements in Hinduism. The mystic Ramakrishna came to the conclusion that "all religions are one" and that all religions are valid. One of Ramakrishna's followers, Narendranath Datta, founded the Ramakrishna Mission. He encouraged community service, helping the poor and he opposed the differences in caste. The Ramakrishna Mission is one of the most important developments in modern reformed Hinduism and has branches all over the world.

Hindu revival movements of the 19th and 20th centuries are closely linked with the growth in Indian nationalism and the struggle for India's independence from Britain. Mahatma Gandhi was a religious leader who became the most important figure in India's struggle for independence. He introduced the reforms in Hinduism to the majority of people and was also against the caste system. He was seen by his followers as the ideal Hindu although many of his ideas were influenced by Western thought.

In 1947 when India gained independence and was divided from Pakistan, nationalist feeling increased, leading to widening divisions between Muslims and Hindus. But the Indian government wanted to establish a non-religious state and later governments have kept to this. Laws have since been passed which make it illegal to discriminate against untouchables, men are only allowed one wife, divorce is allowed, women can inherit, and dowries are forbidden. Although many of the restrictive traditions of Hinduism are dying out, it is still a strong and growing religion.

Women and Hinduism

Hinduism is a strongly male-oriented religion although there are exceptions. A woman is under the authority of her father before marriage, then as a wife she is under the authority of the husband and later under the authority of her sons. It is stated in many sacred texts that a woman cannot be independent. She cannot own property except for jewelry. It is a woman's duty to wait on her husband and she is expected to maintain high standards of decorum and modesty in the company of other men. However Hinduism does stress that women should be treated with honor.

Since 1955 laws have been passed giving women more rights. Widows are now allowed to remarry and do not have to die with their husbands (*suttee*) or lead a life of withdrawal. Dowries are no longer necessary for girls and more women are being educated.

Essential Sikh beliefs

6436 Sikhism is monotheistic, holding there is only one God.

Sikhs follow the teachings, scriptures, and example of the Gurus. They adopt some of the Hindu beliefs, such as the theory of *samsara* - birth, death, and rebirth of the soul, and *karma* where the nature of one's life is determined by actions in a previous life. However, they maintain that God, known by many names and beyond comprehension, is the one and only reality, all else is illusion. Through the repetition of his name, singing hymns, and meditation under the guidance of a guru, Sikhs believe they can approach God. They oppose the structure of the Hindu caste system.

Sikhism forbids God being shown in pictures and forbids the worship of idols. Only the *Adi Granth* has become an object of intense reverence.

Reciting *nama* is important to Sikhs. The constant repetition of God's name and the divine hymns of the Gurus cleanse the soul, Sikhs believe, and conquers the ego. The taming of the ego is vital to overcome lust, anger, greed, attachment, and pride. Nama calms the wandering mind and creates stillness, it opens a channel through which divine light can enter the body. A person can then attain a state of absolute bliss.

Work, worship, and charity are the fundamental ideals of Sikh life and behavior.

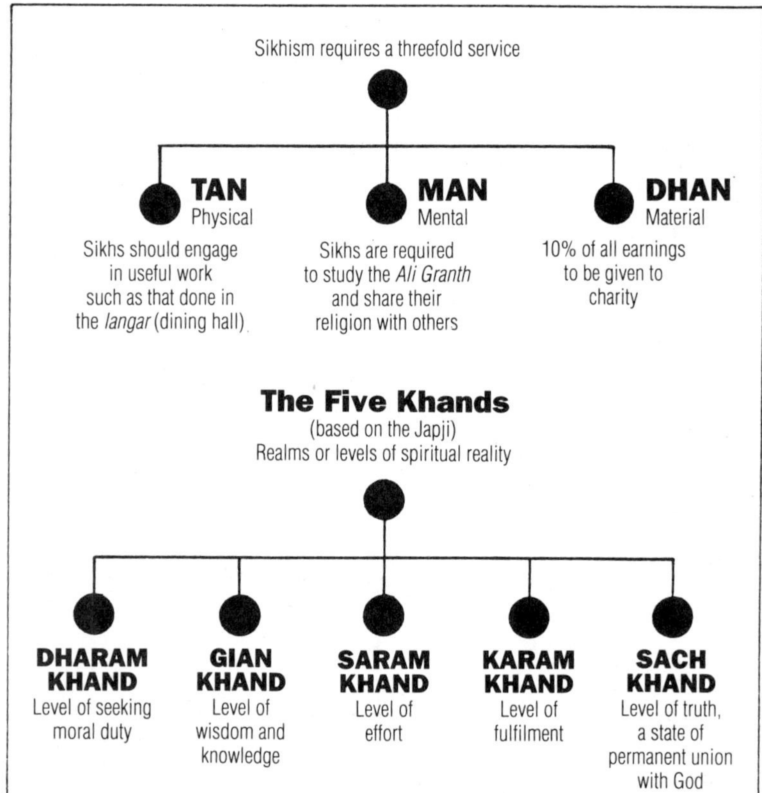
Sikhism requires a threefold service
TAN
Physical
Sikhs should engage in useful work such as that done in the *langar* (dining hall)
MAN
Mental
Sikhs are required to study the *Ali Granth* and share their religion with others
DHAN
Material
10% of all earnings to be given to charity
The Five Khands
(based on the Japji)
Realms or levels of spiritual reality
DHARAM KHAND
Level of seeking moral duty
GIAN KHAND
Level of wisdom and knowledge
SARAM KHAND
Level of effort
KARAM KHAND
Level of fulfilment
SACH KHAND
Level of truth, a state of permanent union with God

The Mool Mantra: root belief of Sikhism

The opening lines of the morning prayer *Japji* are called the *Mool Mantra*. The *Mool Mantra* sums up the beliefs of Sikhism taught by Guru Nanak.

There is one God,
Eternal Truth is His name;
Maker of all things,
Fearing nothing and at enmity with nothing
Timeless in His Image;
Not begotten, being of His own Being
By the grace of the Guru, made known to men.

Ik Oankar
"God is one being"

The *Mool Mantra* written in the Gurumurkhi script

ੴ ਸਤਿਨਾਮੁ ਕਰਤਾਪੁਰਖੁ ਨਿਰਭਉ ਨਿਰਵੈਰੁ
ਅਕਾਲ ਮੂਰਤਿ ਅਜੂਨੀ ਸੈਭੰ ਗੁਰ ਪ੍ਰਸਾਦਿ ॥

644 SACRED TEXTS

Hindu texts

6441 There are many sacred writings which have contributed to Hinduism's fundamental beliefs. They have developed over 1, 500 years and were written in Sanskrit, the ancient language of India. They are older than the sacred writings of any other religion.

The *Vedas* are the oldest Hindu scriptures. There are four *Vedas*, the *Rig Veda*, the *Sma-Veda*, the *Yajur Veda*, and the *Atharva Veda*. These have parts. First the *Samhitas* which contain prayers and hymns and are regarded as the most important part. Second the *Brahamanas* which concern ritual theology and include explanation of the *Samhitas*. Third, the *Upanishads* which are teachings and works of philosophy written in the form of a dialogue. A move away from rituals to philosophy particularly the doctrine of reincarnation.

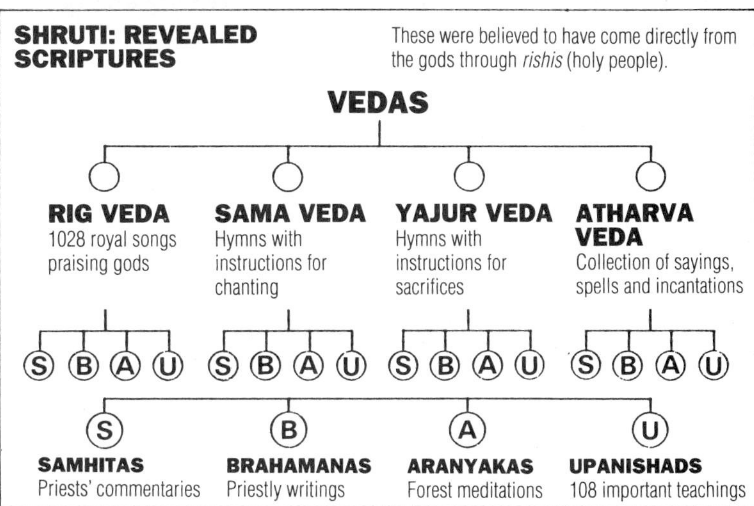

OTHER WRITINGS

The Puranas
The *Puranas* comprise long verse stories about important Hindu myths, gods, goddesses, and Hindu heroes.

The Ramayana
The *Ramayana* tells the story of Prince Rama and Sita his wife.

The Mahabharata
The *Mahabharata* is the great Indian story of a battle between the Pandavanas and the Kauravas.

The Bhagavad-Gita
The *Bhagavad-Gita* is a philosophical work which forms part of the *Mahabharata* and which discusses the meaning and nature of existence.

The Manu Smriti
The *Manu Smriti*, or *The Code of Manu*, is a basic source of Hindu religion and social law. One section explains the basis of the caste system.

Sikh texts

6442 **Adi Granth**
The most sacred book of the Sikh religion is the *Adi Granth* meaning the "first book." It was compiled in 1604 by the fifth Guru, Arjun. There are three versions, the one that is considered authentic was revised by Gobind Singh in 1704. The book contains nearly 6,000 hymns composed by the first five Gurus and hymns of the Bhakta saints and Muslim Sufis. It is placed on an altar in temples.

The Dasam Granth
This means "tenth book." It is a collection of writings said to be by Gobind Singh. There is disagreement as to the authenticity of this book. It is not considered as holy as the *Adi Granth*.

The Vars
The *Vars* are heroic ballads composed by Bhai Gurdas, who died in 1626.

The Rahatnamas
The Rahatnamas, or codes of conduct, contain traditions of the Khalsa.

645 PEOPLE

Aditi the unbound. Old Vedic goddess of the open sky, mother of all gods.
Agni old Vedic god. The life-force, god of fire and of sacrifice.
Ashoka Mauryan ruler of India from c. 265–238 BC. Buddhist but respected and recognized brahmans.
Banda Singh Bahadur Sikh military leader executed in 1716.
Bhakta saints Bhaktas were devotees or followers of the Hindu Vaisnava Bhakti movement between 1017 and 1137. The Bhaktas believed that God was beyond comprehension but that he was the only reality and that all else was illusion. The best way of approaching God was thought to be by chanting his name, singing hymns, and by doing good deeds. Bhaktas opposed the caste system. Sikhism has maintained many of their beliefs.
Bhindranwala, Jarnail Singh Sikh fundamentalist and militant leader in the 1970s. Died at Amritsar in 1984.
Brahma the creator of the world, the embodiment of ultimate reality. Brahma is not often worshipped as he is the One and the All.
Gandhi, Indira 1917–1984, Indian Prime Minister from 1966–77 and from 1980–4. Daughter of Jawaharlal Nehru, India's first prime minister after partition. Mrs Gandhi sought to fight mass poverty and limit population growth by encouraging birth control. Her modern views alienated some of the older members of the Congress Party.
Gandhi, Mahatma 1869–1948 religious leader with deep political beliefs. Thought of as a saint by many Indians. He lived an austere life, fasting and dressing in simple cloth. He was against the caste system, and discrimination against untouchables and women. He became leader of Indian National Congress and believed in Indian independence. Killed by a Hindu fanatic in 1948 amid tension between Hindus and Muslims.
Ganesha the elephant-headed god. A divinity of scribes and commerce. A god who both places obstacles before humans and removes them.
Hanuman the monkey god.
Kali the black goddess. She is the cruel and bloodthirsty wife of Shiva. Kali is also known as Durga. She is also called Parvati or Uma and as such represents the goddess of motherhood.

Gurus, Ten these are the ten Gurus, or religious leaders. Sikhs follow their teachings. The Gurus are:
Guru Nanak 1469–1539
Guru Angad 1539–52
Guru Amar Das 1469–1574
Guru Ram Das 1534–81
Guru Arjan 1563–1606
Guru Hargobind 1595–1644
Guru Har Rai 1630–61
Guru Har Krishan 1656–64
Guru Tegh Bahadur 1622–75
Guru Gobind Singh 1666–1708

Indra god of war, storm, and fertility. Old Vedic god who is now forgotten.
Krishna one of the most widely worshipped of Hindu gods, the greatest of the incarnations of Vishnu. He is a warrior, cowherd, lover, slayer of dragons. Through devotion to Krishna salvation is possible for everyone regardless of caste.

continued

People continued

645 **Lakshmi** goddess of beauty, wealth, and luck; wife of Vishnu.
Narendranath Datta follower of Ramakrishna. He assumed the religious name of Vivekananda. After lecturing in the USA and England he set up the Ramakrishna Mission in India.
Prajapati old Vedic god. Creator of the world and all life forms, later a title for Brahma.
Rama or Ramachandra heroic prince of the Ramayana epic. He is worshipped as an incarnation of Vishnu.
Ramakrishna Paramahamsa 1836–86, brahman given to mystic trances and visions in which he saw God in "everything." Studied other religions and announced that "all religions are one." Helped growth of Hinduism and raised national religious consciousness.
Ranjit Singh first Sikh maharaja of the Punjab.
Rudra Vedic god of the jungle, wild beasts, and disease. Later merged with Shiva.
Saravasti river goddess and consort of Brahma. Also goddess of knowledge and truth. Deity of writers and poets.
Sati first wife of Shiva. She began the practice of *suttee* in which widows burned themselves alive on their husbands' funeral pyres.
Shiva the destroyer of the universe. Male god who is the inspiration for good and evil acts and thoughts. He is the great ascetic deity sitting in meditation on the slopes of the Himalaya Mountains. He signifies eternal rest and ceaseless activity when he is shown as Natarjee, Lord of the Dance.
Surya old Vedic god of the Sun, the eye of Varuna. Later merged with Vishnu.
Varuna Vedic god of daylight, sky, and nature. Later became god of waters.
Vishnu preserver of the universe. Originally a Sun god, the decider of human destiny. Vishnu is believed to have appeared in many incarnations including human ones. There have been nine human incarnations of Vishnu, including both Rama and Krishna. Another final incarnation of Vishnu is expected when he will return to destroy the wicked and end the present age, to start a new golden age.

646 CALENDAR

Hindu calendar

6461 Hindu festivals vary widely according to location. Even the New Year celebration may take place on different days in different areas because some people use a lunar calendar and others use a solar calendar. The various deities may be worshipped in individual ways, resulting in a god's different aspects being celebrated at different times. Some festivals are only celebrated by a single village.

Festival of Diwali
Diwali means a garland of lights. It falls in the month of Karttika (October/November) and traditionally marks the beginning of the New Year in Gujarat. Lakshmi, the goddess of wealth, is remembered and thanked for her prosperity over the last year. Many Hindus look on the festival as celebrating the happy ending of the epic *Ramayana*, in which Rama and the monkey god, Hanuman, rescue Rama's wife Sita from Ravanna, the demon of darkness.
1 Rama
2 Sita
3 Hanuman
4 Lakshmi
5 Diva (small oil lamp)

	Hindu months	Festivals	
January	Magha	MAKER SANKRANTI Winter solstice festival and time for peace making	
February	Phalguna	SARASWATI PUJA Beginning of Spring dedication to Goddess Saraswati	MAHASHIVRATRI Great Shiva night
March	Chaitra	HOLI Spring festival	CHAITRA Regional New Year festival
April	Vaisakha	RAM NAVAMI Birthday of Rama, 7th avatar of Vishnu	
May	Jyestha		
June	Ashadha	RATHA YATRA Celebration of Krishna as Jagannatha, Lord of the Universe	
July	Sravana		
August	Bhadrapada	RAKSHA BANDHAN Holiday for brothers and sisters	JANAMASHTAMI Celebration of Krishna's birth
September	Asvina	NAVARATRI DURGA PUJA DUSSEHRA Commemorates Rama's victory over Ravanna	
October	Karttika	DIWALI New Year festival and festival of lights	
November	Margasirsha		
December	Pausa		
January			

1

2

3

4

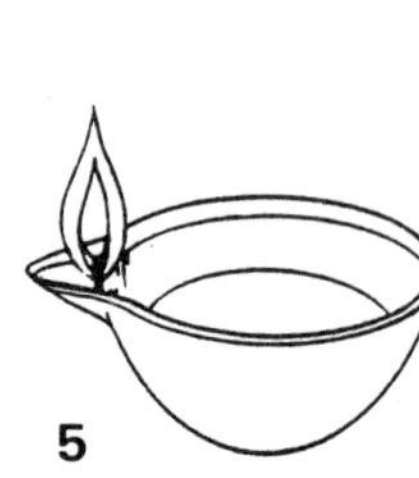
5

Sikh calendar

6462 **Baisakhi: New Year festival**

Baisakhi marks the beginning of the Sikh New Year. It falls on 13 or 14 April. On Baisakhi in 1699, Guru Gobind Singh founded the Khalsa fellowship at Anandpur and the five Ks were adopted. Sikhs also took additional names: Singh (meaning lion) for men and Kaur (meaning princess) for women. The festival has three major functions as charted here.

RELIGIOUS

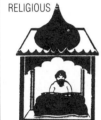

Faith renewed

Khalsa foundation commemorated and new members initiated

A complete reading of the *Adi Granth*

SOCIAL

Annual fairs

Livestock sold

Start of corn harvest

POLITICAL

Nisan Sahib flag replaced at each temple

Rally at the Jallianwala Bagh to mark 1919 Amristar massacre of Sikhs

	Sikh calendar	Festivals	
January	**Magh**	MAGHI	
February	**Phalgan**	HOLA MOHALLA (Day of military power)	
March	**Chait**		
April	**Vaisakh**	BAISAKHI (New Year)	
May	**Jaith**	Martyrdom of Guru Arjun	
June	**Har**	Birthday of Guru Har Krishan	
July	**Sawan**		
August	**Bhadro**	RAKHSHA BANDHAN	
September	**Asun**	Installation of Guru Granth Sahib	Birthday of Guru Ram
October	**Katik**	Birthday of Guru Nanak	DIWALI (Release of Guru Hargobind)
November / December	**Magar**	Martyrdom of Guru Tegh Bahardur	
January	**Poh**	Birthday of Guru Gobind Singh	LOHRI

647 DISTRIBUTION

Hindus

There are about 600 million Hindus in India. Sri Lanka also contains a sizable Hindu population. Minor Hindu populations are found in Bali, east Africa, parts of the Caribbean and South-east Asia.

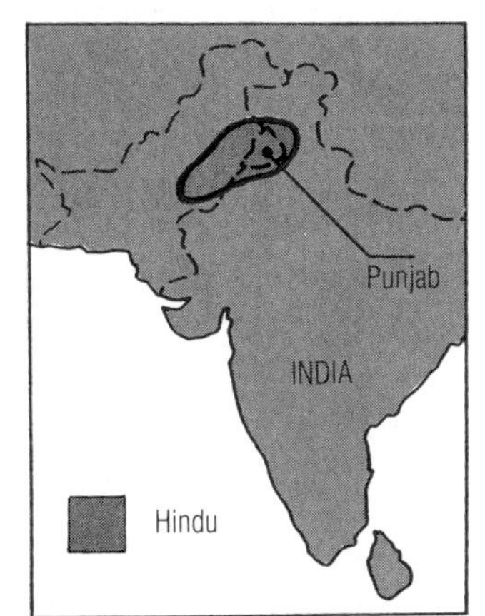

Sikhs

There are approximately 14 million Sikhs living in India. They live predominantly in north India in the Punjab State.

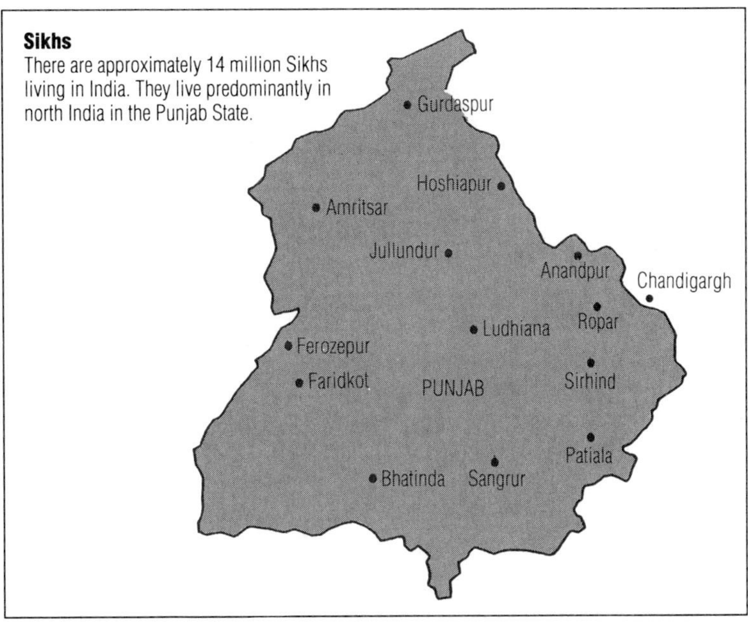

648 CEREMONIAL AND HOLY OBJECTS

Hindu ceremonial and holy objects

6481 **arati deep** For performance of the *arati* ceremony. This includes five wicks symbolizing the five elements (earth, fire, water, air, and space). Light symbolizes enlightenment, removal of darkness and ignorance, and is a symbol of the presence of God.
bell Rung to call the attention of the believers to worship and to concentrate their minds on prayer.
conch shell Blown in a temple to attract the attention of the worshippers and to concentrate their minds. Also a symbol of worship.
diwali deep Diva lamps filled with vegetable oil or ghee (clarified butter) and cotton wicks. Lit at Diwali festival.
garlands Used to decorate and honor deities and worn by Hindus at festivals.
incense burner To make a pleasing smell for the deity.
mandala Means circle. It is a visual representation of a sacred truth about the universe and the mystic forces it contains.
moorti images Gods are seen as incarnations of Brahman, revealing different sides of the One Reality. *Moorti* are placed at the center of shrines.
offerings These are presents to the gods. They may be sweets, flowers, or money.
prayer beads An aid to meditation and prayer. There are 108 beads.
puja tray *Puja* takes place in the home and in the temple. The objects on the tray are a bell, a diva, an incense holder, a water pot, and spoon, and a dish for sandalwood paste.
sandalwood paste Paste used to mark the forehead of the deity and the followers.
water pot Symbolizes cleaning and purification. Spoon used to offer water to the god and the followers.

Sikh ceremonial and holy objects

6482 ***Adi Granth*** The holy book is regarded as an eternal guru and is treated as a living teacher.
bata and khanda Iron bowl used to hold sweet water called *amrit* which is stirred with the *Khanda*, or double-edged sword. The *amrit* is sprinkled on Sikh initiates as they join the Sikh brotherhood.
chakkara An energy circle (*see* circle on Khanda badge) worn on turban.
chola/ bana Traditional tunic.
ek onkar Symbol of belief in one God.
keski Small under-turban.
khanda symbol Double-edged sword that represents the oneness of God. The two kirpans, or swords, represent spiritual and temporal justice. The circle represents the unity of God. This is the symbol of Sikhism.
nishan sahib Saffron-colored flag flown outside the Gurdwara. The symbol of the *khanda* is shown on it.
Nit Nem Gutka A book of prayers and hymns used in the home and Gurdwara.
patka A square peice of cloth worn by Sikh boys until they are capable of tying their own turban.
romalla Beautiful material used to cover the *Adi Granth* in the gurdwara. Dedicated by the congregation.
simran mala prayer beads 108 beads used to repeat the God, Waheguru, "Wonderful Lord, The Vast Creator."
turban Length of muslin cloth, traditionally white, black, blue, or saffron. Usually about 16 x 3 ft (5 x 1 m) and regarded as a spiritual crown. It is a distinct identification of a Sikh.

Five Ks Worn by any baptized Sikh either male or female. They are:
- **Kach** shorts worn for ease of movement, a symbol of modesty and high moral character
- **Kanga** wooden comb used for hair and to rid the wearer of impurities of thought
- **Kada** an iron bangle worn on the wrist as a reminder of a Sikh's unity with God, the Guru, and the Khasa brotherhood. Symbol of restraint and a reminder to do good
- **Kesh** uncut hair. This shows acceptance of God's will and teaches humility and acceptance
- **Kirpan** a sword. A symbol of honour, bravery, courage, dignity, duty, justice, and self-sacrifice. A reminder to defend and protect the weak and uphold the truth

649 GLOSSARY

Adi Granth Sikh sacred book.
Aryans Ancient invaders of India and founders of the Hindu religion.
atman Essence or principle of life: reality in individual forms.
Bhagavad-Gita Philosophical work forming part of *Mahabharata*.
Brahma The all-pervading power.
brahman Priest or teacher.
caste A system of class differentiation based on Hindu scriptures.
cow All cows are seen as sacred or holy and are the subject of worship.
dharma Moral and religious duty. Right way of living.
Diwali Four-day New Year festival.
Ganges Hinduism's sacred river.
guru Spiritual leader who embodies the teachings of his order and the founder-deity and receives pupils in his ashram.
gurdwara A Sikh temple.
Hare Krishna Movement This is another name for the International Society for Krishna Consciousness which was founded by Swami Prabhupada in 1965 following the teachings of a 16th-century holy man, Chaitanya.
Indian National Congress Established in 1885 and the party which took up the fight for Indian independence. Later, the governing party in India for most of the years after partition in 1947.
khalsa Baptized Sikhs. The word means "pure ones."
kharma Literally "action." Moral law of cause and effect governing the future. Bad actions lead to rebirth in the lower orders. Good behavior leads to rebirth in the higher orders.
Mahabharata Great story of battle between Pandavas and the Kauravas.
moksha Release, liberation from continuous rebirth.
monotheistic Believing in one god only.
Om or **aum** The symbol of Hinduism and of Hindu *dharma*. It represents Brahman and is the first sound which began creation. By chanting *om*, Hindus identify themselves as part of the whole of creation.
puja A performed ceremony and prayer.
Punjab Region that lies between India and Pakistan.
samsara The endless cycle of life, death, and rebirth governed by law and kharma.
Sanskrit Ancient language of India, considered to be sacred.
untouchables Members of no caste. They are considered impure and treated as outcasts.
Vedas Four books forming the Hindu sacred texts.

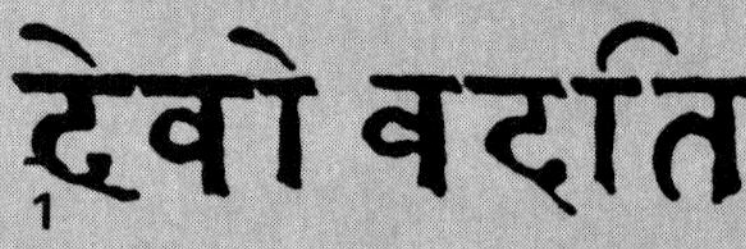

Sanskrit (1) Ancient language of India, considered to be sacred.

651 HISTORY

Buddhism: timeline

6511 **c. 563–483 BC** Buddha alive. Spread of Buddhism in India.
4th century BC Spread of Theravada Buddhism. Spread of Buddhism to Nepal.
3rd–2nd centuries Spread of Buddhism in Sri Lanka.
c. 274–236 BC Spread of Buddhism by Emperor Ashoka in India
1st century BC Spread of Mahayana Buddhism and spread of Buddhist religion to China.
3rd century AD Spread of Buddhism to Korea.
AD 402 Pure Land Buddhism.
5th–6th centuries Spread of Buddhism to Japan.
6th–7th centuries Buddhism spreads to Tibet.
7th century Spread of Buddhism to Thailand.
1191 Zen Buddhism.
1253 Nichiren Buddhism.
14th–15th century Rise of Tibetan Buddhism, sometimes called Lamaism.
16th century Spread of Buddhism to Mongolia.
18th century Buddhism spreads to Europe and America.
1959 Annexation of Tibet by China.

Buddha

6512 Buddha is the name given to the founder of Buddhism, Siddhartha Gautama. He lived around 563-483 BC and he was born in the part of India which is now Nepal. There is almost no real historical information about his life. The Buddha's followers spread his story which has an important place in Buddhism.

He grew up at his father's palace, the warrior Prince Suddodhana, and later Gautama married the Princess Yasodhara. When he was 29 he had a series of four visions. In the first he saw an old man, in the second he saw a sick man, and in the third he saw a corpse. In the fourth he met a wandering holy man. The first three visions convinced Gautama that life involved aging, sickness, and death. The vision of the holy man led him to leave his wife and son to seek religious enlightenment which would free him from the suffering of life.

Gautama became a wandering monk for six years, seeking enlightenment by suffering extreme self-denial and self-torture. He lived in filth and sometimes ate only a grain of rice. Finally, Gautama gave this up, deciding that this did not lead to enlightenment. One day he wandered into a village near Gaya and sat under a bodhi tree to meditate, determined to remain there until he gained enlightenment. This occured at dawn. People learned of the event and called him the Buddha, which means Enlightened One. The Buddha learned from his enlightenment that it was possible to escape from life's suffering.

For the rest of his life the Buddha preached the message of how to overcome suffering, which is called *dharma*, or the saving truth. The Buddha preached his first sermon to five holy men in Varanasi (Benares) and this has become one of the most important Buddhist events.

The Buddha preached the *dharma* all over northern India, gradually drawing more followers. He organized them into a religious community of monks, nuns, and laity. Fame of the Buddha's powers, religious insight, and compassion increased and spread. At 80 the Buddha became ill and died. His disciples burned his body and distributed his bones as holy relics which many followers still believe retain the Buddha's powers.

Sacred places and symbols associated with the life of Buddha

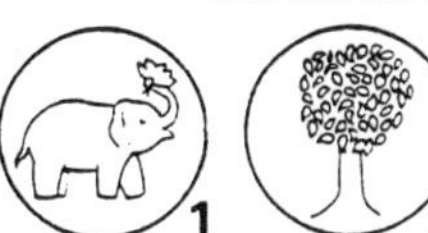

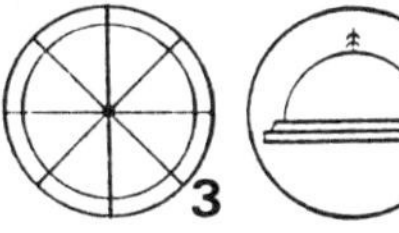

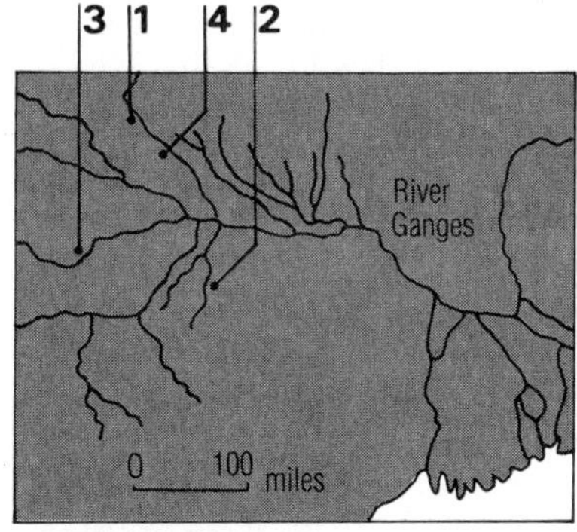

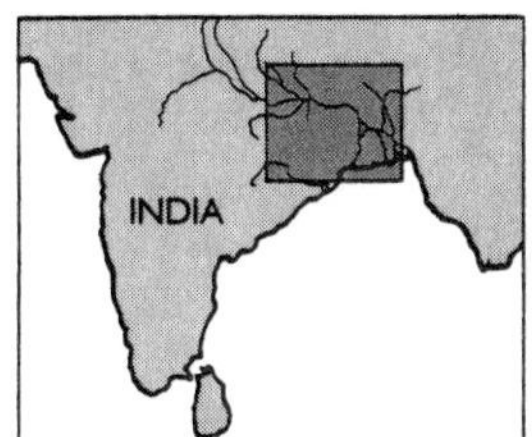

	1	2	3	4
Modern	Rummindei	Bodh-Gaya	Varanasi	Kusinagara
Old name	Lumbini	Buddha-Gaya	Sarnath	Kusinara
Symbol	White elephant	Bodhi tree	Dharma wheel	Stupa
Meaning	Birth	Enlightenment	First sermon	Death

Spread of Buddhism

6513 **Buddhism in China**

In the period from AD 150–1000 Buddhism spread widely in China through the study of the *Sutras* in translation. This is due to Indian culture expanding into central Asia and China and important political and trade links. During the 4th century Buddhism was the dominant religion in China. Although there were wars throughout this century and the northern area was overrun by barbarians, many of the barbarian chiefs were converted to Buddhism. Gentlemen of the imperial court were also converted.

In the 5th century the earliest examples of Chinese Buddhist art appeared. The 8th–9th centuries saw the spread of the Pure Land Sect. In the 13th–14th century the Mongols ruled China and accepted Buddhism. China remained Buddhist until the overthrow of the Manchurian dynasty in 1911. In 1931 China became Communist and Buddhism has only survived in a restricted form. In 1950 Communist China moved into Tibet, later absorbing it. The Dalai Lama and many of his followers fled to India. Monastery lands are now restricted and Buddhists have been mistreated.

Buddhism in Japan

Buddhism first arrived from Korea in the 6th century and it dominated cultural life in Japan until the 17th century. During the 7th century, under a series of Buddhist rulers, Buddhism became well established and during the 8th century Buddhist monks became an important part of the imperial administration. Between 1150 and 1300 Buddhism became the religion of the Japanese people. Before this it had been a religion of the upper classes. Zen Buddhism, which was known in the 9th century, became established around 1200. The Nichiren Sect was also founded around this time and gained a large following. It is still a large sect in Japan today. From 1603 to 1863 the Tokugawa regime restricted Buddhist preaching. But today Japan is still mainly Buddhist and is probably the best educated and richest of the Buddhist countries.

Jainism: timeline

6514

Along with Hinduism and Buddhism, Jainism is one of the three most ancient of India's religions still in existence. Although Jainism has less followers than Hinduism and Sikhism it has had an influence on Indian culture for over 2,500 years, making significant contributions in philosophy, logic, art and architecture, grammar, mathematics, astronomy, astrology, and literature. Jainism is based on the teachings of Vardhamana who is called Mahavira, or the great hero. He is regarded as the last of a line of about 24 holy and spiritually enlightened beings, the Tirthankaras.

6th century BC Vardhamana born in east India. He was the son of a chieftain and a contemporary of the Buddha. At the age of 30 he renounced his princely status to take up an ascetic life and he began his teachings. With his 11 disciples he founded monastic orders.
3rd century BC Split occurs and two sects are created, the Svetambaras (white-robed) and the Digambaras (sky-clad, or naked). The two sects argue over proper monastic attire and whether or not a soul can obtain liberation from a female body.
4th–5th centuries AD Four councils are held to formulate, preserve, and codify teachings of Mahavira in written form. Further split over texts occurs. Irrevocable split in the two communities.
AD 320–c. 600 Gupta dynasty. Jainas retain patronage of Gupta emperors of Magadha. They become stronger in central and western India.
500–1100 The Digambara community in the south flourishes under various dynasties.
1100–1800 Period of great influence from 6th to 12th century. Jaina monks stop being wandering ascetics and tend to become dwellers at temples and monasteries.
1400–1800 Digambara Jainism loses significant royal support and influence. Reform within its community begins.
late 16th century Layman and poet Banarasidas attacks ritualism and behavior of religious leaders.
1800–present Svetambara Jainism is stronger, with a larger monastic community and more effective organization than the Digambara. Both committed to *ahimsa* (non-violence.)

652 ORGANIZATION

Buddhist schools

6521

Various Buddhist schools have developed in India and other Asian countries, including the Theravada, the Mahayana, the Mantrayana, and the Zen.

Theravada Buddhism

Theravada means "way of the elders." This is the only early school of Buddhism which has survived. In some parts of South-east Asia, in Sri Lanka and Thailand it is the main form of Buddhism. Theravada Buddhism emphasizes the Buddha's historical importance, strict observance of monastic life and the authority of the *Tripitaka*.

Mahayana Buddhism

Most followers of Mahayana Buddhism live in Japan and east Asia. Mahayana means "greater vehicle." The followers of this type of Buddhism believe in the existence of many Buddhas. Attention is often focused on buddhas in heaven and the goal of religious practice is Buddahood, becoming a buddha. Mahayana followers believe that these buddhas can save people's lives through grace and compassion. Mahayana Buddhists have their own scriptures which they believe reveal a higher level of truth. The Mahayana school encourages everyone to follow the ideal of a *bodhisattva* who is a person who vows to become a buddha by leading a virtuous life.

The Mantrayana school

Mantrayana means holy recitation. The majority of followers of this sort of Buddhism are in the Himalayas, Mongolia, and Japan, where it is called Shingon. Mantrayana Buddhism accepts most of the ideas and beliefs of the Mahayana school. It also emphasizes a close relationship between a spiritual leader and a small group of disciples. Much of the disciples' time is spent reciting chants called mantras, dancing, and meditating. Many followers believe in devils, goblins and other gods. Magic also plays a part in the teachings and rituals of Mantrayana Buddhism. Some branches of Mantrayana Buddhism use sexual symbolism and believe sex should be used for holy purposes.

Zen Buddhism

Zen Buddhism is practiced mainly in Japan, although it originated in China and was called Chan. Zen Buddhism accepts most of the beliefs of the Mahayana school and emphasizes a close relationship between master and disciples. Zen has also developed its own practices to lead to a state of spiritual enlightenment, called *satori*. Some believers think *satori* is reached suddenly, while others believe it is a gradual process.

Buddhist monks and nuns

6522

Sangha refers to the order of Buddhist monks and nuns and to the community of monks, nuns, and laity. It sometimes also refers to the ideal Buddhist community consisting of those who have reached the higher stages of spiritual development.

Since the origins of Buddhism, monks, and nuns have played an important part in preserving and spreading the faith, and the monasteries have become centers of Buddhist learning. Within their communities the monks and nuns act as examples to the lay members and teach morality.

The monasteries also offer a monk an opportunity to retreat from the world. Many Buddhist groups believe that the discipline of monastic life is necessary for those who want to attain *nirvana*. In most Buddhist countries monks are expected to live a life of poverty, meditation, chastity, and study.

Some Buddhists only join the *sangha* for short periods, they are not monks or nuns for life. Monks wear special robes and are a common sight in all Buddhist countries.

The laity also plays an important part in the role of the *sangha*. They are expected to honor the Buddha, follow basic moral rules, and to support the monks.

Monks and nuns are called *bikkhu* (meaning beggar.) They do not beg and may only accept gifts such as food from people wishing to donate it as a noble act. They do not own anything except:

Three pieces of cloth for robes

Alms bowl to collect gifts of food; the lid is used as a plate

A piece of rope (girdle) for holding robes together

A water strainer

A razor

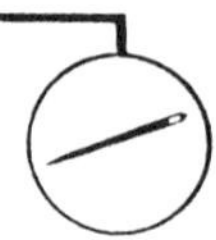

A needle

Places of worship

6523 There are three main types of Buddhist building. The first is the *stupa* which is a commemorative relic mound. The second is a *caitya* – a temple including a *stupa* or an image of Buddha. The *vihara*, or monastery, is a place for monks. It is a non-religious building but often a *stupa* or images are enclosed in the monastery making it a religious place.

The *stupa*
The *stupa* is the most important Buddhist monument and focus for devotion. It was built to house the Buddha's relics or those of his disciples or to remember a place in Buddhist history. It is a dome resting on a base which is surrounded by a fence. A square railing or boxlike structure rests on the top of the dome from which rises a pole or steeple. In some places the *stupa* is of a slightly different shape. The pagodas of China and Japan are *stupas*. Their shape may have developed from the Chinese watchtowers or from tall *stupas* in India.

The *caitya*
Caitya means temple. In the past it was used to refer to holy objects. A *caitya* usually consists of a hall which contains a sacred object such as a small *stupa* or an image of Buddha.

The *vihara*
The *vihara*, or monastery was first built in a rectangular or square shape with a central courtyard used for teaching. It contained chapels for images and sometimes the courtyard contained a *stupa*. The whole monastery was usually surrounded by a wall. But the monasteries vary in design because of weather conditions, local building styles, and the number of members. In Tibet the monasteries are large high rectangular buildings. North Indian monasteries are almost all surrounded by walls. The *huha* is a monastery built in a cave and can be found all over southern and western India as well as China.

Jaina sects

6524 The two main sects in Jainism are the Digambara and the Svetambara.

The Digambara
The name of these monks means "sky-clad" because of their vow of nudity. They renounce and reject all earthly possessions including clothes and believe that enlightenment is impossible for women.

The Svetambara
This means "white-robed." The monks and nuns renounce all earthly possessions except clothes and believe that women may obtain enlightenment. They focus on the writings of the *Agama*.

A Jaina monk must take the following vows:
- No injury or killing of any living thing
- No stealing
- No lying
- No sexual intercourse
- No possession of property

The laity support monks and nuns and obey less strict rules of conduct. They are not allowed to engage in the killing of anything. A majority of them follow business activities to avoid being involved in military careers. They prepare to be monks and nuns in a future life.

Jaina temple worship

6525 Gods are worshipped and this action is supposed to help the discipline of the believer. Worship takes place daily in the morning and in the evening. It is conducted by a temple priest, or *pujari*. Almost every village in a Jaina area will have its own temple where names of the Jinas are recited and idol worship practiced. Offerings might be made to the image.

Sacred places in Asia

6526 **1** Sanchi, the Great Stupa begun c. 250 BCE by Emperor Ashoka
2 Potala and Chorten, palace of Dalai Lamas and funeral pyre
3 Phra Pathom Chedi, the tallest Thai Stupa 380 ft (116 m) begun c. 500 CE (west of Bangkok)
4 Wild Goose Pagoda at an old imperial capital
5 Ruvanveliseya Dagoba, pre-760 CE temple in the old Sinhalese capital
6 Shwe Dagon pagoda, gold-covered 326 ft (99 m) focal point of the Burmese capital and center of Burma's religious life
7 Borobudur stupa built c. 800 CE, unique eight-terraced temple mountain with 72 Buddhas in the circular terraces
8 Horyuji pagoda built 607 CE, oldest of the Seven Great Temples of the Southern Capital (Nara)

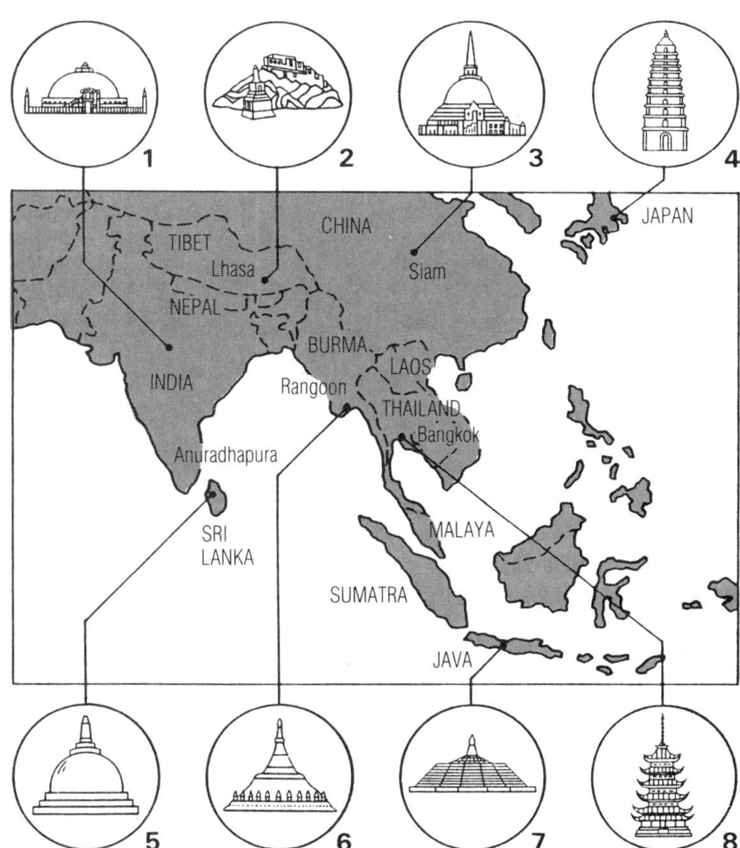

653 BELIEFS

Buddhist beliefs

6531 All Buddhists believe the *triratna*, meaning the Threefold Refuge or Three Jewels which commit a follower to achieving a certain way of life. The Threefold Refuge consists of:
1 Belief in the Buddha
2 Belief in the Buddha's teachings, called the *dharma*
3 Belief in the *sangha*, the religious community founded by Buddha

Buddhism also lists traditional moral guides which must be followed. A Buddhist who is not a monk or a nun must not kill, steal, behave improperly in sexual matters, must not lie or drink alcohol. People who are training to become monks or nuns or who are committed to a stricter way of life must also not eat at forbidden times which is after midday, not take part in singing, dancing, or other amusements, wear any decoration, perfume, or cosmetics, must not live in a luxurious way, and must not accept money for themselves.At every Buddhist shrine and meeting of Buddhists, belief in the Buddha is confirmed by repeating:

"To the Buddha for refuge I go
To the Dharma for refuge I go
To the Sangha for refuge I go."

The Buddhist dharma

6532 Buddhists believe that the self is not permanent but subject to change and decay. Existence is a continuing cycle of death and life. Each person's position is determined by behavior in previous lives. Good deeds may lead to rebirth as a wise or wealthy person. Bad deeds may lead to rebirth as a poor or ill person or even in hell. The Buddha taught that as long as man remained in the cycle of death and rebirth he could never be free of pain and suffering. In the Four Noble Truths Buddha acknowledges suffering. It is attachment to earthly things, which are impermanent, that causes delusion, suffering, greed. By ridding themselves of such earthly attachments people could gain perfect peace and happiness. This is called *nirvana*. Buddha said that those who were willing to follow the Middle Way and the Noble Eightfold Path will conquer their attachment of worldly things and achieve nirvana.

The Middle Way
This is a way of life which steers a middle path between the uncontrolled satisfaction of human desires and extreme forms of self-denial.

The Four Noble Truths
The Buddha acknowledged the existence and source of suffering in the Four Noble Truths. He showed the way out of this by following the Eightfold Path. The four Noble Truths consist of:
- The noble truth of suffering. All suffering is part of life on Earth
- The noble truth of the origin of suffering. Suffering arises from craving and desire
- The noble truth of the end of desire. To stop desire means to stop suffering
- The noble truth of the way to the end of desire. The end of desire comes by following the Noble Eightfold Path

The Noble Eightfold Path
The Noble Eightfold Path consists of:
- Right understanding. Knowledge of the truth
- Right purpose. The intention to resist evil
- Right speech. Saying nothing to hurt others
- Right action
- Right livelihood. Having a job that does not harm others
- Right effort. Trying to free one's mind of evil thoughts
- Right thought. Controlling one's feelings and thoughts
- Right concentration. Practicing proper forms of concentration

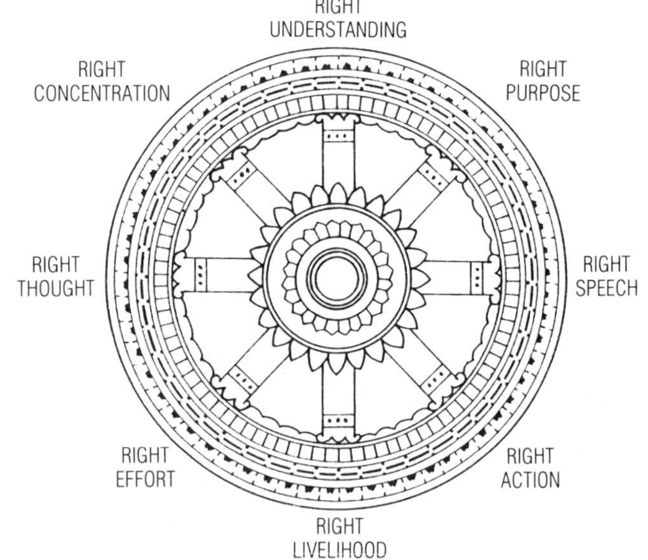

Jaina beliefs

6533 The ultimate religious goal of the Jainist is salvation by complete perfection and purification of the soul. In Jainism there is no diety. It is a monastic, ascetic religion. The great preachers are honored but not worshipped as gods. Basic beliefs are:

1 Every living thing (including earth, water, wind) consists if an eternal soul, the *jiva*, and a temporary physical body
2 The eternal *jiva* is trapped in the body by worldly activities
3 To free the *jiva* we must avoid worldly activities as much as possible
4 Each *jiva* is reincarnated in different bodies before it is finally liberated
5 If the *jiva* is freed it will exist eternally in a perfect state.

The most important figures in Jaina legend are the 24 Tirthankaras. These perfected human beings appear from time to time to preach, teach, and embody the Jaina religious path. Mahavira was the 24th and last.

Ahimsa
Ahimsa is the Jaina doctrine of non-injury to any life form. It is very strictly followed. A monk may hold a mask over his mouth in order not to kill any insect. He may also carry a broom to sweep the path in front of his feet in order not to harm insects as he walks. Jainism orders avoidance of all forms of injury whether committed by body, mind, or speech.

The Three Jewels
The Three Jewels, or *ratnatraya*, are the basis of Jaina ethics. Right knowledge, faith, and conduct must be encouraged together.
- Right faith leads to calmness, kindness, and the rejection of pride of birth, beauty of form, health, prowess, and fame
- Right knowledge consists of clear distinction between the self and the non-self, knowledge of scriptures and inner self. The mind must be purged by right faith and conduct. Ignorance must be eliminated and teachings understood
- Right conduct is attained gradually through following the doctrine of *ahimsa* and self-control, ideally by keeping the five great vows required of monks and nuns

654 SACRED TEXTS

Buddhist texts

6541 After the Buddha's death his followers collected the traditions which had developed around the *dharmas*. The oldest Buddhist school compiled a scripture called the *Tripitaka* which means three baskets. The writings date from the 2nd through the 6th centuries. The *Tripitaka* contains three parts. The first is the *Vinaya Pitaka*, or the basket of discipline, and it contains rules of conduct governing the life of a Buddhist monk or nun. The second book, the *Sutta Pitaka*, is called the basket of doctrine. It contains mainly Buddha's dialogues and teachings. The *Abhidamma Pitaka* is the last book and is called the basket of higher *dharma*. It contains higher teachings or philosophy.

The Mahayana Buddhists also have their own scriptures called the *Prajnaparamita Sutras*. They are a guide to perfect wisdom, the *Saddharmapundarika* which means the lotus of the good law, the *Lankavatara* which means the revelation of the teaching in Lanka, and the *Sukhavativyuha*, a desription of the paradise of Sukhavati.

Some scriptures of the Theravada (Way of Elders) or Southern School of Buddhism

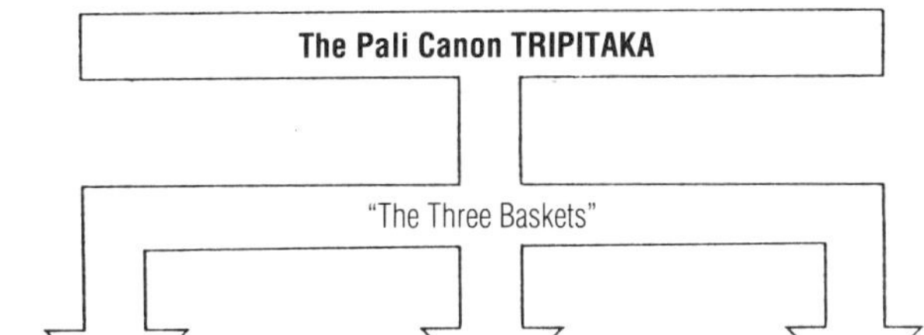

VINAYA PITAKA
Discipline
Discipline or rules of conduct governing the way of life of Buddhist monks and nuns

SUTTA PITAKA
Doctrine
The oldest dialogues or teachings given by the Buddha

ABHIDAMMA PITAKA
Philosophy
Higher teachings or philosophy, included in the Pali Canon

Some scriptures recognized by Mahayana Buddhists:

Prajnaparamita Sutras
Guide to perfect wisdom

Saddharmapundarika Sutra
The Lotus of the Good Law

Lankavatara Sutra
Revelation of the teaching in Lanka

Sukhavativyuha
Description of the Paradise of Sukhavati

Jaina holy books

6542 Scriptures do not belong to a single period as they have been revised and had additions made at various times. The Svetambaras follow a large canon, the *agama*, which is based on compilations by Mahavira's disciples of his talks. There are around 45 texts in the canon.

The Digambara give canonical status to two works, the *Karmaprabhrta* and the *Kasayaprabhrta*. The former deals with the doctrine of *karman*, a phenomenon linked together in a universal chain of cause and effect. All events have a definite cause. The latter deals with the passions that defile and bind the soul.

655 PEOPLE

Ashoka 265–238 BC, Indian emperor who made Buddhism a national religion.
Banarasidas 16th-century layman and poet who brought about reform in Jainism.
Bodhisattvas Bodhisattva (bodhi = enlightened; sattva = a being) is an enlightened being. In Theravada Buddhism, bodhisattvas often embody ideals of life and compassion for the help of lesser beings as opposed to Theravada self-salvation. Bodhisattva figures vary according to the country of origin. The one shown (**1**) is a prominent Mahayana bodhisattva, Avalokitesvara, who looks down with compassion.
Dalai Lama A lama in Tibetan Buddhism is a spiritual leader. Some lamas are thought to be reincarnations of their predecessors. Other lamas have gained their position because of the high level of spiritual development they have achieved. The Dalai Lama is the highest of the reincarnated lamas. He was also the temporal ruler of Tibet until 1959 when he went into exile.
Nichiren 1222–82, founder of the Nichiren sect of Buddhism in Japan. Nichiren said all other sects should be suppressed. He was banished and chased from place to place but he gained a large following due to his prophesies.
Rahula the Buddha's son.
Tirthankara meaning ford-maker. These are the Jinas. They are the revealers of the Jaina religious path, who have crossed over life's streams of rebirths and set a clear example to follow.
Vardhamana known as Mahavira the "great hero." The 24th Tirthankara of the current age and founder of Jainism.
Yasodhara the Buddha's wife.

1

656 CALENDAR

The Buddhist calendar

6561 The Buddhist year is based on the lunar calendar. Each month ends on a full moon and festivals are celebrated on full moon days. Followers of Theravada Buddhism and Mahayana Buddhism do not always celebrate festivals at the same time. For example, in Japan and other places where Mahayana Buddhism is followed, the Buddha's birth, enlightnement and death are celebrated on three different days.

Western month	Buddhist month	Significance of full moon day
April	**CITTA**	Celebration of Buddha's role as peacemaker
May	**VESAKHA**	Birth, Enlightenment and Death of the Buddha
June	**JETTHA**	Commemorates spread of Buddhism
July	**ASALHA**	Buddha's departure from home and his first sermon remembered
August	**SAVANA**	Start of the rains: retreat season for monks and nuns
September	**POTTHAPADA**	
October	**ASSAYUIA**	
November	**KATTIKA**	End or the rains retreat. Commemoration of first Buddhist missionaries
December	**MAGGASIRA**	First community of nuns founded by Theri Sanghamitta in Sri Lanka
January	**PHUSSA**	Celebrates Buddha's first visit to Sri Lanka
February	**MAGHA**	Assembly of Buddha's disciples and Buddha's renunciation of his life
March	**PHAGGUNA**	Buddha's return home and conversion of his family to Buddhism

Jaina festivals

6562 The major Jaina festivals are connected with five major events in the life of each Tirthankara. The most popular festival is Paijusana in the month of Bhadrapada (August-September). An occasion of forgiving and giving to the poor.

Twice a year for nine days (in March-April and September-October) a fasting ceremony takes place, known as Oli.

On the full-moon day of the month of Karttika (October-November), at the same time that Hindus celebrate Diwali, Jaina followers remember the Nirvana of Mahavira by lighting lamps.

Mahavira Jayanti celebrates Mahavira's birthday in March or early April. Jainas also celebrate some festivals in common with Hindus such as Holi and Navaratra.

657 DISTRIBUTION

Buddhism
Buddhism has about 300 million followers worldwide. Many Buddhist live in Sri Lanka, South-east Asia, and Japan.

Jainism
Well over two million people are followers of Jainism. The majority live in India, but some are scattered throughout the world.

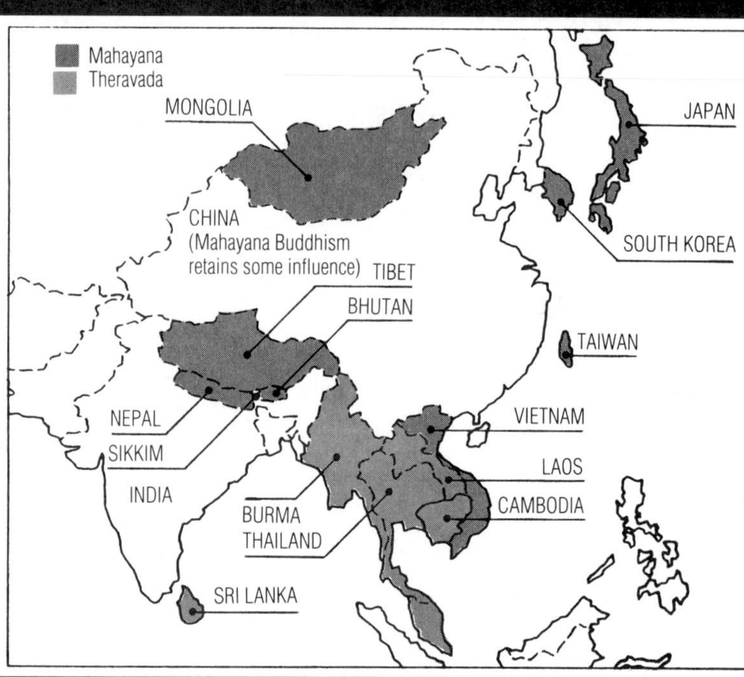

658 CEREMONIAL OBJECTS

Buddhist holy objects and symbols

6581

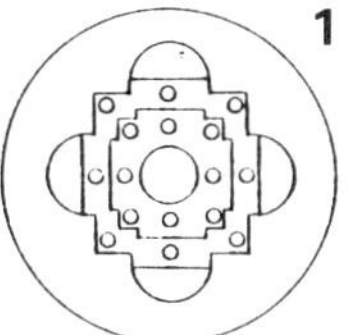

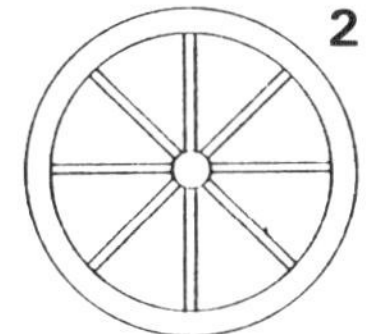

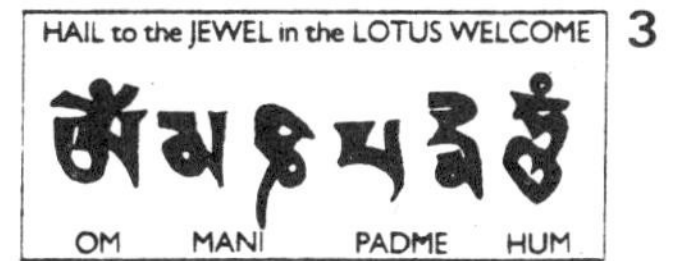

1 Mandala
2 Symbol of Wheel of Law
3 Mantra
4 *Vajra* or *dorje*
5 *Thorbu*
6 Tibetan hand prayer wheel
7 Prayer beads

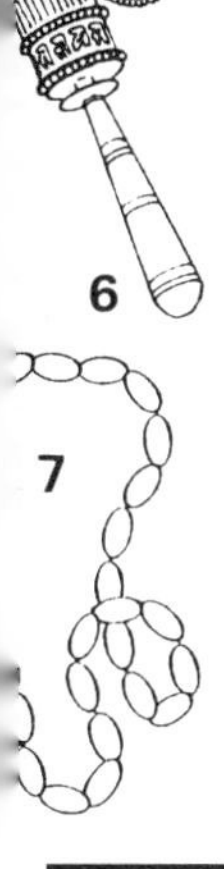

bell A bell is rung in services. It represents emptiness.
bodhisattvas Images of Buddhist saints, enlightened beings. They represent aspects of the path to enlightenment.
incense Given as an offering lit and unlit.
mandala A mandala is a symbol surrounded by a circle. It symbolizes perfection and wholeness for Buddhists. It is a symbol for zero and signifies the end or completion. Monks draw mandalas on the wall or the floor to help them meditate.
offering bowls These are seven bowls holding water or offerings of flowers, incense, food, music, or light. The bowls are arranged on a shrine and used in worship.
padme Word meaning lotus flower which stands for wisdom. It is also a symbol used in meditation.
prayer wheel used to generate or gather positive *karma.* It contains mantras.
rupas Symbolic statues representing Buddhas in different poses.
Shakyamuni Buddha Representation of the historical Buddha and always found on a shrine.

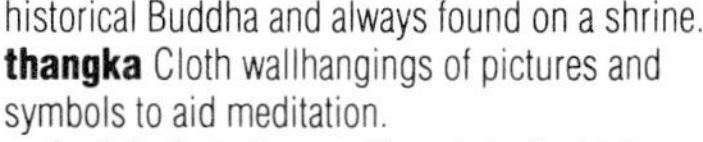

thangka Cloth wallhangings of pictures and symbols to aid meditation.
vajra/ dorje A diamond thunderbolt which represents wisdom cutting through ignorance. It is used in religious services.
wheel of life This is the symbol of Buddhism.
yantra Means instrument. It is a geometric mandala. The *shri yantra* has nine linked triangles with four entrances. It symbolizes wholeness and also the union of male and female.

mudras Hand positions which represent different qualities of the enlightened mind.
1 Dhyana mudra The posture of concentration in yogic meditation.
2 Bhumisparsha mudra After attaining Enlightenment Gautama called the earth to witness by touching it with the fingertips of his right hand.
3 Dharmachakra mudra Buddha taught the *dharma*, the Wheel of Life, symbolized by the fingers imitating the motion of the wheel.
4 Vitarka mudra Upraised hand used as an expression of reasoning and appeasement.
5 Abhaya mudra Protection and assurance.
6 Vara mudra Compassion, vow fulfilling, and granting of favors.

1 2 3 4

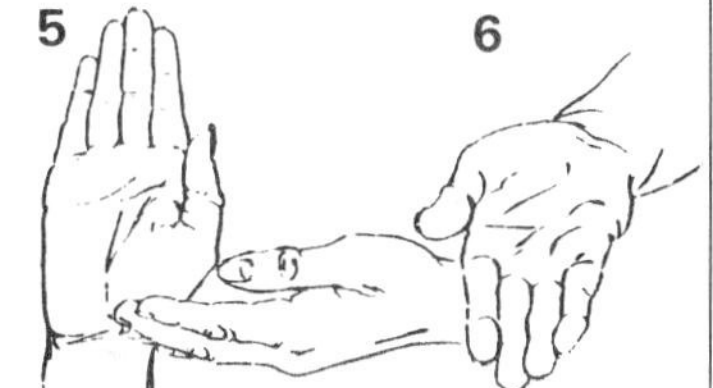

Jaina holy objects and symbols

6582

cave temples Some dating as far back as the 2nd century BC have been found.
donations of copies of religious manuscripts are regarded as pious acts.
flowers, fruit, perfume, and lamps are offered and used in idol worship.
pillars surrounded by elephants are a common symbol of Jaina.
sculptures of Jina seated like the Buddha.
shrines Most towns and villages with Jaina followers have at least one shrine.

659 GLOSSARY

agama Canon of holy work.
ahisma Jaina doctrine of nonviolence and noninjury to any form of life.
ajiva A non-soul, or nonliving substance.
bodhi tree also called a bo tree. The Buddha sat under the shade of this tree to meditate until he gained enlightenment.
bodhisattva A person who vows to become a Buddha by leading a virtuous and wise life. At the highest level this is a person who postpones entering *nirvana* by doing charitable work.
buddha A word meaning awakened or enlightened one. It is a title and not a proper name. Buddhists believe that there have been many buddhas and that there will be many buddhas in the future.
canon A list of sacred books officially recognized as being genuine.
dharma Saving truth. The Buddha's message of how to overcome suffering.
Digambara Jaina sect who go naked on the final stages of their spriritual journey.
gompa A Tibetan word for a meditation room which contains a shrine, *thangkas*, meditation cushions, and desks for sacred books.
jatakas Stories of the Buddha's past lives before he was born as Gautama.
jina A victor or conqueror also a Tirthankara, a title given to the great Jaina teachers such as Mahavira.
jiva A living soul, or living substance.
karman A tenet of Jaina doctrine that all phenomena are linked together in a universal chain of cause and effect.
laity People who are not clergy or part of a religious order.
nirjana A process consisting of fasting, not eating certain kinds of food, control over taste, modesty, study, and meditation, and renunciation of the ego.
ratnatraya Jaina ethics of right knowledge, faith, and conduct. A Jaina follower must try to achieve and follow all three together.
relic A part of the body or something used or associated with a saint or other very important religious figure such as the Buddha.
shrine A cabinet or table which contains representations of the Three Jewels. These are a statue, the holy books wrapped in cloth and a *stupa*. The shrine also contains offering bowls, pictures of gurus, flowers, lights, statues of other buddhas. In Tibetan Buddhism the shrines are very ornate.
Stupa A three-dimensional mandala used on a shrine. It represents the Buddha's mind.
sutra The Buddha's words or a guru's commentary on the Buddha's words.
Svetambaras One of the two Jaina sects. Their name means "white robed."
Tirthankaras Revealers of the Jaina religious path, also called Jinas, who have set the example that all disciples of Jainism must follow.

661 TAOISM

Timeline

6611 Along with Confucianism, Taoism is one of the two major religions or philosophies which originated in China and which have influenced Chinese life for over 2,000 years. Taoist ideas lie behind many aspects of Chinese life and other Asian cultures, especially in Vietnam, Japan, and Korea.

Taoist painting of Chinese philosopher Lao-tzu riding a water buffalo

369–286 BC Chang-tzu writes the great Taoist work the *Chang-tzu*. Lao-tzu is mentioned in it as being one of Chang-tzu's teachers and the book contains many of his speeches. It also contains Lao-tzu's meeting with Confucius.
350–300 BC Lao-tzu's book of mainly verse *Lao-tzu's Five Thousand Words*. It is also called the *Tao Te Ching*. Huang-lao masters in eastern China, followers of Lao-tzu. They regard Lao-tzu as a sage whose book gives instructions for perfect government. From the court of the King of Ch'i, the Huang-lao masters spread their teachings throughout learned and official circles.
AD 34–156 In western China, Chang Tao Ling is called the First Celestial Master. Organized religious Taoism is seen to start from this, the Way of the Celestial Masters.
184 Yellow Turban Rebellion against the Han dynasty in eastern China. Taoists lead failed peasant rising. Taoism in eastern China has around 360,000 followers .
late 2ND century T'ien-shih Tao, descendants of Chang Tao Ling, lead a religious-political organization. They have authority over the western region, and temporal and religious powers join. The Way of the Celestial Masters also becomes known as the Way of the Five Pecks of Rice after a tax contributed by each household of five pecks of rice.
215 The Celestial Master Chang Lu submits to the Han general Ts'ao Ts'ao.
220 Fall of Han dynasty. Ts'ao Ts'ao founds Wei dynasty which officially recognizes Taoism.
220–618 Taoism flourishes in a China which is not politically united and many of the most powerful families in northern China support Taoism.
364–70 Highest Pure or Mao Shan sect emphasize meditation.
c. 397 Ko Ch'ao-fu begins composing *Classic of the Sacred Jewel*. The Sacred Jewel sect introduces practices which are adopted by followers of the Way of the Celestial Masters and later by all orthodox sects.
504 All Taoist sects are banned except the Mao Shan sect.
618–907 Wide spread of Taoism throughout the vast T'ang dynasty. Taoism reaches Japan, Tibet, Kashmir.
960–1279 Sung dynasty.
1016 First printing of the Taoist canon.
c. 1126 Retreat of the Sung government south of the Yangtze River. A number of new Taoist sects are founded in the north which soon gain impressive followings.
1329 Treatise on Mao Shan includes hagiographies, history, and mountain topography.
1949 63rd Celestial Master takes refuge in Taiwan.
1957 Chinese Taoist Association officially founded in Beijing.
1980 Chinese state pays for the repair of the largest Taoist temple in Beijing.

Religious and philosophical Taosim

6612 Taosim includes both a philosophy and a religion. The two forms are related although there are many points in which they oppose each other. Most of the Taoist texts are philosophical works. The most important are the *Tao Te Ching* and the *Chang-tzu*. Philosophical Taoism and its texts became established during 481-221 BC while religious Taoism did not develop until the 2nd century AD. It became a movement of organized religious communities.

Taoist thought

This emphasizes non-action, naturalness, spontaneity, and passivity along with peace and meditation. Chang-tzu saw Tao as the quiet spirit in everything. A Taoist should cultivate complete peace. These ideas became part of religious Taoism.

Religious Taoism

Religious Taoism adopted many ideas from philosophical Taoism, especially from the *Tao Te Ching* and the idea of *yin-yang*. It also follows ideas on the search for immortality, mental and physical discipline, healing and exorcism, and belief in many gods and spirits.

Spiritual techniques

These are connected with gaining immortality. They did not always agree with philosophical Taoism, although the texts seemed to hint at immortality and protection for all those who followed the *Tao*. The lives of such perfected ones, or immortals called the *hsien* became the models for religious Taoism. Lao-tzu was seen as a god and savior as he had revealed sacred texts. In the 3rd and 4th centuries AD the preoccupation with the search for immortality moved toward finding the miracle drug through alchemy. This had already been tried in previous centuries.

Philosophical Taoism

In philosophical Taoism the universe is viewed as a whole and every part of it reflects the whole. Man is a small universe whose body is a miniature of the wider universe. In meditation the religious Taoist would see the thousands of gods that inhabit the human body which reflect the gods inhabiting the universe.

In some Taoist sects, temples, and monasteries are important. These are looked after by Taoist priests. Although Taoism has been discouraged in China since the Cultural Revolution, it continues to be popular in Taiwan. Today there are approximately 190 million Taoists around the world.

Taoist symbols and signs

6613 **Yin and yang**

Yin and yang means the dark side and the sunny side of a hill. It means the balance of opposite pairs. Taoists believe that the universe is kept in balance by the opposite forces of *yin and yang* which work to hold a tension between themselves. *Yin* is considered to be watery and feminine. It is the force of the Moon and rain, which reaches its peak in the winter. *Yang* is considered a strong and masculine force. It is the force in the Sun and Earth and it reaches its peak in the summer.

The interaction of *yin and yang* shape all life.

1 The symbol of Taoism is *T'ai Chi*, the supreme ultimate, which expresses the production of *yin and yang*, complementary and interacting forces of nature – such as male and female, light and dark – to achieve harmony.

2 Lao-tzu's divinal seal, used in Taoist magic.

3 Priest's robe with applied symbols of *T'ai Chi* and the eight mystic trigrams, normally made of gold-patterned satin.

1

2

3

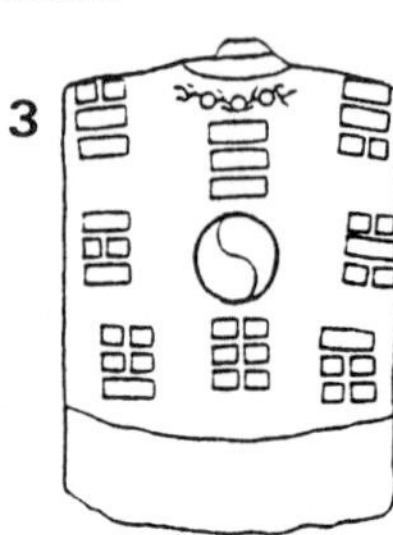

The Tao

6614 The Tao, or Way means the hidden meaning of the universe. A Taoist should aim for a completely harmonious relationship with nature which ensures right behavior and is more important than good deeds. Tao can only be followed by being natural and spontaneous. A person cannot strive to follow the Way and it cannot be taught. Someone who lives by this sees the way in all things. The Tao can only be known by following its calm and simplicity.

Lao-tzu wrote that the Tao is nameless because in ancient Chinese thought the name implied something's worth and placed it in a universe of varying levels. The Tao is outside this system and cannot be named. The Nameless created the universe. The Named and the Not-Named, the Being and the Not-Being are the productive and the passive sides of the Tao. They are all interdependent and grow out of each other. Tao is nameless, beyond understanding and can only be understood by seeing it as the One, the opposite to the endless number of living things. Tao was the creator of all life. Health and sickness, life and death, pleasure and pain are all different aspects of the same reality. We should treat all these opposing pairs alike so that health and sickness are the same.

Te
Tao is emptiness, not-being and non-action but Te is the efficacy of the Tao. Te is the mysterious power of the Tao and shows that Tao is the potentiality of all-being. Te is the extension of Tao into each individual thing. It leads to all living things being linked by one unity. The Te in things turns inward, so the movement of Tao is to turn backward.

The Trinity
The One is the personification of the Tao and it is the greatest god of Taoism. The Greatest One was introduced into Taoist worship between 206 BC and AD 8 and was later called the Celestial Venerable of the Mysterious Origin. Later still, this title was replaced with the Pure August. The Tao was made into a Trinity as Tao had entered into creation in three stages.

1

2

3

Each stage was personified as a different aspect of the Tao. This idea of a chain of Heavenly Masters has continued over the centuries to the present. As well as this Trinity there were a great many Taoist gods and saints, and their number increased over the centuries.
1 The Celestial Venerable of the Mysterious Origin
2 The August Ruler of the Tao
3 The August Old Ruler. Lao-tzu was held to be an incarnation of this god

Taoist texts

6615 **Tao Te Ching**
Tao Te Ching means The Way and its Power, and it is thought to have been written by Lao-tzu. It is the basic and most important text of Taoist philosophy and religion. It describes a quiet, effortless way of life, free from desire. This can be achieved be following the Tao, the universe's
creative and spontaneous life force.

Tao Tsang
The Taoist canon is called the *Tao Tsang*. It was gathered in its present form in 1436. It had previously been longer but the order was disrupted when Kublai Khan, the Mongol leader, ordered it to be burned in 1281. The *Tao Tsang* consists of the *San Tung* (the Three Vaults) and the *Ssu Fu* (the Four Supplements.)

662 CONFUCIANISM

Timeline

6621 Perhaps the best way to view Confucianism is as an all-encompassing humanism concerned primarily with how we live in this life. However, it never denies heaven neither does it slight it. It has influenced east Asian spiritual life as well as political culture. Its theories and practice have affected government, society, education, and family life, particularly in China, for many centuries. It is based on the teachings, philosophy and beliefs of K'ung-fu-tzu, Master K'ung 552-479 BC, known in Western societies as Confucius.

551 BC Confucius is born.
532 BC Confucius marries, has a son and two daughters.
517 BC He meets Taoist teacher Lao-tzu.
501 BC Confucius becomes prime minister of Lu but eventually resigns.
497–484 BC Confucius travels from state to state where he tries to advise rulers on good government, ethics, and correct knowledge. He gathers disciples from all classes.
484 BC He returns to Lu where he teaches and begins to write the history of Lu since 722.
479 BC Confucius dies.
371–289 BC Confucian philosopher and second sage Mencius also tries to advise rulers. His work reinforces Confucian ethics of goodness, stressing moral cultivation.
298–230 BC Confucian rationalist philosopher Hsun Tzu argues that human beings are born evil but they can be improved with good education and moral training.
213 BC All books of Confucian ritual in schools burnt by decree; some saved in archives
202 BC–AD 220 Over the long reign of the Han dynasty Confucianism is made into a state cult.
140–87 BC Emperor Wu Ti educated by Confucians.
136 BC Confucianism established as state ideology.
124 BC First imperial university founded to study the *Five Classics* (the major part of the Confucian canon of writings) and select civil servants.
59 Emperor Ming orders sacrifices to Confucius in all public schools. He sacrifices personally at the shrine of Confucius.
600 Buddhism spreads in China. Confucianism spreads to Japan.
768–824 Han Yu asserts the superiority of Confucianism and its separateness from Buddhism and Taoism.
960–1279 The years of the Sung dynasty. Neo-Confucianism becomes a strong movement.
1392 Confucianism becomes Korean state religion.
1603–1867 Japanese Tokugawa shoguns adopt Neo-Confucianism.
1911 Chinese revolution overthrows Confucian imperial system.
1949 Communist Chinese People's Republic declares all religions "counter revolutionary."
1974–76 Mao's anti-Confucius campaign versus military leadership and intellectuals.
1985 Estimated 150 million Confucians (UN figure.)

Organization

6622

Organization
Confucianism is not organized like other religions. It is a philosophy for good government, good conduct, education, public life, and family life. It suggests a traditional view of life, and has provided a code of manners for the Chinese gentry for 2,000 years. Confucius considered himself to be a teacher and his theories were based on the study of past rulers whom he admired for their conduct and morality, and their success.

Sacrifices were made at Confucian shrines but they were not addressed to personal gods. They were aimed at natural phenomena and men of the past.

Distribution
Communism in China has broken the Confucian tradition. However, there are still followers among the population there and the Chinese populations of South-east Asia and North America. There are also adherents in Taiwan.

Confucian beliefs

6623

Confucianism is essentially secular in its outlook, the main concern being "this world" and our conduct and practices in it. It emphasizes the moral duty of man to his fellows. However, Confucius clearly regarded heaven (*T'ien*) as a positive and personal force in the universe. He was not an agnostic or a sceptic. In his studies he looked back to the Chou dynasty whose rulers believed they had permission from heaven to govern. Heaven or the "supreme ancestor" (*Shang Ti*) was believed to govern the universe, fix seasons, give fertility to people and animals, and order the cycle of death and renewal. This world, which inspired Confucius, was regulated by spirits of dead kings (*ti*,) ancestors, nature gods, and guardian spirits. The ancient traditions of reverence toward heaven and ancestors are where Confucius searched for answers.

Hsaio
This is filial piety to parents and ancestors. It is the strongest of Confucian duties. A son must obey his father absolutely not only in childhood but until his father's death. Then he is supposed to mourn for 25 months. From this developed the five relationships:
1 Between father and son
2 Between older and younger brothers
3 Between husbands and wives
4 Between elder and younger
5 Between ruler and subject

Five cardinal virtues
Confucianism recognizes five cardinal virtues: *Jen, Yi, Li, Chih, Hsin.* The attainment of moral perfection for the individual and moral and social order for society can be attained by the practice of *chung* – being true to the principles of one's nature and *shu* – the application of those principles in relation to others.

Five cardinal virtues

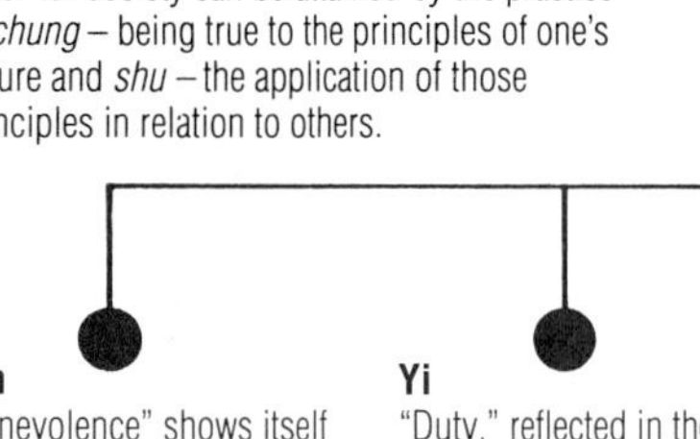

Jên
"Benevolence" shows itself in the feeling of sympathy for others, unselfishness, courtesy, and loyalty to family and prince.

Yi
"Duty," reflected in the feeling of shame after a wrong action.

Li
"Manners," propriety or good form, reflected in the feeling of deference. The code of gentlemanly conduct.

Chih
"Wisdom" is a sense of right and wrong.

Hsin
"Faithfulness," (loyalty.)

People

6624

Hsun-tzu Confucian philosopher who transformed Confucianism into a realistic and systematic inquiry into the human condition, paying special attention to ritual and authority. He taught that human beings are born evil and that humans' instincts must be suppressed for the public good. Human beings can be improved by moral training and education.
Lao-tzu Taoist teacher and philosopher who, according to legend, Confucius met around 517 BC.
Mencius 371–289 BC the great Confucian philosopher and Second Sage. He brought Confucian moral idealism to fruition. He taught that humans are basically good and emphasized moral cultivation.
Neo-Confucians emerged as an identifiable movement during the Sung dynasty (960–1126), initially as a Confucian response to the teachings of Taoism and Buddhism.

Some objects associated with Confucianism

6625

1 The Temple of Heaven in Beijing was the largest temple ever built for ancestral worship.
2 The Temple of Confucius was built around the 13th century. It houses tablets which commemorate Confucius and his disciples.
3 Ancestral tablets show the name of the ancestor, the name of the king, and the name of the son or person who erected it.

1
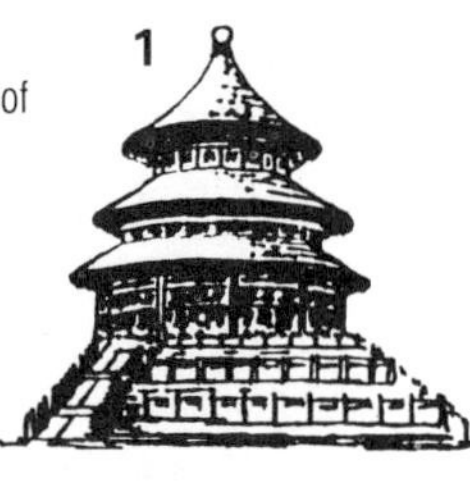

2

3

Confucian texts

662**6**

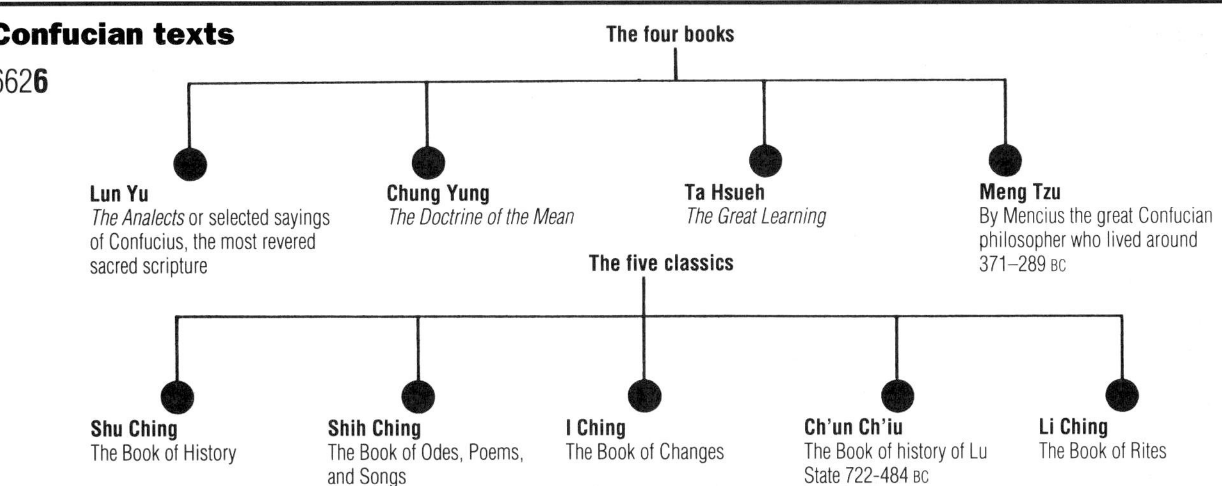

663 SHINTOISM

History

663**1** Shinto literally means "the way of *Kami*" (the "way of the gods"). *Kami* can mean mystical, superior, but generally it is sacred or divine power. It came into use so that Japanese beliefs could be distinguished from Buddhist ideas which were introduced into Japan in the 6th century AD. Shinto is closely bound to the life of the Japanese and their personal motivations, their value system and the people's ways of thinking and acting. It is for many Japanese a basic attitude toward life. There are no founder, no official sacred scriptures, and no dogma. But Shinto has evolved with Japanese society and people over centuries.

The majority of Japanese people are Buddhist and Shintoist at the same time. The population of Japan is around 124,000,000.

3rd–2nd century BC Yayoi culture developed in the northern area of the island of Kyushu. This was directly related to future Japanese culture and therefore Shinto. Agricultural rites were performed and shamanism practiced.
5th century AD Confucianism is believed to have reached Japan.
538 Buddhism first introduced into Japan.
7th century Confucianism spreads among the people along with Taoism and *yin-yang* philosophy. Myths of various clans were mixed and reorganized into a pan-Japanese mythology with the Imperial household at its center. During the 7th century the *Kojika* was written to preserve Shinto legends.
8th century A tendency develops to interpret Shinto from a Buddhist viewpoint.
10th century 3,000 shrines throughout Japan are receiving state offerings to *Kami*.
1192–1333 The Kamakura period. Theories of Shinto-Buddhist amalgamation are formulated.
1603 Neo Confucianism begins to influence Shinto. Neo-Confucianism becomes an official subject of study for warriors.
1867 The fall of the Tokugawa Shogunate. New religious movements emerge out of the social confusion and unrest. Sectarian Shinto groups are formed during the Meiji period 1868-1912. Stimulated by restoration Shinto, 13 groups are created. The government begins to treat Shinto like a state religion and revives the system of national shrines.
1889 Japanese constitution guarantees freedom of faith under certain conditions. Priority is given to Shinto.
1945 After Japanese defeat in World War II, Shinto Directive is issued by occupation forces abolishing state Shinto.

Organization

663**2** Any person who goes through certain training processes may be a priest (or priestess) though in reality many priests are still from the families of hereditary Shinto priests.

There are no weekly religious services. People visit shrines at their own convenience. Some might visit shrines on the first and 15th of each month and when rites and festivals take place. Pious devotees pay their respects to shrines every morning. Shinto shrines are not places where people congregate to meet or worship in union. Each shrine is a house for a god.

Sects
Confucian sects These combine Confucian ideas and Shinto.
Faith healing sects These include a number of groups. One which believes in one God and the universal brotherhood and love of all men. The other which teaches the spiritual nature of sickness and evil and advocated purification rituals as a cure. These are believed to have the most members.
Folk, or Minzoku Shinto This is an aspect of folk belief closely connected with other types of Shinto. It is centered on the veneration of small roadside images and in the agricultural rites of rural families.
Mountain sects These groups, formed around a charismatic founder, believe that their gods live in sacred mountains.
Pure Shinto This emphasizes loyalty to the throne and the worship of ancestors.
Purification sects These groups perpetuate the tradition of water purification to cultivate the body and mind.
Sect, or Kyoha Shinto There are 13 branches of Sect Shinto which are divided into five groups. They all originated in Japan during the 19th century. Most of these bodies are organized around a founder or a systematizer.
Shrine, or Jinja Shinto This has been in existence from the beginning of Japanese history. It is the main current of Shinto tradition. For many years it did include state Shinto but that is now defunct.

Shinto beliefs

663**3** At the core of Shinto beliefs is *Kami*, a mysterious creating and harmonizing power (*musubi*) which can never be fully explained in words because *Kami* transcends the mental capabilities of humans. *Kami* can be found in many forms and things, hence, there are thousands of gods in Shinto. Some of them are local, particular to a village, and some are national. Pious followers can understand *Kami* through faith and then recognize different *Kami* in many forms.

The truthful way or will – *Makoto* – is revealed to people through *Kami*, and shrine worshippers believe that their *Kami* will respond to truthful prayers.

The most important *Kami* is the Sun *Kami*, Amaterasu Omikami. It is believed that human history began when Ninigi, grandchild of the Sun *Kami*, descended to the lower regions.

continued

Shinto beliefs continued

6633

It was his great grandson Jimmu Tenno who became first emperor of a unified Japan. Shinto's holiest shrine is at Ise, near Kyoto. There in the temple of the Sun *Kami* is preserved in the mirror that she is said to have given to Jimmu, the first emperor, in the 7th century BC.

Sacred sites of Japan

6634

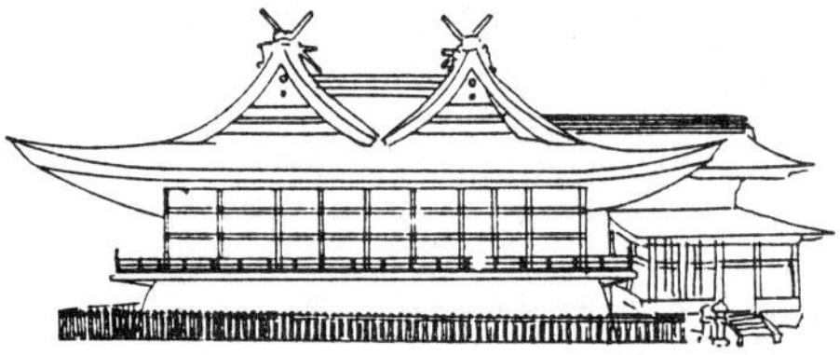

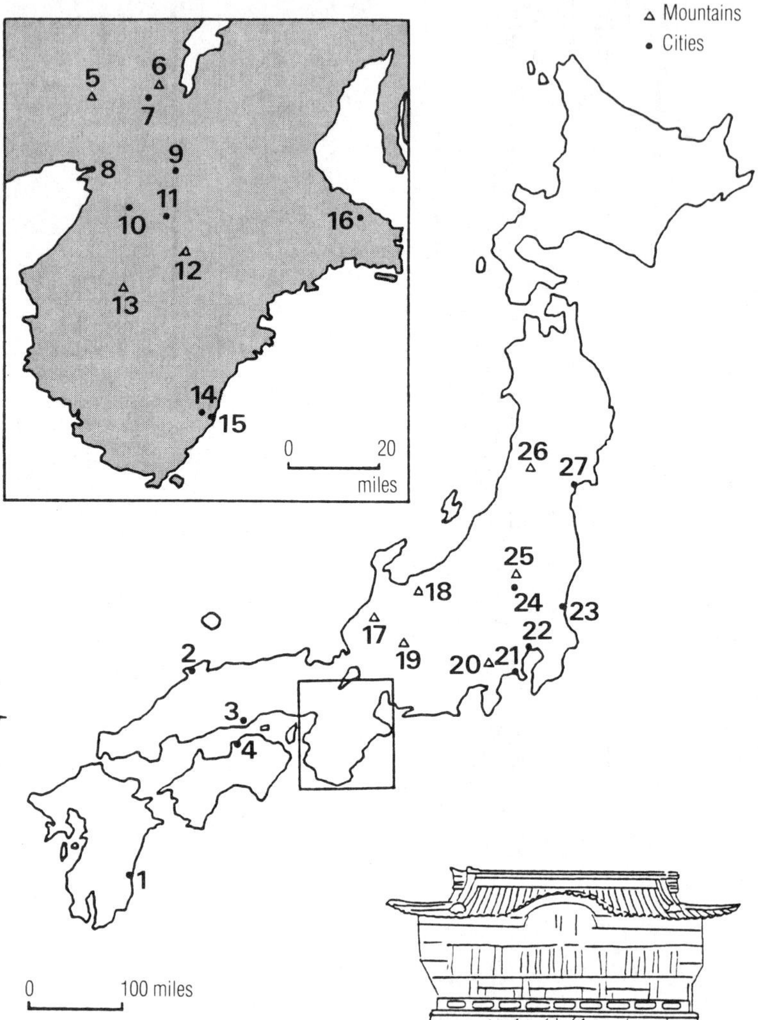

△ Mountains
• Cities

0 20 miles

0 100 miles

1 Miyakazi shrine (first emperor)
2 Izumo shrine, oldest temple site. Main shrine rebuilt 1744
3 Kibitsu shrine, the largest
4 Kotohira-gu shrine, 19th century
5 Mt Mino
6 Mt Hiei
7 Kyoto, old capital
8 Sumiyoshi shrine, Osaka, rebuilt 1810.
9 Kasuga shrine, Nara
10 Tashi-cho, Prince Shotoku (fl. 594–607), Buddhist saint, buried
11 Kashihara, early emperors' tombs and built 1889 shrine
12 Mt Kimbusen
13 Mt Koya
14 Nachi Waterfalls shrine
15 Kumano shrine
16 Ise shrine. Rebuilt every 20 years since 4th century.
17 Mt Hakusan
18 Mt Tateyama
19 Mt Ontake, second most sacred
20 Mt Fuji, most sacred and highest mountain 12,388 ft (3,776 m)
21 Kamakura, bronze Great Buddha (1252)
22 Yasukumi shrine (fallen soldiers), Tokyo
23 Mito, shrines
24 Toshugu shrine, Nikko, for Tokugawa shoguns, begun 1634
25 Mt Nantai
26 Mt Haguro
27 Shiogama shrine, site of annual sea festival

Some Shinto rites

6635 **Newborn babies** Babies are taken to the shrine 30 to 100 days after birth.
Shichi-go-San Seven, Five, Three festival on November 15th is an occasion for boys of five years and girls of three and seven years of age to visit the shrine and give thanks for the protection of *Kami*. They also pray for healthy growth.
Adults' Day On January 15th the youth in a village used to join the local men's association. At present it is the commemoration day for Japanese who have attained their 20th year.
Rites of purification These were also performed for the launching of a ship, the consecration of a building, or the opening of a bridge.
Funerals are mainly in the Buddhist style.
Altars A traditional Japanese household will have two family altars. One Shinto for their tutelary Kami and the goddess Amaterasu Omikami. The other Buddhist for family ancestors.

A Shinto grand festival usually follows a certain order of rituals.
1 Purification rites (harare)
2 Adoration. All the congregation bow to the altar
3 Opening the door of the inner sanctuary (usually carried out by the chief priests)
4 Presentations of food offerings – rice, saki wine, rice cakes are among the foods offered. No animal meat is offered
5 Prayer. The chief priest recites prayers (*norito*)
6 Sacred music and dance
7 A general offering. Participants make symbolic offerings using little branches of the evergreen sacred tree to which strips of white paper are tied
8 Taking offerings away
9 Shutting the door of the inner sanctuary
10 Final adoration
11 Feast (*naorai*) takes place

Sacred texts

6636 Shinto has no founder and no official text. However, two books are revered: the *Kojiki*, the "records of ancient matters," and the *Nihon-gi*, or *Nihon Shoki*, the "chronicles of Japan." These are both regarded in a sense as the sacred books of Shinto. They were compiled between AD 712 and 720 from the oral traditions of ancient Shinto. The books also cover the history, topography, and literature of ancient Japan. They describe religious practices and myths.

Calendar

6637 Each Shinto shrine has several major festivals each year including: spring festival, *Haru Matsuri*, or *Toshigoi Matsuri*, the Prayer for Good Harvest festival; autumn festival, *Aki Matsuri*, or *Niiname-sae*, a harvest festival; an annual festival, *Rei-sai;* and the Divine Procession, *Shinko-sai*.

Sacred objects

6638 **grand shrine of Ise** The most respected shrine dedicated to the Sun goddess.
sacred treasures The mirror, the sword, and jewels, symbols of the imperial throne.
the sakaki The holy tree with flowers which are yellowish white and berries yellowish brown.
shintai Mirrors, jewels, swords, wooden statues wrapped in silk and kept in a container in inner sanctuary. Only chief priest sees them.
tori The symbol of Shinto.
torii The sacred gates of shrines built to mark holy places. An example is Torii (gate) of Iesukushima shrine, Miyajima Island (**1**).

664 GLOSSARY OF TAOISM, CONFUCIANISM, AND SHINTO

664 **alchemy** A sort of magical chemistry which tried to turn base metals into gold and tried to find a potion or substance to make people immortal.
Amaterasu Omikami The most important divinity in Shinto mythology, the Sun goddess and ancestress of the imperial household. Her descendants unified the Japanese people.
hagiography Writings about the lives of saints, biographies of saints. Hagiographies can also be writings which idealize the person being written about.
Han dynasty Chinese dynasty of rulers 206 BC–AD 220 who overthrew the preceeding Qin dynasty. The Emperor Wu Ti completed the conquest of a vast empire. Confucianism was recognized as the state philosophy.
Jimmu Tenno The first emperor of a unified Japan.
kami This means mystical, superior or divine. It is a sacred and divine power assigned to various gods and dieties, but *Kami* can be found in many things.
kojiki Means "records of ancient matters." It is one of the sacred Shinto scriptures.
makoto The truthful way or will of *Kami*. Something which is only revealed to people through *Kami*.
musubi The mysterious creating and harmonizing power of *Kami*.
Nakoto no Kokoro "Heart of truth" or Magokoro "true heart." It can mean sincerity, uprightness, pure heart, of person doing their best in life at work or in relationships.
nihon shoki "Chronicles of Japan" important, in some sense, sacred Shinto scripture.
shinto Literally means the "way of *Kami*," the "way of the gods," or "way of higher forces." The word was used in the 6th century to distinguish traditional religions from Buddhism.
shogun Hereditary military title held by three families in Japan. The shoguns were the rulers of Japan at different times in history.
Sung dynasty A dynasty (960–1279) founded in North China by Zhao Guang Yin.
tutelary dieties The guardian gods, tutors, particular to parishioners of a shrine or community.
Yayoi A Japanese culture which originated in the northern area of the island of Kyushu 3rd or 2nd century BC.

671	**Ecumenical movement**	**6733**	Unification Church
672	**Pentecostal movement**	**6734**	Jesus Movement
673	**New religions of the west**	**6735**	Children of God
6731	Hare Krishna movement	**674**	**New movements in Africa**
6732	Meditative movements	**675**	**Rosicrucians**

671 ECUMENICAL MOVEMENT

The ecumenical movement is a movement to promote closer contact and understanding between Christian Churches. Earlier this century it involved mainly Protestants, but it has now become of interest to many Christians.

The movement started in 1910 with the International Missionary Conference in Edinburgh. In 1948 the World Council of Churches was formed by Protestant leaders and still meets. It aims to reduce differences in doctrine and to encourage Christian unity. The Roman Catholic, Eastern Orthodox, and Pentecostal Churches also take part, which provides a wide view of different forms of Christianity. Church councils are also common at more local or national levels.

Over the past 50 years the main Christian Churches have increasingly discussed theology, tried to be more understanding and cooperative towards each other. Union between some Churches has been achieved but remains difficult among others. Divisions are not always caused by traditional differences in theology. Often it is between more conservative members and the more radical ones within Churches.

672 PENTECOSTAL MOVEMENT

Pentecostalism began in the USA in 1906. Its name comes from the Holy Spirit which came down to the Apostles at Pentecost. The movement grew out of the "holiness movement" which developed among Methodists and other Protestant groups, and it has spread to Europe, Africa, and South America.

Pentecostal Churches include the Elim Foursquare Gospel, the Church of God in Christ and the Assemblies of God, which is the largest. Since the 1960s charismatic movements which resemble Pentecostalism have appeared in both the Roman Catholic and the Protestant Churches.

Church services include enthusiastic sermons and hymns. Adult baptism is practiced and communion is shared by the congregation. Followers believe in the second coming of Christ, baptism by the Holy Spirit, and faith healing. A characteristic feature of Pentecostalism is speaking in "tongues." This is speaking either in an unintelligible speech or perhaps speaking in a way which has similarity to existing languages but which the speaker does not know.

There are approximately 3.5 million followers worldwide.

673 NEW RELIGIONS OF THE WEST

Many new religious movements began to appear in the west during the 1960s and some saw them as a phenomenon of the 1970s. They flourished in North America, and also existed in parts of Europe, Australia, and New Zealand, although they did not appear in southern and eastern Europe and Scandinavia.

The growth of these movements may be due to a reaction to contemporary society. They may meet the spiritual and psychological need of inadequate or very religious people. Some of the movements are thought to brainwash new converts or use mind control techniques. Many of the new movements have a strong or even messianic leader. Some of the new movements believe that the end of the world is near, others believe in ideal societies or the enlightened individual.

Of these new groups some have their origins in India such as the Hare Krishna movement, or Rajneesh Meditation. Others are based on Christian traditions such as the Unification Church. Some of the movements demand complete devotion from their followers requiring them to give up property and careers, and to live in a community together.

Some of the new sects which have emerged, especially in the last 30 years, have aroused concern because of their practices. They have been criticized for such matters as brainwashing, dividing the family, exploiting followers, and leaders making personal fortunes. The mass suicide in 1978 of members of the People's Temple, and the death of about 86 members of the "Davidian sect" in 1993, have shown that perhaps there is cause for anxiety.

Hare Krishna movement

6731

The Hare Krishna movement is also called the International Society of Krishna Consciousness (ISKCON.) It was started by his Divine Grace A.C. Bhaktivedanta Swami Prabhupada in the USA in 1965.

The movement is based on the *Bhagavadgita*, the most popular book in Hindu scriptures, as translated by their master. The followers' frequent chant of "Hare Krishna, Hare Krishna...." has given them their popular name, the Hare Krishnas. Serious members on moving into Temple are forbidden narcotics and alcohol, eat specially prepared vegetarian food, and must lead celibate lives unless they want to have children once they are married.

The Hare Krishna movement has become well known because groups of believers were often seen in city streets. They are dressed in saffron-colored robes, the men with their heads shaved, apart from a small tuft of hair. They sing and dance through the streets, selling records, books or magazines about their faith in order to support their community.

Meditative movements

6732

Rajneesh Meditation

Meditation centers were established in various western countries to spread the "chaotic meditation" and teachings of the Shree Rajneesh whose center was in India. He called himself *Bhagwan,* which is Hindi for "God." The *Bhagwan*'s beliefs were a mixture of traditions from the east and the west. Followers see themselves as ascetics and wear orange robes and carry prayer beads. They are not prohibited any particular things but they are expected to be guided by their instincts with regards to correct behaviour.

Transcendental Meditation

This can be considered as a technique or as a religion depending on viewpoint. Transcendental Meditation was introduced to the west by Maharishi Mahesh Yogi. It gained a wide following in the west during the 1970s after the Beatles converted to the religion.

The Science of Creative Intelligence started in 1970. Many people claimed the benefit of Transcendental Meditation techniques. The movement aims to improve the individual and the state of society and the world. When people begin meditating they are given a *mantra*, a mystical charm, verse or spell to recite over and over. The meditation is supposed to relieve stress and provide relaxation.

Unification Church

6733 The Unification Church is also called the Holy Spirit Association for the Unification of World Christianity, or the "Moonies." The Church is associated with various groups. The movement was founded in Korea by the Reverend Sun Myung Moon in 1954. The movement spread to Japan and later to the west but there are probably not more than 200,000 members worldwide.

Many of the members of the Unification Church join when they are about 20 years old. They live in communities in the west, but spend much time fund-raising in the streets. Moon suggests marriage partners, and mass weddings are held. This is the most important rite.

The Unification Church's beliefs are among some of the most comprehensive and developed of the new religions. The Church believes in a period of 1,000 years when Jesus Christ will rule on the Earth. The *Divine Principle* is the key book of the Church, written by Moon. It gives an interpretation of the Bible and also revelations which Moon claims to have received from God. The Church sees history as a battle to return the Earth to the state which God created it. Jesus' mission failed so he was only able to offer spiritual salvation and not physical salvation. The Lord of the Second Advent is now supposed to be on the Earth. Most followers believe Moon to be a messiah.

The Unification Church has attracted much hostility from parents, the media, and the Anti-cult Movement. It has been accused of brainwashing, splitting up families, exploiting the followers and making the leader rich, and of using deception.

Jesus Movement

6734 The Jesus Movement or the Jesus Revolution as it was called by some, is not a separate religion but rather a term used to describe the many conservative evangelical groups which appeared in the 1960s. Many of the groups were within the Evangelical or Pentecostal Churches but new groups also formed. Some of these are regarded as dangerous and suspicious, such as the Children of God. One of the original and very active groups in California was the Christian World Liberation Front.

Members of these groups were called Jesus freaks as they publicly displayed their "rediscovery" of Jesus. They displayed posters, stickers, clothing, and other accessories, often with "Jesus loves me" written on them.

Children of God

6735 The Children of God started as part of the Jesus Movement. The group, which later called itself the Family of Love, was founded in 1968 by David Berg in California. He later called himself Moses David or simply Mo.

Members of the Children of God are mainly young people who give up their careers to live in communities or colonies together. They spend much of their time selling religious literature on the streets and trying to make new converts. The group became known for some of its conversion techniques involving sex.

The Children of God believe that the world is ending and that these are the "last days." The survivors will be those who have committed themselves to a godly life.

The movement is based on Evangelical Christianity but it is highly critical of the established Church. The main text which members follow are the *Mo Letters*. These are written by the leader David Berg and they cover a wide range of topics. Some of these are prophecies of doom, others give information on health and sexual practices.

674 NEW MOVEMENTS IN AFRICA

Africa has produced around 8,000 different religious movements through its interaction with Christianity but not with Islam. About 9 million people belong to these movements. Some of the movements try to revive traditional religions while borrowing from Christianity. Most of the movements are independent Churches as they use the Bible and call themselves Christian. The Churches are mainly of two types, Ethiopian Churches and Zionist Churches.

Ethiopian Churches There are African independent Churches which started around the 1880s in Nigeria, Ghana, and South Africa. They have developed from earlier missions or Churches which stood on the same site, and the new Church follows many of the traditions and patterns of the old Church with some African variations.

The Zionist Movement This describes Churches which are slightly unorthodox or more Pentecostal than the Ethiopian Church. They are more African in their worship and emphasize the power of the Holy spirit. Zionist Churches include spiritualist movements and prophet-healing Churches, which have been more common since the 1920s.

Some other large and influential movements have been the Harris Movement and the Kimbanguist Church.

The Harris Movement This was the largest movement toward Christianity in west Africa. It was started by William Wade Harris who between 1913 and 1915 led about 120,000 people in the Ivory Coast and Ghana to abandon traditional religion and adopt a basic Christianity. Many followers later joined the Methodist Church but about 100,000 still follow the original movement.

The Kimbanguist Church was started by Simon Kimbangu in 1921. After about 30 years persecution, it is now the largest independent Church in Africa with about 3 million members. It is now led by Kimbangu's three sons.

675 ROSICRUCIANS

The Rosicrucians are a mystical brotherhood who are described in two anonymous manifestos which appeared in Germany in 1614–15. Their main goal was to cure the sick and to travel and disseminate knowledge. They announced a return to learning and piety and invited people to join the order of the Rose Cross, which was founded by Christian Rosencreutz. He had brought knowledge about science and alchemy back from the east. The manifestos attracted much interest because members take vows of secrecy. They seemed not to exist. Belief in their existence has continued and many occult organizations say they originate from Rosicrucianism. Some are described below.

Rosicrucianism is a modern movement founded in 1878 by R.W. Little. It claims to have links to the older Society of the Rose Cross begun in 1413 by Christian Rosencreutz.

The Ancient and Mystical Order Rosae Crucis (AMORC) was founded in San Jose, California in 1915 by H. Spencer Lewis. It is an international organization which teaches its members by correspondence course.

The Rosicrucian Brotherhood was founded in Quakertown, Pennsylvania in 1902 by Reuben Swinburne Clymer. This sect and AMORC can be seen as either religious or fraternal organizations. They both claim to give their members the power of cosmic forces by revealing secret knowledge about nature.

676 NATIVE AMERICAN CHURCH

The Native American Church developed from the Peyote cult. This was a religious movement originating in 19th century North America among the tribes of the southern plains. It is based on the use of the peyote cactus which is hallucenogenic. Peyotism spread rapidly and in 1918 it developed into the Native American Church. It aims to combine Christianity with traditional beliefs and traditions such as drumming, singing, visions, and the use of the sacred pipe. There are now about 100,000 followers from many different North American tribes.

677 RASTAFARIANS

Rastafarianism was founded in the 1930s in Jamaica among poor landless men who were inspired by Marcus Garvey's "Back to Africa" movement. The Rastafarian movement is named after Ras Tafari who became Emperor of Ethiopia as Haile Selassie I. He is still regarded as a messiah of the black race and it is believed that they are the true Jews waiting to be saved.

Rastafarianism is more a way of life than a religion. It is guided by the culture and traditions of Ethiopia and unity and pride in African heritage. Followers meet weekly to discuss community business and spirituality. There is no church, but chaplains are elected for one year, and song, prayer, and music are important. Personal dignity is considered important and smoking marijuana is considered a mystical and peaceful experience.

White culture and Christianity are not accepted although the Bible's Old Testament is accepted. Rastafarians believe that Haile Selassie is the one true God, and that they will eventually return to the ancestral home Africa, to be freed from Babylon which is the western world and to destroy oppression.

Rastafarians must keep their hair uncut and natural as a sign of physical and moral strength, and they must not eat meat.

Festivals revolve around the Ethiopian calendar. Special days are set apart to celebrate Haile Selassie and Marcus Garvey.

Most Rastafarians are found in Jamaica, the Caribbean islands, North America, and Britain.

678 GLOSSARY OF 20TH CENTURY RELIGIONS

charismatic Divinely given power or talent. Word often used to describe sect leaders for being capable of inspiring or influencing people.

evangelical A word used to describe Christian Protestant groups who place an emphasis on the infallibility of the Bible, importance of conversion, and faith in reconciliation with God because of the death of Christ for man's salvation.

millenarianism A belief in a period in the future of 1,000 years when Jesus will come and rule the Earth. Millenarianism has produced sects which date the "end" and others which want to prepare people for Jesus' coming by spreading religion.

occult Magical or hidden. Supernatural or mystical happenings or acts which do not form part of a recognized religion. Witchcraft, divination, magic, Satanism are all considered to be part of the occult.

681 PHILOSOPHERS

Pre-Socratics

6811 **Anaxagoras** 500–428 BC, Greek. Suggested that all matter contains all known qualities. Differences are explained by the balance of qualities in different objects. In glass, the glassy quality predominates, although others, like softness and flexibility are there in minute proportions. Change consists of adding and subtracting qualities.

Anaximander 611–547 BC, Greek. Pupil of Thales, he argued that the universe is spherical, that the Earth rests at its center and that the first principle and element of matter is the infinite.

Anaximander

Anaximenes 588–524 BC, Greek. Studied under Anaximander. Argued that the prime substance is air, which becomes wind, water, earth, and stone when made more dense, and fire as it becomes finer.

Democritus c. 460–c. 370 BC, Greek. Together with Leucippus, the founder of atomism, held the belief that matter is made up of small units of indivisible, unalterable stuff. Reality consists of atoms and empty space. Sensations and appearances occur when atoms combine and act on each other.

Empedocles c. 495–435 BC, Greek. Developed the theory that matter is made up of four elements: earth, water, fire, and air, and two forces: love and strife. This countered the monism of Parmenides, while preserving the claim that nothing can be created or destroyed. Change is simply an alteration in the balance of elements.

Heraclitus 533–475 BC, Greek. Believed that the world of appearances is in some ways illusory, and that reality is in a state of constant change. A single thing contains opposite qualities, e.g. a road may go up and down simultaneously. Some of his ideas were later developed by Plato.

Heraclitus

Leucippus fl. c. 440 BC, Greek. With Democritus, the founder of atomism.

Parmenides c. 515 – c. 440 BC, Greek. Distinguished between types of philosophical investigation. He separated what is from what is not, and both of these from what human beings believe. Argued that all matter is one. These distinctions shaped the course of Greek philosophy.

Protagoras c. 490–421 BC, Greek. Argued that perception equals knowledge. Two people swimming may percieve the water as warm or cold, but neither is wrong. All truth is relative to the individual.

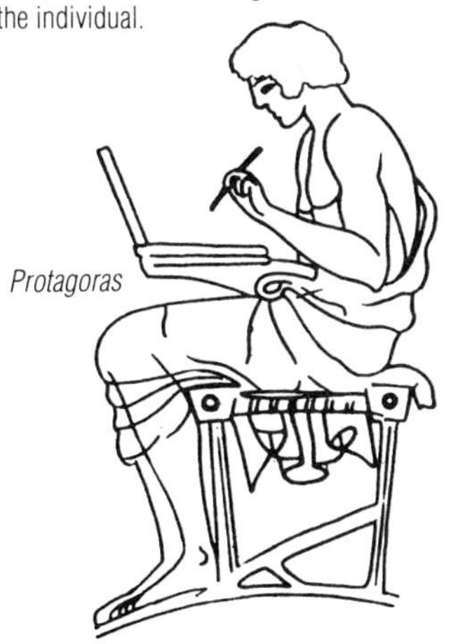
Protagoras

Pythagoras 582–507 BC, Greek. The founder of a secretive sect which recognized certain mathematical influences in the physical world, and held that understanding them was the road to salvation. Perhaps most influential in introducing the concept of the soul into philosophy.

Pythagoras

Thales c. 636–546 BC, Greek. The first thinker to try to account for natural phenomena using natural explanations, rather than the actions of the gods. He argued that the prime substance, from which all natural phenomena arise, is water.

Zeno of Elea 490–430 BC. A follower of Parmenides, he argued that the common sense perception of reality as being made up of lots of things in motion and flux is wrong, and that there is only one unchanging, eternal reality.

Zeno

Classical

6812 **Aristotle** 384–322 BC, Greek (**1**). A pupil of Plato and a teacher of Alexander the Great. His writings cover an enormous range of topics, from ethics and logic to cosmology, psychology, and biology. Among his most influential ideas are his cosmological ones, which dominated the medieval world, thanks to the way they dovetailed with Christian doctrine.

Aristotle's view of the universe
Aristotle saw the universe as consisting of a series of concentric spheres, each sphere being made of crystal and revolving round the Earth at differing speeds. The motions of these spheres was thought to be controlled by the *Primum Mobile*, the outermost sphere. It was not until Copernicus that Aristotle's view of the universe seriously came into question, and it was upheld in the west until this time.

1 Ocean, partly covering the Earth
2 The Firmament
3 Water
4 Air
5 Fire
6 The planetary spheres
7 The fixed stars
8 The *Primum Mobile*

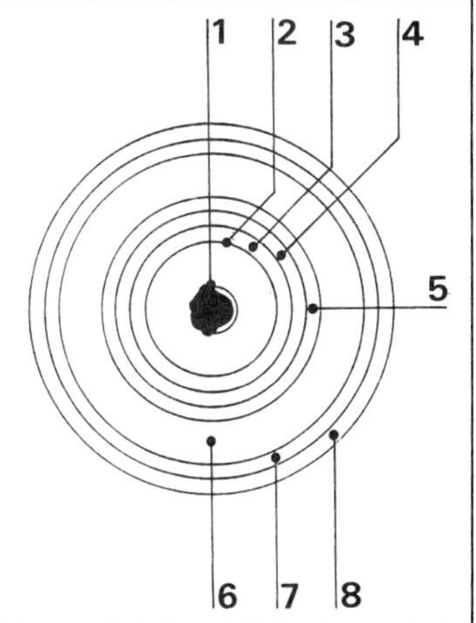

continued

Classical continued

6812 **Plato** c. 427–c. 347 BC, Greek (**1**). One of western civilization's most important philosophers. He proposed a model for a just society, and distinguished between the world of appearances and the world of Forms. While there are many good deeds, there is only one Form of the Good, of which the many are pale reflections. Such ideas have influenced the whole course of western philosophy.

1

2

Socrates 470–399 BC, Greek (**2**). Unlike any of his predecessors, Socrates' chief concern was with ethics. He left no written works and is only known through the works of others, especially Plato. He sought to know the nature of concepts such as justice by gathering many examples of what is meant by it and taking from them a definition. This inductive method was highly influential. He was eventually tried for religious heresy, found guilty, and executed by self-administered poisoning.

Hellenistic and Roman

6813 **Epicurus** 341–270 BC, Greek (**1**). Epicureanism was a reaction to the other-worldliness of Plato. Epicurus regarded sensation as the criterion of truth, and developed the belief that the business of humanity is the avoidance of physical and mental suffering. He placed a high value on pleasure and friendship.

Plotinus AD 205–270, Hellenized Egyptian (**2**). The founder of neoplatonism, which tried to reconcile the thought of Plato with later work by introducing some Aristotelian ideas. The end of man is to seek mystical union with the central sphere of existence, the Good or the One.

Pyrrho of Elis c. 360–270 BC, Greek. Founder of a kind of scepticism which held that since we do not know the real nature of things, we should suspend our judgement and find peace of mind in the thought that all we know is how things appear to us.

Zeno of Citium c. 334–262 BC, Greek (**3**). The founder of stoicism, the central tenet of which is that the world is ordered by divine reason, and that the wise accept their place in this order cheerfully.

1

2

3

Early medieval

6814 **Averroës** 1126–1198, Spanish Arab. Rejected the views of Avicenna and argued that the intellect is universal. Influential in the west, he highlighted the problem of "double-truth:" when rational argument and revelation are at odds, which is to be believed?

Averroës

Avicenna 980–1037, Persian. Leading Muslim philosopher and physician whose significance lies in preserving and developing parts of Aristotelean thought. Made a distinction between existence and essence, God being pure essence. This was taken up by Thomas Aquinas.

St Augustine AD 354–430, Roman. Adapted the ideas of Plato and Plotinus to form a theoretical framework for Christian belief.

Boethius AD 480–524 Roman. Discussed the nature of universals, general terms for groups of particulars resembling each other. Earlier philosophers had held them to be either over and above particulars or inherent in them. Boethius argued that only likenesses of thought are in fact universal, physical likeness being a physical attribute.

An official in the government of Theodoric the Ostrogoth, Boethius was later imprisoned as a traitor. While he was awaiting execution, Boethius wrote *The Consolation of Philosophy* (title page shown here is from a 13th-century copy.)

Maimonides Moses 1135–1204, most important Jewish philosopher of the Middle Ages, Maimonides' work focused on the problem of reconciling Jewish beliefs with the Greek philosophical tradition.

Scholastics

6815 **Abelard, Peter** 1079–1142, French. Abelard's position on the question of universals was that they exist in language only, physical reality being reserved for particulars.

Aquinas, St Thomas 1225–74, Italian. The leading Scholastic philosopher and the most influential thinker of the Middle Ages. He reconciled Christian doctrine with Greek philosophy, particularly that of Aristotle. His work dominated the thinking of the Catholic Church for centuries.

Bacon, Roger c. 1214–92 English Franciscan who placed a new emphasis on empiricism.

Late Middle Ages and Renaissance

6816 **Cusanus, Nicolaus** 1401–64, German. Argued that while God is infinite, and mirrored in all things, human intelligence is finite, and so cannot grasp the infinite except by means of mystical union with it.

Ockham, William of 1285–1349, English Franciscan (**1**), who was excommunicated for challenging Aristotle's supremacy and advocating empiricism. Known for his "Ockham's razor," the principle that "entities are not be multiplied beyond necessity," in other words that simple explanations are best.

1

Scotus, John Duns 1270–1308, Scottish Franciscan dubbed "the subtle doctor" for his clever reconciliation of Aristotelianism with the requirements of the Church.

Early modern

6817 **Arnauld, Antoine** 1612–94, French priest who criticized Descartes and published an influential book rejecting the ideas of Malebranche. Conducted a correspondence with Leibniz, which helped the German clarifiy his ideas.

Bacon, Francis 1561–1626, English. Published a vigorous rejection of Aristotelean "word-spinning" and devised a system, based on empiricism and induction, for advancing science for the benefit of humanity.

Bacon

Descartes, René 1596–1650, French. Sought to re-establish the whole of philosophy from first principles. He argued that God had created two substances, matter and mind, and that consciousness is the only basis for philosophical certainty – hence "I think therefore I am." He placed great emphasis on empiricism and mathematics.

Descartes

Gassendi, Pierre 1592–1655, French priest who sought to reconcile science and religion, and challenged Descartes' mathematical rationalism.

Hobbes, Thomas 1588-1679, English materialist and atheist who argued that the natural state of matter is motion. From this he argued that human beings are "natural machines" while society is an artificial machine. Power in society is not the result of divine rights but of a social contract.

Hobbes

Leibnitz, Gottfried Wilhelm 1646–1716, German. Argued that matter is constituted of created individual substances he called monads, which are "souls." He invented the differential calculus independently of Newton. His view that this world is the best of all possible was lambasted by Voltaire in his *Candide*.

Leibnitz

Locke, John 1632–1704, English empiricist who argued that knowledge about the world comes from sense data called Perceptions, and from Ideas, which the mind forms from its Perceptions. At birth the mind is blank sheet, a *tabula rasa*. Founded a vigorous school of British empricist philosophy which thrived throughout the 18th century.

Locke

Malebranche, Nicholas 1638–1715, French. Took his starting-point from Descartes, but argued that mind cannot be known in the same way as matter. Mind is only known from experience. All causation emanates from God, who has to work hard to keep the world going.

Spinoza, Baruch 1632–77, Dutch lens grinder by profession, Spinoza disputed Descartes' claim that mind and body are different substances, suggesting they are different aspects of the same substance, which is closely identified with God. His metaphysics formed the basis of an influential ethical system.

682 18TH-CENTURY PHILOSOPHERS

Berkeley, George 1685–1753, Irish (**1**). Argued against Descartes and Locke that matter does not exist, all perceptions coming to us from God. Science only gives us knowledge about what God intends, only metaphysics can give us knowledge of reality.
Etienne de Condillac 1715–80, French. Sought to build on the philosophy of Locke, and argued that all knowledge is reducable to "sense-impressions." Vivid sensations create attention, if they are lasting they generate memory, if two occur that are related they foster judgment.
Fichte, Johann Gottlieb 1762–1814, German. His work nearly followed Kant, later he advocated an early form of socialism and proposed a three-step account of knowledge called Dialectics.
Hume, David 1711–76, Scottish empriricist (**2**) who brought empiricism into ethics by arguing that cause and effect are not inherent in the external world but only in the mind. Good and evil are generalized conceptions which originate in the mind out of personal experience.
Kant, Immanuel 1724–1804, German (**3**). Kant built on the work of Hume, arguing that all knowledge comes from experience, except *a priori* insights into the rational mind itself. He argued that there is free will only in our moral choices, all else being determined, and while his philosophy leaves no room for God, he himself tried to soften this implication of his work.
Reid, Thomas 1710–96, Scottish cleric who opposed the idealism of Descartes, Locke, and Hume, by arguing that common sense as expressed in everyday language is the best guide concerning the origin of ideas and knowledge.
Rousseau, Jean-Jacques 1712–78, French-Swiss (**4**). His ideas about the "social contract" between citizen and state formed a reaction to Enlightenment philosophy and part of the ideological background to the French Revolution.
Vico, Giambattista 1668–1744, Italian. Argued against the Enlightenment view of history, and in favor of the primacy of historical knowledge, and the importance of understanding the growth of language in understanding history.

683 19TH-CENTURY PHILOSOPHERS

Hegel, Georg Friedrich 1770–1831, German (**1**). Using the notion of "being" as the most general available, Hegel proceeded to all other concepts using the dialectical method. Especially influential are his ideas about historical processes, moving through distinct cultural phases with the goal of a perfectly rational social order.
James, William 1842–1910, American. Developed Peirce's notion of "pragmatism," and applied it, especially to religious experience.
Kierkegaard, Soren 1813–55, Danish (**2**). Opposed to the ideas of philosophy, he is regarded as the founder of modern existentialism. Held truth to be highly individual, and that people make choices based on no criterion.
Mill, John Stuart 1806–73, English (**3**) Developed a system of logic based on induction as the only method of gaining knowledge about the world. In social questions this method led him to conclude that society should be governed by the principle that actions should bring the greatest good to the greatest number, known as utilitarianism.
Nietzche, Friederich 1844–1900, German. Argued that the will to power rules the world, and that those who overcome their weakness can become "supermen." Mistaken as a precursor of fascism, he was strongly opposed to nationalism.
Peirce, Charles S. 1839–1914, American (**4**). Founder of "pragmatism," the view that the meaning of an assertion is in its practical consequences. Knowledge is gained through science, the criterion of truth being scientific consensus.
Schopenhauer, Arthur 1788–1831, German Romantic philosopher (**5**) who argued that the will is the prime force in the world.

684 20TH-CENTURY PHILOSOPHERS

Bergson, Henri 1859–1941, French. Argued that psychological time is different from time as dealt with in physics, and is the realm of morality and free will. His greatest influence was on the novelist Marcel Proust.
Carnap, Rudolf 1891–1970, German. Leading logical positivist who held various positions on what it is that makes something meaningful, and tried to construct a formal language for science, which would exclude all ambiguity.
Dewey, John 1859–1952, American. A pragmatist, Dewey is best known for his thinking about the nature of education and his argument that morality must be based on experience.

Dewey

Husserll, Edmund 1859–1938, Austrian. Founder of phenomenology, a system of detailed logical description of conscious experience, without attempt at explanation and without drawing on metaphysical assumptions or traditional philosophical questions. His insights into the intentional nature of thought influenced followers.
Heidegger, Martin 1889–1976, German. Studied under Husserl, and succeeded him to become Germany's leading existentialist.
Jaspers, Karl 1883–1969, German psychiatrist and philosopher who developed an existentialist position based on Husserl's phenomenology. He divided existence into the objective, the subjective, and the absolute.
Moore, George 1873–1958, British. He rejected naturalism in ethics, attacking J.S. Mill for confusing "non natural" qualities such as "goodness" with "natural" ones such as "pleasure." He admitted later that he had no adequate explanation of why goodness should be "non natural."

Moore

Ryle, Gilbert 1900–76, British. Chiefly known for his book *The Concept of MInd*, in which he attempts to show that experience is not a mental phenomenon at all and rejects the mind-matter opposition.
Russell, Bertrand 1872–1970, British Grandson of a Victorian Prime Minister, Russell worked with Whitehead on *Principia Mathematica*, in which they explored the relation between logic and mathematics. Best known as a popularizer of philosophy.
Sartre, Jean-Paul 1905–80, French atheist and existentialist writer who argued that human beings are free to create their characters and can decide everything for themselves. He defined Hell as "other people."

Sartre

Russell

Whitehead, A.N. 1861–1947, British mathematician and philosopher who collaborated with Russell on the *Principia Mathematica*, and developed a holistic philosophy of science which was influenced by contemporary theories in physics.
Wittgenstein, Ludwig 1889–1951, British. Austrian born, Wittgenstein studied with Russell, and his contribution to philosophy is in studying the relationship between language, thought, and reality. He influenced logical positivism, but later rejected his own early work.

Wittgenstein

685 GLOSSARY OF IDEAS IN PHILOSOPHY

absolute What exists without depending in any way on other things; the opposite of relative.
atomism In Greek philosophy, the notion that matter is made up particles of solid matter moving in empty space.
cartesianism The philosophy of Descartes and his supporters which emphasized a radical division between matter and mind.
cynics A Greek school of thought which held that nothing can be known; it became associated with the disregard of material things.
determinism The theory that all events are caused, and that there is no free will.
dialectic In Greek philosophy, the art of testing whether assertions hold true. In Hegel, a system of logic proceeding from thesis to antithesis to synthesis.
dualism Any theory which distinguishes between two fundamentally different things, such as good and evil, mind and matter, etc.
empiricism The view that knowledge proceeds from experience.
epistemology The critical investigation of knowledge and its validity.
ethics The philosophical study of morality in human conduct, and of the rules which ought to govern it.
existentialism A practical philosophical tendency centered on the concrete realities of human life, rather than generalized abstractions.
free will Opposed to determinism, the belief that physical causes do not entirely shape the world, and that mental processes can act to influence things.
hedonism The belief that pleasure and the avoidance of pain constitute the highest good.
humanism A view originating in the Renaissance that reason must be autonomous from authorities such as the Church.
hypothesis A suggested explanation for events and phenomena.
idea An object in the mind. For Plato, the metaphysical pattern of which real objects are pale reflections.
idealism The notion that the objects of reality do not have independent existence but are constructs of the mind, or made up of ideas.
innate ideas Ideas which exist, pre-formed, in the mind at birth.
materialism The doctrine that all phenomena are explained by physical laws alone.
metaphysics Branch of philosophy dealing with questions of being.
mind-body problem The philosophical question of how mind and body are related, and whether mind is a non-physical substance.
monism The belief that all things are unified, or that they are all explained ultimately on one single principle or law.
neoplatonism Various schools of philosophy which took the philosophy of Plato as their starting-point.
nominalism The view that universals such as "the true" exist in name only and do not actually exist.
paradox Statements which seem to contradict themselves or lead to absurdity.
phenomenology A philosophical doctrine established by Husserl; the science of appearances.
pluralism The belief that there are more than one or two substances in the world, such as mind and matter.
positivism Philosophical doctrine that we can only have knowledge of things we experience through the senses.
pragmatism An American philosophical school; the view that the meaning of things is in

continued

Glossary of ideas in philosophy continued

685 their practical relation to people.
realism A medieval doctrine that universals such as "the good" have real existence.
reality Whatever is accepted as having objective existence, independent of thought or language.
reductionism The attempt to explain complex phenomena in terms of simple laws or principles.
relativism The view that there are no absolute truths or values.
scepticism The view that there is no certain knowledge without justification.
scholasticism A term for the medieval philosophy taught in schools, and exemplified by Thomas Aquinas.
sensationalism The theory that all our knowledge derives ultimately from the senses
socratic Pertaining to the philosophical method and teachings of Socrates.
utilitarianism A philosophical school of thought arguing that ethics must be based on whatever brings the greatest amount of good to the greatest number of people.

686 ECONOMICS

Economists

6861 **Friedman, Milton** b. 1912, winner of the Nobel Prize for economics. Former president of the American Economic Association. A central figure in a school of thought known as Monetarism or the Chicago School of Economics. Much of Friedman's work has been concerned with studying money supply and developing the Quantity Theory of Money. Friedman has been a passionate supporter of the free market which, he believes, "provides economic freedom" and "promotes political freedom." Friedman is professor of economics at the University of Chicago.
Fisher, Irving 1867–1947, trained as a mathematician, Fisher was the author of a formulation of the Quantity Theory of Money which has played a crucial role in Monetarist economic thought.
Galbraith, John Kenneth b. 1908, American political economist. Former Ambassador to India, personal adviser to President Kennedy and president of the American Economics Association. Galbraith has consistently challenged orthodox economic thinking. He argues that conventional economic theories ignore the clever marketing and advertizing of large corporations which exert power over consumers by manipulating public taste. Although strongly criticized by other economists Galbraith is a great popularizer and is the most widely read modern economist in the world.
Keynes, John Maynard 1883–1946, English economist. In 1936, in the midst of the Great Depression, Keynes published *The General Theory of Employment, Interest and Money*, which challenged the classical school's ideas on unemployment and depression. It was one of the first systematic treatments of macroeconomics and its influence on both economists and governments has been profound. Keynes played a major part in the Bretton Woods Agreement, which lead to the establishment of the International Monetary Fund.
Malthus, Thomas 1766–1834, British social scientist of the 19th century. His main thesis was that population growth increases at a faster rate than growth in the supply of food. Malthus advocated sexual restraint to prevent food shortages in the future. He also argued that an economy might over-produce leading to a glut of unsold commodities, a notion which influenced Keynes.

Malthus

Marshall, Alfred 1842–1924 British economist. Professor of economics at Cambridge, Marshall was the leading member of the Neoclassical school of economics. Developed and expanded microeconomics.
Marx, Karl 1818–83, born in Germany and banished for his radical political activities. Settled in London where he continued his writing in great poverty until his death. Much of Marx's economics was derived from the writings of the classical school. However, unlike the classical school, Marx placed great emphasis on a knowledge of history for understanding current economics. Marx was critical of capitalism which he felt created much injustice and unhappiness. He also emphasized that economic systems are not static but develop through time. He predicted that these developments would lead to the collapse of capitalism. Wrote *Das Kapital* 1867;1885;1895.
Quesnay, François 1694–1774, French economist who advocated *laissez-faire* capitalism. Quesnay is also famous for inventing a model of the circular flow of income in the economy.
Ricardo, David 1772–1823, British economist. In 1817 Ricardo's *The Principals of Political Economy and Taxation* was published. This made a valuable contribution to the theory of wage determination and prices as well as introducing the law of comparative advantage.
Smith, Adam 1723–90, Scottish economist whose book *An Inquiry into the Nature and Causes of the Wealth of Nations* published in 1776 became the foundation upon which the school of Classical economics was built. Covered in the book were the importance of the division of labor and free trade for a nation's wealth. Smith also argued that the economy was a harmonious system which could guide itself as if by an invisible hand. Government interference in the working of the economy should be kept to a minimum. Smith's proposals on taxation were adopted by the British government.

Smith

Schools of economic thought

6862 **Classical school** (1750–1850) In general, classical economists tended to believe that markets were harmonious systems with their own powers of self-regulation and if possible they should be left free from outside interference. Includes: Adam Smith, David Ricardo, Jeremy Bentham, John Stuart Mill.
Marxist economics (1840s onward) A diverse school of economic thought with its roots in the writings of Karl Marx. Marxist economists generally focus on the long term development of the capitalist economic system, paying particular attention to the interaction of social classes. Marxists also tend to believe that capitalism will one day collapse and be replaced by another system.
Keynsian economics (1930s onward) A body of economic theory emanating from the British economist John Maynard Keynes. Keynes challenged the Classical school's belief that the economy could guide itself without outside intervention and that periods of unemployment and recession were only temporary. For Keynes the economy might slump for very long periods. Under such circumstances Keynes advocated stimulating the demand for goods and services through government spending.
Monetarism (1960s onward) Monetarists believe that changes in the money supply are a major cause of economic instability and the main role of the government, in managing the economy, is to keep the money supply constant. Monetarists have revived many of the ideas of the Classical economists, such as the belief that the economy should, as far as possible, be left free from government interference. Unlike Keynesians, monetarists regard government spending as ineffectual and possibly a harmful way in which to control the economy. Includes: Milton Friedman, Irving Fisher.
Neoclassical school (1880s–1930s) Not so much a well defined school as a loose amalgam of sub-schools centring around leading

continued

Schools of economic thought continued

6862 economists such as Alfred Marshall in England, Leon Walras in France and Carl Menger in Austria. Neoclassical economists followed in the tradition of Classical economics but have concentrated primarily on microeconomics, leading to major developments in this field.

supply-side economics (1970s onward) This stresses the importance of the supply of goods and services in determining the state of the economy. It contrasts with many other schools of economic thought, such as Keynsian economics, which have laid emphasis on the importance of the demand for goods and services. Supply-side economists tend to argue that markets should be made competitive and that there should be incentives to encourage work, such as tax cuts. Supply-side economics can be viewed as a further development of Monetarism, and monetarists such as Milton Friedman also advocate supply-side policies.

Glossary of key economic terms

6863 **arbitration** The appointment of an impartial individual to settle a dispute, for example between unions and management.
asset A company's assets are everything it owns that has a money value, e.g. factories, offices, machinery, bank deposits.
balance of payments A country's balance of payments is the difference between the amount it receives for its exports and the amount it pays to other countries for its imports. The balance of payments is divided into: visible items, which are goods, e.g. cars, coffee, oil, and invisible items which are services, e.g. banking, insurance, shipping.
barter The exchanging of goods and services without using money.
bear market A market in which prices are falling.
big bang Refers to events in 1986 when, in the course of one day, the London stock exchange was deregulated and new computing technology brought in.
black economy Economic activities which take place without the paying of taxes.
bond Bonds are issued by private companies or by governments in order to borrow money. A bond is a piece of paper which states when the person loaning the money will be repaid and how much interest they will receive.
budget An estimate of government spending and government revenue for the coming year. If government spending is higher than government revenue, there is a budget deficit. If government spending is lower than government revenue, there is a budget surplus.
bull market A market in which prices are rising.
business cycle The tendencies of some economies to fluctuate regularly between boom and depression.
capital Consists of all goods and services which are used in the production of other goods and services, e.g. machinery, factories, education, and training. Capital can also mean the money value of a company's assets.
capitalism A social system in which capital is privately owned and work is performed under free contract for personal reward.
cartel An agreement between firms within an industry that it is in their interests to collude rather than to compete.
central bank A bank for banks, the central bank can lend other banks money in the last resort; it can also exercise some control over their activities. Central banks tend to work closely with the government. The US central banking system is the Federal Reserve.
closed shop A firm which allows only union members to be employed operates a closed shop.
closed union A union which restricts its membership.
collective bargaining Negotiations between people representing the employers and trade union officials.
command economy An economy in which the state has a large role in deciding what goods and services are produced, how they are produced, and how they are distributed.
commercial bank Bank which is used by the general public.
commodity 1 A general name which covers both goods, e.g. bananas, televisions, and services, e.g. hairdressing, banking. **2** A raw material or primary product, e.g. tea, rubber, tin.
commodity market A market in which commodities (raw materials) are bought and sold. It is not necessary for the commodities to actually be exchanged, pieces of paper carrying the rights of ownership are sufficient. Commodities also can be bought in the futures market. *See* futures
common stock Any kind of share where the owners receive their dividend of company profit only after payments have been made to other shareholders with priority such as those with preferred stocks. Preferred stocks have a stated rate of dividend payment.
consumer price index A measurement of how much money can buy in terms of a selection of goods and services typically consumed by the average household. If there has been inflation a dollar will buy less than it did previously.
creeping inflation *see* inflation
deflation 1 A policy pursued by a government aimed at reducing inflation. **2** A fall in the general level of prices.
depreciation The fall in value of capital, such as machinery, due to wear and tear, old age, obsolescence, or a fall in the market price.
deregulation The abolition or reduction of state controls and supervision over private economic activities.
devaluation Reducing the value of a currency against other curriencies.
direct taxes *see* taxation
disposable income The money an individual has left to spend after all direct taxes have been deducted.
division of labour The division of production into separate processes each of which is performed by different people. Under the division of labour, work becomes more and more specialized, and this allows a higher level of skill to develop.
economics The study of the arrangements that societies make concerning the use and development of the limited resources on our planet.
econometrics The use of mathematical and statistical methods to test economic theories.
entrepreneur Someone who risks their own capital in a business enterprise.
exchange rate The price at which one currency can be exchanged for another currency, or for gold. To prevent fluctuations in the rate of exchange, exchange rates can be fixed or controlled. Exchange rates which are left free to market forces are known as floating exchange rates.
fiscal policy The government's plan for taxation and government spending. Fiscal policy is one way in which a government can attempt to control the economy. Another way is through monetary policy which attempts to guide the economy by controlling the money supply.
fixed costs Those costs a firm has which do not vary with every change in output, e.g. the cost of machinery or buildings. These contrast with variable costs which do vary with output, e.g. the amount spent on materials used in the production process.
fixed exchange rates *see* exchange rate
free market Trade which flows freely between countries without barriers such as tariffs and quotas.
floating exchange rate *see* exchange rate
foreign exchange market The market in which one foreign currency is exchanged for another.
futures An agreement to buy goods at a fixed date in the future at a fixed price. Futures are sold where the price of goods fluctuates, for example, there are futures for commodities such as fruit and also it is possible to buy futures in foreign currencies. If the price fluctuates, above the amount agreed the buyer gains; if the price fluctuates below, the buyer loses. Futures are a hedge against uncertainty.
galloping inflation *see* inflation
gold standard A system in which the value of a currency is legally fixed in terms of how much gold it is worth.
gross national product The money value of all the goods and services produced in a country during a period of one year.
incomes policy A government policy of keeping wage increases under control in order to reduce or prevent inflation.
indirect taxes *see* taxation
inflation A rise in the general level of prices. Galloping inflation (or hyperinflation) is an inflation which precedes at a high rate but perhaps for only a brief period. The rate of inflation generally increases during a galloping inflation. Creeping inflation is an inflation which lasts for a long time at a fairly steady pace.
insider dealing The illegal use of privileged information when trading on the stock market. For example, if someone knows that a takeover bid is about to be launched and starts buying

continued

Glossary of key economic terms continued

6863 shares because they think this will cause the value to increase.
integration Firms within an industry are horizontally integrated if they all specialize in a single process, for example making tin cans. Firms within an industry are vertically integrated if each firm tends to carry through the production of a commodity from the raw material stage right up to the finished product. An industry in which the firms brewed beer, bottled it and sold it in their own bars would be an example of vertical integration.
interest A payment by a borrower for the use of a sum of money.
investment bank A bank that provides money for industry, generally by buying shares in companies.
invisibles *see* balance of payments
laissez-faire The theory that government intervention in industry and commerce should be kept to a minimum.
limited liability If a company goes bankrupt and has limited liability, the owners of the company (the shareholders) are only obliged to pay back company debts with the money they have already invested in the firm. They will not be forced to sell their personal possessions to help pay debts.
liquidity The ease with which an asset can be converted into money. Cash is perfectly liquid but shares in a company are less liquid because they must be sold first before money is obtained. Assets such as property are even less liquid because they are harder to sell than shares.
M1, M2, M3 *see* money supply
macroeconomics That branch of economics which studies the economy as a whole, e.g. the level of output, the level of employment, the level of inflation.
market Any area of business where buyers and sellers are in contact with each other and where prices in one area affect prices in another area. A market need not be confined to a particular place, it could refer to an area of the economy, for example, the market for factory machinery or the market for foreign exchange.
merger The joining together of two or more firms to form a single company.
microeconomics A branch of economics dealing with the study of units within the economy, e.g. firms, markets, and individual consumers.
monetary policy *see* fiscal policy
money supply The amount of money in an economy at a given moment. There are various ways in which the money supply can be defined. Narrowly defined, the money supply can mean the coins and bank notes in circulation and bank deposits where money can be withdrawn at short notice. A broader definition will also include savings accounts at banks and possibly bonds and shares. The terms M1, M2, and M3 have been used to indicate narrow and broad definitions of the money supply. The precise definitions vary from country to country and are often revised.
monopoly A company which is the only producer of a commodity.
national debt Governments create a national debt when they borrow money from people and institutions inside their country's borders. One way a government can borrow is through the issuing of government bonds.
national income The total amount of income earned by all the people and institutions within a country from the production of goods and services (usually measured over a period of one year).
nominal income *see* real income
oligopoly A market where there are few large firms selling a particular product.
open market operations The buying and selling of securities in order to control the money supply. This is normally done by the central bank. If the central bank wants to increase the money supply it will buy securities (in this case pieces of paper carrying the promise to repay the money) from the commercial banks giving the banks extra money. If the central bank wants to decrease the money supply it will sell securities to the commercial banks leaving them with less money.
opportunity cost The benefit that is sacrificed by choosing one course of action rather than the next best alternative, e.g. the opportunity cost sacrificed in building a road might be use of the land for farming.
planned economy *see* command economy
preferred stock *see* common stock
price mechanism The balancing of the forces of supply and demand in a market to produce a price.
privatization Transfering state-owned assets and services into private hands. Term usually applied to the transfer of nationalized industries.
real wages Wages which are in terms of the goods and services money will buy as distinct from nominal wages which are simply wages in terms of money. If there is an inflation real wages may fall while nominal wages may rise.
securities A general term covering both shares and bonds.
stagflation Rising prices combined with rising levels of unemployment.
shares Pieces of paper which testify the ownership of part of a corporation. If 10,000 shares are issued and someone owns 100 shares, they own 1% of the company and they are entitled to 1% of company profits and 1% of the votes in the election of corporate officers or on corporate policy.
stocks A synonym for shares.
stock exchange A market where shares in companies are bought and sold.
takeover When one company takes control over another company by buying more than 50% of its shares. This gives it a majority of votes in the election of corporate offices or on corporate policy.
tariffs A tax on imports.
taxation Compulsory payments by companies or individuals to the state. Direct taxes are on income and indirect taxes are taxes on commodities.
variable costs *see* fixed costs
quota Places a limit on the amount of a good that can be imported into a country, e.g. no more than 2 million oranges a year.

Key dates in economic history

6864 **The era of the merchants 1400–1764**

- European trade greatly increased as merchants aided by the gun-carrying ships and improved navigation, opened up new trade routes in the east and the American continent.
- The activities of the merchants also helped create many of the financial institutions of the modern world.
- The first companies were founded to organize and finance merchant voyages, e.g. Muscovy Company 1555, The Dutch East India Company 1602.
- Banking was revived first in Italy and then in northern Europe providing loans to the merchants.
- Meeting places for merchants, bankers and businessmen developed into the first stock exchanges.

The first wave of industrialization 1764–1877

- New technology led to a huge increase in output. Home-based rural crafts such as spinning and weaving were replaced by factories in the growing towns.
- The old economic ideas of monopoly, warfare and protectionism began to give way to new ideas of competition in free markets, the importance of peace and free trade. Adam Smith expressed this new philosophy in his book *Inquiry into the Nature and Causes of the Wealth of Nations.*
- Industrialization caused considerable hardship, with many people working long hours in appalling conditions and not everyone shared Smith's optimism about the capitalist system. Karl Marx argued that capitalism would one day collapse and be replaced by a better system but his ideas did not have a significant impact until the 20th century.

continued

Key dates in economic history continued

6864 **The second wave of industrialization 1877 onward**

- During this period advances in communication and transportation have led to the growth of much larger companies, some of which have become giant multinationals.
- Economies have become far more interconnected at a global level and there has been a growth of international organizations and agreements such as the IMF, the World Bank, the European Community, and GATT.
- Communism, based on the ideas of Marx, spread rapidly during the 20th century and communist governments have given a large role to the state in managing the economy. However, state-managed economies have often failed to generate the same level of economic growth as capitalist economies and partly in response to this failing the former Soviet Union and Eastern Europe have recently begun to move toward a market economy.
- Pollution of the planet becomes a major international concern.
- The gap in wealth between countries of the developed and developing world increases.

1492 Christopher Columbus travels to America.
1498 The Portuguese explorer Vasco de Gama travels to India.
1588 Spanish Armada defeated by the British.
1600 British East India Company formed.
1611 Amsterdam Stock Exchange created, strengthening Amsterdam's importance as a financial center.
1763 Treaty of Paris, Britain emerges as the dominant world power, ending a long period of intense military rivalry within Europe.
1764 Spinning Jenny invented by Hargreaves.
1776 American Declaration of Independence. First successful steam engine patented by James Watt. Adam Smith publishes his Inquiry into the Nature and Causes of the Wealth of Nations.
1785 The power loom invented by Cartwright.
1804 First steam powered train.
1846 British Corn Laws repealed permitting foreign grain to be imported into Britain.
1848 Marx and Engels publish the Communist Manifesto. Revolutions in Europe.
1860 Cotton still represents two thirds of US exports.
1877 Telephone (Bell.)
1885 Radio (Marconi.)
1900 USA is the largest producer of coal, iron, and steel, and the world's leading economic power.
1903 First airplane flight (Wright brothers.)
1914–1918 First World War.
1917 Revolution in Russia. This eventually led to the establishment of the world's first socialist state-managed economy.
1923 German hyperinflation $1 = 1 trillion marks.
1929 American stock market in Wall Street crashes.
1932–39 Unemployment and recession in America and Europe known as the Great Depression.
1939–45 Second World War.
1944 Bretton Woods conference leads to the creation of the IMF and the World Bank.
1945–48 State managed socialist economies established in Poland, Czechoslovakia, Romania, Hungary, Bulgaria, Albania, Yugoslavia, and East Germany.
1947 The USA aids war-torn economies in a scheme known as the Marshall Plan.
1949 Establishment of a state-managed socialist economy in China.
1950 The European Community created.
1950–73 Period of increasing economic prosperity in USA and Europe.
1973 OPEC oil embargo.
1974 World recession. USA output declines and inflation and unemployment increase.
1989 Berlin Wall pulled down. Communism challenged in Eastern Europe and the Soviet Union which move toward market economies.

6877 SOCIOLOGY

Sociologists

6871 • Major works

Compte, August 1798–1857, French philosopher and social theorist who invented the term sociology. Believed the sciences formed a hierarchy, the pinnacle of which was crowned with sociology. With Saint Simon (an early social philosopher) he formulated the "law of three stages of social development." This theory proposed that human thought progressed from a religious stage to a philosophical stage and finally to a positive (or scientific) stage. This corresponded to society's development from a military to a legal and finally an industrial stage.
- *The Positive Philosophy of August Compte* (1896)

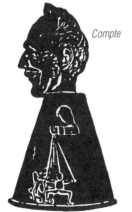

Compte

Dahrendorf, Ralf b. 1929, born in Germany the son of a politician. Imprisoned in a concentration camp 1944–6. Studied sociology at the London School of Economics. Taught in German Universities in the 1950s and 60s. Became involved in German politics. Appointed parliamentary state secretary for foreign affairs 1969. Became director of the London School of Economics 1974. Awarded an honorary knighthood in 1982. Dahrendorf revised Marx's definition of class. For Dahrendorf classes are defined not by whether they own property but by whether they can exercise authority. Has also written extensively on why democracy failed in Nazi Germany, on higher education, modernization, and the third world.
- *Class and Conflict in Industrial Society* (1957)
- *Society and Democracy in Germany, Homo Sociologicus* (1958)

Durkheim, Emile 1858–1917, born in France. Graduated at the Ecole Normale. Taught sociology at the University of Bordeaux. Lectured in sociology in the Sorbonne from 1902. A founder of modern sociology. Concerned with the social forces which hold societies together. For Durkheim, religion served an essential social function in gluing the social fabric together. Durkheim considered what happens when the social norms break down or conflict, a state he called "anomie." In *Suicide* he argues that during periods of disruption when the social norms were weakened or in conflict, the suicide rate increases. Anomie was for Durkheim a cause of suicide as well as being an unhealthy element in modern industrial society.

In the *Rules of Sociological Method* Durkheim argues that social phenomena could be explained in terms of their function in the social system. For example, religion has the function of enhancing social unity. Because of this, Durkheim is regarded as one of the originators of functionalism.

Toward the end of his life Durkheim wrote *The Elementary Forms of Religious Life* and using material on Australian aborigines and Native Americans formulated a theory on how knowledge developed socially. This influenced the structuralist school of anthropological thought.
- *Division of Labour* (1893)
- *Rules of Sociological Method* (1894)
- *Suicide* (1897)
- *The Elementary Forms of Religious Life* (1912)

Durkheim

Evans-Pritchard, Sir Edward Evan 1902–73, professor of social anthropology at Oxford University 1946–70. Disputed the notion

continued

Sociologists continued

6871 that anthropology was a science. He rejected attempts to formulate laws or general theories of society and believed that the main task of social anthropology was to accurately describe and interpret other cultures. He felt that an understanding of history was very important to this task.
- *Witchcraft, Magic and Oracles among the Azande* (1937)
- *The Nuer* (1940)
- *Essays in Social Anthropology* (1964)

Foucault, Michel 1926–84, French social philosopher. Professor of systems of thought, taught at the College de France from 1970. Concerned with the history of knowledge and theories of power. Also carried out detailed studies on prisons and the history of sexuality.
- *Madness and Civilization* (1967)
- *The Archaeology of Knowledge* (1969)
- *The Order of Things* (1970)
- *The History of Sexuality* (1976)

Garfinkel, Harold b. 1917, born in New Jersey, USA. Taught at University College of California and Los Angeles. His work on how people use everyday knowledge about the world led to the founding of a new school of sociology known as ethnomethodology
- *Studies in Ethnomethodology* (1967)

Goffman, Ervine 1922–82, born in Canada. Studied at the Universities of Toronto and Chicago. Professor of sociology at Berkley and the University of Pennsylvania. Became president of the American Sociological Association 1981. *The Presentation of Self in Everyday Life* was based on a study of the Shetland Islands off the coast of Britain. Has written extensively on deviance. His later work concerns patterns of human communication.
- *The Presentation of Self in Everyday Life* (1956)
- *Frame Analysis* (1974)
- *Forms of Talk* (1981)

Lévi-Strauss, Claude b. 1908, French social anthropologist and origninator of structuralist anthropology (structuralism). His work had a widespread influence on sociology and anthropology during the 1970s when structuralist thought successfully challenged established methods of investigation.
- *Structural Anthropology* (1958)
- *The Savage Mind* (1962)
- *Mythologiques* (4 vols 1964–72)

Malinowski, Bronislaw Kasper 1884–1942, Polish-born anthropologist. Became a professor of anthropology at the London School of Economics. Malinowski's study of the Trobiand Islands pioneered a new method of anthropological research in which the anthropologist studied a society at first hand and in depth. Opposed earlier evolutionary approaches to anthropology which tended to view modern day primitive societies as examples of the early stages in the evolution of man. A pioneer of functionalism, Malinowski argued that society should be studied as wholes and not broken into segments.
- *Argonauts of the Western Pacific* (1922)
- *Crime and Custom in Savage Society* (1926)
- *Sex and Repression* (1927)
- *Magic, Science and Religion* (1928)

Mannheim, Karl 1893–1947, born in Hungary. Professor of sociology at Frankfurt. Forced into exile by the Nazis in 1933. Taught sociology at the London School of Economics. One of the founders of the sociology of knowledge.
- *Ideology and Utopia* (1929)
- *Man and Society* (1940)
- *Freedom, Power and Democratic Planning* (1950)

Marx, Karl 1818–83 German social scientist and revolutionary (**1**). Did much work on economics also. Marx put forward a view of history known as historical materialism. This proposed that technology and economics formed the base of the social system which then influenced the political, intellectual, religious, and artistic features of society. Argued that technological change intensifies class antagonism and from this struggle a new social and economic system emerges. He predicted that under capitalism the struggle between the proletariat and the bourgeoisie will lead to the collapse of the system and its replacement by socialism. Although class struggle under capitalism has not intensified in the way in which Marx predicted, Marx's version of historical materialism has shattered the assumption that our political, intellectual, religious, and artistic lives are separate from our economic existence. It demonstrated that many aspects of "human nature" which were previously thought to be fixed are in fact subject to historical change. His analysis of classes has played a large part in the development of sociological theory.
- *The German Ideology* (1845–46)
- *The Communist Manifesto* (1848)
- *Capital Volume I* (1867)
- *Capital Volume II* and *III* (not completed during his lifetime)

Marx

Mead, Margaret 1901–78 American cultural anthropologist whose work stresses the importance of culture in determining personality. Has done much to popularize anthropology and make it more relevant to contemporary problems, especially the role of women in society.
- *Coming of Age in Samoa* (1949)
- *New Lives for Old* (1936)
- *Male and Female* (1950)

Merton, Robert King b. 1910, American sociologist educated at Temple University and Harvard. Lectured in sociology at Columbia until 1979. A founder of the sociology of science. Argued that economic and military necessities (such as the need for better means of navigation) as well as Puritan religious beliefs were important forces behind scientific discovery. Some of Merton's terms such as "self-fulfilling prophecy," are now widely used.
- *Science, Technology and Society in Seventeenth Century England* (1935)
- *Social Theory and Social Structure* (1968)
- *The Sociology of Science: Theoretical and Empirical Investigations* (1973)

Morgan, Lewis Henry 1818–81, an American lawyer whose interest in Iroquois Indian led him to write one of the first modern anthropological studies of native people *League of the Iroquois*. He also established kinship and marriage as essential areas of anthropological research. In *Ancient Society* he developed a theory of cultural evolution which had a strong influence on Marx and Engels.
- *League of the Iroquois* (1851)
- *Ancient Society* (1877)

Parsons, Talcott 1902–79, American sociological theorist and leading member of the functionalist school which dominated American sociology from the 1940s through 1960s.
- *The Structure of Social Action* (1937)
- *Towards a General Theory of Action* (1951)
- *The Social System* (1951)

Radcliff-Brown, Alfred Reginald 1881–1955, British anthropologist who, together with his contemporary Malinowski, was responsible for the development of British social anthropology. Like Malinowski he felt it was important to study societies first hand from field work and he studied societies in the Andman Islands and in Australia. He also advocated a form of functionalism.
- *The Andman Islanders* (1922)
- *A Natural Science of Society* (1957)

Spencer, Herbert 1820–1903, British social theorist. One of the first exponents of evolutionary theory. Spencer proposed a theory of evolution which covered both biological and social systems. Founder of a school of thought known as social darwinism and coined the phrase "the survival of the fittest" to refer to evolutionary competition.
- *Systems of Synthetic Philosophy* (1862-96)

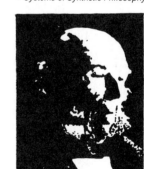

Spencer

Tylor, Sir Edward Burnett 1832–1917, founding father of British anthropology who studied Mexico and other tropical regions. He proposed that some customs and beliefs in modern societies are relics of an ancient past. Also argued that animism formed the basis of primitive religion. He pioneered the first cross-cultural analysis.
- *Primitive Culture* (1871)
- *Anahuac* (1861)
- *Researches into the Early History of Mankind* (1865)

continued

Sociologists continued

6871 • *Anthropology* (1896)
Weber, Max 1864–1920, born in Germany into a Protestant family. Preoccupied with the question of what caused the rise in capitalism in certain Western European countries. In his famous essay *The Protestant Ethic and the Spirit of Capitalism,* Weber argued that the growth of the Protestant religion was a crucial factor in the development of capitalism. The reason for this lay in the Calvinist belief that wordly success was a sign of being chosen by God. For Weber this provided people with an incentive to work harder and save rather than squander wealth. Also concerned that western culture was gradually becoming more and more rationalized and as part of this process he felt that bureaucracy would grow. Known for his use of the word "charismatic" which entered the popular language in the 1960s.
• *The Protestant Work Ethic and the Spirit of Capitalism* (1904–5)
• *Economy and Society* (published after his death)

Weber

Glossary of sociology

6872 **anthropology** The study of the human race. Known in Britain as social anthropology. Anthropology differs from sociology largely because it developed from a different intellectual tradition. Early anthropologists were motivated by a desire to study primitive societies. On the other hand, the founding fathers of sociology (such as Compte, Durkheim, Weber, and Marx) were more concerned with an analysis of industrial societies. Sociology is the study of society. As the boundaries between both subjects have now blurred, we have chosen to include both anthropological and sociological terms in this glossary.
alienation A concept first introduced by Marx and since used in a variety of contexts. Loosely defined it means the separation of the individual from important aspects of the external world accompanied by a feeling of powerlessness or lack of control. A person may feel alienated from themselves or from society as a whole.
animism A belief in the existence of spirits dwelling in natural phenomena such as animals, tree, mountains, or storms.
anomie A term introduced by Durkheim to refer to a situation where the conditions for happiness are absent. Durkheim argued that one of the conditions for happiness was that there should be clear norms governing social behavior. The absence of these norms resulted in anomie and unhappiness.
aristocracy A ruling class which inherits wealth, special privileges, and titles. Typically they are accompanied by a monarchy.
bourgeoisie A class of people who, in the capitalist system, own the means of production, i.e. those things which are used to produce commodities such as factories, machinery, and finance. According to Marx, as society moved from feudalism to capitalism the bourgeoisie replaced the aristocracy as the real power holders. A distinction is sometimes made between the *petite bourgeoisie* (small property owners such as tradesmen, shopkeepers, and craftsmen) and the *haute bourgeoisie* (large scale property owners such as company owners.)
caste A rigid class system based on common acceptance of a religious principle. For example, the ancient Indian caste system. Castes were defined in the Hindu religion. Membership of caste depends on birth and movement between castes is only possible in some instances through marriage. The system was widely accepted by those involved.
charisma A term introduced by Max Weber to describe an ability to lead and inspire through force of personality and without the aid of material incentives, coercion, or the authority of office. Jesus was a purely charismatic leader since he did not coerce, had no wealth, and no office.
clan A group of people who claim to be descended from the same ancestor through either male or female links or both. It may be impossible to trace these links.
class Karl Marx defined two classes: the bourgeoisie and the proletariat. Sociologists have since defined class to include such factors as power and education.
critical theory/critical sociology *See* Frankfurt School
cult A type of religious organization or movement which deviates from the established religious tradition in the community.
cultural anthropology *See* anthropology
deviance Divergence from the accepted social norms of behaviour. deviance can be beneficial to society if unorthodox behaviour leads to creativity or innovation. Alternatively deviance may be harmful as in the case of crime.
endomy The practice of marrying within a particular group such as a tribe or social class.
estate A form of social stratification which is recognized by the legal system. Commonly estates were formed around the following groups: the nobility, the clergy, the peasants.
ethnocentrism Word invented by W.G. Summer to mean a "view of things in which one's own group is the center of everything and all others are scaled and rated with reference to it."
ethnography Branch of anthropology which gives a descriptive account of the way of life in a particular society usually as the result of an in-depth study through personal contact.
ethnology Branch of anthropology which focuses on classifying people and cultures and explaining how these groups became distributed.
ethnomethodology Associated with the sociologist Harold Garfinkel. Ethnomethodology studies the ways in which people use everyday knowledge to interpret and understand the world and communicate with other people.
exomany The practice of marrying outside the social group such as the tribe or village.
extended family Family group which consists of parents and children and other relatives living together or in close contact. The extended family is larger than the nuclear family.
feudalism Term used to describe the social order in Europe from medieval times. Essentially the system consisted of an unarmed peasant population who were subservient to noblemen and warriors. Some sociologists have used the term feudalism to describe historical periods in other cultures, such as Japan.
Frankfurt school Term referring to members of the Frankfurt Institute of Social research founded in 1923. Forced into exile during the Hitler years the school returned in the 1950s. The institute draws on the work of early Marx, Freud, and Hagel to produce an approach to the social sciences and philosophy which is known as critical theory. The following have also been part of the Frankfurt institute: Horkheimer, Marcuse, Adorno, Habermas.
functionalism A school of sociological and anthropological thought which considers social institutions such as religion within the context of the social system as a whole. Some functionalists have drawn a biological analogy seeing society like an organism which is composed of many different parts but which neverthless has its own identity. This contrasts with other methods of inquiry in which investigators study the components of the social system individually and then make cross-cultural comparisons of these components.
hermeneutics The study of the way in which we interpret and attempt to understand phenomena such as texts, works of art, actions, and gestures. Although originally part of philosophy, hermeneutics has recently had an important influence on the study of sociology.
hunter-gatherer Human societies which depend on the hunting of animals, fishing, and gathering of wild fruits and seeds for survival. Hunter-gatherer societies represent at least 90% of human history. The development of societies which have used agriculture as a major food source is relatively recent.
ideology Any system of ideas and beliefs. These beliefs may be true or they may be false. Many writers, such as Marx, use the term to refer to a distorted system of beliefs and ideas.
institutions Patterns of behavior which become established over the course of time. This term can be used to refer to large organizations such as hospitals, monasteries, and army training camps which contain established codes of behavior. It can also refer to important social entities such as the state, the church, the family, and the law, which, like organizations, operate along set patterns of behavior.
kinship Branch of anthropology which studies the way in which people are related by birth or

continued

Glossary of sociology continued

6872 through marriage in different societies.
matriarchal A society in which the positions of power or dominance are held mainly by women. No historical proof of a truly matriarchal society has been found.
matrilineal Descent which is traced through women.
monogamy A rule which permits men and women to have only one marriage partner at a time.
norms Social norms are standards of behavior or ideas which are common to a group. Conforming to social norms increases a group's identity.
nuclear family Family group which consists of just parents and children living together or in close contact without other relatives.
petite bourgeoisie *see* bourgeoisie
physical anthropology Branch of anthropology which studies the biological characteristics of man, such as genetic make up, blood types and bone structure. Among other things, physical anthropologists have been concerned with how physical characteristics vary between humans geographically, between the sexes and between people and other animals.
polygamy Marriage to more than one person at the same time. The most common form of polygamy is polygyny where a man has several wives. A less common form is *polyandry* where a woman has several husbands.
proleteriat A class of people who sell their labor and who do not own the means of production in a capitalist society.
rationality People, organizations, and systems which achieve their goals by operating according to rules of logic can be said to be rational.
rites of passage Rituals which accompany the passage of an individual from one social status to another, e.g. the transition from adolescence to full adulthood.
shamanism A shaman is a religious specialist but unlike a priest a shaman does not belong to a Church. Personal mystical experience forms the basis of the shaman's spiritual knowledge such as healing, protecting through magic, and offering spiritual guidance. The term originally comes from Siberia but anthropologists have used it to describe certain individuals in cultures all round the world.
social anthropology Branch of anthropology concerned with the study of linguistics, archaeology, ethnography, and ethnology.
socialization The shaping of human behavior through experience in social institutions.
social darwinism Term originated with Herbert Spencer (1820-1903) who applied Darwin's theory of evolution to the social sphere. This postulated that natural selection allows those members of society who are well adapted to their social environment to flourish while the others fall by the wayside.
sociology *See* anthropology
social stratification The ranking of social groups in a hierarchy. Castes, classes, and estates are all forms of social stratification.
society A group of people who form a system of relationships and have their own culture.
sociobiology Study of the biological basis for human behavior.
sorcery *See* witchcraft
soul Something which inhabits the body, brings life to it and animates it. There may be one soul or many and sometimes soul may be separate from body. Each culture has its own interpretation of the soul.
structuralism Stemming from the writing of the Swiss linguist Ferdinand de Saussure (1857–1914), structuralism influenced anthropology principally through the work of Claude Lévi-Strauss (b. 1908). Structural anthropologists see cultural forms (e.g. customs, language, and tools used by man) as projections into this world of the inner workings of the human mind. The task of anthropology is to decode these cultural forms to reveal the principles through which the human mind operates.
taboo A word of Polynesian/Melanesian origin which is used in anthropology to refer to an action, object, or space which society regards as forbidden. For exampe, in many societies incest is taboo.
totemism Originally a North American term, totemism is used by anthropologists to refer to a mystical or ritual relationship between a social group and a class of objects such as a species of plant or animal.
voodoo A religious cult practiced in Haiti and in parts of the Caribbean, Brazil, and the southern states of America. Voodoo mixes beliefs and rites of Africa with elements from the Catholic religion.
witchcraft The use of supernatural forces to harm people. Witchcraft is similar to sorcery except that witchcraft is performed by someone who is permanently engaged in using magic for destructive purposes, whereas sorcery is performed by someone who only uses magic for these ends occasionally.

691 CLASSICAL RELIGIONS

Greek gods

6911 **Aphrodite** goddess of love and beauty. Daughter of Zeus and Dione. She was the mother of Aeneus and of Eros.
Apollo god of the Sun and of youth. He is a symbol of manly beauty and reason. The son of Zeus and Leto. Apollo is one of the 12 Olympian gods.
Ares god of war. Son of Zeus and Hera. Father of Eros.
Artemis twin sister of Apollo. Goddess of the Moon and hunting.
Athena goddess of war and wisdom, also a patron of arts and crafts. Daughter of Zeus and Melis. The city of Athens is named after her.
Dardanus son of Zeus and Electra and founder of Troy.
Demeter goddess of agriculture and corn. Mother of Persephone. She searched for her daughter who had been taken away to the Underworld.
Dionysus god of wine. Son of Zeus and Semele. He was snatched by Zeus from Semele's dead body and taken to Mount Nysa in India where he was brought up by nymphs.
Eros god of love. Son of Aphrodite and Ares. He is pictured with a bow and arrows and was thought to be cruel to his victims.
The Fates three daughters of Zeus and Themis. Lachesis, decided men's destinies at birth. Clotho, spun the thread of life. Atropos cut the thread at the moment of death.
The Graces Agalia, Euphrosyne, and Thalia, daughters of Zeus. The three Graces personify beauty, charm, and grace as well as favor and gratitude. They are often shown waiting on Aphrodite.
Hades god of the Underworld. One of the three sons of Kronos and husband of Persephone.
Helen daughter of Zeus and Leda. She was hatched from an egg with her brothers, the twins Castor and Pollux. Helen is half sister to Clytemnestra and famous for her beauty.
Hephaestus blacksmith of the gods and god of fire. Son of Zeus and Hera. He was said to have been thrown from heaven in one of Zeus and Hera's quarrels and to have landed on the island of Lemnos, which caused his limp.
Hera queen of the gods. Wife and sister of Zeus as both were children of Kronos. Jealous and cruel to rivals for Zeus' love.
Herakles most popular of Greek heroes. Son of Zeus and Alcmene. Famous for his exploits, especially the 12 labours, which derive from his strength and courage.
Hermes messenger of the gods. Son of Zeus and Maia. He is often shown with winged sandals and a wide-brimmed hat.
Hestia goddess of home.
Kronos god of time. One of the Titans and the youngest son of Heaven (Uranus) and Earth (Gaea). To gain the throne, Kronos castrated his father. Kronos married Rhea and swallowed his children.
Minos early king of Crete. Son of Zeus and Europa and husband of Pasiphaë.
The Muses daughters of Zeus and Mnemosyne. The Muses judged the contest between Apollo and Marsyus. Each muse presided over one of the arts or sciences: Calliope – heroic epic; Clio – history; Euterpe – flutes and music; Terpischore – lyric poetry and dancing; Erato – hymns; Melopomene – tragedy; Thalia – comedy; Polyhymnia – mime; Urania – astronomy. The Muses embody the highest intellectual and artistic pursuits.
Perseus son of Zeus and Danaë. He is famous for killing the gorgon Medusa and for rescuing Andromeda.
Poseidon god of earthquakes and later of the sea. One of Kronos' three sons. Father of Theseus.
Zeus king of the gods. He dethroned Kronos, his father, in the battle against the Titans which represents the triumph of the Olympian gods over the pre-Greek gods.

1 Zeus
2 Apollo
3 Ares
4 Poseidon
5 Hermes
6 Hephaestus
7 Dionysus
8 Eros
9 Hades/Pluto
10 Kronos
11 Hera
12 Demeter
13 Artemis
14 Athena
15 Aphrodite
16 Hestia

Roman gods

6912 **Aesculapius** god of health and medicine. He was originally a Greek hero and the god of healing. He was brought to Rome after a plague in 293 BC.
Apollo god of sun and youth. Also one of the Greek gods. A symbol of light, youthful manly beauty and reason. He was associated with music, archery, medicine, the care of flocks and herds, and with prophecy.
Aurora goddess of the dawn. She is often depicted driving her chariot and horses through the sky.
Bacchus god of wine. He is normally depicted as a youth crowned with vine leaves and grapes.
Ceres goddess of agriculture. Ancient Italian corn-goddess.
Concordia goddess of unity.
Cupid god of love. For the Romans, Cupid was mainly the playful winged putto as well as a symbol of carnal love and life after death.
Diana goddess of the moon and hunting. An indigenous Italian goddess associated with wooden places, women, childbirth.
Faunus god of woods and shepherds. An Arcadian god generally represented as having goat's horns, ears, and legs. He was also a fertility god and amorous toward both sexes. A patron of pastoral poets from classical times.
Fortuna goddess of fate and good luck.
Furiae the three furies. Originally Greek spirits of vengeance. They largely avenged wrongs, particularly murder within the family.
Flora goddess of spring.
Gratiae the three graces. They personified beauty, charm, and grace. Daughters of Zeus.
Hercules god of strength. Originally one of the most popular Greek heroes. He was popular at Rome as a defender against evil. He was idealized by Stoic philosophers for his endurance, courage, and his service to men.
Janus god of doorways, beginnings, harbors, and travel.
Juno queen of the gods. Early Italian goddess associated with women and childbirth. She later became associated with Hera, wife of the Greek god Zeus, and therefore women and marriage.

continued

Roman gods continued

691**2** **Jupiter** king of the gods. Originally the Italian sky-god connected with rains, storms, and thunder, who was later identified with the Olympian god, Zeus.
Luna goddess of the moon. Like Aurora, the dawn, she was given horses to drive across the sky.
Mars the god of war and patron god of the city of Florence before Christianity flourished.
Mercury the messenger of the gods. The Roman equivalent of Hermes. He was given this name to mark his patronage of merchants.

Minerva the goddess of wisdom. She was associated with wisdom and the arts and also identified with the Greek goddess Athene. Therefore also a goddess of war.
Neptune the god of the sea. Italian god of water later identified with the sea.
Parcae the three fates. One assigned man's lot at birth, one spun the thread of life and the other cut the thread at the moment of death and could not "be turned."
Pax goddess of peace.
Pluto god of the Underworld. Favors were not expected from him. No temples dedicated to him.
Pomona goddess of fruit and trees.
Proserpina goddess of the Underworld. She was carried off by Pluto and forced to spend half the year underground.
Saturn the god of time. Early Italian god of agriculture later identified with the Greek god Kronos. He was the husband of Rhea and the father of Jupiter.
Sol the god of the sun.
Tellus the goddess of the earth.
Venus the goddess of love, beauty, and reproduction.
Vesta goddess of the home. Generally worshipped in every Roman home.
Vulcan blacksmith for the gods. The Roman god of fire.

1 Janus
2 Bellona
3 Venus
4 Penates
5 Fortuna
6 Silvanus
7 Pomona
8 Ops
9 Terminus
10 Vertumnus
11 Concordia
12 Bona Dea
13 Pax
14 Spes
15 Flora

Greek-Roman equivalents

691**3**

Greek	Roman	Position
Aphrodite	Venus	Goddess of love and beauty
Apollo	Apollo	God of the sun, youth, and reason
Artemis	Diana	Goddess of the moon and hunting
Ares	Mars	God of war
Asclepius	Aesculapius	God of health and medicine
Athene	Minerva	Goddess of wisdom
Demeter	Ceres	Goddess of agriculture
Dionysus	Bacchus	God of wine
Eos	Aurora	Goddess of the dawn
Erinyes	Furiae	The Furies
Eros	Cupid	God of love
Gaea	Tellus	Goddess of the Earth
Graces	Gratiae	The Three Graces
Hades	Pluto	God of the Underworld
Helios	Sol	God of the sun
Hephaestus	Vulcan	Blacksmith for the gods
Hera	Juno	Queen of the gods
Hermes	Mercury	Messenger of the gods
Herakles	Hercules	God of strength
Hestia	Vesta	Goddess of the home
Kronos	Saturn	God of time
Moerae	Parcae	The Three Fates
Pan	Faunus	God of the woods and sheperds
Persephone	Proserpina	Goddess of the Underworld
Poseidon	Neptune	God of the sea
Selene	Luna	Goddess of the moon
Tyche	Fortuna	Goddess of good luck
Zeus	Jupiter	King of the gods

Roman religious objects

691**4** **1** A legion's eagle (silver or gold) standard
2 Household shrine with Lar, and oil lamp suspended above
3 Statuette of a household guardian (Lar)
4 Sacred staff or littus of an augur (priest who took auspices)
5 Ritual rattle (sistrum) used in the worship of Isis
6 Incense vessel
7 Stone basin for libations

continued

Roman religious objects continued

6914

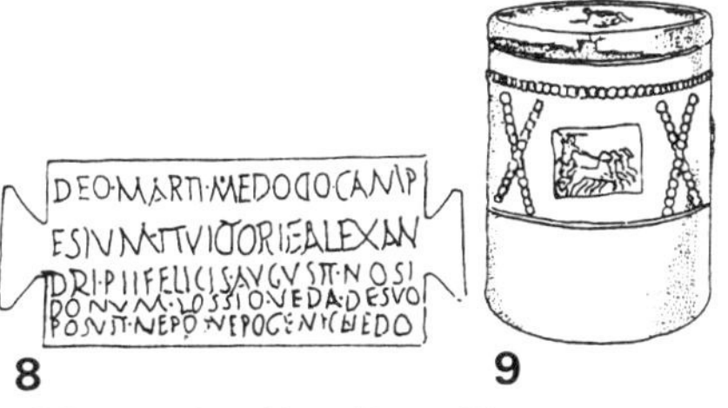

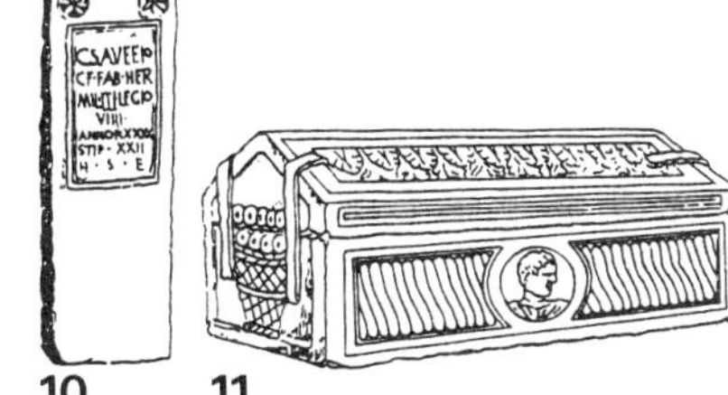

8 Bronze votive tablet to Mars and Emperor Alexander Severus (222–235 CE)
9 Canister with gold Sol (driving chariot) for glass urn and ashes, found outside London
10 Tombstone of a Roman legionary
11 Stone coffin from London (5 ft/1.5 m long)
12 Altar decorated with plane leaves (late BCE or early CE)

Places

6915

Mountains
1 Mount Olympus, home of the gods
2 Pelion, home of the centaurs
3 Parnassus, home of Apollo and the Muses
4 Mount Ida was where Zeus grew up
Oracles
5 Dodoma, place of Zeus' oracle and the most ancient known
6 Delphi, site of the most important oracle, presided over by Apollo
7 Lebadea (Trophonius)
8 Didyma (Apollo)
Shrines
9 Brauron, the most important shrine to Artemis
10 In Sparta Artemis merged with the goddess Orthia
11 Ithaca, home of Odysseus and where he was left sleeping in the nymphs' cave
12 Delos, sacred island of Apollo; his birthplace

● Temples

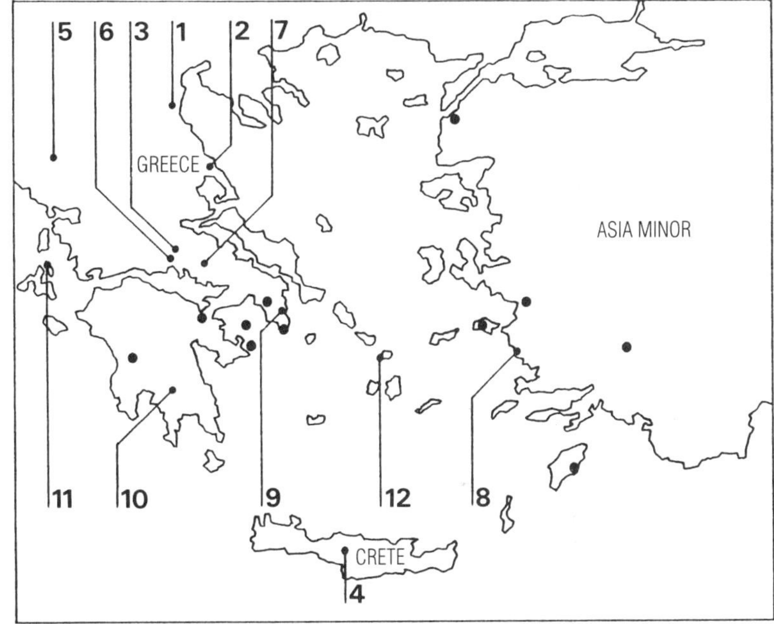

692 MIDDLE EASTERN GODS

Egyptian gods

6921

Amon-Re king of the gods. Creator of the universe, lord of Karnak and father of the pharoahs. He became the supreme deity in Egypt and was part of the triad of Thebes with his wife Mut and Khensu.
Anubis god of the dead. Presiding over the embalming of the dead. He is represented with a jackal's head and holding an ankh, the key of life.
Apep snake god and manifestation of Seth. Lord of the powers of darkness. Enemy of Re and the Sun gods and also enemy of the dead who could only return through his defeat.
Bast goddess of pleasure. Bast had a cat's head and was also known as Little Cat and goddess of fire. Sister of Sekhmet.
Bes god of recreation and childbirth. Shown as a bandy-legged dwarf.
Hathor goddess of women, love, and festivity. She was guardian of the cemeteries of the dead. As mother-goddess she is cow-headed with a sun disk between her horns.
Horus god of light and of Lower Egypt. Son of Osiris and Isis. Hawk-headed and father of the canoptic gods, Amset, Hapi, Duamutef, and Qebhsneuf who protected the liver, lungs, stomach, and intestines.
Isis principal goddess of Egyptian pantheon. Osiris's wife and mother of Horus. She could transform herself into any shape or form.
Khensu human-headed moon god. Son of Amon-Re and Mut. Khensu had seven forms.
Khnum god of creation and the Nile cataracts. He had a ram's head and was associated with Maat, Ptah, and Thoth in creation. Khnum is a potter-god and shaped man from his potter's wheel.
Maat goddess of truth and justice. She wore a large upright feather in her hair to symbolize justice. Daughter of Re, a lady of heaven, queen of the Earth and mistress of the Underworld. Maat sat in the Judgment Hall of Osiris to judge the dead.
Mut goddess of Thebes and wife of Amon-Re. Shown as a vulture or with a vulture headdress. Mother of the gods.
Nephtys goddess of death. Osiris and Isis's sister, wife of Seth and mother of Anubis. A great magician like Isis, Nephtys knew the words of power to raise the dead. Because of this she was considered a protector of the dead.
Osiris god of the Underworld and husband of Isis. Brother and rival of Seth. Osiris had a white crown and carries a scepter and wand.
Ptah god of fertility and creation. God of Memphis. Shaven-headed and carrying a scepter.
Re Sun god, with a falcon's head and carrying a solar disk on his head. Re sailed across the sky in his Sun boat by day and through the Underworld at night. He became associated with Amon-Re.
Sebek god of water, fertility and evil. Sebek had a crocodile's head.

continued

Egyptian continued

6921

Sekhmet goddess of war. She had a lion's head and was Bast's sister.
Seth Sun god who was in conflict with Horus over Re's throne. Mammal-headed. Later became known as lord of the powers of evil.
Thoth god of writing and counting. Thoth had the head of a crested ibis and carried an inscription. He was arbiter of the gods and knew the magic formulae needed by the dead to pass safely through the Underworld.

Egyptian Gods
1 Amon-Re
2 Anubis
3 Bast
4 Bes
5 Hathor
6 Horus
7 Isis
8 Khnum
9 Maat
10 Mut
11 Osiris
12 Ptah
13 Re
14 Sebek
15 Thoth

Mesopotamian gods

6922

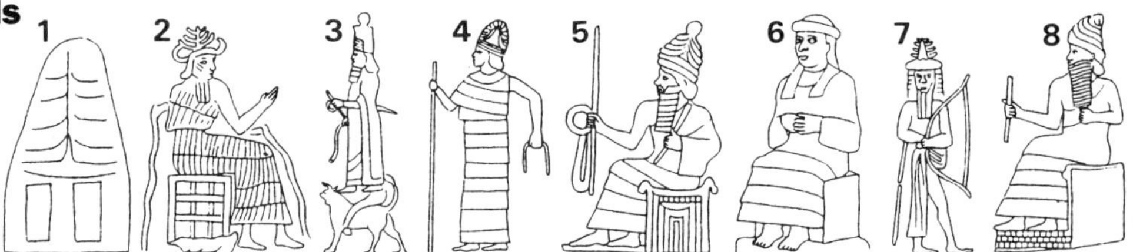

SUMERIAN GODS
1 Anu supreme god of heaven and sky. Chief of the great triad of gods with Enlil and Ea. Father of the gods and ruler of destiny. One of the most ancient of divinities.
2 Ea god of water and Underworld. First of the Babylonian new order of gods, defeating and replacing Apsu and Mommu. Ea was the champion of purity.
3 Enlil supreme god of Earth and air. Son of Anu. Assyrian winged bulls are thought to represent him.
4 Inanna Sumerian goddess of the morning star and of war and also called Ishtar by the Babylonians.
5 Nannar Moon god of Ur which was the center of Nannar worship son of Enlil.
6 Ningal goddess of the Moon and mother of Shamash.
7 Ninurta god of war and hunting and solar deity.
8 Shamash god of Sun and war. He was also known as Chemosh of the Old Testament and Heres of the Canaanites.

BABYLONIAN GODS
Ishtar prominent goddess of Assyro-Babylonic pantheon. Goddess of the moon and evening, and in certain periods goddess of war and love.
Marduk (**1**) supreme Babylonian god, God of the spring Sun, Bel of the Old Testament and head of the Babylonian pantheon. Son of El and Damkina and champion of the gods in their fight against Tiamat, an older goddess.
Nabu (**2**) god of writing, science, vegetation, wisdom, and justice. Son of Marduk. Nabu was a scribe and messenger of the gods and guardian of the Tablets of Wisdom.

ASSYRIAN GODS
1 Adad god of weather and thunder. Formed part of the second triad of gods with Sin and Shamash.
2 Ashtur supreme Assyrian god, holding a similar position to Marduk.
3 Gula goddess of healing.
4 Nusku fire god.

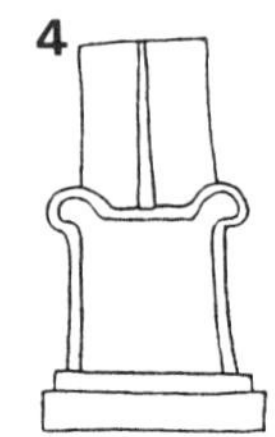

ZOROASTRIAN GODS
Anahita included in Zoroastrian creation legends. She is the mother goddess and river goddess. In the *Aresta*, the Zoroastrian sacred text, she is portrayed as one of the helpers of Ahura-Mazda.
Ahura Mazda supreme god and wise lord of Zoroastrianism.
Zervan Akarana father of Ahura Mazda. In Zoroastrian religion eternal time or destiny. He was the power of good and Anra Maiyu the leader of the powers of evil.

Holy places

6923 **Places in Egypt**
This map shows some of the sacred sites on the Nile.
1 Abu Simbel site of the Great Temple of Rameses II.
2 Abydos is the home of the god Osiris.
3 Dendera site of Temple of Hathor c. 110 BCE–117 CE.
4 Giza is the site of the Great Pyramid of Cheops and Sphinx c. 2560 BCE.
5 Karnak on the River Nile, is the site of the Great temple of Amon c. 1520 BCE–c. 37CE.
6 Memphis center of worship for Ptah and the capital of ancient Egypt.
7 Philae site of Temple of Isis c. 380 BCE–c. 300 CE.
8 Saqqara near Memphis is the site of the Step Pyramid of Djoser c. 2680 BCE.

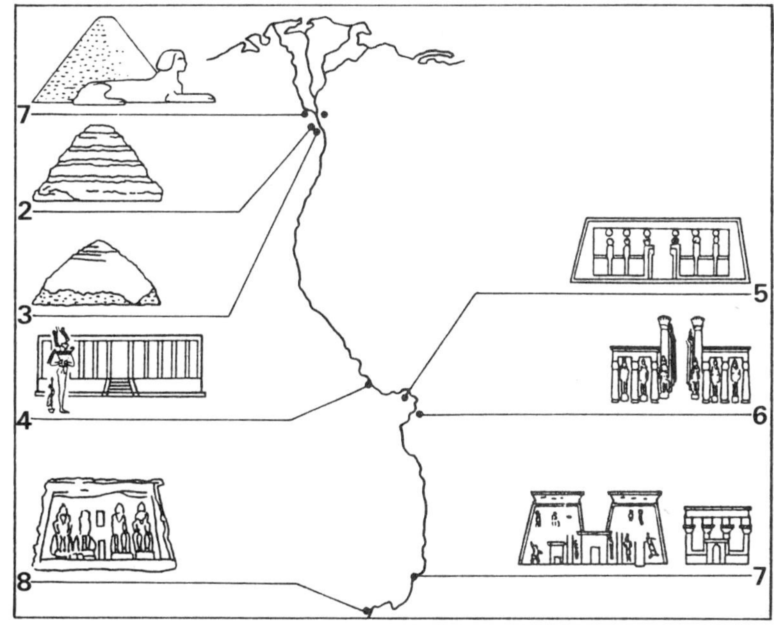

Sacred sites in Turkey
Ararat in Turkey is the place where Noah's Ark is said to have come to rest after the Biblical Flood abated.

Ziggurats in Mesopotamia 3000–707 BCE
Dots on this map show locations of sacred sites around the rivers Euphrates and Tigris in Iraq. One such site is Borsippa (**a**), a ziggurat built around 2500 BC is known as the Tower of Babel and is one of the oldest ziggurats. These were temple towers with a shrine to a god at the top.

Here we show examples of two types of ziggurat:
1 Ashur (three) c. 1114–1076
2 Ur and Eridu c. 2100

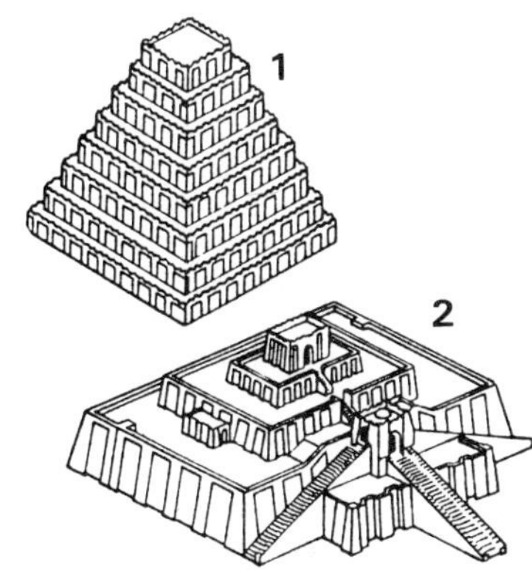

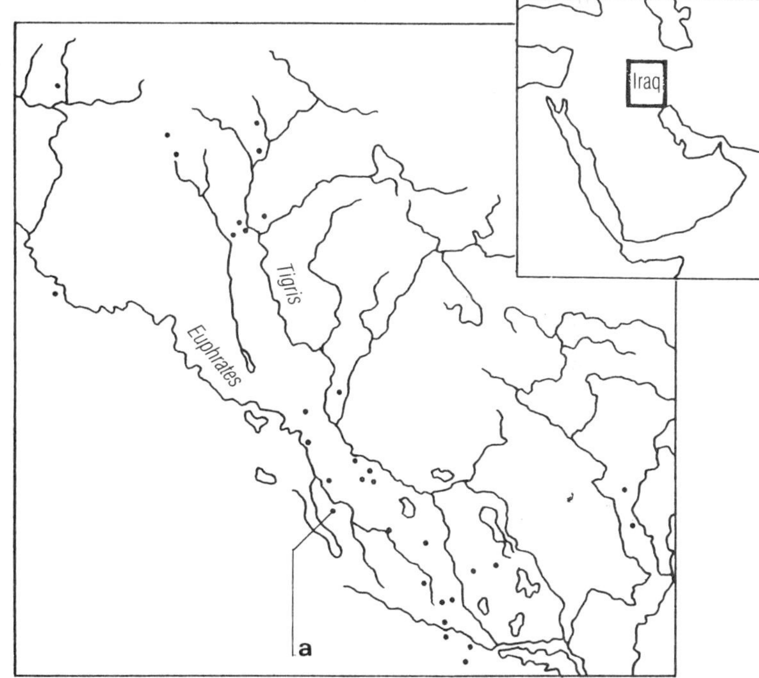

693 NORDIC GODS AND PLACES

Nordic gods

6931 **Balder** god of light. The son of Odin and Frigga.
Bragi the god of poetry and music, and patron of bards.
Frey son of Njord. He had a ship built by dwarfs and a sword which rendered him invincible.
Freya wife of Odin. She traveled on a chariot drawn by two cats and received half of the dead slain in battle.
Heimdall the god of light. One of the Aesir (the group of leaders forming the entourage of Odin.)
Hoenir the god of creation. One of the Aesir, described as fair, tall, and fleet of foot.
Loki the god of evil and fire. His role was that of a malicious magician.
Njord the god of the seashore and father of Frey and Freya. In Nordic myth, one of the Vanir sent to the Aesir as a hostage.
Odin chief god of the Nordic pantheon. God of the dead, cunning, and poetry, and bringer of victory. He became leader of the Aesir and the hero of warriors particularly those of an aristocratic background.
Thor the god of thunder and war and Odin's eldest son. Thor was strong and brutal with gross appetites. Famous for his hammer, belt of power, his chariot, and his iron gloves. He was the hero of the lower orders.
Tyr the god of war, son of Odin who lost his hand in a fight.
Ull/Ullur the god of magic and magnificence. A minor hero.
Vali the son of Loki.
Valkyries the priestesses of Freya accredited with bringing the souls of the slain to Odin.
Vidar the god of silence and the son of Odin.

continued

Nordic gods continued

6931 **1** Balder
2 Odin
3 Thor
4 Valkyrie

Places

6932 **1 Stonehenge** built c. 1500 BC in south west England. It holds the largest stones of any such megalithic structure. A ditch and an earth bank surround the stone circle. Other stone circles are found in France and Britain.

2 Remains of ship burials by ancient Nordic people have been found around Scandinavia.
3 Rune stones these have been found on islands around Britain and in Scandinavia. They are carved with inscriptions. The stones were thought to hold magical powers and were used for grave memorial purposes.

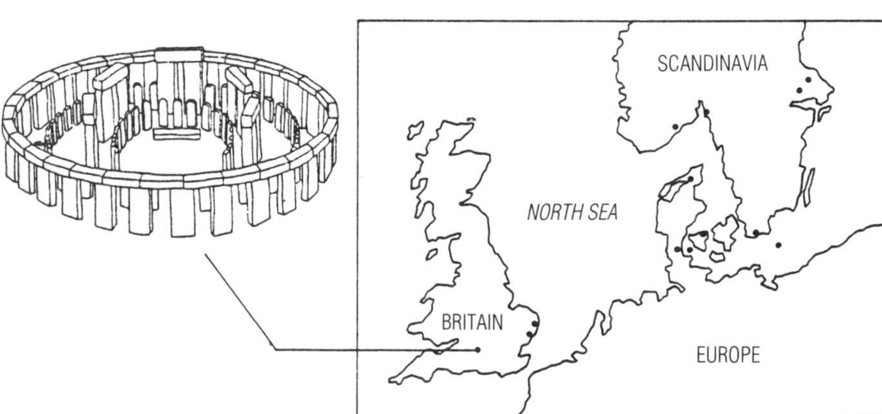

694 EARLY AMERICAN RELIGIONS

American gods

6941 **Cahntico** goddess of fire and hearth.
Chalchuihuitlicue Aztec water goddess. Wife of Tlaloc and known as the Emerald Lady. She was lord of the third hour of the day and the sixth hour of the night.
Huehuecoyotl the old god. A name occasionally given to the Aztec fire god, Xinhtecutli.
Itzapapalotl Aztec butterfly goddess.
Mictlantecuhtli god of death. Lord of the eleventh hour of the day and husband of Mictlantecuhtl, who was also goddess of death.

Patecatl god of medicine and drink.

Quetzacoatl culture hero of Toltecs and absorbed into the Aztec pantheon of gods. Aztec feathered serpent and god of learning, priestly functions, and of the wind.
Teczistecatl Aztec moon goddess.
Tepeyollotl god of Earth. Aztec puma god. Lord of the eighth hour of the night.
Tezacatlipoca or "Smoking Mirror." Chief god of the Aztec pantheon and chief god of Texacoco. Lord of the tenth hour of the day. Identified with Itzacoliuhqui, the carved obsidian knife god. Tezacatlipoca commanded Nata to build a ship to save himself from the deluge in the Aztec creation myth.
Tlaloc god of rain and moisture. One of the most important members of the Mexican pantheon of gods. Father of the Tlalocs, the minor rain gods. Lord of the eighth hour of the day and the ninth hour of the night. Large numbers of children were sacrificed to him each year.
Tlazolteotl Aztec Earth mother, fertility goddess and mother of Centiotl. Lord of the fifth hour of the day and of the seventh hour of the night.
Tonacatecuhtli god of maize. Aztec creator god, husband of Tonacacihuatl.

Tonatiuh Sun god and lord of the fourth hour of the day.
Xipetotec god of springtime and fertility.
Xochiquetzal goddess of flowers and of craftsmen. Mother of Quetzacoatl. Considered to be the first woman.

Xolotl early Aztec cultural hero who became the mythological twin of Quetzacoatl.
Xiuhecuhtli fire god and lord of the year. Lord of the first hours of the day and night.
Xochipilli god of pleasure.

Sacred sites of Central America

6942 **1** Teotihuacán "City of the Gods" c. 1–650 CE
2 Tula Temple of Quetzalcoatl, Toltec capital c. 950–1170 CE
3 Tenochtitlán, Aztec capital 1345-1521 CE
4 Cholula Pyramid c. 100–1519 CE
5 El Tajín, Pyramid of the Niches

Olmec ritual centers
6 Tres Zapotes, flourished to 323 BCE
7 La Venta c. 900–300 BCE
8 San Lorenzo c. 1200–900 BCE

9 Monte Albán, Zapotec Temple of Dancers c. 500 BCE

Maya cult cities c. 300 BCE–1500 CE
10 Palenque
11 Piedras Negra
12 Uaxactun
13 Tikal
14 Naranjo
15 Quirigua
16 Copán
17 Uxmal
18 Mayapan
19 Chichén Itzá
20 Cobá
21 Tulum

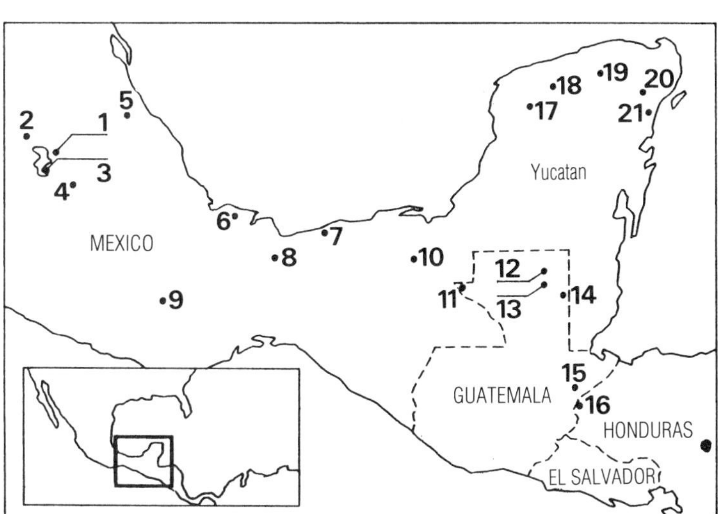

695 TYPES OF SACRED BUILDING

barrow An earth mound over a tomb.
cenotaph A monument to those who are buried elsewhere.
colossus A large statue, usually of a god.
dolmen A stone formation thought to be a megalithic burial mound.
mastaba An ancient Egyptian structure built above tombs. Thought to be from where the pyramids developed.
mausoleum A large grand tomb comprising a separate structure or building.
monolith A single large standing stone.
obelisk A single large needle-like stone with square or rectangular base and tapering toward a pyramid-shaped top.
pantheon A temple to all the gods.
pyramid (**1**) In early Egypt a royal tomb of pyramid shape.
rune stones Nordic single standing stone with religious or magical inscriptions.
shrine A sacred altar.
stela An upright slab of stone usually with an inscription.
temple A place of worship.
tholos A circular domed building.
towers of silence (**2**) Circular buildings to house the dead of those of Zoroastrian faith.
tumuli A megalithic barrow.
ziggurat (**3**) A stepped pyramid with terraces of decreasing size and with a temple or shrine at the top.

1

2

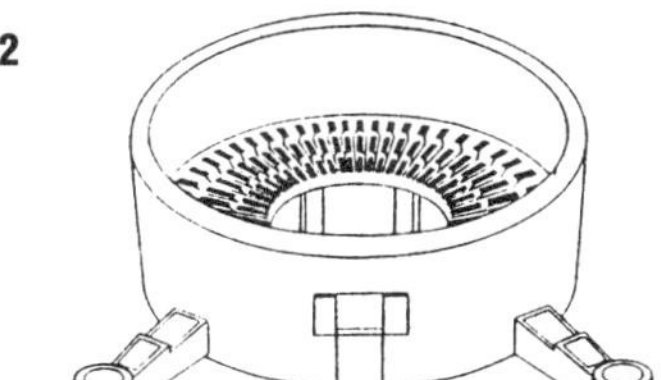

3

696 MYTHICAL CREATURES

1 Griffins huge beasts, with the head and wings of an eagle, the ears of a horse, and the body of a lion. They were often thought to guard a hoard of gold.
2 Unicorns reputedly a lithe, powerful combination of a horse's body and head with an antelope's legs, a lion's tail, and a fearsome spiral horn on the forehead. Only the virtue of a young maiden could tame a unicorn.
3 Cyclops man-eating hairy giants with only one eye, set centrally in the forehead. The biggest and most famous cyclops, Polyphemus, lived in a cave and grazed sheep.
4 Satyrs these had the torso and head of a man, but the horns and hindequarters of a goat. They were woodland creatures, associated with fertility.
5 Harpies said to have the head and torso of a woman, pale, thin, with dirty matted hair, but with the wings and feet of a vulture. They were immortal, although always on the point of starvation.
6 Centaurs they had the upper body of a man and legs of a horse. They were very civilized, being famous for their noble nature and knowledge of medicine.

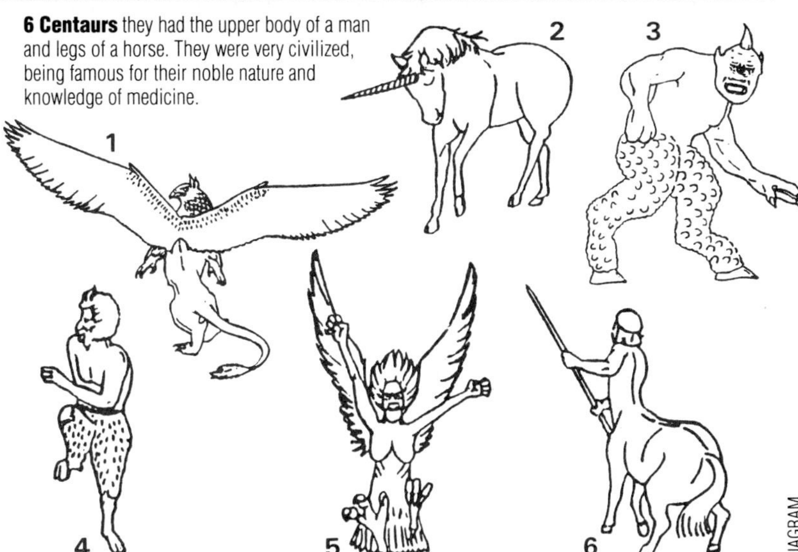

711 BODY SYSTEMS

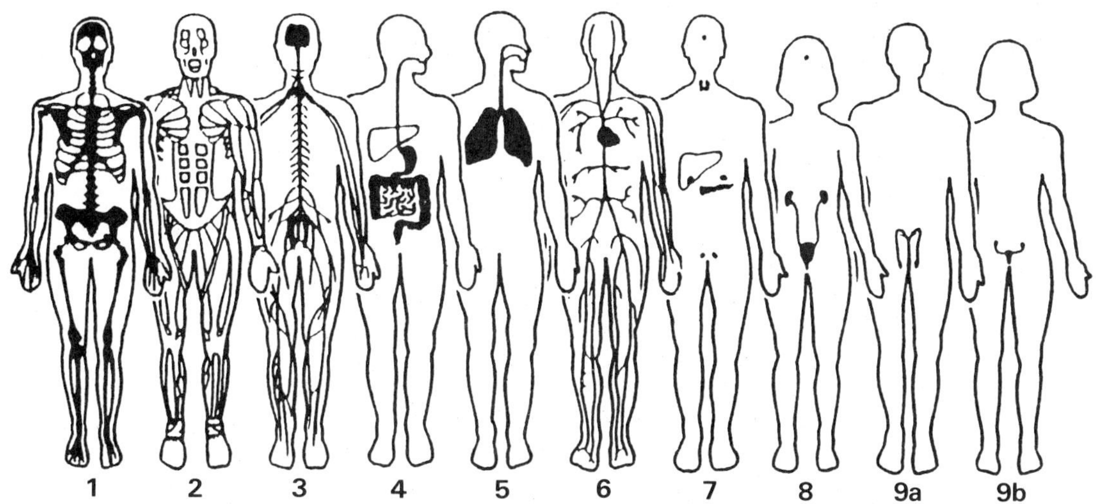

These diagrams show the main body systems. More facts and figures about these systems appear later in this book.

1 Skeletal system This is the body's framework of bones

2 Muscular system This makes it possible for different parts of the body to move

3 Nervous system Consists of the brain, spinal cord, and nerves. It transmits and receives electrochemical messages around the body

4 Digestive system This processes food for the body's nutrition and gets rid of solid waste

5 Respiratory system This takes oxygen into the body and gets rid of waste carbon dioxide

6 Cardiovascular system Consisting of the heart, blood vessels, and blood, this forms the body's main transport system

7 Endocrine system This consists of glands, which produce hormones – chemical messengers that control specific body functions.

8 Urinary system This forms urine, the means of getting rid of the body's waste fluids

9 Reproductive systems of the male (**a**) and the female (**b**). These make possible sexual intercourse and reproduction and also produce sex hormones

712 SKELETAL SYSTEMS

Principal bones

7121 Identified here are the most important human bones. Common names are given in brackets.

1 Cranium (skull)
2 Mandible (jawbone)
3 Clavicle (collarbone)
4 Scapula (shoulder blade)
5 Sternum (breastbone)
6 Ribs
7 Vertebrae (spine or backbone)
8 Pelvis or pelvic girdle

Arm
9 Humerus
10 Radius
11 Ulna
12 Carpals (wrist bones)
13 Metacarpals
14 Phalanges (finger and toe bones)

Leg
15 Femur (thigh bone)
16 Patella (kneecap)
17 Tibia (shin bone)
18 Fibula
19 Tarsals
20 Metatarsals

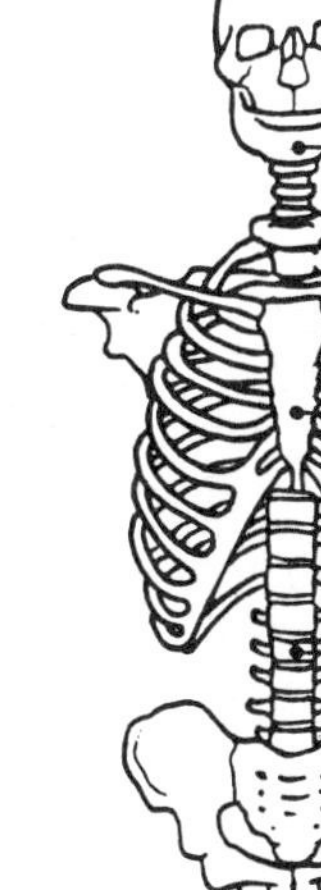

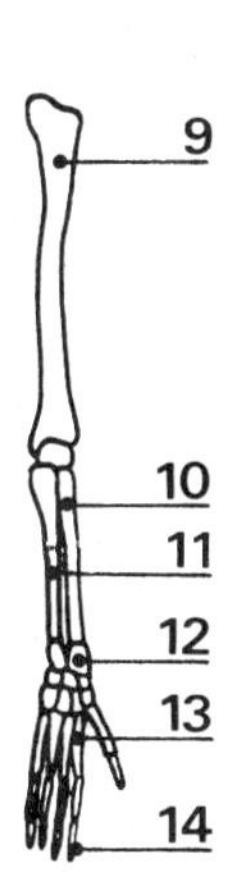

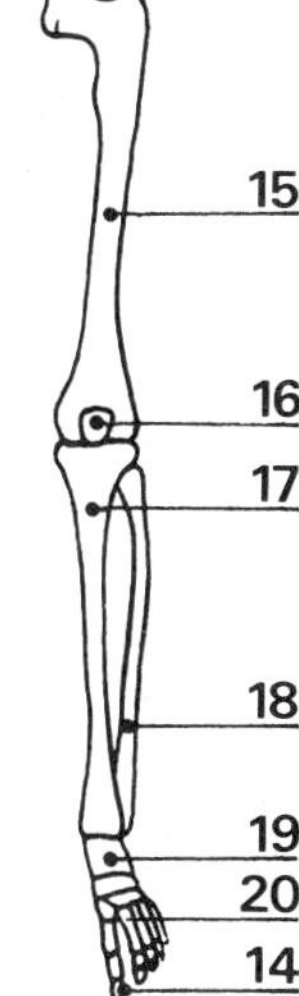

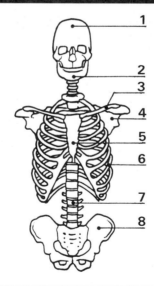

Parts of bone

7122

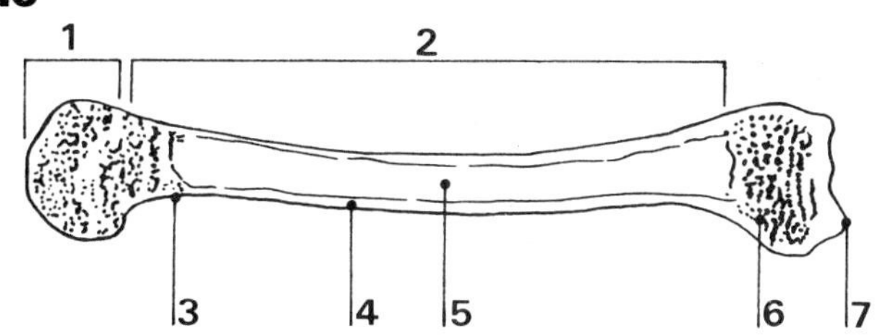

This cross section of a long bone shows a fairly complex structure
1 Head
2 Shaft
3 Periosteum (thin coating)
4 Hard, dense bone
5 Soft, spongy bone
6 Marrow cavity
7 Cartilage

Types of joint

7123

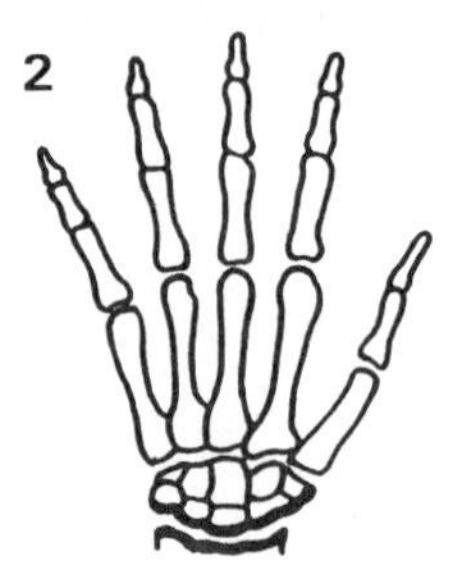

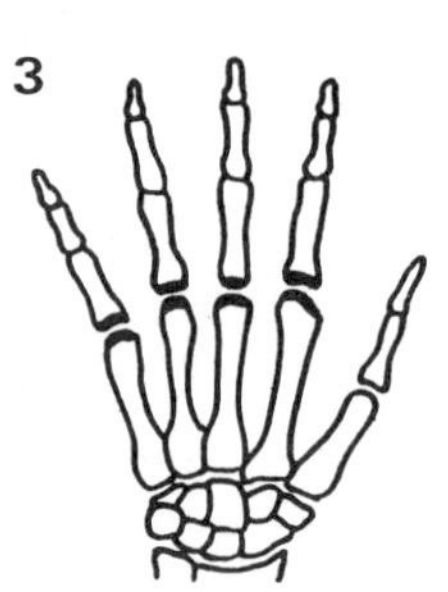

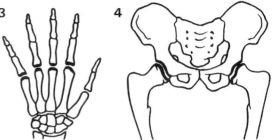

Joints vary greatly in complexity and range of movement from a simple junction between two bones, as between skull bones, to the intricacy of, for example, the elbow. The four principal types are:

1 Hinge joint (e.g. elbow)
2 Gliding joint (e.g. wrist)
3 Saddle joint (e.g. finger)
4 Ball and socket joint (e.g. hip)

Teeth: types

7124

Humans have four basic kinds of teeth, designed to meet different eating requirements.
1 Incisors: chisel-shaped teeth for cutting food
2 Canines: pointed teeth for grasping and tearing food
3 Premolars: grooved teeth for slicing and grinding food
4 Molars: large, grooved teeth for grinding food

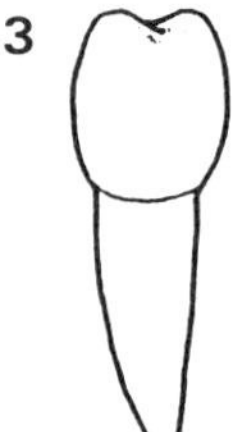

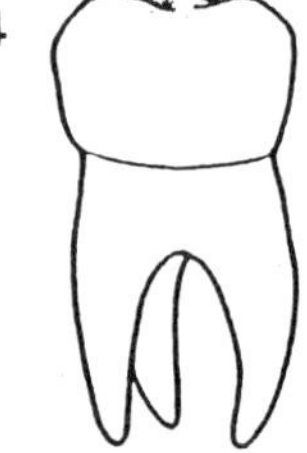

Teeth: structure

7125

1 Crown: jutting from the jaw; the part visible from the gum
2 Root: embedded in the jaw
3 Neck: between crown and root
4 Enamel: covering and protecting the crown, the hardest substance in the body
5 Dentin: the main bulk of the tooth, similar to bone
6 Cementum: a hard, rough coating around the root
7 Pulp: soft tissue containing nerves and blood vessels

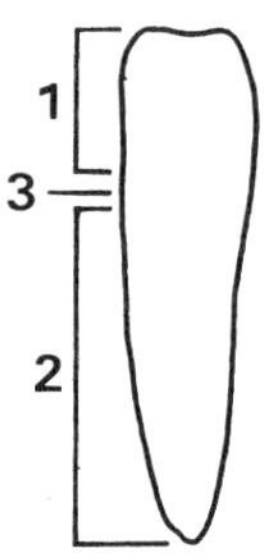

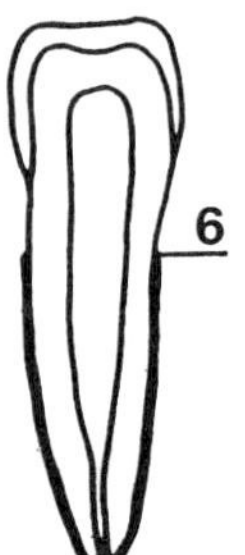

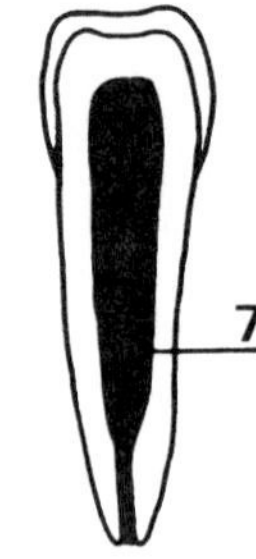

Teeth: sets

7126

In a human there are two successive sets of teeth

Temporary teeth

1 These are also called deciduous or milk teeth. A full set is made up of 20 teeth, as follows:
a Eight incisors
b Four canines
c Eight molars

These teeth appear in stages, usually between the ages of 6 and 30 months. They usually fall out between the age of 7 and 12 years, and are replaced by the permanent teeth.

Permanent teeth

2 A full set of permanent or adult teeth consists of 32 teeth, as follows:
a Eight incisors
b Four canines
c Twelve molars
d Eight bicuspids

First to appear are the first (front) molars, at age six to seven years. Last are the third molars, or wisdom teeth, usually between the ages of 17 and 25 years.

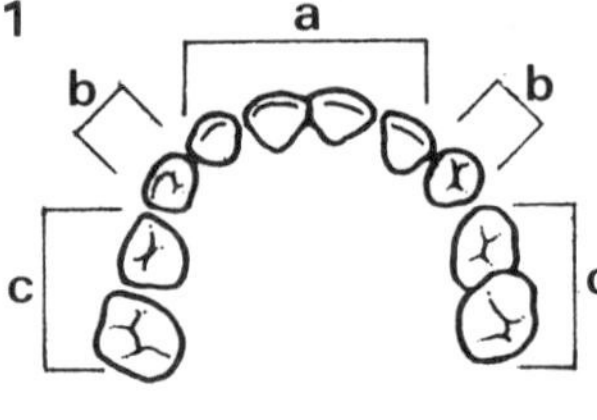

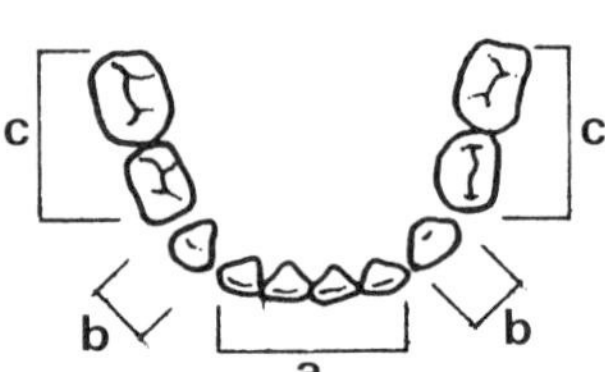

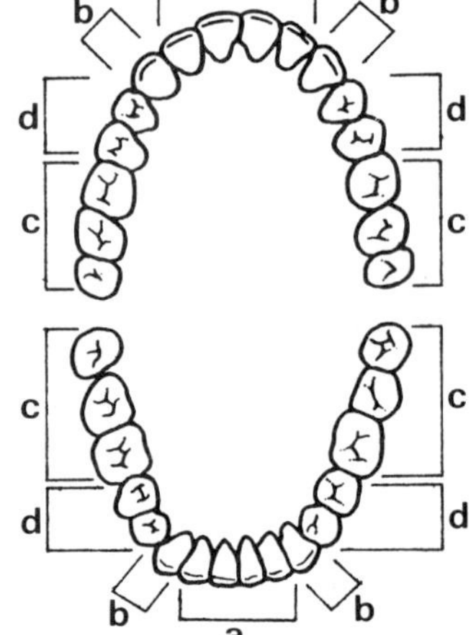

713 THE MUSCULAR SYSTEM

Principal muscles

7131 The principal muscles of the human body are shown from the front (**1**) and the back (**2**). Only the right side of the body is shown.

a Sternomastoid
b Trapezius
c Deltoid
d Pectoralis major
e Biceps
f Triceps
g Latissimus dorsi
h Obliquus Externus
i Gluteus maximus
j Vastus lateralis
k Biceps femoris
l Rectus femoris
m Gastrocnemius
n Tibialis anterior

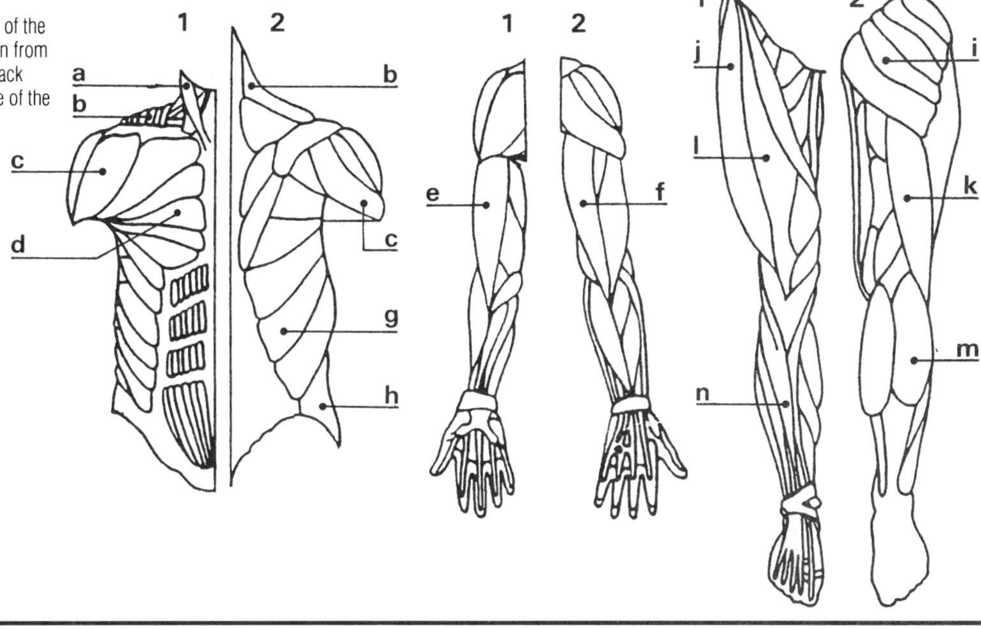

Types of muscle

7132 There are three basic types of muscle tissue:
1 Smooth (also called plain, unstriated, unstriped, or involuntary) muscle - as found in the intestine walls
2 Cardiac (heart) muscle
3 Skeletal (or striated, striped, or voluntary) muscle, which causes the skeleton to move

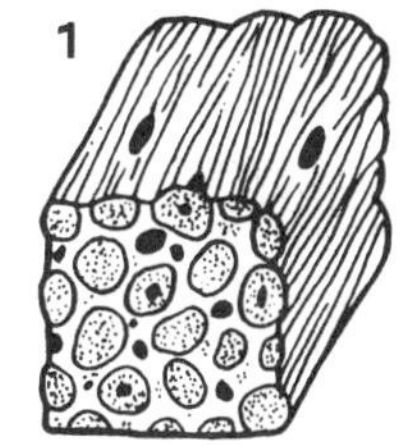

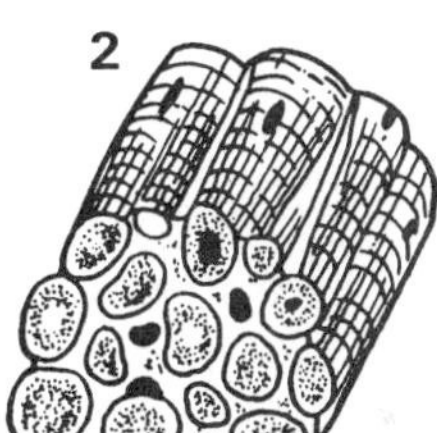

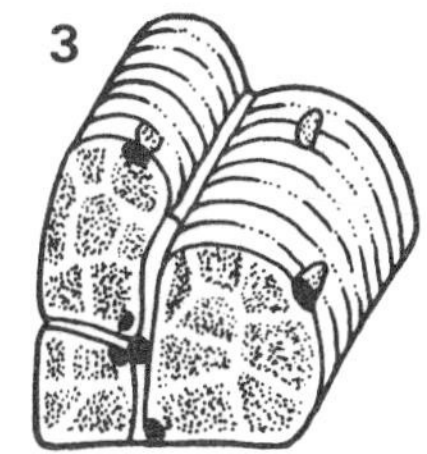

How muscles work

7133 Most muscles work in pairs, allowing movement in two or more directions. To bend the arm at the elbow (**1**), the triceps (**a**) relaxes and the biceps (**b**) contracts.
To straighten the arm at the elbow (**2**), the triceps (**a**) contracts and the biceps (**b**) relaxes.

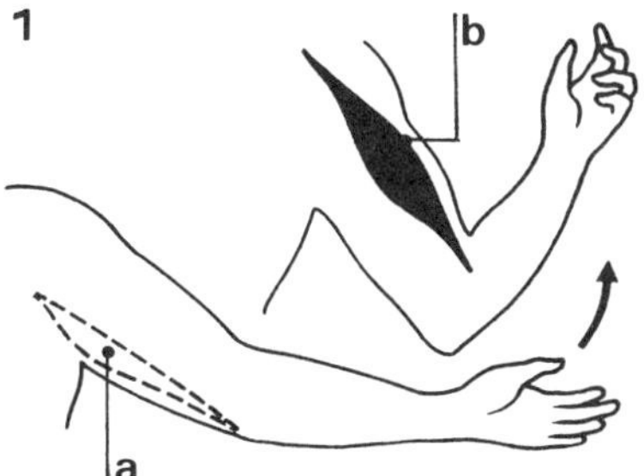

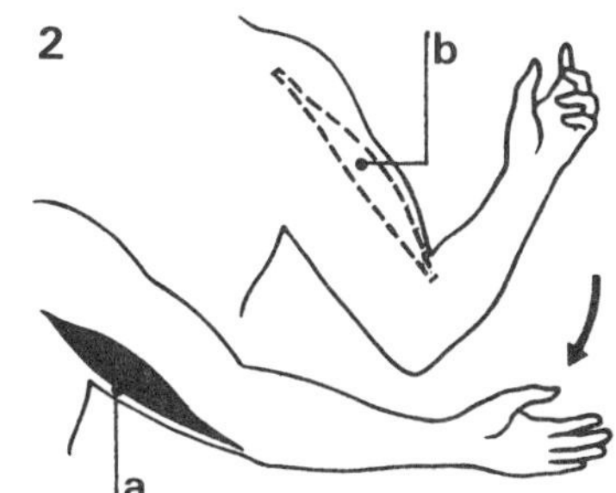

714 THE NERVOUS SYSTEM

Components

7141 There are three components to the nervous system:
1 Central nervous system This consists of the brain (**a**) and spinal cord (**b**). It is the control center for all conscious and unconscious body actions.
2 Peripheral nervous system This is a complex network of nerves that links every part of the body to the central nervous system.
3 Autonomic nervous system This directs unconscious body actions such as heartbeat, breathing, digestion, and blinking.

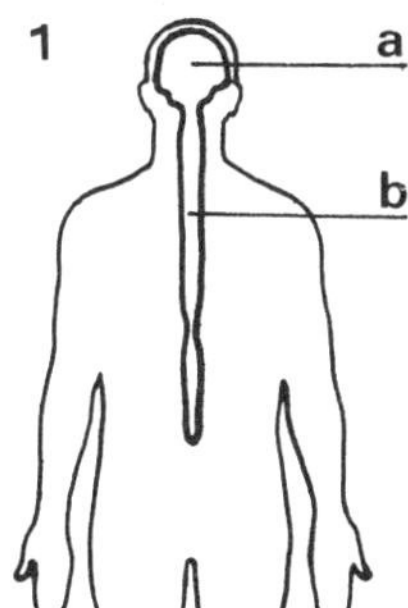

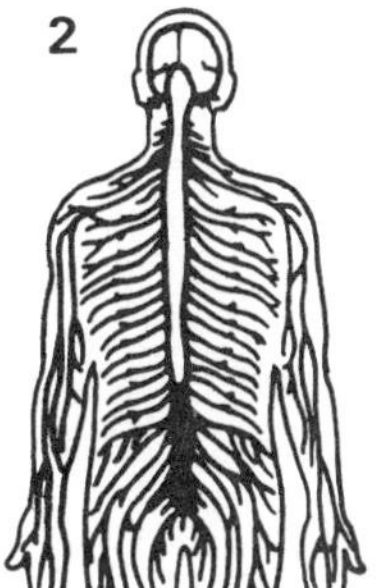

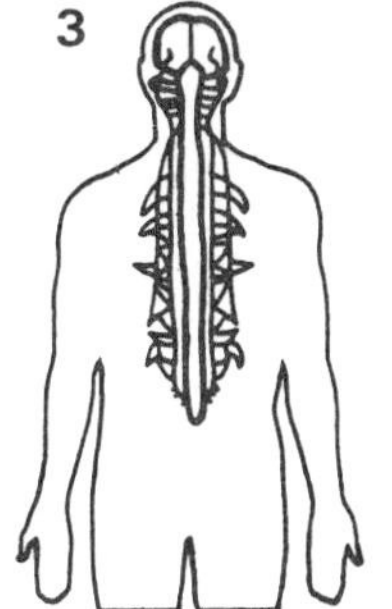

7142 Nerve cells
7143 The brain
7144 The senses
7145 Smell
7146 Sight

Nerve cells

7142 These vary in size and shape according to the job they do. Cells taking information to the central nervous system are called sensory neurons; cells taking information away from it are called motor neurons.
Parts of a motor neuron:
1 Cell body
2 Nucleus
3 Dendrites: these gather information into the cell
4 Axon: this sends out messages
5 Sheath: a fatty covering
6 Terminal (end) processes

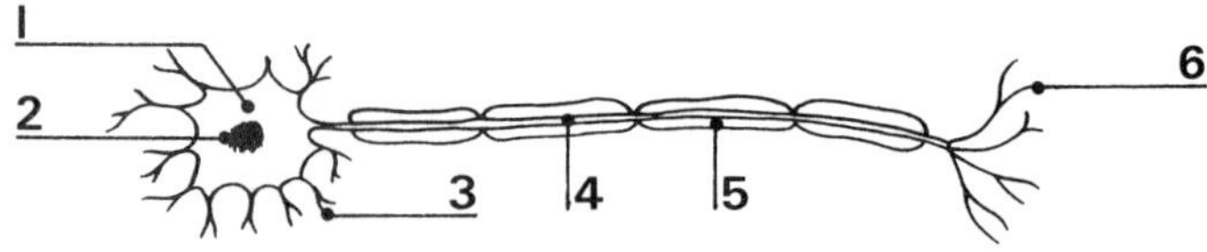

The brain

7143 **Brain: structure**
Three main regions
1 Forebrain (shown here cut through the middle.) Memory and intelligence are based here
a Cerebral hemisphere
b Corpus callosum (linking the right and left cerebral hemispheres)
c Thalamus
d Hypothalamus
2 Midbrain (the top part of the brainstem, **e**.) Mainly a relay station for messages to and from the brain
3 Hindbrain coordinating complex body movements, especially of arms and legs.
Each of these regions comprises several parts:
f Pons (brainstem)
g Medulla oblongata (brainstem)
h Cerebellum

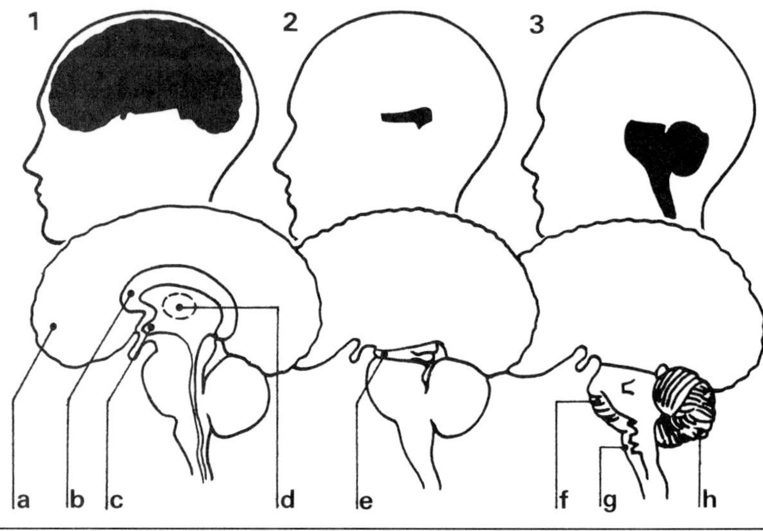

Brain: protection
This cross section shows the five layers that protect the brain and help to shape it.
1 Scalp, with hair, skin, fat, and other tissue
2 Cranium, the part of the skull housing the brain. Its inner network of bony struts and domelike shape give this structure its strength
3 Dura mater, the tough, unstretchable outer membrane enveloping the brain and spinal column
4 Arachnoid, an elastic "skin" enclosing the so-called subarachnoid space
5 Pia mater, a thin "skin" that clings closely to the brain's irregular surface

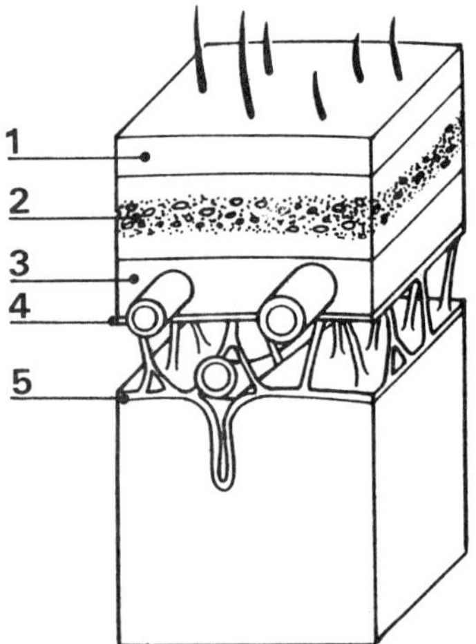

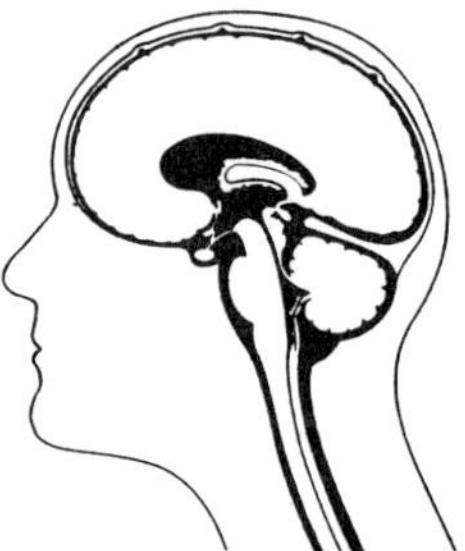

Cerebrospinal fluid
Cerebrospinal fluid (CSF) is produced in and fills four cavities within the brain, known as ventricles, and also flows around the brain's outer rim. It protects the brain, buffering it from shock. The diagram shows a cross section of the head, with areas shaded black showing the cavities in which CSF is present.

Brain: function
The illustration of the left side of a human brain show areas involved with the following important functions. The left side of the brain controls movement on the right side of the body and vice versa.
1 Movement of body parts
2 Speech
3 Receiving body sensations
4 Hearing
5 Sight

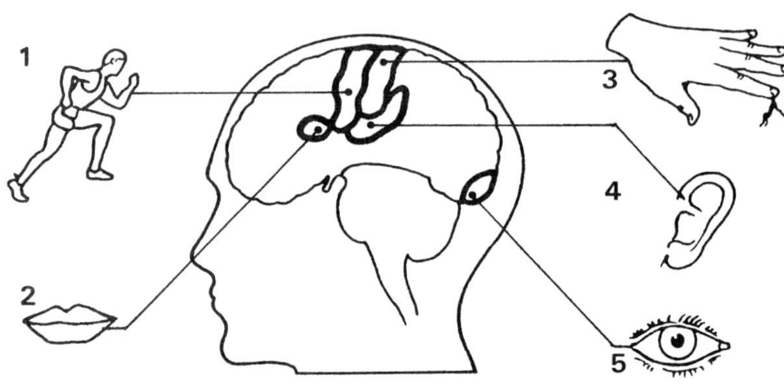

The senses

7144

There are five sense, four of which are located in the head, the fifth in the surface sensitive nerves covering the body. The five senses are:

1 Smell
2 Sight
3 Hearing
4 Taste
5 Touch

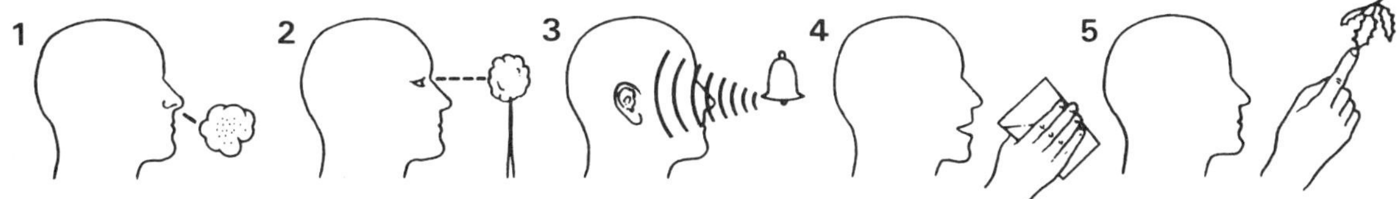

Smell

7145

One of the keenest senses, smell is also a vital part of the taste process. It can distinguish more odors than the ear can distinguish sounds, but its precise mechanism remains a mystery. One attempt to classify odors divides them into four categories – fragrant, burnt, acidic, and – and suggests that all smells are a blend of these.

We smell substances whose molecules are breathed into the roof of each nasal cavity (**1**) and dissolved on a patch of olfactory membrane (**2**) armed with 100 million smell receptor cells equipped with tiny sensitive "hairs." Scent molecules react with these to stimulate nerve impulses in the receptor cells.

Olfactory nerves transmit thses signals to olfactory bulbs (**3**) then via olfactory tracts (**4**) to the smell center (**5**) in the limbic system deep in the brain.

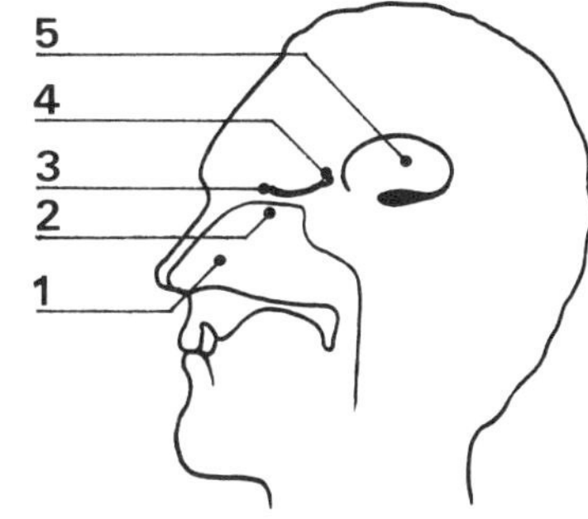

Sight

7146

Front view of an eye
1 Eyelid: protects the eye
2 Lashes: also protect the eye
3 Tear duct: drains away tears
4 Pupil
5 Iris
6 White

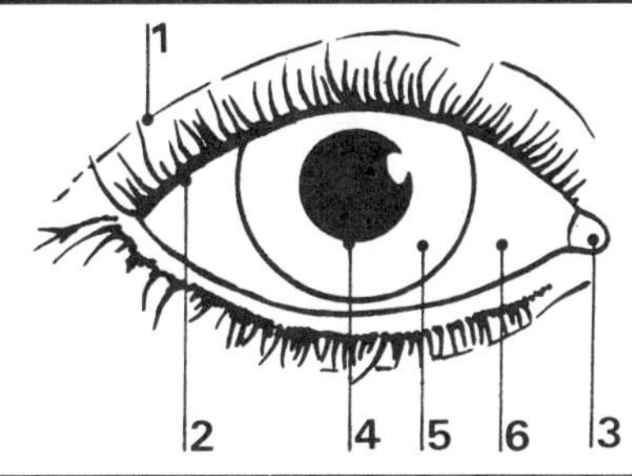

Muscles of the eye
Six occular muscles attached to the outside of the sclera, or tough outer layer, move the eyeball in different ways. Arrows indicate in which direction the muscles (shaded black) move the eyeball.

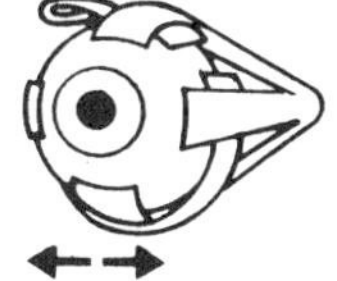

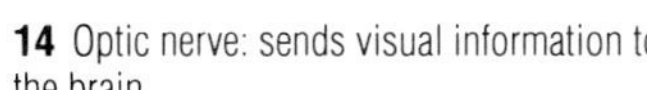

Section through an eye
1 Lachrimal (tear) gland: produces tears to wash the eye
2 Conjunctiva: thin protective membrane (tissue layer)
3 Aqueous humor: watery liquid
4 Cornea: transparent disk at front of eyeball. Refracts light
5 Iris: colored disk that adjusts size of pupil
6 Pupil: aperture in iris through which light passes
7 Lens: soft and transparent, focuses images in the eye
8 Suspensory ligaments: hold lens in place
9 Ciliary muscles: alter lens shape
10 Vitreous humor: transparent jelly-like substance
11 Sclera: tough outer layer
12 Choroid layer: very dark layer, stops light being reflected around the eye
13 Retina: light-sensitive layer (containing rod and cone cells). Images are received here. Rod cells detect light and cone cells detect color.
14 Optic nerve: sends visual information to the brain.

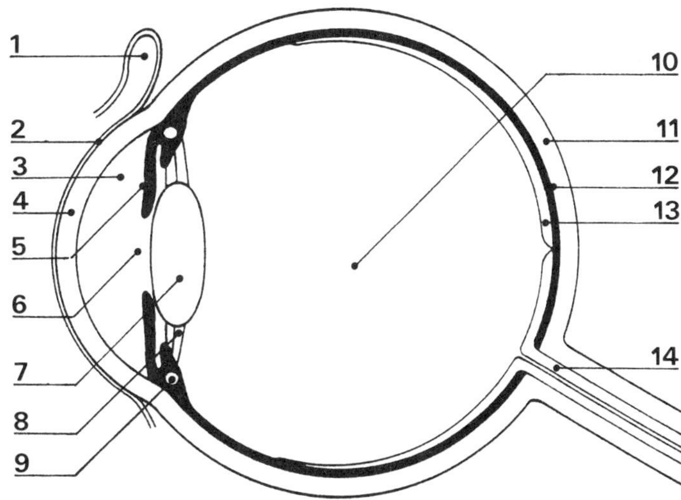

continued

Sight continued

7146 **Focusing**

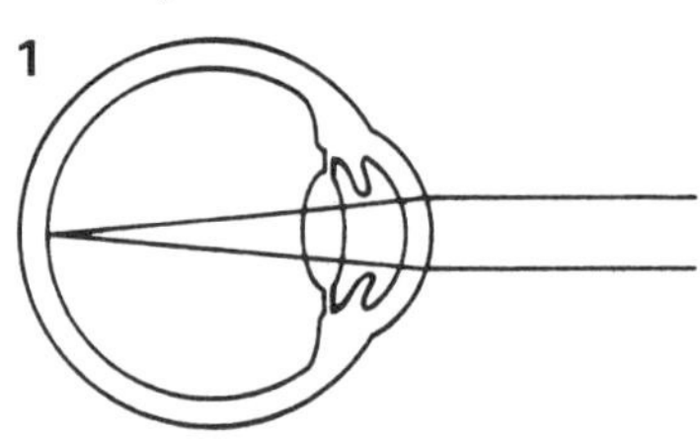

These diagrams show how the lens of the eye focuses far and near objects.
1 Light rays from a distant object are almost parallel when they reach the eye. The lens needs to bend them only slightly to focus them on the retina.
2 Rays from a near object are diverging (moving apart) when they reach the eye. The lens must bulge and so become stronger to bring them into focus.

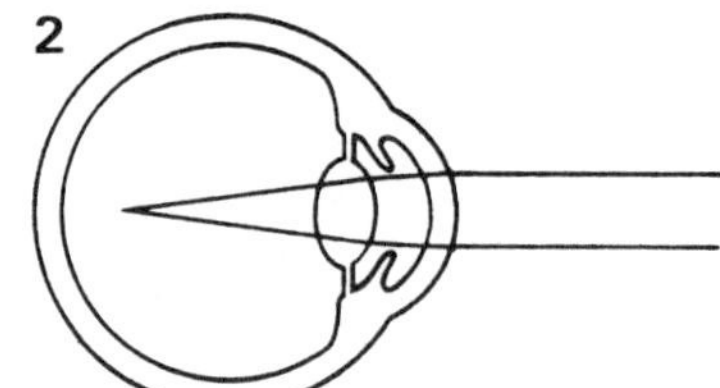

Near and far sight

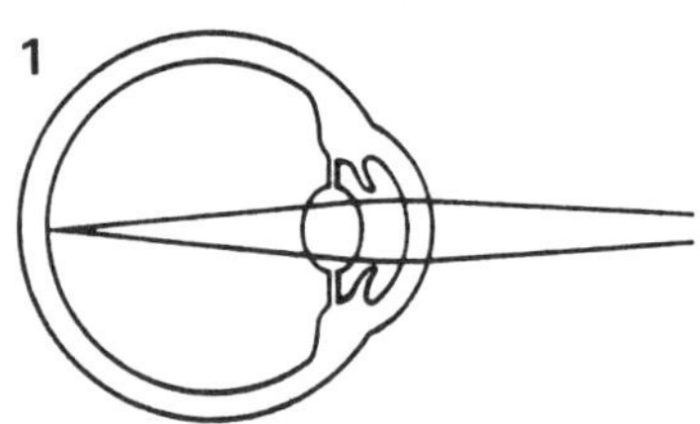

1 Nearsightedness (myopia) is due to the eyeball being too long, or sometimes to the eye's refractive power being too strong. Light rays become focused in front of the retina, and the image is blurred. Concave corrective lenses are needed to focus on distant objects.
2 Farsightedness (hyperopia) is due to the eyeball being too short, or to the eye's focusing power being too weak. Light rays are focused behind the retina, and the image is blurred. Convex corrective lenses are needed for close work such as reading.

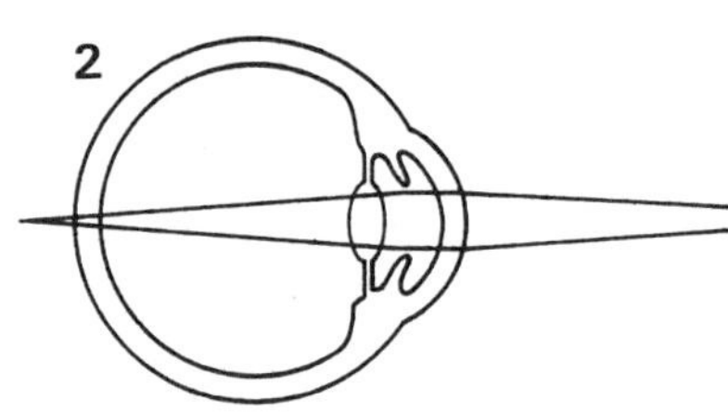

Composite view
A single close object is seen slightly differently by the left eye (**1**) and the right eye (**2**). The brain combines these two images into a composite view (**3**).

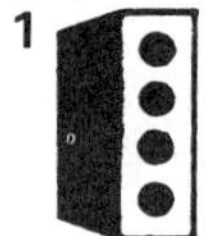

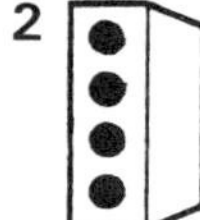

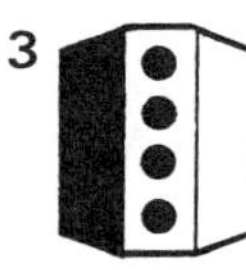

Hearing

7147 **Parts of the ear and hearing**
There are three main regions of the ear, each with various parts, doing different things.
1 Outer ear
a Pinna (ear flap): a cartilage flap on the outside of the head that gathers in sounds. In some animals, it helps to concentrate and direct vibrations into the ear and to judge direction of sound
b Auditory canal: hollow tube through skull bone. It carries sound waves to the middle ear and prevents dirt entering
2 Middle ear
c Tympanic membrane: vibrating in ear canal makes membrane vibrate, making hammer vibrate and passing sound inward. The ossicles are three tiny bones which strengthen and transmit sound waves to the inner ear. They are the malleus (hammer, **d**), the incus (anvil, **e**), and the stapes (stirrup, **f**)
g Middle ear cavity: air-filled cavity
h Eustachian tube: leading to the throat, this keeps air pressure inside the ear equal to air pressure outside
3 Inner ear
i Oval window: opening to inner ear. Passes on vibrations to fluid in inner ear, not visible
j Vesticular canals act as organs of balance. Fluid-filled cavities sensitive to movement, speed, acceleration, and rotation
k Cochlea: a fluid-filled spiral. Converts sound vibrations to nerve impulses using special cells
l Round window: works in conjunction with oval window
m Auditory nerve: sends information to the brain

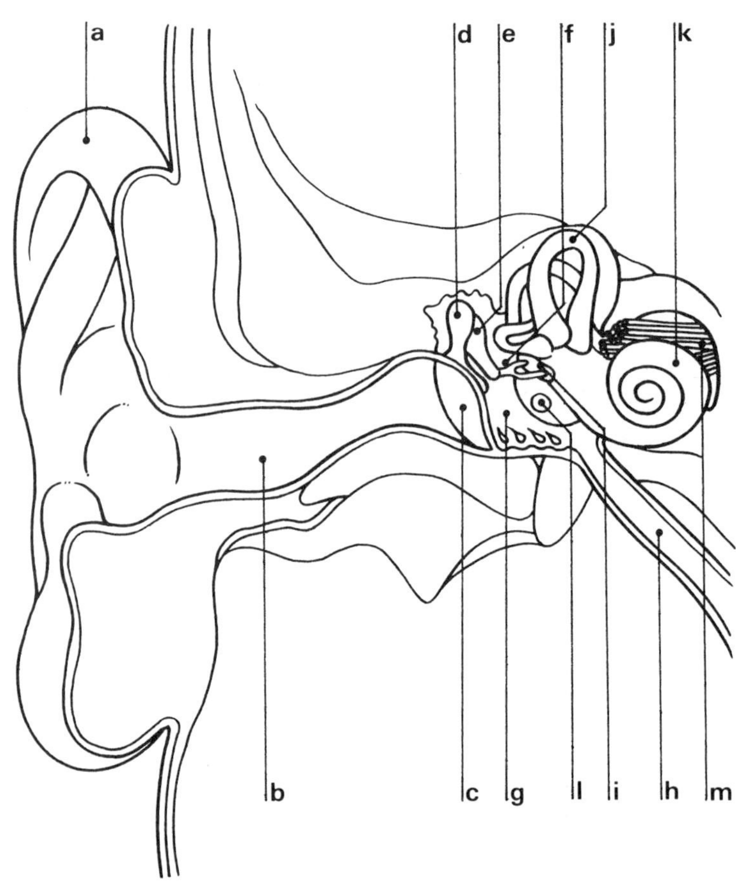

continued

Hearing continued

7147 **Balance**

The organs that are most important to monitoring body position and so maintaining equilibrium are the semicircular canals of the inner ear (**1**). Connected by one large and three small reservoirs, the three fluid-filled canals are set at right-angles to each other in different planes, thus covering every possible dimension of body movement.

How balance is monitored

Stability of the body when sitting or standing is the responsibility of the part of the brain called the cerebellum, which also relies on evidence from the eyes and from a number of receptors in the skin and muscles around the body. But the major sources of information on body position are the semicircular canals, within which fluid flows past hundreds of tiny hair cells and a much smaller number of cells of a jellylike substance. A flow past some of the hair cells measures speed of body movement or direction of gravity; a flow past others indicates angular positioning of the head; nerve fibers relay the information to the brain.

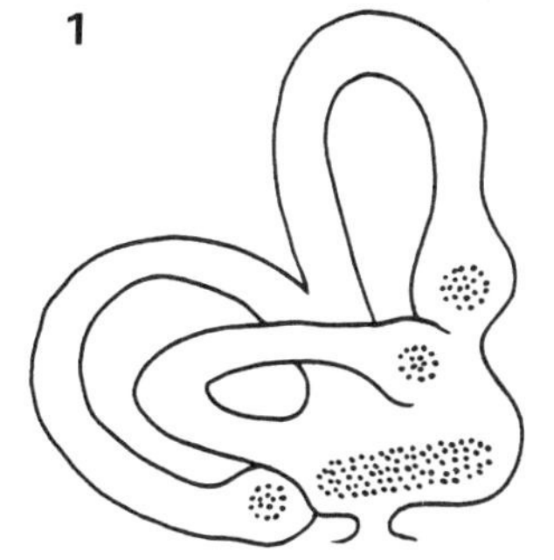

Taste

7148 The sense of taste (helped by the sense of smell) enables us to identify suitable foods. Taste buds (most of them in the tongue) contain special nerve cells that send taste information to the brain. Foods' flavors are partly smells detected by the olfactory membrane in the nasal cavity. Tastes, though, depend on the tongue. To taste dry food we must moisten it with saliva in the mouth. Particles of food dissolved in the saliva stimulate taste buds (**1**) in the sides of the papillae (**2**): up to 9,000 tiny "pimples" on the tongue's surface. The taste buds' taste-sensitive hairs pass nerve signals to nerve fibers and these transmit taste signals to the brain.

A taste map of the tongue

Different areas of the tongue (**3**) respond to different kinds of taste.

a Sweet
b Salt
c Sour
d Bitter

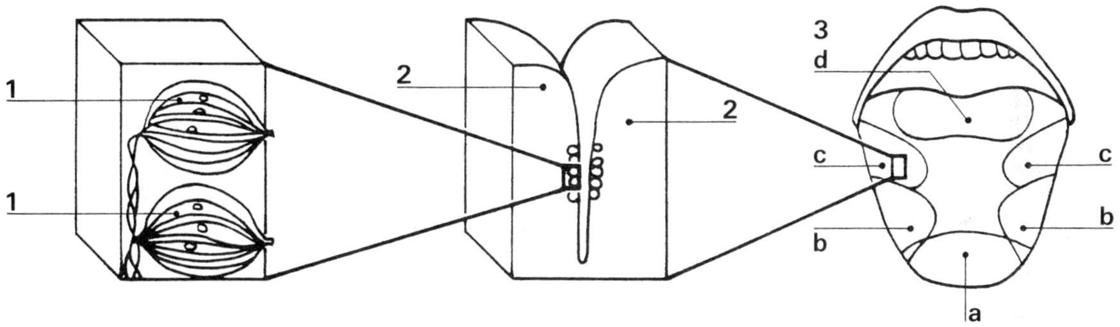

Touch

7149 **Nerve cells**

Sense receptors lying under the surface of the skin convey the sense of touch. Some parts of the body are more sensitive to touch than others because of the number of sense receptors they contain: the fingertips, for example, have a great many, as do the lips. Some nerve endings respond to pressure, others to temperature.

If you step on a pin, for example, a nerve in your foot (**1**) sends a message to a signal nerve (**2**). Nerve cell (**3**) registers pain and sends a further message to nerve cells (**4**) and (**5**), telling them to either relax (**6**) or contract (**7**) muscles in your leg in order to remove your foot from the pin.

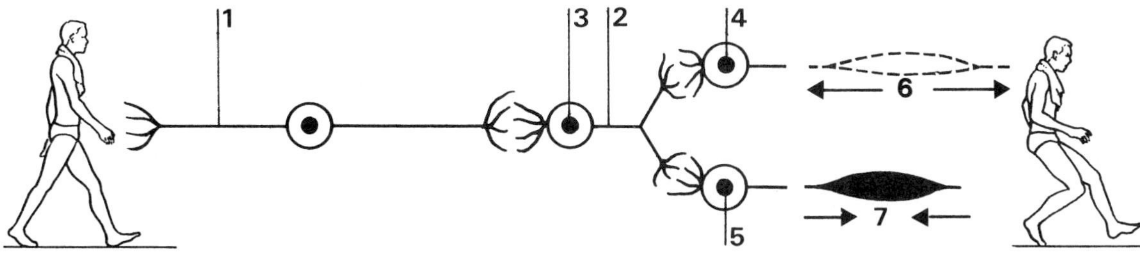

Nerve endings in the skin

Specialized nerve endings in the skin send signals that the brain identifies as touch, pain, pressure, heat, or cold.

1 Free nerve endings (pain)
2 Merkel's disks (touch)
3 Meissner's corpuscles (touch)
4 Beaded nerve net (pain)
5 Krause's end bulbs (cold)
6 Ruffini corpuscles (heat)
7 Pacinian corpuscles (pressure, stretching, and vibration)
8 Hair organs (touch)

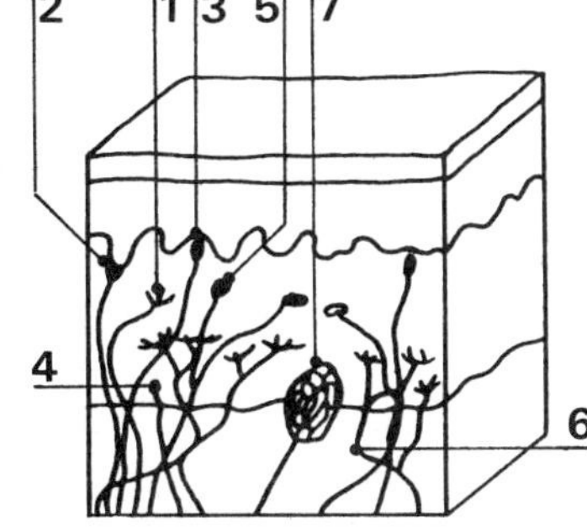

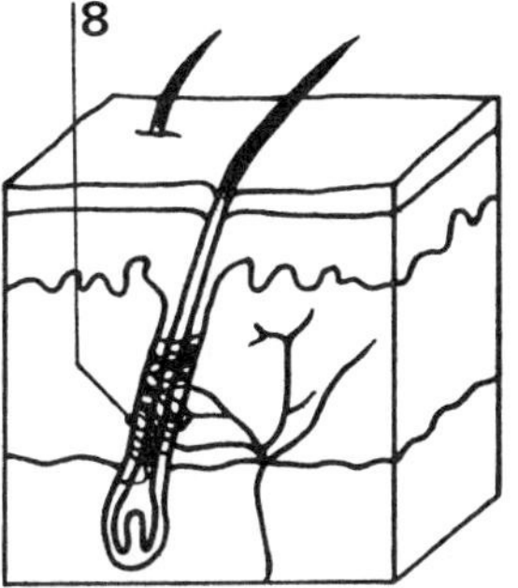

715 THE DIGESTIVE SYSTEM

Components

7151

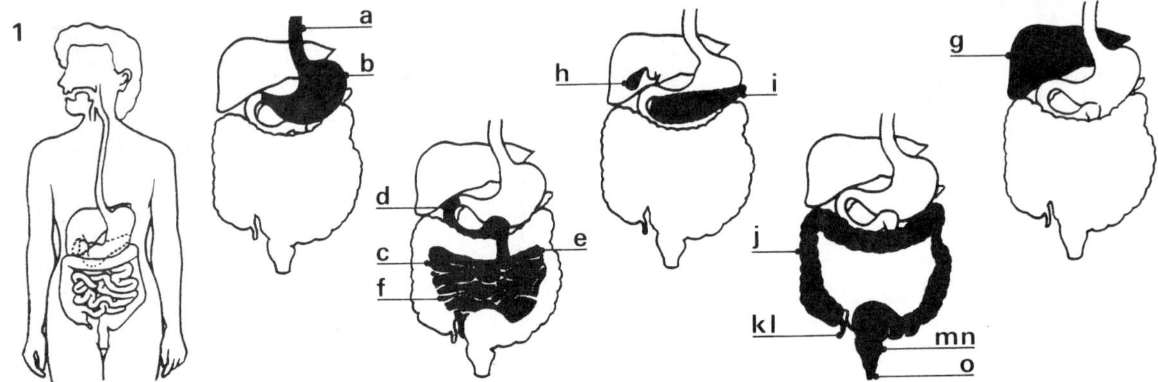

The digestive system (**1**) consists of the digestive tract, and various other body organs that produce juices used to break down food.
a Esophagus: this is a muscular tube about 10 in (25 cm) long and 1 in (15–20 mm) wide that takes food from the pharynx to the stomach
b Stomach: this varies in size and shape depending on how much food is in it. Its maximum capacity is around 3 US pints (1.6 liters). After being mixed with gastric juices containing hydrochloric acid, food is released a little at a time from the stomach into the small intestine
c Small intestine: this is a looped tube about 21 ft (6.5 m) long and up to 1.5 in (35 mm) wide. There are three sections: the duodenum (**d**), the jejunum (**e**), and the ileum (**f**)
g Liver: this produces an alkaline digestive juice called bile
h Gall bladder: this stores bile
i Pancreas: this produces juices used in digestion
j Large intestine: this is about 6 ft (1.8 m) long and up to 2 in (50 mm) wide. It has three main sections: the cecum (**k**) - which includes the appendix (**l**) - the colon (**m**) and the rectum (**n**)
o Anus: this is the opening from the rectum

Swallowing

7152 a

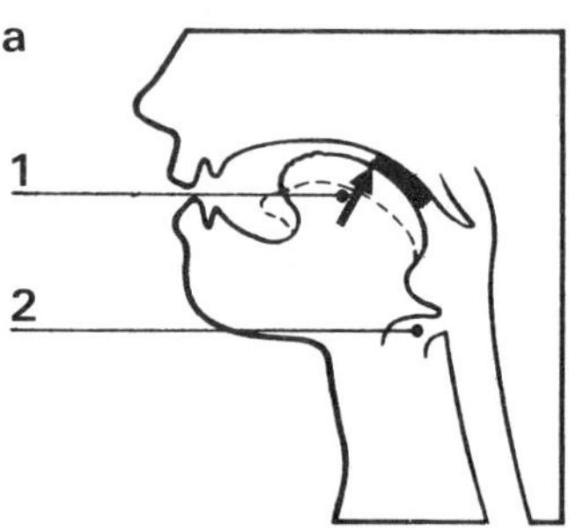

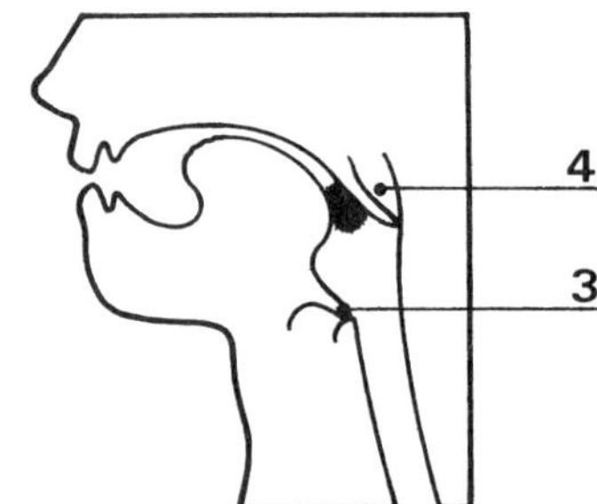

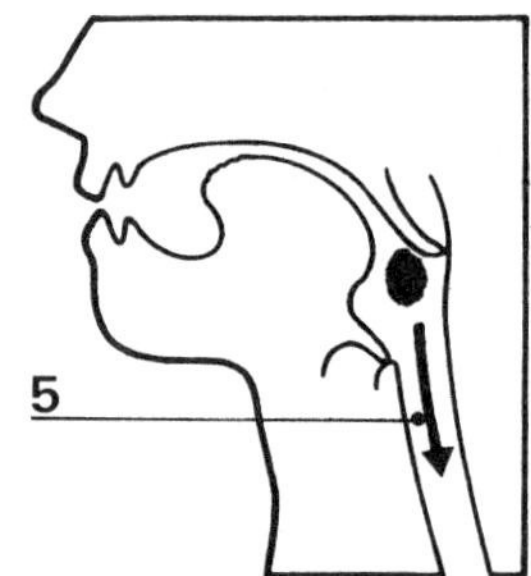

In order to swallow food (**a**):
1 The tongue moves up and back to push the food into the throat
2 The larynx rises
3 The epiglottis drops down and blocks off the trachea (windpipe)
4 The false palate (the soft part of the mouth's roof) moves back to block the airway to the nose
5 Food goes down the esophagus

716 THE RESPIRATORY SYSTEM

Components

7161

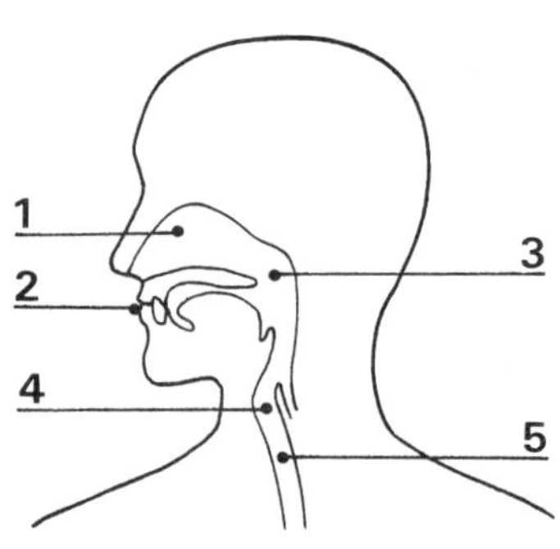

Here we show the main parts of the human respiratory system.
1 Nasal (nose) cavity: here air is warmed and moistened
2 Mouth: an additional airway
3 Pharynx (throat)
4 Larynx (voice box): its vocal cords make sounds for speech
5 Trachea (windpipe): a ridged tube about 9 in (22.5 cm) long which takes air to and from the lungs
6 Lungs: two pink, spongy organs
7 Bronchi: two tubes, one leading to each lung
8 Bronchioles: smaller branches leading off the bronchi
9 Diaphragm

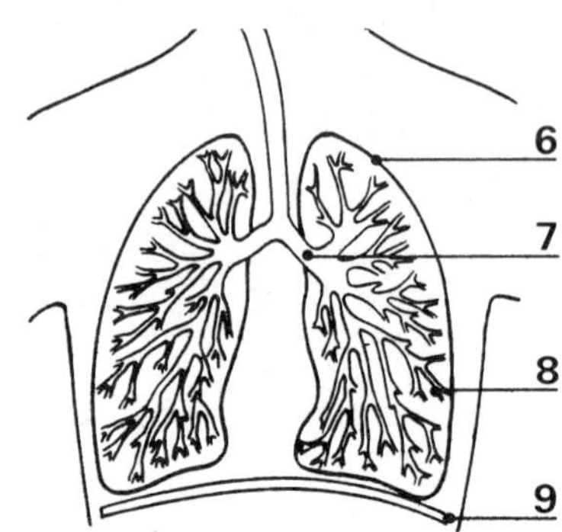

continued

Components continued

7161

Parts of a bronchiole
1 Alveoli (air sacs): here, the gases oxygen and carbon dioxide are exchanged
2 Alveolar ducts: tiny tubes leading to the alveoli

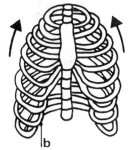

Breathing

7162

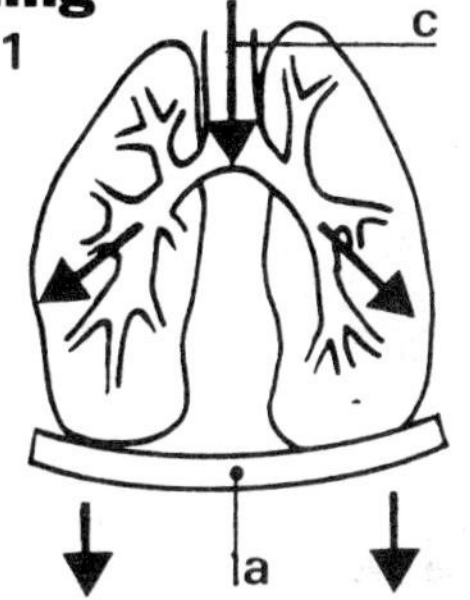

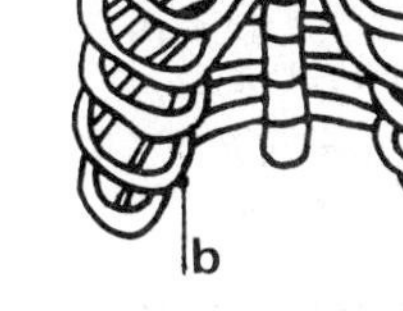

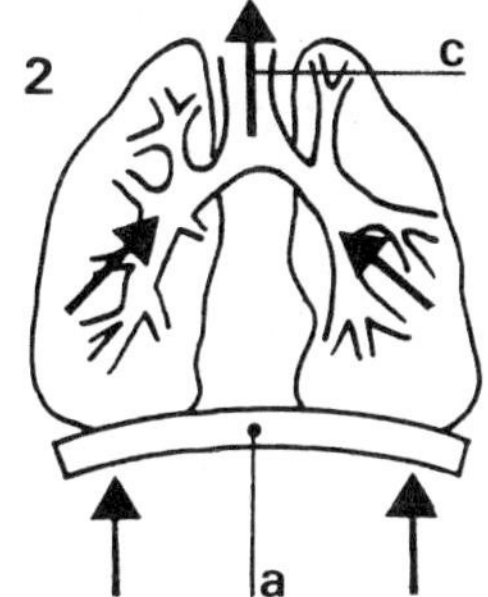

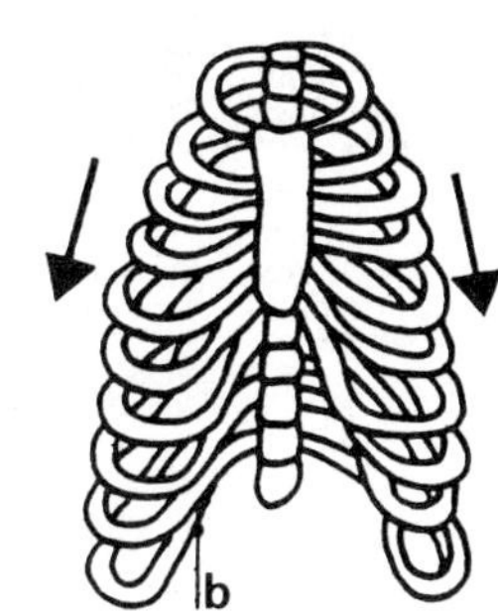

1 Breathing in The diaphragm (**a**) is pulled down, the ribs (**b**) move outward, the chest cavity becomes larger, air pressure in the chest cavity is reduced, and air enters the lungs (**c**).
2 Breathing out The diaphragm (**a**) rises, the ribs (**b**) move inward, the chest cavity becomes smaller, pressure increases, and air (**c**) is forced out of the lungs.

Exchange of gases

7163

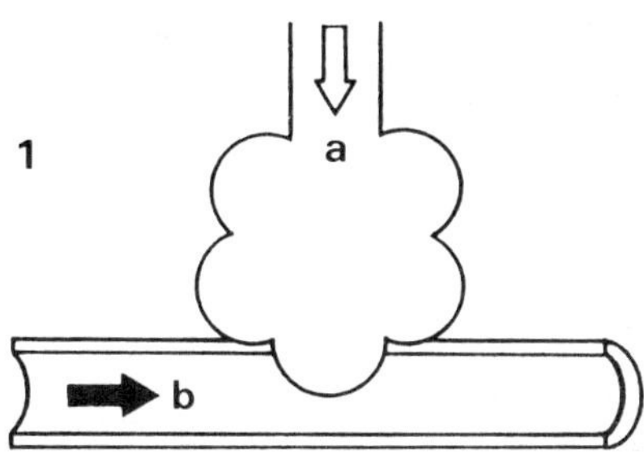

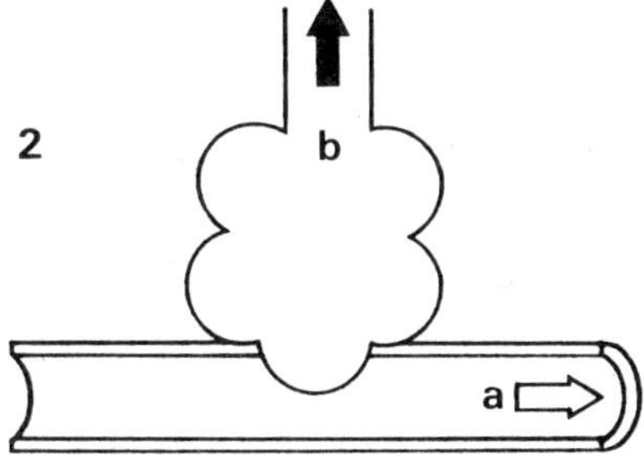

Air we breathe out typically contains nearly 4% more carbon dioxide and nearly 4% less oxygen than the air we breathe in. This gas exchange occurs in the lungs.
1 Oxygen enters air sacs (**a**) during breathing in; and carbon dioxide is carried to the lungs in blood vessels (**b**).
2 Oxygen has entered the blood (**a**); and carbon dioxide is breathed out (**b**).

717 THE CARDIOVASCULAR SYSTEM

Blood

7171

Most adults have about 10 US pints (5 liters) of blood. It consists of an almost colorless fluid, called plasma, and three types of cell:
1 Red corpuscles (blood cells or erythrocytes): disks with an indentation in the middle
2 White corpuscles (leukocytes): spherical with nuclei of different shapes (**a**), (**b**), (**c**)
3 Platelets (thrombocytes): colorless, oval or irregularly shaped, with no nuclei

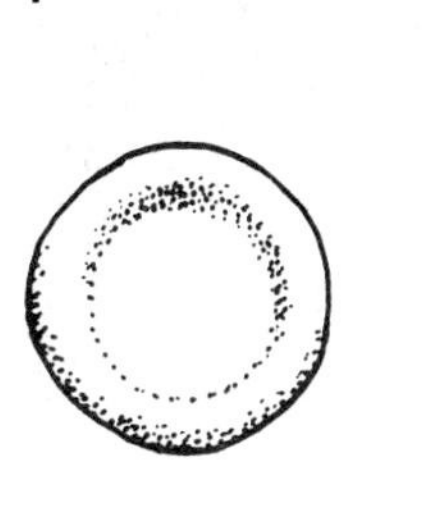

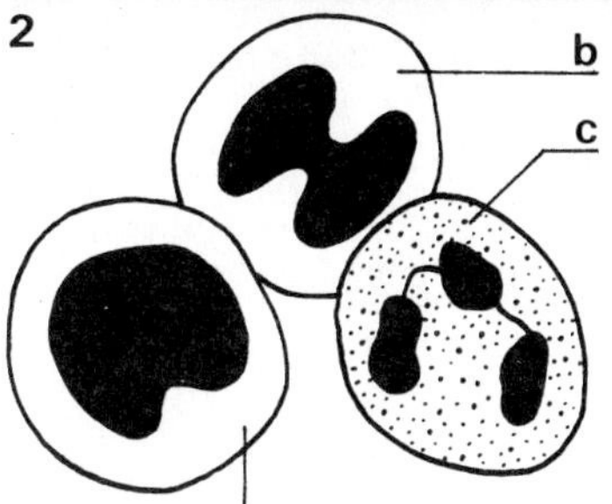

Functions of blood
• Red corpuscles contain iron-rich hemoglobin which carries oxygen to all parts of the body. (Blood-carrying oxygen is red in color; deoxygenated blood is purplish.)
• White corpuscles destroy disease organisms such as bacteria
• Platelets repair blood vessels and form clots to stop bleeding after injury
• Plasma carries protein and clotting factors
• Blood helps to maintain body temperature by transporting heat
• Blood carries carbon dioxide and other waste products

Blood vessels

7172 There are three types of blood vessel: arteries, veins, and capillaries. Arteries carry oxygenated blood from the heart to all parts of the body. They have strong elastic walls that squeeze the blood along with waves of contraction. After profuse branching the blood passes through the tissues of the body in tiny capillaries, where nutritive substances and oxygen are exchanged for waste products. The blood is then conveyed back to the heart through the veins. These have thinner walls than the arteries, and contain valves to prevent a backflow of blood.

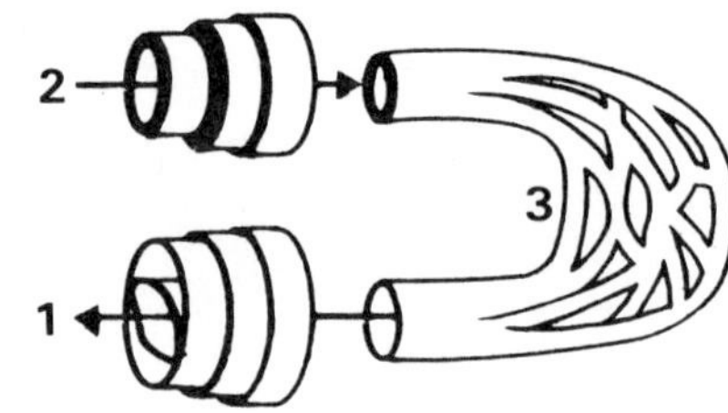

1 Artery
2 Capillary
3 Vein

Arteries and veins

1

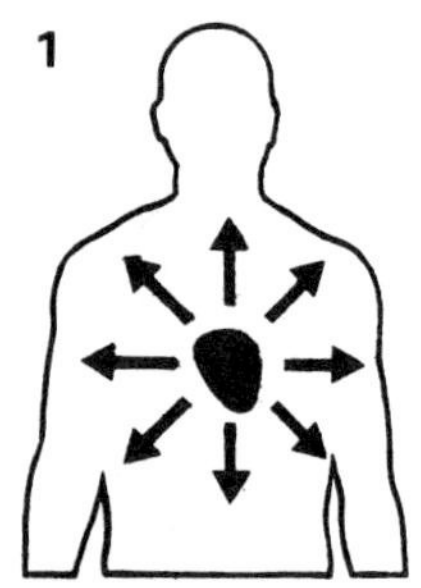

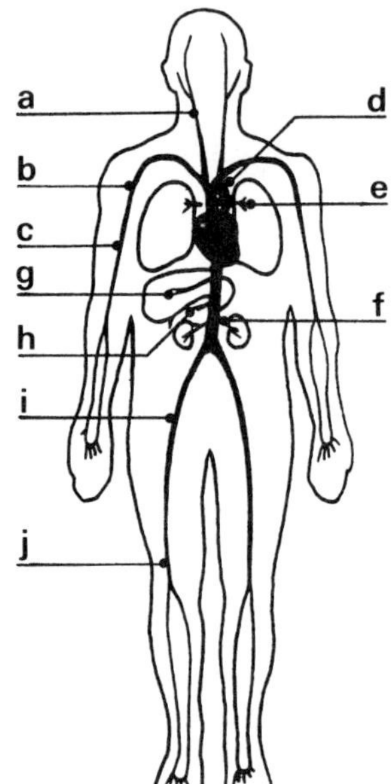

Important arteries
1 These carry blood from the heart to other parts of the body:
a Carotid artery: to head
b Subclavian artery: to arm
c Brachial artery: in arm
d Pulmonary artery: to lung
e Aorta (the largest artery): from heart to rest of body
f Renal artery: to kidney
g Hepatic artery: to liver
h Gastric artery: to stomach
i Iliac artery: to leg
j Femoral artery: in leg

2

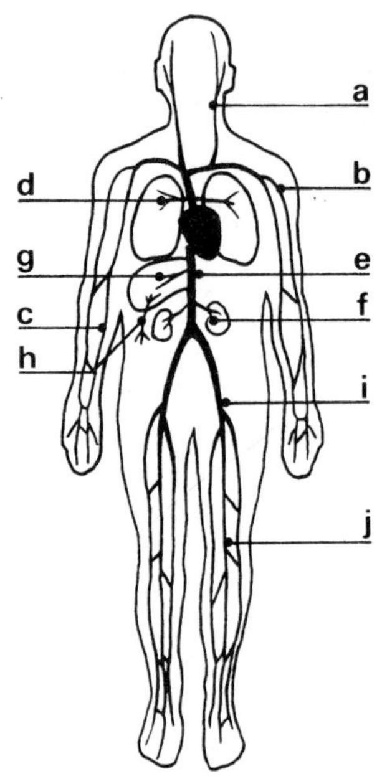

Important veins
2 These carry blood to the heart from other parts of the body:
a Jugular vein: from head
b Subclavian vein: from arm
c Brachial vein: in arm
d Pulmonary vein: from lung
e Vena cava: from body to heart
f Renal vein: from kidney
g Hepatic vein: from liver
h Hepatic portal vein: from intestines to liver
i Iliac vein: from leg
j Femoral vein: in leg

The heart

7173 **Structure**
1 Superior vena cava
2 Valve (prevents backflow of blood)
3 Right atrium
4 Inferior vena cava
5 Right ventricle
6 Left ventricle
7 Left atrium
8 Pulmonary vein
9 Pulmonary artery
10 Aorta

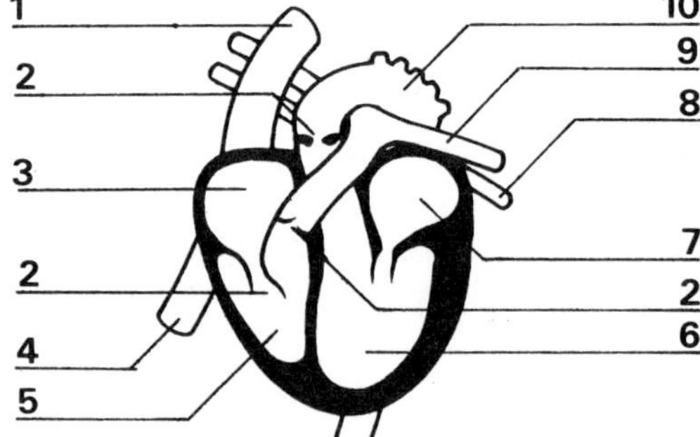

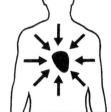

Bloodflow through the heart
1 Deoxygenated blood enters the right atrium through the vena cava.
2 Deoxygenated blood passes from the right atrium to the right ventricle and then to the pulmonary artery.
3 Deoxygenated blood travels to the lungs via the pulmonary artery.
4 Oxygenated blood from the lungs goes by way of the pulmonary vein to the left atrium.
5 Oxygenated blood goes from the left atrium to the left ventricle.
6 Oxygenated blood leaves the heart via the aorta to travel around the body.

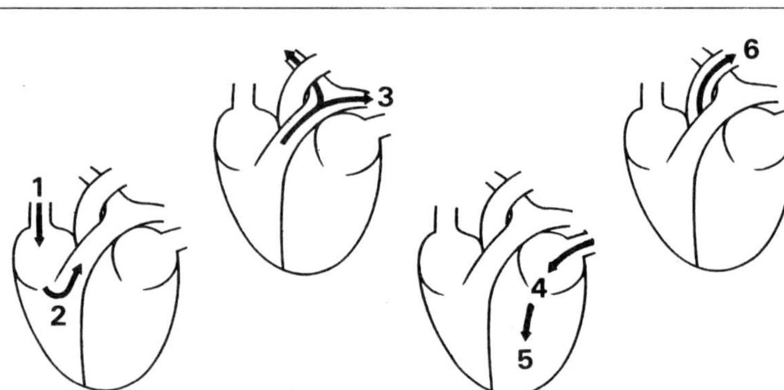

continued

The heart continued

7173

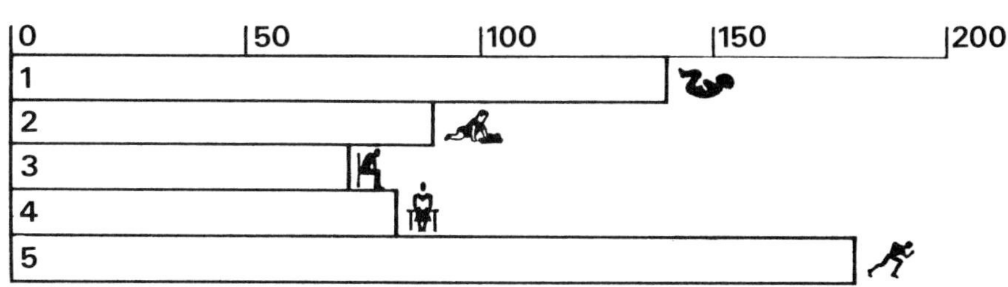

Heart beats
Typical numbers of beats per minute are as follows:
1 Newborn baby: 140
2 10-year-old: 90
3 Man at rest: 70-72
4 Woman at rest: 78-82
5 At vigorous exercise: 140-180

Circulation

7174 **The heart-lung system**
The heart (**1**) is really two pumps. One pump recieves blood from the body (**2**) and sends it out to the lungs (**3**), where the waste product, carbon dioxide, is exchanged for fresh oxygen. The other pump receives back the oxygenated blood (**4**) from the lungs, and speeds it on its way to the rest of the body.

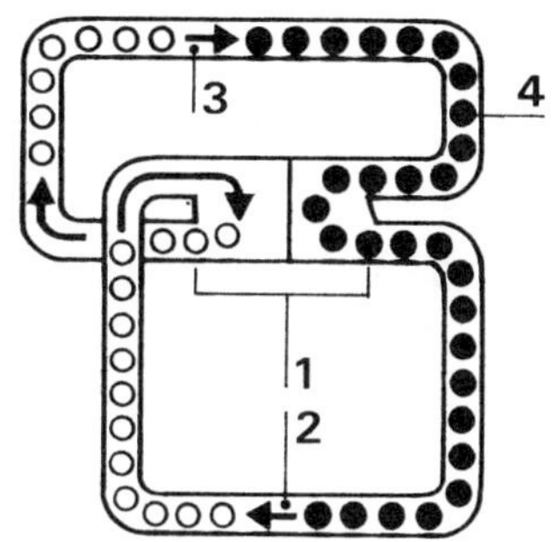

Capillary networks
In body organs, blood from an artery (**a**) passes through a capillary network (**b**), where it releases oxygen and food, and leaves the organ in a vein (**c**).

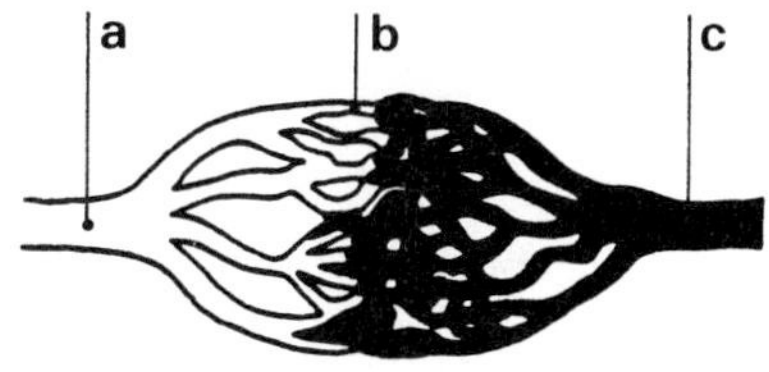

Where the blood goes
This diagram shows the relative distribution of blood to the various organs of the body, when at rest. During exertion, the distribution changes. At rest, the heart-lung-heart route takes six seconds, the heart-brain-heart route, eight seconds, and the heart-toes-heart route, 16 seconds.
1 Heart blood vessels 5%
2 Skin, skeleton, etc. 10%
3 Brain 15%
4 Muscles 15%
5 Kidneys 20%
6 Intestines 35%

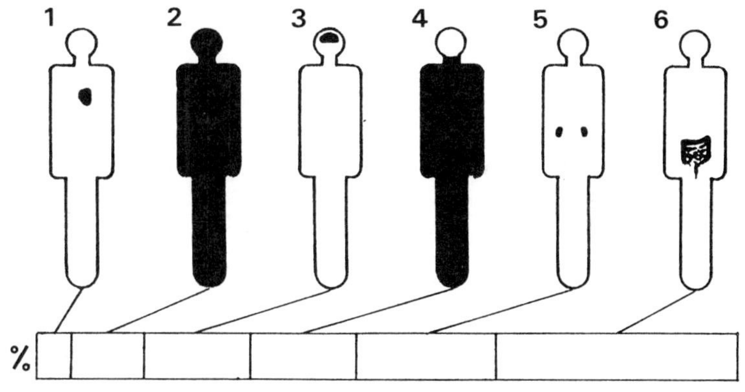

718 THE ENDOCRINE SYSTEM

Principal endocrine glands

7181 The endocrine system is made up of hormone-secreting glands. It acts as the body's regulating system, coordinating and controlling all activity. The following are the body's principal glands:
1 Pituitary gland the body's "master gland." Its hormones control many body activities including general body growth, use of stored fat, amount of water in the urine, and production of milk. Other pituitary hormones work indirectly by stimulating the thyroid, adrenal, and sex glands.
2 Thyroid gland This produces a hormone that controls growth rate and the rate at which the body uses stored energy.
3 Parathyroid glands Four tiny glands embedded in the thyroid. Their hormones control the body's use of calcium and phosphorus.

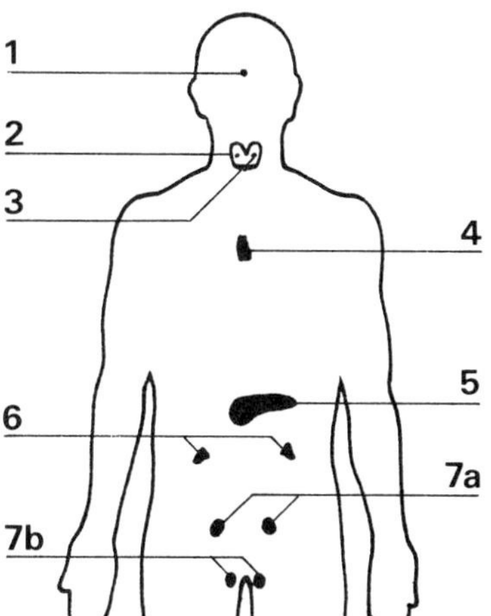

4 Thymus In young children, this helps the body fight infection.
5 Pancreas Cells called Islets of Langerhans produce the hormone insulin, which controls the body's sugar use.
6 Adrenal glands One above each kidney. Their hormone adrenalin controls physical effort and prepares the body to face danger.
7a Ovaries In women, these produce hormones involved in sexual development and in the menstrual cycle (monthly periods).
7b Testes and testicles In men, these produce hormones for male sexual development.

continued

Principal endocrine glands continued

7181 **Liver: the largest gland**
This has a maximum dimension of about 8 x 7 x 5 in (21.5 x 19 x 14 cm) in an average adult. It produces a liquid called bile, which passes via a tube to the small intestine, where it is needed to digest fats. The liver also makes heparin, which stops the blood from clotting.

Lymph glands (nodes)
These are found mainly in the neck, underarms and groin (where legs and trunk meet at the front). They produce leukocytes – a type of white blood cell that fights infection. Because they produce cells and not chemicals, they are more correctly known as lymph nodes rather than lymph glands.

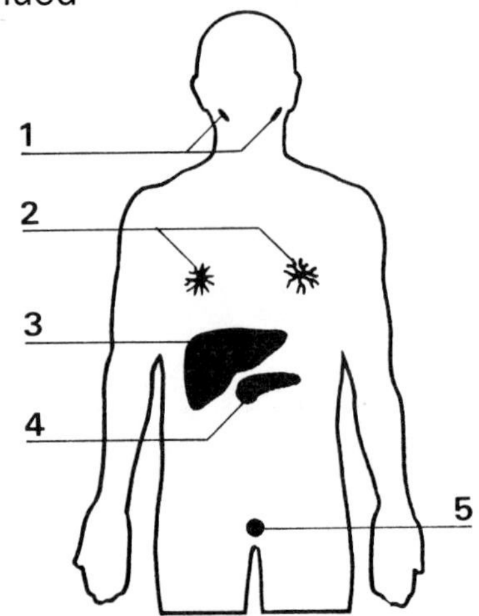

Exocrine glands
Exocrine glands produce substances which are secreted through ducts to the rest of the body. The glands include the sebaceous and sweat glands in the skin and the various glands in the digestive, respiratory, and reproductive systems, as well as those shown here: salivary glands (**1**); milk glands (**2**); liver (**3**); pancreas, which is both an exocrine and endocrine gland (**4**); prostate (**5**).

719 URINARY SYSTEM

Components

7191

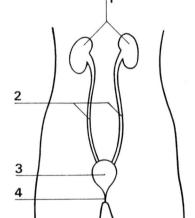

The urinary system consists of those organs that produce and excrete urine:
1 A pair of kidneys Dark red, bean-shaped organs, in similar positions in both sexes, about 4 in (10 cm) long, 2 in (6 cm) wide, 1 in (2.5 cm) thick and 5 oz (150 g) in weight.
2 A pair of ureters Muscular tubes about 10–12 in (24-30 cm) long, carrying urine from the kidneys to the bladder.
3 Bladder A hollow, muscular bag, forming a reservoir for about 1 US pint (0.5 liter) of urine. A muscular ring (sphincter) surrounds the exit from the bladder into the urethra. When this is contracted, it prevents leakage of urine out of the bladder. Upon urination the sphincter is relaxed, and the urine passes into the urethra.
4 Urethra A muscular tube about 8 in (20 cm) long in men and 1–2 in (3–4.5 cm) long in women, taking urine from the bladder to outside the body.

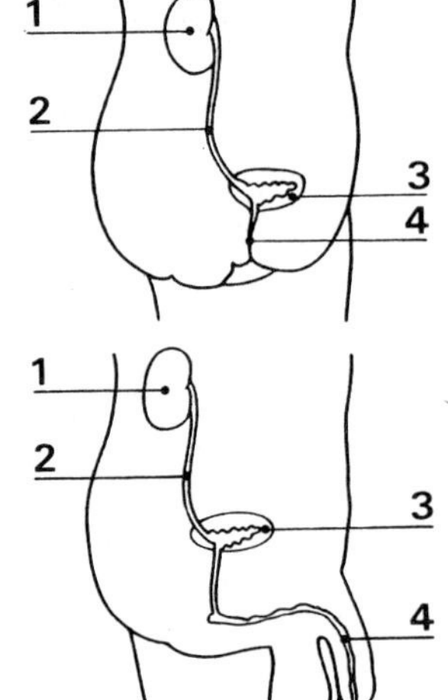

Structure of a kidney
The kidneys are located on either side of the spine, in the region of the middle back. The right kidney lies slightly lower than the left. They consist of the following parts:
1 Capsule: protective skin
2 Cortex: outer region, where blood enters filter units
3 Medulla: its pyramid-shaped structures contain filter loops
4 Renal pelvis: collects urine
5 Renal artery: brings blood
6 Renal vein: removes blood
7 Ureter: drains off urine

How kidneys work
The kidneys are chemical processing works. In them, waste matter in the blood – both solid and liquid – is filtered off under pressure, through more than two million tiny filtering units called glomeruli. This waste matter is called urine. The kidneys filter the entire blood supply about 30 times daily. Blood for processing enters the medulla from the renal artery (**5**). Inside the medulla and cortex, the artery splits into tiny coiled blood vessels. Each coiled vessel is called a glomerulus (**8**). Almost completely surrounding this lies a pinhead-sized sac called Bowman's capsule (**9**). Pressure in the glomerulus forces water and dissolved chemicals from the blood in the glomerulus into the Bowman's capsule. The filtered liquid then continues through a tubule (**10**) surrounded by capillaries (**11**). These tiny blood vessels reabsorb into the blood most of the water and useful chemicals such as amino acids. The treated blood then leaves the kidney via the renal vein (**6**). Meanwhile, wastes remaining in the convoluted tubule flow on via a collecting tubule to the kidney's pelvis. These wastes now form urine. From the kidney's pelvis, urine leaves the kidney through a tube called a ureter.

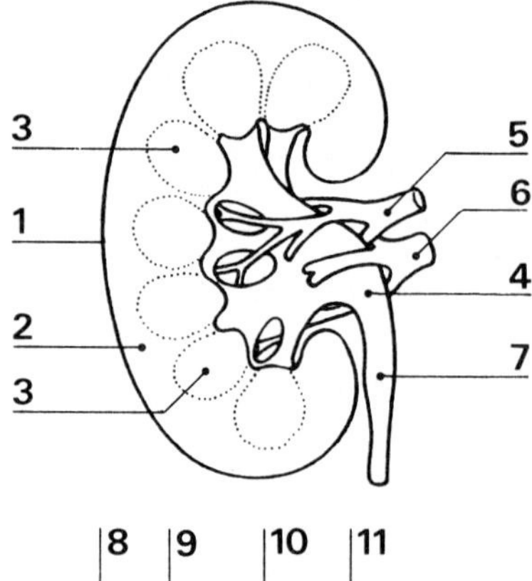

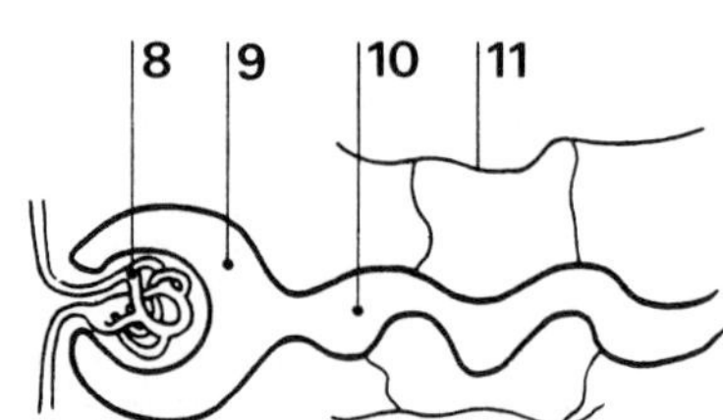

721 SKIN

Skin covers the surface of the body. It is the largest organ of the body, accounting for about 16% of total weight. The skin of an average adult man (**1**) covers an area of about 20 sq ft (1.86 sq m); that of an average woman (**2**) about 17.5 sq ft (1.63 sq m).

1 sq ft

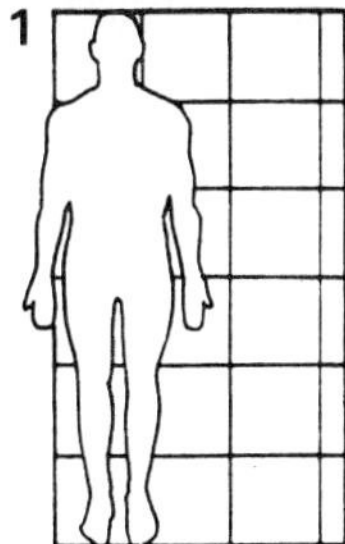

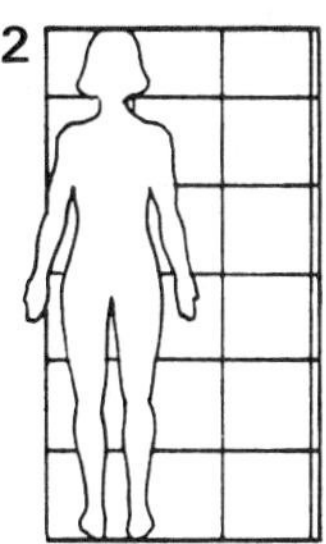

Structure

7211 Skin is made up of several layers of different cells. The top layer is made of dead, flattened cells bound together to form a tough, flexible, and waterproof surface that is constantly being rubbed off and replaced by the living layers below. The lower layers contain hair roots ("follicles"); sweat and "sebaceous" glands; nerves; blood vessels; and fat.

1 Epidermis: outer skin layer, with dead cells on the outside and living ones below
2 Dermis: inner skin layer
3 Sebaceous (grease) gland
4 Nerve
5 Subcutaneous ("under skin") fat
6 Hair
7 Erector muscle: makes the hair stand up
8 Blood vessel
9 Sweat gland

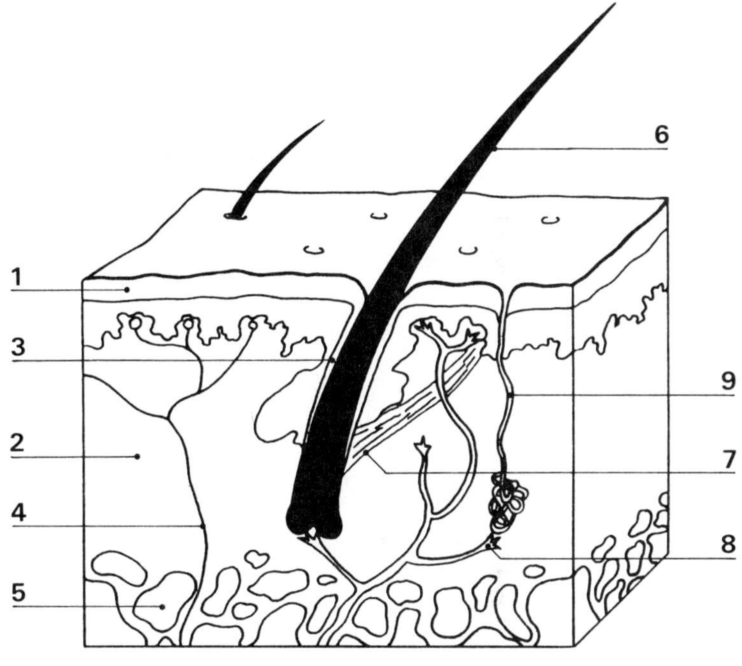

Thickness and elasticity

The skin is generally about $^1/_{16}$ in (1-2 mm) thick, but only about $^1/_{32}$ in (0.5 mm) on the eyelids and up to $^1/_5$ in (6 mm) on palms and soles, where it is dense and ridged to increase gripping powers. Skin is attached to the deeper tissues by elastic fibers, so that it can move about to a certain extent and allow the joints to function. Skin grows constantly with the body but in old age the body bulk shrinks and the skin loses its elasticity, causing bagginess and wrinkles.

Function

7212 The skin acts as a protective barrier against the environment. It stops the evaporation of the water that makes up 60% of the body. It also stops bacteria from entering the body. Wounds are healed quickly by an antiseptic liquid which is secreted from glands in the skin.

The skin also protects the delicate tissues below from the sun's harmful ultraviolet rays. This is done by producing melanin, a dark pigment which forms a layer to absorb the rays.

Populations exposed to extensive sunlight have adapted by producing more melanin and thus developing darker skin. People who have no melanin in their skin have white hair and skin and very pale eyes. The skin of these albinos will not brown in sunlight and is very sensitive to the Sun's rays.

Temperature control

1 In hot weather skin helps to cool down the overheating body. Sweat glands (**a**) release sweat onto the skin. When it evaporates it cools the skin. Blood capillaries dilate (**b**), and radiate heat through the skin.
2 In cold weather the skin can stop the body losing heat. Sweat glands (**a**) close up. Blood capillaries constrict (**b**), and hairs grow erect (**c**), trapping a thick layer of still air that insulates the skin.

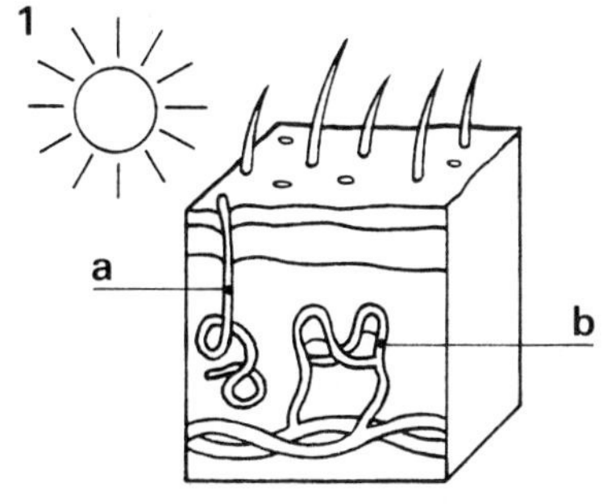

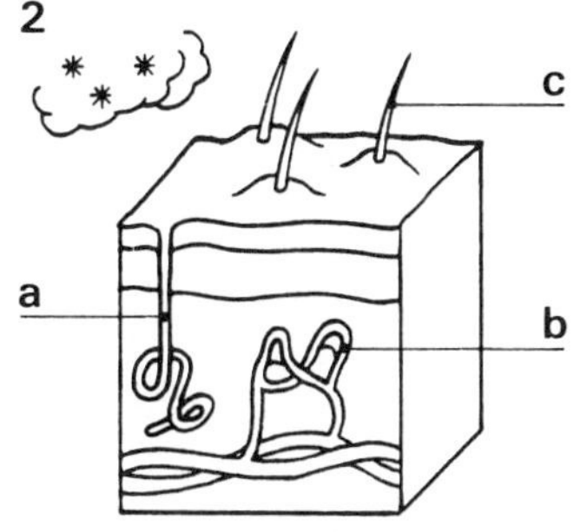

722 HAIR

Structure

7221 A cross section through a hair shows:
1 Shaft: hair above the skin
2 Root: hair embedded in skin
3 Follicle: pit in the skin from which the hair grows
4 Papilla: the growth point
5 Medulla: hollow central core
6 Cortex: main part of the hair, determines color and hair type
7 Cuticle: a hard, colorless, coating
8 Sebaceous (oil) gland, keeps hair shiny and waterproof
9 Erector muscle: raises the hair
10 Blood vessel

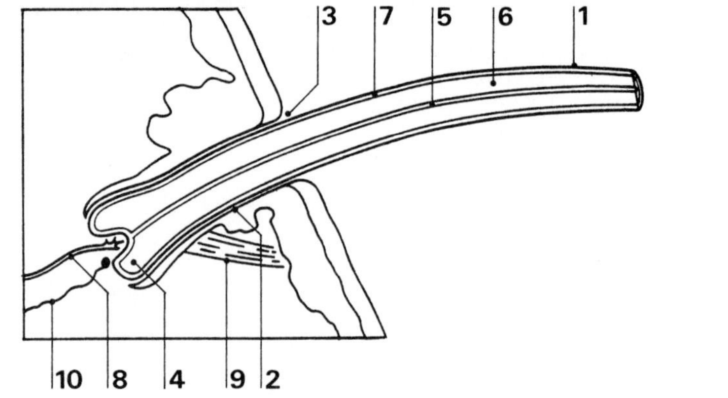

Types

7222 Hair grows over the entire surface of the human body except the palms, soles of the feet, and parts of the genitals. There are three types of hair — scalp hair, body hair, and sexual hair.

Scalp hair resembles the body hair of other animals. Human body hair is very fine and usually less pigmented than animal hair. Sexual hair develops around the genitals, the armpits and (in men) the face. Its growth is dependent on the male sex hormones produced by both sexes during puberty. The number of hairs on the body varies between individuals, but on average there are about 100,000 hairs on the head.

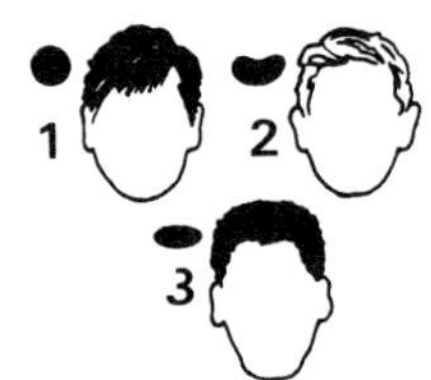

Individual hair types
There are three hair types: oriental, caucasian and negroid. Oriental hair (**1**) is round in cross section, and straight. Caucasian hair (**2**) is kidney-shaped in cross-section, and usually wavy, the degree being dependent on the extent of the curve of the follicle. In negroid hair (**3**) a highly curved follicle gives the hair a flattened oval shape in cross section, and causes it to be extremely curly.

Color
Pigment production in the hair follicle slows down with age and often ceases, so that the hair becomes colorless. A grey hair has colorless sections mixed in with colored sections; when all the hair is colorless it appears white. The tendency to "go grey" is inherited and some people go grey sooner than others. There is no known way to stimulate pigment production once it has ceased.

Function

7223 Hair acts as a protective barrier. The eyelashes protect the eyes, and hair in the nostrils and outer ears prevent the entry of foreign bodies into these organs.The eyebrows prevent sweat dripping into the eyes.

Hair also acts to conserve heat. Air trapped between hairs insulates the skin and stops heat loss. Attached to each hair follicle is a strip of erector muscle which when it contracts, makes the hair stand on end causing "goose-flesh." These muscles are stimulated by cold or emotional stress.

Growth

7224 Hair is made out of keratin, a tough type of protein that also makes nails. It grows out of follicles in the skin. These follicles are established at birth and no new ones are formed later in life.

The hair we see is actually dead. The root of the hair is the only live part of the hair: it grows and pushes the dead hair shaft out of the skin.

Hair growth is cyclical with a growth phase followed by a rest phase in which the hair is loosened. A new hair then pushes it out. In an adult scalp the growth phase is about 2–6 years and the rest phase is 3 months. 30–100 hairs are lost from the scalp each day. About 85% of hair grows while 15% rests. Head hair rarely exceeds 3 ft (90 cm) in length.

723 NAILS

Nail formation

7231 Nails are found at the end of each finger and toe. They are made of the hard, flat, transparent protein keratin, which is also found in the hair. The nail root lies under a fold of skin and grows outward over the nail bed. Fingernails grow quicker than toenails. The average growth rate of nails is 1.5 in (about 4 cm) a year. Nails protect the tips of the fingers and toes and can be used as weapons.

Nails form before birth. Certain epidermal cells in toes and fingers divide (**1**) and the upper cells accumulate hard keratin which produces a nail plate (**2**). This plate grows out of the nail groove (**3**) and over the skin, forming a fingernail or toenail.

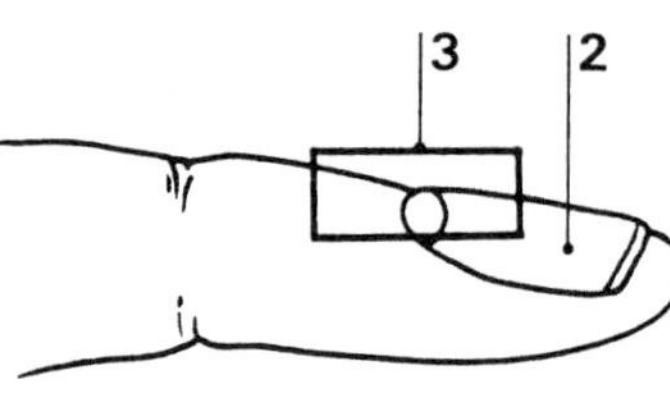

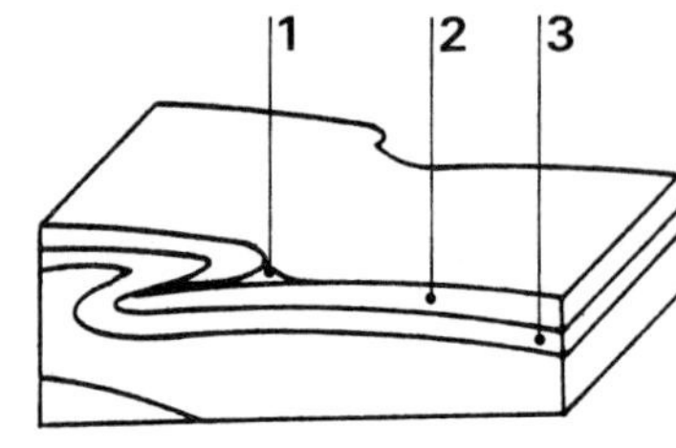

731 REPRODUCTIVE SYSTEMS

Male

7311 **1** A man's reproductive organs are here shown from the side (**1**) and front (**2**).

a Scrotum Skin pouch that holds the testes and keeps them cooler than the rest of the body.
b Testes (or testicles) Two egg-shaped glands which produce sperm and male sex hormones including testosterone.
c Epididymis Tubes through which sperm travel; lying beside the testes, they store sperm while they mature.
d Vas deferens Two tubes that transmit sperm from the testes to the prostate gland.
e Seminal vesicles These produce the seminal fluid which carries sperm out of the body.
f Prostate gland: A chestnut-shaped gland about 2 in (5 cm) in diameter, it produces additional seminal fluid.
g Urethra: Also part of the urinary system, this 7 in (20 cm) tube carries sperm and seminal fluid (together called semen) to the penis tip for ejaculation.
h Penis In adult males, this averages 3–4 in (8–11 cm) in length when limp and about 5–7 in (12.5–18 cm) when erect. It is the organ through which sperm are released.

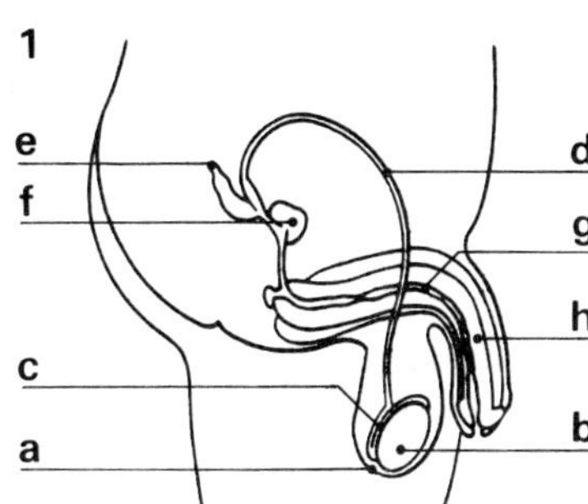

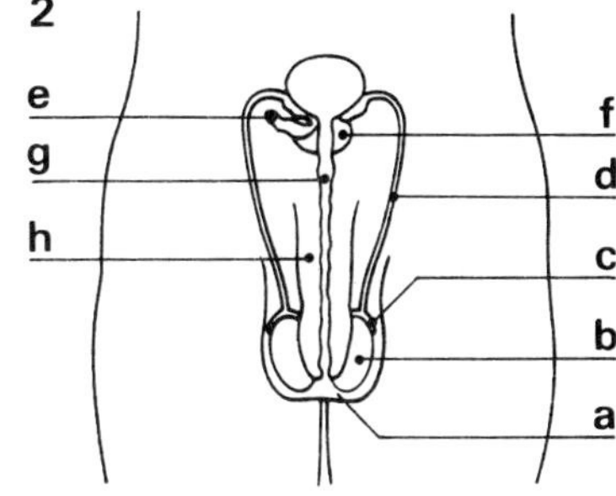

Female

7312 **2** A woman's reproductive organs are here shown from the side (**1**) and front (**2**).

a Ovaries Two female sex glands about 1 x 1 x 1/3 in which produce eggs (ova) and the female sex hormones estrogen and progesterone.
b Fallopian tubes Two tubes about 4 in (11 cm) long, through which ripe eggs pass for possible fertilization by a man's sperm.
c Uterus (womb) This is where fertilized eggs are implanted and develop into babies; it is about the size and shape of a pear in non-pregnant women. The walls expand as a baby grows.
d Cervix Neck of the womb.
e Vagina A 4–5 in (10–12.5 cm) tube leading to the uterus; it receives the man's penis in intercourse and is the route through which babies are born.

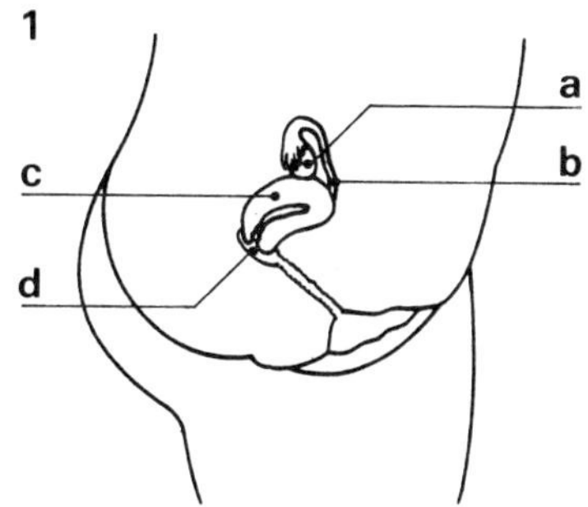

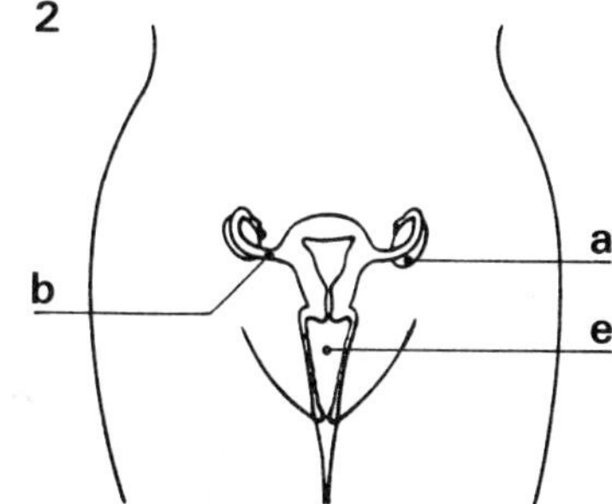

Menstruation

7313 **3** The start of menstruation is the most obvious indication of the onset of puberty in a female. This diagram shows the role of different hormones during the monthly cycle. Changing levels of FSH (**a**), estrogen (**b**), LH (**c**), and progesterone (**d**) produce the cycle's features: the maturing and releasing of an egg (**e**), changes in the quantity and character of cervical mucus (**f**) which is abundant, thin and clear at the time of ovulation, and the building up of the uterus lining or endometrium (**g**) to receive a fertilized egg, and its breaking down and shedding at menstruation (**h**) which occurs if no egg is fertilized.

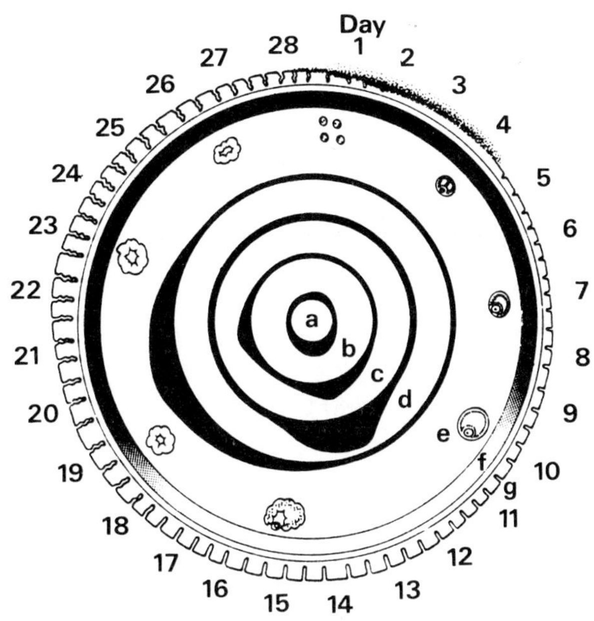

732 INTERCOURSE AND CONCEPTION

Eggs and sperm

7321 A new life starts when a sperm fertilizes an egg. During sexual intercourse, a man's penis releases millions of sperm in seminal fluid, or ejaculate, into a woman's vagina. Lashed along by their tails, the microscopic sperm wriggle through the cervix into the womb or uterus.

Fewer than 3,000 sperm survive to continue into the two Fallopian tubes, many being killed in the vagina. Sperm can survive up to three days in a woman's body until they die or an egg is released. If a woman has recently ovulated (released an egg, or ovum from an ovary) one sperm may meet it for fertilization.

1 Egg follicles mature in the ovary
2 Ovulation (release of egg)
3 Ejaculation of sperm into vagina
4 Arrival of sperm at cervix (neck of womb)
5 Sperm reach uterus (womb)
6 Sperm enter the Fallopian tubes
7 Sperm journey to the ovum (egg)
8 Fertilization occurs

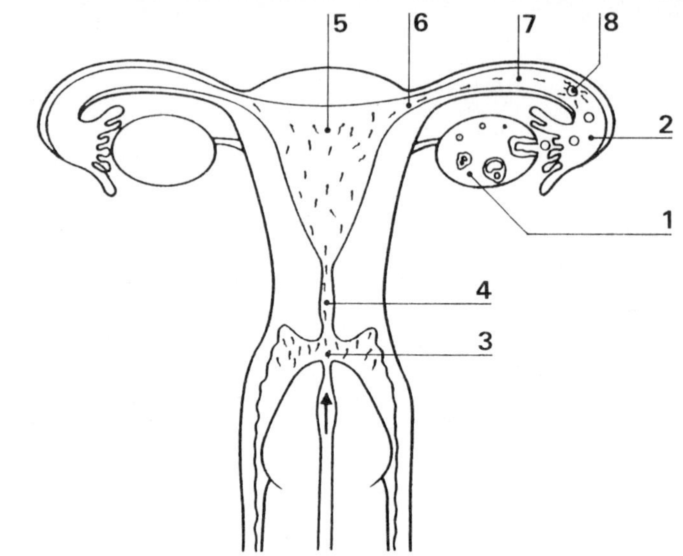

Fertilization

7322 Hugely magnified, a tadpole-like sperm (**1**) fertilizes an egg or ovum (**2**) much larger than itself. The sperm's tail will fall off but its head or nucleus will fuse with the ovum nucleus. The egg then develops an outer wall to keep out other sperm.

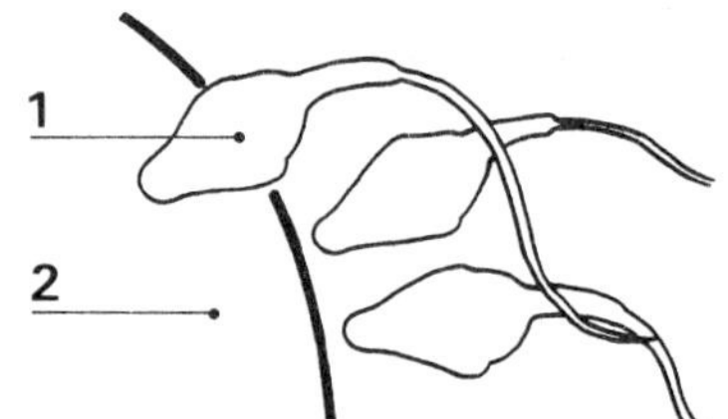

From puberty to old age, men's testes produce 10-30 billion sperm a month. Women are born with perhaps 350,000 total immature eggs. Between puberty and menopause, at least one egg matures in an ovary each month and is released for possible fertilization. Only some 375 eggs mature throughout a lifetime.

733 GENETICS

Chromosomes

7331 Each of two parents contributes to the "blueprint" that determines how their baby grows and develops. This blueprint lies in chromosomes, structures that control each body cell. Each chromosome contains genes, which carry inherited characteristics. Each cell has 46 chromosomes in 23 pairs. Cells divide to multiply for tissue growth or repair. Before division, a cell's chromosomes double, so each daughter cell receives 23 pairs. But doubling does not occur in the sex cells that combine for sexual reproduction. Instead, male (**1**) and female (**2**) "parent" cells with 46 chromosomes divide to form sperm (**3**) and ova (**4**) with 23 chromosomes. A sperm and an ovum fuse to produce a fertilized egg (**5**) with 46 chromosomes, 23 from each parent. So the resulting baby will inherit characteristics from both its mother and father.

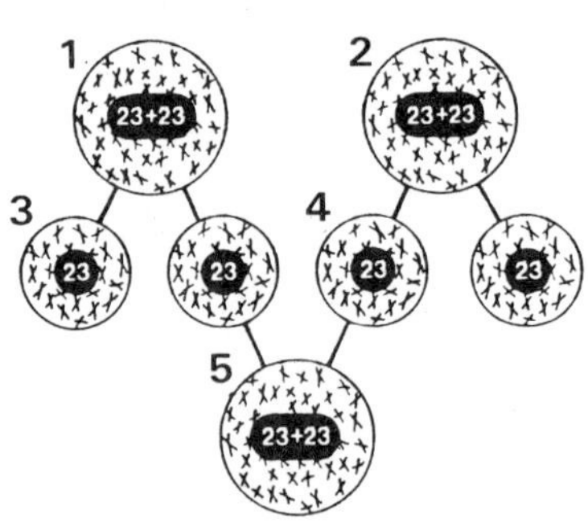

Sex determination

7332

 X chromosome inherited
 X chromosome not inherited
Y chromosome inherited
Y chromosome not inherited

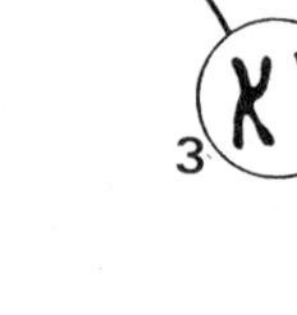
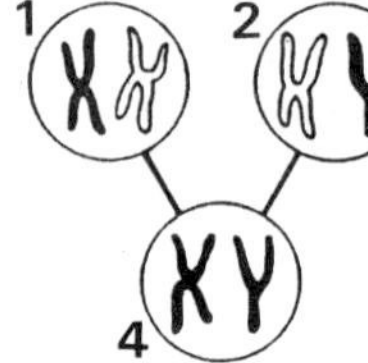
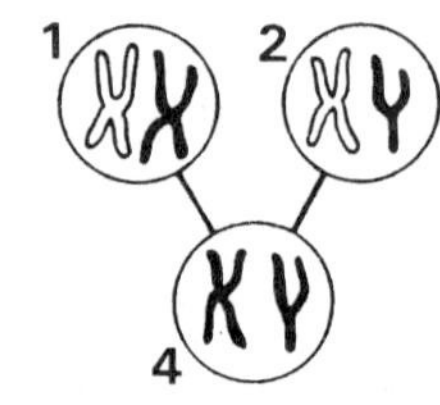

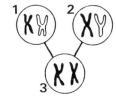

A baby's sex depends upon special chromosomes that it inherits. Each body cell in its mother included a pair of X-shaped sex chromosomes. Each body cell in its father included one X and one Y sex chromosome. A baby inherits only one sex chromosome from each parent. If the baby inherits two Xs it will be female. If it inherits one X and one Y it will be male. Here we show four ways by which a mother (**1**) and father (**2**) can hand on sex cells to produce a daughter (**3**) or son (**4**).

Inherited traits

7333 **Eye color**

From parents we inherit aspects of temperament and physical appearance. Such things as color of the eyes and hair are coded in the genes located on chromosomes. Each type of gene occurs in pairs, and each pair that we inherit contains one gene from each parent. In an inherited pair a dominant gene will "overpower" a recessive gene. Diagrams show the gene for brown eyes (**a**) dominating the gene for blue eyes (**b**) in four of five examples.

a Brown-eye gene ■ Brown eyes
b Blue-eye gene □ Blue eyes

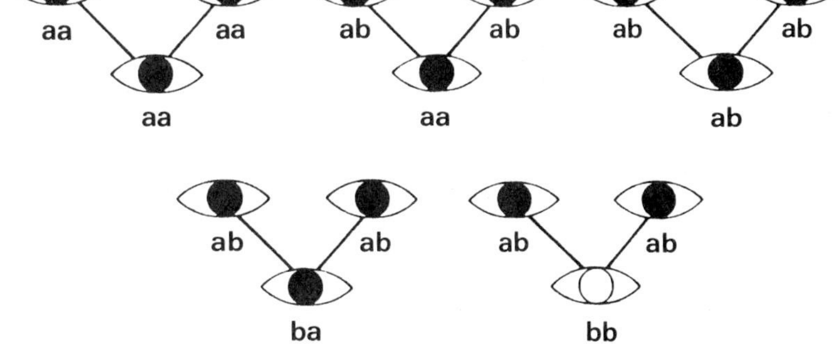

Hair color

Recessive genes can pass through several generations before they reappear. For example, the brown-hair gene (**a**) dominates the red-hair gene (**b**). But as these diagrams show, generations of two families of brown-haired people can unknowlingly hand on a red-haired gene. The gene handed on is circled in the diagram. Only when an individual inherits two of these recessive genes will that person have red hair. Thus in some ways some of us resemble our own parents less than we resemble our grandparents or even our great grandparents.

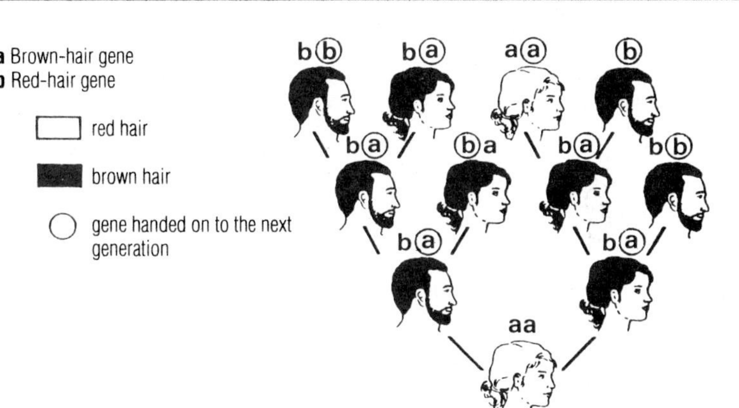

Blood groups

Genetics (the science of heredity) reveals that people inherit various types of blood. Blood donors' and patients' blood groups are an important factor in blood transfusions, where compatability is vital. Also, in paternity cases, a blood-group mismatch between a man and a child helps to prove that the man could not have been the father of the child.

Presence or absence of two factors known as A and B give rise to four blood groups: A, B, AB, and 0. A and B blood each contain one factor. AB blood has both factors. 0 has neither.

This diagram shows the four possible blood groups of the father when the mother and baby have the blood groups shown.

	Baby's blood group			
	0	A	AB	B
Mother's blood group 0	0, A, B	0, A, B		0, A, B
A	A, AB	0, A, AB, B	0, A, AB, B	A, B
AB		AB, B	A, AB, B	A, AB
B	AB, B	AB, B	0, A, AB, B	0, A, AB, B

734 PREGNANCY AND CHILDBIRTH

Stages of pregnancy

7341 Pregnancy is generally divided into three distinct stages, each lasting three months (and thus called a trimester.) The third trimester is really continuous with the second, and perhaps the third division should be considered to begin with labor, as birth commences.

Development of a baby

7342 **The embryo** At conception the fertilized egg comprises a single cell, known as a zygote. The fertilized egg undergoes rapid cell division as it passes down the oviduct and into the uterus, becoming a small bundle of cells that then implants in the lining of the uterus. Fingerlike projections known as villi grow from the embryo into the uterus lining and absorb nourishment. The villi are not part of the embryo, they develop into the placenta, an organ which supplies the embryo with food and oxygen. The placenta becomes a large disk of tissue adhering to the uterine lining.

The uterus extends as the embryo grows. This enlarges the abdomen and displaces the organs to some extent. The uterine lining develops a rich supply of blood vessels and the walls become increasingly muscular because of the hormones estrogen and progesterone. The cells of the embryo divide repeatedly to form tissues and later, organs.

The embryo depends on the mother's blood for food and oxygen but its circulatory system is not directly linked with the maternal blood vessels. The membranes separating the mother and the embryo's blood vessels are very thin so dissolved oxygen, glucose, amino acids, and salts in the mother's blood can pass to the embryo's blood vessels, and carbon dioxide and nitrogenous waste from the embryo can pass in the opposite direction. The membrane also stops harmful material from reaching the embryo and passing into the placenta. The capillaries in the placenta are connected to an artery and vein which run inside the umbilical cord to the embryo.

Throughout the pregnancy the embryo floats in amniotic fluid which fills the amniotic cavity created by the membrane. The fluid protects the embryo from damage and helps maintain its body temperature. Throughout the pregnancy it is known that the developing child drinks the amniotic fluid.

The drawings below show how an embryo becomes a fetus within the mother's uterus (womb), and also show how the mother's body adapts and changes for gestation, and for the events of birth and nursing.

During the first month Rapid growth of the fertilized egg takes place. The embryo's heart pulsates and pumps blood. The backbone and spinal canal are forming. The digestive system is beginning to form and small buds that will eventually become limbs are present.

By week 8 The fetus is $1\frac{1}{8}$ in (29 mm) long and weighs about $\frac{1}{30}$ oz (0.1 g.) The face and features are forming, the eyelids are fused. Limbs are beginning to show distinct division into arms, elbows, forearms, hands, legs, and feet. A distinct umbilical cord has formed. Long bones and internal organs are developing.

By week 16 The fetus is 6–7 in (16–18 cm) long and weighs about 4 oz (100 g). It has a strong heartbeat and active muscles. Its skin is bright pink, transparent and covered with fine downlike hair. Most bones are clearly indicated throughout the body. The head is disproportionately large and eyes, ears, nose, and mouth are nearing their final appearance.

By week 24 The fetus measures 11–14 in (28–35 cm) long and may weigh from $1\frac{1}{4}$–$1\frac{1}{2}$ lb (560–680 g.) The skin is quite wrinkled and red and covered with a protective creamy coating. The eyelids are separated and eyelashes have formed. Fingernails now reach to the end of the fingers.

By week 28 The fetus is about 15 in (38 cm) long and weighs about $2\frac{1}{2}$ lb (1.14 kg). It is still quite red and wrinkled. The fetus may be moving less because it has less room. The eyes open now and there is good hair development.

By week 32 Growth and full development of the fetus are very important in the last two months. The bones of the head are soft and flexible.

By week 36 The baby is fully formed after 36 weeks and measures about 18 in (46 cm) and weighs little more than 5 lb (2.3 kg.) The fetus spends all its time maturing, building up fat tissue to provide it with warmth after birth.

Week 40 This is the approximate time calculated for the date of delivery. The baby is ready and waits for some unknown signal to begin labor. At birth the average baby weighs 7 lb (3.2 kg) and is 19 in (48 cm) long.

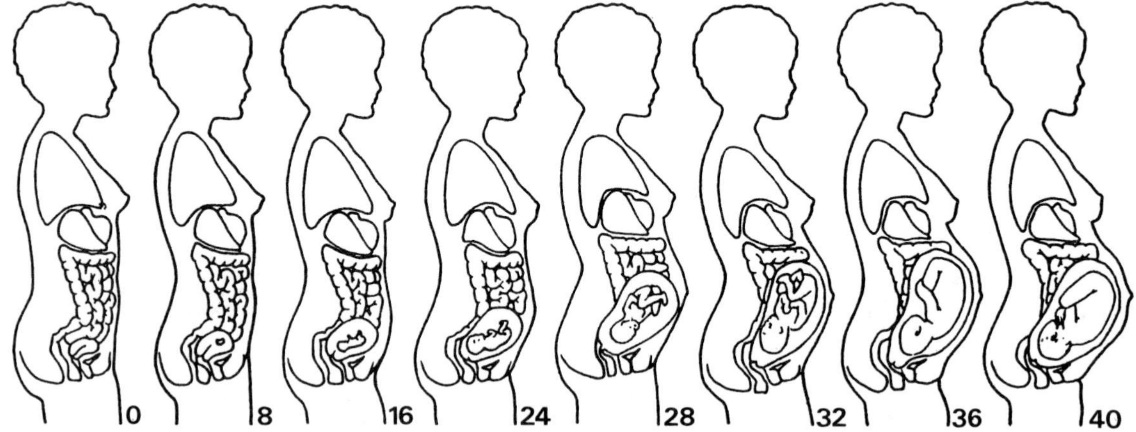

Childbirth

7343 **The three stages of labor**

Stage 1

Technically, the first stage of labor begins at the onset of contractions: gentle spasms of the uterus, becoming regular and strong as the cervix (the neck of the womb) starts to open. In fact, the cervix may begin to dilate a day or so before the actual rhythmic contractions commence at a rate of three or four times an hour. At the end of this stage the cervix is fully dilated, and there will have been a consequent small discharge of blood and mucus from the vagina, followed by a usually more liberal discharge that represents the voiding of the now unnecessary amniotic fluid. The first stage may last for between three and 15 hours altogether, by which time contractions are occurring at a rate of once every two or three minutes lasting 30 to 90 seconds, and are accompanied by an urge to "push" out the baby.

Stage 2

During the second stage, contractions continue and assist the baby to make his or her way down the birth canal. This stage can last up to two or more hours.

Stage 3

The third stage of labor is the final painless expulsion of the remains of the umbilical cord and the placenta from the uterus. It generally lasts for no more than 20 minutes.

Calculating the birth date

7344 **Conception to birth date**

The length of the average pregnancy is approximately 266 days. As the exact estimate of the ovulation is usually not known, an estimate of the date is made using the date of the last menstrual period. This is usually 14

continued

Calculating the birth date continued

7344 days before ovulation, so 14 days is added to the figure of 266, making a total of 280 days, or 40 weeks.
The usual way in which doctors estimate the expected delivery date is to count back 3 months from the first day of the last menstrual period and adding 7 days. For example if the last menstrual period began on May 5 the expected delivery would be February 12 (May 5 minus 3 months = February 5 plus 7 days = February 12)
The table below shows conception (**a**) and birth date (**b**).

a January	1	2	3	4	5	6	7	8	9	10	11	12	13	14	15	16	17	18	19	20	21	22	23	24	25	26	27	28	29	30	31	January
b October	8	9	10	11	12	13	14	15	16	17	18	19	20	21	22	23	24	25	26	27	28	29	30	31	1	2	3	4	5	6	7	November
February	1	2	3	4	5	6	7	8	9	10	11	12	13	14	15	16	17	18	19	20	21	22	23	24	25	26	27	28				February
November	8	9	10	11	12	13	14	15	16	17	18	19	20	21	22	23	24	25	26	27	28	29	30	1	2	3	4	5				December
March	1	2	3	4	5	6	7	8	9	10	11	12	13	14	15	16	17	18	19	20	21	22	23	24	25	26	27	28	29	30	31	March
December	6	7	8	9	10	11	12	13	14	15	16	17	18	19	20	21	22	23	24	25	26	27	28	29	30	31	1	2	3	4	5	January
April	1	2	3	4	5	6	7	8	9	10	11	12	13	14	15	16	17	18	19	20	21	22	23	24	25	26	27	28	29	30		April
January	6	7	8	9	10	11	12	13	14	15	16	17	18	19	20	21	22	23	24	25	26	27	28	29	30	31	1	2	3	4		February
May	1	2	3	4	5	6	7	8	9	10	11	12	13	14	15	16	17	18	19	20	21	22	23	24	25	26	27	28	29	30	31	May
February	5	6	7	8	9	10	11	12	13	14	15	16	17	18	19	20	21	22	23	24	25	26	27	28	1	2	3	4	5	6	7	March
June	1	2	3	4	5	6	7	8	9	10	11	12	13	14	15	16	17	18	19	20	21	22	23	24	25	26	27	28	29	30		June
March	8	9	10	11	12	13	14	15	16	17	18	19	20	21	22	23	24	25	26	27	28	29	30	31	1	2	3	4	5	6		April
July	1	2	3	4	5	6	7	8	9	10	11	12	13	14	15	16	17	18	19	20	21	22	23	24	25	26	27	28	29	30	31	July
April	7	8	9	10	11	12	13	14	15	16	17	18	19	20	21	22	23	24	25	26	27	28	29	30	1	2	3	4	5	6	7	May
August	1	2	3	4	5	6	7	8	9	10	11	12	13	14	15	16	17	18	19	20	21	22	23	24	25	26	27	28	29	30	31	August
May	8	9	10	11	12	13	14	15	16	17	18	19	20	21	22	23	24	25	26	27	28	29	30	31	1	2	3	4	5	6	7	June
September	1	2	3	4	5	6	7	8	9	10	11	12	13	14	15	16	17	18	19	20	21	22	23	24	25	26	27	28	29	30		September
June	8	9	10	11	12	13	14	15	16	17	18	19	20	21	22	23	24	25	26	27	28	29	30	1	2	3	4	5	6	7		July
October	1	2	3	4	5	6	7	8	9	10	11	12	13	14	15	16	17	18	19	20	21	22	23	24	25	26	27	28	29	30	31	October
July	8	9	10	11	12	13	14	15	16	17	18	19	20	21	22	23	24	25	26	27	28	20	30	31	1	2	3	4	5	6	7	August
November	1	2	3	4	5	6	7	8	9	10	11	12	13	14	15	16	17	18	19	20	21	22	23	24	25	26	27	28	29	30		November
August	8	9	10	11	12	13	14	15	16	17	18	19	20	21	22	23	24	25	26	27	28	29	30	31	1	2	3	4	5	6		September
December	1	2	3	4	5	6	7	8	9	10	11	12	13	14	15	16	17	18	19	20	21	22	23	24	25	26	27	28	29	30	31	December
September	7	8	9	10	11	12	13	14	15	16	17	18	19	20	21	22	23	24	25	26	27	28	29	30	1	2	3	4	5	6	7	October

735 CONTRACEPTION

Methods

7351 The following list gives types of contraceptive most commonly practiced, both male and female.

Cervical cap Similar to the diaphragm but not as widely used in the US as in Europe. The cervical cap is a thimble-shaped rigid rubber or plastic cap. It fits directly over the cervix. The cap should be used in conjunction with a spermicide.

Condom Also known as a sheath, rubber, or French letter, this is worn by the man over his erect penis and prevents sperm entering the vagina.

Contraceptive pill Known as The Pill. Taken by the woman, this contains the hormones estrogen and progesterone, or simply progesterone and acts by preventing ovulation. There are often side-effects, and a woman should always seek medical guidance before taking this form of contraception. A male pill is currently being developed.

Diaphragm A rubber cap that is inserted by the woman to fit across her cervix, acting as a barrier to sperm. They should be used in conjunction with a spermicide.

Female sterilization This involves cutting, tying, or removing all or part of the Fallopian tubes so that eggs cannot pass from the ovaries to the uterus and sperm cannot reach the egg. A hysterectomy (complete removal of the uterus) is not generally recommended for the purposes of birth control.

IUD (intrauterine device) Also known as the coil, or loop, this small plastic device is inserted in the uterus by a doctor and left in place for several years. It alters the lining of the uterus and prevents implantation of the fertilized egg.

The mucus method requires recognition of natural changes in the nature of cervical mucus during a woman's menstrual cycle, in order to recognize "safe" days. It is not one of the more reliable methods.

Postcoital methods These include a "morning-after" pill, consisting of large doses of synthetic estrogen to be taken within 72 hours of intercourse; insertion of an IUD up to 5 days after intercourse, and menstrual extraction, which is in effect an early form of abortion.

Rhythm method The calendar method requires that a couple avoid intercourse during those days of the menstrual cycle when a woman is most likely to conceive. The temperature method requires checking the small rise in basal temperature that a woman has when ovulation occurs. Both methods are unreliable on the whole, particularly if menstruation is not regular.

Skin implant (Norplant) This is an under-the-skin implant that prevents pregnancies for up to five years. Norplant is a highly effective contraceptive as it contains only the hormone progesterone, and eliminates the side-effects of estrogen. Minor surgery is needed to place and remove Norplant.

continued

Methods continued

7351 **Spermicides** These chemical products are inserted into the woman's vagina before intercourse and either kill sperm or create a barrier. They come as creams, jellies, foaming tablets, C-film, or suppositories, and should be used with the diaphragm or condoms.

Sponge This spermicide-impregnated sponge is inserted in the vagina prior to intercourse and left in place for six hours afterward.

Vasectomy This simple surgical procedure involves the cutting and tying of both vas deferens in the male so that semen ejected no longer contains sperm. It is not immediately effective, and rarely reversible.

Withdrawal This is the oldest method of birth control, in which the male takes his penis out of the vagina prior to ejaculation. It is not considered a reliable or satisfactory method.

Efficiency

7352 Given here are failure rates for different types of contraception. Figures, based on US surveys, refer to pregnancies per 100 users during the first year of use. Theoretical rates are given first, with actual use rates given in (parenthesis) wherever appropriate.

a Tubal ligation (tying the fallopian tubes) 0.04
b Vasectomy 0.15
c IUD 1.3 (5)
d Combined pill (contraceptive pill containing both estrogen and progesterone) 0.34 (4-10)
e Minipill (contraceptive pill containing progesterone only) 1-1.5 (5-10)
f Condom 3 (10)
g Diaphragm and spermicide 3 (17)
h Rhythm (temperature) 7 (10)
i Rhythm (calender) 13 (21)
j Rhythm (mucus) 2 (25)
k Spermicides 3 (20-25)
l withdrawal 9 (20-25)

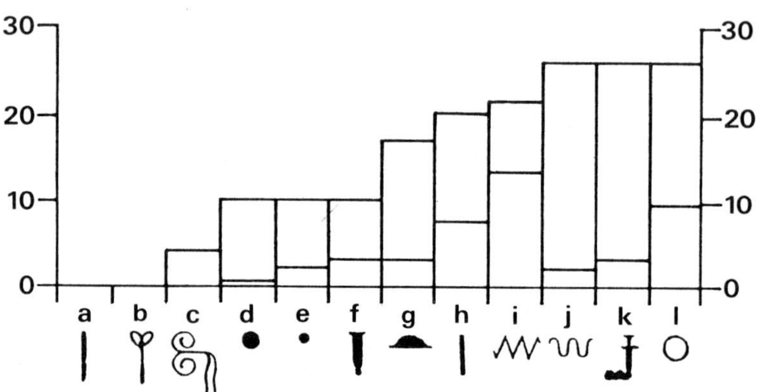

736 SEXUALLY TRANSMITTED DISEASES

Types

7361 **Gonorrhea** This is a common infectious disease, with maybe 200 million cases worldwide. It is rarely fatal, but sometimes has serious complications, mainly in women and children. It spreads by direct genital, oral, and anal intercourse. Men first notice a discharge from the penis and a burning sensation on urinating. Only 20% of infected women show symptoms; usually a vaginal discharge with pain on urinating. At birth, babies can get infected eyes from a mother's vagina. In both sexes, the infection can spread through the sexual organs, and long-standing infection invading the bloodstream can affect skin, joints, and even the brain. Treatment usually involves one large dose of penicillin, boosted by probenecid.

Syphilis This is now relatively rare in the developed world. It is highly infectious and can be transmitted by kissing if the skin of the mouth is broken. Mothers with syphilis can pass it on to their unborn babies. Untreated syphilis passes through four stages. The first, second, and final stages show active signs of the disease. But the third or latent stage lacks symptoms and starts six months to two years after infection, lasting up to 30 years. The primary syphilis sore most often occurs on a man's penis or foreskin, or on a woman's vulval lips or clitoris. It starts as a small red spot that grows moist and eroded, with a hard base like a button. It may be almost too small to see or the size of a fingernail. Penicillin or other antibiotic may be used to treat the disease.

Cervical cancer While there may be other causative factors at work, experts now believe that a recognized virus establishes the nature of cervical cancer as a sexually transmitted disease. Men can spread the virus among different partners. Cervical smears (Pap tests) are an important part of the screening program enabling the disease to be caught in its early stages.

AIDS (Acquired immune deficiency syndrome) The HIV virus attacks the body's immune system and is present in body fluids such as blood, saliva, semen, or vaginal secretions from an infected person. It can be transmitted through sexual activity, as a result of transfusions using infected blood, or via injection with infected needles. It cannot be caught through ordinary social contact. High-risk groups include male homosexuals, drug users, prostitutes, and hemophiliacs who may have received transfusions of infected blood. The virus can, however, also be passed on heterosexually. Synthetic latex condoms provide a very important degree of protection.
Blood tests to detect infection with HIV are available, and after about 12 weeks it is usually possible to say whether or not someone has contracted the virus. To be diagnosed as HIV-positive is not an immediate "death sentence." One survey has shown, for instance, that 75% of HIV-positive men were well and symptom-free two years after diagnosis. AIDS (**1**) does not develop immediately. Being affected with the AIDS virus (**2**), HIV, is not the same as having AIDS. Many people who carry the virus do so unknowingly, without showing any symptoms. It may be that they have not developed the disease. Other HIV-carriers suffer intermediate illnesses, such as Persistent Generalized Lymphadenopathy (PGL) (**3**).

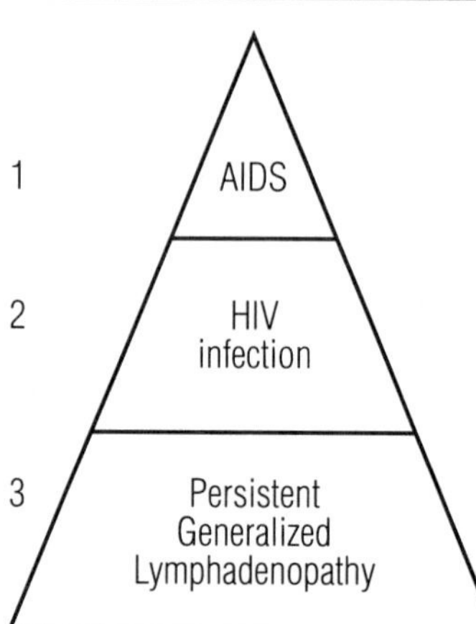

continued

Types continued

7361 **HIV infection** Full-blown AIDS does not develop immediately after infection with the HIV virus. There are several stages through which the disease may evolve. Even if symptoms never show themselves, someone who is HIV-positive may still infect others.

Genital herpes Symptoms include a feeling of being generally unwell, a stinging sensation, a high temperature, and contagious blisters or small ulcers. Ulcers present at the end of pregnancy can cause a life-threatening infection in the newborn. Many forms of medication are available, but the condition may recur. To avoid spread of infection, sexual contact should be avoided. A condom will not provide complete protection.

Non-specific urethritis (NSU) One of the most common sexual disorders in men, with symptoms resembling those of gonorrhea – principally discharge and discomfort on urinating. It can be treated with antibiotics.

Genital warts May appear on the genitals or around the anus, and are due to a virus appearing 1-6 months after sexual contact. Treatment may involve repeated use of a resin application. There is now thought to be a link with cancer of the cervix.

Candidiasis

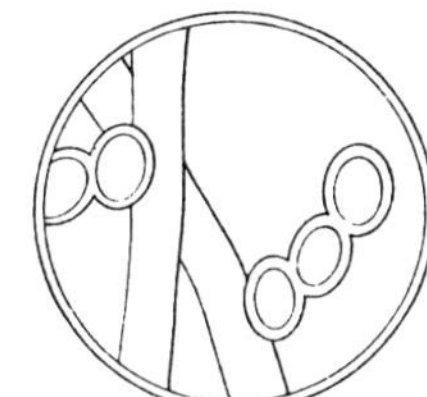

Also called moniliasis and thrush, in women this can give an itchy swollen vulva; curdy vaginal discharge; and pain on urination and intercourse. Men may have a red, spotty penis and inner foreskin, with a burning sensation. The cause is a yeast-like fungus, treated by fungal pessaries in the vagina or creams on the vulva or penis.

Trichomoniasis

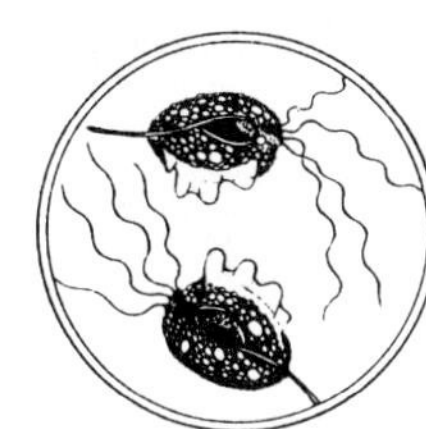

"Trich" involves a foul-smelling greenish, foamy vaginal discharge, and inflammation of vagina and vulva with pain on intercourse and perhaps urination. Most infected men suffer no symptoms but can still spread the disease. Its cause is a microscopic one-celled animal parasite. The cure is a course of oral drugs.

Infestations

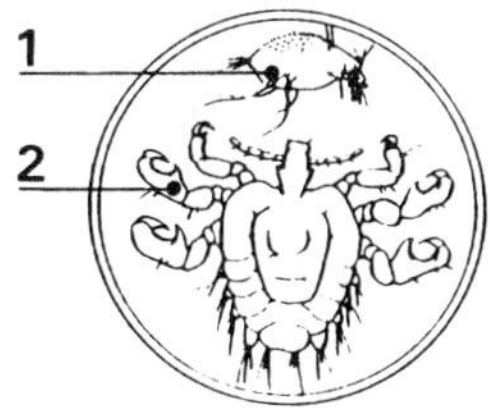

Are sometimes passed sexually. Pubic lice (**1**), for example, are genital versions of mites that can also occur elsewhere on the body. Treatment involves painting the area with appropriate chemicals. Scabies (**2**), meanwhile, takes the form of small itchy lumps caused by a tiny mite. It, too, is easily treated chemically.

Signs and symptoms

7362 **Signs and symptoms on the genitals (1)**
- A sore, ulcer, or rash on the penis, vagina, or vulval lips
- A sore, ulcer, or rash on or near the anus
- Swollen glands in the groin
- A burning sensation or pain on urination
- An itchy or sore vagina or an itchy penis tip
- Pain on intercourse
- Unusual discharge from the penis or vagina
- A frequent urge to urinate

Signs and symptoms elsewhere (2)
a Patchy hair loss
b Eye infection
c A sore, ulcer, or rash on the mouth or on the lips
d A sore throat after oral sex
e Body rash
f Sores in soft skin folds
g A rash, sore, or ulcer on finger or hand

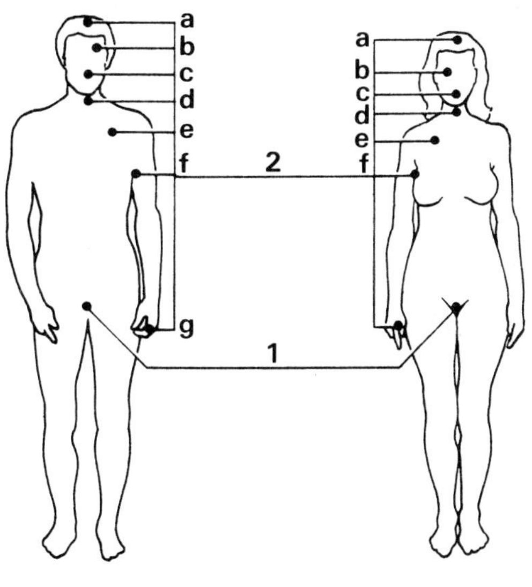

741 BODY TYPES

Body shapes

7411

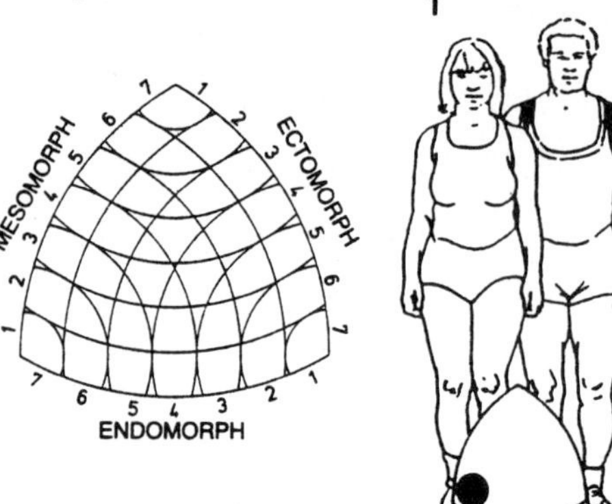

1

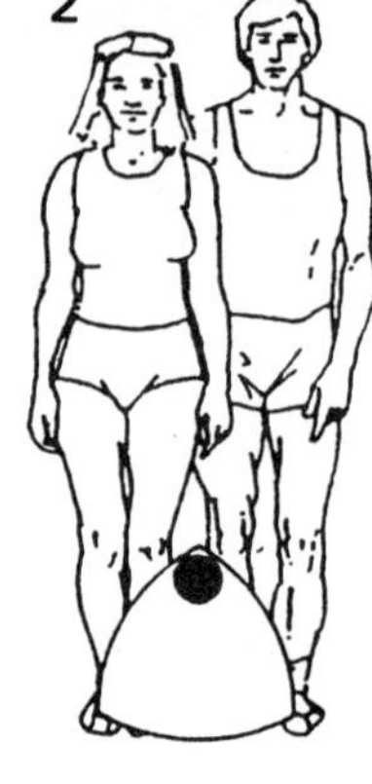

2

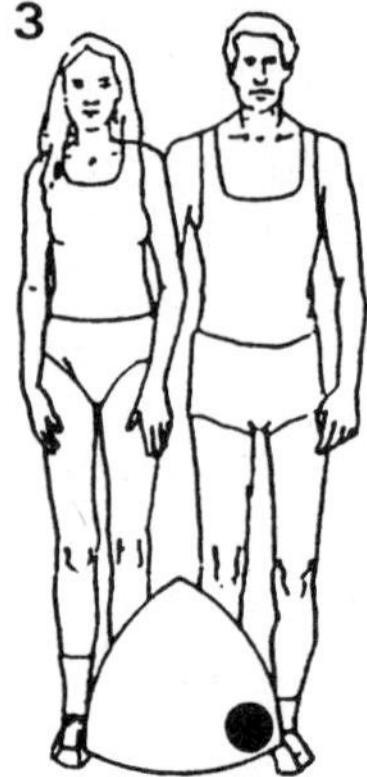

3

4

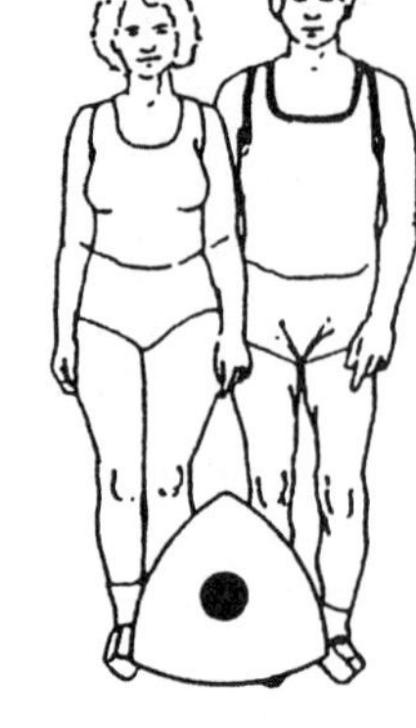

In the 1940s an American psychologist identified three extreme body types or somatotypes: endomorph (soft and rounded), mesomorph (muscular), and ectomorph (linear.) An individual's tendency toward each body type is scored from 1 through 7 and plotted on a shield where the three corners represent the three somatotypes. Each body type relates to high or low physical performance in five categories: strength; power; endurance; body support; and agility.

1 Endomorph (711): low in all categories
2 Mesomorph (171): high in strength, power, endurance, body support, and agility
3 Ectomorph (117): high in agility, endurance, and body support
4 Average individual (444): moderate performances

Height and weight

7412 People eating no more than their bodies need have an ideal weight that varies with their sex and height. Weight often increases with middle age, largely because people eat the same amount as before but tend to exercise less. They therefore burn up fewer calories and store the surplus calories as fat. These tables show ideal weights for the main height ranges of women (**1**) and men (**2**) of large frame (**a**), medium build (**b**), and small frame (**c**), at any age.

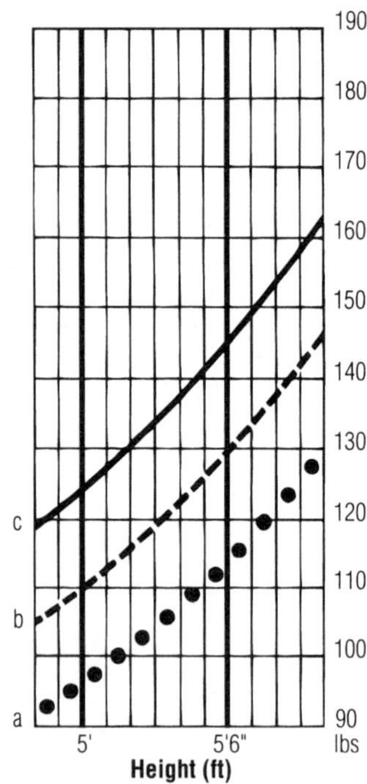

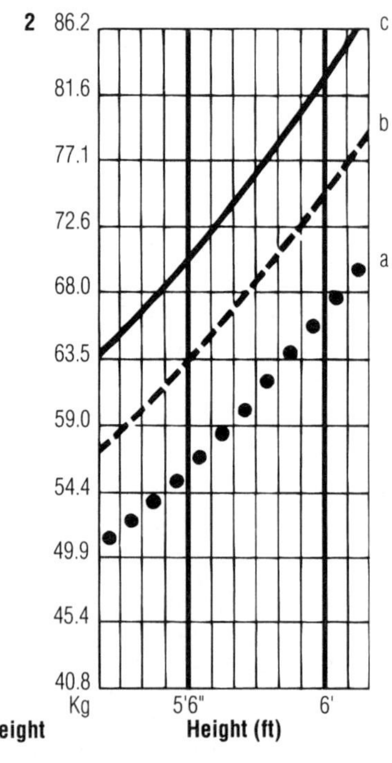

Normal growth patterns in children

7413 At birth, a newborn's legs make up only some 35% of its total height; after puberty, the legs may account in the same individual for as much as half of his or her total height.

Height and weight in both boys and girls tend to show a steady increase until the onset of puberty. At the same time, genetic factors retain considerable influence – a child of parents of relatively short, thin stature is unlikely even while very young to match the overall growth of a child of much taller, heavier parents. Environmental factors may also be significant (especially in areas where nutrition is poor.) But within these constraints, growth is most often in proportion.

The major difference with the growth of boys and girls, then, is the timing of puberty. In girls it begins at about age 11 and lasts until about age 14. In boys it begins at about age 13 and goes on until about age 17. During this period the so-called "growth-spurt" takes place, but in different individuals the event may commence at different times or be spread over a different duration. The growth hormone is responsible for all such changes in the body. It is produced and secreted by the pituitary gland in the brain.

742 FITNESS

Fitness components

7421 The fitter your body the more efficiently it works. Fit individuals complete their daily tasks and still have energy to spare.

Fitness involves five factors (others include agility, balance, coordination, and speed.)

1 Body composition Fat content, proportions, shape, and weight/size ratio (partly inherited, partly determined by diet and exercise.)

2 Flexibility Range of movement around a joint.

3 Strength The force contracting muscles can apply to move a load (the rate at which muscles move a load is muscle power.)

4 Muscular endurance How long specific muscles can perform a task before fatigue sets in.

5 CR (cardiovascular and respiratory) fitness The ability of the heart and lungs to supply oxygen to muscles and remove waste products. CR fitness arguably matters more than all the rest.

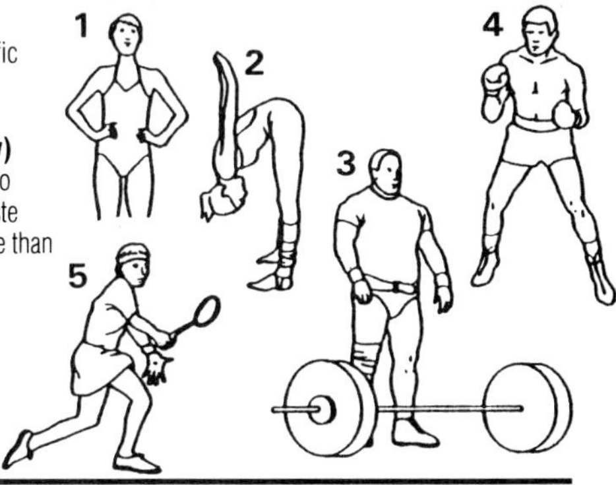

Your pulse

7422 Your pulse is the measure of your heartbeat – its speed, strength, and regularity. The best place to feel the pulse is at the wrist, and you should learn to take your pulse there as a ready assessment of your fitness and also as a check against exercising too strenuously.

Place the first three fingers of your right hand on the inside of your left wrist, and count the number of beats for 30 seconds; multiply by two for the rate per minute.

Maximum recommended pulse rates
This diagram shows a selection of maximum recommended pulse rates for various ages. (**1**) shows the typical pulse rate for people at rest; (**2**) shows pulse ratings by age for people unused to exercise; and (**3**) shows the maximum levels to which you should raise your pulse when you get more fit.

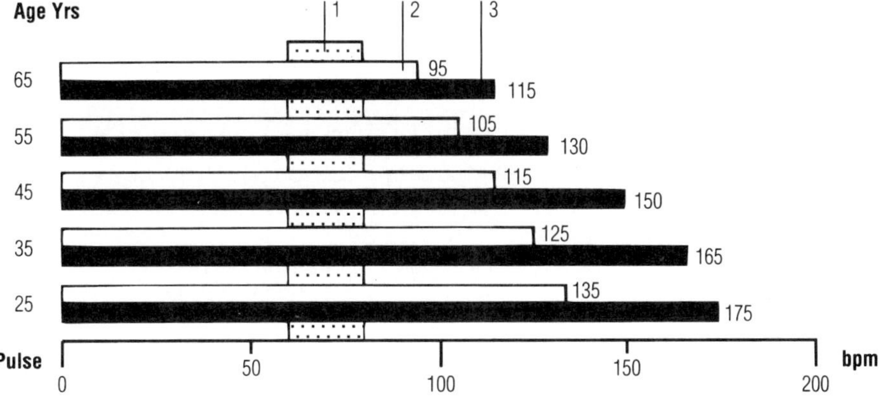

Blood pressure

7423 Blood pressure is generally measured by means of a sphygmomanometer – a device that comprises an inflatable cuff attached to a pump, and a scale for recording the air pressure exerted. The cuff is place around the patient's upper arm and inflated with the bulb pump until blood flow through the arm is heard through a stethoscope to have halted. The pressure is then reduced until the pulsing blood flow is heard to restart: the systolic reading is taken at this point. The pressure is further reduced until the flow is constant, without a beat: the diastolic reading is taken at this point. The two readings together constitute the measure of the blood pressure. A healthy young adult's pressure at rest might be measured as 110/75; at age 60 a measure of about 130/90 at rest is more normal.

Blood pressure rises with exertion and with any condition that narrows the arteries (such as heart disease and smoking tobacco.)

A fit heart

7424 Exercise makes the heart and lungs work harder to meet the muscles' needs for extra blood and oxygen. At rest an unfit heart has only a small reserve capacity, so beats much faster during exercise. After exercise an unfit heart takes a long time to slow down to normal.

A heart made fit by exercise grows stronger, bigger and more efficient. A fit heart pumps more blood with every stroke, so it beats more slowly than an unfit heart. It also has a large reserve capacity, and after exercise soon slows down to normal.

Temperature

7425 The part of the brain responsible for temperature regulation is the hypothalamus. It is the hypothalamus that stimulates shivering when body temperature falls, and promotes perspiration when the body overheats.

Taking a temperature
Body temperature is most commonly taken by putting a thermometer under the tongue for a short time. However, patients in a hospital may well be asked to place a thermometer under the armpit, where in fact the temperature registers about 0.5° F lower. Children may alternatively have their temperature taken in the rectum, where the temperature is about 0.5° F higher than under the tongue.

continued

Temperature continued

7425 **Normal temperature variations**
Everyone's body temperature varies considerably hour by hour - although the range is generally between 98° F (36.5° C) and 99° F (37.2° C). It all depends on the environmental heat, the amount of exertion, the time of day (for body temperature has its own rhythm) and other factors (such as the person's age). Women are more subject to temperature fluctuation than men, because their menstrual patterns cause lower body temperature at menstruation and higher body temperature at ovulation.

743 SLEEP

Sleep is a rest period during which we become unaware of our surroundings, our muscles relax, and our breathing rate and heartbeat slow down. Sleep helps to revitalize the nervous system. Without sleep, people soon lose energy and concentration and grow irritable. In orthodox, or deep sleep (75% of total sleep) the body is relaxed. During paradoxical, or shallow sleep (25% of total sleep) dreams occur.

Sleep patterns

7431

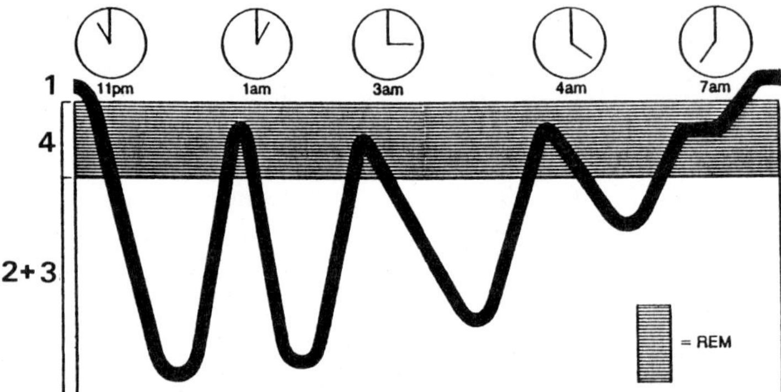

Sleep follows a standard pattern:
1 Consciousness We are aware of our surroundings.
2 Shallow orthodox sleep We are aware of our surroundings.
3 Deep orthodox sleep Body building and repair processes reach their peak.
4 Paradoxical or REM (rapid eye movement) sleep Breathing and heartbeat grow irregular, eyes move back and forth behind shut lids, brain activity increases, and we dream. There are five REM phases in eight hours sleep, so we dream about five times a night.

744 FOOD AND NUTRITION

Food requirements

7441

1

2

3

We need food for three reasons:
1 Fuel providers
To provide the fuel that creates the energy needed to work, play, and to stay alive. Energy comes from carbohydrates (starch and sugar), fats, and to a small extent from protein. Starch comes from cereals, seeds and root vegetables, and foods made from them. Sugar (glucose, fructose, and galactose) is made from sugar beet, cane or maple and is found in fruit, honey, sweet foods and in drinks like beer, sherry, and cider. A third supplier of energy is fat – animal and vegetable. Sources include butter, oils, milk, cereal, meat, and nuts. Protein and alcohol also provide fuel for the body, though to a lesser extent.

2 Raw material suppliers
To supply the raw materials from which the body takes what it needs to build and repair itself. These are the foods which give the body the materials – particularly proteins – it needs to rebuild parts that get used up or deteriorate in the course of living. Protein is part of every one of the millions of cells from which the body is built – it forms our building blocks. No food is pure protein, but some are more protein-rich than others. These include fish, meat, poultry, cheese, milk, yogurt, nuts, beans, and cereals. Bread is also important as a protein provider because it is a significant part of the Western diet.

3 Vital chemicals
To make available the chemicals that are the basis of the reactions and processes which make the body's self-maintenance possible. The body also needs a number of chemicals and minerals to aid its chemical processes and to help energy and material foods work properly. Carbohydrates cannot be converted into energy without vitamin B1. Most vitamins cannot be made by the body, so they must be supplied by food. Minerals are needed too, usually in tiny amounts. While the average diet provides most of these chemicals it may also give too much carbohydrate or too little of some of the minerals and vitamins.

PROTEINS
These build and repair body cells. They are made up of amino acids – chemical compounds combining nitrogen, carbon, hydrogen, and oxygen. Eight of these amino acids are considered essential for adults. They cannot be made in the body and must be provided by the diet. Good sources of protein are meat, fish, eggs, milk, cheese, beans, grains, and nuts.

continued

Food requirements continued

7441 **CARBOHYDRATES**
Provide energy for rapid use. They include sugars in fruits, sugar cane, and sugar beet, and starches in potatoes, cereals, and other vegetables. Many foods rich in carbohydrates are also good sources of vitamins.

FATS
These are concentrated stores of energy, found in butter, margarines, edible oils, meat, eggs, etc. They are also important in carrying soluble vitamins such as A, D, E, and K.

VITAMINS
In tiny quantities these help regulate chemical processes inside the body. Different vitamins occur in fats and oils, fresh fruits and vegetables, and other substances.
Vitamin A This maintains the eyes' ability to adapt to the dark and keeps skin in good condition. Deficiency can damage the eyes and cause blindness. Taken in excess it can accumulate in the liver and poison the body. It is not widely distributed in food, the best sources being fish-liver oils followed by animal liver, kidney, dairy produce, and eggs.
Vitamin B complex This includes thiamin, riboflavin, folic acid, and biotin. Eight of the vitamins in this category are regarded as essential nutrients for humans, each one having a different function. They are all water-soluble and tend to occur in the same types of food so that a deficiency of one of them is unlikely. Good sources are yeast extracts, whole grains, offal such as liver and kidney, green vegetables, eggs, and milk.
Vitamin C This is needed to maintain healthy skin, ligaments, and bones. It also promotes the absorption of iron and can help ward off a cold. It occurs in citrus fruits, blackcurrants, brussel sprouts, and strawberries in relatively high concentrations. However, it is easily lost when fruit and vegetables are cooked.
Vitamin D This promotes the absorption of calcium for the formation of normal bones. Infants and children who suffer from vitamin D deficiency develop weak bones; they may be deformed as a result. But too much vitamin D can damage the kidneys. The Sun creates vitamin D by acting on natural fats beneath the skin. Other sources include fish-liver oil, herring, and eggs.
Vitamin E The function of this is not yet fully understood. As most foods contain some vitamin E and it is easily stored in the body, deficiency problems are unlikely. Good sources are eggs and oils derived from cereals such as wheat-germ oil, maize oil, and cottonseed oil.
Vitamin K This is known as the anti-hemorrhagic vitamin because it is essential for the proper clotting of blood. It occurs in a wide range of foodstuffs of which green vegetables and fish-liver oils are perhaps the most important. Deficiency is very unlikely.

MINERALS
It is not certain what role some minerals play, and the amount of a mineral that is taken up from food when we eat may depend on the way we combine our foods.
Calcium Needed for strong bones and teeth. Deficiency leads to tetany (muscular twitching) and rickets (stunted and malformed bones). Rickets can also occur if there is a lack of vitamin D in the body. Calcium is also needed to prevent osteoporosis (brittle bones). Best sources are milk, cheese, yogurt, sardines (in the bones,) and white flour (to which it is added by government regulation.)
Iron Essential for healthy blood. Deficiency results in anemia. Best sources are liver, meat, and eggs. More is absorbed if there is plenty of vitamin C in the diet.
Sodium Common salt, or sodium chloride, is a vital constituent for the body fluids. Too little can result in cramps, while too much is associated with high blood pressure. Foods rich in salt include cheese, bacon, butter.
Phosphorus Primarily a "bone and teeth" mineral. Essential for the formation of cells and for the production of energy within them. It is present in all living matter.
Magnesium This is needed for bone development. It is found in vegetables, although all foods contain it.
Potassium An important ingredient in the fluids of the body cells which work in conjunction with sodium, potassium is found in vegetables, fruits, nuts, fish, meat, and yeast extract. Deficiency may occur following the use of diuretics or purgatives.

Energy expenditure

7442 Scientists measure food energy in calories. Our need for these depends on age, sex, and level of acitivity. Here we show the number of calories per hour used by a woman performing different acitivities. (A man's calorie requirements would be greater.)

= 100 calories per hour

1 Sleeping
2 Sitting
3 Standing
4 Walking
5 Running
6 Climbing stairs

1
2
3
4

Here we show numbers of calories required per day by "typical" males and females in temperate climates.

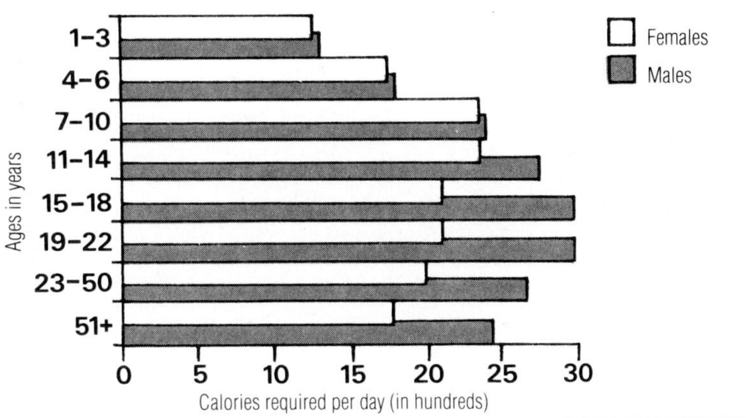

745 SYMPTOMS AND POSSIBLE CAUSES

THESE POINTERS OFFER NO SUBSTITUTE FOR THOROUGH MEDICAL DIAGNOSIS

Head

7451

GENERAL
Dizziness *see* **Eyes**
Facial pallor Anemia; Faintness; Hemorrhaging; Jaundice; Kidney disorder; Lack of sleep; Shock
Facial rash Allergy; Bites or stings; Chicken pox; Dermatitis; Eczema; Hemorrhaging; Hives (Urticaria); Impetigo; Measles; Other infections; Prickly heat
Facial spots/zits Acne; Bites or stings; Burn; Infection; Pimple/Pustule; Shingles; Wart
Facial tic Anxiety; Bell's palsy; Lack of sleep; Nerve disorder
Fainting Anemia; Diabetes; Epilepsy; Hypotension; Injury; Menstruation; Puberty; Shock
Hair loss Eczema; Natural baldness; Ringworm
Headache Allergy; Altitude sickness; Common cold; Concussion; Diabetes; Drug overdose; Eye strain; Hangover; Head injury; Menstruation; Migraine; Neuralgia; Shingles; Sinusitis; Stress
Lump on skin Abscess; Bite or sting; Boil; Bruise; Cyst; Dental disorder; Gland, swollen; Hives (Urticaria); Injury; Mumps; Wart

EARS
Deafness, sudden Common cold; Ear infection; Flu (Influenza); Mumps; Scarlet fever; Wax
Discharge Boil; Ear infection; Wax
Earache Boil; Chilblain; Cold (Hypothermia) Common cold; Ear infection; Sinusitis; Throat infection; Wax

NOSE
Blocked nose Adenoid problem; Common cold; Drug habit; Flu (Influenza); Polyp; Sinusitis
Nosebleed Anemia; Head injury; Hypertension; Puberty; Shock/Stress; Violent sneezing
Running nose Allergy; Common cold; Dusty environment; Flu (Influenza); Hay fever; Measles

EYES
Blindness, sudden Concussion; Detached retina; Diabetes; Glaucoma; Head injury; Nerve damage; Stroke
Blurred vision Cataract; Conjunctivitis; Detached retina; Diabetes; Focusing problem; Migraine
Dizziness Concussion; Detached retina; Ear infection; Epilepsy; Hypertension; Hypotension; Migraine; Pneumonia; Vertigo
Pain Blocked tear duct; Cold (Hypothermia); Conjunctivitis; Injury
Pain in light Hay fever; Migraine
Watery Allergy; Common cold; Conjunctivitis; Foreign body; Hay fever; Stye
Lump Mole; Stye; Wart
Pain Bruise; Inflammation; Stye
Tic Allergy; Anxiety; Lack of sleep; Nerve damage

MOUTH
Bad breath Poor hygiene; Sinusitis; Tobacco smoking; Tonsillitis; Tooth decay
Cracking lips Anemia; Common cold; Infection
Pain Cold sore; Infection; Inflammation; Mouth injury; Mouth ulcer
Taste, peculiar Common cold; Gastritis; High temperature; Nausea; Severe thirst
Tongue, sore Inflammation; Tobacco smoking
Tooth problems Abscess; Gum disease; Impacted teeth; Mouth injury; Tooth decay

THROAT
Cough Bronchitis; Common cold; Flu (Influenza); Lung disorder; Pneumonia; Throat infection; Tobacco smoking; Tracheitis; Tuberculosis; Whooping cough
Sore throat Common cold; Flu (Influenza); Glandular fever; Mumps; Sinusitis; Throat infection; Tonsillitis

Torso

7452

NECK AND SHOULDERS
Swelling on neck Boil; Cyst; Gland swollen; Goiter
Shoulder pain Arthritis; Cramps; Displacement; Frozen shoulder; Injury; Rheumatism; stiffness

BACK
Back pain Arthritis; Bedsore; Dysmenorrhea; Fibrositis; Lumbago; Osteoporosis; Overweight; Pregnancy; Sciatica; Slipped disk; Stiffness; Strain

STOMACH AND DIGESTION
Burping Gastritis; Hiatus hernia; Indigestion
Stomach pain Cirrhosis; Heartburn; Hiatus hernia; Indigestion; Peptic ulcer; Stomach disorder
Vomiting Acid stomach; Altitude sickness; Anorexia nervosa; Anxiety; Appendicitis; Diabetes; Drug overdose; Ear infection; Food poisoning; Gallstone; Gastroenteritis; Hiatus hernia; Kidney disease; Migraine; Motion sickness; Pancreatitis; Peptic ulcer; Pregnancy; Pyloric stenosis; Tonsillitis; Travel sickness; Whooping cough

continued

Torso continued

7452 **ABDOMEN**
Abdominal pain Appendicitis; Bladder disorder; Colic; Colitis; Diverticulitis; Ectopic pregnancy; Food poisoning; Gastroenteritis; Indigestion; Intestinal problem; Kidney stone; Menstruation; Ovulation; Peritonitis; Pleurisy; Pregnancy; Salpingitis
Abdominal rash Allergy; Bites or stings; Chicken pox; Dermatitis; Eczema; Hemorrhaging; Hives (Urticaria); Impetigo; Measles; Other infections; Prickly heat

CHEST
Breast pain Breast abscess; Breast disorder; Cyst; Discharging nipple; Menstrual problem
Breathlessness Anemia; Angina pectoris; Anxiety; Asthma; Common cold; Drug overdose; Emphysema; Heart attack; Heart disease; Hypertension; Lung disorder; Overweight; Pneumonia; Shock; Stress; Tobacco smoking
Chest constriction Angina pectoris; Anxiety; Asthma; Common cold; Heart attack; Heart disease; Lung disorder; Shock
Chest pain Abscess; Boil; Cyst; Gallstone; Heartburn; Heart disease; Hiatus hernia; Indigestion; Lung disorder; Pleurisy; Pneumonia; Shingles
Chest rash Allergy; Bites or stings; Chicken pox; Dermatitis; Eczema; Hemorrhaging; Hives (Urticaria); Impetigo; Measles; Other infections; Prickly heat

LOIN AND HIPS
Loin pain Abscess; Diverticulitis; Hernia; Kidney stone
Hip pain Arthritis; Bruise; Displacement; Rheumatism; Sciatica

Limbs

7453 **ARMS AND HANDS**
Arm, lump Boil; Bruise; Cyst
Arm pain Arm injury; Arthritis; Bursitis; Elbow injury; Fibrositis; Heart disease; Muscle disorder; Nerve disorder; Osteoarthritis; Pulled muscle; Rheumatism; Stiffness
Arm or hand, rash Allergy; Bites or stings; Chicken pox; Dermatitis; Eczema; Hemorrhaging; Hives (Urticaria); Impetigo; Measles; Other infections; Prickly heat
Hand, discolored Bruise; Mole; Wart
Hands, itchy Allergy; Cramps; Dermatitis; Scabies
Hands, shaking Alcoholism; Anxiety; Drug habit; Hypertension; Parkinsonism; Thyrotoxicosis
Hand or finger, lump Boil; Cyst; Rheumatoid arthritis; Wart

LEGS AND FEET
Ankle pain Arthritis; Edema; Gout; Kidney disease; Pregnancy; Rheumatism; Sprain; Tendinitis; Vein inflammation
Foot, itchy Athlete's foot; Other infections; Ringworm; Sweating
Foot pain Allergy; Arthritis; Bruise; Bunion; Chilblains; Corn; Ingrowing toenail; Plantar wart; Pregnancy; Shingles; Tight footwear; Ulcer; Wart
Knee pain Abrasion; Arthritis; Bruise; Bursitis; Cartilage problem; Displacement; Gout; Rheumatism; Sprain
Leg and thigh pain Bruise; Cramps; Muscle disorder; Osteomyelitis; Pulled muscle; Thrombosis; Varicose vein
Leg rash Allergy; Bites or stings; Chicken pox; Dermatitis; Eczema; Hemorrhaging; Hives (Urticaria); Impetigo; Measles; Other infections; Prickly heat

Reproductive system

7454 **Menstrual difficulty** Adolescence; Anxiety; Cervicitis; Contraception; Fibroids; Menarche; Menopause; Menorrhagia; Premenstrual syndrome; Salpingitis; Uterine infection
Menstruation, ceased Anorexia nervosa; Contraception; False pregnancy; Malnutrition; Menopause; Pregnancy
Penis discharge Bladder disorder; Incontinence; Infection; Sexually-transmitted disorder
Penis pain Chancre; Chancroid; Herpes simplex; Infection; Prostate disorder; Sexually-transmitted disorder; Ulcer
Scrotum pain Cyst; Epididymitis; Hernia; Hydrocele; Orchi(di)tis; Ringworm; Sexually-transmitted disorder
Sexually-transmitted disorders *see* 736.
Vaginal discharge Cervicitis; Ovulation; Salpingitis; Sexually-transmitted disorder; Urethritis; Uterine infection; Vaginal infection
Vaginal pain Fibroids; Infection; Rough intercourse; Sexually-transmitted disorder; Uterine prolapse
Vulval pain Chancre; Chancroid; Infection; Sexually-transmitted disorder; Ulcer; Vaginal prolapse

Excretory system

7455 **Anal bleeding** Anal fissure; Anxiety; Colitis; Constipation; Diverticulitis; Dysentery; Hemorrhoids; Parasitic worms; Polyp; Sexually-transmitted disorder; Straining
Anal itching Hemorrhoids; Parasitic worms; Scabies; Wart
Anal pain: Abscess; Anal fissure; Anal prolapse; Hemorrhoids; Proctitis
Diarrhea Alcoholism; Anxiety; Change of diet; Colitis; Diverticulitis; Dysentery; Food poisoning; Gastroenteritis; Hepatitis; Thyrotoxicosis; Tonsillitis
Urethral itching Bladder disorder; Cystitis; Sexually-transmitted disorder
Urination, decreased Anxiety; Bladder disorder; Dehydration; High temperature; Kidney disease; Pregnancy; Prostate problem; Strangury
Urination, increased Alcoholism; Anxiety; Bladder disorder; Cystitis; Diabetes; Kidney disease; Pregnancy; Prostate problem
Urine discolored Bladder disorder; Cystitis; Hematuria; Hepatitis; Jaundice; Kidney disease; Parasitic worms; Prostate problem; Porphyria

751 GLOSSARY OF MEDICAL CONDITIONS

abscess Pus-filled cavity; in the skin known as a pimple, pustule, or boil depending on size or position.
acid stomach Effect of surplus digestive juices in the stomach.
allergy Extra sensitivity to a substance or circumstance, causing effects that vary from a mild rash to a dangerous coma.
anal fissure Painful tear in the anal sphincter (and often rectal lining).
anemia Deficiency of red cells or of hemoglobin in the blood.
angina pectoris Temporary heart pain caused by localized oxygen starvation.
anorexia nervosa Mental illness in which dieting becomes obsessive.
appendicitis Inflammation of the appendix; cured usually by removing the appendix.
arteriosclerosis Thickening of the walls of, and thus narrowing of the channel within, the arteries.
arthritis Joint inflammation, causing loss of mobility, pain, and swelling.
asthma Condition, most often resulting from allergy or respiratory infection, in which breathing becomes strained.
ataxia Lack of coordination of the muscles.
athlete's foot Irritant fungal infection between the toes.
atrophy Wasting away; withering.
blackhead Plug of grease in a blocked skin pore; mostly appear on the face.
boil *see* abscess
Bornholm disease (or pleurodynia). Viral infection that causes pain and overall swelling; requires long convalescence.
bronchitis Inflammation of the air channel to/from the lungs; the usual cause is infection or tobacco smoking.
bunion Distortion of the joint of the big toe, caused by extreme bursitis.
bursitis Inflammation of the bursa – the fluid-filled sac within a joint that acts to cushion friction.
cancer Uncontrolled growth of cells, mostly constituting a tumor. May be benign (harmless) or malignant (harmful and liable to spread). There are two main types: carcinoma (cancer of the skin and the linings of the internal organs) and sarcoma (cancer of the connective tissue, including bone, blood, and lymph).
candidiasis *see* moniliasis
cataract Opaque area within eye lens.
celiac disease Sensitivity to gluten, a protein in cereals; it prevents the normal absorption of fats and necessitates a special diet for life.
cerebral palsy Effect of brain damage at birth; the symptoms depend on severity.
cervicitis Inflammation of the neck of the womb, perhaps through infection.
chancre Painless ulcer, which is often a symptom of the sexually-transmitted disease syphilis.
chancroid Bacterially inflamed sore caused by sexually-transmitted disease.
chicken pox Virus infection of the whole body; the rash starts on the back and chest. The disease may cause shingles in adults.
cholera Severe bacterial infection common in the tropics, transmitted in food or drink that has been contaminated by feces.
cirrhosis of the liver Growth of permanent fibrous areas and lumps in the liver; mostly caused by alcoholism or hepatitis.
cold sore Recurring viral blister on the face, caused by herpes simplex.
colic Abdominal pain through temporary intestinal obstruction.
colitis Inflammation of the lower intestinal tract
common cold (or coryza). Virus disease caught through airborne droplets; symptoms appear 48 hours after exposure, and can be treated, however the cause cannot.
concussion Effect of brain injury after harsh head contact, whiplash, or jarred spine; may be serious.
conjunctivitis Inflammation of the transparent surface of the eyeball.
cyst Abnormal fluid-filled sac in skin or tissues; many causes and types.
cystic fibrosis Inherited disorder in which thickened mucous secretions may affect lung and liver functions.
cystitis Inflammation of the bladder, causing frequent and painful urination.
dermatitis Inflammation of the skin, usually through infection.
diabetes Two serious disorders: Diabetes mellitus is a disorder of sugar metabolism which may require constant supplements of insulin. Diabetes insipidus affects the kidneys' water absorption and also requires hormone supplements.
dislocation *see* displacement
displacement (or dislocation). Separation of a bone from its socket at a joint, stretching surrounding muscles.
diverticulitis Inflammation of a pouch formed within the intestinal tube.
dysentery Bacterial or amebic infection causing bloody diarrhea, transmitted by contaminated food or water.
ear infections (or otitis). Middle and inner ear infections may seriously disrupt both hearing and balance.
eczema Skin inflammation that is red, itchy, scaling, and may "weep."
edema Swelling through excess fluids in body tissues.
elephantiasis Infestation of the lymph vessels by parasitic worms that are transmitted by a mosquito bite; causes gross swelling.
embolism Formation of a blood clot that is dangerously mobile in the circulation.
emphysema Leakage of air into body tissues, especially the lung lining.
encephalitis Inflammation of the brain, causing severe symptoms.
epilepsy Complex condition in which the brain undergoes periodic dysfunction; the two types involve either partial seizures or generalized seizures.
fibroids Fibrous knots in the muscle tissue of uterus or vagina.
fibrositis Imprecise term for muscular pain, particularly in the back.
flu (or influenza). Viral infection much like a severe cold, but may also infect throat and ears.
gangrene Death of tissue through lack of blood supply; may spread to surrounding tissue.
gastritis Inflammation of the stomach lining through infection or through sensitivity to stomach contents.
gastroenteritis Inflammation of the stomach and intestines, commonly through virus infection.
glandular fever (or infectious mononucleosis). Infection by a herpes virus that results in symptoms such as lethargy or malaise that last for a long time.
glaucoma Condition in which pressure mounts within the fluid of the eyeball.
goiter Bulge in the neck caused by a thyroid gland enlarged through insufficiency of iodine.
gonorrhea Highly contagious bacterial infection that is transmitted sexually; antibiotic treatments rapidly effective.
hay fever Allergic reaction to pollen and other forms of airborne dust.
heart attack (or myocardial infarct) Death of part of the heart muscle through blockage of its blood supply.
heartburn Pain caused by acid in the esophagus, rising from the stomach as a result of indigestion.
hematuria Blood in the urine.
hemophilia Inherited disorder of males passed on by females, in which clotting factor VIII is missing from the blood.
hemorrhoids (or piles). Distended and broken veins in and around the anus.
hepatitis Inflammation of the liver. This serious condition has many causes, one form (B) that is sexually transmitted.
hernia Protrusion of a loop of intestine through a weakened section of surrounding body tissue.
herpes simplex Virus that causes cold sore – also the name of the virus that causes similar sores on the genitals, which are transmitted sexually.
hiatus hernia Loop of stomach protruding upward through the hole in the diaphragm used by the esophagus.
high blood pressure *see* hypertension
hives (or urticaria). Red eruptions or lumps on the skin, usually caused by allergy but sometimes by infection.
hydrocele Accumulation of fluid in a body cavity, especially the scrotum.
hypertension High blood pressure, often caused by stress, arteriosclerosis, and/or heart disease.
hyperthyroidism *see* thyrotoxicosis
hypotension Low blood pressure; may cause faintness on standing suddenly.
hypothyroidism Effect of shortfall of hormones produced by the thyroid gland.
impetigo Bacterial skin disease.
infection Effect of attack by viruses, bacteria, amebas or fungi; attack by parasites is called infestation. All forms of infection except viral can be treated effectively with drugs.
infectious mononucleosis *see* glandular fever
inflammation Hot, reddened swelling as the body's immune system fights intrusion or friction.
influenza *see* flu
ischemia Reduced blood supply to a part of

continued

Glossary of medical conditions continued

751 the body or to an organ, especially the brain.
jaundice Excess of the pigment bilirubin, the effect is to yellow the whites of the eyes.
kwashiorkor Effects of long term malnutrition on a child: emaciation, loss of skin color, bloated stomach.
labyrinthitis Inflammation of the inner ear; usual cause is infection.
laryngitis Inflammation of the vocal cords; the usual causes are tobacco smoking, shouting, infection, alcohol.
Legionnaires' disease Pneumonia-like bacterial infection caught through inhaling airborne droplets in watery atmosphere.
leishmaniasis Infestation by parasitic protozoa transmitted by sandfly bites.
leukemia Cancer of the white blood cells; affects blood-forming tissues, especially bone marrow.
low blood pressure *see* hypotension
lumbago Low backache of any cause.
mastitis Inflammation of the breast through infection or hormonal factors.
ME *see* myalgic encephalomyelitis
measles Common name for both rubeola and rubella (also called German measles), two similar viral diseases that produce an irritant rash over the whole body, starting at the head. Vaccination is available against both forms.
meningitis Inflammation of the membranes that protect the brain; the usual cause is infection and the effects can be serious unless treatment is administered immediately.
migraine Severe headache with visual symptoms that occurs periodically in some people; onset influenced by diet and stress. Rest in darkness may alleviate the symptoms.
moniliasis (or candidiasis, thrush). Fungal infection of moist skin areas.
motor neuron disease Progressive degeneration of brain or spinal cord tissue; cause unknown.
multiple sclerosis This disease is caused by damage to nerves of the brain and spinal cord; the cause of the damage is unknown but it may be progressive.
mumps Virus infection of the salivary glands around the cheeks. Adults may suffer complications. Vaccine in use.
myalgic encephalomyelitis (ME) Condition of malaise, fatigue, and stress. The cause is unknown but it may be associated with recent lung or stomach infection.
myocardial infarct *see* heart attack
nephritis Inflammation of a kidney.
neuralgia Pain in a nerve, usually caused by injury or inflammation.
orchi(di)tis Inflammation of a testis.
osteoarthritis Erosion of cartilage and deformation of the bones at a joint through long-term friction; there is pain, but no inflammation.
osteomalacia Softening of the bones through erosion of calcium and dietary shortfall of vitamin D.
osteomyelitis Inflammation of bone and bone marrow; mostly through bacterial infection. May cause bone abscess.
osteoporosis Shrinkage and brittleness of bones through erosion of bone.
otitis *see* ear infections
pancreatitis Inflammation of the pancreas (the digestive gland).
Parkinsonism Tremors, faltering movement, and halting speech; named for the effects of Parkinson's disease – a disease of the nervous system.
peptic ulcer Erosion of a hole in the stomach lining by over-concentration of stomach acids, mostly caused by stress.
peritonitis Infection of the lining of the abdominal cavity; now rare.
pertussis *see* whooping cough
piles *see* hemorrhoids
plantar wart Wart forced by pressure into the sole of the foot.
pleurisy Inflammation of the lining of the chest cavity surrounding the lungs; causes include infection and injury.
pleurodynia *see* Bornholm disease
pneumonia Bacterial, viral, or fungal infection of at least one lung.
poliomyelitis (polio). Virus infection of groups of muscles, with severe symptoms. Vaccine available.
polyp Small tumor (usually benign) with a stalk, situated on a mucous membrane.
porphyria Group of disorders that all cause excess of the nitrogenous factors in hemoglobin (which transports oxygen) in the blood. The symptoms are severe.
premenstrual tension (or premenstrual syndrome). Mental and physical stress felt by women as menstruation nears.
prickly heat Fine rash caused by dead skin cells blocking sweat gland pores.
proctitis Inflammation of the anus and rectum; causes include intestinal infection, injury, anal sex, and allergy.
prolapse Displacement of the lining of a hollow body into the next cavity.
psoriasis Recurrent serious skin condition of unknown cause, which also produces psychological effects; may be inherited.
pyloric stenosis Narrowing or blocking of the digestive channel transporting digesting food from the stomach to the duodenum.
rabies Serious virus infection transmitted through animal bites; symptoms severe. Immunization available.
rheumatic fever Serious allergic reaction to bacterial infection (usually tonsillitis); the symptoms are severe.
rheumatism Pain in the muscles at the joints; there are many types and many causes of this disease.
rheumatoid arthritis Inflammation of a joint and the surrounding muscles, involving bone erosion and deformation.
ringworm Highly contagious fungal infection; attacks mostly hands and feet, groin, and scalp.
rubella *see* measles
salpingitis Inflammation of Fallopian tube, generally caused by infection.
scabies Infestation of mites that burrow into the skin (of the hands, feet, or groin) causing an allergic reaction.
scarlet fever Severe bacterial infection giving rise to body rash and hair loss.
sciatica Pain from buttock to thigh through pressure on the sciatic nerve.
shingles Severe and painful form of chicken pox suffered mostly by adults aged over 50; the disease demands a lengthy convalescence.
shock Technically, the effect of the lack of blood following injury; more generally, the psychological effect of an unwelcome, sudden event.
sinusitis Inflammation of the sinuses, channels behind and above the nose inside the skull; the main cause is infection.
slipped disk Rupture and displacement of a vertebral disk causing pain and stiffness.
strangury Obstruction of the flow through a vessel caused by outside pressure – especially through the intestine at the point of a hernia.
stroke Effect of a fault in the blood flow through the brain; caused either by a burst blood vessel or by an obstruction to the blood supply. Recovery of faculties may be protracted.
stye Painful, red, bacterial infection around the stem of an eyelash.
syphilis Highly contagious bacterial infection that is transmitted sexually; antibiotic treatments are rapidly effective.
tendinitis Inflammation of a tendon.
tetanus Serious bacterial infection requiring hospitalization for possible surgery to maintain breathing.
thrombosis Formation of a blood clot (thrombus) within a blood vessel.
thrush *see* moniliasis
thyrotoxicosis Excessive production of thyroid hormones by the thyroid gland.
tonsillitis Bacterial or viral infection of the tonsils in the throat.
tracheitis Inflammation of the trachea (the windpipe in the throat).
tuberculosis Bacterial infection that starts in the lungs but spreads; it can be very serious. Vaccination is available.
typhoid fever Bacterial infection of the intestines; rash, fever, and diarrhea may lead to pneumonia. Vaccine in use.
typhus Various serious disorders characterized by fever, rashes and headaches, and caused by Rickettsia microorganisms.
urethritis Inflammation of the urethra, mainly caused by infection.
urticaria *see* hives
varicose vein Vein swollen and twisted by internal pressure.
vertigo Sensation that the world is spinning; main medical causes are ear disorders, eye disorders, or drugs.
wart Small viral growth on the skin.
whooping cough (or pertussis). Bacterial infection of the throat and lungs, causing breathlessness and severe cough attacks. Vaccination is available.
worms Parasitic worms include tapeworms (cestodes), roundworms (nematodes), and flukes (trematodes). All infest specific body organs but drugs are effective against most.
yellow fever Serious virus infection transmitted by mosquito bites; the symptoms are severe. Vaccination is available.

752 Glossary of drug types
7521 Recreational drugs
753 Glossary of alternative medicine

752 GLOSSARY OF DRUG TYPES

amebicidal drugs These prevent or treat amebic infections.
amphetamines Drugs which stimulate the brain, and are used to treat drowsiness or hyperactive children; they are potentially addictive.
anabolic steroids These are synthetic hormones that promote an increase in muscle size.
analgesics A class of drugs that relieve pain.
androgen The name for the male sex hormone.
anesthetics Reduce or numb sensation, and promote painless sleep.
anorectics Reduce appetite; most are potentially addictive and their use is now rare.
antacids Neutralize stomach acidity; prolonged use inadvisable.
antiarrhythmic drugs Improve the regularity of the heartbeat.
antibacterial drugs Prevent or treat bacterial infections.
antibiotics Prevent or treat infection by various agents; most are ineffective against viral infections, however.
anticholinergic drugs Inhibit certain nerves from relaxing groups of muscles; some side effects.
anticoagulants Reduce or prevent blood clotting.
anticonvulsants Reduce or prevent convulsive seizures, such as those caused by epilepsy.
antidepressants Reduce or treat mental depression: two main types are MAO inhibitors and tricyclic antidepressants.
antidiuretics Reduce or prevent the formation or output of urine.
antiemetics Prevent nausea and thus vomiting; mainly used by travelers.
antifungal drugs Prevent or treat fungal infections, locally (on the skin) or systemically.
antihelminthics Prevent or treat infestation by parasitic worms.
antihypertensive drugs Prevent or treat high blood pressure, and thus heart and circulatory disease.
antimalarial drugs Prevent or treat the various forms of malaria.
antinauseants *see* antiemetics
antipruritics Reduce or prevent itching of the skin or mucous membranes.
antipsychotic drugs Calm patients who are psychologically disturbed.
antipyretics Reduce high body temperature (fever).
antirheumatics Reduce or relieve the effects of rheumatism.
antiserums These are inoculations containing antibodies to a specific infection.
antispasmodics Prevent the contraction of smooth muscle, and are used mainly to treat bronchial and bladder disorders.
antitubercular drugs These are used in combination to treat tuberculosis.
antitussives Reduce or prevent coughing; some contain opiates.
antivenins Serums containing specific antibodies used to treat snakebite.
antiviral drugs These treat infections by individual groups of viruses.
anxiolytic drugs These relieve the anxiety states of medically diagnosed patients.
appetite suppressants These are occasionally used to treat obesity; most are potentially addictive and are therefore rarely administered.
barbiturates Group of potentially addictive sedatives and anesthetics, with severe side effects; many were formerly used as tranquilizers. Best known are pentobarbital, phenobarbital, and amobarbital (all subject to abuse).
benzodiazepines Large group of drugs that affect the brain; some are used as sedatives or anxiolytics, others as muscle relaxants or anti-convulsants. Best known are diazepam, nitrazepam, and loprazolam.
beta blockers These drugs inhibit the body's normal reaction to stress, and are thus used mostly as antihypertensives.
beta receptor stimulants These drugs increase the body's normal reaction to stress, and are mostly used to strengthen the heartbeat or to widen respiratory passages.
bronchodilators These act to widen the bronchioles.
cephalosporins Antibiotics related to penicillin, used to treat bacterial infections.
chelating agents These are used to treat metal poisoning by absorbing metals in the bloodstream.
contraceptives Used to prevent conception; there are several types which may be taken orally.
corticosteroids Natural or synthetic hormones that assist metabolism, act in relation to stress, or maintain the salt-and-water balance in the body.
cytotoxic drugs Used to destroy cells, mainly in cancer chemotherapy.
decongestants Reduce mucus in the air passages of the nose.
depressants Reduce reactions in the body and relax muscles.
diuretics Increase the output of urine and so reduce body fluid levels.
emetic drugs These are used to promote vomiting.
estrogens The name for the female sex hormone.
hemostatic drugs Prevent or reduce bleeding; they are mostly injected or infused.
hormone supplements Prescribed to make up for a lack of natural hormones.
hypnotics Act on the brain to promote sleep.
imidazoles Group of antifungal drugs, used mainly to treat infections of the skin and mucous membranes.
keratolytic drugs Treat scaly, horny areas of skin in conditions such as psoriasis and eczema.
laxatives Promote easy defecation.
MAOI drugs (monoamine oxidase inhibitors). Group of antidepressants; highly effective, they require dietary precautions.
mucolytic drugs Promote the coughing up of sputum, so clearing air passages.
muscle relaxants Reduce or paralyse muscles; much used during surgery.
mydriatic drugs These drugs dilate the pupils of the eyes and are useful to oculists.
narcotics Technically, any drugs that cause stupor; the term is used also of sedatives and hypnotics, particularly the opiates; in law, however, the term describes illegal recreational drugs.
NSAIDs (nonsteroidal anti-inflammatory drugs). Treat or reduce inflammation; "nonsteroidal" means they do not contain hormones, as do other anti-inflammatory drugs.
opiates Derivatives of opium.
parasympathomimetics Relieve the body's stress reactions, slowing the heart, widening the blood vessels, etc.
penicillins Group of antibiotics used to treat bacterial infections.
progestogens Synthetic female sex hormones.
Rauwolfia alkaloids Drugs used as antihypertensives; also once used as antipsychotic drugs.
respiratory stimulants Promote breathing in severely traumatized patients.
scabicides Used to treat infestations by itchmites.
sedatives These are used to calm patients and make drowsy. Many are hypnotics used in smaller doses; some are potentially addictive.
sulfonamides Prevent the growth of bacteria and are used mainly to treat urinary infections.
sulfonylureas Reduce blood levels of glucose and are used to treat diabetes mellitus.
sympathomimetics Evoke the body's stress reactions, speeding up the heart, constricting blood vessels, etc.
tetracyclines Group of antibiotics that treat conditions caused by a range of infective organisms.
thiazides Group of diuretics.
tranquilizers A class of drugs ranging from sedatives to antipsychotic drugs.
uricosuric agents Reduce the uric acid in the body, and so are used to treat gout.
vaccines These oblige the body to create its own antibodies to specific infections.
vasoconstrictors These narrow the blood vessels and so increase blood pressure.
vasodilators These widen the blood vessels and so reduce blood pressure.
Vinca alkaloids Cytotoxic drugs that prevent cell replication.

Recreational drugs

7521 **acid** Nickname for LSD, *see* hallucinogens.
adam Nickname for MDMA, a synthetic "designer drug."
alcohol Found in beer, wine, and spirits. Acts as a depressant when used in large quantities. Psychologically and physically addictive.
amphetamines Stimulants, sometimes prescribed medically as appetite-suppressants to control weight. Commonly abused and psychologically addictive. Nicknames: pep pills, uppers, bennies (benzedrine).
antidepressants Drugs prescribed to treat severe depression. Of two types: tricyclic and MAOI (monoamine oxidase inhibitors). Lithium is commonly used medically to control mood swings.
barbiturates Sedatives, formerly prescribed to relieve anxiety and aid sleep, but, after widespread abuse, now strictly controlled and replaced medicinally with benzodiapines (*see* tranquilizers). Barbiturates can be very addictive. Nicknames: barbs, candy, goofballs, downers, blues (amobarbital), yellows (pentobarbital), reds (secobarbital), goofers (diazepam).
barbs Nickname for barbiturates.
base Nickname for crack.
bennies Nickname for benzadrine, and amphetamine.
blues Nickname for amobarbital, a barbiturate.
caffeine A stimulant found in coffee, tea, cocoa, and many cola drinks.
cannabis Also called marijuana, produced from the *Cannabis sativa* plant. Usually smoked, either in its dried form – called grass – or as a hashish resin – called hash – in a pipe or joint ("reefer"). Can also be mixed with food and eaten. Nicknames: pot, Mary Jane, weed.
candy Nickname for barbiturates.
china white A synthetic "designer drug" similar to heroin.
cocaine A white powder produced from the coca plant, found mainly in South America. Usually "snorted," cocaine acts as a stimulant and is psychologically addictive. Formerly used as a mild local anesthetic but, after widespread abuse, it has been largely replaced by safer anesthetics. Also called coke or snow.
codeine A narcotic prescribed medically as a painkiller. Most often found in cough syrup and mixed with aspirin or acetaminophen. No longer available over the counter.
coke Nickname for cocaine.
crack Cocaine that is freebased – dissolved in water and heated, separating the cocaine base from the salt. Usually smoked, in a pipe, cigarettes, or a piece of tin foil. Highly addictive. Nicknames: wash, base, rock.
crystal Nickname for methadrine, an amphetamine. Also known as meth.
designer drugs Synthetic chemical substances with effects similar to more common drugs. MPP and china white are synthetic versions of heroin. MDMA, also known as Adam or ecstasy, has features of both hallucinogens and amphetamines.
downers Nickname for barbiturates.
ecstasy Nickname for MDMA, a synthetic "designer drug."
glue *see* solvents
goofers Nickname for barbiturates, especially diazepam; also called goofballs.
grass Nickname for cannabis, or marijuana.
H Nickname for heroin.
hallucinogens Also called psychedelics, illegal drugs that induce vivid dream-like visions. The most famous is LSD (lysergic acid diethylamide), also known as acid, which can be injected but which is usually taken orally. *See also* mescaline and mushrooms.
hash Form of cannabis, or marijuana.
heroin A narcotic derived from morphine. Chemically known as diacetylmorphine, it is a white or gray-brown powder that is usually dissolved in water and injected, but can also be smoked or snorted. Highly addictive. Also known as H, horse, and smack.
horse Nickname for heroin.
joint Nickname for cigarette in which cannabis or marijuana is smoked.
Mary Jane Nickname for cannabis, or marijuana.
mescaline or mesc, a hallucinogen produced from the peyote cactus. Mescaline is usually taken orally but can be injected.
methadone A synthetic narcotic resembling morphine and used most often to relieve withdrawal symptoms of morphine and heroin addicts.
morphine The main active constituent of opium. Used medicinally as a painkiller.
mushrooms Some types of mushroom induce hallucinations when eaten. They include fly agaric and Psilocybin mexicana, which produces psilocybin. DMT (dimethyltryptammine), STP, and DOM are other hallucinogenic amphetamines. Nickname: magic mushrooms.
narcotics Opiates, or substances derived from opium. These include, heroin, codeine, and morphine, as well as opium itself. They all act as depressants, and in large doses, can induce a sense of contentment and euphoria. They all have addictive effects and are controlled substances.
nicotine A stimulant found in tobacco. Legal and highly addictive.
opium The dried juice from the seeds of the poppy plant. Usually smoked in a pipe, it can also be injected or taken orally. Opium and its derivatives are known as narcotics.
pep pills Nickname for amphetamines.
red Nickname for secobarbital, a barbiturate.
reefer Nickname for a cannabis (marijuana) cigarette or "joint."
rock Nickname for crack.
smack Nickname for heroin.
snow Nickname for cocaine.
solvents Glue, gasoline, paint thinner, and other fluids whose fumes, when inhaled, induce a high that can include hallucinations.
speed Nickname for methadrine, an amphetamine.
steroids Anabolic steroids produce similar effects to the male hormone testosterone. They help to build tissue, strengthen bone, and aid muscle recovery – widely abused by athletes as a result.
tranquilizers Sedative drugs – medicinally known as benzodiazepines – prescribed to relieve anxiety and to aid sleep. Among the most common are diazepam. Although addictive, these "minor tranquilizers" have largely replaced barbiturates in prescriptions.
uppers Nickname for amphetamines.
wash Nickname for crack.
weed Nickname for cannabis, or marijuana.
yellows Nickname for pentobarbital, a barbiturate.

753 GLOSSARY OF ALTERNATIVE MEDICINE

acupuncture Application of fine needles to certain points on the skin in order to stimulate selected nerve-endings and thus relieve pain or cure disease.
Alexander technique Realigning the body through improved posture and movement.
anthroposophical medicine Theory of health as tied to one's awareness of the unity of mind and body; addresses posture and movement.
aromatherapy Use of essential plant oils to speed healing and enhance moods.
Bach flower remedies Method of healing using flower essences to counter mental and emotional conflicts.
biogenetics Use of exercises to relieve muscle tension and release emotions.
chiropractic Manipulation of joints in the spine to relieve pain and restore normal nerve function.
color therapy Using color to affect emotional responses.
Faldenkrais exercises Precise movements that help realign the spine.
herbalism Use of plant extracts to treat illness.
homeopathy Treatment based on the theory that symptoms reflect the body's natural healing power. Consequently, small amounts of a drug which produces symptoms similar to that of the disease are administered.
hydrotherapy The use of water exercises and massages to build up muscles and to help ease stiff joints.
hypnosis A trance-like state that is induced to reduce inhibitions, including the sensation of pain.
kinesiology Treatment using nutritional diagnosis and the measurement of muscle tone.
macrobiotics Healing and illness prevention method based on diet of grains, brown rice, and vegetables.
mesmerism Using magnetic forces of the moon and planets for healing purposes.
naturopathy Theory that illness is caused by poor diet and posture.
osteopathy Manipulating the vertebrae of the spine in order to ease pain, particularly that caused by back troubles.
polarity therapy Stimulating the charge of the body's polar opposites in order to heal.
psionic medicine Using dowsing and

continued

Glossary of alternative medicine continued

753

psychic techniques to diagnose and treat illness.
radionics Healing from a distance.
reflexology Use of foot massage to treat various illnesses.
reifing Use of deep massage to soften tight tissue.
shiatsu Applying finger pressure to certain parts of the body to prevent or cure disease.
zone therapy A form of reflexology, involving the massaging of parts of the feet and hands that correspond to verticle and horizontal zones elsewhere in the body.

754 GLOSSARY OF MEDICAL SPECIALISMS

allergist Conditions resulting from extreme sensitivity to substances or environments.
anesthesiologist The science and administration of anesthesia.
cardiologist Conditions and diseases related to the heart and circulation.
dentist Care and treatment of the teeth and gums.
dermatologist Conditions and diseases affecting the skin.
endocrinologist Conditions and diseases of the hormonal glands – e.g. pituitary, thyroid, pancreas, ovaries, testicles.
gastroenterologist Diseases related to the digestive system.
genetic counselor Specialist adviser on the chances of a child inheriting genetic malformation.
gerentologist Specialist in the effects and problems of old age.
gynecologist Conditions and diseases of the female body, particularly the reproductive system.
hematologist Specialist in the composition and analysis of blood.
histologist Specialist in the size, shape, and constitution of cells.
nephrologist Conditions related to the kidney.
neurologist Specialist in treatment of the nervous system.
obstetrician Pregnancy and related conditions (often also experienced in gynecology).
oncologist Specialist in the nature and treatment of cancer.
ophthalmologist Conditions and diseases related to the eyes.
optician Fitting and adjusting glasses and contact lenses.
optometrist Testing eyes and prescribing lenses to correct vision.
orthodontist Branch of dentistry for treatment of crooked or misaligned teeth
orthopedist Conditions and diseases of the bones, joints, and spine.
osteologist Specialist in the structure and diseases of bone.
otorhinolarynologist Conditions of the ear, nose, and throat.
pathologist Specialist in the structural and functional changes caused by disease.
pediatrician Specialist in the diseases and disorders of babies and children.
peridontist Branch of dentistry for treatment of conditions of the supporting structures of the teeth.
physiotherapist Specialist in the promotion of mobility in those handicapped by illness.
podiatrist Conditions and diseases related to the foot.
pulmonologist Conditions and diseases of the lungs.
radiologist Specialist in the use and interpretation of X-ray photography.
rheumatologist Conditions and diseases of the muscles and skeletal system, especially the joints.
urologist Conditions and diseases of the genitourinary system.

755 MEDICINE AND PHYSIOLOGY: BIOGRAPHIES

Avicenna (Arabic name: Ibn Sina) 980–1037, Arab philosopher and physician renowned for his precocious and prodigious learning. Author of some 200 works on science, religion, and philosophy. His medical textbook, *Canon of Medicine*, long remained a standard work.
Bernard, Claude 1813–78, French physiologist who researched on the action of the secretions of the alimentary canal, connection between liver and nervous system, the changes of blood temperature, and the presence of oxygen in arterial and venous blood. His *Introduction to the Study of Experimental Medicine* (1865) is a scientific classic.
Boerhaave, Hermann 1668–1738, Dutch physician and botanist whose fame rests chiefly on two works, *Institutiones Medicae* (1708) and *Aphorismi de Cognoscendis et Curandis Morbis* (1709). His *Elementa Chemiae* (1724) is also a classic. Patients came to him from all over Europe.
Borelli, Giovanni Alfonzo 1608–79, Italian "mathematician" and physiologist who founded iatrophysical school of medicine, which sought to explain all bodily functions by physical laws.
Celsus, Aulus Cornelius 1st century AD, Roman writer who compiled encyclopedia on medicine, rhetoric, history, philosophy, war, and agriculture. Only surviving portion is *De Medicina*, one of the first medicinal works to be printed (1478).
Chauliac, Guy de c. 1300–68, French surgeon – the most famous in the Middle Ages, who wrote *Chirurgia Magna* (1363). This famous text was used as a manual by generations of doctors.
Frank, Johann Peter 1745–1821, German physician, medical reformer and author. His pioneering *System of a Complete Medical Police*, describes comprehensive system of medical care which, in combining preventative and curative medical services, gives an early vision of the welfare state.
Galen, or Claudius Galenus c. 130–c. 201, Greek physician. Prolific writer who, for many centuries, was considered the standard authority on medical matters. Careful dissector of animals, and first to diagnose by feeling the pulse.
Haller, Albrecht von 1708–77, Swiss anatomist, botanist, physiologist, and poet. Organized botanical garden, anatomical museum and theater, and an obstetrical school, helped to found Academy of Sciences, and wrote anatomical and physiological works.
Harvey, William 1578–1657, English physician (**1**) and discoverer of the circulation of blood, as described in celebrated *Exercitatio Anatomica de Motu Cordis et Sanguinis* (1628). Book on animal reproduction, *Exercitationes de Generatione Animalium*, appeared in 1651.
Hippocrates c. 460–c. 377 BC, Greek physician, known as "father of medicine," and associated with the medical professions' "Hippocratic Oath." Believed that four fluids or humors of body (blood, phlegm, and yellow and black bile) are the primary seats of disease.
Hopkins, Frederick Gowland 1861–1947, English biochemist. Pioneer in study of accessory food factors, now called vitamins.
Hunter, John 1728–93, Scottish physiologist and surgeon, "founder of scientific surgery." His *Natural History of Human Teeth* (1771-78) revolutionized dentistry. Investigated wide range of subjects, from venereal disease and embryology to blood, inflammation, and gunshot wounds.
Imhotep c. 2980 BC, Egyptian physician highly revered for his knowledge of medicine. During the Saite period (500 BC), he was worshipped as life-giving son of Ptah, god of

1

Medicine and physiology: biographies continued

Memphis. Greeks identified him with Asclepios, their own god of healing.

Jenner, Edward 1749–1823, English physician, and discoverer of vaccination (**2**). Studies of cowpox after 1775 convinced him it was efficacious as protection against smallpox. In crucial experiment (1792), he vaccinated a boy with cowpox matter, then inoculated him with smallpox.

Koch, Robert 1843–1910, German physician and pioneer bacteriologist. Work on wounds, septicemia, and splenic fever gained him a seat on the imperial board of health in 1880. Discovered tuberculosis bacillus (1882) and the cholera bacillus.

Leeuwenhoek, Anton van 1632–1723, Dutch scientist. Famous microscopist who made discoveries in support of the circulation of blood, and concerning blood corpuscules, spermatozoa, etc. First to detect fibrils and striping of muscle, structure of hair and ivory, and scales of epidermis.

Lind, James 1716–94, Scottish physician and "father of naval hygiene" who stressed cleanliness in prevention of fevers. His work on scurvy persuaded the Admiralty in 1795 to issue an order supplying the navy with lemon juice. His *A Treatise of the Scurvy* (1753) is a medical classic.

Lister, Joseph, Lord 1827–1912, English surgeon (**3**) and "father of antiseptic surgery." In addition to important observations on coagulation of blood, inflammation, etc., Lister's great contribution was the introduction of the antiseptic system in 1867, which revolutionized modern surgery.

3

Ludwig, Karl Friedrich Wilhelm 1816–95, German physiologist who pioneered research on glandular secretions. His invention of the mercurial blood-gas pump revealed the role of oxygen and other gases in the bloodstream. Also invented kymograph (1847).

Mechnikov, Ilya Ilich 1845–1916, Russian biologist. Conducted research into transparent larvae of starfish at Medina in Italy (1882-6), where he discovered phagocytes, the cells which devour infective organisms.

Morgagni, Giovanni Battista 1682–1771, Italian physician and pathologist. In his writings, he correlated pathological lesions with symptoms in over 700 cases, and is traditionally considered to be the foremost pioneer of morbid anatomy.

Muller, Johannes Peter 1801–58, German physiologist who studied nervous system and comparative anatomy. His *Handbuch der Physiologie des Menschen* (1833–40; translated 1840–9) was extremely influential.

Paracelsus Name coined for himself by Theophrastus Bombastus von Hohenheim, 1493–1541, German alchemist and physician. Paracelsus encouraged research, observation and experiment, and revolutionized medical methods. He improved pharmacy and therapeutics, and established the role of chemistry in medicine.

Paré, Ambroise c. 1510–90, French doctor regarded as the pioneer of modern surgery. Improved treatment of gunshot wounds, and substituted ligature of arteries for cauterization with red-hot iron after amputation. His *Cinq Livres de Chirurgie* (1562), and other writings greatly influenced surgery.

Rhazes or Rszi, 9th century, Persian physician and alchemist. Considered the greatest physician of the Arab world. Wrote many medical works, some of which were translated into Latin and had considerable influence on medical science in the Middle Ages. Distinguished smallpox from measles.

Sherrington, Charles Scott 1861–1952, English physiologist whose researches on reflex action, and especially *The Integrative Action of the Nervous System* (1906), constitute a landmark in modern physiology.

Sydenham, Thomas 1642–89, English physician, "the English Hippocrates." Distinguished symptoms of venereal disease (1675), recognized hysteria as distinct disease and gave name to mild convulsions of children – "Sydenham's chorea" – and to medicinal use of liquid opium – "Sydenham's laudanum."

Sylvius, Franciscus, or Franz de la Boë, 1614–72, German physician. Sylvius was the first to treat the pancreatic, saliva, and other body juices chemically. Also described the relationship between tubercule and phthisis, and helped to found the iatrophysical school.

Versalius, Andreas 1514–64, Belgian anatomist whose great work *De Human Corporis Fabrica* (1543) greatly advanced the science of biology with its excellent descriptions and drawings of bones and nervous system. One of the first dissectors of human cadavers.

Virchow, Rudolph 1821–1902, German pathologist and politician, and founder of cellular pathology, whose *Cellularpathologie* (1858) established that every morbid structure contained cells derived from previous cells. Contributed to study of tumors, leukemia, hygiene, and sanitation.

2

761 THE MIND

Psychology is the study of mental processes. Psychologists examine areas of the mind such as perception, learning, thought, intelligence, memory, creativity, emotions, and personality.

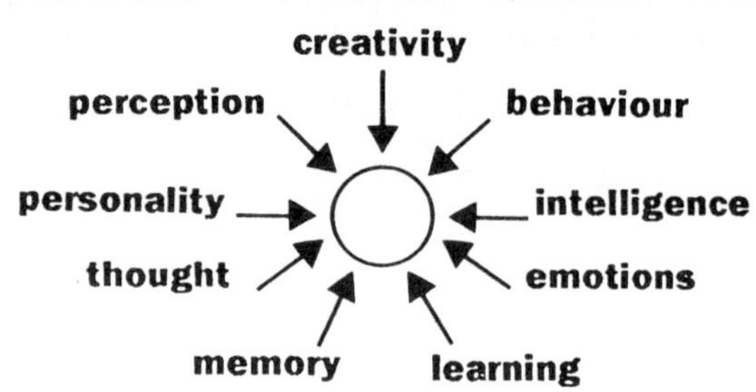

Functions

7611 Different parts of our brain work to control different activities. Generally, however, the right side of the brain controls one type of activity, and the left side of the brain controls another. In most people, the left hemisphere of the brain is dominant over the right hemisphere. There are many differences between the functions of each side, some of them more subtle than others; but in general when you write or speak, you probably do so with the dominant hemisphere. If you are left-handed, however, it is the right half of the brain that is dominant.

Verbal ideas (**1**), complex use of words (**2**), writing and speech (**3**), and complex calculations (**4**) are functions of the left hemisphere, if it is dominant. Whilst the right hemisphere controls concepts (**5**), simple use of words (**6**), ability to perceive touch (**7**) and the ability to do simple calculations (**8**).

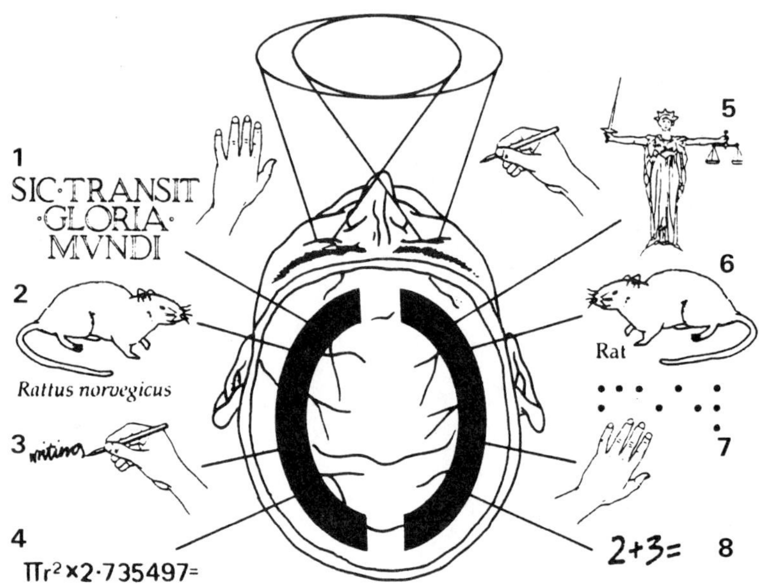

Perception

7612 To perceive an object seen by the eyes, the brain takes the signals of light and movement encoded by neurons at the back of the brain and relates them to neurons dealing with memory and often emotion. In this way how we perceive what we do depends at least partly on our experience. If we do not receive enough information the mind becomes confused. For example, a revolving cube eventually gives us enough clues for the brain to make out its form. It is unlikely that anyone looking at images (**1**) and (**2**) would instantly recognize this shape as a cube.

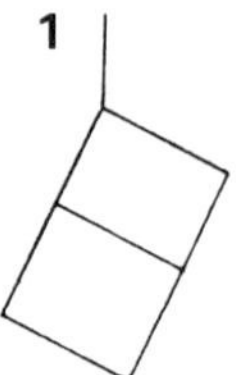

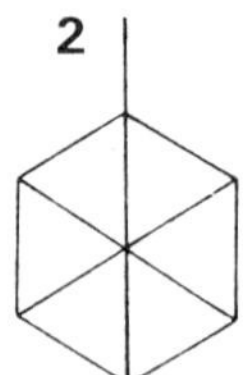

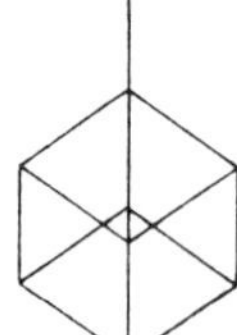
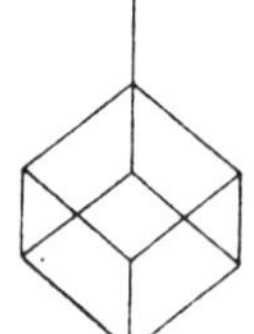
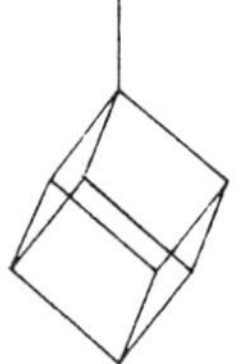

Fooling the brain

How we perceive the world around us depends on several factors, some inborn, some learned. The inborn tendency of nerve cells to tire and give false readings can make the same thing appear quite different to us at different times. If sensory nerves send messages to the brain saying the same thing for a long time, the brain cells eventually become tired, and when the stimulus stops, the cells registering opposite sensations influence our perception. For example, hands immersed in hot or cold water for a while think that tepid water is either colder or hotter than it really is.

continued

Perception continued

7612 **Ambiguous pictures**
The brain can only see one image at a time. The illustration (**1**) is therefore seen either as two peoples' heads or as a vase. Similarly, because we rely on memory to help us identify objects, the three-pronged figure (**2**) is difficult to understand as a whole because we are unable to make sense of the parts of it when we call on our model-making memory.

1

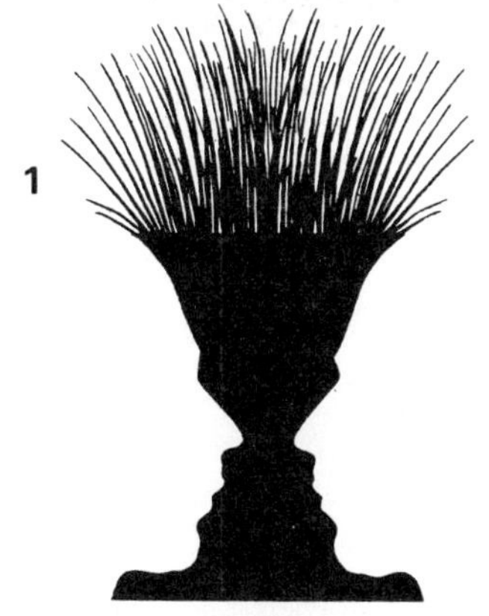

2

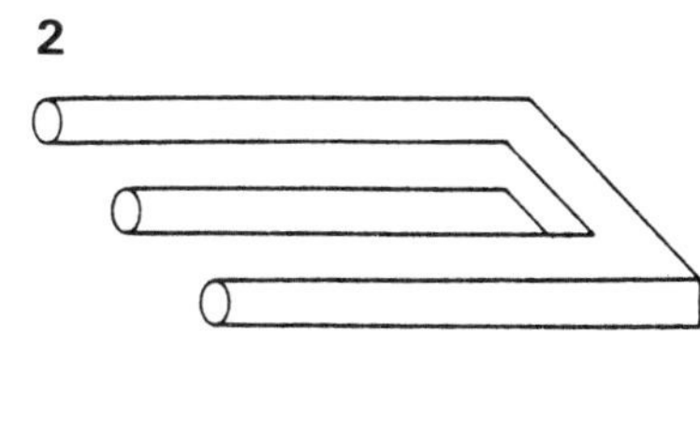

Ink blot tests
The Swiss psychiatrist Hermann Rorschach felt that response to a random image can reveal much about personality, and went on to develop a sequence of ink blot tests. Subjects are shown ten different ink blots, some colored and some black and white, and asked about images and ideas provoked by each. There is no right or wrong answer; but results may provide clues to an individual's personality traits or to a temporary state of mind.

Learning

7613 Learning depends on the brain associating a stimulus with a response. Russian psychologist Ivan Pavlov found, for instance, that dogs not only salivated at the sight of food, they also learned to salivate at the sound of a bell rung just before the food appeared. He called this a conditioned reflex, and argued that it forms the basis for all learned behavior.

Operant conditioning
In 1930, the American psychologist B.F. Skinner described the process of operant conditioning. Unlike Pavlov's classical conditioning, which involved persistent change in reflex activity, Skinner's technique caused change in voluntary behavior. Rats accidentally pressing a lever learned to do this deliberately if that act produced food. This showed that a reward reinforces response to a stimulus. But Skinner's opponents believe that intelligence produces motivations too complex for human learning to be explained merely in terms of rewards or punishments.

Thought

7614 Scientists have not agreed about what thinking means. All we know is that thought involves knowledge, which in turn implies forming and integrating mental concepts at various levels of complexity. Thought involves close, almost simultaneous coordination between many brain regions.

Intelligence

7615 Most psychologists agree that the key ingredient in intelligence is the ability to make and use symbols – to construct a mental model of the world outside. This involves memory, perception; and other attributes coordinated in the higher levels of the cerebrum. Psychologists have designed tests for all ages and every mental level to probe specific abilities.

Number puzzles
These tests assess arithmetic reasoning. The participant is asked to deduce the next number in a series.

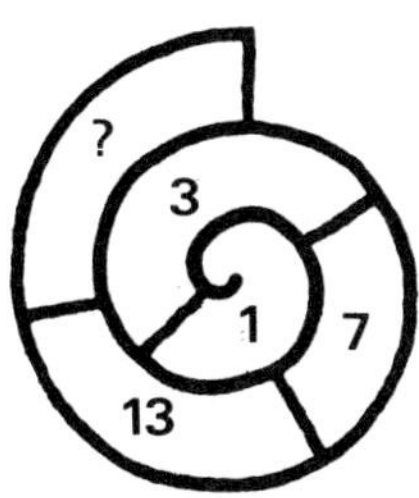

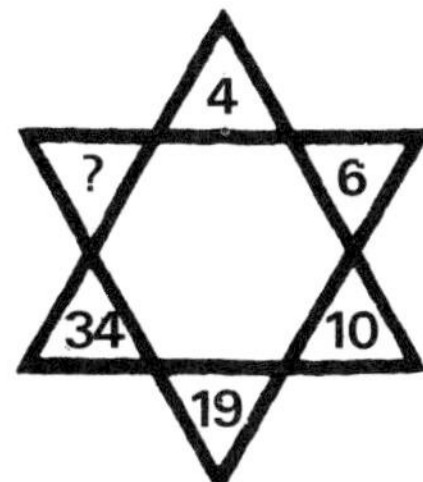

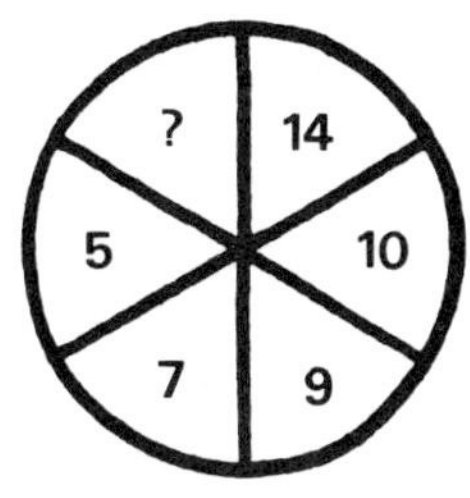

continued

Intelligence continued

7615 **Visuospatial ability testing**
This type of test examines the participant's ability to find the odd one out in a series of shapes. Examples are shown here.

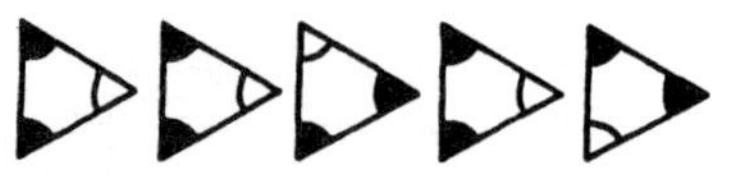

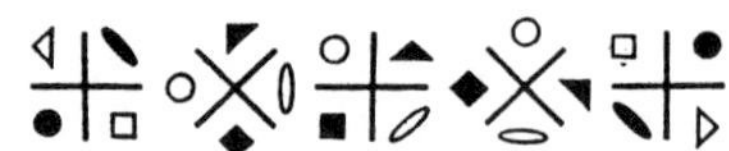

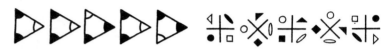

IQ
Scores in intelligence tests are standardized so that 100 is the average IQ (intelligence quotient). Generally, 67% of the population have an IQ between 85 and 115; fewer than 1% have an IQ over 150; and 3%, with an IQ of under 70, are considered subnormal. IQ tests seem to reveal that heredity accounts for 80% of an individual's intelligence, but devising questions free of cultural bias is problematic.

IQ tests reveal sexual differences, too. Women outperform men in memory, detail, and verbal reasoning, but men excel in numerical reasoning and mechanical aptitude, as well as motor skills.

Memory

7616 The shaded areas on these illustrations represent those areas of the brain responsible for memory. Certain parts of the brain appear to be involved with different types of memory.

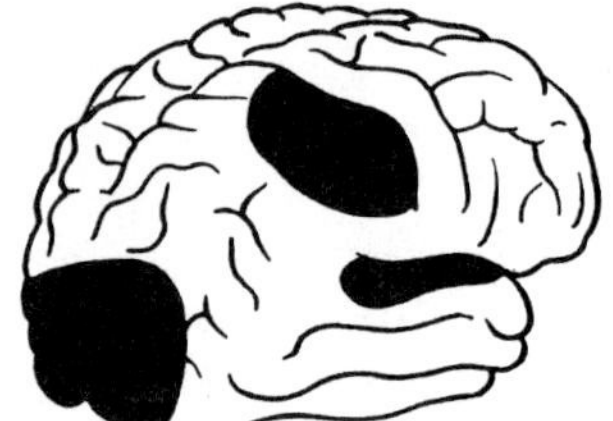

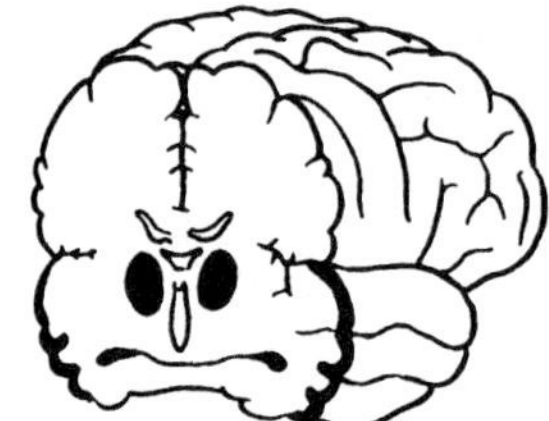

Retention of memory
These two graphs, relating to short-term memory (**1**) and long-term memory (**2**), show the effectiveness of each over an appropriate time scale. Items in the short-term memory are constantly being replaced by incoming data; and so, unless transferred to long-term memory, they are seldom recalled for more than 20 seconds. Items that have been learned and transferred to the long-term memory are also subject to the forgetting process, but the percentage of information retained depends on its nature; the more meaningful and organized the material, the more readily it will be remembered.

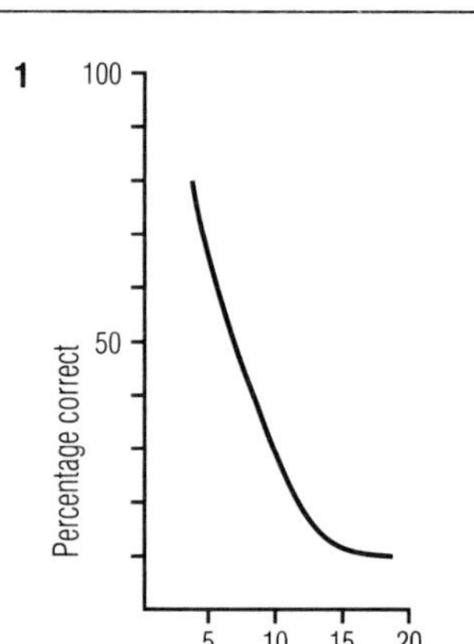

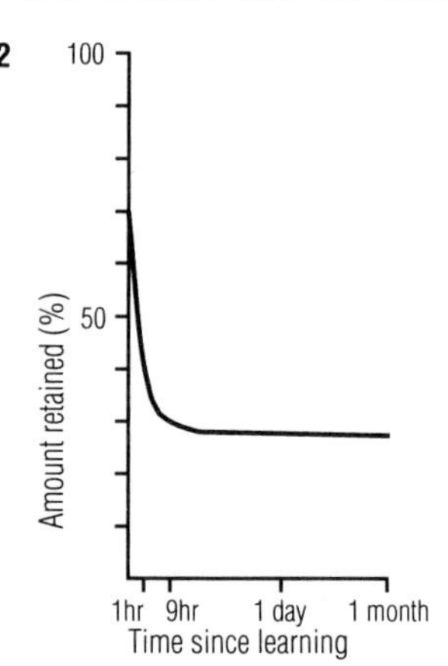

How memory works
The diagram shows how some scientists think that memory works. Our senses convert outside stimuli into signals sent to a temporary storage area where the brain decides how they should be handled. Some items go to the short-term memory where they enter a "rehearsal" loop until they are processed. But some impressions go straight from temporary storage to long-term memory. Most information, however, has to go through elaborate processes by which it is categorized and interfiled with previously stored material.

Impressions not dealt with
Outside stimuli
Outside stimuli
TEMPORARY STORAGE
Rehearsal
Elaborative process
Retrieval
LONG TERM MEMORY
SHORT TERM MEMORY
Decay: lost
Forgetting: permanently lost
Forgetting: lost but possibly recoverable

Creativity

7617 Creativity may owe much to the behavior of specific brain cells. Yet it implies more than a mind teeming with ideas. There must be judgment and selection, too.

Tests developed by psychologists during the late 1950s and early 1960s reveal a good deal about the sort of thinking involved in creativity. One such type of test (**1**) involves suggesting as many uses as possible for some common object – a brick or barrel, for example.

Another test (**2**) is to draw as many objects as possible from the starting point of a circle.

Inventing a story around a given picture (**3**) is a further favorite creativity test. This can distinguish "divergent" thinkers who give spontaneous and nonconformist replies, and "convergent" thinkers who approach matters logically.

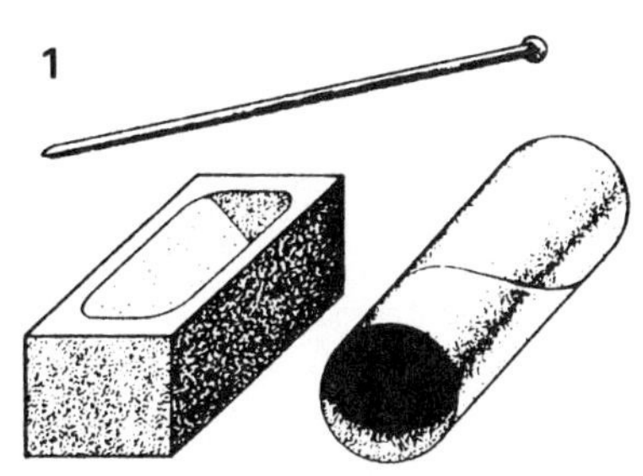

Emotions

7618 The part of the brain generally thought to be responsible for emotions is the hypothalamus. The capacity to experience and recognize a wide variety of emotions is not present at birth, but develops through increased experience of emotional stimuli. The more subtle the distinctions between emotions, the later a child experiences them. This chart shows what age a child experiences a variety of emotions.

1 Distress 2½ weeks
2 Excitement 1½ months
3 Anger 4 months
4 Disgust 5 months
5 Elation 6 months
6 Fear 6½ months
7 Affection 10½ months
8 Jealousy 15 months

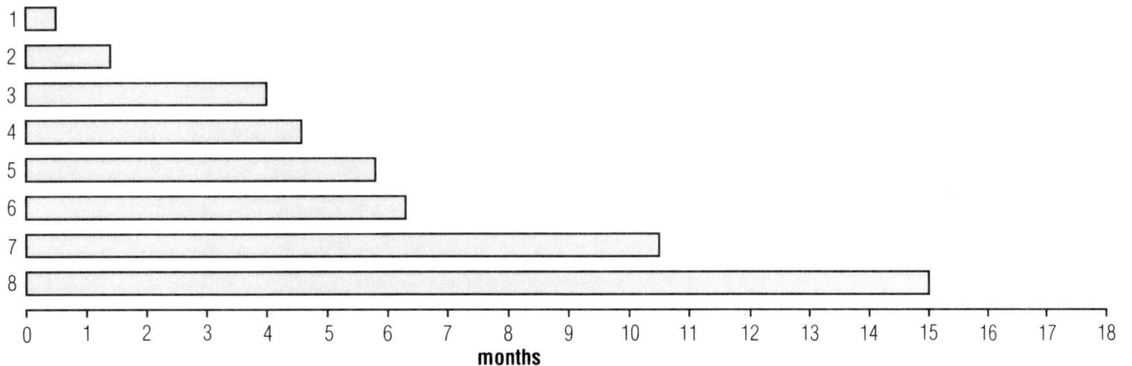

Personality

7619 From the beginnings of psychological science there have been several theories relating to the development and nature of personality.

The psychologist – later described as psychoanalyst – Sigmund Freud theorized that personality develops as a child passes through five distinct stages, four of which correspond to an interest in a specific area of the body: oral, anal, phallic (then a latent period), and genital.

He believed that the personality of an adult involves a tug-of-war between three components:

- the selfish, pleasure-seeking id
- the moral and perfectionist superego or conscience
- the realistic ego, which seeks a balance.

Alfred Adler argued for self-imposed goals and social relationships as influences on personality. Carl Jung developed the idea of a personality scale: shy, introverted people at one end, and outgoing extroverted individuals at the other. H.J.Eysenck suggests that inhibitory brain cells outnumber excitatory signals in introverts whereas in extroverts the imbalance is the other way around.

762 PARAPSYCHOLOGY

Many scientists and researchers attribute other powers to the mind, powers that may for example affect physical objects at a distance (telekinesis) or somehow transmit or receive information in an unknown way (telepathy or ESP: extra-sensory perception.) So far, however, there is no genuine record of any such power that is consistently available, or even measurable, under conditions that permit scientific proof. Probably the most manifest form of psychic power is the poltergeist, an entity that throws household objects around and disrupts furniture, but that occurs most often in households where a teenager is undergoing a particularly difficult stage in puberty.

763 MENTAL DISTURBANCE

Types

7631 There are many forms of mental disturbance, from the state of mild anxiety that we may all suffer from time to time, to the much more serious and debilitating conditions of mental illness that require constant care in an institutional environment. The four major forms of mental illness that require professional therapy are:
1 Neurosis, including hysterical states, phobias, and dissociative states
2 Psychosis, including schizophrenia and manic-depressive illness
3 Personality disorders, including psychopathy
4 Mental illnesses stemming from organic malfunctions or injury, mostly forms of dementia

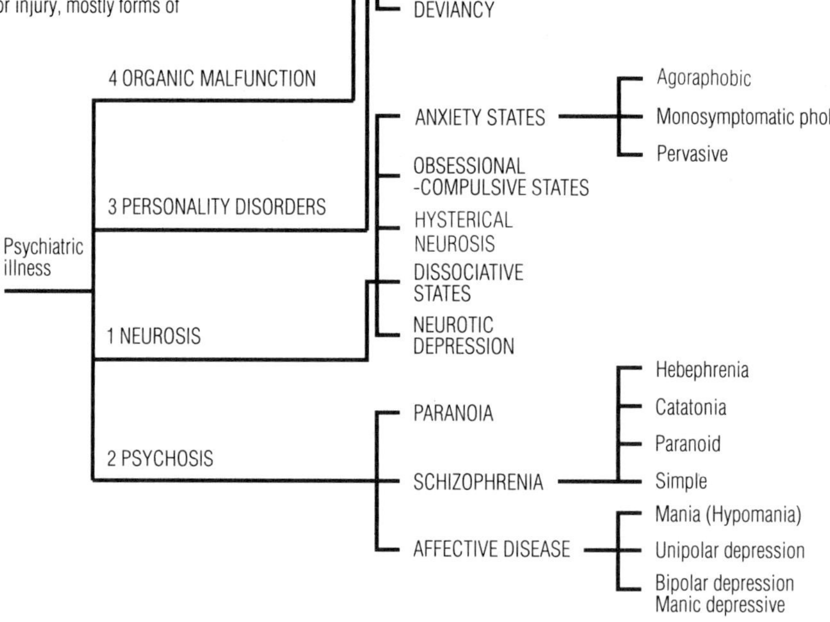

Neurosis

7632

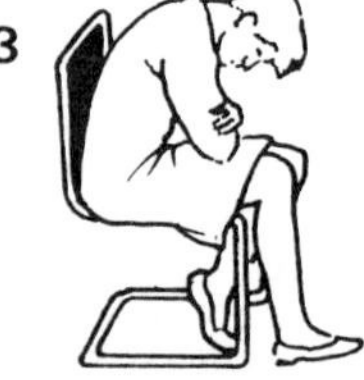

Fairly mild mental disturbances, neuroses are often due to emotional conflict involving a blocked impulse. They are often classified into four main types:
1 Anxiety neuroses These comprise overreaction to an everyday event, such as seeing a particular animal or standing in a confined space.
2 Hysterical neuroses These involve the shutting down of some part of the body's system, such as one of the senses or motor control, so that the individual does not have to confront the object of fear.
3 Obsessive neuroses Involving inappropriate repetitions of certain thoughts or actions.
4 Depressive neuroses Involving inappropriately severe feelings of inadequacy in response to emotional stress or minor failures.

Psychosomatic disorders

7633 A psychosomatic illness is one that produces physical symptoms although the underlying cause is anxiety or some other form of mental disturbance. Such symptoms are surprisingly common and in very mild form often appear, for example, when a schoolchild fears an imminent examination, or an executive fears a meeting with the boss. But in less ordinary circumstances, stress and emotional disturbance have been shown to aggravate such disorders as:

- asthma attacks
- high blood pressure
- heart disease
- stomach problems
- diabetes mellitus
- arthritis
- dental problems

Eating disorders

7634

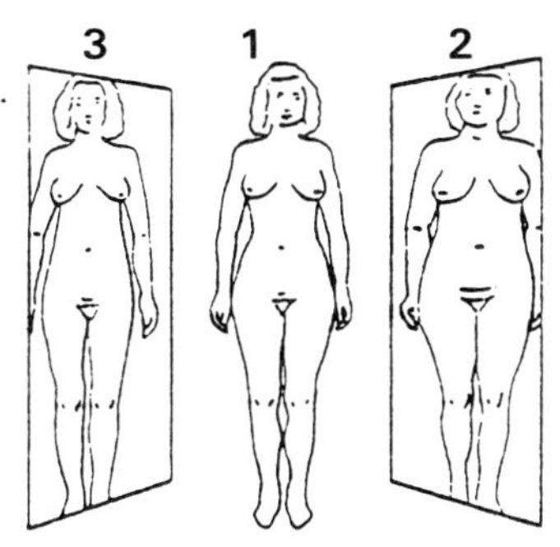

The conditions anorexia nervosa and bulimia nervosa involve a patient's distorted view of his or her (almost always her) own body proportions. In anorexia, the patient (**1**) sees herself as hideously and grossly overweight (**2**), even when in fact the mirror shows her to be of average build (**3**), or even seriously malnourished.

The condition tends to arise at puberty, when the patient suddenly refuses to eat and may in a matter of weeks become semistarved (**4**) while noticing no difference in the mirror (**5**). In bulimia, the patient binges and then induces vomiting to regurgitate the food she has just eaten. Both anorexics and bulimics have a terrific fear of being fat.

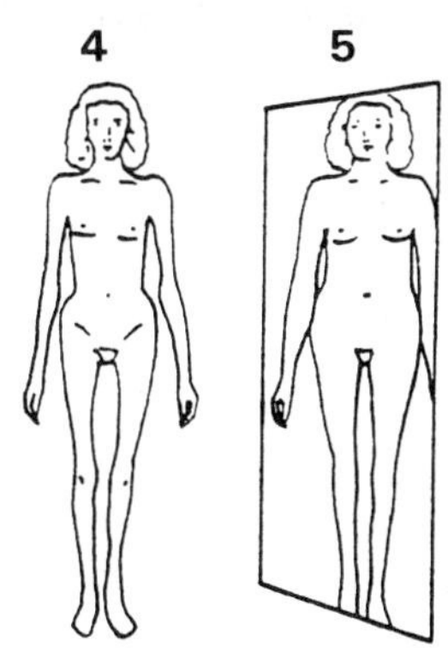

Phobias

7635 Phobias can be classified into four main types: animal phobias; other specific phobias such as fear of water or of heights; social phobias such as fear of specific types of people; and fear of the outdoor world. Psychotherapists have noted that animal phobias (**1**) tend to begin at around age four, while other types of phobia generally have much later onsets. Social phobias (**2**) begin at an average age of 19, other specific phobias (**3**) at around age 23, and agoraphobia (fear of the outdoor world) at about age 24 (**4**).

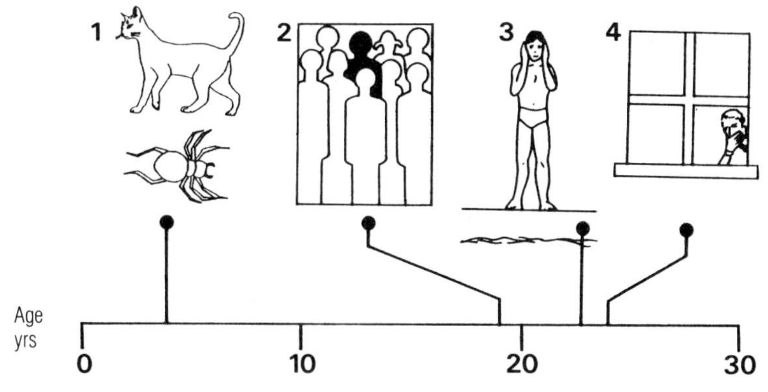

Type	Fear of
Achluophobia	Night, darkness
Acrophobia	Sharpness (pinnacles)
Aerophobia	Flying, air
Agoraphobia	Open spaces
Aichurophobia	Points
Ailourophobia	Cats
Alektorophobia	Chickens
Algophobia	Pain
Altophobia	Height
Amathophobia	Dust
Amaxophobia	Vehicles
Ancraophobia	Wind
Androphobia	Men
Anthophobia	Flowers
Anthropophobia	Human beings
Antlophobia	Flood
Apiphobia	Bees
Arachnophobia	Spiders
Astraphobia	Lightning
Automysophobia	Being dirty
Autophobia	Being alone, being egotistical
Bacilliphobia	Microbes
Bacteriophobia	Bacteria
Ballistophobia	Missiles
Basiphobia	Walking
Batophobia	Passing high objects
Batrachophobia	Reptiles
Belonophobia	Needles
Bibliophobia	Books
Blennophobia	Slime
Brontophobia	Thunder
Carcinophobia	Cancer
Cardiophobia	Heart condition
Chaetophobia	Hair
Cheimatophobia	Cold
Chionophobia	Snow
Chrometophobia	Money
Chromophobia	Color
Claustrophobia	Enclosed spaces
Cnidophobia	Stings
Cryophobia	Ice, frost
Crystallophobia	Crystals
Cynophobia	Dogs
Demonophobia	Demons
Demophobia	Crowds
Dendrophobia	Trees
Dermatophobia	Skin
Dermatosiophobia	Skin diseases
Doraphobia	Fur
Dromophobia	Crossing streets
Ecclesiaphobia	Churches
Eisoptrophobia	Mirrors
Electrophobia	Electricity
Enetephobia	Pins
Entomophobia	Insects
Eosophobia	Dawn
Ergasiophobia	Surgical operations
Ergophobia	Work
Erotophobia	Physical love
Erythrophobia	Blushing
Frigophobia	Cold
Gamophobia	Marriage
Genophobia	Sex
Gynophobia	Women
Hadephobia	Hell
Haematophobia	Blood
Harpaxophobia	Robbers
Heliophobia	Sun
Helminthophobia	Worms
Hippophobia	Horses
Hodophobia	Travel
Homichlophobia	Fog
Hydrophobia	Water
Hypegiaphobia	Responsibility
Hypnophobia	Sleep
Ichthyophobia	Fish
Iophobia	Rust
Kakorraphiaphobia	Failure
Katagelophobia	Ridicule
Keraunophobia	Thunder
Koniphobia	Dust
Limnophobia	Lakes
Linonophobia	String
Lyssophobia	Insanity
Maieusiophobia	Pregnancy
Mechanophobia	Machinery
Melissophobia	Bees
Metallophobia	Metals
Microphobia	Bacteria
Musicophobia	Music
Musophobia	Mice
Mysophobia	Dirt, infection
Myxophobia	Slime
Necrophobia	Corpses
Nelophobia	Glass
Nephophobia	Clouds
Nomatophobia	Names
Nosemaphobia	Illness
Nosophobia	Disease
Nyctophobia	Darkness/night
Ochlophobia	Crowds
Ochophobia	Vehicles
Odontophobia	Teeth
Odynophobia	Pain
Ombrophobia	Rain
Ommetaphobia	Eyes

continued

Phobias continued

7635

Type	Fear of
Oneirophobia	Dreams
Ophidiophobia	Snakes
Ornithophobia	Birds
Paediphobia	Children
Pantophobia	Everything
Parthenophobia	Young girls
Pathophobia	Disease
Peccatophobia	Sinning
Pediculophobia	Lice
Pediophobia	Dolls
Peniaphobia	Poverty
Pharmacophobia	Drugs
Phasmophobia	Ghosts
Phengophobia	Daylight
Phobophobia	Fears
Phthisiophobia	Tuberculosis
Phyllophobia	Leaves
Pnigerophobia	Smothering, choking
Pogonophobia	Beards
Potamophobia	Rivers
Potophobia	Drink, alcohol
Psychrophobia	Cold
Pteronophobia	Feathers
Pyrophobia	Fire
Satanophobia	Satan
Scholionophobia	School
Sciophobia	Shadows
Scopophobia	Being looked at
Selaphobia	Flashes
Siderodromophobia	Traveling by train
Siderophobia	Stars
Sitophobia	Food
Spermophobia	Germs
Spheksophobia	Wasps
Stygiophobia	Hell
Tachophobia	Speed
Taphophobia	Burial alive
Teratophobia	Monsters
Terdekaphobia	Number 13
Thalassophobia	Sea
Thanatophobia	Death
Theophobia	God
Toxiphobia	Poison
Traumatophobia	Wounds, injury
Tremophobia	Trembling
Triskaidekaphobia	Number 13
Trypanophobia	Inoculations, injections
Zenophobia	Foreigners
Zoophobia	Animals

Psychoses

7636 These are serious mental illnesses affecting the entire personality, and with far more disabling effects than neuroses. The most common are schizophrenia and depressive illness.

Schizophrenia The personality disintegrates and there is loss of contact with reality. Schizophrenics often show a lack of appropriate emotional response, suspect others of hostility, and hide real feelings. They may also express a string of unrelated thoughts. Some doctors believe that a disturbed or stressed family background may be associated with schizophrenia; others, that it coincides with too much of the neurotransmitter dopamine in the brain's limbic system.

Recent research into schizophrenia has suggested that some sufferers may have abnormalities of the corpus callosum, the bridge between the two halves of the brain. Scans and other tests on a small number of schizophrenics have revealed that each corpus callosum is thickened, damaged, or nonfunctioning. If this proved to be the case with most schizophrenics, it might be possible in the future to provide screening so that preventative treatment could be given.

Manic depression Manic depressives suffer attacks involving violent mood swings from sadness through to extreme elation. They have been helped with long-term use of the drug lithium carbonate.

Severe depressive illness This illness is a more severe and debilitating version of the common form of depression through which most people pass unscathed. In susceptible people, depression may run deep until eventually recognized as a true illness requiring prompt treatment. Situations involving emotional stress often act as catalysts in the development of severe depression and may include the following:

- The death of a spouse or close relative
- The emotional and social upheaval of a divorce
- Becoming unemployed, shocking the system of someone truly career-minded

Brain scans
Brain scans of schizophrenic patients have shown decreased glucose consumption in some areas (**1**), while scans of manic-depressives (**2**) showed increased consumption during the manic phase compared to the brain scan of a person showing a normal glucose consumption (**3**).

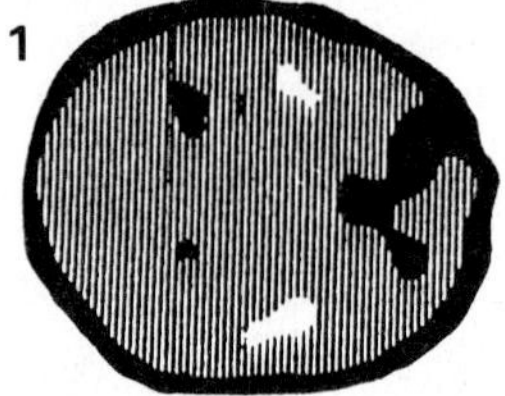

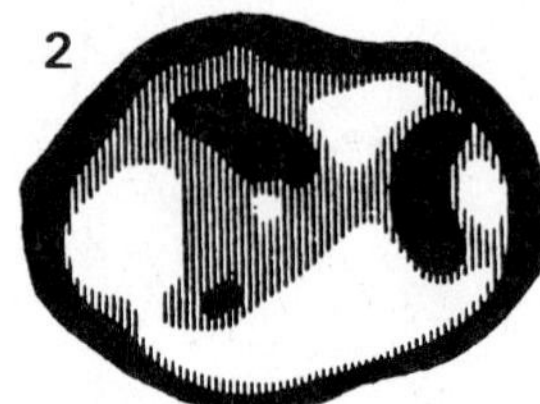

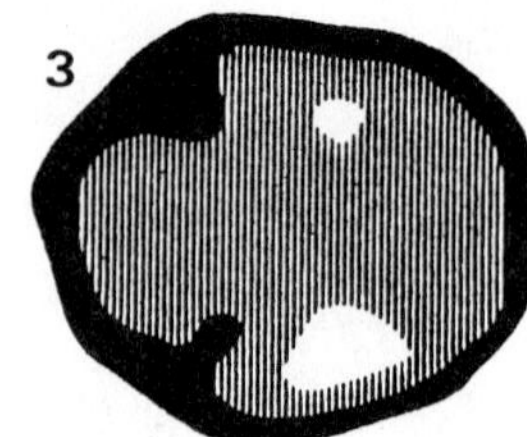

Treatment of psychological disorders

7637 **Psychotherapy**
Some of the most widely used psychotherapeutic techniques used to treat those with emotional problem are:

- A patient's thoughts roam freely while the therapist (usually a psychoanalyst) listens for clues to the cause of conflict.
- Rebirthing technique; a subject is encouraged to reenact birth trauma; and in primal therapy
- A patient is encouraged to release tension built up by a lifelong backlog of emotional pain.
- Transactional therapy looks at response in terms of the parent, child, and adult in us.
- Gestalt therapy aims to help patients discover and utilize repressed aspects of personality.

continued

Treatment of psychological disorders continued

7637 **Family therapy and self-help**
Family therapy involves a counselor working with other members of the family as well as the patient. The use of self-suggestion and self-hypnosis methods can also be helpful in some instances.

Biofeedback
This is a mind control technique in which subjects develop a relaxed mental state by passive concentration, and are wired to electronic devices which feed back data concerning such physical indicators as blood pressure.

Hypnotism

Only the most suggestible can be deeply hypnotized. Unwilling subjects remain unaffected. The subject relaxes while watching a swinging ball or listening to the hypnotist's voice monotonously inducing the hypnotic state. Afterward, the subject may remain responsive to ideas put forward by the hypnotist. The method has proved helpful where a subject wishes to stop smoking or lose weight, for example. The effect can be shown in brain wave traces. (**1**) is the trace of someone awake; (**2**) is the trace of a hypnotized subject and shows a different frequency.

Electroconvulsive therapy
Some doctors consider ECT to be helpful in the trreatment of certain psychological disorders where other treatment has failed. The patient is given a drug to relax the muscles, and a general anesthetic. An electric current (**1**) is then applied to the brain through electrodes (**2**) taped to the scalp. This results in furious electrical activity in the brain. The patient wakes soon after and may suffer from a temporary loss of memory. The treatment is repeated over a few weeks.

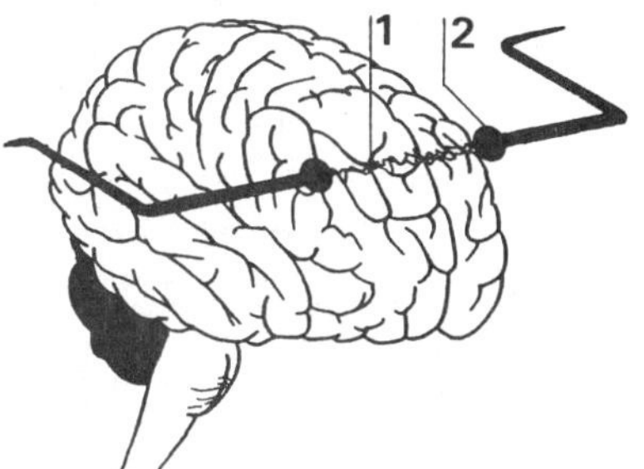

Radioactive implants
This technique involves placing radioactive seeds (**1**) within the frontal lobes of the brain. These destroy a limited area of tissue with minimal effect on the rest of the brain. The procedure aims to help the patient suffering from severe depression or some other incapacitating mental state, and is only used as a last resort when drug and ECT treatments have failed.

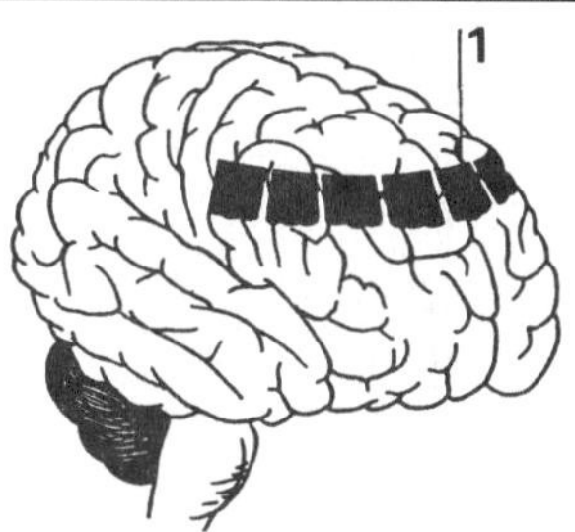

Psychotherapeutic drugs
Drugs are used to treat a whole range of mental conditions.

Minor tranquilizers, such as the benzodiazepines, are often prescribed for anxiety, for example, and antidepressants, are prescribed for depression. However, such drugs do not always cure the underlying problem.

Most tranquilizers, which are used to sedate very disturbed patients, work by affecting the transfer of messages between neurons; sedatives, for example, slow down the brain, and so may calm patients with schizophrenia. Some drugs affect the reticular formation (**1**), which helps to regulate consciousness and the level of activity in the rest of the brain.

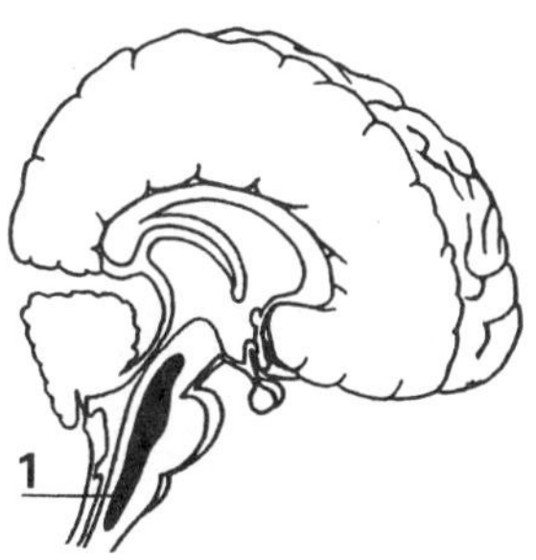

Frontal labotomy
This is an operation which severs fibers connecting frontal lobes to the limbic system or, more crudely, destroys areas of the lobes themselves. Most doctors now feel that we still know too little about the workings of the brain to carry out such invasive surgical techniques.

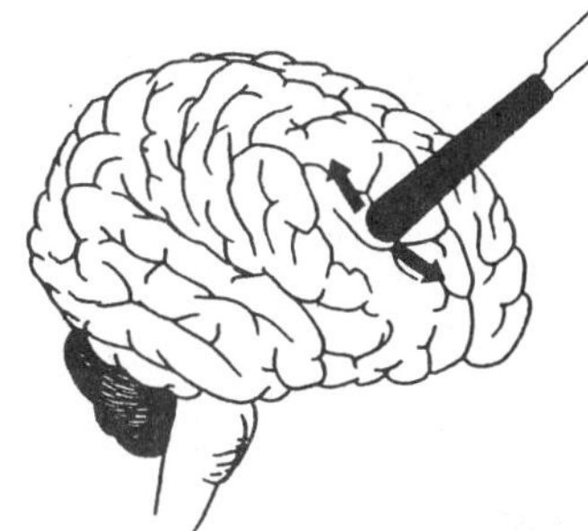

764 PSYCHOLOGY GLOSSARY

amnesia Memory loss, sometimes due to a blow on the head or some other damage to brain function, or to neurotic disorder as a result of inner conflict.
analytical psychology The process of attempting to explain or relieve disturbance by looking into the unconscious forces governing behavior. The term is also used more specifically to refer to the school of Carl Jung.
archetype Jung used this term to refer to such universal concepts as the "here," which he saw as part of the collective unconscious – that part of the mind inherited from the experience of previous generations and common to us all.
association The technique of association involves reading out a list of words and encouraging subjects to respond with the first word coming to mind.
autism Children suffering from this condition appear withdrawn, as if lost in fantasy. No cause or cure has yet been found; but specialized teaching has enabled many to lead relatively normal lives.
autosuggestion Theory that if individuals can suggest a belief to themselves, they will come to believe it.
behaviorism School of psychology that places great importance on learned behavior and conditioned reflexes.
castration complex A child's fear that he will lose his genitals as a punishment for fantasizing about them is often the basis of a castration complex, and the root of neurosis in some cases.
catalepsy A state of muscular rigidity maintained for long periods.
catatonia An extreme form of schizophrenia characterized by muscular rigidity or catalepsy, stereotyped mannerisms, refusal to communicate, and stupor.
catharsis As a subject begins to talk about problems during analysis, the process of catharsis begins, and pent-up feelings and repressed emotions are released.
complex An idea which is partly or wholly repressed, but which determines your opinion of yourself, may produce a complex. A woman may not consciously recall being teased as a child for being fat, for instance, but the idea may remain in her unconscious and as a result she may develop a complex about her appearance, whatever her adult build.
compulsion Irresistible urge, often a neurotic reaction, taking such forms as having to wash one's hands every few minutes or touching certain objects before leaving a room.
conversion reaction Form of hysteria in which repressed conflict is converted into symptoms such as deafness, blindness, or paralysis, without actual physical cause.
death wish According to Freud, in addition to a "drive to survive," we also have certain impulses known collectively as the death wish.
depersonalization Pathological loss of contact with reality.
deviation Conduct departing from the norm. Specifically, it is used to describe sexual perversions, such as a fetish or sadism.
displacement The man who gets angry at the office but is afraid to lose his temper there, may arrive home and let out all that pent-up aggression on the family. In a process known as displacement, he has directed his anger to a handy substitute.
double-bind Two contradictory responses from the child. Some schools hold that this is sometimes a root cause of schizophrenia.
ego That aspect of the mind most in touch with reality.
Electra complex A daughter's fixation on her father.
extroversion Uninhibited, the extrovert is far more concerned with things outside than with his or her own thoughts and feelings. Jung first devised the term "extroversion – introversion" as a dimension along which people can be divided into psychological types.
folie à deux This mental disorder, present in two closely associated individuals at once, most commonly occurs in a husband and wife.
free association In this method, sometimes used in psychoanalysis, subjects are encouraged to let their thoughts wander, the final chain of associations often providing clues to the underlying disturbance.
id Part of the mind or personality that is governed by the pleasure principle, and which demands gratification.
individual psychology This school, founded by Alfred Adler, aims to reach an understanding of mental disturbance through the examination of early feelings of inferiority and subsequent compensatory activity, and to improve patterns of reaction.
industrial psychology Working conditions, stress, morale, and rewards can all influence efficiency, and are the concern of the industrial psychologist.
inferiority complex Unconscious feelings of insignificance and insecurity are hidden by excessively aggressive or other compensatory behavior.
inhibition Mental blockage occurring when the superego or voice of conscience prevents the individual from behaving in a particular way.
introversion Tendency to turn inward, first examined by Jung, which often results in avoidance of social contact, isolation and loneliness.
kleptomania Compulsive stealing, symbolic of an unconscious need, often sexual in origin.
libido The sex instinct or erotic desire.
masochism A disorder in which pleasure is derived from having pain, whether mental or physical, inflicted on oneself; it is sometimes associated with sexual activity.
megalomania Arising from exaggerated valuation of oneself, this state is characterized by delusions of grandeur.
nervous breakdown Any mental condition prohibiting normal functioning.
obsession Dominating idea or thought which takes over an individual.
Oedipus complex The repressed desire of a boy or man for a sexual relationship with his mother.
paranoia Psychotic disorder marked by imaginary persecution.
penis envy Repressed female desire to possess a penis as part of their own anatomy.
phantom limb Imagined sensations in a limb that has been amputated. These result from nerve ends in the stump which continue to convey misleading messages to the brain.
phrenology This pseudo-science developed in the 19th century and holds that certain characteristics – such as wit, normality, aggression or benevolence – are related to particular parts of the brain and can be recognized by bumps on the contour of the head.
pleasure principle The immediate satisfaction of urges and desires is, according to psychoanalytical theory, an overriding principle which remains with us even in adulthood to a marked degree.
psychiatrist Practitioner specializing in the diagnosis and treatment of mental and nervous disorders.
psychoanalysis System of psychology aiming to discover and address the unconscious motivation for certain types of behavior.
psychodrama The acting out of relationships or feelings in an attempt to release and identify repressed emotions.
psychologist Practitioner who studies behavior and the way in which the mind actually works.
psychopath Unstable individual who is unable to adjust to society.
psychosomatic Physical disorders resulting at least partly from psychological factors.
psychotherapy Treatment that sets out to help a subject adjust to daily life.
reflexes Acts that occur involuntarily – such as blinking – are the result of a reflex response.
regression This term implies a return to an earlier stage of psychological development. In the course of therapy, regression hypnosis is sometimes used in order to uncover the possible root of some current problem.
repression Involuntary ejection of shameful emotions and memories from consciousness because they are too painful to bear; it may sometimes result in neurotic symptoms.
sadism Form of perversion, often sexual, involving pleasure through inflicting pain on another. Sado-masochism implies a tendency toward both sadism and masochism.
subconscious This term describes any mental process of which we are only dimly aware.
sublimation Freud first described this unconscious process whereby an instinctive urge is transformed so that it is more socially acceptable.
superego That part of the personality that exercises a prohibitive role, acting as the voice of conscience.
transference Psychoanalytical theory holds that through the process of transference, healing may take place. So it is that the psychoanalyst becomes the object of a patient's suppressed emotions – either love or hatred – while the transference is resolved.
unconscious This part of the mind is cut off from consciousness and is believed to be the seat of repressed emotions.

765 LANDMARKS IN PSYCHOLOGICAL RESEARCH

1800s French physiologist Claude Bernard shows that the nervous system can control blood flow in the body.
1870 German researcher Gustav Fritsch and Eduard Hitzig finds that electric shocks to one of a dog's cerebral hemispheres produce movement on the other side of its body.
1874 German neurologist Karl Wernicke discovers the brain area concerned with understanding words.
1879 Sir William Macewen, a Scot, pioneers successful brain surgery.
1800s Jean Martin Charcot of Paris helps separate neuroses from psychoses, and shows where brain damage causes paralysis and epilepsy.
1892 Britain's Sir Francis Galton pioneers the scientific study of the nature of intelligence.
1890s Austrian physician Sigmund Freud pioneers psychoanalysis.
1900s Russian physiologist Ivan Pavlov discovers conditioned reflexes in dogs.
1900s French psychologist Alfred Binet devised tests that make him the "father of modern intelligence testing."
1911 Austrian psychoanalyst Alfred Adler breaks away from Freud and founds his school of individual psychology, based on the theory that we all have feelings of inadequacy for which we strive to compensate.
1912 Swiss psychoanalyst Carl Jung breaks with Freud's way of thinking and founds his school of analytical psychology, stressing the importance of the collective unconscious, comprising memories common to us all.
1914 American psychologist John Watson launches behaviorism with the theory that brain activity comprises response to outside stimuli.
1920s Canadian neurosurgeon Wilde Penfield uses microelectrodes to map parts of the human cerebral cortex with different functions.
1930 American psychologist Burrhus (B.F.) Skinner (inventor of teaching machines) describes operant conditioning (learned behavior.)
1949 In Illinois, Giuseppe Moruzzi and Horace Magoun show that brain stem signals keep the whole brain awake.
1953 American researcher James Olds discovers a pleasure center in the brain.
1960s Swiss psychologist Jean Piaget discovers the chronological stages of intellectual development. American psycholinguist Noam Chomsky claims that the human brain is born "programed" for learning.
1965 Geoffrey Harris and other British researcher show that sexual drive is built into the hypothalamus.
1970s American neurophysiologist Karl Pribram suggests that brain activity resembles holography, a photographic-like process. Researchers in the US and Scotland discover brain chemicals that block transmission of pain signals.
1981 American psychobiologist Roger Sperry shares a Nobel Prize for discoveries concerning the right and left spheres of the cerebrum.
1982 In Canada, Martin Benfev and Albert Aguayo show that damaged brain cells can be persuaded to regrow.

766 PSYCHOLOGISTS

Adler, Alfred 1870–1937, Austria pioneer (**1**) psychiatrist who became a prominent member of Freud's psychoanalytical group, but later developed his own "Individual Psychology." Contributed concept of "inferiority complex", as well as treatment of neurosis as "exploitation of shock."
Bell, Sir Charles 1774–1842, Scottish anatomist and surgeon famous for neurological discoveries. In 1807, he distinguished between the sensory and motor nerves in the brain. Facial paralysis known as "Bell's Palsy" is named after him. Said to have been the inspiration for the character of Sherlock Holmes.
Binet, Alfred 1857–1911, French psychologist, and founder of "Intelligence Tests," which he first used on his children. In 1905, with Théodore Simon, he expanded the tests to encompass measurement of relative intelligence amongst deprived children (Binet-Simon tests).
Charcot, Jean Martin 1825–93, French pathologist and neurologist who helped separate neuroses from psychoses, and demonstrated how brain damage causes paralysis and epilepsy. Made important studies of hypnotism. Freud was among his pupils.
Chomsky, Avril Noam b. 1928, American linguist and political activist; one of the founders of the concept of transformational generative grammar. Anti-empiricist who regards language and other facets of human cognitive behavior to be a result of innate cognitive structures built into the mind.
Eccles, Sir John Carew b. 1903, Australian neurophysiologist who shared 1963 Nobel prize with Hodgkin and Huxley for research into mechanisms of nerve impulse transmission.

Freud, Sigmund 1856–1939, Austrian (**2**) neurologist and founder of psychoanalysis who developed the technique of "free association." His *The Interpretation of Dreams* (1900) argues that dreams, like neuroses, are disguised manifestations of repressed sexual desires. Later, after his break with Jung, Freud elaborated theories of division of unconscious mind into "Id," "Ego," and "Super-Ego."
Gall, Franz Joseph 1758–1828, German physician and co-founder of the pseudo-science of phrenology who also dissected the brain, thus laying the foundations for modern neurology. Evolved theories by which he traced talents and other qualities to particular areas of brain and the shape of the skull overlying them.
Galton, Sir Francis 1822–1911, English scientist who devoted himself later in life to heredity, founding and endowing the study of eugenics. His researches into color blindness and mental imagery were of great value. Devised system of fingerprint identification.
Gibson, James Jerome 1904–79, American psychologist. Developed concept of "direct perception" of "invariant" attributes of visual world, transcending any sensory processes. Stressed role of vision as handmaiden for bodily action rather than as means of achieving awareness of surroundings.
Horney, Karen 1885–1952, Norwegian-Dutch psychoanalyst, writer, teacher. Stressed social and environmental factors in determining personality. Studied child behavior. Works include *The Neurotic Personality of Our Time* (1937).
Jackson, John Hughlings 1835–1911, English neurologist who investigated unilateral epileptiform seizures, and discovered that certain regions of the brain are associated with certain movements of the limbs.
Jung, Carl Gustav 1875–1961, Swiss psychiatrist (**3**) who broke away from Freud's

continued

Psychologists continued

76**6** psychoanalytical circle to develop "analytical psychology.".Introduced term "complex," and concepts of "introvert" and "extrovert" personalities, as well as theory of "collective unconscious" with its archetypes of man's basic psychic nature.

3

Köhler, Wolfgang 1887–1967, German psychologist, and co-founder with Koffka of Gestalt school of psychology. Director of anthropoid research station in Canary Islands (1913-20), where he became authority on problem-solving in animals.
Langley, John Newport 1852–1925, English physiologist noted for research on sympathetic nervous system. Coined term "autonomic nervous system" in 1898.
Lucas, Keith 1879–1916, British physiologist who demonstrated the "all or none" response of stimulated neurons.
Luria, Alexandr Romanovich 1902–77, Russian psychologist and co-founder of neuropsychology – the application of theories and methods of experimental psychology to the understanding of neurological disorders. Discovered functional defects produced by local brain damage.

4

Mesmer, Friedrich Anton or Franz 1734–1815, Austrian physician (**4**), and founder of mesmerism, who promoted the idea that there exists a power which he called "animal magnetism." Created sensation in Paris by curing diseases at séances, but was denounced in 1785 as imposter by a learned commission.
Pavlov, Ivan Petrovich 1849–1936, Russian physiologist (**5**). Worked on physiology of circulation and digestion, but is most famous for his study of "conditioned" or "acquired" reflexes, each associated with some part of brain cortex. Regarded brain function as a mere coupling of neurones to produce reflexes.

5

Penfield, Wilder Graves 1891–1976, American-born Canadian. An outstanding practical neurosurgeon, Penfield became even more famous for experimental work on the exposed brains of living human beings, which helped in understanding the higher functions of brain as well as the causes and symptoms of brain diseases such as epilepsy.
Piaget, Jean 1896–1980, Swiss psychologist and pioneer in study of child intelligence. Best known for research on the development of cognitive functions (perception, intelligence, logic), for intensive "case study" methods of research, and for postulating "stages" of cognitive development.
Rogers, Carl Ransom 1902–87, American psychotherapist, and originator of client-centered therapy. This therapy attempts to elicit and resolve a neurotic person's problems by allowing the patient to talk out their problems under the supervision of a passive, non-doctrinaire therapist.
Sherrington, Sir Charles Scott 1857–1952, English physiologist who made major advances in the understanding of inborn reflexes and showed that the central nervous system involves the integration of different "levels." Awarded 1932 Nobel prize with Lord Adrian.
Skinner, Burrhus Frederic 1904–90, American psychologist and radical behaviorist. A prolific writer, his ideas led to the development and proliferation of "programmed learning," techniques, which seek to tailor teaching to the needs of each individual, and to reinforce learning by regular and immediate feedback.
Sperry, Roger Wolcott b. 1913, American neuroscientist who, in the 1950s and 1960s, pioneered the behavioral investigation of "split-brain" animals and humans, arguing that two separate realms of consciousness could coexist inside one skull. Believes mind is an "emergent property" arising from the very complexity of the physical system that constitutes the brain. Shared 1981 Nobel prize with Hubel and Wiesel.
Watson, John Broadus 1878–1958, American psychologist (**6**). Leading exponent of behaviorism, who holds that scientific psychology can only study what is directly observable – i.e. behavior. Published *Behavior: An Introduction to Comparative Psychology* (1914).

6

Wernicke, Carl, 1848-1905, German neurologist who studied brain damage leading to aphasia or dysphasia (loss of certain kinds of language ability). "Wernicke's area" is the name now given to the area in the brain that is concerned with understanding words.
Wundt, Wilhelm Max 1832–1920, German physiologist and psychologist, founder of experimental psychology. Made studies of nervous system and senses, relations of physiology and psychology, logic, and other subjects. Works include *Human and Animal Psychology* (1863) and *Folk Psychology* (1900-20).

811 TYPES OF SPORT

Athletics

8111 TRACK AND FIELD

decathlon Ten-event combined competition for men over two days: 100 m, long jump, shot-put, high jump, 400 m, 110 m hurdles, discus, pole vault, javelin, and 1,500 m.
discus Throwers spin in a large cage (enclosed area) to hurl a saucer-shaped wooden discus with a metal rim as far as possible into a marked sector.
heptathlon Combined seven-event competition for women held over two days. It is made up of high hurdles, high jump, shot-put, 200 m, long jump, javelin, and 800 m.
hammer Throwers in a large cage (enclosed area) whirl around their heads a heavy metal ball attached to a steel wire, and try to hurl it as far as possible within a marked sector.
high jump Competitors jump over a crossbar between two uprights. Height is raised after each round, and three consecutive failures result in elimination.
hurdles, high Track event in which competitors sprint over barriers (usually ten). Men run 110 m with hurdles 42 in (107 cm) high. Women, 100 m with 33 in (84 cm) hurdles.
hurdles Four hundred metre international hurdle race; men jump hurdles 36 in (91 cm) high; women jump 30 in (76 cm) hurdles.
javelin Competitors run up to a foul line and hurl a spear of wood or metal as far as possible into a marked sector.
long distance Covers three different events, 3,000 m, 5,000 m, and 10,000 m.
long jump Competitors leap from a take off board into a sand landing area. Each competitor has three attempts, the competitor who jumps the furthest is the winner.
marathon Competitors race on roads for 26 mi 385 yds (42.195 km), with the start and finish usually in a stadium.
middle distance races Track races of 800 m, 1500 m, and a mile.
modern pentathlon Olympic combined event for individuals and three-member teams made up of riding, fencing, shooting, swimming, and cross-country running.
pole vault Competitors use flexible fiberglass pole to vault over a crossbar held high between two uprights.
relay races Usually 100 m and 400 m. Teams of four runners compete, each individual carrying a baton over a quarter of the distance and then passing it over to a teammate to run the next quarter.
shot-put Competitors rest a heavy metal ball between neck and shoulder and putt (push) it as far as possible.
sprints Track races of 100 m, 200 m, and 400 m.
steeplechase Track race of 3,000 m that includes 28 sturdy hurdle jumps and seven water jumps.
triple jump Competitors sprint down a runway to hop and step in sequence, then jump from a take-off board into a sandpit for distance.
walking races Track or road, covering 20 km or 50 km. Walkers must maintain unbroken contact with the ground.

OTHER

cross-country running Winter sport in which individuals and teams run over marked courses in open country.
fell running British sport confined to highland areas. Resembles cross-country running but involves longer, steeper, and more rugged ground.
orienteering Individuals or teams, armed with map and compass, traverse rough country on foot. Winner is the first to locate all checkpoints.

Ball

8112 STICK

bandy Game resembling ice hockey, with teams of 11 players on a larger ice rink, and no play behind goals.
baseball Two opposing teams of nine players compete with bat and ball, on a field with four bases forming a diamond. Runs are scored by batting a pitched ball and running around the bases.
camogie A version of hurling played by women only. It involves less body contact than the game played by men. See hurling.
cricket Outdoor bat-and-ball game between two opposing teams of 11 players. Runs are scored by batting the ball and running between two facing wickets without being bowled or caught out.
hockey, field Two opposing teams of 11 players on a field use curved sticks to try to drive a ball into the opponents' goal.
hockey, ice Two opposing teams of six players on an ice rink, equipped with sticks, knock a small rubber disk into the opposing goal.
hockey, indoor European game for teams of up to seven players in which the ball may be pushed but not hit.
hockey, roller Game similar to hockey. Two opposing teams of five players on roller skates play in an enclosed wood-floor rink with a colored ball and curved sticks.
hurling Gaelic field game played by two opposing teams of 15. The ball may be struck with or carried on the hurley (curved stick with a broad blade) or handled or kicked toward goal.
lacrosse Two opposing teams of 10 men or 12 women use long-handled sticks fitted with nets to catch, carry or throw a ball into the opposing goal. Box lacrosse is a Canadian version, played on ice-hockey rinks covered with matting.
rounders British game similar to baseball. Batter hits a thrown ball and runs around a marked area for a "rounder."
shinty Gaelic field game in which two opposing teams of 12 men use a caman (club) to hit a ball and score goals.
softball Variation of baseball in which players use a larger, softer ball and pitch underhand.

TARGET

billiards Any of several games such as carom, pool, and snooker. Two opponents play on a green, baize-covered table, using a cue to drive colored balls against each other or into pockets.
boules French game similar to lawn bowls, played with metal bowls on rough, hard surfaces.
bowling Any of several related games such as tenpin, fivepin, ninepin, or duckpin bowling, and skittles, in which players roll balls down an alley at a target.
croquet Two or four players on a lawn drive wooden balls through iron hoops with mallets in order to hit a peg.
curling Two opposing teams of four players slide heavy round stones with handles across ice toward a target.
golf Players, using clubs on a large open obstacle course, sink a small ball into each one of usually 18 holes in as few strokes as possible.
lawn bowls Two opponents or opposing teams roll heavy wooden biased bowls in turn on a smooth lawn. Flat green bowls uses a "level" rink. Crown green bowls uses a green rising gently from the edges to center.

TEAM

American football Outdoor North American game between two opposing teams of 11 players, in which one side at a time tries to run or pass an oval ball over the opposing goal line.
Australian rules football Game resembling rugby football in which two teams of 18 men play with an oval ball on an oval pitch. They score by kicking the ball.

continued

Ball games continued

8112 between four goalposts at each end.
basketball Two opposing teams of five men or six women play on an indoor court and score by tossing the ball through a raised metal hoop at each end.
Canadian football Differs from American football in that the pitch is larger, the goals are at the front of the end zones, and there are 12 players a side. Also, different rules for scrimmages, kicked balls, and scoring.
canoe polo Two opposing teams of five canoeists use their paddles to draw a ball over the water and score goals.
cycle polo Two teams of five players on bicycles aim to hit a ball into the opponents' goal using a mallet. Indoor cycle polo is a two-a-side European version played by women.
Gaelic football Irish game similar to rugby football, with 15 men a side, a spherical ball, and the lower half of each goal netted.
korfball Dutch game resembling basketball, in which two opposing teams of 12 (six men and six women) try to throw the ball into the opponents' basket.
netball Seven-a-side game, similar to basketball, played usually by women. Scoring is by throwing the ball through an elevated ring at each end.
pato Argentine basketing-scoring game, played on horseback between two teams of four men, involving windsock-shaped "baskets," and a ball with six leather handles.
polo Two opposing teams of four players on polo ponies use mallets to knock a ball through the opponents' goals.
polo crosse Horseback hybrid of polo and lacrosse, with six players-a-side. The object is to propel a rubber ball into the opponents' goal by galloping with it, or passing it to another team-member to score.
rugby football Two opposing teams of 13 (rugby league) or 15 (rugby union) players score tries (goals) by planting an oval ball over the opposing goal line. Forward passing is not allowed.
soccer (Association Football) Football in which two teams of 11 kick or head the ball goalward. Only goalkeepers may handle the ball.
speedball North American version of football between two opposing teams of 11 in which they may catch, throw, or kick the ball, but not carry it or pick it up from the ground. Scoring is by kicking goals, and by touchdowns.
tchouk-ball two teams, and one (six a side) or two (nine a side) rebound a ball off nets ("goals"). A team scores if a shot hits the net and is not caught on the rebound by the opposing side.
team handball Two opposing teams of seven players on a marked pitch try to score goals by passing or dribbling the ball with their hands.
touchball Also known as Finnish rugby. Two opposing teams of five players must release the ball if touched on the back by an opponent. Kicking the ball is not allowed. Scoring is by touchdowns.
volleyball Two opposing teams of six on an indoor court hit a leather ball over a high net with hands or arms. The ball must be volleyed at all times. A junior version has three players a side.
water polo Two opposing teams of seven swimmers propel a ball with their hands to score goals in a pool.

COURT
badminton Racket game for two or four players in which a shuttle of cork and feathers is hit over a high net dividing a court.
court (real) tennis An ancient game featuring a slack net, lopsided rackets, and a court with a number of special features, including ingenious hazards. Played as singles or doubles.
court handball Two or four players hit a small, hard rubber ball with their hands against a wall or walls.
jai alai A version of pelota played by two or four players. This is played in the US. See Pelota..
lawn tennis Racket game in which two or four opposing players hit a light elastic ball back and forth over a low net on a court of grass, clay, wood, etc.
paddleball Walled-court game played with paddle (short-handled "bat").
paddle tennis Game resembling lawn tennis where players use wooden paddles on a half-size court to knock a sponge-rubber ball over a low net.
pelota Any of several fast Spanish or Latin American games in which two players use a basket strapped to their wrist to knock a ball against a marked wall.
platform tennis Variation of paddle tennis. Players play on a wooden platform enclosed by a wire fence.
raquetball Two or four opposing players hit a small ball with rackets (not hands as in handball) against the four walls and ceiling of an indoor court.
rugby fives British game in which two players with padded gloves hit a small, hard rubber ball against a wall in a roofless court with three walls.
squash Two or four players in a four-walled court use light, long-handled rackets to knock a small rubber ball against the walls to score.
table tennis Miniature version of lawn tennis played on a table top with small paddles and a small, light, hollow plastic ball.

Combat

8113 **aikido** Japanese unarmed fighting sport embodying various styles in which a defender tries to catch the attacker off balance.
boxing Two fighters with padded gloves battle each other with their fists in a roped-off area called a ring.
fencing Swordmanship between two opponents using one of three blunted weapons: foil, *épée*, or saber.
judo Developed form of Japanese unarmed self-defense system of jujitsu that aims to throw and hold an opponent to the ground, using minimum force.
karate Japanese unarmed combat using kicks, smashes, and chops with hands, feet, legs, and elbows. In sport, blows are pulled back before contact.
kendo Japanese form of fencing with bamboo staves between two contestants wearing protective clothing.
kung fu Chinese martial art that combines the principles of karate and judo.
tae kwon do Korean martial art that combines spinning kicks with punching, jumping, blocking, and dodging.
wrestling Two contestants try to throw each other and pin the opponent's shoulders to the floor. Greco-Roman, freestyle, Sambo, and Japanese sumo figure among more than 50 different styles of wrestling.

Display

8114 AIR
aerial skiing Involves acrobatic leaps from prepared snow jumps. Skiers are judged on their performance of the maneuver, the height achieved, and the style of takeoff and landing.
aerobatics Pilots perform maneuvers in single-engined light aircraft, and are judged for skill and versatility during free and compulsory programs.
hang gliding Pilot hangs from a harness attached to a glider with a triangular frame and a sail, controling with a control bar.
helicopter flying Covers precision flying

continued

Display continued

8114 (arriving at a specified airfield, or just following a line on the ground), navigation, and observation (answering questions about surprise route).

parasailing "Human kites" are towed into the air on a line pulled by a land vehicle or watercraft. The aim is to touch down at the center of a target.

skydiving (sport parachuting) Parachutists fall several thousand feet (or meters) in free fall before opening their parachutes to perform geometric patterns (in a group) or aim for a ground target (singly).

ANIMAL

carriage driving Teams of four horses pull a four-wheeled carriage. Areas of competition include presentation/dressage, obstacle driving, driving marathon, and combined events.

dressage Riders guide their horses through movements at a walk, trot, and canter.

show jumping Horse and rider face a course of jumps of various heights, spreads, and designs, in an indoor arena or on an outdoor course.

three-day event Equestrian discipline occurring on three consecutive days, and comprising dressage, endurance, and show jumping.

GYMNASTICS

artistic (Olympic) gymnastics Name for area in which competitors perform a series of balletic and acrobatic movements either within a set floor area or on various pieces of fixed apparatus.

asymmetrical (uneven parallel) bars Women swing between two wooden bars, one higher than the other.

beam Women leap and do handstands, somersaults, flips, and cartwheels on a long wooden beam about 4 in (10 cm) wide.

floor exercises Men and women display a continuous series of movements involving balance, agility, and strength. Women perform their routine to a musical accompaniment.

horizontal bar Men swing around a flexible steel bar about 100 in (250 cm) above the floor without coming to a full stop.

horse vault Men vault across the length of the "horse" (padded apparatus on legs) after a run and jump from a low springboard. Women vault across the horse's width.

parallel bars Men perform handstands, swings, twists, etc, on two long wooden bars about 65 in (165 cm) high and a little more than shoulder width apart.

pommel horse Men swing their legs and support their weight with their hands on a "horse" with two pommels (wooden handles) on top.

rhythmic gymnastics Floorwork performed to music with ropes, hoops, balls, clubs, or ribbon.

ring Men perform various maneuvers from two wooden rings suspended from cables, keeping the rings still.

sports acrobatics Sequences of somersaults, tumbling routines, balance routines, and jumps.

trampolining Single gymnasts bounce on a trampoline (tough canvas sheet suspended by springs or cords) and perform aerial tumbling maneuvers.

ON WHEELS

roller skating Men, women, and teams race counterclockwise around an oval track. Artistic skating includes figure, pair, and dance.

skateboarding In bowl riding, a concrete bowl or pool is used in which to perform acrobatic feats. In flatland freestyle skateboarding, tricks such as headstands, flying turns, and flips are performed.

WATER

diving Competitors perform a set number of voluntary and compulsory dives from springboard and highboard, scoring for performance and difficulty.

ski jump Jumpers take off down a sloping channel known as an in-run. The jumper awarded the most points for distance and style wins.

surfing Competitors ride the crest of a wave toward the shore while standing on a surfboard. They score points for complex maneuvers and length of ride.

synchronized swimming Competing teams form patterns in the water using their bodies.

water skiing A powerboat tows skiers on one or two skis. Events include jumping by means of a ramp; slalom, swinging across six buoys; and trick riding on a straight course. Barefoot water skiing is also an event.

water ski jump Water skiers are pulled onto a ramp by powerboats at set maximum speeds (men, 36 mph (58 km/h); women, 30 mph (48 km/h)), and jump off the end to cover the greatest distance.

OTHER

ballet skiing Skiers perform a free program of maneuvers (such as jumps, spins, and somersaults) on smooth, firm snow, in harmony with their choice of music.

baton twirling Individuals or teams compete at twirling and tossing a baton (a rubber-tipped, thin metal rod). Twirlers often enliven sports events during intermissions.

ice skating Includes single, pair, and precision skating (teams in formation), and ice dancing. Marks are awarded for artistry and technique.

mogul skiing Skiers perform maneuvers off the tops of bumps, or "moguls". on a steep snow slope.

ski jumping Competitors on skis jump from a specially constructed hill down a snow course and are judged on style, technique, and distance covered.

Racing

8115 AIR

air racing Pilots race aerobatic aircraft (any of five different classes) for several laps around courses marked by colored pylons.

ballooning Pilot and crew (up to six) ascend in hot-air balloons competing for altitude, duration, or distance.

gliding Pilots ascend on thermals (currents of warm air) in aircraft without engines to compete for distance, duration, and height.

continued

Racing continued

8115 ANIMAL

camel racing Popular in the Middle East. The racing camel is the dromedary, an Arabian (one humped) camel bred for the purpose.
greyhound racing Betting event in which dogs dash out of traps to chase a mechanical hare around an oval track for up to 1200 yds (1.1 km).
harness racing Horses pull a driver in a sulky (light two-wheeled vehicle). Horses are classified as trotters or pacers, according to their gait.
horse racing Jockeys on thoroughbred horses race either around flat courses or over jumps. Steeplechases have fences, hurdle races have hurdles.
ostrich racing Popular racing in North Africa and the Middle East.
pigeon racing Homing pigeons, tagged with a rubber ring, fly from a common release point up to 600 mi (970 km) to their own lofts, and are timed.
show jumping Riders steer their horses around a course with obstacles that have to be jumped. Winners clock the fastest time with the fewest faults.
sled-dog racing Harnessed dog teams drag a sled and driver over a long course of ice and snow. They start at intervals and are timed.

AUTOMOBILE

autocross Cars in various classes compete against the clock over short stretches of rough surfaces. In autograss events, up to 25 cars race at one time.
drag racing High-speed cars sprint over a 440 yd (402 m) paved drag strip to clock the shortest time.
drag racing (motorcycles) Similar to car drag racing, with riders racing in pairs along a straight 440 yd (402 m) track on modified machines.
Formula One (**Grand Prix**) Competition for the World Drivers' Championship and the World Constructors' Championship. Drivers race high-speed cars built to a standard set of specifications.
hill climb Cars compete singly to drive up a tarmac-surfaced hill in the shortest time.
hill trials Cars in three classes drive as far as possible up a steep hill with a passenger "bouncing" the vehicle.
indy car racing Cars resemble Formula One machines, with single seat and open cockpit. Named after Indianapolis 500 in which the first car around 200 laps wins.
karting Karts are the smallest racing vehicles. Drivers race around one of three types of approved track: permanent, round-the-houses or temporary.
off-road racing A wide range of vehicles races for one to 30 hours on courses often located in remote areas.
rallycross Up to six cars from three different groups race against the clock over 1 $^{7}/_{8}$ – 3 mi (3–6 km) on an asphalt, grass, gravel, and loose earth circuit.
rallying Specialy adapted sedan cars race over stages in long routes on public roads. Each car carries a driver and a navigator.
slalom Production and special cars compete in maneuverability, forward, and reverse, through markers on a course.
soap box derby Coasting race for small racing cars without engines, built by the contestants. Age limits 10–15.
sportscar racing Events for production sports cars and special sports-racing cars, usually held on roads or combined roads and tracks. They include endurance races such as Le Mans 24-hour race.
stock car racing Specialy modified, powerful, late-model sedans race around an oval track. UK stock car racing allows contact between vehicles.

MOTORCYCLE

grasstrack racing Solo and sidecar variants of speedway or road racing on grass.
ice racing Individual and team event similar to speedway, on ice. Steel spurs on rear wheels grip the ice.
motocross (scrambles) Motorcycle solo and sidecar events carried out on rough surfaces and tarmac.
speedway Motorcyclists ride around an oval track of ash or shale on light machines up to 500 cc without brakes.
sprint races Races less than 1 mile (1.6 km) long for solo and sidecar machines in a straight line from point to point on a level surface.
trials Events for solo and sidecar machines to test skill rather than speed. Held in stages on roads and rough ground.

WATER

canoe sailing One-person canoes equipped with mast and sails race around a marked triangular course.
canoe slalom Individuals and teams with kayaks and canoes negotiate a rapid river course with hazards.
canoeing Individuals and crews with kayaks and canoes paddle over courses 550 yd (502 m), 1100 yd (1,006 m), and 11,000 yd (10,058 m) long.
Channel swimming Swimmers swim across the English Channel from England to France or vice versa, or both ways nonstop, to clock the shortest time.
powerboat racing Individuals and crews race sportsboats on inland waters, and various types of powerboat at sea.
rowing Individuals and crews propel boats with oars. Sculling, each oarsman has two oars; sweep-oar rowing, each oarsman has one oar. Regattas are knockout competitions; head of the river races are processional.
sailing Cruising or racing in various classes of boats fitted with 1 or more sails, ranging from dinghies of 7.5 ft (2.3 m) to yachts of 80 ft (24 m) or more.
swimming Individuals and teams race over predetermined distances in freestyle, breastroke, butterfly, and backstroke categories, or a medley.
waterskiing Three sections make up a waterskiing competition: jumping, slalom, and trick riding. Individuals compete in all three events.

WINTER

Alpine skiing Includes downhill, slalom, and giant slalom races. Downhill is straight down with control gates; slalom and giant slalom involve twisting courses marked by pairs of flags ("gates").
biathlon Cross-country ski racing combined with marksmanship. Skiers, individual or relay, fire at five targets over courses 4.7 mi (7.5 km) to 12 mi (20 km) long.
bobsleigh racing Teams of two or four men race down a steep icy course, at least 1,640 yd (1,500 m) long with at least 15 banked curves, in racing sleds.
iceboating Competitors race in light craft, that look like sailboats with runners, over smooth stretches of ice about 1 mile (1.6 km) long.
Nordic skiing Includes cross-country and ski jumping. Cross-country races are held over courses from 3 mi (5 km) to 30 mi (50 km) long.
skibob racing Competitors on skibobs (vehicles made of two short skis with handles and seat) race down a marked snow course as fast as possible.
snowmobiling Competitors on snowmobiles (sled-sized vehicles on two short skis powered

continued

Racing continued

8115 by a small rear engine) race over snow-covered tracks.
speed skating Two skaters race counterclockwise on an oval ice track over varying distances. Fastest time wins.
tobogganing Coasting downhill, over snow or ice, on toboggans (sleds without runners).

OTHER
cycle racing Road races may be over 1,800 miles (3,000 km), raced in stages. Track racing machines have no free wheel, gears, or brakes.
grass skiing Rules as for Alpine skiing. Competitors race on short skis fitted with rollers or caterpillar tracks.
roller-cycling Roller-cyclists ride normal, but stationary, bicycles mounted on rollers. The rollers turn to record the "distance" the cyclist has traveled.
skateboarding In the slalom, competitors race downhill and negotiate lines of cones. In downhill events, skateboarders race one another directly over any distance from a few hundred yards (or meters) to several miles (or kilometers).

Target

8116 **crossbow archery** Archery that involves shooting square-headed arrows from a crossbow (a small bow fitted across a wooden stock).
darts Old English "pub" game with many variants. Competitors score points by throwing darts at a dartboard divided into numbered wedges and rings.
field archery Competitors walk around an open field and shoot at butts (woven straw mats) from various distances.
horseshoe pitching Two, three, or four players pitch horseshoes at stakes planted at alternate ends of a court, and score by getting closest to the stake.
pistol shooting Marksmen and women fire 60 shots at five targets from 27 yd (25 m) using 0.22 caliber automatic pistols or revolvers.
practical shooting Events recreate hostile encounter situations, and include rapid-fire exercises, and assault courses, and are shot in the fastest possible time. Pistols, rifles, and shotguns are used.
quoits Two or four players toss quoits (metal rings) to get nearest to a mott (peg) which is level with the ground and surrounded by a white target.
rifle shooting Competitors fire shots at targets to record the highest score. Weapons used may be smallbore, bigbore, or air rifles, and positions may be prone, kneeling, or standing.
target archery Competitors shoot a certain number of arrows from different distances at targets marked with concentric color zones for scoring.
tournament casting Competitors use various forms of angling equipment to cast at a circular target set on the ground 20–80 ft (6–24 m) away.
trapshooting (clay pigeon or shotgun shooting) Competitors shoot at clay discs or "pigeons" thrown into the air by a machine. Rules vary according to skeet, Olympic trench, or down-the-line shooting.

Miscellaneous

8117 **rafting** Crews of up to six float down river, often on white water, usually in inflatable rubber rafts.
birling Lumberjacks spin floating logs with their feet.
bullfighting Contest, popular in Spanish-speaking countries and Portugal, in which a bullfighter and assistants, sometimes mounted on horseback, bait and usually kill a bull.
caber tossing The competitor cradles the base of a section of tree trunk (the "caber"), makes a run, and tries to pitch it so that it will land with the base pointing away from the thrower.
caving, or spelunking Climbing in caverns below the ground.
falconry Keeping and training falcons, hawks, or eagles to hunt game. Birds are trained to return to the falconer's fist or a lure.
fishing (angling) Catching fish with baited hook, line, and rod. Includes game fishing (salmon and trout), coarse fishing (carp family), sea fishing (in shallow waters), and big-game fishing (deep water for shark, tuna, etc.).
foxhunting (riding to hounds) Men and women on horseback follow a pack of foxhounds across open country, chasing foxes by scent.
frisbee In ultimate frisbee, a team tries to pass the frisbee to a player who is across the opponents' goal line. In guts, the frisbee is thrown back and forth, and a team scores if the opponents make a bad throw, or fail to catch a good one.
hiking Walking alone or with others, especially in the country, for an hour or two or up to several weeks. Backpacking hikers carry food, clothing, and shelter on their backs.
hunting Hunters use rifles to shoot wild animals such as bears, moose, wild boar, birds, and deer. Specialy trained gundogs sometimes help to retreive. Most countries impose strict quotas.
mountaineering Climbing and exploring mountains (including rock climbing), which calls for skill, daring, and equipment such as nylon ropes, crampons, and special clothing.
powerlifting Men of similar body weights attempt to lift the heaviest weighted bar by one of three lifts: squat, bench press, or dead lift.
ringette Team sport for girls and women similar to hockey. Opposing teams of six players on skates try to drive a hollow rubber ring into a goal.
shuffleboard Two opposing players or teams use cues (long-handled sticks) to push plastic discs into numbered scoring sections at each end of a flat, slick court.
skin diving Snorkeling usually includes face mask, swim fins, and snorkel (breathing tube); scuba diving uses portable metal tanks of compressed air.
spearfishing Hunting fish underwater with a gun that shoots a spear. Other equipment includes a face mask, snorkel (breathing tube), and swim fins.
steel strandpulling Competitors stretch a set of coiled steel strands using handles attached at each end. There are 20 official "pulls" using this equipment.
tug of war Teams of eight members tug at opposite ends of a long rope, each trying to pull the other out of position. The winner is decided on the best of three pulls.
weightlifting Athletes of similar body weights compete to lift the heaviest weighted bar by one of two methods: the snatch, and the clean and jerk.

821 ATHLETICS

History

8211 The first Olympic Games in Greece in 776 BC featured a foot race as the only event. Track and field was introduced into England in the 1100s, but the sport did not gain popularity until the 1800s. In 1868, the New York Athletics Club sponsored the first US amateur meet indoors. In 1896, the first modern Olympic Games took place in Athens, Greece. In 1912, 12 countries formed the International Amateur Athletic Federation (IAAF) to govern men's track and field athletics.

Rules

8212 **Objectives** To run or walk fastest, throw or jump farthest, or jump highest, according to the event.
Equipment Baton for relay races; hurdles for hurdle races and steeplechase; discus and safety cage for discus throw; hammer and safety cage for hammer throw; bar and uprights for high jump and pole vault (and pole for the latter); javelin for javelin throw, sand pits for long jump and triple jump; shot for shot-put; spiked running shoes for running races; numbered shirts; starting pistol; tape for finishing line; electronic timing apparatus; starting blocks.

The athletics arena

8213 Races of different lengths end at the same point (**F**) on a standard 400 m (438 yd) track and so must start at different points.

Sprints
1 110 m (120 yd)
2 100 m (109 yd)
3 200 m (219 yd)
Middle-distance races
4 400 m (437 yd)
5 800 m (875 yd)
6 1,500 m (1,641 yd)
Long-distance races
8 3,000 m (3,282 yd) and 5,000 m (5,468 yd)
9 10,000 m (10,940 yd)
Hurdles
2 100 m (109 yd)
1 110 m (120 yd)
7 3,000 m steeplechase (3,281 yd)
Relay
4 4 x 100 m (4 x 109 yd)
Walking races and marathons These start and finish in the stadium but are mainly run outside.
Field event locations
10 Pole vault
11 Hammer
12 Discus
13 Shot put
14 High jump
15 Javelin
16 Long jump and triple jump
F Finish for all races

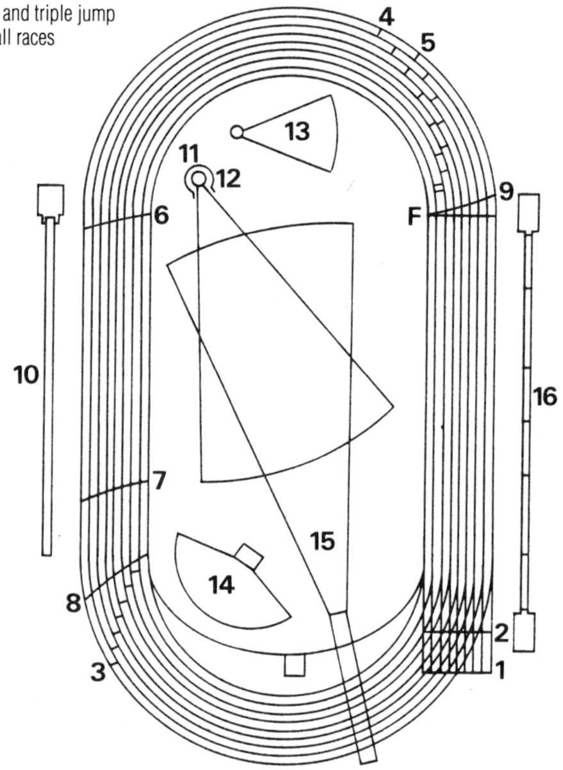

Types

8214 TRACK
Athletes start from a crouched position with their feet against running blocks. Programs are made up of:
hurdle events In hurdle events there are ten hurdles over which the competitors must jump to complete the race. The Olympic steeplechase is a men's event in which participants must jump 28 hurdles and seven water jumps.
long distance races Races run at 3,000 m, 5,000 m, and 10,000 m.
middle distance races Races run at 800 m, and 1,500 m.
relay races In relay races a team has four members, each of whom runs a stage of the race, and then hands on a smooth, hollow baton to the next teammate.
sprint events Races run at 100 m, 200 m, and 400 m.
walking events These are held on tracks or roads. The walker's rear foot must not leave the ground until the front one touches the ground. The leg must briefly straighten while the foot is on the ground.

FIELD
Programs involve throwing events and jumping for distance and height, and include:
Discus Disc-shaped object thrown from a circle to try for the longest throw.
Hammer Metal ball weighing at least 16 lb (7.26 kg), attached to a steel wire, is whirled around the thrower's head three or four times and then released to try for the longest throw.
High jump Jumper jumps over a thin crossbar held between two upright posts. He or she tries to jump the greatest height without knocking the crossbar down.
Javelin The thrower runs down a short runway to hurl a spear for the longest throw. He or she must not cross the throwing line and the spear must land point first.
Long jump Jumper sprints down a long runway and leaps off a take off board into a sandpit for the longest jump.
Pole vault Vaulter, with the aid of a long, flexible pole, tries to clear a high crossbar held between two rigid uprights.
Shot-put Athlete presses against the neck a metal ball, weighing at least 16 lb (7.26 kg) for men and 8lb 13oz (4 kg) for women, and thrusts it forward and upward for the greatest distance.
Triple jump Jumper sprints down a long runway and jumps from a take off board, then hops, skips, and jumps in one continous movement into a sandpit. Formerly called "hop, skip and jump."

Combined events

8215 Combined events competitions are made up of a number of events. The decathlon is a men's competition of ten events, and the heptathlon a women's competition of seven events. Competitors score points for their performance in each event.

Decathlon
First day
1 100 m
2 Long jump
3 Shot put
4 High jump
5 400 m

Second day
6 110 m hurdles
7 Discus
8 Pole vault
9 Javelin
10 1,500 m

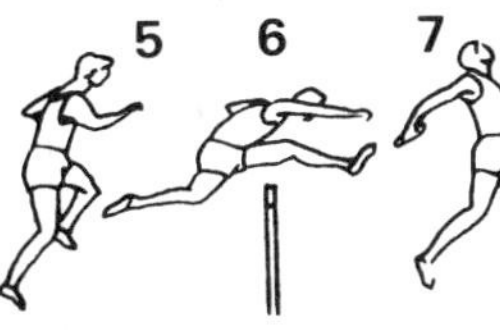

Heptathlon
First day
1 100 m hurdles
2 High jump
3 Shot put
4 200 m
Second day
5 Long jump
6 Javelin
7 800 m

Participants

8216 Listed here are the main athletics events. The chart shows in which of them men and women participate.

Sprints

	men	women
100m	●	●
200m	●	●
400m	●	●

Middle distance

	men	women
800m	●	●
1500m	●	●

Long distance

	men	women
3000m		●
5000m	●	
10 000m	●	●

Relays

	men	women
4x100m	●	●
4x400m	●	●

Hurdle

	men	women
100m		●
110m	●	
400m	●	●

Steeplechase

	men	women
3000m	●	

Road races

	men	women
Marathon	●	●

Walks

	men	women
10km		●
20km	●	
50km	●	

Throwing events

	men	women
Javelin	●	●
Shot	●	●
Discus	●	●
Hammer	●	

Jumping events

	men	women
High jump	●	●
Pole vault	●	
Long jump	●	●
Triple jump	●	

Combined events

	men	women
Decathlon	●	
Heptathlon		●

Key words

8217 **baton** Short bar carried by runners in a relay race.
cage A net cage within which discus and hammer events are undertaken.
cat jump An early style of high jumping.
eastern cut-off An old style of high jumping in which a jumper twists the top part of the body to face the bar as he or she goes over it.
final Last round of any event.
Fosbury flop The modern style of high jumping in which an athlete jumps head first over a bar, with the back to the bar.
heats Preliminary races to eliminate slower runners in crowded events.
lap One circuit of the track.
leg The distance run by each competitor in relay.
mile Only non-metric race still featured in many major meets.
no-jump A disallowed trial in the jumping events.
octathlon Indoor contest for men, consisting of eight events.
"spikes" Popular name for spiked athletic shoes used to improve grip. The number and size of spikes is strictly controlled.
split times Times taken at different stages of a race to determine whether the winning team will be fast or slow.
staggered start For races run around bends, starts are staggered so that all runners cover the same distance.
starting blocks Rigid blocks positioned at the start of each race in each lane from which competitors must begin their race.
steeplechase A men's 3,000 m race in which runners must clear hurdles and water jumps.
straddle An old style of high jumping in which a jumper takes off from the foot nearest to the bar, crossing it stomach downward in a draped position.
take-over zone An area in relay racing in which the baton must change hands.
trial An attempt to jump or throw; also qualifying rounds for inclusion in, for example, an Olympic team.
western roll A high jumping style in which the jumper crosses the bar, facing it, with the side of the body.

831 BOXING

History

8311 Modern boxing evolved from brutal bare-knuckle contests held in England from the 1600s onward. Such fights became popular in the United States in the 1800s, although they were usually illegal. In the 1860s, England's Marquess of Queensbury sponsored a more civilized code of 12 boxing rules that is still in use today. In 1920, the Walker Law legitimized the sport in the US.

Rules

8312 **Number of boxers** Two.
Objective To win the bout on points by punching more effectively than the opponent, to force him to give up the fight, or to knock him down for at least 10 sec. At the same time, a boxer tries to protect his head and body from the opponent's punches.
Equipment Gloves of padded leather weighing 8 or 10 oz (227 or 283.5 g). Lightweight boots. Cup (athletic protector) to protect the sex organs. Gumshield (rubber mouthpiece) to protect the teeth. Amateurs wear undershirt and shorts and protective, padded headgear; professionals fight bare-chested.
Duration Professionals: 3 min each round, championships usually lasting 12 rounds. Amateurs: usually 2 to 3 min each round, bouts lasting three rounds. There is a 1 min rest period between rounds.

Professional weight categories
Flyweight: up to 112 lb (51 kg)
Bantamweight: up to 118 lb (53 kg)
Featherweight: up to 126 lb (57 kg)
Lightweight: up to130 lb (59 kg)
Welterweight: up to 147 lb (67 kg)
Middleweight: up to 160 lb (73 kg)
Light heavyweight: up to 175 lb (79 kg)
Heavyweight: more than 195 lb (88 kg)

The ring

8313 Early boxers fought surrounded by spectators with nothing separating the two. In the frenzy aroused by the money bet on the fight, crowds often interrupted fights. To stop this, elevated, roped-off rings were introduced in the 18th century. Modern rings – at least 16 ft (4.9 m) square for amateurs, 14 ft (4.3 m) for professionals, 20 ft (6 m) maximum – have three or four ropes and a canvas-covered floor underlaid with rubber felt.
Officials
A referee (**1**) enforces rules, cautions for offenses, and ensures each boxer is fit to box. Judges (**2**), score the boxers' fighting skills. A timekeeper (**3**) starts and ends bouts. Amateur boxers have an official second (**4**) and an assistant to encourage and coach in intervals; up to four seconds may aid a professional. Seconds may not coach during bouts, and must leave the ring if instructed to do so by the referee; seconds may administer certain types of first aid during intervals.

Key words

8314

below the belt Foul punch below the waistline, especially in the groin area.
break Come out of a clinch.
canvas The floor of the ring.
clinch Holding on to an opponent.
cross Counter-punch crossing over the opponent's head.
decision Official verdict to determine the winner.
distance The full number of rounds.
hook Bent-arm punch thrown from the side at close range (**1**).
infighting Close-range fighting.
jab Light, straight punch by the leading arm (**2**).
knockout (KO) End of the fight, when one boxer is knocked unconscious or is floored for at least 10 sec.
neutral corner One of two corners not used for resting between rounds. When one boxer is floored, his opponent must retire to neutral corner while the referee counts.
points win Victory by scoring more points (more punches landing on the target area).
purse Prize money for the boxers.
rabbit punch Foul punch landing on the back of the neck (**3**).
reach Length of a boxer's arms.
ring Three-roped square platform with a post at each corner.
round One of several periods of boxing during a bout.
southpaw Left-handed boxer who leads with his right hand and right foot forward.
spar To practice boxing, or threaten punches.
target area Any part of the front or sides of the head or body above the belt line.
technical knockout (TKO) Referee's decision to stop the fight because one boxer can no longer defend himself.
throw in the towel Act of throwing a towel into the ring by a boxer's seconds in order to stop the fight and save him further punishment.
uppercut Bent-arm punch delivered upward to the chin (**4**).
weigh-in Weighing of boxers before a fight to check that they are within the correct limits.

832 ORIENTAL MARTIAL ARTS

History

8321 The main forms of Japanese armed and unarmed combat have been developed from jujitsu, the fighting art of an ancient warrior caste known as the samurai. These include judo, karate, aikido, and kendo. Kung fu, a Chinese form of self-defense, is closely related to karate. Most of these forms of combat are associated with distinct philosophies.

Judo was developed in the late 1800s by Professor Joigoro Kano. Karate originated with a Buddhist priest in the AD 400s and later surfaced on the Japanese island of Okinawa in the 1600s. Aikido developed in the 1100s from the *daitoryu* school of jujitsu. Professor Morihei Uyeshiba established the modern school of aikido in the early 1900s. The origins of kendo date back to the 400s, and 20th century exponents still wear the traditional dress of the samurai period. Kung fu, or Chinese karate, was popularized by the US actor Bruce Lee in the 1960s.

Weapons

8322 In sport karate and judo the main scoring "weapons" are:
1 The knuckles of the first and middle fingers of the fist
2 The heel
3 The side of the foot
4 The ball of the foot
5 The instep

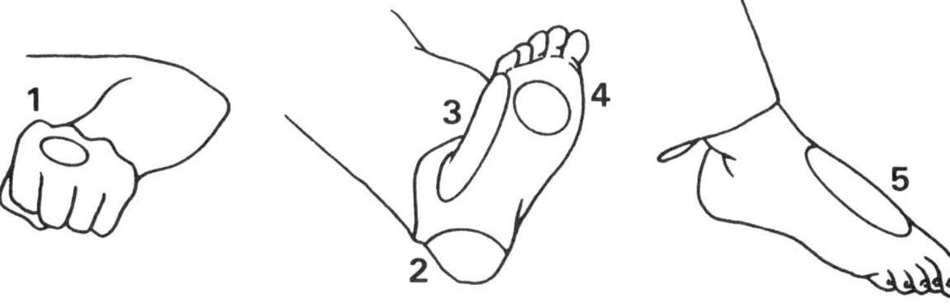

Karate

8323 RULES

Number of contestants Two individuals or teams.

Objective To be the first to score one full point by controlled techniques of punches, blows, strikes, and kicks having a focus within 2 in (5 cm) of the target area, although light bodily contact is permitted.

Equipment White costume with colored belt. Identified by white or red string fastened to the belt.

Duration Usually 2 min but may be extended to 3 or 5 min.

MATCH AREA

The match area is a flat surface, 26 ft (8 m) square, with two starting lines marked on the match area.
1 Competitors' starting lines
2 Referee
3 Judges
4 Arbitrator(s), record keeper(s), timekeeper(s) and caller(s).

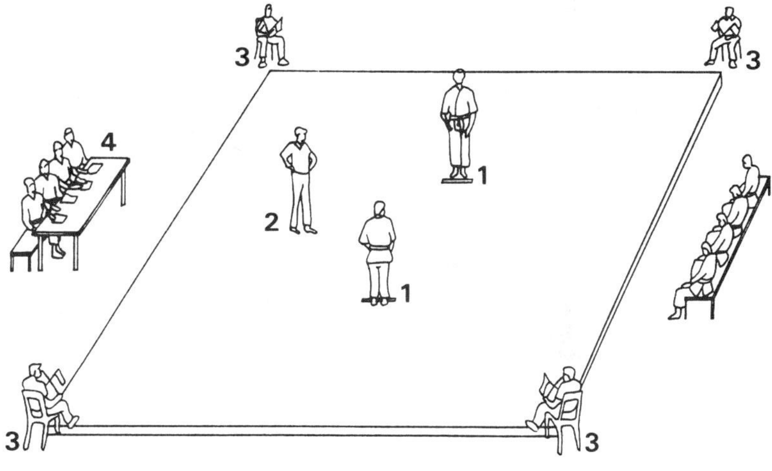

SCORING

To win, a fighter must score three ippons (three full points) or six waza-ari (six half points). An ippon-winning blow (**1**, **2**, **3**) must have vigor, correct timing and distancing, good attitude, and constant alertness. No ippon is awarded (**4**, **5**, **6**) if an attacker does not deliver a blow the moment he or she throws or seizes an opponent, or if fighters score at the same time.

KEY WORDS

belt Beginners wear white belts. They graduate through yellow, orange, green, blue, and brown to black (expert).
dan One of 12 top grades for proficiency.
dojo Practice hall.
hanteigachi Superiority of a contestant.
karate-gi White costume.
yame referee's call for temporary halt.

Judo

8324 RULES

Number of contestants Two.
Objective To hold or throw the opponent by means of superior strength and balance.
Equipment White or off-white costume of jacket with loose sleeves, loose trousers, long belt, and white or red sash.
Scoring By half points and points. One whole point means an outright win. Penalties are imposed for fouls.
Duration Minimum 3 min, maximum 20 min.

THE MAT

In international competitions the contest area (shiajo) is a 33 x 33 ft (10 x 10 m) or 29 x 29 ft (9 x 9 m) mat (**1**) around which there is a red danger area (**2**). This is surrounded by a safety area of green matting (**3**) to prevent injuries.

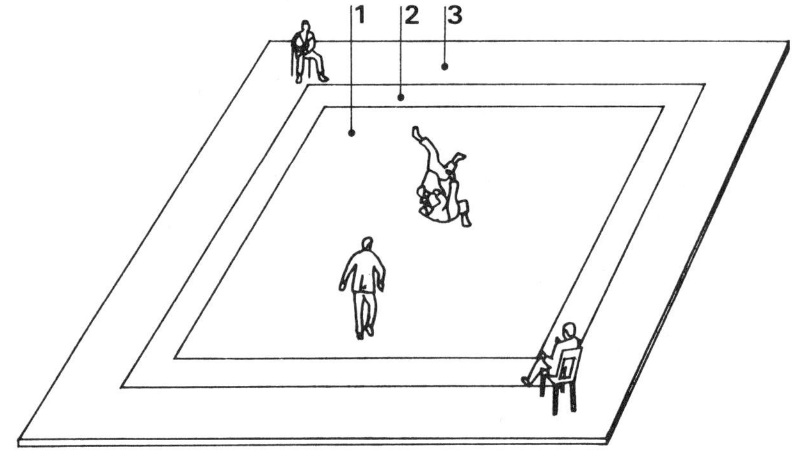

SCORING

Contestants are judged on throwing technique (negewaza) and holding technique (katemewaza). Violations are also a determining factor. By achieving an ippon (one point) a competitor wins outright. Ippon is awarded for:
1 A throw of considerable force
2 Lifting the opponent from the mat to shoulder height
3 Making an effective stranglehold or lock; maintaining a hold for 30 seconds.

KEY WORDS

atemiwaza Technique of striking or kicking to disable the opponent.
belt Color of belts show proficiency of contestants.
chui One of four penalties awarded for infringements.
dan One of 12 top grades for proficiency.
dojo Practice hall.
hajime refereee's call to start the match.
hansokomake Disqualification.
judogi Costume.
judoka Learners.
kanstsuwaza Joint lock.
kata Two fighters display routine of attack and defense in formal competition.
katamewaza Holding technique.
keioku One of four penalties for infringements.
matte Referee's call for a temporary halt.
nagewaza Throwing technique.
ne-waza Ground technique.
randori Free fighting.
shai A contest.
shiaijo Contest area.
shido Minor penalty for infringement.
sono-mama Referee's command to "freeze."
tachiwaza Standing or throwing techniques.
yame Referee's call for temporary halt.
tsurikomishi-ashi Footsweep maneuver.
utsuri-goshi A maneuver known as countering.

Aikido

8325 RULES

Consists of four kinds of competition. Kata, a formal event; ninin dori, tanto randori, randori kyoghi are three types of fighting event.
Number of contestants Two or three.
Objective To score points either as attacker or defender by strikes, throws, or avoiding action.
Equipment As for judo. In tanto randori the attacker is armed with a rubber knife.
Scoring By half points and points. One whole point means an outright win, Penalties are imposed for fouls.
Duration Minimum 3 min, maximum 5 min per bout.

AREA

The aikido area is at least 29 ft (9 m) square.
1 Senior judge
2 Assistant judges
3 Scorer
4 Timekeeper

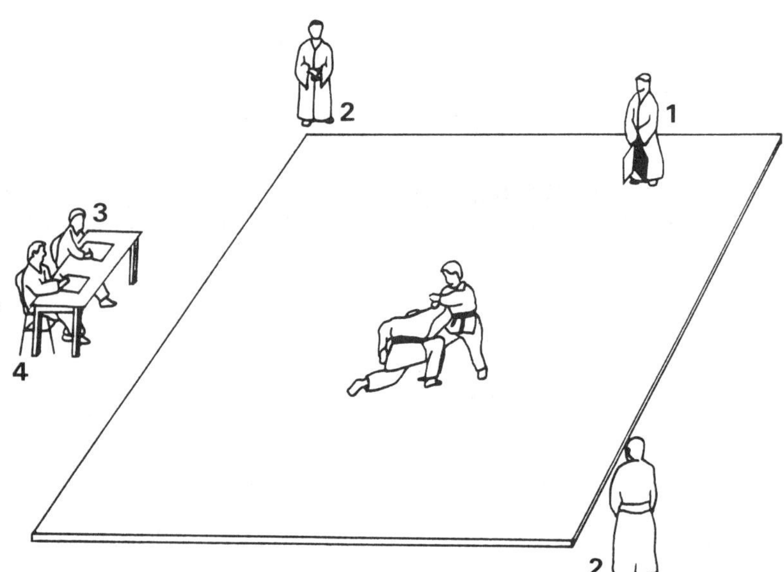

continued

Aikido continued

8325 KEY WORDS

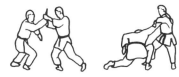

hajime Referee's call to start the match.
hikiwake A draw.
kata Two fighters display routine of attack and defense in formal competition (**1**).
matte Referee's call for a temporary halt.
ninin dori Three contestants in a mock fight (**2**).
randori kyoghi Free fighting for one round between two unarmed contestants.
score-made Finish of a round or a fight.
tanto randori Free fighting between two contestants (**3**).
tomiki Free contests, armed and unarmed.
uyeshiba Formalized exhibition with no competition.
waza-ari Half a point.
yame Referee's call for temporary halt.

1

2

3

Kendo

8326 RULES

Number of contestants Two.
Equipment Bamboo swords, mask, gauntlets, breastplate, apron, shirt, long divided skirt, toweling headcloth.
Objective To score the most points, which are awarded for correctly delivered sword cuts.
Scoring Winner is the first to score two points.
Duration 3 or 5 min.

AREA
Kendo is fought on a smooth wooden floor, with an area 32 ft 9 in or 36 ft (10 m or 11 m) square bordered by two lines and a wide space (**1**). Two starting lines are marked on the floor (**2**) and a cross or circle marks the center (**3**).

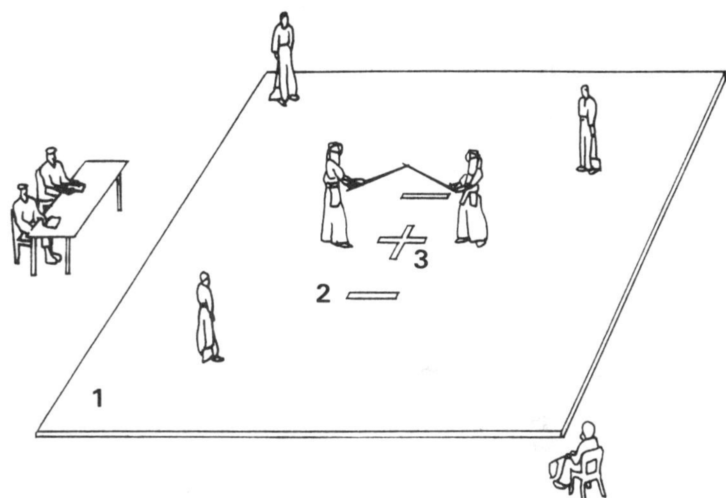

KEY WORDS
do Breastplate.
hachimaki Toweling headcloth.
hajime Refereee's call to start the match.
hikiwake A draw.
keikogi Shirt.
kote Gauntlets.
men mask.
nikomme Re-start after one point has been scored.
shinai Bamboo sword.
shobu Re-start after each contestant has won one point.
tare Apron.

833 WRESTLING

History

8331 Murals in French caves, some 20,000 years old, show wrestlers in action. Wrestling was also a favorite Egyptian sport around 2000 BC. The sport was introduced into the ancient Olympic Games in the early 700s BC, and was regarded as a knightly pastime in the Middle Ages. Amateur wrestling, both freestyle and Greco-Roman, has formed part of the modern Olympic Games since 1904. Professional wrestling is today largely a predetermined exhibition of highly skilled clowning.
Wrestling is a male sport, but sambo (Russian wrestling) is open to women.

Rules

8332 The two main styles are freestyle and Greco-Roman. In Greco-Roman, contestants are not allowed to seize their opponents below the hips nor to grip with the legs.
Number of wrestlers Two, dressed in red or blue, respectively.
Objective To win the bout by a fall (pinning both the opponent's shoulders simultaneously on the mat) or on points. Points are awarded for placing an opponent in danger (of a fall) or for obtaining a correct hold. Penalty points are given for passivity, foul holds, and other infringements.
Equipment A 39 ft 3 in (12 m) square mat enclosing a circular contest area 29 ft 6 in (9 m) in diameter. Within the contest area is a small center circle 39 in (1 m) in diameter. Bouts start from the center of the mat. Dress consists of red or blue leotards, athletic support, shoes without heels or buckles; no oil or grease on the bodies.
Duration The bout is 5 min without a break.
Officials Four: a referee, mat chairman, judge, and timekeeper. The mat chairman is the chief official with the final decision.

The mat

8333 The ring (**3**) in the middle of an international contest mat is 29 ft 6 in (9 m) in diameter. The mat may be raised on a platform (**1**). The two diagonaly opposite corners (**2**) of the 39 ft (12 m) square mat are red and blue. A circle, 3 ft 3 in (1 m) in diameter, is marked in the center of the ring (**5**), enclosed by a 23 ft (7 m) wide rim (**4**).

Amateur wrestling weight limits (kg)

Light flyweight	106 lb	(48 kg)
Flyweight	115 lb	(52 kg)
Bantamweight	126 lb	(57 kg)
Featherweight	137 lb	(62 kg)
Lightweight	150 lb	(68 kg)
Welterweight	163 lb	(74 kg)
Middleweight	181 lb	(82 kg)
Light heavyweight	198 lb	(90 kg)
Heavyweight	220 lb	(100 kg)
Heavyweight plus	over 220 lb	(over 100 kg)
Superheavyweight	287 lb	(130 kg)

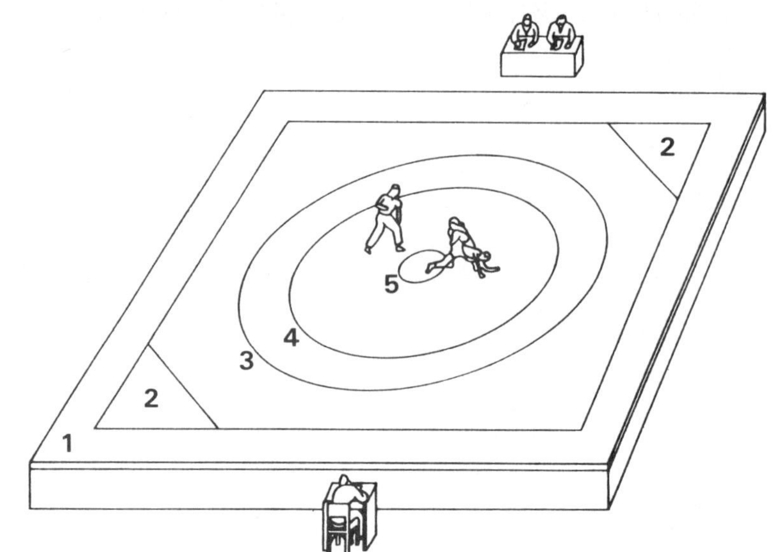

Maneuvers

8334 **Sparring positions** The starting stance (**1**).
Tie-up Two wrestlers come to grips in a standing position (**2**); a common way of starting a bout.
Drag and trip A contestant rolls down his opponent's arm (**3**), catches it in his hand, trips his opponent with his leg, and pushes him over one leg (**4**).
Reverse half nelson A contestant locks his leg around his opponent's (**5**), pulls his oppnent's arm over his head (**6**), and lies back (**7**) to turn his opponent's shoulders onto the mat for a fall (**8**).
Pull-by A contestant grabs his opponent's arm (**9**), turns as he pulls him in (**10**) and drags him down with one arm (**11**). He grasps his opponent's thigh with his other arm (**12**) and hooks a leg over his opponent's other leg as he swings him over (**13**).

Key words

8335 **all-in (catch-as-catch-can)** Type of professional wrestling that allows many holds and tricks forbidden in the amateur sport, and which relies largely on showmanship and entertainment value.
catch-as-catch-can See All-in.
Cumberland and Westmorland Style of English wrestling in which the contestants clasp their hands around each other's bodies and hold on. The loser is the one who breaks his hold or touches the ground with any part of his body except his feet.
passivity zone Red strip 1 yd (1 m) wide inside the 10-yd (9 m) wrestling circle to show the wrestlers that they are close to the outer limits of the circle.
pin (fall) Holding the opponent's shoulders on the mat, thus ending the contest.
ride One of a number of methods by which a wrestler attempts to control the movements of his opponent.
sambo Russian style of jacket wrestling similar to judo. The only form of wrestling open to women.
sumo Japanese style of wrestling in which two giants try to force each other out of the 15 ft (4.6 m) ring, or push any part of the opponent's body except his feet onto the mat.
switch A swift method of changing defense into offense through arm leverage.
Take-down Any move that brings a wrestler down onto the mat from a standing position.

841 GYMNASTICS

History

8411 Gymnastics derives from the Greek word *gymnos* (naked), and the word "gymnasium" originally meant a public place or building where Greek youths exercised. Most of the current competitive exercises may be attributed to the German, Jahn, but the origin of the sport can be traced back to the ancient civilizations of China, Persia, and India, as well as Greece. Gymnastics became a true world-wide sport after the Second World War, with the introduction of women's events and the staging of the biennial world and European championships. The sport has been dominated by Russia, Japan, the former Czechoslovakia, and, since the 1960s, East Germany (now part of Germany).

Rules

8412 **Officials** Four judges score each event independently, supervised by one superior judge (two in men's individual finals).
Scoring Highest and lowest scores of four judges discarded, and middle two scores averaged to give recorded score. Each exercise scored from 1 to 10, with deduction of whole, half, and one-tenth points. All disciplines, except for sports acrobatics, involve compulsory exercises, set for a period of four years, and designed to test gymnasts' control, and mastery of specific skills. Further voluntary exercises give gymnast opportunity to display his or her own area of expertise.
In team competition, the six members of each team perform a compulsory and optional exercise on each apparatus. The five highest scores are added to give the team total (maximum points: men 600, women 400). In individual combined events (all-around) competition, the 36 leading gymnasts in the team competition perform an optional exercise on each apparatus (maximum points: men 60, women 40). In individual events competitions, the eight competitors with the highest total on each individual apparatus from the team competition compete again for the individual apparatus title. The maximum score for both men and women is 10.

Disciplines

8413 Each discipline has its own specific requirements in terms of apparatus, style of performance, and judging criteria.
Artistic gymnastics Women use vault, asymmetric bars, balanced beam, and floor. Men use floor, side or pommel horse, rings, vault, parallel bars, and horizontal or high bar. Competitors perform compulsory and optional movements on each apparatus.
Rhythmic gymnastics Floorwork only, performed to music with or without ropes, hoops, clubs, and ribbons. Gymnasts may perform individually or in groups. Individual exercises must include jumps and leaps, balances, pivots, and flexibility (fundamental groups of body movements), as well as various methods of traveling, skips and hops, swings and circles, turns, and waves (other groups). In group work, groups of six gymnasts perform together using either six pieces of identical apparatus, or three pieces of one type of apparatus and three of another, e. g., three hoops and three ropes. Judges assess gymnasts on the basis of body movement and specific apparatus, in addition to exchanges of apparatus, and changes of formation of gymnasts.
Sports acrobatics Governed by separate International Federation for Sports Acrobatics (IFSA), founded in 1973. Comprises two main sections: tumbling, for women and men; and pair and group work: men's and women's pairs, mixed pairs (one man/one woman), women's trio, and men's four. There are two basic routines for pair and group work: balance and tempo routines. The combined routine contains elements from both these categories. Except for the men's four balance, all routines are performed to music.

Equipment

8414 **1 Rings** Two rings suspended at same height from frame 19 ft 2 in (575 cm) high.
2 Reuther board Springboard used with horse.
3 Side or pommel horse Stands at 3 ft 10 in (115 cm), with two grips on top.
4 Horse Vaulting apparatus, 4 ft (120 cm) high for women (with springboard placed in line with short axis of horse), and 4 ft 5 in (135 cm) high for men (with springboard placed in line with long axis of horse).
5 Parallel bars Two wooden laminated bars placed parallel to each other and at same height.
6 Horizontal or high bar Equipment made of high tensile steel, and 8 ft 2 in (275 cm) high.
7 Uneven bars Two wooden laminated bars placed parallel to each other and at different heights.
8 Balance beam Suede-covered beam 16 ft x 3 in x 4 in (5 m x 7.5 cm x 10 cm), standing at 3 ft 11 in (120 cm).
9 Rope Made of hemp or similar synthetic material, without handles and proportionate to size of gymnast.
10 Ribbon Made up of stick attached to ribbon. Stick made of wood, plastic, or fiberglass, length: 20–24 in (50–60 cm); diameter: 0.5 in (1 cm) maximum at widest part. Ribbon made of satin or similar material, length: 20 ft (6 m); width: 1–2 in (4–6 cm); weight: 1.25 oz (35 g) minimum.
11 Hoop Made of wood or plastic. Interior diameter: 31–35 in (80–90 cm).
12 Ball Made of rubber or similar synthetic. Interior diameter: 7–8 in (18–20 cm); weight: 14 oz (400 g) minimum.
13 Clubs Made of wood or synthetic material. Length: 16–20 in (40–50 cm); weight: 5 oz (150 g) minimum for each club.

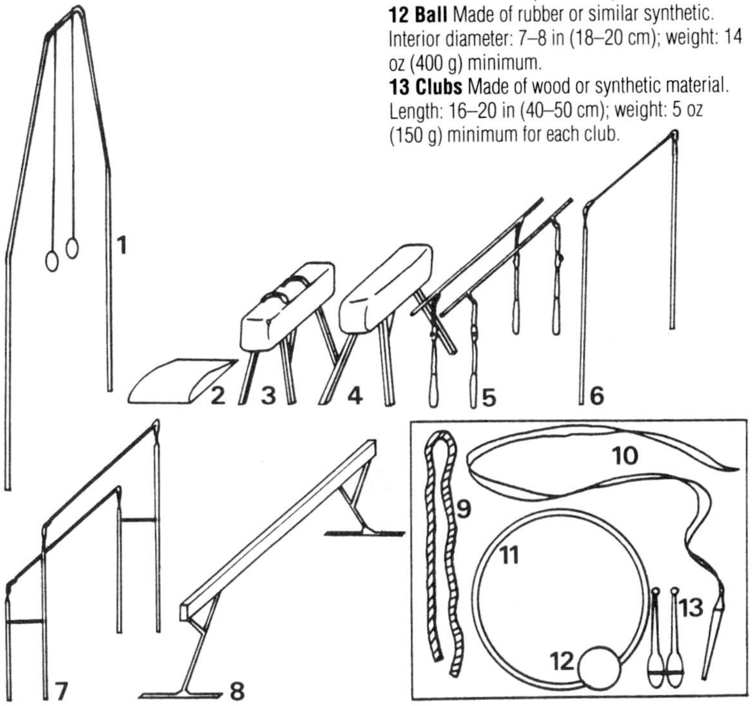

Artistic gymnastics (women)

8415 **Women's vault**
Gymnasts perform one compulsory vault followed by two optional vaults. Vaults are graded for difficulty and divided into eight groups by style. Each vault is divided into four phases for the purposes of evaluation.

Women's uneven bars
Within any routine the gymnast must not perform more than four consecutive exercises on any bar: she must change bar, touch the other bar, or dismount. Routines must involve pirouettes, saltos, swings forward and back, Hecht elements, grip change, flight elements, and kips.

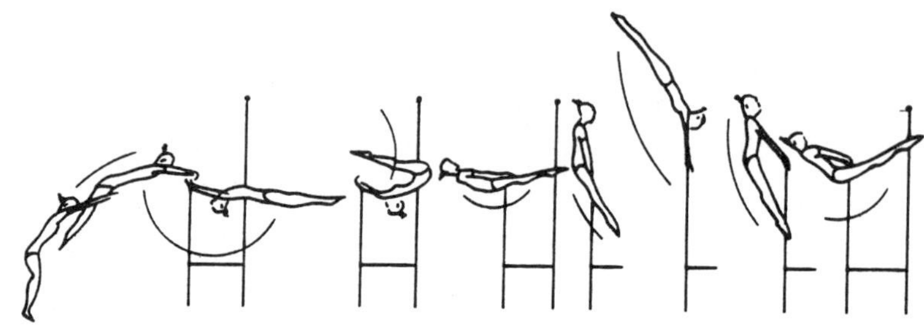

Women's beam
Gymnasts are required to perform a balanced routine of movements lasting between 1 min 10 sec and 1 mi 30 sec and including acrobatic, strength, gymnastic, and dance elements.

Women's floor exercises
Performed to music, the gymnast must complete one compulsory set of exercises followed by an optional routine. Each must include acrobatic, strength, gymnastic, and dance elements.

Artistic gymnastics (men)

8416 **Men's floor exercises**
These are shorter in duration than women's floor exercises and are not performed to music. They must include acrobatics, strength, and a balance exercise on one arm or one leg.

Men's rings
The exercise on rings should be composed of strength, swing, and held positions in about equal proportions. Competitors first perform a compulsory exercise, followed by an optional exercise.

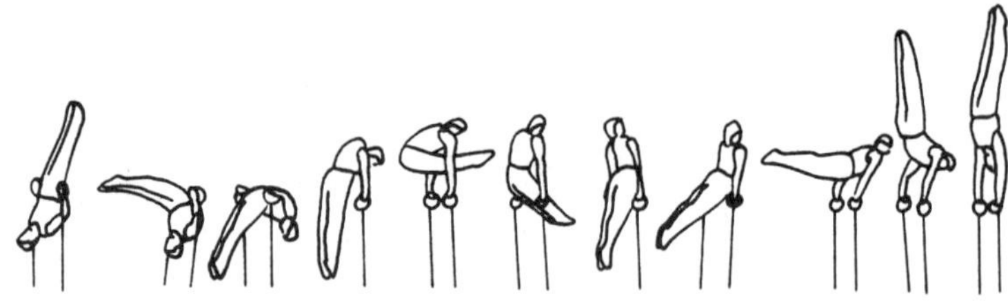

Men's vault
Competitors must select and perform a vault from a list of vaults graded for difficulty.

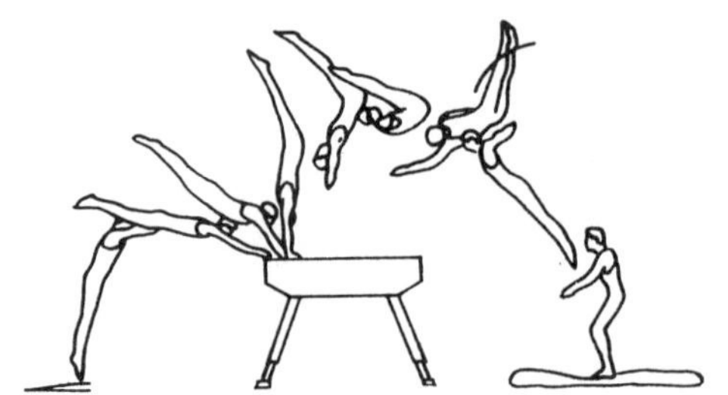

continued

Artistic gymnastics (men) continued

8416 **Men's parallel bars**
Participants perform one compulsory exercise and one optional exercise. Both must consist of support, hang, swing, and balance movements.

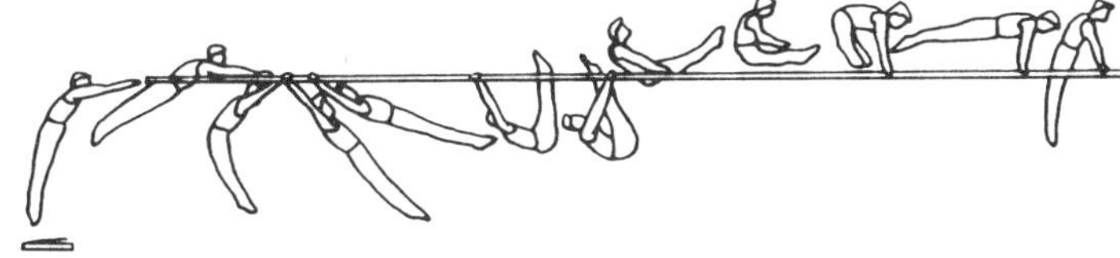

Men's horizontal bar
Competitors perform one compulsory routine, followed by an optional routine. Both must comprise uninterrupted swinging movements both back and forth, and near and far from the bar, and must involve some flighted elements.

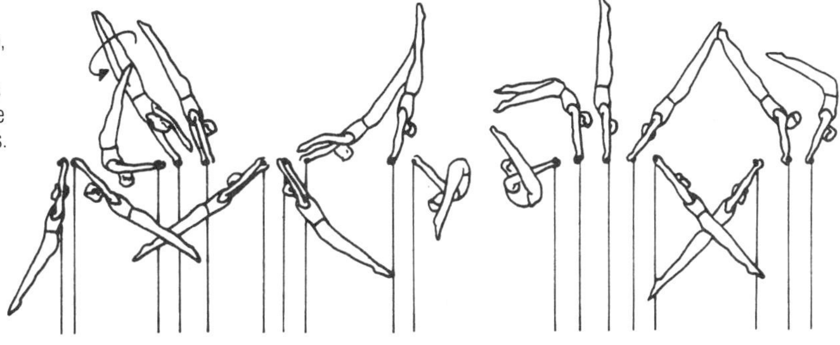

Men's pommel horse
Competitors perform one compulsory exercise followed by an optional exercise. Both must involve swinging motions of the legs, and include at least two scissor movements and a one-handle-only exercise.

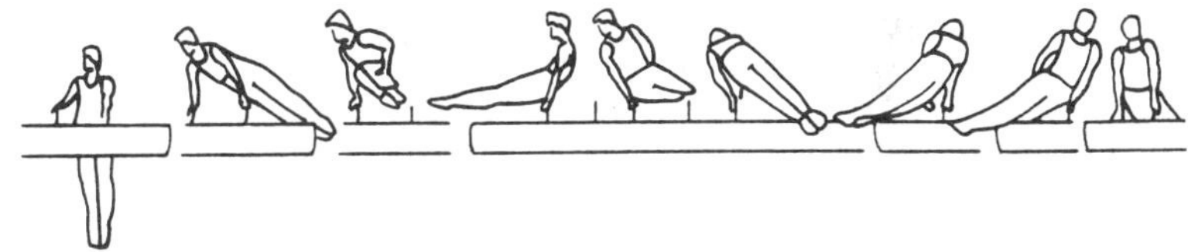

Rhythmic

8417 **1 Rope** Exercises include jumps, leaps, skips, hops, swings, circles, rotations, figure eights, and throws.
2 Hoop Exercises include rolls on floor or body exercises, swings, circles, and figure eights, passing through or over the hoop, and throws.
3 Ball Includes throws, active bouncing, free rolls over body or on floor, circles, spirals, and figure eight movements.
4 Club Exercises involve small circles with clubs, mills, rotations of clubs during flight of apparatus, throws, asymmetric movements, swings, circles, and tapping.
5 Ribbon These exercises include snakes in different planes, swings and circles in different planes, figure eights, throws, and small tosses.

Sports acrobatics

8418 There are two basic routines for sports acrobatics:
Balance routine This consists of elements without a flight phase; pyramids; handstands; balances; individual elements; choreographic, and combination elements (**1**).
Pair tempo routine Consists of elements with a flight phase; turns; somersaults; individual elements; choreographic elements, and a tumbling series, and includes at least two elements in which the partner is caught.

Key words

8419

balance routine Routine consisting of elements without flight phase; pyramids; handstands; balances; individual elements; choreographic, and combination movements.
pirouettes Turns around longitudinal axis of body.
saltos Turns around short axis of body.
tempo routine Routine consisting of elements with flight phase; turns; somersaults; including at least two elements where partner is caught; individual elements; choreographic element, and a tumbling series.
tsukahara Men's vault exercise, named after Japanese gymnast who first performed it.
yamashita Women's vault exercise.

842 FIGURE SKATING

History

8421

Ice-skating is believed to have originated in Scandinavia before the birth of Christ, and developed as a means of transport throughout northern Europe. The first skates were made from animal bones. The first skating club was formed in Edinburgh, Scotland, in 1742, and the sport was introduced into America and Canada by the British in the 19th century. The first American skating club was founded in Philadelphia in 1849. The first all-iron skate was invented by Bushnell of Philadelphia in 1850, and in 1859 the first skating rink to be regularly maintained was opened on the lake in Central Park, New York.
Figure skating developed in Scandinavia in the 1880s and was developed by H.E. Vandervell, Chairman of the National Skating Association of Great Britain, in 1880. Free skating emerged in Vienna and Britain later in the century.

Rules

8422

Music In both single and pair skating, the music is selected by the competitors.
Officials There must be two referees, a maximum of nine judges for both figure skating and ice dancing; one announcer; two secretaries; one timekeeper; and supplementary officials as necessary.
Duration In both single and pair skating, the original programs and the free skating sections have specified time limits. The skater must finish within 10 sec before or after the specified time.
Sequence The compulsory dances are skated first, followed by the original program or dance, and then the free skating or dancing.
Dress Costumes for ISU (International Skating Union) championships must be modest, dignified and appropriate for athletic competition.
Skates These usually have a single steel blade about 1/10 in (3 mm) wide. The blade is hollow-ground on the bottom to give two skating edges; figures are skated on the inside or the outside edge.

Disciplines

8423

Single skating This consists of an original program, including compulsory movements (this section is omitted from some competitions), and free skating.
Pair skating This also consists of an original program, including compulsory movements, and free skating. The pair must consist of a man and a woman, and must give a united, harmonious performance.
Ice dancing This consists of compulsory dances, an original dance and free dancing.
In compulsory dances, competitors skate two dances drawn from three groups of dances:
1 The Westminster, Viennese, Starlight, and Ravensberger Waltzes
2 The Kilian, Quickstep, Paso Doble, and Yankie Polka
3 The Blues, Rhumba, Argentine Tango, and Tango Romantica.
The original dance is treated as a separate part of the event. Each couple chooses its own music, tempo, and composition, but the rhythm is announced annually by the ISU Ice Dance Committee. The free dance consists of non-repetitive combinations of dance movements composed into a 4-min program displaying the dancers' personal ideas in concept and arrangement. Competitors choose their own music.

The rink

8424

The rink area for free skating and short programs is rectangular and is equipped with a music reproduction system. Maximum size: 197 x 98 ft (60 x 30 m); minimum size: 184 x 85 ft (56 x 26 m).
1 Free skating arena
2 Compulsory figures arena

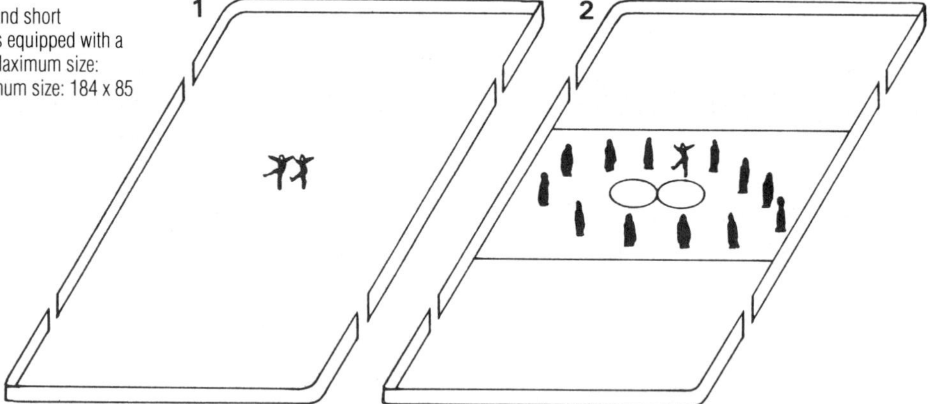

Scoring

8425

The scale of marks for each performance runs from one to six (to one decimal place). Marks are awarded for technical merit (composition) and artistic impression (presentation). At the end of each part of the competition, each judge places the competitors according to the total points he or she has awarded. The judges mark each competitor individually, and the winner in each part is the skater or pair or dance couple placed first by the majority of judges. The other

continued

Scoring continued

8425 places are similarly decided. After the result in each part of the competition has been determined, the placing obtained by each competitor is multiplied by the appropriate factor, as follows:

Dance	Factor
Compulsory dances	20% (0.4)
Original/set pattern	30% (0.6)
Free dance	50% (1.0)
Singles	Factor
Technical program	33% (0.5)
Free skating	67% (1.0)

Pairs	Factor
Technical program	33% (0.5)
Free skating	67% (1.0)

Jumps and spins

8426 **Free skating** The skater selects movements, jumps (Axel-Paulsen, double Lutz, regular double Salchow, etc), spins (sit, camel, upright, etc), steps, and other linking movements. This program should be executed with a minimum of two-footed skating, and in harmony with the music.

Spins
4 Camel spin
5 Sit spin
6 Upright spin

Jumps
1 Double Lutz jump
2 Regular double Salchow jump
3 Axel-Paulsen jump

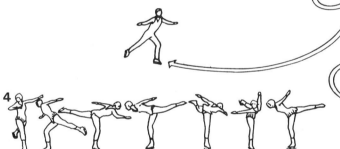

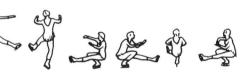

843 AEROBATICS

History

8431 Aerobatics originated during the early years of the 20th century. The first aerobatic maneuver (a loop) was carried out by a Russian, Lt. Nesterov of the Emperial Russian Air Service, but the real founder was a Frenchman, Adolphe Pégoud. He gave the earliest display of aerobatic flying in 1913. In its early years, aerobatics was the preserve of rich amateurs and military pilots, but as airplanes became less expensive, the sport took off in terms of accessibility and popularity. What began as a crowd-pleasing entertainment has evolved into a highly disciplined sport making high demands on the skill and expertise of the participants.

Rules

8432 **Aircraft type** Single-engined light aircraft are usually used. World championships and most international competitions are open to piston-engined aircraft only. They are usually 180–360 hp, and may be biplanes or monoplanes. An aircraft may be replaced by another at any time during the contest, provided the change is officially recommended by the technical commission and approved by the jury. If an aircraft is damaged during flight, the flight may be repeated if the jury agrees.

Daily briefing The competitors, officials, judges, and jury members must attend.

Height In world championships and most international competitions, competitors must not fly lower than approx. 330 ft (100 m) or higher than approx. 3,300 ft (1,000 m). In competitions involving less experienced pilots, the minimum height specified will often be between 990 ft and 1,650 ft (300 m and 500 m).

Judges For world championships and international competitions, there is a board consisting of a chief judge, seven to ten international judges with their assistants, four positioning judges – placed at each corner of the performance zone – and an administrative secretary.

Jury For world championships, there is an international jury consisting of seven members elected by the Fédération Aéronautique

continued

Rules continued

8432 Internationale (FAI) commission, plus the chief judge, who has no vote. They are responsible for ensuring that the championships are conducted in accordance with the regulations.
Performance zone Flights must be performed within a zone of approx. 1,100 yd x 1,100 yd (1,000 m x 1,000 m) which must be clearly marked on the ground.
Radio sets These may be used only for safety reasons in international competitions.
Teams These vary according to the rules of each competition. Solo entries are also allowed. Competitors may be substituted only before the contest begins. For world championships, a team comprises up to five pilots; there may be women's and men's teams. Other team members may include a chief delegate, a team manager, a judge, two assistants, a trainer, a doctor, up to three mechanics, and an interpreter.
Technical commission Inspects aircrafts and certifies them airworthy.
Training flights A flight of up to 15 minutes – the time limit for the flight program – may be made by each competitor in order to familiarize himself or herself with local conditions in the performance zone.
Weather conditions For world championships, the cloud base must be at least 165 ft (50 m) above the maximum height at which competing aircraft will fly, and visibility must be at least 3 mi (5 km), otherwise the jury may halt flying. At other competitions, the minimum weather conditions required for contest may be determined by regional weather patterns.

Figures

8433 Illustrated here are some of the flying figures commonly displayed in aerobatics. They show both positive and negative flight figures.
1 Horizontal slow roll
2 Inverted ("negative") flight
3 Vertical half roll
4 Stall turn ("hammer head")
5 Loop
6 Vertical eight

1

2

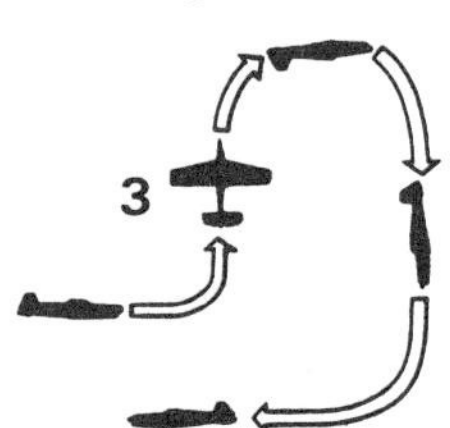

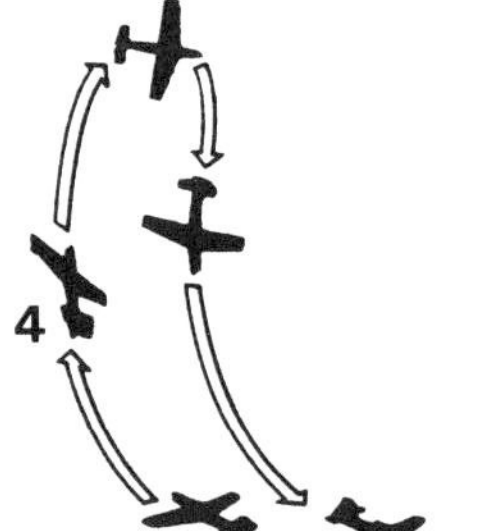

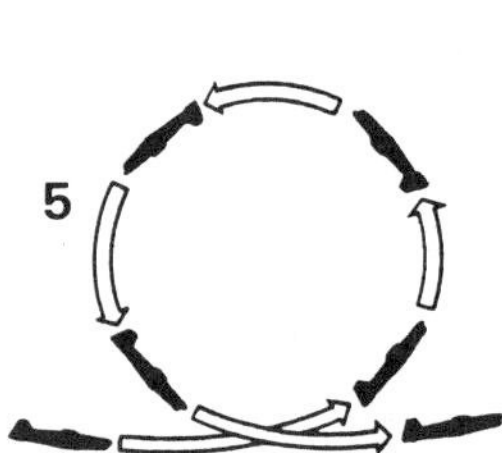

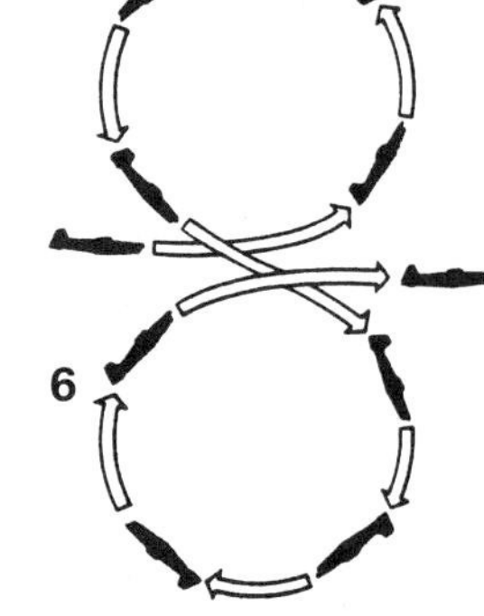

World championship programs

8434 Pilots fly three programs:
Program 1 The known compulsory program. This is composed of figures in both normal and inverted ("negative") flight, and is published in advance for all competitors.
Program 2 The free program. This consists of up to 18 figures which are selected by the computer from the aerobatic catalogue. The figures must be within criteria governing versatility and repetition.
Program 3 The unknown compulsory program. This consists of at least 15 figures chosen by the heads of delegations, and arranged by the jury into a sequence.
After completing these three programs, the highest-placed third of the men and half of the women respectively may then compete in a fourth, which carries a separate title, and lasts for 4 min exactly. Any number of figures may be flown within that limit.
Scoring For programs 1, 2, and 3, every judge rates the quality of each figure flown, taking precision and smoothness into account, and gives it a mark between 0 and 10. The score for each figure is multiplied by a difficulty factor (between 1 and about 35) for that figure. In the freestyle program, each judge rates the total performance, taking into account the difficulty and versatility of the complete sequence rather than marking individual figures. The final score in each program for each competitor is found by means of a computer program which has the effect of removing bias through statistical averaging.
Penalties Any figures flown after the 15 minute limit in the first three programs are not marked. Any deviation by more than 5 sec from the 4 min allowed for program 4 is penalized by 10 penalty points per sec.
Penalties are also incurred when pilots fly too high or too low or outside the performance zone, when they interrupt the program to correct their course, or when they climb to regain height.
Results In the world championships, there is a male and female winner in each of the four programs. The overall champions are the man and woman who gain the highest total number of points in the three qualifying programs. There are also men and women team champions.

844 PARACHUTING

History

8441 Parachuting was popular as a pastime and as professional entertainment long before it was used for saving lives. The first successful parachute descent was made by Anoré Garnerin, a Frenchman, in 1797.
In the US, parachuting from balloons was a popular spectacle in the 1880s, and sporting competitions began in Russia in the 1930s.
World championiship competition originated in Yugoslavia in 1951. A para-theater, the first of its kind, was built at Orange, Massachusetts in 1962.

Rules

8442 **Clothing and accessories** Each competitor must wear a protective helmet, and must have suitable life saving equipment if the jumps are made over or near water. Generally, competitors wear one-piece coveralls (jumpsuits), goggles, and gloves. Oxygen equipment must be carried for jumps from heights above 14,750 ft (approx. 4,500 m), and an altimeter which can be read must be worn for any fall involving a delayed opening of 10 sec or more.
Parachutes Both main and reserve parachutes must be worn, of any type approved by a national authority.
Aircraft These can be of any type, including microlight-craft, suitably prepared for the purpose in accordance with each country's regulations. Pilots must must be experienced in solo flying, and must undergo training in dropping techniques.

continued

Rules continued

8442 **Competitors** Only qualified parachutists registered with a national air club, of age, and certified medically fit may take part in international or world championships.
Weather Wind at ground level must not exceed 29.5 ft/sec or 23 ft/sec (9 m/sec or 7 m/sec) for accuracy jumps.
Briefing This occurs before the start of a competition. All parachutists must attend.
Jump and opening altitude: the minimum jump altitude above ground level for free fall jumps is 2,296.5 ft (700 m) for an individual, and 2,624.7 ft (800 m) for a team jump.
Training jump One training jump is permitted before a championship begins, either by an individual or by a group.
Officials Consist of a drop zone controller, who keeps the target area free of hazards, personally watches all descents, and keeps a check on wind and weather conditions; the international jury, consisting of at least three members of the CIP (the international parachuting committee of the FAI); and a panel of international judges – at least seven for world, and at least five for international, championships.
Ground signals These are made with colored panels in red, orange, yellow, or white.
A full cross Conditions are safe.
"T": conditions are unsafe for any but experienced parachutists.
"I": all parachuting is temporarily suspended.
"L": paracuhting is suspended and aircraft must land.
Disqualification This may be ordered for misconduct, or for failing to have the parachute open by at least 1,310 ft (400 m) above the ground.

Events

8443 **Accuracy events**
Individual parachutists or teams attempt to land on, or as close as possible to, the center of a target. Performance is based on the number of consecutive landings on the central disc, plus the distance of the next jump not on the disc. Individual accuracy jumps are made from an altitude of 2,625 ft (800 m). Team jumps are made from an altitude of 6,309 ft (1,100 m). The competitor/team with the lowest aggregate score for the rounds completed is the winner.

Target area
a 2 in (5 cm) disc on 6 in (16 cm) electronic pad in sand or fine gravel (10 ft (3m circle))
b Clearly marked circle (16 ft (5 m))
c Rounded gravel (16 ft (5 m))
d Clearly marked circle (115 ft (35 m))

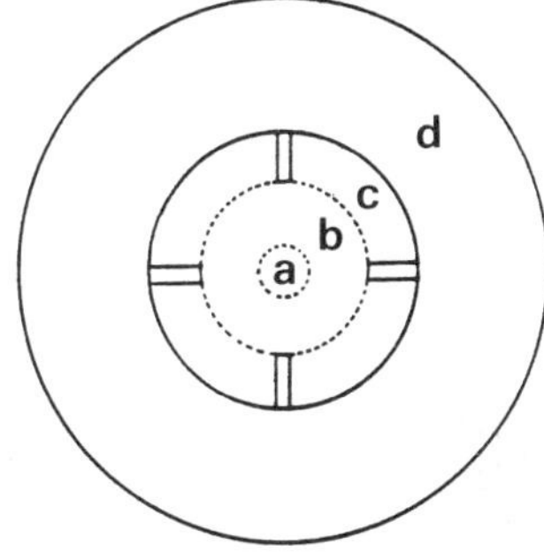

Style events
Individuals perform a series of individual maneuvers in freefall. Jumps are made from an altitude of 7,218 ft (2,200 m), or 6,562 ft (2,000 m) if meteorological conditions do not allow. The competitor with the lowest total time, including penalties, for all jumps is the winner.

Relative work
Teams perform a formation of sequences in free fall – including, for example, the zig–zag (**1**), and the star (**2**).
The four-way event This involves teams of four jumpers including the team captain; the exit altitude is 9,500 ft (2,950 m), the working time 35 sec.
The eight-way event This involves teams of eight jumpers including the team captain; the exit altitude is 11,500 ft (3,500 m), the working time 50 sec.

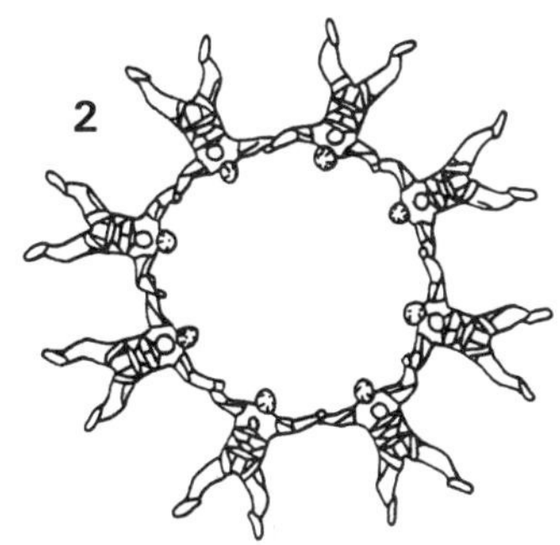

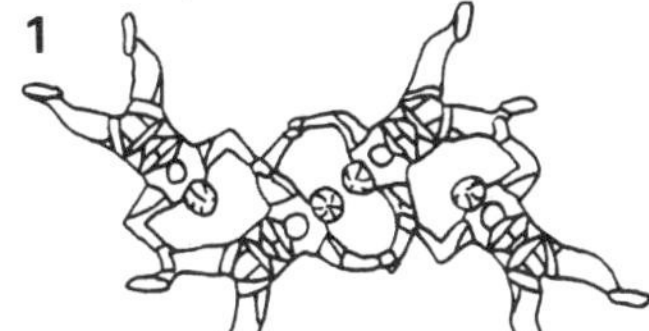

Canopy relative work events
Teams perform a canopy formation, such as Stacking (**3**), or a sequence of canopy formations, during descent under open canopy. The parachutists are linked together by grips. All parachutes are fully open and under control. For the eight-way speed formation event, the exit altitude is 6,000 ft (1,800 m), and the working time is 120 sec; for the four-way rotation event, 6,000 ft (1,800 m) and 120 sec; and for the four-way sequential event, 6,600 ft (2,000 m) and 180 sec. The winners in canopy relative work events are the team that accumulate the highest number of points for timing and technique in the completed round. Rejumps are permitted in both accuracy events and canopy relative work events, if a fault occurs in the main canopy.

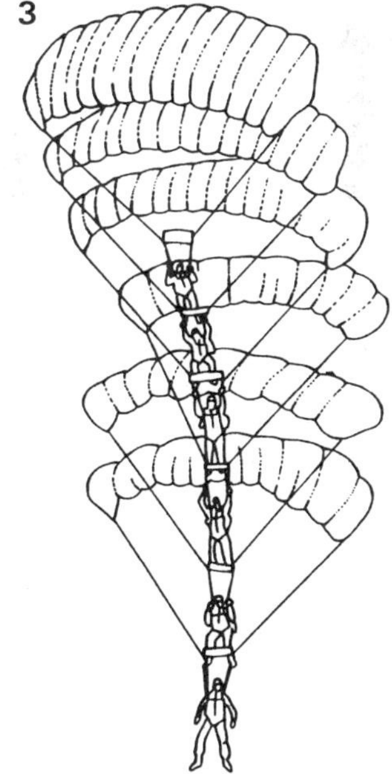

Key words

8444 **anemometer** Device, installed in the most appropriate position in the drop zone, indicating the speed of the wind in m/sec.
canopy The part of a parachute that opens up and catches the air.
drop zone (DZ) Area of ground, required for all competitive parachuting, into which parachutists may be safely dropped.
target area Circular area comprising 2 in (5 cm) disc on 6 in (16 cm) electronic pad in sand or fine gravel which is at the center, followed by a clearly marked circle 16 ft (5 m), a further ring of rounded gravel 16 ft (5m), and finally a second clearly marked circle 115 ft (35m).
wind sock A cylindrical device, 19 ft 6 in (6 m) long, used to indicate wind direction at ground level. It must be able to show the wind direction when the wind speed is 6.5 ft/sec (2 m/sec) or more. For accuracy events, the judges determine the position of the windsock, which is located approx. 164.1 ft (50 m) from the target.

851 DARTS

History

8511 The Romans are known to have competed in a similar game by throwing short iron javelins at a target and at each other. Centuries later, Anne Boleyn presented King Henry VIII with a set of darts. The Pilgrim Fathers played darts on the *Mayflower*, sailing to the New World in 1620. The modern dartboard, with its arbitrary numbering system, evolved in England during the reign of Queen Victoria.

Rules

8512 **Number of players** Individuals, teams, or any number.
Objective To throw three darts each in turn into various scoring areas of the board in order to reduce a starting score (usually 501) to exactly zero before the opponent does so.
Equipment Dartboard made of cork, bristle, or elm, hung on a wall with a scoreboard to one side. The dartboard is divided by wires into 20 equal segments (alternately colored black and buff), numbered from 1 to 20 but not in numerical order. A narrow outer wire ring and a similar inner ring mark double and triple scoring areas, respectively. At the center of the target is the bull's-eye surrounded by a small ring called the semicenter or outer bull. Three darts for each player, made of brass or nickel tungsten and balanced by three plastic flights each.

Key words

8513 **bull's-eye** Small disc in the center of the board; scores 50 points.
bust To score more points than needed to win. The player forfeits the rest of his or her turn and the points thus scored.
check-out To finish.
double ring Outer ring on the board; scores double the value of its respective segment.
double top Double 20, the number located at the top of the board.
flights Three pieces of plastic or polyester that balance the dart in flight.
oche (toe line) Line from behind which the player throws. It is 7ft 9 in (2.4 m) from the board.
semicenter (outer bull) Small ring that encircles the bull's-eye; scores 25 points.
toe the oche To begin play.
triple ring Inner ring on the board; scores triple the value of its respective segment.
wire dart Dart that hits the board and bounces back; does not score.

The dartboard

8514 The dartboard is usually made from cork, bristle, or elm, with the divisions marked by wires. Adjacent sectors are differentiated by color. The board is always hung so that the 20 sector is vertically above the bull.
The playing area
The dartboard is hung on a wall, with the scoreboard to one side. The toe line (**1**) is marked either on a mat or on the floor.

The scoreboard
This is a slate or black-painted board. Each side's score is recorded in chalk.

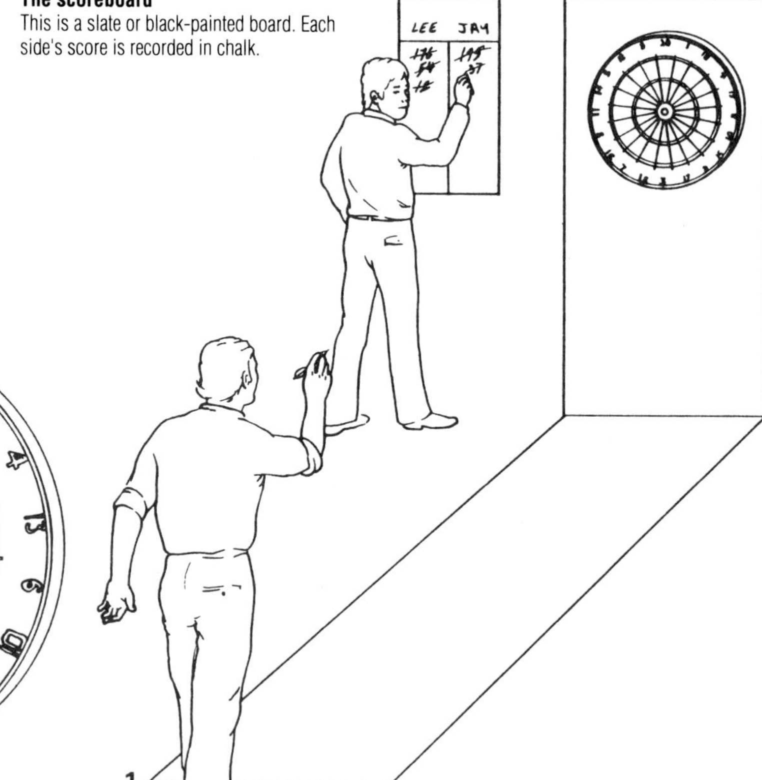

852 GOLF

History

8521 Modern golf was originally developed in Scotland, and the first organized club was founded there in 1744. The Royal and Ancient Golf Club of St Andrews came into being ten years later and set the standard course of 18 holes. Several US clubs were founded in the 1880s. In 1916, US professionals formed the Professional Golfers' Association of America (PGA), which today offers more than $14 million in prizes.

Rules

8522 **Number of players** Two to four.
Equipment Each player has a set of clubs made up of woods, irons, and putters, and a rubber-cored ball weighing not more than 1.62 oz (45.9 g) with a diameter of not less than 1.68 in (4.27 cm).

Objective To hit the ball from each tee into each hole on the course with as few strokes as possible.
Scoring In match play, the game is played by holes. A hole is won by the side that holes the ball in fewer strokes. The side that wins the most holes wins the match. In stroke play, the winner is the player who completes the round or rounds in the fewest strokes.
Duration In match play, the match is ended when one player leads by more holes than there are holes left to play. Most professional tournaments use stroke play over 72 holes (four rounds).

The course

8523 Courses range from about 6,500 to 7,000 yd (5,900 to more than 6,400 m) in length. They have 18 holes, the distance from tee to hole ranging from 100 to 600 yd (90 to 540 m). Each course has a number of hazards.

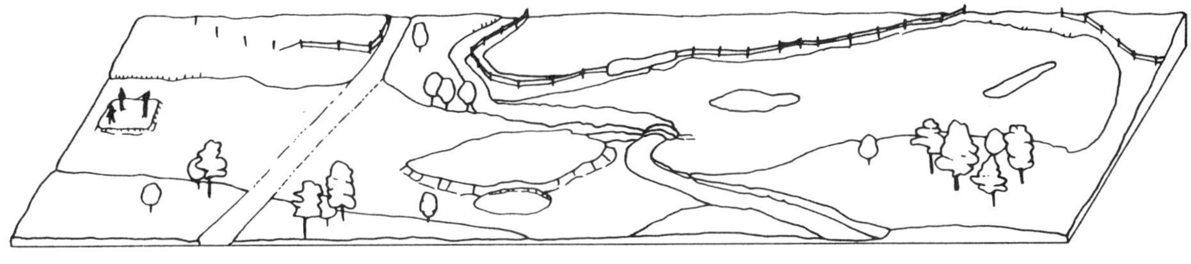

Clubs and trajectories

8524 Players may use up to 14 clubs, woods, and irons. There are normally three clubs, four woods, and nine irons. They are usually referred to by number, but some have names.

1 Clubs	**2 Irons**
a Putter	**3 Woods**
b Pitching wedge	**a** driver
c Sand wedge	**b** brassie
	c spoon
	d 4 wood

1

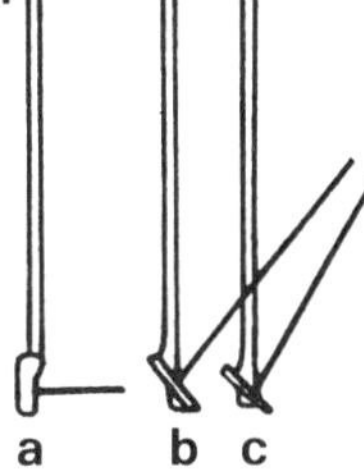

2

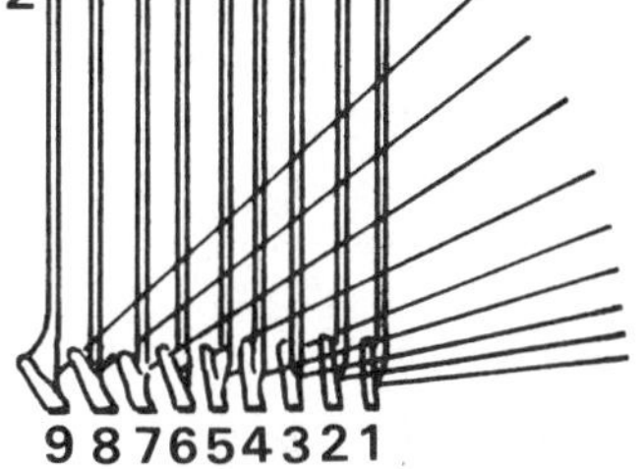

3

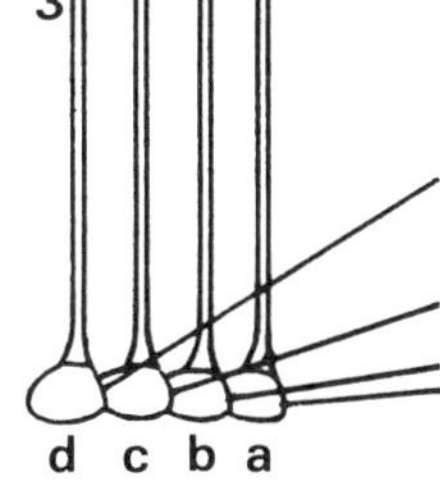

8525

address A player's stance before hitting the ball.
albatross Three under par for a hole.
approach shot Iron shot or long putt to the hole.
birdie One under par for a hole.
bogey One over par for a hole.
borrow Slope on a putting green.
bunker A type of hazard, usually a sandfilled hollow. Also called sand trap.
caddie Person who carries a player's clubs and gives advice.
chip Short, lofted approach shot.
divot Piece of turf dug out by a properly played iron shot; it should be replaced.
dogleg Hole with a sharp bend in it between tee and green.
draw A hook executed deliberately.
drive A golfer's first stroke from the tee (**1**).
driver Wooden club with which the player drives the ball.
eagle Two under par for a hole.
fade A slice executed deliberately.
fairway Smooth turf between tee and green.
fore! Warning shout by a player about to play a shot.
green Area around the hole closely mown for putting.
halved hole A hole in which opponents make the same score.
handicap A way of equalizing competition by allowing a certain number of strokes to a golfer playing against a better opponent.
hazard Obstacle on the course, usually a bunker or an area of water.
hole-in-one Occurs when a player's tee shot goes straight into the hole; a rare feat.
hook A badly executed drive that results in the ball curling to the left (in a right handed shot) or to the right (in a left-handed shot).
iron Club with a metal head.
lie The position in which the ball lies on the course after a stroke.
nineteenth hole Slang name for the bar in the clubhouse.
par Estimated standard score for a hole or course based on the ability of a first-class player.
pin Flagpole marking the hole on a green.
play through Pass slower players in front by playing a hole before they do.
putter Club used for putting.
putting Strokes played on the green to try to roll the ball into the hole (**2**).
rough Untrimmed grass bordering the fairway.
slice A badly executed drive that results in the ball curving to the right (in a right-handed shot) or to the left (in a left-handed shot).
tee Slighlty elevated area from which a player drives the ball; also the peg on which the ball is placed.
wedge Wedge-shaped club used for lofting the ball.
wood Wooden club used for longer shots.

853 HORSESHOE PITCHING

History

8531 Horseshoe pitching dates from about AD 100, when Roman soldiers played the game to relieve boredom in their camps. It has been a favorite pastime in the US and Canada for many years, but formal rules were not established until 1914. The National Horseshoe Pitchers' Association of America, the leading organization, emerged in 1920.

Rules

8532 **Number of players** Two or three competing individually, or four in two competing teams of two.
Objective To throw shoes as near as possible to the target stake.
Equipment A pitching court (see diagram); two horseshoes with calks for each player; two steel or iron stakes, one at each end of the pitching court.
Scoring There are two types of scoring: cancellation and count-all. All shoes must land within 6 in (15 cm) of the stake to score. All ringers count three points.

Key words

8533 **calks** Rolled-down edges at the toe and heel ends of the horseshoe.
cancellation A type of scoring in which each shoe closer to the stake than an opponent's counts one point. Opposing ringers and shoes equally close cancel each other out. First to reach 50 points wins.
count-all Each shoe within 6 in (15 cm) of the stake scores one point regardless of the opponent's shoe. A game consists of 25 innings.
foul line A line marking the front end of the pitching box behind which the pitcher must stand when throwing the shoe.
horseshoe Flat, U-shaped piece of iron (**1**) specially made for pitching, with calks at toe and heels.
innings Two throws by each player.
leaner Shoe that leans against the stake (worth one point).
pitching box Area at each end of the pitching court from which contestants pitch the shoes.
pitching court Rectangular box of moist clay with a pitching box and stake at each end. Men pitch 40 ft (12.2 m), women 30 ft (9.1 m).
ringer A shoe that encircles the stake so that a straight edge can touch the two prongs without touching the stake.
stakes Two iron or steel stakes (**2**) standing 14 in (36 cm) above the ground with a 3 in (7.5 cm) tilt toward the opposite stake.

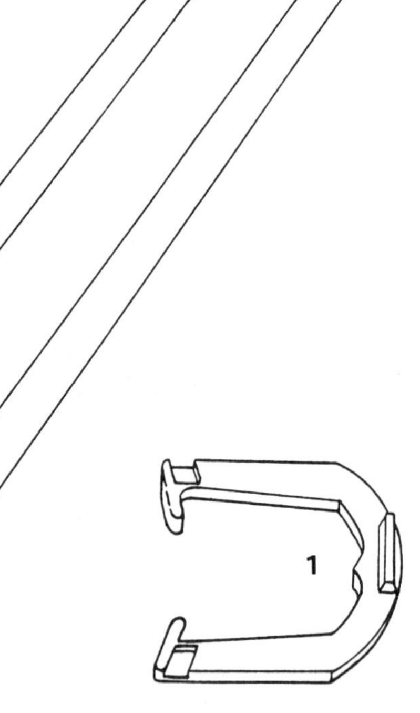

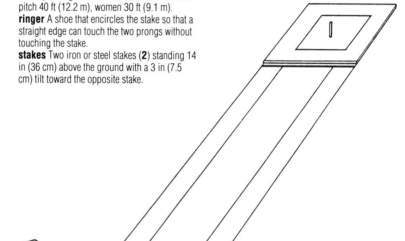

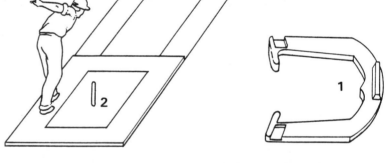

854 BOWLING (TENPIN)

History

8541 Tenpin bowling is a modern, highly competitive, and commercialized version of a simple game which involved throwing a ball at a target. In Germany during the 3rd and 4th centuries AD members of the church congregation would set up a *kegel*, representing a "Heathen One," as a target. In England, early bowlers met with a mixed reception - bowling was banned by Edward III and condemned by Henry VIII. The sport did not become properly organized until the formation of the American Bowling Congress (ABC) in 1895. This body gave the game rules and standardized equipment. The British Tenpin Bowling Association was formed in 1961.

Rules

8542 **Number of players** One to five players, or teams of up to five a side.
Equipment Bowling lane (**1**), 60 ft (18.3 m) long and 3 ft 6 in (1.01 m) wide, with gutters on either side to catch badly aimed balls. The lane's surface is made of wood or plastic. At least 15 ft (4.6 m) must be allowed before the foul line to give bowlers sufficient approach space. Most bowling lanes have automatic machinery to replace the pins (**2**) and return the ball (**3**). The pins, numbered from 1 to 10, are made of maple wood and are plastic-coated. Their height is 1 ft 3 in (38.1 cm), and their weight from 3 lb 6 oz (1.53 kg) to 3 lb 10 oz (1.65 kg). The ball weighs not more than 16 lb (7.26 kg), measures 8 in (21.59 cm) in diameter, is made of hard rubber, plastic or urethane, and has finger holes for gripping. Bowling shoes have soft soles so as not to scar the approach surface.
Objective The ball is propeled underarm down the lane, usually in a four-step delivery, with the aim of knocking down the ten pins, positioned in a triangle at the end of the lane. Every player bowls twice in every frame, unless he or she achieves a strike on the first ball.
Scoring The winning player or team has the highest score at the end of ten frames. One point is scored for every pin knocked over, with a bonus for a strike or spare.
Officials For major competitions, a foul judge is appointed, unless there is an automatic foul-detecting device. Official matches must be played on two lanes.

Bowling lane

8543

Key words

8544 **foul line** Line which the bowler must not touch or cross during or after bowling, or the ball is illegal. Any pins knocked down by that ball do not score. If the first ball in a frame is foul, all the pins are reset. If they are then all knocked down by a legal second ball, a spare, not a strike, is scored. If the foul ball is the second in a game, only those pins knocked down with the first ball are counted.
frame A game consists of ten frames.
spare When a player knocks down all ten pins with both balls in a frame, he or she scores 10 points, plus the score from the next ball bowled.
strike When a player knocks down all ten pins with his first ball of a frame, he or she scores 10 points, plus the score from the next two balls bowled.

Ready for first ball

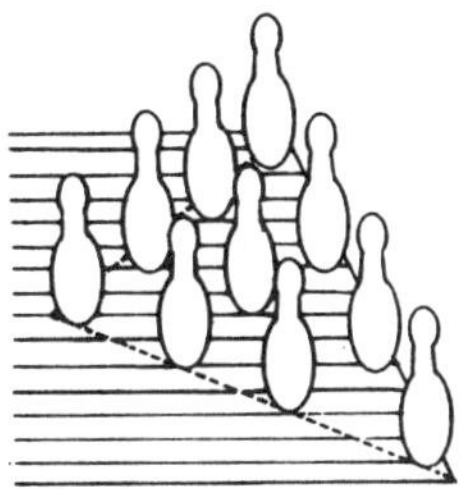

First ball   o Strike   Second ball   oo Spare

855 SKITTLES

History

8551 Modern skittles derived from the German peasants' habit of throwing stones at a flat-bottomed club or *kegel,* stood on end, which represented a sin or temptation. In 1541, the game of *loggats*, another forerunner, was forbidden, and the game has had a chequered legal career. Skittles is now widely played in Europe.

Rules

8552 **Number of players** Any even number of players from 2 to 24. As a team game, it is usually played five a side.
Objective Participants roll or throw a ball or thick, flat disc (**1**) at nine skittles (**2**) at the end of an alley (**3**), and score a point for each one knocked down. If a player knocks down all the skittles before completing the throw, they are set up again. The scores for each player are aggregated and the side with the higher total wins the leg. Alternatively, a chalk is decided by the number of throws needed to knock down all nine skittles, five throws being the maximum number. A game ends when one team has completed seven chalks. The match is then played over five games.
The player The player must stand with the heel of one foot at least 21 ft (6.4 m) from the frame. He or she is allowed one step forward before releasing the cheese or ball.
Foul If the cheese or ball hits the side of the alley before hitting the skittle, it is a foul throw.
Officials Competitive matches are played under the complete control of a referee.
Equipment The alley or run is 3 ft (0.91 m) wide and must be 21 ft (6.4 m) long. Each skittle, made of wood, weighs between 8 lb (3.86 kg) and 9 lb (4.31 kg) and measures 1 ft 2 in (36.8 cm) high, 3 in (7.62 cm) in diameter at the base, and 6 in (17.2 cm) in diameter at its widest part.
The skittles rest on circular metal plates.

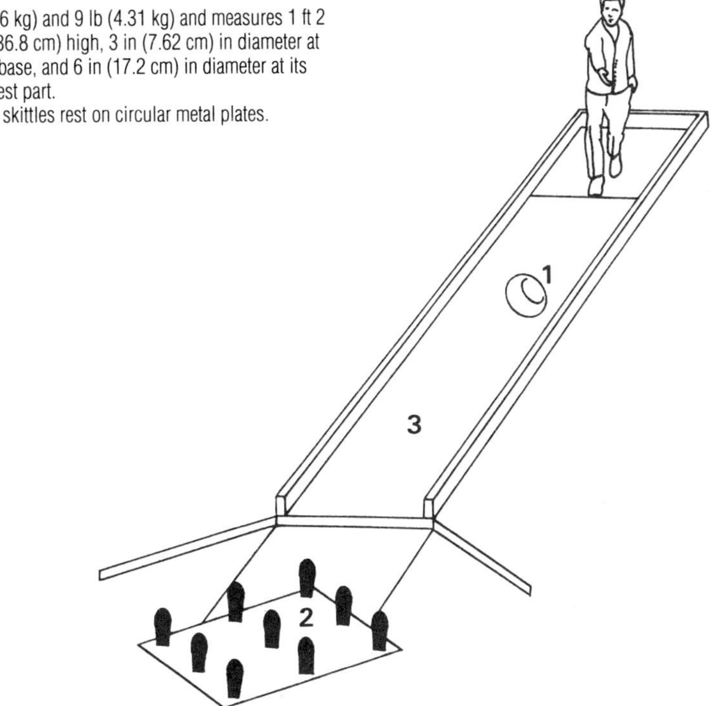

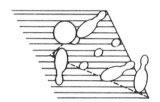

Key words

8553 **chalk** Each player has three throws, a "chalk," with a maximum score of 27.
cheese Thick, flat disc, usually made of lignum vitae (a very hard wood), weighing between 10 lb (4.54 kg) and 12 lb (5.44 kg).
floorer Occurs when all nine skittles are knocked down by striking the head pin with considerable force at exactly the correct angle.
frame The platform for the skittles, made of hornbeam.
leg Three chalks from each player constitute a leg.
match Best of three legs.
setter-up The team member who sets up the pins at the end of a chalk and removes the cheese or ball after a foul throw.

856 BILLIARDS

History

8561 The origin of billiards is unknown and the first recorded mention of the game was in France in 1429. In later years it was played by many famous people, including Mary Queen of Scots, Mozart, and Queen Victoria. Balls were originally made of wood, and the cue was a long wooden shovel called a mace. The Billiards Congress of America in Chicago supervises US play.

Rules

8562 **Number of players** Two, or sometimes opposing pairs.
Objectives In agreed length of time, the first to achieve the agreed number of points.
Equipment Table with slate bed and covered with green baize, fitted with pockets. Cue for each player. Two cue balls (white and spot white, an all-white ball is used by one player; a white ball distinguished by a black spot by the other). Mechanical bridges or rests. Chalk for chalking cue tip. Scoreboard.

The table

8563 **1** Cushion
2 Top pocket
3 Center pocket
4 Bottom pocket
5 The spot
6 Center spot
7 Pyramid spot
8 Balk line
9 Balk line spot
10 The "D"
11 The balk area

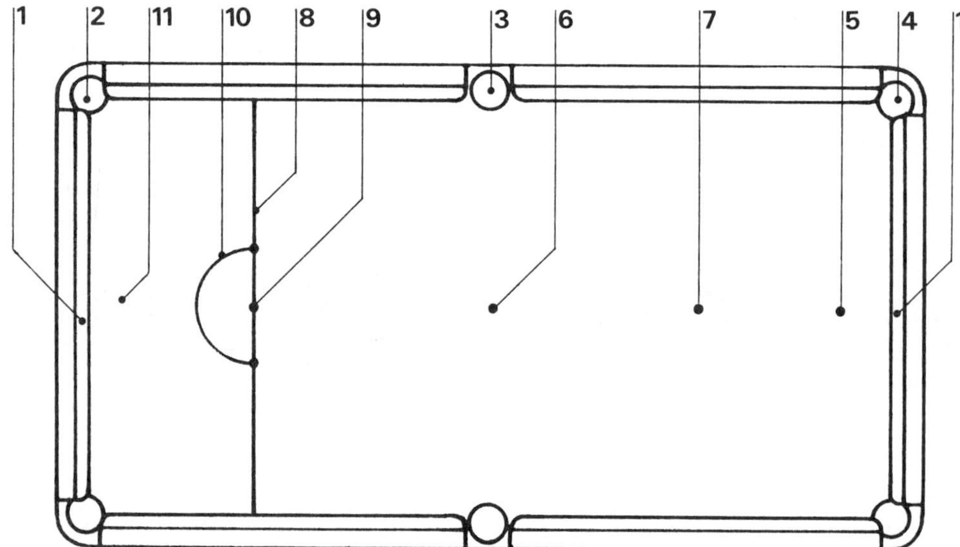

Balls and positions

8564 **1 The balls are:**
a Cue ball (player 1)
b Cue ball-spot (player 2)
c Red ball
2 Starting positions:
d Cue ball starts in the "D"
c Red ball starts on the spot

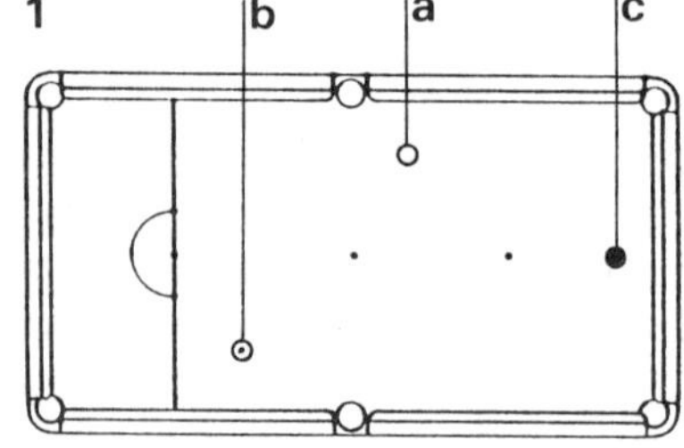

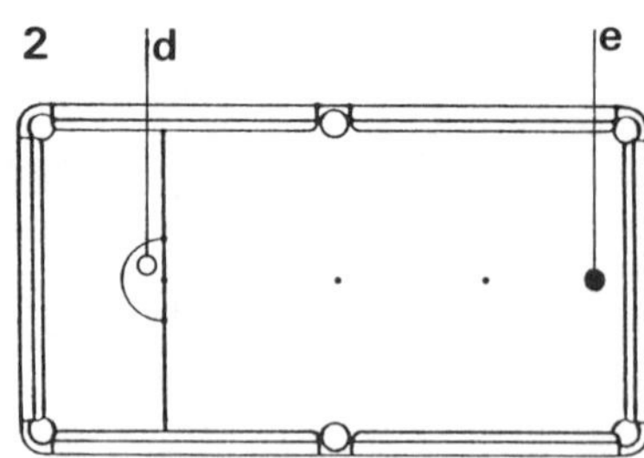

Scoring

8565 The striker scores points for winning hazards, losing hazards, and cannons. All points accumulated in a shot are counted.
Winning hazards
1 Two points if the cue ball hits the other white ball into a pocket.
2 Three points if the cue ball hits the red into a pocket.

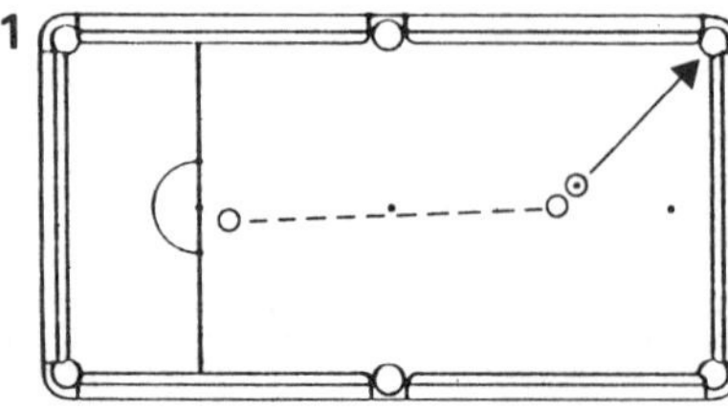

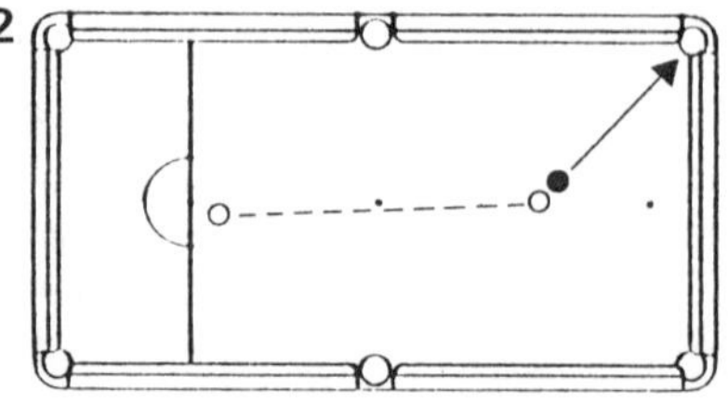

continued

Scoring continued

8565 **Losing hazards**
1 Two points if the cue ball is pocketed "in off" the white.
2 Three points if the cue ball is pocketed 'in off' the red.
Only 15 consecutive hazards may be scored, whether winning, losing, or both.

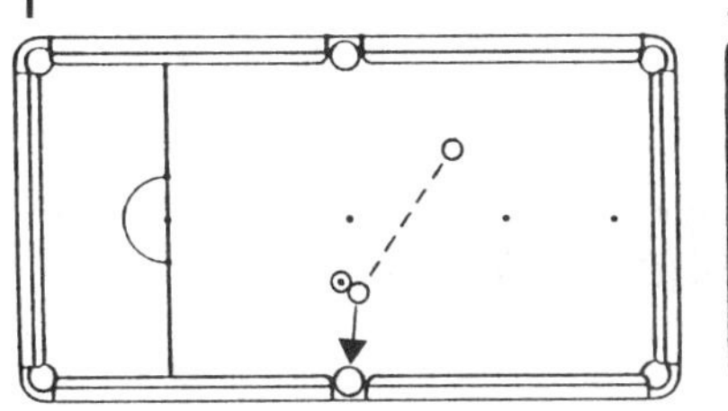

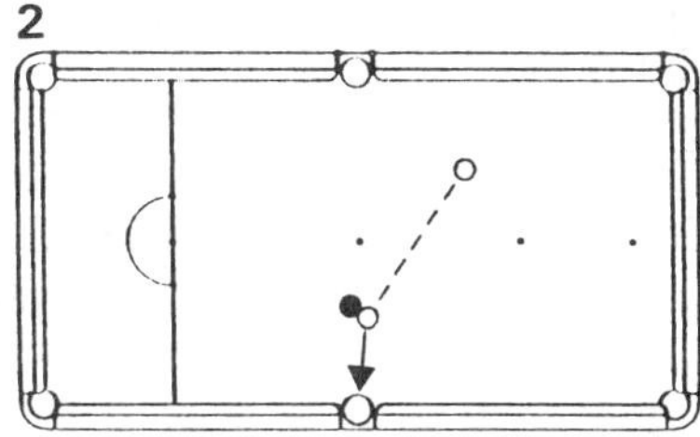

Cannons
1 Two points are scored when the cue ball strikes both other balls.
2 If the cue ball goes into a pocket after a cannon, it scores an additional two points if the white ball, or three points if the red ball, was struck first.
Cannons may be scored consecutively.

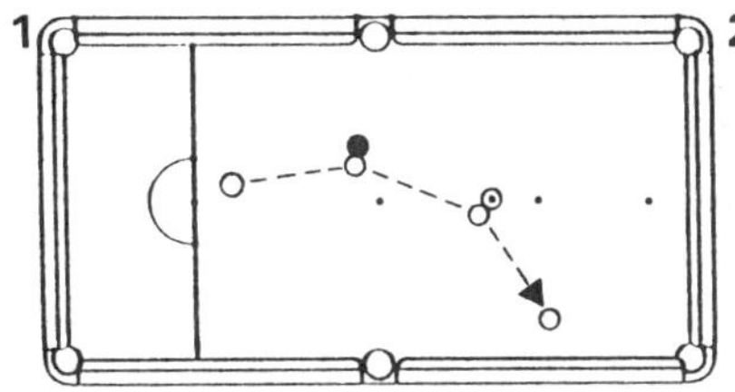

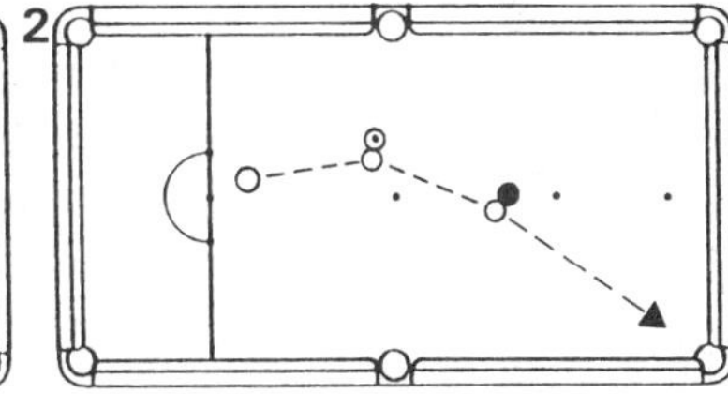

Key words

8566 **balk line** Line at the top of the table.
break Opening shot.
bridge Position of the hand on which the cue rests.
cannon Hitting both object balls.
cue Long tapered stick with a leather tip used for striking the cue ball.
cue ball White ball struck by the cue and propeled on to an object ball.
"D" A semicircle centered on the balk line from within which the cue ball is struck at the start of a game.
in-off Scoring stroke in billiards, foul stroke in snooker, when the cue ball goes into a pocket after striking the object ball.
mechanical bridge Rod with a metal bridge on which the cue slides. Also called rest.
object ball Ball aimed at.
pot Scoring stroke in which the object ball is knocked into a pocket.
rest Mechanical bridge.
snooker A layout of balls in which the path from the cue ball to the object ball is blocked by one or more other balls.
winning hazard A pot.

857 SNOOKER

History

8571 The origin of the game is not known for certain. The earliest snooker reference mentions British army officers playing a form of the game in late 19th century India, and in 1900 the Billiards Association published a set of snooker rules. An English amateur championship began in 1916, but snooker was a very minor sport until the 1920s, and would probably still be virtually unknown but for the effort of one man – billiards champion Joe Davis. Singlehanded, he developed the complex positional strategies and techniques of the modern game. Pushed by Davis, the Billiards Association and Control Council (BACC) held the first world snooker championship in 1927, which Davis won. In November 1970, the World Professional Billiards and Snooker Association was formed.

The table

8572 **Cushions**
1 Top cushion
2 Bottom cushion

Spots
3 Center (blue) spot
4 Pyramid (pink) spot
5 The spot (black)
6 Balk line
7 The "D"
8 Balk area
9 Pockets

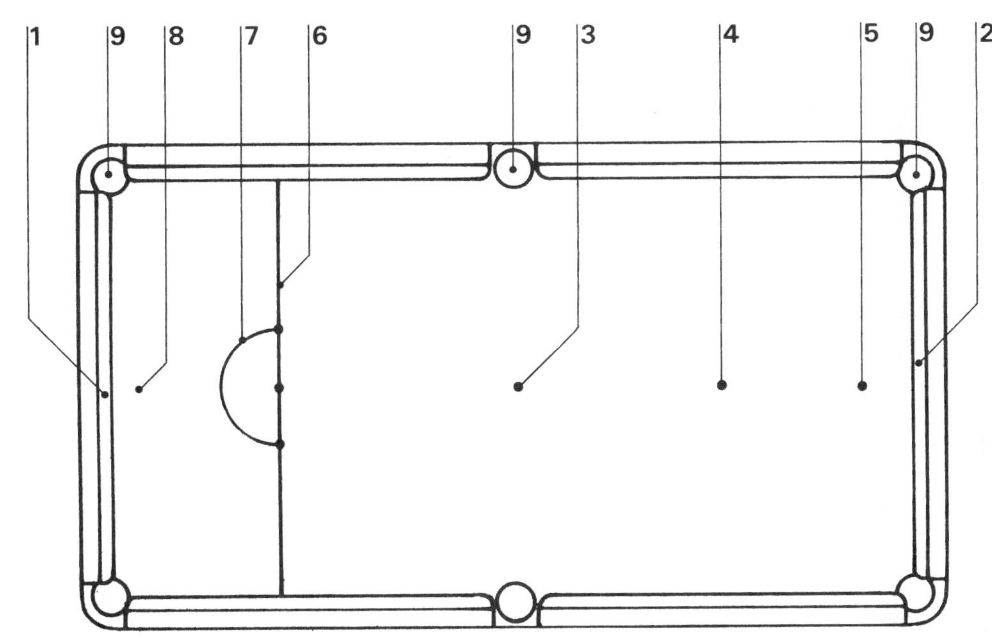

Rules

8573 **Number of players** Two persons, or two pairs, or two teams.
Equipment A standard pocket billiard table. 22 balls: 15 red, six colored - yellow, green, brown, blue, pink, black - and a white cue ball, all of equal size and weight. A triangular rack used to position the red balls for the start of play. Cues and rests as for English billiards.
Objectives The winner is the player with the highest score when all balls have been cleared from the table. Points are scored by potting the "on," or object, balls, and by forcing the opponent to give away points through "snookers."
The initial object ball of each turn is a red, so long as any red remains on the table. A striker who succeeds in potting a red scores that ball, which stays pocketed, and continues by attempting to pot any non red nominated ball. If a ball is potted, the player continues playing, alternately, a red and a nominated colored ball. When all the reds have been potted, the colored balls are potted in strict ascending order of scoring value. Once potted, they are not put back on the table. A break ends when a player fails to pocket either a red or, if no reds remain, the colored ball of the lowest value left on the table. It also ends when the cue ball is potted, after which it is next played from the "D".
Fouls and penalties After any foul shot, the striker loses that turn plus any score he or she may have made on that shot. The opponent receives the appropriate penalty score, and has the option of playing the balls where they have come to rest or of asking the other player to do so. The minimum penalty score is four points, incurred when the cue ball is pocketed.
The score is recorded on a board showing units, tens, and hundreds.

Ball values and positions

8574 **1** 15 Reds: 1 point each
2 Yellow: 2 points
3 Green: 3 points
4 Brown: 4 points
5 Blue: 5 points
6 Pink: 6 points
7 Black: 7 points

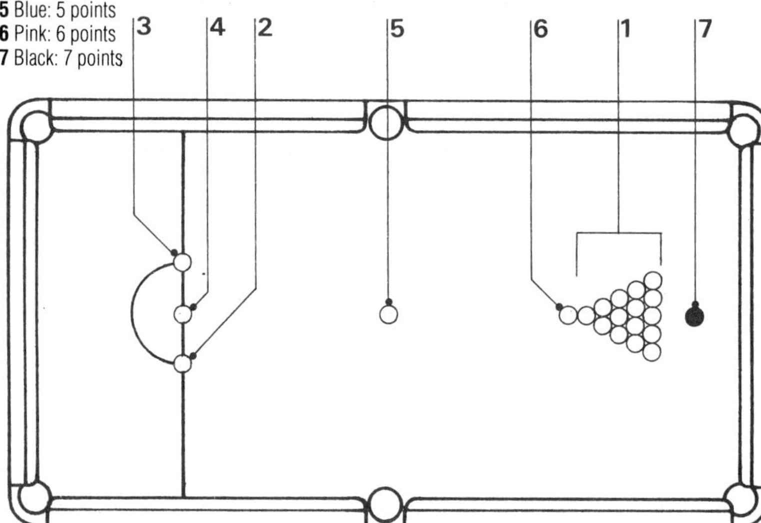

Racking
At the start of play, the red balls are racked as shown and placed with the apex of the triangle touching the pyramid (pink) spot (**6**).

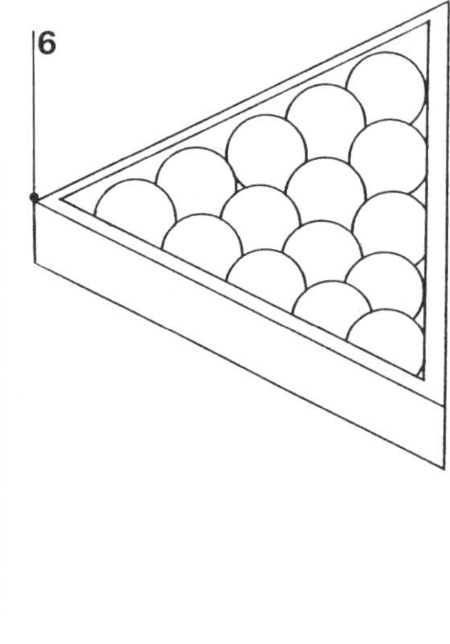

Scoring

8575 **Fouls and penalties**
Examples:
1 For pocketing the cue ball
2 For missing all the balls
3 For striking simultaneously, or pocketing with one shot, two balls other than two reds, or the "on" ball.
4 For a push stroke or jump shot.

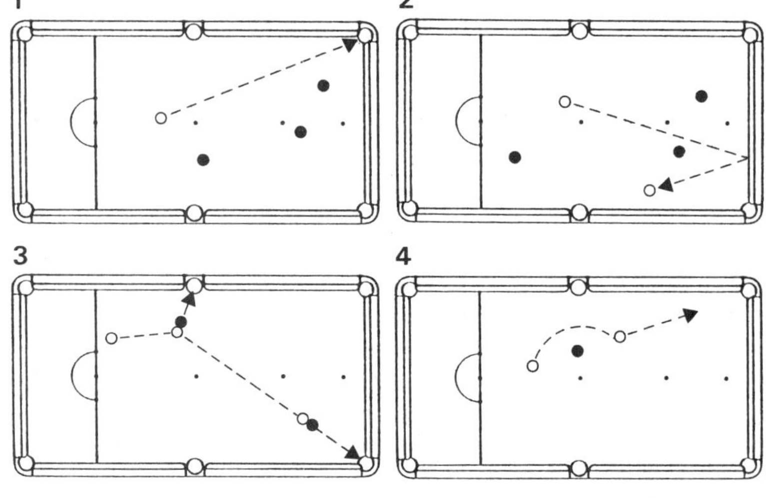

continued

Scoring continued

8575 **A snooker**
A player is snookered when a ball he or she must not play obstructs a straight line between the cue ball and the ball that is "on."
The player must attempt the shot, and will be penalized for missing the "on" ball or first hitting any other ball.

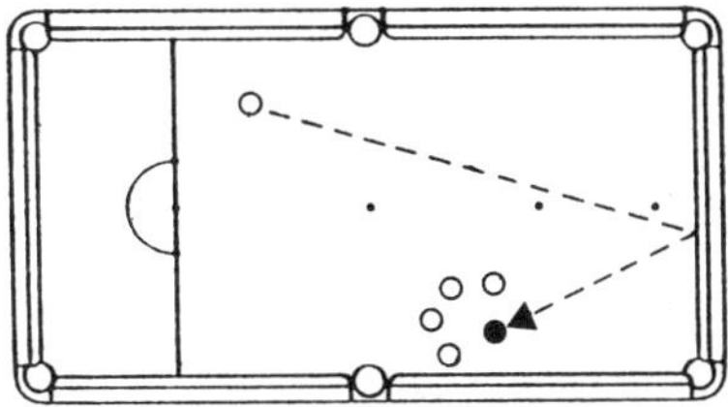

A player who is snookered by an opponent's foul stroke may play any ball he or she nominates. If the player pockets it, the ball is treated as a red, unless all reds are off the table, in which case it is treated as the "on" ball from which the player is snookered.

Key words

8576 **balk line** A line drawn across the width of the table marking the top quarter. The "D" is marked on this line.
break (also Billiards) Sequence of scoring shots.
bridge Position of the hand on which the cue rests.
cue Long tapered stick with a leather tip used for striking the cue ball.
cue ball White ball struck by the cue and propeled on to an object ball.
"D" (also Billiards) Semicircle, centered on the balk line, from within which the cue ball is struck at the start of a frame.
frame A complete game.
in-off Foul stroke where the cue ball goes into a pocket after striking the object ball.
mechanical bridge Rod with a metal bridge on which the cue slides. Also called rest.
"on" or object ball (also Billiards) Ball that is next to be struck.
pot (also Billiards) Scoring stroke in which the object ball is knocked into a pocket.
rest Mechanical bridge.

858 POOL

History

8581 Pool – or championship pocket billiards – is the most popular form of billiard table game played in North and South America. The game's greatest growth occurred between 1890 and 1920, when a billiard saloon appeared in almost every American town. Pool's chief propagandist was the child prodigy Willie Mosconi, who dominated the game from 1941 to 1957. It was he who presented the game as a test of nerve and skill, and not just a gambling exercise.

Rules

8582 **Number of players** Two persons, pairs, or teams.
Equipment Pool is played on tables of American design measuring 9 ft (2.74 m) by 4 ft (1.22 m), with six pockets, those at the four corners measuring between 4 $^{7}/_{8}$ in (12.38 cm) and 5 $^{5}/_{8}$ in (14.29 cm). The plastic balls are consecutively numbered – balls from 1 to 8 are in solid colors, while those from 9 to 15 are striped – and there is a white cue ball. The game begins with the 15 balls racked in a triangle, as shown, and the cue ball anywhere behind the head string (scratch line).
Objective The aim of the game is for a player or side to make a continuous run of 14 balls, leaving the fifteenth on the table. The 14 balls are then racked again and the striker attempts to pocket the last ball and scatter the racked balls to continue the run. The first player or side to score 150 points wins. Players "call" or nominate each ball and pocket in advance, and score one point for each ball pocketed.
penalties Failure to break properly involves a penalty of two points. Scratching the cue ball into the pocket – snooker's equivalent of going "in off" – or causing the cue ball to leave the table – involves a penalty of one point.
safety shots Permissible if the player calls "safe" prior to striking and causes an object ball to hit a cushion. Failure to do so involves a one-point penalty.
variations There are many other varieties of pool. One of the most popular is "rotation," in which the aim is to pocket the 15 object balls in numerical order.

The table

8583 **1** Foot cushion
2 Foot string
3 Foot spot
4 Center string
5 Center spot
6 Head string
7 Head spot
8 Head cushion
9 Long string
10 Side rails
11 Pocket

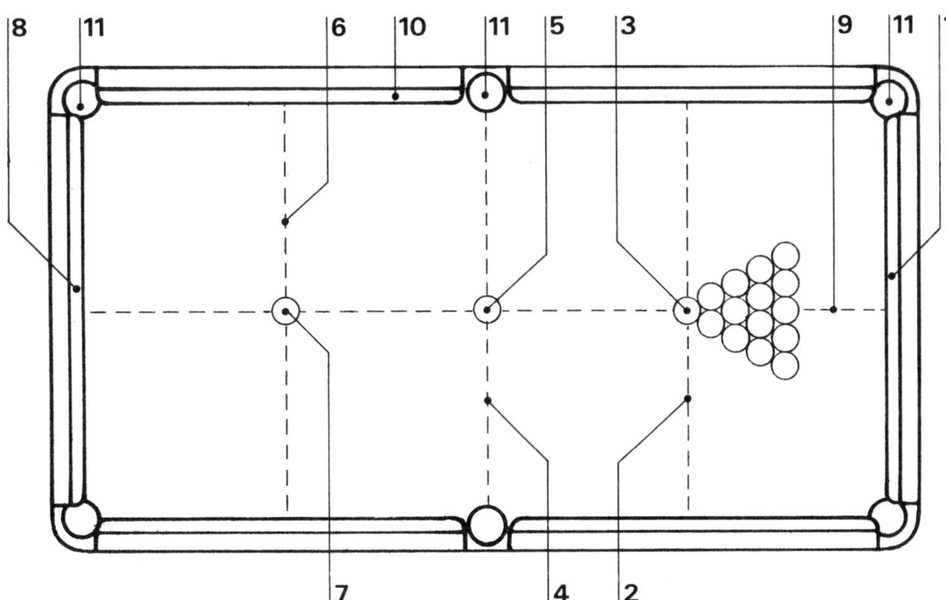

Key words

8584

block Segment of a match played to an agreed point requirement – usually 150 in title matches.
break shot Opening shot.
bridge Position of the hand on which the cue rests.
cue Long tapered stick with a leather tip (**1**) used for striking the cue ball.
cue ball White ball (**2**) struck by the cue and propeled onto an object ball.
foot spot Position on the table marking the apex of the racked 15-ball triangle.
head string (scratch line) Line at the top of the table behind which the cue ball is placed to start the game.
jump shot Player causes the cue ball to rise from the bed of the table.
mechanical bridge Rod with a metal bridge on which the cue slides (**3**). Also called rest.
racked Fifteen balls arranged in a triangle at the foot spot.
rest Mechanical bridge.
safety play A safety shot allows a player to end his or her turn without penalty. The cue ball must contact a cushion after sriking an object ball, or drive an object ball into a cushion.
strings Imaginary lines through the spots on a table and parallel to the ends of the table.

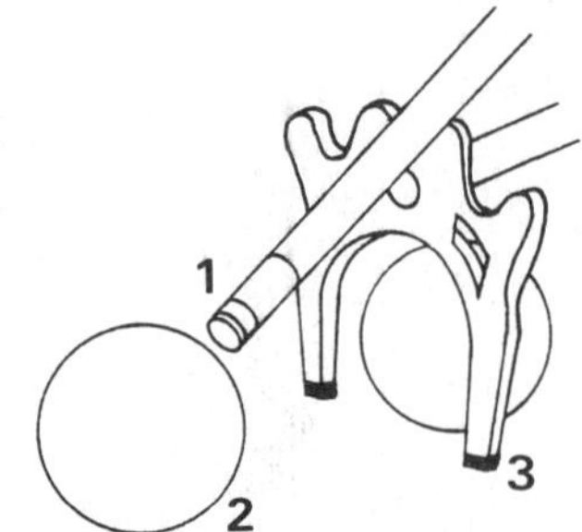

Balls and positions

8585

Racking
At the start of play the object balls (**1**) are placed within a triangle (**2**). The balls are arranged in a certain order within the triangle positioned at the top of the table. The position of the cue ball (**3**) is shown in the diagram. The triangle is removed when play starts.

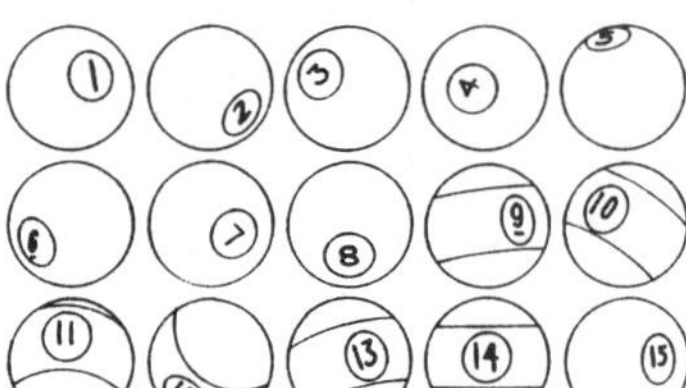

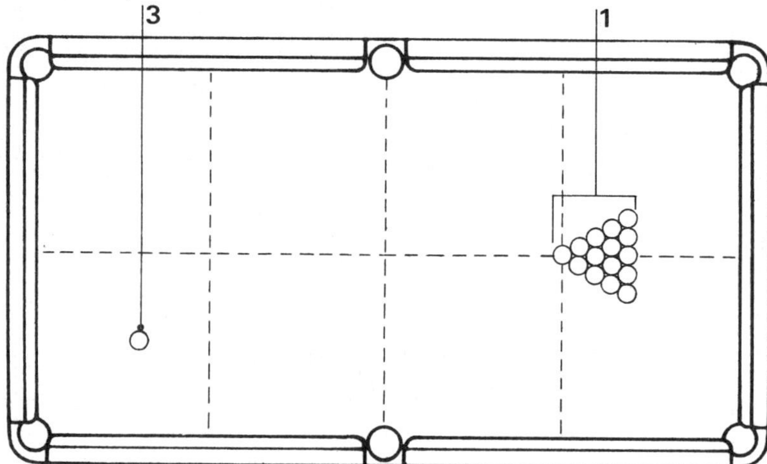

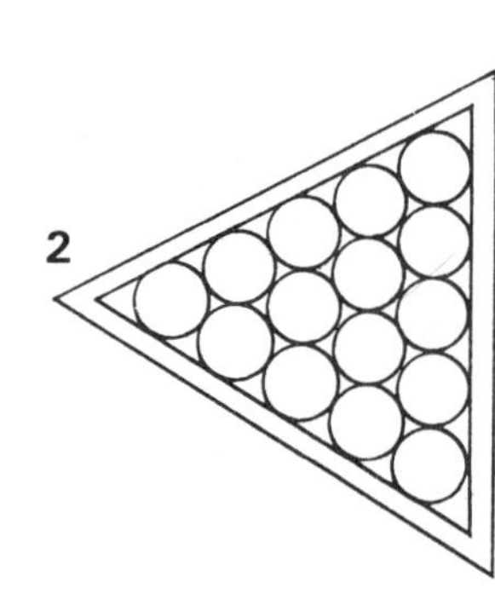

The break

8586

Types of break:
1 Pocket designated ball

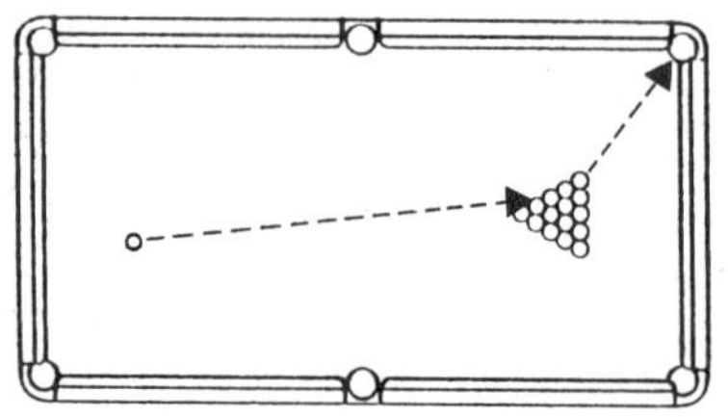

2 Drive cue ball and two object balls onto cushion

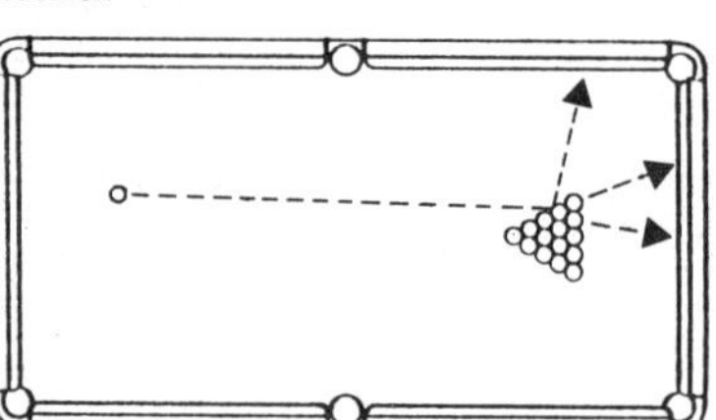

3 Drive two object balls to cushion and scratch into pocket with cue ball

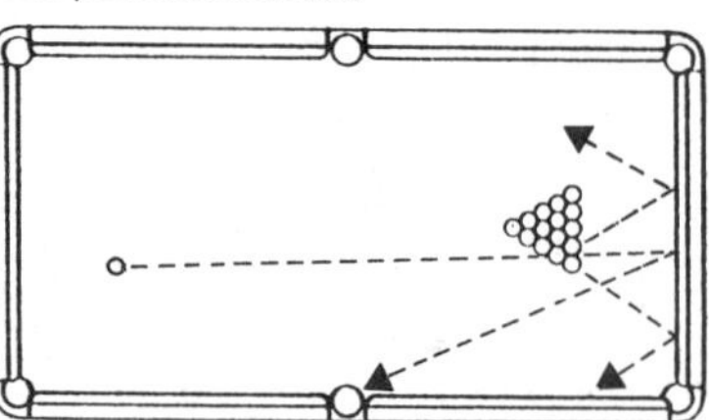

Safety play

8587

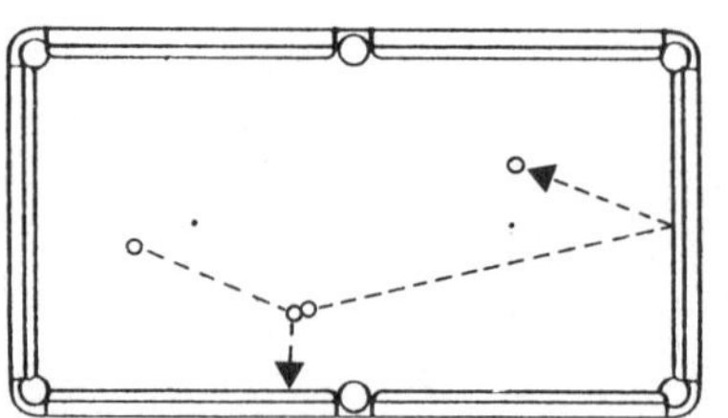

In attempting a safety, a player must either:
1 Drive an object ball onto a cushion

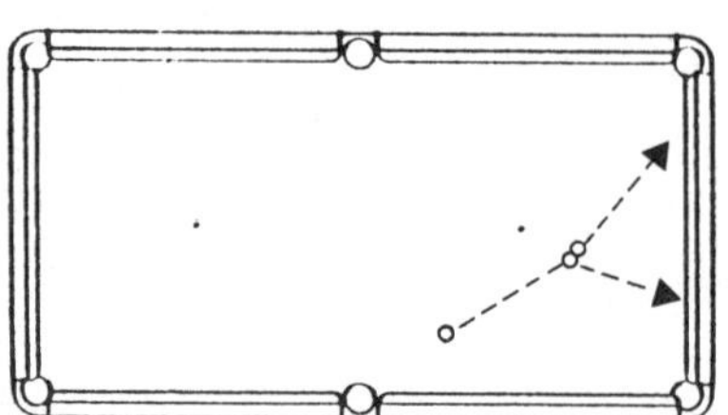

2 Cause the cue ball to strike a cushion, after contacting an object ball

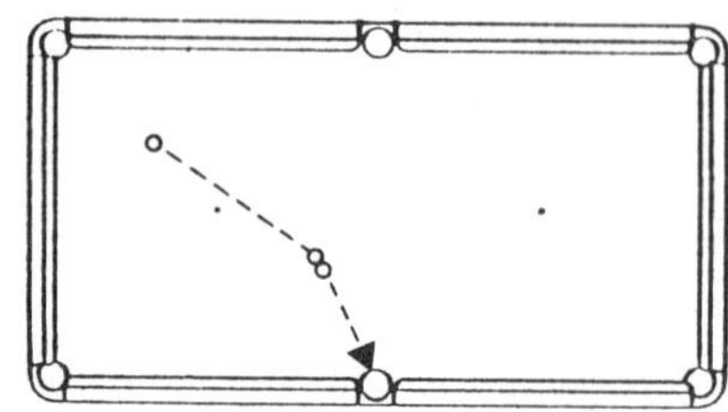

3 Pocket an object ball

861 LAWN TENNIS

History

8611 Tennis is a racket-and-ball game played on a flat surface of grass or a hard material. An Englishman, Major Walter Wingfield, founded the modern game on grass in the 1870s. The first major lawn tennis tournament took place at Wimbledon, in England, in 1877. The first US men's championship tournament took place in 1881 in Rhode Island. Since 1968 lawn tennis has been mainly a professional sport.

Rules

8612 **Number of players** One a side (singles), two a side (doubles), or opposing pairs of a man and a woman (mixed doubles).
Equipment Rackets of wood, steel, or composition frames; gut or synthetic strings; weight usually 13–14 oz (368.5–396.9 g). Balls have a hollow rubber core covered with a white or yellow felt fabric; diameter $2\frac{1}{5}$–$2\frac{5}{8}$ in (6.35–6.67cm); weight 2–$2\frac{1}{16}$ oz (56.7–58.5 g).
Objectives To hit the ball over the net so that it falls inside the opponent's court and cannot be returned into the player's court.
Duration A match consists of a maximum of five sets for men and three for women. A set is won by the first side to win six games and at least two more games than an opponent e.g. 6–4, 7–5. A game is won by the first side to win four points. The score for one point is 15, two points 30, three points 40. Four points is a game. If both players have the same score it is called "all" e.g. 30–all. When both players reach the same score of 40 (40–all), it is called deuce. The next point scored will be "advantage." If the same player wins the following point he or she wins the game.
The court The surface may be grass, a variety of asphalt, clay, porous concrete, or other composition. It is marked out with white lines as shown in the diagram. The lines are included within the limits of the court.
1 Base line
2 Service line
3 Right court
4 Left court
5 Singles sideline
6 Doubles sideline
7 Center line
8 Center mark

Doubles

8613 The doubles game is played within a wider playing area. Except for the order of service, the same rules apply as for singles.
Service
The pair (**1, 2**) about to serve in the first game decides which player will serve for that game. The opposing pair (**3, 4**) decides similarly for the second game.
The player in the first pair who did not serve in the first game serves in the third game, while the fourth player (**4**) serves in the fourth game. The same order is kept throughout each set.
Receiving
The pair about to receive in the first game (**3, 4**) decides which player shall receive the first service (**3**).That player then receives all the first services in the odd games of that set. Similarly, the pair due to receive in the second game (**1, 2**) makes a choice, and the chosen player (**2**) receives the first service in the even games of that set.
In each game, partners receive the service alternately. During a rally each pair plays the ball alternately, either partner of each pair being allowed to return the ball.

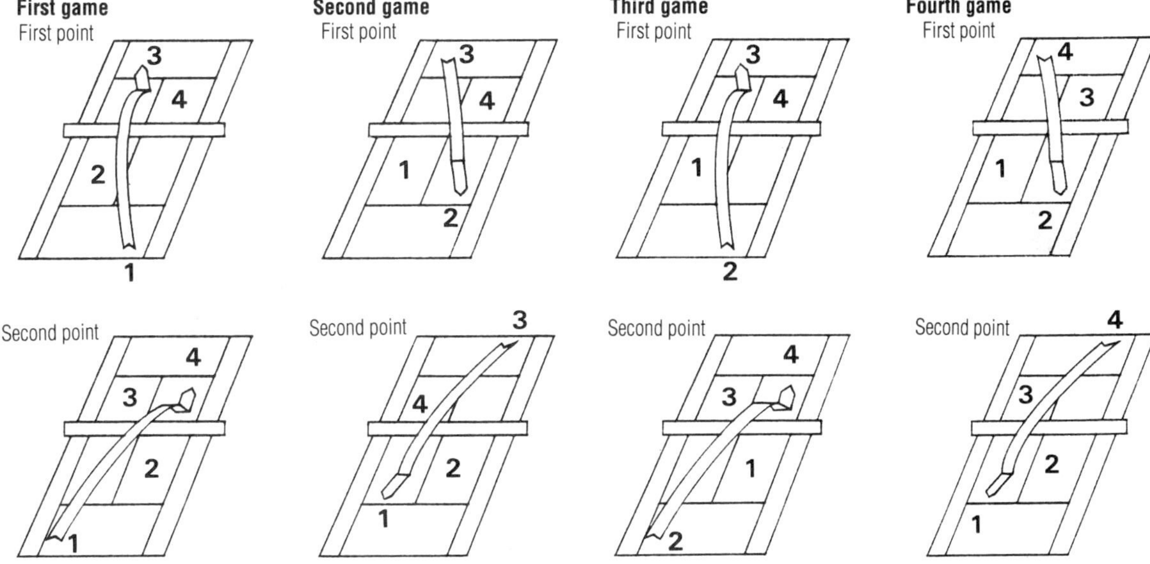

Strokes

8614

1 Service
2 Lob
3 Forehand drive
4 Half volley
5 Backhand drive
6 Smash

Key words

8615 **ace** A service winner that the receiver is unable to touch.
advantage The first point served after deuce.
deuce The score after each player has scored three points (40–all). Deuce is also the score of any tied result after 40–all in the same game. If both players score advantage, the score is deuce once more until one player wins two consecutive points to win a game.
fault A service that lands in the net or outside the receiver's service court.
foot fault An illegal move. The server is on or over the base line, or walks or runs while serving.
grand slam The winning of the four major championships in one year (Wimbledon, US Open, French Open, and Australian Open).
ground stroke Any stroke played after the ball has bounced once on the court.
let A service that touches the net before dropping into the proper service court. It does not count and has to be replayed.
love A score of zero.
receiver The player receiving service.
seeding The placing of the best players in separate sections of a draw so that they do not meet until the later rounds.
service The stroke that starts each point, played from behind the base line into the service court diagonally opposite.
tie-breaker A method of deciding the winner of a set that is tied (usually at 6–all) by playing a certain number of extra points.

862 TABLE TENNIS

History

8621 No precise date of origin or inventor is known, but the game seems to have resulted from efforts to miniaturize tennis for the house, undertaken at about the same period of the 19th century as the efforts to adapt it for outdoor play on the lawn. Equipment for an early manufactured form is mentioned in a sports goods catalogue in 1884. The name ping-pong refers to the sound made by a celluloid toy ball picked up in the US by Gibb, holder of the four-mile record in 1887, and used for domestic play. The pimple-rubber covering for the wooden blade was first used by Goode of Putney, England, in around 1903. The International Table Tennis Federation (ITTF) was founded in 1926.

Rules

8622 **Number of Players** Two (singles) or four (doubles).
Officials Play is controlled by an umpire, whose decision is final on any question of fact.
Equipment Table 9 ft (2.74 m) long, 5 ft (1.52 m) wide, 2 ft 6 in (76 cm) high. A net 6 in (15.25 cm) high, suspended across the center of the table. Rackets of any size, weight or shape, with the blade made of wood and covered with rubber of a total thickness not exceeding $^{1}/_{8}$ in (4 mm). The ball is of celluloid or similar plastic, white or yellow, with a matt surface and weighing 0.09 oz (2.5 g).
Objective The aim is to win points by making shots that an opponent is unable to return.
Serving The ball is thrown nearly vertically upward from the palm of the free hand, without imparting spin, rises at least 6.3 in (16 cm), and is struck on descent, from behind the end of the table, first to touch the server's court and then, passing directly over or around the net, to touch the service area within the receiver's court. In doubles, the ball must touch the right-hand half of the court on the serving side and then the diagonaly opposite court, within the service line.
Returning service The ball, after bouncing once only, is struck to pass directly over or around the net to touch the opponent's court. The ball must not be struck by a player more than once consecutively. The ball goes out of play when it touches any object other than the playing surface, the net or its supports, the racket or the racket hand below the wrist.
Change of service In singles and doubles, service passes from one player to another after every five points scored, unless both sides score 20 points, when the service changes after every point. In doubles, the second server is the player who receives first, the third server is the partner of the player who served first, and the fourth server the partner of the player who received first, a sequence repeated until the end of the game.
Expedite system Introduced if a game is unfinished 15 minutes after the start, and applying thereafter to all remaining games of the match. Each player serves in turn. If the service and 12 successive strokes of the server are returned by the receiver, the server loses a point.

The table

8623

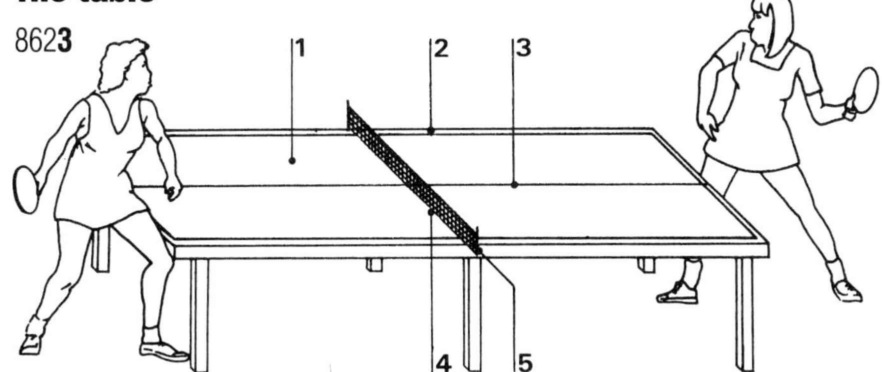

The table may be of any material but is normally of wood. It must give a bounce of about 23 cm to a standard ball, when the ball is dropped from a height of 30 cm. The playing surface (**1**) should be dark coloured, preferably green, and matt, with white marking lines. A white line (**2**), 2 cm wide, marks the edges of the table. the sides of the table top are not concidered part of the playing surface. For doubles, the playing surface is divided into halves by a 3 mm white line (**3**). The net (**4**), 1.83 cm long, is suspended across the center of the table by a cord attached to a post (**5**) at either end. The playing area is only defined for international competition, where the minimum area required is about 2.75 m at esch side and 5.5 m at the ends. The minimum height is 3.5 m.

Key words

8624

game Won by the player or pair first scoring 21 points, unless both have scored 20 points, when the winner is the first to score two points more than the opposition.
let When no point is scored, for example, when the ball touches the net in service.
match Best of three or five games.
rally Period when the ball is in play.
receiver Player who strikes the ball second in a rally.
server Player who strikes the ball first in a rally.

863 BADMINTON

History

8631

Badminton derives its name from the seat of the Duke of Beaufort in Gloucestershire, England, where the game is supposed to have developed about 1870 from the ancient children's game of battledore and shuttlecock. From the outset it gained popularity with army officers who took it to India and played it out of doors. The first laws were drawn up in Poona in the mid-1870s.

The Badminton Association was founded at Southsea, Hampshire, in 1893. It was the prime mover in 1934 in founding the International Badminton Federation (IBF), which now has over 50 member countries.

Rules

8632

Number of players Two (singles) or four (doubles).
Equipment Court 44 ft (13.40 m) by 20 ft (6.10 m), with a net 5 ft (1.52 m) high. Rackets, light and usually made of metal or carbon fiber, and weighing 3–4.94 oz (85–140 g). A shuttle, made of 16 feathers fixed in a cork base (in lower class play, synthetic materials are used), weighing 0.17–0.19 oz (4.74–5.50 g). Dress may be colored. Rubber-soled shoes are worn.
Officials The umpire is in charge of the match, the court and its immediate surroundings. A service judge and line judges may also be appointed.
Objective The aim of the game is to hit the shuttle to the floor on the opponent's side of the net.
Singles If the server's score is even, he or she serves from the right-hand court; if odd, from the left-hand court. The shuttle is served into the service court diagonaly opposed to the server.
Doubles If the server wins the first point, he or she then serves into the opponent's left service court from his or her own left service court. When the serve is lost, it passes to the opponent who was in the right service court at the start of the rally. After the service has thus changed ends at the start of each game, the receiving side must win two rallies to retrieve it. The first opponent to serve does so from alternate courts until he or she loses a rally. Then the opponent's partner takes over, serving from the court he or she was in at the start of the rally. The partner serves from alternate courts until he or she loses a rally. The service then passes across the net, and both of that pair serve.
Scoring Only the serving side can score a point. A game consists of 15 points in doubles and men's singles, and of 11 points in women's singles. The players change ends after every game and during the third game, when the leading player's score reaches eight points in a game of 15 points, or six points in a game of 11 points.

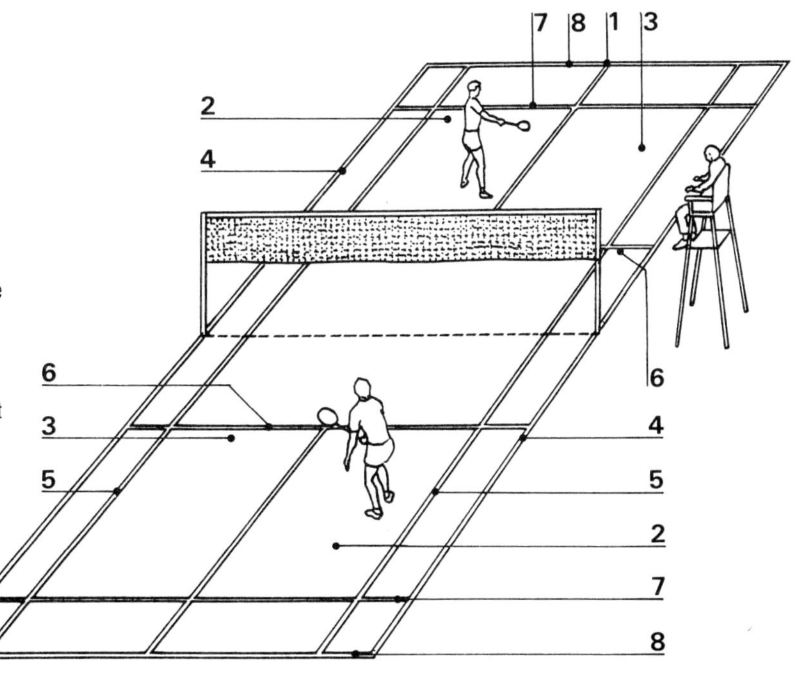

1 Center
2 Right service court
3 Left service court
4 Doubles sideline
5 Singles sideline
6 Short service line
7 Long service line doubles
8 Long service line singles

Key words

8633

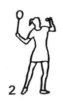

1 Short service
2 High service

faults Infringements that end a rally. If the server commits a fault, the serve passes to the opponents. If the non-server does so, the server wins a point.
let Allows a rally and resulting score to be disregarded. Lets are declared by the umpire without appeals from the players.
match Generally consists of the best of three games.
receiver Player who receives the service.
server Player who opens the rally.
setting If both players or sides reach the same score during the last stages of a game, play may be extended by "setting" a new deciding score. The player or side entitled to "set" the game must decide to do so before the next service is taken when the score first reaches the "setting" score. The score reverts to 0–0 and proceeds to 2, 3, or 5 as appropriate. The final score is the total number of points scored in the game.

864 JAI A LAI (PELOTA)

History

8641 Jai a lai or *pelota*, or *pelote Basque*, is a generic name for numerous hand, glove, racquet, or bat-and-ball games adapted originally from the ancient French *jeux de paume*, and first - and still mainly - played in the Basque areas of France and Spain, though pelota in one or more of its varieties is now played all over the world.

Rules

8642 **Number of players** Two, or several teams. The game can be played as singles, doubles or triples.
Officials Three judges, standing opposite lines 4, 7 and 11, carrying rackets to protect themselves from the ball.
Equipment Three-walled court (fronton) divided into 15 numbered areas along the lateral wall. The serving zone is the space between areas 4 and 7. A ball (pelota) with a hard rubber core and covered with a layer of linen thread and two layers of goatskin, diameter 2 in (5 cm), weight 4.5 oz (127.58 g). Wicker basket (cesta) with a chestnut frame, covered with woven reed. The player's hand is inserted into a leather glove sewn to the outside of the cesta, and a long tape is wrapped around the glove to keep it on the hand. Players wear white trousers, a colored sash or belt, a colored shirt with number, white rubber-soled shoes and a helmet.
Objective Players try to hit the pelota with the wicker basket against the front wall so that their opponents will be unable to return it and will therefore lose a point.
Play The ball must be served against the frontis wall so that it returns within the serving zone. It must be caught in the cesta and thrown in a continuous motion, and may be returned before it bounces or after bouncing once. The ball must be returned to the frontis, and must be played within the shaded areas on the walls.
Scoring A match is played for a score of 7 to 35, points gained when the opponent returns the ball after it has bounced more than once; misses the ball; does not return the ball on to the frontis; fails to catch the ball and throw it in a continuous motion.

The court

8643

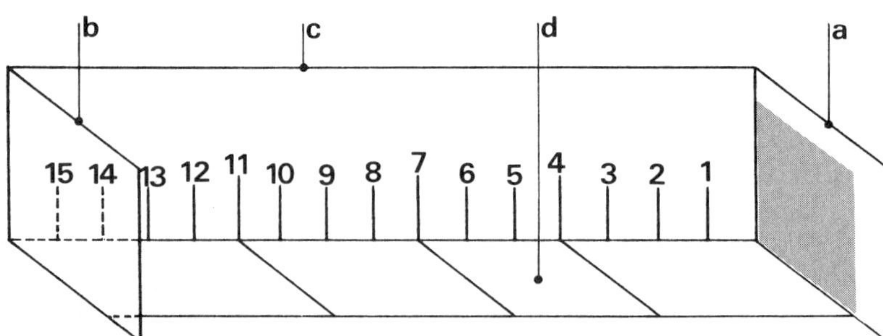

The court has three walls. The fronf wall is called the frontis (**a**), the back wall is called the rebote (**b**), the side wall is called the lateral (**c**). The frontis is made of granite blocks; the rabote, lateral, and floor are made of gunite, a pressurised cement. The fourth side of the court has a clear screen through which the spectators watch the game. The court is divided into 15 numbered areas. The serving zone (**d**) is in the space between areas 4 and 7.

1 Cesta
2 Pelota

Key words

8644 **frontis** Front wall of the playing court, made of granite blocks.
lateral Side wall of the playing court, made of a pressurized cement, gunite.
quiniela (betting) Version of the game played as singles or doubles with a maximum of eight teams of one or two players. The first two players or teams begin with the first side serving. Play continues until one of the teams loses a point. The losing team returns to the end of the players' bench and is replaced by the next team to play (the third side). The game continues in this way, with the winning team always remaining on court, until one side wins the match by scoring the specified number of points. There is a play-off in case of a tie.
rebote Back wall of the playing court, made of a pressurized cement, gunite.
seven-points system In games in which eight teams or players are playing for seven points, one point is scored for each win in the first round (i.e., until all eight players or teams have played once) and two points for each win in subsequent games.

871 BASEBALL

History

8711 Baseball was originally derived from an old English game called rounders, although many people believe that it was invented by Abner Doubleday, an American, in 1839. The game began in the US in the mid-1800s. In 1845, Alexander Cartwright founded a club called the Knickerbocker Base Ball Club of New York. Two major leagues of professional players, the American League and the National League, each made up of 14 clubs, eventually emerged. The US champions are decided by the World Series, a series of games played each fall between the winners of the major leagues.

Rules

8712 **Number of players** Nine in each of two teams. American League teams use a tenth player, known as a "designated hitter."
Objectives To score more runs than the opponents. A game consists of nine innings (turns at bat). Extra innings are played if scores are tied after nine. Visitors bat first. The pitcher throws the ball to the batter to try to get the batter out. The batter scores by hitting the ball in such a way as to be able to run the circuit of all four bases successfully. This equals one run. A player can also hit safely to reach base and later get home off a subsequent player's hit.
Equipment A rounded wooden bat up to 42 in (106 cm) long and up to $2^3/_4$ in (7 cm) in diameter. A hard round ball with a cork center encased in rubber, yarn, and cowhide, $9–9^1/_4$ in (23–23.5 cm) in circumference, weighing $5–5^1/_2$ oz (142–156 g.) Gloves and padding to protect players.
Duration When three players are out, regardless of how many are on base, the side is retired and the opponents go in to bat. An inning finishes when each side has had three players retired.
Substitutes A substitute may take the place of any player on the field when the ball is dead.

The playing area

8713 The playing field is composed of the infield and the outfield. In the infield is the area bounded by the four bases. The outfield is the area beyond this section bounded by the extension of the two foul lines.
Home plate This is a five-sided slab of whitened rubber, while the other three bases are marked by white canvas bags. The pitcher's plate is a rectangular slab of whitened rubber usually set on a raised mound of earth.
Fielding positions
1 Pitcher
2 Catcher
3 First baseman
4 Second baseman
5 Third baseman
6 Shortstop
7 Left fielder
8 Center fielder
9 Right fielder

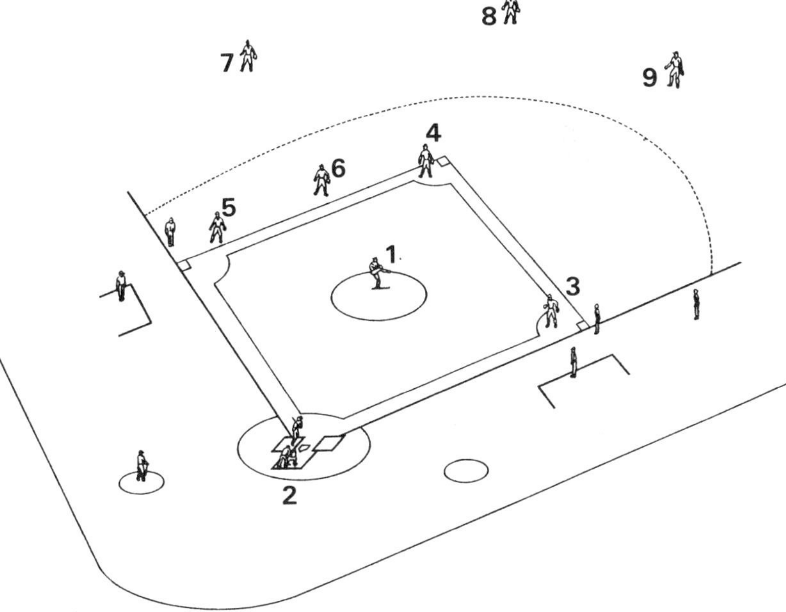

Key words

8714

balk An illegal act by the pitcher while one or more runners are on base. Any runner may then walk on to the next base.
ball A pitch outside the strike zone that is not struck at by the batter.
bases Located at the home plate and the other three corners of the infield, where they are canvas bags pegged to the ground.
batter's box Area to left and right of the home plate in which the batter stands.
bunt A batted ball hit softly within the infield (**1**).
diamond Nickname for the infield.
double A hit for two bases.
double play Two players put out on the same pitch (**2**).
fair territory The area formed by the 90° angle between home plate and first and third bases.
force play When a runner is forced to move on to the next base because the batter has become a runner.
home plate Slab of whitened rubber sunk into the ground in front of the catcher.
home run A hit that allows the batter to get around all the bases in one turn.
infield A square area with a base at each corner.
outfield Grass-covered area between the infield and the fences or walls farthest from home plate.
pinch-hitter Substitute batter.
pitcher's mound Mound near the center of the infield from which the pitcher throws the ball.
run Scored by a batter who progressively reaches first, second, third, and home bases without being put out.
single A hit for first base.
squeeze play The batter bunts the ball so that a runner on third base can get home.
steal The advance by a runner from one base to another when no hit has been made, usually while the pitcher is pitching (**3**).

continued

Key words continued

8714 **strike** Called by the umpire when the batter misses a legal pitch or does not swing at a pitch in the strike zone.
strike out Three strikes on the batter, which is an out.
strike zone Area over the home plate between the batter's armpits and knees (**4**).

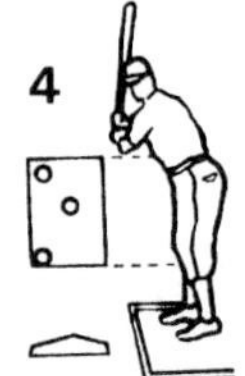

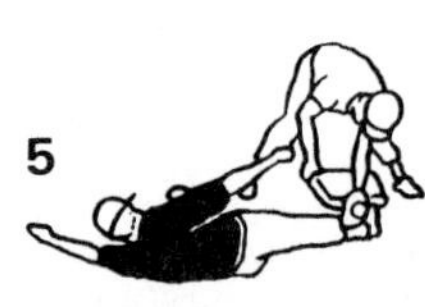

tagging Putting out a runner who is off a base by a fielder touching the base with a foot while holding the ball, or by touching the runner with the ball (**5**).
triple A hit for three bases.
Umpire: One of four officials stationed round the bases. The home plate umpire stands behind the catcher and calls balls and strikes.

872 BASKETBALL

History

8721 Basketball was invented in 1891 by James Naismith, a physical education instructor at a college in Springfield, Massachusetts. Asked to devise an indoor sport for playing in winter, he used a soccer ball and two empty peach boxes hanging from a balcony 10 ft (3 m) up. The game improved as baskets replaced the boxes and soon it was being played by colleges, clubs, and professionals throughout the US and Canada. The National Basketball Association (NBA) was formed in 1949.

Rules (NBA)

8722 **Number of players** Two teams of five players.
Equipment One round, inflated, leather ball; a basket and backboard; sleeveless numbered shirt, shorts, white socks, lightweight sports shoes with rubber soles.
Objective To score more points than the opponents by advancing the ball down the court and shooting it into the oppponents' basket; and to stop the opponents from scoring.
Substitutes Up to five or seven, who may come on the court at any time the ball is not in play.
Officials Three referees, one or two scorekeepers, one or two timekeepers.
Duration Four 12-min quarters with a $1^1/_2$-min break between each quarter, and 15 min between halves. If scores are tied at the end of regulation time, 5-min overtime sessions are played until one team wins.
The court This must have a hard surface (not grass). Its width may vary by 6.5 ft (2 m) and its length by 13 ft (4 m), but the proportions must be kept. The ceiling must be at least 23 ft (7 m) high. Lighting must be uniform and must not hinder players from throwing for a goal.

Baskets These consist of white cord nets to hold the ball briefly as it drops through. They are suspended from orange metal rings attached rigidly at right angles to the backboards.

1 Backboard
2 Basket
3 End line
4 Center line
5 Side line
6 Free throw line
7 Umpires
8 Players

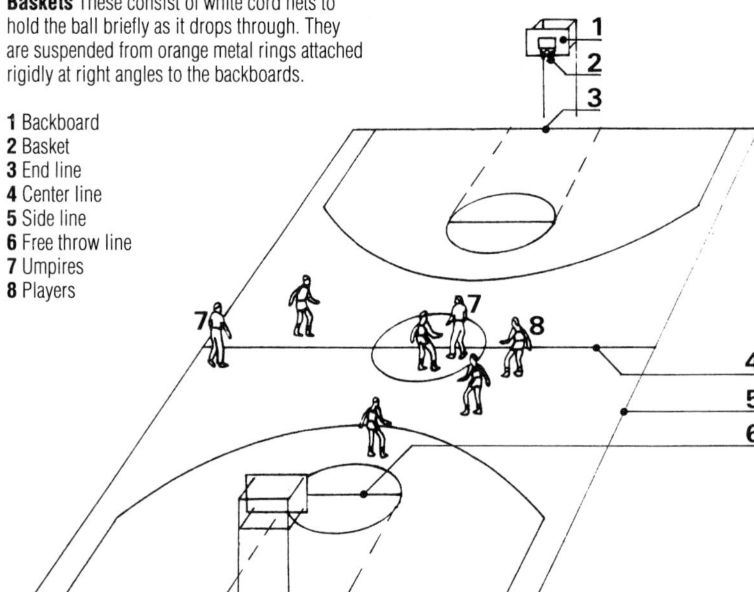

Key words

8723

assist A pass that leads directly to a basket being scored.
backcourt A team's defensive half of the court.
basket The target for shooting the ball, consisting of a metal hoop with a loose, open string net hanging down. The basket is fixed to a backboard.
backboard Rectangular board of clear fiberglass or metal to which the basket is attached.
center Usually the tallest and most important player of a team, playing between the two forwards; must be good on the rebound.
center jump Method of starting a game. An official tosses the ball into the air (**2**) between opposing centers standing in the center circle; they jump up and try to tap it to a teammate.
delay Offensive strategy to use up time by denying the ball to the opponents and thus preserve a lead.
double-team (trap) Defensive maneuver in which two players converge on the player with the ball, hoping to force the player into an error.
dribble To move the ball by repeatedly tapping it with the hand (**1**).
dunk A field goal made by jumping very high and stuffing the ball through the basket from above the rim.
fake To feign.
fast break An attempt to score quickly after the offensive team gains possession of the ball.
field goal A successful shot by any offensive player from anywhere on the floor during normal play. Counts three points if taken from behind a 3-point line, otherwise two points.
free throw Uncontested shot from behind the free throw line (**3**), as a penalty after certain fouls; scores one point.
front court The offensive team's half of the court.
goaltending Illegal interference with a field goal attempt when the ball is above the basket.
guards Two good dribblers and passers who direct the offense.
Harlem Globetrotters A dazzling all-black professional team that dominated the game in the 1930s and later switched to exhibition matches.

continued

Key words continued

8723 **held ball** Ball held and claimed by two opposing players simultaneously; possession is determined by a jump ball between the two players.
lay-up A shot attempted close to the basket.
National Basketball Association (NBA) US professional body formed in 1949 by the merger of the National Basketball League (NBL) and the Basketball Association of America (BAA).
personal foul Committed by a player who pushes, holds, or charges into an opponent or hits an opponent when in the act of shooting.
pick (screen) The legal blocking of a defensive player in order to free a teammate for a shot.
post The position played by the center on offense.
rebound Ball that bounces back into play off the backboard or rim of the basket after an unsuccessful shot.
screen See pick.
steal Interception of a pass, or other legal means of gaining possession of the ball from the offense.
technical foul Usually called for unsportsmanlike conduct toward an official.
three-point play Takes place when a player is fouled while making a successful shot and then goes on to score from the free throw.
three-point shot A basket scored from behind the 3-point line.
time out Legal stoppage of play, usually to discuss tactics. Seven "time outs" of 90 sec each are allowed during a game. Each team is also allowed one 20-sec "time out" in each half.
tip-in A field goal scored by tipping a rebound into the basket.
trap See double-team.
turnover Loss of possession by the offensive team without taking a shot.
violations Minor offenses such as ball-handling errors, usually by the offensive team; penalty is usually loss of possession.

873 CRICKET

History

8731 Cricket may first have been played in England in the 1300s. By the 1700s, it had become a popular sport, the first printed rules appearing in 1744. The rules are now made and published by the Marylebone Cricket Club (MCC). Test matches are played between Australia, England, India, New Zealand, Pakistan, Sri Lanka, and the West Indies.

Rules

8732 **Number of players** Two teams of 11 players each.
Equipment One ball, two bats, two wickets; white or cream shirt and long trousers, optional sweater, cricket boots; optional helmet with face guard, gloves for batsmen and wicket keeper; white padded leg and optional arm guards for batsmen; abdomen protector.
Objective To score the most runs.
Duration From one to five days (for test matches); prescribed by time or a certain number of overs. There are intervals for lunch, tea, and between innings.
Substitutes These may replace injured or sick players provided they do not bat or bowl.
Officials Two umpires who control the game: one at the bowling wicket, the other standing square to the batting wicket.
Pitch This is the area between the two bowling creases 22 yd (20 m) long and extending 5 ft (1.5 m) in width on either side of a line joining the center of the wickets. The pitch, of grass (or approved matting), is prepared before the game to be level and with the grass trimmed short. In first class cricket, regulations govern when and how often the pitch is to be rolled, mown, watered, or covered. The rest of the area is enclosed by a boundary line. The wicket at each end of the pitch is composed of three vertical stumps on top of which are placed two horizontal bails.
The return and popping creases are unlimited in length.

10 3 6 2

1 Bowler
2 Wicket keeper
3 Striking batsman
4 Non-striking batsman
5 Umpire
6 Wicket
7 Bowling crease
8 Popping crease
9 Return crease
10 The pitch

Fielding positions

8733 There are 11 players in a team.
Fielding positions (for a right handed batsman):

1 Bowler
2 Wicket keeper
3 Slips
4 Leg slip
5 Backward short leg
6 Square short leg
7 Forward short leg
8 Silly point
9 Gully
10 Silly mid off
11 Silly mid on
12 Midwicket
13 Square leg
14 Backward point
15 Point
16 Cover
17 Short extra cover
18 Extra cover
19 Deep extra cover
20 Mid off
21 Deep mid off
22 Mid on
23 Deep mid on
24 Short fine leg
25 Deep fine leg
26 Short third man
27 Third man
28 Long leg
29 Deep square leg
30 Deep midwicket
31 Long on
32 Long off

Key words

8734

Ashes, the Trophy competed for by England and Australia in test matches, comprising the remains of a burnt cricket stump in a small urn.
bails Two small pieces of wood that rest horizontally in grooves on top of the stumps.
bouncer Ball bowled short so that it bounces high and fast at the batsman as it pitches.
boundary When a batsman strikes the ball over the boundary of the field, scoring four runs. If the ball clears the boundary without bouncing, the score is six runs.
bowler Must deliver the ball with the back foot between the return creases.
bowling crease White line, 8 ft 8 in (2.64 m) long, drawn through the stumps.
bye A run not struck by the bat and allotted to extras.
declaration Voluntary closure of an innings announced by the batting team's captain before all ten wickets have fallen.
duck A score of zero by a batsman who has lost a wicket.
extras Runs scored not by the bat but by errors in the fielding side.
follow-on Immediate second innings forced on a team that has failed to score a prescribed total of runs in the first innings.
full toss Ball that does not bounce before reaching the batsman.
hat-trick Three wickets taken with three successive balls.
howzat! ("How's that!") A shouted appeal to the umpire by the fielders, meaning "Is the batsman out?"
innings The batting turn of a team or player, ended when ten batsmen are dismissed or the captain makes a declaration. Matches may be of one or two innings per team.
leg Side of the field to the left of and behind a right-handed batsman facing the bowler.
leg before wicket (lbw) A way in which a batsman may be out if any part of the body except the hands prevents the ball from hitting the wicket, provided the ball has not first touched the bat or a hand (**1**).
legbreak Ball that breaks from leg to off when it pitches.
leg bye Run scored when the ball misses the bat but touches any other part of the batsman's body except the hands (**2**).
long hop Short-pitched ball that is easy to hit.
Lord's A major cricket ground in London, headquarters of the Marylebone Cricket Club (MCC).
maiden over An over in which no runs are scored.
national championships Series held to determine the best national teams. They include the County Championships (England); Sheffield Shield (Australia); Plunket Shield (New Zealand); Currie Cup (South Africa); Shell Series (West Indies), and the Ranji Trophy (India).
no-ball A ball judged illegal because of some infringement by the bowler. The batting side scores one run unless the batsman hits it (**3**).
nonstriker Batsman at the wicket opposite to that of the striker.
off Part of the field to which the batsman presents the bat when taking strike; i.e., the right-hand side for a right-hander.
off-break Ball that breaks from off to leg when it hits the ground.
over Series of six or sometimes eight balls bowled from one end by the same bowler.
over the wicket Bowling with the bowler's arm nearest the wicket.
popping crease White line drawn 4 ft (1.2 m) in front of the bowling crease. The bowler must deliver the ball with some part of the front foot behind the popping crease. A batsman cannot be stumped or run out if a foot or the bat is behind the popping crease.
return creases Lines drawn from each end of the bowling crease, extending forward to the popping crease and back at least 4 ft (1.2 m) behind the bowling crease.
round the wicket Bowling with the bowler's arm farthest from the wicket.
run Score usually achieved after one batsman has hit the ball and each batsman has run safely to reach the opposite wicket.
seamer Medium pace bowler who moves the ball by angling the seam of the ball.
striker Batsman standing at the far end from the bowler and receiving the ball from him.
stump Upright wooden stick, three in a line form a wicket.
test matches International competitions at the highest level between seven nations (see History.)
wicket Three wooden stumps and two bails that rest on top of the stumps, 9 in (23 cm) wide, 2 ft 4 in (81.5 cm) high.
wicket keeper Member of the fielding side who stands behind the batsman and the wicket to catch or stop the ball from the bowler.
wide A ball bowled so wide or high that the batsman cannot reach it. A run is added to the score and an extra ball added to the over.
yorker Ball that pitches just under or just behind the bat.

874 AMERICAN FOOTBALL

History

8741

A soccerlike game, with a round ball, developed in the Eastern US. in the mid-1800s. After a Canadian team from McGill University introduced the English game of rugby to Harvard University, Americans began to play rugby-style football, with an oval ball. Games became increasingly hectic and violent, but by the early 1900s, new rules were introduced to make the sport more orderly, safer, and more exciting.

Rules

8742

Number of players Two teams of 11.
Equipment Leather or plastic helmet; plastic face mask; jersey in team color; number on chest and back; chest and shoulder padding; pants; below-the-belt padding; shin padding; lightweight shoes.
Objective To score more points than the opponents by kicking or putting the ball behind the opponents' goal line by passing or running with it.
Duration Sixty min playing time divided into two halves and four quarters. A 15-min interval separates the halves. After a tie, there is a 15-min sudden-death period.
Substitutes Unlimited, but allowed on the field only after the ball is dead.
The field The area between the end lines and the side lines is the field of play.

The field is divided between the goal lines by parallel yardlines, 5 yd (4.6 m) apart. These are intersected by short inbound lines 70 ft 9 in (21.5 m) from each sideline. Between the inbound lines there are marks at 1 yd (91 cm) intervals. Sidelines and end lines are out of bounds; goal lines signify the start of end zones.

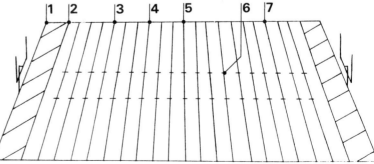

1 End line
2 Goal line
3 20 yd line
4 35 yd line
5 50 yd line
6 Inbound lines
7 Yardlines

Players and positions

8743 **backfield formation** This is made up of the four backs.
backs four players consisting usually of one quarterback, two halfbacks, and one fullback.
blocking back Fullback used as a blocker.
center One of five interior linemen.
cornerbacks In Canadian football, two players who, with two safeties, make up a defensive unit called the secondary.
defensive tackles Two of the four-man line called the front four in a defensive team.
ends Two of the seven linemen of an offensive team whose main job is to block.
flanker In Canadian football, offensive halfback who lines up on the flank behind the line of scrimmage, mainly as a pass receiver.
fullback One of the four backs that make up the backfield of the offensive team.
guards Two interior linemen next to the center.
halfbacks Two of the four backs who make up the backfield.
interior linemen Five of the seven linemen: a center, two guards and two tackles.
linebacker Defensive player who lines up behind the line of scrimmage. He tackles running plays through the line.
quarterback One of the four backs of an offensive team. He initiates all the attacks and directs play.
secondary In Canadian football, one of three principal units in the defensive team, made up of two cornerbacks and two safeties.
wingback In Canadian football, another name for flanker.

Scrimmage position for American football

Team with ball (attacking)
C Center
G Guard
T Tackle
E End
Q Quarterback
B Back

Team defending
A Defensive tackle
F Defensive end
L Linebacker
D Defensive back

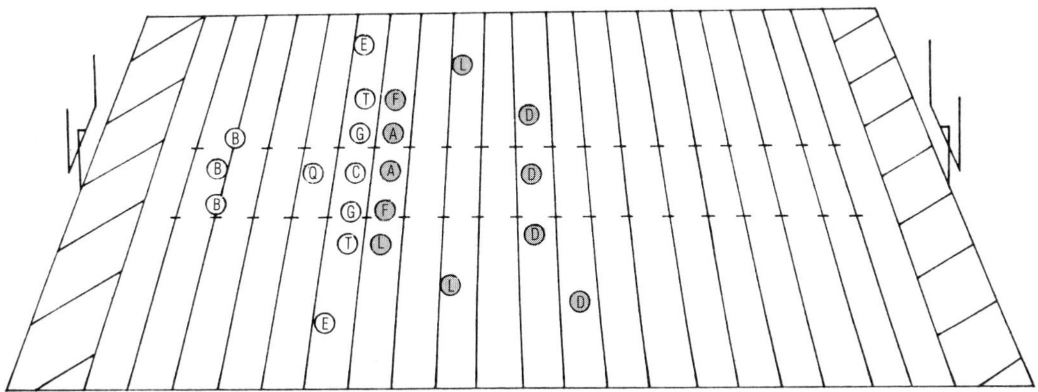

Comparison of types

8744 CANADIAN AND AMERICAN FOOTBALL
American football has 11 players a side. One side at a time runs with, passes, or kicks an oval ball in short "plays." Points are won by touchdowns behind the defense's goal line or by kicking the ball over the goal crossbar. Defenders can tackle the ball carrier. Playing time is 60 min, with one long interval and two brief ones.
Canadian football This resembles American football but there are 12 players a side. Also, the field is larger, with a "dead-line" 25 yd (22.5 m) behind each goal line, and some of the rules are different. For instance, there is an extra means of scoring one point. Playing time is 60 min, with one long interval and two brief ones.

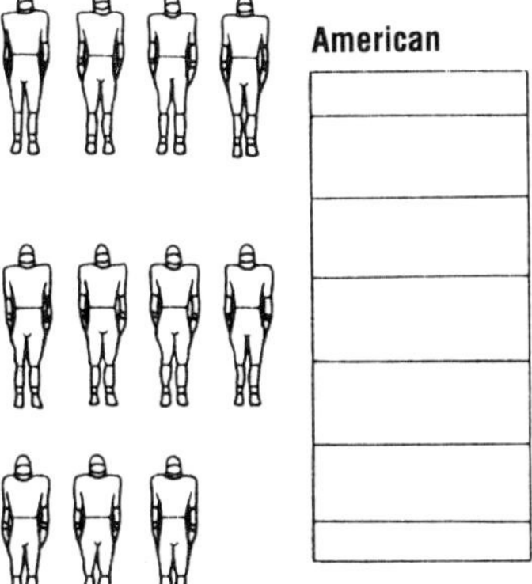

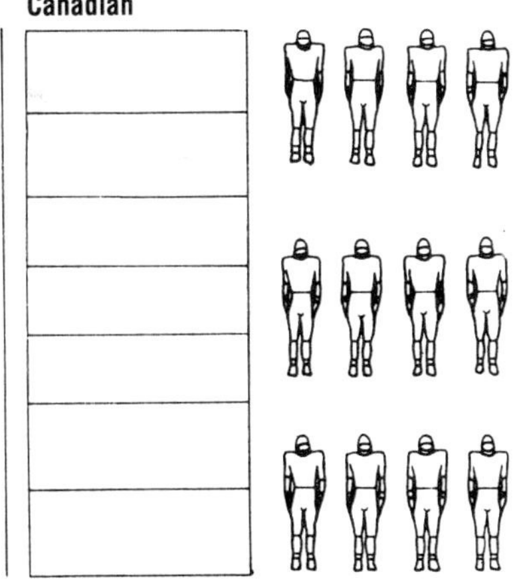

COLLEGE AND PROFESSIONAL FOOTBALL	COLLEGE FOOTBALL	PROFESSIONAL FOOTBALL
The field	Same overall dimensions as those for the professional game, but the sidelines are only 53 ft 4 in (16.3 cm) in from the sidelines, and the goal line is the equivalent of the end line on the professional field	Inbounds lines are 70 ft 9 in (21.5 m) in from the sidelines.
Goalposts (width between goalpost uprights)	24 ft 4 in (7 m)	18 ft 6 in (5.6 m)
Ball	Rubber or composition-cover ball if agreed beforehand. Dimensions as for professional except that the short circumference must be 21–21.25 in (53–54 cm)	Leather. Short circumference 21.25–21.5 in (54–54.5 cm)
Number of officials	5–6	7
Kick off	Players kick from the 40 yd (36.6 m) line	Players kick from the 35 yd (32 m) line

continued

Comparison of types continued

8744

	COLLEGE FOOTBALL	PROFESSIONAL FOOTBALL
Point-after-touchdown	Players are awarded one point for kicking the ball through the posts and two points for running or passing it over the goal line.	One point is awarded for kicking
If the game ends after four periods in a tie score	The result of the game is a tie.	A sudden death overtime period of 15 min is provided. Whichever team scores first is the winner.
Fumbles	When a fumble touches the ground, only the team that has fumbled can advance the ball.	A fumble may be picked up and advanced by any player in either team.
Penalty for holding an opponent	10 yd (9.1 m).	15 yd (13.7 m).
Inbounds	The player must have one foot inbounds at the time of the catch.	Player must have both feet inbounds while in possession of the ball.
Player on the ground	Player may not advance if any part of his body except his hands and feet touches the ground.	A running back or receiver, with the ball, may continue to run after he slips to the ground without being tackled.
Missed field goals	Ball returned to the 20 yd (18.3 m) line.	Ball is returned to where kick was made (line of scrimmage), or to the 20 yd (18.3 m) line.
Uniformed players	As many players in uniform as wanted for a home game, 90 or more, and travel with 60 or more.	Limited to 45.

Key words

8745

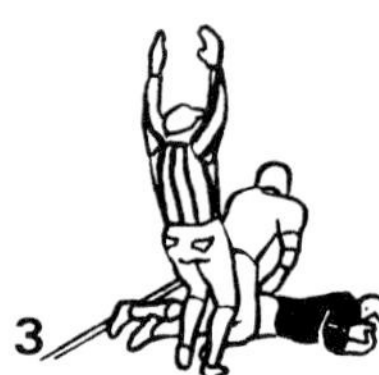

blitz Rush by defensive linebackers to tackle the opposing quarterback before he can get rid of the ball.
clipping Violation by an offensive player who blocks a defensive player from behind beyond the line of scrimmage.
conversion Score (one point) immediately after a touchdown by place-kicking the ball over the crossbar and between the goalposts. Two points scored, in Canadian football after a touchdown by ball-carrying or passing play.
dead ball Ball kicked beyond the end zone, or one caught by the kick returner in the end zone while touching the ground with his knee.
defensive team Team without the ball defending against the offensive team.
down Any of four attempts by the offense (three in Canadian football) to advance the ball at least 10 yards (9.1 m) by passing or running.
draw Play in which the quarterback drops back to feign pass then hands the ball to a running back.
fair catch Catch of a kicked ball by a player who signals by raising a hand at arm's length above his head. He may not advance the ball and may not be tackled.
field goal Score (three points) made by place-kicking or drop-kicking the ball over the crossbar during ordinary play.
field position Location of the ball on the field.
flag Yellow cloth thrown in the air by an official to signal a violation.
forward pass Thrown ball from behind the line of scrimmage to any one of five possible receivers.
fumble Occurs when a runner loses the ball before being tackled; results in a free ball.
gridiron The football field, marked with white lines.
hash marks In Canadian football, two rows of lines that run down the field across the yard lines; called inbound lines in American football.
I-formation Offensive formation in which the running backs line up directly behind the quarterback.
interference Occurs when the pass receiver or pass defender is tackled, blocked or pushed while the ball is still in the air.
kick-off Kick that puts the ball into play (**1**). Ball must travel at least 10yd (9.1 m) after a kick off. Either team may then recover it.
line of scrimmage Imaginary line passing through the end of the ball nearest a team's own goal line. Each team has its own line. It marks the position of the ball at the start of each down.
National Football League The only major professional football league in the US, made up of 28 teams.
neutral zone Area between the two lines of scrimmage.
offensive team Team with the ball.
offside This occurs when a player crosses the line of scrimmage before the ball is snapped.
onside kick Short kick-off that travels just far enough to be recoverable by the kicking team.
option Offensive maneuver in which a back may choose to pass the ball or run with it.
rollout Maneuver in which a passer retreats behind the line of scrimmage and runs to the left or right before passing the ball.
rouge or single point In Canadian football, one point scored when the ball is played into the opposition goal area and becomes dead in the opponents' posession; touches or crosses the boundary lines, or touches the ground or a player beyond those lines,
roughing Foul committed against a passer or kicker.
running back Halfback who carries the ball.
sack The tackle of a quarterback before he can pass the ball.
safety Score (two points)made by the defense when it tackles the ball carrier in his own end zone.
screen pass Occurs when the quarterback behind the line of scrimmage passes the ball to a receiver behind several blockers.
scrimmage Period from the moment the ball goes into play until the moment it is declared dead.
snap This occurs when a center quickly puts the ball in play from its position on the ground by passing it through his legs to a teammate behind (**2**).
Super Bowl Game played each January for the National Football League title.
T-formation Offensive formation with two running backs lined up side by side behind the quarterback.
time out A period of $1\frac{1}{2}$ minutes during which play is suspended. Each team is allowed up to three time outs in each half. In Canadian football, can be requested only during the last three minutes of a half and the last minute of extra time, and last 30 sec.
touchback Play in which a ball is put down by a player behind his own goal line after an opposing player has put it across the goal line. The ball is then put in play on the receiving team's 20-yd (18.2 m) line.
touchdown Score (six points) by running the ball or catching a pass over the opposing team's goal line (**3**).
trap Play in which player is allowed to cross the line of scrimmage and then blocked from the side; the ball carrier then runs through the resulting gap.
yard lines White lines marked across the field every 5 yd (4.6 m).
zone coverage System of defense in which each back is responsible for a certain area.

875 SOCCER

History

8751 A ball game similar to soccer was played in China, Greece, Rome, and England many hundreds of years ago. The Football Association was founded in England in 1863. In 1913, the US Soccer Federation was founded. The World Cup Championship is held every four years. The United States was chosen to host the 1994 tournament.

Rules

8752 **Number of players** 22 (11 a side).
Equipment A ball of leather or other approved material, weighing 14–16 oz (396 –453 g), inflated to 0.6–1.1 atmosphere (600–1,100 g/sq cm²); numbered shirt, shorts, socks, boots with cleats; optional shin guards.
Objective To try to kick the ball into the opponents' goal. The winning team is the one that scores most goals.
Duration Two halves of 45 min each, with a 5-min rest before teams change ends.
Substitutes Not more than two for each side, except in "friendly" matches.
Officials A referee and two linesmen (one on each touchline (**5**) to help the referee.
The field The soccer field, 50–100 yd (46–91 m) wide and 100–130 yd (91–119 m) long, is rectangular with a goal at either end, 24 ft (7.32 m) wide and 8 ft (2.44 m) high. Touchlines and goal lines are part of the playing area. There are flags at each corner of the field and sometimes at the center line too.

1 Goal line
2 Penalty area
3 Penalty spot
4 Center circle
5 Touchline
6 Referee
7 Linesmen

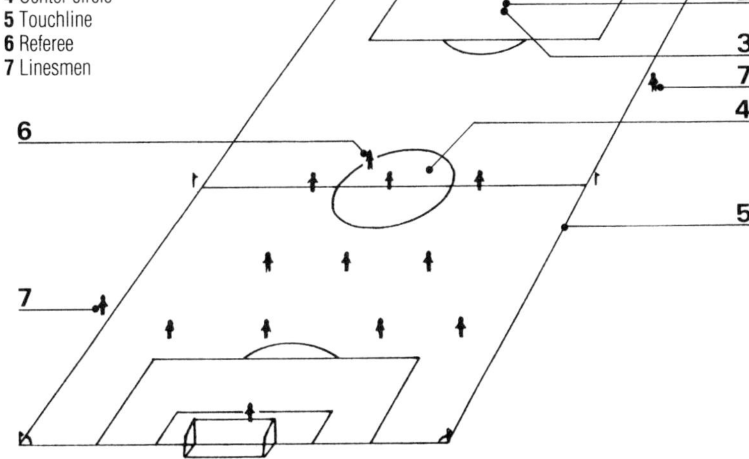

Key words

8753 **center** Another name for cross.
corner kick Awarded to the attacking team after the defending team has played the ball over its own goal line. A player from the attacking team kicks the ball from the quarter circle at a corner of the pitch.
cross Ball kicked into the penalty area from near the touchline. Also called center.
dead ball Ball kicked from a stationary position such as a corner, free kick, etc.
defenders Defensive players who try to stop goals being scored by the opposing team.
dribbling Trying to beat opponents by running with the ball at the feet.
far post Goal post farthest away from the player in possession.
free kick Kick awarded to a team for a foul committed by the opponents. A direct free kick is awarded for any of nine specific offenses. A goal cannot be scored from an indirect free kick without first being touched by a second player.
forwards Offensive players whose job is to score goals
full backs Defenders who patrol the side areas of the field
goal kick Kick taken by the defending team after the attackers have kicked the ball over the goal line but not into the goal.
handball Foul committed by a player who deliberately touches the ball with a hand or arm.
heading Striking the ball with the forehead.
kicking Ball is struck by the foot, also called shooting
killing the ball Rendering the ball stationary (**1**).
linesman Two linesmen patrol the side of the perimeter field. Their job is to indicate with a flag when the ball goes outside the perimeter. They also give offside decisions
marking Staying within playing distance of an opponent.
midfield player Player staying mostly in the central areas of the field, linking defense and offense.
near post Goal post nearest to the player in possession.
offside An offensive player is offside if, when the ball is played, he is nearer the opposing goal than two opponents, or level with them; unless he is in his own half of the field or an opponent was the last player to touch the ball.
overhead kick Also known as the bicycle kick due to the cycling movement involved. As the body falls back into a horizontal position, the ball is hooked over the head (**2**).
over the top Foul play involving running over the top of the ball and kicking the opponent.
penalty kick Kick awarded for one of nine specific fouls within the penalty area, taken from the penalty spot. All players except the kicker and the goalkeeper must stand outside the penalty area.
red card Displayed by the referee to a player for violent conduct or for a serious foul after having already been cautioned by a yellow card; the player is then sent off the field and no substitute allowed.
referee Arbitor who officiates the game, he is also the time keeper
save Made by the goalkeeper or another player to stop the ball from entering the goal.
set piece Corner, free kick, throw-in , etc., in which predetermined tactical moves can be carried out.
shoulder charges Legal charges, shoulder to shoulder.
sliding tackle A tackle performed by sliding in feet first to rob the opponent of the ball.
stopper One of two centerbacks.
striker An offensive player who normally stays forward in an attempt to score goals.
sweeper A player operating behind the defensive line of four, sweeping up loose balls.
throw-in Return of the ball to play after it has crossed the touchline to go out of play. The throw must be taken with both hands from behind and over the head.
volleying Kicking a ball when it is in the air
wall Line-up of defending players between the ball and the goal to block a free kick at goal. All opponents must be at least 29.5 ft (9m) from the ball.
winger Offensive player who attack down the side areas of the fild
yellow card Displayed by the referee to a player guilty of a serious foul or persistent lesser fouling; constitutes a caution.

1

2

876 FIELD HOCKEY

History

8761 Ancient Greek carvings show men playing a similar game to field hockey. The first English hockey club for men was formed in 1861. The All England Women's Hockey Club was established in 1889. Men's field hockey first featured in the Olympic Games in 1908. The US Field Hockey Association (USFHA) for women was organized in 1922. The Field Hockey Association of America (FHAA) for men came into being in 1930.

Rules

8762 **Number of players** Two teams of 11 players each.
Equipment A curved stick for each player, flat on one side, rounded on the other. Only the flat side is used to hit the ball. A small, hard, round ball, covered with leather or plastic.
Objective To score more points than the opponents. Players propel the ball, using only their sticks, until they reach their opponents' shooting circle (striking circle), and from there try to shoot the ball into the goal. Each goal counts one point. Bodily contact is prohibited, as are dangerous hitting and playing the ball above shoulder height. No player except the goalkeeper may stop or deflect the ball with any part of his or her body.
Duration Two periods of 35 min each, with a 5 to 10 min break between them.
Substitutes Up to two for the men's game.
Officials Two umpires, one in each half of the field.

The field The hockey field is 100 yd (91.5 m) long and 60 yd (54.9 m) wide with a goal at each end.

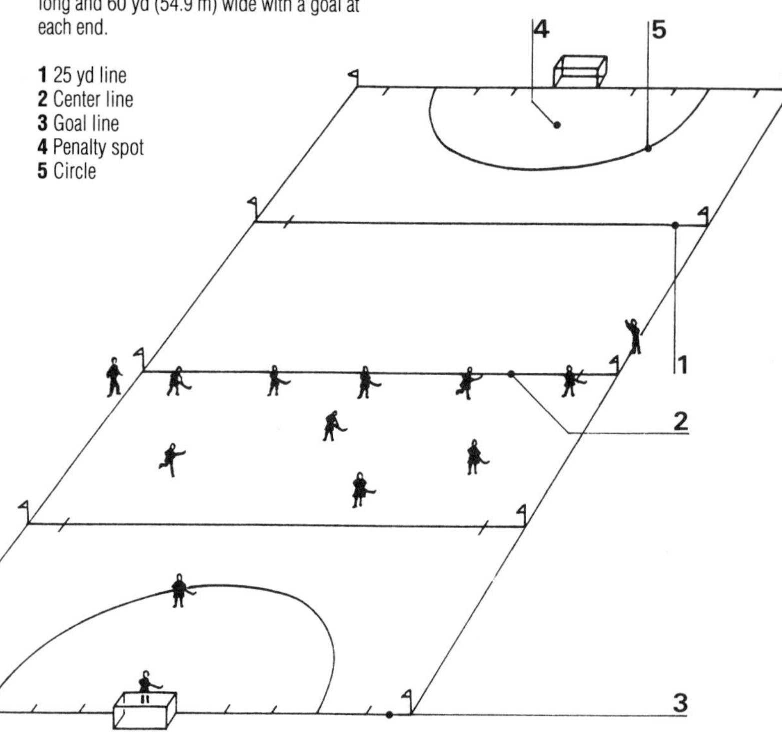

Key words

8763 **bully** Played on the spot where an incident or accident occured to restart the game. A player taps the stick first on the ground on his/her own side of the ball, then against his/her opponent's stick above the ball. This is done three times after which one player must strike the ball.
charging A player deliberately pushing an opposition player out of the way when playing the ball (**1**).
corner Awarded to the non-offending side when a defender sends the ball unintentionally over his or her own goal line. The ball must be hit along the ground from a spot on the goal line within 3 yd (2.7 m), or (5 yd (4.6 m) for women, of the corner flag.
dangerous play When the ball or stick rises above shoulder level when hit (**2**).
offside A player is offside when within his or her opponents' half when the ball is played by a teammate further from the goal-lin, and when there are fewer than two opponents nearer the goal line.
free hit Awarded to the non-offending side for infringements committed outside the shooting circle.
hit in When the ball is hit out of play over a side line a player of the opposing team may push or hit the ball from the side.
passback A player from one team knocks the ball back to a teammate; this is used to start the game and re-start after a goal.
penalty corner (short corner) Awarded to the non-offending side when an opponent deliberately plays the ball over the goal line, or for offenses within the shooting circle. Taken from anywhere on the goal line at least 10 yd (9.1 m) from the goal post.
penalty stroke Awarded against defenders in the circle for an intentional foul, an unintentional foul preventing a goal, or deliberate positioning infringement at penalty corners. Taken by an attacker from a spot 7 yd (6.4 m) in front of the center of the goal.
push-in (men), roll-in (women) Awarded to the opposition when a player hits the ball over the sideline.
reverse stick Turning the stick over in order to play the ball on the other side of the body.
roll-in See push-in.
short corner See penalty corner.
shooting circle (striking circle) A wide arc extending from the goal line in front of each goal.

877 ICE HOCKEY

History

8771 Ice hockey, derived from field hockey, was first played in Canada by British soldiers in the mid-1800s. It was played on unmarked rinks, and players wore little protective clothing because the game was gentler than it is today. The universities of Yale and Johns Hopkins organized the first US hockey matches about 1895. Professional hockey began at Houghton, Michigan, in 1903. The World Hockey Championships started in 1924.

Rules

8772 **Number of players** Two teams of six players each.
Equipment A hard, black rubber disk called a puck, 1 in (2.5 cm) thick and 3 in (7.6 cm) in diameter; a stick; skates; and protective clothing.
Objective To try to score points by knocking the puck into a goal cage located at each end of a rink 200 ft (61 m) long and 100 ft (30.5 m) wide.
Duration Three 20-min periods separated by two 15-min intervals. Each team is also allowed one 30-sec time out in each game.

The rink
Rinks for international matches have:
1 Center line
2 Center circle
3 Zone marking
4 Face-off circle
5 Goal crease
6 Goal judge's box
7 Team benches
8 Penalty bench
9 Boards

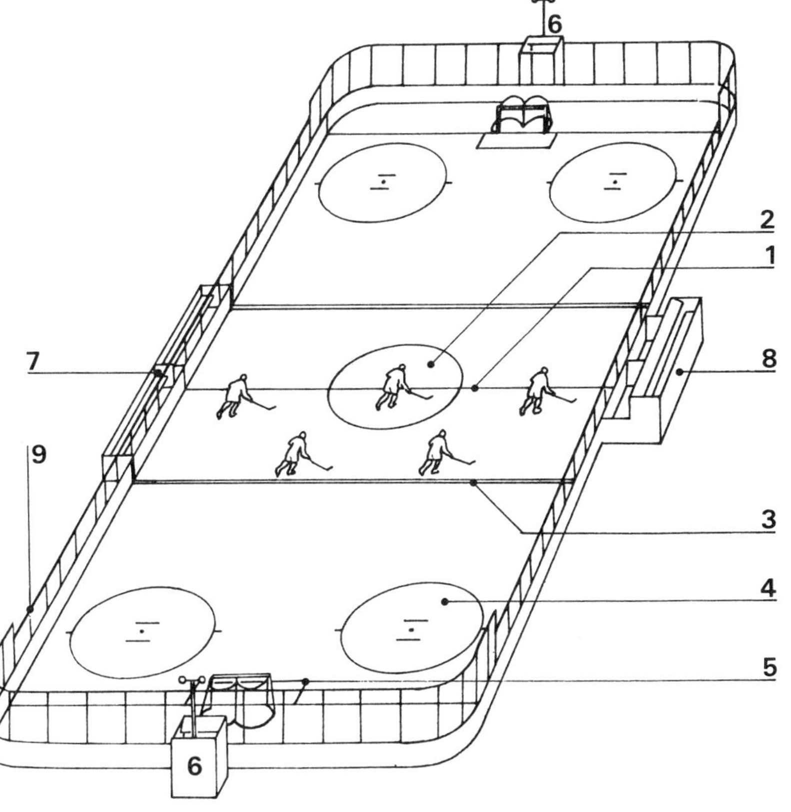

Key words

8773 **assist** The passing of the puck by another player to the goal-scorer.
back-checking Defensive tackling to break up an attack.
blocker One of the goalie's leather gloves with a large pad on the back.
boarding Forcing an opponent into the boards at the edge of the rink.
body-checking A hip or shoulder charge against an opponent to try to block his progress or unbalance him.
butt-ending Striking an opponent with the end of a stick; a major penalty.
drop pass Leaving the puck behind to be collected by a teammate.
face-off An official drops the puck between two opponents in order to start play at any time.
flip pass A pass to a teammate that rises off the ice.
fore-checking Tackling an opponent who has the puck in his own defending zone.
high-sticking Carrying the stick above shoulder level.
hooking A minor penalty is omposed on a player who impedes or tries to impede an opponent by hooking with the stick.
icing the puck Illegal defensive move called when a player shoots the puck from his own half across the opponents' goal line; or when the player attempted to pass the puck to a teammate who failed to touch it .
interference A minor penalty is imposed if a player interferes with or impedes the progress of an opponent not in possession of the puck.
offside An illegal move that occurs when a player enters his team's attacking zone ahead of the puck; or when the puck is passed from the defending zone to a teammate beyond the centerline.
penalty box Area by the side of the rink to which players who break the rules are temporarily banished.
penalty killers Substitutes sent on to keep opponents away from the danger zone in front of goal by forming a square.
penalty shots Awarded for infringements, they are free shots at goal defended only by the goalie.
power play Occurs when a team sends all its players except the goalie in a drive against the opponents' goal.
screening Blocking the goalie's view.
shut-out Achieved by a goalie who survives a match or period without allowing a goal.
stick checking Using the stick to hook the puck away from an opponent's stick.

878 RUGBY

History

8781 **RUGBY UNION**
In 1823, William Webb Ellis, a boy at Rugby School in England, was playing soccer when suddenly he picked up the ball and ran with it, instead of kicking it. That, allegedly, was the origin of rugby football. This winter game later spread to other schools and universities and, in 1871, the Rugby Football Union was formed. The sport eventually became popular in other countries, mainly Australia, New Zealand, South Africa, and France.
Rugby is usually played by men, but women's teams have been formed in recent years.

RUGBY LEAGUE
In 1893, northern Rugby Union clubs in England broke away over a dispute about paying their players to compensate them for money lost through time off work. They formed the Northern Union in 1895. A year later, they cut the team size from 15 to 13 players and introduced different laws from the Rugby Union game. In 1922, the Northern Union changed its name to Rugby League. All professionals are now part-time players. Great Britain plays France twice each season, and also plays against touring sides from Australia, New Zealand, and Papua New Guinea.

Rules

8782

RUGBY UNION
Number of players Two amateur teams of 15 players each.
Equipment An oval ball of leather or other approved material played on a grass outdoor field. Players wear jerseys, shorts, socks, and boots, with optional headbands or scrum caps.
Objective To score more points than the opposition by placing the ball over the opponents' goal line (a try), or kicking it over the crossbar (a goal). A try scores four points; a conversion two points; a drop goal three points; a penalty goal three points.
Play Players may run and carry the ball and kick it anywhere, but they must not knock or throw it toward the opponents' goal line. Any player holding the ball may be tackled and brought down.
Substitutes Not more than two injured players may be replaced at any time, and then only in international matches.
Duration Two halves of 40 min each separated by a 5-min break, after which teams change ends.

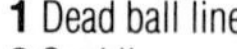

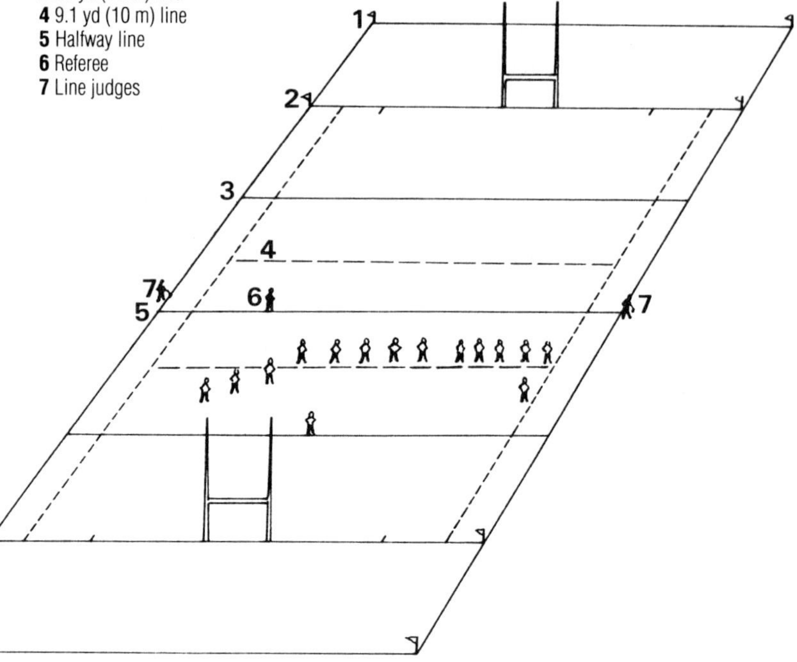

RUGBY LEAGUE
Number of players Two teams of 13 players each.
Equipment Similar to Rugby Union, but the ball is slightly smaller and thinner.
Objective As in Rugby Union, to collect more points than the opponents by scoring tries and goals. A try scores three points; a conversion two points; a drop goal three points in England, one point elsewhere; a penalty goal two points.
Play Similar to Rugby Union but with some important exceptions. Each team can only retain the ball for the duration of six tackles. After that, a scrum is formed and the tackle count starts again with whichever team gains possession. A player who is tackled stands up facing his opponent and plays the ball back with his heel to a teammate behind him. This is known as play-the-ball. When the ball goes out of play, the game is restarted with a scrum 10 yd (9.1 m) inside the touchline from where the ball went out.
Substitutes See Rugby Union.
Duration See Rugby Union.

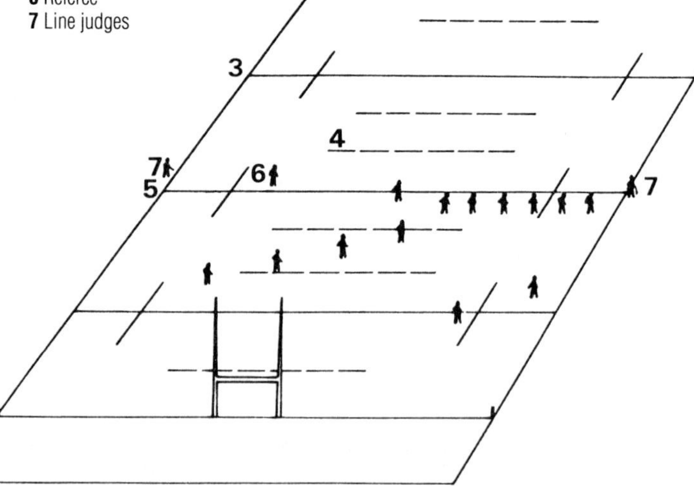

Key words

8783

All Blacks Members of New Zealand's international team, so-called because of their black outfits.
backs The seven players who are not forwards. Made up of scrum halfback, stand-off or outside halfback, four three-quarter halfbacks, and fullback.
blind side The side of the scrum nearest to touch.
British Lions International touring team made up of the best players from England, Scotland, Wales, and Ireland.
Calcutta Cup Prize awarded to the winner of the international match between England and Scotland.
conversion The act of kicking a goal following the scoring of a try; worth an extra two points in addition to the four points (three points in Rugby League) for the try (**1**).
dead ball Ball out of play.
drop goal Goal scored by drop-kicking the ball over the crossbar; worth three points.

continued

Key words continued

8783 **drop-kick** A ball dropped and kicked on the bounce (**2**).
drop-out A drop-kick taken from between the posts or from the center of the 24 yd (22 m) line to bring the ball back into play.
dummy The pretense of passing the ball while still holding on to it.
fair catch See mark.
Five Nations Championship The most important competition, played between England, Scotland, Wales, Ireland, and France.
forward pass A throw toward the opponents' goal line; an illegal move. All passes must be made laterally or backward.
forwards The eight large, strong players who force the play. In a scrum they are made up of a front row of a hooker flanked by two props, backed by a second row of two lock forwards flanked by two wing forwards, and a solitary No 8 forward at the rear.
five meters scrum A scrum formed 5 m (5.5 yd) from the goal line opposite the place where an infringement has occurred.
free kick An unimpeded kick awarded for a mark.
goal Scored when the ball is kicked over the crossbar.
hand-off Method used by a player carrying the ball to push away a tackling opponent with the palm of his hand.
hooker The central forward in the front row of the scrum whose main job it is to hook the ball with his heel to a teammate.
in-goal Area behind the posts that lies between the goal line and the dead ball line.
knock-on In Rugby League, an infringement of playing the ball forward with hand or arm, earning the opponents a scrum.
line-out A set piece in Union play, for re-starting play after the ball has gone into touch. Some or all of the opposing forwards form two parallel lines at right angles to the touchline and jump for the ball when it is thrown in (**3**).
loose scrum See ruck.
mark (fair catch) In Union play, the act of a player, standing with both feet on the ground within his 24 yd (22 m) line, who catches the ball cleanly from an opponent's kick and simultaneously shouts "Mark!", for which he is awarded a free kick.
maul In Union play, a crowd of opposing players pushing against each other and closing around a player who is carrying the ball. The ball must not touch the ground.
no side The end of the game.
offside A player is offside when he is in front of a teammate who has played the ball.
pack Collective name for the forwards.
penalty goal Goal scored direct from a penalty kick; worth three points.
penalty kick Awarded to the non-offending side for an infringement; the opponents must retire at least 10 yd (9.1 m).
penalty try Awarded when a player is illegally stopped from scoring a certain try; worth four points in Rugby Union, three in Rugby League.
place kick Made by kicking the ball after it has been placed on the ground for that purpose (**4**).
punt A ball dropped from the hands and kicked before it touches the ground.
Ranfurly Shield Trophy competed for by the top teams in New Zealand.
ruck (loose scrum) Similar to a maul but with the ball being kicked on the ground; it must not be handled.
scrum (scrummage in Union play) Formation in which the forwards link themselves together tightly, lower their heads, and push against the opposing pack. The non-offending side tosses the ball into the tunnel between the packs and the respective hookers try to heel it back to a teammate (**5**).
strike Act of hooking the ball in the front row of the scrum.
strike against the head In the scrum describes the opponents' winning of the ball from the opposition.
touch Out of play beyond a touchline.
Triple Crown Imaginary prize, part of the Five Nations Championship, awarded to the home international side of England, Scotland, Wales, or Ireland that wins all three of its matches against the other home teams.
try Scored when a player runs through the defense to touch a ball down in the opponents' in-goal area; worth four points in Rugby Union, three in Rugby League (**6**).
up-and-under A ball kicked toward the opponents' goal line high enough to allow the kicking side to rush after it and be underneath it when it comes down.

879 POLO

History

8791 The Persian poet Firdausi described a polo match between the Persians and Turkomans in about 600 BC. The name polo comes from *pulu*, the willow root from which the balls were and are made in the East. The game was discovered by visiting British officers, who began to establish polo clubs in India.
Captain Sherer first organized the game in Assam, India, in the 1850s, and was thus the father of modern polo. The game was introduced to the US by James Gordon Bennett. By 1914, it was known all over the world.

Rules

8792 **Number of players** Two teams of four players, mounted on horseback.
Officials The game is controlled by two mounted umpires. A referee, whose decision is final, stands off the field. Two goal judges stand behind each goal area and report to the umpires in cases of doubt or incidents near their goal. The timekeeper signals the end of each period, and also keeps the score.
Equipment Ground comprising the playing

continued

Rules continued

8792 area, 160 yd (146.4 m) by 300 yd (275 m), and a safety zone around it. Boards, extending along either length of the playing area, designed to direct low balls back into play. Goalposts, 10 ft (3.05 m) high, of light construction, designed to break if collided with. A stick, for each player, with mallet heads covered in sycamore, ash, bamboo, or vellum. A ball made of ash or bamboo, weighing 4.25–4.6 oz (120–130 g). A polo helmet or cap, polo boots, and knee pads worn by all players. The ponies ridden must be calm in temperament, and able to see with both eyes. Distinguishing colors must be worn by both teams.

Duration A match is divided into eight 7 min periods or "chukkas," amounting to 56 min playing time. There is a 3 min interval between each period, and a 5 min interval when half the periods have been played. Ends are changed at halftime: after the fourth period in a seven-period match, and after the third period in a five-period match.

Objective Each team attempts to score goals by striking a ball with its sticks between the opponents' goalposts. Players must control their ponies with the left hand, as the stick may be held only in the right hand. The winning team is the one to score the greater number of goals.

Starting play Opposing sides line up facing the umpire in the center of the ground, each team on its own side of the half-way "T" mark. The umpire bowls the ball underhand between the two stationary ranks of players at a distance of not less than 5 yd (4.57 m). Ends are changed at halftime, and after every goal.

Out of play The ball is out of play when it is hit over the boards or sidelines; when it is hit over the back line by either the attacking or the defending side; when the ball becomes damaged, or lodged in a player's clothing.

Accidents and loss of equipment The umpire stops the match if a player is injured or a pony goes lame, or if a pony's equipment is so damaged as to be a danger to other players and ponies. If a player fallsfrom a pony without injury, the match will not be stopped. If a player is injured, 15 min are allowed for the player's recovery. If the player is unable to continue after that interval, the game is restarted with a substitute player.

Misuse of the stick A player must not: reach across or under an opponent's pony to strike the ball; hit into the legs of an opponent's pony; use the stick dangerously, or hold it in such a way as to interfere with another player or pony.

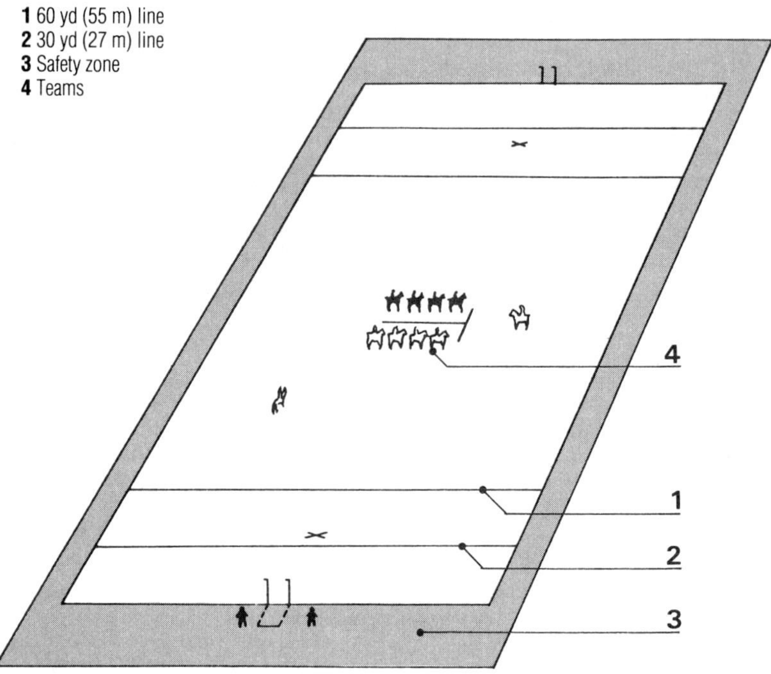

1 60 yd (55 m) line
2 30 yd (27 m) line
3 Safety zone
4 Teams

Key words

8793 **penalty goal** Awarded if the umpire considers that a goal would have been scored but for a foul by the defending side.

penalty hit Awarded at an appropriate distance by the umpire, according to the gravity of an offense. Failure to carry out penalty hits corrrectly may result in: a penalty goal; allowing members of the team that did not commit the fault to position themselves where they wish; retaking the hit, unless a goal was scored or awarded.

Unnecessary delay in taking a free hit may result in the umpire bowling the ball from the same spot.

riding off – or Bumping between players riding in the same direction – is permitted, though not at angles which may be dangerous to other players or their ponies.

right of way One of polo's most important principles. Right of way is held by the player(s) following the ball on its exact line, or at the smallest angle to it, and taking it on the offside. It is a foul for another player to cross or pull up in the right of way, thereby making a player with the right of way check pace.

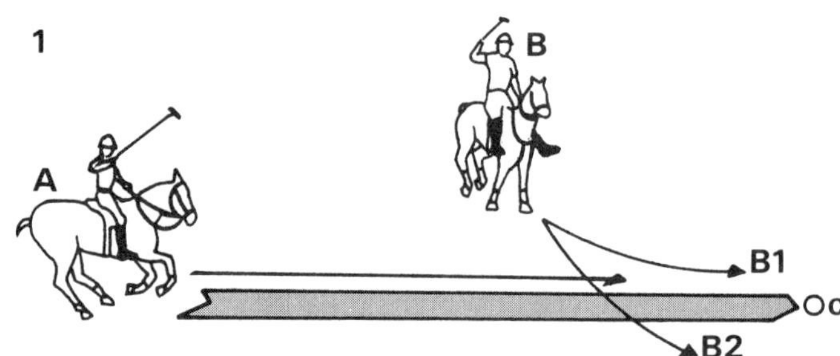

1 Example of right of way
Player **A** hits the ball to **c**, follows its line, and assumes the right of way. If player **B** can reach the ball at **c** without interfering with **A**'s play, **B** assumes the right of way and may strike the ball at **B1**. **B** must pull up if he can reach **c** only at the risk of fouling **A**.Provided he keeps out of **A**'s way throughout. **B** may then swerve and take a nearside backhander at **B2**.

881 SWIMMING

HISTORY

8811 People in ancient Middle Eastern lands swam for exercise and recreation many hundreds of years ago. The sport declined from the AD 400s to the 1500s because of fear of water pollution. It revived from the mid-1800s onward. The first Olympic Games in 1896 marked the start of international swim meets.

Rules

8812 **Number of swimmers** Individual and team competitors; up to ten swimmers in one event.
Equipment Men, swimming trunks; ladies, one-piece costume with shoulder straps from front to back. Swimwear must be non-transparent. Caps and goggles optional.
Pool Long-course 164 ft (50 m) long, divided into six, eight or ten lanes, each 8 ft (2.4 m) wide. Short-course 75 ft (22.88 m) long, divided into six or eight lanes, each 7 or 8 ft (2.1 m or 2.4 m) wide. Water at least 4 ft (1.2 m) deep at about 78°F (26°C).
Objective To be the first to cover a predetermined distance.
Duration A race usually lasts seconds or minutes, depending on the distance covered.
The pool Competitions are held in pools of varying lengths but in the Olympic games, where swimming is the second largest sport, a 55 yd (50 m) pool is used. The pool is divided into eight lanes, each swimmer must remain in his or her lane. In all events except backstroke, swimmers begin the race by diving from starting blocks.

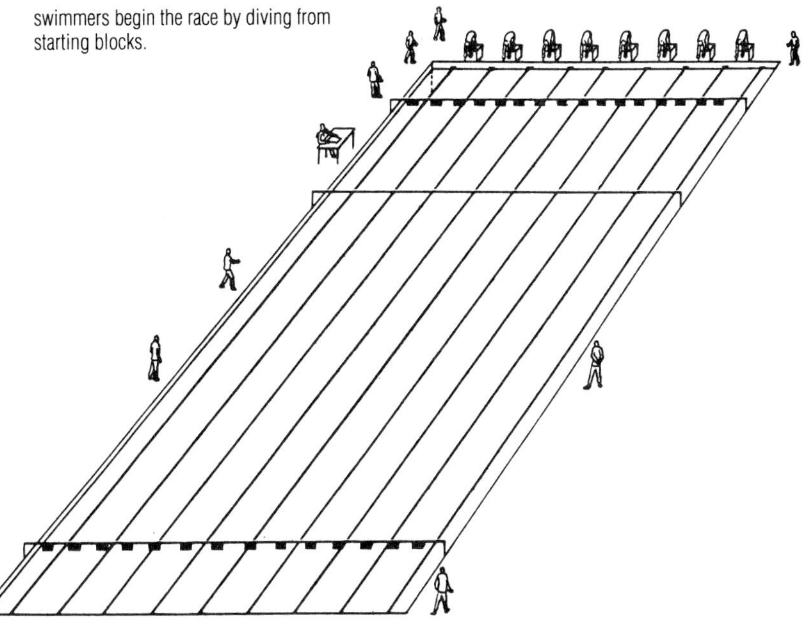

Key words

8813 **backstroke** Swum on the back, with each arm moving alternately in a circular motion; legs do a flutter kick (**1**).
breaststroke Arms are extended in front of the head and swept back on either side; legs do a breaststroke kick (**2**).
butterfly Arms plunge forward together in large circular movements; legs make two dolphin kicks with each stroke (**3**).
dog paddle Cupped hands rotate in a circular motion under water; legs do a flutter kick.
dolphin kick Both legs move up and down together.
flip turn Underwater somersault to reverse direction after touching the end of the pool.
flutter kick Legs move up and down alternately with a bend at the knees.
freestyle race Race in which swimmers may use any strokes they choose.
front crawl Arms reach forward alternately and pull back through the water; legs use the flutter kick (**4**).
medley events Races in which individual competitors swim an equal distance for each of four strokes – butterfly, backstroke, breaststroke and freestyle. In medley relays, each swimmer swims one stroke for the set distance – backstroke, breaststroke, butterfly or freestyle.
scissors kick One leg moves forward as the other bends back; they then come together in a scissors-like action.
sidestroke Swum on the side with arms thrusting downward and backward alternately; legs do a scissors kick.

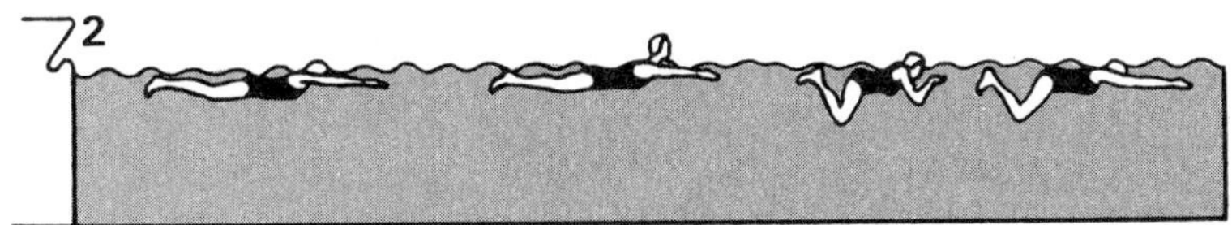

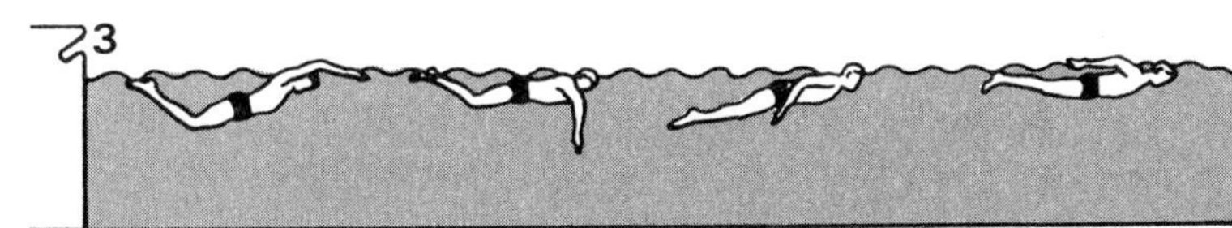

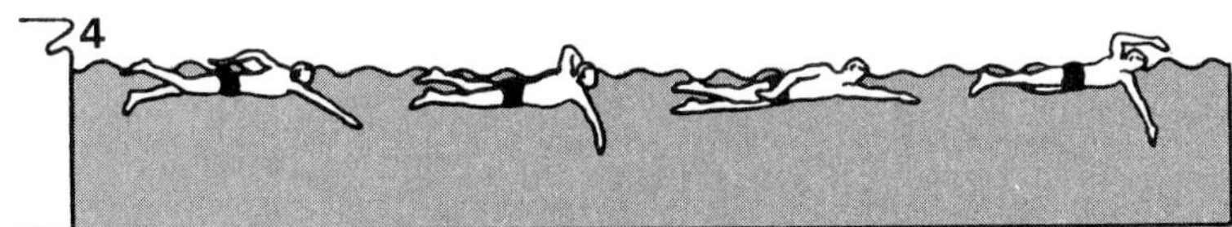

spearhead principle In each event, the competitor with the fastest entry time swims in the center lane, with other competitors placed left and right in descending order of speed.
survival bobbing Method of indefinite survival by means of floating on one's front while bobbing up and down on the water's surface.
synchronized swimming Graceful, rhythmic water sport in which swimmers match rhythm and mood to music. A women only sport.

882 SAILING

History

Competitive sailing as a sport dates back at least to the reign of King Charles II of England in the 1600s. The sport grew in the early 1900s when commercial sailing craft had largely been superseded by steamships. In the 1920s and 1930s, small boats were raced by amateurs. The sport really took off from 1945, largely because of marine plywood and resin glues developed during World War II.

8822 Rules
8823 Types of sailboat
8824 Olympic yacht classes
8825 Parts of a sailboat

Rules

8822 **Equipment** Varies according to classes of boats and types of race. Generally includes an anchor; life-saving equipment; identifying inscriptions on sails; signal flags; radio; certificate of conformity to class rules.
Objective To cross the finishing line first with fewest infringements. In team races, two or more teams or two or more yachts compete. Leading craft receives lowest points, and points are added for infringements. Lowest score wins.
Duration Anything from a few minutes for a short race to a few months for round-the-world races.
Courses Marked by buoys, which must be rounded or passed on the correct side and in the correct order.

Types of sailboat

8823

1

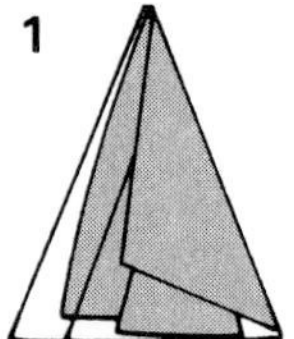

2

3

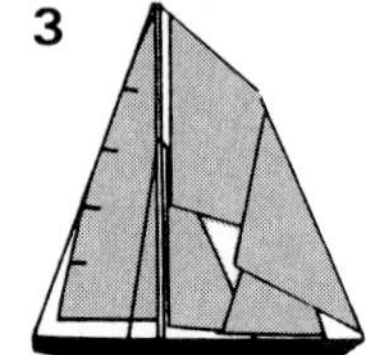

4

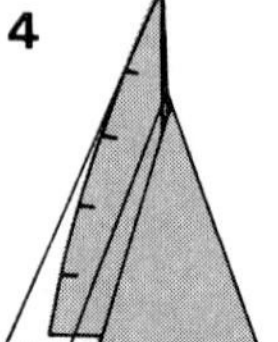

5

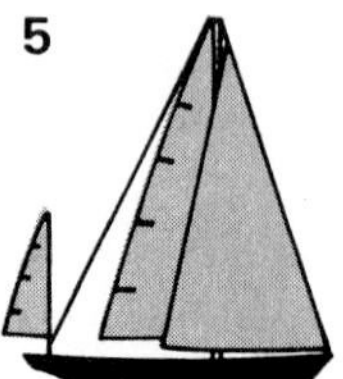

auxiliary Sailboat with an engine.
Bermuda rig Fore-and-aft rig with a tall mast and pointed sail.
canoe sailing Canoes equipped with sails race around an equilateral course marked by three buoys.
catamaran Sailboat with twin hulls.
catboat Small boat with one sail and one mast forward in the bow. Also called sailing dinghy.
cutter Large sloop with two jibs (**1**).
Flying Dutchman Fast Olympic class, two-person centerboard dinghy of molded plywood or fiberglass.
inland scow Lake sailing boat. Light, fast, usually sloop-rigged, flat-bottomed with rounded bow and square stern.
ketch Two-masted boat with three or more sails and mizzenmast in front of the rudder post (**2**).
one-design class One of three internationally recognized classes of sailboat in which all boats must be identical.
pram Small, lightweight, flat-bottomed boat with a squared-off bow.
schooner Large boat with many sails. It has at least two masts and one or more jibs (**3**).
sloop Boat with one mast near the middle and two sails – mainsail and jib (**4**).
Soling Olympic class, very fast three-person sloop made of fiberglass.
Star Olympic class two-person keel-boat, oldest of all the designs.
Tempest Olympic class keel-yacht made of fiberglass, with a crew of two.
Tornado Olympic class plywood or fiberglass catamaran with a crew of two.
Windglider Fiberglass windsurfer with a 14 ft 9 in (4.5 m) mast on a 12 ft (3.6 m) surfboard.
Yawl Large boat with at least three sails. The mizzenmast stands behind the rudder post (**5**).

Olympic yacht classes

8824 In the Olympic Games there may be events for the following eight yacht classes:
1 470; two-woman dinghy, one-man dinghy
2 Finn; one-woman dinghy
3 International Europe Class centerboard dinghy
4 Flying Dutchman; two-man dinghy
5 Lechner 390 sailboard
6 Soling; three-person keelboat
7 Star; two-person catamaran
8 Tornado; two-person high performance dinghy

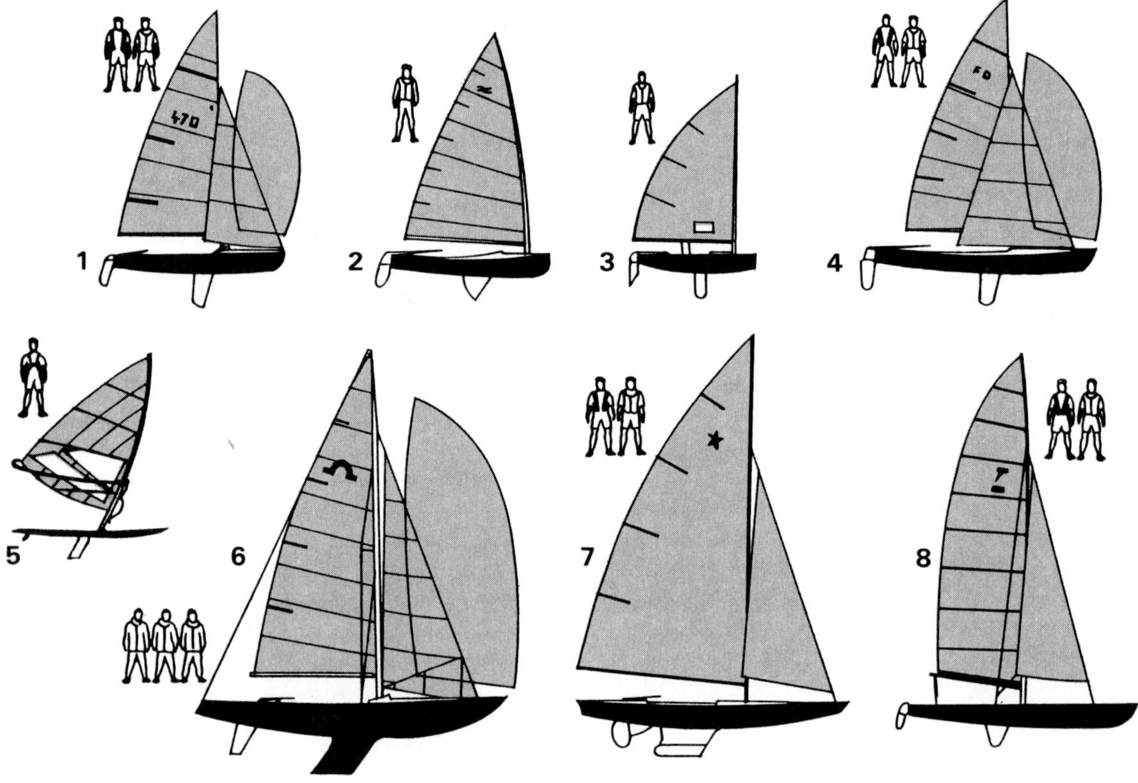

Parts of a sailboat

8825

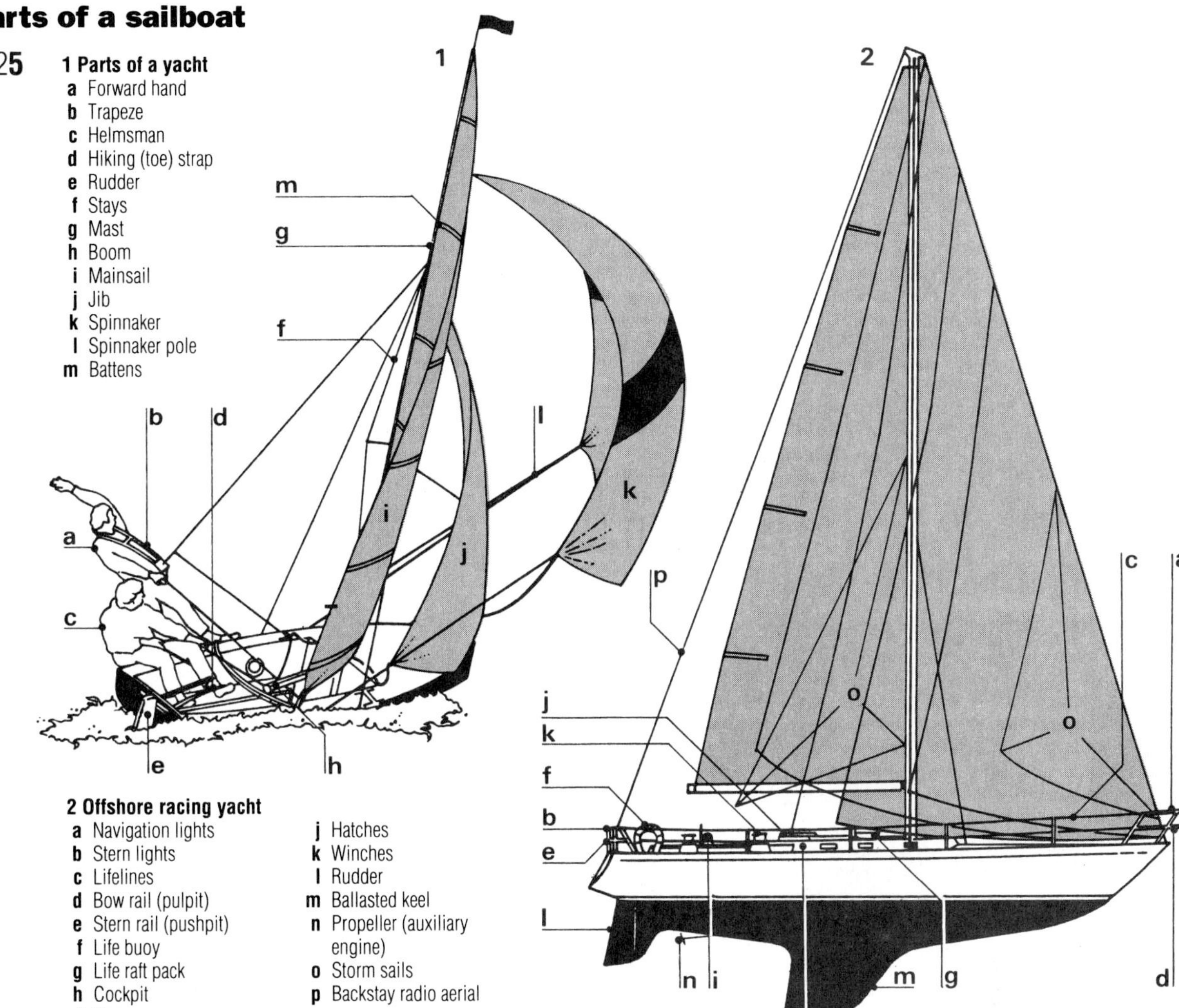

1 Parts of a yacht

- **a** Forward hand
- **b** Trapeze
- **c** Helmsman
- **d** Hiking (toe) strap
- **e** Rudder
- **f** Stays
- **g** Mast
- **h** Boom
- **i** Mainsail
- **j** Jib
- **k** Spinnaker
- **l** Spinnaker pole
- **m** Battens

2 Offshore racing yacht

- **a** Navigation lights
- **b** Stern lights
- **c** Lifelines
- **d** Bow rail (pulpit)
- **e** Stern rail (pushpit)
- **f** Life buoy
- **g** Life raft pack
- **h** Cockpit
- **i** Compass
- **j** Hatches
- **k** Winches
- **l** Rudder
- **m** Ballasted keel
- **n** Propeller (auxiliary engine)
- **o** Storm sails
- **p** Backstay radio aerial

backstay A rope from the masthead to the stern.
bilge Part of the underwater hull of a boat with vertical sides curving inwards to form the bottom.
bilge boards Two finlike projections located one on either side of the bilge for stability.
block Pulley through which a rope or chain passes over a grooved wheel.
boom Horizontal pole attached to the foot of a sail to hold it straight out.
bow The forward end or part of a boat.
burgee Triangular or swallow-tailed flag flown from the masthead to show the colors of a club or organization.
centerboard Type of keel that can be raised or lowered through a slot in the hull.
cleat T-shaped piece of wood or metal used to secure rope.
crosstrees Two wooden or metal braces at a masthead to spread the shrouds.
finn Single-handed centerboard dinghy, smallest of the Olympic classes.
foremast Mast nearest the bow on the boats with two or more masts.
470 Small, fast, Olympic class two-person centerboard dinghy, with spinnaker and trapeze.
gaff Pole extended at right angles to the mast to hold the sail straight out; usually at the top of the sail.
Genoa jib Large triangular foresail that overlaps the mast and reaches back to the mainsail.
halyards Ropes that raise and lower the sails.
helm Tiller or wheel controlling the rudder by which the boat is steered.
hull Body of the boat.
jib Small triangular sail in front of the mainmast.
keel Flat piece of wood or metal extending into the water from the bottom of the hull to provide lateral stability.
leeward Side of a boat farthest away from the wind.
lines Ropes.
luff Leading edge of a fore-and-aft sail. To luff is to sail a boat into the wind so that its sails flap.
mainmast Mast that holds the largest sail.
mainsail Largest sail on a boat, fastened to the back of the mainmast.
mizzenmast Short mast or a yawl or ketch located toward the stern.
painter Rope fastened to the bow of a dinghy for tying it up.
pennant Length of wire or rope fastened to a pole and having the lower end attached to a block or other fitting.
port Left side of a boat when facing the bow.
quarter After-part of the side of a boat.
rudder Fin extending into the water at the stern and used to steer the boat.
running Sailing before the wind.
sheets Ropes used to trim the sails.
shrouds Wires used to support the mast.
spars Poles, including booms, gaffs, and masts, that support the sails.
spinnaker Large, light, triangular racing sail set from the foremast for extra speed when sailing with the wind.
spreaders Another name for crosstrees.
standing rigging Permanent ropes that support the masts.
starboard Right side of a boat when facing the bow.
stay Wire rope used to support the mast.
stern The rear of a boat.
tiller Long handle used to turn the rudder.
trapeze Sling attached to a wire, used by a crew member, who hangs over the side to balance the boat.

The course

8826 Marks (usually buoys) must be rounded or passed in the correct order and on the required side. If necessary, because of foul weather or insufficient wind, flag signals are used to denote that the course is shortened or reversed, or that the race is cancelled, postponed, or abandoned.
The start The starting line may be between two marks (usually buoys), a mark and a sighting post, or an extension from two sighting posts.
The finish The line is marked in the same way as the starting line. There may be a time limit for finishing a race.

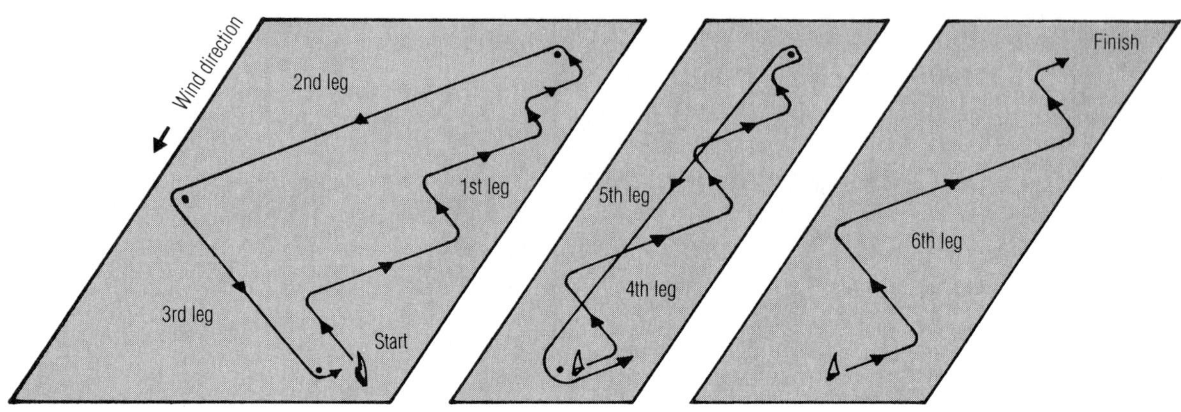

Maneuvers

8827 **beam reach** Sailing with the wind at right angles to the boat.
bear away Alter course away from the wind or to avoid a collision (**2**).
boating to windward Also called tacking to windward or sailing into the wind. The boat zigzags at a 45° angle to the wind.
close-hauled Sailing with the sails flat, close to where the wind is blowing from.
coming about When sailing into the wind, turning the bow so that the wind crosses it.
downwind In the direction from which the wind is blowing.
ease To slacken a rope.
fetch Sail a course that does not require a boat to tack.
goosewinged Boat sailing before the wind with sail set on both sides.
harden in Haul in the sails.
headsail Sail set forward of the mast.
jibing With the wind behind, turn bringing the wind to the other side of the boat, so that the mainsail crosses the center line (**6**).
luffing Altering course toward the wind until head to wind (**1**).
ooching Lunging forward and stopping abruptly; a prohibited maneuver in racing.
overlapping yacht When a yacht overtakes, it must allow the other yacht ample room to keep clear (**4**).
port tack Sailing with the wind blowing on a boat's left side.
pumping Frequent rapid trimming of the sails to fan the air; a prohibited maneuver in racing.
reefing Reducing sail area.
rigging Network of ropes on a boat.
rocking Persistently rolling a boat from side to side; a prohibited maneuver in racing.
running rigging Ropes used to adjust the booms and sails.
slacking off Letting out the sails so that some of the wind spills from them.
tacking When sailing into the wind, turning the boat so the wind comes from the opposite side (**5**).
trimming Adjusting the sails to take full advantage of the wind.
yacht clear astern Sailing so as to keep clear of a yacht ahead (**3**).

Key words

8828 **aback** When the wind blows on the wrong side of the sail, preventing forward motion.
abeam At right angles to the length and center of a boat.
aft Toward or at the rear of stern.
America's Cup World's oldest international sailing competition, first won in 1851 by the schooner *America*.
athwart Across the width of a boat.
berth Place reserved for a boat at mooring.
buoys Shaped and colored floats, anchored to the seabed, to indicate channels, obstructions, or moorings.
helmsman Person at the wheel or tiller.
knot One nautical mile (1.852 km) per hour.
leeward Facing the direction toward which the wind is blowing.
marina Docking facility for sailboats and other pleasure craft.
Olympic classes Seven classes of sailboat eligible for competition in the Olympic games: Finn, Flying Dutchman, 470, Soling, Star, Tornado, Windglider.
twelve-meter formula Complex formula governing a yacht's eligibility for entry into the America's Cup competition.
waterline Line where a boat's hull meets the surface of the water.
windsurfing Sailing across the water while standing on a surfboard equipped with mast and sail.
windward Side of a boat against which the wind blows.

883 SKIING

History

8831 Hunters and travelers in Scandinavia and parts of Asia moved on skis some 5,000 years ago. Alpine racing was pioneered by British skier Sir Arnold Lunn, who organized the world's first downhill race in Switzerland, in 1911. Among other pioneers, the American Hannes Schneider introduced the Arlberg technique, which is still in use today. In 1948, Gretchen Fraser became the first American to win an Olympic gold medal in the sport.

Rules

8832 **Number of competitors** Individual entries except for Nordic cross-country relay races. Not more than 100 competitors in the slalom.
Equipment Skis, sticks (poles), boots, bindings, warm waterproof clothing, goggles or sunglasses.
Objective To complete a variety of courses in the shortest possible time, or to jump the greatest distance.
Duration Races can last from seconds to hours, depending on the distance covered.

The course

8833 **1 Alpine (downhill)** The snow must be as smooth and compact as possible. Snow banks, straw, nets, etc. are used for protection against hazards. Smaller obstacles are removed from the course. There must be direct communication between the start and the finish.
2 Slalom Slalom courses test a wide variety of ski techniques. Traverses across the slope are interspersed with runs down it, and courses include turns that allow maximum speed, precision, and neat execution. The snow must be as hard as possible.

a = men's
b= women's

The course is at least 131 ft (40 m) wide, if two runs are set on the same slope. In world and Olympic championships the course is set on slopes with a gradient of 20 to 27 new degrees (= 33 to 45%). There are four types of alpine skiing race: Downhill (**1**); Slalom (**2**); Giant slalom (**3**); and Super. G (**4**).

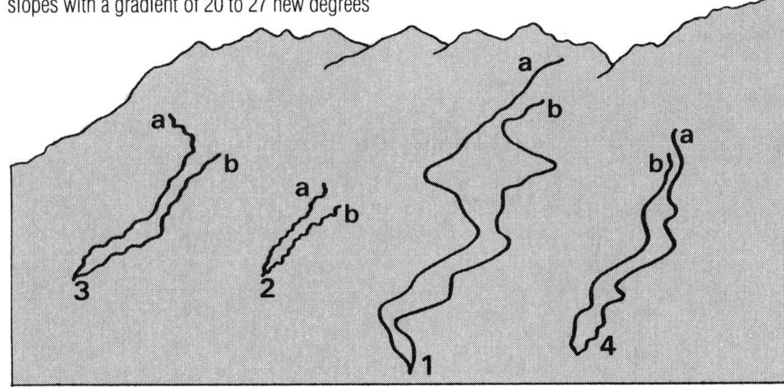

Techniques

8834 **diagonal stride** Basic movement for cross-country skiing (**4**).
edging Tilting skis at an angle to the slope.
herringboning Method of climbing a slope with ski tips far apart.
parallel turn Turn with skis kept parallel and close together (**3**).
schussing Skiing straight down the fall line.
snowplough Another name for wedge.
stem christie A turn that is begun with a stem but completed by bringing the skis parallel, half way to a parallel turn.
stemming Pushing out the back of the ski closest to the top of the slope to create an angle to the direction of movement.
traversing Skiing across a slope at an angle to the fall line (**2**).
vorlage Ski jumper's forward lean in mid-air.
wedge Maneuver for slowing down or stopping; also called snowplough (**1**).

1

2

3

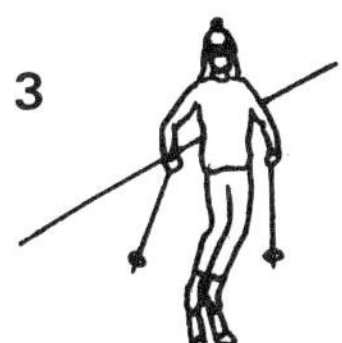

4

Key words

8835 **Alpine skiing** Type of skiing that includes downhill, slalom and giant slalom races.
cross-country skiing Form of Nordic skiing, usually over long distances up and down hills and on flat ground.
fall line Most direct route to the bottom of a slope.
gates Two solid uniform flagpoles, alternately blue or red with flags of the same color; used in slaloms to define twisting courses.
giant slalom A longer kind of slalom with gates farther apart and competitors free to choose their own line between the gates.
jumping Form of Nordic skiing in which competitors take off from a specially constructed hill; each jumps twice to try for the greatest distance.
mogul Snow mound usually formed by many skiers turning in the same place.
Nordic skiing Type of skiing made up of cross-country skiing and ski jumping.
piste Prepared downhill trail.
sitzmark Impression left in the snow by a fallen skier.
slalom Form of alpine skiing made up of two different downhill runs for each competitor over a winding course marked by gates.
waxing Wax applied to ski bottoms for greater control.

884 LUGE TOBOGGANING

History

8841 The origins of lugeing are believed to be older than those of skiing, and it is probable that in the times when the ancient Greeks celebrated their original Olympic Games, sled-like vehicles were used by the inhabitants of the Alpine region of Europe for transport and rereation. The development of lugeing as a racing sport is traceable to the middle of the 19th century, when British tourists started sled-racing on snowbound mountain roads in the Alps. A big advance came in the 1930s, when Tietze of Austria invented the flexible sled. In 1955, the first world championships were staged in Oslo, Norway, and the sport was first included in the Olympic Games in 1964.

Rules

8842 **Teams** For the Olympics, a maximum of three men and three women entering for the individual events, two for men's doubles. For other events, teams may include twice these numbers. Competitors must be amateurs, and members of a national association affiliated to the FIL (Fédération Internationale de Luge de Course).
Officials The race director, starting and finishing officials, and timekeepers. Control is exercised by the jury, the chairperson, technical delegates, and the FIL representative.
Training Systematic training comprises a tour of the course under the guidance of the race director. Nonstop training ideally involves at least four runs for each competitor. Under adverse conditions, every competitor must have at least one run for the race to take place. Both kinds of training are compulsory.
Events Men's and women's individual races; men's doubles race; team event (world championship and European championship). The race consists of four runs for singles and two runs for doubles in the Olympic Games; three for singles, two for doubles in world cup events; two for all categories and a team competition in the world championships.
The start A sitting start is compulsory for all events. Only one toboggan may be on the course at a time. The competitor has 30 sec (singles) or 45 sec (doubles), after the "track is clear" signal, in which to push off from the start handles.
Steering The competitor lies flat, with the body from the waist upward over the back of the toboggan. Slight shoulder, hand and foot pressures on the respective parts of the sled transmit steering force through the bridges and runners to the steels.

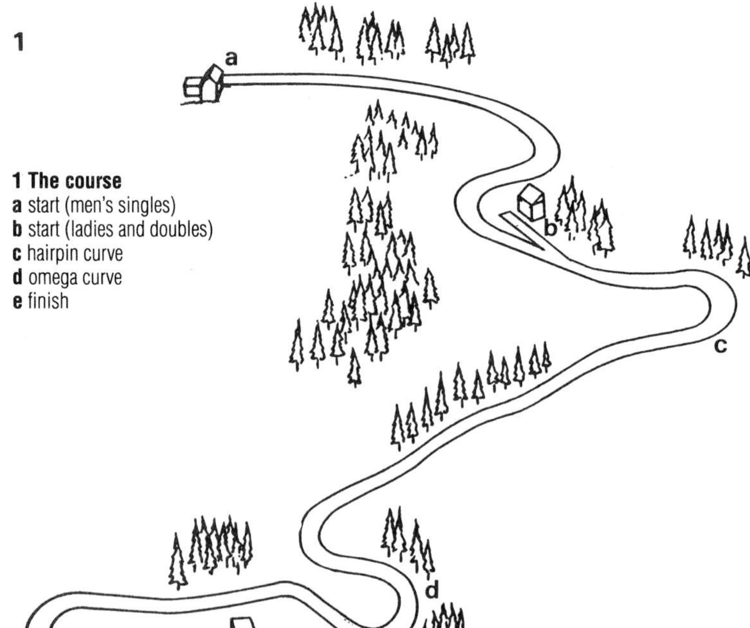

1 The course
a start (men's singles)
b start (ladies and doubles)
c hairpin curve
d omega curve
e finish

2 Cross section through wall of course
a Ice layer
b Refrigeration pipes
c Reinforced concrete
d Insulation

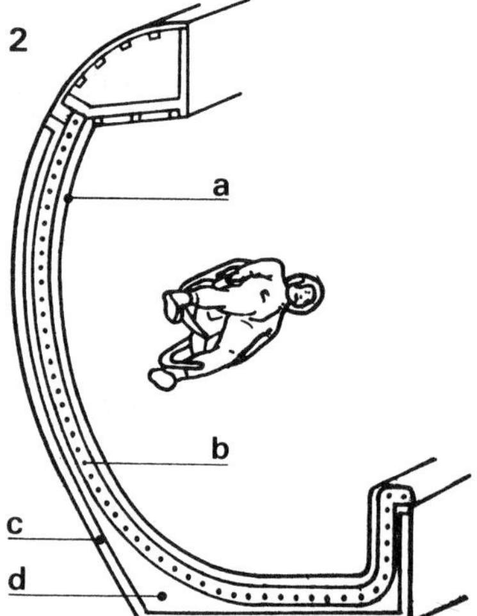

False start If this was due to a technical error, a new start is compulsory. If the competitor is at fault, he/she is disqualified.
Offenses Include warming toboggan runners before a race; adding ballast, or wearing weighted clothing, to bring the toboggan over the allowed weight; pushing, or allowing another person to push, the toboggan at the start of or during a race; training outside the approved hours. Penalties vary from exclusion from a particular race to total disqualification, depending on the gravity of the offense.
Course All courses are artificial with a cement infrastructure. Courses should feature a left-hand bend, a right-hand bend, an S bend, a hairpin bend, and some straight sections.
Timing Electronic timing apparatus, accurate to $^1/_{100}$th of a second, is compulsory for Olympic and international races. At least two hand stopwatches are used as a check in case of a failure of the electronic apparatus.

885 BOBSLED

History

8851 Although various forms of sled-riding on ice have been popular for centuries, bobsled – as a recognized sport, distinct from tobogganing – originated in Switzerland in 1888, when an Englishman, Wilson Smith, connected two sleighs with a board to travel from St Moritz to Celerina. The world's first separate bob run was built in 1902. The world administration, now called the International Bobsleigh Federation, was formed in 1923. The first world title for two-person crews was contested in 1931 at Oberhof, Germany, and this category became an Olympic event the following year at Lake Placid, NY.

Rules

8852 **Team** The team of two consists of a driver and brakeman, who provide the initial impetus at the start before mounting the bob; once in the bob, they work together, transferring their bodyweight when cornering, and keeping as low as possible in order to achieve maximum aerodynamic performance. A team of four consists of two side pushers, in addition to the driver and brakeman. Competitors must be amateur, and must hold an up-to-date FIBT (Fédération Internationale de Bobsleigh et de Tobogganing) license.
Officials Appointed by the FIBT. They normally consist of a jury, a president, and a minimum of two jury members. They ensure strict adherence to FIBT rules. Control station personnel ensure that the run is clear before each heat, and keep spectators informed of a bobsled's progress.
Equipment Bobsled track, usually of artificial construction, formed from concrete with refrigeration pipes passing below the surface. The ice layer must be at least 0.75 in (19 mm) thick. For championship events, the course must be at least 1,312 yd (1,200 m) in length, with a gradient of 8–15%.
Bobsleds These are made of steel, and fitted with an aerodynamic cowling.
Steering This is achieved by pulling on ropes connected to a centrally pivoted front axle. Attached to both front and rear axles are runner carriers onto which are bolted steel runners; the rear axle is fixed. Maximum weight for a two-person team and bob is 860 lb (390 kg); for a four-person team and bob, 1,389 lb (630 kg). Crash helmets are compulsory. In addition, goggles, elbow guards, and gloves are worn. For racing, teams usually wear skintight racing suits.
Training For world championships, teams must train for four days on the track, with two training runs per day. Teams must achieve three good runs (i.e. without crashing) to qualify for the competition.
Events Include the Olympic Games, the World Cup, and international and junior international competitions. All competitions include two-person and four-person events which usually consist of four runs, or heats, for each team.
The start When the track is clear, a light changes from red to green, and at the same time a buzzer sounds. Teams then have one minute in which to start, or else they are disqualified. They must do so under their own efforts, without any mechanical or extra human assistance.
The race Teams must achieve all competition runs in order to gain a placing in the overall race. The winner is the team with the lowest aggregate of times, taken, using electronic equipment, to the nearest 1/100th of a second.

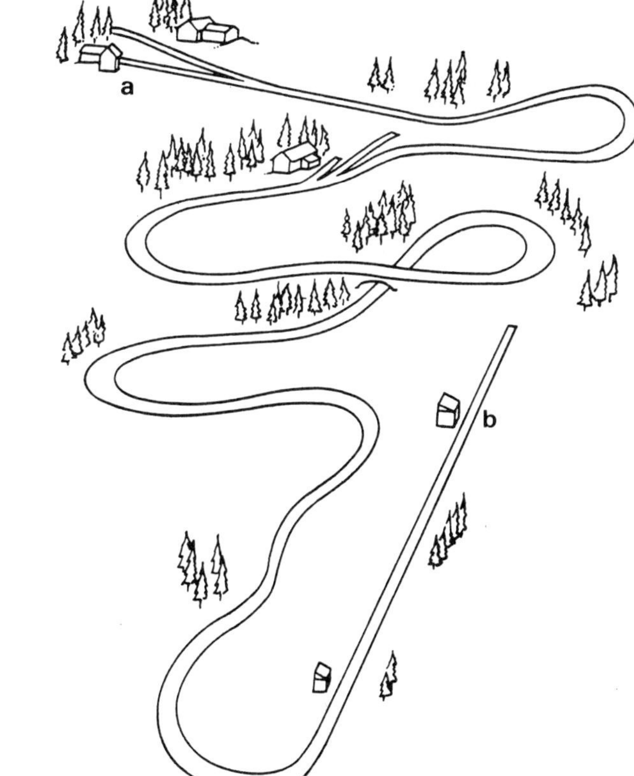

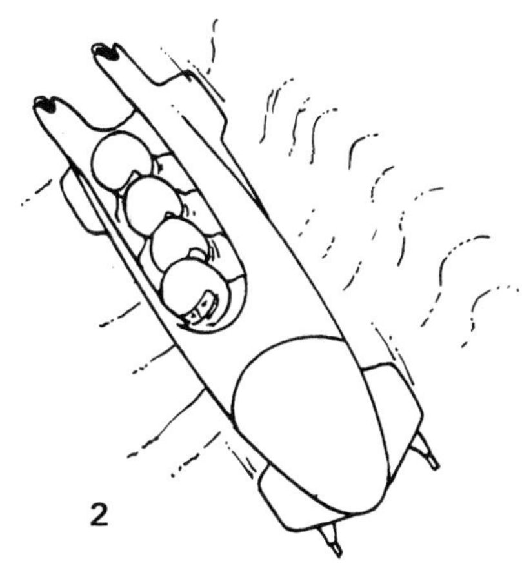

1 Bobsled course
a Start
b Finish
2 Four-man bob

Key words

8853 **brakeman** Slows the bob down by the use of a harrow type brake which digs into the ice.
braking straight Area after the finish clock used by the brakeman to slow down the bob before the finish exit.
control station Located at critical points on the course, and connected by telephone and radio to the control building.
start area Area before the start clock, of at least 49.2 ft (15 m) in length, which is used by the teams to build up momentum. A block of wood, frozen into the ice but protruding 3–4 in (7.6–10 cm) above it, is used by the brakeman (and side pushers, in a four-person bob) as a stop for the initial start effort.

886 Automobile racing
8861 History
8862 Circuit racing rules
8863 Circuits
8864 Single seater racing
8865 Stock car racing
8866 Sedan and sports car racing
8867 Karts

886 AUTOMOBILE RACING

History

8861 Automobile racing began in the 1890s on open public roads. The first event took place in 1895, organized by the Automobile Club de France. It covered a 732-mile (1,178 km) round trip between Paris and Bordeaux, and the winners averaged 15 mph (24 km/hr). The Vanderbilt Cup races began in 1904, on Long Island, New York. The first Grand Prix race was staged near Le Mans, France, in 1906. The first Indianapolis race took place five years later.

Circuit racing rules

8862 **Circuits** They range from short, banked speedways to 14-mi (22.5 km) circuits with hairpin bends.
Vehicles Must not have more than four road wheels; be in perfect safe and sound mechanical and bodily running order; and be fitted with special types of protection listed for the various classes of car.
Equipment Drivers must have a competition license, approved crash helmet, and protective clothing covering the body.
Starting All cars start together from the starting grid, the fastest in practice starting in front, the slowest behind.
Objective To cross the finishing line first or be in the lead when a certain time has elapsed.
Duration A set number of laps or a certain length of time.

Circuits

8863 Grand Prix races are the most famous international road races. Each year, streamlined, rear-engined, single-seaters compete for the FIA Formula One World Championship on a series of circuits in a number of countries. Each Grand Prix race is named after the country where it is held. Drivers score points for every race, and each year the winner of the World Championship is the driver with the highest number of points. The shape of the 21 circuits regularly used in Grand Prix racing are shown. Their lengths and the countries where they are located are given. (Australia, Hungary, Japan, Mexico, Portugal and San Marino have Grand Prix circuits too.)

Circuit	Country	Circuit length mi	km
1 Brands Hatch	UK	2.61	4.2
2 Hockenheim	Germany	4.22	6.79
3 Watkins Glen	US	3.38	5.44
4 Imola	Italy	3.13	5.04
5 Jarma	Spain	2.06	3.31
6 Buenos Aires	Argentina	3.71	5.97
7 Paul Ricard	France	3.61	5.81
8 Monza	Italy	3.6	5.8
9 Long Beach	US	2.02	3.25
10 Silverstone	UK	2.93	4.72
11 Spa Francorchamps	Belgium	4.31	6.94
12 Nurburgring	Germany	2.82	4.54
13 Zandvoort	Netherlands	2.64	4.25
14 Zolder	Belgium	2.65	4.26
15 Detroit	US	2.5	4.02
16 Dijon-Prenois	France	2.36	3.8
17 Montreal	Canada	2.74	4.41
18 Kyalami	S Africa	2.55	4.10
19 Monte Carlo	Monaco	2.06	3.31
20 Rio de Janeiro	Brazil	3.31	5.03
21 Österreichring	Austria	3.69	5.94

Le Mans Circuit in France is 8.47 mi (13.63 km) long. The 24-hour Le Mans endurance race marks the high point in the World Sports Car Manufacturers' Championship.
The Indianapolis in the United States is 2.5 mi (4.02 km) long and is famous for a 500 mi (805 km) endurance race named the Indianapolis 500.
Monte Carlo This circuit has sharp bends which make it one of the slowest circuits used in the Formula One World Championship (**19**).

Single seater racing

8864

Formula One racing International events for Grand Prix cars up to 3,500 cc unsupercharged, or 1,500 cc supercharged.

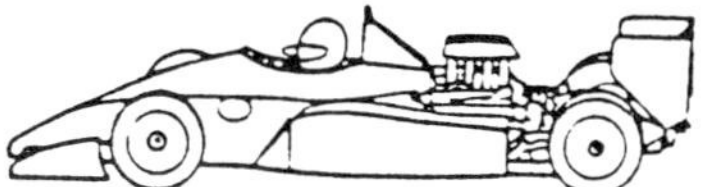

Formula 3000 Introduced in 1985 to replace Formula Two as the final rung on the ladder to F1 racing. Engines normally 3,000 cc with a maximum of 12 cylinders.

Formula Three racing International events for cars up to 2,000 cc with engines developed as four-cylinder production engines.

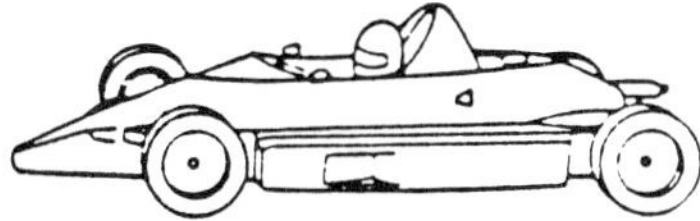

Formula Ford (Formula F) racing International events for cars with production 1600GT Cortina engines, with minimum modifications.

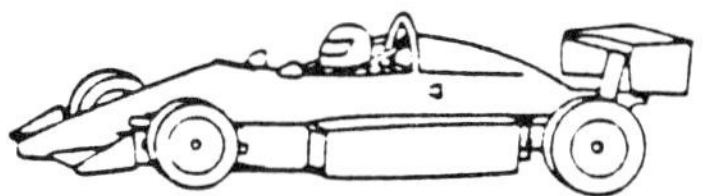

Formula Vauxhall Lotus European single seater formula for identical Reynard-built chassis, powered by two-liter, 156 bhp GM.

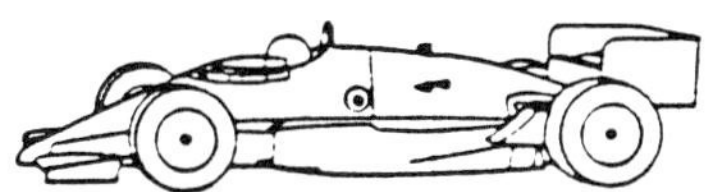

CART Indianapolis type cars up to 2,999 cc supercharged or 4,490 cc unsupercharged.

Stock car racing

8865 Events for highly modified stock production models on oval tracks. Restricted to US cars. In Britain, stock cars are stripped down for crashing on small tracks.

1

2

1 Hillclimb Cars race around a tarmac®-surfaced hill to complete the course in the fastest time. Sprints are similar to hillclimbs but the course is over a flat section of track.

2 Slalom A test of maneuverability. Cars are required to weave in and out of markers and back in and out of garages.

3

4

5

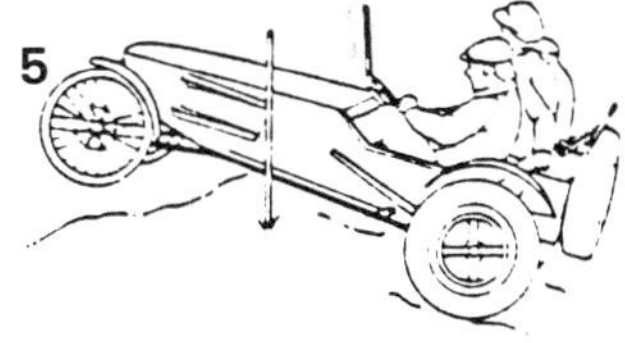

3 Autocross Cars race over grass or other rough surface to complete the course in the fastest time.

4 Rallycross Race for sedan or production sports cars on rough surfaced or tarmaced® roads but not public roads.

5 Hill trials Cars attempt to climb fastest up a steep hill. In grasstrack, all cars start together and race over an unsealed or grass course.

Sedan and sports car racing

8866 1

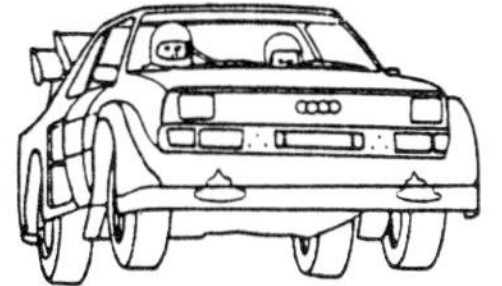

2

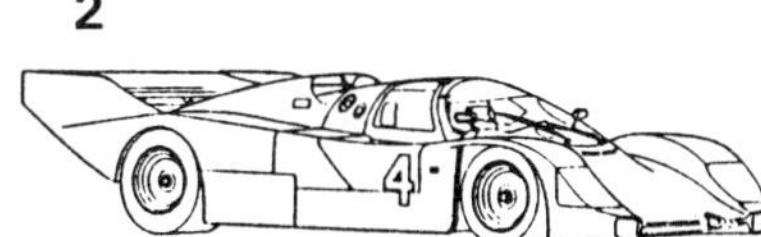

3

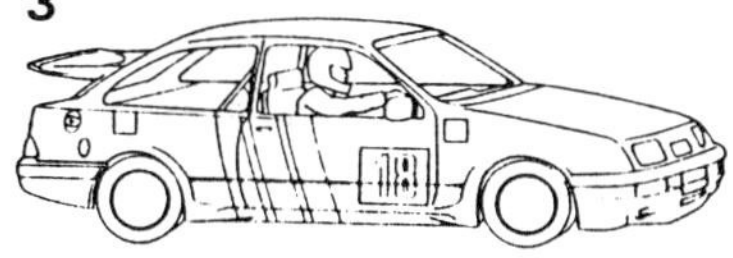

Events held on road-racing courses or oval tracks, or both, for production or specially built sports cars.

1 Group A Series Production touring cars, of which 5,000 must be built over the same 12 months period.

2 Group C World Sports Prototype Championship formula for closed, two-seater sports cars.

3 Group N Series Production touring cars, almost identical to the cars you might see in a dealer's showroom window.

Karts

8867 **Kart racing** Events for go-karts (small, single-seater open cars for children and adults).

Le Mans Annual 24-hour sports car race in western France.

Midgit cars Slightly larger versions of go-karts, racing on steeply banked tracks 0.25 mi (0.4 km) long.

Key words

8868

drag racing High speed events to record the fastest time over a given distance. Cars compete in pairs on a straight paved track called a drag strip at speeds that may top 260 mph (420 km/hr).
endurance racing Sports car events such as Le Mans lasting 3 to 24 hours. First to complete the distance or cover the most laps in the time wins.
Fédération International de l'Automobile (FIA) Organization established in 1904 to supervise international automobile racing.
fuel cell Safety petrol container in a leak-resistant metal or plastic tank.
Grand Prix "Large Prize" events for Formula One cars, which compete for the World Drivers' Championship.
Indianapolis 500 Race for Indy (Indianapolis) cars, which resemble Formula One cars. It takes place on the 2-mi (4.02 km) Indianapolis Motor Speedway.
monocoque Racing car design whose central structure is a shell of strong, lightweight material such as aluminum or carbon fiber, with no separate chassis and body.
off-road racing Long distance events over rough, desert courses, usually for small trucks.
oval tracks Racing tracks, usually from about 0.25 mi (0.4 km) to more than 2 mi (4 km) long, with straightways and banked curves.
pits Special areas along racing tracks for refueling and servicing the cars.
power-to-weight formula Formula that allows cars of inferior horsepower to weigh less than competing cars with more powerful engines.
rallies Long-distance events for production models with driver and navigator, usually held on public roads.
road-racing courses Courses that resemble country roads, with hills, straightways, and unbanked curves.
roll bar Protective metal bar that arches over the driver in an open cockpit.
roll cage Structure of steel tubes in an enclosed car that supports the roof should the car overturn.
round-the-houses Events, such as in Monaco, held on temporarily cleared city streets.
sprint cars Cars, slightly bigger than midgit cars, with a tall, narrow body, front engine, and open wheels, which race on oval tracks.
superspeedways Tracks with wide corners and high banking for speeds of up to 200 mph (320 km/h.)
super Vee Cars with a Volkswagen engine, which resemble small Formula One cars. Raced usually by aspiring young drivers.
Trans-Am Championship Series of road races in US and Canada for top production sports cars.
turbocharging Increasing the power of a small engine by means of a turbine driven by the engine's exhaust gases.

887 MOTORCYCLE RACING

History

8871

There are many types of competition for motorcycles, with a wide variety of machines competing on various types of course. The first motorcycle races were unspecialized, and began in Europe with events open to cars and motorcycles. However, in 1907, a new type of race, designed for motorcycles only, was organized over a closed circuit by the Auto Club de France. The parallel development of highly specialized motorcycles for closed-circuit racing in relatively small areas was virtually complete in England and France by 1903. The oldest motorcycle racing circuit still in use is the Snaefell mountain course, over which the Isle of Man Tourist Trophy (TT) races are run. Road racing – on specially built circuits or sometimes on ordinary roads – has the largest following at international level.

Rules

8872

Number of riders Determined, in a solo machine race, by the type of course.
Officials Up to five stewards are responsible for supervising a meeting, and adjudicating any protests. The clerk of the course is responsible for the meeting, and organizes the events. The clerk supervises the entries, starters, judges, and timekeepers, and the scrutineers, who ensure, before the start of a race, that all machines conform to required legal and safety standards.
Equipment The track should have a nonskid surface if possible, with warning signs placed in advance of any corners on the course. Riders must wear protective clothing, plus an all-enveloping full-face style helmet, or an open-face type with goggles or visors. The usual classes are for motorcycles with an engine capacity of 125 cc, 250 cc, 350 cc, 500 cc, and 750 cc (single, twin, twin, four, and four cylinders, respectively), plus an unlimited class (501–1300 cc). For all motorcycles: at least one brake on each wheel; tires at least 16 in (40 cm) in diameter; number plates on both sides, the rear, and the front; handlebars no less than 15.75 in (40 cm); clutch and brake levers, with an integral ball end at least 0.75 in (1.9 cm) in diameter; fixed footrests; a guard preventing the drive chain or shaft being touched accidentally; an exhaust pipe that does not project behind the machine or its bodywork; oil drain plugs, tightly locked in position.
The start Signaled by the lowering of a flag. Starting positions may be arranged by means of a grid, and be allocated according to the rider's known ability or to the rider's total time for preceding heats. A false start occurs when a rider moves forward from the start position before the signal is given. A 1-min penalty is usually added to the offending rider's total time for the race.
Riding conduct Any rider found guilty of riding in a foul, unfair or dangerous manner must leave the track as soon as possible.
The finish Signaled by the waving of a checkered flag as the leading rider completes the last lap. All riders are flagged off the track at the finish line.

Disciplines

8873

Drag Racing Riders race in pairs over a straight 440 yd (408 m) track or "strip." The fastest rider in each pair goes into the next round. There must be a braking area at least 800 yd (731 m) long at the end of the track. Competitors preheat and clean out their tires before the race. The race procedure is generally the same as for drag car racing. The main classes are street solo and competition solo.

Speedway Riders on special speedway machines race, usually over four laps, each of 350 yd (320 m) in length, around an ash- or shale-surfaced oval track. A special riding technique is needed, as the machines have no brakes and riders are forced to broadside their machines through the bends at speeds of up to 70 mph (109 km/h). There are individual and team events.

Sprint From point to point in a straight line on an approximately level, metaled surface. They are more or less than 1 mi in length, and held between two or more competitors, or individually against time. There are races for solo machines and for sidecar combinations. Sprints are popular in the UK, Australia, and parts of Europe.

continued

Disciplines continued

8873 **Ice racing** Similar to speedway. There are individual events and team events of seven or eight riders, and the riders race around an ice track. Motorcycles have steel spikes attached to their wheels to grip the ice surface. Events are divided into heats, and points are awarded for the first three places in each heat.

Engine capacities

8874 Motorcycles compete in classes determined by engine capacity. Class divisions for different events are shown in the diagram; solo motorcycle classes on the immediate right (**1**), and sidecar classes on the far right (**2**).

□ 2- stroke engine
▽ 4- stroke engine
O all engines

Engine capacities (cc)

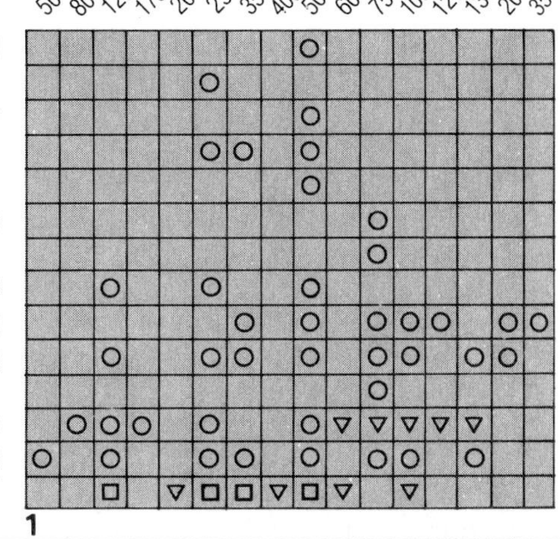

1

	50	80	125	175	200	250	350	400	500	600	750	1000	1200	1300	2000	3500
Ice racing									O							
Short track						O										
Speedway									O							
Grass track						O	O		O							
Long track									O							
TT steeplechase											O					
Flat track											O					
Motocross			O			O			O							
Drag racing							O		O		O	O	O		O	O
Sprinting			O			O	O		O		O	O		O	O	
Dirt track											O					
Enduro		O	O	O		O			O	▽	▽	▽	▽	▽		
Road racing	O		O			O	O		O		O	O		O		
Formula TT			□		▽	□	□	▽	□	▽		▽				

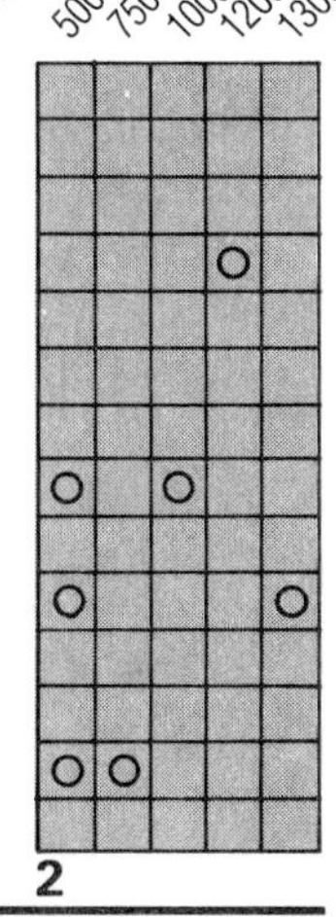

2

	500	750	1000	1200	1300
Ice racing					
Short track					
Speedway					
Grass track				O	
Long track					
TT steeplechase					
Flat track					
Motocross	O		O		
Drag racing					
Sprinting	O				O
Dirt track					
Enduro					
Road racing	O	O			
Formula TT					

Tracks and circuits

8875

Event	Length of track yd/mi	m
1 Ice racing	328–437 yd	300–400
2 Short track	440 yd	402
3 Speedway	300–470 yd	275–430
4 Grass track	492–1,422	450–1,300
5 Long track	1,093 yd	1,000
6 TT steeplechase	660–1,320 yd	604–1,207
7 Flat track	0.5 mi or 1 mi	805 or 1.609
8 Motocross	1–3 mi	1,609–4,827
9 Drag racing	440 yd	402
10 Sprint racing	0.25–1 mi	402–1,609

Circuit	Country	Length mi	Length km
a Daytona	US	2.5	4.02
b Brands Hatch	UK	2.61	4.21
c Monza	Italy	3.6	5.8
d Van Drethene Assen	Neth	4.78	7.68
e Dunford	N Ireland	7.5	12.0
f Francorchamps	Belgium	8.74	14.12
g Nurburgring	Germany	14.19	22.84
h Isle of Man TT	UK	37.73	60.71

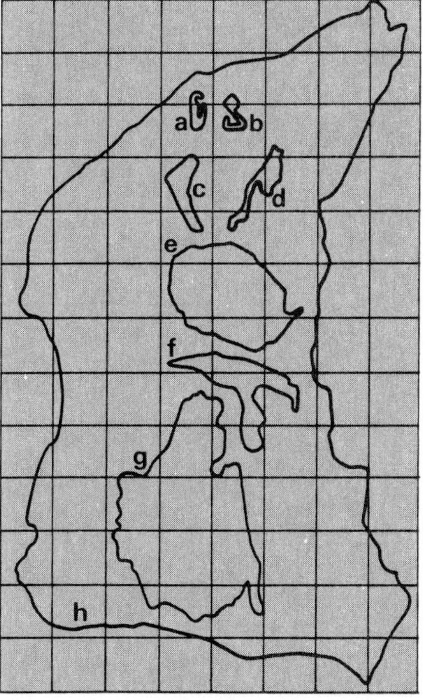

888 CYCLE RACING

History

8881 The bicycle was designed as a means of sport and recreation rather than a mode of transport. Its forerunner was the célerifère, or vélocifère, built for the French Comte de Sivrac and demonstrated in the gardens of the Palais Royale, Paris, France, in 1719. It had no steering mechanism, and was propeled by the rider pushing the ground with alternate feet. In 1817, the German engineer Baron von Drais de Sauerburn introduced a pivoting front wheel which enabled him to steer his machine by means of a handlebar. A method of propulsion involving treadles connected by levers and cranks directly to the rear wheel was developed in 1839 by Macmillan, a Scottish blacksmith, and by 1879, Lawson's Bicyclette had been developed, with a chain-wheel drive to the rear wheel. The first cycle race took place at the Parc de St Cloud, in the suburbs of Paris, on May 31 1868. The sport is now broadly divided into track and road racing.

Rules

8882 **Competitors** Must be licensed by their clubs in accordance with national regulations.
Officials A referee (a chief judge in the UK) with one or more assistants, timekeepers, machine examiners, lap scorers, and starters, if needed. A chief commissaire (referee) and at least one assistant commissaire are necessary at a road-race meeting.
Banned substances Any competitor found to be taking any substance likely to affect performance is liable to suspension. A rider is also barred from competition if he or she takes banned substances in the course of medical treatment.
Starts For road races, at the drop of a flag, and may be made either standing or rolling.
Dismounting A rider who has dismounted may complete the course carrying, dragging or wheeling the machine, but must not receive assistance.
Refreshments Competitors may accept food and drink that are handed to them at specified feeding stations.
Sanctions Include, in order of severity, a warning, a reprimand, a fine, relegation, disqualification, suspension, and withdrawal of license. Amateurs may not be fined.

Road races

8883 **Regulations** Races run in conformity with the law of the country in which they are run, and with regard to the local traffic regulations. Riders may exchange machine equipment, food and drink. The results of races are settled at road meetings by the commissaires. Pacing by another rider is not allowed in individual time trials, but is permissible in other road races and team time trials. Illegal riding includes pushing another rider, and crossing in front of another rider to prevent him or her from moving on.
Equipment Any kind of cycle, provided it is propeled only by human forces, has no streamlining, and does not exceed specified dimensions. It must have brakes, lights and reflectors if ridden at night, and, for long rides, a pump, a spare tube, and one or two feeding bottles mounted in cages attached to the frame.

TYPES
The road surface used is any that is suitable for vehicles but that is not a purpose-built cycle track. It may be a public highway (either open or closed to other traffic), or a course may be marked out on an airfield or motor racing circuit.
1 Road time trials Cyclists are racing against the clock. Each individual or team aims to be the fastest over a set distance: as they start at timed intervals, they must be able to judge their own pace as they cannot know how fast their competitors are traveling.
2 Hill climb A specialized form of time trial. The cyclist is still racing against the clock, but the course is always uphill.
3 Massed start races The cyclists race each other: the first rider past the finishing post wins.
4 Stage races The most famous stage race is the Tour de France. Each of these events is a series of massed start road races, but may also include time trials, special mountain stages, and criterium and kermesse races (see track races).

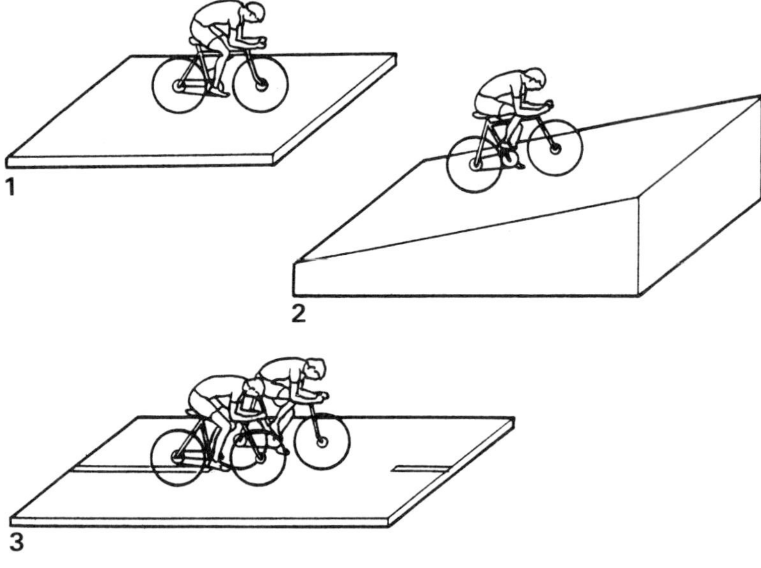

Track races

8884 **Equipment** Tracks are usually hard-surfaced, but may be on grass. Markings include lines to mark handicap starts, finishing lines, and starting points for various standard distances. The sprinters' line is a red line 35.43 in (90 cm) from the inside edge of the track. No overtaking is allowed inside this line if the rider ahead is on or inside this line. Machines with free-wheel gears, brakes, and quick-release wheels are usually prohibited. Cycles must be fitted with a fixed wheel.
EVENTS
Sprints These are races between two or more riders over one or more laps of a track up to 3,280 ft (1,000 m). The earlier part of the race is devoted to tactical maneuvering. Handicap races are over short distances generally not more than 3,280 ft (1,000 m). At the start, riders are positioned on the track according to their handicaps, held upright, and given a push-off.
Individual pursuit This is a world championship event in which two riders start on opposite sides of the track. If one rider does not catch the other rider, the rider with the fastest time wins.
Australian pursuit (a variant) This has up to eight riders on the track.
Team pursuit This is like individual pursuit, but with two teams of four riders. Victory is decided on the times of the first three riders from each team to finish. Italian pursuit is between two or more teams of up to five riders. The leading rider from each team drops out after each lap, and the finishing time of the last rider of each team decides the race.
Point to point This is a bunch race awarding points to the highest-placed riders in each lap or group of laps. Scratch races are longer races over distances from 3 to 62 mi (5 to 100 km).
Madison racing This is a form of delay racing in which a pair of riders race, with one in the race and one slowly circling the track and resting. The relays are effected by the outgoing rider pushing his or her partner into the racing group of riders.
Cyclo-cross Events take place in winter over open country. The maximum recommended distance is 15 mi (24 km). Hill climbs generally do not exceed 3 mi (5 km), and may be much

continued

Track races continued

8884 shorter depending on the gradient of the hill. In time trials, competitors set off at 1-min intervals and race against the clock to cover a set distance in the least possible time.

Roller races Take place on sets of rollers geared to dials that indicate the "distance" covered by the rider.
Pacing Human pacing may be allowed, but only one pacer may be on the track for each competitor, except during a changeover. Events of over 6.2 mi (10 km) may be motor-paced, with each stayer preceded by a motorcyclist who sets the pace and affords some shelter from the wind.

Circuits

8885 TRACKS
Many cycle races are held on circuits, which may be road routes or special tracks. Listed here are the lengths of various racing circuits
1 Criterium This is a circuit road race, or series of races, held in a town or along the roads connecting a group of villages. The roads are closed to other traffic, and the cyclists race each other over a set number of laps.
2 Cyclocross This is cross-country cycle racing. Only one third of the course may be road: the rest will include plowed land, woods, streams, gates, hedges, and similar obstacles. Competitors ride whenever possible, or run carrying their cycles.
3 Kermesse Like the criterium event, this is a massed start road race held on an urban circuit. The difference is in the size of the circuit: the criterium circuit is at least four times as long as the one used in the kermesse.
4 BMX (bicycle motocross) Here the cyclist is again racing over different terrain, but, unlike the cyclocross circuit, the BMX track is purpose-built with a smooth, sandy soil. After a steep, downhill start, the circuit includes banked curves ("berms"), tabletop jumps several feet high, and double jumps over raised mounds in the track ("whoop-de-doos").
5 Track Another, but very different, purpose-built circuit. The smooth oval track is banked all around, more steeply on the curves than on the straight sections. The surface of an indoor track is usually wood: outdoor tracks may be concrete or asphalt. The wide range of events held on the track includes: time trials; sprint races; pursuit races; and points races.
6 Speedway Here again the cyclist races over a purpose-built oval track, but this time unbanked, and with a shale or dirt track surface.

Circuit	Length mi/yd	km/m
1 Criterium	2–4 mi	3.2–6.4 km
2 Cyclocross	1.8 mi	3 km
3 Kermesse	0.5 mi	0.8 km
4 BMX	0.25–0.5 mi	0.4–0.8 km
5 Track (championship size)	364.5 yd	333.33 m
6 Cycle speedway	350 yd	320 m

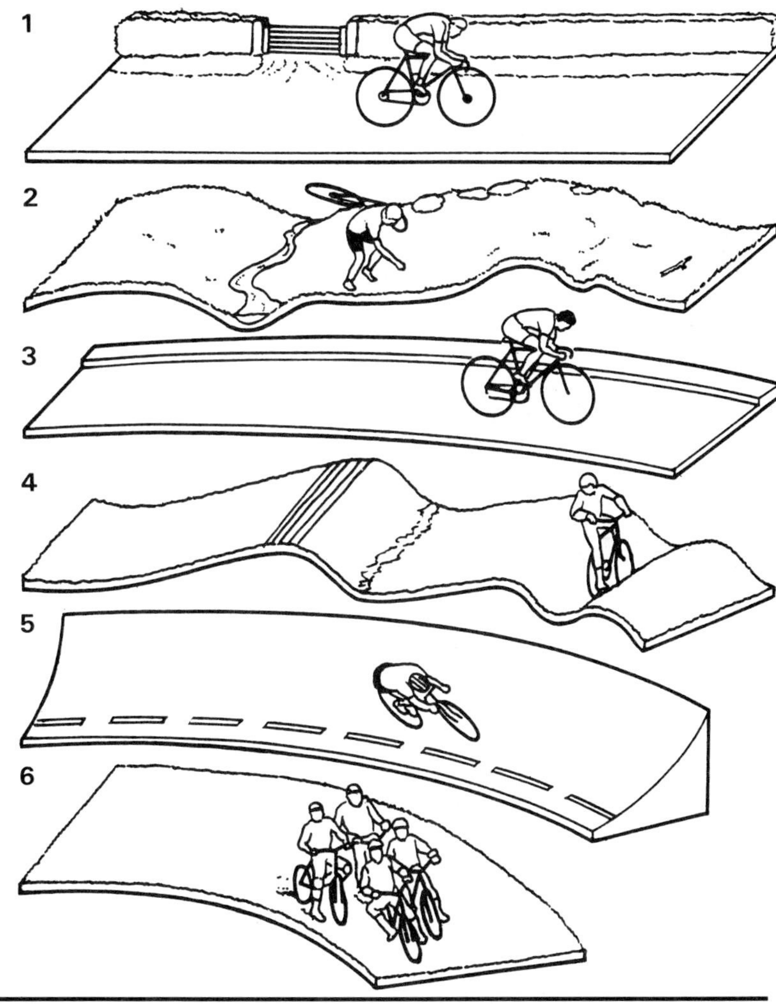

Key words

8886 **box** Tactic by which a rider rides just behind and to one side of another, and thus prevents a third rider from overtaking without swinging right out.
break-away Getting clear of the field.
circuit races (criterium) Road race consisting of several laps over a circuit of roads. Races vary in length up to 62.14 mi (100 km).
control points (pits) Set up on long road-race events for feeding and repairs.
Course des primes A race with intermediate prizes ("primes") at specified laps, or other points along the course.
demi-fond A middle-distance, paced track event.
domestique A team rider in road racing, whose job it is to help the team leader to win.
King of the mountains The title given to the winner of most points in hill climbs as part of a road, circuit, or stage race.
lanterne rouge (red lantern) A booby prize for the last rider in a stage race.
maillot jaune (yellow jersey) Worn by the current leader of the Tour de France and some other major events.
musette Cotton bag in which food is handed up to a rider in a road race.
omnium A track event in which the competitors ride in several races of different types.
peleton The main bunch of riders in a road race.
repêchage A kind of "second chance" race to allow losers from the heats an additional opportunity to qualify for the next round of the series in a progressive race.
sag wagon One of the last following vehicles in road events used to pick up riders who have dropped out.
stayer A track rider in a motor-paced race.

891 Olympic games
8911 History and organization
8912 Summer games
8913 Winter games
8914 Other games events

891 OLYMPIC GAMES

History and organization

8911 The first games took place at Olympia in western Greece in 776 BC. They were staged every four years until abolished in AD 393 by Emperor Theodosius I of Rome. The modern Games were revived in 1896 in Athens by French educator Baron Pierre de Coubertin. The winter games began in 1924.

Governing body
The Games are governed by the International Olympic Committee (IOC). It selects the host cities six years in advance, schedules events, and decides the types and numbers of sports, and the numbers of eligible athletes. Summer and winter games traditionally take place in the same year. From 1994, they will occur on four-year cyles, two years apart; e.g.; Winter Games will occur in 1994 and 1998, and Summer Games in 1996 and 2000.

Finance
Athletes are technically amateurs, but professionals are eligible for some sports. Others receive expenses and compensation for loss of normal earnings. Most host nations defray expsenses with government funds.

Olympic symbol Five interlocking rings, representing Africa, Asia, Australia, Europe, and North and South America. Rings are black, blue, green, red, and yellow.

Summer Olympics

Year	Venue	Countries	Year	Venue	Countries
1896	Athens, Greece	13	1948	London, England	59
1900	Paris, France	22	1952	Helsinki, Finland	69
1904	St Louis, US	13	1956	Melbourne, Australia	67
1908	London, England	22	1960	Rome, Italy	83
1912	Stockholm, Sweden	28	1964	Tokyo, Japan	93
1916	Not held	—	1968	Mexico City, Mexico	112
1920	Antwerp, Belgium	29	1972	Munich, West Germany	122
1924	Paris, France	44	1976	Montreal, Canada	92
1928	Amsterdam, Netherlands	46	1980	Moscow, USSR	81
1932	Los Angeles, US	37	1984	Los Angeles, US	140
1936	Berlin, Germany	49	1988	Seoul, South Korea	160
1940	Not held	—	1992	Barcelona, Spain	172
1944	Not held	—			

Summer Games

8912 **Ceremony** Held every four years in a major city in various summer months. Athletes from Greece enter the stadium first, followed by each nation alphabetically; host nation enters last. Doves, symbolizing peace, are released as the Olympic flag is raised. A lighted torch from the valley of Olympia, Greece, is carried for four weeks by relays of runners to the stadium, and there lights the Olympic Flame. It remains alight throughout the Games.

Sports From 15 to 23. Men only: boxing, judo, soccer, weight lifting, wrestling, and modern pentathlon. Separate men's and women's events include archery, basketball, canoeing and kayaking, cycling, fencing, field hockey, gymnastics, rowing, shooting, swimming and diving (water polo for men, synchronized swimming for women), table tennis, team handball, tennis, track and field, and volleyball. Events for men and women in the same team include equestrian sports and yachting.

Numbers Almost 10,000 athletes take part.

Medals Top three athletes in each event win medals; the next five receive certificates. The first two medals are silver, the winner's coated with gold; third is bronze. Duration 16 days.

Winter Games

8913 **Preparation** Held every four years in a winter resort in January or February. An outdoor stadium houses the opening ceremony and speed skating races. Figure skating and ice hockey take place in an indoor stadium. Ski trails are laid for cross-country, downhill, and slalom competitions. Two high ski jumps are needed for ski jumping.

Sports Seven, including biathlon, bobsledding, and ice hockey for men only. Figure skating, luge, skiing and speed skating have separate competitions for men and women.

Numbers About 1,200 athletes take part.

Medals As for Summer Games.

Duration About 15 days.

Other games events

8914 **Pan-American Games** Series of athletic contests strated after World War II to increase goodwill among the American peoples. Held every four years, usually in the summer before the Olympic Games. Thirty-eight Western Hemisphere nations take part.

Commonwealth Games Series of athletic events, patterned after the Olympic Games, for members of the Commonwealth of Nations. Held every four years in a different country each time. They started in 1930, in Hamilton, Canada, and were called the British Empire Games. The name was changed in 1974.

Asian Games Athletics competition for men and women from all Asian countries affiliated to the International Amateur Athletic Federation (IAAF). The Games began in New Delhi, India, in 1951, and have been held every four years since 1954. They cover a full Olympic program of track and field events, with Japan dominating.

National Collegiate Athletic Association (NCAA) Chanpionship US Championship events in 19 sports for men and women in college sports. Founded in 1906, the NCAA has a membership of more than 990 schools. It establishes athletic standards and official playing rules for all college sports.

Marathon Long-distance running race held in various cities (e.g., Boston, New York, London) at various times of the year. Named after the Greek soldier who ran from the Battle of Marathon to Athens with news of victory, today's race has no official world record because courses vary. The official distance is 26 mi 385 yd (42.195 km), covered in a best time of just over 2 hr. It is also an Olympic event.

Special Olympic Games International competition to train mentally retarded children and adults to compete as athletes. Local and regional contests, based on age and ability, lead to an international final. The first of these was held in the US in 1968.

Paraplegic Games Also known as the "Paralympics" and the "Wheelchair Olympics," but correctly designated the International Stoke Mandeville Games.The contests are named after the Stoke Mandeville hospital in Berkshire, England, for paralyzed and semi-paralyzed patients. Started in 1948 and held annually to encourage disabled men and women, contests are held in various cities and include sports such as archery, swimming, fencing, table tennis, discus, and basketball.